June 6–8, 2011
San Jose, California, USA

**Association for
Computing Machinery**

Advancing Computing as a Science & Profession

PODC'11

Proceedings of the 2011 ACM Symposium

Principles of Distributed Computing

Sponsored by:

ACM SIGOPS & ACM SIGACT

Supported by:

Microsoft Research & Google

Association for
Computing Machinery

Advancing Computing as a Science & Profession

The Association for Computing Machinery
2 Penn Plaza, Suite 701
New York, New York 10121-0701

Notice to Past Authors of ACM-Published Articles
ACM intends to create a complete electronic archive of all articles and/or other material previously published by ACM. If you have written a work that has been previously published by ACM in any journal or conference proceedings prior to 1978, or any SIG Newsletter at any time, and you do NOT want this work to appear in the ACM Digital Library, please inform permissions@acm.org, stating the title of the work, the author(s), and where and when published.

ISBN: 978-1-4503-0719-2

Additional copies may be ordered prepaid from:

ACM Order Department
PO Box 30777
New York, NY 10087-0777, USA

Phone: 1-800-342-6626 (USA and Canada)
+1-212-626-0500 (Global)
Fax: +1-212-944-1318
E-mail: acmhelp@acm.org
Hours of Operation: 8:30 am – 4:30 pm ET

ACM Order Number: 536110

Printed in the USA

Foreword

This volume contains 34 extended abstracts and 31 brief announcements selected for the 30th Annual ACM SIGACT-SIGOPS Symposium on Principles of Distributed Computing (PODC), held on June 6-8, 2011, in San Jose, California, USA, as part of the 5th Federated Computing Research Conference (FCRC). The program committee selected these papers among 129 regular submissions, and 34 additional brief announcements submissions. The selection of the papers was done electronically using Easychair, in two phases. During the first phase, which lasted slightly more than one month, each paper was reviewed by at least three program committee members, with the help of external referees. During the second phase, which lasted more than two weeks, the papers have been discussed and compared, until the program committee eventually converges to the final list.

It is expected that many of these papers will appear in more polished form in refereed scientific journals. A selection of papers has been invited to appear in the Journal of the ACM, and to a special issue of Distributed Computing dedicated to PODC 2011. The program committee has delivered the PODC 2011 Best Paper Award to the paper "The Space Complexity of Long-Lived and One-Shot Timestamp Implementations" by Maryam Helmi, Lisa Higham, Eduardo Pacheco and Philipp Woelfel. The PODC 2011 Best Student Paper Award has been delivered to the paper "Distributed Deterministic Edge Coloring using Bounded Neighborhood Independence" by Leonid Barenboim and Michael Elkin.

On behalf of the program committee, I would like to thank the many authors who submitted their work for consideration by the conference. As it is often the case, the decision of the committee was made difficult by the large number of very good submissions. We thus look forward to seeing many of the papers that were not able to fit into PODC 2011 appearing in other venues. We hope that the authors of these submissions will continue to be interested in PODC, and that they will see their work appear in future PODC.

I would like to express my deep thanks to all members of the program committee, with whom it has been a great pleasure to work.

Pierre Fraigniaud
PODC 2011 Program Chair
CNRS and University Paris Diderot

Table of Contents

Session 5: Best Papers
Session Chair: Yehuda Afek *(Tel-Aviv University)*

Session 6: Compact or Sparse Distributed Structures
Session Chair: Amos Korman *(CNRS and Univ. Paris Diderot)*

Session 7: Security and Consistency
Session Chair: Dahlia Malkhi *(Microsoft Research Silicon Valley)*

Session 8: Brief Announcements
Session Chair: Phillip Gibbons *(Intel Labs Pittsburgh)*

Session 12: Self-* Systems
Session Chair: Boaz Patt-Shamir *(Tel Aviv University)*

Session 13: Brief Announcements
Session Chair: Pierre Fraigniaud *(CNRS and Univ. Paris Diderot)*

Session 14: Information Dissemination
Session Chair: Fabian Kuhn *(University of Lugano)*

PODC 2011 Conference Organization

General Chair: Cyril Gavoille *(LaBRI, University of Bordeaux, France)*

Program and Proceedings Chair: Pierre Fraigniaud *(CNRS and University of Paris Diderot, France)*

Publicity Chairs: Yuval Emek *(ETH Zurich, Switzerland)*
Seth Gilbert *(EPFL, Switzerland)*

Treasurer: Darek Kowalski *(University of Liverpool, UK)*

Steering Committee Chair: Andrzej Pelc *(Université du Québec en Outaouais, Canada)*

Steering Committee: Lorenzo Alvisi *(University of Texas Austin, USA)*
Pierre Fraigniaud *(CNRS and University Paris Diderot, France)*
Cyril Gavoille *(University of Bordeaux, France)*
Rachid Guerraoui *(EPFL, Switzerland)*
Darek Kowalski *(University of Liverpool, UK)*
Andrzej Pelc *(Université du Québec en Outaouais, Canada)*
Jennifer Welch *(Texas A&M University, USA)*

Program Committee: Yehuda Afek *(Tel-Aviv University, Israel)*
James Aspnes *(Yale University, USA)*
Petra Berenbrink *(Simon Fraser University, Canada)*
Anat Bremler-Barr *(IDC, Israel)*
Edith Cohen *(AT&T Research, USA)*
Michael Elkin *(Ben-Gurion University, Israel)*
Faith Ellen *(University of Toronto, Canada)*
Pierre Fraigniaud *(CNRS and University Paris Diderot, France)*
Phillip Gibbons *(Intel Labs Pittsburgh, USA)*
Amos Korman *(CNRS and University Paris Diderot, France)*
Fabian Kuhn *(University of Lugano, Switzerland)*
Dahlia Malkhi *(Microsoft Research Silicon Valley, USA)*
Laurent Massoulie *(Technicolor, France)*
Mark Moir *(Sun Labs at Oracle, USA)*
Yoram Moses *(Technion, Israel)*
Boaz Patt-Shamir *(Tel Aviv University, Israel)*
David Peleg *(Weizmann Institute of Science, Israel)*
Harald Raecke *(University of Warwick, UK)*
Michel Raynal *(IRISA, Université de Rennes, France)*
Jared Saia *(University of New Mexico, USA)*
Nir Shavit *(Sun Labs at Oracle and Tel-Aviv University, Israel)*
Sam Toueg *(University of Toronto, Canada)*
Mark Tuttle *(Intel, USA)*

Additional reviewers:

Ittai Abraham
Marcos Aguilera
Hoda Akbari
Jeffrey Alexander
Hagit Attiya
Chen Avin
Hillel Avni
Eitan Bachmat
Leonid Barenboim
Hervé Baumann
Petra Berenbrink
François Bonnet
Ran Canetti
Armando Castaneda
Keren Censor-Hillel
Shiri Chechik
Andrea Clementi
Alex Cornejo
Artur Czumaj
Robert Danek
Ajoy K. Datta
Ajoy Kumar Datta
Carole Delporte
Bilel Derbel
David Dice
Robert Elsaesser
Yuval Emek
Matthias Englert
Funda Ergun
Guy Even
Ittay Eyal
Rui Fan
Hugues Fauconnier
Alexandra Fedorova
Matthias Fitzi
Paola Flocchini
Leszek Gasieniec
Cyril Gavoille
Chryssis Georgiou
George Giakkoupis
Wojciech Golab
Dov Gordon
Maria Gradinariu Potop-Butucaru
Maxim Gurevich
Vassos Hadzilacos
Magnus M. Halldorsson
Avinatan Hassidim

Danny Hendler
Maurice Herlihy
Amir Herzberg
Avni Hillel
Eshcar Hillel
Martin Hoefer
Thomas Holenstein
Yuval Ishai
Prasad Jayanti
Colette Johnen
Jussi Kangasharju
Michal Kapalka
Jonathan Katz
Idit Keidar
Kamyar Khodamoradi
Valerie King
Jeff Knockel
Gillat Kol
Guy Kortsarz
Adrian Kosowski
Michal Koucky
Dariusz Kowalski
Danny Krizanc
Shay Kutten
Doug Lea
Hyonho Lee
Christoph Lenzen
Huijia Lin
Yaroslav Litus
Zvi Lotker
Victor Luchangco
Virendra Marathe
Alex Matveev
Alexander May
Moti Medina
Yves Metivier
Alessia Milani
Pradipta Mitra
Neeraj Mittal
Michael Mitzenmacher
Ossi Mokryn
Adam Morrison
Dabid Movshovitz
Rotem Oshman
Rafail Ostrovsky
Alessandro Panconesi
Saurav Pandit

Additional reviewers:

Gopal Pandurangan
Sriram Pemmaraju
Dima Perelman
Benny Pinkas
David Pointcheval
Giuseppe Prencipe
Sergio Rajsbaum
Dror Rawitz
Tzachy Reinman
Andrea Richa
John Michael Robson
Liam Roditty
Adi Rosen
Eric Ruppert
Thomas Sauerwal
Michael Schapira
Christian Scheideler
Ulrich Schmid
Johannes Schneider
Michael Scott
Marco Serafini

Jean-Sébastien Sereni
Nir Shavit
Alex Shraer
Haya Shulman
Christian Sommer
Troels Bjerre Sorensen
Jukka Suomela
Tami Tamir
Gadi Taubenfeld
Andreas Tielmann
Denis Trystram
Martin Vechev
Laurent Viennot
Berthold Voecking
Marko Vukolic
Oren Weimann
Jennifer Welch
Philipp Woelfel
Maxwell Young
Akka Zemmar
Piotr Zielinski

PODC 2011 Sponsors & Supporters

Sponsors:

Supporters:

Coordinated Consensus in Dynamic Networks

Fabian Kuhn
Faculty of Informatics,
University of Lugano
6904 Lugano,Switzerland
fabian.kuhn@usi.ch

Yoram Moses
Department of Electrical
Engineering, Technion
Haifa, 32000, Israel
moses@ee.technion.ac.il

Rotem Oshman
Computer Science and
Artificial Intelligence Lab, MIT
Cambridge, MA 02139, USA
rotem@csail.mit.edu

ABSTRACT

We study several variants of coordinated consensus in dynamic networks. We assume a synchronous model, where the communication graph for each round is chosen by a worst-case adversary. The network topology is always connected, but can change completely from one round to the next. The model captures mobile and wireless networks, where communication can be unpredictable.

In this setting we study the fundamental problems of eventual, simultaneous, and Δ-coordinated consensus, as well as their relationship to other distributed problems, such as determining the size of the network. We show that in the absence of a good initial upper bound on the size of the network, eventual consensus is as hard as computing deterministic functions of the input, e.g., the minimum or maximum of inputs to the nodes. We also give an algorithm for computing such functions that is optimal in every execution. Next, we show that simultaneous consensus can never be achieved in less than $n - 1$ rounds in any execution, where n is the size of the network; consequently, simultaneous consensus is as hard as computing an upper bound on the number of nodes in the network.

For Δ-coordinated consensus, we show that if the ratio between nodes with input 0 and input 1 is bounded away from 1, it is possible to decide in time $n - \Theta(\sqrt{n\Delta})$, where Δ bounds the time from the first decision until all nodes decide. If the dynamic graph has diameter D, the time to decide is $\min\{O(nD/\Delta), n - \Omega(n\Delta/D)\}$, even if D is not known in advance. Finally, we show that (a) there is a dynamic graph such that for every input, no node can decide before time $n - O(\Delta^{0.28} n^{0.72})$; and (b) for any diameter $D = O(\Delta)$, there is an execution with diameter D where no node can decide before time $\Omega(nD/\Delta)$. To our knowledge, our work constitutes the first study of Δ-coordinated consensus in general graphs.

Categories and Subject Descriptors:
F.2.2 [Analysis of Algorithms and Problem Complexity]:
Non-numerical Algorithms and Problems—*computations on discrete structures*
G.2.2 [Discrete Mathematics]: Graph Theory—*network problems*
General Terms: Algorithms, Theory
Keywords: distributed algorithms, dynamic networks, consensus, coordination, common knowledge

1. INTRODUCTION

Coordinating the actions of distributed computing devices or mobile agents is an essential distributed task. Applications of coordination for instance abound in robotics and swarm protocols, where many mobile agents cooperate to jointly accomplish some global objective. In such examples, nodes must jointly agree to execute some common action (movement, data collection, or even something so simple as resetting their clocks or starting a protocol) at the same or almost the same time.

Global coordination is a challenging task, made all the more difficult in dynamic settings, where the agents move around and the communication links between them can behave unpredictably. In this paper we study the problems of consensus, simultaneous consensus, and Δ-coordinated (i.e., "almost simultaneous") consensus in dynamic networks. Our goal is to characterize the time complexity of these tasks, as well as to investigate the relationship that they bear to higher-level tasks, such as computing functions of inputs to the nodes and determining the number of nodes.

We study the above problems in the dynamic network model of [18]. The model is round-based; in each round, the communication network is an adversarially-chosen graph over a vertex set V of size n. The set V of network nodes is assumed to be fixed throughout an execution, although we do not assume that the participants know V (or even n, in some cases). The communication graph is assumed to be connected, but it can change completely from one round to the next. Nodes communicate by broadcasting messages to their immediate neighbors. Similar dynamic network models have previously been considered in, e.g., [1, 16, 17, 22], and many others.

Our main objective in this paper is to understand the complexity of consensus and of coordinating actions and decisions in dynamic networks. We begin by studying *eventual consensus*, in which each node receives an initial input, and all nodes must eventually agree on the input to one of the nodes. We show that eventual consensus is closely related to knowing when a node has been causally influenced by all nodes in the graph; namely, in certain settings, no node can decide on an output value until it has been causally influenced by all nodes. Although the decision value in a consensus protocol is not a deterministic function of the inputs, our result implies that in many settings it is equivalent in difficulty to computing a deterministic function such as the minimum or maximum of inputs. We also give an optimal criterion for determining when a node knows it has been causally influenced by all nodes, and so can decide.

Next we turn our attention to the problem of *simultaneous consensus*, where nodes are required to output their decision value simultaneously. Simultaneous coordination is a useful primitive, as many distributed protocols assume that all nodes begin executing the protocol at the same time; without simultaneous coordination, it is not possible to execute such a protocol soon after some other protocol completes (that is, the protocols cannot be sequentially composed). It is known that achieving simultaneous consensus is tightly related to obtaining common knowledge in a distributed system [8, 15]. Informally, a fact φ is common knowledge whenever φ is known to all nodes, and everyone knows that everyone knows φ, and (everyone knows)[3] φ, and so on (a more rigorous definition is presented in Section 2). When nodes must execute an action at the same time, the fact that the action is being performed must be common knowledge. We show that achieving common knowledge is costly in dynamic networks: it always requires $n-1$ rounds. This holds even in executions where the communication graph is well-behaved, e.g., when it is static and has a small diameter. In particular, this result implies that simultaneous consensus can never be achieved before time $n-1$, even if n is known a priori. (Compare to eventual consensus, which can be solved in two rounds if the graph is fully-connected.) If the number of nodes is *not* known a priori, then n rounds are required. This implies that solving simultaneous consensus in this model is as hard as computing an upper bound on the size of the network: given a protocol for simultaneous consensus, we can obtain an upper bound on n by simply having each node output the round number in which it decides.

In light of the cost of simultaneous consensus, it is desirable to find a trade-off between the time it takes to achieve coordination and the quality of coordination achieved. We show that such a trade-off exists by considering Δ-*coordinated consensus*, a variant of consensus in which all nodes are required to output their decision values within Δ rounds of each other. In particular, simultaneous consensus is equivalent to 0-coordinated consensus, and eventual consensus to ∞-coordinated consensus.

One might initially expect that a protocol for Δ-coordinated consensus would not be able to improve upon the running time of a simultaneous consensus protocol by more than Δ rounds, and indeed we show that this is true in the worst-case: for some input and some execution, Δ-coordinated consensus requires $n-\Delta-1$ rounds. However, surprisingly, there are many cases in which even 1-coordinated consensus can decide significantly faster than simultaneous consensus. For example, we give a protocol that halts in $n-\Theta(\sqrt{n\Delta})$ rounds if the ratio of the number of zeroes to the number of ones in the input is bounded away from 1, and we give another protocol that halts in $\min\{O(nD/\Delta), n-\Omega(n\Delta/D)\}$ rounds in graphs where each message takes no more than D rounds to traverse the network (we call D the *dynamic diameter* of the network). Hence, for the purpose of achieving coordinated consensus, having a small-diameter network does help significantly, whereas for simultaneous consensus it does not help at all.

On the negative side, we show that there is a static network such that for every Δ-coordinated consensus algorithm and every input assignment, no node decides before time $n-O(\Delta^{0.28}n^{0.72})$. The network we construct in this lower bound has a diameter of $\Theta(n)$, which makes it inherently "difficult". To complete the picture, we also show that for every $D=O(\Delta)$, there is a static network of diameter D such that for all algorithms and inputs, no node decides before time $\Omega(nD/\Delta)$. Both lower bounds use a novel variation on the standard proof technique used in, e.g., [8] to obtain lower bounds on the time to acquire common knowledge. In [8], one freely moves between indistinguishable points (configurations); in contrast, here we pay a cost each time we move to some new indistinguishable point, and our goal is to minimize the total number of points involved in the proof.

In these two lower bounds we exhibit *static* networks in which solving Δ-coordinated consensus is hard (i.e., it requires many rounds). The hardness arises from the *potential* for dynamic behavior: although in practice the network topology does not change

during the execution, the nodes do not know in advance that this will be the case, and informally, they must assume the worst-case dynamic behavior. We note also that the three lower bounds we give in this paper are in some sense incomparable with each other.

- The $n-\Delta-1$ lower bound asserts, in a non-constructive manner, the existence of a particular combination of dynamic network and input assignment for which Δ-coordinated consensus is hard.
- In the $n-O(\Delta^{0.28}n^{0.72})$ lower bound we construct a specific network in which *every* input assignment is hard. This network has diameter $\Theta(n)$.
- The $\Omega(nD/\Delta)$ lower bound also gives a specific network in which every input assignment is hard. While the bound is smaller than the previous one, it applies to every diameter $D=O(\Delta)$.

1.1 Related work

Consensus and knowledge. Consensus is a central topic in distributed computing, initiated by the seminal paper by Pease, Shostak and Lamport [23]. Most of the literature on the subject in the context of message-passing systems assumes that the network is a complete graph, with direct channels connecting every pair of nodes. For more general networks, there has been work on the connectivity requirements for reaching consensus under various failure models (see, e.g., [7]), as well as work on implementing consensus in bounded-degree networks with special properties, such as expanders [14, 9]. We are not aware of a study of the efficiency of consensus protocols in general graphs. The current paper considers an even weaker network model, where the graph can possibly change completely from one round to the next.

While most of the literature on consensus is concerned with tolerating node failures, in the dynamic network model that we consider here the nodes themselves are assumed to be reliable, but the protocol must overcome potentially drastic changes in topology between rounds. Santoro and Widmayer studied consensus in the context of edge failures [24], and showed that it is unsolvable if more than $n-2$ (arbitrarily chosen) edges can be down in every round. The dynamic network model allows a much broader set of executions, since almost all (in fact, all but $n-1$) edges can be down in every round, and their choice is almost arbitrary. The only requirement is that the network in each round be connected.

Some of our results concern cases in which the number of nodes in the network is unknown, or in which there is a rough but inexact bound on the number of nodes. These are unusual assumptions in the context of consensus. A number of standard consensus protocols (e.g., [2]) can easily be modified to handle such assumptions, but this is only due to the fact that the network there is a complete graph, so that a node hears from all correct nodes in every round.

Simultaneous coordination has been shown to be closely related to the notion of common knowledge [15, 10]. Thus, for example, in a simultaneous consensus protocol [8, 21], when the nodes decide on v, it must be common knowledge that some initial value is v. This is much stronger than for regular consensus, in which a node deciding v must (individually) know that one of the initial values was v. It has been shown that deciding in simultaneous consensus (and in a large class of simultaneous coordination tasks) can be reduced to the problem of computing when facts (and which facts) are common knowledge at any given point in an execution. For simultaneous tasks, this enables the design of protocols that are *all-case* optimal: for *every* behavior of the adversary, in the execution of the all-case optimal protocol, nodes decide as fast as they do for that behavior under any other protocol. (All-case optimality does not exist for eventual consensus, as shown in [21].)

Part of our analysis centers on the problem of Δ-coordinated consensus, in which decisions must be taken at most Δ rounds apart. In the standard literature, many protocols for eventual agreement are 1-coordinated in this sense: because the network is assumed to be fully-connected, once some correct node v decides, all other correct nodes find out about v's decision in the next round; it is then safe for all correct nodes to decide v as well. For networks that are general graphs, we know of no work developing Δ-coordinated consensus protocols. As in the case of simultaneous coordination, the property of Δ-coordination has a natural counterpart in knowledge theory, called Δ-common knowledge. Very roughly speaking, if u knows that a fact is Δ-common knowledge, then within Δ rounds everyone will know that this is the case. In order to decide, a node must know that the decision value is Δ-common knowledge [15, 10]; the analysis in Section 6 is the first case in which such coordination is analyzed and nontrivial bounds are obtained as a result.

Dynamic networks. In an increasingly networked world, in which various kinds of computing devices of all sizes are connected to form large networks, understanding dynamic networks has become all the more important. It is thus not surprising that in recent years there has been a significant amount of work on dynamic network algorithms, for a large variety of different dynamic network models. Our discussion here is restricted to models similar to the one we consider in the current paper; we refer the interested reader to [19] for a discussion of a few alternative models.

Some initial results on distributed computations in completely adversarial dynamic networks were obtained in [22]. The model as studied in this paper was introduced in [18], where the complexity of basic computation and communication tasks such as determining the size of the network or exchanging information among all the nodes was studied. In [1], Avin et al. study the behavior of random walks in a very similar dynamic network model. Some basic information dissemination tasks, such as globally broadcasting a message, have also been considered in a probabilistic version of the graph model in which edges are independently formed and removed according to a simple random process; e.g., [3, 5, 6]. Another problem related to distributed coordination is clock synchronization. In [16, 17], the problem of clock synchronization was investigated in a partially-synchronous variant of the dynamic graph model we study here. Related dynamic network models were also considered in, e.g., [4, 11, 12, 13], and others.

2. MODEL AND DEFINITIONS

We now formally introduce the dynamic graph model, originally introduced in [18]. As explained above, we consider a synchronous-round based model of computation, in which the set of nodes (processes) is not known *a priori*. The set of nodes that participate in a given execution is, however, fixed for the duration of the execution, and each of them has a unique identifier (UID). The nodes share a global clock, which starts at 0 and advances in unit steps.

Communication proceeds in synchronous rounds; we think of round k (for $k = 1, 2, \ldots$) as taking place between time $k - 1$ and time k. Round k proceeds as follows: first, each node generates a single message to broadcast, based on its local state at time $k - 1$. The adversary then selects a communication graph (i.e., a set of edges) for round k, and delivers each message to the sender's neighbors in accordance with the edges it chose. The communication graph for each round is assumed to be connected, but this is

the only constraint on the adversary.[1] After messages are delivered, each node processes the messages it received, and transitions to a new state (its state at time k). Then the next round begins.

The adversary's behavior in a given execution is described by a *dynamic graph* $G = (V, E, \sigma)$, where $|V| > 2$ is a set of nodes (or processes), $E : \mathbb{N}^+ \to \binom{V}{2}$ is a *dynamic edge function* which assigns to each round r a set $E(r)$ of undirected edges over V, and σ is the *signature* of the execution. The signature is an assignment of a unique identifier (UID) and an input (or initial value) to each node in V. If nodes have access to an upper bound on the count $|V|$, this upper bound is also part of the signature σ. In particular, if σ always includes the exact number of nodes, then we say that the count is known *a priori*. We are frequently concerned only with the dynamic network topology; in this case we omit the signature σ from our notation.

A dynamic graph $G = (V, E)$ induces a *causal order*, denoted $(u, t) \leadsto_G (v, t')$, where (u, t) and (v, t') are *time-nodes* representing the states of nodes u and v at times t and t', respectively. Informally, the causal order captures the idea that a time-node (u, t) can only influence another time-node (v, t') in a given execution if there is a chain of messages starting from u at time t and ending at v at time t'. Formally, the causal order is defined in the usual way: it is the transitive and reflexive closure of the order $(u, t) \to_G (v, t + 1)$, which holds iff either $u = v$ or $\{u, v\} \in E(t + 1)$. We omit the subscript G when it is clear from the context.

At time t, node u has direct information only about the states of nodes v at time t' such that $(v, t') \leadsto (u, t)$. This motivates the next definition, which defines all the information a node can possibly acquire about an execution.

DEFINITION 1 (VIEW). *The view of node u at time t in dynamic graph G, denoted $\mathsf{view}_{(G,u,t)}$, is defined as the restriction of G to the time-nodes and edges along paths from time 0 nodes to (u, t) in G (see Fig. 1). In particular, $\mathsf{view}_{(G,u,t)}$ includes the states of all nodes v at time t' such that $(v, t') \leadsto_G (u, t)$.*

In particular, node u cannot know the input value of any node v such that $(v, 0) \not\leadsto (u, t)$. A common strategy in consensus lower bounds and impossibility proofs is to create a situation where $(v, 0) \not\leadsto (u, t)$, and then flip the input value of v, without node u being able to tell the difference (at least until time t). Thus we are often interested in the set of nodes whose input values u can potentially know at time t (see Fig. 1 for an illustration.)

DEFINITION 2 (PAST SET). *The past set of a time-node (u, t) from time t' in graph G is defined by*

$$\mathsf{past}_{(G,u,t)}(t') := \{ v \mid (v, t') \leadsto (u, t) \}.$$

If $v \in \mathsf{past}_{(G,u,t)}(0)$ (i.e., if $(v, 0) \leadsto_G (u, t)$), then we say that at time t node u has *heard from* node v. As usual, we omit the subscript G from our notation where it is clear from the context.

In static networks, the performance of distributed algorithms often depends on the *diameter* of the network. In a dynamic network, the diameter of the communication graph can change from round to round, and is not a good measure of the amount of time required for information to spread through the network (see [19] for discussion). Thus, we use a more general definition, which explicitly captures the amount of time required for any node to hear from any other node:

DEFINITION 3 (DYNAMIC DIAMETER). *We say that dynamic graph $G = (V, E)$ has a dynamic diameter of D up to time t if for all $t' \le t$ and $u, v \in V$ we have $(u, \max\{0, t' - D\}) \leadsto (v, t')$.*

---

[1] This assumption was called *1-interval connectivity* in [18].

3

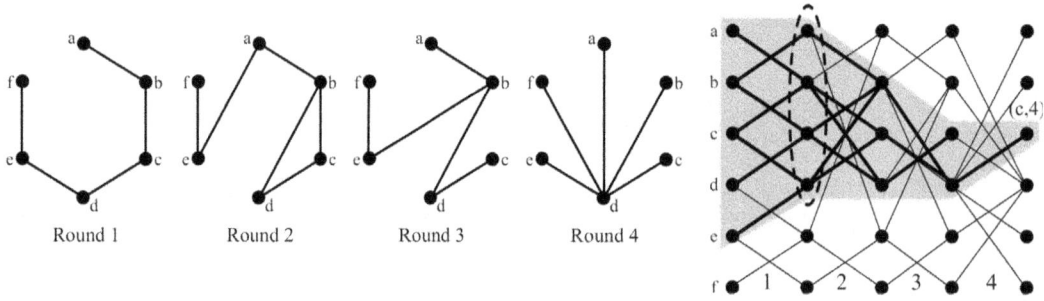

Figure 1: 4 rounds of a 6-node dynamic graph: The nodes and edges in the gray area together form $\text{view}_{(c,4)}$, the 4 nodes inside the dashed ellipse are the nodes in the set $\text{past}_{(c,4)}(1)$.

(In other words, for any time $t' \leq t$ and any node $u \in V$, we have $\text{past}_{(u,t')}(t' - D) = V$.)

In our lower bounds and knowledge analysis we assume that nodes execute a *full information protocol*, where the state of each node u at time t is exactly $\text{view}_{(u,t)}$. This state is then broadcast by u at time t, allowing u's neighbors v to combine the views they receive and compute $\text{view}_{(v,t+1)}$. Any lower bound on full information protocols extends, of course, to protocols that are not full information. Our upper bounds typically require nodes to send at least the inputs of all the nodes they have heard from, and sometimes more information as well.

2.1 Knowledge and Common Knowledge

Knowledge theory, and specifically the notion of common knowledge and its variants, is central to the study of coordinated actions. This connection has been developed and described in [8, 10, 15, 20, 21]. This literature shows, in particular, that simultaneous coordination is closely related to common knowledge. In this section we review the basic definitions, focusing on the elements needed for our analysis of dynamic networks. For a more complete exposition of knowledge theory see [10].

Given a distributed protocol P, let $\mathcal{R} = \mathcal{R}(P)$ be the set of all runs (executions) of P. A *point of* $\mathcal{R}$ is a pair (G, t), representing the global state of the execution at time t when protocol P is executed in dynamic graph G.

The fundamental notion underlying the concept of knowledge is *indistinguishablity* among points. We write $(G, t) \sim_u (G', t)$ and say that the two points are *indistinguishable to node* u, if node u's view is the same in both runs, that is, $\text{view}_{(G,u,t)} = \text{view}_{(G',u,t)}$. (Recall from Section 2 that a node's view represents all the information it can possibly acquire about the execution.) Notice that two points may be indistinguishable to u even though the runs are quite different; for example, the number of nodes may differ between the two runs, as well as the inputs and UIDs of some of the nodes. The points (G, t) in a system $\mathcal{R}$, and the individual indistinguishability relations $\sim_u$ for all nodes that appear in the runs of $\mathcal{R}$, define an undirected, edge-labelled graph that is called the *similarity graph* for $\mathcal{R}$. We are particularly interested in the connected components of the similarity graph; we denote $(G, t) \sim (G', t)$ if points (G, t) and (G', t) are in the same connected component, that is, there is a sequence $u_0, \ldots, u_k$ such that $(G, t) = (G_0, t) \sim_{u_0} (G_1, t) \sim_{u_1} \ldots \sim_{u_k} (G_{k+1}, t) = (G', t)$. (Note that for $i = 0, \ldots, k - 1$ we must have $u_i \in V_i \cap V_{i+1}$, where V_i is the node set of G_i.)

Intuitively, node u will *know* a fact φ at (G, t) exactly if φ holds at all points (G', t) such that $(G, t) \sim_u (G', t)$. In other words, a fact is known by u if u's view implies that the fact must be true. ode u knows a given fact iff the node's information implies that the fact is true. We now formalize this intuition with a minimal amount of logical notation.

Given a system $\mathcal{R} = \mathcal{R}(P)$ (that is, a collection of all runs of some protocol P), we start out with some set Φ of *basic facts* of interest; each basic fact is associated with a set of points (G, t) in which it is satisfied. We use $(\mathcal{R}, G, t) \vDash \varphi$ to denote the satisfaction of fact φ in (G, t).

Now let $K_u \varphi$ stand for the fact that *node u knows that φ holds*. We call $K_u \varphi$ a *knowledge formula*, and its satisfaction is formally defined as follows:

$$(\mathcal{R}, G, t) \vDash K_u \varphi \quad \text{iff}$$
$$(\mathcal{R}, G', t) \vDash \varphi \text{ holds for all } (G', t) \sim_u (G, t).$$

Note that φ does not have to be a basic formula; it can itself be a knowledge formula. For example, the formula $K_u K_v \psi$ asserts that "node u knows that node v knows ψ".

It is convenient to define additional knowledge operators E and C, which can also be combined and nested. The operator E stands for *everyone knows*, and it is formally defined by

$$(\mathcal{R}, G, t) \vDash E\varphi \quad \text{iff}$$
$$(\mathcal{R}, G, t) \vDash K_u \varphi \text{ holds for all } u \in V,$$

where V is the node set of G.

The operator C stands for *common knowledge*: a fact φ is common knowledge if φ holds, and everyone knows that φ holds, and everyone knows that everyone knows that φ holds, and so on. The C operator can be formally defined as a fixpoint (see [10]), but here we give a more semantic definition, in terms of the similarity graph:

$$(\mathcal{R}, G, t) \vDash C\varphi \quad \text{iff}$$
$$(\mathcal{R}, G', t) \vDash \varphi \text{ holds for all } (G', t) \sim (G, t).$$

According to this definition, a fact φ is *not* common knowledge at (G, t) whenever there is a graph (G', t) such that $(G', t) \nvDash \varphi$, and a chain $u_0, \ldots, u_k$ such that $(G, t) = (G_0, t) \sim_{u_0} (G_1, t) \sim_{u_1} \ldots \sim_{u_k} (G_{k+1}, t) = (G', t)$. Informally this means that φ is not common knowledge if some node u_0 suspects that some node u_1 suspects that... some node u_k suspects that φ might not hold. (Here "u_i suspects ψ" is to be formally understood as $\neg K_{u_i} \neg \psi$, that is, u_i does not know that ψ is not true.)

Common knowledge is known to be closely related to simultaneous coordination. For example, in simultaneous consensus, a node cannot decide v before it is common knowledge that v is the input to some node. In general, any action a that must be performed simultaneously can only be performed when it is common knowledge that a is being performed. The simultaneity of a implies that whenever a is performed *everyone knows* that a is performed; a straightforward induction on the length of paths in the similarity graph shows that a is common knowledge, that is, a is performed at all points in the connected component of the similarity graph. We review the argument relating common knowledge and simultaneous consensus in Section 6.1.

3. CAUSALITY IN DYNAMIC GRAPHS

As we saw in the previous section, at time t a node u can only know the input of another node v if $v \in \mathsf{past}_{(u,t)}(0)$, i.e., if $(v,0) \rightsquigarrow (u,t)$. Globally-sensitive functions, such as the minimum or maximum of inputs to all nodes, require a node to know when it has *heard from everyone*; node u is only guaranteed that it has the true answer at time t if $\mathsf{past}_{(u,t)}(0) = V$.[2] In this section we give an optimal condition that allows a node to test when it has heard from all nodes in the graph, even if it does not know *a priori* how many nodes there are.

The problem of determining when a node has heard from everyone was already considered in [18], and an $\Theta(n)$-round algorithm was presented. While $\Omega(n)$ is a trivial lower bound on the problem, the algorithm of [18] has the drawback of *always* requiring $\Theta(n)$ rounds, even when the network has small dynamic diameter. Here we give an algorithm which is all-case optimal, and in particular, requires $O(D)$ time in networks with dynamic diameter D.

The test is surprisingly simple; it only requires the node to keep track of its past sets from time 0 and from time 1.

LEMMA 3.1. *Node u knows at time t that $\mathsf{past}_{(u,t)}(0) = V$ iff $\mathsf{past}_{(u,t)}(0) = \mathsf{past}_{(u,t)}(1)$.*

PROOF. First, suppose that $\mathsf{past}_{(u,t)}(0) = \mathsf{past}_{(u,t)}(1)$. This implies that $\mathsf{past}_{(u,t)}(1) = V$: if $V \setminus \mathsf{past}_{(u,t)}(1)$ is non-empty, connectivity in round 1 implies that there is some edge $\{v, w\} \in E(1)$ such that $v \in \mathsf{past}_{(u,t)}(1)$ and $w \notin \mathsf{past}_{(u,t)}(1)$. But this means that $(w,0) \rightsquigarrow (v,1) \rightsquigarrow (u,t)$, and hence $w \in \mathsf{past}_{(u,t)}(0)$ and $\mathsf{past}_{(u,t)}(0) \neq \mathsf{past}_{(u,t)}(1)$. Thus, $\mathsf{past}_{(u,t)}(1) = V$, which also implies that $\mathsf{past}_{(u,t)}(0) = V$.

For the other direction, suppose $\mathsf{past}_{(u,t)}(0) \neq \mathsf{past}_{(u,t)}(1)$. This does not necessarily imply that $\mathsf{past}_{(u,t)}(0) \neq V$; however, there is some node $v \in \mathsf{past}_{(u,t)}(0) \setminus \mathsf{past}_{(u,t)}(1)$ that u has not heard from since time 0. At time 0, no communication rounds have occurred yet, so v does not yet know who its neighbors will be. The adversary can conceal arbitrarily many nodes from (u,t) by connecting them only to node v throughout the execution. Since u never hears from v from time 1 onwards, it cannot distinguish (for example, in the graph from Fig. 1, node (c) cannot tell whether node (f) is part of the network or not). Therefore node u cannot *know* it has heard from everyone (even if in fact it has). □

We remark that if $\mathsf{past}_{(u,t)}(0) \neq V$ and u has no *a priori* upper bound on the count, then u has no upper bound on $|V|$ at time t: as we saw above, any node v from which u has not heard could be "concealing" arbitrarily many other nodes that are connected to the rest of the graph only through v. Thus, if $\mathsf{past}_{(u,t)}(0) \neq V$, then at time t node u cannot know the value of a wide class of functions, including majority, minimum or maximum with unbounded inputs, and in general any function $f : (\bigcup_{n=1}^{\infty} D^n) \to D$ (where D is the data domain) satisfying the following condition: for any input assignment $I \in D^n$ there exists a size $n' > n$ and an extension $I' \in D^{n'}$ of I, such that $f(I) \neq f(I')$. For each such function,

Lemma 3.1 yields an all-case optimal algorithm: by forwarding all input values (or sufficient information about them to allow f to be computed), and stopping as soon as $\mathsf{past}_{(u,t)}(0) = \mathsf{past}_{(u,t)}(1)$, we obtain an algorithm that cannot be beaten by any other algorithm in any execution.

In fact, it turns out that knowing when $\mathsf{past}_{(u,t)}(0) = V$ is crucial not only for computing deterministic functions of the input but also for eventual consensus, as we show below.

4. CONSENSUS AND CAUSALITY

In this section we show that when nodes do not have an initial upper bound on the count that is tight to within a factor of 2 of the true count, eventual consensus is in some sense equivalent to knowing when $\mathsf{past}_{(u,t)}(0) = V$. Specifically, for either the all-zero or all-one input assignment (or both), no node can decide until it hears from all the other nodes.

For simplicity, the statement we include here applies only to *comparison-based* algorithms, in which nodes can only compare UIDs to each other (but they cannot, e.g., execute a different program based on the UID they are assigned).

For $i \in \{0, 1\}$, let $\sigma_{V,i}$ denote the signature where all nodes in V receive i as their input, and the upper bound on the count is $2n$.

THEOREM 4.1. *If nodes are given an upper bound on the count that is loose to a factor of at least 2, then for any comparison-based algorithm there is an $i \in \{0, 1\}$ such that in any execution $G = (V, E, \sigma_{V,i})$, no node u can decide at time t if $\mathsf{past}_{(G,u,t)}(0) \neq V$.*

PROOF SKETCH. Suppose not. Then there exist executions $G_i = (V_i, E_i, \sigma_i)$ for $i = 0, 1$, such that σ_i assigns to all nodes of V_i input i, the sets of UIDs used in σ_0 and σ_1 are disjoint, and there exist nodes u_i, v_i and times t_i such that u_i decides at time t_i, even though $v_i \notin \mathsf{past}_{(G_i, u_i, t_i)}(0)$ (that is, u_i does not hear from v_i before it decides).

Because u_0 and u_1 do not hear from all the nodes in their respective executions, we can "stitch together" G_0 and G_1 without these nodes noticing. Consider the execution $H = (V_0 \cup V_1, E_H, \sigma_0 \cup \sigma_1)$, where for all $s \geq 1$ we set $E_H(s) := E_0(s) \cup E_1(s) \cup \{v_0, v_1\}$. In H, nodes are provided $2n$ as an upper bound on the count. Because u_0 and u_1 do not hear from v_0 and v_1 respectively, they cannot distinguish H from G_0 and G_1 respectively, and they each decide the same as they would in the original execution. But in G_0 all nodes must decide 0, including u_0, and in G_1 all nodes must decide 1, including u_1; therefore agreement is violated in H. □

The assumption that the upper bound provided to the nodes is loose to within a factor of 2 is nearly tight: if nodes have access to an upper bound $N < 2(n-1)$, then the claim no longer holds, and nodes can halt without being causally influenced by everyone on both the all-zeroes and all-ones input assignments. One simple protocol illustrating this is the one where nodes decide on the majority input. To know that it has the true majority value v, it is sufficient for a node to hear of $\lfloor N/2 \rfloor + 1$ copies of v in the input; when $N < 2(n-1)$ we have $\lfloor N/2 \rfloor + 1 < n$, so a node can sometimes decide before it has heard from all the nodes, even in the case of the all-zeroes or the all-ones input assignment.

5. COMPUTING COMMON KNOWLEDGE

As noted in Section 2, simultaneous coordination is closely related to common knowledge: a simultaneous action can only be performed when it is common knowledge that it is being performed. To understand simultaneous consensus in dynamic networks, we characterize the time required to achieve common knowledge.

---

[2]This assumes that inputs are unbounded. If inputs are bounded from above or below, then a node knows it has the true minimum or maximum if it has heard the smallest or largest possible value (respectively). However, if this smallest or largest value is not present then the node cannot halt until it hears from everyone.

The results in this section hold for common knowledge in general; see Section 6.1 for a discussion of how they apply to simultaneous consensus. Roughly speaking, we prove the following:

- Even if n is known *a priori*, it takes $n - 1$ rounds to acquire common knowledge of any fact that is not "trivially common knowledge".[3]

- If n is not known *a priori*, then it takes n rounds to acquire common knowledge of any fact about time 0 that is not initially common knowledge (such as n itself).

For simplicity, we focus here on facts pertaining to time 0, such as the inputs to consensus. However, the result holds for other times as well; any fact about time t cannot become common knowledge until time $t + n - 1$.

Recall that a fact is common knowledge in (G, t) iff it holds at all points $(H, t) \sim (G, t)$ in the similarity component of (G, t). To prove the result above, we show that we can change any aspect of the dynamic graph G at times $0, \dots, n - 2$ (and in particular, in rounds $1, \dots, n - 2$) while still remaining inside the similarity component of (G, t). Formally, we show the following.

THEOREM 5.1. *For every full-information protocol and all dynamic graphs G and H,*

1. $(G, t) \sim (H, t)$ *for all $t \leq n - 2$; and*

2. *If n is not known a priori then in addition, $(G, n - 1) \sim (H, n - 1)$.*

PROOF SKETCH. The main concept in the proof is *hiding*: given a set $X \subseteq V$, times $t' \leq t$ and a node $u \in V$, we say that X at time t' can be hidden from (u, t) if there is a point $(G', t) \sim (G, t)$ such that $\text{past}_{(G', u, t)}(t') \cap X = \varnothing$. Hiding X at time t' means that we move inside the similarity component of (G, t) to a point $(G', t) \sim (G, t)$ where node u knows nothing about the states of the nodes in X from time t' onwards. Once we have done this, we can add or remove any edges adjacent only to nodes in X in round t', while still remaining in the similarity component of (G, t), because u does not learn of these changes by time t.

To prove the theorem, we show by induction on $k \leq n - 2$ that for any set X of size at most $n - k - 1$ and for any node $u \notin X$, set X at time $t - k$ can be hidden from (u, t), without altering any round preceding time $t - k - 1$. We hide sets of *decreasing size* as we go back in time; essentially, we "use up" one node for each round we go back. The case where $k = n - 2$ yields the theorem, since it shows that we can hide any single node at time $t - (n - 2)$, and then change its state. In particular, we can hide any node at time 0 from any other node at time $n - 2$, so the state of no node is common knowledge at time $n - 2$. Moreover, if n is not known *a priori*, then we can hide any node w at time 1 from some node $u \neq w$ at time $n - 1$ and proceed to add more nodes to the network, as in the proof of Lemma 3.1. By adding more nodes we can increase the dynamic diameter of the network to more than $n - 1$, which again shows that the state of no node is common knowledge (nor is the size of the network common knowledge).

To hide a set X at time $t - k$ we must remove all edges from nodes in X to node u and to other nodes that u is causally influenced by in rounds $t - k + 1, t - k + 2, \dots, t$. ("Removing" here means that we move to a point $(G', t) \sim (G, t)$ where these edges do not exist, by first hiding both endpoints of the edge at time $t - k + 1$ from some node at time t.) To ensure that connectivity is preserved,

---

[3]For example, the current round number is trivially common knowledge.

before we remove edges we choose some node $w \notin X \cup \{u\}$ and add edges between w and all nodes in the graph. Then we remove all edges from nodes in X to all nodes except $X \cup \{w\}$. In the resulting graph, only nodes in $X \cup \{w\}$ hear from nodes in X in round $t - k + 1$. Our final step is to use the induction hypothesis to hide $X \cup \{w\}$ at time $t - k + 1$ from (u, t), so that we have $\text{past}_{(u, t)}(t - k) \cap X = \varnothing$. □

An immediate consequence of Theorem 5.1 is that all initial values become common knowledge precisely at time $n - 1$ if n is known *a priori*. Thus, a simultaneous consensus protocol that is all-case optimal can be designed. It decides at time $n - 1$ in all executions, and no protocol for this task can ever decide earlier. In fact, Theorem 5.1 implies that simultaneously acting based on any nontrivial function of the initial values can be done at time $n - 1$ (when n is known), and this is all-case optimal.

We also note that Theorem 5.1 implies that solving simultaneous consensus is as hard as computing an upper bound on the count, because a simultaneous consensus protocol can only decide at time t if $t \geq n$ represents an upper bound on the count.

6. Δ-COORDINATED CONSENSUS

Since simultaneous consensus is expensive and requires $n - 1$ rounds even in very well-behaved executions, it is interesting to consider a trade-off between the performance of the consensus algorithm and the degree of coordination it achieves. To this end we consider the following problem:

DEFINITION 4 (Δ-COORDINATED CONSENSUS). *A protocol solves Δ-coordinated consensus if it solves consensus, and in addition, all nodes decide no later than Δ rounds after the first node decides.*

In the sequel we assume, unless stated otherwise, that the count is initially known. (An upper bound on the count can be used instead, or one can combine the algorithm in this section with the criterion from Section 3.)

One might expect that Δ-coordinated consensus should not be much easier than simultaneous consensus. For example, when $\Delta = 1$, we require all nodes to decide within one round of each other; it seems that if we can achieve this, then simultaneous coordination can be achieved at not much extra cost (a cost of Δ additional rounds, perhaps). Indeed, in the worst case this expectation is borne out by the following theorem.

THEOREM 6.1. *For any Δ-coordinated consensus algorithm, there exists an execution in which no node decides before round $n - \Delta - 1$, even when n is known a priori.*

PROOF. Suppose that there exists a Δ-coordinated consensus algorithm $\mathcal{A}$, such that in every execution some node decides before time $R < n - \Delta - 1$. Then in $\mathcal{A}$, *all* nodes decide no later than time $R + \Delta < n - 1$ in every execution. We can obtain an algorithm for simultaneous consensus in fewer than $n - 1$ rounds by simply having each node run $\mathcal{A}$ and output $\mathcal{A}$'s decision value at time $R + \Delta < n - 1$, contradicting the lower bound from Section 5. □

This result shows the existence of only one "bad" execution where no node can decide until time $n - \Delta - 1$. Given the general similarity between Δ-coordinated consensus and simultaneous consensus, one might expect that a Δ-coordinated consensus protocol would *never* be able to decide before time $n - \Delta - 1$ (just as simultaneous consensus can never decide before time $n - 1$). However, we now show that even in 1-coordinated consensus, nodes can sometimes decide significantly earlier than time $n - \Delta - 1$. Consider the following protocol.

Clear-Majority Protocol. Fix some integer $k_{\max}$, and for each $k = 1, \ldots, k_{\max}$, let $t_k := n - k \cdot \Delta - 1$. In each round the nodes forward the set of all node UIDs they have heard from so far, along with the input to each node. At time t_k, an undecided node decides v iff it has heard of at least $\lfloor n/2 \rfloor + 1 + \binom{k}{2}\Delta$ inputs equal to v. Finally, at time $n - 1$, all the nodes know all the inputs; at this point any undecided node decides on the majority input (breaking ties in some consistent way if there is no majority).

LEMMA 6.2. *The clear-majority protocol solves Δ-coordinated consensus. Furthermore, when the fraction of identical inputs is at least $(1/2 + \epsilon)n$ for some constant ϵ, and if $\Delta \leq (\epsilon n - 1)/2$, all nodes can decide after $n - \Theta(\sqrt{n\Delta})$ rounds.*

PROOF. Agreement and validity follow immediately from the fact that nodes always decide on the majority value (or, if there is no majority value, all nodes reach time $n - 1$ and decide in some consistent way). To show that the protocol is Δ-coordinated, suppose that in some execution, the earliest node u decides on value v at time t_k. We must show that all nodes decide no later than time $t_k + \Delta = t_{k-1}$.

Because the communication graph in every round is connected, for all $s \leq n - 1$, at time $n - s - 1$ in the execution each node has heard all but at most s of the inputs. In particular, by time $t_{k-1} = n - (k - 1)\Delta - 1$ each node has heard all but $(k - 1)\Delta$ of the inputs. Since u decides v at time t_k, the input assignment contains at least $\lfloor n/2 \rfloor + 1 + \binom{k}{2}\Delta$ values equal to v, and hence by time t_{k-1} each node hears at least $\lfloor n/2 \rfloor + 1 + \binom{k}{2}\Delta - (k - 1)\Delta = \lfloor n/2 \rfloor + 1 + \binom{k-1}{2}\Delta$ inputs equal to v. Thus, all nodes that do not decide at time t_k decide v at time $t_{k-1} = t_k + \Delta$, as required.

Now suppose that for some constant ϵ, the input assignment contains at least $(1/2 + \epsilon)n$ copies of some value v. By time $t_k = n - k \cdot \Delta - 1$ each node hears all but $k \cdot \Delta$ of the input values, i.e., at least $(1/2 + \epsilon)n - k \cdot \Delta$ copies of v. If $\Delta \leq (2\epsilon n - 1)/4$, we set $k_{\max} = \lfloor \sqrt{(2\epsilon n - 1)/\Delta} - 1 \rfloor$, and then simple algebra shows that $(1/2 + \epsilon)n - k_{\max} \cdot \Delta \geq \binom{k_{\max}}{2} + \lfloor n/2 \rfloor + 1$; thus, by time $t_{k_{\max}}$, each node hears sufficiently many copies of v to decide. For this value of $k_{\max}$ we have $t_{k_{\max}} = n - \Theta(\sqrt{n\Delta})$. $\qquad\square$

The clear-majority protocol can be viewed as an instance of a more general scheme, in which nodes decide as soon as they know that everyone else will decide the same value within Δ rounds. Using this abstract scheme, any eventual consensus algorithm can be transformed into a Δ-coordinated consensus protocol as follows. Let "$\mathcal{A} = v$" stand for the formula that asserts that (G, t) is v-valent with respect to algorithm $\mathcal{A}$ (that is, in any possible extension of the first t rounds of G, all nodes decide v). Let $K_u^{@t}\varphi$ denote the formula that means "node u knows that at time t fact φ will hold", and let $E^{@t}\varphi := \bigwedge_{u \in V} K_u^{@t}\varphi$. Now we can state the protocol:

The Δ-Ladder. Given an eventual consensus algorithm $\mathcal{A}$ in which all nodes decide no later than round $n - 1$, we first transform $\mathcal{A}$ into a full-information algorithm $\mathcal{A}'$. Nodes execute $\mathcal{A}'$, but do not immediately output its decisions. Instead, each undecided node u evaluates the following decision rules at each decision point $t_k = n - \Delta \cdot k - 1$ (the rules are given here in reverse order w.r.t. the time each rule is evaluated):

- Decide v at time $n - 1$ if $(\mathcal{R}(\mathcal{A}'), G, n - 1) \models K_u (\mathcal{A}' = v)$, that is, if it is known that the run is v-valent for $\mathcal{A}'$.

- Decide v at time $n - \Delta - 1$ if
$$(\mathcal{R}(\mathcal{A}'), G, n - \Delta - 1) \models K_u E^{@(n-1)} (\mathcal{A}' = v),$$

that is, if it is known that everyone will decide v no later than time $n - 1$.

- Decide v at time $n - 2\Delta - 1$ if
$$(\mathcal{R}(\mathcal{A}'), G, n - 2\Delta - 1) \models K_u E^{@(n-\Delta-1)} E^{@(n-1)} (\mathcal{A}' = v),$$

that is, if it is known that everyone will know at time $n - \Delta - 1$ that everyone will decide v no later than time $n - 1$.

$\ldots$

In general, at time $n - k \cdot \Delta - 1$, a node decides v if it has not decided already and
$$(\mathcal{R}(\mathcal{A}'), G, n - k \cdot \Delta - 1) \models K_u E^{@(n-(k-1)\Delta-1)} \ldots$$
$$E^{@(n-\Delta-1)} E^{@(n-1)} (\mathcal{A}' = v).$$

It is easy to see that any instantiation of this scheme satisfies Δ-coordinated consensus; this is in some sense the optimal strategy. However, it requires nodes to keep track of information about the full dynamic graph, and to evaluate complex knowledge criteria; the clear-majority protocol uses less precise rules, but they are simpler and easier to evaluate. In general, any approximation for the knowledge criteria above can be used, as long as the same approximation is applied consistently at each decision point $n - k \cdot \Delta - 1$.

Approximate Δ-Ladder. Let $\mathcal{A}$ be an eventual consensus algorithm with round complexity at most $n - 1$, let $k_{\max} \in \mathbb{N}$, and fix a collection $\left\{ \Phi_u^{k,v} \right\}_{u \in V, k \in [k_{\max}], v \in \{0,1\}}$ of *local* knowledge formulas, such that u can evaluate the satisfaction of $\Phi_u^{k,v}$ based on its local state. These formulas represent the decision rules, and they must satisfy:

(a) **Consistency:** for all u,
$$\mathcal{R}(\mathcal{A}) \models \Phi_u^{0,0} \to (\mathcal{A} = 0) \text{ and } \mathcal{R}(\mathcal{A}) \models \Phi_u^{0,1} \to (\mathcal{A} = 1).$$

(b) **Timeliness:** for all executions G,
$$(\mathcal{R}(\mathcal{A}), G, n - 1) \models \Phi_u^{0,0} \vee \Phi_u^{0,1}.$$

(c) **Coordination:** for all $1 \leq k \leq k_{\max}$ and $v \in \{0,1\}$, if $(\mathcal{R}(\mathcal{A}), G, n - k \cdot \Delta - 1) \models K_u \Phi_u^{k,v}$, then
$$(\mathcal{R}(\mathcal{A}), G, n - (k-1)\Delta - 1) \models \bigwedge_{w \in V} K_w \Phi_w^{k-1,v}.$$

Then a protocol for Δ-coordinated consensus is given by the following: the nodes simulate algorithm $\mathcal{A}$ with their local inputs, but do not output $\mathcal{A}$'s decisions immediately. Instead, for each $k = k_{\max}, \ldots, 1$, a node u (which has not decided already) decides v at time $n - k \cdot \Delta - 1$ if $(\mathcal{R}, n - k \cdot \Delta - 1) \models K_u \Phi_u^{k,v}$.

LEMMA 6.3. *Any instantiation of the Δ-ladder protocol solves Δ-coordinated consensus.*

Finally, let us give another instantiation of the approximate Δ-ladder, which decides quickly in graphs where all nodes hear from everyone quickly.

Dynamic Diameter-Based Protocol. Let $f : \{0,1\}^n \to \{0,1\}$ be any function that satisfies $f(0^n) = 0$ and $f(1^n) = 1$. Nodes always forward their full view of the execution so far. At time $n - k \cdot \Delta - 1$, a node decides $f(\bar{x})$ if it knows that the input assignment is $\bar{x}$, and it knows that there exists some D such that the dynamic graph had a dynamic diameter of at most D until time $(k-1)D$ (where $(k-1)D \leq n - k \cdot \Delta - 1$).

To see that this decision rule is consistent with the requirements, suppose that the rule for deciding at time $n - k \cdot \Delta - 1$ holds at node u, i.e., u knows the input assignment and dynamic diameter of the graph is at most D until time $(k-1)D$. If $k \geq 2$, then for any two nodes w, w' we have $(w, (k-2)D) \rightsquigarrow (w', (k-1)D)$; consequently at time $(k-1)D$, all nodes know that the dynamic graph had diameter at most D up to time $(k-2)D$ and all nodes know the input assignment. When time $n - (k-1)\Delta - 1$ arrives the decision rule for $k-1$ is satisfied. If $k = 1$, then the decision rule for time $n - (k-1)\Delta - 1 = n-1$ holds trivially, because it only requires nodes to know the input assignment.

The value we choose for $k_{\max}$ should satisfy $(k_{\max} - 1)D < n - k_{\max} \cdot \Delta - 1$, otherwise the decision rule for time $t_{k_{\max}}$ would be unsatisfiable. If we choose $k_{\max} \geq \lfloor n/(D+\Delta) \rfloor$, nodes can stop as early as time $n - k_{\max} \cdot \Delta - 1 < n(1 - \Delta/(D+\Delta)) + \Delta = nD/(D+\Delta) + \Delta$. For example, if the communication graph is always a clique, then the running time is slashed by a factor of Δ. Note that the algorithm does not commit in advance to some diameter D; nodes always evaluate the stopping condition with respect to all D, and check if some bound D satisfies the requirement.

6.1 Lower Bounds

In the following, we prove two lower bounds that complement the upper bounds from the previous section.

In Section 5 we proved a lower bound on common knowledge. Viewed through the lens of simultaneous consensus, we can interpret our strategy as follows: to show that simultaneous consensus cannot decide in (G, t), we showed that there exist two points (G_0, t) and (G_1, t) such that

(a) In G_0 the input to all nodes is 0, and in G_1 the input to all nodes in 1; and

(b) $(G_0, t) \sim (G, t) \sim (G_1, t)$.

To briefly review the argument, suppose that some node decides v in (G, t). Consider the path between (G, t) and (G_{1-v}, t) in the similarity graph; denote this path by

$$(G, t) = (H_0, t) \sim_{u_1} (H_1, t) \sim_{u_2} \ldots \sim_{u_\ell} (H_\ell, t) = (G_{1-v}, t).$$

We show that some node decides v in (G_{1-v}, t), violating validity, by employing the following argument at each step $i = 1, \ldots, \ell$ along the path:

1. Some node w decides v in (H_i, t); therefore,
2. From simultaneity and agreement, node u_i decides v in (H_i, t); therefore,
3. Node u_i also decides v in (H_{i+1}, t), because it cannot distinguish (H_{i+1}, t) from (H_i, t).

This argument hinges on simultaneity, and we cannot employ it as-is to prove lower bounds on Δ-coordinated consensus. However, Δ-coordination allows us to make the following weaker argument:

1. Some node w decides v in (H_i, t); therefore,
2. **From Δ-coordination and agreement, node u_i decides v in $(H_i, t + \Delta)$;**[4] therefore,
3. If $(H_i, t + \Delta) \sim_{u_i} (H_{i+1}, t + \Delta)$, node u_i also decides v in $(H_{i+1}, t + \Delta)$, because it cannot distinguish $(H_{i+1}, t + \Delta)$ from $(H_i, t + \Delta)$.

The key difference is that unlike before, now we have to pay for each step we take in the similarity graph; our lower bound is weakened by Δ rounds at each step, as we move forward in time.

---

[4]Technically, there exists some $t' \leq t + \Delta$ such that u_i decides v in (H_i, t'). The essential property is that by time $t + \Delta$ node u_i has already decided v in H_i.

This reasoning, applied repeatedly, yields the following lemma.

LEMMA 6.4. *Let G, G_0, G_1 be runs, where in G_0 and G_1 all nodes receive input 0 and 1, respectively. Assume that for some $\ell \geq 1$ and time t, the following two sequences of steps (i.e., edges) exist in the similarity graph:*

$$(G, t + \Delta) \sim_{u_1} (H_1, t + \Delta),$$
$$(H_1, t + 2\Delta) \sim_{u_2} (H_2, t + 2\Delta),$$
$$\ldots$$
$$(H_{\ell-1}, t + \ell\Delta) \sim_{u_\ell} (G_0, t + \ell\Delta)$$

and

$$(G, t + \Delta) \sim_{u_1'} (H_1', t + \Delta),$$
$$(H_1', t + 2\Delta) \sim_{u_2'} (H_2', t + 2\Delta),$$
$$\ldots$$
$$(H_{\ell-1}', t + \ell\Delta) \sim_{u_\ell'} (G_1, t + \ell\Delta);$$

Then in any Δ-coordinated consensus algorithm, no node can decide by time t in G.

PROOF SKETCH. As outlined above, if some node decides v in (G, t), we show by induction on the path length (ℓ) that some node decides v in $(G_{1-v}, t + \ell\Delta)$, violating validity. $\square$

The condition of Lemma 6.4 involves many different times, $t + \Delta, t + 2\Delta, \ldots, t + \ell\Delta$. A simpler condition that implies the lemma can be obtained by replacing all times with the last time, $t + \ell\Delta$ (to still obtain a lower bound for time t). We show the existence of the following two walks in the similarity graph:

$$(G, t + \ell\Delta) = (H_0, t + \ell\Delta) \sim_{u_1} (H_1, t + \ell\Delta) \sim_{u_2} \ldots$$
$$\sim_{u_\ell} (H_\ell, t + \ell\Delta) = (G_0, t + \ell\Delta), \text{ and}$$
$$(G, t + \ell\Delta) = (H_0', t + \ell\Delta) \sim_{u_1'} (H_1', t + \ell\Delta) \sim_{u_2'} \ldots$$
$$\sim_{u_\ell'} (H_\ell', t + \ell\Delta) = (G_1, t + \ell\Delta).$$

This only strengthens the condition, since $(G, t) \sim_u (G', t)$ implies $(G, t') \sim_u (G', t')$ for all $t' \leq t$. Thus the existence of these walks is sufficient to apply Lemma 6.4.

When a full-information protocol is used, all information about the input becomes common knowledge at time $n - 1$; therefore we cannot hope to have $t + \ell\Delta > n - 1$ when we apply (the simplified version of) Lemma 6.4. In order to maximize t and obtain the strongest possible lower bound, we must minimize ℓ; that is, we must find short walks in the similarity graph. Since our ultimate goal is to span between G and two runs where the inputs are 0 and 1 (respectively), the walk should allow us to flip the inputs of as many nodes as possible in each step.

Lower bound for static paths. We now apply the strategy described above to obtain an $n - O(\Delta^{0.28} n^{0.72})$ lower bound in static paths of length n. A path is a natural candidate for proving strong lower bounds: we can flip the inputs of nodes at one end of the path, and the nodes at the other end do not find out for a long time. However, to use Lemma 6.4, we must be able to flip the inputs of *all* the nodes in the network, not just the nodes at the ends of the path. Thus, we start with some path $u_1, \ldots, u_n$, and flip the inputs in some prefix $u_1, \ldots, u_\beta$ of the path; node u_n cannot distinguish the two cases until time roughly $n - \beta$. Then we find a short walk in the similarity graph from our original path $u_1, \ldots, u_n$ to a new path, $u_{\beta+1}, \ldots, u_{n+\beta}$ (i.e., we preserve the order of nodes, but we rotate the path so that now it starts at $u_{\beta+1}$;

8

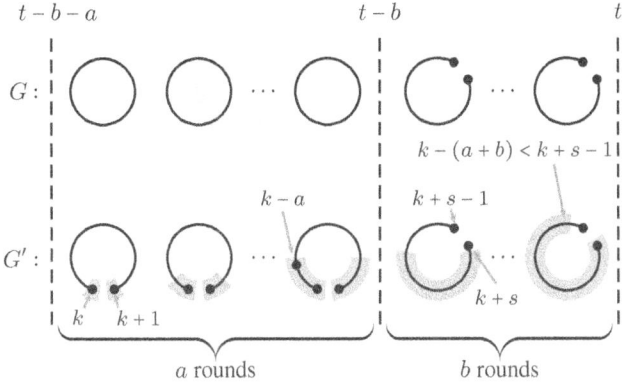

Figure 2: Illustration of Lemma 6.5. The shaded arcs indicate which nodes can distinguish G from G'. Switching from P_k to P_{k+s} "cuts off" the spread of information about the missing edge, and prevents it from reaching node $k + s - 1$.

note that here and in the sequel, node indices are given modulo n. The parameter β will be fixed later). Now we can flip the inputs of nodes $u_{\beta+1}, \ldots, u_{2\beta}$; node $u_\beta = u_{n+\beta}$, located at the end of the new path, cannot distinguish until time roughly $n - \beta$. We require at most $\lceil n/\beta \rceil$ such steps to flip any input assignment into either the all-zero or the all-one input assignment.

The strength of the lower bound is determined by the length of the walk from one path, $u_{i \cdot \beta + 1}, \ldots, u_{n + i \cdot \beta}$, to the next path, $u_{(i+1) \cdot \beta + 1}, \ldots, u_{n+(i+1) \cdot \beta}$. To construct the walk we use an intricate recursion. During the walk between paths we do not change any input values; in the sequel we focus on the dynamic graph and assume some fixed signature for all the executions we consider.

Let $P_k := u_{k+1}, \ldots, u_{n+k}$ denote the path starting at node u_{k+1}, and let C denote the cycle $u_1, \ldots, u_n, u_1$. It is convenient to use the cycle C to bridge between paths: we cannot remove any edge of a path without violating connectivity, but a cycle is 2-vertex connected, so we can drop any of its edges. Intuitively, to move from a path P_k to a different path P_{k+s} (for $s \neq 0$), we first close P_k to form the cycle C, then drop edge $\{v_{k+s}, v_{k+s+1}\}$ to obtain P_{k+s}. The following lemma shows how we can move from a path to the cycle while ensuring that some node cannot distinguish the two executions; it represents an intermediate step which will be used later to move between two paths.

LEMMA 6.5. *Let* $k \in \{0, \ldots, n-1\}$, $s \in \mathbb{Z}$, *and let* $0 \leq a \leq |s|$ *and* $b \geq 0$ *satisfy* $a + b < n - s$. *Fix a time* $b < t \leq n - 1$. *Consider two graphs* G, G' *that agree on the first* $\max\{0, t - b - a\}$ *rounds, such that*

- *In rounds* $r \in [t - b - a + 1, t - b]$, $G(r) = C$ *and* $G'(r) = P_k$;
- *In rounds* $r \in [t - b + 1, t]$, $G(r) = G'(r) = P_{k+s}$.

Then $(G, t) \sim_{u_{k+s-1}} (G', t)$.

PROOF SKETCH. Assume that $s \geq 0$ (the other case is symmetric). At each time $r = (t - b - a + 1) + i$ for $i = 1, \ldots, a$, only nodes $u_{k-i}, \ldots, u_{k+i+1}$ might have learned of the missing edge, $\{u_k, u_{k+1}\}$. Thus, at time $t - b$, only nodes $u_{k-a}, \ldots, u_{k+a+1}$ can distinguish G from G'. Next, both graphs switch to P_{k+s} where the distance between any node $u_{k-a}, \ldots, u_{k+a+1}$ and node $u_{k+s-1} = u_{k-(n-s+1)}$ is at least $n - s - a$. Since $b < n - s - a$, node u_{k+s-1} does not learn of the difference by time t (see Fig. 2). □

Next, we show how to use Lemma 6.5 to recursively transform a suffix of the execution from one path P_k to a different path P_{k+s}.

(Our eventual goal is to transform the entire execution from one path to another.) Let $d((G, t), (G', t))$ denote the distance between (G, t) and (G', t) in the similarity graph.

LEMMA 6.6. *Fix a time* $0 \leq t \leq n - 1$ *and a value* $1 \leq \beta \leq n - 1$. *Let* G, G' *be dynamic graphs that agree up to time* $t - (n - 1 - \beta)$, *such that in rounds* $r \in [t - (n - 1 - \beta) + 1, t]$, $G(r) = P_k$ *and* $G'(r) = P_{k'}$ *(for some* k, k'). *Then* $d((G, t), (G', t)) \leq 9(n/\beta)^{\log_2 3}$.

PROOF SKETCH. Define $\ell_\beta := \lceil \log_2(n/\beta) \rceil$. We show by induction on ℓ_β that $d((G, t), (G', t)) \leq 3^{\ell_\beta + 1} - 1$. The claim then follows, because

$$3^{\ell_\beta + 1} - 1 \leq 3^{\log_2(n/\beta) + 2} = 9\left(\frac{n}{\beta}\right)^{\log_2 3}.$$

Let us denote $d_\beta := 3^{\ell_\beta} + 1$. Note that we are transforming the suffix $[t - (n - 1 - \beta) + 1, t]$ of the execution; hence, smaller values of β (or equivalently, larger values of ℓ_β) are "harder" because they require us to transform a longer suffix.

The induction base is straightforward; it is omitted here. For the step we use Lemma 6.5. Set $a = \beta$ and $b = n - 1 - 2\beta$. Given static graphs H_1, H_2, let $G[H_1, H_2]$ be the dynamic graph defined by

$$G[H_1, H_2](r) := \begin{cases} G(r) & r \leq t - (n - 1 - \beta), \\ H_1 & t - (n - 1 - \beta) < r \leq t - b, \\ H_2 & t - b < r \leq t. \end{cases}$$

Since $b = n - 1 - 2\beta$ and $\ell_{2\beta} = \ell_\beta - 1$, the induction hypothesis shows that for any graph H and for any two paths $P_q, P_{q'}$ we have $d((G[H, P_q], t), (G[H, P_{q'}], t)) \leq d(2\beta)$. Further, Lemma 6.5 shows that $d((G[P_q, P_{q+\beta}], t), (G[C, P_{q+\beta}], t)) = 1$ for any q (because these points are indistinguishable to some node). Thus, we construct the following walk (see Fig. 3):

$$(G, t) = (G[P_k, P_k], t) \overset{d(2\beta)}{\underset{\text{I.H.}}{\to}} (G[P_k, P_{k+\beta}], t) \overset{1}{\underset{\text{Lem. 6.5}}{\to}}$$

$$(G[C, P_{k+\beta}], t) \overset{d(2\beta)}{\underset{\text{I.H.}}{\to}} (G[C, P_{k'+\beta}], t) \overset{1}{\underset{\text{Lem. 6.5}}{\to}}$$

$$(G[P_{k'}, P_{k'+\beta}], t) \overset{d(2\beta)}{\underset{\text{I.H.}}{\to}} (G[P_{k'}, P_{k'}], t) = (G', t).$$

The length of the walk is at most $3d(2\beta) + 2 = 3(3^{\ell_\beta} - 1) + 2 = 3^{\ell_\beta + 1} - 1$. □

THEOREM 6.7. *In the static line graph, for any input assignment, no* Δ-*coordinated consensus algorithm can decide by time* $n - O(\Delta^{\frac{1}{2 + \log_2 3}} n^{1 - \frac{1}{2 + \log_2 3}}) \approx n - O(\Delta^{0.28} n^{0.72})$.

PROOF SKETCH. Let σ be any signature, and let σ_0, σ_1 be the corresponding signatures where all nodes receive input 0 or 1, respectively. Let $P^{k,\tau}$ denote the dynamic graph defined by $P^{k,\tau}(r) = P_k$ for all r, using signature $\tau \in \{\sigma, \sigma_0, \sigma_1\}$. Also set $t := n - 2\beta - 1$.

For $v \in \{0, 1\}$, we span between $(P^{1,\sigma}, t)$ and $(P^{n-\beta,\sigma_v}, t)$ by repeating the following steps $O(n/\beta)$ times:

1. Flip the inputs of the leftmost β nodes on the path to v in one move (the endpoint of the line cannot distinguish),

2. Applying Lemma 6.6, move from our current point $(P^{k,\tau}, t)$ to $(P^{k+\beta}, t)$ in $O((n/\beta)^{\log_2 e})$ steps.

The total length of the walk is $\ell = O((n/\beta) \cdot (n/\beta)^{\log_2 e}) = O((n/\beta)^{1 + \log_2 3})$. Now, fix β such that $\beta \geq c \cdot \Delta \cdot (n/\beta)^{1 + \log_2 e}$. For this setting of the parameters, Lemma 6.4 shows that no node decides by time $t - \ell\Delta = n - O(\Delta^{\frac{1}{2 + \log_2 3}} n^{1 - \frac{1}{2 + \log_2 3}})$. □

9

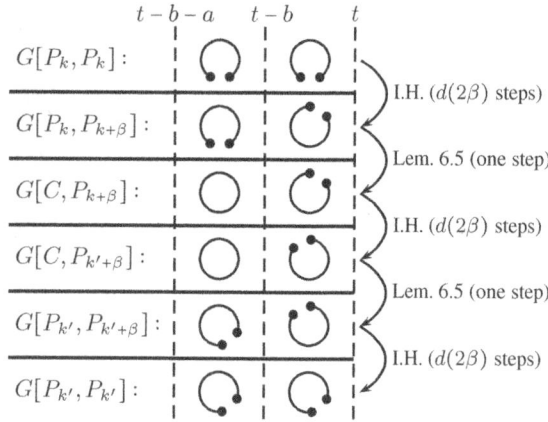

Figure 3: The recursion from Lemma 6.6. The two graphs shown for each step represent the communication graph for rounds $t - b - a, \ldots, t - b$ and for rounds $t - b + 1, \ldots, t$.

The final theorem states that the dynamic diameter-based protocol is asymptotically optimal for diameters $D = O(\Delta)$, even for static executions. The proof uses Lemma 6.4 with $t + \ell\Delta \approx n/2$, that is, we construct a short walk in the indistinguishability graph for time roughly $n/2$ (recall that t is the time for which we wish to show the lower bound, and ℓ is the length of the walk we construct in the similarity graph). We start with an execution whose first t rounds are a static graph with diameter D, and the remaining $n/2 - t$ are a static path. This $(n/2 - t)$-round suffix means that the nodes at the end of the path require roughly n rounds to learn what the communication graph was in each of the first $n/2 - t$ rounds. In $\ell = O(t/D)$ steps in the similarity graph, we move from this execution to a static path. Because we need only maintain indistinguishability until time roughly $n/2$, once we have reached the static path we can flip the inputs of nodes $1, \ldots, n/2$ on the path in one step; node n does not find out by time $n/2$. By repeating this process twice we can flip all the inputs. Since we have $\ell = O(t/D)$ and we are constrained by $t + \ell\Delta \leq n/2$ (as indistinguishability is only maintained until time $n/2$), we can apply Lemma 6.4 to obtain the lower bound at time $t = \Omega(nD/\Delta)$.

THEOREM 6.8. *For every $D = O(\Delta)$, there is a static graph $H = (V, E_H)$ with diameter at most D such that for every Δ-coordinated consensus algorithm, every input σ and every dynamic graph $G = (V, E, \sigma)$ with $E(r) = E_H$ for all rounds r until the first node decides, no node can decide at a time before $\Omega(nD/\Delta)$.*

7. REFERENCES

[1] C. Avin, M. Koucky, and Z. Lotker. How to explore a fast-changing world (cover time of a simple random walk on evloving graphs). In *Proc. 35th Coll. on Automata, Lang. and Programming (ICALP)*, pages 121–132, 2008.

[2] A. Bar-Noy and D. Dolev. Consensus algorithms with one-bit messages. *Distributed Computing*, 4:105–110, 1991.

[3] H. Baumann, P. Crescenzi, and P. Fraigniaud. Parsimonious flooding in dynamic graphs. In *Proc. 28th Symp. on Principles of Distributed Computing (PODC)*, pages 260–269, 2009.

[4] A. Casteigts, P. Flocchini, W. Quattrociocchi, and N. Santoro. Time-varying graphs and dynamic networks. *CoRR*, abs/1012.0009, 2010.

[5] A. Clementi, C. Macci, A. Monti, F. Pasquale, and R. Silvestri. Flooding time in edge-markovian dynamic graphs. In *Proc. 27th Symp. on Principles of Distributed Computing (PODC)*, pages 213–222, 2008.

[6] A. E. F. Clementi, A. Monti, F. Pasquale, and R. Silvestri. Broadcasting in dynamic radio networks. *J. Comput. Syst. Sci.*, 75(4):213–230, 2009.

[7] D. Dolev, C. Dwork, O. Waarts, and M. Yung. Perfectly secure message transmission. *J. ACM*, 40(1):17–47, 1993.

[8] C. Dwork and Y. Moses. Knowledge and common knowledge in a Byzantine environment: crash failures. *Information and Computation*, 88(2):156–186, 1990.

[9] C. Dwork, D. Peleg, N. N Pippenger, and E. Upfal. Fault tolerance in networks of bounded degree. In *Proc. 8th Symp. on Theory of Computing (STOC)*, pages 370–379, 1986.

[10] R. Fagin, J. Y. Halpern, Y. Moses, and M. Y. Vardi. *Reasoning about Knowledge*. MIT Press, Cambridge, MA, 2003.

[11] A. Fernández Anta, A. Milani, M. A. Mosteiro, and S. Zaks. Opportunistic information dissemination in mobile ad-hoc networks. In *Proc. 24th Conference on Distributed Computing (DISC)*, pages 374–388, 2010.

[12] A. Ferreira. Building a reference combinatorial model for MANETs. *IEEE Network Magazine*, 18(5):24–29, 2004.

[13] A. Ferreira, A. Goldman, and J. Monteiro. Performance evaluation of routing protocols for MANETs with known connectivity patterns using evolving graphs. *Wireless Networks*, 16(3):627–640, 2010.

[14] J. A. Garay and R. Ostrovsky. Almost-everywhere secure computation. In *Proc. 27th EUROCRYPT*, pages 307–323, 2008.

[15] J. Y. Halpern and Y. Moses. Knowledge and common knowledge in a distributed environment. *J. ACM*, 37(3):549–587, 1990.

[16] F. Kuhn, C. Lenzen, T. Locher, and R. Oshman. Optimal gradient clock synchronization in dynamic networks. In *Proc. 29th Symp. on Principles of Distributed Computing (PODC)*, pages 430–439, 2010.

[17] F. Kuhn, T. Locher, and R. Oshman. Gradient clock synchronization in dynamic networks. In *Proc. 21st Symp. Paralellism in Algorithms and Architectures (SPAA)*, pages 270–279, 2009.

[18] F. Kuhn, N. Lynch, and R. Oshman. Distributed computation in dynamic networks. In *Proc. 42nd Symp. on Theory of Computing (STOC)*, pages 513–522, 2010.

[19] F. Kuhn and R. Oshman. Dynamic networks: models and algorithms. *SIGACT News*, 42:82–96, March 2011.

[20] T. Mizrahi and Y. Moses. Continuous consensus via common knowledge. *Distributed Computing*, 20(5):305–321, 2008.

[21] Y. Moses and M. R. Tuttle. Programming simultaneous actions using common knowledge. *Algorithmica*, 3:121–169, 1988.

[22] R. O'Dell and R. Wattenhofer. Information dissemination in highly dynamic graphs. In *Proc. 9th Joint Workshop on Foundations of Mobile Computing (DIALM-POMC)*, pages 104–110, 2005.

[23] M. Pease, R. Shostak, and L. Lamport. Reaching agreement in the presence of faults. *J. ACM*, 27(2):228–234, 1980.

[24] N. Santoro and P. Widmayer. Time is not a healer. In *Proc. 6th Symp. on Theoretical Aspects of Computer Science (STACS)*, pages 304–313. Springer-Verlag, 1989.

Error-Free Multi-Valued Consensus with Byzantine Failures

Guanfeng Liang
Dept. of Electrical and Computer Engineering,
and Coordinated Science Laboratory
University of Illinois at Urbana-Champaign
Urbana, Illinois, USA
gliang2@illinois.edu

Nitin Vaidya
Dept. of Electrical and Computer Engineering,
and Coordinated Science Laboratory
University of Illinois at Urbana-Champaign
Urbana, Illinois, USA
nhv@illinois.edu

ABSTRACT

In this paper, we present an efficient *deterministic* algorithm for consensus in presence of Byzantine failures. Our algorithm achieves consensus on an L-bit value with communication complexity $O(nL + n^4 L^{0.5} + n^6)$ bits, in a network consisting of n processors with up to t Byzantine failures, such that $t < n/3$. For large enough L, communication complexity of the proposed algorithm becomes $O(nL)$ bits, linear in the number of processors. To achieve this goal, the algorithm performs consensus on a long message (L bits), in multiple *generations*, each generation performing consensus on a part of the input message. The failure-free execution of each generation is made efficient by using a combination of two techniques: error detection coding, and processor clique formation based on matching input values proposed by the processors. By keeping track of faulty behavior over the different generations, the algorithm can ensure that most generations of the algorithm are failure-free. With parameterization, our algorithm is able to achieve a large class of validity conditions for consensus, while maintaining linear communication complexity. With a suitable choice of the error detection code, and using a clique of an appropriate size, the communication cost can be traded off with the strength of the validity condition. The proposed algorithm requires no cryptographic techniques.

Categories and Subject Descriptors

F.2.2 [**Theory of Computation**]: Analysis of Algorithms and Problem Complexity—*Nonnumerical Algorithms and Problems*

General Terms

Theory

Keywords

Byzantine agreement, consensus, distributed computing

1. INTRODUCTION

The Byzantine consensus problem considers n processors, namely $P_1, ..., P_n$, of which at most t processors may be *faulty* and deviate from the algorithm in arbitrary fashion. Each processor P_i is given an L-bit input value v_i. The basic version of the consensus problem considered here requires that the following properties to be satisfied.

- *Termination*: every fault-free P_i eventually decides on an output value v_i',

- *Consistency*: the output values of all fault-free processors are equal, i.e., for every fault-free processor P_i, $v_i' = v'$ for some v',

- *Validity*: if every fault-free P_i holds the same input $v_i = v$ for some v, then $v' = v$.

These properties have been used as the requirements for consensus in previous literature as well [9]. Other characterizations of the *validity* condition above are also of potential interest in practice. For instance, we may want the processors to agree on a value v if at least $\lceil \frac{n+1}{2} \rceil$ processors have input value equal to v. With suitable parameterization, our algorithm satisfies such more general validity conditions as well (Section 4). Algorithms that satisfy the desired properties in *all* executions are said to be *error-free*. We are interested in the communication complexity of error-free consensus algorithms. *Communication complexity* of an algorithm is defined as the maximum (over all permissible executions) of the total number of bits transmitted by all the processors according to the specification of the algorithm. This measure of complexity was first introduced by Yao [24], and has been used widely (e.g., [8, 9, 21]).

System Model: We assume a synchronous fully connected network of n processors. Every pair of processors is connected by a pair of directed point-to-point communication channels. Each processor correctly knows the identity of the processors at the other end of its channels. Whenever a processor receives a message on such a directed channel, it can correctly assume that the message is sent by the processor at the other end of the channel. We assume a Byzantine adversary that has complete knowledge of the state of the processors, including the L-bit input values. No secret is hidden from the adversary. The adversary can take over up to t processors ($t < n/3$) at any point during the algorithm. These processors are said to be *faulty*. The faulty processors can engage in any "*misbehavior*", i.e., deviations from the algorithm, including collusion. The remaining processors are *fault-free* and follow the algorithm.

It has been shown that error-free consensus is impossible if $t \geq n/3$ [20]. $\Omega(n^2)$ has been shown to be a lower bound on the number of messages needed to achieve error-free consensus [7]. Since any message must be of at least 1 bit, this gives a lower bound of $\Omega(n^2)$ bits on the communication complexity of any binary (1-bit) consensus algorithm.

The problem of achieving consensus on a single L-bit value may be solved using L instances of a 1-bit consensus algorithm. However, this approach will result in communication complexity of $\Omega(n^2 L)$, since $\Omega(n^2)$ is a lower bound on communication complexity of 1-bit consensus. Fitzi and Hirt [9] proposed a probabilistically correct multi-valued consensus algorithm which improves the communication complexity to $O(nL)$ for sufficiently large L, at the cost of allowing a non-zero probability of error. Since $\Omega(nL)$ is a lower bound on the communication complexity of consensus on an L-bit value [9], this algorithm has optimal complexity. We present a deterministic error-free consensus algorithm with communication complexity of $O(nL)$ bits for sufficiently large L. For smaller L, the communication complexity of our algorithms is $O(nL + n^4 L^{0.5} + n^6)$. The proposed algorithm is also able to satisfy more general *validity* conditions (with parameterization), while still achieving communication complexity linear in n.

2. ALGORITHM OVERVIEW

The goal of the proposed consensus algorithm is to achieve consensus on an L-bit value (or message). The algorithm is designed to perform efficiently for large L. Consequently, our discussion will assume that L is "sufficiently large" (how large is "sufficiently large" will become clearer later in the paper). We now briefly describe the salient features of the consensus algorithm, with the detailed algorithm presented later in Sections 3 and 4.

2.1 Execution in Multiple Generations

To improve the communication complexity, consensus on the L-bit value is performed "in parts". In particular, for a certain integer D, the L-bit value is divided into L/D parts, each consisting of D bits. For convenience of presentation, we will assume that L/D is an integer. A sub-algorithm is used to perform consensus on each of these D-bit values, and we will refer to each execution of the sub-algorithm as a "generation".

2.2 Memory Across Generations

If during any one generation, misbehavior by some faulty processor is detected, then additional (and expensive) diagnostic steps are performed to gain information on the potential identity of the misbehaving processor(s). This information is captured by means of a *diagnosis graph*, as elaborated later. As the sub-algorithm is performed for each new generation, the *diagnosis graph* is updated to incorporate any new information that may be learned regarding the location of the faulty processors. The execution of the sub-algorithm in each generation is adapted to the state of the diagnosis graph at the start of the generation.

2.3 Bounded Instances of Misbehavior

With Byzantine failures, it is not always possible to immediately determine the identity of a misbehaving processor. However, due to the manner in which the diagnosis graph

is maintained, and the manner in which the sub-algorithm adapts to the diagnosis graph, the t (or fewer) faulty processors can collectively misbehave in at most $t(t+1)$ generations, before all the faulty processors are exactly identified. Once a faulty processor is identified, it is effectively isolated from the network, and cannot tamper with future generations. Thus, $t(t+1)$ is also an upper bound on the number of generations in which the expensive diagnostic steps referred above may need to be performed.

2.4 Low-Cost Failure-Free Execution

Due to the bounded number of generations in which the faulty processors can misbehave, it turns out that the faulty processors do not tamper with the execution in a majority of the generations. We use a low-cost mechanism to achieve consensus in failure-free generations, which helps to achieve low communication complexity. In particular, we use an *error detecting code*-based strategy to reduce the amount of information the processors must exchange to be able to achieve consensus in the absence of any misbehavior (the strategy, in fact, also allows detection of potential misbehavior). The error detection code is used to efficiently identify a a large enough *clique* of processors that "propose" an identical value. Clique formation helps reduce communication cost by ensuring that the non-clique processors, whose input value is not going to correspond to the final consensus, do not interfere with the correct consensus. The algorithm can satisfy a large range of *validity* conditions, without changing the algorithm structure, simply by changing the level of redundancy in the error detecting code used by the algorithm, while still maintaining low failure-free overhead.

2.5 Consistent Diagnosis Graph Maintenance

A copy of the diagnosis graph is maintained locally by each fault-free processor. To ensure consistent maintenance of this graph, the *diagnostic information* (elaborated later) needs to be distributed consistently to all the processors in the network. This operation is performed using an error-free 1-bit Byzantine broadcast algorithm that tolerates $t < n/3$ Byzantine failures with communication complexity of $O(n^2)$ bits [6, 3]. This 1-bit broadcast algorithm is referred as *Broadcast_1_Bit* in our discussion. While *Broadcast_1_Bit* is expensive, its cumulative overhead is kept low by invoking it a relatively small number of times.

The structure above is inspired by prior work on fault-tolerant computing and communications theory, which is discussed in Section 6. It turns out that the "dispute control" approach used in the work on multi-party computation (MPC) has also used this structure [1], and its variation called *player elimination* has been used to design an error-free linear complexity Byzantine *broadcast* algorithm [2].

We now elaborate on the error detecting code used in our algorithm, and also describe the *diagnosis graph* in some more detail.

2.6 Error Detecting Code

We will use Reed-Solomon codes in our algorithm (potentially, other codes may be used instead). Consider a (m, d) Reed-Solomon code in Galois Field $\mathrm{GF}(2^c)$, where c is chosen large enough (specifically, $m \leq 2^c - 1$). This code encodes d data symbols from $\mathrm{GF}(2^c)$ into a codeword consisting of m symbols from $\mathrm{GF}(2^c)$. Each symbol from $\mathrm{GF}(2^c)$ can be represented using c bits. Thus, a data vector of d symbols contains dc bits, and the corresponding codeword contains mc bits. Each symbol of the codeword is computed as a linear combination of the d data symbols, such that every subset of d coded symbols represents a set of linearly independent combinations of the d data symbols. This property implies that any subset of d symbols from the m symbols of a given codeword can be used to determine the corresponding data vector. Similarly, knowledge of any subset of d symbols from a codeword suffices to determine the remaining symbols of the codeword. So d is also called the *dimension* of the code. The (m, d) code has the Hamming distance of $m - d + 1$, and can always detect up to $m - d$ errors. We will denote a code with dimension d as C_d, and the encoding/decoding operations as $Z = C_d(v)$ and $v = C_d^{-1}(Z)$ for a data vector v and the corresponding codeword Z.

In our algorithm, we also assume the availability of a null ($\perp$) symbol that is distinguished from all other symbols. For an m-element vector V, we denote $V[j]$ as the j-th element of the vector, $1 \leq j \leq m$. Given a subset $A \subseteq \{1, \ldots, m\}$, denote $V|A$ as the ordered list of elements of V at the locations corresponding to elements of A. For instance, if $m = 5$ and $A = \{2, 4\}$, then $V|A$ is equal to $(V[2], V[4])$. We will say that $V|A \in C_d$ if $V|A$ contains at least d non-null ($\neq \perp$) elements, and there exists a codeword $Z = C_d(v)$ for some v such that the non-null elements of $V|A$ are equal to the corresponding elements of $Z|A$. When such Z and v exist, by generalizing the decoding operation, we define $C_d^{-1}(V|A) = v$. If no such Z and v exist, we will say that $V|A \notin C_d$.

For our algorithm, we use a $(n, q-t)$ distance-$(n-q+t+1)$ code C_{q-t}, for a suitable q such that $t + 1 \leq q \leq n - t$, and ensure that there are at least $q - t$ non-null elements in the argument to C_d^{-1} (when the decoding function is used at a fault-free processor).

2.7 Diagnosis Graph

The fault-free processors' (potentially partial) knowledge of the identity of the faulty processors is captured by a diagnosis graph. A diagnosis graph is an undirected graph with n vertices, with vertex i corresponding to processor P_i. A pair of processors are said to "trust" each other if the corresponding pairs of vertices in the diagnosis graph is connected with an edge; otherwise they are said to "accuse" each other.

Before the start of the very first generation, the diagnosis graph is initialized as a fully connected graph, which implies that all the n processors initially trust each other. During the execution of the algorithm, whenever misbehavior by some faulty processor is detected, the diagnosis graph will be updated, and one or more edges will be removed from the graph, using the diagnostic information communicated using the *Broadcast_1_Bit* algorithm. The use of *Broadcast_1_Bit* ensures that the fault-free processors always have a consistent view of the diagnosis graph. The evolution of the diagnosis graph satisfies the following properties:

- If an edge is removed from the diagnosis graph, at least one of the processors corresponding to the two endpoints of the removed edge must be faulty.

- The fault-free processors always trust each other.

- If more than t edges at a vertex in the diagnosis graph are removed, then the processor corresponding to that vertex must be faulty.

The last two properties above follow from the first property, and the assumption that at most t processor are faulty.

3. MULTI-VALUED CONSENSUS

In this section, we describe a consensus algorithm that satisfies the properties listed in Section 1, and present a proof of correctness. Algorithm parameterization to satisfy more general *validity* requirements will be discussed in Section 4.

The L-bit input value v_i at each processor is divided into L/D parts of size D bits each, as noted earlier. These parts are denoted as $v_i(1), v_i(2), \cdots, v_i(L/D)$. The algorithm for achieving L-bit consensus consists of L/D sequential executions of Algorithm 1 presented in this section. Algorithm 1 is executed once for each generation. For the g-th generation ($1 \leq g \leq L/D$), each processor P_i uses $v_i(g)$ as its input in Algorithm 1. Each generation of the algorithm results in processor P_i deciding on g-th part (namely, $v_i'(g)$) of its final decision value v_i'.

The value $v_i(g)$ is represented by a vector of $n - 2t$ symbols, each symbol represented with $D/(n - 2t)$ bits. For convenience of presentation, assume that $D/(n - 2t)$ is an integer. We will refer to these $n - 2t$ symbols as the *data symbols*.

An $(n, n - 2t)$ distance-$(2t + 1)$ Reed-Solomon code, denoted as C_{n-2t}, is used to encode the $n - 2t$ data symbols into n coded symbols. We assume that $D/(n-2t)$ is large enough to allow the above Reed-Solomon code to exist, specifically, $n \leq 2^{D/(n-2t)} - 1$, which implies that $D = \Omega(n \log n)$. This condition is met only if L is large enough (since $L > D$). As we will see later, C_{n-2t} is used only for error detection. To detect t faults, a more efficient code of dimension $n - t$ suffices. We will discuss this improvement in Section 7.

Let the set of all the fault-free processors be denoted as P_{good}. Algorithm 1 for each generation g consists of three stages. We summarize the function of these three stages first, followed by a more detailed discussion:

1. Matching stage: Each processor P_i encodes its D-bit input $v_i(g)$ for generation g into n coded symbols, as noted above. Each processor P_i sends one of these n coded symbols to the other processors *that it trusts*. Processor P_i trusts processor P_j if and only if the corresponding vertices in the diagnosis graph are connected by an edge. Using the symbols thus received from each other, the processors attempt to identify a "matching set" of processors (denoted P_{match}) of size $n - t$ such that the fault-free processors in P_{match} are guaranteed to have an identical input value for the current generation. If such a P_{match} is not found, it can be determined with certainty that all the fault-free processors do not have the same input value – in this case, the fault-free processors decide on a default output value and terminate the algorithm.

2. Checking stage: If a set of processors P_{match} is identified in the above matching stage, each processor $P_j \notin P_{match}$ checks whether the symbols received from processors in P_{match} correspond to a valid codeword. If such a codeword exists, then the symbols received from P_{match} are said to be "consistent". If any processor finds that these symbols are not consistent, then misbehavior by some faulty processor is detected. Else all the processors are able to correctly compute the value to be agreed upon in the current generation.

3. Diagnosis stage: Whenever misbehavior is detected, the diagnosis stage is performed, to learn (possibly partial) information regarding the identity of the faulty processor(s). For fault diagnosis, the processors in P_{match} are required to *broadcast* the coded symbol they sent in the matching stage, using the *Broadcast_1_Bit* algorithm. Using the information received during these broadcasts, the fault-free processors are able to learn new information regarding the potential identity of the faulty processor(s). The *diagnosis graph* (called *Diag_Graph* in Algorithm 1) is updated to incorporate this new information.

In the rest of this section, we discuss each of the three stages in more detail. Note that whenever algorithm *Broadcast_1_Bit* is used, all the fault-free processors will receive the broadcast information identically. One instance of *Broadcast_1_Bit* is needed for each bit of information broadcast using *Broadcast_1_Bit*.

3.1 Matching Stage

The line numbers referred below correspond to the line numbers for the pseudo-code in Algorithm 1.

Line 1(a): In generation g, each processor P_i first encodes $v_i(g)$, represented by $n-2t$ symbols, into a codeword S_i from the code C_{n-2t}. The j-th symbol in the codeword is denoted as $S_i[j]$. Then processor P_i sends $S_i[i]$, the i-th symbol of its codeword, to all the other processors *that it trusts*. Recall that P_i trusts P_j if and only if there is an edge between the corresponding vertices in the diagnosis graph (referred as *Diag_Graph* in the pseudo-code).

Line 1(b): Let us denote by $R_i[j]$ the symbol that P_i receives from a trusted processor P_j. If a processor P_i does not trust some processor P_j, then P_i sets $R_i[j]$ equal to null ($\perp$). Messages received from untrusted processors are ignored.

Line 1(c): Flag $M_i[j]$ is used to record whether processor P_i finds processor P_j's symbol consistent with its own local value. Specifically, the pseudo-code in Line 1(c) is equivalent to the following:

- When P_i trusts P_j:
  If $R_i[j] = S_i[j]$, then $M_i[j] =$ **true** ;
  else $M_i[j] =$ **false** .

- When P_i does not trust P_j: $M_i[j] =$ **false** .

Line 1(d): As we will see later, if a fault-free processor P_i does not trust another processor, then the other processor must be faulty. Thus entry $M_i[j]$ in vector M_i is **false** if (i) P_i believes that processor P_j is faulty, or (ii) the input value at processor P_j appears to differ from the input value at P_i. Thus, entry $M_i[j]$ being **true** implies that, as of this time, P_i believes that P_j is fault-free, and that the value at P_j is possibly identical to the value at P_i. Processor P_i uses *Broadcast_1_Bit* to broadcast M_i to all the processors. One instance of *Broadcast_1_Bit* is needed for each bit of M_i.

Lines 1(e) and 1(f): Due to the use of *Broadcast_1_Bit*, all fault-free processors receive identical vector M_j from each processor P_j. Using these M vectors, each processor P_i attempts to find a set P_{match} containing $n-t$ processors such that, for every pair $P_j, P_k \in P_{match}$, $M_j[k] = M_k[j] =$ **true** . Since the M vectors are received identically by all the fault-free processors (using *Broadcast_1_Bit*), they can compute identical P_{match}. However, if such a set P_{match} does not exist, then the fault-free processors conclude that

all the fault-free processors do not have identical input – in this case, they decide on a default value, and terminate the algorithm.

It is worth noting that finding P_{match} is, in fact, equivalent to identifying a clique of size $n-t$ in an undirected graph of size n, whose edges are defined by the M vectors. Specifically, an edge exists between j and k in this graph, if $M_j[k] = M_k[j] =$ **true** . Finding a clique of a certain size in general graphs is NP-Complete. It turns out that, with a slight modification, the algorithm can perform correctly even if P_{match} is not a clique in the graph induced by M vectors. Instead it suffices if P_{match} includes at least $n-2t$ fault-free processors with identical input for the current generation. In other words, the subgraph induced by M and P_{match} will contain a clique of size $n-2t$ corresponding to fault-free processors. Such a P_{match} can be found with polynomial computational complexity (please refer the Appendix). However, for simplicity, in our proofs, we will assume that P_{match} indeed corresponds to a clique of size $n-t$.

In the following discussion, we will show the correctness of the *Matching Stage*. In the proofs of Lemmas 1, 2, and 3, we assume that the fault-free processors (that is, the processors in set P_{good}) always trust each other – this assumption will be shown to be correct later in Lemma 4.

LEMMA 1. *If for each fault-free processor $P_i \in P_{good}$, $v_i(g) = v(g)$, for some value $v(g)$, then a set P_{match} necessarily exists (assuming that the fault-free processors trust each other).*

PROOF. Since all the fault-free processors have identical input $v(g)$ in generation g, $S_i = C_{n-2t}(v(g))$ for all $P_i \in P_{good}$. Since these processors are fault-free, and trust each other, they send each other correct messages in the matching stage. Thus, $R_i[j] = S_j[j] = S_i[j]$ for all $P_i, P_j \in P_{good}$. This fact implies that $M_i[j] =$ **true** for all $P_i, P_j \in P_{good}$. Since there are at least $n-t$ fault-free processors, it follows that a set P_{match} of size $n-t$ must exist. $\square$

Observe that, although the above proof shows that there exists a set P_{match} containing only fault-free processors, there may also be other such sets that contain some faulty processors as well. That is, all the processors in P_{match} cannot be assumed to be fault-free. The converse of Lemma 1 implies that, if a set P_{match} does not exist, it is certain that all the fault-free processors do not have the same input values. In this case, they can correctly agree on a default value and terminate the algorithm. Thus Line 1(f) is correct.

In the case when a set P_{match} is found, the following lemma is useful.

LEMMA 2. *All processors in $P_{match} \cap P_{good}$ have identical input in generation g.*

PROOF. $|P_{match} \cap P_{good}| \geq n-2t$ because $|P_{match}| = n-t$ and there are at most t faulty processors. Consider any two processors $P_i, P_j \in P_{match} \cap P_{good}$. Since $M_i[j] = M_j[i] =$ **true** , it follows that $S_i[i] = S_j[i]$ and $S_j[j] = S_i[j]$. Since there are $n-2t$ fault-free processors in $P_{match} \cap P_{good}$, this implies that the codewords computed by these fault-free processors (in Line 1(a)) contain at least $n-2t$ identical symbols. Since the code C_{n-2t} has dimension $(n-2t)$, this implies that the fault-free processors in $P_{match} \cap P_{good}$ must have identical input in generation g. $\square$

Algorithm 1 Multi-Valued Consensus (generation g)

---

1. **Matching Stage:**

Each processor P_i performs the matching stage as follows:

(a) Compute $(S_i[1], \ldots, S_i[n]) = C_{n-2t}(v_i(g))$, and *send* $S_i[i]$ to every trusted processor P_j

(b) $R_i[j] \leftarrow \begin{cases} \text{symbol that } P_i \text{ receives from } P_j, \text{ if } P_i \text{ trusts } P_j; \\ \bot, \text{otherwise} \end{cases}$

(c) If $S_i[j] = R_i[j]$ then $M_i[j] \leftarrow$ **true** ; else $M_i[j] \leftarrow$ **false**

(d) P_i broadcasts the vector M_i using *Broadcast_1_Bit*

Using the received M vectors:

(e) Find a set of processors P_{match} of size $n - t$ such that
$$M_j[k] = M_k[j] = \textbf{true} \text{ for every pair of } P_j, P_k \in P_{match}$$

(f) If P_{match} does not exist, then decide on a default value and terminate;
else enter the Checking Stage

2. **Checking Stage:**

Each processor $P_j \notin P_{match}$ performs steps 2(a) and 2(b):

(a) If $R_j | P_{match} \in C_{n-2t}$ then $Detected_j \leftarrow$ **false** ; else $Detected_j \leftarrow$ **true** .

(b) Broadcast $Detected_j$ using *Broadcast_1_Bit*

Each processor P_i performs step 2(c):

(c) Receive $Detected_j$ from each processor $P_j \notin P_{match}$ (broadcast in step 2(b)).
If $Detected_j =$ **false** for all $P_j \notin P_{match}$, then decide on $v'_i(g) = C^{-1}_{n-2t}(R_i | P_{match})$;
else enter Diagnosis Stage

3. **Diagnosis Stage:**

Each processor $P_j \in P_{match}$ performs step 3(a):

(a) Broadcast $S_j[j]$ using *Broadcast_1_Bit*

Each processor P_i performs the following steps:

(b) $R^\#[j] \leftarrow$ symbol received from $P_j \in P_{match}$ as a result of broadcast in step 3(a)

(c) For all $P_j \in P_{match}$,
if P_i trusts P_j and $R_i[j] = R^\#[j]$ then $Trust_i[j] \leftarrow$ **true** ;
else $Trust_i[j] \leftarrow$ **false**

(d) Broadcast $Trust_i | P_{match}$ using *Broadcast_1_Bit*

(e) For each edge (j, k) in $Diag\_Graph$, such that $P_j \in P_{match}$
remove edge (j, k) **if** $Trust_j[k] =$ **false** or $Trust_k[j] =$ **false**

(f) If $R^\# | P_{match} \in C_{n-2t}$ then
if for any $P_j \notin P_{match}$,
$Detected_j =$ **true** , but no edge at vertex j was removed in step 3(e)
then remove all edges at vertex j in $Diag\_Graph$

(g) If at least $t + 1$ edges at any vertex j have been removed so far,
then processor P_j must be faulty, and all edges at j are removed.

(h) Find a set of processors $P_{decide} \subset P_{match}$ of size $n - 2t$ in the updated $Diag\_Graph$,
such that every pair of $P_j, P_k \in P_{decide}$ still trust each other

(i) Decide on $v'_i(g) = C^{-1}_{n-2t}(R^\# | P_{decide})$

NOTE: Instead of performing steps 3(h) and 3(i), Algorithm 1 may be repeated for generation g again after the diagnosis graph has been updated in step 3(g). This alternative does not affect algorithm correctness.

3.2 Checking Stage

When P_{match} is found during the matching stage, the checking stage is entered.

Lines 2(a), 2(b): Each fault-free processor $P_j \notin P_{match}$ checks whether the symbols received from the trusted processors in P_{match} are consistent with a valid codeword: that is, check whether $R_j | P_{match} \in C_{n-2t}$. The result of this test is broadcast as a 1-bit notification $Detected_j$, using *Broadcast_1_Bit* . If $R_j | P_{match} \notin C_{n-2t}$, then processor P_j is said to have detected an *inconsistency*.

Line 2(c): If no processor announces in Line 2(b) that it has detected an inconsistency, each fault-free processor P_i chooses $C^{-1}_{n-2t}(R_i | P_{match})$ as its output for generation g.

The following lemma argues correctness of Line 2(c).

LEMMA 3. *If no processor detects inconsistency in Line 2(a), all fault-free processors $P_i \in P_{good}$ decide on the identical output value $v'(g)$ such that $v'(g) = v_j(g)$ for all $P_j \in P_{match} \cap P_{good}$.*

PROOF. We assume that the fault-free nodes trust each other. Observe that size of set $P_{match} \cap P_{good}$ is at least $n - 2t$, and hence the decoding operations $C^{-1}_{n-2t}(R_i | P_{match})$

---

and $C_{n-2t}^{-1}(R_i|P_{match} \cap P_{good})$ are both defined at fault-free processors.

Since fault-free processors send correct messages, and trust each other, for all processors $P_i \in P_{good}$, $R_i|P_{match} \cap P_{good}$ are identical. Since no inconsistency has been detected by any processor, every $P_i \in P_{good}$ decides on $C_{n-2t}^{-1}(R_i|P_{match})$ as its output. Also, $C_{n-2t}^{-1}(R_i|P_{match}) = C_{n-2t}^{-1}(R_i|P_{match} \cap P_{good})$, since C_{n-2t} has dimension $(n-2t)$. It then follows that all the fault-free processors P_i decide on the identical value $v'(g) = C_{n-2t}^{-1}(R_i|P_{match} \cap P_{good})$ in Line 2(c). Since $R_j|P_{match} \cap P_{good} = S_j|P_{match} \cap P_{good}$ for all processors $P_j \in P_{match} \cap P_{good}$, $v'(g) = v_j(g)$ for all $P_j \in P_{match} \cap P_{good}$. $\quad\square$

3.3 Diagnosis Stage

When any processor that is not in P_{match} announces that it has detected an inconsistency, the diagnosis stage is entered. The algorithm allows for the possibility that a faulty processor may erroneously announce that it has detected an inconsistency. The purpose of the diagnosis stage is to learn new information regarding the potential identity of a faulty processor. The new information is used to remove one or more edges from the diagnosis graph $Diag\_Graph$ – as we will soon show, when an edge (j,k) is removed from the diagnosis graph, at least one of P_j and P_k must be faulty. We now describe the steps in the Diagnosis Stage.

Lines 3(a), 3(b): Every fault-free processor $P_j \in P_{match}$ uses $Broadcast\_1\_Bit$ to broadcast $S_j[j]$ to all processors. Let us denote by $R^\#[j]$ the result of the broadcast from P_j. Due to the use of $Broadcast\_1\_Bit$, all fault-free processors receive identical $R^\#[j]$ for each processor $P_j \in P_{match}$. This information will be used for diagnostic purposes.

Lines 3(c), 3(d): Every fault-free processor P_i uses flag $Trust_i[j]$ to record whether it "believes", as of this time, that each processor $P_j \in P_{match}$ is fault-free or not. Then P_i broadcasts $Trust_i|P_{match}$ to all processors using $Broadcast\_1\_Bit$. Specifically,

- If P_i trusts P_j **and** $R_i[j] = R^\#[j]$, then set $Trust_i[j] =$**true** ;

- If P_i does not trust P_j **or** $R_i[j] \neq R^\#[j]$, then set $Trust_i[j] =$**false** .

Line 3(e): Using the $Trust$ vectors received above, each fault-free processor P_i then removes any edge (j,k) from the diagnosis graph such that $Trust_j[k] =$ **false** or $Trust_k[j] =$ **false** . Due to the use of $Broadcast\_1\_Bit$ for distributing $Trust$ vectors, all fault-free processors will maintain an identical view of the updated $Diag\_Graph$. Note that edges may only be removed from $Diag\_Graph$.[1]

Line 3(f): As we will soon show, in the case $R^\#|P_{match} \in C_{n-2t}$, a processor $P_j \notin P_{match}$ that announces that it has detected an inconsistency, i.e., $Detected_j =$**true** , must be faulty if no edge attached to vertex j was removed in Line 3(e). Such a processor P_j is "isolated", by having all edges attached to vertex j removed from $Diag\_Graph$, and the fault-free processors will not communicate with it anymore in subsequent generations.

Line 3(g): As we will soon show, a processor P_j must be faulty if at least $t+1$ edges at vertex j have been removed. The identified faulty processor P_j is then isolated.

---

[1] If the system allows "repair" of faulty processors, then edges will need to be added back to $Diag\_Graph$.

Lines 3(h) and 3(i): Since $Diag\_Graph$ is updated only with information broadcast with $Broadcast\_1\_Bit$ ($Detected$, $R^\#$ and $Trust$), all fault-free processors maintain an identical view of the updated $Diag\_Graph$. Then they can compute an identical set $P_{decide} \subset P_{match}$ containing exactly $n-2t$ processors such that every pair $P_j, P_k \in P_{decide}$ trust each other. Finally, every fault-free processor chooses $C_{n-2t}^{-1}(R^\#|P_{decide})$ as its decision value for generation g.

LEMMA 4. *Every time the diagnosis stage is performed, at least one edge attached to a vertex corresponding to a faulty processor will be removed from $Diag\_Graph$, and only such edges will be removed.*

PROOF. We prove this lemma by induction. For the convenience of discussion, let us say that an edge (j,k) is "*bad*" if at least one of P_j and P_k is faulty.

Consider a generation g starting with any instance of the $Diag\_Graph$ in which only bad edges have been removed. Suppose that a processor $P_i \notin P_{match}$ "claims" that it detects a failure by broadcasting $Detect_i =$**true** in Line 2(b). This implies that, if P_i is fault-free, $R_i|P_{match}$ cannot be a valid codeword, i.e., $R_i|P_{match} \notin C_{n-2t}$.

The symbols broadcast by processors of P_{match} in Line 3(a), i.e., $R^\#|P_{match}$, can either be a valid codeword of C_{n-2t} or not. We consider the two possibilities separately:

- $R^\#|P_{match} \in C_{n-2t}$: In the case, if P_i is actually fault-free, $R^\#[k] \neq R_i[k]$ must be true for some faulty processor $P_k \in P_{match}$, which is trusted by P_i. Thus, $Trust_i[k] =$ **false** and the bad edge (i,k) will be removed in Line 3(e). The converse of this argument implies that if $Detected_i =$**true** but no edge attached to vertex i is removed in Line 3(e), then P_i must be faulty. As a result, all bad edges at vertex i are removed in Line 3(f).

- $R^\#|P_{match} \notin C_{n-2t}$: There are always at least $n-2t$ fault-free processors in $P_{match} \cap P_{good}$, and $R_j|P_{match} \in C_{n-2t}$ is true for every $P_j \in P_{match} \cap P_{good}$. Thus, if $R^\#|P_{match} \notin C_{n-2t}$, then $R^\#|P_{match} \neq R_j|P_{match}$ must be true for every $P_j \in P_{match} \cap P_{good}$. Similar to the previous case, $R^\#[k] \neq R_j[k]$ must be true for some faulty processor $P_k \in P_{match}$ which is trusted by every processor $P_j \in P_{match} \cap P_{good}$. As a result, $Trust_j[k] =$ **false** and the bad edge (j,k) will be removed in Line 3(e), for all $P_j \in P_{match} \cap P_{good}$.

At this point, we can conclude that by the end of Line 3(f), at least one new bad edge has been removed. Moreover, since $R_i[k] = R^\#[k]$ for every pair of fault-free processors $P_i, P_k \in P_{good}$, $Trust_i[k]$ remains **true** , which implies that the vertices corresponding to the fault-free processors will remain fully connected, and each will always have at least $n-t-1$ edges. This follows that a processor P_j must be faulty if at least $t+1$ edges at vertex j have been removed. So all edges at j are bad and will be removed in Line 3(g).

Now we have proved that for every generation that begins with a $Diag\_Graph$ in which only bad edges have been removed, at least one new bad edge, and only bad edges, will be removed in the updated $Diag\_Graph$ by the end of the diagnosis stage. Together with the fact that $Diag\_Graph$ is initialized as a complete graph, we finish the proof. $\quad\square$

The above proof of Lemma 4 shows that all fault-free processors will trust each other throughout the execution of the algorithm, which justifies the assumption made in the proofs of the previous lemmas. The following lemma shows the correctness of Lines 3(h) and 3(i).

LEMMA 5. *By the end of diagnosis stage, all fault-free processors $P_i \in P_{good}$ decide on the same output value $v'(g)$, such that $v'(g) = v_j(g)$ for all $P_j \in P_{match} \cap P_{good}$.*

PROOF. First of all, the set P_{decide} necessarily exists since there are at least $n - 2t \geq t + 1$ fault-free processors in $P_{match} \cap P_{good}$ that always trust each other. Secondly, since the size of P_{decide} is $n - 2t \geq t + 1$, it must contain at least one fault-free processor $P_k \in P_{decide} \cap P_{good}$. Since P_k still trusts all processors of P_{decide} in the updated $Diag\_Graph$, $R^{\#}|P_{decide} = R_k|P_{decide} = S_k|P_{decide}$. The second equality is due to the fact that $P_k \in P_{match}$. Finally, since the size of set P_{decide} is $n - 2t$, the decoding operation of $C_{n-2t}^{-1}(R^{\#}|P_{decide})$ is defined, and it equals to $v_k(g) = v_j(g)$ for all $P_j \in P_{match} \cap P_{good}$, as per Lemma 2. □

We can now conclude the correctness of the Algorithm 1.

THEOREM 1. *Given n processors with at most $t < n/3$ are faulty, each given an input value of L bits, Algorithm 1 achieves consensus correctly in L/D generations , with the diagnosis stage performed for at most $t(t+1)$ times.*

PROOF. Lemmas 1 to 5 imply that consensus is achieved correctly for each generation g of D bits. So the termination and consistency properties are satisfied for the L-bit outputs after L/D generations. Moreover, in the case all fault-free processors are given an identical L-bit input v, the D bits output $v'(g)$ in each generation g equals to $v(g)$ as per Lemmas 1, 3 and 5. So the L-bit output $v' = v$ and the validity property is also satisfied.

According to Lemma 4 and the fact that a faulty processor P_j will be removed once more than t edges at vertex j have been removed, it takes at most $t(t+1)$ instance of the diagnosis stage before all faulty processors are identified. After that, the fault-free processors will not communicate with the faulty processors. Thus, the diagnosis stage will not be performed any more. So it will be performed for at most $t(t+1)$ times in all cases. □

3.4 Communication Complexity

Let us denote by B the complexity of broadcasting 1 bit with one instance of *Broadcast_1_Bit*. In every generation, the complexity of each stage is as follows:

- Matching stage: every processor P_i sends at most $n-1$ symbols, each of $D/(n-2t)$ bits, to the processors that it trusts, and broadcasts $n-1$ bits for M_i. So at most $\frac{n(n-1)}{n-2t}D + n(n-1)B$ bits in total are transmitted by all n processors.

- Checking stage: every processor $P_j \notin P_{match}$ broadcasts one bit $Detected_j$ with *Broadcast_1_Bit*, and there are t such processors. So tB bits are transmitted.

- Diagnosis stage: every processor $P_j \in P_{match}$ broadcasts one symbol $S_j[j]$ of $D/(n-2t)$ bits with *Broadcast_1_Bit*, and every processor P_i broadcasts $n-t$ bits of $Trust_i|P_{match}$ with *Broadcast_1_Bit*. So the complexity is $\frac{n-t}{n-2t}DB + n(n-t)B$ bits.

According to Theorem 1, there are L/D generations in total. In the worst case, P_{match} can be found in every generation, so the matching and checking stages will be performed for L/D times. In addition, the diagnosis stage will be performed for at most $t(t+1)$ time. Hence the communication complexity of the proposed consensus algorithm, denoted as $C_{con}(L)$, is then computed as

$$
\begin{aligned}
C_{con}(L) &= \left(\frac{n(n-1)}{n-2t}D + n(n-1)B + tB \right)\frac{L}{D} \\
&\quad + t(t+1)\left(\frac{n-t}{n-2t}D + n(n-t) \right)B. \quad (1)
\end{aligned}
$$

For a large enough value of L, with a suitable choice of $D = \sqrt{\frac{(n^2 - n + t)(n - 2t)L}{t(t+1)(n-t)}}$, we have

$$
\begin{aligned}
C_{con}(L) &= \frac{n(n-1)}{n-2t}L + t(t+1)n(n-t)B \\
&\quad + 2BL^{0.5}\sqrt{\frac{(n^2 - n + t)t(t+1)(n-t)}{n-2t}}. \quad (2)
\end{aligned}
$$

Error-free algorithms that broadcast 1 bit with communication complexity $\Theta(n^2)$ bits are known [3, 6]. So we assume $B = \Theta(n^2)$. Then the complexity of our algorithm for $t < n/3$ becomes

$$
\begin{aligned}
C_{con}(L) &= \frac{n(n-1)}{n-2t}L + O(n^4 L^{0.5} + n^6) \\
&= O(nL + n^4 L^{0.5} + n^6). \quad (3)
\end{aligned}
$$

For $L = \Omega(n^6)$, the communication complexity becomes $O(nL)$. (This requirement can be improved to $L = \Omega(n^5)$ if we use a technique from [1] in the Diagnosis stage.[2])

4. OTHER VALIDITY CONDITIONS

Algorithm 1 satisfies the validity conditions stated in Section 1. As noted earlier, other validity conditions may also be desirable in practice. Algorithm 1 is flexible in the sense that, with proper parameterization, it can achieve other (reasonable) validity properties. In particular, q-validity property defined below can be achieved for $t+1 \leq q \leq n-t$:

- q-Validity: If at least q fault-free processors hold an identical input v, then the output v' agreed by the fault-free processors equals input v_j for some fault-free processor P_j. Furthermore, if $q \geq \lceil \frac{n+1}{2} \rceil$, then $v' = v$.

In order to achieve q-validity, we need to change the error detecting code and the size of P_{match} in Algorithm 1 as follows (q is said to be the parameter of the algorithm):

- Throughout the algorithm, we replace the $(n, n - 2t)$ distance-$(2t+1)$ code C_{n-2t} with a $(n, q - t)$ distance-$(n - q + t + 1)$ code, denoted as C_{q-t}. Since $q \geq t + 1$, $q - t \geq 1$. Thus C_{q-t} always exists.

- Line 1(e): Choose a set of q processors P_{match} such that $M_j[k] = M_k[j] = \textbf{true}$ for every pair of $P_j, P_k \in P_{match}$.[3]

---

[2] We would like to thank Martin Hirt for suggesting this improvement.

[3] The validity condition achieved can be made stronger, particularly for $q \leq n/2$, by choosing the largest possible set P_{match} with size at least q.

- **Lines 3(h) and 3(i):** For the more general validity conditions, instead of performing steps 3(h) and 3(i), as stated in the NOTE at the end of Algorithm 1, the algorithm can be repeated for generation g with the updated diagnosis graph. For $q > 2t$, we also have the alternative of retaining steps 3(h) and 3(i), but the size of the chosen P_{decide} must be $q - t$.

Similar to Lemmas 1 through 5, we can prove that

1. If at least q fault-free processors $P_i \in P_{good}$ hold the same input $v_i(g) = v(g)$ for some $v(g)$, then a set P_{match} of size q necessarily exists.

2. There are at least $q - t \geq 1$ fault-free processors in P_{match} and all the fault-free processors in P_{match} have the same input for generation g.

3. If no processor detects inconsistency in Line 2(a), all fault-free processors $P_i \in P_{good}$ decide on the identical output value $v'(g)$ such that $v'(g) = v_j(g)$ for all $P_j \in P_{match} \cap P_{good}$. Furthermore, when $q \geq \lceil \frac{n+1}{2} \rceil$, and at least q fault-free processors have identical input v, at least one of these fault-free processors is bound to be in P_{match}, and therefore, $v'(g) = v$.

4. In case (for $q > 2t$) steps 3(h) and 3(i) are used, by the end of diagnosis stage, all fault-free processors $P_i \in P_{good}$ decide on the same output value $v'(g)$, such that $v'(g) = v_j(g)$ for all $P_j \in P_{match} \cap P_{good}$. Otherwise, the algorithm is repeated for generation g with the updated diagnosis graph.

Then it can be concluded that Algorithm 1 achieves q-validity for $t + 1 \leq q \leq n - t$ with the aforementioned parameterization. The communication complexity for achieving q-validity is

$$
\begin{aligned}
C_{con}^q(L) &= \frac{n(n-1)}{q-t}L + O(n^4 L^{0.5} + n^6) \\
&= O(nL + n^4 L^{0.5} + n^6), \text{ if } q - t = \Omega(n).
\end{aligned}
$$

When $q < \lceil \frac{n+1}{2} \rceil$, there may be more than one choice for P_{match} in Line 1(e). For example, there can be two disjoint cliques, one containing q fault-free processors with the same input v, and the other containing $q - t$ fault-free processors with input u ($v \neq u$) and t faulty processors that pretend to have input u. It is possible that the second clique is picked to be P_{match} and the consensus value ends up being u. So in this case, even though at least q fault-free processors hold the same input, we can only guarantee agreement on the input of *some* fault-free processors, but not necessarily equal to the q identical inputs. However, when $q \geq \lceil \frac{n+1}{2} \rceil$, it is guaranteed that, if at least q inputs at the fault-free processors equals to v, then the agreed output equals v.

5. MULTIPLE CONSENSUS

In the above discussion, we considered consensus on a single long L-bit value. An alternate view of the problem is likely to be more relevant in practice. In particular, let us consider the problem of performing g instances of consensus, with each processor receiving a D-bit input for each instance (in particular, the input for P_i is $v_i(g)$ for instance g). Then the consensus properties need to be satisfied for each instance *separately*. We assume that the identity of faulty processors remains fixed across the different instances.

Then it should not be difficult to see that Algorithm 1 solves the multiple consensus problem, with the algorithm for g-th generation essentially performing the g-th instance of the consensus problem for D-bit values.

Let us denote the *average* complexity for performing g instances of consensus on D-bit values as $\overline{C}_{con}(g, D)$. Similar to the analysis in Section 3.4, for $g \geq t(t+1)$, we have

$$
\begin{aligned}
\overline{C}_{con}(g, D) &= \frac{n(n-1)}{n-2t}D + n(n-1)B + tB \\
&\quad + \frac{t(t+1)}{g}\left(\frac{n-t}{n-2t}D + n(n-t)\right)B \quad (4) \\
&= O\left(\left(n + \frac{n^4}{g}\right)D + n^4 + \frac{n^6}{g}\right). \quad (5)
\end{aligned}
$$

From Eq.5, we can conclude that we only need $D = \Omega(n^3)$ and $g = \Omega(n^3)$ instances of D-bit consensus for the per consensus complexity to reduce to $O(nD)$. In other words, when the goal is to sequentially perform a large number $(\Omega(n^3))$ of instances of consensus, the input size for each instance only needs to be $\Omega(n^3)$ in order to achieve complexity linear in n, rather than $\Omega(n^6)$ as discussed in Section 3.4.

6. RELATED WORK

Binary agreement: Binary agreement corresponds to $L = 1$ in our notation. For binary agreement, optimal error-free algorithms with $O(n^2)$ communication complexity have been proposed [3, 6]. King and Saia [11] introduced a randomized *consensus* algorithm with communication complexity of $O(n^{1.5})$, allowing a non-zero probability of error.

Multi-valued agreement: Fitzi and Hirt [9] proposed a multi-valued *consensus* algorithm in which an L-bit value (or message) is first reduced to a much shorter message, using a universal hash function. Byzantine consensus is then performed for the shorter hashed values. Given the result of consensus on the hashed values, consensus on L bits is then achieved by requiring processors whose L-bit input value matches the agreed hashed value deliver the L bits to the other processors jointly. By performing initial consensus only for the smaller hashed values, this algorithm is able to achieve linear communication complexity for large L and up to $t < n/2$ failures, with a non-zero error probability. Our algorithm can also probabilistically tolerate more than $n/3$ failures if $Broadcast\_1\_Bit$ is replaced by any 1-bit broadcast algorithm that is probabilistically correct up to the desired number of faults.

Beerliova-Trubiniova and Hirt have presented an error-free linear communication complexity multi-party computation algorithm, which uses a linear complexity Byzantine *broadcast* algorithm as a sub-algorithm [2]. This algorithm achieves linear complexity using a *player elimination* framework, which is motivated by the *dispute control* framework proposed in [1]. When two processors disagree with each other (or, *do not trust* each other, in our terminology), one of the two processors must be fault-free. In player elimination, both the processors are removed from the system, and the underlying algorithm is performed on the smaller system, which must now tolerate one fewer faulty processor, with two fewer processors. This approach has also been adopted by asynchronous Byzantine agreement algorithms (e.g. [19]). While it may be possible to also use *player elimination* to achieve consensus, we believe that our approach, in general, can more efficiently achieve stronger validity properties than approaches that may be designed using player elimination.

In designing the proposed algorithm, we drew inspiration from well-known ideas in prior work, as summarized next.

System-level diagnosis: Preparata, Metze and Chien [23] introduced the system *diagnosability* problem in their 1967 paper. Since then there has been a large body of work exploring different variations of the problem (e.g., [18]). The work on system-level diagnosis considers a (un)directed *diagnosis graph* (or a *test graph*), wherein each (un)directed edge represents a *test*: in essence, when node X tests node Y, it may declare Y as *faulty* or *fault-free*, with a faulty tester providing potentially erroneous test outcomes. The goal then is to use the results of the tests to either exactly identify the faulty nodes, or identify a small set of nodes that contains the faulty nodes. The past work differ in the nature of tests being performed, and the nature of the faults being diagnosed. In the system-level diagnosis jargon, our faults are *intermittent* [17], and the tests are *comparison-based* [4]. We interpret the test outcome *fault-free* (*faulty*) as equivalent to the corresponding two processors trusting (not trusting) each other. In our work, we strengthen the comparison-based system-level diagnosis approach by incorporating an error detection code, which provides additional structure to our "comparison test" outcomes. This structure can be exploited for computational efficiency as well (see Appendix).

Linear coding and block coding: A standard mechanism for improving efficiency of information transmission is to use *block codes*, meaning that a "block" (or multiple bits) of data is encoded together in a single codeword. Our specific approach for using linear error detecting (block) codes for consensus is motivated by the rich literature on network coding, particularly, multicasting in the presence of a Byzantine attacker (e.g., [25, 5, 10]). Application of such an approach to Byzantine consensus or broadcast in an arbitrary point-to-point networks under per-link capacity constraints is non-trivial [14, 15]. However, under the *communication complexity* model, the problem is simpler, as the algorithm in this paper demonstrates. Essentially, the simplification arises from the ability to treat each point-to-point link identically, resulting in a solution that has a certain symmetry (such a symmetric solution is generally not optimal when the different links have different capacities).

Make the common case fast: In fault-tolerant systems, a common trick to improve average system performance (or reduce average overhead of fault-tolerance) is to make the "common case", namely, the failure-free execution, efficient, with the possibility of much higher overhead when a failure does occur. This approach works well when failure rates are low. There are many instances of the application of this idea, but some examples include error detection followed by retransmission for link reliability, and checkpointing and rollback or roll-forward recovery after failure detection [22].

7. FURTHER RESEARCH

Algorithm 1 has complexity $\frac{n(n-1)}{n-2t}L$ (ignoring the terms sub-linear in L). We have recently developed another algorithm with communication complexity $\frac{n(n-1)}{n-t}L$ [16] (when $q = n - t$), which can be twice as efficient as Algorithm 1 when t gets close to $n/3$. (A Byzantine broadcast algorithm with the same communication complexity is introduced in our earlier report [12].) While the new algorithm may not be better in terms the *order* of the communication complexity, in practice, a factor of 2 reduction in communication overhead is quite significant. Whether this algorithm is optimal for arbitrary t and n ($t < n/3$) remains an open question. What we do know, however, is that the degenerate version of the algorithm for $t = 0$ with complexity $(n - 1)L$ is not optimal for all n (when $t = 0$, the consensus problem with $q = n - t$ reduces to the problem of checking *equality* of the inputs at all the processors, which are necessarily fault-free [13]). In [16], we also introduce a consensus algorithm that achieves q-validity with $O(nL)$ communication complexity for all $t+1 \leq q \leq n-t$, not just when $q-t = \Omega(n)$ (as is the case for the solution in Section 4). In particular, while the solution in Section 4 has $O(nL)$ complexity for $q = t+\Omega(n)$, the complexity is quadratic in n for $q = t+1$. The algorithm in [16] achieves linear complexity even for $q = t+1$ (and can also achieve lower complexity for some other values of q).

Another related research direction of interest is multiple agreements under the constraints of the communication network capacity. In our related work [14, 15], we have studied the Byzantine broadcast and consensus problems in networks where each communication channel has a finite capacity. We proved upper bounds for the throughput of agreement in such networks, and showed their tightness in some (substantially) restricted classes of topologies. The problem is still open in general networks.

8. CONCLUSION

In this paper, we present an efficient error-free Byzantine consensus algorithm for long messages. The algorithm requires $O(nL)$ total bits of communication for messages of L bits for sufficiently large L. The algorithm makes no cryptographic assumptions. With proper parameterization, the proposed algorithm also satisfies a range of validity properties, while still achieving complexity linear in n. The choice of the parameter (called q in the paper) affects the choice of error detecting code used to achieve consensus, and also the size of a processor *clique* that the algorithm attempts to identify. With a suitable choice of the error detection code, and using a clique of an appropriate size, the algorithm can trade-off communication cost with the strength of the validity condition.

9. ACKNOWLEDGMENTS

We thank the referees for their insightful comments and asking interesting questions. In particular, the referees asked whether strong forms of validity conditions can be satisfied, and whether the clique required in our algorithm can be determined efficiently. Section 4 and the Appendix address these questions. We thank Martin Hirt (ETH) for his encouraging feedback on our prior related work, and for pointing us to some of the relevant literature on multi-party computation. Thanks also to Manoj Prabhakaran (UIUC) and Ashish Chaudhury (ISI-Kolkata) for their feedback, and to Jennifer Welch for answering our many questions on distributed algorithms. This research is supported in part by Army Research Office grant W-911-NF-0710287 and National Science Foundation award 1059540. Any opinions, findings, and conclusions or recommendations expressed here are those of the authors and do not necessarily reflect the views of the funding agencies or the U.S. government.

10. REFERENCES

[1] Z. Beerliova-Trubiniova and M. Hirt. Efficient multi-party computation with dispute control. In *TCC*, 2006.

[2] Z. Beerliova-Trubiniova and M. Hirt. Perfectly-secure MPC with linear communication complexity. In *TCC*, 2008.

[3] P. Berman, J. A. Garay, and K. J. Perry. Bit optimal distributed consensus. *Computer science: research and applications*, 1992.

[4] D. Blough and A. Pelc. Complexity of fault diagnosis in comparison models. *IEEE Trans. Comp.*, 1992.

[5] N. Cai and R. W. Yeung. Network error correction, part ii: Lower bounds. *Communications in Information and Systems*, 2006.

[6] B. A. Coan and J. L. Welch. Modular construction of a byzantine agreement protocol with optimal message bit complexity. *Inf. Comput.*, 97(1):61–85, 1992.

[7] D. Dolev and R. Reischuk. Bounds on information exchange for byzantine agreement. *J. ACM*, 1985.

[8] D. Dolev and H. R. Strong. Authenticated algorithms for byzantine agreement. *SIAM J. on Comp.*, 1983.

[9] M. Fitzi and M. Hirt. Optimally efficient multi-valued byzantine agreement. In *ACM PODC*, 2006.

[10] S. Jaggi, M. Langberg, S. Katti, T. Ho, D. Katabi, and M. Medard. Resilient network coding in the presence of byzantine adversaries. In *IEEE INFOCOM*, 2007.

[11] V. King and J. Saia. Breaking the $o(n^2)$ bit barrier: scalable byzantine agreement with an adaptive adversary. In *ACM SIGACT-SIGOPS PODC*, 2010.

[12] G. Liang and N. Vaidya. Complexity of multi-valued byzantine agreement. *Tech-Report, UIUC*, June 2010.

[13] G. Liang and N. Vaidya. Multiparty equality function computation in networks with point-to-point links. *Tech-Report, UIUC*, October 2010.

[14] G. Liang and N. Vaidya. Capacity of byzantine agreement with finite link capacity. In *IEEE INFOCOM*, 2011.

[15] G. Liang and N. Vaidya. Capacity of byzantine consensus with capacity limited point-to-point links. *Tech-Report, UIUC*, March 2011.

[16] G. Liang and N. Vaidya. New efficient error-free multi-valued consensus with byzantine failures. *Tech-Report, UIUC*, under preparation (as of March 2011).

[17] S. Mallela and G. Masson. Diagnosable systems for intermittent faults. *IEEE Trans. Comp.*, 1978.

[18] G. M. Masson, D. M. Blough, and G. F. Sullivan. *System diagnosis.* Fault-Tolerant Computer System Design. Prentice Hall, 1996.

[19] A. Patra and C. P. Rangan. Communication optimal multi-valued asynchronous byzantine agreement with optimal resilience. Cryptology ePrint Archive, 2009.

[20] M. Pease, R. Shostak, and L. Lamport. Reaching agreement in the presence of faults. *J. ACM*, 1980.

[21] B. Pfitzmann and M. Waidner. Information-theoretic pseudosignatures and byzantine agreement for $t \geq n/3$. *Technical Report, IBM Research*, 1996.

[22] D. Pradhan and N. Vaidya. Roll-forward and rollback recovery: performance-reliability trade-off. *IEEE Trans. Comp.*, 1997.

[23] F. P. Preparata, G. Metze, and R. T. Chien. On the connection assignment problem of diagnosable systems. *IEEE Trans. Electr. Comput.*, 1967.

[24] A. Yao. Some complexity questions related to distributive computing. In *STOC*, 1979.

[25] R. W. Yeung and N. Cai. Network error correction, part i: Basic concepts and upper bounds. *Communications in Information and Systems*, 2006.

APPENDIX

To make the algorithm computationally more efficient, we need to modify Algorithm 1 slightly, as elaborated later in this appendix. With this change, the algorithm only looks for a set P_{match} of size $n - t$ such that all the fault-free processors in $P_{match} \cap P_{good}$ have the same input in generation g. The algorithm's response when such a P_{match} is not found is now somewhat different, as sketched below. A complete description and the proof of correctness of the modified algorithm is omitted for brevity.

P_{match} is found as follows. We maintain a set Q that contains the largest set of processors that appear to have identical input up to the previous generation. Initially, Q is the set of all n processors. The matching stage is performed as it is in Algorithm 1, up to Line 3(d). The subsequent steps of the matching stage are different.

(i) Determine the largest set $Q' \subseteq Q$ such that all the processors in set Q' have M vectors that contain at least $n - t$ **true** entries. If $|Q'| < n - t$, then the fault-free processors must have different L-bit inputs, and the algorithm terminates with the decision being a default value. If $|Q'| \geq n-t$, the proceed to the following steps.

(ii) For every pair $P_i, P_j \in Q'$ that trusts each other, if there are more than t distinct processors not trusted by P_i or P_j, then one of P_i and P_j must be faulty. Remove edge (i, j) in the diagnosis graph, set $M_i[j] = $ **false** and $M_j[i] = $ **false** , and go back to step (i) above.

(iii) For every pair $P_i, P_j \in Q'$ (that now trust the same set of at least $n-t$ processors), check whether $M_i[k] = M_j[k]$ for each P_k that is trusted by both P_i and P_j. If this check fails, then either $v_i(g)$ and $v_j(g)$ are different (or, pretending to be different, in case one of these processors is faulty), or P_k has sent different symbols to P_i and P_j. In this case, go to step (iv); otherwise it can be proved that $v_i(g) = v_j(g)$ if P_i and P_j are both fault-free. If all these checks pass, then P_{match} can be chosen as any subset of Q' of size $n-t$, and it always contains a clique of at least $n-2t$ fault-free processors that have the same input for the current generation. Then proceed to the Checking stage as in Algorithm 1.

(iv) If misbehavior, or difference in processor inputs, is detected in step (iii) above, some additional steps are needed: All processors in Q' broadcast their inputs for generation g. Q is then updated as the largest subset of Q' that broadcast the same value. If $|Q| < n - t$, then terminate and decide on a default output. If $|Q| \geq n-t$, then decide on the value broadcast by processors in Q. Additionally, diagnosis is also performed to remove an edge from the diagnosis graph, if misbehavior has indeed occurred.

Byzantine Agreement with Homonyms

Carole Delporte-Gallet *
University Paris Diderot

Hugues Fauconnier
University Paris Diderot

Rachid Guerraoui
Ecole Polytechnique Fédérale
de Lausanne

Anne-Marie Kermarrec
INRIA Rennes-Bretagne
Atlantique

Eric Ruppert
York University

Hung Tran-The
University Paris Diderot

ABSTRACT

So far, the distributed computing community has either assumed that all the processes of a distributed system have distinct identifiers or, more rarely, that the processes are anonymous and have no identifiers. These are two extremes of the same general model: namely, n processes use ℓ different authenticated identifiers, where $1 \leq \ell \leq n$. In this paper, we ask how many identifiers are actually needed to reach agreement in a distributed system with t Byzantine processes.

We show that having $3t + 1$ identifiers is necessary and sufficient for agreement in the synchronous case but, more surprisingly, the number of identifiers must be greater than $\frac{n+3t}{2}$ in the partially synchronous case. This demonstrates two differences from the classical model (which has $\ell = n$): there are situations where relaxing synchrony to partial synchrony renders agreement impossible; and, in the partially synchronous case, increasing the number of *correct* processes can actually make it harder to reach agreement. The impossibility proofs use the fact that a Byzantine process can send multiple messages to the same recipient in a round. We show that removing this ability makes agreement easier: then, $t + 1$ identifiers are sufficient for agreement, even in the partially synchronous model.

Categories and Subject Descriptors

D.1.3 [**Programming Techniques**]: Concurrent Programming—*Distributed programming*

General Terms

Algorithms, Reliability, Theory

Keywords

agreement, Byzantine failures, consensus, identifiers, lower bounds, synchrony

*This work is partially supported by the ERC Starting Grant project 204742 and the ANR VERSO SHAMAN.

1. INTRODUCTION

We consider a distributed system in which ℓ distinct identifiers are assigned to n processes, where $1 \leq \ell \leq n$. Several processes may be assigned the same identifier, in which case we call the processes *homonyms*. The identifiers are authenticated: if a process p receives a message from a process q with identifier i, p knows that the message was not sent by a process with identifier $i' \neq i$, but p does not know whether the message was sent by q or another process q' having the same identifier i. A process cannot direct a message it sends to a particular process, but can direct the message to all processes that have a particular identifier.

This model generalizes the classical scheme where processes have distinct identifiers (i.e., $\ell = n$), and the less classical scheme where processes are anonymous (i.e., $\ell = 1$). Studying systems with homonyms provides a better understanding of the importance of identifiers in distributed computing, and there are two additional motivations for the new model. Firstly, assuming in systems such as Pastry or Chord [19, 22] that all processes have unique (unforgeable) identifiers might be too strong an assumption in practice. We may wish to design protocols that still work if, by a rare coincidence, two processes are assigned the same identifier. This approach is also useful if security is breached and a malicious process can forge the identifier of a correct process, for example by obtaining the correct process's private key. Secondly, in many cases, users of a system may wish to preserve their privacy by remaining anonymous. However, in a fully anonymous system where no identifiers are used, very few problems are solvable. (In particular, Okun observed that Byzantine agreement is impossible in the fully anonymous model [15], even with a single faulty process.) With a limited number of identifiers, more problems become solvable, and some level of anonymity can be preserved by hiding, to some extent, the association between users and identifiers. For example, users of a distributed protocol might use only their domain names as identifiers. Others will see that some user within the domain is participating, but will not know exactly which one. If several users within the same domain participate in the protocol, they will behave as homonyms.

We ask in this paper how many distinct identifiers are needed to reach *agreement* in a system of n processes, up to t of which can be Byzantine. We need only to consider systems where $n > 3t$: this assumption is known to be a requirement for solving Byzantine agreement, even when $\ell = n$ [14, 18], and it thus applies also for systems with homonyms. For the synchronous case, we prove using a scenario argument that $3t + 1$ identifiers are necessary. The

	Synchronous	Partially synchronous
Innumerate processes	$\ell > 3t$	$\ell > \frac{n+3t}{2}$
Numerate processes	$\ell > 3t$ ($\ell > t$ for restricted Byzantine processes)	$\ell > \frac{n+3t}{2}$ ($\ell > t$ for restricted Byzantine processes)

Table 1: Necessary and sufficient conditions for solving Byzantine agreement in a system of n processes using ℓ identifiers and tolerating t Byzantine failures. In all cases, n must be greater than $3t$.

matching synchronous algorithm is obtained by a simulation that transforms any synchronous Byzantine agreement algorithm designed for a system with unique identifiers to one that works in a system with $\ell > 3t$ identifiers. For the partially synchronous case, we prove using a partitioning argument that the lower bound becomes $\ell > \frac{n+3t}{2}$. (Note that $\frac{n+3t}{2}$ is strictly greater than $3t$ because $n > 3t$.) We show that this bound is also tight by giving a new partially synchronous Byzantine agreement algorithm. This bound is somewhat surprising because the number of required identifiers ℓ depends on n as well as t. Counter-intuitively, increasing the number of correct processes can render agreement impossible. For example, if $t = 1$ and $\ell = 4$, agreement is solvable for 4 processes but not for 5. Another difference from the classical situation (where $\ell = n$) is that the condition that makes Byzantine agreement solvable is different for the synchronous and partially synchronous models.

To strengthen our results, we show that (a) both the synchronous and partially synchronous lower bounds hold even if correct processes are *numerate*, i.e., can count the number of processes that send identical messages in a round and (b) the matching algorithms are correct even if processes are *innumerate*. In systems with unique identifiers, senders can append their identifier to all messages, making it trivial for the receiver to count copies of messages. This is not possible in systems with homonyms, so the distinction between numerate and innumerate processes is important.

What has more impact, however, is the ability for a Byzantine process to send multiple messages to a single recipient in a round. In a classical system with unique identifiers, the Byzantine process has no advantage in doing this: algorithms could simply discard such messages. In systems with homonyms, there is a clear advantage. In fact, we prove that if each Byzantine process is restricted to sending a single message per round to each recipient (and processes are numerate), then $t + 1$ identifiers are enough to reach agreement even in a partially synchronous model. We also show this bound is tight using a valency argument: $t + 1$ identifiers are needed even in the synchronous case. The fact that $t + 1$ identifiers are sufficient to reach agreement with restricted Byzantine processes has some practical relevance: In some settings, it is reasonable to assume that Byzantine processes are simply malfunctioning ordinary processes sending incorrect messages, and not malicious processes with the additional power to generate and send more messages than correct processes can.

The results are summarized in Table 1. Section 2 describes our models and recalls the specification of Byzantine agreement. Section 3 considers the synchronous case and Section 4 considers the partially synchronous one. Section 5 gives our results for restricted Byzantine processes. Section 6 provides some concluding remarks. Due to space limitations, details of some proofs and algorithms appear in [8].

2. DEFINITIONS

We consider a distributed message-passing system with $n \geq 2$ processes. Each process has an authenticated identifier from the set $\mathcal{L} = \{1, ..., \ell\}$. We assume that $n \geq \ell$ and that each identifier is assigned to at least one process. Thus, the parameter ℓ measures the number of different identifiers that are actually assigned to processes. In the case where $n > \ell$, one or more identifiers will each be shared by several processes. In the case where $\ell = 1$, all processes have the same identifier, and they are therefore anonymous. We assume algorithms are deterministic. Thus, the actions of a process are entirely determined by the process's initial state and the messages it receives. Processes with the same identifier execute the same code but processes with different identifiers may behave differently. In our proofs, we sometimes refer to individual processes using names like p, but these names cannot be used by the processes themselves in their algorithms.

A *correct* process does not deviate from its algorithm specification. A process that is not correct is called *Byzantine*. The maximum possible number of Byzantine processes is denoted t (where $0 < t < n$). We need only consider systems where $n > 3t$: this assumption is known to be a requirement for solving Byzantine agreement, even when $\ell = n$ [14, 18], and it thus also applies to systems with homonyms. A Byzantine process may choose to send arbitrary messages (or no message) to each other process. However, we assume Byzantine processes cannot forge identifiers: each message is authenticated with its sender's identifier. Given a message m, we denote by $m.val$ its *value* (or content) and by $m.id$ the identifier of the sender. If a correct process receives m, then at least one process p with identifier $m.id$ sent m.

In the *synchronous model*, computation proceeds in rounds. In each round, each process can send a message to each other process and then receive all messages that were sent to it during that round.

For the *partially synchronous model* we use the definition of Dwork, Lynch and Stockmeyer [10]: computation proceeds in rounds, as in the synchronous model, except that in each execution, a finite number of messages might not be delivered to all of their intended recipients. There is no bound on the number of messages that can be dropped. As argued in [10], this basic partially synchronous model is equivalent to other models with partially synchronous communication. More specifically, the model in which message delivery times are eventually bounded by a known constant and the model in which message delivery times are always bounded by an unknown constant can both simulate the basic partially synchronous model. Conversely, each of these models can be simulated by the basic partially synchronous model. Thus, our characterization of the values of n, ℓ and t for which Byzantine agreement can be solved applies to the other models with partially synchronous communication too.

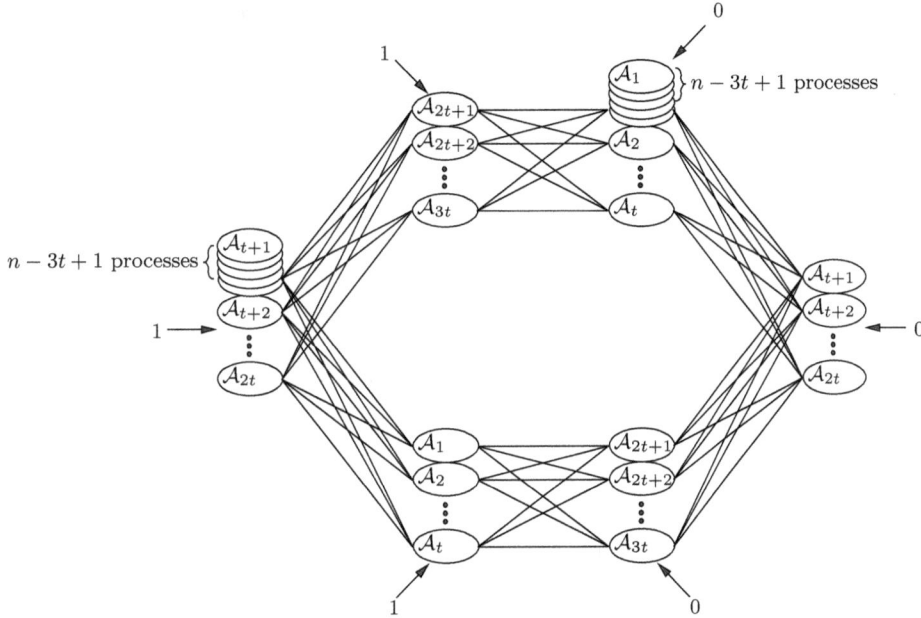

Figure 1: System used in proof of Proposition 1

As mentioned in the introduction, we also consider variants of the models in which each Byzantine process is *restricted* to sending at most one message to each recipient in each round. In general, we consider unrestricted Byzantine processes unless the restriction is explicitly mentioned. We also distinguish the cases where processes are *innumerate* from the case where they are *numerate*. We say that a process is innumerate if the messages it receives in a round form a set of messages: the process cannot count the number of copies of identical messages it receives in the round. We say that a process is numerate if the messages it receives in a round form a multiset of messages: the process can count the number of copies of identical messages it receives in the round. (As we shall show, the numerate model is more powerful than the innumerate model against restricted Byzantine processes.)

The goal of an agreement algorithm is for a set of processes proposing values to decide on exactly one of these values. We consider the classical *Byzantine agreement* problem [11,18], defined by the following three properties.

1. *Validity:* If all correct processes propose the same value v, then no value different from v can be decided by any correct process.

2. *Agreement:* No two correct processes decide different values.

3. *Termination:* Eventually, each correct process decides some value.

An algorithm solves Byzantine agreement in a system of n processes with ℓ identifiers tolerating t failures if these three properties are satisfied in every execution in which at most t processes fail, regardless of the way the n processes are assigned the ℓ identifiers. (Recall that each identifier must be assigned to at least one process.)

3. SYNCHRONOUS MODEL

Here, we prove that having $\ell > 3t$ is necessary and sufficient for solving synchronous Byzantine agreement, regardless of whether the processes are numerate or innumerate. To show that the condition $\ell > 3t$ is sufficient to reach agreement, we design a simulation, where each group of processes with a common identifier cooperatively simulate a single process.

3.1 Impossibility

We prove the condition $\ell > 3t$ is necessary using a scenario argument, in the style of Fischer, Lynch and Merritt [11].

Proposition 1 *Synchronous Byzantine agreement is unsolvable even with numerate processes if $\ell \leq 3t$.*

PROOF. It suffices to prove there is no synchronous algorithm for Byzantine agreement when $\ell = 3t$. To derive a contradiction, suppose there was an n-process synchronous algorithm $\mathcal{A}$ for Byzantine agreement when $\ell = 3t$. Let $\mathcal{A}_i(v)$ be the algorithm executed by a process with identifier i when it has input value v.

Imagine setting up a system as shown in Figure 1. Every process correctly executes the algorithm $\mathcal{A}_i$ assigned to it. The two stacks of processes shown in the diagram each have $n - 3t + 1$ processes, so there are a total of $2n$ processes in this system. All processes within a stack have the same identifier, and execute the same algorithm $\mathcal{A}_i$, as shown. Inputs to each of the $2n$ process are indicated by the arrows.

Consider the $n - t$ processes that run $\mathcal{A}_{t+1}(1), \ldots, \mathcal{A}_{3t}(1)$. These $n - t$ processes cannot distinguish this execution from an execution in an n-process system where the remaining identifiers, $1, \ldots, t$ are each assigned to a single Byzantine process. (Here, we use the fact that each Byzantine process can send multiple messages to each correct process in a single round.) By validity, the $n - t$ processes must output 1.

By a symmetric argument, the $n - t$ processes running $\mathcal{A}_1(0), \ldots, \mathcal{A}_{2t}(0)$ must output 0.

Now, consider the $n - 2t$ processes that run $\mathcal{A}_1(0), \ldots, \mathcal{A}_t(0)$ and the t processes that run $\mathcal{A}_{2t+1}(1), \ldots, \mathcal{A}_{3t}(1)$. These $n - t$ processes cannot distinguish this execution from an n-process execution where each of the remaining identifiers, $t+1, \ldots, 2t$ are each assigned to a single Byzantine process. By agreement, the $n - t$ processes must output the same value, contradicting the previous two paragraphs $\qquad\square$

3.2 Algorithm

Next, we present an algorithm that solves Byzantine agreement assuming $\ell > 3t$. Our agreement algorithm is generic: given any synchronous Byzantine agreement algorithm for ℓ processes with unique identifiers (such algorithms exist when $\ell = n > 3t$, e.g., [14]), we transform it into an algorithm for n processes and ℓ identifiers, where $n \geq \ell$. Without loss of generality, we assume that the algorithm to be transformed uses broadcasts: a process sends the same message to all other processes. (If a process wishes to send a message only to specific recipients, it could include the recipient's identifier in the broadcasted message.)

In our transformation, we divide processes into groups according to their identifiers. Each group simulates a single process. If all processes within a group are correct, then they can reach agreement and cooperatively simulate a single process. If any process in the group is Byzantine, we allow the simulated process of that group to behave in a Byzantine manner. The correctness of our simulation relies on the fact that more than two-thirds of the simulated processes will be correct (since $\ell > 3t$), which is enough to achieve agreement.

Proposition 2 *Synchronous Byzantine agreement is solvable even with innumerate processes if $\ell > 3t$.*

PROOF SKETCH. We transform any Byzantine agreement algorithm $\mathcal{A}$ for the classical model with unique identifiers into an algorithm $\mathcal{T}(\mathcal{A})$ for systems with homonyms. Consider any such $\mathcal{A}$ (Figure 2) for a system with ℓ processes $\{p_1, \ldots, p_\ell\}$. $\mathcal{A}$ can be specified by: (1) a set of local process states, (2) a function $init(i, v)$ that encodes the initial state of process p_i when p_i has input value v, (3) a function $M(s, r)$ that determines the message to send in state s in round r, (4) a transition function $\delta(s, r, R)$ that determines the new state to which the process moves from state s after receiving a set of messages R in round r, and (5) a decision function $decide(s)$ which is the decision in state s, or $\perp$ if there is no decision yet (once a correct process has decided in a state s, $decide(s')$ remains equal to this decision in all states s' reachable from s).

Let $G(i)$ be the set of processes with identifier i. We name such a set a *group*. We say that the group $G(i)$ is correct if all processes in $G(i)$ are correct. At most t of the ℓ groups are not correct.

In our new algorithm $\mathcal{T}(\mathcal{A})$, shown in Figure 3, three rounds simulate one round of $\mathcal{A}$. We call these three rounds a *phase*. Each phase consists of a *selection round*, a *deciding round* and a *running round*. In the selection round (line 3 to 5) of a phase r, the processes within each group agree on a state for phase r. For each i, if $G(i)$ is correct, then in each round the selected state will be the same for the processes

---

Code for process p_i

Variable:

```
1   s = init(i, v)              /* v is the value proposed by p_i */
```

Main code:

```
2   for all r from 1 to ∞
3       if decide(s) ≠ ⊥ then decide the value decide(s)
4       send(M(s, r)) to all processes
5       receive(R)   /* receive messages sent this round */
6       s = δ(s, r, R)
```

Figure 2: Synchronous Byzantine agreement algorithm $\mathcal{A}$ with ℓ processes and ℓ identifiers.

in this group. In deciding rounds (line 6 to 9), if there is a value decided by $t + 1$ processes with different identifiers then the process can decide that value. At least one of these identifiers refers to a correct group and gives the decision. The deciding rounds are useful for correct processes that belong to a group with a Byzantine process. In running rounds (line 10 to 15), each process executes one step of algorithm $\mathcal{A}$ with the state chosen in the preceding selection round and the messages received in the round.

Let α_H be an execution of $\mathcal{T}(\mathcal{A})$. For all phases r, at the end of the r-th selection round (line 5), all processes in a correct group $G(i)$ have the same value for the state s, and therefore for $M(s, r)$ and $decide(s)$. Let s_i^r be the value of state s for the processes in group $G(i)$ after the rth selection round. Note that s_i^1 is the initial state of at least one process in $G(i)$.

By induction on r, we prove that there is an execution α_S of $\mathcal{A}$ such that for all r and for all processes in each correct group $G(i)$: $s_i^r = st_i^r$ (and hence $M(s_i^r, r) = M(st_i^r, r)$), where st_i^r is the value of p_i's variable s at the beginning of round r in α_S. In α_S, p_i is correct for all identifiers i such that $G(i)$ is correct in α_H.

We sketch the key idea of the inductive step that proves this claim. In each running round, messages sent by the processes in a correct group $G(i)$ are identical and indistinguishable from a single message from a unique correct process with identifier i. On the other hand, if $G(i)$ is not correct, the processes in $G(i)$ may send different messages to a process p (in which case p ignores the messages at line 14) or they may all send the same (arbitrary) message to p. Either way, their collective behaviour is indistinguishable from a unique Byzantine process with identifier i (which could either send nothing or an arbitrary message to p).

As $\mathcal{A}$ is a synchronous Byzantine agreement algorithm that tolerates t Byzantine failures, all correct processes eventually decide some value v in α_S. It follows from the claim above that in α_H, eventually for all correct groups $G(i)$, s_i^r is a state where $decide(s_i^r)$ is v. As $\ell > 3t$, at least $t + 1$ groups $G(i)$ are correct and all processes in these groups eventually send v in the deciding rounds. Thus, each correct process in α_H eventually decides, even if it is in a group with a Byzantine process. Furthermore, if a correct process decides in α_H, it decides the value it received from $t + 1$ groups, at least one of which is a correct group, so it must decide v. Thus, the agreement, validity and termination

Code for processes with identifier i

Variable:

```
1    s = init(i, v)                                              /* v is the value proposed by the process */
```

Main code:

```
2    for all r from 1 to ∞
3        send(s) to all processes                               /* get groups to agree on their state */
4        receive(R)                                             /* receive the messages of the round */
5        s = deterministic choice of some element x.val such that x ∈ R and x.id = i

6        send(decide(s)) to all processes          /* deciding round replaces decision line of original algorithm */
7        receive(R)                                             /* receive the messages of the round */
8        if there is a v ≠ ⊥ such that |{d ∈ R : d.val = v}| ≥ t + 1
9            then decide such a v

10       send(M(s, r)) to all processes                         /* almost identical to original algorithm */
11       receive(R)                                             /* receive the messages of the round */
12       for all j in L                                   /* eliminate messages from known Byzantine groups */
13           if there is more than one different message from identifier j in R
14               then remove all of them from R
15       s = δ(s, r, R)
```

Figure 3: Synchronous Byzantine agreement algorithm $T(A)$ with n processes and ℓ identifiers.

properties for α_H follow from the agreement, validity and termination properties for α_S. □

If the algorithm in Figure 2 is known to terminate within k rounds, the algorithm in Figure 3 need only be run for $k + 1$ iterations of the loop. (The extra iteration provides an additional deciding round to ensure correct processes in incorrect groups decide.)

Proposition 1 states that $\ell > 3t$ identifiers are required to solve synchronous Byzantine agreement, even if processes are numerate. Proposition 2 states that $\ell > 3t$ identifiers are sufficient, even if processes are innumerate. Thus, we have the following theorem.

Theorem 3 *Synchronous Byzantine agreement is solvable if and only if $\ell > 3t$.*

4. PARTIALLY SYNCHRONOUS MODEL

Here we prove that having $\ell > \frac{3t+n}{2}$ is necessary and sufficient for solving Byzantine agreement in a partially synchronous system, regardless of whether the processes are numerate or innumerate. Intuitively, this condition means that at least $3t + 1$ of the identifiers must each be assigned to a single process (since $2\ell - n > 3t$). We shall see in Section 4.2 that having this many non-homonym processes will be crucial in proving the correctness of the algorithm that we design.

4.1 Impossibility

We prove the necessity of the condition $\ell > \frac{n+3t}{2}$ using a partitioning argument. We show that if there are too few identifiers, and messages between two groups of correct processes are not delivered for sufficiently long, then the Byzantine processes can force processes in the two groups to decide different values.

Proposition 4 *Partially synchronous Byzantine agreement is unsolvable even with numerate processes if $\ell \leq \frac{n+3t}{2}$.*

PROOF. Byzantine agreement is impossible when $\ell \leq 3t$, even in the fully synchronous model, by Proposition 1. So, it remains to show that agreement is impossible when $\ell > 3t$ and $\ell \leq \frac{n+3t}{2}$. To derive a contradiction, assume a Byzantine agreement algorithm A does exist for such a system. In our proof, we construct three executions of this algorithm, α, β and γ.

In α, process identifiers are assigned as shown in the upper left portion of Figure 4. In this diagram, a process labelled A_i has identifier i and runs the algorithm A correctly, and a process labelled B_i has identifier i and is Byzantine. Note that there are n processes in total. The t Byzantine processes send no messages and all messages sent by correct processes are delivered. All correct processes have input 0 in α and must therefore decide 0 by some round r_α.

Execution β is defined similarly, as shown in the upper right portion of Figure 4. Again, the t Byzantine processes send no messages and all messages sent by correct processes are delivered. All correct processes have input 1, and must therefore decide 1 by some round r_β.

In γ, the n processes are assigned identifiers as shown in the bottom half of Figure 4. (Here, we use the assumption that $\ell \leq \frac{n+3t}{2}$, so that $n \geq 2\ell - 3t$.) The inputs to each group of correct processes is also shown in the diagram. The t Byzantine processes $B_1, B_2, \ldots, B_t$ send to each correct process with input 0 the same messages as that process receives in α and they send to each correct process with input 1 the same messages as that process receives in β. (This requires the ability of Byzantine process B_1 to send more than one message to each recipient per round.) All messages sent across the edges shown in the diagram are delivered. All other messages are not delivered for the first $r = \max(r_\alpha, r_\beta)$ rounds. The correct processes with input 0 cannot distinguish γ from α for the first r rounds, so they must decide 0 by round r. The correct processes with input 1 cannot distinguish γ from β for the first r rounds, so they must decide 1 by round r. This contradicts the assumption that A satisfies agreement. □

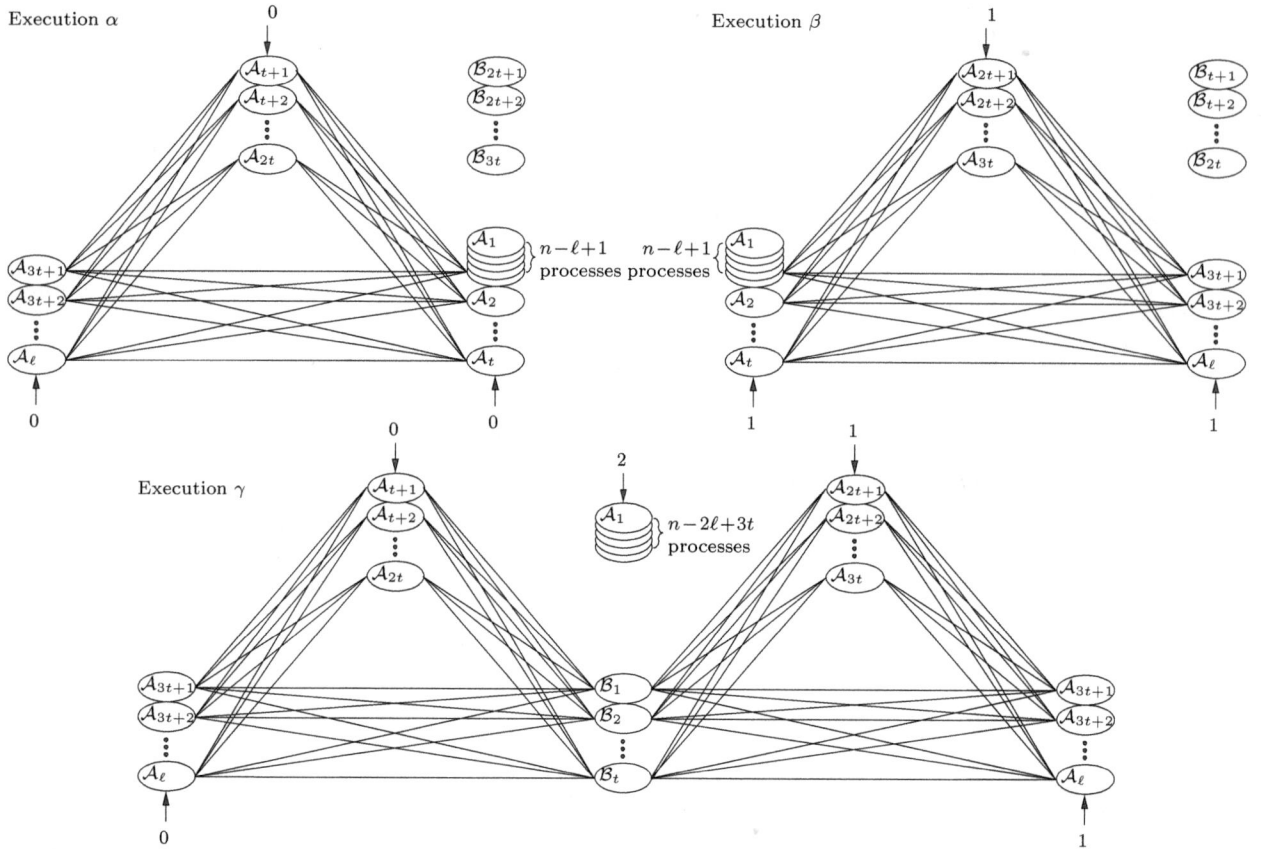

Figure 4: System used in proof of Proposition 4

4.2 Algorithm

We now describe an algorithm that solves Byzantine agreement in the basic partially synchronous model when $\ell > \frac{n+3t}{2}$. Our algorithm is based on the algorithm given by Dwork, Lynch and Stockmeyer [10] for the classical case where $n = \ell$, with several novel features. Generalizing the algorithm is not straightforward. Some of the difficulty stems from the following scenario. Suppose two correct processes share an identifier and follow the traditional algorithm of [10]. They could send very different messages (for example, if they have different input values), but recipients of those messages would have no way of telling apart the messages of the two correct senders, so it could appear to the recipients as if a single Byzantine process was sending out contradictory information. Thus, the algorithm has to guard against inconsistent information coming from correct homonym processes as well as malicious messages sent by the Byzantine processes.

Proposition 5 *Partially synchronous Byzantine agreement is solvable even with innumerate processes if $\ell > \frac{n+3t}{2}$.*

We think of an execution as being divided into superrounds, where each superround consists of two consecutive rounds. Let T be the first superround such that all messages sent during or after superround T are delivered. We begin with an *authenticated broadcast* primitive based on [21]. This primitive allows processes to perform BROADCAST(m) com-

mands. Once a process receives sufficient evidence that a process with identifier i has performed a BROADCAST(m), it performs an ACCEPT(m,i) action. This is guaranteed to happen for broadcasts from correct processes after superround T. (In the case where a process with identifier i is Byzantine, processes will at least eventually agree on which messages to accept from identifier i.) Our version of authenticated broadcast for homonymous systems satisfies the following three properties.

1. *Correctness*: If a process with identifier i performs BROADCAST(m) in superround $r \geq T$, then every correct process performs ACCEPT(m,i) during superround r.

2. *Unforgeability*: If all processes with identifier i are correct and none of them perform BROADCAST(m), then no correct process performs ACCEPT(m,i).

3. *Relay*: If some correct process performs ACCEPT(m,i) during superround r, then every correct process performs ACCEPT(m,i) by superround $\max(r+1, T)$.

Proposition 6 *It is possible to implement authenticated broadcasts satisfying the correctness, unforgeability and relay properties in the basic partially synchronous model, provided $\ell > 3t$.*

PROOF SKETCH. The implementation is a straightforward generalization of the ones given in [10, 21] for systems with

26

Code for process with identifier $i \in \{1, \ldots, \ell\}$

```
1   locks = ∅
2   ph = 0                                                              /* phase number */
3   proper = {v}                                     /* v is the value proposed by the process */
4   Note: in each round, proper is updated as described on page
5   while true
6       /* beginning of superround 1 of phase */
7       let V be the set of values v ∈ proper such that there is no pair (w,*) ∈ locks for any w ≠ v
8       BROADCAST(⟨propose V, ph⟩)                                        /* superround 1 */
9       /* beginning of superround 2 of phase */
10      if i = (ph mod ℓ) + 1 and there is some value v_lock such that the process has performed ACCEPT(⟨propose V_j, ph⟩, j)
11          from ℓ − t different identifiers j with v_lock ∈ V_j
12          then send ⟨lock v_lock, ph⟩ to all processes                 /* round 1 of superround 2 */
13      /* beginning of superround 3 of phase */
14      if there is some value v for which the process received ⟨lock v, ph⟩ from identifier (ph mod ℓ) + 1 and
15          has performed ACCEPT(⟨propose V_j, ph⟩, j) for ℓ − t different identifiers j with v ∈ V_j
16          then choose one such v and perform BROADCAST(⟨vote v, ph⟩)    /* superround 3 */
17      /* beginning of superround 4 of phase */
18      if for some v, the process has performed ACCEPT(⟨vote v, ph⟩, j) from ℓ − t different identifiers j
19          then    add (v, ph) to locks and remove any other pair (v,*) from locks
20                  send ⟨ack v, ph⟩ to all processes                    /* round 1 of superround 4 */
21      if i = (ph mod ℓ) + 1 and the process has received ⟨ack v_lock, ph⟩ from ℓ − t different identifiers in this round
22          then decide v_lock (but continue running the algorithm)
23      if the process has already decided some value v
24          then send ⟨decide v⟩ to all processes                        /* round 2 of superround 4 */
25      if for some v, the process has received ⟨decide v⟩ from t + 1 different identifiers j in this round
26          then decide v (but continue running the algorithm)
27      for each (v_1, ph_1) ∈ locks
28          if for some v_2 ≠ v_1 and ph_2 > ph_1, the process has performed ACCEPT(⟨vote v_2, ph_2⟩, j) for ℓ − t
29              different identifiers j
30              then remove (v_1, ph_1) from locks
31      ph = ph + 1
```

Figure 5: Byzantine agreement algorithm for the partially synchronous model.

unique identifiers. To perform BROADCAST(m) in superround r, a process sends a message $\langle$init $m \rangle$ in the first round of superround r. Any process that receives this message from identifier i sends $\langle$echo $m, r, i \rangle$ in the following round, which is the second round of superround r, and in all subsequent rounds. In each round after superround r, any process that has so far received $\langle$echo $m, r, i \rangle$ from $\ell - 2t$ distinct identifiers sends a message $\langle$echo $m, r, i \rangle$. If, at any time, a process has received the message $\langle$echo $m, r, i \rangle$ from $\ell - t$ distinct identifiers, the process performs ACCEPT(m, i). □

We now describe the Byzantine agreement protocol. Each process keeps track of a set of *proper* values, which are values that can be output without violating validity. Initially, only the process's own input value is in this set. Each process appends its *proper* set to each message it sends. If a process receives *proper* sets containing v in messages from $t + 1$ different identifiers, it adds v to its own *proper* set. Also, if a process has received *proper* sets from $2t + 1$ different identifiers and no value appears in $t + 1$ of them, it adds all possible input values to its own *proper* set. (This can be done because $t + 1$ of the *proper* sets are from correct processes, so there are at least two different inputs to correct processes.)

The Byzantine agreement algorithm is shown in Figure 5. Whenever a correct process sends a message, it sends it to all processes. The execution of the algorithm is broken into phases, each of which lasts four superrounds. Processes

assigned the identifier $(ph \bmod \ell) + 1$ are the *leaders* of phase ph. In each phase, each process first performs a BROADCAST of a proposal containing the set of values it would be willing to decide (line 8). These are the values in its *proper* set, unless it has already locked a value, as described below, in which case it can only send its locked value. Each phase leader chooses a value that appears in proposals the leader has accepted from $\ell - t$ different identifiers (if such a value exists) and sends out a request for processes to lock that value (line 12) during superround 2 of the phase. Then, in superround 3 of the phase, all processes vote on which lock message to support, using a BROADCAST (line 16). In the third superround of the phase, each process that performed ACCEPT for votes for a particular value v from $\ell - t$ different identifiers sends $\langle$ack $v \rangle$ back to the leaders (line 20) and locks the value v (by adding the value to its *locks* set, along with the phase number associated with the lock). A leader that receives $\ell - t$ ack messages for the value it wanted locked can decide that value (line 22). Finally, each process that has decided sends a message to others (line 23); if any process receives such a message with the same decision value from $t + 1$ identifiers, it can also decide that value (line 26). At the end of a phase, a process releases old locks (line 30) if it has accepted enough votes for a later lock request.

To cope with homonyms, our algorithm differs from the original algorithm of [10] in the following three ways. (1) The new algorithm uses a set of processes with $\ell - t$ different identifiers as a quorum (e.g., for vote messages). The key property of these quorums is that any two such sets must both contain a process that is correct and does not share its identifier with any other process, as shown in Lemma 7, below. (2) The vote messages are needed to ensure agreement in the case where several leaders ask processes to lock different values, something which could not occur in the original algorithm of [10], since each phase in that algorithm has a unique leader. (3) The decide messages are used to ensure that a correct process that shares its identifier with a Byzantine process can eventually decide. (This is similar to the mechanism used in Section 3.2.) We begin by proving the property of quorums used by the algorithm.

Lemma 7 *Assume $\ell > \frac{n+3t}{2}$. If A and B are sets of identifiers and $|A| \geq \ell - t$ and $|B| \geq \ell - t$, then $A \cap B$ contains an identifier that belongs to only one correct process and no Byzantine processes.*

PROOF. At most $n - \ell$ identifiers belong to more than one process. At most t identifiers belong to Byzantine processes. Thus, any set that has more than $n - \ell + t$ identifiers must contain an identifier that belongs to only one correct process and no Byzantine processes. Since $2\ell - 3t > n$, we have $|A \cap B| = |A| + |B| - |A \cup B| \geq |A| + |B| - \ell \geq (\ell - t) + (\ell - t) - \ell = 2\ell - 3t - \ell + t > n - \ell + t$. $\square$

In the original algorithm of [10], each phase has a unique leader. In our algorithm, there may be several leaders. The new voting superround ensures this cannot cause problems, as shown in the following lemmas.

Lemma 8 *If the messages $\langle ack\ v, ph \rangle$ and $\langle ack\ v', ph \rangle$ are sent by correct processes, then $v = v'$.*

PROOF. Suppose a correct process p sends $\langle ack\ v, ph \rangle$ and a correct process p' sends $\langle ack\ v', ph \rangle$. (We may have $p = p'$.) According to line 18, there is a set A of $\ell - t$ identifiers j for which p performs ACCEPT($\langle vote\ v, ph \rangle, j$). Similarly, there is a set B of $\ell - t$ identifiers j for which p' performs ACCEPT($\langle vote\ v', ph \rangle, j$). By Lemma 7, $A \cap B$ contains an identifier j that belongs to only one correct process and no Byzantine processes. By unforgeability, the correct process with identifier j performed BROADCAST($\langle vote\ v, ph \rangle$) and BROADCAST($\langle vote\ v', ph \rangle$). Thus, $v = v'$. $\square$

Lemma 9 *If two correct processes decide on line 22 in the same phase, then they decide the same value.*

PROOF. Suppose two correct processes p and p' decide values v and v', respectively, during some phase ph. Then, process p received $\langle ack\ v, ph \rangle$ from $\ell - t > t$ different identifiers, so some correct process must have sent $\langle ack\ v, ph \rangle$. Similarly, some correct process must have sent $\langle ack\ v', ph \rangle$. By Lemma 8, $v = v'$. $\square$

The remainder of the proof of correctness of the algorithm is similar to the proof for the original algorithm of [10]. It is given in [8], using the following lemmas.

Lemma 10 *Suppose there is a value v and a phase ph such that processes with $\ell - t$ different identifiers sent an $\langle ack\ v, ph \rangle$ message in phase ph. Then, at all times after phase ph, each correct process that sent $\langle ack\ v, ph \rangle$ has a pair (v, ph') with $ph' \geq ph$ in its locks set.*

Lemma 11 *At the end of any phase ph_3 that occurs after T, if (v_1, ph_1) is in the locks variable of a correct process p_1 and (v_2, ph_2) is in the locks variable of a correct process p_2, then $v_1 = v_2$.*

Lemma 12 *Let p be a correct process. Let ph be a phase such that $(ph \mod \ell) + 1$ is the identifier of p and phase $ph - 1$ occurs after T. Then, p will send a lock message in superround 2 of phase ph.*

Combining Proposition 4 and 5 yields the following theorem (for numerate or innumerate processes).

Theorem 13 *Partially synchronous Byzantine agreement is solvable if and only if $\ell > \frac{n+3t}{2}$.*

5. RESTRICTED BYZANTINE PROCESSES

We now consider the effect of restricting the Byzantine processes so that each Byzantine process can send at most one message to each recipient in each round. We prove that this restriction reduces the number of identifiers needed to reach agreement if processes are numerate but does not help if processes are innumerate.

5.1 Numerate Processes

First, we consider the model where processes can count copies of identical messages. We prove the following two theorems for this model.

Theorem 14 *Synchronous Byzantine agreement is solvable with numerate processes against restricted Byzantine processes if and only if $\ell > t$.*

Theorem 15 *Partially synchronous Byzantine agreement is solvable with numerate processes against restricted Byzantine processes if and only if $\ell > t$.*

Both of these theorems follow from Proposition 16 and 18, below.

Proposition 16 *Synchronous Byzantine agreement is unsolvable with numerate processes against restricted Byzantine processes if $\ell \leq t$.*

PROOF SKETCH. To derive a contradiction, assume that there exists an algorithm $\mathcal{A}$ that solves Byzantine agreement with $\ell \leq t$. In the argument below, we consider only executions of $\mathcal{A}$ with some fixed set of ℓ Byzantine processes, chosen so that each of the ℓ identifiers is held by one Byzantine process.

We consider configurations of the the algorithm $\mathcal{A}$ at the end of a synchronous round. Such a configuration can be completely specified by the state of each process. A configuration C is *0-valent* if, starting from C, the only possible decision value that correct processes can have is 0; it is *1-valent* if, starting from C, the only possible decision value that correct processes can have is 1. C is *univalent* if it is either 0-valent or 1-valent; C is *multivalent* if it is not univalent.

The following lemma encapsulates a Byzantine agent's ability to influence the decision value.

Lemma 17 *Let C and C' be two configurations of $\mathcal{A}$ such that the state of only one correct process is different in C and C'. Then, there exist executions α and α' that start from C and C', respectively, which both produce the same output value.*

PROOF. Let p be the correct process whose state is different in C and C' and let i be the identifier assigned to p. Let s and s' be the state of p in C and C', respectively. Let b be a Byzantine process that has identifier i.

Let α be the execution from C in which b starts in state s' and follows p's algorithm, and all other Byzantine processes send no messages. Let α' be the execution from C' in which b starts in state s and follows p's algorithm, and all other Byzantine processes send no messages. No correct process other than p can distinguish between α and α', since p and b send the same messages in α as b and p send in α'. Thus, each correct process other than p must output the same decision in α and α'. $\square$

The remainder of the proof of Proposition 16 is a standard valency argument (see [8]). We sketch it here. By validity, the initial configuration where all inputs are 0 is 0-valent. We can obtain a sequence of initial configurations by changing the correct process's inputs to 1, one at a time. By validity, the final configuration in this sequence is 1-valent. By Lemma 17 successive configurations in this sequence are capable of leading to the same output. It follows that some initial configuration in this sequence is multivalent.

A similar argument can be used to show that every multivalent configuration must have a multivalent successor configuration, again using Lemma 17. Hence, we can construct an infinite execution of multivalent configurations in which no process ever decides, violating termination. This contradiction establishes Proposition 16. $\square$

Proposition 18 *Partially synchronous Byzantine agreement is solvable with numerate processes against restricted Byzantine processes if $\ell > t$.*

The algorithm used to prove this proposition is similar to the one presented in Section 4.2. Details may be found in [8]. Like the algorithm in Section 4.2, it uses an authenticated broadcast primitive, but here ACCEPT actions have an extra parameter indicating the multiplicity of the accepted message. More precisely, this multiplicity is greater than the number of correct processes that sent the message and does not exceed the number of correct processes by more than the actual number of Byzantine processes in the execution. Furthermore, all correct processes agree eventually on the multiplicity of each message.

This authenticated broadcast with multiplicity is used to ensure the agreement property. As $\ell > t$, at least one identifier is assigned only to correct processes. This property is used to ensure the termination property of the agreement algorithm.

5.2 Innumerate Processes

Theorem 19 *Synchronous Byzantine agreement is solvable with innumerate processes against restricted Byzantine processes if and only if $\ell > 3t$.*

PROOF SKETCH. (See [8] for a detailed proof.) By Proposition 2, there is an algorithm if $\ell > 3t$, even against (unrestricted) Byzantine processes, so the same algorithm would work against restricted Byzantine processes. To prove that $\ell > 3t$ is necessary, we use a simulation. If it were possible to solve the problem when $\ell \leq 3t$, this algorithm would work, in particular, when $n - \ell + 1$ of the processes are all assigned the same identifier and input, and all receive exactly the same messages from the Byzantine agents. In this situation, the $n - \ell + 1$ processes would behave as clones, taking exactly the same sequence of steps. This would imply that the same algorithm would solve Byzantine agreement when $n = \ell \leq 3t$, which is known to be impossible. $\square$

Theorem 20 *Partially synchronous Byzantine agreement is solvable with innumerate processes against restricted Byzantine processes if and only if $\ell > \frac{n+3t}{2}$.*

PROOF. By Proposition 5, there is an algorithm if $\ell > \frac{n+3t}{2}$, even against (unrestricted) Byzantine processes, so the same algorithm would work against restricted Byzantine processes. The impossibility result can be proved in exactly the same way as Proposition 4. In that proof, only the Byzantine process denoted $\mathcal{B}_1$ must send multiple messages to a single recipient in execution γ. Consider the messages $\mathcal{B}_1$ must send to $\mathcal{A}_t(0)$ in γ. It must send the same messages as the entire stack of processes running $\mathcal{A}_1$ send to $\mathcal{A}_t(0)$ in α. However, all processes in that stack behave identically in α, so $\mathcal{B}_1$ must simply send $n - \ell + 1$ copies of a message to $\mathcal{A}_t(0)$. Since we are now considering a model where $\mathcal{A}_t(0)$ is innumerate, $\mathcal{B}$ can simply send one copy of the message to $\mathcal{A}_t(0)$ instead. (A symmetric argument applies to the messages sent by $\mathcal{B}_1$ to each other process in γ.) $\square$

6. CONCLUDING REMARKS

Since the pioneering work of [1], the question of what can be computed in a totally anonymous distributed systems has been extensively studied. Some results depended on properties of the communication graph (e.g., [4, 23]). Some work considered shared memory for the "wake up" problem [13], others considered consensus [3]. The power of anonymous broadcast systems, in comparison with anonymous shared-memory systems has also been studied [2]. None of these considered process failures. Anonymous processes with crash failures have been considered more recently [5, 6, 9, 12, 17, 20]. In [16], Byzantine agreement was studied in a model with a restricted kind of anonymity: processes have no identifiers, but each process has a separate channel to every other process and a process can detect through which channel an incoming message is delivered. It was shown that Byzantine agreement can be solved in this model when $n > 3t$.

This paper is the first to study a distributed system model with homonyms, *i.e.*, with a limited number of identifiers. The model unifies both classical (non-anonymous) and anonymous models and is interesting from both a theoretical and a practical viewpoint. We completely characterized the solvability of Byzantine agreement in this model, precisely quantifying the impact of the adversary, with some surprising results. We focused however on agreement and many other problems would be interesting to consider. We also focused on computability and complexity is yet to be explored.

29

Acknowledgments.

We are grateful to Christian Cachin for his useful comments on our model with homonyms. A small subset of our results was presented in a preliminary form in [7]. Eric Ruppert received funding from the Natural Sciences and Engineering Research Council of Canada.

7. REFERENCES

[1] Dana Angluin. Local and global properties in networks of processors (extended abstract). In *Proc. 12th ACM Symposium on Theory of Computing*, pages 82–93. ACM, 1980.

[2] James Aspnes, Faith Ellen Fich, and Eric Ruppert. Relationships between broadcast and shared memory in reliable anonymous distributed systems. *Distributed Computing*, 18(3):209–219, February 2006.

[3] Hagit Attiya, Alla Gorbach, and Shlomo Moran. Computing in totally anonymous asynchronous shared memory systems. *Information and Computation*, 173(2):162–183, 2002.

[4] Paolo Boldi and Sebastiano Vigna. An effective characterization of computability in anonymous networks. In *Proc. 15th International Conference on Distributed Computing*, volume 2180 of *LNCS*, pages 33–47. Springer, 2001.

[5] François Bonnet and Michel Raynal. The price of anonymity: Optimal consensus despite asynchrony, crash and anonymity. In *Proc. 23rd International Symposium on Distributed Computing*, volume 5805 of *LNCS*, pages 341–355. Springer, 2009.

[6] Harry Buhrman, Alessandro Panconesi, Riccardo Silvestri, and Paul M. B. Vitányi. On the importance of having an identity or, is consensus really universal? *Distributed Computing*, 18(3):167–176, February 2006.

[7] Carole Delporte-Gallet, Hugues Fauconnier, Rachid Guerraoui, and Anne-Marie Kermarrec. Brief announcement: Byzantine agreement with homonyms. In *Proc. 22nd ACM Symposium on Parallelism in Algorithms and Architectures*, pages 74–75, 2010.

[8] Carole Delporte-Gallet, Hugues Fauconnier, Rachid Guerraoui, Anne-Marie Kermarrec, Eric Ruppert, and Hung Tran-The. Byzantine agreement with homonyms. Technical Report hal-00580133, CNRS, France, 2011.

[9] Carole Delporte-Gallet, Hugues Fauconnier, and Andreas Tielmann. Fault-tolerant consensus in unknown and anonymous networks. In *Proc. 29th IEEE International Conference on Distributed Computing Systems*, pages 368–375. IEEE Computer Society, 2009.

[10] Cynthia Dwork, Nancy A. Lynch, and Larry Stockmeyer. Consensus in the presence of partial synchrony. *Journal of the ACM*, 35(2):288–323, April 1988.

[11] Michael J. Fischer, Nancy A. Lynch, and Michael Merritt. Easy impossibility proofs for distributed consensus problems. *Distributed Computing*, 1(1):26–39, January 1986.

[12] Rachid Guerraoui and Eric Ruppert. Anonymous and fault-tolerant shared-memory computing. *Distributed Computing*, 20(3):165–177, October 2007.

[13] Prasad Jayanti and Sam Toueg. Wakeup under read/write atomicity. In Jan van Leeuwen and Nicola Santoro, editors, *Proc. 4th International Workshop on Distributed Algorithms*, volume 486 of *LNCS*, pages 277–288. Springer, 1990.

[14] Leslie Lamport, Robert Shostak, and Marshall Pease. The Byzantine generals problem. *ACM Transactions on Programming Languages and Systems*, 4(3):382–401, July 1982.

[15] Michael Okun. Agreement among unacquainted Byzantine generals. In *Proc. 19th International Conference on Distributed Computing*, volume 3724 of *LNCS*, pages 499–500. Springer, 2005.

[16] Michael Okun and Amnon Barak. Efficient algorithms for anonymous Byzantine agreement. *Theory of Computing Systems*, 42(2):222–238, February 2008.

[17] Michael Okun, Amnon Barak, and Eli Gafni. Renaming in synchronous message passing systems with Byzantine failures. *Distributed Computing*, 20(6):403–413, April 2008.

[18] Marshall Pease, Robert Shostak, and Leslie Lamport. Reaching agreement in the presence of faults. *Journal of the ACM*, 27(2):228–234, April 1980.

[19] Antony I. T. Rowstron and Peter Druschel. Pastry: Scalable, decentralized object location, and routing for large-scale peer-to-peer systems. In *Middleware*, volume 2218 of *LNCS*, pages 329–350, 2001.

[20] Eric Ruppert. The anonymous consensus hierarchy and naming problems. In *Proc. Principles of Distributed Systems, 11th International Conference*, volume 4878 of *LNCS*, pages 386–400. Springer, 2007.

[21] T. K. Srikanth and Sam Toueg. Simulating authenticated broadcasts to derive simple fault-tolerant algorithms. *Distributed Computing*, 2(2):80–94, 1987.

[22] Ion Stoica, Robert Morris, David R. Karger, M. Frans Kaashoek, and Hari Balakrishnan. Chord: A scalable peer-to-peer lookup service for internet applications. In *ACM SIGCOMM*, pages 149–160, 2001.

[23] Masafumi Yamashita and Tsunehiko Kameda. Computing on anonymous networks: Part I-characterizing the solvable cases. *IEEE Transactions on Parallel and Distributed Systems*, 7(1):69–89, 1996.

Distributed Graph Coloring in a Few Rounds

Kishore Kothapalli[*]
Center for Security, Theory, and Algorithmic
Research
International Institute of Information Technology
Hyderabad, India 500 032.
kkishore@iiit.ac.in

Sriram Pemmaraju[†]
Department of Computer Science
The University of Iowa
Iowa City, IA 52242, USA.
sriram@cs.uiowa.edu

ABSTRACT

This paper considers the question of how many colors a distributed graph coloring algorithm would need to use if it had only k rounds available, for any positive integer k. In our main result, we present an algorithm that runs in $O(k)$ rounds for any k bounded below by $\Omega(\log \log n)$ and bounded above by $O(\sqrt{\log n})$, and uses $O(a \cdot n^{1/k})$ colors to color a graph with arboricity a. This result is optimal since the palette size matches the lower bound of Barenboim and Elkin (*PODC 2008*). This result is achieved via the use of several new results developed in this paper on coloring graphs whose edges have been acyclically oriented. For example, suppose that G is an n-vertex, acyclically oriented graph with maximum out-degree Δ_o. We present an algorithm that, for any $k \geq 2 \log \log n$, runs in $O(k)$ rounds on G to produce an (i) $O(\Delta_o)$-coloring when $\Delta_o \in \Omega(\max\{kn^{2/k^2} \log^{1+1/k} n, 2^k\})$ and an (ii) $O(\Delta_o \cdot n^{2/k^2})$-coloring when $\Delta_o \in \Omega(\max\{k \log^{1+1/k} n, 2^k\})$. These results are useful in any setting where it is possible to efficiently compute acyclic orientations of a graph with $\Delta_o \ll \Delta$. We derive non-trivial bounds on the palette size even when $k < 2 \log \log n$.

Our main technical contributions can be summarized as: (i) developing a k-round version of the algorithm of Kothapalli et al. (*IPDPS 2006*) which computes an $O(\Delta)$-coloring of a graph in $O(\sqrt{\log n})$ rounds, and (ii) developing an oriented version of the Brooks-Vizing coloring result of Grable and Panconesi (*SODA 1998*).

Categories and Subject Descriptors

G.2.2 [**Graph Theory**]: [Graph Algorithms]

General Terms

Algorithms, Theory

[*]Partially supported by the IBM Hybrid Multicore Center of Excellence, IIIT Hyderabad.
[†]Partially supported by NSF Grant CCF 0915543.

Keywords

Graph coloring, distributed algorithms, symmetry breaking, oriented graphs

1. INTRODUCTION

In this paper we answer the following question: if we have only a few rounds at our disposal, how many colors might a distributed algorithm need for coloring a graph? More specifically, we assume that we have a budget of about k rounds, for k typically much smaller than $\Theta(\log n)$, and our goal is to design distributed algorithms that run in $O(k)$ rounds and use as small a color palette as possible. We expect the number of colors to be an increasing function of graph parameters such as n (number of vertices), and Δ (maximum vertex degree), and a decreasing function of k. Recently this line of investigation, that studies the interplay between the number of rounds k and the quality of the solution computed by a k-round algorithm has been quite fruitful for classical combinatorial optimization problems such as minimum dominating set, facility location, and vertex cover [13, 18, 22]. Distributed algorithms that use very few rounds are important for wireless ad hoc and sensor networks that operate in environments characterized by heavy churn. In such settings, it is important to arrive at a feasible solution very quickly, even if the solution is poor relative to the optimal solution, so that higher-order tasks such as routing and scheduling are minimally affected.

Graph coloring is one of the most widely studied problems in distributed computing (not to mention, graph theory), not only because of its myriad applications to resource allocation and scheduling, but also because graph coloring nicely abstracts fundamental challenges of distributed computing such as contention resolution and symmetry breaking. Distributed graph coloring has a rich history starting with Linial's seminal work [15]. Significant advances continue to be made in the area with two ground breaking papers appearing in PODC 2010, one advancing the state of the art for *randomized* distributed coloring [23] and, the other [2] solving a 20 year old question due to Linial on the existence of a *deterministic* distributed graph coloring algorithm that uses $o(\Delta^2)$ colors, yet runs in $O(\text{polylog}(n))$ rounds. The most well-known distributed graph coloring algorithm is randomized and is based on Luby's maximal independent set (MIS) algorithm [16]. This algorithm yields a $(\Delta + 1)$-coloring in $O(\log n)$ rounds with high probability (w.h.p.). If one wants to use fewer rounds, the algorithm of Kothapalli et al. [11] computes an $O(\Delta)$-coloring in $O(\sqrt{\log n})$ rounds w.h.p.; this was the first evidence that

$O(\Delta)$-coloring is possible in sublogarithmic rounds. If one wants to use even fewer colors, the best results are from the recent work of Schneider and Wattenhofer [23], where randomized algorithms that run in $O(\log \log n)$ rounds, $O(\log^* n)$ rounds, and $O(1)$ rounds are described. See Table 1 for a summary of these results.

Table 1: Fewest colors that distributed coloring algorithms with various running times $k = O(\log n)$ use. Here c is some positive integer constant and $\log^{(c)} n$ is obtained by applying the $\log$ function c times to n.

Running time	Number of colors	Source
$O(\log n)$	$\Delta + 1$	[16]
$O(\sqrt{\log n})$	$O(\Delta)$	[11]
$O(\log \log n)$	$O(\Delta + \log n)$	[23]
$O(\log^* n)$	$O(\Delta + \log^{1+1/\log^* n} n)$	[23]
$O(1)$	$O(\Delta \log^{(c)} n + \log^{1+1/c} n)$	[23]

In our work, we focus on *arboricity*, rather than on the maximum degree Δ, as a parameter for measuring the number of colors used. Let the *density* of a graph $G = (V, E)$, $|V| \geq 2$, be the ratio $\lceil |E|/(|V| - 1) \rceil$. Let the density of a single-vertex graph be 1. The *arboricity* of a graph $G = (V, E)$, denoted $a(G)$, can be defined as $a(G) := \max\{$density$(G') \mid G'$ is a subgraph of $G\}$. By the celebrated Nash-Williams decomposition theorem [20], the arboricity of a graph is exactly equal to the minimum number of forests that its edge set can be decomposed into. The arboricity of a graph seems to more finely calibrate (as compared to Δ) the number of colors a graph might need. For example, graphs with constant arboricity – planar graphs are a simple example – can be easily colored by a sequential greedy algorithm with constant number of colors, despite having vertices with arbitrarily high degree. In fact, it is not hard to see that for a graph with constant arboricity, there is a distributed $O(1)$-coloring algorithm that runs in $O(\log n)$ rounds (see [1] for a far more general result). The general question we ask is this: if we want to color a graph in a distributed fashion, using $k \leq \log n$ rounds, what is the minimum number of colors we need, expressed as a function of $a(G)$. A specific instance of this question might be: how many colors might we need to color constant-arboricity graphs if we have $k = \sqrt{\log n}$ rounds at our disposal. It is tempting to wonder if an $O(1)$-coloring of constant-arboricity graphs in $O(\sqrt{\log n})$ rounds is possible. Unfortunately, a lower bound due to Linial [15], and extended by Barenboim and Elkin [1], quickly dashes these hopes.

THEOREM 1.1 (**Barenboim and Elkin** [1]). *Given a graph with n vertices and with arboricity a and a parameter $q = O(\sqrt{n}/a^2)$, an $O(a^2 \cdot q)$-coloring requires $\Omega(\frac{\log n}{\log(aq)} + \log^* n)$ time.*

The lower bound can be restated in a language more convenient to us as follows.

THEOREM 1.2. *For any k and $a \leq n^{1/2-1/k}$, coloring an n-vertex arboricity-a graph with $O(a \cdot n^{1/k})$ colors needs $\Omega(k)$ rounds.*

From this lower bound it is immediate that an $O(a)$-coloring for graphs with arboricity a cannot be computed in $o(\log n)$ rounds. In this paper we present algorithms that show that this lower bound can be matched exactly for a wide range of values of k.

1.1 Our Techniques and Results

One of our main technical contribution is in extending the approach of Kothapalli et al. [11] in two directions. This paper [11] starts by assuming that the edges of the given network G have been *oriented*, i.e., each undirected edge $\{u, v\}$ is replaced by the directed edge (u, v) or (v, u). Each vertex starts with a palette of size $O(\Delta)$ and runs a "Luby-like" coloring algorithm in which it only pays attention to color choices made by its out-neighbors. By a "Luby-like" algorithm we mean one that has the following general form: each vertex makes a tentative color at random from its palette; then the vertex makes this choice permanent if none of its neighbors have made the same tentative choice; finally, the vertex updates its color palette by deleting all colors that have been permanently chosen by neighbors in the current round. There are many different variants on this general theme. For example, Grable and Panconesi [9] use a version of this algorithm in which in each round each vertex first decides probabilistically whether to participate in that round or not. For more background on Luby-like algorithms, we refer the reader to [7]. The aforementioned algorithm of Kothapalli et al. [11] can be viewed as yet another variant, one in which each vertex resolves contention for colors only with out-neighbors. Kothapalli et al. [11] show that w.h.p. after $O(\sqrt{\log n})$ rounds the vertices that are still color-free induce a subgraph in which the maximum length of an oriented path is $O(\sqrt{\log n})$. If the initial edge orientation of the input graph is acyclic then the subgraph induced by the color-free vertices can be colored in a deterministic, level-by-level fashion in $O(\sqrt{\log n})$ rounds. An acyclic orientation is easy to obtain, for example, by using vertex IDs and therefore the algorithm of Kothapalli et al. [11] colors an arbitrary graph in $O(\sqrt{\log n})$ rounds using $O(\Delta)$ colors.

In one direction we derive and analyze a version of the Kothapalli et al. algorithm that runs in $O(k)$ rounds, for any k, instead of in $O(\sqrt{\log n})$ rounds. In another direction, we show how this algorithm could use only $O(\Delta_o)$ colors (under certain circumstances) instead of $O(\Delta)$ colors, where Δ_o is an upper bound on the out-degree of vertices in the oriented graph G. Managing with $O(\Delta_o)$ colors requires a fundamental rethinking of the Kothapalli et al. algorithm and more generally "Luby-like" coloring algorithms. This is because a vertex can no longer respond to colors chosen by in-neighbors by deleting these colors from its palette. Such deletions may cause the palette of a vertex to empty out rapidly since the number of in-neighbors of the vertex may be quite large relative to its palette size (which is proportional to its out-degree). We deal with this using several new techniques. First, we allow the construction of an improper coloring, which is then rectified by a "Palette Inflation" technique. In order to keep the number of new colors introduced by Palette Inflation down, we use techniques from the distributed computation of Brooks-Vizing colorings due to Grable and Panconesi [9]. These techniques are designed for sparse, i.e., triangle-free graphs, but we show how despite the presence of triangles, we get the appropriate behavior due to edge-orientations. In our first main result, we prove the following theorem.

THEOREM 1.3. *Let G be an edge-oriented n-vertex graph with maximum vertex out-degree Δ_o.*

(i) *For any positive integer k, G can be colored using*
$$O(k \cdot \Delta_o^{1+1/k} \cdot n^{2/k^2}) \text{ colors in } O(k) \text{ rounds.}$$

(ii) *If $k \geq 2 \log \log n$ and $\Delta_o = \Omega(\max\{k \cdot n^{2/k^2} \cdot \log^{1+1/k} n, 2^k\})$, G can be colored using $O(\Delta_o)$ colors in $O(k)$ rounds.*

(iii) *If $k \geq 2 \log \log n$ and $\Delta_o = \Omega(\max\{k \cdot \log^{1+1/k} n, 2^k\})$, G can be colored using $O(\Delta_o \cdot n^{2/k^2})$ colors in $O(k)$ rounds.*

(iv) *If $k < 2 \log \log n$ and $\Delta_o \geq 2^{2^k} \cdot \log n$, then G can be colored using $O\left(n^{2/k^2} \cdot \Delta_o^{1+1/k} \cdot \frac{1}{2^{2^k}}\right)$ colors in $O(k)$ rounds.*

Item (i) in the above theorem is our basic result, while items (ii)-(iv) are improvements over (i) for certain ranges of values of k and Δ_o. Since for any edge orientation of a graph $\Delta_o \leq \Delta$, all of the above results hold when Δ_o is replaced by Δ. However, it is worth noting that our result is incomparable to results (e.g., [23]) that use $\Theta(\Delta)$ or more colors. Our result may be relatively weak when $\Delta_o = \Delta$, but it is designed to be particularly useful when $\Delta_o \ll \Delta$. In such situations, our algorithm can rapidly construct colorings with far fewer colors than $\Theta(\Delta)$, something that is not possible with earlier results.

Item (ii) tells us that for "high" out-degree graphs an $O(\Delta_o)$ coloring is possible in very few rounds. It is instructive to consider specific instances of this result for two two extreme values of k. At $k = \sqrt{\log n}$, one can simplify the lower bound on Δ_o to $\Omega(2^{\sqrt{\log n}})$ and therefore this instance of our result is an $O(\Delta_o)$-coloring in $O(\sqrt{\log n})$ rounds when $\Delta_o = \Omega(2^{\sqrt{\log n}})$. At the other end of the spectrum, when $k = 2 \log \log n$, Δ_o can be bounded below by $\Omega(n^{c/(\log \log n)^2})$ for some constant $c > 2$ and therefore this instance of our result is an $O(\Delta_o)$-coloring in $O(\log \log n)$ rounds when $\Delta_o = \Omega(n^{c/\log \log n})$. Note that items (ii) and (iii) are identical for $k = \Theta(\sqrt{\log n})$ and this result — $O(\Delta_o)$-coloring in $O(\sqrt{\log n})$ rounds — subsumes the result of Kothapalli et al. [11] for large enough Δ_o and is much stronger whenever $\Delta_o \ll \Delta$.

The above theorem is particularly useful in settings in which "good" edge orientations are easily obtained. One such setting is identified by Barenboim and Elkin [1], who show that the edges of a graph G with arboricity a can be oriented in $O(k)$ rounds so that $\Delta_o = O(a \cdot n^{1/k})$. Our final result is obtained by using the Barenboim-Elkin orientation as a first step followed by the algorithm corresponding to Theorem 1.3.

THEOREM 1.4. *Let G be an n-vertex graph with arboricity a.*

(i) *For any k, $2 \log \log n \leq k \leq \sqrt{\log n}$, G can be colored with $O(a \cdot n^{1/k})$ colors in $O(k)$ rounds.*

(ii) *For any $k < 2 \log \log n$, G can be colored using*
$$O\left(a^{1+1/k} \cdot n^{\frac{1}{k} + \frac{3}{k^2}} \cdot \frac{1}{2^{2^k}}\right) \text{ colors in } O(k) \text{ rounds.}$$

Item (i) in the above theorem provides an upper bound that exactly matches the lower bound in Theorem 1.2, for values of k sandwiched between $\Omega(\log \log n)$ and $O(\sqrt{\log n})$. The orientation of Barenboim and Elkin [1] mentioned above can be obtained via deterministic means and is similar to decomposition techniques used by Czygrinow et al. [3, 4, 6]. As pointed out by Barenboim and Elkin [1], using these decomposition techniques, one can obtain an $O(q \cdot a^2)$-coloring on an n-vertex graph with arboricity a and parameter $q \geq 1$ in $O(\frac{\log n}{\log q} + \log^* n)$ rounds. For $k = \Omega(\log^* n)$ this translates to an $O(a^2 \cdot n^{1/k})$-coloring algorithm in $O(k)$ rounds. For constant values of the arboricity a, this result obtained via a *deterministic* algorithm matches our result (Item (i) of Theorem 1.4) and also matches the lower bound. However, for larger values of a the power of randomization seems to come into play and as the value of a grows, the coloring promised by Theorem 1.4 uses a factor-a fewer colors relative to the result of Barenboim and Elkin [1].

1.2 Related Work

There is a vast body of literature on distributed graph coloring and we do not review this work here, instead referring the reader to "Related Work" sections in [2, 23]. Our work is inspired by two recent trends in distributed algorithms, one that focuses on graph arboricity as a parameter of interest and another that seeks to design k-round algorithms for very small k, with a possible concomittant loss in the quality of the solution.

The work of Barenboim and Elkin [1] on coloring graphs with bounded arboricity has already been discussed. In addition to the coloring problem, this paper also considers the maximal independent set (MIS) problem and presents an algorithm that runs in $O(\frac{\log n}{\log \log n})$ rounds for graphs with constant arboricity. Also worth mentioning is a recent paper by Lenzen and Wattenhofer [14] on distributed approximation algorithms for the minimum dominating set problem on bounded arboricity graphs. The algorithm in this paper computes an $O(a^2)$-approximation for MDS in $O(\log n)$ rounds on graphs with arboricity a. Another example is the work of Czygrinow et al. [5] on distributed maximum matching algorithms on bounded arboricity graphs.

There is recent interest in designing distributed algorithms that run in a fixed number, say k, rounds and compute non-trivial solutions despite having a tiny budget of communication rounds. Kuhn and Wattenhofer [13] seem to have been the first to ask whether one can design a k round distributed algorithm that can compute a non-trivial approximation to MDS even when $k = O(1)$. They answered this question in the affirmative and their approach of using LP relaxation techniques was subsequently generalized and extended to other problems [12, 18]. More recently, Pandit and Pemmaraju [21, 22] have shown that such k-round algorithms for MDS and facility location can also be derived using primal-dual techniques, sometimes yielding better results.

2. PRELIMINARIES

2.1 Model and Notations

Our algorithms run on the standard distributed computing model in which a graph G represents the network, with vertex set $V = V(G)$ representing the computational entities and edge set $E = E(G)$ representing the communication links. Computation proceeds in synchronous rounds, and in each round, each node can, (i) receive a (possibly) different message from each neighbor, (ii) perform some finite amount of local computation, and (iii) send a (possibly) different message to each neighbor. We assume that all the communication links are undirected and hence bidirectional. Our algorithms will usually assume that the edges of G are *oriented*, even though the underlying network consists of bidirectional links. When the edges of the graph G are oriented, for each $v \in V$, we denote by $d_o(v)$, the *out-degree* of v, i.e., the number of neighbors w of v such that the edge $\{v, w\} \in E$ is oriented from v to w. We call such neighbors as the *out-neighbors* of v. We define $\Delta_o(G) := \max_{v \in V} d_o(v)$.

2.2 The Oriented Graph Coloring Algorithm

Our algorithms and the corresponding analysis use edge-orientation in a critical way. Consider two neighbors v and w such that w is an out-neighbor of v. Consider a Luby-type coloring algorithm in which each node independently and tentatively picks a color from its palette and then coordinates with neighbors to resolve conflicts in color choices. In a round of this algorithm, suppose that both nodes v and w tentatively choose the same color c. After one round of communication, node v detects an out-neighbor with a conflicting color choice and uncolors itself. Node w however, ignores choices made by in-neighbors and can finalize its choice of color c provided it has no out-neighbor that has chosen color c in this round. Thus, the resolution of color conflicts is different from what happens in standard distributed coloring algorithms (see for example [16, 10]) in which both v and w would have remained uncolored. In fact, nodes ignore their in-neighbors to the extent that they do not even update their color palette in response to in-neighbors making a permanent color choice. Specifically, suppose that in some round, node v permanently colors itself c. Color c is not deleted from w's palette and in a subsequent round w may decide to color itself c also, thereby leading to an improper coloring (at least temporarily). Our main idea is to use orientation to quickly produce a partial, improper coloring and then repair it using a separate algorithm. Our algorithm `OrientedRandColor` for vertex coloring oriented graphs is shown in Figure 1. At an arbitrary node u, this algorithm takes two arguments, k, a positive integer specifying the number of rounds the algorithm should run for, and C_u, an initial palette of colors. The algorithm is similar to well-known randomized distributed graph coloring algorithms [17, 10], the main difference being in how color conflicts are resolved. Note that in Steps 3 and 7 node u sends its color choice only to in-neighbors because its out-neighbors are not interested in its actions. Also, in Step 4 node u only considers color choices made by out-neighbors in figuring out whether to color itself permanently. When `OrientedRandColor` terminates, the coloring may be *partial*, i.e., not all nodes may have been assigned a color because k rounds may not suffice to color all vertices in G. Furthermore, as mentioned earlier, the coloring may also be *improper*, i.e., neighbors in G may be assigned the same color.

3. A SLIGHTLY LOOSE ANALYSIS

All edge-orientations we work with are assumed to be *acyclic*. This is mainly for ease of exposition. In subsequent remarks we will point out that the presence of oriented cycles

is not a problem, provided the cycles are not small. In Lemmas 3.1 and 3.3 we prove properties of the partial, improper coloring constructed by `OrientedRandColor` and later show how to repair this coloring quickly.

3.1 A Partial Improper Coloring

We first show a useful property of neighbors that are assigned the same color.

LEMMA 3.1. *If* `OrientedRandColor` *assigns the same color to two neighbors in G, then it does so in different rounds.*

PROOF. Suppose that u and v are neighbors in G with edge $\{u, v\}$ oriented from u to v. Further suppose that u and v are both assigned the same color, say c, by `OrientedRandColor`. Consider the round t in which u was permanently assigned c. Node v could not have been assigned color c in any round earlier than t because that would mean that c is absent from u's color palette at the beginning of round t. Node v could not have been assigned color c in round t, because that would mean that both u and v picked color c tentatively in round t and in such a situation node u would defer to its out-neighbor and remain uncolored. Therefore, node v is assigned a color permanently in a round that comes after round t. □

In Lemma 3.3, we show that w.h.p. there are no long, oriented, uncolored paths after `OrientedRandColor` has terminated. But before we get to this lemma, we need a technical lemma that helps us upper bound the joint probability of certain, possibly dependent, events.

LEMMA 3.2. *Let S be a subset of vertices of G that have remained uncolored in the first $i - 1$ rounds of* `Oriented-RandColor`. *Let E_S denote the event that all vertices in S remain uncolored in round i and let E_v denote the event that a vertex $v \in S$ has remained uncolored in round i. Then,*

$$\Pr(E_S) \leq \prod_{v \in S} \Pr(E_v).$$

PROOF. Let $S = \{v_1, v_2, \dots, v_t\}$. We can write $\Pr(E_S)$ as

$$\Pr(E_S) = \prod_{v_j \in S} \Pr(E_{v_j} | \wedge_{\ell=1}^{j-1} E_{v_\ell}).$$

We will now show that

$$\Pr(E_{v_j} | \wedge_{\ell=1}^{j-1} E_{v_\ell}) \leq \Pr(E_{v_j}), \qquad (1)$$

which will yield the inequality claimed in the theorem.

Define a *configuration* as the tentative color choice made in round i by all the vertices in G that did not color themselves in rounds 1 through $i - 1$. Fix a configuration C and for any $v \in S$ let $N_o^C(v)$ denote the set of out-neighbors of v that have been assigned the same color as v in the configuration C. The set of all configurations that satisfy $\wedge_{\ell=1}^{j-1} E_{v_\ell}$ can be partitioned into two subsets:

(i) Those configurations C in which for every v_ℓ, $1 \leq \ell \leq j - 1$, $N_o^C(v) - N_o(v_j) \neq \emptyset$

(ii) The rest of the configurations, i.e., those configurations C in which for some v_ℓ, $1 \leq \ell \leq j - 1$, $N_o^C(v_\ell) \subseteq N_o(v_j)$.

With respect to the configurations of Type (i), the probability of E_{v_j} is equal to its unconditional probability. It

```
Algorithm OrientedRandColor(k, C_u)
Comment: C_u is node u's palette of colors
Begin-Algorithm
1.    for i := 1 to k do
2.        Node u chooses a color c_u from C_u, uniformly at random.
3.        Node u sends c_u to all of its uncolored in-neighbors
4.        if every color received by node u from an out-neighbor is distinct from c_u, then
5.            u makes c_u its permanent color. Otherwise node u remains uncolored.
6.        if u is permanently colored in Step 5 then
7.            u sends it color choice to all uncolored in-neighbors
8.        Node u deletes from C_u all colors assigned permanently to out-neighbors
9.    end-for
End-Algorithm
```

Figure 1: Coloring oriented graphs via a Luby-like algorithm.

is possible that in some configurations of Type (ii), two or more out-neighbors of v_j are required to have the same color. Therefore, with respect to configurations of Type (ii), the probability of E_{v_j} is at most the unconditional probability of E_{v_j}. Combining these observations about both types of configurations, we obtain Inequality (1). $\square$

In the rest of the paper we will use Δ_o as a shorthand for $\Delta_o(G)$ whenever G is apparent from the context.

LEMMA 3.3. *Suppose that initially $|C_u| \geq \Delta_o^{1+1/k} \cdot n^{2/k^2}$ for all nodes u. After* OrientedRandColor *has terminated, w.h.p., every oriented uncolored path in G has length at most k.*

PROOF. Fix an oriented path $P = (v_1, v_2, \ldots, v_{k+1})$ of length $k+1$. For any integer j, $1 \leq j \leq k+1$ and nonnegative integer i, let $E_{v_j,i}$ denote the event that vertex v_j remains uncolored after the first i rounds and let $E_{P,i}$ denote the event that *all* of the vertices in path P remain uncolored after the first i rounds. We first compute an upper bound on the conditional probability $\Pr(E_{v_j,i}|E_{P,i-1})$.

$E_{P,i-1}$ implies that v_j is not colored at the end of round $i-1$. Suppose that v_j's palette has lost some t colors over the course of the first $i-1$ rounds. This means that the number of uncolored out-neighbors of v_j has shrunk by at least t, i.e., $d_o(v_j) - t$ is an upper bound on the number of uncolored out-neighbors of v_j after the first $i-1$ rounds. Then the probability that v_j is not colored in round i (conditioned on $E_{P,i-1}$) is equal to the probability that it picks the same color as an out-neighbor. And this is at most

$$\frac{d_o(v_j) - t}{|C_{v_j}| - t} \leq \frac{d_o(v_j)}{|C_{v_j}|} \leq \frac{\Delta_o}{\Delta_o^{1+1/k} \cdot n^{2/k^2}} \leq \frac{1}{\Delta_o^{1/k} \cdot n^{2/k^2}}.$$

Let E_P be shorthand for the event $E_{P,k}$. Then,

$$\Pr(E_P) = \prod_{i=1}^{k} \Pr(E_{P,i}|E_{P,i-1}).$$

Using the definition of $E_{P,i}$ and Lemma 3.2, we obtain

$$\begin{aligned}
\Pr(E_{P,i}|E_{P,i-1}) &= \Pr(\wedge_{j=1}^{k+1} E_{v_j,i}|E_{P,i-1}) \\
&\leq \prod_{j=1}^{k+1} \Pr(E_{v_j,i}|E_{P,i-1}) \\
&\leq \left(\frac{1}{\Delta_o^{1/k} \cdot n^{2/k^2}}\right)^{k+1}.
\end{aligned}$$

Hence,

$$\Pr(E_P) \leq \left(\frac{1}{\Delta_o^{1/k} \cdot n^{2/k^2}}\right)^{k(k+1)} \leq \frac{1}{\Delta_o^{k+1} \cdot n^2}.$$

There are at most $n \cdot \Delta_o^{k+1}$ oriented paths of length $k+1$ and therefore, using the union bound we see that the probability that there exists an uncolored, oriented path of length $k + 1$ is at most

$$n \cdot \Delta_o^{k+1} \cdot \frac{1}{\Delta_o^{k+1} \cdot n^2} = \frac{1}{n}.$$

$\square$

3.2 Repairing the Coloring

Even though the coloring constructed by OrientedRand-Color is partial and improper, the properties established in Lemmas 3.1 and 3.3, allow us to "repair" the coloring in k additional rounds with an accompanying inflation of the palette by factor k.

Palette Inflation.

Let c_u denote the color assigned by OrientedRandColor to node u. We recolor each node u with the color (c_u, t_u), where t_u is an integer satisfying $1 \leq t_u \leq k$ that denotes the round in which u was permanently assigned a color by OrientedRandColor. Since Lemma 3.1 tells us that any two neighbors which are assigned the same color by Oriented-RandColor are assigned colors in distinct rounds, we see that neighbors in G now have distinct colors. Furthermore, using the round numbers in this way to disambiguate the colors inflates the palette size by a factor of k.

Deterministic Completion.

Lemma 3.3 allows us to color the nodes not colored by OrientedRandColor by using a simple deterministic algorithm. In the each round, all uncolored nodes with no uncolored out-neighbors are assigned an arbitrary color from their palette. Note that this step is well-defined as long as the initial palette size $|C_u|$ is at least $\Delta_o + 1$ for all vertices u. By definition, the set of nodes considered in each round forms an independent set and therefore no coordination is needed while making color choices. Lemma 3.3 tells us that every oriented uncolored path has length at most k. After one round of the Deterministic Completion algorithm, every oriented uncolored path in G has length at most $k - 1$. It is easy to see via an inductive argument that after t rounds, $1 \leq t \leq k$, of the Deterministic Completion algorithm, every oriented uncolored path in G has length at most $k - t$. Hence, OrientedRandColor augmented by Palette Inflation and followed by Deterministic Completion leads to the following theorem.

THEOREM 3.4. *Let k be any positive integer. Given a graph G with an acyclic orientation with maximum out-degree Δ_o, a $(k \cdot \Delta_o^{1+1/k} \cdot n^{2/k^2})$-coloring of G can be achieved in $2k$ rounds.*

This result appears as item (i) in Theorem 1.3 in the "Introduction."

Remark.

We use the acyclic orientation of G in the Deterministic Completion Step. Such an orientation guarantees that the subgraph induced by uncolored vertices does not contain any oriented cycles and therefore this subgraph can be processed in a level-by-level fashion. It is worth noting that an acyclic orientation is stronger than what we need; it would suffice to have an orientation that did not have any cycles of length k or less.

4. A TIGHTER ANALYSIS

We now use a tighter analysis to improve on Theorem 3.4. We first assume that $k \geq 2 \log \log n$ (in Section 4.1) and in this setting we obtain two results: (i) for large enough Δ_o, we shave off the $\Delta^{1/k} \cdot n^{2/k^2}$-term from the number of colors in Theorem 3.4 and show that we can obtain a $k \cdot \Delta_o$-coloring in $2k$ rounds, and (ii) for smaller values of Δ_o, we shave off the $\Delta_o^{1/k}$-term from the number of colors in Theorem 3.4 and obtain a $k \cdot \Delta_o \cdot n^{2/k^2}$-coloring in $2k$ rounds. Subsequently (in Section 4.2) we deal with the case when $k < 2 \log \log n$.

4.1 When $k \geq 2 \log \log n$

We use "Phase I" to denote the first $k/2$ rounds of the `OrientedRandColor` algorithm and first bound the "effective" maximum out-degree of vertices in G after Phase I in Section 4.1.1. We use "Phase II" to denote the last $k/2$ rounds and analyze this phase separately in Section 4.1.2.

4.1.1 Phase I: Reducing Δ_o Quickly

We define the *effective out-degree* of a vertex v as the number of uncolored out-neighbors of v. In the following analysis, we show that the effective out-degree of every vertex in G decays quite rapidly (at an inverse doubly exponential rate) and this allows us to claim a lot of progress even in $O(\log \log n)$ rounds. This analysis is similar to that used in certain balls-and-bins problems (see Problem 3.4 in [19]) and has been used in other papers [9, 11]. The analysis also requires the use large deviation inequalities due to Grable [8]. We start with the following lemma that shows the progress made by the algorithm in Phase I. The proof of this lemma is similar to the proof of [11, Lemma 4.1].

LEMMA 4.1. *Suppose that $|C_u| \geq 3\Delta_o$ for all $u \in V$. At the end of Phase I, the effective out-degree of every vertex in G is at most $\min\{\log n, \Delta_o\}$ w.h.p.*

PROOF. Let us denote by $d_o^i(v)$ the effective out-degree of v at the start of round i. Let $d_o^i = \max_v d_o^i(v)$ and let C_u^i denote u's palette at the beginning of round i. Then,

$$\begin{aligned} P_u^i &:= \quad \text{Pr}(u \text{ does not get colored in round } i) \\ &\leq \quad \sum_{j=1}^{d_o^i(v)} \frac{1}{|C_u^i|} \\ &\leq \quad \frac{d_o^i}{2\Delta_o}. \end{aligned}$$

Let $N_o^i(v)$ denote the set of uncolored out-neighbors of vertex v at the beginning of round i. Using the above upper

bound on P_u^i we obtain

$$\text{Ex}(d_o^{i+1}(v)) = \sum_{u \in N_o^i(v)} P_u^i \leq \frac{(d_o^i)^2}{2\Delta_o}.$$

Using large deviation arguments from [8], it can be shown that $d_o^{i+1}(v)$ exceeds its expectation by more than $\sqrt{cd_o^i \log n}$ (for some constant c) with probability less than $1/n^2$. This means that w.h.p. the d_o^i-values satisfy the following recurrence:

$$d_o^{i+1} \leq \frac{(d_o^i)^2}{2\Delta_o} + \sqrt{cd_o^i \log n}$$

Thus, w.h.p., $d_o^i \leq \frac{d_o^1}{2^{2^i}} = \frac{\Delta_o}{2^{2^i}}$. □

The above lemma guarantees that after Phase I, i.e., the first $k/2$ rounds of `OrientedRandColor`, every vertex has at most $\log n$ uncolored out-neighbors.

4.1.2 Phase II : Breaking Long Uncolored Paths

Suppose that all nodes start Phase II with palettes of size at least $t \cdot \Delta_o$ for a parameter t to be specified later. As in Lemma 3.3, we argue that w.h.p. after Phase II, every oriented path of length at least $(k + 1)$ has at least one colored node. However, in the current lemma, the fact that Phase I has caused a significant reduction in the effective out-degree plays a critical role.

LEMMA 4.2. *Suppose that initially $|C_u| \geq t \cdot \Delta_o \geq n^{2/k^2} \cdot \log^{1+1/k} n$ for all nodes u. After `OrientedRandColor` has terminated, w.h.p., every oriented uncolored path in G has length at most k.*

PROOF. This proof is similar to the proof of Lemma 3.3 and so we borrow notation from that proof and only provide a sketch here.

Fix an oriented path $P = (v_1, v_2, \ldots, v_{k+1})$ of length $k+1$. Then,

$$\text{Pr}(E_{v_j,i} | E_{P,i-1}) \leq \frac{d_o(v_j)}{|C_{v_j}|} \leq \frac{\log n}{t \cdot \Delta_o}.$$

Using this and following the calculations in the proof of Lemma 3.3, we see that

$$\text{Pr}(E_P) \leq \left(\frac{\log n}{t \cdot \Delta_o} \right)^{k(k+1)}.$$

There are at most $n \cdot \log^{k+1} n$ oriented paths of length $k+1$ and therefore, using the union bound we see that the probability that there exists an uncolored, oriented path of length $k + 1$ is at most

$$n \cdot \log^{k+1} n \cdot \left(\frac{\log n}{t \cdot \Delta_o} \right)^{k(k+1)} \tag{2}$$

For this expression to be at most $1/n$, we require that

$$(t \cdot \Delta_o)^{k(k+1)} \geq n^2 \log^{(k+1)^2} n.$$

The requirement in the lemma that $t \cdot \Delta_o \geq n^{2/k^2} \cdot \log^{1+1/k} n$ ensures this. □

4.1.3 Completing the Coloring

Since Phase II requires a palette of size at least $t\Delta_o \geq n^{2/k^2} \cdot \log^{1+1/k} n$, we can distinguish between two cases for Phase II.

- When $\Delta_o \in \Omega(n^{2/k^2} \cdot \log^{1+1/k} n)$, we can choose $t = O(1)$.

- When $\Delta_o \in \Omega(\log^{1+1/k} n)$, we have to choose $t = O(n^{2/k^2})$.

Phase I needs an additional $O(\Delta_o)$ colors. At the end of Phase II, we have a situation that is similar to what was considered by Lemma 3.3. As in the proof of Theorem 3.4, we can use Palette Inflation and Deterministic Coloring to arrive at a proper coloring. Putting everything together, we have the following theorems.

THEOREM 4.3. *Let G be a graph with an acyclic orientation satisfying $\Delta_o \in \Omega(n^{2/k^2} \cdot \log^{1+1/k} n)$. Then G can be properly colored in $2k$ rounds, for any $k \geq 2 \log \log n$ rounds, using $O(k\Delta_o)$ colors.*

THEOREM 4.4. *Let G be a graph with an acyclic orientation satisfying $\Delta_o \in \Omega(\log^{1+1/k} n)$. Then G can be properly colored in $2k$ rounds, for any $k \geq 2 \log \log n$ rounds, using $O(k\Delta_o \cdot n^{2/k^2})$ colors.*

Theorems 4.3 and 4.4 are improvements over Theorem 3.4 for wide ranges of values of Δ_o and k, however they are a factor-k away from what was promised in Theorem 1.3.

4.2 When $k < 2 \log \log n$

When $k < 2 \log \log n$, we can use calculations that are very similar to those above, to prove the following theorem.

THEOREM 4.5. *Given a graph G with an acyclic orientation satisfying $\Delta_o \geq 2^{2^k} \cdot \log n$, the vertices of G can be properly colored w.h.p. in $O(k)$ rounds, for any $k < 2 \log \log n$ rounds, using $O(k \cdot n^{2/k^2} \cdot \Delta_o^{1+1/k} \cdot \frac{1}{2^{2^k}})$ colors.*

PROOF. Our proof for this theorem follows the proof of Theorem 4.3. Since $\Delta_o > 2^{2^k} \cdot \log n$, using the argument of Lemma 4.1 we can show that at the end of $k/2$ rounds of Phase I the effective out-degree of every vertex in G is at most $\Delta_o/2^{2^k}$. During this phase, vertices use a palette of size $3\Delta_0$ as in the Proof of Lemma 4.1. Now, suppose that vertices start Phase II of OrientedRandColor with $t \cdot \Delta_o$ colors. Using calculations similar to those in Lemma 4.2, we can see that at the end of Phase II, w.h.p., every uncolored path has length at most k, provided

$$n \cdot \left(\frac{\Delta_o}{2^{2^k}}\right)^{k+1} \cdot \left(\frac{\Delta_o/2^{2^k}}{t\Delta_o}\right)^{k(k+1)} \leq \frac{1}{n} \quad (3)$$

Setting $t = n^{\frac{2}{k^2}} \Delta_o^{\frac{1}{k}} \cdot \frac{1}{2^{2^k}}$ guarantees that Phase II will complete successfully. Palette Inflation to fix possible improprieties in the coloring causes the extra factor-k to appear in the palette size. Deterministic completion leads to an additional k rounds. The total number of colors required is $O(kt\Delta_o)$ which is $O(k \cdot n^{2/k^2} \cdot \Delta_o^{1+1/k} \cdot \frac{1}{2^{2^k}})$. $\square$

5. AVOIDING PALETTE INFLATION VIA BROOKS-VIZING-TYPE COLORINGS

Applying the Palette Inflation technique from Section 3.2 results in the color palettes being inflated by a factor k for algorithms that run in $O(k)$ rounds. In this section we show how to get rid of this extra factor k in the palette size.

Consider the result in Theorem 4.3 which shows how to color G using $O(k\Delta_o)$ colors in $2k$ rounds, when Δ_o is sufficiently large. One approach to removing the extra factor k from the number of colors and obtaining an $O(\Delta_o)$-coloring is to try and use only $O(\Delta_o/k)$ colors prior to Palette Inflation; then when the palette is inflated by a factor k, we end up with an $O(\Delta_o)$-coloring. In this section, we show how to obtain an $O(\Delta_o/k)$-coloring of G that is improper, but can be rectified via the use of Palette Inflation. Our result employs techniques due to Grable and Panconesi used in the distributed computation of Brooks-Vizing colorings [9] in sparse, i.e., *triangle-free* graphs. Our graphs are not triangle-free, but we can still use certain parts of the Grable-Panconesi approach. In particular, the fact that edges are oriented plays a key role in ensuring that our claims go through despite the presence of triangles in the graph. The main result of Grable and Panconesi [9] is the following.

THEOREM 5.1 (GRABLE AND PANCONESI [9]). *Let G be a Δ-regular triangle-free graph. For any $k = O(\log \Delta)$, G can be colored in $O(k + \frac{\log n}{\log \Delta})$ rounds using $O(\frac{\Delta}{k})$ colors.*

The algorithm that leads to this theorem has two phases: a *dozing phase*, and a *trivial phase*. In both phases the algorithm is essentially similar to Luby's algorithm. Each node starts the dozing phase with the palette $\{1, 2, \ldots, \Delta/k\}$. In each round, each as yet uncolored node chooses to wake up with a probability p and if the node wakes up, it picks a tentative color from amongst the available colors in its palette uniformly at random and independent of the choices of other nodes. Color conflicts are resolved in the usual manner and palettes are updated. The dozing phase runs for $O(k)$ rounds. The key innovation of Grable and Panconesi is to start the wake-up probability p at $1/k$ and then increase it in each round. This ensures that in each round an appropriate fraction of the vertices are competing for the colors in the color palettes. Furthermore, in each round the size of the palette relative to the number of uncolored neighbors of a node grows, allowing p to grow from round to round. The manner in which p increases ensures that p equals 1 in $e \cdot k$ rounds and this brings the algorithm to the trivial phase. For a more detailed description of the algorithm, we refer the reader to [9]. The following lemma [9] describes the progress made during the dozing phase.

LEMMA 5.2 (GRABLE AND PANCONESI [9]). *Under the hypothesis of Theorem 5.1, at the end of the dozing phase involving $e \cdot k$ rounds, the number of uncolored neighbors reduces to $O(\Delta/k)$ w.h.p.*

By modifying the dozing phase suitably for oriented graphs, we show a similar result (see Lemma 5.5) — at the end of $O(k)$ rounds, the number of uncolored *out-neighbors* of every vertex has shrunk to at most Δ_o/k. Once this state is reached, we can use OrientedRandColor with a palette size that is a factor $1/k$ smaller.

Let us now trace important steps of the proof of the above lemma from [9]. First define the following quantities: (i) $s_i(u)$ denotes the size of the palette for node u in round i, (ii) $d_i(u, c)$ denotes the number of uncolored neighbors of u which have color c in their palette in round i, and (iii) $D_i(u)$ denotes the number of uncolored neighbors of u at round i

Now consider the following recurrence relations:

$$s_{i+1}(u) = s_i(u) \cdot e^{-1/e},$$
$$d_{i+1}(u,c) = d_i(u)\left(1 - \frac{s_i(u)}{d_i(u)}\frac{1}{e}\right) \cdot e^{1/e}, \text{ and} \qquad (4)$$
$$D_{i+1}(u) = D_i(u)\left(1 - \frac{s_i(u)}{d_i(u)}\frac{1}{e}\right).$$

Grable and Panconesi [9] show that these recurrence relations respectively describe the behavior of the random variables $s_i(u)$, $d_i(u,c)$, and $D_i(u)$ for all vertices u, rounds i, and colors c. It is first shown that the random variables satisfy these recurrences in expectation and then via the use of concentration inequalities, it is established that the recurrences are also satisfied w.h.p.

To establish the above recurrences, the work of [9] relies on the hypotheses of Lemma 5.2 which require that the graph be (i) triangle-free, and (ii) regular. The triangle-free property of the graph is required for the following reason. To understand the change in the palette size $s_i(u)$ at a node u as it changes from round to round, we need to understand the rate at which colors disappear from u's palette. Fix a round and suppose that at the beginning of the round, u is not yet colored and it has color c in its palette. Let $E_{u,c}$ denote the conditional event (c disappears from u's palette in the round| u does not get colored in the round). Let $N_{u,c}$ be the neighbors of u that are awake in the round and have c in their palette. Then, $\Pr(E_{u,c}) = 1 - \Pr(\forall v \in N_{u,c} : v$ does not get colored c in the round $|u$ does not get colored in the round). Let $F_{v,c}$ denote the event (v does not get colored in the round $|$ u does not get colored in the round). The probability on the right-hand side of the equation for $\Pr(E_{u,c})$ can be expressed as the product $\prod_{v \in N_{u,c}} \Pr(F_{v,c})$ if the events $F_{v,c}$ were independent. And one way to guarantee independence is to ensure that G contains no 3-cycles or 4-cycles (i.e., girth is at least 5). And in fact when the $F_{v,c}$ events are independent, it is not too hard to show that $\Pr(E_{u,c}) \approx 1 - exp(e^{-1})$.

The presence of 4-cycles however does pose a problem since this allows two vertices $v, v' \in N_{u,c}$ to have common neighbors besides u. Grable and Panconesi [9] deal with this problem by showing that the events $F_{v,c}$ are positively correlated and as a result $\Pr[\forall v \in N_{uc} : v$ does not get colored c in the round $|u$ does not get colored in the round] is at least $\prod_{v \in N_{u,c}} \Pr(F_{v,c})$.

As a result, $\Pr(E_{u,c})$ falls relative to its value in the absence of 4-cycles. Also, now (i.e., in the presence of 4-cycles) $\Pr(E_{u,c})$ can be quite different at different vertices u. To fix this, Grable and Panconesi [9] introduce an additional step in their algorithm. Each vertex maintains a complete description of its neighborhood out to distance 2. This allows each vertex u to compute, for each color c in its palette, the natural probability $p_{u,c}$ of decay. This is done before tentative colors are chosen. The round proceeds as before and at the end each color c that was not naturally removed is artificially removed with a certain probability that depends on $p_{u,c}$. This artificially shrinks the palette at each vertex and ensures that the palette sizes remain balanced and decay at the rate specified by the recurrence relation in Equation (4).

In Lemma 5.3 we show that the positive correlation that holds among events $F_{v,c}$ in the absence 3-cycles also holds when we do oriented coloring. Before we state and prove this lemma, we show the Algorithm DozeOff in Figure 2, which is the dozing off phase of the Grable-Panconesi algorithm, modified for oriented graphs.

```
Algorithm DozeOff(k, C_u)
Begin-Algorithm
1.     p := 1/k
2.     for i := 1 to e · k do
3.         state(u) := awake with probability p
4.         if state(u) = awake then
5.             Node u chooses a tentative color c_u uniformly
               at random from C_u
6.             Node u sends c_u to all of its uncolored
               in-neighbors
7.             if every color received by node u from an
               out-neighbor is distinct from c_u, then
8.                 u makes c_u its permanent color.
9.             Otherwise node u remains uncolored.
10.            if u is permanently colored in Step 8 then
11.                u sends its color choice to all uncolored
                   in-neighbors
12.                Node u deletes from C_u all colors assigned
                   permanently to out-neighbors
13.            end-if
14.            p := 1/(1/p - 1/e)
15.        end-if
16.    end-for
End-Algorithm
```

Figure 2: Algorithm DozeOff. The argument k satisfies $k = O(\log \Delta_o)$ whereas vertex u's color palette C_u is $\{1, 2, \ldots, \Delta_o/k\}$.

LEMMA 5.3. *Let G be an acyclically oriented graph with out-degree bounded by Δ_o. Fix a round of Algorithm Doze-Off and consider an uncolored node u and a color c that is available in the palette of u at the beginning of the round. Then,*

$$\Pr(E_{u,c}) \le 1 - \prod_{i=1}^{k} \Pr(F_{v_i,c})$$

where $N_{u,c} = \{v_1, v_2, \cdots, v_k\}$ denotes the set of uncolored out-neighbors of u that also have the color c in their palette.

PROOF. Consider a round r, an uncolored node u and a color c. We wish to compute the probability that in this round, the color c disappears from the palette of u given that node u does not color. Therefore,

$$\Pr(E_{u,c}) = 1 - \Pr(\forall_{v \in N_{u,c}} v \text{ is not } c\text{-colored in round } r \mid u \text{ is not colored in round } r)$$
$$= 1 - \prod_{i=1}^{k} \Pr(v_i \text{ is not } c\text{-colored in round } r \mid u \text{ is not colored}, v_1, \ldots, v_{i-1} \text{ are not } c\text{-colored in round } r).$$

Let us denote by C_{v_i} the above conditional event. To compute $\Pr(C_{v_i})$, we first order the v_i's so that for $1 \le i \le k$, no out-neighbors of v_i are in the set $\{v_1, v_2, \cdots, v_{i-1}\}$. This is possible as long as the out-neighbors of u do not induce an oriented cycle. The assumption that we are considering an acyclic orientation of G clearly ensures that this is the case. Recall that F_{v_i} is the event that v_i fails to get colored with color c conditioned just on the event that u does not get colored. We now show that the events C_{v_i}, $1 \le i \le k$ are positively correlated.

Let us denote by a configuration C the tentative choices of all uncolored neighbors in this round. The set of all configurations $\mathcal{C}$ that satisfy the condition that $u, v_1, v_2, \ldots, v_{i-1}$ are not colored, can be partitioned into two sets $\mathcal{C}_1$ and $\mathcal{C}_2$ as follows. The set $\mathcal{C}_1$ contains all configurations in which there exists a vertex v_j, $1 \leq j \leq i-1$, so that v_i and v_j share an uncolored out-neighbor w and the tentative choice of w is c. The set $\mathcal{C}_2$ is the remaining set of configurations.

It can be noted that with respect to configurations in $\mathcal{C}_1$, the probability that v_i fails to color with c is 1, as w's tentative choice of c overrides the tentative choice of v_i. In the second set of configurations, the failure of v_i to get colored with c is independent of the events C_{v_i} is conditioned on. Therefore, $\Pr(C_{v_i}) \geq \Pr(F_{v_i})$. Since the above holds for every i, $1 \leq i \leq k$, we have that $\prod_{i=1}^{k} \Pr(C_{v_i}) \geq \prod_{i=1}^{k} \Pr(F_{v_i})$. Due to the above observations, we can say that:

$$\Pr(E_{u,c}) = 1 - \prod_{i=1}^{k} \Pr(E_{v_i}) \leq 1 - \prod_{i=1}^{k} \Pr(F_{v_i}).$$

$\square$

The hypothesis of Lemma 5.2 also requires that the graph be regular. The regularity condition ensures that $d_0(u) = D_0(u) = \Delta$ for all vertices u and this uniform initial condition is critical in ensuring that the recurrence relations shown in Equation (4) hold. In Lemma 5.4, we show how to convert a given oriented graph with maximum out-degree Δ_o to a Δ_o–regular oriented graph, so that the out-degree of *every* vertex is equal to Δ_o. The fact that the in-degrees are not relevant makes this construction relatively easy. The one thing to watch out for is the introduction of oriented cycles; in particular, in the proof of Lemma 5.3 we use the fact that the out-neighbors of a vertex do not induce an oriented cycle. Our construction guarantees this property. In Lemma 5.5, we show the degree reduction result that we obtain via Algorithm DozeOff.

LEMMA 5.4. *Let G be an oriented graph with the out-degree bounded by Δ_o. Then, we can construct a graph G' such that G' is regular with each vertex having an out-degree of Δ_o.*

PROOF. Let every vertex of G be a vertex in G'. Every edge of G is added to $E(G')$. In addition, for each vertex $v \in V(G')$ such that $d_o(v) < \Delta_o$, let $b(v) = \Delta_o - d_o(v)$. For each such vertex v, we add additional vertices and edges to G' as follows. Let H_v be a graph with a vertex set that is a union of 4 sets $S_1(v), S_2(v), S_3(v), S_4(v)$ where each such set has Δ_o vertices. Each vertex in $S_i(v)$ is made a neighbor of every vertex in $S_{i+1}(v)$ for $0 < i < 4$. Each such edge with $u \in S_i(v)$ and $v \in S_{i+1}(v)$, the edge uv is oriented from u to v. Each vertex in $S_4(v)$ is also made a neighbor of every vertex in $S_1(v)$ with edges oriented from vertices in $S_4(v)$ to vertices in $S_1(v)$. Further, from the vertex v, $b(v)$ edges are added to from v to *any* $b(v)$ vertices in $S_1(v)$. The graph G' can therefore be defined as $G' = G \bigcup \left(\cup_{v \in V(G)} H_v \right)$. It can be seen that $\max_{v \in V(G')} d_o(v) = \Delta_o$. $\square$

LEMMA 5.5. *Let G be an oriented graph with out-degree bounded above by Δ_o and let $k \in O(\log \Delta_o)$ be a positive integer. There is a distributed algorithm running in $O(k)$ rounds that uses Δ_o/k colors to properly color (some of) the vertices of G such that after the execution of this algorithm every vertex of G has at most Δ_o/k uncolored neighbors w.h.p.*

PROOF. Let us construct the graph G' as described in Lemma 5.4. Then, using the result of Lemma 5.3 and the techniques of [9], it holds that after the execution of the

DozeOff algorithm on G', every vertex of G' has at most Δ_o/k uncolored neighbors with high probability. Note that Algorithm DozeOff uses a palette of size Δ_o/k. Since our network is the graph G and not G', we simulate the execution of Algorithm DozeOff on G with each vertex v in G simulating the actions of all vertices in H_v in G'. Note that this is easy since vertices in H_v has edges only amongst themselves or to v. After the simulation of the algorithm, vertices in G simply inherit the color they might have been assigned during the execution of Algorithm DozeOff on G'. $\square$

Algorithm BudgetColor(G, k)
Begin-Algorithm
1. **for** every node u, $C_u = \{1, 2, \cdots, \Delta_o/k\}$;
2. Call DozeOff(k, C_u) for every node u;
3. Call OrientedRandColor(k, C_u) at every node u of G
End-Algorithm

Figure 3: Algorithm BudgetColor. The argument k is required to satisfy $k = O(\log \Delta_o)$.

We are now ready to show our final result, Theorem 1.3 restated below for convenience.

THEOREM 5.6. *Let G be a graph with an acyclic orientation whose out-degree is bounded by Δ_o. Then,*

(i) *If $k \geq 2 \log \log n$ and $\Delta_o = \Omega(\max\{k \cdot n^{2/k^2} \cdot \log^{1+1/k} n, 2^k\})$, G can be colored using $O(\Delta_o)$ colors in $O(k)$ rounds.*

(ii) *If $k \geq 2 \log \log n$ and $\Delta_o = \Omega(\max\{k \cdot \log^{1+1/k} n, 2^k\})$, G can be colored using $O(\Delta_o \cdot n^{2/k^2})$ colors in $O(k)$ rounds.*

(iii) *If $k < 2 \log \log n$ and $\Delta_o \geq k \cdot 2^{2^k} \cdot \log n$, then G can be colored using $O\left(\Delta_o^{1+\frac{1}{k}} \cdot n^{2/k^2} \cdot \frac{1}{2^{2^k}}\right)$ colors in $O(k)$ rounds.*

PROOF. The algorithm that we use to arrive at the stated theorem is shown in Figure 3. We only discuss (i); (ii) and (iii) are very similar. We first appeal to Lemma 5.5. Notice that since $\Delta = \Omega(2^k)$ is part of the hypothesis of the current lemma, $k = O(\log \Delta_o)$ as required by the hypothesis of Lemma 5.5. The algorithm implied by Lemma 5.5 runs in $O(k)$ rounds, uses Δ_o/k colors, and produces a proper, *partial* coloring of G such that the number of uncolored vertices of every vertex is at most Δ_o/k, w.h.p. We take the subgraph of G induced by the uncolored vertices and apply Theorem 4.3, with the out-degree bound being Δ_o/k rather than Δ_o. At the end of $O(k)$ rounds of the algorithm implied by this theorem, we use an additional $k \cdot \Delta_o/k = \Delta_o$ colors to complete the coloring. $\square$

6. OBTAINING OPTIMAL COLORINGS IN TERMS OF GRAPH ARBORICITY

By combining Theorem 5.6 with a result of Barenboim and Elkin [1] on distributed graph decomposition, we obtain our final result. As mentioned in the introduction, Barenboim and Elkin [1] showed the following result.

THEOREM 6.1. *For a graph G with arboricity $a(G) = a$, and any parameter q, $q > 2$, there is a deterministic, distributed algorithm that partitions the edges of G into at most $(2 + q) \cdot a$ forests within $O(\frac{\log n}{\log q})$ rounds. Further, the edges of G can be acyclically oriented so that the out-degree of each vertex is bounded by $O((2 + q) \cdot a)$.*

This theorem can be restated in a more convenient form as follows.

THEOREM 6.2. *For a graph G with arboricity $a(G) = a$, and any positive integer $k < \log n$, there is a deterministic, distributed algorithm that constructs an acyclic orientation of G in $O(k)$ rounds so that the out-degree of each vertex is bounded by $O(a \cdot n^{1/k})$.*

PROOF. If we set $k = \frac{\log n}{\log q}$, we obtain that $q = n^{1/k}$. Requiring that $k < \log n$ guarantees that $q > 2$. □

By combining this with Theorem 5.6 we obtain item (ii) of Theorem 1.4 as shown below. Items (i) and (iii) of Theorem 1.4 similarly follow.

COROLLARY 6.3. *Let G be an n-vertex graph with arboricity a. For any k, $2 \log \log n \leq k \leq \sqrt{\log n}$, G can be properly colored with $O(a \cdot n^{1/k})$ colors in $O(k)$ rounds.*

PROOF. We first use the Barenboim-Elkin algorithm to obtain an acyclic orientation of G with $\Delta_o(G) \in O(a \cdot n^{1/k})$. To apply Theorem 5.6, we require that $k \geq 2 \log \log n$ and also require that $a \cdot n^{1/k} = \Omega(2^k)$ and $a \cdot n^{1/k} = \Omega(k \cdot n^{2/k^2} \cdot \log^{1+1/k} n)$. When $k \leq \sqrt{\log n}$, we have

$$n^{1/k} \geq n^{1/\sqrt{\log n}} \geq c \cdot 2^{\sqrt{\log n}} \geq c \cdot 2^k,$$

for some constant c. This ensures that when $k \leq \sqrt{\log n}$, we have $a \cdot n^{1/k} = \Omega(2^k)$. Also, for some constants c_1, c_2, and c_3, we have

$$k \leq c_1 \cdot n^{1/3k}; n^{2/k^2} \leq c_2 \cdot n^{1/3k}; \log^{1+1/k} n \leq c_3 \cdot n^{1/3k},$$

for all $k \leq \sqrt{\log n}$. This implies that when $k \leq \sqrt{\log n}$, we have that $a \cdot n^{1/k} = \Omega(k \cdot n^{2/k^2} \cdot \log^{1+1/k} n)$ Hence the hypothesis of Theorem 5.6 is satisfied and we obtain an $O(a \cdot n^{1/k})$ coloring of G in $O(k)$ rounds. □

The above corollary restricts k to be in the range $2 \log \log n \leq k \leq \sqrt{\log n}$ in order to obtain an optimal coloring. However, for smaller values of k a slightly suboptimal coloring can be obtained via the use of item (iii) in Theorem 5.6.

COROLLARY 6.4. *Let G be an n-vertex graph with arboricity a. For any $k < 2 \log \log n$, G can be properly colored with $O(a^{1+1/k} \cdot n^{1/k+3/k^2} \cdot \frac{1}{2^{2^k}})$ colors in $O(k)$ rounds.*

The two corollaries above correspond to Theorem 1.4 in the "Introduction."

7. REFERENCES

[1] BARENBOIM, L., AND ELKIN, M. Sublogarithmic distributed MIS algorithm for sparse graphs using nash-williams decomposition. In *ACM Symp. on Principles of Distributed Computing (PODC)* (2008), pp. 25–34.

[2] BARENBOIM, L., AND ELKIN, M. Deterministic distributed vertex coloring in polylogarithmic time. In *ACM Symp. on Principles of Distributed Computing (PODC)* (2010), pp. 410–419.

[3] CZYGRINOW, A., AND HAŃĆKOWIAK, M. Distributed almost exact approximations for minor-closed families. In *European Symposium on Algorithms* (2006), pp. 244–255.

[4] CZYGRINOW, A., AND HAŃĆKOWIAK, M. Distributed approximation algorithms for weighted problems in minor-closed families. In *COCOON: 13th Annual International Conference on Computing and Combinatorics* (2007), pp. 515–525.

[5] CZYGRINOW, A., HAŃĆKOWIAK, M., AND SZYMANSKA, E. Fast distributed alogrithm for the maximum matching problem in bounded arboricity graphs. In *20th International Symposium on Algorithms and Computation (ISAAC 2009)* (2009), vol. 5878/2009, pp. 668–678.

[6] CZYGRINOW, A., HANCKOWIAK, M., AND WAWRZYNIAK, W. Fast distributed approximations in planar graphs. In *International Symposium on Distributed Computing* (2008), pp. 78–92.

[7] FINOCCHI, I., PANCONESI, A., AND SILVESTRI, R. Experimental analysis of simple, distributed vertex coloring algorithms. In *ACM SODA* (2002), pp. 606–615.

[8] GRABLE, D. A. A large deviation inequality for functions of independent, multi-way choices. *Comb. Probab. Comput. 7*, 1 (1998).

[9] GRABLE, D. A., AND PANCONESI, A. Fast distributed algorithms for brooks-vizing colorings. *J. Algorithms 37*, 1 (2000), 85–120.

[10] JOHANSSON, O. Simpled distributed $\Delta + 1$ coloring of graphs. *Information Processing Letters 70* (1999), 229–232.

[11] KOTHAPALLI, K., SCHEIDELER, C., ONUS, M., AND SCHINDELHAUER, C. Distributed coloring in $O(\sqrt{\log n})$ bit rounds. In *In International Parallel and Distributed Processing Symposium, (IPDPS)* (2006).

[12] KUHN, F., MOSCIBRODA, T., AND WATTENHOFER, R. The price of being near-sighted. In *SODA '06: Proceedings of the seventeenth annual ACM-SIAM symposium on Discrete algorithm* (New York, NY, USA, 2006), ACM, pp. 980–989.

[13] KUHN, F., AND WATTENHOFER, R. Constant-time distributed dominating set approximation. *Distributed Computing 17*, 4 (2005), 303–310.

[14] LENZEN, C., AND WATTENHOFER, R. Minimum dominating set approximation in graphs of bounded arboricity. In *International Symposium on Distributed Computing (DISC)* (2010), pp. 510–524.

[15] LINIAL, N. Locality in distributed graph algorithms. *SIAM Journal of Computing 21* (1992), 193–201.

[16] LUBY, M. A simple parallel algorithm for the maximal independent set problem. In *Proc. of ACM Symposium on Theory of Computing* (1985), pp. 1–10.

[17] LUBY, M. Removing randomness in parallel without processor penalty. *Journal of Computer and System Sciences 47*, 2 (1993), 250–286.

[18] MOSCIBRODA, T., AND WATTENHOFER, R. Facility location: distributed approximation. In *Proc. ACM symposium on Principles of distributed computing* (2005), pp. 108–117.

[19] MOTWANI, R., AND RAGHAVAN, P. *Randomized Algorithms.* Cambridge University Press, 1995.

[20] NASH-WILLIAMS, C. Decompositions of finite graphs into forests. *J. London Math 39*, 12 (1964).

[21] PANDIT, S., AND PEMMARAJU, S. Return of the primal-dual: distributed metric facilitylocation. In *Proceedings of the 28th ACM symposium on Principles of distributed computing* (2009), pp. 180–189.

[22] PANDIT, S., AND PEMMARAJU, S. V. Rapid randomized pruning for fast greedy distributed algorithms. In *ACM Symp. on Principles of Distributed Computing (PODC)* (2010), pp. 325–334.

[23] SCHNEIDER, J., AND WATTENHOFER, R. A new technique for distributed symmetry breaking. In *ACM Symp. on Principles of Distributed Computing (PODC)* (2010), pp. 257–266.

MIS on Trees

Christoph Lenzen
Computer Engineering
and Networks Laboratory
ETH Zurich
Switzerland
lenzen@tik.ee.ethz.ch

Roger Wattenhofer
Computer Engineering
and Networks Laboratory
ETH Zurich
Switzerland
wattenhofer@tik.ee.ethz.ch

ABSTRACT

A maximal independent set on a graph is an inclusion-maximal set of mutually non-adjacent nodes. This basic symmetry breaking structure is vital for many distributed algorithms, which by now has been fueling the search for fast local algorithms to find such sets over several decades. In this paper, we present a solution with randomized running time $\mathcal{O}(\sqrt{\log n \log \log n})$ on trees, improving roughly quadratically on the state-of-the-art bound. Our algorithm is uniform and nodes need to exchange merely $\mathcal{O}(\log n)$ many bits with high probability. In contrast to previous techniques achieving sublogarithmic running times, our approach does not rely on any bound on the number of independent neighbors (possibly with regard to an orientation of the edges).

Categories and Subject Descriptors

G.2.2 [**Discrete Mathematics**]: Graph Theory—*graph algorithms, trees*; F.2.2 [**Analysis of Algorithms and Problem Complexity**]: Nonnumerical Algorithms and Problems—*computations on discrete structures*

General Terms

Algorithms, Theory

Keywords

symmetry breaking, optimal bit complexity, maximal independent set, asymptotic analysis

1. INTRODUCTION & RELATED WORK

In graph theory, two nodes are independent if they are not neighbors. A set of nodes is independent if the nodes in the set are pairwise independent. And a maximal independent set (MIS) is an independent set that is not a proper subset of any other independent set; in other words, an MIS cannot be extended. Finding an MIS is a most basic form of *symmetry breaking*, and as such widely used as a building block in distributed or parallel algorithms.

Not surprisingly, obtaining an MIS quickly is one of the fundamental questions in distributed and parallel computing. More surprisingly, despite all the research, the state-of-the-art algorithm was discovered in the 1980s. Several research groups [1, 6, 10] more or less concurrently presented the same simple randomized *marking* algorithm that finds an MIS in time $\mathcal{O}(\log n)$ *with high probability*[1] (w.h.p.) Deterministic algorithms tend to be much slower; Panconesi and Srinivasan [13] presented an algorithm with running time $2^{\mathcal{O}(\sqrt{\log n})}$, based on a network decomposition. In contrast, the strongest lower bound proves that $\Omega(\sqrt{\log n})$ time is required, even for randomized algorithms on line graphs [8]. Arguably, reducing this complexity gap is one of the most important open problems in distributed computing.

In the last 25 years, a lot of work went into understanding special graph classes. One line of work shows that the MIS problem can be solved in time $\Theta(\log^* n)$ on rooted trees [4], graphs of bounded degree [5], and bounded-growth graphs [14]. The upper bounds are deterministic and the matching lower bound [9] can be extended to randomized algorithms [12]. Another common technique is to compute a coloring first and subsequently gradually augment an independent set by concurrently adding all feasible nodes of a given color. Using deterministic $(\Delta + 1)$-coloring algorithms with running time (essentially) linear in the maximum degree Δ [2, 7], this reduction yields $\mathcal{O}(\Delta + \log^* n)$-time solutions suitable for small-degree graphs. However, all these results work on graphs with restricted degrees, sometimes explicitly, sometimes implicitly. In rooted trees, for instance, each node just deals with one single neighbor (the parent) and in bounded-growth graphs the number of independent neighbors is bounded.

In other words, finding an MIS seems to be difficult mostly in graphs with an unbounded number of independent neighbors. Until recently, even on (non-rooted) trees no better algorithm than the randomized marking algorithms from the 1980s was known. This was changed by Barenboim and Elkin [3], who devised a deterministic algorithm with running time $o(\log n)$ for graphs with arboricity[2] $o(\sqrt{\log n})$. Their algorithm first computes a forest decomposition and subsequently efficiently colors the graph. Again, the key ingredient of the coloring step is that nodes can restrict their attention to the small number of parents they have in the de-

---

[1] That is, with probability $1 - 1/n^c$ for an arbitrary, but fixed constant c.

[2] A forest decomposition is a partitioning of the edge set into rooted forests. The arboricity of a graph is the minimum number of forests in a forest decomposition.

composition. However, even on graphs of constant arboricity (in particular trees) the improvement is marginal, i.e., their algorithm has a time complexity of $\Theta(\log n/\log\log n)$. An accompanying lower bound shows that even randomized algorithms require $\Omega(\log n/\log f)$ rounds to compute a forest decomposition into f forests, while the computed coloring uses $\Omega(f)$ colors. Hence, their technique is limited to a factor $\mathcal{O}(\log\log n)$ gain in time complexity. What is more, their algorithm is non-uniform, as it needs an upper bound of $\mathcal{O}(A)$ on the arboricity A of the graph or a polynomial upper bound on the number of nodes as input.

In this work, we present a much faster, uniform algorithm running on arbitrary forests. Our approach guarantees termination within $\mathcal{O}(\sqrt{\log n \log\log n})$ rounds w.h.p. This is achieved by fusing several techniques into a single algorithm and devising a novel analysis. Initially, we employ a recent variation by Métivier et al. [11] of the traditional randomized marking algorithm. The authors show how their algorithm can be implemented with optimal bit complexity of $\mathcal{O}(\log n)$ w.h.p. This is not an inherent property of their approach, as also the classic algorithms can be adapted to exhibit the same bit complexity; we demonstrate how to obtain the same bound for our technique. However, their algorithm appeals by its simplistic elegance: In each phase, each eligible node picks a random value and joins the independent set if its value is a local maximum. As a positive side effect of this subroutine, our algorithm will also succeed to obtain an MIS on arbitrary graphs within $\mathcal{O}(\log n)$ rounds w.h.p. However, we make use of the technique with a different goal. The logarithmic time complexity of the randomized marking algorithm follows from the argument that in expectation a constant fraction of the edges is removed in each phase. Thus, by itself, the algorithm might also on trees exhibit a logarithmic running time. The key observation we make is that on trees—up to maybe a few exceptions—nodes of high degree will not survive more than $\mathcal{O}(\sqrt{\log n \log\log n})$ phases of this algorithm. Moreover, (in essence) it can be shown that on trees the maximum node degree falls exponentially until it becomes $\mathcal{O}(\sqrt{\log n})$. From this point on, we utilize deterministic coloring [2, 7] to clear most of the remaining subgraph consisting of nodes that are still eligible to join the independent set. Afterwards, the diameter of connected components will be sufficiently small such that iteratively removing isolated nodes and leaves will complete the task quickly. Although the presented proof is tailored to trees, the main ingredient is that in trees probabilistic dependencies are scarce. Therefore, one might hope that our result can be extended to more general sparse graph classes, e.g. graphs of bounded arboricity.

2. MODEL & PRELIMINARIES

We employ the standard synchronous message passing model of distributed computation. The (non-faulty) system is modelled as a simple graph $G = (V, E)$, where nodes represent computational devices and edges represent bidirectional communication links. In each synchronous round, nodes may perform arbitrary finite local computations, and send (receive) a message to (from) each neighbor. The set of neighbors of a node $v \in V$ is denoted by $\mathcal{N}_v := \{w \in V \mid \{v, w\} \in E\}$. The *degree* of $v \in V$ is $\delta_v := |\mathcal{N}_v|$. Initially, each node knows its neighbors and the (local part) of the input of the problem. For deterministic MIS algorithms, the latter is typically an initial coloring of polynomially many

(in $n := |V|$) colors. If randomization is permitted, nodes have access to an infinite source of unbiased and independent random bits. In this case, an initial coloring can be generated w.h.p. (without any communication) and verified in one round by exchanging the colors between neighbors. The *time* and *bit complexity* of an algorithm are the maximum number of rounds any node requires to terminate and the maximum number of bits sent over any edge, respectively.

Throughout our analysis, we will make frequent use of Chernoff type bounds. For reference, we state here the variants we use.

THEOREM 2.1. *For N independent 0–1 random variables $X_1, \ldots, X_N$, define $X := \sum_{i=1}^{N} X_i$. Then*

(i) $X \in E[X] + \mathcal{O}\left(\log n + \sqrt{E[X]\log n}\right)$ *w.h.p.*

(ii) $E[X] \in \mathcal{O}\left(\frac{1}{\sqrt{\log n}}\right) \Rightarrow X \in \mathcal{O}\left(\sqrt{\frac{\log n}{\log\log n}}\right)$ *w.h.p.*

(iii) $P[X = 0] \leq e^{-E[X]/2}$

(iv) $E[X] \geq 8c\log n \Rightarrow X \in \Theta(E[X])$ *w.h.p.*

(v) $E[X] \in \omega(\log n) \Rightarrow X \in (1 \pm o(1))E[X]$ *w.h.p.*

3. ALGORITHM

In this section, we introduce our MIS algorithm for trees. For the sake of simplicity, we (i) present a non-uniform variant, (ii) assume that the algorithm makes use of uniformly random real numbers, and (iii) use a generic term of $\Theta(R)$ in the description of the algorithm. In Theorem 4.10, we will show how to remove the first two assumptions, and it will turn out that for the uniform algorithm the precise choice of the constants in the term $\Theta(R)$ is (up to a constant factor) irrelevant for the running time of the algorithm.

The algorithm seeks to perpetually increase the number of nodes in the independent set I until it finally is maximal. Whenever a node enters I, its inclusive neighborhood is removed from the graph and the algorithm proceeds on the remaining subgraph of G. It consists of three main steps, each of which employs a different technique to add nodes to I. It takes a single parameter R, which ideally is small enough to guarantee a small running time of the first two loops of the algorithm, but large enough to guarantee that the residual nodes can be dealt with quickly by the final loop of the algorithm.

We proceed by describing the parts of the algorithm in detail, whose pseudocode is given in Algorithm 1. In the first part, the following procedure is repeated $\Theta(R)$ times. Each active node draws uniformly and independently at random (u.i.r.) a number from $[0, 1] \subset \mathbb{R}$ and joins I if its value is a local maximum.[3] This and similar techniques have been known for long and ensure to reduce the number of edges in the graph exponentially w.h.p.; however, in our case we have the different goal of reducing the maximum degree in the graph rapidly. Once degrees become small, we cannot guarantee a quick decay of degrees w.h.p. anymore, therefore the employed strategy is changed.

---

[3] A random real number from $[0, 1]$ can be interpreted as infinite string of bits of decreasing significance. As nodes merely need to know which one of two values is larger, it is sufficient to generate and compare random bits until the first difference occurs.

Algorithm 1: Fast MIS on Trees.

input : $R \in \mathbb{N}$
output: maximal independent set I
$I := \emptyset$
for $i \in \{1, \dots, \Theta(R)\}$ **do** // reduce degrees
  for $v \in V$ *in parallel* **do**
    $r_v :=$ u.i.r. number from $[0, 1]$
    if $r_v > \max_{w \in \mathcal{N}_v} \{r_w\}$ **then**
      $I := I \cup \{v\}$
      delete $\mathcal{N}_v \cup \{v\}$ from G

for $i \in \{1, 2\}$ **do** // remove nodes of small degree
  $H :=$ subgraph of G induced by nodes of degree
  $\delta_v \leq R$
  $(R + 1)$-color H
  for $c \in \{1, \dots, R + 1\}$ **do**
    for $v \in V$ *with color c in parallel* **do**
      $I := I \cup \{v\}$
      delete $\mathcal{N}_v \cup \{v\}$ from G

while $V \neq \emptyset$ **do** // clean up
  for $v \in V$ *in parallel* **do**
    if $\delta_v = 0$ **then** // remove isolated nodes
      $I := I \cup \{v\}$
      delete $\mathcal{N}_v \cup \{v\}$ from G
    if $\delta_v = 1$ **then** // remove leaves
      $\{w\} := \mathcal{N}_v$
      if $\delta_w \neq 1$ **then** // true leaf
        $I := I \cup \{v\}$
        delete $\mathcal{N}_v \cup \{v\}$ from G
      else // pair of degree-1 nodes
        $r_v :=$ u.i.r. number from $[0, 1]$
        if $r_v > r_w$ **then**
          $I := I \cup \{v\}$
          delete $\mathcal{N}_v \cup \{v\}$ from G

Consequently, the second part of the algorithm aims at dealing with small-degree nodes by means of a deterministic scheme. Though it might be the case that not all nodes of degree larger than R could be removed during the first loop, we will show that if R is large enough, most nodes will not have more than R neighbors of degree larger than R in their neighborhood. Thus, removing all nodes of degree at most R for *two* times will thin out the graph considerably. To this end, we first $(R + 1)$-color the subgraph induced by all nodes of degree at most R and then iterate through the colors, adding all nodes sharing color c concurrently to I.

Yet, a small fraction of the nodes may still remain in the graph. In order to deal with these nodes, we repeat the step of removing all leaves and isolated nodes from the forest until all nodes have terminated.

As evident from the description of the algorithm, iterations of the first and third loop can be implemented within a constant number of synchronous distributed rounds. The second loop requires $\mathcal{O}(R)$ time plus the number of rounds needed to color the respective subgraph; for this problem deterministic distributed algorithms taking $\mathcal{O}(R + \log^* n)$ time are known [2, 7]. In Theorem 4.9 we will show that for some $R \in \mathcal{O}(\sqrt{\log n \log \log n})$, the third loop of the algorithm will complete in $\mathcal{O}(R)$ rounds w.h.p. Thus, for an ap-

propriate value of R, the algorithm computes an MIS within $\mathcal{O}(\sqrt{\log n \log \log n})$ rounds.

4. ANALYSIS

For the purpose of our analysis, we will make use of the notion of a *rooted* tree. A tree becomes rooted by choosing a node $r \in V$ as root. The parent $p \in \mathcal{N}_v$ of a node $V \setminus \{r\}$ then is its neighbor which is closer to the root, while its children $\mathcal{C}_v := \mathcal{N}_v \setminus \{p\}$ are the remaining neighbors. In all lemmas, w.l.o.g. we take for granted that G is a rooted tree. Note that this assumption is introduced to simplify the presentation. To execute the algorithm, nodes do not require knowledge of an orientation of the edges and the proof trivially generalizes to forests.

The lion's share of the argumentation will focus on the first loop of Algorithm 1. We will call an iteration of this loop a *phase*. By $\delta_v(i)$ we denote the degree of node v at the beginning of phase i in the subgraph of G induced by the nodes that have not been deleted yet; similarly, $\mathcal{N}_v(i)$ and $\mathcal{C}_v(i)$ are the sets of neighbors and children of v still active at the beginning of phase i, respectively.

We start our analysis with the observation that, in any phase, a high-degree node without many high-degree children is likely to be deleted in that phase, *independently* of the behaviour of its parent.

LEMMA 4.1. *If at the beginning of phase i it holds for a node v that half of its children have a degree of at most $\delta_v(i)/16 \ln \delta_v(i)$, then v is deleted with probability at least $1 - 5/\delta_v(i)$ in that phase, independently of the random number of its parent.*

PROOF. Observe that the probability that v survives phase i is increasing in the degree $\delta_w(i)$ of any child $w \in \mathcal{C}_v(i)$ of v. Thus, w.l.o.g., we may assume that all children of v of degree at most $\delta := \delta_v(i)/16 \ln \delta_v(i)$ have exactly that degree.

Consider such a child w. With probability $1/\delta$, its random value $r_w(i)$ is larger than all its children's. Denote by X the random variable counting the number of children $w \in \mathcal{C}_v(i)$ of degree δ satisfying that

$$\forall u \in \mathcal{C}_w(i) : \; r_w(i) > r_u(i). \tag{1}$$

Thus, for the random variable X counting the number of such nodes it holds that

$$E[X] = \sum_{\substack{w \in \mathcal{C}_v(i) \\ \delta_w(i) = \delta}} \frac{1}{\delta} \geq 8 \ln \delta_v(i).$$

Since the random choices are independent, applying Chernoff's bound yields that

$$P\left[X < \frac{E[X]}{2}\right] < e^{-E[X]/8} \leq \frac{1}{\delta_v(i)}.$$

Node v is removed unless the event $\mathcal{E}$ that $r_v(i) < r_w(i)$ for all the children $w \in \mathcal{C}_v(i)$ of degree δ satisfying (1) occurs. If $\mathcal{E}$ happens, this implies that $r_v(i)$ is also smaller than all random values of children of such w, i.e., $r_v(i)$ is smaller than $\delta E[X]/2 \geq \delta_v(i)/4$ other independent random values. Since the event that $X \geq E[X]/2$ depends only on the order of the involved random values, we infer that $P[\mathcal{E} \mid X \geq E[X]/2] < 4/\delta_v(i)$. We conclude that v is deleted with probability at least

$$P\left[X \geq \frac{E[X]}{2}\right] P\left[\bar{\mathcal{E}} \,\middle|\, X \geq \frac{E[X]}{2}\right]$$
$$> \left(1 - \frac{1}{\delta_v(i)}\right)\left(1 - \frac{4}{\delta_v(i)}\right)$$
$$> 1 - \frac{5}{\delta_v(i)}$$

as claimed. Since we reasoned about whether children of v join the independent set only, this bound is independent of the behaviour of v's parent. □

Applied inductively, this result implies that in order to maintain a high degree for a considerable number of phases, a node must be the root of a large subtree. This concept is formalized by the following definition.

DEFINITION 4.2 (DELAY TREES). *A delay tree of depth $d \in \mathbb{N}_0$ rooted at node v is defined recursively as follows. For $d = 0$, the tree consists of v only. For $d > 0$, node v satisfies at least one of the following criteria:*

(i) *At least $\delta_v(d+1)/4$ children $w \in \mathcal{C}_v$ are roots of delay trees of depth d with $\delta_w(d) \geq \delta_v(d+1)/16 \ln \delta_v(d+1)$.*

(ii) *Node v is the root of a delay tree of depth $d-1$ and it holds that $\delta_v(d) \geq \delta_v(d+1)^2/(81 \ln \delta_v(d+1))$.*

In order to bound the number of phases for which a node can have a significant chance to retain a large degree, we bound the depth of delay trees rooted at high-degree nodes.

LEMMA 4.3. *Assume that $R \geq 2\sqrt{\ln n \ln \ln n}$ and also that $\delta_v(d) \geq e^R$. Then for a delay tree of depth $d-1$ rooted at v it holds that $d \in \mathcal{O}(\sqrt{\log n/\log \log n})$.*

PROOF. Assume w.l.o.g. that $d > 1$. Denote by $s_i(\delta)$, where $i \in \{0, \ldots, d-1\}$ and $\delta \in \mathbb{N}$, the minimal number of leaves in a delay tree of depth i rooted at some node w satisfying $\delta_w(i+1) = \delta$.

We claim that for any δ and $i \leq \ln \delta/(2\ln(81 \ln \delta))$, it holds that

$$s_i(\delta) \geq \prod_{j=1}^{i} \frac{\delta}{(81 \ln \delta)^{j-1}},$$

which we will show by induction. This is trivially true for $i = 1$, hence we need to perform the induction step only.

Observe that because any node is a delay tree of depth zero, the number of leaves in a delay tree of depth one equals the degree of the root. Moreover, as δ is sufficiently large, we have for any $x' \geq \delta/(81 \ln \delta)^i$ that the derivative of the function $x/(81 \ln x)$ at x' is at least one. Hence, for any $C \geq 1$, we have that

$$s_i(C\delta') \geq C s_i(\delta')$$

because the minimal number of leaves s_i in the tree must grow at least linearly in the argument no matter which of the two possible conditions in the recursive definition of a delay tree is satisfied.

Consequently, for any $i \in \{2, \ldots, \lfloor \ln \delta/(2\ln(81 \ln \delta)) \rfloor\}$, the assumption that the claim is true for $i-1$ and the re-

cursive definition of delay trees yield that

$$s_i(\delta) \geq \min\left\{\frac{\delta}{4} s_{i-1}\left(\frac{\delta}{16 \ln \delta}\right), s_{i-1}\left(\frac{\delta^2}{81 \ln \delta}\right)\right\}$$
$$\geq \delta \, s_{i-1}\left(\frac{\delta}{81 \ln \delta}\right)$$
$$> \delta \prod_{j=1}^{i-1} \frac{\delta}{(81 \ln \delta)^j}$$
$$= \prod_{j=1}^{i} \frac{\delta}{(81 \ln \delta)^{j-1}}.$$

Thus the induction step succeeds, showing the claim.

Now assume that v is the root of a delay tree of depth $d-1$. As $\delta_v(d) \geq e^R$, we may insert any $i \in \{1, \ldots, \min\{d-1, \lfloor R/(2 \ln 81R) \rfloor\}\}$ into the previous claim. Supposing for contradiction that $d-1 \geq \lfloor R/(2 \ln 81R) \rfloor$, it follows that the graph contains at least

$$\prod_{j=1}^{\lfloor R/(2 \ln 81R) \rfloor} \frac{e^R}{(81R)^{j-1}}$$
$$> \prod_{j=1}^{\lfloor R/(2 \ln 81R) \rfloor} e^{R/2}$$
$$\in e^{R^2/((4+o(1)) \ln R)}$$
$$\subseteq n^{2-o(1)}$$

nodes. On the other hand, if $d-1 < \lfloor R/(2 \ln 81R) \rfloor$, we get that the graph contains at least $e^{(d-1)R/2}$ nodes, implying that $d \in \mathcal{O}(\sqrt{\ln n/\ln \ln n})$ as claimed. □

With this statement at hand, we infer that for some $R \in \Theta(\sqrt{\log n \log \log n})$, it is unlikely that a node has degree e^R or larger for R phases.

LEMMA 4.4. *Suppose that $R \geq 2\sqrt{\ln n \ln \ln n}$. Then, for any node $v \in V$ and some number $r \in \mathcal{O}(\sqrt{\log n/\log \log n})$, it holds with probability at least $1 - 6e^{-R}$ that $\delta_v(r+1) < e^R$. This statement holds independently of the behaviour of v's parent.*

PROOF. Assume that $\delta_v(r) \geq e^R$. According to Lemma 4.1, node v is removed with probability at least $1 - 5/\delta_v(r)$ in phase r unless half of its children have at least degree $\delta_v(r)/16 \ln \delta_v(r)$.

Suppose the latter is the case and that w is such a child. Using Lemma 4.1 again, we see that in phase $r-1$, when $\delta_w(r-1) \geq \delta_w(r) \geq \delta_v(r)/16 \ln \delta_v(r)$, w is removed with probability $1 - 5/\delta_w(r-1)$ if it does not have $\delta_w(r-1)/2$ children of degree at least $\delta_w(r-1)/16 \ln \delta_w(r-1)$. Thus, the expected number of such nodes w that do not themselves have many high-degree children in phase $r-1$ but survive until phase r is bounded by

$$\frac{5\delta_v(r-1)}{\delta_w(r-1)} \leq \frac{80\delta_v(r-1) \ln \delta_v(r)}{\delta_v(r)}.$$

Since Lemma 4.1 states that the probability bound for a node $w \in \mathcal{C}_v(r-1)$ to be removed holds independently of v's actions, we can apply Chernoff's bound in order to see that

$$\frac{(80 + 1/2)\delta_v(r-1) \ln \delta_v(r)}{\delta_v(r)} + \mathcal{O}(\log n)$$

44

of these nodes remain active at the beginning of phase r w.h.p. If this number is not smaller than $\delta_v(r)/4 \in \omega(\log n)$, it holds that $\delta_v(r-1) \in \delta_v(r)^2/((80+1/2+o(1))\ln \delta_v(r))$. Otherwise, at least $\delta_v(r)/2 - \delta_v(r)/4 = \delta_v(r)/4$ children $w \in \mathcal{C}_v(r-1)$ have degree $\delta_w(r-1) \geq \delta_v(r)/16\ln \delta_v(r)$. In both cases, v meets one of the conditions in the recursive definition of a delay tree. Repeating this reasoning inductively for all $r \in \mathcal{O}(\sqrt{\log n/\log\log n})$ rounds (where we may choose the constants in the $\mathcal{O}$-term to be arbitrarily large), we construct a delay tree of depth at least r w.h.p.

However, Lemma 4.3 states that $r \in \mathcal{O}(\sqrt{\log n/\log\log n})$ provided that $\delta_v(r) \geq e^R$. Therefore, for an appropriate choice of constants, we conclude that w.h.p. the event $\mathcal{E}$ that both half of the nodes in $\mathcal{C}_v(r)$ have degree at least $\delta_v(r)/16\ln \delta_v(r)$ and $\delta_v(r) \geq e^R$ does not occur. If $\mathcal{E}$ does not happen, but $\delta_v(r) \geq e^R$, Lemma 4.1 gives that v is deleted in phase r with probability at least $1 - 5e^{-R}$.

Thus, the total probability that v is removed or has sufficiently small degree at the beginning of phase $r+1$ is bounded by

$$P\left[\bar{\mathcal{E}}\right] \cdot P\left[v \text{ deleted in phase } r \,\Big|\, \bar{\mathcal{E}} \text{ and } \delta_v(r) \geq e^R\right]$$
$$> \left(1 - \frac{1}{n}\right)\left(1 - \frac{5}{e^R}\right)$$
$$> 1 - 6e^{-R},$$

where we used that $R < \ln n$ because $\delta_v \leq n - 1$. Since all used statements hold independently of v's parent's actions during the course of the algorithm, this concludes the proof. $\square$

For convenience reasons, we rephrase the previous lemma in a slightly different way.

COROLLARY 4.5. *Provided that $R \geq 2\sqrt{\log n \log\log n}$, for any node $v \in V$ it holds with probability $1 - e^{-\omega(R)}$ that $\delta_v(R) < e^R$. This bound holds independently of the actions of a constant number of v's neighbors.*

PROOF. Observe that $R \in \omega(r)$, where r and R are as in Lemma 4.4. The lemma states that after r rounds, v retains $\delta_v(r+1) \geq e^R$ with probability at most $6e^{-R}$. As the algorithm behaves identically on the remaining subgraph, applying the lemma repeatedly we see that $\delta_v(R) < e^R$ with probability $1 - e^{-\omega(R)}$. Ignoring a constant number of v's neighbors does not change the asymptotic bounds. $\square$

Since we strive for a sublogarithmic value of R, the above probability bound does not ensure that all nodes will have degree smaller than e^R after R phases w.h.p. However, on paths of length at least $\sqrt{\ln n}$, at least one of the nodes will satisfy this criterion w.h.p. Moreover, nodes of degree smaller than e^R will have left a few high-degree neighbors only, which do not interfere with our forthcoming reasoning.

LEMMA 4.6. *Assume that $R \geq 2\sqrt{\log n \log\log n}$. Given a path $P = (v_0, \ldots, v_k)$, define for $i \in \{0, \ldots, k\}$ that C_i is the connected component of G containing v_i after removing the edges of P. If $\delta_{v_i}(R) < e^R$, denote by $\bar{C}_i$ the connected (sub)component of C_i consisting of nodes w of degree $\delta_w(R) < e^R$ that contains v_i. Then, with probability $1 - e^{-\omega(\sqrt{\ln n})}$, we have that*

(i) $\delta_{v_i}(R) < e^R$ and

(ii) nodes in $\bar{C}_i$ have at most $\sqrt{\ln n}$ neighbors w of degree $\delta_w(R) \geq e^R$.

This probability bound holds independently of anything that happens outside C_i.

PROOF. Corollary 4.5 directly yields Statement (i). For the second statement, let u be any node of degree $\delta_u(R) < e^R$. According to Corollary 4.5, all nodes $w \in \mathcal{C}_u(R)$ have $\delta_w(R) < e^R$ with independently bounded probability $1 - e^{-\omega(R)}$. In other words, the random variable counting the number of such nodes having degree $\delta_w(R) \geq e^R$ is stochastically dominated from below by the sum of $\delta_u(R)$ independent Bernoulli variables attaining the value 1 with probability $e^{-\omega(R)} \subset e^{-\omega(\sqrt{\ln n})}$. Applying Chernoff's bound, we conclude that w.h.p. no more than $\sqrt{\ln n}$ of u's neighbors have too large degrees. By means of the union bound, we thus obtain that with probability $1 - e^{-\omega(\sqrt{\ln n})}$, both statements are true. $\square$

Having dealt with nodes of degree e^R and larger, we need to show that we can get rid of the remaining nodes sufficiently fast. As a first step, we show a result along the lines of Lemma 4.1, trading in a weaker probability bound for a stronger bound on children's degrees.

LEMMA 4.7. *Given a constant $\beta > 0$, assume that in phase i for a node v we have that at least $e^{-\beta}\delta_v(i)$ of its children have degree at most $e^{\beta}\delta_v(i)$. Then v is deleted with at least constant probability in that phase, regardless of the random value of its parent.*

PROOF. As in Lemma 4.1, we may w.l.o.g. assume that all children with degree at most $\delta := e^{\beta}\delta_v(i)$ have exactly that degree. For the random variable X counting the number of nodes $w \in \mathcal{C}_v(i)$ of degree δ that satisfy Condition (1) we get that

$$E[X] \geq \sum_{\substack{w \in \mathcal{C}_v(i) \\ \delta_w(i)=\delta}} \frac{1}{\delta} > e^{-2\beta}.$$

Since the random choices are independent, applying Chernoff's bound yields that

$$P[X=0] \leq e^{-E[X]/2} < e^{-e^{-2\beta}/2} =: \gamma.$$

Provided that $X > 0$, there is at least one child $w \in \mathcal{C}_v$ of v that joins the set in phase i unless $r_v(i) > r_w(i)$. Since $r_w(i)$ is already larger than all of its neighbors' random values (except maybe v), the respective conditional probability certainly does not exceed $1/2$, i.e.,

$$P[v \text{ is deleted in phase } i \,|\, X > 0] \cdot P[X > 0] \geq \frac{1-\gamma}{2}.$$

Since we reasoned about whether children of v join the independent set only, this bound is independent of the behaviour of v's parent. $\square$

We cannot guarantee that the maximum degree in the subgraph formed by the active nodes drops quickly. However, we can show that for all but a negligible fraction of the nodes this is the case.

LEMMA 4.8. *Denote by $H = (V_H, E_H)$ a subgraph of G still present in phase R in which all node degrees are smaller than e^R and for any node there are no more than $\mathcal{O}(\sqrt{\log n})$*

neighbors outside H still active in phase R. If $R \geq R(n) \in \mathcal{O}(\sqrt{\log n \log \log n})$, it holds that all nodes from H are deleted after the second for-loop of the algorithm w.h.p.

PROOF. For the sake of simplicity, we consider the special case that no edges to nodes outside H exist first. We claim that for a constant $\alpha \in \mathbb{N}$ and all $i, j \in \mathbb{N}_0$ such that $i > j$ and $e^{R-j} \geq 8ec \ln n$, it holds that

$$\max_{v \in V} \left\{ \left| \left\{ w \in \mathcal{C}_v(R + \alpha i) \, | \, \delta_w(R + \alpha i) > e^{R-j} \right\} \right| \right\}$$
$$\leq \max \left\{ e^{R-2i+j}, 8c \ln n \right\}.$$

w.h.p. For $i = 1$ we have $j = 0$, i.e., the statement holds by definition because degrees in H are bounded by e^R. Assume the claim is established for some value of $i \geq 1$.

Consider a node $w \in H$ of degree $\delta_w(R + \alpha i) > e^{R-j} \geq 8ec \ln n$ for some $j \leq i$. By induction hypothesis, w.h.p. the number of children of w having degree larger than $e^{R-(j-1)}$ in phase $R + \alpha i$ (and thus also subsequent phases) is bounded by $\max\{e^{R-(2i-(j-1))}, 8c \ln n\} \leq e^{R-(j+1)}$, i.e., at least a fraction of $1 - 1/e$ of w's neighbors has degree at most factor e larger than $\delta_w(R + \alpha i)$ in phase $R + \alpha i$. According to Lemma 4.7, this implies that w is removed with constant probability in phase $R + \alpha i$. Moreover, as long as w keeps such a high degree, also in subsequent phases there is at least a constant probability that w is removed. This constant probability bound holds independently from previous phases (conditional to the event that w retains degree larger than e^{R-j}). Furthermore, due to the lemma, it applies to all children w of a node $v \in H$ independently. Hence, applying Chernoff's bound, we get that in all phases $k \in \{\alpha i, \alpha i + 1, \ldots, \alpha(i+1) - 1\}$, the number $|\{w \in \mathcal{C}_v(k) \, | \, \delta_w(k) > e^{R-j}\}|$ drops by a constant factor w.h.p. (unless this number is already smaller than $8c \ln n$). Consequently, if the constant α is sufficiently large, the induction step succeeds, completing the induction.

Recapitulated, after in total $\mathcal{O}(R)$ phases, no node in H will have more than $\mathcal{O}(\log n)$ neighbors of degree larger than $\mathcal{O}(\log n)$. The previous argument can be extended to reduce degrees even further. The difficulty arising is that once the expected number of high-degree nodes removed from the respective neighborhoods becomes smaller than $\Omega(\log n)$, Chernoff's bound does no longer guarantee that a constant fraction of high-degree neighbors is deleted in each phase. However, as used before, for critical nodes the applied probability bounds hold in each phase independently of previous rounds. Thus, instead of choosing α as a constant, we simply increase α with i.

Formally, if j_0 is the greatest index such that $e^{R-j_0} \geq 8ec \ln n$, we define

$$\alpha(i) := \begin{cases} \alpha & \text{if } i \leq j_0 \\ \lceil \alpha e^{i-j_0} \rceil & \text{otherwise.} \end{cases}$$

This way, the factor e loss in size of expected values (weakening the outcome of Chernoff's bound) is compensated for by increasing the number of considered phases by factor e (which due to independence appears in the exponent of the bound) in each step. Hence, within

$$\sum_{i=\lceil \ln \sqrt{\log n} \rceil}^{R} \alpha(i)$$
$$\in \mathcal{O} \left(R + \sum_{i=\lceil \ln \sqrt{\log n} \rceil}^{\lceil \ln(8ec \ln n) \rceil} \frac{\ln n}{e^i} \right)$$
$$= \mathcal{O} \left(R + \frac{\ln n}{\sqrt{\log n}} \right)$$
$$= \mathcal{O}(R)$$

many phases w.h.p., no node in H will have left more than $\mathcal{O}(\sqrt{\log n})$ neighbors of degree larger than $\mathcal{O}(\sqrt{\log n})$. Assuming that constants are chosen appropriately, this is the case after the first for-loop of the algorithm.

Recall that in the second loop the algorithm removes all nodes of degree at most R in each iteration. Thus, degrees in H will drop to $\mathcal{O}(\sqrt{\log n})$ in the first iteration of the loop, and subsequently all remaining nodes from H will be removed in the second iteration. Hence, indeed all nodes from H are deleted at the end of the second for-loop w.h.p., as claimed.

Finally, recall that no node has more than $\mathcal{O}(\sqrt{\log n})$ edges to nodes outside H. Choosing constants properly, these edges contribute only a negligible fraction to nodes' degrees even once they reach $\mathcal{O}(\sqrt{\log n})$. Thus, the asymptotic statement obtained by the above reasoning holds true also if we consider a subgraph H where nodes have $\mathcal{O}(\sqrt{\log n})$ edges leaving the subgraph, concluding the proof. □

We are now in the position to prove our bound on the running time of Algorithm 1.

THEOREM 4.9. *Assume that G is a forest and the coloring steps of Algorithm 1 are performed by a subroutine running for $\mathcal{O}(R + \log^* n)$ rounds. Then the algorithm eventually terminates and outputs a maximal independent set. Furthermore, if $R \geq R(n) \in \mathcal{O}(\sqrt{\log n \log \log n})$, Algorithm 1 terminates w.h.p. within $\mathcal{O}(R)$ rounds.*

PROOF. Correctness is obvious because (i) adjacent nodes can never join I concurrently, (ii) all neighbors of nodes that enter I are immediately deleted, (iii) no nodes from $V \setminus \bigcup_{v \in I}(\mathcal{N}_v \cup \{v\})$ get deleted, and (iv) the algorithm does not terminate until $V = \emptyset$. The algorithm will eventually terminate, as in each iteration of the third loop all leaves and isolated nodes are deleted and any forest contains either of the two.

Regarding the running time, assume that the value $R \in \mathcal{O}(\sqrt{\log n \log \log n})$ is sufficiently large, root the tree at a node v_0, and consider any path $P = (v_0, \ldots, v_k)$ of length $k \geq \sqrt{\ln n}$. Denote by C_i, $i \in \{0, \ldots, k\}$, the connected component of G containing v_i after removing the edges of P and—provided that $\delta_{v_i}(R) < e^R$—by $\bar{C}_i$ the connected (sub)component of C_i that contains v_i and consists of nodes w of degree $\delta_w(R) < e^R$ (as in Lemma 4.6). Then, by Lemma 4.6, with probability independently lower bounded by $1 - e^{-\omega(\sqrt{\ln n})}$, we have that

(i) $\delta_{v_i}(R) < e^R$ and

(ii) nodes in $\bar{C}_i$ have at most $\sqrt{\ln n}$ neighbors w of degree $\delta_w(R) \geq e^R$.

Hence, each of the $\bar{C}_i$ satisfies with a probability that is independently lower bounded by $1 - e^{-\omega(\sqrt{\ln n})}$ the prerequisites of Lemma 4.8, implying that w.h.p. all nodes in $\bar{C}_i$ are deleted by the end of the second for-loop. Since Property (i) implies that $\bar{C}_i$ exists, we conclude that independently of all $v_j \neq v_i$, node v_i is *not* deleted until the end of the second loop with probability $e^{-\omega(\sqrt{\ln n})}$. Thus, the probability that no node from P gets deleted is at most

$$\left(e^{-\omega(\sqrt{\ln n})} \right)^k \subseteq e^{-\omega(\ln n)} = n^{-\omega(1)}.$$

In other words, when the second loop is completed, w.h.p. no path of length $k \geq \sqrt{\ln n}$ exists in the remaining graph, implying that w.h.p. any of its components has diameter at most $\sqrt{\ln n}$. Consequently, it will take at most $\sqrt{\ln n}$ iterations of the third loop until all nodes have been deleted.

Summing up the running times for executing the three loops of the algorithm, we get that it terminates within $\mathcal{O}(R + (R + \log^* n) + \sqrt{\ln n}) = \mathcal{O}(R)$ rounds w.h.p. $\square$

We complete our analysis by deducing a uniform algorithm that features the claimed bounds on time and bit complexity.

THEOREM 4.10. *There exists a uniform MIS algorithm that terminates w.h.p. within $\mathcal{O}(\log n)$ rounds on general graphs and $\mathcal{O}(\sqrt{\log n \log \log n})$ rounds on forests. It can be implemented with a bit complexity of $\mathcal{O}(\log n)$ w.h.p.*

PROOF. Instead of running Algorithm 1 directly, we wrap it into an outer loop trying to guess a good value for R (i.e., $R(n) \leq R \in \mathcal{O}(R(n))$, where $R(n)$ as in Theorem 4.9). Furthermore, we restrict the number of iterations of the third loop to R, i.e., the algorithm will terminate after $\mathcal{O}(R)$ steps, however, potentially without producing an MIS.[4] Starting e.g. from two, with each call R is doubled. Once R reaches $R(n)$, according to Theorem 4.9 the algorithm outputs an MIS w.h.p. provided that G is a forest. Otherwise, R continues to grow until it becomes logarithmic in n. At this point, the analysis of the algorithm of Métivier et al. [11] applies to the first loop of the algorithm, showing that it terminates and return an MIS w.h.p. Hence, as the running time of each iteration of the outer loop is (essentially) linear in R and R grows exponentially, the overall running time of the algorithm is $\mathcal{O}(\sqrt{\log n \log \log n})$ on forests and $\mathcal{O}(\log n)$ on arbitrary graphs w.h.p.

Regarding the bit complexity, consider the first and third loop of Algorithm 1 first. In each iteration, a constant number of bits for state updates (entering MIS, being deleted without joining MIS, etc.) needs to be communicated as well as a random number that has to be compared to each neighbor's random number. However, in most cases exchanging a small number of leading bits is sufficient to break symmetry. Overall, as shown by Métivier et al. [11], this can be accomplished with a bit complexity of $\mathcal{O}(\log n)$ w.h.p. Essentially, for every round their algorithm generates a random value and transfers the necessary number of leading bits to compare these numbers to each neighbor only. Using Chernoff's bound, comparing $\mathcal{O}(\log n)$ random numbers between neighbors thus requires $\mathcal{O}(\log n)$ exchanged bits w.h.p., as

in expectation each comparison requires to examine a constant number of bits. Thus, if nodes do not wait for a phase to complete, but rather continue to exchange random bits for future comparisons in a stream-like fashion, the bit complexity becomes $\mathcal{O}(\log n)$.

However, in order to avoid increasing the (sublogarithmic) time complexity of the algorithm on trees, more caution is required. Observe that in each iteration of the outer loop, we know that $\Theta(R)$ many random values need to be compared to execute the respective call of Algorithm 1 correctly. Thus, nodes may exchange the leading bits of these $\Theta(R)$ many random values concurrently, without risking to increase the asymptotic bit complexity. Afterwards, for the fraction of the values for which the comparison remains unknown, nodes send the second and the third bit to their neighbors simultaneously. In subsequent rounds, we double the number of sent bits per number repeatedly. Note that for each single value, this way the number of sent bits is at most doubled, thus the probabilistic upper bound on the total number transmitted bits increases at most by a factor of two. Moreover, after $\log \log n$ rounds, $\log n$ bits of each single value will be compared in a single round, thus at the latest after $\log \log n + \mathcal{O}(1)$ rounds all comparisons are completed w.h.p. Employing this scheme, the total time complexity of all executions of the first and third loop of Algorithm 1 is (in a forest) bounded by

$$\mathcal{O}\left(\sum_{i=1}^{\lceil \log R(n) \rceil} 2^i + \log \log n \right)$$
$$\subseteq \mathcal{O}(R(n) + \log R(n) \log \log n)$$
$$= \mathcal{O}\left(\sqrt{\log n \log \log n} \right)$$

w.h.p.

It remains to show that the second loop of Algorithm 1 does not require the exchange of too many bits. The number of transmitted bits to execute this loop is determined by the number of bits sent by the employed coloring algorithm. Barenboim and Elkin [2] and Kuhn [7] independently provided deterministic coloring algorithms with running time $\mathcal{O}(R + \log^* n)$. These algorithms start from an initial coloring with a number of colors that is polynomial in n (typically one assumes identifiers of size $\mathcal{O}(\log n)$), which can be obtained w.h.p. by choosing a random color from the range $\{1, \dots, n^{\mathcal{O}(1)}\}$. Exchanging these colors (which also permits to verify that the random choices indeed resulted in a proper coloring) thus costs $\mathcal{O}(\log n)$ bits.[5] However, as the maximum degree of the considered subgraphs is $R + 1$, which is in $\mathcal{O}(\log n)$ w.h.p., subsequent rounds of the algorithms deal with colors that are of (poly)logarithmic size in n. As exchanging coloring information is the dominant term contributing to message size in both algorithms, the overall bit complexity of all executions of the second loop of Algorithm 1 can be kept as low as $\mathcal{O}(\log n + R(n) \log \log n) = \mathcal{O}(\log n)$. $\square$

5. REFERENCES

[1] N. Alon, L. Babai, and A. Itai. A Fast and Simple Randomized Parallel Algorithm for the Maximal

---

[4]There is no need to start all over again; one can build on the IS of previous iterations, although this does not change the asymptotic bounds.

[5]To derive a uniform solution, one again falls back to doubling the size of the bit string of the chosen color until the coloring is locally feasible.

Independent Set Problem. *Journal of Algorithms*, 7(4):567 – 583, 1986.

[2] L. Barenboim and M. Elkin. Distributed ($\Delta + 1$)-Coloring in Linear (in Δ) Time. In *Proc. 41st annual ACM symposium on Theory of computing (STOC)*, pages 111–120, 2009.

[3] L. Barenboim and M. Elkin. Sublogarithmic Distributed MIS algorithm for Sparse Graphs using Nash-Williams Decomposition. *Distributed Computing*, 22(5–6):363–379, 2009.

[4] R. Cole and U. Vishkin. Deterministic Coin Tossing with Applications to Optimal Parallel List Ranking. *Information and Control*, 70(1):32–53, 1986.

[5] A. Goldberg, S. Plotkin, and G. Shannon. Parallel Symmetry-Breaking in Sparse Graphs. In *In Proc. 19th Annual ACM Conference on Theory of Computing (STOC)*, pages 315–324, 1987.

[6] A. Israeli and A. Itai. A Fast and Simple Randomized Parallel Algorithm for Maximal Matching. *Information Processing Letters*, 22(2):77 – 80, 1986.

[7] F. Kuhn. Weak Graph Coloring: Distributed Algorithms and Applications. In *In Proc. 21st ACM Symposium on Parallelism in Algorithms and Architectures (SPAA)*, 2009.

[8] F. Kuhn, T. Moscibroda, and R. Wattenhofer. Local Computation: Lower and Upper Bounds. *Computing Research Repository*, abs/1011.5470, 2010.

[9] N. Linial. Locality in Distributed Graph Algorithms. *SIAM Journal on Computing*, 21(1):193–201, 1992.

[10] M. Luby. A Simple Parallel Algorithm for the Maximal Independent Set Problem. *SIAM Journal on Computing*, 15(4):1036–1055, 1986.

[11] Y. Métivier, J. M. Robson, N. Saheb Djahromi, and A. Zemmari. An optimal bit complexity randomised distributed MIS algorithm. In *Proc. 16th Colloquium on Structural Information and Communication Complexity (SIROCCO)*, pages 323–337, 2009.

[12] M. Naor. A Lower Bound on Probabilistic Algorithms for Distributive Ring Coloring. *SIAM Journal on Discrete Mathematics*, 4(3):409–412, 1991.

[13] A. Panconesi and A. Srinivasan. On the Complexity of Distributed Network Decomposition. *Journal of Algorithms*, 20(2):356–374, 1996.

[14] J. Schneider and R. Wattenhofer. A Log-Star Distributed Maximal Independent Set Algorithm for Growth-Bounded Graphs. In *Proc. of the 27th Annual ACM Symposium on Principles of Distributed Computing (PODC)*, 2008.

Toward More Localized Local Algorithms: Removing Assumptions Concerning Global Knowledge

[Extended Abstract]

Amos Korman[*]
CNRS & Univ. Paris Diderot
Paris
France
Amos.Korman@liafa.jussieu.fr

Jean-Sébastien Sereni[†]
CNRS
Paris
France
sereni@kam.mff.cuni.cz

Laurent Viennot[‡]
INRIA & Univ. Paris Diderot
Paris
France
Laurent.Viennot@inria.fr

ABSTRACT

Numerous sophisticated local algorithm were suggested in the literature for various fundamental problems. Notable examples are the MIS and $(\Delta + 1)$-coloring algorithms by Barenboim and Elkin [6], by Kuhn [22], and by Panconesi and Srinivasan [33], as well as the $O(\Delta^2)$-coloring algorithm by Linial [27]. Unfortunately, most known local algorithms (including, in particular, the aforementioned algorithms) are *non-uniform*, that is, they assume that all nodes know good estimations of one or more global parameters of the network, e.g., the maximum degree Δ or the number of nodes n.

This paper provides a rather general method for transforming a non-uniform local algorithm into a *uniform* one. Furthermore, the resulting algorithm enjoys the same asymptotic running time as the original non-uniform algorithm. Our method applies to a wide family of both deterministic and randomized algorithms. Specifically, it applies to almost all of the state of the art non-uniform algorithms regarding MIS and Maximal Matching, as well as to many results concerning the coloring problem. (In particular, it applies to all aforementioned algorithms.)

To obtain our transformations we introduce a new distributed tool called *pruning algorithms*, which we believe may be of independent interest.

[*]Supported in part by a France-Israel cooperation grant ("Mutli-Computing" project) from the France and Israel Ministries of Science, by the ANR projects ALADDIN and PROSE, and by the INRIA project-team GANG.

[†]CNRS (LIAFA, Université Denis Diderot), Paris, France and Department of Applied Mathematics (KAM), Faculty of Mathematics and Physics, Charles University, Prague, Czech Republic. Supported in part by the French *Agence Nationale de la Recherche* under reference ANR 10 JCJC 0204 01.

[‡]INRIA project-team GANG, supported by the european STREP project EULER, and the ANR project PROSE.

Categories and Subject Descriptors

G.2.2 [**Discrete Mathematics**]: Graph Theory—*Graph algorithms, Graph labeling, Network problems*

General Terms

Algorithms

Keywords

Distributed algorithm, global knowledge, parameters, MIS, coloring, Maximal matching

1. INTRODUCTION

1.1 Background and motivation

Distributed computing concerns environments in which many processors, located at different sites, must collaborate in order to achieve some global task. One of the main themes in distributed network algorithms concerns the question of how to cope with *locality* constrains, that is, the lack of knowledge about the global structure of the network (cf., [34]). On the one hand, information about the global structure may not always be accessible to individual processors and the cost of computing it from scratch may overshadow the cost of the algorithm using it. On the other hand, global knowledge is not always essential, and many seemingly global tasks can be efficiently achieved by letting processors know more about their immediate neighborhoods and less about the rest of the network.

A standard model for capturing the essence of locality is the $\mathcal{LOCAL}$ model (cf., [34]). In this model, the network is modeled by a graph $G = (V, E)$, where the nodes of G represent the processors and the edges represent the communication links. To perform a task, nodes are woken up simultaneously, and computation proceeds in fault-free synchronous rounds during which every node exchanges messages with its neighbors, and performs arbitrary computations on its data. Since many tasks cannot be solved distributively in an anonymous network, symmetry breaking must be addressed. The typical way to address this issue is by assuming that a unique identity $Id(v)$ is initially provided to each node v in the network, and encoded using $O(\log n)$ bits, where n is the number of nodes in the network. A *local algorithm* operating in such a setting must return an output at each node such that the collection of outputs satisfies the required task. For example, in the Maximal Independent Set (MIS) problem, the output at each node v is a bit $b(v)$ indicating whether v belongs to a selected set $S \subseteq V$ of nodes, and it is required that S forms a MIS of G. The *running time* of a local algorithm is the number of rounds needed for the algorithm to complete its operation at each node, taken in the worst case scenario. This is typically evaluated with respect to some parameters of the underlying graph. The common parameters used are the number of nodes n in the graph and the maximum degree Δ of a node in the graph.

To ease the computation, it is often assumed that some kind of knowledge about the global network (e.g., the number of nodes) is provided to each node *a priori*. Actually, the amount and type of such information may have a profound effect on the design of the distributed algorithm. Obviously, if the whole topology of the network is known to each node in advance, then the distributed algorithm can be reduced to a central one. In fact, the whole area of *computation with advice* [9, 12, 13, 14, 15, 20, 21] is dedicated to studying the amount of information known to nodes and its effect on the performances of the distributed algorithm. For instance, Fraigniaud *et al.* [15] showed that if each node is provided with only a constant number of bits then one can locally construct a BFS-tree in constant time, and can locally construct a MST in $O(\log n)$ time, while both tasks require diameter time if no knowledge is assumed. As another example, Cohen *et al.* [9] showed that $O(1)$ bits, chosen judiciously at each node, can allow a finite automata to distributively explore every graph. As a matter of fact, from a radical point of view, for many questions (e.g., MIS, Maximal Matching), additional information may push the question at hand into absurdity: even a constant number of bits of additional information per node is enough to compute a solution—simply let the additional information encode the solution!

When dealing with locality issues, it is desired that the amount of information that is known to nodes regarding the whole network is minimized. A local algorithm that assumes that each node initially knows merely its own identity is often called *uniform*. Unfortunately, there are only few local algorithms in the literature that are uniform (e.g., [11, 25, 28, 29, 36]). In contrast, most known local algorithms assume that all nodes know upper bounds on the values of some global parameters of the network. Moreover, it is often assumed that all nodes agree on their candidates for being these upper bounds. Furthermore, typically, not only the correct operation of the algorithm requires the knowledge of the upper bounds, but also its running time is actually a function of the upper bound estimations and not of the actual value of the parameters. Hence, it is desired that the known upper bounds are not significantly larger than the real values of the parameters.

Some attempts to transform a non-uniform local algorithm into a uniform one were made by examining the details of the algorithm at hand and modifying it appropriately. For example, Barenboim and Elkin [6] first gave a non-uniform MIS algorithm for the family of graphs with arboricity $a = O(\log^{1/2 - \delta} n)$, for some constant $\delta \in (0, 1/2)$, running in time $O(\log n / \log \log n)$. At the cost of increasing the running time to $O(\frac{\log n}{\log \log n} \log^* n)$, the authors show how to modify their algorithm to not require the knowledge of a. (Nevertheless, their algorithm still requires nodes to agree on an upper bound on n.)

In this paper, we present a rather general method for transforming a non-uniform local algorithm into a uniform one without increasing the asymptotic running time of the original algorithm. Our method can apply to a wide family of both deterministic and randomized algorithms. In particular, our method can apply to all of the state of the art non-uniform algorithms regarding MIS and Maximal Matching, as well as to several of the best known results concerning the coloring problem.

Our transformations are obtained using a new type of local algorithms termed *pruning algorithms*. Informally, the basic property of a pruning algorithm is that it allows one to iteratively apply a sequence of local algorithms (whose output may not form a correct global solution) one after the other, in a way that "always progresses" toward a solution. In a sense, a pruning algorithm is a combination of a gluing mechanism and a *local checking* algorithm (cf., [16, 31]). A local checking algorithm for a problem Π runs on graphs with an output value at each node (and possibly an input too), and can locally detect whether the output is "legal" with respect to Π. That is, if the instance is not legal then at least one node detects this, and raises an alarm. (For example, a local checking algorithm for MIS is trivial: each node in the set S, which is suspected to be a MIS, checks that none of its neighbors belongs to S, and each node not in S checks that at least one of its neighbors belongs to S. If the check fails, then the node raises an alarm.) A pruning algorithm needs to satisfy an additional *gluing* property not required by local checking algorithms. Specifically, if the instance is not legal, then the pruning algorithm must carefully choose the nodes raising the alarm (and possibly modify their input too), so that a solution for the subgraph induced by those alarming nodes can be well glued to the previous output of the non-alarming nodes, in a way such that the combined output is a solution to the whole initial graph.

We believe that this new type of algorithms may be of independent interest. Indeed, as we show, pruning algorithms have several types of other applications in the theory of local computation, besides the aforementioned issue of designing uniform algorithms. Specifically, they can be used also to transform a local Monte-Carlo algorithm into a Las Vegas one, as well as to obtain an algorithm that runs in the minimum running time of a given set of uniform algorithms.

1.2 Previous work

MIS and coloring: There is a long line of research concerning the two related classical $(\Delta + 1)$-coloring and MIS problems [3, 10, 17, 18, 23, 24, 27]. Recently, Barenboim and Elkin [4] and independently Kuhn [22] presented two elegant $(\Delta + 1)$-coloring and MIS algorithms running in $O(\Delta + \log^* n)$ time on general graphs. This is the current best bound for these problems on low degree graphs. For graphs with a large maximum degree Δ, the best bound is due to Panconesi and Srinivasan [33], who devised an algorithm running in $2^{O(\sqrt{\log n})}$ time. The aforementioned algorithms are non-uniform. Specifically, all three algorithms require that all nodes know and agree on an upper bound on n and the first two also require an upper bound on Δ.

For bounded-independence graphs, Schneider and Wattenhofer [36] designed uniform deterministic MIS and $(\Delta + 1)$-coloring algorithms running in $O(\log^* n)$ time. Barenboim and Elkin devised [6] a deterministic algorithm for the MIS problem on graphs of bounded arboricity that requires time $O(\log n / \log \log n)$. More specifically, for graphs with ar-

Problem	Parameters	Time	Ref.	This paper (uniform)	Theorem
Det. MIS and $(\Delta+1)$-coloring	n, Δ	$O(\Delta + \log^* n)$	[4, 22]	$\min\left\{O(\Delta + \log^* n), 2^{O(\sqrt{\log n})}\right\}$	Th. 1 Th. 2
	n	$2^{O(\sqrt{\log n})}$	[33]		
Det. MIS (arboricity $a = o(\sqrt{\log n})$)	n, a	$o(\log n)$	[6]	$o(\log n)$	Th. 1
Det. MIS (arboricity $a = O(\log^{1/2-\delta} n)$)	n, a	$O(\log n / \log \log n)$	[6]	$O(\log n / \log \log n)$	Th. 1
Det. $\lambda(\Delta+1)$-coloring	n, Δ	$O(\Delta/\lambda + \log^* n)$	[4, 22]	$O(\Delta/\lambda + \log^* n)$	Th. 3
Det. $O(\Delta)$-edge coloring	n, Δ	$O(\Delta^\epsilon + \log^* n)$	[7]	$O(\Delta^\epsilon + \log^* n)$	Th. 4
Det. $O(\Delta^{1+\epsilon})$-edge coloring	n, Δ	$O(\log \Delta + \log^* n)$	[7]	$O(\log \Delta + \log^* n)$	Th. 4
Det. Maximal Matching	n or Δ	$O(\log^4 n)$	[19]	$O(\log^4 n)$	Th. 5
Rand. MIS	uniform	$O(\log n)$	[29, 1]		
Rand. $(2, 2(c+1))$-ruling-set	n	$O(2^c \log^{1/c} n)$	[35]	$O(2^c \log^{1/c} n)$	Th. 6

Table 1: **Comparison of $\mathcal{LOCAL}$ algorithms with respect to global parameter knowledge. "Det." stands for deterministic, and "Rand." for randomized.**

boricity $a = o(\sqrt{\log n})$, they show that a MIS can be computed deterministically in $o(\log n)$ time, and whenever $a = O(\log^{1/2-\delta} n)$ for some constant $\delta \in (0, 1/2)$, the same algorithm runs in time $O(\log n / \log \log n)$. At the cost of increasing the running time by a multiplicative factor of $O(\log^* n)$, the authors show how to modify their algorithm to not require the knowledge of a. Nevertheless, all their algorithms require all nodes to know and agree on an upper bound on the value of n. Deterministic non-uniform coloring algorithms with number of colors and running time corresponding to the arboricity parameter were given by Barenboim and Elkin [5, 6].

Concerning the problem of coloring with more than $\Delta + 1$ colors, Linial [26, 27], and subsequently Szegedy and Vishwanathan [37], described $O(\Delta^2)$-coloring algorithms with running time $\Theta(\log^* n)$. Barenboim and Elkin [4] and, independently, Kuhn [22] generalized this by presenting a tradeoff between the running time and the number of colors: they devised a $\lambda(\Delta + 1)$-coloring algorithm with running time $O(\Delta/\lambda + \log^* n)$, for any $\lambda \geqslant 1$. All these algorithms require the knowledge of upper bounds on both n and Δ.

Efficient deterministic algorithms for the edge-coloring problem can be obtained from [5, 7, 32]. The state of the art results are due to Barenboim and Elkin [7]. Specifically, they design an $O(\Delta)$-edge coloring algorithm running in time $O(\Delta^\epsilon) + \log^* n$, for any $\epsilon > 0$, and an $O(\Delta^{1+\epsilon})$-edge coloring algorithm running in time $O(\log \Delta) + \log^* n$, for any $\epsilon > 0$. Both these algorithms require the knowledge of upper bounds on both n and Δ.

Randomized algorithms for MIS and $(\Delta + 1)$-coloring running in expected time $O(\log n)$ were initially given by Luby [29] and, independently, by Alon et al. [1]. Recently, Schneider and Wattenhofer [35] constructed the best known non-uniform $(\Delta + 1)$-coloring algorithm, which runs in time $O(\log \Delta + \sqrt{\log n})$. They also provide random algorithms for coloring using more colors. For integral $c > 0$, a randomized algorithm for $(2, 2(c + 1))$-ruling-set in time $O(2^c \log^{1/c} n)$ is also presented. All these algorithms in [35] are non-uniform and require the knowledge of an upper bound on n.

Maximal Matching: Schneider and Wattenhofer [36] designed a uniform deterministic maximal matching algorithm on bounded-independence graphs running in $O(\log^* n)$ time. For general graphs, however, the state of the art maximal matching algorithm is non-uniform: Hanckowiak et al. [19] presented a non-uniform deterministic algorithm for maximal matching running in time $O(\log^4 n)$. This algorithm assumes the knowledge of an upper bound for n (for some parts of the algorithm, the nodes can ignore n provided they know Δ).

1.3 Our results

The main conceptual contribution of the paper is the introduction of a new type of algorithms called *pruning algorithms*. Informally, the fundamental property of this type of algorithms is to allow one to iteratively run a sequence of algorithms (whose output may not necessarily be correct everywhere) so that the global output does not deteriorate, and it always progresses toward a solution.

Our main application for pruning algorithm concerns the problem of locally computing a global solution while minimizing the necessary global knowledge known to nodes. Addressing this, we provide a rather general method for transforming a non-uniform local algorithm into a uniform one without increasing the asymptotic running time of the original algorithm. Our method applies to a wide family of both deterministic and randomized algorithms; in particular, it applies to many of the best known results concerning classical problems such as MIS, Coloring, and Maximal Matching. (See table 1.2 for a summary of some of the uniform algorithms we obtain and the corresponding state of the art existing non-uniform algorithms.)

In another application, we show how to transform a Monte-Carlo local algorithm into a Las Vegas one. Finally, given several uniform algorithms for the same problem whose running times depend on different parameters—which are unknown to nodes—we show a general method for constructing a uniform algorithm solving the problem, that on every instance runs asymptotically as fast as the fastest algorithm among those given algorithms. In particular, we obtain the following theorems.

THEOREM 1. *There exists a uniform deterministic algorithm solving MIS on general graphs in time*

$$\min\left\{O(\Delta + \log^* n), 2^{O(\sqrt{\log n})}, f(a)\right\},$$

where $f(a) := o(\log n)$ for graphs of arboricity $a = o(\sqrt{\log n})$, and $f(a) := O(\log n / \log \log n)$ for arboricity $O(\log^{1/2-\delta} n)$, for some constant $\delta \in (0, 1/2)$ (otherwise, $f(a) := n$).

THEOREM 2. *There exists a uniform deterministic algorithm solving $(\Delta + 1)$-coloring problem on general graphs in time $\min\{O(\Delta + \log^* n), 2^{O(\sqrt{\log n})}\}$.*

THEOREM 3. *There exists a uniform deterministic algorithm solving the $\lambda(\Delta+1)$-coloring problem on general graphs and running in time $O(\Delta/\lambda + \log^* n)$, for any $\lambda \geqslant 1$, such that Δ/λ is either a constant or a moderately increasing function. In particular, there exists a uniform deterministic algorithm solving the $O(\Delta^2)$-coloring problem in time $O(\log^* n)$.*

THEOREM 4. *(1) There exists a uniform deterministic $O(\Delta)$-edge coloring algorithm for general graphs running in time $O(\Delta^\epsilon + \log^* n)$, for any $\epsilon > 0$. (2) There exists a uniform deterministic $O(\Delta^{1+\epsilon})$-edge coloring algorithm for general graphs that runs in time $O(\log \Delta + \log^* n)$, for any $\epsilon > 0$.*

THEOREM 5. *There exists a uniform deterministic algorithm solving the maximal matching problem in time $O(\log^4 n)$.*

THEOREM 6. *For a constant integral $c > 0$, there exists a uniform randomized algorithm solving the $(2, 2(c+1))$-ruling-set problem in time $O(2^c \log^{1/c} n)$.*

2. PRELIMINARIES

General definitions: For two integers a and b, we let $[a, b] := \{a, a+1, \cdots, b\}$. Let $G = (V(G), E(G))$ be an undirected and unweighted graph. The *degree* $\deg_G(v)$ of a node $v \in V(G)$ is the number of neighbors of v in G. The *maximum degree of G* is $\Delta_G := \max\{\deg_G(v) \mid v \in V(G)\}$. The *distance* $\text{dist}_G(u, v)$ between two nodes $u, v \in G$ is the number of edges on a shortest path connecting them. Given a node u and an integer r, the *ball* of radius r around u is the subgraph $B_G(u, r)$ of G induced by the collection of nodes at distance at most r from v. The *neighborhood* $N_G(u)$ of u is the set of neighbors of u, i.e., $N_G(u) := B_G(u, 1) \setminus \{u\}$. In what follows, we may omit the subscript G from the previous notations when there is no risk of confusion.

Functions: Fix an integer k. A function $f : \mathbf{R}^k \to \mathbf{R}$ is *non-decreasing* if $f(x_1, x_2, \cdots, x_k) \leqslant f(y_1, y_2, \cdots, y_k)$ for any two sequences $(x_1, x_2, \cdots, x_k)$ and $(y_1, y_2, \cdots, y_k)$ where $x_i \leqslant y_i$ for each $i \in [1, k]$. An *ascending* function is a non-decreasing and unbounded function $f : \mathbf{R} \to \mathbf{R}^+$ (by unbounded, we mean that $\lim_{x \to \infty} f(x) = \infty$). A function $f : (\mathbf{R}^+)^\ell \to \mathbf{R}^+$ is called *additive* if $f(x_1, \cdots, x_\ell) = \sum_{i=1}^\ell f_i(x_i)$ and f_i is ascending for each $i \in [1, \ell]$.

A function $f : \mathbf{R}^+ \to \mathbf{R}^+$ is *moderately-increasing* if it is increasing and there exists a positive integer α such that $f(\alpha i) > 2f(i)$ and $\alpha f(i) > f(2i)$ for every integer $i \geqslant 2$. Note that $f(x) = x^{k_1} \log^{k_2}(x)$ is a moderately-increasing function for every non-negative constants k_1 and k_2 (such that $k_1 + k_2 > 0$).

Problems and instances: Given a set of nodes V, a *vector* for V is an assignment $\mathbf{x}$ of a bit string $\mathbf{x}(v)$ to each $v \in V$, i.e., $\mathbf{x}$ is a function $\mathbf{x} : V \to \{0, 1\}^*$. A *problem* is defined by a collection of triplets: $\Pi = \{(G, \mathbf{x}, \mathbf{y})\}$, where $G = (V, E)$ is a (not necessarily connected) graph, and $\mathbf{x}$ and $\mathbf{y}$ are *input* and *output* vectors for V, respectively. We consider only problems that are closed under disjoint union, i.e., if G_1 and G_2 are two vertex disjoint graphs and $(G_1, \mathbf{x}_1, \mathbf{y}_1), (G_2, \mathbf{x}_2, \mathbf{y}_2) \in \Pi$ then $(G, \mathbf{x}, \mathbf{y}) \in \Pi$, where $G = G_1 \cup G_2$, $\mathbf{x} = \mathbf{x}_1 \cup \mathbf{x}_2$ and $\mathbf{y} = \mathbf{y}_1 \cup \mathbf{y}_2$. An *instance*, with respect to a given a problem Π, is a pair $(G, \mathbf{x})$ for which there exists an output vector $\mathbf{y}$ satisfying $(G, \mathbf{x}, \mathbf{y}) \in \Pi$. In what follows, whenever we consider some collection $\mathcal{F}$ of instances, we always assume that $\mathcal{F}$ is closed under inclusion. That is, if $(G, \mathbf{x}) \in \mathcal{F}$ and $(G', \mathbf{x}') \subseteq (G, \mathbf{x})$ (i.e., G' is a subgraph of G and $\mathbf{x}'$ is the input vector $\mathbf{x}$ restricted to $V(G')$) then $(G', \mathbf{x}') \in \mathcal{F}$. Informally, given a problem Π and a collection of instances $\mathcal{F}$, the goal is to design an efficient distributed algorithm that takes an instance $(G, \mathbf{x}) \in \mathcal{F}$ as input, and produces an output vector

$\mathbf{y}$ satisfying $(G, \mathbf{x}, \mathbf{y}) \in \Pi$. The reason why we require Π to be closed under disjoint union is that a distributed algorithm operating on an instance $(G, \mathbf{x})$ behaves separately and independently on each connected component of G. Let $\mathcal{G}$ be a family of graphs closed under inclusion. We define $\mathcal{F}(\mathcal{G})$ to be the set of pairs $\{(G, \mathbf{x}) \mid G \in \mathcal{G}, \mathbf{x} \text{ is arbitrary}\}$.

We assume that each node $v \in V$ is provided with a unique integer referred to as the *identity* of v, and denoted $\text{Id}(v)$, encoded using $O(\log |V|)$ bits; by unique identities, we mean that $\text{Id}(u) \neq \text{Id}(v)$ for every two distinct nodes u and v. (In some works on coloring, the assumption that the identities are unique is relaxed and the collection of assigned identities is only required to be a coloring, i.e., every two neighboring nodes have different identities.) For ease of exposition, we consider the identity of a node to be part of its input.

We consider classical problems such as coloring, (α, β)-ruling set (and in particular MIS, which is $(2, 1)$-ruling set) and maximal matching. Informally, viewing the output of a node as a *color*, the requirement of *coloring* is that the colors of two neighboring nodes must be different. In *MIS* (for Maximal Independent Set), the output at each node is Boolean, and indicates whether the node belongs to a set S that must form a MIS, that is, S must is independent: no two neighboring nodes are in S, and must be maximal: if all neighbors of a node v are not in S then $v \in S$. In (α, β)-ruling set, the set S of selected nodes must satisfy: (1) two nodes that belong to S must be at distance at least α from each other, and (2) if a node does not belong to S, then there is a node in the set at distance at most β from it. (Observe that MIS is precisely $(2, 1)$-ruling set.) Finally, given a triplet $(G, \mathbf{x}, \mathbf{y})$, two nodes u and v are called *matched* if $(u, v) \in E$, $\mathbf{y}(u) = \mathbf{y}(v)$ and $\mathbf{y}(w) \neq \mathbf{y}(u)$ for every $w \in (N_G(u) \cup N_G(v)) \setminus \{u, v\}$. In MM (for Maximal Matching) it is required that each node u is either matched to one of its neighbors or that every neighbor v of u is matched to one of v's neighbors.

Parameters: Fix a problem Π and let $\mathcal{F}$ be a collection of instances for Π. A *parameter* $\mathbf{p}$ is a non-decreasing positive valued function $\mathbf{p} : \mathcal{F} \to \mathbf{N}$. By non-decreasing, we mean that if $(G', \mathbf{x}') \in \mathcal{F}$ and $(G', \mathbf{x}') \subseteq (G, \mathbf{x})$ then $\mathbf{p}(G', \mathbf{x}') \leqslant \mathbf{p}(G, \mathbf{x})$.

Let $\mathcal{F}$ be a collection of instances. A parameter $\mathbf{p}$ for $\mathcal{F}$ is called a *graph-parameter* if $\mathbf{p}$ is oblivious of the input, that is, if $\mathbf{p}(G, \mathbf{x}) = \mathbf{p}(G, \mathbf{x}')$ for every two instances $(G, \mathbf{x}), (G, \mathbf{x}') \in \mathcal{F}$ such that the input assignments $\mathbf{x}$ and $\mathbf{x}'$ preserve the identities, i.e., the inputs $\mathbf{x}(v)$ and $\mathbf{x}'(v)$ contain the same identity $\text{Id}(v)$ for every $v \in V(G)$. For example, in what follows, we will focus on the following graph-parameters: the number n of nodes of the graph G, i.e., $|V(G)|$, the maximum degree $\Delta = \Delta(G)$ of G, i.e., $\max\{\deg_G(u) \mid u \in V(G)\}$, and the arboricity $a = a(G)$ of G, i.e., the least number of edge-disjoint forests whose union is G.

Local algorithms: Consider a problem Π and a collection of instances $\mathcal{F}$ for Π. An algorithm for Π and $\mathcal{F}$ takes as input an instance $(G, \mathbf{x}) \in \mathcal{F}$ and must terminate with an output vector $\mathbf{y}$ such that $(G, \mathbf{x}, \mathbf{y}) \in \Pi$. We consider the $\mathcal{LOCAL}$ model (cf., [34]). During the execution of a *local* algorithm $\mathcal{A}$, all processors are woken up simultaneously and computation proceeds in fault-free synchronous rounds, i.e., it occurs in discrete rounds. In each round, every node may send messages of unrestricted size to its neighbors and may perform arbitrary computations on its data. A message that is sent in a round r, arrives to its destination before the next round $r+1$ starts. It must be guaranteed that after a finite number of rounds, each node v terminates with some output value $\mathbf{y}(v)$. (It is required that a node knows that its output is indeed its final output.) The algorithm $\mathcal{A}$ is *correct* if for every instance $(G, \mathbf{x}) \in \mathcal{F}$, the resulted output vector $\mathbf{y}$ satisfies $(G, \mathbf{x}, \mathbf{y}) \in \Pi$.

Let $\mathcal{A}$ be a local deterministic algorithm for Π and $\mathcal{F}$. The *running time* of $\mathcal{A}$ over a particular instance $(G, \mathbf{x}) \in \mathcal{F}$, denoted $T_{\mathcal{A}}(G, \mathbf{x})$, is the number of rounds from the beginning of the execution of $\mathcal{A}$ until all nodes terminate. The running time of $\mathcal{A}$ is typically evaluated with respect to a collection of parameters $\Lambda = \{\mathbf{q}_1, \mathbf{q}_2, \cdots, \mathbf{q}_\ell\}$. Specifically, it is compared to a function $f : \mathbf{N}^\ell \to \mathbf{R}^+$; we say that f is an upper bound for the running time of $\mathcal{A}$ with respect to Λ if $T_{\mathcal{A}}(G, \mathbf{x}) \leqslant f(\mathbf{q}_1^*, \mathbf{q}_2^*, \cdots, \mathbf{q}_\ell^*)$ for every instance $(G, \mathbf{x}) \in F$ with parameters $\mathbf{p}_i^* := \mathbf{p}_i(G, \mathbf{x})$ for $i \in [1, \ell]$.

A remark about running an algorithm after another: Many $\mathcal{LOCAL}$ algorithms happen to have different termination times at different nodes. On the other hand, most of the algorithms rely on a simultaneous wake up of all nodes. This becomes a problem when one wants to run an algorithm $\mathcal{A}$ and subsequently an algorithm $\mathcal{B}$ taking the output of $\mathcal{A}$ as input. Indeed, this problem amounts to running $\mathcal{B}$ with non-simultaneous wake up: a node u starts $\mathcal{B}$ when it terminates $\mathcal{A}$.

As observed (e.g., by Kuhn [22]), one can use a synchronizer [2] to run a synchronous local algorithm in an asynchronous system, with the same asymptotic time complexity. Hence, the synchronicity assumption can actually be removed. Although the standard asynchronous model introduced still assumes simultaneous wake up, it can be easily verified that the technique still applies with non-simultaneous wake up times if a node can buffer messages received before it wakes up, which is the case when running an algorithm after another. However, we have to adapt the notion of running time. We define it as the number of time units elapsed between the last wake up time of a node and the last termination time of a node. We let $\mathcal{A}; \mathcal{B}$ be the process of running $\mathcal{B}$ after $\mathcal{A}$. Note that the running time of $\mathcal{A}; \mathcal{B}$ is bounded by the sum of the running times of $\mathcal{A}$ and $\mathcal{B}$. In the sequel we implicitly assume that the simple α synchronizer is used when running a sequence $\mathcal{A}_1; \mathcal{A}_2; \cdots; \mathcal{A}_k$ of algorithms.

Local algorithms requiring parameters: Fix a problem Π and let $\mathcal{F}$ be a collection of instances for Π. Let $\Gamma = \{\mathbf{p}_1, \mathbf{p}_2, \cdots, \mathbf{p}_r\}$ be a collection of parameters and let $\mathcal{A}$ be a local algorithm. We say that $\mathcal{A}$ *requires* Γ if, in order to execute $\mathcal{A}$ on an instance $(G, \mathbf{x}) \in \mathcal{F}$, all nodes must agree on a value $\tilde{\mathbf{p}}$ for each parameter $\mathbf{p} \in \Gamma$. The value $\tilde{\mathbf{p}}$ is called a *guess* for $\mathbf{p}$. A collection of guesses for the parameters in Γ is denoted by $\tilde{\Gamma}$. An algorithm $\mathcal{A}$ that requires Γ is denoted by $\mathcal{A}^\Gamma$. An algorithm that does not require any parameter is called *uniform*.

Consider an instance $(G, \mathbf{x}) \in \mathcal{F}$, a collection Γ of parameters and a parameter $\mathbf{p} \in \Gamma$. A guess $\tilde{\mathbf{p}}$ for $\mathbf{p}$ is termed *good* if $\tilde{\mathbf{p}} \geqslant \mathbf{p}(G, \mathbf{x})$, and the guess $\tilde{\mathbf{p}}$ is called *correct* if $\tilde{\mathbf{p}} = \mathbf{p}(G, \mathbf{x})$. We typically write correct guesses and collection of correct guesses with a star exponent, that is $\mathbf{p}^*$ and $\Gamma^*(G, \mathbf{x})$, respectively. When $(G, \mathbf{x})$ is clear from the context, for simplicity, we may use the notation Γ^* instead of $\Gamma^*(G, \mathbf{x})$.

An algorithm $\mathcal{A}^\Gamma$ *depends* on Γ if for every instance $(G, \mathbf{x})$

$\in \mathcal{F}$, the correctness of $\mathcal{A}^\Gamma$ over $(G, \mathbf{x})$ is guaranteed when $\mathcal{A}^\Gamma$ uses a collection $\tilde{\Gamma}$ of good guesses.

Consider an algorithm $\mathcal{A}^\Gamma$ that depends on a collection of parameters $\Gamma = \{\mathbf{p}_1, \mathbf{p}_2, \cdots, \mathbf{p}_r\}$ and fix an instance $(G, \mathbf{x})$. Observe that the running time of $\mathcal{A}^\Gamma$ over $(G, \mathbf{x})$ may be different for different collections of guesses $\tilde{\Gamma}$, in other words, the running time over $(G, \mathbf{x})$ is a function of $\tilde{\Gamma}$. Recall that when we consider an algorithm that does not require parameters, we still typically evaluate its running time with respect to a collection of parameters Λ. We generalize this to the case where the algorithm depends on Γ as follows.

Consider two collections of parameters $\Gamma = \{\mathbf{p}_1, \mathbf{p}_2, \cdots, \mathbf{p}_r\}$ and $\Lambda = \{\mathbf{q}_1, \mathbf{q}_2, \cdots, \mathbf{q}_\ell\}$. Some parameters may belong to both Γ and Λ. Without loss of generality, we shall always assume that $\{\mathbf{p}_{r'+1}, \mathbf{p}_{r'+2}, \cdots, \mathbf{p}_r\} \cap \{\mathbf{q}_{r'+1}, \mathbf{q}_{r'+2}, \cdots, \mathbf{q}_\ell\} = \emptyset$ for some $r' \in [0, \min\{r, \ell\}]$ and $\mathbf{p}_i = \mathbf{q}_i$ for every $i \in [1, r']$. Notice that $\Gamma \setminus (\Gamma \cap \Lambda) = \{\mathbf{p}_{r'+1}, \mathbf{p}_{r'+2}, \cdots, \mathbf{p}_r\}$. A function $f : (\mathbf{R}^+)^\ell \to \mathbf{R}^+$ *upper bounds* the running time of $\mathcal{A}^\Gamma$ with respect to Γ and Λ if the running time $T_{\mathcal{A}^\Gamma}(G, \mathbf{x})$ of $\mathcal{A}^\Gamma$ for $(G, \mathbf{x}) \in \mathcal{F}$ using a collection of good guesses $\tilde{\Gamma} = \{\tilde{\mathbf{p}}_1, \tilde{\mathbf{p}}_2, \cdots, \tilde{\mathbf{p}}_r\}$ is at most $f(\tilde{\mathbf{p}}_1, \tilde{\mathbf{p}}_2, \cdots, \tilde{\mathbf{p}}_{r'}, \mathbf{q}_{r'+1}^*, \cdots, \mathbf{q}_\ell^*)$, where $\mathbf{q}_i^* = \mathbf{q}_i(G, \mathbf{x})$ for $i \in [r', \ell]$. Note that we do not put any restriction on the running time of $\mathcal{A}^\Gamma$ over $(G, \mathbf{x})$ if some of the guesses in $\tilde{\Gamma}$ are not good. In fact, in such a case, the algorithm may not even terminate.

For simplicity of presentation, in this extended abstract, we always assume that the function $f : (\mathbf{R}^+)^\ell \to \mathbf{R}^+$ is additive. In the full paper we show how to obtain similar results for other types of functions; we note that this extension may sometimes require overheads in the running time.

For simplicity of notation, when Γ and Λ are clear from the context, we say that f upper bounds the running time of $\mathcal{A}^\Gamma$, without writing that it is with respect to Γ and Λ.

The set Γ is *weakly-dominated* by Λ if for each $j \in [r'+1, r]$, there exists an index $i_j \in [1, \ell]$ and an ascending function g_j such that $g_j(\mathbf{p}_j(G, \mathbf{x})) \leqslant \mathbf{q}_{i_j}(G, \mathbf{x})$ for every instance $(G, \mathbf{x}) \in \mathcal{F}$. (For example, $\Gamma = \{\Delta\}$ is weakly-dominated by $\{\Lambda\} = n$, since $\Delta(G, \mathbf{x}) \leqslant n(G, \mathbf{x})$ for any $(G, \mathbf{x})$.)

3. PRUNING ALGORITHMS

Consider a problem Π in the centralized setting and an efficient randomized Monte-Carlo algorithm $\mathcal{A}$ for Π. A known method for transforming $\mathcal{A}$ into a Las Vegas algorithm is based on repeatedly doing the following. Execute $\mathcal{A}$ and, subsequently, execute an algorithm that checks the validity of the output. If the checking fails then continue, and otherwise, terminate, i.e., break the loop. This transformation can yield a Las Vegas algorithm whose expected running time is similar to the running time of the Monte-Carlo algorithm provided that the checking mechanism used is efficient.

If we wish to come up with a similar transformation in the context of locality, a first idea would be to consider a local algorithm that checks the validity of a tentative output vector. This concept has been studied in several forms (e.g., [16, 21, 31]). However, such fast local checking procedures can only guarantee that faults are detected by at least one node, whereas to restart the Monte-Carlo algorithm, all nodes should be aware of a fault. This notification can take diameter time and will thus violate the locality constraint.

Instead of using local checking procedures, we introduce the notion of *pruning algorithms*. Informally, this is a mechanism that identifies "valid areas" where the tentative output vector $\hat{\mathbf{y}}$ is valid and *prunes* these areas, i.e., takes them out of further consideration. A pruning algorithm $\mathcal{P}$ must satisfy two properties, specifically, (1) *gluing*: $\mathcal{P}$ must make sure that the current solution on these "pruned areas" can be extended to a valid solution for the remainder of the graph, and (2) *solution detection*: if $\hat{\mathbf{y}}$ was a valid global solution to begin with then $\mathcal{P}$ should prune all nodes.

Now, given a Monte-Carlo algorithm $\mathcal{A}$ and a pruning algorithm $\mathcal{P}$ for the problem, we can transform $\mathcal{A}$ into a Las Vegas algorithm by iteratively executing the pair of algorithms $(\mathcal{A}; \mathcal{P})$ in iterations, where each iteration i is executed on the graph G_i induced by the set of nodes that where not pruned in previous iterations (G_1 is the initial graph G). If, in some iteration i, Algorithm $\mathcal{A}$ solves the problem on the graph G_i, then the solution detection property guarantees that the subsequent pruning algorithm will prune all nodes in G_i and hence at that time all nodes are pruned and the execution terminates. Furthermore, using induction, it can be shown that the gluing property guarantees that the correct solution to G_i combined with the output of previously pruned nodes forms a global solution for G.

We now formally define pruning algorithms. Fix a problem Π and a family of instances $\mathcal{F}$ for Π. A *pruning* algorithm $\mathcal{P}$ for Π and $\mathcal{F}$ takes as input a triplet $(G, \mathbf{x}, \hat{\mathbf{y}})$, where $(G, \mathbf{x}) \in \mathcal{F}$ and $\hat{\mathbf{y}}$ is some tentative output vector, and returns a bit $b(v)$ and an updated input $\mathbf{x}'(v)$ at each node v. The bit $b(v)$ indicates whether v belongs to some selected subset $W \subseteq V(G)$ of nodes to be pruned. (Recall that the idea is to assume that nodes in W have a satisfying tentative output value and that they can be excluded from further computations.) Let G' be the subgraph of G induced by the nodes in $V(G) \setminus W$. The pruning algorithm does not change the input of the nodes in W, i.e., $\mathbf{x}'(v) = \mathbf{x}(v)$ whenever $b(v) = 1$ (that is, $v \in W$). On the other hand, the pruning algorithm may change the input for the rest of the nodes, i.e., those in G'. (Informally, this is because after $\mathcal{P}$ pruned the set W, it may need to adjust the remaining nodes for further use.) Thus, Algorithm $\mathcal{P}$ takes a triplet $(G, \mathbf{x}, \hat{\mathbf{y}})$ as input, where $(G, \mathbf{x}) \in \mathcal{F}$, and returns a pair $(G', \mathbf{x}')$. The pruning algorithm must guarantee that $(G', \mathbf{x}') \in \mathcal{F}$.

Consider now an output vector $\mathbf{y}'$ for the nodes in $V(G')$. The *combined* output vector $\mathbf{y}$ of the vectors $\hat{\mathbf{y}}$ and $\mathbf{y}'$ is the output vector that is a combination of $\hat{\mathbf{y}}$ restricted to the nodes in W and $\mathbf{y}'$ restricted to the nodes in G', i.e., $\mathbf{y}(v) \coloneqq \hat{\mathbf{y}}(v)$ if $v \in W$ and $\mathbf{y}(v) \coloneqq \mathbf{y}'(v)$ otherwise. A pruning algorithm $\mathcal{P}$ for a problem Π must satisfy the following properties.

- **Solution detection:** $(G, \mathbf{x}, \hat{\mathbf{y}}) \in \Pi \iff \mathcal{P}$ outputs $W = V(G)$.
- **Gluing:** if $\mathcal{P}(G, \mathbf{x}, \hat{\mathbf{y}}) = (G', \mathbf{x}')$ and $\mathbf{y}'$ is a solution for $(G', \mathbf{x}')$, i.e., $(G', \mathbf{x}', \mathbf{y}') \in \Pi$, then the combined output vector $\mathbf{y}$ is a solution for $(G, \mathbf{x})$, i.e, $(G, \mathbf{x}, \mathbf{y}) \in \Pi$.

The pruning algorithm $\mathcal{P}$ is *monotone with respect to a parameter* p if $\mathsf{p}(G, \mathbf{x}) \geqslant \mathsf{p}(G', \mathbf{x}')$, for every $(G, \mathbf{x}) \in \mathcal{F}$, where $\mathcal{P}(G, \mathbf{x}, \hat{\mathbf{y}}) = (G', \mathbf{x}')$, for some $\hat{\mathbf{y}}$. The pruning algorithm $\mathcal{P}$ is *monotone with respect to a collection of parameters* Γ if $\mathcal{P}$ is monotone with respect to every parameter $\mathsf{p} \in \Gamma$. In such a case, we may also say that $\mathcal{P}$ is Γ-*monotone*. The following assertion follows from the definition of a parameter.

Observation 3.1 *Let $\mathcal{P}$ be a pruning algorithm. Then (1) Algorithm $\mathcal{P}$ is monotone with respect to any graph-parameter, and (2) If $\mathcal{P}$ does not update the inputs of the unpruned nodes,*

i.e., $\mathbf{x}'(v) = \mathbf{x}(v)$ for every $v \in V \setminus W$, then $\mathcal{P}$ is monotone with respect to any parameter.

For simplicity, in this extended abstract, we restrict the running time of a pruning algorithm $\mathcal{P}$ to be constant. In the full paper, we consider the more general case where $\mathcal{P}$ is a uniform algorithm whose running time may depend on some parameters. We note that this generalization may incur an overhead in the running time of our transformations, as these repeatedly use $\mathcal{P}$.

We now give examples of (constant time) pruning algorithms for several problems, namely, $(2, \beta)$-Ruling set for a constant integer β (recall that MIS is precisely $(2, 1)$-Ruling set), and maximal matching. These pruning algorithms do not change the input at nodes outside W (in fact, the input is ignored in these problems, and can be assumed to be empty). Thus, by Observation 3.1, they are monotone with respect to any parameter.

The $(2, \beta)$-ruling set pruning algorithm: Let β be a (constant) integer. We define a pruning algorithm $\mathcal{P}_{(2,\beta)}$ for the $(2, \beta)$-ruling set problem as follows. Given a triplet $(G, \mathbf{x}, \hat{\mathbf{y}})$, let W be the set of nodes u satisfying one of the following two conditions.

- $\hat{\mathbf{y}}(u) = 1$ and $\hat{\mathbf{y}}(v) = 0$ for all $v \in N(u)$, or
- $\hat{\mathbf{y}}(u) = 0$ and $\exists v \in B_G(u, \beta)$ such that $\hat{\mathbf{y}}(v) = 1$ and $\hat{\mathbf{y}}(w) = 0$ for all $w \in N(v)$.

Observation 3.2 *Algorithm $\mathcal{P}_{(2,\beta)}$ is a pruning algorithm for the $(2, \beta)$-ruling set problem, running in time $1 + \beta$. Furthermore, $\mathcal{P}_{(2,\beta)}$ is monotone with respect to any parameter.*

The interested reader can check that this pruning algorithm is not implementable through simple combinations of the classical local check procedure for $(2, \beta)$-ruling set even though it has a similar flavor.

The maximal matching problem: We define a pruning algorithm $\mathcal{P}_{\text{MM}}$ as follows. Given a tentative output vector $\hat{\mathbf{y}}$, recall that u and v are matched when u and v are neighbors, $\hat{\mathbf{y}}(u) = \hat{\mathbf{y}}(v)$ and $\hat{\mathbf{y}}(w) \neq \hat{\mathbf{y}}(u)$ for every $w \in (N_G(u) \cup N_G(v)) \setminus \{u, v\}$. Set W to be the set of nodes u satisfying one of the following conditions.

- $\exists v \in N(u)$ such that u and v are matched, or
- $\forall v \in N(u)$, $\exists w \neq u$ such that v and w are matched.

Observation 3.3 *Algorithm $\mathcal{P}_{\text{MM}}$ is a pruning algorithm for MM whose running time is 3. Furthermore, $\mathcal{P}_{\text{MM}}$ is monotone with respect to any parameter.*

4. A GENERAL METHOD

We now turn to the main application of pruning algorithms discussed in this paper, that is, the construction of a transformer taking a non-uniform algorithm A^Γ as a black box and producing a uniform one that enjoys the same (asymptotic) time complexity as the original non-uniform algorithm.

The basic idea is very simple. Consider a problem for which we have a pruning algorithm $\mathcal{P}$, and a non uniform algorithm $\mathcal{A}$ that requires the knowledge of upper bounds on some parameters. To obtain a uniform algorithm, we execute the pair of algorithms $(\mathcal{A}; \mathcal{P})$ in iterations, where each iteration executes $\mathcal{A}$ using a specific set of guesses for the parameters. Typically, as iterations proceed, the guesses for the parameters grow larger and larger until we reach an iteration i where all guesses are larger than the actual value of the parameters. In this iteration, the operation of $\mathcal{A}$ on G_i using such guesses guarantees a correct solution on G_i. As mentioned before, the properties of the pruning algorithm guarantee that the execution terminates in this iteration and that at that time, the output of all nodes combines to a global solution on G. To bound the running time, we will make sure that the total running time is dominated by the running time of the last iteration, and that this last iteration is relatively fast.

There are various delicate points when using this general method. For example, in iterations where incorrect guesses are used, we have no control over the behavior of the non-uniform algorithm $\mathcal{A}$ and, in particular, it may run for too many rounds, perhaps even indefinitely. To overcome this obstacle, we allocate a prescribed number of rounds for each iteration; if Algorithm $\mathcal{A}$ reaches this time bound without outputting at some node u, then we force it to terminate with an arbitrary output. Subsequently, we run the pruning algorithm and proceed to the next iteration.

Obviously, this simple approach of running in iterations and increasing the guesses from iteration to iteration is hardly new. It was used, for example, in the context of wireless networks to compute estimates of parameters (cf., e.g., [8, 30]). One of the main contributions of this current paper is the formalization and generalization of this technique, allowing it to be used for a wide varieties of problems and applications. Interestingly, note that we are only concerned with getting rid of the knowledge of some parameters, and not with obtaining estimates for them (in particular, when our algorithms terminate, the vertices have no way of knowing whether they have upper bounds on these parameters).

To illustrate the method, let us consider the non-uniform MIS algorithm of Panconesi and Srinivasan [33]. This algorithm $\mathcal{A}$ assumes the knowledge of an upper bound $\tilde{n}$ on the number of nodes n, and runs in time at most $f(\tilde{n}) = 2^{O(\sqrt{\log \tilde{n}})}$. Consider a pruning algorithm $\mathcal{P}_{\texttt{MIS}}$ for MIS (such an algorithm is given by Observation 3.2). The following sketches our method for obtaining a uniform MIS algorithm. For each integer i, let n_i be the largest integer a such that $f(a) \leqslant 2^i$. In Iteration i, for $i = 1, 2, \cdots$, we first execute Algorithm $\mathcal{A}$ using the guess n_i (as an input serving as an upper bound for the number of nodes) for precisely 2^i rounds. Subsequently, we run the pruning algorithm $\mathcal{P}_{\texttt{MIS}}$. When the pruning algorithm terminates, we execute the next iteration $i + 1$ on the non-pruned nodes. Let s be the integer such that $2^{s-1} < f(n) \leqslant 2^s$, where n is the number of nodes of the input graph. By the definition, $n \leqslant n_s$. Therefore, the application of $\mathcal{A}$ in Iteration s uses a guess n_s that is indeed larger than the number of nodes. Moreover, this execution of $\mathcal{A}$ is completed before the prescribed deadline of 2^s expires because its running time is at most $f(n_s) \leqslant 2^s$. Hence, we are guaranteed to have a correct solution by the end of Iteration s. The running time is thus at most $\sum_{i=1}^s 2^i = O(f(n))$.

This method can sometimes be extended to simultaneously remove prior knowledge concerning several parameters. For example, consider the MIS algorithm of Barenboim and Elkin [4] (or that of Kuhn [22]), which requires the knowledge of upper bounds $\tilde{n}$ and $\tilde{\Delta}$ on n and Δ, respectively, and runs

in time $f(\tilde{n}, \tilde{\Delta}) = f_1(\tilde{n}) + f_2(\tilde{\Delta})$, where $f_1(\tilde{\Delta}) = O(\tilde{\Delta})$ and $f_2(\tilde{n}) = O(\log^* \tilde{n})$. The following sketches our method for obtaining a corresponding uniform MIS algorithm that runs in time $O(f(n, \Delta))$. For each integer i, let n_i (respectively Δ_i) be the largest integer a (respectively, b) such that $f_1(a) \leqslant 2^i$ (respectively, $f_2(b) \leqslant 2^i$). In Iteration i, for $i = 1, 2, \cdots$, we first execute Algorithm $\mathcal{A}$ using the guesses n_i and Δ_i, but this time the execution lasts for precisely $2 \cdot 2^i$ rounds. (The factor 2 in the running time of an iteration follows from the fact that we consider two parameters here, namely n and Δ. In general, if we consider r parameters, Iteration i will run for $r \cdot 2^i$ rounds.) Subsequently, we run the pruning algorithm $\mathcal{P}_{\texttt{MIS}}$, and as before, when the pruning algorithm terminates, we execute the next iteration $i + 1$ on the non-pruned nodes. Now, let s be the integer such that $2^{s-1} < f(n, \Delta) \leqslant 2^s$. By the definition, $n \leqslant n_s$ and $\Delta \leqslant \Delta_s$. Hence, the application of $\mathcal{A}$ in Iteration s uses guesses that are indeed upper bounds on the real values. This execution of $\mathcal{A}$ is completed before the prescribed deadline of 2^{s+1} expires because its running time is at most $f_1(n_s) + f_2(\Delta_s) \leqslant 2^{s+1}$. Thus, the algorithm consists of at most s iterations. Since the running time of the whole execution is dominated by the running time of the last iteration, the total running time is $O(2^{s+1}) = O(f(n, \Delta))$.

The following theorem formalizes the above discussion. It considers a single set of parameters $\Gamma = \{\mathtt{p}_1, \mathtt{p}_2, \cdots, \mathtt{p}_r\}$, and assumes that the given non-uniform algorithm $\mathcal{A}^\Gamma$ both depends on Γ as well as that its running time is evaluated according to the parameters in Γ. Recall that in such a case, we say that a function $f : \mathbf{N}^r \to \mathbf{R}^+$ upper bounds the running time of $\mathcal{A}^\Gamma$ with respect to Γ if the running time $T_{\mathcal{A}^\Gamma}(G, \mathbf{x})$ of $\mathcal{A}^\Gamma$ for every $(G, \mathbf{x}) \in \mathcal{F}$ using a collection of good guesses $\tilde{\Gamma} = \{\tilde{\mathtt{p}}_1, \tilde{\mathtt{p}}_2, \cdots, \tilde{\mathtt{p}}_r\}$ for $(G, \mathbf{x})$ is at most $f(\tilde{\mathtt{p}}_1, \tilde{\mathtt{p}}_2, \cdots, \tilde{\mathtt{q}}_r)$. Recall also that this extended abstract focuses on the case that the function f is additive. The proof of the theorem below follows using similar arguments to the ones discussed in the aforementioned examples and is therefore omitted.

THEOREM 7. *Consider a problem Π and a family of instances $\mathcal{F}$. Let $\mathcal{A}^\Gamma$ be a deterministic algorithm for Π and $\mathcal{F}$ depending on $\Gamma := \{\mathtt{p}_1, \mathtt{p}_2, \cdots, \mathtt{p}_r\}$. Suppose that the running time of $\mathcal{A}^\Gamma$ is upper bounded by an additive function $f := \sum_{i=1}^r f_i(\mathtt{p}_i)$. Assume there exists a Γ-monotone pruning algorithm $\mathcal{P}$ for Π and $\mathcal{F}$. Then there exists a uniform deterministic algorithm for Π and $\mathcal{F}$ whose running time is $O(f(\Gamma^*)) = O(\sum_{i=1}^r f_i(\mathtt{p}_i^*))$.*

Theorem 5 follows directly by applying Theorem 7 to the maximal matching algorithm of Hanckowiak *et al.* [19], and using Observation 3.3. In addition, using Observation 3.2, Theorem 7 allows us to transform each of the MIS algorithms in [4, 22, 33] into a uniform one with asymptotically the same time complexity. That is, we obtain the following.

COROLLARY 1. *(1) There exists a uniform deterministic algorithm solving MIS on general graphs in time $O(\Delta + \log^* n)$, and (2) there exists a uniform deterministic algorithm solving MIS on general graphs in time $2^{O(\sqrt{\log n})}$.*

Some complications arise when the correctness of the given non-uniform problem depends on the knowledge of one set of parameters Γ, while its running time is evaluated by another set of parameters Λ. For example, it may be the case that an upper bound on a parameter $\mathbf{p}$ is required for the correct operation of an algorithm, yet the running time of the algorithm does not depend on $\mathbf{p}$. In this case, it is not clear how to choose the guesses for $\mathbf{p}$. (This occurs, for example, in the MIS algorithms of Barenboim and Elkin [6], where the knowledge of n and the arboricity a are required, yet the running time f is a function of n only.) Such complications can be solved when there is some relation between the parameters in Γ and those in Λ; specifically, when Γ is weakly-dominated by Λ. (See the definition of weakly-dominated in Section 2.) This issue is handled in the following theorem. Due to the lack of space, the proof is deferred to the full paper.

THEOREM 8. *Consider a problem* Π, *a family of instances* $\mathcal{F}$ *and two sets of parameters* Γ *and* $\Lambda = \{q_1, q_2, \cdots, q_\ell\}$, *where* Γ *is weakly-dominated by* Λ. *Let* $\mathcal{A}^\Gamma$ *be a deterministic algorithm depending on* Γ *whose running time is upper bounded by some additive function* $f := \sum_{i=1}^\ell f_i(q_i)$. *Let* $\mathcal{P}$ *be a* $\Lambda \cup \Gamma$*-monotone pruning algorithm for* Π *and* $\mathcal{F}$. *Then there exists a* uniform *deterministic algorithm for* Π *and* $\mathcal{F}$ *whose running time is* $O(f(\Lambda^*)) = O(\sum_{i=1}^\ell f_i(q_i^*))$.

The following corollary follows by applying the theorem above to the work of [6], by setting $\Gamma = \{a, n\}$ and $\Lambda = \{n\}$.

COROLLARY 2. *There exists a uniform deterministic algorithm solving* MIS *on general graphs in time* $O(f(a))$, *where* $f(a) = o(\log n)$ *for graphs with arboricity* $a = o(\sqrt{\log n})$, *and* $f(a) = O(\log n / \log \log n)$ *for graphs with arboricity* $a = O(\log^{1/2-\delta} n)$, *for some constant* $\delta \in (0, 1/2)$ *(otherwise,* $f(a) = n$).

To illustrate the topic of the next theorem, consider the best known non-uniform algorithms for MIS, namely the algorithms of Barenboim and Elkin [4] and that of Kuhn [22], which run in time $O(\Delta + \log^* n)$ and require the knowledge of n and Δ, and the algorithm of Panconesi and Srinivasan [33], which runs in time $2^{O(\sqrt{\log n})}$ and requires the knowledge of n. Furthermore, consider the MIS algorithm of Barenboim and Elkin [6], which is very efficient for graphs with bounded arboricity a (let $f'(a)$ be the running time of their algorithm). If n, Δ and a are known to all nodes, then one can compare the running times of these algorithms and use the fastest one. That is, there exists a non-uniform algorithm $\mathcal{A}^{\{n,\Delta,a\}}$ that runs in time $T'(n, \Delta, a) := \min\{2^{O(\sqrt{\log n})}, O(\Delta + \log^* n), f'(a)\}$.

Unfortunately, Theorem 8 does not allow us to transform $\mathcal{A}^{\{n,\Delta,a\}}$ into a uniform one—the reason being that the running time $T(n, \Delta, a)$ does not satisfy the running time requirements as specified in Theorem 8. On the other hand, as mentioned in Corollary 1, Theorem 7 does allow us to transform each of the algorithms in [4, 22, 33] into a uniform one—with asymptotically the same time complexity. Moreover, as mentioned in Corollary 2, we can also transform the algorithm in [6] into a uniform one running in time $f(a)$. Nevertheless, since n, Δ and a are unknown to the nodes, it is not clear how to obtain from these transformed algorithms a uniform algorithm running in time $T(n, \Delta, a) := \min\{2^{O(\sqrt{\log n})}, O(\Delta + \log^* n), f(a)\}$. The following theorem solves this problem.

THEOREM 9. *Consider a problem* Π, *a family of instances* $\mathcal{F}$. *Let* Λ_1 *and* Λ_2 *be two sets of parameters. Suppose that there exists a* $\Lambda_1 \cup \Lambda_2$*-monotone pruning algorithm* $\mathcal{P}$ *for* Π *and* $\mathcal{F}$. *Consider two uniform algorithms* $\mathcal{U}_1$ *and* $\mathcal{U}_2$

whose running times are bounded by non-decreasing functions $f_1(\Lambda_1^*)$ *and* $f_2(\Lambda_2^*)$, *respectively. Then there is a uniform algorithm with running time* $O(f_{\min})$, *where* $f_{\min} := \min\{f_1(\Lambda_1^*), f_2(\Lambda_2^*)\}$.

The basic idea behind the proof of theorem above is to run in iterations, such that each iteration i consists of running the quadruple $(\mathcal{U}_1; \mathcal{P}; \mathcal{U}_2; \mathcal{P})$, where $\mathcal{U}_1$ and $\mathcal{U}_2$ are executed for precisely 2^i rounds each. Hence, a correct solution will be produced in Iteration $s := \lceil \log f_{\min} \rceil$ or before. Since each iteration i lasts for roughly 2^{i+1} rounds (recall that the running time of $\mathcal{P}$ is constant), the running time is $O(f_{\min})$. Due to the lack of space we defer the detailed proof to the full paper.

Theorem 1 follows as a direct corollary of Theorem 9, using Corollaries 1 and 2. A standard trick (cf., [27, 29]) allows us to transform an efficient MIS algorithm for general graphs into one for $(\Delta + 1)$-coloring. This is based on the observation that $(\Delta + 1)$-colorings of G and MISs of $G' = G \times K_{\Delta+1}$ are in one-to-one correspondence. This known transformation, however, uses the knowledge of Δ. Nevertheless, it is straightforward to check that a similar correspondence holds when G' is defined as follows. For each node $u \in V(G)$, take a clique of size $\deg_G(u) + 1$ with vertices $u_1, u_2, \cdots, u_{\deg_G(u)+1}$. Now, for each $(u, v) \in E(G)$ and each $i \in [1, 1 + \min\{\deg_G(u), \deg_G(v)\}]$, let $(u_i, v_i) \in E(G')$. The graph G' can be constructed locally without any global knowledge, hence we obtain Theorem 2 as a corollary of Theorem 1.

In the full paper we show how to extend Theorem 8 to the randomized setting. More specifically, we replace the given deterministic Algorithm $\mathcal{A}^\Gamma$ in Theorem 8 by a non-uniform Monte-Carlo algorithm A^Γ and produce a uniform Las Vegas one running in the same asymptotic running time as A^Γ. This transformer is more sophisticated than the one given in Theorem 8, and requires the use of sub-iterations for bounding the expected running time and probability of success of the resulting Las-Vegas algorithm. Theorem 6 follows by applying this extended theorem to the ruling-set algorithm of Schneider and Wattenhofer [35], and using the pruning algorithm given by Observation 3.2.

5. MORE COLORING ALGORITHMS

As mentioned, some uniform $(\Delta + 1)$-coloring algorithms can be obtained from our uniform MIS algorithms using a known technique. In general, however, we could not apply directly the aforementioned transformers to obtain other uniform coloring algorithms. The main reason is that we could not find an efficient pruning algorithm for the coloring problem. Another difficulty in coloring is that, often, the number of colors to be used depends on unknown parameters.

In this section, we present a method for transforming non-uniform algorithms into uniform ones, tailored particularly to the coloring problem. We begin with the following definitions. An *instance for the coloring problem* is a pair $(G, \mathbf{x})$ where G is a graph and $\mathbf{x}(v)$ contains a color $c(v)$ such that the collection $\{c(v) \mid v \in V(G)\}$ forms a coloring of G. (The color $c(v)$ can be the identity $\text{Id}(v)$.) For a given family of graphs $\mathcal{G}$, we define $\mathcal{F}(\mathcal{G})$ to be the collection of instances $(G, \mathbf{x})$ for the coloring problem, where $G \in \mathcal{G}$.

Recall that many coloring algorithms consider the identities as colors, and relax the assumption that the identities are unique by replacing it with the weaker requirement that the set of initial colors forms a coloring. Given an instance $(G, \mathbf{x})$, let $m = m(G, \mathbf{x})$ be the maximum integer i such that all identities (initial colors) are taken from $[1, i]$. Without loss of generality, we may assume that $m > \Delta$. Note that m is a graph-parameter.

Recall the $\lambda(\tilde{\Delta} + 1)$-coloring algorithm of [4, 22] (which generalizes the $O(\tilde{\Delta}^2)$-coloring algorithm in [27]). We would like to point out that, in fact, everything works similarly in these algorithms if one replaces n with m. That is, the $\lambda(\tilde{\Delta} + 1)$-coloring algorithms in [4, 22] can be viewed as requiring m and Δ and running in time $O(\tilde{\Delta}/\lambda + \log^* \tilde{m})$. The same is true for the edge-coloring algorithms of Barenboim and Elkin [7].

The following theorem implies that these algorithms can be transformed into uniform ones. In the theorem, we consider two sets of graph-parameters Γ and Λ such that (1) Γ is weakly-dominated by Λ, and (2) $\Gamma \subseteq \{\Delta, m\}$. Such a pair of sets of parameters is said to be *related*. Also, the function $g(x)$ governing the number of colors is assumed to satisfy (1) $g(x) > x$, (2) $g(x)$ is moderately-increasing, and (3) $g(x)$ is upper bounded by a polynomial in x. Such a function is called *moderately-fast*.

THEOREM 10. *Let $\mathcal{A}^{\Gamma}$ be a $g(\tilde{\Delta})$-coloring algorithm with running time bounded by $f := \sum_{i=1}^{|\Lambda|} f_i$, where Γ and Λ are related collections of graph parameters. If*

1. *$g(x)$ is a moderately-fast function,*
2. *the dependence of f on m is bounded by a polylog, and*
3. *the dependence of f on Δ is moderately-increasing,*

then there exists a uniform $O(g(\Delta))$-coloring algorithm whose running time is $O(\sum_{i=1}^{|\Lambda|} f_i(\mathsf{q}_i^*))$.

Proof sketch: Our first goal is to transform $\mathcal{A}^{\Gamma}$ into a uniform algorithm that solves the following problem.

The *strong list-coloring* (SLC) problem: A pair $(G, \mathbf{x}) \in \mathcal{F}(\mathcal{G})$ is a configuration for the SLC problem if the following holds. For every $v \in V(G)$, the input $\mathbf{x}(v)$ contains (in addition to $\mathrm{Id}(v)$) a *degree-estimation* $\hat{\Delta}$, such that $\hat{\Delta} \geqslant \Delta$ (the estimate $\hat{\Delta}$ being the same for all nodes) and a list $L(v) \subseteq [1, g(\hat{\Delta})] \times [1, \hat{\Delta} + 1]$ of colors, such that

$$\forall k \in [1, g(\hat{\Delta})], \quad |\{j \mid (k, j) \in L(v)\}| \geqslant \deg_G(v) + 1.$$

Given a configuration $(G, \mathbf{x}) \in \mathcal{F}(\mathcal{G})$, an output vector $\mathbf{y}$ is a *solution* for SLC if it forms a coloring and if $\mathbf{y}(v) \in L(v)$ for every node $v \in V(G)$.

We first transform $\mathcal{A}^{\Gamma}$ into an algorithm $\mathcal{B}^{\Gamma'}$ that depends on $\Gamma' = \Gamma \setminus \{\Delta\}$ and solves SLC. Specifically, Algorithm $\mathcal{B}^{\Gamma'}$ consists of executing $\mathcal{A}^{\Gamma}$ using a good guess $\tilde{\Delta} = \hat{\Delta}$ for the parameter Δ. Furthermore, if $\mathcal{A}^{\Gamma}$ outputs at v a color c, then $\mathcal{B}^{\Gamma'}$ outputs the color (c, j) where $j := \min\{s \mid (c, s) \in L(v)\}$. Observe that Algorithm $\mathcal{B}^{\Gamma'}$ depends on Γ' and solves SLC.

If $\Delta \in \Lambda$ then set $\Lambda' := \Lambda \setminus \Delta \cup \hat{\Delta}$, and otherwise, $\Lambda' := \Lambda$. ($\hat{\Delta}$ is viewed here as a parameter). It can be shown that the running time of $\mathcal{B}^{\Gamma'}$ is bounded by $f(\Lambda')$ (the dependency of f on Δ is replaced by the dependency on $\hat{\Delta}$).

For SLC we can design the following pruning algorithm $\mathcal{P}$. Consider a triplet $(G, \mathbf{x}, \hat{\mathbf{y}})$, where $(G, \mathbf{x})$ is a configuration for SLC and $\hat{\mathbf{y}}$ is some tentative assignment of colors. The set W to be pruned is the set of nodes u satisfying $\hat{\mathbf{y}}(u) \in L(u)$ and $\hat{\mathbf{y}}(u) \neq \hat{\mathbf{y}}(v)$ for all $v \in N_G(u)$. Algorithm $\mathcal{P}$ modifies the input for the nodes outside W as follows: the input at a node $u \in V \setminus W$ is changed so that the new list of available colors $L'(u)$ contains precisely $L(u)$ minus the colors assigned to those neighbors of u in G that belong to W. Let $(G', \mathbf{x}')$ be the output of $\mathcal{P}$. Note that if we start with a configuration $(G, \mathbf{x})$ for SLC then the output $(G', \mathbf{x}')$ of the pruning algorithm $\mathcal{P}$ is also a configuration for SLC. This is because, for every node v and every k, at most $\deg_W(v)$ pairs (k, j) were removed from the list $L(v)$ of v, where $\deg_W(v)$ is the number of neighbors of v that belong to W. On the other hand, the degree of v in G' is reduced by $\deg_W(v)$.

Assume without loss of generality that f_1 is the function corresponding to Δ in f (i.e., that $\mathsf{q}_1 = \Delta$). Having the sets of parameters Γ' and Λ' in mind, Algorithm $\mathcal{B}^{\Gamma'}$, and the aforementioned pruning algorithm $\mathcal{P}$ for SLC, we apply Theorem 8 and obtain a uniform algorithm $\mathcal{B}$ for SLC and $\mathcal{F}(\mathcal{G})$ whose running time is $O(f_1(\hat{\Delta}) + \sum_{i=2}^{\ell} f_i(\mathsf{q}_i^*))$ if $\Delta \in \Lambda$, and $O(\sum_{i=1}^{\ell} f_i(\mathsf{q}_i^*))$ otherwise.

We are now ready to specify a uniform $O(g(\Delta))$-coloring algorithm. We inductively define integers D_i for $i \in \mathbf{N}$ as follows. $D_1 := 1$, and $D_{i+1} := \min\{\ell \mid g(\ell) \geqslant 2g(D_i)\}$ for $i \geqslant 1$. Given an initial configuration $(G, \mathbf{x})$, we partition it by node degrees as follows. For $i \in \mathbf{N}$, let G_i be the subgraph of G induced by the set of nodes $v \in G$ with $\deg_G(v) \in [D_i, D_{i+1} - 1]$. Let $\mathbf{x}_i$ be the input $\mathbf{x}$ restricted to the nodes in G_i. The configuration $(G_i, \mathbf{x}_i) \in \mathcal{F}(\mathcal{G})$ is referred to as *layer i*. Note that nodes can figure out locally which layer they belong to. Observe also, that $D_{i+1} - 1$ is an upper bound on node degrees in layer i.

The algorithm proceeds in two phases. In the first phase, each node in layer i is assigned the list of colors $C_i'' := [1, g(D_{i+1})] \times [1, D_{i+1} + 1]$, and the degree estimation $\hat{\Delta}_i := D_{i+1}$. Each layer is now an instance of SLC and we execute Algorithm $\mathcal{B}$ in parallel on all layers. If Algorithm $\mathcal{B}$ assigns a color (c, j) to a node v in layer i then we change this color to $(g(D_{i+1}) + c, j)$. Hence, each layer i is colored with colors taken from $C_i' := [g(D_{i+1}) + 1, 2g(D_{i+1})] \times [1, D_{i+1} + 1]$.

Note that the number of colors in C_i' is $O(D_{i+1}g(D_{i+1}))$. Note also that nodes in different layers have disjoint colors. Hence, we obtain a global coloring. Since g and f_1 are moderately increasing it can be shown that this first phase of the algorithm terminates by time $O(\sum_{j=1}^{|\Lambda|} f_i(\mathsf{q}_i^*))$, and that the total number of colors used in this phase is $O(\Delta g(\Delta))$.

The second phase consists of running a second algorithm to change the set of possible colors of nodes in layer i from C_i' to $C_i := [g(D_{i+1}) + 1, 2g(D_{i+1})]$. Specifically, on layer i, we execute $\mathcal{A}^{\Gamma}$ using the guess $\tilde{\Delta} = D_{i+1}$ for the parameter Δ and the guess $\tilde{m} = O(D_{i+1}g(D_{i+1}))$ for the parameter m (recall that $\Gamma \subseteq \{\Delta, m\}$). This colors each layer with colors taken from the range $[1, g(D_{i+1})]$. Let v be in layer i and let $c(v)$ be the color assigned to v by $\mathcal{A}^{\Gamma}$. The final color of v given by our desired algorithm $\mathcal{A}$ is $g(D_{i+1}) + c(v)$. Thus, the colors assigned to the nodes in layer i belong to $[g(D_{i+1}) + 1, 2g(D_{i+1})]$, and are therefore disjoint on different layers. The algorithm is executed on each layer independently, all in parallel, and hence, we obtain a coloring. Moreover, since g is moderately-increasing, the total number of colors used is $O(g(\Delta))$. Finally, using the assumptions on g, and on the dependencies of f on Δ and m, it can be shown that the running time of the second phase is $O(\sum_{i=1}^{\ell} f_i(\mathsf{q}_i^*))$.

Combining this with the running time of the first phase, we obtain the theorem. □

Theorem 3 now follows as a direct corollary of the Theorem 10. Regarding edge-coloring, observe that Barenboim and Elkin [7] obtain their edge-coloring algorithm on general graphs by running a vertex-coloring algorithm on the line-graph of the given graph. This vertex-coloring algorithm assumes the knowledge of m and Δ and uses the same number of color and time complexity as the resulted edge-coloring algorithm. Using Theorem 10, we can transform that vertex-coloring algorithm [7] designed for the family of line graphs into a uniform one, having the same asymptotic number of colors and running time. Hence, Theorem 4 follows.

6. REFERENCES

[1] N. ALON, L. BABAI, AND A. ITAI, *A fast and simple randomized parallel algorithm for the maximal independent set problem.*, J. Algorithms, 7 (1986), pp. 567–583.

[2] B. AWERBUCH, *Complexity of network synchronization*, J. ACM, 32 (1985), pp. 804–823.

[3] B. AWERBUCH, M. LUBY, A. V. GOLDBERG, AND S. A. PLOTKIN, *Network decomposition and locality in distributed computation*, in FOCS, 1989, pp. 364–369.

[4] L. BARENBOIM AND M. ELKIN, *Distributed $(\Delta + 1)$-coloring in linear (in Δ) time*, in STOC, 2009, pp. 111–120.

[5] ——, *Deterministic distributed vertex coloring in polylogarithmic time*, in PODC, 2010, pp. 410–419.

[6] ——, *Sublogarithmic distributed mis algorithm for sparse graphs using nash-williams decomposition*, Distrib. Comput., 22 (2010), pp. 363–379.

[7] ——, *Distributed deterministic edge coloring using bounded neighborhood independence*, in PODC, 2011. Available at http://arxiv.org/abs/1010.2454.

[8] J. L. BENTLEY AND A. C.-C. YAO, *An almost optimal algorithm for unbounded searching*, Inf. Process. Lett., 5 (1976), pp. 82–87.

[9] R. COHEN, P. FRAIGNIAUD, D. ILCINKAS, A. KORMAN, AND D. PELEG, *Label-guided graph exploration by a finite automaton*, ACM Trans. Algorithms, 4 (2008), pp. 42:1–42:18.

[10] R. COLE AND U. VISHKIN, *Deterministic coin tossing and accelerating cascades: micro and macro techniques for designing parallel algorithms*, in STOC, 1986, pp. 206–219.

[11] B. DERBEL, C. GAVOILLE, D. PELEG, AND L. VIENNOT, *On the locality of distributed sparse spanner construction*, in PODC, 2008, pp. 273–282.

[12] D. DERENIOWSKI AND A. PELC, *Drawing maps with advice*, in DISC, Springer-Verlag, 2010, pp. 328–342.

[13] P. FRAIGNIAUD, C. GAVOILLE, D. ILCINKAS, AND A. PELC, *Distributed computing with advice: information sensitivity of graph coloring*, Distrib. Comput., 21 (2009), pp. 395–403.

[14] P. FRAIGNIAUD, D. ILCINKAS, AND A. PELC, *Communication algorithms with advice*, J. Comput. Syst. Sci., 76 (2010), pp. 222–232.

[15] P. FRAIGNIAUD, A. KORMAN, AND E. LEBHAR, *Local mst computation with short advice*, in SPAA, 2007, pp. 154–160.

[16] P. FRAIGNIAUD, A. KORMAN, AND D. PELEG, *Local distributed decision*. Submitted for Publication.

[17] A. V. GOLDBERG AND S. A. PLOTKIN, *Efficient parallel algorithms for $(\Delta + 1)$-coloring and maximal independent set problem*, in STOC, 1987, pp. 315–324.

[18] A. V. GOLDBERG, S. A. PLOTKIN, AND G. E. SHANNON, *Parallel symmetry-breaking in sparse graphs*, SIAM J. Discrete Math., 1 (1988), pp. 434–446.

[19] M. HAŃĆKOWIAK, M. KAROŃSKI, AND A. PANCONESI, *On the distributed complexity of computing maximal matchings*, SIAM J. Discrete Math., 15 (2001/02), pp. 41–57.

[20] A. KORMAN AND S. KUTTEN, *Distributed verification of minimum spanning trees*, Distrib. Comput., 20 (2007), pp. 253–266.

[21] A. KORMAN, S. KUTTEN, AND D. PELEG, *Proof labeling schemes*, Distrib. Comput., 22 (2010), pp. 215–233.

[22] F. KUHN, *Weak graph colorings: distributed algorithms and applications*, in SPAA, 2009, pp. 138–144.

[23] F. KUHN, T. MOSCIBRODA, AND R. WATTENHOFER, *What cannot be computed locally!*, in PODC, 2004, pp. 300–309.

[24] F. KUHN AND R. WATTENHOFER, *On the complexity of distributed graph coloring*, in PODC, 2006, pp. 7–15.

[25] C. LENZEN, Y. OSWALD, AND R. WATTENHOFER, *What can be approximated locally?: case study: dominating sets in planar graphs*, in SPAA, 2008, pp. 46–54.

[26] N. LINIAL, *Distributive graph algorithms global solutions from local data*, in FOCS, 1987, pp. 331–335.

[27] ——, *Locality in distributed graph algorithms*, SIAM J. Comput., 21 (1992), p. 193.

[28] Z. LOTKER, B. PATT-SHAMIR, AND A. ROSÉN, *Distributed approximate matching*, SIAM J. Comput., 39 (2009), pp. 445–460.

[29] M. LUBY, *A simple parallel algorithm for the maximal independent set problem*, SIAM J. Comput., 15 (1986), pp. 1036–1053.

[30] K. NAKANO AND S. OLARIU, *Uniform leader election protocols for radio networks*, IEEE Trans. Parallel Distrib. Syst., 13 (2002), pp. 516–526.

[31] M. NAOR AND L. STOCKMEYER, *What can be computed locally?*, SIAM J. Comput., 24 (1995), pp. 1259–1277.

[32] A. PANCONESI AND R. RIZZI, *Some simple distributed algorithms for sparse networks*, Distrib. Comput., 14 (2001), pp. 97–100.

[33] A. PANCONESI AND A. SRINIVASAN, *On the complexity of distributed network decomposition*, J. Algorithms, 20 (1996), pp. 356–374.

[34] D. PELEG, *Distributed computing. A locality-sensitive approach.*, SIAM Monographs on Discrete Mathematics and Applications, SIAM, 343 p. , 2000.

[35] J. SCHNEIDER AND R. WATTENHOFER, *A new technique for distributed symmetry breaking*, in PODC, 2010, pp. 257–266.

[36] ——, *An optimal maximal independent set algorithm for bounded-independence graphs*, Distrib. Comput., 22 (2010), pp. 1–13.

[37] M. SZEGEDY AND S. VISHWANATHAN, *Locality based graph coloring*, in STOC, 1993, pp. 201–207.

The Complexity of Robust Atomic Storage

Dan Dobre[*]
TU Darmstadt
Darmstadt, Germany
dan@cs.tu-darmstadt.de

Rachid Guerraoui
EPFL
Lausanne, Switzerland
rachid.guerraoui@epfl.ch

Matthias Majuntke
TU Darmstadt
Darmstadt, Germany
majuntke@cs.tu-darmstadt.de

Neeraj Suri
TU Darmstadt
Darmstadt, Germany
suri@cs.tu-darmstadt.de

Marko Vukolić
EURECOM
Sophia-Antipolis, France
marko.vukolic@eurecom.fr

ABSTRACT

We study the time-complexity of robust atomic read/write storage from fault-prone storage components in asynchronous message-passing systems. Robustness here means wait-free tolerating the largest possible number t of Byzantine storage component failures (optimal resilience) without relying on data authentication. We show that no single-writer multiple-reader (SWMR) robust atomic storage implementation exists if (a) read operations complete in less than *four* communication round-trips (rounds), and (b) the time-complexity of write operations is constant. More precisely, we present two lower bounds. The first is a read lower bound stating that *three* rounds of communication are necessary to read from a SWMR robust atomic storage. The second is a write lower bound, showing that $\Omega(log(t))$ write rounds are necessary to read in three rounds from such a storage. Applied to known results, our lower bounds close a fundamental gap: we show that time-optimal robust atomic storage can be obtained using well-known transformations from regular to atomic storage and existing time-optimal regular storage implementations.

Categories and Subject Descriptors

C.2.4 [**Computer-Communication Networks**]: Distributed Systems; D.4.1 [**Operating Systems**]: Process Management—*concurrency, multiprocessing / multiprogramming / multitasking, synchronization*; D.4.5 [**Operating Systems**]: Reliability—*Fault-tolerance*

General Terms

Algorithms, Performance, Reliability, Theory

[*]Dan Dobre is currently also with NEC Laboratories Europe, Kurfürsten-Anlage 36, 69115 Heidelberg, Germany

Keywords

Lower bounds, Storage emulations, Arbitrary failures, Optimal resilience, Time-complexity

1. INTRODUCTION

1.1 Background

Variable sharing is critical to modern distributed and concurrent computing. The *atomic* read/write register abstraction [18] is essential to sharing information in distributed systems; it abstracts away the complexity incurred by concurrent access to shared data by providing processes an illusion of sequential access to data. This abstraction is also referred to as atomic *storage*, for its importance as a building-block in practical distributed storage and file systems (see e.g., [24, 25]). Besides, its read/write API, despite being very simple, is today the heart of modern "cloud" key-value storage APIs (e.g., [5]).

In this paper, we study atomic storage implementations in asynchronous message-passing systems in which a set of reader and writer processes (*clients*) share data leveraging a set of storage *object* processes. We consider fault-tolerant, *robust* [3] storage implementations characterized by: a) wait-freedom [17], i.e., the fact that read/write operations invoked by correct clients always eventually return, and b) ensuring correctness despite the largest possible number t of object failures (optimal resilience). We allow for the most general type of failures, arbitrary, also called Byzantine [19] failures[1], without assuming authenticated (also called self-verifying [23]) data to limit the adversary (by relying on e.g., digital signatures).

In this model, we ask a fundamental question: what is the optimal worst-case complexity of robust atomic storage implementations? Our complexity metric is an important one: time-complexity, or *latency*, measured in number of *communication round-trips* (or simply *rounds*) between a client and objects. The relevance of the question we ask extends beyond theoretical. Namely, with the growth in storage outsourcing driven by the advent of cloud computing, the arbitrary failure model becomes increasingly relevant in absence of the full trust in the cloud [6]. In addition, the number of

[1]In the Byzantine failure model, optimal resilience corresponds to using $3t + 1$ objects to tolerate t failures [23].

interactions with the remote cloud storage needed to access the data, maps to our latency metric and is often directly associated with the monetary cost; this obviously increases further the practical relevance of the question we ask.

Perhaps surprisingly and despite the wealth of literature exploring latency-optimal storage implementations, this question has not been answered. It is known that the worst-case latency of *writing* into robust storage is at least 2 rounds [1]. In this paper, we show that the optimal worst-case latency of *reading* from *scalable* robust atomic storage is 4 (four) rounds. Here, the notion of scalability captures two basic criteria: a) support for any number of readers, and b) constant write-latency. Our results close a fundamental gap, showing that latency-optimal scalable and robust atomic storage, combining 2-round writes and 4-round reads, can be achieved (in the case of single-writer multi-reader (SWMR) storage) using standard transformations from weaker, regular [18] registers to the atomic ones [4,20].

Our contribution goes through proving two lower bounds. To help fully appreciate our contributions, we first discuss how the scope of this paper fits into related work.

1.2 Related work

Several papers have explored the time-complexity metric in the context of a read/write register abstraction. A seminal crash-tolerant robust atomic SWMR register implementation assuming a majority of correct processes was presented in [3]. In [3], all write operations complete in a single round; on the other hand, read operations always take two rounds between a client and objects.

The problem of modifying [3] to enable single round reads was explored in [9], which showed that such *fast* atomic implementations are possible albeit they come with the price of limited number of readers and suboptimal resilience. Moreover, the reader in [9] needs to write (i.e., modify the objects' state) as dictated by the lower bound of [12] which showed that every atomic read must write into at least t objects. [10] extends the result of [9] to the Byzantine failure model assuming authenticated (i.e., digitally signed) data and established the impossibility of fast crash-tolerant multi-writer multi-reader (MWMR) atomic register implementations. This result is in line with classical MWMR implementations such as [22] that have read/write latency of at least 2 rounds. The limitation on the number of readers of [9], was relaxed in [13], where a crash-tolerant robust SWMR atomic register implementation was presented, in which most of the reads complete in a single round, yet a fraction of reads is permitted to be slow and complete in 2 rounds.

In the Byzantine context, optimizing latency is particularly interesting when data is assumed to be unauthenticated, which we also assume here. [1] showed that any Byzantine-tolerant storage employing at most $4t$ storage objects has at least some write operation complete in 2 rounds. Moreover, [1] showed a tight lower bound of $t+1$ rounds from reading from robust SWMR safe [18] storage, with the constraint that readers are precluded from writing. However, allowing readers to write helps improve latency as shown in [15], through a 2-round tight lower bound on reading from robust SWMR *regular* [18] storage. This bound was circumvented in [8], assuming secret values used to detect concurrent operations, where reads are expedited to complete in a single round. However, none of these papers dealt with

optimal worst-case latency of reading from robust *atomic* storage, which is precisely the scope of our paper.

On the other hand, few papers have explored the *best-case* complexity of Byzantine-tolerant optimally resilient atomic storage. Here, "best-case" encompasses synchrony, no or few object failures and the absence of read/write concurrency. In this context, [14] presented the first robust atomic storage implementation in which both reads and writes are fast in the best-case (i.e., complete in a single round-trip). Furthermore, [16] considered robust atomic storage implementations with the possibility of having fast reads and writes gracefully degrade to 2 or 3 rounds, depending on the size of the available quorum of correct objects. Unlike these papers, we are interested here with the unconditional, *worst-case* latency of atomic storage.

Finally, the worst-case read latency in existing Byzantine-tolerant robust atomic storage implementations for unauthenticated data (e.g., [2,14,16,23]) is either unbounded or $\Omega(t)$ rounds at best [2].

1.3 Contributions

We present two lower bounds (impossibility results) on time-complexity of reading from robust atomic storage for unauthenticated data, implemented from storage objects prone to Byzantine faults. Together, our lower bounds imply that *there is no* scalable robust atomic storage implementation in the Byzantine unauthenticated model in which all reads complete in less than 4 rounds.

- The first lower bound, referred to as the *read lower bound*, demonstrates the impossibility of reading from robust SWMR atomic storage in two rounds. More precisely, we show that if the number of storage objects S is at most $4t$ and if the number of readers R is greater than 3, then no SWMR atomic implementation may have all reads complete in two rounds.

  Our proof scheme resembles that of [9] and relies on sequentially appending reads on a write operation, while progressively deleting the steps of a write and preceding read operations, exploiting asynchrony and possible failures. This deletion ultimately allows reusing readers and reaching an impossibility with as few as $R = 4$ readers. As none of these appended operations are concurrent under step contention, the impossibility also holds in the stronger data model of [8], in which the adversary is unable to simulate step contention among operations, making use of secret values.

- Our second lower bound, referred to as the *write lower bound*, shows that if read operations are required to complete in three communication rounds, then the number of write rounds k is $\Omega(log(t))$. More precisely, we show that if the number of storage objects is at most $3t + \lfloor t/t_k \rfloor$ and $R \geq k$, then no implementation of a SWMR atomic storage may have all reads complete in three rounds and all writes in $k \leq \lfloor \log(\lceil \frac{3t_k+1}{2} \rceil) \rfloor$ rounds. In a sense, our lower bound generalizes the write lower bound of [1], which proves our result for the special case of $k = 1$.

  While using a similar approach, the write lower bound proof is much more involved and differs from our read lower bound proof in several key aspects. Due to the additional third read round, read steps cannot be entirely deleted, which prohibits the reuse of readers. Consequently, the number of supported readers R and the number of write rounds k are related ($R \geq k$). Furthermore, the proof relies on a set of malicious objects that forges critical steps of the write and of prior reads with respect to subsequent reads. This set grows with the number of appended reads, relating the number of faulty objects t and the number of readers (which is at least k). At the heart of the proof we use a recurrent formula that relates t and k, similar to a Fibonacci sequence, which describes the exact relation between the two parameters. In its closed form, the formula transforms to the log function ($k = \Omega(log(t))$).

The rest of the paper is organized as follows. In Section 2 we give our model and definitions. Sections 3 and gives the proof of our read lower bound. [2] Section 4 gives the proof of our write lower bound. Section 5 concludes the paper by discussing modular implementations that match our lower bounds.

2. MODEL

2.1 Basics

The distributed system we consider consists of three *disjoint* sets of processes: a set *objects* of size S containing processes $\{s_1, ..., s_S\}$ and representing the base register elements; a singleton *writer* containing a single process $\{w\}$; and a set *readers* of size R containing processes $r_1, ..., r_R$. The set *clients* is the union of the sets *writer* and *readers*. We assume that every client may communicate with any process by message passing using point-to-point reliable communication channels. However, objects cannot communicate among each other, nor send messages to clients other than in reply to clients' messages.

Here we define only the notions we use in our proofs; model details can be found in [20]. A distributed algorithm A is a collection of automata [21], where automaton A_p is assigned to process p. Computation proceeds in steps of A; each step is denoted by a pair of process id and a set of messages received in that step $\langle p, M \rangle$ (M might be $\emptyset$). A run is an infinite sequence of steps of A. A partial run is a finite prefix of some run. A (partial) run r extends some partial run pr if pr is a *prefix* of r. At the end of a partial run, all messages that are sent but not yet received are said to be *in transit*. In any run, any client can fail by crashing and up to t objects may be malicious faulty, exhibiting arbitrary behavior. The non-faulty objects are also called correct. An algorithm that assumes $S = 3t + 1$ is said to be optimally resilient.

2.2 Atomic Storage

A register abstraction is a read/write data structure. It provides two operations: write(v), which stores v in the register, and read(), which returns the value from the register. We assume that each client invokes at most one operation at a time (i.e., does not invoke the next operation until it

receives the response for the current operation). Only readers invoke read operations and only the writer invokes write operations. We further assume that the initial value of a register is a special value $\perp$, which is not a valid input value for a write operation. We say that an operation op is complete in a (partial) run if the run contains a response step for op. In any run, we say that a complete operation op_1 precedes operation op_2 (or op_2 succeeds op_1) if the response step of $op1$ precedes the invocation step of op_2 in that run. If neither op_1 nor op_2 precedes the other, then the operations are said to be concurrent.

An algorithm implements a register if every run of the algorithm satisfies *wait-freedom* and *atomicity* properties. Wait-freedom states that if a process invokes an operation, then eventually, unless that process crashes, the operation completes (even if all other client processes have crashed). Here we give a definition of atomicity for the single-writer registers. In the single-writer setting, the writes in a run have a natural ordering which corresponds to their physical order. Denote by wr_k the kth write in a run ($k \geq 1$), and by val_k the value written by the kth write. Let $val_0 = \perp$. We say that a partial run satisfies atomicity if the following properties hold: (1) if a read returns x then there is k such that $val_k = x$, (2) if a read rd is complete and it succeeds some write wr_k ($k \geq 1$), then rd returns val_l such that $l \geq k$, (3) if a read rd returns val_k ($k \geq 1$), then wr_k either precedes rd or is concurrent with rd, and (4) if some read rd_1 returns val_k ($k \geq 0$) and a read rd_2 that succeeds rd_1 returns val_l, then $l \geq k$.

Time-complexity.

We measure the time-complexity of an atomic register implementation in terms of communication round-trips (or simply rounds). A round is defined similar to [9, 11, 13, 22]:

DEFINITION 1. *Client c performs a communication round during operation* op *if the following conditions hold:*

1. *The client c sends messages to all objects. (This is without loss of generality because we can model the fact that messages are not sent to certain objects by having these objects not change their state or reply.)*

2. *Objects, on receiving such a message, reply to the client before receiving any other messages (as dictated by our model).*

3. *When the invoking client receives a sufficient number of such replies, the round (rnd) terminates, and the operation* op *either completes or moves to the next round.*

Note that, since any number of clients can crash, we can construct partial runs in which no client receives any message from any other client. In our proofs in Section 3 and 4 we focus, without loss of generality, on such partial runs.

Since up to t objects might be faulty, ideally, in every round rnd the invoking client can only wait for reply messages from correct objects (at least $S-t$). In fact, we require that if in a partial run pr, a round rnd terminates without the reply from some object s_i, then either (a) s_i is faulty or (b) there is partial run pr' indistinguishable from pr, and in which s_i is faulty.

Each round attempts to invoke operations on *all* objects. If on some correct object s_i there is a pending invocation (of an earlier round), then the new invocation awaits the

---

[2]An extension to the model of [26] using distinct thresholds for malicious and crash objects' faults can be found in our full paper [7].

completion of the pending one. Note that this is equivalent to the round model of [1].

3. THE READ LOWER BOUND

In this section we prove the following proposition.

PROPOSITION 1. : *If $S \leq 4t$ and $R > 3$, then no read implementation I of a multi-reader (SWMR) atomic register exists that completes in two rounds.*

Overview.

The idea behind the proof is to start with a complete write that writes 1 into the storage, after which a complete read is appended. By atomicity, the read returns 1. Then, further reads by distinct readers are appended one after the other such that the last appended read returns 1. At the same time, steps of the write and the previous reads are progressively deleted. After appending the fourth read, the final round of the write is deleted from the storage. Moreover, similar to a circular buffer, all steps of the first read are erased, and the read ca be "recycled". By atomicity, the last appended read returns 1. The next iteration starts by reusing the first read, which in turn frees the second read. The proof proceeds through a sequence of such iterations. In each iteration, the last appended read frees the first appended read, and deletes another round of the write. After the last iteration, all steps of the write are deleted, meaning that no write is invoked. However, the last appended read returns 1, violating atomicity.

Preliminaries.

In the proof w denotes the writer, r_i for $1 \leq i \leq 4$ denote the readers, and s_i for $1 \leq i \leq S$ denote objects. Suppose by contradiction that $R = 4$ and there is an atomic register implementation I that uses at most $4t$ objects, such that in every partial run of I every *read* operation completes in two rounds.

We partition the set *objects* into four disjoint subsets (which we call *blocks*), denoted B_1, B_2, B_3 and B_4. Blocks B_1, B_2 and B_3 are of size exactly $t \geq 1$ and the size of B_4 is at least 1 and at most t. We refer to the initial state of every correct block B_j as σ_0^j. For simplicity we simply write σ_0, where the block name is implicit.

We say that a round rnd of an operation op *skips* a set of blocks BS in a partial run, (where $BS \subseteq \{B_1, \ldots, B_4\}$), if (1) no object in any block $BL \in BS$ receives any message in round rnd from op in that partial run; (2) all other objects receive all messages in round rnd from op and reply to the messages, and (3) in case round rnd is terminated, the invoking client has received all these reply messages or, in case rnd is not terminated, all these reply messages are in transit. We say that an operation op skips a set of blocks BS in a partial run if every round of op skips BS.

To show a contradiction, we construct a partial run of the implementation I that violates atomicity: a partial run of I in which no value is ever written and some read returns 1.

Partial writes.

Throughout the proof there is only one write operation write(1) by w that writes value 1. Consider a partial run wr in which w completes write(1) on the register and let k be the number of rounds invoked by w in wr. We denote the state of every correct block B_j after it has replied to the messages of the write during round 1 to i where $1 \leq i \leq k$ as σ_i, where j is again implicit. The write operation skips blocks B_4. We define a series of partial runs containing an incomplete write(1) invocation, each being a prefix of wr. For $1 \leq i \leq k$ and $1 \leq j \leq 4$, we define wr_j^i as the partial run in which (1) rounds 1 to $i-1$ are terminated and skip B_4; (2) round i is not terminated and skips all blocks $\{B_l \mid 1 \leq l \leq j-1\} \cup \{B_4\}$, and (3) all objects are correct. We make two observations: (1) partial run wr_1^k differs from wr only at w and (2) partial run wr_4^1 differs from a run in which write(1) is never invoked only at w.

Block diagrams.

We illustrate the proof in Figure 1 (a)-(n). We depict a round rnd of an operation op through a set of rectangles arranged in a single column. In the column corresponding to some round rnd of op we draw a rectangle in a given row, if all objects in the corresponding block BL have received the message from the client in round rnd of op and have sent reply messages, i.e., if round rnd of op does not skip BL. We write "@" in the row corresponding to BL iff BL is malicious.

Appending reads.

Partial run pr_1 extends wr by appending a complete read rd_1 by r_1 that skips B_2 in round one and B_1 in round two (see Figure 1 (a)). Note that when the second round is started, there is a pending first round invocation on B_2. Therefore in the second round, rd_1 waits for both first *and* second round replies from B_2. For ease of presentation, the late first round replies are not illustrated.

In pr_1, all objects in block B_1 are malicious, and forge their state to σ_{k-1} before replying to rd_1. By atomicity rd_1 returns 1. Observe that r_1 cannot distinguish pr_1 from some partial run Δpr_1 that extends wr_2^k by appending rd_1, and where all objects are correct (see Figure 1 (b)). Note that Δpr_1 is obtained from pr_1 by deleting the crossed steps.

Partial run pr_2 extends Δpr_1 by appending a complete read rd_2 by r_2 that skips B_3 and B_2 in round one and two respectively (see Figure 1 (c)). In pr_2, all objects in block B_2 are malicious, and forge their state to σ_{k-1} before replying to rd_2. By atomicity rd_2 returns 1. Observe that r_2 cannot distinguish pr_2 from some partial run Δpr_2, that extends wr_3^k by appending an incomplete rd_1 and a complete rd_2, and where all objects are correct (Figure 1 (d)). Δpr_2 is obtained from pr_2 by deleting the crossed steps.

Partial run pr_3 extends Δpr_2 by appending a complete read rd_3 by r_3 that skips B_4 in round one and B_3 in round two (Figure 1 (e)). In pr_3, all objects in block B_3 are malicious, and forge their state to σ_{k-1} before replying to rd_3. By atomicity rd_3 returns 1. Let σ_1^r denote the state of the objects in block B_4 in run pr_3 before replying to rd_2. Observe that r_3 cannot distinguish pr_3 from some partial run Δpr_3, that extends wr_4^k by appending incomplete reads rd_1 and rd_2 and a complete read rd_3 and in which (1) all objects in B_4 are malicious and (2) they forge their state to σ_1^r before replying to rd_2 (Figure 1 (f)).

Note that in pr_3, rd_3 completes the second round based on replies from all correct objects, and similarly in Δpr_3, the first round misses replies only from faulty objects. Since r_3 cannot distinguish pr_3 and Δpr_3, it cannot wait for additional replies (in any of the two runs).

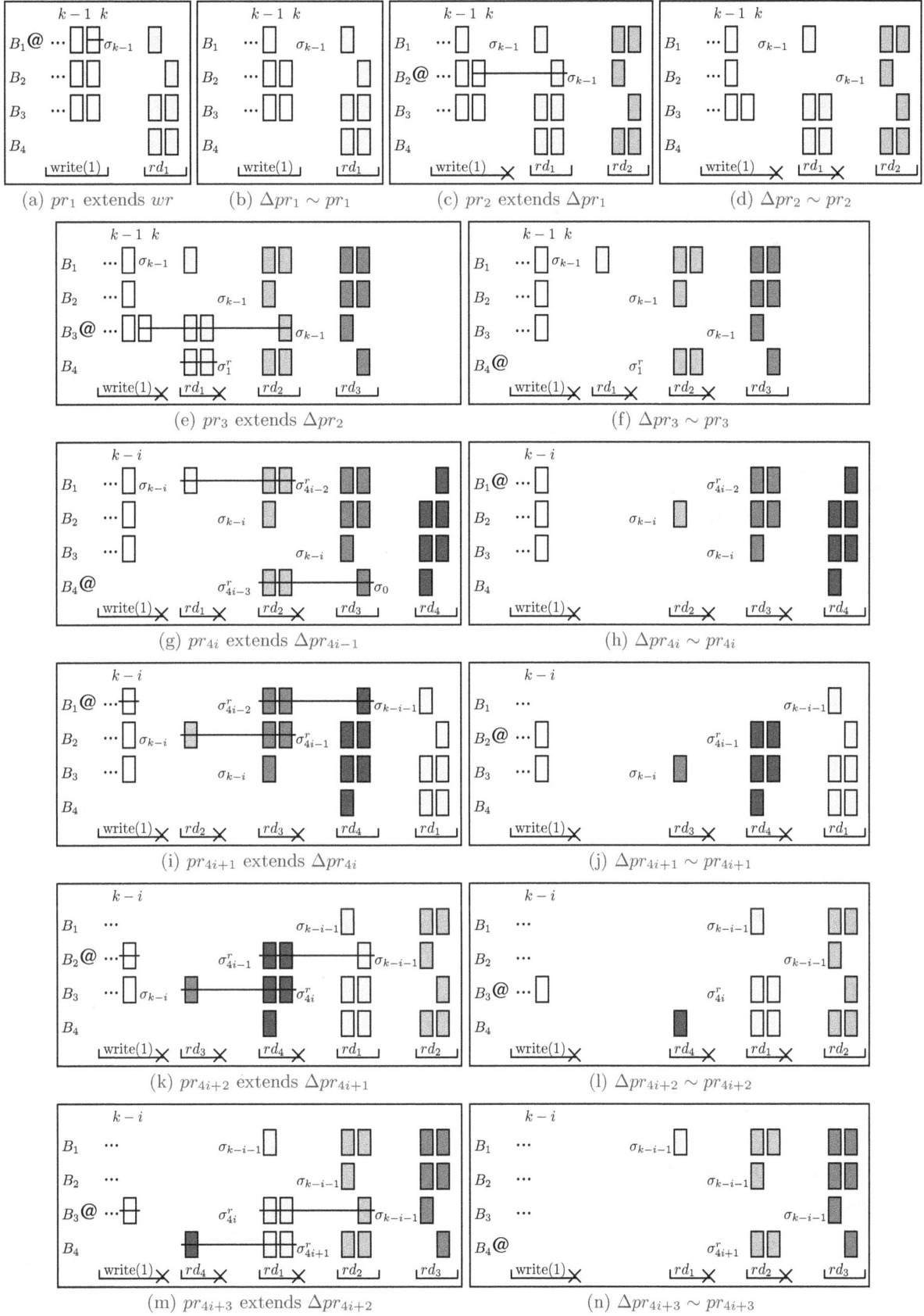

(a) pr_1 extends wr

(b) $\Delta pr_1 \sim pr_1$

(c) pr_2 extends Δpr_1

(d) $\Delta pr_2 \sim pr_2$

(e) pr_3 extends Δpr_2

(f) $\Delta pr_3 \sim pr_3$

(g) pr_{4i} extends Δpr_{4i-1}

(h) $\Delta pr_{4i} \sim pr_{4i}$

(i) pr_{4i+1} extends Δpr_{4i}

(j) $\Delta pr_{4i+1} \sim pr_{4i+1}$

(k) pr_{4i+2} extends Δpr_{4i+1}

(l) $\Delta pr_{4i+2} \sim pr_{4i+2}$

(m) pr_{4i+3} extends Δpr_{4i+2}

(n) $\Delta pr_{4i+3} \sim pr_{4i+3}$

Figure 1: Illustration of the runs used in the proof of Proposition 1 ($1 \le i \le k-1$)

Partial run pr_4 (illustrated in Figure 1 (g)) extends Δpr_3 by appending a complete read rd_4 by r_4 that skips B_1 in round one and B_4 in round two. In pr_4, all objects in block B_4 are malicious and forge their state (1) to σ_1^r before replying to rd_2 and (2) to σ_0 before replying to rd_4. By atomicity rd_4 returns 1. Let σ_2^r denote the state of the objects in block B_1 before replying to rd_3. Observe that r_4 cannot distinguish pr_4 from some partial run Δpr_4, that extends wr_1^{k-1} by appending incomplete reads rd_2, rd_3 and a complete read rd_4, and in which (1) all objects in B_1 are malicious and (2) they forge their state to σ_2^r before replying to rd_3 (Figure 1 (h)). Note that in partial run pr_4, rd_4 receives second round replies from all correct objects. Similarly in Δpr_4, rd_4 receives first round replies from all objects except the faulty ones. Since r_4 cannot distinguish pr_4 and Δpr_4, rd_4 cannot wait for additional replies without violating termination.

After appending rd_4 and constructing Δpr_4 by deleting all steps from pr_4 which are not visible to rd_4, we notice that we have erased all steps in column k of write(1) as well as, deleted all steps of rd_1. Thus, we can recycle r_1 by appending rd_1 again and start deleting the steps in column $k-1$.

Starting from Δpr_4 we iteratively define the following partial runs for $1 \leq i \leq k-1$ and $1 \leq j \leq 4$ (see Figure 1 (g)-(n)). Partial run $pr_{4i+(j \bmod 4)}$ extends $\Delta pr_{4i+(j \bmod 4)-1}$ by appending rd_j. In $pr_{4i+(j \bmod 4)}$, all objects in block B_j are malicious and they forge their state (1) to $\sigma_{4i+(j \bmod 4)-3}^r$ before replying to rd_{j-2}[3] and (2) to $\sigma_{((j \bmod 4)/j)(k-i-1)}$ before replying to rd_j. Let $\sigma_{4i+(j \bmod 4)-2}^r$ denote the state of the objects in block $B_{(j \bmod 4)+1}$ before replying to rd_{j-1}. Observe that r_j cannot distinguish $pr_{4i+(j \bmod 4)}$ from some partial run $\Delta pr_{4i+(j \bmod 4)}$, that extends $wr_{(j \bmod 4)+1}^{k-i}$ by appending incomplete reads rd_{j-2} and rd_{j-1} and a complete read rd_j, and in which (1) all objects in $B_{(j \bmod 4)+1}$ are malicious, and (2) they forge their state to $\sigma_{4i+(j \bmod 4)-2}^r$ before replying to rd_{j-1} (Figure 1 (h),(j),(l),(n)). In run $\Delta pr_{4i+(j \bmod 4)}$ and $pr_{4i+(j \bmod 4)}$, rd_j receives first and second round replies from all correct objects respectively. As r_j cannot distinguish $\Delta pr_{4i+(j \bmod 4)}$ and $pr_{4i+(j \bmod 4)}$, rd_j cannot wait for additional replies without blocking.

Read rd_4 in Δpr_4 returns 1. Since pr_5 extends Δpr_4 by appending rd_1, by atomicity, rd_1 in pr_5 returns 1. However, as r_1 cannot distinguish pr_5 from Δpr_5, rd_1 in Δpr_5 returns 1. In general, since $pr_{4i+(j \bmod 4)}$ extends $\Delta pr_{4i+(j \bmod 4)-1}$ by appending rd_j (for $1 \leq i \leq k-1$ and $1 \leq j \leq 4$), and r_j cannot distinguish $pr_{4i+(j \bmod 4)}$ from $\Delta pr_{4i+(j \bmod 4)}$, it follows by induction that rd_j in $\Delta pr_{4i+(j \bmod 4)}$ returns 1. In particular, rd_3 reads 1 in Δpr_{4k-1}. By our construction, Δpr_{4k-1} extends wr_4^1 and wr_4^1 is indistinguishable from a run in which write(1) is never invoked. Hence, rd_3 returns 1 even if no write is invoked, violating atomicity. $\square$

4. THE WRITE LOWER BOUND

In this section we prove the following proposition.

PROPOSITION 2. : *If* $S \leq 3t + \lfloor t/t_k \rfloor$ *and every read completes in three rounds then no* write *implementation* I *of a multi-reader atomic register exists that completes in* $\min\{R, \lfloor \log(\lceil (3t_k+1)/2 \rceil) \rfloor\}$ *rounds.*

---

[3] By rd_{j-c}, we denote the cth last read prior to rd_j. Formally, $rd_{4-((c-j) \bmod 4)}$.

We first prove the following key lemma. In the effort of making its involved proof easier to follow we first proceed through a careful proof setup that we found worthwhile. To further help follow the proof, we also visualize runs we use in the proof in Figure 2.

LEMMA 1. *Let* $k \geq 1$, $t_{-1} = t_0 = 0$ *and* $t_k = t_{k-1} + 2t_{k-2} + 1$. *There is no implementation* I *of a* k-*reader atomic storage with* $3t_k + 1$ *objects and* t_k *faults such that the* write *completes in* k *rounds and the* read *completes in three rounds.*

Overview.

The idea of the proof consists of having a complete write that writes 1 into the storage, after which we append a sequence of read operations. We use patterns of concurrency and failures such that the first read in the sequence cannot distinguish if it overlaps with or succeeds the write. In each case, by atomicity, it must return 1. For each of the following reads we use the same indistinguishability argument such that the last read in the sequence cannot tell if it is concurrent with or follows after the preceding read. In both cases, by atomicity, the last appended read has to return 1.

To derive a contradiction, for each appended read, we progressively delete one of the k rounds of the write and rounds of the previous reads. As a consequence, the kth appended read returns 1 in a run in which 1 is never written. To reduce the information about the write propagated via the 3rd read round, as more reads are appended, a monotonically increasing set of base object present forged information. Consecutive read operations increasingly skip these faulty objects together and therefore overlap in an increasing number of correct objects. If two rounds of consecutive reads, both skip the same set of x faulty objects, then they overlap in $2x+1$ correct objects. To derive a contradiction for the kth appended read, the set of faulty objects consists of those needed to derive a contradiction for the $k-1^{\text{st}}$ read plus the $2x+1$ objects in the intersection of the 3rd round of the $k-1^{\text{st}}$ read and the first round of the kth read. In fact, x equals the number of faulty objects needed to derive a contraction for the $k-2^{\text{nd}}$ read. Together, this leads to the recursive formula used throughout the proof.

Preliminaries.

Recall that w denotes the writer, r_i for $1 \leq i \leq k$ denote the readers, and s_i for $1 \leq i \leq S$ denote the objects. The initial value of the register is $\perp$. In the proof, there is only one write operation write(1) by w that writes value 1. We know from [1] that the lemma is true for $k=1$; hence, we assume $k \geq 2$. Suppose by contradiction that there is an implementation I that uses at most $3t_k+1$ objects, such that in every partial run of I every write (resp., read) completes in k (resp. 3) rounds.

We partition the set *objects* into $2k+2$ distinct blocks, $B_0, \ldots, B_{k+1}$ and $C_1, \ldots, C_k$ such that $|\bigcup_{j=0}^{k+1} B_j| = 2t_k+1$ and $|\bigcup_{j=1}^{k} C_j| = t_k$. Block B_0 contains a single object. For $1 \leq l \leq k$, the size of B_l is $t_l - t_{l-2}$ and the size of B_{k+1} is $2t_k + 1 - |\bigcup_{j=0}^{k} B_j| = t_k - t_{k-1}$. For $1 \leq l \leq k-1$, the size of C_l is $t_{l-1} - t_{l-2}$ and the size of C_k is $t_k - |\bigcup_{j=1}^{k-1} C_j| = t_k - t_{k-2}$. It is important to note that C_1 is empty. Towards a uniform presentation of the result, we will refer to C_1

wherever appropriate. Also, we use the abbreviation $BL_{i,j}$ to denote the set $\{BL_i, BL_j\}$, for some $BL \in \{B, C\}$.

We also define three sets of blocks called *superblocks*: the "malicious" superblock $\mathcal{M}_l$, the "parity" superblock $\mathcal{P}_l$ and the "correct" superblock $\mathcal{C}_l$. Superblock $\mathcal{M}_l$ contains all blocks with index at most l. Formally, for $-1 \leq l \leq k-1$ we define $\mathcal{M}_l := \{B_j \mid 0 \leq j \leq l\} \cup \{C_j \mid 1 \leq j \leq l\}$. For instance, $\mathcal{M}_{-1} = \emptyset$ and $\mathcal{M}_2 = \{B_0, B_1, C_1, C_2\}$. Superblock $\mathcal{P}_l$ contains all blocks B_j with index $j \geq l \geq 1$ such that j and l have the same parity. More formally, for $1 \leq l \leq k$, we define $\mathcal{P}_l := \{B_j \mid l \leq j \leq k+1 \ \wedge \ j \equiv (l \bmod 2)\}$. For instance, if k is even then $\mathcal{P}_1 = \{B_1, B_3, \ldots, B_{k-1}, B_{k+1}\}$ and $\mathcal{P}_2 = \{B_2, B_4, \ldots, B_{k-2}, B_k\}$. Finally, superblock $\mathcal{C}_l := \{C_j \mid l \leq j \leq k\}$.

Given the size of the individual blocks, we can determine the cardinality of the union of all elements of a superblock. Namely, if $\mathcal{S} \in \{\mathcal{M}_l, \mathcal{P}_l, \mathcal{C}_l\}$, then we define the union of its elements as $\bigcup \mathcal{S} = \{s \in BL \mid BL \in \mathcal{S}\}$. Having in mind that $t_k = t_{k-1} + 2t_{k-2} + 1$ (Def.) and $t_{-1} = t_0 = 0$, we have:

$$\left|\bigcup \mathcal{M}_l\right| = t_l + 2t_{l-1} + 1 \stackrel{(Def.)}{=} t_{l+1} \quad \text{for } 0 \leq l \leq k-1 \quad (1)$$

$$\left|\bigcup \mathcal{P}_l\right| = t_k - t_{l-2} \quad \text{for } 1 \leq l \leq k+1 \quad (2)$$

$$\left|\bigcup \mathcal{C}_l\right| = t_k - t_{l-2} \quad \text{for } 1 \leq l \leq k \quad (3)$$

Block diagrams.

Figure 2 illustrates the proof for $R = k = 4$. Reader r_i invokes read rd_l, $1 \leq l \leq k$. In the column corresponding to some round rnd of op we draw a rectangle in a given row, iff round rnd of op does not skip[4] the corresponding block BL. We write "@" in the row of BL iff BL is malicious.

Read patterns.

We first characterize a *complete* read rd_l for $1 \leq l \leq k-1$. A complete rd_l skips (1) $\mathcal{M}_{l-2} \cup \mathcal{P}_{l+1}$ in round one and two, and (2) $\mathcal{M}_{l-2} \cup \mathcal{C}_{l+1}$ in round three. Read rd_k skips $\mathcal{M}_{k-2} \cup \mathcal{P}_{k+1}$. Observe that by equations (1), (2) and (3), a read skips exactly t_k objects in each round.

Consider the example in Figure 2. Complete reads rd_1, rd_2 and rd_3 skip (respectively): (1) $\{B_{2,4}\}$, $\{B_0\} \cup \{B_{3,5}\}$ and $\{B_{0,1}\} \cup \{B_4\}$ in rounds one and two, and (2) $\{C_{2,3,4}\}$, $\{B_0\} \cup \{C_{3,4}\}$ and $\{B_{0,1}\} \cup \{C_4\}$ in round three. Read rd_4 skips $\{B_{0,1,2}, C_2\} \cup \{B_5\}$.

We further define three types of *incomplete* reads $inc1$, $inc2$ and $inc3$, depending on the read's progress. For $1 \leq l \leq k$, read rd_l is of type $inc1$ if the first round is not terminated and skips all blocks *except* $\mathcal{P}_l$. For $1 \leq l \leq k-1$, read rd_l is of type (1) $inc2$ if the first round is terminated, and the second round is not terminated and skips all blocks *except* $\mathcal{C}_l$, and (2) $inc3$ if the second round is terminated and the third round is not terminated and skips $\mathcal{M}_{l-2} \cup \mathcal{C}_{l+1} \cup \mathcal{P}_{l+1}$.

Consider our example in Figure 2 (c) that illustrates partial run Δpr_2 (after deleting the crossed out steps). Observe that (1) rd_2 is incomplete of type $inc3$ (its third round skips $\{B_0\} \cup \{C_{3,4}\} \cup \{B_{3,5}\}$), (2) rd_1 is incomplete of type $inc2$ (its second round skips all blocks except $\{C_{2,3,4}\}$) and (3) rd_3 (resp., rd_4) is incomplete of type $inc1$; its first round skips all blocks except $\{B_{3,5}\}$ (resp., $\{B_4\}$).

---

[4]The definition of *skipping* extends here from Sec. 3.

Towards a contradiction, we construct a partial run of the atomic register implementation I that violates atomicity. More specifically, we exhibit a partial run in which some read returns a value that was never written.

Initialization.

Consider a partial run pr_{init} in which (1) all blocks are correct and (2) pr_{init} extends the empty run by appending incomplete reads rd_l by r_l of type $inc1$, for $1 \leq l \leq k$, one after the other. In pr_{init}, there is no write operation. We refer to the state of each correct block $BL \in \mathcal{P}_l$ after replying to rd_l as σ_0^l. Thus, the state of B_l at the end of pr_{init} corresponds to σ_0^l for $1 \leq l \leq k$. Further, B_{k+1} is in state σ_0^{k-1}. To see why, note that B_{k-1} and B_{k+1} have the same parity and there are only k reads.

Consider our example Figure 2 (a). At the end of pr_{init}, block B_1 (resp., B_2; $B_{3,5}$; B_4) replied to rd_1 (resp., rd_2; rd_1 and rd_3; rd_2 and rd_4); thus, at the end of the run its state is σ_0^1 (resp., σ_0^2; σ_0^3; σ_0^4).

Partial writes.

We extend pr_{init} to a partial run wr^k by appending a complete write(1) that completes in k rounds and skips superblock $\mathcal{C}_1$. Moreover, we define a series of partial runs each being a prefix of wr^k. For $1 \leq i \leq k$, let wr^{k-i} be the partial run which extends pr_{init} by appending an incomplete write(1) such that (i) round 1 to $k-i$ are terminated and (ii) round $k-i+1$ is not terminated and skips $\mathcal{C}_1$ and all B_j's such that $j > 0$ and i and j have the same parity, i.e., $\mathcal{C}_1 \cup \mathcal{P}_{2-(i \bmod 2)}$ (Fig. 2 (a) and (c)). We refer to the state of the blocks $B_l \in \mathcal{P}_{2-(i \bmod 2)}$ at the end of wr^{k-i} as σ_{k-i}^l for $1 \leq l \leq k$. If $B_{k+1} \in \mathcal{P}_{2-(i \bmod 2)}$, then we refer to its state at the end of wr^{k-i} as σ_{k-i}^{k-1}. Note here that σ_{k-i}^l results from σ_0^l by appending $k-i$ rounds of the write. When the context is clear, for simplicity we refer to these states using the implicit notation σ_{k-1}^*. Finally, we refer to the state of B_0 at the end of runs wr^k and wr^{k-1} as σ_k.

We refer to our example in Figure 2 (a),(c),(e) and (g) for illustrations of the runs wr^3 to wr^0 and the corresponding states. For instance Figure 2 (a), illustrates wr^3 as an extension of pr_{init}. The states of the blocks B_0, B_1 and $B_{3,5}$ at the end of wr^3 are σ_4 (4 rounds of write), σ_3^1 and σ_3^3 (3 rounds of write).

Appending Reads.

Partial run pr_1 extends wr^{k-1} by appending the missing steps of a complete read rd_1. In pr_1 all objects are correct and thus rd_1 receives replies from $S - t_k$ correct objects. After receiving the third round replies, rd_1 completes and returns value x. We now show that $x = 1$. We define a partial run $@pr_0$, (Fig. 2(b)) which is *identical* to wr^k except that in $@pr_0$ (1) no read by r_1 occurs and (2) superblock $\mathcal{P}_1$ is malicious and mimics the occurrence of rd_1 by forging its initial state to σ_0^1. By equation (1), the malicious objects in $@pr_0$ amount to t_k. Partial run pr_1^C (Fig. 2(b)) is defined as an extension of $@pr_0$ by appending a complete read rd_1. Read rd_1 cannot distinguish pr_1^C from pr_1 because $\mathcal{P}_1$, which is malicious in pr_1^C, mimics pr_1. Specifically, $\mathcal{P}_1$ forges its state to σ_0 before replying to rd_1's first round, and then to σ_{k-1}^* before replying to rd_1's second round. In pr_1^C, by atomicity rd_1 returns 1. Since pr_1^C and pr_1 are indistinguishable to reader r_1, $x = 1$.

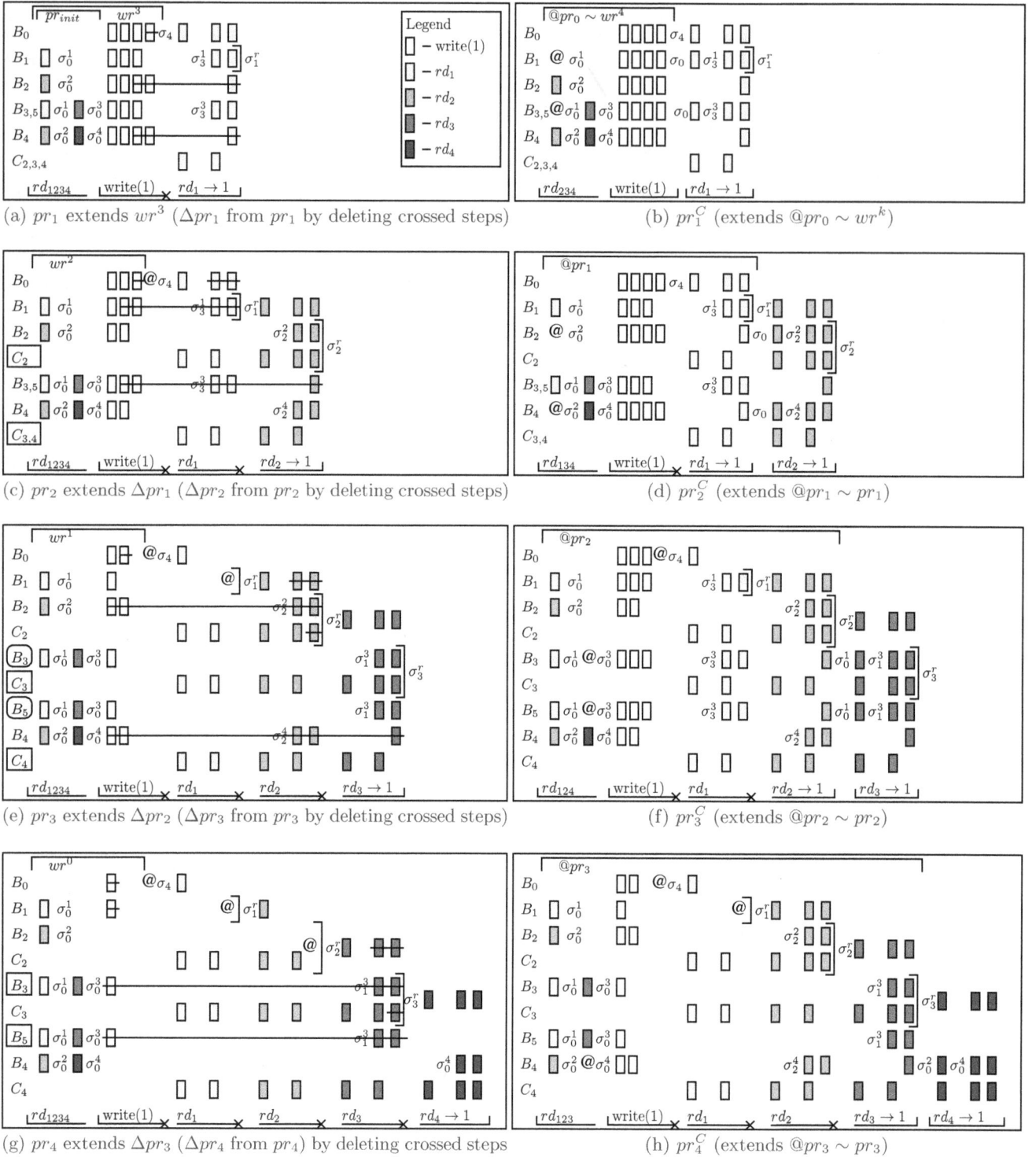

(a) pr_1 extends wr^3 (Δpr_1 from pr_1 by deleting crossed steps)

(b) pr_1^C (extends $@pr_0 \sim wr^k$)

(c) pr_2 extends Δpr_1 (Δpr_2 from pr_2 by deleting crossed steps)

(d) pr_2^C (extends $@pr_1 \sim pr_1$)

(e) pr_3 extends Δpr_2 (Δpr_3 from pr_3 by deleting crossed steps)

(f) pr_3^C (extends $@pr_2 \sim pr_2$)

(g) pr_4 extends Δpr_3 (Δpr_4 from pr_4) by deleting crossed steps

(h) pr_4^C (extends $@pr_3 \sim pr_3$)

Figure 2: Instance of the proof with $k = 4$.

Next, we define partial run Δpr_1 obtained from pr_1 by deleting the steps of the read and the write as illustrated in Figure 2 (a). More specifically, Δpr_1 extends wr^{k-2} by appending the missing steps of an incomplete read rd_1 of type $inc3$, after which rd_1 crashes. In Δpr_1, $\mathcal{M}_0 = \{B_0\}$ is malicious and forges its state to σ_k before replying to rd_1.

Observe that at the end of pr_1 and Δpr_1, every correct block is in the same state, except $\mathcal{P}_2$. We refer to the state of B_1 at the end of Δpr_1 as σ_1^r.

Starting from Δpr_1 we iteratively define the following partial runs for $2 \leq l \leq k$ (see Fig. 2). Partial run pr_l extends Δpr_{l-1} by appending the missing steps of a complete read rd_l. In pr_l, superblock $\mathcal{M}_{l-2}$ is malicious and all other blocks are correct. Since rd_l does not receive any messages from $\mathcal{M}_{l-2}$, it completes only on the basis of replies from correct objects (at least $S - t_k$ by equation (1)). At the end of pr_l, rd_l completes and returns value x. To show that $x = 1$, we define a partial run $@pr_{l-1}$ which is identical to pr_{l-1} except that in $@pr_{l-1}$ (1) there is no read by r_l and (2) and (in addition to $\mathcal{M}_{l-3}$), superblock $\mathcal{P}_l$ is malicious and forges its state to σ_0^l, simulating the occurrence of rd_l as in pr_{l-1}. The count of malicious objects in $@pr_{l-1}$ is exactly t_k. To see why, notice that by equation (1) and (2) the malicious objects in $@pr_{l-1}$ amount to $|\bigcup \mathcal{P}_l| + |\bigcup \mathcal{M}_{l-3}| = t_k - t_{l-2} + t_{l-2} = t_k$.

Then, partial run pr_l^C extends $@pr_{l-1}$ by appending rd_l. Note that rd_l cannot distinguish pr_l^C from pr_l because superblock $\mathcal{P}_l$, which is malicious in pr_l^C, mimics pr_l. In particular, $\mathcal{P}_l$ forges its state to σ_0 before replying to rd_l's first round and then to σ_{k-l}^* before replying to rd_l's second round. By atomicity, rd_l returns 1 in pr_l^C. Since pr_l^C and pr_l are indistinguishable to reader r_l, $x = 1$.

Next, we define partial run Δpr_l. For $2 \le l < k$, Δpr_l is obtained from pr_l by deleting steps of rd_l, rd_{l-1} and the write (see Fig. 2 (c) and (e)). In Δpr_l, superblock $\mathcal{M}_{l-1}$ is malicious, all other block are correct, and blocks $\{B_{l-1}, C_{l-1}\} \in \mathcal{M}_{l-1}$ forge their state to σ_j^r before replying to rd_l.[5] In more detail, Δpr_l extends wr^{k-l-1} by appending the missing steps (1) of incomplete reads $rd_1, \ldots, rd_{l-1}$ of type $inc2$, and (2) of an incomplete rd_l of type $inc3$. B_0 forges its state to σ_k before replying to rd_1 and for $1 \le j \le l-1$, $\{B_j, C_j\}$ forge their state to σ_j^r before replying to rd_{j+1}. Observe that at the end of pr_l and Δpr_l, every correct block is in the same state, except $\mathcal{P}_{l+1}$. We refer to the state of $\{B_l, C_l\}$ at the end of Δpr_1 as σ_l^r.

Finally, partial run Δpr_k is obtained analogously from pr_k, except that in Δpr_k, (a) no write is invoked and (b) read rd_k is complete and skips $\mathcal{M}_{k-2} \cup \mathcal{P}_{k+1}$ (see Fig. 2 (g) for $k = 4$). In particular, in Δpr_k, $\mathcal{M}_{k-1}$ is malicious and blocks $\{B_{k-1}, C_{k-1}\} \in \mathcal{M}_{k-1}$ forge their state to σ_{k-1}^r before replying to rd_k. By equation (1) the malicious objects amount to $|\bigcup \mathcal{M}_{k-1}| = t_k$. Partial runs pr_k and Δpr_k differ only at $\mathcal{P}_{k+1}$, and rd_k completes without receiving any message from $\mathcal{P}_{k+1}$. Thus, rd_k cannot distinguish Δpr_k from pr_k and returns 1 in Δpr_k, a contradiction, as no write was invoked. □

LEMMA 2. : *If $S \le 3t + 1$ and every read completes in three rounds then no* write *implementation I of a multi-reader (SWMR) atomic register exists that completes in* $\min\{R, \lfloor \log(\lceil(3t + 1)/2\rceil)\rfloor\}$ *rounds.*

PROOF. Let $k = \min\{R, \lfloor \log(\lceil(3t + 1)/2\rceil)\rfloor\}$, i.e., $R \ge k$ and $k \le \lfloor \log(\lceil(3t + 1)/2\rceil)\rfloor$. By Lemma 1, there exists no optimally resilient k-reader atomic register implementation with $t_k = t_{k-1} + 2t_{k-2} + 1$ faulty objects, where the read completes in three rounds and the write completes in k rounds. Observe that this is valid even with $R \ge k$ readers and $t \ge t_k$ faults. Writing t_k in closed form results in $t_k = \frac{1}{6}(2^{k+2} - (-1)^k - 3)$. Thus, we have that $t \ge \frac{1}{6}(2^{k+2} - (-1)^k - 3)$. Solving for k results in $k \le \lfloor \log(\lceil(3t + 1)/2\rceil)\rfloor$. □

Finally, we generalize our result to a resilience of $3t + \lfloor t/t_k \rfloor$ for $t \ge t_k$, proving Proposition 2.

PROOF. Without loss of generality we can assume that $t \ge t_k$ because every implementation is subject to the resilience lower bound of $S \ge 3t + 1$. The observation is that if we multiply each of the blocks in the proof of Lemma 1 with a constant c, then the result holds for $S' = cS = 3ct_k + c$ objects and ct_k faults. By carefully choosing $c = t/t_k$, we obtain a lower bound proof for $S' = 3t + \lfloor t/t_k \rfloor$ and t faults. □

5. CONCLUSION

In this paper, we show that no single-writer multiple-reader (SWMR) robust atomic storage implementation exists if (a) read operations complete in less than *four* communication round-trips (rounds), and (b) the time-complexity of write operations is constant.

However, we observe that a matching implementation can simply be obtained by a) reusing the SWMR regular storage implementation of [15] which features the worst-case time complexity of 2 rounds for both reads and writes, and b) transforming it to the SWMR atomic implementations using a standard SWMR regular – SWMR atomic transformation technique [4, 20].[6] This yields a sought SWMR atomic implementation in which write operations complete in 2 rounds whereas reads complete in 4 rounds.

Furthermore, in the stronger authentication model that allows for secret values [8], regular storage of [15] can be replaced in the above transformation with the corresponding time-optimal regular implementation [8], yielding a 2-round write 3-round read atomic storage, which is optimal in this model. In both models, multi-writer atomic storage can be implemented by applying the standard transformations further [4, 20].

In summary, we present two lower bounds. The first is a read lower bound stating that *three* rounds of communication are necessary to read from a SWMR robust atomic storage. The second is a write lower bound, showing that $\Omega(\log(t))$ write rounds are necessary to read in three rounds from such a storage. Our results close a fundamental gap: we show that time-optimal, 2-round write 4-round read (resp. 3-round read in the secret value model) robust atomic storage can be obtained using well-known transformations from regular to atomic storage and existing time-optimal regular storage implementations.

6. REFERENCES

[1] Ittai Abraham, Gregory Chockler, Idit Keidar, and Dahlia Malkhi. Byzantine disk paxos: optimal resilience with byzantine shared memory. *Distributed Computing*, 18(5):387–408, 2006.

[2] Amitanand S. Aiyer, Lorenzo Alvisi, and Rida A. Bazzi. Bounded wait-free implementation of optimally resilient byzantine storage without (unproven) cryptographic assumptions. In *Proceedings of the 21st International Symposium on Distributed Computing*, pages 7–19, September 2007.

---

[5]The states are different and are indexed by the object's id, which for simplicity of presentation is made implicit.

---

[6]In short, this transformation employs $R + 1$ regular registers, one dedicated to the writer and R additional ones, one per reader, in which a given reader writes back the read value.

[3] Hagit Attiya, Amotz Bar-Noy, and Danny Dolev. Sharing memory robustly in message-passing systems. *Journal of the ACM*, 42(1):124–142, 1995.

[4] Hagit Attiya and Jennifer Welch. *Distributed Computing. Fundamentals, Simulations, and Advanced Topics.* McGraw-Hill, 1998.

[5] AWS Simple Storage Service. http://aws.amazon.com/s3/.

[6] Christian Cachin, Idit Keidar, and Alexander Shraer. Trusting the cloud. *SIGACT News*, 40(2):81–86, 2009.

[7] Dan Dobre, Rachid Guerraoui, Matthias Majuntke, Neeraj Suri, and Marko Vukolić. The Complexity of Robust Atomic Storage. Technical Report TR-TUD-DEEDS-06-01-2010, 2010.

[8] Dan Dobre, Matthias Majuntke, Marco Serafini, and Neeraj Suri. Efficient robust storage using secret tokens. In *Proceedings of the 11th International Symposium on Stabilization, Safety, and Security of Distributed Systems*, pages 269–283, 2009.

[9] Partha Dutta, Rachid Guerraoui, Ron R. Levy, and Arindam Chakraborty. How fast can a distributed atomic read be? In *Proceedings of the 23rd annual ACM symposium on Principles of distributed computing*, pages 236–245, July 2004.

[10] Partha Dutta, Rachid Guerraoui, Ron R. Levy, and Marko Vukolic. Fast access to distributed atomic memory. *SIAM J. Comput.*, 39(8):3752–3783, 2010.

[11] Burkhard Englert, Chryssis Georgiou, Peter M. Musial, Nicolas C. Nicolaou, and Alexander A. Shvartsman. On the efficiency of atomic multi-reader, multi-writer distributed memory. In *Proceedings of the 13th International Conference on Principles of Distributed Systems*, pages 240–254, 2009.

[12] Rui Fan and Nancy Lynch. Efficient replication of large data objects. In *Proceedings of the 17th International Symposium on Distributed Computing*, pages 75–91, October 2003.

[13] Chryssis Georgiou, Nicolas C. Nicolaou, and Alexander A. Shvartsman. Fault-tolerant semifast implementations of atomic read/write registers. *J. Parallel Distrib. Comput.*, 69(1):62–79, 2009.

[14] Rachid Guerraoui, Ron R. Levy, and Marko Vukolić. Lucky read/write access to robust atomic storage. In *Proceedings of the International Conference on Dependable Systems and Networks*, pages 125–136, 2006.

[15] Rachid Guerraoui and Marko Vukolić. How fast can a very robust read be? In *Proceedings of the twenty-fifth annual ACM symposium on Principles of distributed computing*, pages 248–257, New York, NY, USA, 2006. ACM.

[16] Rachid Guerraoui and Marko Vukolić. Refined quorum systems. In *Proceedings of the twenty-sixth annual ACM symposium on Principles of distributed computing*, pages 119–128, 2007.

[17] Maurice Herlihy. Wait-free synchronization. *ACM Transactions on Programming Languages and Systems*, 13(1):124–149, January 1991.

[18] Leslie Lamport. On interprocess communication. *Distributed computing*, 1(1):77–101, May 1986.

[19] Leslie Lamport, Robert E. Shostak, and Marshall C. Pease. The Byzantine generals problem. *ACM Transactions on Programming Languages and Systems*, 4(3):382–401, 1982.

[20] Nancy A. Lynch. *Distributed Algorithms.* Morgan-Kaufmann, 1996.

[21] Nancy A. Lynch and Mark R.Tuttle. An introduction to input/output automata. *CWI Quarterly*, 2(3):219–246, 1989.

[22] Nancy A. Lynch and Alexander A. Shvartsman. Rambo: A reconfigurable atomic memory service for dynamic networks. In *Proceedings of the 16th International Conference on Distributed Computing*, pages 173–190, London, UK, 2002. Springer-Verlag.

[23] Jean-Philippe Martin, Lorenzo Alvisi, and Michael Dahlin. Minimal Byzantine storage. In *Proceedings of the 16th International Conference on Distributed Computing*, pages 311–325, October 2002.

[24] Yasushi Saito, Svend Frolund, Alistair Veitch, Arif Merchant, and Susan Spence. Fab: building distributed enterprise disk arrays from commodity components. *SIGOPS Oper. Syst. Rev.*, 38(5):48–58, 2004.

[25] Frank Schmuck and Roger Haskin. GPFS: A shared-disk file system for large computing clusters. In *Proceedings of the 1st USENIX Conference on File and Storage Technologies*, pages 231–244, Berkeley, CA, USA, 2002. USENIX Association.

[26] Philip M. Thambidurai and You-Keun Park. Interactive consistency with multiple failure modes. In *Symposium on Reliable Distributed Systems*, pages 93–100, 1988.

Resilience of Mutual Exclusion Algorithms to Transient Memory Faults

Thomas Moscibroda
Microsoft Research
Redmond, WA
moscitho@microsoft.com

Rotem Oshman
Computer Science and AI Laboratory, MIT
Cambridge, MA
rotem@mit.edu

ABSTRACT

We study the behavior of mutual exclusion algorithms in the presence of unreliable shared memory subject to transient memory faults. It is well-known that classical 2-process mutual exclusion algorithms, such as Dekker and Peterson's algorithms, are not fault-tolerant; in this paper we ask what degree of fault tolerance can be achieved using the same restricted resources as Dekker and Peterson's algorithms, namely, three binary read/write registers.

We show that if one memory fault can occur, it is not possible to guarantee both mutual exclusion and deadlock-freedom using three binary registers; this holds in general when fewer than $2f + 1$ binary registers are used and f may be faulty. Hence we focus on algorithms that guarantee (a) mutual exclusion and starvation-freedom in fault-free executions, and (b) only mutual exclusion in faulty executions. We show that using only three binary registers it is possible to design an 2-process mutual exclusion algorithm which tolerates a single memory fault in this manner. Further, by replacing one read/write register with a test&set register, we can guarantee mutual exclusion in executions where one variable experiences unboundedly many faults.

In the more general setting where up to f registers may be faulty, we show that it is not possible to guarantee mutual exclusion using $2f + 1$ binary read/write registers if each faulty register can exhibit unboundedly many faults. On the positive side, we show that an n-variable single-fault tolerant algorithm satisfying certain conditions can be transformed into an $((n - 1)f + 1)$-variable f-fault tolerant algorithm with the same progress guarantee as the original. In combination with our three-variable algorithm, this implies that there is a $(2f + 1)$-variable mutual exclusion algorithm tolerating a single fault in up to f variables without violating mutual exclusion.

Categories and Subject Descriptors:

D.4.1 [Operating Systems]: Process Management–*mutual exclusion*

D.4.5 [Operating Systems]: Reliability–*fault tolerance*

General Terms: Algorithms, Theory

Keywords: mutual exclusion, fault tolerance, transient memory faults

1. INTRODUCTION

Mutual exclusion is among the most important and well-studied problems in distributed computing. It is used in concurrent programming to avoid the simultaneous use of shared data structures by pieces of computer code called critical sections. In a shared memory environment, synchronization among processes trying to access a critical section is achieved via a small set of shared variables that can be accessed by the processes. Existing mutual exclusion algorithms are based on the underlying assumption that these shared variables are reliable: if a process sets a shared variable to a certain value x, any subsequent read access to the variable will return x, until some other process overwrites the value.

In this paper we study the implications of relaxing this assumption, and consider mutual exclusion algorithms in the presence of unreliable shared memory. Our motivation for this relaxation is the observation that due to faster clock rates, increasing on-chip transistor density, decreasing voltages and smaller hardware feature sizes, the likelihood of encountering *transient memory faults* is non-negligible in today's computer systems, and is bound to rapidly increase in future systems. A transient memory fault, also known as a *soft error*, is a temporary hardware failure that alters a signal transfer, a register value, or some other processor component. Transient faults can occur due to many reasons; there are several recent examples where they have caused substantial reliability problems, leading to costly failures in industrial high-end systems.

In the context of mutual exclusion algorithms, the possibility of sudden changes to shared memory variables is particularly problematic, since it could result in a violation of the mutual exclusion property. Indeed, none of the well-known existing mutual exclusion algorithms (e.g., Dekker's algorithm, Peterson's algorithm, or Lamport's Bakery algorithm) is designed to be *resilient* to transient faults. Each of these algorithms may fail to maintain mutual exclusion if a shared variable used for communication among the processes suddenly changes. In fact, this holds even when processes always execute the entry and exit sections of the mutual exclusion algorithms all by themselves (that is, no other process can take steps when some process is in the entry or exit section).

Motivated by these observations, this paper investigates the extent to which 2-process mutual exclusion algorithms can withstand transient memory faults. The paper is divided into three parts. In the first part (Section 4) we give a basic characterization of fault-resilient 2-process mutual exclusion algorithms. One basic observation is that any f-fault-resilient 2-process mutual exclusion algorithm must satisfy the following structural property: when a process p_i executes the critical section by itself while the other process is in the remainder, p_i must change $f + 1$ shared variables before it enters the critical section. We use this observation to show that any algorithm that uses $2f + 1$ binary read/write registers must exhibit either deadlock or mutual exclusion violation in f-fault executions.

In the second part of the paper (Sections 5–7), we show that a certain level of fault-resilience to transient faults comes "for free". We present a new starvation-free algorithm that, like Dekker's or Peterson's algorithms, uses three binary read/write shared variables; unlike Dekker and Peterson's algorithm, our algorithm guarantees mutual exclusion even in the presence of a single memory fault. The algorithm only guarantees progress in fault-free executions; it may deadlock in executions where memory faults occur. However, given the above impossibility result, this is in some sense the best one can do. Given the choice between guaranteeing mutual exclusion or guaranteeing deadlock-freedom in faulty executions, we choose the former in this paper. This seems to be the more natural choice in the context of mutual exclusion algorithms, and in many systems, deadlocks are arguably easier to detect and break, and their consequences less severe than mutual exclusion violations.

In fact, this is the best we can do in more than one sense. In Section 6 we prove a lower bound showing that $2f + 1$ binary variables are not sufficient to guarantee mutual exclusion when f of the variables can experience unboundedly many faults. Translated to the 3 variable case, this implies that no algorithm that uses 3 binary read/write registers can tolerate a single "Byzantine variable" which can flip unboundedly many times.

Given this gap, it is natural to ask if there is some relaxation of the model that would allow us to achieve unbounded fault-resilience. In Section 7, we give an answer to this question, by presenting a mutual exclusion algorithm which uses test&set register instead of one of the read/write registers, and is able to withstand unbounded faults to one variable. Both this and the above algorithm are non-trivial, and their structure is quite different from that of existing mutual exclusion algorithms.

One reason we are interested in understanding the possibilities and limitations of fault-resilience in the 3-variable, 1-fault setting is that these results have implications for the ratio of faulty variables that can be tolerated in general. It is reasonable to expect that the number of faults will increase with the amount of memory used, and hence this ratio is interesting to study. In the third part of the paper (Section 8), we show that our results for the 3-variable case imply more general results for m-variable algorithms tolerating f faults. We show that using $(n - 1)f + 1$ variables, of which f can be faulty, one can simulate a "well-behaved" n-variable algorithm that tolerates one fault. "Well-behaved" here means that the algorithm contains no data races, and that if one process attempts to read from a variable, the other process eventually stops writing to it. This property, which is satisfied by many existing mutual exclusion algorithms (including Dekker's algorithm and the algorithms we present in this paper), allows us to use a simple and lightweight simulation of n variables with one faulty variable from $(n-1)f+1$ variables of which f can be faulty. In conjunction with the 3-variable algorithm from Section 5, this implies the existence of a mutual exclusion algorithm using $2f + 1$ variables and tolerating f faulty variables, each of which can flip once. Moreover, the same simulation can be used to transform Dekker's algorithm into a $3(f + 1)$-variable algorithm tolerating f "Byzantine" faulty variables, which can each flip unboundedly many times.

Due to lack of space, the full proofs for some of the claims in the paper are omitted here. The algorithms presented in Sections 5 and 7 were model-checked using the NuSMV2 finite-state model checker (in addition to a manual proof of correctness), to verify both starvation-freedom in fault-free executions and mutual exclusion in faulty executions.

2. BACKGROUND & RELATED WORK

Transient faults. Transient faults (or "soft errors") can occur in different parts of the hardware stack in a computer system, and arise for various reasons, such as energetic particles that strike a transistor and cause it to change its state. In memory, for instance, alpha particles emitted by traces of radioactive elements present in the packaging materials of the device can penetrate the die and generate a high density of holes and electrons in its substrate, thereby creating an imbalance in the electrical potential distribution and causing stored data to be corrupted. A single alpha particle that possesses enough energy can cause a soft error all by itself. Transient faults are usually random and non-recurring, and their rate of occurrence depends on circuit sensitivity and the alpha flux emitted by the device. Such faults have led to costly failures in high-end systems in recent years. For example, they are known to have caused crashes at Sun's major customer sites including America Online and eBay [4], and HP's Los Alamos Labs supercomputers [21].

Unfortunately, while transient errors already cause substantial reliability problems, current trends in hardware design suggest that fault rates will further increase in the future. Faster clock rates, increasing transistor density, decreasing voltages and smaller feature sizes all contribute to increasing fault rates, e.g. [3, 22]. In fact, fault rates in modern processors have been increasing at a rate of approximately 8% per generation [5]. To counter soft errors, computer architects and compiler researchers have proposed various solutions, which usually involve adding redundancy to computations in one way or another. For instance, there are proposals involving hardware-only solutions such as error-correcting codes, watchdog co-processors or redundant hardware threads (e.g. [16, 17]) as well as software-only techniques that use both single and multiple cores (e.g. [20, 18]). These solutions are typically "heavy-weight" and quite costly in terms of memory and performance.

Resilient algorithms. In the area of algorithms, designing resilient algorithms for unreliable memories has also attracted interest. Problems such as fault-resilient selection, sorting, and matrix computations in various failure models have attracted a lot of interest in recent years (see [10] for a survey). Faulty memory has also been studied in multiprocessors. There is significant research in the parallel computing literature devoted to deliver general simulation mechanisms of fully operational parallel machines on their faulty counterparts, e.g. [7, 8].

Fault-tolerant simulations. In the shared memory distributed computing literature, the problem of implementing fault-tolerant registers (and other objects) from faulty objects under various fault models was studied, e.g. in [1, 2, 13]. With regard to our simulation in Section 8, the most relevant results are the ones given in [1] and [13] on implementing various read/write registers from faulty registers in the arbitrary, responsive failure mode.[1] For example, in combination with earlier work [19, 24], it is shown that one *safe* read/write register can be implemented from $2f + 1$ safe faulty registers, and one *atomic* read/write register using $6f + 3$ ($8f + 4$) safe registers and $24f + 12$ ($16f + 8$) safe binary registers, respectively, if the f faulty registers can have infinitely many faults. A relevant result from [1] shows that one reliable atomic register can be implemented from $20f + 8$ atomic registers if at most f are faulty. In our context, however, the simulation in Section 8 serves a different purpose; we do not seek to mask faults completely, as the high-level

---

[1] Much better results are known for more benign failure modes, e.g. [13, 11]

mutual exclusion algorithm that uses the objects can tolerate some degree of faulty behavior. Instead, we seek to reduce f faults to a single fault, which can then be handled by the algorithm. Together with the fact that we make assumptions about the behavior of the algorithm and do not require liveness in faulty executions, this allows us to get away with a very lightweight simulation, where $2f + 1$ low-level registers simulate three high-level registers of which at most one is faulty.

Fault-tolerant mutual exclusion. The issue of fault-tolerance in mutual exclusion algorithms was one of the principal themes of Lamport's paper on non-atomic algorithms [14]. Several failure models are considered. Among many other malfunctions, one failure type studied are transient faults, which allows arbitrary changes to the shared memory (and local) variables of the algorithm. A mutual exclusion algorithm tolerating all these types of failures was presented in [25], but it required 17 binary shared variables. This was subsequently improved to 8 binary variables for 2-process mutual exclusion in [23]. These algorithms require more shared variables than the algorithms we present here, but they do not deadlock in faulty executions.

3. MODEL & DEFINITIONS

Mutual exclusion algorithms. We represent a 2-process mutual exclusion algorithm as follows. Let PC_0, PC_1 be the control locations (code lines) for processes 0 and 1 respectively, and let Var be the set of shared variables (in the current paper we assume that the shared variables are binary). We assume that PC_0, PC_1 each include two distinguished locations N, C, representing the remainder and the critical section, respectively. [2]

A *configuration* of the algorithm is a triplet $(\ell_0, \ell_1, \bar{v})$, where $\ell_0 \in PC_0$ and $\ell_1 \in PC_1$ are the control locations of p_0 and p_1 respectively, and $\bar{v} \in 2^{Var}$ represents the state of the shared variables Var. A *step* of the algorithm is a transition from one global configuration to another, in which some process p_i executes either a $\mathsf{read}(x)$ or a $\mathsf{write}(x, v)$ operation on some shared variable x, and transitions to a new control location. If the control location of a process is N or C, it can also take null-transitions, in which its location and the values in shared memory do not change.

An *execution* of the algorithm is a sequence $\sigma_0 \sigma_1 \ldots$ of configurations, starting from the initial configuration σ_0, in which each configuration is obtained from the previous configuration by either a step of p_0 or p_1, or by a *memory fault*, in which the value of some shared variable $x \in Var$ changes from 0 to 1 or vice-versa. In an (f, c)-*fault execution*, at most f shared variables experience at most c memory faults each; in a *fault-free execution* there are no memory faults. We are concerned only with *admissible* executions, in which both processes take infinitely many steps. (This includes idle steps in which a process that is currently in the remainder stays in the remainder.)

The algorithms we present in this paper are *starvation-free*: for each process p_i, if p_i begins executing the entry section, then p_i eventually enters the critical section. For our lower bounds we typically assume *deadlock-freedom*, a weaker progress condition which asserts that if some process p_i is in the entry section, then eventually some process (either p_i or p_{1-i}) enters the critical section.

---

[2]For convenience we assume that the algorithm is memoryless, and each process has a single control location that it returns to whenever it goes into the remainder. However, this assumption is not necessary for our lower bounds.

Fault-tolerant mutual exclusion. In the current paper we are concerned with algorithms that guarantee mutual exclusion in the face of memory faults. We say that an algorithm is (f, c)-*resilient* if it guarantees mutual exclusion in (f, c)-fault executions, and deadlock-freedom (or starvation-freedom) in admissible fault-free executions. In the remainder of the paper, when we refer to deadlock- or starvation-freedom, these are restricted to fault-free executions (unless otherwise stated).

Notation and terminology. A *schedule* is a finite sequence $\alpha \in (\{p_0, p_1\} \cup \{\mathsf{flip}(x) \mid x \in Var\})^*$ of process identifiers, interspersed with memory faults $\mathsf{flip}(x)$ in which a variable x changes its value. A schedule is p_i-*only* if it does not contain any steps of p_{1-i}. We use $exec(\sigma, \alpha)$ to denote the execution fragment obtained by letting the system take the steps in α starting from configuration σ, and we use $config(\sigma, \alpha)$ to denote the final configuration reached in $exec(\sigma, \alpha)$.

A common lower bound technique is to maneuver the system into a configuration σ where the next step of some process p_i is to write to a register x, obliterating whatever value was stored there previously. In this case we say that p_i *covers* x in σ.

A configuration $\sigma = (\ell_0, \ell_1, \bar{v})$ is *indistinguishable to* p_i from $\sigma' = (\ell'_0, \ell'_1, \bar{v}')$, denoted $\sigma \sim_{p_i} \sigma'$, if $\ell_i = \ell'_i$ and $\bar{v} = \bar{v}'$. It can be shown by induction on the length of the schedule that if $\sigma \sim_{p_i} \sigma'$, then for any p_i-only schedule α we also have $config(\sigma, \alpha) \sim_{p_i} config(\sigma', \alpha)$.

4. BASIC IMPOSSIBILITY RESULTS

In this section, we derive a set of results that characterize the resilience of mutual exclusion algorithms to a single memory fault. These results have implications throughout the remainder of the paper. We begin by observing that any $(1, 1)$-resilient algorithm must have the following property.

DEFINITION 4.1 (HAMMING DISTANCE 2 PROPERTY, **HD2**). *Suppose that* $\sigma = (\ell_0, \ell_1, \bar{v})$ *and* $\sigma' = (\ell'_0, \ell'_1, \bar{v}')$ *are reachable configurations such that* σ *is an idle configuration* $(\ell_0 = \ell_1 = N)$ *and for some* $i \in \{0, 1\}$, $\ell'_i = C$ *and* $\ell'_{1-i} = N$. *Then the Hamming distance between* $\bar{v}$ *and* $\bar{v}'$ *must be at least 2.*

Algorithms that do not have the **HD2** property can violate mutual exclusion when a single memory fault occurs: if σ and σ' are configurations as in the definition above, whose Hamming distance is smaller than 2, then we can flip a single bit in σ' to obtain a configuration τ that is indistinguishable to p_{1-i} from σ. Since σ is idle, when we let p_{1-i} run by itself from τ (which p_{1-i} cannot distinguish from σ) it must eventually enter the critical section, violating mutual exclusion.

If there are only two shared variables, then in order to satisfy the **HD2** property each process must modify both variables when it executes its entry section by itself; it can be shown that no algorithm can accomplish this.

THEOREM 4.1. *No deadlock-free mutual exclusion algorithm that uses two binary variables can satisfy the **HD2** property.*

This result is similar in spirit to the lower bound of [6], which shows that n shared variables are necessary for n-process mutual exclusion; each process must have a variable that it "owns". Technically, however, the proof of Theorem 4.1 shares very little with the lower bound of [6], because in our case the number of shared variables does match the number of processes. The proof of Theorem 4.1 is quite similar to the proof of Theorem 6.1 in Section 6, and it is omitted here. In general, no f-binary variable mutex algorithm can satisfy the **HD-f** property (the proof is again similar to that of Theorem 6.1).

It follows from Theorem 4.1 that two binary variables cannot be used to guarantee $(1, 1)$-resilience, even if only deadlock-freedom is required, and even in executions where neither process takes steps while the other process is in the entry or exit section. In Section 5 we show that three binary variables suffice to guarantee $(1, 1)$-resilience and starvation-freedom in fault-free executions.

Impossibility of achieving both safety and liveness. Our definition of *resilience* focuses on algorithms that guarantee mutual exclusion, but sacrifice liveness in faulty executions; one might ask whether it is possible to guarantee mutual exclusion *and* deadlock-freedom or even starvation-freedom. Unfortunately, for the case of 3 variables and one fault, the answer is negative. The following theorem shows that in general, when fewer than $2f + 1$ registers are used, liveness in faulty executions comes at the cost of violating mutual exclusion. If starvation-freedom is desired in fault-free executions, then $2f + 1$ registers are also insufficient. This result motivates our definition of resilience. Unlike the other negative results in this paper, the following theorem is not restricted to binary registers, if one assumes that in the multi-valued case a faulty register's value can flip to any other value.

THEOREM 4.2. *Let $\mathcal{A}$ be an m-variable deadlock-free mutual exclusion algorithm. If $m \leq 2f$, or if $m \leq 2f + 1$ and $\mathcal{A}$ is also starvation-free, then $\mathcal{A}$ fails to satisfy either deadlock-freedom or mutual exclusion in some $(f, 1)$-fault execution in which no process takes steps while the other process is in the entry or exit section.*

PROOF. Consider an execution fragment in which starting from the initial configuration σ_0, we let p_0 run solo until it enters the critical section. Let σ_C be the resulting configuration. If $m \leq 2f$, then for any two states $\bar{v}, \bar{v}' \in \{0, 1\}^m$ of the shared memory, there is a third state $\bar{u}$ whose Hamming distance from both $\bar{v}$ and $\bar{v}'$ is at most f. Thus, we can flip no more than f registers from σ_C, and obtain a configuration τ whose Hamming distance from both σ_0 and σ_C is no more than f (see Fig. 1).

Because the Hamming distance of the shared memory in τ from that in σ_0 is no more than f, p_1 cannot distinguish τ from a configuration τ' obtained from σ_0 by flipping no more than f variables. In τ' both processes are idle, so if the algorithm satisfies deadlock-freedom in $(f, 1)$-fault executions where processes are not interleaved in the entry and exit sections, when we let p_1 run by itself from τ' it will eventually enter the critical section. But $\tau \sim_{p_1} \tau'$, so the same is true for τ, and mutual exclusion is violated.

Next, suppose that the algorithm guarantees starvation-freedom in fault-free executions, and $m \leq 2f + 1$. Let σ be a reachable idle configuration such that when p_0 runs by itself from σ, eventually σ occurs again. Then there must exist some register x that p_0 does not write to in its solo run from σ: if there is no such register, then we can let p_1 begin the entry section as well, but each time p_1 covers some register y, we let p_0 run until it covers y as well. Then we let p_1 write to y, followed immediately by p_0. All evidence that p_1 is in the entry section is erased from the shared memory, so p_0 cannot distinguish this execution from the one in which it runs solo from σ. Continuing in this manner, we can construct an infinite admissible execution in which p_1 remains in the entry section forever. Thus there must be some register to which p_0 does not write.

Since $m \leq 2f + 1$, p_0 writes to at most $2f$ registers when it runs solo from σ. We can repeat the argument we used for $m \leq 2f$ to show again that either deadlock-freedom or mutual exclusion must

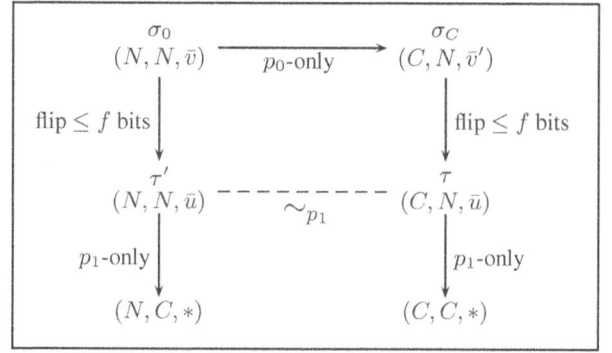

Figure 1: Illustration for the proof of Thm. 4.2

be violated in some $(f, 1)$-fault execution where process steps are not interleaved when a process is in the entry or exit section. □

5. A (1,1)-RESILIENT THREE-VARIABLE ALGORITHM

In this section we give a starvation-free mutex algorithm, Algorithm HANDSHAKE, that uses three binary read/write registers and guarantees mutual exclusion in the face of one memory fault. The algorithm satisfies the Hamming Distance 2 property: when a process executes the entry section solo, it sets two of the shared variables to 1.

As in the Peterson and Dekker algorithms, two of the shared variables, c_0 and c_1, serve as flags indicating whether p_0 and p_1 are active. However, the function of the third variable is different. The Peterson and Dekker algorithms achieve starvation-freedom by using the third shared variable as a "turn variable", but the Hamming Distance 2 property precludes this strategy; the third variable must now be used more like a *lock*: processes set it to 1 when they enter the critical section by themselves and reset it to 0 when they leave. Thus, if process p_i executes its entry section by itself, before it enters the ciritical section it sets both its flag c_i and the third variable *lock* to 1, protecting itself by two bits in case of a single memory fault. We use a different mechanism to guarantee fairness.

One major difficulty a $(1, 1)$-resilient algorithm must face is the following. Suppose that the two processes begin executing their entry section in lockstep, until the first time they write to the shared memory. Assume they write to different variables (as eventually they must); now the state of the shared memory is 110. Both processes are in the entry section, but neither process can distinguish this configuration from the one in which the other process is in the critical section and the third variable (*lock*) has flipped to 0. Therefore neither process can enter the critical section until it has verified that the other process is not in the critical section, by interacting with the other process in a sequence of reads and writes that we call a *handshake*. The handshake is designed so that even if a memory fault occurs, a process can never reach the end of the handshake if the other process is in the critical section. This is achieved by having each process p_i go through a sequence of writes to shared memory, leaving a unique footprint in shared memory that is never encountered elsewhere in the algorithm; in particular, it cannot be "faked" by the adversary using a memory fault, or by having p_i go in and out of the critical section.

The handshake comprises lines 008–010 for p_0 and lines 104–106 for p_1. At the end of the handshake, p_0 enters the critical section, and p_1 waits in line 107 for a signal from p_0. When p_0

Algorithm HANDSHAKE: code for process 0

```
001  c_0 := 1
002  wait until lock = 0
003  while c_1 = 1 do
004   |  if c_0 = 0 then goto 009
005  lock := 1
006  if c_1 = 1 then
007   |  lock := 0
008   |  wait until c_0 = 0
009   |  c_0 := 1
010   |  wait until c_1 = 0
         (enter critical section)
011   |  c_0 := 0
012   |  c_1 := 1
013   |  lock := 1
014  else
015   |  if c_0 = 0 then // A fault occurred
016   |   |  lock := 0
017   |   |  goto 002
         (enter critical section)
018   |  c_0 := 0
019   |  lock := 0
```

Algorithm HANDSHAKE: code for process 1

```
101  c_1 := 1
102  wait until lock = 0
103  if c_0 = 1 then
104   |  c_0 := 0
105   |  wait until c_0 = 1
106   |  c_1 := 0
107   |  wait until c_1 = 1
108   |  wait until lock = 1
109  else
110   |  lock := 1
111   |  if c_0 = 1 then
112   |   |  lock := 0
113   |   |  goto 104
114   |  if c_1 = 0 then // A fault occurred
115   |   |  lock := 0
116   |   |  goto 102
         (enter critical section)
117  lock := 0
118  c_1 := 0
```

exits the critical section, it hands the critical section over to p_1 by setting both c_1 and $lock$ to 1. Notice that (a) p_1 must observe both c_1 and $lock$ change to 1 in order to enter the critical section, so that a single memory fault cannot cause it to enter; and (b) we achieve starvation-freedom, because whenever p_0 and p_1 contend in the entry section, eventually both processes enter the critical section.

The overall strategy for both processes is as follows:

(1) Set the flag, c_i (lines 001 and 101).

(2) Check if the other process is present (lines 003 and 103), and if so, try to engage in a handshake with it.

(3) If the other process is not around, set $lock$ (lines 005, 110).

(4) Check again if the other process is present (lines 006, 111) if so, release $lock$ and engage in a handshake.

(5) If the other process is still not around, enter the critical section.

The reason we require (4) is that if p_{1-i} begins the entry section when p_i is executing (2) or (3), p_{1-i} may see either $lock = 0$ or $lock = 1$ when it executes its second line (line 002 or 102), depending on the specific interleaving of process steps. If $lock = 1$, then p_{1-i} becomes stuck in the second line; if $lock = 0$ then p_{1-i} falls through the second line and attempts to participate in a handshake. Significantly, p_i cannot tell what p_{1-i} saw when it checked $lock$. Thus, to make sure that p_{1-i} does not get stuck waiting for a handshake that is never reciprocated, p_i releases $lock$, allowing p_{1-i} to fall through the second line (if it has not done so already). Then both processes engage in a handshake.

There are a few subtleties beyond this basic pattern. First, note that p_0 does not necessarily engage in a handshake if it sees $c_1 = 1$ in line 003 (it can fall through to line 005), but p_1 always executes a handshake if it sees $c_0 = 1$ in line 103. This ties in to the different order of writes in the processes' exit sections, lines 018–019 and 117–118: when p_0 exits, it releases first its flag and then $lock$, whereas p_1 releases $lock$ first and then c_1.

Informally, we want p_0 to release $lock$ last to make sure that p_1 cannot get past line 102 until p_0 has finished the exit section, otherwise the sequence "observe $c_0 = 1$, set $c_0 := 0$, observe $c_0 = 1$", which gets p_1 through lines 103–105, can also be created by p_0 being in the exit section (having already released $lock$) and later beginning the entry section again and setting $c_0 := 1$. That creates mis-coordination from which the algorithm cannot recover. On the other hand, if p_1 were to set $lock$ to 0 after it sets c_1 to 0, then we would have a dangerous situation in which p_1 has already set c_1 to 0, erasing this evidence of its presence, and is covering $lock$, about to write 0. If c_0 experiences a memory fault and flips to 0, this situation can arise when p_0 is in the entry section, has already set $lock$, and believes that it is protected by both $c_0 = 1$ and $lock = 1$. But when we let p_1 take its next step, it writes 0 to $lock$, erasing all evidence of p_0's presence and freeing p_1 to enter the critical section even though p_0 is already critical. Consequently we must ensure that whenever p_1 is about to set $lock$ to 0, we allow p_0 to see that this may be the case by having $c_1 = 1$.

As a consequence of the different write order, when p_0 sees $c_1 = 1$ in line 003, there are two cases: either p_1 is in the entry section (but has either not set $lock$ yet, or has set $lock$ and later released it), or p_1 is in the exit section, about to execute line 118. Thus, p_0 waits to see what p_1 does: if p_1 sets c_0 to 0 then it is in the entry section and wants to execute a handshake, and if p_1 sets c_1 to 0 then it is in the exit section. In this last case p_0 continues as though it never saw $c_1 = 1$ when it executed line 003. As for p_1, because it cannot get past line 102 (where it waits to see $lock = 0$) until p_0 has finished the exit section and gone into the remainder, if p_1 sees $c_0 = 1$ in line 103 then there is only one possibility: p_0 is in the entry section and will engage in a handshake.

Finally, when the processes believe they are about to enter the critical section uncontended (line 015 for p_0 and line 114 for p_1), they perform one final test, which is to check that their own flag c_i has not flipped after they set it in the first line of the entry section. If the test succeeds, it guarantees that the process has managed to secure both c_i and $lock$ before the other process started its entry section, so that if one of the two variables were to flip, the other variable would remain non-faulty and block the other process from entering the critical section. If the test fails, then a memory fault has occurred; the process releases $lock$ and starts the entry section from the beginning.

THEOREM 5.1. *There is a two-process* $(1,1)$-*resilient mutual exclusion algorithm that uses three binary read/write registers, and guarantees starvation-freedom in fault-free executions.*

The correctness proof of algorithm HANDSHAKE is quite tedious, and we do not include it here. In addition to the manual proof, the NuSMV2 model-checker was used to verify that the algorithm is starvation-free and $(1,1)$-resilient.

6. IMPOSSIBILITY OF (f, ∞)-RESILIENCE WITH $2f + 1$ REGISTERS

We have shown that using three binary registers it is possible to achieve $(1,1)$-resilience; next we show that it is not possible to guarantee $(1, \infty)$-resilience using three variables. More generally, we show that no algorithm using $2f + 1$ binary registers can be (f, ∞)-resilient.

We begin by giving a characterization of f-resilience that is similar to the **HD2** property defined in Section 4; we show that in a $(f, 1)$-resilient algorithm, each process must use $f + 1$ variables to protect itself whenever it enters the critical section. These variables must be written when the process enters the critical section by itself, and restored to their initial value when the process exits the critical section by itself.

DEFINITION 6.1 (FLAG REGISTERS). *We say that register* x *is a* flag register *for* p_i *in* σ *if*

(a) σ *is an idle configuration,*

(b) *When* p_i *runs by itself from* σ *in a fault-free execution it eventually writes both 0 and 1 to* x, *and*

(c) *When* p_i *runs by itself from* σ *in a fault-free execution, the system eventually returns to configuration* σ.

As with the HD2 property we saw in Section 4, in any algorithm that tolerates f faulty variables (even restricted to a single fault in each variable), each process that enters the critical section by itself must protect itself by $f + 1$ bits.

LEMMA 6.1. *In any* $(f, 1)$-*resilient algorithm, for each process* p_i *there is an idle configuration* σ *that is reachable in a fault-free execution, such that* p_i *has at least* $f + 1$ *flag registers in* σ.

PROOF. From any idle configuration σ, if we let p_i run by itself until it enters the critical section, it must change the values of at least $f + 1$ shared registers; otherwise, once p_i enters the critical section, we could flip the values of all shared registers that p_i modifies back to their values in σ, and obtain a configuration σ'_C that is indistinguishable to p_{1-i} from σ. If we let p_{1-i} run by itself from σ'_C, it must eventually enter the critical section (as it would from σ), violating mutual exclusion.

Since there are only finitely many configurations, there exists an idle configuration σ, reachable by a fault-free execution fragment, such that if we let p_i run by itself in a fault-free execution from σ then eventually configuration σ occurs again. But p_i changes the values of at least $f + 1$ registers from their values in σ on its way into the critical section, and when we return to σ these registers have returned to their values in σ. Therefore p_i must write both 0 and 1 to each of these $f + 1$ registers at some point in its solo run from σ before σ occurs again. $\square$

THEOREM 6.1. *No 2-process mutex algorithm using* $2f + 1$ *binary read/write registers is* (f, ∞)-*resilient.*

PROOF. Suppose for the sake of contradiction that an (f, ∞)-resilient algorithm that uses at most $2f + 1$ registers does exist.

Let σ be the idle configuration whose existence is guaranteed by Lemma 6.1, such that p_1 has at least $f + 1$ flag registers in σ. Let Y denote the set of p_1's flag registers in σ.

If we let p_0 run solo from σ it must eventually enter the critical section. Let $\ell_0 \ell_1 \ldots \ell_m \in PC_0^*$, where $\ell_0 = N$ and $\ell_m = C$, be the sequence of control locations that p_0 passes through on its way into the critical section in a solo run from σ. We show by induction on k that for all $0 \le k \le m$, there is a configuration σ_k such that

(a) In σ_k we have $pc_0 = \ell_k$,

(b) σ_k is reachable from σ in an execution fragment where all the register in Y are non-faulty, and

(c) $\sigma_k \sim_{p_1} \sigma$.

In other words, we can "sneak p_0 into the critical section" step by step, without p_1 being able to distinguish any step from the idle configuration σ. The contradiction follows immediately.

The base of the induction is $k = 0$, for which the claim holds trivially. For the step, suppose that we have already shown that there is a reachable configuration σ_k in which $pc_0 = \ell_k$ and such that $\sigma_k \sim_{p_1} \sigma$. Consider the step that p_0 takes to reach location ℓ_{k+1} from location ℓ_k. We will show that this step can be simulated by an execution fragment from σ_k in which we do not corrupt any register in Y (see Fig. 2 for an illustration).

There are two types of steps that p_0 can take. The first is a write; this operation has no return value, and control always passes to ℓ_{k+1} (i.e., the code does not branch at ℓ_k). In this case we must ensure that p_1 does not observe p_0's write. On the other hand, p_0 can execute a read operation, and then branch on the result. In this case we must ensure that the value p_0 reads is the "right" value, the one that will cause it to reach ℓ_{k+1}.

Let us first handle the cases where p_0 accesses a variable $x \notin Y$, which we are allowed to corrupt. If the step is a read(x) step which is expected to return v, then we simulate the step by flipping x to v (if its value is not already v), letting p_0 take its read step, and flipping x back to its previous value. Similarly, if the step is a write(x, v), then we let p_0 take the step, and flip x back to its previous value before the write. Let σ_{k+1} be the resulting configuration. In both cases the values in shared memory are the same in σ_k and in σ_{k+1}, and p_1 does not take any steps between σ_k and σ_{k+1}, so $\sigma_{k+1} \sim_{p_1} \sigma_k \sim \sigma$.

Now suppose that some variable $y \in Y$ is accessed. If the step is a read(y) step expected to return v, then we simulate the step as follows. Because y is a flag register of p_1 in σ, we know that there is some p_1-only schedule α such that the last step in $exec(\sigma, \alpha)$ is write(y, v), and there is another p_1-only schedule β such that $config(\sigma, \alpha\beta) = \sigma$ (that is, β returns us to configuration σ). Because $\sigma_k \sim_{p_1} \sigma$, the last step in $exec(\sigma_k, \alpha)$ is also a write(y, v) by p_1. Now we let p_0 take its read(y) step, which returns v, and does not change the shared memory. Because $config(\sigma_k, \alpha) \sim_{p_1} config(\sigma_k, \alpha p_0)$, if we append β to the schedule αp_0, we obtain a configuration σ_{k+1} in which $pc_0 = \ell_{k+1}$, such that $\sigma_{k+1} \sim_{p_1} \sigma$.

Finally, if the step is a write(y, v) such that $y \in Y$, then we proceed as follows. Since y is a flag register of p_1 in σ, there is a p_1-only schedule α such that in $config(\sigma, \alpha)$, p_1 covers y. Since $\sigma_k \sim_{p_1} \sigma$, the same holds for $config(\sigma_k, \alpha)$. Thus, from σ_k, we let p_1 run until it covers y; then we let p_0 take its write(y, v) step, followed by p_1's step, which overwrites y. The resulting configuration σ'_k is indistinguishable to p_1 from $config(\sigma, \alpha p_1)$, so there is some p_1-only schedule β which returns p_1 to σ ($config(\sigma, \alpha p_1 \beta) = \sigma$). We have $config(\sigma_k, \alpha p_0 p_1 \beta) \sim_{p_1} \sigma$, as required.

We have now shown that from σ, which is reachable in a fault-free configuration, there is an execution fragment in which no register in Y is corrupted, and mutual exclusion is violated. Since $|Y| \geq f+1$, the number of faulty variables is at most $2f+1-(f+1) = f$. Hence the algorithm is not (f, ∞)-resilient. $\square$

We remark that the proof of Theorem 6.1 does not extend to registers that can take more than two values. The majority of the proof relies only on the fact that the algorithm must have the **HD-$(f+1)$** property, i.e., any process that enters the critical section uncontended must write to at least $f+1$ registers; this holds for multi-valued registers as well as for binary ones. The one part of the proof that fails is the case in the induction step where p_0 reads a variable $y \in Y$, which we cannot corrupt. In the proof we handle this case by maneuvering p_1 into writing the value that p_0 expects to read from y. In the multi-valued case we cannot do this, as there is no necessity for a process to write all possible values into its flag variables (it still must write at least two different values, but now there can exist values it does not write at any point). In fact, p_0 can detect p_1's presence by writing some unique value which is never written by p_1 into a flag register $y \in Y$. On its way into the critical section (and possibly back out), p_1 must then write some different value into y. If p_0 later checks y again, it can detect that it is not alone, because its value has been overwritten. Thus it is entirely conceivable that an (f, ∞)-resilient algorithm using $2f+1$ multi-valued registers does exist.

7. A $(1, \infty)$-RESILIENT THREE-VARIABLE ALGORITHM USING TEST&SET

As we saw above, there does not exist a $(1, \infty)$-resilient algorithm that uses three binary read/write registers. In particular, Algorithm HANDSHAKE also does not tolerate more than a single fault in any variable. For example, consider an execution where

1. p_0 runs by itself until it enters the critical section.
2. p_1 begins the entry section, and becomes stuck in line 102.
3. The value of c_1 flips from 1 to 0.
4. p_0 exits the critical section and releases $lock$.
5. p_1 progresses to line 105, where it waits for p_0 to begin its part of a handshake by setting c_0 to 1.
6. p_0 starts the entry section again, setting c_0 to 1 in line 001. This is mis-interpreted by p_1 as the start of a handshake.
7. p_0 continues to run until it enters the critical section (recall that c_1 has flipped to 0, so p_0 does not see p_1), and p_1 runs until it reaches the **wait** statement in line 107.
8. The value of c_1 flips from 0 to 1, freeing p_1 to enter the critical section and violate mutual exclusion. (Note that $lock = 1$, because p_0 sets $lock$ in line 005.)

This scenario illustrates two problems that render Algorithm HAND-SHAKE susceptible to multiple faults. First, the processes can "sneak past each other": it is possible for a process p_i to complete its entry section without p_{1-i} noticing that p_i has taken any steps. Indeed, the proof of Theorem 6.1 shows that this is unavoidable if only read/write registers are used. Therefore we replace $lock$ with a test&set register, and have processes test&set $lock$ instead of writing 1 to it. In the original algorithm, both processes set $lock$ during the entry section only when they believe they are about to enter the critical section uncontended; in particular, the value of $lock$ should always be 0 when a process writes 1 to it. Thus, if p_i tries to test&set $lock$ and fails, p_i backs off and re-starts the entry section.

Replacing $lock$ with a test&set register does not resolve the error scenario above, due to a second problem with Algorithm HAND-SHAKE: a change of $lock$ from 0 to 1 is interpreted by p_1 (in line 108) as a signal to enter the critical section. This seems like

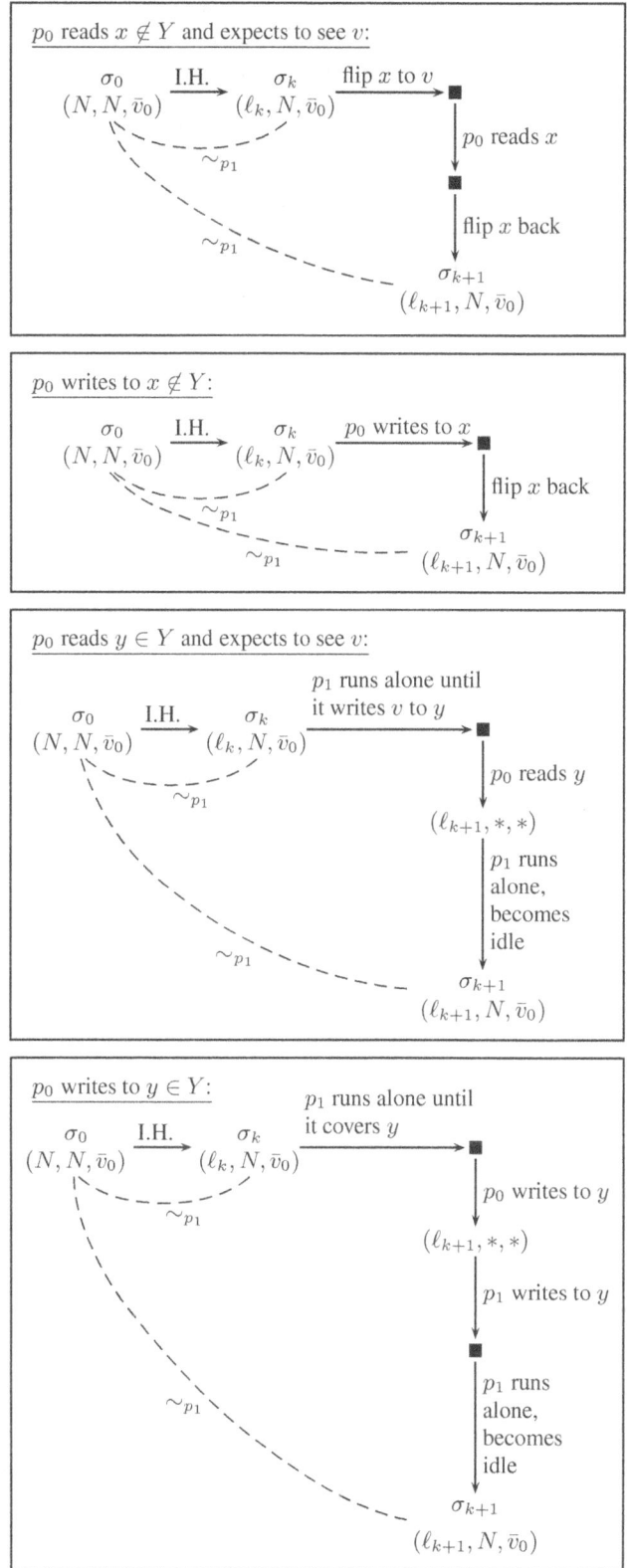

Figure 2: The induction step in the proof of Thm. 6.1. The figures illustrates the four possibilities for the step that p_0 takes to move from location ℓ_k in its code to location ℓ_{k+1}. Here, "I.H." stands for the execution fragment whose existence is guaranteed by the induction hypothesis.

a bad idea, because a value of $lock = 1$ generally indicates that p_0 is interested in the critical section (and may already believe it has secured access to it, as in the trace above). We can get away with it when only one fault is possible; with multiple faults we must be more careful. Thus, we modify the handshake so that p_1 must observe $lock = 0$ before it can enter the critical section.

These changes yield Algorithm T&S-HANDSHAKE, given below. The algorithm incorporates an extended handshake in which p_1 test&sets $lock$ before it enters the critical section. Unfortunately, there is a cost to having p_1 set $lock$ itself instead of waiting for p_0 to do so: we cannot allow p_0 to exit into the remainder until it observes $lock$ change to 1, to ensure that two bits (c_1 and $lock$) witness p_1's presence in the critical section. Hence, replacing one read/write register with a test&set register is not the only price we pay for the extra degree of resilience; the $(1, \infty)$-resilient algorithm also does not have a wait-free exit section.

Finally, the algorithm also incorporates a number of further "sanity checks" in which processes verify that a variable's value has not changed when they were not expecting it to. For example, if the processes execute the entry section without observing the other process's presence, in lines 025 and 119 (respectively) they check that their flag has not been reset since they began the entry section.

THEOREM 7.1. *There is a two-process $(1, \infty)$-resilient mutual exclusion algorithm that uses two binary read/write variables and one test&set variable, and guarantees starvation-freedom in fault-free executions.*

The code uses the test&set(x) atomic instruction. If $x = 0$, the instruction sets x to 1 and returns 1; otherwise x is left unchanged and a value of 0 is returned. We assume that in addition to the test&set operation, test&set registers can be read and written like a read/write register.

8. TRANSFORMING 1-RESILIENCE INTO f-RESILIENCE

So far we have focused on algorithms that tolerate a single faulty variable, using as few variables as possible. We now turn to consider the more general case of f faulty variables. We show that under a certain "well-behavedness" condition on the algorithm, a $(1, c)$-resilient algorithm using n variables (for $c \in \mathbb{N} \cup \{\infty\}$) implies an (f, c)-resilient algorithm using $(n-1)f + 1$ registers. Further, even a non-resilient (but correct) mutual exclusion algorithm that is "well-behaved" can be transformed into an (f, ∞)-resilient using $(f + 1)n$ registers. The property we require of the original 1-resilient or non-resilient algorithm is the following. (The results in this section apply to general m-process mutual exclusion algorithms, but for simplicity we present the results for two processes.)

DEFINITION 8.1 (BOUNDED INTERFERENCE). *An algorithm is said to have the* bounded-interference *property if in all configurations reachable in a fault-free execution,*

(a) *Both processes never cover the same register, and*

(b) *If one process p_i is about to read from a register x_i, then the other process p_{1-i} can only write to x_i a bounded number of times before p_i executes its read.*

Many mutual exclusion algorithms (e.g., Dekker and Burns' algorithms) enjoy the bounded-interference property; however, not all do. For example, Peterson's algorithm and Lamport's fast mutual exclusion algorithm both contain a data race, violating requirement (a). We are not aware of examples in which requirement (b) is violated. The algorithms we present in this paper do have bounded

---

Algorithm T&S-HANDSHAKE: code for process 0

```
001  c₀ := 1
002  wait until lock = 0
003  while c₁ = 1 do
004  │  if c₀ = 0 then goto 010
005  if test&set(lock) = 0 then
006  │  goto 001
007  if c₁ = 1 then
008  │  lock := 0
009  │  wait until c₀ = 0
010  │  c₀ := 1
011  │  wait until c₁ = 0
012  │  if test&set(lock) = 0 then
013  │  │  goto 001
014  │  if c₀ = 0 then
015  │  │  lock := 0
016  │  │  goto 002
017  │  if c₁ = 1 then
018  │  │  lock := 0
019  │  │  goto 002
     │  (enter critical section)
020  │  lock := 0
021  │  c₀ := 0
022  │  wait until lock = 1
023  │  c₁ := 1
024  else
025  │  if c₀ = 0 then // A fault occurred
026  │  │  lock := 0
027  │  │  goto 002
     │  (enter critical section)
028  │  c₀ := 0
029  │  lock := 0
```

---

interference, and this allows us to use a simple simulation (instead of, e.g., a linearizable snapshot object, which would require much more memory and may itself be vulnerable to memory faults).

The idea of the simulation is to implement one high-level register x using f low-level registers $x_1, \ldots, x_f$, in such a way that x only exhibits a fault if $x_1, \ldots, x_f$ all experience a memory fault. In the sequel we use Read and Write to denote high-level operations on x (as opposed to low-level operations on $x_1, \ldots, x_f$).

To be useful, our implementation should be *linearizable* [12]: the operations invoked on x should appear to take place instantaneously, as though the algorithm were accessing an atomic faulty read/write register. However, unlike many fault-tolerant simulations (see Section 2), the simulation we give here exposes some subset of the low-level faults, instead of masking them completely. The standard notion of linearizability does not completely characterize the behavior we require. A linearizable implementation takes high-level operations as external input, and maps them into low-level operations; in contrast, with memory faults, we wish to take the *low-level* faults of $x_1, \ldots, x_f$ as (adversarially controlled) input and generate *high-level* faults of x as output. To complicate matters further, we wish to expose only a subset of faults. To capture this behavior we introduce the following definition.[3]

---

[3] It is also possible to take a more ad-hoc approach and use the standard definition of linearizability, treating low-level faults as high-level operations and high-level faults as low-level operations.

Algorithm T&S-HANDSHAKE: code for process 1

```
101  c₁ := 1
102  wait until lock = 0
103  if c₁ = 0 then
104  │   goto 101

105  if c₀ = 1 then
106  │   c₀ := 0
107  │   wait until c₀ = 1
108  │   c₁ := 0
109  │   wait until c₀ = 1
110  │   if test&set(lock) = 0 then
111  │   │   goto 101
112  │   wait until c₁ = 1

113  else
114  │   if test&set(lock) = 0 then
115  │   │   goto 101
116  │   if c₀ = 1 then
117  │   │   lock := 0
118  │   │   goto 106
119  │   if c₁ = 0 then   // A fault occurred
120  │   │   lock := 0
121  │   │   goto 102

     (enter critical section)
122  lock := 0
123  c₁ := 0
```

DEFINITION 8.2 (FAULT LINEARIZABILITY). *An implementation of a high-level object $\mathcal{O}$ from low-level objects $\mathcal{O}'$ is fault linearizable if in every execution, one can*

(a) *Embed linearization points for all the operations on $\mathcal{O}$ that complete and some subset of the operations that do not complete, and*

(b) *Insert high-level Flip events for $\mathcal{O}$ coinciding with some subset of low-level flip events of $\mathcal{O}'$,*

such that the following conditions are satisfied:

(a) *Each high-level operation of $\mathcal{O}$ is linearized at some point between its invocation and its return (or after its invocation, for operations that do not complete);*

(b) *If c high-level Flip events are inserted, then each low-level $\mathcal{O}'$ object experiences at least c faults in the execution; and*

(c) *The sequential history obtained by the linearization points and Flip events represents a valid history of a faulty $\mathcal{O}$ object.*

LEMMA 8.1. *There is a fault linearizable implementation of a faulty read/write register from f faulty read/write registers, such that when used in an fault-free execution of a bounded-interference algorithm, all operations of the high-level register complete.*

PROOF SKETCH. The implementation is very simple: to write a value v to the high-level register x, a process writes v to each of the low-level registers $x_1, \ldots, x_f$. To read from x, a process reads $x_1, \ldots, x_f$, and if all registers contain the same value, that value is returned as the result of the Read. Otherwise the process reads again, until it makes a full pass over $x_1, \ldots, x_f$ in which all registers are observed to have the same value. This value is then returned as the result of the Read.

To show that the implementation is fault linearizable, fix a low-level register x_i, and divide the execution into segments according

to the points where x_i flips; i.e., each segment ends with a flip of x_i, and does not contain any other flips of x_i. We linearize each high-level operation at the point where it last accesses x_i (or at the only point where it accesses x_i, in case of a Write). Note that the value associated with each high-level operation is the value it reads from or writes to x_i for the last time; since x_i does not flip inside each segment, the linearization points of all the operations linearized in a particular segment form a valid sequential history fragment. To complete the picture we insert a high-level Flip at the end of each segment. It is not hard to verify that the sequential history thus obtained is valid. Note also that the number of Flips inserted is exactly the number of times that x_i flips. If we choose x_i to be one of the registers that display the minimum number of faults in the execution, we obtain a linearization that satisfies condition (b).

A linearization can be viewed as a mapping from low-level executions to high-level executions, which annotates each low-level configuration with a configuration of the high-level algorithm (formally, the linearization induces a trace simulation between the low-level implementation to the high-level algorithm. The relationship between linearizability and refinement was already explored in [12], where the notion of linearizability was first introduced, and it has also been extensively studied in the formal methods community recently, e.g., [9, 15]). We saw above that we can choose any register and linearize all operations when they last access it. In particular, we can choose the last register accessed, x_f. When we embed linearization points using x_f, any low-level configuration where a Write(x, v) operation is in progress corresponds to a high-level configuration where the invoking process covers x.

The implementation does not, in general, guarantee liveness of any sort. However, when the implementation is used by a bounded-interference algorithm in a fault-free execution, we are guaranteed that no two Write operations overlap: if they did, then the configuration where the second Write is invoked corresponds to a configuration of the algorithm where both processes cover x. This guarantees that whenever a Write completes, all low-level registers $x_1, \ldots, x_f$ contain the same value. Furthermore, if a process invokes a Read(x), we are guaranteed that eventually the other process will cease writing to x. Therefore all operations complete. □

Using the implementation above we can transform a $(1, c)$-resilient algorithm using n registers into an (f, c)-resilient algorithm using $(n - 1)f + 1$ registers. In conjunction with Algorithm HAND-SHAKE, we obtain the following general result.

COROLLARY 1. *For any $f \geq 1$, there is a starvation-free $(f, 1)$-resilient mutual exclusion algorithm using $2f + 1$ binary read/write registers.*

PROOF SKETCH. We use $2f$ low-level registers to implement two high-level registers using Lemma 8.1, and the last high-level register is simulated by the remaining single low-level register. Since f faulty low-level registers are required to corrupt either of the first two high-level registers, the adversary cannot cause more than one high-level register to exhibit faulty behavior. Further, if each low-level register flips at most once, then the high-level registers also do not flip more than once. In fault-free executions the simulation guarantees liveness, so the overall algorithm is starvation-free. □

Unfortunately we do not obtain a similar result for the $(1, \infty)$-resilient algorithm, because it uses a test&set register. However, if we use more than f low-level registers to simulate each high-level register, we can use the simulation from Lemma 8.1 to mask faults completely (though the implementation may still deadlock in executions that contain memory faults). In conjunction with, e.g., Dekker's algorithm, we obtain the following result.

COROLLARY 2. *For all $f \geq 1$, there is a starvation-free (f, ∞)-resilient mutex algorithm using $3(f+1)$ binary registers.*

PROOF. We use $f + 1$ low-level registers to simulate each of the three high-level registers used by Dekker's algorithm. The adversary cannot corrupt any simulated register, because $f + 1$ faulty registers are required to do so. As before, in fault-free executions the simulation is live and starvation-freedom is satisfied. □

9. CONCLUSION

There has been a growing interest in various communities to understand the impact of increasingly unreliable hardware on software in general, and on algorithms in particular. Mutual exclusion is a particularly interesting problem, because the consequences of failure could be dramatic. Off-the-shelf solutions, such as error-correcting codes and specialized hardware, tend to be heavy-weight, and it is not clear that the extra cost is always necessary.

In this paper we have introduced a new variant of fault-tolerance, *safe* fault-tolerance, under which an algorithm must be safe even when memory faults occur, but not necessarily live. The consequences of violating liveness are often less sever than those of violating safety, and in many cases there are already systems in place to detect and resolve deadlock. Sacrificing liveness in faulty executions allowed us to design two-process mutual exclusion algorithms that tolerate a faulty variable, at the cost of no extra memory.

It is clear that our work is only a first step; many problems remain open. Our results in this paper focus mostly on the two-process case; in follow-up work we intend to extend the results to n-processes. Also, we focus in this paper primarily on binary shared variables, i.e., the type of variable used in Peterson's and Dekker's algorithms. Our results show that even in this restricted setting, a significant degree of fault-resilience can be achieved; nevertheless, it is interesting to consider whether the lower bound from Section 6 continues to hold for general multi-valued registers, or whether a $(2f + 1)$-variable (f, ∞)-resilient algorithm exists.

Acknowledgement. We are indebted to John Douceur and to Karthik Pattabiraman for fruitful early discussions on the problem.

10. REFERENCES

[1] Y. Afek, D. S. Greenberg, M. Merritt, and G. Taubenfeld. Computing with Faulty Shared Memory. In *Proceedings of Symposium on Principles of Distributed Computing (PODC)*, 1992.

[2] Y. Afek, D. S. Greenberg, M. Merritt, and G. Taubenfeld. Computing with Faulty Shared Objects. *Journal of the ACM*, 1995.

[3] R. C. Baumann. Soft Errors in Advanced Semiconductor Devices – Part I: The Three Radiation Sources. *IEEE Transactions on Device and Materials Reliability*, 2001.

[4] R. C. Baumann. Soft Errors in Commercial Semiconductor Technology: Overview and Scaling Trends. *IEEE 2002 Reliability Physics Tutorial Notes, Reliability Fundamentals*, 2002.

[5] S. Borkar. Designing Reliable Systems from Unreliable Components: The Challenges of Transistor Variability and Degradation. *IEEE Micro*, 2005.

[6] J. E. Burns and N. A. Lynch. Bounds on shared memory for mutual exclusion. *Inf. Comput.*, 107:171–184, December 1993.

[7] B. S. Chlebus, A. Gambin, and P. Indyk. Shared-Memory Simulations on a Faulty-Memory DMM. In *Proceedings of 23rd Colloquium on Automata, Languages and Programming (ICALP)*, 1996.

[8] B. S. Chlebus, L. Gasieniec, and A. Pelc. Deterministic Computations on a PRAM with Static Processor and Memory Faults. *Fundamenta Informaticae*, 2003.

[9] J. Derrick, G. Schellhorn, and H. Wehrheim. Proving linearizability via non-atomic refinement. In J. Davies and J. Gibbons, editors, *IFM*, volume 4591 of *Lecture Notes in Computer Science*, pages 195–214. Springer, 2007.

[10] I. Finocchi, F. Grandoni, and G. F. Italiano. Designing Reliable Algorithms in Unreliable Memories. In *Proceedings of European Symposium on Algorithms (ESA)*, pages 1–8, 2005.

[11] R. Guerraoui and M. Raynal. From Unreliable Objects to Reliable Objects: The Case of Atomic Registers and Consensus. In *Proceedings of PaCT*, 2007.

[12] M. P. Herlihy and J. M. Wing. Linearizability: a correctness condition for concurrent objects. *ACM Trans. Program. Lang. Syst.*, 12:463–492, July 1990.

[13] P. Jayanti, T. D. Chandra, and S. Toueg. Fault-tolerant wait-free shared objects. *Journal of the ACM*, 1998.

[14] L. Lamport. The Mutual Exclusion Problem: Part II – Statement and Solutions. *Journal of the ACM*, 1986.

[15] Y. Liu, W. Chen, Y. A. Liu, and J. Sun. Model checking linearizability via refinement. In *Proceedings of the 2nd World Congress on Formal Methods*, FM '09, pages 321–337, Berlin, Heidelberg, 2009. Springer-Verlag.

[16] T. N. V. M. Gomaa, C. Scarbrough and I. Pomeranz. Transient-fault Recovery for Chip Multiprocessors. In *Proceedings of 30th Symposium on Computer Architecture (ISCA)*, pages 98–109, 2003.

[17] S. S. Mukherjee, M. Kontz, and S. K. Reinhardt. Detailed Design and Evaluation of Redundant Multithreading Alternatives. In *Proceedings of 29th Symposium on Computer Architecture (ISCA)*, pages 99–110, 2002.

[18] N. Oh, P. P. Shirvani, and E. J. McCluskey. Error Detection by Duplicated Instructions in Super-Scalar Processors. *IEEE Transactions on Reliability*, 2002.

[19] G. L. Peterson. Concurrent Reading while Writing. *Transactions on Programming Languages and Systems*, 1983.

[20] G. A. Reis, J. Chang, and D. I. August. Automatic Instruction-Level Software-Only Recovery Methods. *IEEE Micro Top Picks*, 2007.

[21] N. W. H. B. E. T. S. E. Michalak, K. W. Harris and S. A. Wender. Predicting the Number of Fatal Soft Errors in Los Alamos National Labratory's ASC Q Computer. *IEEE Transactions on Device and Materials Reliability*, 2005.

[22] P. Shivakumar, M. Kistler, S. W. Keckler, D. Burger, and L. Alvisi. Modeling the Effect of Technology Trends on the Soft Error Rate of Combinational Logic. In *Proceedings of the Conference on Dependable Systems and Networks*, pages 389–388, 2002.

[23] B. K. Szymanski. Mutual Exclusion Revisited. In *Proceedings of 5th Jerusalem Conference on Information Technology*, 1990.

[24] J. Tromp. How to Construct an Atomic Variable. In *Proceedings of 3rd Workshop on Distributed Algorithms*, 1989.

[25] K. Truuvert. A Self-Stabilizing First-Come-First-Serve Mutual Exclusion Algorithm with Small Shared Variables. *Technical Note, University of Toronto*, 1989.

Structuring Unreliable Radio Networks

Keren Censor-Hillel[*]
Computer Science and
Artificial Intelligence Lab, MIT
ckeren@csail.mit.edu

Seth Gilbert[†]
Department of Computer
Science, National University of
Singapore
gilbert@comp.nus.edu.sg

Fabian Kuhn[‡]
Faculty of Informatics,
University of Lugano
fabian.kuhn@usi.ch

Nancy Lynch[‡]
Computer Science and
Artificial Intelligence Lab, MIT
lynch@csail.mit.edu

Calvin Newport[§]
Computer Science and
Artificial Intelligence Lab, MIT
cnewport@csail.mit.edu

ABSTRACT

In this paper we study the problem of building a connected dominating set with constant degree (CCDS) in the dual graph radio network model [4,9,10]. This model includes two types of links: *reliable*, which always deliver messages, and *unreliable*, which sometimes fail to deliver messages. Real networks compensate for this differing quality by deploying low-layer detection protocols to filter unreliable from reliable links. With this in mind, we begin by presenting an algorithm that solves the CCDS problem in the dual graph model under the assumption that every process u is provided a local *link detector* set consisting of every neighbor connected to u by a reliable link. The algorithm solves the CCDS problem in $O(\frac{\Delta \log^2 n}{b} + \log^3 n)$ rounds, with high probability, where Δ is the maximum degree in the reliable link graph, n is the network size, and b is an upper bound in bits on the message size. The algorithm works by first building a Maximal Independent Set (MIS) in $\log^3 n$ time, and then leveraging the local topology knowledge to efficiently connect nearby MIS processes. A natural follow up question is whether the link detector must be perfectly reliable to solve the CCDS problem. With this in mind, we first describe an algorithm that builds a CCDS in $O(\Delta \text{polylog}(n))$ time under the assumption of $O(1)$ unreliable links included in each link detector set. We then prove this algorithm to be (almost) tight by showing that the possible inclusion of only a single unreliable link in each process's local link detector set is sufficient to require $\Omega(\Delta)$ rounds to solve the CCDS problem, regardless of message size. We conclude by discussing how to apply our algorithm in the setting where the topology of reliable and unreliable links can change over time.

Categories and Subject Descriptors

F.2.2 [**Analysis of Algorithms and Problem Complexity**]: Non-numerical Algorithms and Problems—*computations on discrete structures*; G.2.2 [**Discrete Mathematics**]: Graph Theory—*graph algorithms*; G.2.2 [**Discrete Mathematics**]: Graph Theory—*network problems*

General Terms

Algorithms, Theory

Keywords

unreliable networks, dual graphs, maximal independent set, connected dominating set

1. INTRODUCTION

In this paper we study the problem of constructing a connected dominating set with constant degree (CCDS) in a radio network. The CCDS problem is important in this setting as it provides a routing backbone that can be used to efficiently move information through the network [15,19]. In more detail, we study this problem in the dual graph network model, which describes static ad hoc radio networks. The dual graph model, previously studied in [4,9,10], includes two types of links: *reliable*, which in the absence of collisions always deliver messages, and *unreliable*, which sometimes fail to deliver messages. This model was inspired by the observation that in real radio network deployments unreliable links are an unavoidable (and much cursed) feature; c.f., [1,2,5–7,16,18,20]. To mitigate the difficulties introduced by such links, most modern ad hoc radio network deployments use low-level link detector protocols (e.g., [2,5–7,20]) or sometimes even specialized hardware (e.g., [1]) that attempt to isolate reliable from unreliable links. We capture this strategy in our model with the new *link detector* abstraction, which provides each process u, at the beginning of each execution, a set of ids that represent an estimate of which neighbors are reliable (i.e., connected to u by a reliable link).

Using this abstraction, we are able to explore two important questions: (1) How can we leverage the link detection information commonly assumed in practice to build efficient solutions to the CCDS problem? (2) How reliable must these link detectors be

[*]Supported by the Simons Postdoctoral Fellows Program.

[†]Partially supported by NUS (FRC) R-252-000-443-133.

[‡]Supported by AFOSR award number FA9550-08-1-0159, NSF award numbers CCF-0726514, CCF-0937274, and NSF-Purdue-STC award number 0939370-CCF.

[§]Supported by Mobile Mesh Networks (Ford-MIT Alliance Agreement January 2008).

for their information to be useful? Our answers potentially extend beyond the realm of theoretical interest and into the realm of practice, where the optimal use of link detection is considered an open problem.

Results.

In this paper, we study the τ-*complete link detector*, $0 \leq \tau \leq n$. A τ-complete link detector, for a given process u, contains the id of every reliable neighbor of u and potentially up to τ additional ids. In other words, τ bounds the number of classification mistakes made by the detector, with 0-complete indicating perfect knowledge of reliable neighbors.[1] Notice, however, that assuming a 0-complete link detector is different than assuming a network with only reliable edges: the completeness of the link detector only describes the quality of knowledge about the network topology, but one still must grapple with the uncertainty caused by the presence of unreliable edges.

As mentioned, practical network deployments seek to accurately filter reliable from unreliable links; i.e., implement a 0-complete link detector [2, 5–7, 20]. With this in mind, in Section 5 we describe a randomized upper bound that uses a 0-complete link detector to construct a CCDS. In more detail, the algorithm constructs a CCDS in $O(\frac{\Delta \log^2 n}{b} + \log^3 n)$ rounds, with high probability, where Δ is the maximum degree in the reliable link graph, b is an upper bound in bits on the message size, and n is the network size. For reasonably large messages ($b = \Omega(\Delta)$), this algorithm terminates in polylogarithmic time. The algorithm works by first building a Maximal Independent Set (MIS) in $O(\log^3 n)$ rounds (the algorithm for which is presented separately, in Section 4), and then leveraging the link detector information to execute a novel *path finding* procedure to identify paths to nearby MIS processes.

A natural follow-up question is whether such accuracy in our link detector is necessary. In other words, can we find efficient solutions to the CCDS problem for some $\tau > 0$? To answer this question, we start by describing, in Section 6, an algorithm that solves the CCDS problem in $O(\Delta \text{polylog}(n))$ rounds, given a τ-complete detector for any $\tau = O(1)$. We then prove in Section 7 that this bound is (almost) tight by showing that with a 1-complete link detector, every algorithm that solves the CCDS problem requires $\Omega(\Delta)$ rounds, regardless of message size. This bound not only defines a separation with the classic radio network model, which assumes only reliable links, but also defines a separation with the $\tau = 0$ case. Concurrent work has identified a CCDS algorithm for the classic model that uses no topology knowledge and requires only $O(\text{polylog}(n))$ rounds [17].

We conclude by discussing, in Section 8, how to apply our algorithm in the setting where the topology of reliable and unreliable links can change over time.

Related Work.

The dual graph model was introduced in [4], where it was called the dynamic fault model, and then later studied in [9, 10] under its current name. These papers show, among other results, that the canonical problem of multihop broadcast is strictly harder in the presence of unreliable links. There are some similarities between the dual graph model and the quasi-unit disk graph model [13], which includes a gray zone distance at which two nodes in a radio network may or may not have a link. Unlike the dual graph model,

---

[1] Notice, these detectors never misclassify reliable neighbors as unreliable. In practice, we suspect such misclassifications would not affect our algorithms' correctness, provided that the correctly classified reliable edges still describe a connected graph. We omit this variant for the sake of conciseness.

however, the quasi-unit disk graph model features uncertainty only in the definition of the topology; once the links have been decided, they behave reliably.

The CCDS problem, along with related coordination problems, have been extensively studied in general graph models (see [12] for a good overview). In the context of radio networks without unreliable links (what we call the *classic radio network model*), [19] describes an $O(n)$ time CCDS algorithm, and [15] describes an $O(\log^2 n)$ time algorithm. The latter algorithm, however, requires that processes know their multihop local neighborhoods so they can construct collision-free broadcast schedules. In our model, for a process to learn its $(h + 1)$-hop neighborhood (of reliable links) would require $\Omega(\Delta^h)$ time, and even then the broadcast schedules constructed in [15] could be thwarted by unreliable links causing collisions. As with our paper, both [19] and [15] assume synchronous starts (i.e., processes start during the same round). Concurrent work has identified a $O(\text{polylog}(n))$-time CCDS solution in the classic radio network model *without synchronous starts* [17].

The MIS problem, which we use as a step in our construction of a CCDS, was studied in the classic radio network model without synchronous starts in [11], which provides a $O(\log^6 n)$ time solution. This was later improved in [14] to $O(\log^2 n)$. The MIS algorithm presented in the main body of this paper requires $O(\log^3 n)$ rounds, and it assumes synchronous starts and a 0-complete link detector. In the full version of this paper, however, we describe a minor variation to the algorithm that works in the same running time in the classic radio network model, without synchronous starts or any topology information. This algorithm is a factor of $O(\log n)$ slower than the result of [14], but trades this decreased speed for increased simplicity in both the algorithm description and proof structure.

2. MODEL

Fix some $n > 2$. We define a network (G, G') to consist of two undirected graphs, $G = (V, E)$ and $G' = (V, E')$, where V is a set of n wireless nodes and $E \subseteq E'$. We assume G is connected. For each $u \in V$, we use the notation $N_G(u)$ to describe the neighbors of u in E, and the notation $N_{G'}(u)$ to describe the neighbors of u in E'. Let Δ be the maximum size of N_G over all nodes and Δ' be the maximum size of $N_{G'}$ over all nodes. To simplify notation we assume in this paper that $\Delta = \omega(\log n)$. We assume that each node in V is embedded in a two-dimensional plane, and use $dist(u, v)$ to denote the distance between nodes u and v in the plane. We assume there exists a *constant* distance $d \geq 1 = O(1)$, such that for all $u, v \in V$ where $dist(u, v) \leq 1$, $(u, v) \in E$, and for all $(u', v') \in E'$, $dist(u', v') \leq d$. Notice, this is a generalization of the unit disk graph model that now captures the (potentially) large *gray zone* of unpredictable connectivity observed in real wireless networks.

We next define an algorithm $\mathcal{A}$ to be a collection of n processes. An execution of an algorithm $\mathcal{A}$ on network (G, G') first fixes some bijection *proc* from processes of $\mathcal{A}$ to V. This bijection represents the assignment of processes to graph nodes. We assume an adversary controls the definition of *proc*. We also assume that each process in $\mathcal{A}$ has a unique identifier from the range 1 to n. We use the notation $id(v)$, $v \in V$, with respect to an execution, to indicate the unique identifier of *proc*(v). For simplicity, throughout this paper we sometimes use the notation *process u*, for some $u \in V$, to refer to *proc*(u) in the execution in question. We also sometimes use the notation *process i*, for some $i \in [n]$, to refer to the process with id i.

An execution proceeds in synchronous rounds, $1, 2, \ldots$, with all nodes starting in the first round. At the beginning of each round,

r, every node v decides whether or not to send a message, as indicated by its process, $proc(v)$. Next, the adversary chooses a *reach set* of edges that consists of E and some subset, potentially empty, of edges in E' but not E. This set describes the links that will behave reliably in this round.[2] Let $B_{v,r}$ be the set of nodes that broadcast in round r and are connected to v by an edge in the reach set for this round. The messages received by v depend on the size of $B_{v,r}$. If node v broadcasts in r then it receives only its own message. If node v does not broadcast and $|B_{v,r}| = 1$, then it receives the message sent by the single broadcaster in $B_{v,r}$. Otherwise, it receives $\perp$; i.e., we assume no collision detection.

We sometimes use the notation $[i]$, for positive integer i, to indicate the sequence $\{1, ..., i\}$. Furthermore, we use the notation w.h.p. (i.e., *with high probability*) to indicate a probability at least $1 - \frac{1}{n^c}$, for some positive constant c. For simplicity we omit the specific constants used in our proofs, and assume only that they are large enough such that the union bounds applied to our various w.h.p. results produce a final probability that is also at least $1 - \frac{1}{n}$.

Link Detectors.

As described in the introduction, real wireless network deployments compensate for unreliability by using low-level protocols and special hardware to differentiate reliable from unreliable links. Because these link detection strategies often make use of information not described in our network model (e.g., properties of the received physical layer signal) we introduce the *link detector* abstraction to capture the functionality of these services.

In more detail, this abstraction provides each process $proc(u)$ a link detector set $L_u \subseteq [n]$. This set, fixed through the entire execution, is an estimate of which neighbors are connected to u by a reliable link. In this paper we study the τ-**complete link detector**, $0 \leq \tau \leq n$. In more detail, we say a link detector set L_u is τ-**complete** if and only if $L_u = \{id(v) : v \in N_G(u)\} \cup W_u$, where $W_u \subseteq \{id(w) : w \in V \setminus N_G(u)\}$, and $|W_u| \leq \tau$. That is, the detector contains the id of every neighbor of u connected by a reliable link, plus up to an additional τ additional neighbors. This makes τ a bound on the number of links that are mistakenly classified as reliable.

3. PROBLEM DEFINITIONS

We define the maximal independent set and constant-bounded connected dominating set problems. In both definitions, we reference the graph $H = (V, E_H)$, defined with respect to a specific execution, where V is the vertex set from G and G', and E_H is the edge set consisting of every edge (u, v) such that: $u \in L_v$ and $v \in L_u$ (that is, u and v are in each other's link detector set). Notice, for a τ-complete link detector, for any value of τ, G is a subgraph of H, and for $\tau = 0$, $H = G$.

Maximal Independent Set.

A maximal independent set (MIS) algorithm has every process eventually output a 0 or a 1, where a 1 indicates the process is in the MIS, and a 0 indicates it is not. We say an execution of an MIS algorithm has *solved the MIS problem* by round r, if and only if the following three conditions hold: (1) **[Termination]** every pro-

[2]This behavior might seem to constrain the adversary, as it requires reliability to be symmetric. In practice, however, this restriction has no noticeable effect. In more detail, the only way to learn about the reliability of a directed link (u, v) is for $proc(u)$ to broadcast and $proc(v)$ to receive (as broadcasters receive only their own messages). Therefore, even if the adversary could specify differing reliability on (u, v) versus (v, u), only the reliability of one of these directions could be assessed in any given round.

cess outputs 0 or 1 by the end of round r; (2) **[Independence]** if processes u and v both output 1, then $(u, v) \notin E$; and (3) **[Maximality]** if process u outputs 0, then there exists a process v such that v outputs 1 and $(u, v) \in E_H$.

Constant-Bounded Connected Dominating Set.

A constant-bounded connected dominating set (CCDS) algorithm has every process eventually output a 0 or a 1, where a 1 indicates the process is in the CCDS, and a 0 indicates it is not. We say an execution of a CCDS algorithm has *solved the CCDS problem* by round r, if and only if the following four conditions hold: (1) **[Termination]** every process outputs 0 or 1 by the end of round r; (2) **[Connectivity]** the set of processes that output 1 is connected in H; (3) **[Domination]** if a process u outputs 0, then there exists a process v such that v outputs 1 and $(u, v) \in E_H$; and (4) **[Constant-Bounded]** there exists a constant δ, such that for every process u, no more than δ neighbors of u in G' output 1.

4. MIS ALGORITHM

In this section, we present an algorithm that solves the MIS problem in $O(\log^3 n)$ rounds, w.h.p. We assume the processes have access to a 0-complete link detector and that the message size b is $\Omega(\log n)$ bits. In Section 5, we use this algorithm as a subroutine in our solution to the CCDS problem. Recall that having a 0-complete link detector is not equivalent to having a network model with only reliable edges. The completeness of the link detector describes the quality of information about the topology; it does not eliminate the negative impact of unreliable edges. In particular, as highlighted by the proofs in this section and the next, one of the main difficulties presented by unreliable edges is that their unpredictable behavior can thwart standard contention-reduction techniques, such as the exponential increase of broadcasting probability.

Algorithm Description.

The algorithm has processes discard messages received from a process not in its link detector set. Therefore, in the following description, when we say that a process *receives a message*, we imply that it is a message sent from a neighbor in E. Each process u maintains a set M_u of MIS process ids (initially empty). The execution is divided into $\ell_E = \Theta(\log n)$ groups of consecutive rounds that we call *epochs*, and which we index $1, \ldots, \ell_E$. At the beginning of each epoch i, each process u declares itself *active* if and only if its MIS set M_u does not include its own id or the id of a process in its link detector set. Only active processes will participate in the epoch.

In more detail, the epoch is divided into $\lceil \log n \rceil$ *competition phases* each of length $\ell_P = \Theta(\log n)$, followed by a single *announcement phase* of the same length. During the first competition phase, in each round, each active process broadcasts a contender message, labeled with its id, with probability $1/n$. If an active process u receives a contender message from another process, process u is knocked out: it sets its status to non-active and does no further broadcasting during this epoch. At each successive competition phase, the remaining active processes double their broadcast probabilities. In the second competition phase they broadcast with $2/n$, in the third $4/n$, and so on, up to probability $1/2$ in the final competition phase.

An active process u that makes it through all $\lceil \log n \rceil$ competition phases without being knocked out adds itself to the MIS set. It outputs 1, adds its own id to M_u, and broadcasts an MIS message labeled with its id, with probability $1/2$, in every round of the announcement phase. Every process v that receives an MIS message from a process u adds u to its MIS set M_v.

Correctness Proof.

As with the MIS solutions presented in [11,14], which are proved for the standard radio model where $G = G'$, we begin by covering the plane with an overlay of disks of radius $1/2$, arranged on an hexagonal lattice to minimize overlap. We index the disks: $D_1, \ldots$. (Notice, because our graph is connected, no more than n disks are required to cover all occupied portions of the plane.) Also following [11,14], we use the notation E_i^r to reference the disk of radius r centered at disk D_i. We introduce the new notation I^r to reference the maximum number of overlay disks that can intersect a disk of radius r. The following fact concerning this overlay, also used in [11,14], will prove useful:

FACT 4.1. *For any $c = O(1)$: $I^c = O(1)$.*

In the following, let $P_i(r) = \sum_{u \in A_i(r)} p(u, r)$, where $A_i(r)$ is the set of active processes in D_i at the beginning of the epoch that contains round r, and $p(u, r)$ is the broadcast probability of process u in round r. The following standard probability facts will prove useful:

FACT 4.2. *For any $p \leq 1/2$ it holds that $(1 - p) \geq (1/4)^p$, and for any $p > 0$ it holds that $(1 - p) < e^{-p}$.*

We continue with an important lemma that bounds the broadcast probability in the network.

LEMMA 4.3. *Fix some epoch. During every round r of this epoch, and every disk index i: $P_i(r) \leq 1$, w.h.p.*

PROOF. Fix some disk D_i. We begin by bounding the probability that D_i is the first disk to have its broadcast sum (P_i) exceed 1. For P_i to exceed 1, there must be some round r, such that r is the first round in which D_i's broadcast probability is greater than 1. Round r must be the first round of a competition phase, as these are the only rounds in which processes increase their broadcast probabilities. Furthermore, r cannot be the first round of the first competition phase, as the broadcast sum of the first phase can never exceed 1, as it has each process broadcasting with probability $1/n$. Combining these observations with fact that broadcast probabilities double between each phase, it follows: there exists a full competition phase before r, such that during every round r' of this preceding phase: $1/2 \leq P_i(r') \leq 1$. Furthermore, by assumption, r was the first round in which *any* disk exceeds a broadcast sum of 1, so we also know that for all disks $j \neq i$, during every round r' of this preceding competition phase, $P_j(r') \leq 1$.

We will now use these two observations to prove that there is a high probability that a single process in D_i broadcasts alone among nearby disks, and therefore knocks out all other active processes in D_i: reducing its broadcast probability to $1/2$ for the remainder of the epoch. To start, fix any round r' of the phase preceding r. Let p_1 be the probability of a single process broadcasting in D_i during this round. Using Fact 4.2 and our our bounds on disk broadcast sums from above, we can bound p_1 as follows: First, note that $p_1 = \sum_{u \in A_i(r')} \left(p(u, r') \prod_{v \in A_i(r'), v \neq u} (1 - p(v, r')) \right)$, which is greater than or equal to

$$\sum_{u \in A_i(r')} \left(p(u, r') \prod_{v \in A_i(r'), v \neq u} \frac{1}{4}^{p(v,r')} \right) \geq \frac{1}{2} \cdot \frac{1}{4}.$$

Next, let D_j be a disk that contains a G' neighbor of a node in D_i, and let probability p_2 be the probability that no process in D_j broadcasts in r'. By the same approach used above, we can bound $p_2 = \prod_{u \in A_j(r')} (1 - p(u, r'))$, which we know is greater than

or equal to: $\prod_{u \in A_j(r')} \frac{1}{4}^{p(u,r')} \geq \frac{1}{4}$. Let $\gamma = I^{d+1/2}$ describe the total number of disks potentially containing G' neighbors of nodes in D_i (recall that $d = O(1)$ is the maximum distance at which a G' edge exists), and let p_3 be the probability that a single process in D_i broadcasts in r', and this message is received by all processes in D_i (an event we call an *uncontested* broadcast). We know: $p_3 \geq p_1 p_2^{\gamma} = \frac{1}{2} \cdot \frac{1}{4}^{(\gamma+1)} = (\frac{1}{4})^{\gamma+1.5}$. (Notice, by Fact 4.1, $\gamma = O(1)$, therefore p_3 is also constant.)

To conclude the proof, we note that the probability that we *fail* to achieve an uncontested broadcasts in D_i in all ℓ_P rounds of this phase is no more than $(1 - p_3)^{\ell_P}$. By Fact 4.2 this is less than $e^{-p_3 \ell_P}$. For sufficiently large constant factors in our definition of ℓ_P, this evaluates to $\frac{1}{n^c}$, with a sufficiently large constant c that we retain high probability even after we perform a union bound over all $O(n)$ occupied disks. The result, is that w.h.p no disk is the first to exceed 1 during this epoch. $\square$

The following lemma leverages the observation that if the broadcast probability in the system is low (as established by Lemma 4.3), then a process about to enter the MIS will have a good probability of both knocking out its G neighbors and announcing to them its new status, during the $\Theta(\log n)$ round final competition phase and subsequent announcement phase.

LEMMA 4.4. *(Independence) For every pair of nodes u and v, $(u, v) \in E$, it is not the case that both output 1, w.h.p.*

PROOF. Fix any epoch in which neither u nor v has yet output 1. Such an epoch must exist in any execution where u and v proceed to both output 1. Assume that Lemma 4.3 holds in this epoch. Under this assumption, we will show that with high probability, either neither process joins the MIS in this epoch, or one process joins and the other outputs 0. Assume that at least one process makes it through the final competition phase (otherwise, we are done). Without loss of generality, assume this is u. Process u broadcasts in this phase with probability $p_1 = 1/2$. Let D_i be the disk containing u, and let p_2 be the probability that no process other than u in a disk intersecting $E_i^{d+1.5}$ broadcasts in r. (This is sufficient to ensure that v would receive any message sent by u, as $E_i^{d+1.5}$ contains all G' neighbors of v.) Under the assumption that Lemma 4.3 holds, we can use Fact 4.2 in a similar manner as in Lemma 4.3 to bound $p_2 \geq \frac{1}{4}^{\gamma'}$, where $\gamma' = I^{d+1.5}$. Let p_3 be the probability that v receives a message from u during this final competition phase, and is therefore knocked out and does not join the MIS. We combine p_1 and p_2 to yield $p_3 \geq \frac{1}{2} \cdot \frac{1}{4}^{\gamma'}$. (By Fact 4.1, $\gamma' = O(1)$, therefore p_3 is also constant.) We note that u fails to knock v in all ℓ_P rounds of the phase with probability no more than $(1 - p_3)^{\ell_P}$. By Fact 4.2 this is less than $e^{-p_3 \ell_P}$. For sufficiently large constant factors in our definition of ℓ_P, this evaluates to $\frac{1}{n^c}$, for any constant c. We can use the same argument to show that u fails deliver its MIS message to v during the subsequent announcement phase with a similarly low probability. For sufficiently large constant factors in our definition of ℓ_P, these probabilities are small enough to retain high probability even after we perform a union bound over all $O(n^2)$ pairs of processes and all $O(\log n)$ epochs, combined with a union bound establishing that Lemma 4.3 holds in each epoch. $\square$

This next lemma, whose proof is deferred to the full version of this paper, leverages the observation that a process u, in each epoch, either joins the MIS or is knocked out by a G neighbor v. If the latter occurs, due to the low amount of contention provided by Lemma 4.3, v has a constant probability of knocking out *all* of its G neighbors, and then continuing uncontested to join the MIS and announce this to u. Over $\Theta(\log n)$ epochs, therefore, u will either output 1 or 0, w.h.p.

LEMMA 4.5. *(Termination) By the end of the last epoch, every process has outputted 0 or 1, w.h.p.*

THEOREM 4.6. *Using 0-complete link detectors, our MIS algorithm generates an execution that solves the MIS problem in $O(\log^3 n)$ rounds, w.h.p.*

PROOF. By definition, the algorithm requires $O(\log^3 n)$ rounds: $O(\log n)$ epochs each consisting of $O(\log n)$ phases each of length $O(\log n)$. To satisfy termination, we note that by Lemma 4.5, every process outputs 0 or 1 by the end of the algorithm, w.h.p. To satisfy independence, we note that by Lemma 4.4, no two processes who are neighbors in E both output 1, w.h.p. And finally, to satisfy maximality, we note that by the definition of the algorithm, a process does not output 0 unless it receives an MIS message from a neighbor in E, and any process that sends an MIS message, outputs 1. To achieve our final high probability we simply use a union bound to combine the two high probability results from above. □

This corollary about the density of the resulting MIS follows from the definition of independence which allows no more than a single MIS node in any disk.

COROLLARY 4.7. *Fix an execution in which the MIS algorithm solves the MIS problem. For any process u and distance r, there are no more than I^r MIS processes within distance r of u.*

5. CCDS ALGORITHM

In this section, we present an algorithm that solves the CCDS problem in $O(\frac{\Delta \log^2 n}{b} + \log^3 n)$ rounds, w.h.p., where b is the bound on message size in bits. This algorithm uses the MIS algorithm from Section 4 as a subroutine. As in that previous section, we assume that $b = \Omega(\log n)$. Without loss of generality, we also assume that $b = O(\Delta \log n)$ (as our algorithm never sends messages of any larger size). Finally, we assume that processes are provided a 0-complete link detector.

At a high-level, the algorithm proceeds in two phases. First, it has processes build an MIS, placing each MIS node in the CCDS. Next, it connects all MIS nodes within 3 hops in G with a path consisting of CCDS nodes. Standard techniques show that the resulting structure satisfies the definition of a CCDS. The core technical novelty of the algorithm is its efficient method for discovering and connecting nearby MIS nodes. In more detail, the simple approach would be to have each MIS node give each of its neighbors a chance to explore whether it is on a path to a nearby MIS node. This would require, however, $O(\Delta)$ explorations. This is too slow given that there are only $O(1)$ nearby MIS nodes to be discovered (a property that follows from Corollary 4.7, which bounds the density of our MIS). The algorithm presented here, by contrast, makes use of a *banned list* data structure to ensure that an MIS node gives a neighbor a chance to explore only if that neighbor is on the path to a nearby MIS node that has not yet been discovered. This reduces the required number of explorations from $O(\Delta)$ to $O(1)$. The $O(\frac{\Delta \log^2 n}{b})$ term in the time bound expression describes the time required to for an MIS node to communicate its banned list to its neighbors. For large message size (i.e., large b), this is fast, and the time to build the MIS and explore dominates the time complexity. For small message size, however, this banned list communication time dominates the time complexity and yields an algorithm no faster than the simple approach of giving each neighbor a chance to explore.

For clarity, we start by presenting and proving the correctness of the subroutines before moving on to the main algorithm.

Subroutine Descriptions.

We start by describing the two subroutines used by our CCDS algorithm. The first subroutine, *bounded-broadcast*, is used by a process to broadcast a message to its G neighbors, given a known bound on contention for this message. The second subroutine, *directed-decay*, assumes an MIS and that each MIS process has a subset of its covered neighbors wanting to send it a message. The subroutine efficiently delivers at least one message to each MIS process.

bounded-broadcast(δ, m): This subroutine, when called by a process u with message m, attempts to deliver m to u's G neighbors.

The subroutine works as follows: A process calling bounded-broadcast(δ, m) broadcasts m with probability $1/2$ for $\ell_{BB}(\delta) = \Theta(2^\delta \log n)$ consecutive rounds.

The following lemma, whose proof is deferred to the full version of this paper, states the property that the above subroutine guarantees.

LEMMA 5.1. *Assume process u calls bounded-broadcast(δ, m), and that during every round of the subroutine, no more than δ other processes within distance $d + 1$ of u are running the subroutine concurrently. It follows that u delivers m to all of its G neighbors, w.h.p.*

directed-decay$(\langle m_1, m_2, ... \rangle)$: This subroutine assumes that the processes have already solved the MIS problem. We will use the terminology *covered processes* to describe the processes that are not in the MIS. It also assumes that all processes call the subroutine during the same round. Covered processes pass the subroutine a vector containing the messages they want to attempt to send—at most one message per neighboring MIS process. We assume each message is labeled with the id of its destination. All other processes pass an empty vector to the subroutine. The subroutine attempts to ensure that for every covered process v with a message to send to MIS neighbor u, u will receive at least one message from one of its neighbors with a message to send to u.

The subroutine works as follows: The subroutine divides time into $\lceil \log n \rceil$ phases of length $\ell_{DD} = \Theta(\log n)$, each associated with an exponentially increasing broadcast probability, starting with $1/n$ and ending with $1/2$. Every covered process with a message to send simulates a unique covered process for each of its messages. Initially all simulated covered processes are *active*. If a simulated covered process with a message starts a phase active, it broadcasts its message with the corresponding probability during every round of the phase. If a process has multiple simulated processes broadcast during the same round, it combines the messages. (No process has more than a constant number of neighbors in the MIS, therefore these messages are of size $O(\log n)$ bits, matching our assumption that $b = \Omega(\log n)$.) At the end of each phase, every MIS process that received a message during the phase runs bounded-broadcast$(d + 2, m)$ to send its neighbors a *stop order*, m, labeled with its id. On receiving a stop order from its message's destination, a simulated covered process sets its status to *inactive* for the remainder of the subroutine.

LEMMA 5.2. *Assume that in some round after the processes have solved the MIS problem, they run the directed-decay subroutine. It follows that by the end of the subroutine, for every covered process v that has a message to send to MIS neighbor u, u will receive at least one message intended for it from a neighboring covered process, w.h.p.*

Main Algorithm Description.

Having described our subroutines we continue by describing the main CCDS algorithm that makes use of these subroutines. Our algorithm begins with the processes executing the MIS algorithm from Section 4. We assume every process not in the MIS knows the ids of the MIS processes that neighbor it in G (the algorithm in Section 4 provides this information). After building the MIS, the algorithm adds every MIS process to the CCDS, then attempts to discover, and add to CCDS, a constant-length path between every pair of MIS processes that are within 3 hops in G.

At a high-level, this path-finding procedure works as follows: Each MIS process u maintains a *banned list*, initially set to contain its id and the id of the processes in its link detector set (i.e., its neighbors in G). Throughout the path-finding procedure, process u will add to its banned list B_u the MIS processes that it discovers as well as the G neighbors of these discovered processes. When a given MIS process asks its neighbors to a nominate a nearby process to explore (i.e., to see if its connected to an MIS), it uses this banned list to prevent exploration of processes that lead to already discovered MIS processes. In other words, an MIS process will ask processes to report any neighbors that are *not* already in its banned list.

We divide the search procedure into *search epochs*. During the first phase of each epoch, process u will transmit its banned list to its neighbors using bounded-broadcast. The time required to do this depends on b: this is the source of the Δ/b term in the final time complexity.

During the second phase, process u asks its reliable neighbors to use directed-decay to nominate one of their reliable neighbors for further exploration (recall, "reliable neighbor" refers to a neighbor connected by a reliable link). The restriction for such a nomination, however, is that the nominated process cannot be in the banned list. Notice, these nominations require that each process knows its set of reliable neighbors: this is where the assumption of 0-complete link detectors proves useful. By the definition of the banned list, any such nominated process must either be an MIS process that u does not know about, or be a neighbor of an MIS process that u does not know about. In both cases, we find a new MIS process within 3 hops if such an MIS process exists.

In the third phase, bounded broadcast is used to talk to the nominated process, find out if it is in the MIS, or if it is a neighbor of a process in the MIS, and then transmit the necessary new information to u to add to its banned list.

This *path finding* process, which ensures that u never explores a path that leads to an MIS process it already knows, is what provides our efficient running time (as long as the message size is large). If we instead had u explore every reliable neighbor, and in turn had these neighbors explore each of *their* neighbors, the running time would be $O(\Delta \text{polylog}(n))$, regardless of the message size.

We continue by describing more details of this path finding procedure: Each MIS process maintains a *banned list* B_u and a *delivered banned list* D_u. B_u is initially set to u's link detector set and D_u is empty. Each non-MIS process v maintains a *replica banned list* B_u^v and a *primary replica banned list* P_u^v, both initially empty, for each MIS process u that neighbors it in G. The algorithm proceeds by dividing groups of consecutive rounds into $\ell_{SE} = O(1)$ *search epochs*. Each search epoch is divided into 3 *search phases*, which we describe below.

Phase 1: Each MIS process u divides $B_u \setminus D_u$ into messages of size $b - \log n$ bits, where b is the maximum message size. It then includes its own id with each message so recipients know its source. Process u sends these messages to its non-MIS neighbors using bounded-broadcast(δ, m), with $\delta = I^{d+1} = O(1)$. Let process v be a non-MIS process that neighbors u in G. This process adds the values received from u to B_u^v. If this is the first search epoch, it also adds these values to P_u^v. At the end of the phase, u sets $D_u = B_u$. The phase is of a fixed length, long enough for the maximum number of calls to bounded-broadcast that might need to be made. As will be clear by the description of subsequent phases, the set $B_u \setminus D_u$ never contains more than Δ ids, therefore we can bound the number of calls by $O(\frac{\Delta \log n}{b})$.

Total Length: $O(\frac{\Delta \log^2 n}{b})$ rounds.

Phase 2: Let N_u be the subset of processes that neighbor MIS process u in G, where each $v \in N_u$ has a neighbor w in its link detector set such that $w \notin B_u^v$. We say w is the neighbor *nominated for u* by v. To do so, the processes run directed-decay to report their nominations to their neighbor MIS processes. With high probability, each MIS process u will hear from one process in N_u, if the set is non-empty. The fixed length of this process is number of rounds required to run directed-decay.

Total Length: $O(\log^2 n)$ rounds.

Phase 3: Let u be an MIS process that heard from a process $v \in N_u$ during the previous phase. Let w be the process nominated for u by v. During this phase, u will initiate an exploration of w. In more detail, using bounded-broadcast, with the same parameters as phase 1, u tells v that it has been selected. Next v uses bounded-broadcast with these same parameters to tell w that it wants to find out more about it. If w is in the MIS, it sends u its neighbor set. If w is not in the MIS, it chooses a neighbor x that is in the MIS, and sends to u the id of x and P_x^w (i.e., x's neighbor set). Finally, v uses bounded-broadcast to pass this information along to u, which adds the new values to its banned set, B_u. Process v and w add themselves to CCDS by outputting 1 if they have not already done so. The fixed length of this phase is set to the number of rounds required for the maximum number of calls that might need to be made to bounded-broadcast, which, as in phase 1, is bounded as $O(\frac{\Delta \log n}{b})$.

Total Length: $O(\frac{\Delta \log^2 n}{b})$ rounds.

The total running time for the MIS algorithm is $O(\log^3 n)$ rounds, and the time required to run $O(1)$ search epochs is $O(max\{\frac{\Delta \log^2 n}{b}, \log^2 n\})$. Combined this provides our final running time of $O(\frac{\Delta \log^2 n}{b} + \log^3 n)$ rounds.

We conclude with our main theorem:

THEOREM 5.3. *Using 0-complete link detectors, our CCDS algorithm generates an execution that solves the CCDS problem in* $O(\frac{\Delta \log^2 n}{b} + \log^3 n)$ *rounds, w.h.p.*

PROOF. Our CCDS algorithm first constructs an MIS using the algorithm presented in 4. It then executes ℓ_{SE} search epochs, each consisting of three phases. The MIS algorithm and the search epoch phases are of fixed length, so the running time of the algorithm follows directly from its definition.

For the remainder of the proof, assume that the MIS algorithm called by the CCDS algorithm solves the MIS problem, and that all $O(n)$ calls to bounded-broadcast and directed-decay during the search epochs satisfy the guarantees of Lemmas 5.1 and 5.2. By a union bound, these assumptions hold w.h.p.

Useful Notation. We begin by defining some useful notation: (a) We say a process v is *covered* by an MIS process u if v and u are neighbors in G. (b) we say an MIS process u has *discovered* an MIS process v ($u \neq v$) if u learned about v and v's G neighbors during phase 3 of a search epoch; (c) we say an MIS process u is *connected* to an MIS process v ($u \neq v$) if there exists a path in the CCDS of length 6 hops or less between u and v in G; and (d) we define U_u, for MIS process u, to be the set of MIS processes (not including u) that are within 3 hops of u and that are *not* connected to u.

Useful Claims. Our goal will be to show that this set U_u becomes empty by the end of the algorithm. To aid this task, we define the following useful claims:

Claim 1: If MIS process u discovers MIS process v, then by the end of the same search epoch it adds a path of length no more than 3 hops between u and v to the CCDS.

Proof. This claim follows from the definition of the algorithm.

Claim 2: Let u be an MIS process. Assume that during phase 2 of some search epoch at least one process covered by u has a neighbor to nominate to u. It follows that u will discover a new MIS process during this epoch.

Proof. Let u' be the process covered by u assumed by the claim. Assume u' is nominating a neighbor v' for u. By definition of the algorithm, v' is not in the banned set B_u for this epoch. It follows that either v' is an MIS process that has not been discovered by u, or none of the MIS neighbors of v' have been discovered by u. At least one such u' succeeds in its call to directed decay. In either case, u discovers a MIS process during phase 3 of this epoch.

Main Proof Argument. By repeated application of Claim 2, it follows that u will keep discovering processes within 3 hops until its neighbors run out of nominations for u. There are two things to note here: first, banned sets are monotonically increasing, so once a process runs out of nominations it will never again have nominations; second, by Corollary 4.7, we know there are no more than $I^{3d} = O(1)$ MIS processes within 3 hops of u, so if we set $\ell_{SE} = I^{3d}$, we have enough search epochs to reach the point where we run out of nominations.

We will now consider the set U_u of processes that are in the MIS, are within 3 hops of u, but are still undiscovered by u after the point where its neighbors have run out of nominations. Our goal is to show that a constant length path in the CCDS between u and these processes will exist by the end of algorithm. We first note that every process $v \in U_u$ must be exactly 3 hops from u: if some v was within 2 hops, it would have been nominated by its common neighbor with u until discovered. Let u, u', v', v be a 3 hop path from u to some $v \in U_u$. Because we assume that no neighbor of u has nominations for u at this point, v' must be in the banned set B_u—otherwise, u' could nominate it. By the definition of the algorithm, it follows that that u must have previously discovered some MIS process w such that w neighbors v'. This, in turn, puts MIS process w within 2 hops of v, on the path w, v', v. As we argued above, however, any MIS processes within 2 hops will eventually discover each other. It follows that by the end of the algorithm w will discover v.

We now have a path from u to w and from w to v. By claim 1, because each path was from a discovery, each is of length 3 hops or less. We can combine these two paths to get a single path, of length 6 hops or less, from u to v.

Assuming our assumptions from the beginning of the proof hold, which occurs w.h.p., we have shown that the algorithm constructs a CCDS consisting of all MIS processes, plus a constant-length path between every pair of MIS processes within 3-hops. By the standard argument (See section 2.6.1 of [8]), this yields a valid CCDS. We are left to show that the CCDS is constant-bounded. To prove this, fix a process u. By Corollary 4.7, there are only a constant number of MIS processes within 1 hop of u in G'. We must also bound, however, the CCDS processes added by connecting nearby MIS processes with a path. Consider every pair of MIS processes (v, w) such that v discovered w and added a path of length 2 or 3 to the CCDS. If v and w are both more than distance $4d$ from u, then

neither v, w, nor any process on their connecting path are within 1 hop of u. By Corollary 4.7, there are at most $x = I^{4d} = O(1)$ MIS processes within distance $4d$ of u, and therefore at most $x^2 = O(1)$ pairs of MIS processes, each contributing no more than 4 processes to the CCDS, for a total of no more than $4x^2 = O(1)$ CCDS processes within 1 hop of u, as needed. $\square$

6. CCDS ALGORITHM FOR INCOMPLETE LINK DETECTORS

In the previous section, we described an algorithm that can solve the CCDS problem with a 0-complete link detector. In this section we consider whether we can still solve the problem with an *incomplete* link detector (i.e., a τ-complete link detector for some $\tau > 0$). In particular, we describe an algorithm that solves the problem in $O(\Delta \text{polylog}(n))$ rounds, when combined with a τ-complete link detector for any $\tau = O(1)$.[3] In the next section, we will show the gap between this algorithm and the algorithm for 0-complete detectors is inherent.

The algorithm follows the same strategy as the CCDS algorithm presented in Section 5—i.e., build a dominating structure then connect nearby dominating processes—but differs in its details. To start, notice that the MIS we get in Section 4 guarantees the maximality condition only in H. For $\tau > 0$, however, $H \setminus G$ can be non-empty: potentially resulting in a process that is far from any other MIS process in terms of G edges. Such an event would thwart attempts to connect nearby MIS process—i.e., the strategy used in Section 5—as a lack of a short path in G can prevent communication between two such processes.

To compensate for this unreliability, we instead use a procedure that sequentially executes $\tau + 1$ iterations of the MIS algorithm from Section 4. A process that outputs 1 in any of these iterations does not participate in subsequent iterations. To ensure that the maximality of each iteration is defined for H, we also have processes label their messages with their local link detector sets. A process u *receiving* a message from process v will keep the message if and only if $v \in L_u$ and $u \in L_v$ (i.e., the two processes are connected in H). This procedure provides the following useful properties:

LEMMA 6.1. *Using a τ-complete link detectors, for any $\tau = O(1)$, the above procedure requires $O(\log^3 n)$ rounds, and w.h.p. it satisfies that (a) every process either outputs 1 or has a G neighbor that outputs 1; and (b) there are no more than $O(1)$ processes that output 1 within G' range of any process.*

PROOF. The number of rounds is easily derived: we run the $O(\log^3 n)$ time procedure of Section 4, $\tau + 1 = O(1)$ times. Theorem 4.6, when combined with our above modification to the MIS algorithm that has processes discard messages from non-H neighbors, proves that a single iteration of our modified MIS algorithm satisfies maximality in H. For a process to *never* output 0 in the iterated procedure, it has to receive $\tau + 1$ such MIS messages from an H neighbor, one in each iteration. These must be sent by distinct processes, since a process that outputs 1 in some iteration does not participate in the subsequent iterations. It follows that if a process outputs 0 for the entire iterated procedure, then it has $\tau + 1$ neighbors in H that outputted 1. Since we are using a τ-complete link detector, at most τ of these neighbors can be in $H \setminus G$, implying that this process must have at least G neighbor that outputs 1: providing property (a) of our lemma.

[3]Solving the problem for larger τ remains an open problem, though our intuition is that the problem will become impossible once the τ grows larger than the bound on neighboring CCDS processes allowed by the constant-bounded condition of the CCDS problem.

To prove (b), we can apply the same argument as in Corollary 4.7. In more detail, we know, w.h.p., that each iteration of the MIS has at most one process per disk (in the disk overlay used in Section 4) output 1. Over $\tau + 1$ iterations, therefore, no more $\tau + 1 = O(1)$ processes output 1 in each disk. Finally, because there are at most a constant number of disks within G' range of any process, there are at most a constant number of processes that output 1 within G' of any process. $\square$

Given the structure obtained by our iterated procedure, we can now build a CCDS. As in our previous algorithm, we want each process that outputs 1 in the procedure to connect to all other such processes that output 1 and are within 3 hops in G. Property (a) of Lemma 6.1 promises that this will create a connected dominating set. To satisfy the constant-bounded property of the CCDS definition, we rely on property (b). We are left, therefore, to connect nearby processes that output 1. The CCDS algorithm of Section 5, which uses a banned list approach to make this process more efficient, does not work in this setting.[4] We replace this banned list approach with something much simpler (and slower): each of the processes that output 1 dedicates time for each of its link detector neighbors to announce its id and master, using the bounded broadcast subroutines of Section 5. Call this phase 1. In phase 2, each of these processes gets another turn, this time announcing everything it learned in the previous phase. After these two phases, each process that output 1 knows about every other such process that is within 3 hops in G, and a path in H. (It might also learn about a constant number of such processes connected in H but not G.) This is sufficient to build the CCDS structure. With $O(\Delta)$ link detector neighbors, each requiring $O(\text{polylog}(n))$ rounds for each of their two phases, the total running time is: $O(\Delta \text{polylog}(n))$. We formalize this below:

THEOREM 6.2. *Using τ-complete link detectors, for any $\tau = O(1)$, the CCDS algorithm described above generates an execution that solves the CCDS problem in $O(\Delta \text{polylog}(n))$ rounds, w.h.p.*

7. LOWER BOUND

In Section 6, we described an algorithm that solved the CCDS problem in $O(\Delta \text{polylog}(n))$ rounds, given a τ-complete detector, for $\tau > 0$. In this section we show the bound to be nearly tight by proving that even with a 1-complete link detectors, constructing a CCDS requires $\Omega(\Delta)$ rounds. This bound holds regardless of message size. Notice that this represents a clear separation between the algorithms for τ-complete detectors with $\tau > 0$, and 0-complete detectors, which for sufficiently large messages can solve the CCDS problem in $O(\text{polylog}(n))$ rounds. Formally:

THEOREM 7.1. *Let $\mathcal{A}$ be a randomized CCDS algorithm such that $\mathcal{A}$ combined with a 1-complete link detector guarantees, w.h.p., to generate an execution that solves the CCDS problem in $f_1(\Delta, n)$ rounds, where Δ is the maximum degree in G and n is the network size. It follows that $f_1(\Delta, n) = \Omega(\Delta)$.*

Our proof strategy is to reduce an easily boundable game to the CCDS problem. This reduction requires a pair of transformations.

First Transformation.

The first transformation is from a CCDS algorithm to a solution to the β-double hitting game, which is defined as follows: There

---

[4]In this setting, with $\tau > 0$, it may be possible, for example, that the banned list of an MIS node includes a neighbor in $H \setminus G$. This neighbor will therefore not be nominated, even though it might be on the path to a nearby MIS process.

are two players, A and B, represented by the synchronous probabilistic automata $\mathcal{P}_A$ and $\mathcal{P}_B$. At the beginning of the game, an adversary chooses two target values $t_A, t_B \in [\beta]$. It then provides t_B as input to $\mathcal{P}_A$ and t_A as input to $\mathcal{P}_B$. The automata execute in rounds. In each round each automaton can output a guess from $[\beta]$. Notice, however, other than the inputs provided by the adversary at the beginning of the execution, these automata have no communication with each other. That is, their executions unfold independently. The players solve the game when either $\mathcal{P}_A$ outputs t_A or $\mathcal{P}_B$ outputs t_B. We continue with the transformation lemma:

LEMMA 7.2. *Let $\mathcal{A}$ be a CCDS algorithm such that $\mathcal{A}$, combined with a 1-complete link detector, guarantees, w.h.p., to generate an execution that solves the CCDS problem in $f_1(\Delta, n)$ rounds, where Δ is the maximum degree in G and n is the network size. There exists a pair of probabilistic automata $(\mathcal{P}_A, \mathcal{P}_B)$ that solve the β-double hitting game in $f_2(\beta, n) = f_1(\beta, n) + O(1)$ rounds, w.h.p., where β is any positive integer.*

Notice, with this transformation we shift from the world of radio network algorithms to the world of abstract games, where players are represented by probabilistic automata. We maintain n as a parameter in the running time function, however, so we can specify "w.h.p." in a consistent manner.

PROOF. Our transformation requires that we construct two player automata, $\mathcal{P}_A$ and $\mathcal{P}_B$, given a CCDS algorithm $\mathcal{A}$. Our strategy is to design our player automata to cooperatively simulate an execution of $\mathcal{A}$ running on a dual graph network of size 2β, where G consists of two cliques, each of size β, that are connected by a single link, and G' is fully connected. Call the two cliques in this network A and B. Automata $\mathcal{P}_A$ simulates processes 1 to β assigned to nodes in clique A, and $\mathcal{P}_B$ simulates processes $\beta + 1$ to 2β assigned to nodes in clique B. Thus we have 2β processes total, each assigned a unique id from $[2\beta]$, as required by our network model.

In this simulation, we want the two target ids, t_A and t_B from the hitting game to correspond to the ids of the processes assigned to the endpoints of the link connecting the two cliques (which we will call the *bridge*). To do so, we must be careful about how we simulate the 1-complete link detectors used by the broadcast algorithm. In more detail, we have $\mathcal{P}_A$ give each of its simulated processes a link detector set consisting of the set $[\beta]$ and the id $t_B + \beta$, and we have $\mathcal{P}_B$ give its simulated processes the set consisting of $\{\beta + 1, ..., 2\beta\}$ and the id t_A. It follows, that each player is simulating their processes receiving a 1-complete link detector set that is compatible with a process assignment that has process t_A (in clique A) and $t_B + \beta$ (in clique B) as the endpoints of the bridge.

We have each of the two player automata simulate each round of the CCDS algorithm as follows: if two or more simulated processes broadcast, or no simulated process broadcasts, then all processes simulated by the automata receive $\bot$. Notice, here we leverage the fact that we are in the dual graph model. Assume, for example, that t_A and one other process, i, broadcast in clique A. In the classic radio network model, t_A's message would be received by process $t_B + \beta$ because i is not connected to $t_B + \beta$. In the dual graph model, however, the adversary can choose in this round to deliver a message on i's G' edge to $t_B + \beta$, causing a collision with t_A's message.

On the other hand, if only one simulated process broadcasts, then all processes simulated by that automata receive the message, and the automata makes a guess at the end of the round. The guessing works as follows: if process i simulated by $\mathcal{P}_A$ broadcasts alone in

86

a simulated round, A guesses i during this round of the game, and if j simulated by $\mathcal{P}_B$ broadcasts alone, B guesses $j - \beta$.

Finally, if the simulated processes in clique A (resp. B) terminate (i.e., they have all outputted 0 or 1), then $\mathcal{P}_A$ (resp. $\mathcal{P}_B$), halts its simulation and guesses i (resp. $i - \beta$), for each simulated process i from its clique that output 1. Because players can only output one value per round, but multiple simulated processes from a clique might join the CCDS, completing this guessing might require multiple rounds. Due to the constant-bounded property of the CCDS, however, no more than $O(1)$ rounds will be needed to complete this guessing.

To conclude this proof, we must now show that this simulation strategy solves the double hitting game. We first notice that the simulations conducted by $\mathcal{P}_A$ and $\mathcal{P}_B$ will remain valid so long as there is no communication required between the cliques. By our model definition, the only scenario in which a message *must* pass between the cliques is if process t_A or $t_B + \beta$ (i.e., the processes at the endpoints of the bridge) broadcasts alone. In this case, however, the player responsible for the solo broadcaster would guess its target, solving the double hitting game.

We now consider the case where the algorithm terminates without communication between the cliques. Assume that the execution under consideration solves the CCDS problem (an event that occurs, by assumption, w.h.p.). Consider the graph H used in the definition of the CCDS problem. In our simulated network, this graph matches G: i.e., cliques A and B connected by a single bridge link. By the domination and connectivity properties of the CCDS problem, the endpoints of this bridge must be included in the CCDS. The processes corresponding to these endpoints are t_A and $t_B + \beta$. Therefore, when the respective players in the double hitting game output the guesses corresponding to their CCDS processes, they will output their targets, solving the game. $\square$

Second Transformation.

Our next transformation is from the β-double hitting game to the β-*single hitting game*, which is defined the same as double hitting game, except there is now only one player and target. That is, the adversary chooses a value from $[\beta]$, and then the synchronous probabilistic automata $\mathcal{P}_{A,B}$ guesses one value per round until it guesses the target value. In the proof of our main theorem statement, we will show that the single hitting game is easily bounded. Note the reason we require a non-trivial transformation from the double hitting game to the single hitting game is because the exchange of input values at the beginning of the double hitting game, allows for subtle cooperative strategies that prevent us from just using one of the automata $\mathcal{P}_A$ or $\mathcal{P}_B$ as our solution to the single player variant. We detail this transformation with the following lemma:

LEMMA 7.3. *Let $(\mathcal{P}_A, \mathcal{P}_B)$ be a pair of automata that solve the β-double hitting game in $f_2(\beta, n)$ rounds, w.h.p., for any positive integer β. We can construct a probabilistic automata $\mathcal{P}_{A,B}$ that solves the β-single hitting game in $f_3(\beta, n) = f_2(2\beta, n)$ rounds, w.h.p., also for any positive integer β.*

PROOF. We are given a pair of automata $\mathcal{P}_A$ and $\mathcal{P}_B$ that solve the 2β-double hitting game in $f_2(2\beta, n)$ rounds, w.h.p. Unwinding the definition of the problem we get the following: for every pair of targets $t_A, t_B \in [2\beta]$, $\mathcal{P}_A$ and $\mathcal{P}_B$ will solve the double hitting game for these targets in no more than $f_2(2\beta, n)$ rounds, w.h.p.

Let us now unwind even more: if we run $\mathcal{P}_A$ with target t_A and input t_B, and run $\mathcal{P}_B$ with target t_B and input t_A, at least one of these two automata will output their target in $f_2(2\beta, n)$ rounds,

w.h.p. To make this argument we must proceed carefully. Recall, we define w.h.p. to be $1 - \frac{1}{n^c}$ for some constant c that is sufficiently large for our needs. In this case, assume it is at least of size 2. Let p_A be the probability that $\mathcal{P}_A$ fails to output t_A in $f_2(2\beta, n)$ rounds given input t_B. And let p_B be the probability that $\mathcal{P}_B$ fails to output t_B in $f_2(2\beta, n)$ rounds given input t_A. Notice, these two probabilities are independent as the player automata execute independently once provided their respective inputs. By our assumption that at least one player succeeds with high probability, we know $p_A p_B \leq \frac{1}{n^c}$. To satisfy this inequality, at least one of these probabilities is no larger than $\frac{1}{n^{c/2}}$. The player automata with this probability therefore solves the game fast, when run with (t_A, t_B), with probability at least $1 - \frac{1}{n^{c/2}}$, which still qualifies as "w.h.p." Call this automata the "winner" for this pair of targets (if both output in the required time with the required probability, default to call automata $\mathcal{P}_A$ as the winner).

With this in mind, we can calculate a $(2\beta \times 2\beta)$-sized table, where each position (x, y) contains either A or B depending on which corresponding automata is the winner for targets $t_A = x$ and $t_B = y$. (Notice, this table is not something constructed by $\mathcal{P}_{A,B}$, it is instead something that can be calculated offline to help construct $\mathcal{P}_{A,B}$.) By a simple counting argument, there must exist either: (a) a column with at least β A's; or (b) a row with a least β B's.

For the remainder of this construction, assume we find some column y such that this column contains at least β A's. The case for a row with β B's is symmetric. Given this column y, we know that there is a subset $S_y \subset [2\beta]$ of size β, such that if we run $\mathcal{P}_A$ with target $t_A \in S_y$ and input $t_B = y$, it will output the target in $f_3(2\beta, n)$ rounds, w.h.p. (e.g., we can define S_y to be the first β rows in column y that contain A.) Let ψ be bijection from S_y to $[\beta]$.

We now define $\mathcal{P}_{A,B}$ as follows: have the automata simulate $\mathcal{P}_A$ being passed input y. If the simulated $\mathcal{P}_A$ outputs a guess x in a round, and $x \in S_y$, $\mathcal{P}_{A,B}$ outputs $\psi(x)$.

We now argue that $\mathcal{P}_{A,B}$ solves the β-single hitting game. Let $t_{A,B} \in [\beta]$ be the target chosen for $\mathcal{P}_{A,B}$ at the beginning of some execution of the single hitting game. By definition, there exists an $x \in S_y$ such that $\psi(x) = t_{A,B}$. By the definition of our table, we know $\mathcal{P}_A$ will output target $t_A = x$, given input $t_B = y$, in $f_2(2\beta, n)$ rounds, w.h.p. It follows that $\mathcal{P}_{A,B}$ simulating $\mathcal{P}_A$ with this input will therefore output $\psi(x) = t_{A,B}$ in this same time with this same high probability, as needed. $\square$

Main Proof.

We can now pull together these pieces to prove Theorem 7.1:

PROOF (OF THEOREM 7.1). Starting with the CCDS algorithm $\mathcal{A}$ provided by the theorem statement, we apply Lemmas 7.2 and 7.3, to produce a solution to the β-single hitting game that solves the game in $f_3(\beta, n)$ rounds. We next note that the β-single hitting game, which requires a player to identify an arbitrary element from among β elements, requires $\Omega(\beta)$ rounds to solve w.h.p. (We formalize this intuitive probability fact as part of the proof for our lower bound on randomized broadcast, presented in [9].) This yields: $f_3(\beta, n) = \Omega(\beta)$. Finally, substituting the running time functions generated by our transformations, we get: $f_3(\beta, n) = f_2(2\beta, n) = f_1(2\beta, n) + O(1)$. It follows from our bound on f_3 that $f_1(2\beta, n) + O(1) = \Omega(\beta)$. There exists a graph in which $\Delta = 2\beta$, and therefore $f_1(\Delta, n) = \Omega(\Delta)$, as needed. $\square$

8. DYNAMIC LINK DETECTORS

This paper has considered building a CCDS as a one-shot problem: processes are provided a static estimate of their reliable neighbors, formalized as a link detector set, and then attempt to build the desired structure as quickly as possible. In long-lived wireless networks, however, link status is not necessarily stable. It is possible for a link that has behaved reliably for a long period to suddenly degrade into unreliability (this could happen, for example, due to a change in the multipath environment). We can capture this setting with a dynamic definition of link detector as a service that provides a set to each process *at the beginning of every round* (a definition more aligned with the classic *failure detector* abstraction [3]). We say a dynamic link detector *stabilizes* at some round r, if in every execution its output matches the definition of the corresponding static link detector at r and never again changes in future rounds.

Given the efficiency of our CCDS solution (at least, under the assumption of large messages), a simple approach to dealing with changing link detector output is to rerun the CCDS algorithm every $\delta_{CDS} = \Omega(\frac{\Delta \log^2 n}{b} + \log^3 n)$ rounds. Call this the *continuous CCDS algorithm*. We can assume that when we rerun the algorithm, processes wait to change their outputs until the very end of the algorithm, so they can transition from the old CDS to the new CCDS all at once. We say that the continuous CCDS algorithm solves the CCDS problem by some round r, if for any round $r' \geq r$, the output solves the CCDS problem, w.h.p. The following theorem follows directly:

THEOREM 8.1. *In any execution of the continuous CCDS algorithm with a 0-complete dynamic link detector that stabilizes by round r, the algorithm solves the CCDS problem by round $r + 2\delta_{CDS}$.*

9. FUTURE WORK

This work motivates a collection of related open problems. For example, our CCDS algorithm for the 0-complete link detector setting requires large messages in order to terminate fast. It remains open whether this is fundamental, or if there exist fast solutions for the small message case. It is also interesting to consider whether there exist CCDS algorithms for non-constant τ. Finally, our τ-complete link detector abstraction is only one possible definition from many different approaches to defining this style of service. We leave the exploration of different definitions as additional future work.

In addition, it remains an interesting open question to explore the dynamic case in more detail. For example, we might want to redefine what it means to solve problems like MIS and CCDS, with respect to the current output of the link detector. We might also want to design efficient *repair* protocols that can fix breaks in the structure in a localized fashion, rather than reusing the entire protocol.

10. REFERENCES

[1] M. Abusubaih. A New Approach for Interference Measurement in 802.11 WLANs. In *Proceedings of the International Symposium on Personal Indoor and Mobile Radio Communications*, 2010.

[2] D. Aguayo, J. Bicket, S. Biswas, R. Morris, B. Chambers, and D. De Couto. MIT Roofnet. In *Proceedings of the International Conference on Mobile Computing and Networking*, 2003.

[3] T. D. Chandra and S. Toueg. Unreliable failure detectors for reliable distributed systems. *Journal of the ACM*, 43(2):225–267, 1996.

[4] A. Clementi, A. Monti, and R. Silvestri. Round robin is optimal for fault-tolerant broadcasting on wireless networks. *Journal of Parallel Distributed Computing*, 64:89–96, 2004.

[5] D. De Couto, D. Aguayo, J. Bicket, and R. Morris. A High-Throughput Path Metric for Multi-Hop Wireless Routing. *Wireless Networks*, 11(4):419–434, 2005.

[6] D. De Couto, D. Aguayo, B. Chambers, and R. Morris. Performance of Multihop Wireless Networks: Shortest Path is Not Enough. *ACM SIGCOMM Computer Communication Review*, 33(1):83–88, 2003.

[7] K. Kim and K. Shin. On Accurate Measurement of Link Quality in Multi-Hop Wireless Mesh Networks. In *Proceedings of the Annual International Conference on Mobile Computing and Networking*, 2006.

[8] F. Kuhn. *The Price of Locality: Exploring the Complexity of Distributed Coordination Primitives*. PhD thesis, ETH Zurich, 2005.

[9] F. Kuhn, N. Lynch, and C. Newport. Brief Announcement: Hardness of Broadcasting in Wireless Networks with Unreliable Communication. In *Proceedings of the International Symposium on Principles of Distributed Computing*, 2009.

[10] F. Kuhn, N. Lynch, C. Newport, R. Oshman, and A. Richa. Broadcasting in Unreliable Radio Networks. In *Proceedings of the International Symposium on Principles of Distributed Computing*, 2010.

[11] F. Kuhn, T. Moscibroda, and R. Wattenhofer. Initializing Newly Deployed Ad Hoc and Sensor Networks. In *Proceedings of the Annual International Conference on Mobile Computing and Networking*, 2004.

[12] F. Kuhn and R. Wattenhofer. Constant-Time Distributed Dominating Set Approximation. *Distributed Computing*, 17(4):303–310, 2005.

[13] F. Kuhn and A. Zollinger. Ad-Hoc Networks Beyond Unit Disk Graphs. In *Proceedings of the Workshop on the Foundations of Mobile Computing*, 2003.

[14] T. Moscibroda and R. Wattenhofer. Maximal independent sets in radio networks. In *Proceedings of the International Symposium on Principles of Distributed Computing*, 2005.

[15] S. Parthasarathy and R. Gandhi. Distributed Algorithms for Coloring and Domination in Wireless Ad Hoc Networks. In *Proceedings of the Conference on the Foundations of Software Technology and Theoretical Computer Science*, 2005.

[16] K. Ramachandran, I. Sheriff, E. Belding, and K. Almeroth. Routing Stability in Static Wireless Mesh Networks. *Passive and Active Network Measurement*, pages 73–82, 2007.

[17] J. Schneider. Personal Communication, ETH Zurich, Jan. 2011.

[18] K. Srinivasan, M. Kazandjieva, S. Agarwal, and P. Levis. The β-Factor: Measuring Wireless Link Burstiness. In *Proceedings of the Conference on Embedded Networked Sensor System*, 2008.

[19] P. Wan, K. Alzoubi, and O. Frieder. Distributed Construction of Connected Dominating Sets in Wireless Ad Hoc Networks. In *Proceedings of the IEEE Conference on Computer Communnications*, 2002.

[20] M. Yarvis, W. Conner, L. Krishnamurthy, J. Chhabra, B. Elliott, and A. Mainwaring. Real-World Experiences with an Interactive Ad Hoc Sensor Network. In *Proceedings of the International Conference of Parallel Processing*, 2002.

The Impact of Memory Models on Software Reliability in Multiprocessors

Alexander Jaffe
University of Washington
ajaffe@cs.washington.edu

Thomas Moscibroda
Microsoft Research
moscitho@microsoft.com

Laura Effinger-Dean
University of Washington
effinger@cs.washington.edu

Luis Ceze
University of Washington
luisceze@cs.washington.edu

Karin Strauss
Microsoft Research
kstrauss@microsoft.com

ABSTRACT

The memory consistency model is a fundamental system property characterizing a multiprocessor. The relative merits of strict versus relaxed memory models have been widely debated in terms of their impact on performance, hardware complexity and programmability. This paper adds a new dimension to this discussion: the impact of memory models on software reliability. By allowing some instructions to reorder, weak memory models may expand the window between critical memory operations. This can increase the chance of an undesirable thread-interleaving, thus allowing an otherwise-unlikely concurrency bug to manifest. To explore this phenomenon, we define and study a probabilistic model of shared-memory parallel programs that takes into account such reordering. We use this model to formally derive bounds on the *vulnerability* to concurrency bugs of different memory models. Our results show that for 2 concurrent threads, weaker memory models do indeed have a higher likelihood of allowing bugs. On the other hand, we show that as the number of parallel, buggy threads increases, the gap between the different memory models becomes proportionally insignificant, and thus the importance of using a strict memory model diminishes.

Categories and Subject Descriptors

F.1.2 [**Computation by Abstract Devices**]: Modes of Computation—*parallelism and concurrency*; G.3 [**Probability and Statistics**]: *Stochastic processes*; B.3.4 [**Memory Structures**]: Reliability, Testing, and Fault-Tolerance

General Terms

Theory, Reliability

Keywords

Memory consistency models, probabilistic analysis, sequential consistency, total store order, weak ordering, software reliability

1. INTRODUCTION

A critically important property of a shared-memory multiprocessor is its *memory consistency model*. There has been an enormous amount of work on this subject, both in industry and academia. The memory consistency model describes which values may be returned by a load operation in a parallel or multi-threaded program. The strongest and most intuitive model is *Sequential Consistency* (SC) [15]. SC imposes two requirements on the execution of parallel programs: first, all processors must see the same *global order* of memory operations, and second, the operations for a particular processor must appear to execute in *program order*. This model is attractive for its high level of programmability, but the strict constraints on memory operation reordering rule out important optimizations such as access buffering, pipelining, or dynamic scheduling, which improve performance by hiding the latency of memory accesses. In order to enable these aggressive optimizations, a wide variety of *relaxed memory models* have been proposed. Relaxed memory models allow the reordering of certain types of memory operations at the cost of increased programming complexity, since programmers need to explicitly encode reordering restrictions to ensure correctness.

Historically, the vast literature on memory consistency models has discussed a three-way trade-off between performance, hardware complexity, and programmability. In this paper, we bring a new axis to this discussion: *software reliability*. Software is inherently unreliable, and is arguably becoming less reliable with pervasive concurrency. Concurrency bugs such as data races and deadlocks are extremely common in practice, and can cause unexpected failures in even production-level code.

In this paper, we investigate to what extent relaxed memory consistency models further contribute to the unreliability of parallel software by increasing the likelihood that concurrency bugs will manifest during an execution. For this purpose, we study a new probabilistic model for the instruction reordering introduced by relaxed memory models, and analyze a canonical buggy program (specifically, an atomicity violation [9, 4, 17]) with respect to this model. We compare three important memory consistency models: Sequential Consistency, Weak Ordering, and Total Store Order. We derive two interesting results for our model:

- We show that for 2 (or any small constant number of) parallel threads, the bug is indeed more likely to manifest under weaker memory models. This is intuitive and follows from the following high-level argument: A typical concurrency bug, such as a data race, can manifest only during a short window of time. The reordering of operations caused by relaxed memory models may increase the size of this critical window, thus making the bug more likely to manifest. In the paper, we give precise bounds on this *vulnerability* of the three memory models.

- On the other hand, we show that as the number of parallel, buggy threads increases, the gap between the different memory models shrinks in proportion to the risk for even the strongest memory model. This implies that *as the number of parallel threads in the system increases, the importance of using a strict memory model diminishes* (with regard to the software reliability metric we study in this paper).

Notice that the latter result could have far-reaching implications on the choice of memory consistency models in future multi-core and massively parallel systems. Intuitively, one might expect that with more and more concurrent threads, stronger memory consistency models should be used in order to counter the generally increased likelihood of bugs. However, our results indicate that the opposite is the case: As the number of threads increase, the relative importance of having stronger memory models reduces to a minimum. The underlying reason is that the larger number of threads causes the likelihood that bugs occur to increase much more quickly than what even the strictest memory model is able to contain. That is, the asymptotic growth fundamentally works against using strict memory models as we increase the number of threads.

The technical content of our paper proceeds as follows. In Section 3, we introduce two distinct random processes, each of which is a natural object of inquiry in isolation. By combining them—treating the output of the first process as the input to the second—we model the end-to-end behavior of program execution. This allows us to answer our central question: how does the probability that a canonical data race manifests vary across memory models and quantity of threads?

The first process models the generation of a random program, and the subsequent randomized reordering of instructions. Specifically, in Section 4, we derive the probability that a certain essential window of vulnerability between two instructions widens. The second process enacts a random series of shifts on a set of heterogenous segments of the integer line. We use the positions of these line segments to model the interleaving of the vulnerable windows of the threads. In Section 5, we estimate the probability that each of these segments is shifted to mutually disjoint positions. Finally, the two processes are combined together in Section 6 to derive overall bounds on the probability of bug manifestation, first for two threads, then for a large number of threads. Due to lack of space, several proofs are omitted and deferred to the full version of this paper.

2. BACKGROUND & RELATED WORK

2.1 Memory Consistency Models

Memory models are a key aspect of the hardware/software interface in shared-memory multicore/multiprocessor systems. They determine what values read memory operations are allowed to return by dictating how memory operations are allowed to be reordered, as well as when writes become visible to other processors. They have major implications on the performance, design complexity and programmability of multiprocessor systems and the programs that run on them. Common misunderstandings about memory models often lead to bugs that are very difficult to find and fix, and can also lead to major performance issues. There exists a vast and rich line of literature on memory models (a good tutorial overview is presented in [1]). Most of the past work has focused on new memory models [11, 2, 13], hardware implementations [10, 12, 7], memory models for popular languages such as Java [18] and C++ [6], and compiler optimizations [16] and their relative merits [1, 5].

Relaxed memory models: The strongest memory model is Lamport's *Sequential Consistency* (SC) [15]. In order to enable important performance optimizations, a number of relaxed memory models have been proposed in the literature, with varying degrees of guarantees. One of the strongest examples is known as *Total Store Order* (TSO) [19]. In TSO, loads may execute before stores that precede them in program order, as long as no data dependency is violated. All other pairs of instructions must maintain strict program order. This model encapsulates the natural case in which stores are observed by remote processors in program order. Some stores may take extra time to be observed after their execution, but the local program is allowed to proceed. A similar, but slightly weaker consistency model is *Partial Store Order* (PSO) [19], which also allows the reordering of stores with respect to each other as long as they access distinct memory locations. A significantly weaker consistency model is *Weak Ordering* (WO) [8, 2]. The opposite extreme from Sequential Consistency, WO allows any memory operations to reorder with one another, as long as no data dependencies are violated. This model allows for an equal amount of optimization as a uniprocessor, but is also the most vulnerable to programmer error, since it requires explicit *fences* to prevent unwanted reorderings. Modern processors typically support relaxed models. For example, the x86 memory model [3, 14] supports a model similar to TSO and the IBM POWER architecture supports a form of WO.

The above memory consistency models follow a pattern: they can be defined by a subset of the four ordered memory operation pairs, specifying which pairs are allowed to reorder: For example, in the WO model, any two memory operations are allowed to be reordered; in SC, no two memory operations are allowed to be reordered; and in the TSO model, no two memory operations are allowed to be reordered, except that loads can reorder before stores (see Table 1).

Note that since in this paper we analyze a concurrency bug involving multiple threads, we ignore store atomicity [5], which is tangential to our present analysis. Moreover, we do not currently handle *fence* operations explicitly,[1] which are used to restrict reorderings and are typically used for synchronization. For that reason, we do not consider models such as Release Consistency (RC) [11], which differs mainly in the types of fences supported. As we discuss in Section 7, it will be interesting to extend our process to distinguish such memory models.

---

[1]However, our shift process in Section 5 can be used to simulate a behavior similar to that arising from the use of fences.

ST/ST	ST/LD	LD/ST	LD/LD	Name
	X			Sequential Consistency
	X			Total Store Order
X	X			Partial Store Order
X	X	X	X	Weak Ordering

Table 1: **Important memory models. A "X" in column** ST/LD **means that the ordering restriction from stores to later loads can be relaxed, i.e., loads can complete before stores that precede them in program order. With regard to our model in Section 3.1.2, this means that a** LD **can settle past (swap with) a preceding** ST**. Other columns are analogous.**

2.2 Race Conditions

A common type of bug in shared-memory multithreaded programming is a *race condition*, which occurs when correctness depends on an assumption about the order in which instructions from two or more threads interleave. In particular, an *atomicity violation* [9] occurs when the programmer assumes that multiple instructions will execute as an atomic unit, but fails to insert the proper synchronization. A recent study showed that atomicity violations are extremely common in "real world" programs [17]. Race conditions are often difficult to identify due to nondeterminism: the program may behave correctly most runs, but fails only for specific thread interleavings.

A canonical example of an atomicity violation is as follows:

Thread 1	Thread 2
1: int loc = x;	1: int loc = x;
2: loc = loc + 1;	2: loc = loc + 1;
3: x = loc;	3: x = loc;

Here x is a shared variable (with x = 0 initially) and loc is local to each thread. Two threads simultaneously try to increment x by loading its value into a local variable, incrementing that local variable, then storing the updated value back to x. The programmer's intent is that x = 2 after both threads finish executing. However, the program has a race condition that can result in the spurious outcome x = 1. For instance, suppose that the two threads interleave as follows: (1) Thread 1 executes Lines 1 and 2; (2) Thread 2 executes Lines 1 and 2; (3) Thread 1 executes Line 3; (4) Thread 2 executes Line 3. This interleaving produces the final result x = 1. We say that the bug *manifests* because the result did not match programmer intent.

The standard solution for race conditions like the example above is to protect the variable x with a lock. However, locking protocols can be extremely complicated in large programs, and in practice, a concurrency bug may easily slip past even the most experienced programmers. Note that such bugs can manifest in any memory model, even Sequential Consistency.

3. MODEL

Our goal is to study how the use of different memory models impacts the likelihood of an error occurring given a canonical atomicity violation. In this section, we describe a model that allows us to formally analyze these likelihoods. It is a probabilistic model of parallel program executions under memory models that may permit reordering. At a high level, we consider two or more threads which execute a simple program containing an atomicity bug. The program

consists of basic memory operations (stores and loads). Depending on the memory model under consideration, the operations in each thread are then independently reordered via a random process we call the *settling process*. Finally, we use a thread interleaving model—the *shift model*— to model the execution of the program by interleaving the instructions of different threads. The probability of the bug manifesting is determined by analyzing how the operations from the threads interleave. We show in this paper that, when executing two threads, this probability crucially depends on the underlying memory model. Yet, perhaps counter-intuitively, we show that as the number of threads grows larger, the relative difference between the memory models becomes smaller and smaller.

3.1 Program Model

We first describe a process for modeling a typical, randomly reordered program. The process proceeds in two phases: program generation and program reordering.

3.1.1 Program Generation

We model an initial program based on the canonical atomicity violation bug described in §2.2. The program is a sequence S of memory operations $x_1, x_2, \ldots, x_m, x_{m+1}, x_{m+2}$, where each x_i has *type* $\tau(x_i) \in \{\mathsf{LD}, \mathsf{ST}\}$. x_{m+1} and x_{m+2} are Lines 1 and 3 of the canonical bug, respectively. Since we are only concerned with memory operations, we omit Line 2 (which accesses only the local variable loc), and we will use the terms *instruction* and *memory operation* synonymously in this paper. We assume for simplicity that that only x_{m+1} and x_{m+2} access the same location.[2] We will call x_{m+1} the *critical load* and x_{m+2} the *critical store*. An *initial program order* S_0 starts with a random sequence of m independently distributed LD and ST operations; $\tau(x_i) = \mathsf{ST}$ with probability p and LD with probability $1 - p$. Furthermore, for convenience in the analysis, it will be useful to approximate a very long program by letting $m \to \infty$.

3.1.2 Instruction Reordering: The Settling Process

Different memory models allow for different forms of instruction reorderings. We model this relaxation of program order using a probabilistic *settling process*. This random process models instruction reordering by taking a (random) initial program order as input, and producing a reordering of that initial program. The settling process takes into account which kinds of reorderings are allowed by the memory consistency model under consideration, and generates a random program order that is allowed to occur given the kinds of reorderings. In this section, we give an informal description of the settling process; a formal definition is given in the full paper. Figure 1 presents a visualization of the settling process.

Given an initial program order S_0, the settling process proceeds in $m+2$ rounds. In the rth round, (1) the program order S_{r-1} from the end of the $(r-1)$st round is taken as the input, and (2) the rth instruction is *settled* in this program order, which (3) creates the new program order S_r. The final output of the settling process is the program order S_{m+2} after settling the critical store x_{m+2}. Settling the rth instruction in round r of the process works as follows. Instruction x_r is recursively reordered (that is, swapped in

---

[2]If two instructions access the same location, they cannot reorder, so this assumption simplifies our analysis.

91

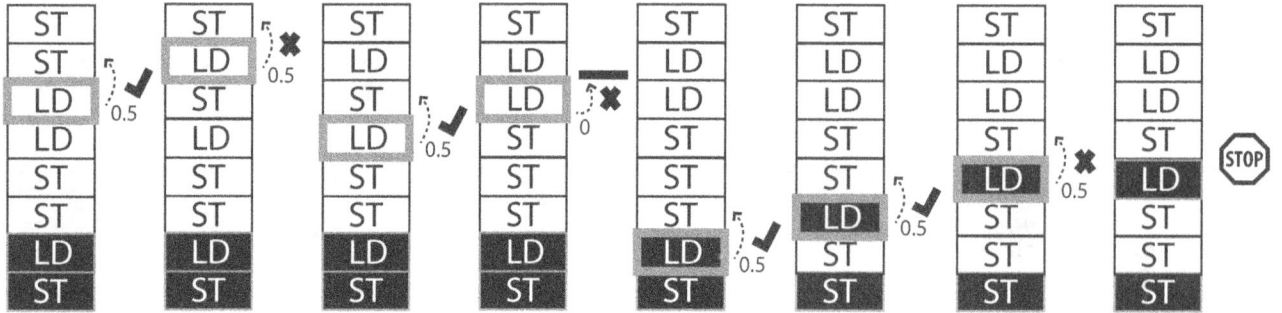

Figure 1: An instantiation of the settling process under TSO. LDs repeatedly settle upward with probability 1/2. If they fail to settle, or encounter another LD, they stop permanently, and the next-lowest LD begins. The black boxes represent the critical instructions. The grey outlines indicate the currently settling instruction. The bottom four instructions in the final order form the *critical window*.

the current program order) with its preceding instruction (initially, this is the instruction at position $r - 1$), until a reordering "fails," in which case x_r remains at its current position in the program order. A reordering always fails if the memory consistency model does not allow two operations of this type to be reordered. Otherwise, the reordering succeeds with some fixed probability s, and fails with probability $1 - s$.[3] When a reordering fails, we move onto the next round.

For ease of exposition, we will set both probabilities p (from program model) and s to be $1/2$ in subsequent sections. However, note that as long as s and p are constant, the key theorems and conclusions derived in this paper remain fundamentally the same (though some of the numerical values change somewhat).

Examples: In SC, no instructions are allowed to be reordered; hence $S_{m+2} = S_0$. In WO, all types of reorderings are allowed, so, starting from instruction 2 in the initial program order, each instruction is settled using a series of swaps with its preceding instructions, until with probability $1 - s$ a swap fails. Then the next instruction is settled, and so forth. TSO relaxes only the ST $\rightarrow$ LD ordering, which in our model implies that a LD may reorder with a preceding ST with probability s, but all other types of reorderings fail.

We will represent the result of a settling process by a permutation on the indices. For thread k, $\pi^{(k)}(i) : [1, 2, \ldots, m+2] \rightarrow [1, 2, \ldots, m+2]$ maps the instruction starting at position i to its final settled position.

The settling process has two key features: (1) memory model constraints are enforced (two operations can reorder only if allowed by the memory model), and (2) reorderings that *are* allowed occur with a fixed likelihood. One effect of the latter property is that in the final program order, most instructions will not to move too far from their position in the initial program order. The critical property of a memory consistency model that we seek to capture is the *degree to which individual instructions can reorder beyond other instructions, and thus move further away from their original position.*

---

[3]A more general form of the settling model allows different nonzero probabilities for different kinds of reorderings, depending on the types of memory operations involved. For example $s_{LD,LD}$ can be different from $s_{LD,ST}$, even if both are nonzero.

3.2 Thread Interleaving Model

We describe a second high-level random process, which is used to determine the interleaving of n threads when they are executed simultaneously on a multiprocessor. In fact, the process is quite general, and may be of independent interest as a probabilistic model. We first describe it in the abstract, then discuss how it will be used to determine the effect of the program model's output on the probability of bug manifestation.

Definition 1. Consider a sequence of n positive line segments originating at 0, having integer lengths $\bar{\gamma} = \gamma_1, \ldots, \gamma_n$. A *shift process* translates the segments by i.i.d. geometric random variables $s_1, \ldots, s_n$. Then the random event of interest, called $A(\bar{\gamma})$, is the event that the segments are shifted such that all are mutually disjoint. That is,

$$A(\bar{\gamma}) := [s_i, s_i + \gamma_i] \cap [s_j, s_j + \gamma_j] = \emptyset \ \forall \ i \neq j.$$

In Section 5, we will analyze the probability of $A(\bar{\gamma})$ for arbitrary segment lengths $\bar{\gamma}$. However, to connect this model to the task at hand, we will go on to think of these segment lengths as the *critical windows* of reordered programs generated by the program model.

Recall that we study a canonical data race, for which correct execution requires that each thread's pair of critical LD and critical ST be executed atomically. We thus refer to the sequence of instructions between the critical LD and ST (inclusively) as the *critical window* of a thread. We let B_γ^k be the event that the final ordering of thread T_k inserts γ instructions between the critical LD and ST, (sometimes referred to as the *critical window growth* of a memory model). Manifestation of the data race corresponds exactly to the event that when the reordered threads are executed in parallel, some pair of critical windows are *not* executed disjointly. We let A refer to the event that critical windows are disjoint. One can then think of $\Pr[B_\gamma^k]$ and $\Pr[A]$ as the two fundamental values we seek to characterize in this paper - each a measure of the vulnerability of a memory model to this canonical data race.

The shift model is used to simulate the parallel execution of the critical windows of each thread, under the following assumptions. All threads are assumed to initially be identical copies of a single program, generated randomly as in Section 3.1.1. Each thread is then independently reordered according the process of Section 3.1.2. We then simulate the parallel execution of the reordered threads by placing the final instruction of each critical window the origin of the number line (here representing time in reverse, with 0 being the final time step of execution), and using the shift model of Definition 1 to model the *varying rates of execution* of each thread. After shifting, the execution of each instruction is assumed to take one unit of time; instructions begin and end synchronously across all threads, in lock-step. We assume that instructions instantaneously read the current state of the system at the beginning of the time step, and instantaneously commit their changes at the end of the time step. In this way we ensure a clear semantics for the state of the system at any given time: when a LD executes, it observes all the effects of any ST that completed in a time step preceding it.

We can now observe the circumstances in which a data race manifests. There must be two threads such that, subsequent to reordering, the final regions of time steps between the critical LD and ST (inclusive) overlap with one another. In this case the data race must manifest, because one of the LDs must observe a value after (or simultaneous to) the other LD being observed, but before the other ST has committed.

A formal definition and a graphical visualization of the shift process is in the full paper.

4. THE CRITICAL WINDOW

In this section, we study what is perhaps the core component of our random process, and the only one that directly distinguishes the memory models: the reordering of instructions within an individual thread. In particular, we are interested in the final distribution of the size of the *critical window* between the critical LD and ST. For the extreme memory models of Sequential Consistency and Weak Ordering, we are easily able to exactly characterize this distribution. The bulk of the technical challenge of this section (and consequently of later sections) is in establishing results for the more subtle model, Total Store Order. By carefully conditioning on several auxiliary random variables, lower bounding complex algebraic terms by their low-indexed values, and utilizing a bound on the *partition number* of certain integers, we derive rather sharp approximations for the distribution of the critical window size. These bounds will in subsequent sections be plugged into derived formulae for the probability of bug manifestation, as a function of the thread *interleaving* process. Though the results in this section are tailored specifically to the thread generation and reordering processes specified in the previous section, it is worthwhile to observe how the asymptotics of the overall bug manifestation probability will not depend delicately on the details of this process.

We will be estimating the critical window growth, $\Pr[B_\gamma^k]$, for a select set of memory models. Recall that B_γ^k is the event that the thread T_k inserts γ instructions between the critical LD and ST in reordering. Because we will be considering a single fixed thread in this subsection, we will refer to the event B_γ^k by B_γ, and the permutation $\pi^{(k)}$ by π. The first two memory models can be considered a warmup, for the substantially more challenging case of Total Store Order. All of these results are captured in the following theorem.

THEOREM 4.1. *The critical window growth behaves according to the following functions:*

- *Sequential Consistency:*

$$\Pr[B_\gamma] = \begin{cases} 1 & \text{if } \gamma = 0, \\ 0 & \text{if } \gamma > 0. \end{cases}$$

- *Weak Ordering:*

$$\Pr[B_\gamma] = \begin{cases} 2/3 & \text{if } \gamma = 0, \\ (2^{-\gamma})/3 & \text{if } \gamma > 0. \end{cases}$$

- *Total Store Order:*

$$\Pr[B_\gamma] = \begin{cases} 2/3 & \text{if } \gamma = 0, \\ (6/7) \cdot 4^{-\gamma} + R(\gamma) \cdot 2^{-\gamma} & \text{if } \gamma > 0, \end{cases}$$

for non-negative approximation term $R(\gamma) \leq \frac{2}{21}$.

Observe that the critical window grows at vastly different rates across the models. Up to lower-order terms, the probability of a window size γ is $2^{-\gamma}$ in Weak Ordering, $(2^{-\gamma})^2$ in Total Store Order, and 0 in Sequential Consistency. It remains to be seen in later sections the extent to which this window size effects bug manifestation.

PROOF (THEOREM 4.1—SEQUENTIAL CONSISTENCY). Under sequential consistency, no instruction is ever allowed to reorder. Hence $\Pr[B_0] = 1$, and $\Pr[B_\gamma] = 0 \ \forall \gamma \neq 0$. □

We next consider the case of intermediate difficulty: Weak Ordering.

PROOF (THEOREM 4.1—WEAK ORDERING). Under weak ordering, all four ordered pairs of instruction types are allowed to pass one another. Recall that we assume a strong normal form, in which all possible swaps occur with probability 1/2. Hence in weak ordering, each subsequent instruction continually moves up with probability 1/2, until it ever fails to swap. This applies to the critical load and critical store as well, with the exception that the critical store will never pass the critical load, (because they access the same address). To calculate the probability, we condition on the resting position of the critical LD, which entails a given resting position for the critical ST, for any $\gamma > 0$.

$$\Pr[B_\gamma] = \Pr[\pi(m+2) - \pi(m+1) = \gamma + 1]$$
$$= \sum_{i=\gamma}^{\infty} \Pr[\pi(m+1) = m+1-i]$$
$$\cdot \Pr[\pi(m+2) = m+2-i+\gamma \mid \pi(m+1) = m+1-i]$$
$$= \sum_{i=\gamma}^{\infty} 2^{-(i+1)} 2^{-(i+1-\gamma)} = \frac{2^{-\gamma}}{3}.$$

We must handle the case of $\gamma = 0$ separately, because here the critical ST stops moving "automatically," when it runs up against the critical LD.

$$\Pr[B_0] = \sum_{i=0}^{\infty} \Pr[\pi(m+1) = m+1-i]$$
$$\cdot \Pr[\pi(m+2) = m+2-i \mid \pi(m+1) = m+1-i]$$
$$= \sum_{i=0}^{\infty} 2^{-(i+1)} 2^{-(i)} = 2/3. \ \square$$

Finally we turn to the far more challenging setting of Total Store Order.

PROOF (THEOREM 4.1—TOTAL STORE ORDER).
One of the strongest and most commonly used relaxed memory models, Total Store Order (TSO) only permits loads to swap with stores. Hence in calculating the distribution of window size, we need only consider the number of stores located directly before the critical load. Those stores will never move themselves, and the critical load can never swap past the first load above it. Moreover, the critical store never swaps with anything, so its final position is fixed.

However, deriving bounds on $\Pr[B_\gamma]$ is difficult. LD *operations may reorder past* ST *operations, thus pushing longer sequences of* ST *operations together*. In this section we derive bounds on the critical window growth for TSO, which is a core technical contribution of this paper. The proof is quite involved. Much difficulty arises in gaining control over the relative positions of LDs and STs. We outline the steps taken to estimate the critical window growth below. The majority of these steps are non-trivial, and often involve a delicate case analyses.

Proof Outline.

1. Express the critical window probability in terms of a series of new random variables, L_μ: the event that the second-to-last reordering leaves exactly μ contiguous STs above the critical LD.

2. To calculate the probability of L_μ, condition on the value of another series of random variables, Ψ_μ: the number of LDs *initially* between the critical LD and the $\mu + 1$th lowest ST.

3. Express the Ψ_μ-conditioned probability of L_μ in terms of the limit of the fraction of STs near the bottom of a reordered thread, and another probability, $\Pr[F_\mu | \Psi_\mu = q]$: the chance of q LDs all reordering out of a region of *at least* μ STs.

4. To estimate $\Pr[F_\mu | \Psi_\mu = q]$, condition on a new random variable, Δ: the sum, over STs, of the number of LDs below each ST. Express the probability of Δ in terms of the weighted sum of several integer *partition numbers*, and estimate these by a simple lower bound.

5. After combining the above elements to bound the probability of L_μ, lower bound an ugly term of this expression by its value at $\mu = 1$, checking via the derivative that this term is increasing in μ.

6. Use the lower bound on the probability of L_μ to finally lower bound the probability of a given window size. To achieve an upper bound, calculate the total probability not attributed to some L_μ in the lower bound, and attribute it to the worst-possible case.

We now move on to execute this plan in detail.

Step 1—Number of contiguous STs above the critical LD: Recall that S_0 (S_{m+2}) denotes the initial (final) instruction order, and that S_m refers to the instruction order just *before* the critical load is settled. For convenience, we define the following basic random events. Let $S_{\mathsf{LD},i}(j)$ be the event that after the jth instruction of S_i is a LD. Furthermore, we define $S_{\mathsf{LD},i}(j,k) = \bigwedge_{\ell=j}^{k} S_{\mathsf{LD},i}(\ell)$ as the event that the entire contiguous range from j to k in S_i consists of LDs. $S_{\mathsf{ST},i}(j)$ and $S_{\mathsf{ST},i}(j,k)$ are defined accordingly.

For $\mu \in \mathbb{N}$, we define L_μ as the event that in S_m, there are exactly μ ST operations immediately preceding the critical LD. In other words,

$$L_\mu = S_{\mathsf{LD},m}(m-\mu) \wedge S_{\mathsf{ST},m}(m-\mu+1,m).$$

The critical LD may only move γ positions if there are at least γ contiguous ST operations above it. Hence for any γ, we have

$$\Pr[B_\gamma] = \sum_{\mu=\gamma}^{\infty} \Pr[B_\gamma | L_\mu] \cdot \Pr[L_\mu].$$

Deriving $\Pr[B_\gamma | L_\mu]$ is straightforward. If $\mu = \gamma$, we have $\Pr[B_\gamma | L_\gamma] = 2^{-\gamma}$, as the critical LD must pass all γ STs. After that, it stops because the next instruction is a LD. For $\mu > \gamma$, we have $\Pr[B_\gamma | L_\mu] = 2^{-(\gamma+1)}$, because the instruction above the γth ST is also a ST. Hence there is only a $1/2$ probability of the reordering completing when it reaches that point.

It remains to derive bounds for $\Pr[L_\mu]$ for all μ. This is the primary technical lemma of the proof.

LEMMA 4.2. *For any* $\mu > 0$, $\Pr[L_\mu] \geq \frac{4}{7} \cdot 2^{-\mu}$. *Moreover,* $\Pr[L_0] = 1/3$ *exactly.*

PROOF. We will approach this lemma by asking (1) how many LDs are interspersed among the first μ STs above the critical LD, and (2) what is the probability that all of those LDs settle such that we are left with μ contiguous STs above the critical LD. Because STs cannot settle past LDs in this model, nothing happens during rounds in which a ST can move; the technical difficulty arises in the motion of the LDs.

Step 2—Number of interspersed LDs: In the initial program order S_0, let Φ_μ refer to the position of the μth-lowest non-critical ST. Formally,

$$\Phi_\mu = \min\{i : |\{j \geq i : S_{\mathsf{ST},0}(j)\}| = \mu + 1\}.$$

Furthermore, let Ψ_μ refer to the number of LD operations above the critical LD but below the μth-lowest non-critical ST. That is,

$$\Psi_\mu = m + 1 - \mu - \Phi_\mu.$$

Note that as the program length goes to infinity, the probability that such a Φ_μ and Ψ_μ exist goes to 1. Now we can express $\Pr[L_\mu]$ as

$$\Pr[L_\mu] = \sum_{q=0}^{\infty} \Pr[L_\mu | \Psi_\mu = q] \cdot \Pr[\Psi_\mu = q]. \tag{1}$$

We have $\Pr[\Psi_\mu = q] = 2^{-\mu} 2^{-q} \binom{\mu+q-1}{q}$ because there are $\binom{\mu+q-1}{q}$ ways to build a string of μ STs and q LDs such that the top instruction is a ST.

Step 3—Probability of interspersed LDs settling out: The difficult part of bound (1) is $\Pr[L_\mu | \Psi_\mu = q]$. This is the probability that

(A) All q LDs between the ST at Φ_μ and the critical LD settle up until they pass the ST at Φ_μ,

(B) but do not settle so far that the settled instruction above the ST at Φ_μ is another ST.

(B) is due to the fact that L_μ specifies that there be *exactly* μ STs above the critical LD. The probability of (B) relies

94

on the instruction directly above Φ_μ in $S_{\Phi_\mu - 1}$. If it is a LD, then (B) holds automatically, since all the LDs must stop settling. However, if it is a ST, then (B) only holds if not all of the q LDs that have passed the ST at Φ_μ also pass the next-highest ST. Hence this is the first property on which we condition.

$$\Pr[L_\mu | \Psi_\mu = q] = \Pr[L_\mu \wedge S_{LD,\Phi_\mu - 1}(\Phi_\mu - 1) | \Psi_\mu = q]$$
$$+ \Pr[L_\mu \wedge S_{ST,\Phi_\mu - 1}(\Phi_\mu - 1) | \Psi_\mu = q].$$

By Bayes' Law,

$$\Pr[L_\mu \wedge S_{LD,\Phi_\mu}(\Phi_\mu - 1) | \Psi_\mu = q]$$
$$= \Pr[S_{LD,\Phi_\mu}(\Phi_\mu - 1) | \Psi_\mu = q]$$
$$\cdot \Pr[L_\mu | S_{LD,\Phi_\mu}(\Phi_\mu - 1) \wedge \Psi_\mu = q].$$

We first consider the latter term. Because the final instruction that settles above Φ_μ will be a LD under these conditions, this depends only on the bottom μ instructions settled above the critical LD being STs. For shorthand, let

$$F_\mu = S_{ST,m}(m - \mu + 1, m).$$

Then

$$\Pr[L_\mu | S_{LD,\Phi_\mu}(\Phi_\mu - 1) \wedge \Psi_\mu = q] = \Pr[F_\mu | \Psi_\mu = q].$$

In contrast, for L_μ to hold given $S_{ST,\Phi_\mu - 1}(\Phi_\mu - 1)$, it does not suffice for the q LDs to move past Φ_μ. They must also not all settle past the next highest instruction. They do so with probability 2^{-q}. Hence

$$\Pr[L_\mu | S_{ST,\Phi_\mu - 1}(\Phi_\mu - 1) \wedge \Psi_\mu = q] =$$
$$\Pr[F_\mu | \Psi_\mu = q] \cdot (1 - 2^{-q}).$$

Putting these expressions together, we find that

$\Pr[L_\mu | \Psi_\mu = q]$
$= \Pr[F_\mu | \Psi_\mu = q] \cdot \Pr[S_{LD,\Phi_\mu - 1}(\Phi_\mu - 1)]$
$\quad + \Pr[F_\mu | \Psi_\mu = q] \cdot \Pr[S_{ST,\Phi_\mu - 1}(\Phi_\mu - 1)] \cdot (1 - 2^{-q})$
$= \Pr[F_\mu | \Psi_\mu = q] \cdot (1 - 2^{-q} \cdot (1 - \Pr[S_{ST,\Phi_\mu - 1}(\Phi_\mu - 1)])).$

We first derive an exact value for $\Pr[S_{ST,i}(i)]$. Though it is difficult to determine the probability that a given instruction is a ST in general, this particular value can be derived exactly through a recurrence relation.

CLAIM 4.3.

$$\lim_{i \to \infty} \Pr[S_{ST,i}(i)] = 2/3.$$

PROOF. After reordering stage i, instruction i can be a ST in one of two ways. Either it can initially be a ST, (in which case it never reorders) or it can initially be a LD, the instruction above it can be settled as a ST, and the two can swap. Hence

$$\Pr[S_{ST,i}(i)] = \frac{1}{2} + \frac{1}{2} \cdot \Pr[S_{ST,i-1}(i-1)] \cdot \frac{1}{2}.$$

This is a recurrence relation of the form $X_i = b + aX_i$, which has the solution $X_i = \frac{b}{1-a} + a^{i-1}(X_1 - \frac{b}{1-a})$. Plugging in $X_1 = 1/2$, $a = 1/4$, $b = 1/2$, we find

$$\Pr[S_{ST,i}(i)] = \frac{1/2}{1 - 1/4} + (1/4)^{i-1} \left(1/2 - \frac{1/2}{1 - 1/4}\right).$$
$$= 2/3 + (1/4)^{i-1}(1/2 - 2/3)$$

The resulting probability is a function of i, but we are interested in the steady-state as the size of the program goes to infinity. Hence the second term falls out.

$$\lim_{i \to \infty} \Pr[S_{ST,i}(i)] = 2/3. \quad \square$$

Now that we know the typical fraction of instructions near the bottom of the program that are STs after reordering, we can derive a bound on $\Pr[F_\mu | \Psi_\mu = q]$.

Step 4—Estimating $\Pr[F_\mu | \Psi_\mu = q]$:

CLAIM 4.4.

$$\Pr[F_\mu | \Psi_\mu = q] \geq \frac{2^{-(q-1)} - 2^{-\mu q}}{\binom{\mu + q - 1}{q}}.$$

PROOF. Everything in this proof is implicitly conditioned on the event $\Psi_\mu = q$. Let the random variable

$$\Delta = \sum_{\Phi_\mu < i \leq m : \tau_{LD,0}(i)} |\{\Phi_\mu \leq j < i : \tau_{ST,0}(j)\}|$$

represent the total number of positions that LDs from Φ_μ to m must move up, in order to leave a sequence of μ STs immediately above the critical LD. It must be that $\Delta \geq q$, because at least instruction Φ_μ is a ST, and $\Delta \leq \mu q$, because no LD can be required to pass more than μ STs. With this definition, we may write $\Pr[F_\mu | \Psi_\mu = q] = \sum_{\delta = q}^{\mu q} \Pr[\Delta = \delta] \cdot 2^{-\delta}$. The exact value of $\Pr[\Delta = \delta]$ can be stated formally, but not in a closed form. Namely, let $\phi(x, y, z)$ be the number of distinct multi-sets of y positive integers summing to x, such that each integer is at most z. This is a variant on the much-studied *partition number* of x. Then $\phi(\delta, q, \mu)$ is exactly the number of arrangements of q LDs and μ STs (beginning with a ST) such that δ is the sum of the number of STs above each of the LDs. (For each LD, we simply select how many STs to place it below—the relative order of the LDs is immaterial.) There are $\binom{m+q-1}{q}$ total arrangements of LDs and STs beginning with a ST. Hence

$$\Pr[\Delta = \delta] = \frac{\phi(\delta, q, \mu)}{\binom{\mu + q - 1}{q}},$$

and

$$\Pr[F_\mu | \Psi_\mu = q] = \sum_{\delta = q}^{\mu q} \frac{\phi(\delta, q, \mu)}{\binom{\mu + q - 1}{q}} \cdot 2^{-\delta}.$$

Simple forms for $\phi(x, y, z)$ are not known. Asymptotic results exist, but are not helpful here because the terms with small parameters have the largest contributions. However, to achieve a good bound it suffices to show that $\phi(\delta, q, \mu) \geq 1$ when $q \leq \delta \leq \mu q$. To show that a partition exists that achieves any number in this range, consider the following construction. Set $\delta \bmod q$ of the integers to $\lceil \delta/q \rceil$, and set the rest of the integers to $\lfloor \delta/q \rfloor$. We can set the integers this large, because $\delta/q \leq (\mu q)/q = \mu$. Then the chosen integers sum to $(\delta \bmod q)\lceil \delta/q \rceil + (q - (\delta \bmod q))\lfloor \delta/q \rfloor$ which can be shown to be exactly δ. Hence we may write

$$\Pr[F_\mu | \Psi_\mu = q] \geq \frac{1}{\binom{\mu + q - 1}{q}} \sum_{\delta = q}^{\mu q} 2^{-\delta} = \frac{2^{-(q-1)} - 2^{-\mu q}}{\binom{\mu + q - 1}{q}}. \quad \square$$

Having derived a bound for $\Pr[F_\mu | \Psi_\mu = q]$, we are now in a position to conclude the proof of Lemma 4.2. First note that $\Pr[L_0] = 1/3$, by Claim 4.3. For values of μ greater than 0, Claim 4.4 will be the central tool in the proof, which is left to the full version of the paper. $\square$

The remainder of the proof of Theorem 4.1, steps 5 and 6, is deferred to the full version of the paper. $\square$

5. SHIFT PROCESS

Here we discuss the next component of our analysis: a "shift process" meant to capture the interleaving of reordered threads. We refer the reader back to the definition in Section 3.2. This process is where the critical windows derived from the reordering process come into effect.

In the analysis that follows, we assume that each critical window's shift is distributed geometrically, representing the intuition that threads are exponentially less likely to execute at progressively increasing offsets from one another. Let $\bar{\gamma} = (\gamma_1, \gamma_2, \ldots, \gamma_n) \in \mathbb{N}^n$ be a sequence of integral "segment lengths." In subsequent sections, γ_k will be used to represent the length of the critical window of thread T_k. We define a shift process on $\bar{\gamma}$ as follows. Consider n segments of the line, of lengths $\gamma_1, \gamma_2, \ldots, \gamma_n$, and let the starting point of each segment be shifted up from 0 by an i.i.d. positive random variable s_i. We are interested in the probability that the resulting set of shifted segments is non-overlapping. In other words, we would like to bound $\Pr[A(\bar{\gamma})]$, where $A(\bar{\gamma})$ is the event that $\forall i \neq j \in \{1, 2, \ldots, n\}$, we have $[s_i, s_i + \gamma_i] \cap [s_j, s_j + \gamma_j] = \emptyset$.

The following theorem states this probability precisely, and as such is not particularly enlightening on its own. However, when the segment lengths are random variables drawn from a well-understood distribution (as they are in the case of reordered random threads), we will be able to state the probability concisely.

THEOREM 5.1.

$$\Pr[A(\bar{\gamma})] = \frac{2^{-\left(\binom{n+1}{2}-1\right)}}{\prod_{i=1}^{n-1}(1 - 2^{-(n+1-i)})} \sum_{\sigma \in Sym_n} \prod_{i=1}^{n-1} 2^{-(n-i)\gamma_{\sigma(i)}},$$

where Sym_n is the symmetric group of degree n: the set of all permutations on n elements.

The following corollary simplifies this expression:

COROLLARY 5.2. For some $c(n) \in [2, 4]$,

$$\Pr[A(\bar{\gamma})] = c(n) \cdot 2^{-\binom{n+1}{2}} \cdot \sum_{\sigma \in Sym_n} \prod_{i=1}^{n-1} 2^{-(n-i)\gamma_{\sigma(i)}}.$$

In particular, $c(2) = \frac{8}{3}$ exactly.

The proof of the corollary is in the full version of the paper. We now turn to the proof of the main theorem. The challenge is to characterize the probability that the next segment is shifted to a position disjoint from all previous segments. At first glance, it is difficult to handle the huge and diverse set of legal placements for a set of segments. Our key insight is to condition on the *relative order* of the magnitude of the shifts. We then consider the probability that each segment is disjoint from the previous threads in this order. In so doing, we are able to exploit the memorylessness of the geometric distribution. Let t be an arbitrary segment, and t' be the segment immediately preceding it in this order. To understand the distribution of disjoint placements for t, we need only know the distribution of the origin of

t'. Then by assuming that the segments are disjoint, we can infer that the origin of t is distributed according the origin of t', plus the length of t', plus an independent geometric random variable.

PROOF (THEOREM 5.1). Let s_i be a geometric random variable with expectation 2 (i.e., $s_i = k$ with probability $2^{-(k+1)}$ $\forall k \in \mathbb{N}$). In order to analyze the probability of $A(\bar{\gamma})$, we will take the following steps. We will first condition on the ordering of the segments. Then for a given ordering, we will use the memorylessness of the shift variables to calculate the probability of each successive segment being disjoint from each previous.

For a permutation σ on $\{1, 2, \ldots, n\}$, let Y_σ be the event that for all i, the ith largest shift occurs on segment $\sigma(i)$. That is, $s_{\sigma(1)} \geq s_{\sigma(2)} \geq \cdots \geq s_{\sigma(n)}$. Then $\Pr[A(\bar{\gamma})] = \sum_{\sigma \in Sym_n} \Pr[A(\bar{\gamma}) \wedge Y_\sigma]$.

We now analyze $\Pr[A(\bar{\gamma}) \wedge Y_\sigma]$. We will refer to this event by $A(\bar{\gamma}, \sigma)$. For all segments to be disjoint, it must be the case that each segment begins after the *end* of every segment that began before it. σ captures exactly the order in which segments begin. So disjointness means that for all i, j s.t. $\sigma(j) > \sigma(i)$, segment j begins after the end of segment i. Hence for each i, we may condition on the shift of the segment with the ith largest shift, and consider the probability that each segment with a smaller shift follows its completion.

$$\Pr[A(\bar{\gamma}, \sigma)] = \sum_{\ell_1=0}^{\infty} \Pr[A(\bar{\gamma}, \sigma) \wedge s_{\sigma(1)} = \ell_1]$$

$$= \sum_{\ell_1=0}^{\infty} \Pr[A(\bar{\gamma}, \sigma) \wedge s_{\sigma(1)} = \ell_1 \wedge \bigwedge_{i=2}^{n} s_{\sigma(i)} \geq \ell_1 + \gamma_{\sigma(1)}]$$

$$= \sum_{\ell_1=0}^{\infty} \Pr[A(\bar{\gamma}, \sigma) | s_{\sigma(1)} = \ell_1 \wedge \bigwedge_{i=2}^{n} s_{\sigma(i)} \geq \ell_1 + \gamma_{\sigma(1)}]$$

$$\cdot \Pr[s_{\sigma(1)} = \ell_1] \cdot \prod_{i=2}^{n} \Pr[s_{\sigma(i)} \geq \ell_1 + \gamma_{\sigma(1)}].$$

The third equality is due to the independence of the shift variables. Let $\bar{\gamma}^i$ refer to the restriction of $\bar{\gamma}$ to the segment indices with the $n - i + 1$ smallest shifts (i.e., $\bar{\gamma}^i = \bar{\gamma}_{|[n] \setminus \bigcup_{j=i}^{n} \sigma(j)}$). Similarly, let σ^i refer to the restriction of σ to the $n - i + 1$ smallest shifts (i.e., $\sigma^i = \sigma_{|[n] \setminus [i-1]}$). We define these structures so that we can express the disjointness event in terms of a new disjointness event on a smaller set of unconditioned segments. In particular, let $A(\bar{\gamma}^i, \sigma^i)$ be the disjointness event for an independent random shift process on segments $\sigma(i), \sigma(i+1), \ldots, \sigma(n)$, with permutation σ^i pointing to the new indices of these segments. We will see that we are permitted to condition on such a prior event, because of the memoryless of the shift variables.

Conditioned on the first segment being disjoint from all the following segments, we need only consider the event $A(\bar{\gamma}^2, \sigma)$. Then due to the memorylessness of the shifts, we have

$$\Pr[A(\bar{\gamma}^i, \sigma^i) | s_{\sigma^i(1)} = \ell_1 \wedge \bigwedge_{j=2}^{n} s_{\sigma^i(j)} \geq \ell_1 + \gamma_{\sigma^i(1)}]$$

$$= \Pr[A(\bar{\gamma}^{i+1}, \sigma^{i+1}) | \bigwedge_{j=2}^{n} s_{\sigma^i(j)} \geq \ell_1 + \gamma_{\sigma^i(1)}]$$

$$= \Pr[A(\bar{\gamma}^{i+1}, \sigma^{i+1})| \bigwedge_{j=2}^{n} s_{\sigma^i(j)} \geq 0] = \Pr[A(\bar{\gamma}^{i+1}, \sigma^{i+1})].$$

We now observe a simple recurrence relation that defines $\Pr[A(\bar{\gamma}^i, \sigma^i)]$.

$$\Pr[A(\bar{\gamma}^i, \sigma^i)] = \sum_{\ell_1=0}^{\infty} \Pr[A(\bar{\gamma}^{i+1}, \sigma^{i+1})] \cdot \Pr[s_{\sigma^i(1)} = \ell_1]$$
$$\cdot \prod_{j=i+1}^{n} \Pr[s_{\sigma^i(j)} \geq \ell_1 + \gamma_{\sigma^i(1)}]$$
$$= \sum_{\ell_1=0}^{\infty} \Pr[A(\bar{\gamma}^{i+1}, \sigma^{i+1})] \cdot \frac{1}{2} 2^{-\ell_1} \cdot \prod_{j=i+1}^{n} \frac{1}{2} \cdot 2^{-(\ell_1 + \gamma_{\sigma^i(1)})}$$
$$= \sum_{\ell_1=0}^{\infty} \Pr[A(\bar{\gamma}^{i+1}, \sigma^{i+1})] \cdot 2^{-(\ell_1 + 1 + (n-i)(\ell_1 + \gamma_{\sigma^i(1)} + 1))}$$
$$= 2^{-1 + (n-i)(\gamma_{\sigma^i(1)} + 1)} \cdot \Pr[A(\bar{\gamma}^{i+1}, \sigma^{i+1})] \sum_{\ell_1=0}^{\infty} (2^{-(n-i+1)})^{\ell_1}$$
$$= \frac{2^{-1 + (n-i)(\gamma_{\sigma^i(1)} + 1)}}{1 - 2^{-(n-i+1)}} \cdot \Pr[A(\bar{\gamma}^{i+1}, \sigma^{i+1})].$$

Moreover, it is clear that $\Pr[A(\bar{\gamma}^n, \sigma^n)] = 1$. Then noting that $\sigma^i(1) = \sigma(i)$, the solution is trivial:

$$\Pr[A(\bar{\gamma}^1, \sigma^1)] = \prod_{i=1}^{n-1} \frac{2^{-(n+1-i)-(n-i)\gamma_{\sigma(i)}}}{1 - 2^{-(n+1-i)}}$$
$$= \frac{2^{-(\binom{n+1}{2}-1)}}{\prod_{i=1}^{n-1}(1 - 2^{-(n+1-i)})} \cdot \prod_{i=1}^{n-1} 2^{-(n-i)\gamma_{\sigma(i)}}.$$

Finally, plugging these terms into the overall probability of disjointness yields the expression in the theorem. We will use this expression in the next section to calculate the probability of bug manifestation. □

6. JOINING THE MODELS

We have now described the two fundamental random processes of our work. Though the two are interesting in isolation, it is by combining them that we will achieve our overall goal: to characterize the probability of the canonical data race manifesting, under various memory models.

Our first observation is to note that Corollary 5.2 can be further simplified, provided the segment lengths are drawn from a distribution with a very weak condition.

THEOREM 6.1. *Let $\bar{\Gamma} = \Gamma_1, \ldots, \Gamma_n$ be a distribution over segment lengths, drawn from $\mathbb{N}^n$. Assume that the marginal distribution of each segment length is identical (i.e., $\Gamma_i \sim \Gamma_j \ \forall \ i \neq j$); they needn't be independent. Then all permutations of segment shifts are equivalent, and*

$$\Pr[A(\bar{\Gamma})] = c(n) \cdot 2^{-\binom{n+1}{2}} \cdot n! \cdot \mathbb{E}_{\bar{\Gamma}}[\prod_{i=1}^{n-1} 2^{-i\Gamma_i}].$$

The proof is given in the full paper. Because the identicality condition holds for the critical window size, the theorem gives an indication of how it is that we can analyze the overall bug manifestation concretely. Recall that the process of Section 4 generates a uniformly random program of STs and LDs, then randomly "settles" each instruction in turn, according to the rules of the memory model. The process of Section 5 applies a random "shift" to a series of line segments, the key event for which is the mutual disjointness of all the segments. We now combine these two processes by letting the line segment lengths of the shift process be distributed as the critical window size of the settling process. An important subtlety is that *we generate a single initial random program, then independently reorder n copies of this program.* Though this makes the analysis more complex, it adds a degree of realism: with n identical threads, it is more natural that the same data race would be present in the same position of every pair of threads. The following two theorems summarize our key results.

THEOREM 6.2. *For $n = 2$ threads, the probability that the canonical data race does not manifest is the following, in each of the three main models.*

Sequential Consistency:	$\Pr[A] \approx 0.1666$
Total Store Order:[4]	$0.1369 > \Pr[A] > 0.1315$
Weak Ordering:	$\Pr[A] \approx 0.1296$

THEOREM 6.3. *As n grows, the probability of successful execution is identical in all models, up to lower order terms in the exponent. In particular, $\Pr[A] = e^{-n^2(1+o(1))}$.*

The first tightly bounds the probability of successful execution for the case of $n = 2$ threads; the second gives an asymptotic bound on this probability for large n. We leave the proofs of these theorems to the full paper. Both proofs are rather technical and build upon the theorems of the previous two sections. The only surprising observation necessary is that, when lower bounding a certain expectation over the critical window for n threads, it suffices to use only a single term of this expectation. Doing so achieves the asymptotic behavior we seek.

Key Observations: Interpreting Theorems 6.2 and 6.3 yields remarkable insights. Though the case of $n = 2$ substantively distinguishes the memory models, we find that as n grows, the probability in all memory models approaches the same value, up to lower order terms in the exponent. This dichotomy is a fundamental take-away for informing computer architecture decisions. Though the use of weaker memory models does increase the risk of program error, as the number of threads grows this risk grows negligibly compared to growth of risk of error in even sequential consistency. This is of particular importance given the trends towards ever larger multicores that enable more and more concurrent threads.

7. DISCUSSION

Limitations and possible extensions: Our analysis assumes that the program consists solely of loads and stores, when real programs include synchronization, arithmetic, etc. These instructions can affect the timing of the program, introduce data dependencies that limit reordering, or disallow certain types of reorderings. An important item for future work is to include acquire/release fences, which are necessary to simulate memory models such as Release Consistency [11]. These fences act as one-way barriers, allowing instructions to reorder into, but not out of, a critical section. This behavior can be easily modeled using settling (§3.1.2). Fences

---

[4]A very similar analysis achieves a similar result for Partial Store Order (PSO). We omit the result for brevity.

make concurrency bugs less likely to manifest, as programs with fences have fewer legal reorderings. However, we conjecture that adding fences will not significantly change the main conclusions derived in this paper.

Optimized implementations of SC: Our model of Sequential Consistency assumes a relatively simple implementation wherein each processor executes only one memory instruction at a time. Many SC implementations use aggressive optimizations such as speculative execution to compete with the performance of weaker memory models [10, 12, 7]. We do not consider this simplifying assumption to be a weakness of our model; rather, we believe our results about weak memory models can be extended to address optimizing implementations of strong memory models. In other words, concurrency bugs are more likely to manifest in an implementation of SC that uses aggressive reordering than in a simple (and slow) implementation.

Generality of Results: In this paper, we propose and study one specific probabilistic process to model program execution and thread interleaving. Clearly, there are other plausible models that can be studied. Our intuition is that the results in this paper have a certain robustness with regard to changes to the parameters in our models as well as to changes in the model. However, future work is required to formally validate this conjecture.

8. CONCLUSION

With the ubiquity of multicore systems and the trend towards integrating every more cores on a single chip, multiprocessor programmability has become one of the key challenges in computer science. Even with improvements in programmability, we are likely to see an increase in software defects, given the inherent difficulty of concurrent programming. Memory consistency models are at the center of the programmability discussion, since they determine the memory access semantics of parallel programs. The debate over memory models has historically revolved around the trade-offs between programmability, performance and complexity. In this paper we bring a new axis to this discussion: *software reliability*. We study an analytical model and show that concurrency bugs are indeed more likely to manifest themselves in relaxed memory models, but surprisingly, that as the number of parallel threads increases, the difference between harsh and weak memory models diminishes. The latter observation can have important consequences on system designers when developing new memory models.

9. REFERENCES

[1] S. V. Adve and K. Gharachorloo. Shared memory consistency models: A tutorial. *IEEE Computer*, 29(12):66–76, December 1996.

[2] S. V. Adve and M. D. Hill. Weak ordering—a new definition. In *Proc. of the 17th International Symposium on Computer Architecture (ISCA)*, 1990.

[3] AMD Corp. *AMD64 Architecture Programmer's Manual - Volume 2: System Programming*, July 2007.

[4] C. Artho, K. Havelund, and A. Biere. High-level data races. *Journal on Software Testing, Verification & Reliability*, 13(4):220–227, 2003.

[5] Arvind and J.-W. Maessen. Memory model = instruction reordering + store atomicity. In *Proc. of*

the 33th International Symposium on Computer Architecture (ISCA), 2006.

[6] H.-J. Boehm and S. V. Adve. Foundations of the C++ concurrency memory model. In *Proc. of the 29th Conference on Programming Language Design and Implementation (PLDI)*, 2008.

[7] L. Ceze, J. Tuck, P. Montesinos, and J. Torrellas. BulkSC: Bulk enforcement of sequential consistency. In *Proc. of the 34th International Symposium on Computer Architecture (ISCA)*, 2007.

[8] M. Dubois, C. Scheurich, and F. A. Briggs. Memory access buffering in multiprocessors. In *Proc. of the 13th International Symposium on Computer Architecture (ISCA)*, 1986.

[9] C. Flanagan and S. Qadeer. A type and effect system for atomicity. In *Proc. of the 24th Conference on Programming Language Design and Implementation (PLDI)*, 2003.

[10] K. Gharachorloo, A. Gupta, and J. Hennessy. Two techniques to enhance the performance of memory consistency models. In *International Conference on Parallel Processing*, 1991.

[11] K. Gharachorloo, D. Lenoski, J. Laudon, P. Gibbons, A. Gupta, and J. Hennessy. Memory consistency and event ordering in scalable shared-memory multiprocessors. In *Proc. of the 17th International Symposium on Computer Architecture (ISCA)*, 1990.

[12] C. Gniady, B. Falsafi, and T. N. Vijaykumar. Is SC + ILP = RC? In *Proc. of the 26th International Symposium on Computer Architecture (ISCA)*, 1999.

[13] J. R. Goodman. Cache consistency and sequential consistency. Technical Report 1006, University of Wisconsin-Madison, 1989.

[14] Intel Corp. *Intel 64 and IA-32 Architectures Software Developer's Manual—Volume 3A: System Programming Guide, Part 1*, December 2009.

[15] L. Lamport. How to make a multiprocessor computer that correctly executes multiprocess programs. *IEEE Transactions on Computers*, 28(9):690–691, September 1979.

[16] J. Lee and D. Padua. Hiding relaxed memory consistency with compilers. In *Proc. of the 9th Conference on Parallel Architectures and Compilation Techniques (PACT)*, 2000.

[17] S. Lu, S. Park, E. Seo, and Y. Zhou. Learning from mistakes—a comprehensive study on real world concurrency bug characteristics. In *Proc. of the 13th Conference on Architectural Support for Programming Languages and Operating Systems (ASPLOS)*, 2008.

[18] J. Manson, W. Pugh, and S. V. Adve. The Java memory model. In *Proc. of the 32th Symposium on Principles of Programming Languages (POPL)*, 2005.

[19] SPARC International, Inc. *The SPARC Architecture Manual—Version 8*, 1992.

On The Power of Hardware Transactional Memory to Simplify Memory Management

Aleksandar Dragojević
EPFL, Switzerland
aleksandar.dragojevic@epfl.ch

Maurice Herlihy
Brown University
mph@cs.brown.edu

Yossi Lev
Oracle Labs
yossi.lev@oracle.com

Mark Moir
Oracle Labs
mark.moir@oracle.com

ABSTRACT

Dynamic memory management is a significant source of complexity in the design and implementation of practical concurrent data structures. We study how hardware transactional memory (HTM) can be used to simplify and streamline memory reclamation for such data structures. We propose and evaluate several new HTM-based algorithms for the "Dynamic Collect" problem that lies at the heart of many modern memory management algorithms. We demonstrate that HTM enables simpler and faster solutions, with better memory reclamation properties, than prior approaches. Despite recent theoretical arguments that HTM provides no worst-case advantages, our results support the claim that HTM can provide significantly better common-case performance, as well as reduced conceptual complexity.

Categories and Subject Descriptors

D.1.3 [**Programming Techniques**]: Concurrent Programming

General Terms

Algorithms,Design,Performance

Keywords

Transactional Memory, Synchronization, Hardware, Memory Management

1. INTRODUCTION

The Java(tm) concurrency libraries [13] provide a number of lock-free data structures that have no counterparts in C++. A key obstacle to porting them to C++ is that Java is garbage-collected, while C++ requires explicit memory management, which can be very difficult. In this paper, we explore our belief that hardware transactional memory (HTM) [12] can significantly simplify the design and implementation of common concurrent data structures and algorithms, particularly with respect to dynamic memory management.

We begin with some anecdotal evidence showing that, by using HTM, we can build a lock-free FIFO queue that is superior to the state-of-the-art implementation in terms of algorithmic complexity, performance, and space requirements. This dramatic example motivates us to explore whether HTM is *fundamentally* more powerful than traditional hardware synchronization primitives for building dynamic-sized concurrent data structures. We argue that the *Dynamic Collect* problem [11] is an appropriate problem to study in exploring this question, and most of this paper focuses on that problem.

In Section 2, we precisely specify the Dynamic Collect variant on which we have focused for this work. In Section 3, we outline a variety of HTM-based Dynamic Collect algorithms that explore various tradeoffs; we present one algorithm in detail in Section 4. In Section 5, we present performance results illustrating the impact of these tradeoffs on different HTM-based implementations, as well as comparing to some implementations that do not use HTM. Broadly, our results show that with HTM it is significantly easier to design correct implementations, and that non-HTM algorithms tend to perform worse, require significantly more space, or both. We discuss how various aspects of HTM designs relate to our algorithms in Section 6, and conclude in Section 7.

1.1 Lock-free FIFO queues

The Michael-Scott queue [15] is one of the best-known and most widely used lock-free data structures. The queue is represented as a linked list of entries that are allocated dynamically as values are enqueued. Any practical implementation of this algorithm must address the question of how the memory for these entries can be reused. This is challenging because the algorithm allows a queue node to be accessed by ongoing operations even after the node has been removed from the queue.

The most straightforward approach is to have each thread keep a thread-local pool of unused entries. When a thread enqueues an item, it allocates an entry from its local pool whenever possible, and when a thread dequeues a value, it returns the dequeued entry to its own pool. Using this approach, once an entry has been allocated, that memory cannot be used for any purpose other than as a queue entry. Therefore, even in a quiescent state, when no method calls are in progress, the memory used for the queue is at least proportional to the *historical* maximal queue size, which is a significant disadvantage.

An alternative is to use a technique such as the "Repeat Offender Problem" ROP [10] or Hazard Pointers [14] to enable the Michael-Scott algorithm to reclaim memory, but this entails significant additional overhead and complexity, as discussed further below. We have implemented a concurrent FIFO queue by enclosing

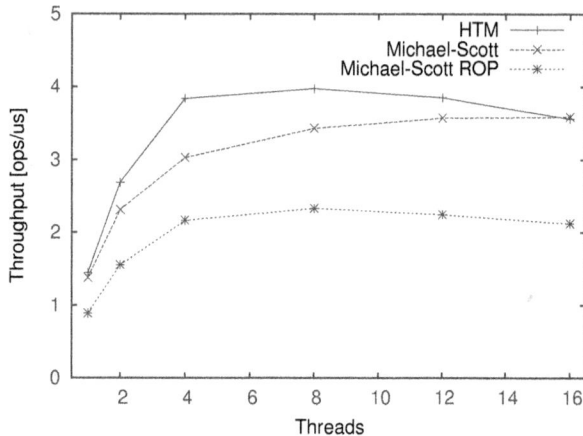

Figure 1: Queue performance

simple sequential code in hardware transactions. A successful dequeue operation frees the dequeued entry's memory to the operating system. No transaction serialized after the dequeue will see a reference to that entry, so the only danger is that a concurrent transaction may try to use it. However, if it does, it is guaranteed to abort.[1] Moreover, the HTM-based algorithm is significantly simpler than the Michael-Scott algorithm, which must deal with certain race conditions that cannot occur when operations are executed within hardware transactions, as well as with the ABA problem [15] that arises due to recycling queue nodes. To roughly quantify the difference in complexity between these algorithms, the HTM-based one would be a reasonable homework exercise for an undergraduate student, while the Michael-Scott algorithm yielded a PODC publication!

Figure 1 compares the throughput of the simple HTM-based queue and the Michael-Scott queue (with and without ROP) when a mix of enqueue and dequeue operations is performed on the queue. The experiment was performed on a 16 core Rock CPU [8]. The HTM-based algorithm can reclaim unused entries and is nonetheless up to 25% faster than the Michael-Scott queue due to its simpler code. The overheads of using ROP for reclaiming memory are significant—between 35% and 75%. This matches our intuition that HTM can enable algorithms that are better in terms of speed, simplicity *and* memory reuse.

1.2 Dynamic Collect problem

Techniques such as Hazard Pointers [14] or the "Repeat Offender Problem" (ROP) [10] can be used to enable concurrent data structures such as the Michael-Scott queue to return memory to the system when it is no longer needed. These techniques require a thread to "announce" its intention to use a reference before using it. Before a thread can free a block of memory, it must check that no other thread has announced an intention to access that block. This check amounts to performing a *collect* [2, 3, 16] over an array of announced references to ensure that the block to be freed is not potentially in use.

While Hazard Pointers and ROP can enable memory reuse, they have memory requirements of their own. In particular, each active thread requires a separate location in which to announce a pointer

---

[1] We assume "sandboxed" HTM such as in Sun's prototype multi-core chip code named Rock [8], in which a transaction that dereferences an illegal reference aborts, but does not otherwise disrupt the thread (say, by causing a segmentation fault).

it intends to access. Unless these locations themselves can be reclaimed and recycled, algorithms that use these techniques inherit another form of historical space requirement: even in a quiescent state, the memory consumption of the data structure is at least proportional to its current size plus the historical maximum number of active threads. To overcome this limitation, Michael [14] and Herlihy et al. [10] propose dynamic versions of their techniques that allow locations used for announcements to be released and recycled. As a result, these memory management techniques encompass *Dynamic Collect* [11] algorithms: a thread announces its intention to dereference a pointer by using the `Register` and/or `Update` operations, and scans for other threads' announcements using the `Collect` operation. Any fundamental limitation of Dynamic Collect algorithms is inherited by any data structure that uses these approaches to manage memory. We therefore believe that studying the impact of synchronization support on Dynamic Collect algorithms provides useful insight into the inherent limitations of the ability of non-HTM systems to support dynamic concurrent data structures.

2. DYNAMIC COLLECT

2.1 Data types and operations

A *Collect object* uses two data types, *handle* and *value*, and supports the following operations:

- $h = $ `Register`(v): binds the value v to an unused handle h, which is returned to the caller.

- `Update`(h, v): binds value v to handle h.

- `DeRegister`(h): removes the current binding to handle h.

- `Collect`(): returns a set of (handle,value) pairs.

2.2 Well-formedness

We say that a handle h is *registered* to a thread t when it is returned by an invocation by t of `Register`(v) for some v, and that it is *deregistered* when `DeRegister`(h) is invoked. A thread may invoke `Update` and `DeRegister` only with a handle that has previously been registered to it, and which it has not since deregistered. Any thread may invoke `Collect` at any time if it is not currently performing another operation on the dynamic collect object.

2.3 Requirements

Following standard definitions, there is a natural partial order on operations: if the invocation event of an operation *op0* occurs after the return event of another operation *op1*, then *op0 follows op1* and *op1 precedes op0*. Otherwise, the operations are said to be *concurrent*.

A call to `Register` by thread t must return a handle that is not registered to any other thread. Together with the well-formedness requirements stated above, this implies that `Register` and `Update` operations for a given handle h are totally ordered by the *precedes* relation. Thus, if any such operations precede an operation *op*, then there is a unique "last" one of them. If this operation exists and there is no `DeRegister`(h) operation that follows it and precedes *op*, then we denote it as *lastbind*(h, op); otherwise *lastbind*(h, op) is not defined.

Informally, a handle-value pair (h, v) may "flicker" during a $h = $ `Register`(v) or `Update`(h, v) call: a concurrent `Collect` call may or may not return it. However, if such an operation completes *before* the invocation of a `Collect` operation, and the handle is not subsequently deregistered, then the `Collect` operation *must* return a value for that handle (either v or another value v' if there is a subsequent Update(h, v') operation). More precisely, a Collect operation *cop* returns a set S of handle-value pairs such that the following conditions hold, for every handle h and value v:

- If $(h, v) \in S$, then either
  - *lastbind*(h, cop) is defined and is a $h = $ Register(v) or Update(h, v) operation, or
  - a $h = $ Register(v) or Update(h, v) call was concurrent with *cop*.

- If *lastbind*(h, cop) is defined and there is no DeRegister(h) operation that is concurrent with *cop*, then $(h, v') \in S$, for some value v'.

Note that this specification is non-deterministic: there may be multiple sets of handle-value pairs that can legitimately be returned by a Collect call. Furthermore, it does not preclude a Collect operation returning multiple pairs for the same handle h. Clients can filter out duplicates if necessary by choosing any one of the pairs for each handle in the returned set.

There are many possible small variations on this specification. For example, an alternative Register might return a handle without binding it to a value, or Collect might omit the handles and simply return a multiset of values. Nonetheless, the above specification is suitable for a variety of use cases, including for use in memory management mechanisms as discussed in Section 1. To our knowledge, these possible minor variations in the specification do not have a significant impact on our findings.

3. ALGORITHMS

Our primary goal has been to explore how the availability of HTM *in general* impacts the ease of dynamic memory management. However, we wanted to be able to implement and experiment with the algorithms using real HTM-enabled hardware, namely Sun's Rock prototype. Thus, we could not ignore certain limitations [8, 9] of Rock's HTM, such as the requirement that transactions do not perform more stores than are accommodated by the store buffer.

Despite these constraints, we have found that the availability of HTM allows us to explore many algorithmic approaches, tradeoffs and optimizations. In contrast, without HTM, it is significantly more difficult to come up with *any* correct algorithm, and there is less flexibility for variants and optimizations. In this section, to illustrate the flexibility HTM enables, we give high-level descriptions of some of the algorithmic techniques we have explored; in the next section, we describe one algorithm in more detail.

3.1 List-based Algorithms

We have developed two kinds of list-based algorithms: *hand-over-hand reference counting* (HOHRC) and *fast collect* (FastCollect); each uses a doubly-linked list with one value per node.

3.1.1 HOHRC

This algorithm uses a per-node reference count to "pin" a node (prevent it from being deallocated) while a Collect is accessing its value. Collect traverses the list, using short transactions to increment the reference count of a node n while atomically confirming that n's predecessor still points to it. As the predecessor has previously been pinned, this ensures that node n is still part of the Collect object. After incrementing n's reference count, Collect reads n's value non-transactionally and copies it to the

result set. It then unpins n's predecessor, using a transaction to decrement its reference count, and, if it becomes zero and the predecessor's "delete marker" has been set, unlinks it from of the list and deallocates it.

Register allocates a new node, uses a transaction to insert it at the beginning of the list, and returns its address. Update nontransactionally stores the new value into the node. DeRegister executes a short transaction to set the delete marker of the node to be deregistered. If this transaction observes that the node's reference count is zero, it unlinks the node from the list and deallocates it after the transaction commits. Otherwise, some ongoing Collect has pinned the node. The last Collect that unpins the node will unlink it and deallocate it. Note that a given node may be continually pinned and thus never reclaimed. However, each Collect pins at most two nodes at a time, so the shared memory used is proportional to the number of active handles plus the number of ongoing Collects.

This description assumes that values stored by Update operations fit into a word that can be written and read by a native machine instruction, a significant advantage when Update operations are frequent. This advantage stems from the fact that the storage for a given handle does not move during the lifetime of the handle. The array-based algorithms described below depend on the ability to move the storage for a handle, thus requiring Update operations to use transactions to confirm the location of the storage.

The main disadvantage of the HOHRC algorithm is the expensive Collect operation, which updates each list node twice, increasing the cost of Collect, causing significant memory coherence traffic, and causing transactions used by Collect operations to conflict with each other. Telescoping (Section 3.4) reduces these effects, but cannot fully eliminate them.

3.1.2 FastCollect

This algorithm aims to improve Collect performance when DeRegister operations are infrequent. It uses the same Register and Update operations as HOHRC. However, it avoids HOHRC's main disadvantage by dispensing with the reference counts: DeRegister uses a transaction to atomically unlink a node n and increment a shared deregister counter dc, and deallocates n immediately afterwards. Collect traverses the list using transactions to atomically read the current value of dc and the next node in the list. If dc has changed since the start of the Collect, the Collect is restarted from the beginning.

The main disadvantage of FastCollect is that Collects can be prevented from making any progress by concurrent DeRegisters. A variety of practical approaches can be used to address this problem, such as adding a mode in which DeRegister operations add nodes to a to-be-freed list that is freed by a Collect operation after it completes. Again, HTM makes it straightforward to integrate such variants.

3.2 Array-based Algorithms

Our array-based algorithms can be categorized based on how they: (1) manage memory, (2) register new handles, and (3) compact (move elements inside) the array.

3.2.1 Managing memory

Our array-based algorithms are either *static* or *dynamic*. The static ones *do not solve* the Dynamic Collect problem: they assume a known bound on the number of handles to be registered, and do not attempt to deallocate unused space. We use these algorithms as a stepping stone towards truly dynamic ones, and to isolate the algorithmic and performance issues related to registering and deregistering handles, collecting only from registered handles, etc., from the issues related to reclaiming unused memory.

The dynamic array-based algorithms can replace the current array with a new one of a different size, employing a level of indirection to identify the current array. We double the array when it is full, that is, when every *slot* (array entry) is in use for a registered handle; and halve it when it is 25% full. This way we avoid excessive resizing while keeping space usage proportional to the number of registered handles.

To resize the array, the algorithms allocate a new one, and install it as the "new" array. The values are then copied from the current array to the new, and the new array is made current. These steps may be performed in cooperation with other threads. While there are small differences in how our algorithms achieve this, the detailed description in the next section is representative.

3.2.2 Registering

The `Register` operation can either *search* for an empty slot or *append* a new element after the last used slot in the array (for example, using the `count` variable in the next section).

3.2.3 Compacting

To reduce or avoid fragmentation, the array can be "compacted" by moving elements within it. Our algorithms either perform *no* compaction, or do so on each *resize* or each `DeRegister`.

Compacting requires slots to be moved by threads other than their owners. This creates a race between one thread moving a slot and another performing a `Update` to it, requiring synchronization between these threads. This is explained in detail in the next section.

Algorithms that compact on resize move slots only when the array is resized. Elements are copied into consecutive locations in the new array.

Algorithms that perform compaction with every `DeRegister` operation use a transaction to move the last used slot into the space used by the slot being deregistered, atomically updating other data such as a count of the number of registered slots, and data used to associate the handle of the moved slot with the memory location in which it is stored. `Collect` operations must access the elements in the array from the last towards the first to avoid missing an element that is moved by a concurrent `DeRegister`. This may lead to multiple values being returned by the same `Collect` operation for the same handle, which is allowed by the specification, whereas missing a handle is not.

3.2.4 Algorithms

Many combinations of these design choices yield meaningful algorithms. We have implemented some of the most interesting choices, naming the algorithms according to the choices for memory management, registering, and compacting, yielding the following algorithms: `ArrayStatSearchNo`, `ArrayStatAppendDereg`, `ArrayDynSearchResize`, and `ArrayDynAppendDereg`.

3.3 Baseline algorithms

We have also implemented two non-HTM-based Collect algorithms for comparison. The Static baseline algorithm uses a fixed-sized array, with threads mapped statically to slots in it (`Register` and `DeRegister` are no-ops). `Update` operations by a thread write directly to the thread's slot, and `Collect` simply scans the entire array and returns the set of non-null values seen. Recall that such static algorithms do not solve the Dynamic Collect problem: we use them merely to put the performance of dynamic algorithms in context.

The Dynamic baseline (Algorithm 2 from [11]) uses a doubly linked list of nodes whose forward pointers are augmented with reference counts *for the pointed-to node*. `Register` searches for a free node, incrementing forward pointer counters on the way. If none is found, a new one is added to the end of the list. The address of the node that is found or added is returned as the handle. `Update` uses the handle to store the value directly into the registered node. `DeRegister` of node n decrements forward pointer counters in all nodes preceding n. If any of the counters reaches zero, the node pointed to by the associated forward pointer is unlinked and deallocated. `Collect` traverses the list, incrementing the forward pointer counters. After reaching the end of the list, it goes back in the opposite direction decreasing the counters, unlinking and deallocating nodes pointed to by forward pointers with zero reference counts.

3.4 Telescoping

The `HOHRC` algorithm can be improved by observing that the net effect of several traversal steps executed in sequence (without activity by other threads) is to increment the reference count of the last node accessed and decrement that of the first because the reference count of each of the intermediate nodes is incremented and subsequently decremented. By combining these steps into a single transaction, we not only amortize the cost of starting and committing a transaction over multiple steps down the list, but we also avoid modifying the intermediate nodes, thereby improving cache behavior. This is safe because the intermediate nodes are accessed inside a transaction that ensures not only that the first node accessed in a transaction is still in the list, but also that the pointers between this node and subsequent ones are intact. We call this technique *telescoping* and the number of nodes accessed in each transaction the *step size*.

The telescoping technique is also applicable to other algorithms. For example, in the `FastCollect` algorithm, each transaction could read dc once, and then access a number of list nodes, thereby amortizing the cost of starting and committing a transaction and of reading dc.

The best choice of step size depends on several factors. Larger step sizes allow fixed transaction costs to be amortized over more steps, but make transactions more vulnerable to abort, depending on the algorithm and limitations of the HTM. In our experiments, we were could not use step sizes greater than 32, which is the size of Rock's store buffer, because each step performs at least one store (to record a value in the result set). Because different step sizes perform best at different contention levels, we developed a simple mechanism for adapting the step size based on the abort rate. This mechanism bases its decisions on the success or failure of the most recent 8 transactions. However, in order to avoid excessive resizing, only transaction attempts since the last resize are relevant to the decision.

Our mechanism maintains a counter that records the difference between the number of commits and the number of aborts amongst the relevant transactions. The counter is maintained by using an 8-bit vector to record the results of the recent transactions, allowing us to "age out" the contribution of the oldest transaction and update the difference counter accordingly. If the value of the counter is higher than 6 after a commit, we double the step size. If it is below -2 after an abort, we halve the step size. These thresholds were determined experimentally.

4. THE `ArrayDynAppendDereg` ALGORITHM

In this section, we present the `ArrayDynAppendDereg` algorithm in more detail. Figure 2 gives pseudocode for the algorithm,

```
 1  public struct slot_t {                          68  void append(slot_t **slot_ref, val_t val) {
 2    val_t val;                                     69    array[count] = slot_t(val, slot_ref);
 3    slot_t **slot_ref;                             70    *slot_ref = &(array[count]);
 4  }                                                71    count = count + 1;
 5                                                   72  }
 6  # shared data                                    73
 7  slot_t array[] = new slot_t[MIN_SIZE];           74  public void Update(slot_t **slot_ref, val_t
 8  int capacity = MIN_SIZE;  // MIN_SIZE >= 1             val) {
 9  int count = 0;                                   75    atomic {
10  slot_t array_new[] = NULL;                       76      (*slot_ref)->val = val;
11  int capacity_new;                                77    }
12  int copied;                                      78  }
13                                                   79
14  bool copying() {                                 80  public void Collect(vector_t ret) {
15    return array_new != NULL;                      81    help_copy();
16  }                                                82    int i = count - 1;
17                                                   83    while(i >= 0) {
18  public slot_t **Register(val_t val) {            84      atomic {
19    slot_t **slot_ref = new (slot_t *);            85        if(i >= count)
20    action_t action = NOTHING;                     86          i = count - 1;
21    while(action != DONE) {                        87        if(i >= 0) {
22      atomic {                                     88          ret.add(array[i].val);
23        if(!copying()) {                           89          i = i - 1;
24          if(count < capacity) {                   90        }
25            append(slot_ref, val);                 91      }
26            action = DONE;                         92    }
27          } else {                                 93  }
28            count_l = count;                       94
29            action = GROW;                         95  void attempt_resize(int count_l, int
30          }                                             capacity_l) {
31        } else {                                   96    slot_t array_tmp[] = new slot_t[count_l*2];
32          if(count < capacity && count <           97    bool free_tmp = true;
               capacity_new) {                       98    atomic {
33            append(slot_ref, val);                 99      if(!copying() && count == count_l &&
34            action = DONE;                                 capacity == capacity_l) {
35          } else                                  100        array_new = array_tmp;
36            action = HELP;                        101        capacity_new = count_l*2;
37        }                                         102        copied = 0;
38      }                                           103        free_tmp = false;
39      if(action == GROW) attempt_resize(count_l,  104      }
             count_l);                              105    }
40      else if(action == HELP) help_copy();        106    if(free_tmp) delete[] array_tmp;
41    }                                             107    help_copy();
42    return slot_ref;                              108  }
43  }                                               109
44                                                  110  void help_copy() {
45  public void Deregister(slot_t **slot_ref) {     111    while(copying()) help_copy_one();
46    action_t action = HELP;                       112  }
47    while(action != DONE) {                       113
48      atomic {                                    114  void help_copy_one() {
49        count_l = count;                          115    slot_t array_to_free[] = NULL;
50        capacity_l = capacity;                    116    atomic {
51        if (count_l*4 == capacity_l && count_l*2  117      if(copying()) {
             >= MIN_SIZE)                           118        if(copied < count) {
52          action = SHRINK;                        119          array_new[copied] = array[copied];
53        else if(!copying()) {                     120          *(array_new[copied].slot_ref) = &
54          count = count_l-1;                                  array_new[copied];
55          **slot_ref = array[count];              121          copied = copied + 1;
56          *(array[count].slot_ref) = *slot_ref;   122        } else {
57          action = DONE;                          123          array_to_free = array;
58        }                                         124          array = array_new;
59      }                                           125          capacity = capacity_new;
60      if(action == SHRINK) {                      126          array_new = NULL;
61        attempt_resize(count_l, capacity_l);      127        }
62        action = HELP;                            128      }
63      } else if(action == HELP) help_copy();      129    }
64    }                                             130    if(array_to_free != NULL) delete[]
65    delete slot_ref;                                     array_to_free;
66  }                                               131  }
67
```

Figure 2: Pseudocode for the ArrayDynAppendDereg algorithm.

using C++-like notation: we use $*$ for declaring and dereferencing pointers, $->$ for accessing a field of a structure through a pointer, and $\&$ for taking the address of a variable. We use `public` to denote all functions and types that are parts of the object interface.

4.1 Dynamic array and resizing mechanism

`ArrayDynAppendDereg` uses a dynamic array of "slots"; each slot can store one value that has been associated with one handle The current array and the number of slots in it are identified by `array` and `capacity`, respectively. To resize the array, a thread allocates a new array (line 96), then atomically stores a pointer to it in `array_new` and its size (in slots) in `capacity_new`, and sets `copied` to zero to indicate that no slots have yet been copied from the old array to the new (lines 100-102). The thread then calls `help_copy`, which copies slots individually from the old array to the new (lines 119–121), and finally makes the new array current and sets `array_new` back to `null` to facilitate subsequent resizing (lines 124–126). Other threads calling `help_copy` may also participate; the one that makes the new array current deallocates the old array (line 130).

The value associated with a handle can be moved, either during resizing or if it is the last value in the current array and is moved to replace a slot being deregistered. To facilitate moving of values, each handle has an associated "slot reference", which points to its associated slot, and the slot has a pointer back to this slot reference. This way, when a value is moved, the slot's pointer to the slot reference can be used to update the slot reference so that it points to the new slot (lines 56 and 120), thus allowing subsequent `Update` operations for that handle to determine its new location.

An interesting observation is that HTM makes it trivial to implement a minor variant on this algorithm that is optimized for `Update` performance at the cost of higher overhead for `Collect` operations. The idea is to store the value associated with a handle together with the slot reference for that handle, rather than in the array slot to which it points. This way, slot references do not move, even if their associated array slots are compacted. Therefore, a `Update` operation can store its value directly and without using a transaction (at least for some common cases; see Section 5.1), rather than through a level of indirection using a transaction. The downside of this choice is that `Collect` operations must now use a transaction to dereference the pointer in each array slot in order to access the associated value. Depending on anticipated workload, this may be an appropriate choice. We have not implemented this variant.

4.2 Operations

`Register` is very simple in the common case: it allocates a new slot reference (line 19) and calls `append` to store the new value and a pointer to the new slot reference in the first unused slot, updates the slot reference to point to the new slot, and increments `count` so that a subsequent `Register` operation will use the next slot (lines 69–71). The `DeRegister` operation is also straightforward in the common case: it copies the last used slot to the slot being deregistered, updates the slot reference for the moved slot to point to its new location (line 56), decrements `count` to make the last used slot available again (line 54), and frees the slot reference associated with the deregistered handle (line 65).

The more complicated cases for the `Register` and `DeRegister` operations arise because of resizing the array. First, if a new array is being installed (lines 23 and 53), these operations call `help_copy` to ensure that the new array become current before trying again. (There is one exception in `Register` that we discuss later.) Furthermore, these operations perform additional steps in order to keep the space used by the array proportional to the number of registered slots (while ensuring a non-zero minimum number of slots). Specifically, we maintain the following invariant: $max($`count`$, MIN\_SIZE) \leq$ `capacity` $\leq 4 *$ `count`. `Register` checks if there is still room in the current array (line 24), and if not initiates an attempt to grow the array (line 39). Similarly, `DeRegister` checks if decrementing the number of slots used would violate the invariant, and if so initiates an attempt to shrink the array (line 61). Both procedures pass the values of `count` and `capacity` seen in the transaction to the `attempt_resize` procedure. The resize attempt is abandoned if either of these variables differs from the previously observed value (line 99), as this indicates that either there is no longer any risk of violating the above invariant, or the array has already been resized. Furthermore, if copying is already in progress, the resize attempt is abandoned, and the thread helps to complete the current resizing if necessary (lines 99 and 107).

The new array size chosen when resizing—whether shrinking or growing—is twice the value of `count`; this way, after a successful resize, `count` is in the middle of the range of values that satisfy the above invariant, so further resizing will occur only when the number of registered handles either halves or doubles.

Interestingly, a `Register` operation can complete even while resizing is in progress, provided there is enough space for the newly registered element in both the old and new arrays (line 32). This is because the same transaction that determines that the last element has been copied (line 118) also installs the new array. Thus, if a `Register` operation succeeds in claiming a slot in the current array during resizing, it is guaranteed that the slot will be copied to the new array before the new array becomes current.

It remains to describe the `Collect` operation. It would be trivial to satisfy the requirements of the `Collect` by reading values from all registered slots in one hardware transaction. However, this is not practical: existing HTM implementations do not support transactions of unbounded size, and even if they did, we would be attempting to read many locations in a transaction that would conflict with any concurrent `Update` operation, causing excessive aborts. Therefore, the algorithm presented in Figure 2 reads only a single slot in each hardware transaction. As discussed in Section 3.4, the `Collect` could copy more than one slot per transaction to reduce the overheads of starting and committing the transactions. That is, lines 87–90 can be executed multiple times in the same transaction; we experiment with different "step sizes" (number of elements copied within each transaction) in the next section.

Even using multiple transactions, `Collect` is quite simple, but there are some subtle issues. First, for the reason explained in Section 3.2, `Collect` reads slots in reverse order.

Second, a `Collect` operation can proceed despite concurrent resizing and compacting. This is because any slot that is continually registered during the `Collect` either stays at the same index in the current array, or moves to a lower one due to a concurrent `DeRegister` operation. Thus, because `Collect` reads from the slot of the current array for each index below the value of `count` observed at the beginning of the `Collect` in *reverse* order, a slot will not be missed even if it is moved to a new array during the `Collect`.

However, there is one exception. If a resize were in progress when a `Collect` operation began, then the `Collect` could copy a value from a slot that had already been copied to the new array. An `Update` operation could have updated such a slot in the new array before the `Collect` operation began, but the `Collect` would fail to return the new value, which would be incorrect. To eliminate this possibility, a `Collect` operation begins by calling `help_copy`, which ensures that there is no copy in progress before it returns. While `Collect` may still miss `Update`s performed during *subsequent* resizes, these `Update`s are concurrent with the `Collect` operation, and therefore the specification allows them to be missed.

Finally, we note that `Collect` checks that the index from which it is about to read is still valid (lines 85), "advancing" the index down to `count-1` if not, to avoid reading deregistered slots.

4.3 Impact of HTM on algorithm complexity

Transactions make it easy to maintain simple invariants. For example, `capacity` always contains the size of `array`, and similarly for `capacity_new` and `array_new`. Access-after-free errors are easily avoided as we only deallocate arrays that are not referenced by either `array` or `array_new`, and accesses to slots in arrays are always performed inside transactions that confirm that the array is identified by either of these variables. Similarly, ensuring that a handle's slot reference always points to its slot makes it easy to move slot data without the risk of an `Update` operation accessing the old location. Without hardware transactions, these simple relationships cannot be maintained, as variables involved in them must be updated individually, which significantly complicates the algorithm.

We included the optimization of allowing a `Register` operation to complete despite ongoing resizing in order to illustrate the power of HTM to facilitate such changes. In our experience, nonblocking algorithms designed using only traditional hardware support for synchronization are delicate and inflexible, making such optimizations infeasible or too complicated. For the sake of simplicity, we have foregone a number of other optimizations that would be similarly straightforward.

5. EXPERIMENTAL RESULTS

In this section, we present results of experiments performed on a 16-core Rock system [8]. We used the `libumem` malloc implementation. Each graph point represents the average of 10 runs. Unless stated otherwise, we show the results for the best telescoping step size and indicate it in the graphs. We used several microbenchmarks to evaluate different aspects of the algorithms.

5.1 Update latency

We measured the latency of `Update` operations at about 215ns for the `ArrayStatAppendDereg`, `ArrayDynSearchResize`, and `ArrayDynAppendDereg` algorithms, and about 135ns for the remaining algorithms. This is explained by the fact that the remaining algorithms all perform `Update` operations directly to an address determined by the handle, whereas the algorithms named above all require a level of indirection through the handle to determine the address to write.

Although this seems like a significant difference, we believe that in many workloads of interest, `Update` operations will account for a small fraction of application runtime. Furthermore, the ability of some of the algorithms to perform `Update` operations using naked store instructions depends on the values being stored fitting within a single machine word, as in our experiments. For larger values, synchronization (HTM-based or not) would be needed to prevent `Collect` from returning partial values, which would largely close the gap in `Update` performance. Also, as discussed later, it is straightforward to reduce the frequency of `DeRegister` and `Register` operations in workloads in which they are invoked frequently enough to dominate performance. Therefore, the rest of our evaluation concentrates on `Collect` performance.

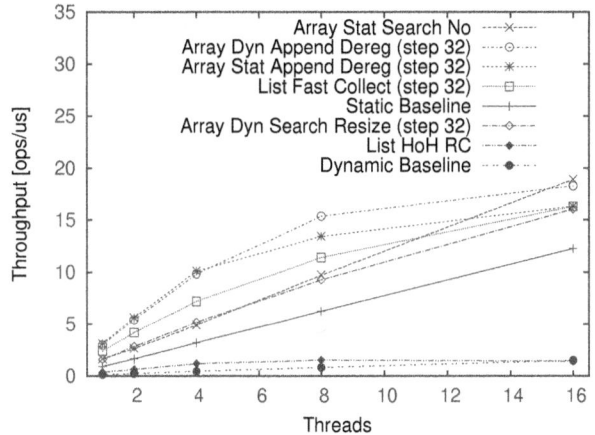

Figure 3: Collect-dominated

5.2 Collect-dominated benchmark

In this benchmark, threads randomly perform operations, with the following distribution: `Collect` 90%, `Update` 8%, `Register` 1%, `DeRegister` 1%. Each thread t maintains a queue of at most n_t slots, where the n's are chosen to spread a total of 64 evenly amongst the threads used. Before measurement begins, the threads register a total of 32 slots, spread evenly between them.

A thread ignores `Register` operations when its queue is full and ignores `DeRegister` and `Update` operations when the queue is empty. Otherwise, for a `Register` operation, a thread registers a new slot and adds it to its queue; for a `DeRegister` operation, it removes a slot from its queue and deregisters it; and for an `Update` operation, the thread stores to the least recently used slot in the thread's queue.

As shown in Figure 3, the Dynamic baseline and `HOHRC` performed significantly worse than all other algorithms due to poor cache performance caused by modifying each node in the list while traversing it. These two algorithms were similarly outperformed by large margins in all experiments involving `Collect` operations and are therefore omitted from the rest of our results to allow easier comparison of the remaining algorithms.

`ArrayDynAppendDereg` and `ArrayStatAppendDereg` perform best up to 8 threads. They outperform even the Static baseline because its `Collect` traverses the entire array, which is on average only half full, whereas the Append algorithms scan only registered slots.

With higher thread counts, the `Collect` transactions restart more often due to higher contention, and the Append-Dereg algorithms become slower than `ArrayStatSearchNo` with 16 threads (recall that this algorithm does not solve the Dynamic Collect problem). Even so, both algorithms are consistently among the best. The two Append-Dereg algorithms have roughly the same performance up to 4 threads, but diverge slightly thereafter. Upon further investigation, we determined that this difference is caused by idiosyncrasies of Rock's microTLB, not algorithmic differences. Similar experiences were reported in [9].

5.3 Collect-Update benchmark

This benchmark evaluates `Collect` performance under contention from concurrent `Update`s. One thread performs `Collect`s while 15 others execute `Update`s (Figure 4). `Update` threads perform `Update` operations no more often than the *update period*, which we vary in order to control contention. Before measurement

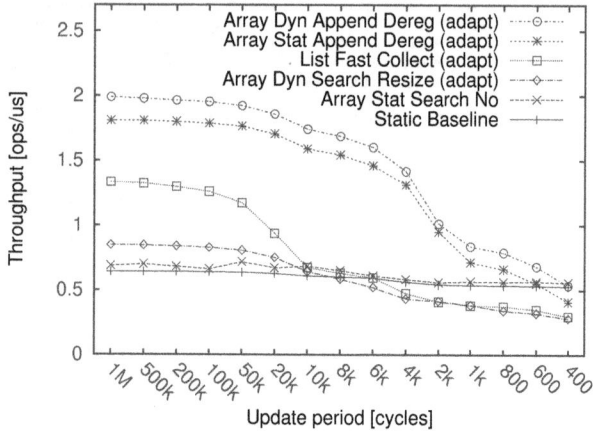

Figure 4: Collect-Update

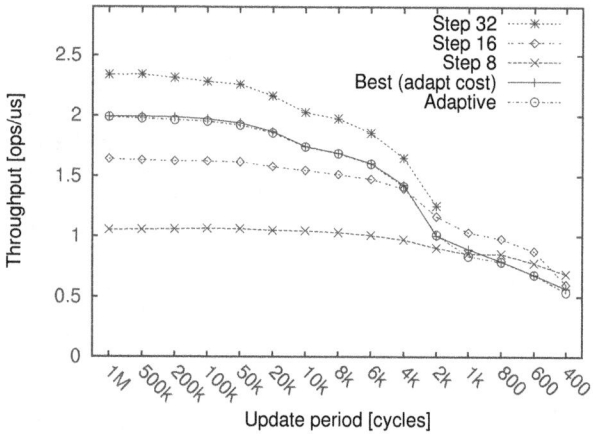

Figure 6: Step size distribution for `ArrayDynAppendDereg`

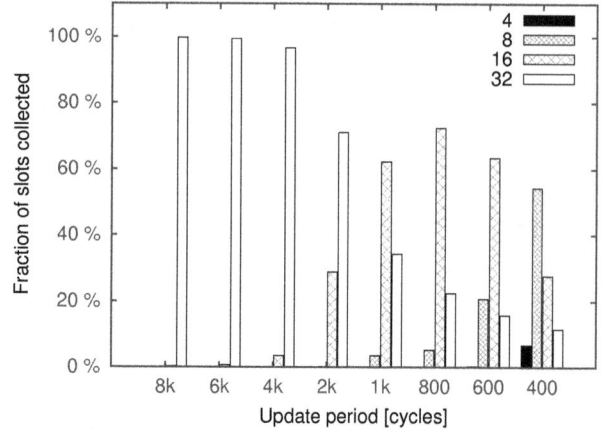

Figure 5: Adapting step size for `ArrayDynAppendDereg`

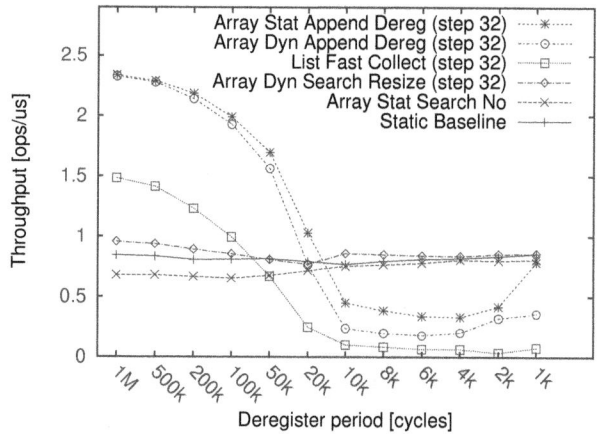

Figure 7: Collect-(De)Register

begins, the `Update` threads register a total of 64 handles. Each `Update` thread uses the same one of its handles for all operations; the rest of the handles are unused; we register them only to keep the total number of registered slots in this experiment independent of the number of threads.

The performance of Static baseline and `ArrayStatSearchNo`—whose `Collect` operations do not use transactions—are affected only slightly by more frequent `Updates`, due to an increase in cache misses. For the other algorithms, performance degrades more significantly because the `Collect` transactions abort more often with higher contention. The two Append-Dereg variants perform best for all update periods except 400 cycles. Even at this point, the Append-Dereg algorithms perform only slightly worse than Static baseline and `ArrayStatSearchNo`, which do not solve the Dynamic Collect problem, and easily outperform all algorithms that do. Thus, the Append-Dereg algorithms are the clear winners for this benchmark.

Figure 5 examines the need for and effectiveness of an adaptive step size using `ArrayDynAppendDereg`. The tradeoff discussed in Section 3.4 is apparent: larger step sizes result in lower overhead for successful transactions, but larger transactions are more likely to abort as contention increases. `Collect` operations that use step size of 32 do not complete for update periods less than 2000 cycles.

Each point on the "Best (adapt cost)" curve shows the through-

put for the best-performing step size for that threading level with the *collection* (but not use) of data to enable adaptive step size. It shows overhead of between 20% and 30% for collecting this data. These overheads could be reduced or eliminated with simple hardware support to track recent transaction attempts. The adaptive algorithm performs close to "Best (adapt cost)" for all update periods, showing that it chooses the step size effectively and that most of its overhead stems from collecting the additional data. In some cases, the adaptive algorithm even performs better than "Best (adapt cost)", because it manages to commit a fraction of transactions with larger step size. Figure 6 shows the fraction of slots collected using common step sizes, and confirms that the adaptive algorithm is effective in finding the best step size to use.

5.4 Collect-(De)Register

Next, we evaluate the performance of `Collect` under contention from concurrent `Registers` and `DeRegisters` (Figure 7). One thread executes `Collects`, while 15 others execute `Register`-`DeRegister` pairs with delays between them. We call the delay between the start of a `DeRegister` and the start of the following `Register` operation the *register period*, and the delay between the start of the `Register` and the start of the following `DeRegister` operation the *deregister period*. We fix the register period to 20,000 cycles and vary the deregister period. Initially, the total number of

106

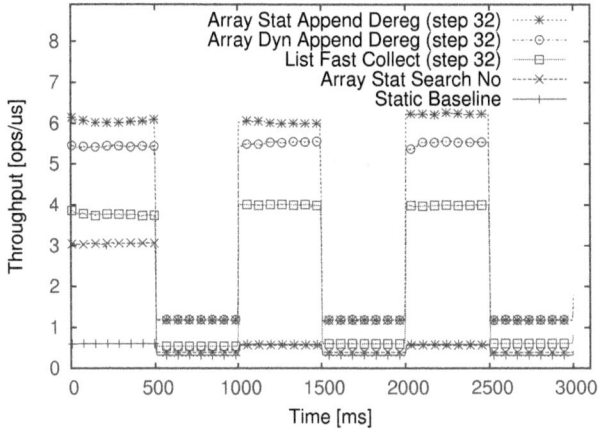

Figure 8: Collect performance with varying number of registered slots

registered slots is 64, evenly spread across the register/deregister threads. The threads start the experiment by first deregistering a slot, so the total number of registered slots is always at most 64.

With long deregister periods, algorithms in which `Collect` traverses only the registered slots perform best. The others perform worse because they either traverse all slots (Static baseline) or frequently traverse more slots than are registered due to infrequent compaction (`ArrayDynSearchResize`) or no compaction (`ArrayStatSearchNo`).

As the deregister period decreases, the algorithms that perform best with large deregister periods begin to degrade due to increased abort rates because of more frequent `Register` and `DeRegister` operations. The performance of `ArrayStatAppendDereg` and `ArrayDynAppendDereg` degrade significantly due to higher abort rates. `FastCollect` also degrades significantly, due to increased `DeRegister` frequency resulting in increased contention on the deregister count, causing `Collect` operations to start over from the beginning.

Interestingly, several of the algorithms exhibit noticeable performance *gains* at the shortest deregister periods. This is because a shorter deregister period results in fewer handles being registered at a time, so `Collect` operations are both shorter *and* less likely to conflict with a concurrent `DeRegister` operation.

For applications that perform frequent `Register` and `DeRegister` operations, it may make sense to *defer* deregistering handles, allowing them to be reused by subsequent `Register` operations. This could improve performance of many of the algorithms for such workloads, particularly `FastCollect`, because `Collects` conflicts on the deregister count would be less frequent and thus cause fewer aborts.

5.5 Varying the number of registered slots

Finally, we examine `Collect` performance as the number of registered slots varies. One thread performs `Collects`, while 15 others perform `Updates` with update period of 20,000 cycles. Initially, the number of registered slots is 16. The experiment proceeds in phases, with the `Update` threads alternately increasing and decreasing the number of registered handles every 500ms.

Figure 8 shows the throughput of the `Collect` operations for 3 seconds. As expected, the performance of `Collect` operations for Static Baseline is not significantly affected by the number of registered slots. The throughput varies slightly because the `Collect` copies less data when there are fewer registered slots.

`ArrayStatSearchNo` initially performs significantly better than the Static baseline. However, when the number of registered slots increases (at 500ms, for example), its performance degrades significantly and becomes similar to that of Static baseline. Furthermore, it does not improve when the number of registered slots decreases at 1s because `Collect` traverses the maximum *historical* number of registered slots. The performance of Append-Dereg algorithms and `FastCollect` is also reduced at 500ms because the number of registered slots increases. However, when it decreases again at 1s, the performance of both algorithms becomes as good as it was initially. This clearly shows the benefit of algorithms that adapt to the number of registered slots. The best performing algorithms in this experiment are, again, the two Append-Dereg variants.

6. DISCUSSION

In this section, we discuss how various details about the HTM implementation affect our algorithms. A similar discussion appears in [7], so here we only briefly mention specific issues that are relevant to the algorithms in this paper. First, as noted in Section 1, our algorithms rely on *sandboxing* [7].

Rock's memory consistency model is like TSO [17], with transactions being treated as both loads and stores, similarly to the way atomic instructions such as CAS are treated. This model is sufficient to support our algorithms without additional memory barriers. Depending on the memory consistency model implemented by other (future) architectures that support HTM, additional memory barriers may be required.

Some of our algorithms depend on the ability to eventually commit at least some small transactions, which Rock does not guarantee. We hope that future HTMs will make such guarantees (see [1], for example). It is not difficult to modify our algorithms so that they do not need this guarantee, at the cost of making the algorithms block occasionally, by using the TLE technique [6]. The key idea is to make all transactions read a lock variable and confirm that it is not held before proceeding. This way, if a transaction fails repeatedly, its effects can be applied nontransactionally while holding the lock. Note that, in the absence of any guarantees for completion of transactions, the lock would have to be acquired using nontransactional synchronization, for example using compare-and-swap (CAS).

Some of our algorithms perform concurrent transactional and nontransactional accesses to the same variable. That is, they rely on *strong atomicity* [5]. This dependence could be avoided, at the cost of some additional overhead and code complexity, by replacing such nontransactional accesses with short transactions.

The observations of the two previous paragraphs together imply that, in order to support our algorithms, HTM must provide either strong atomicity or guarantees that certain "small" transactions will eventually commit (at least in the absence of contention). The best algorithms can be built with HTMs that provide *both* features.

Some of our algorithms, including the one presented in detail in Section 4, have been complicated somewhat by our efforts to avoid memory allocation within transactions. Because we have used standard malloc implementations that use instructions such as CAS, which are not supported in transactions on Rock, modifications that naturally belong in one transaction had to be split into multiple transactions; this complicates control flow as well as synchronization. We emphasize that this complication is due to a combination of idiosyncrasies of Rock's HTM and not using a TM-aware allocator. It is *not* a fundamental limitation of HTM in general. Nonetheless, future HTMs could simplify software by allowing the use of instructions such as CAS in transactions.

As discussed in Section 4, Rock's bounded transactions did not impose much complexity on our algorithms, because we would want to avoid large transactions even if unbounded transactions were supported. However, in some cases we believe we could have achieved better performance if we could use larger transactions. In other cases, feedback about transaction failure reasons appeared to indicate a store buffer overflow, but it was difficult to understand why, even examining assembly code in detail. This experience suggests that support for larger or unbounded transactions may still make programming easier. Relatedly, the ability to capture more detailed information about a transaction and the reason it failed would be helpful too.

7. CONCLUDING REMARKS

We have shown that hardware transactional memory (HTM) can facilitate dynamic sized concurrent data structures that are superior in terms of simplicity, flexibility, performance, and space usage, compared to those that do not use HTM. Our results add to a growing body of practical evidence that HTM has the potential to make effective concurrent programming significantly easier [7, 8].

Known limitations of Rock have complicated our algorithms to some extent. We expect future HTM implementations to have fewer limitations, making it even easier to achieve similar results.

Some have argued that HTM provides little or no inherent benefits for concurrent data structures. However, the theoretical results on which these arguments rest focus on issues of secondary practical importance: strong progress properties such as wait-freedom, worst-case time complexity under extreme contention, and fully asynchronous models that preclude common practical techniques such as back-off.

In particular, Attiya and Hendler [4] have used such results to argue that HTM does not help to solve the "adaptive collect" problem. Despite the similarity in names, this problem is fundamentally different from the Dynamic Collect problem, and seems to have little bearing on practical issues of dynamic memory management. Specifically, because it does not allow threads to dynamically allocate and release handles, the problem *specification* implies knowledge of the number of threads in the system, and time and space complexity that depend on this number. We therefore believe that studying (variants of) our Dynamic Collect problem is more likely to provide useful insight into the impact of HTM on practical concurrent programming, especially with respect to dynamic memory management. Finally, Attiya and Hendler acknowledge that their results have no bearing on the critical issue of programming complexity, whereas our results demonstrate that HTM indeed facilitates simpler and more flexible algorithm designs.

References

[1] Advanced Micro Devices. Advanced synchronization facility proposed architectural specification, March 2009. Publication # 45432, Revision: 2.1.

[2] Y. Afek, H. Attiya, D. Dolev, E. Gafni, M. Merritt, and N. Shavit. Atomic snapshots of shared memory. *Journal of the ACM*, September 1993.

[3] H. Attiya, A. Fouren, and E. Gafni. An adaptive collect algorithm with applications. *Distributed Computing*, April 2002.

[4] H. Attiya and D. Hendler. Time and space lower bounds for implementations using k-cas. *IEEE Transactions on Parallel and Distributed Systems*, February 2010.

[5] C. Blundell, E. C. Lewis, and M. Martin. Deconstructing Transactions: The Subtleties of Atomicity. In *the 4th Annual Workshop on Duplicating, Deconstructing, and Debunking*, 2005.

[6] D. Dice, M. Herlihy, D. Lea, Y. Lev, V. Luchangco, W. Mesard, M. Moir, K. Moore, and D. Nussbaum. Applications of the adaptive transactional memory test platform. Transact 2008 workshop. http://research.sun.com/scalable/pubs/ TRANSACT2008-ATMTP-Apps.pdf.

[7] D. Dice, Y. Lev, V. J. Marathe, M. Moir, D. Nussbaum, and M. Oleszewski. Simplifying concurrent algorithms by exploiting hardware transactional memory. In *Proceedings of the 22nd ACM symposium on Parallelism in algorithms and architectures*, SPAA '10, 2010.

[8] D. Dice, Y. Lev, M. Moir, and D. Nussbaum. Early experience with a commercial hardware transactional memory implementation. In *Proceeding of the 14th international conference on Architectural support for programming languages and operating systems*, ASPLOS '09, 2009.

[9] D. Dice, Y. Lev, M. Moir, D. Nussbaum, and M. Olszewski. Early experience with a commercial hardware transactional memory implementation. Technical Report TR-2009-180, Sun Microsystems Laboratories, 2009.

[10] M. Herlihy, V. Luchangco, P. Martin, and M. Moir. Nonblocking memory management support for dynamic-sized data structures. *ACM Transactions on Computer Systems*, May 2005.

[11] M. Herlihy, V. Luchangco, and M. Moir. Space and time adaptive non-blocking algorithms. *Electronic Notes in Theoretical Computer Science*, April 2003.

[12] M. Herlihy and J. E. B. Moss. Transactional memory: architectural support for lock-free data structures. In *Proceedings of the 20th annual international symposium on Computer architecture*, ISCA '93, 1993.

[13] JSR166: Concurrency Utilities. http://gee.cs.oswego.edu/dl/concurrency-interest/.

[14] M. Michael. Hazard pointers: Safe memory reclamation for lock-free objects. *IEEE Transactions on Parallel and Distributed Systems*, June 2004.

[15] M. M. Michael and M. L. Scott. Simple, fast, and practical non-blocking and blocking concurrent queue algorithms. In *Proceedings of the 15th annual ACM symposium on Principles of distributed computing*, PODC '96, 1996.

[16] M. Saks, N. Shavit, and H. Woll. Optimal time randomized consensus making resilient algorithms fast in practice. In *Proceedings of the 2nd annual ACM-SIAM symposium on Discrete algorithms*, SODA '91, 1991.

[17] Sparc International, Inc. The SPARC architecture manual, version 8, 1991.

A Complexity Separation Between the Cache-Coherent and Distributed Shared Memory Models

Wojciech Golab[*]
Hewlett-Packard Labs
Palo Alto, California, USA
wojciech.golab@hp.com

We consider asynchronous multiprocessor systems where processes communicate by accessing shared memory. Exchange of information among processes in such a multiprocessor necessitates costly memory accesses called *remote memory references* (RMRs), which generate communication on the interconnect joining processors and main memory. In this paper we compare two popular shared memory architecture models, namely the *cache-coherent* (CC) and *distributed shared memory* (DSM) models, in terms of their power for solving synchronization problems efficiently with respect to RMRs. The particular problem we consider entails one process sending a "signal" to a subset of other processes. We show that a variant of this problem can be solved very efficiently with respect to RMRs in the CC model, but not so in the DSM model, even when we consider amortized RMR complexity.

To our knowledge, this is the first separation in terms of amortized RMR complexity between the CC and DSM models. It is also the first separation in terms of RMR complexity (for asynchronous systems) that does not rely in any way on wait-freedom—the requirement that a process makes progress in a bounded number of its own steps.

Categories and Subject Descriptors: B.3.2 [Memory Structures]: Design Styles, *Shared memory*; F.2.2 [Analysis of Algorithms and Problem Complexity]: Nonnumerical Algorithms and Problems.

General Terms: Algorithms, theory.

Keywords: Shared memory models, remote memory references, complexity.

1. INTRODUCTION

Shared memory multiprocessors in the form of multi-core chips can be found in most servers and desktop computers

---

[*]This research was conducted mostly during a postdoctoral fellowship at the University of Calgary, under the supervision of Prof. Philipp Woelfel. Author partially supported by the Natural Sciences and Engineering Research Council (NSERC) of Canada.

today, as well as many embedded systems. Due to the large gap between memory and processor speed, such systems rely heavily on architectural features that mitigate the relatively high cost of accessing memory. Two models of such architectures, illustrated in Figure 1, are the cache-coherent (CC) model and the distributed shared memory (DSM) model [3]. Cache-coherent systems are most common in practice, and often use a shared bus as the interconnect between processors and memory. Memory references that can be resolved entirely using a processor's cache (e.g., in-cache reads) are called *local* and are much faster than ones that traverse the interconnect (e.g., cache misses), called *remote memory references* (RMRs). The fact that any memory location can be cached by any process simplifies greatly the design of efficient algorithms in the CC model. In contrast, in the DSM model memory is partitioned into modules that are tied to specific processors. Different memory modules can be accessed in parallel by those processors using separate memory controllers, which provides superior memory bandwidth. As in the CC model, we can classify memory references in the DSM model as fast local references versus more costly RMRs. The classification in the DSM model is based only on the memory location (as opposed to the state of caches): A reference to a memory location in a processor's own memory module is local, and a reference to another processor's memory module is an RMR.

In this paper we consider efficient algorithms for solving synchronization problems in asynchronous multiprocessors that conform to either the CC or DSM model. In particular, we consider algorithms that use *blocking synchronization*, whereby processes may busy-wait by repeatedly reading the values of shared variables. In this context, RMR complexity has been shown to be a meaningful indicator of real world performance (e.g., [4]). The fundamental technique in the design of RMR-efficient algorithms is to co-locate variables with processes that access them most heavily. Unfortunately such techniques are specific to a shared memory model. Consequently, an algorithm that is very RMR-efficient in one model is not necessarily efficient with respect to RMRs in another model (e.g., see Section 5 of [3]).

An interesting open problem is to compare the relative power of the CC and DSM models for solving synchronization problems efficiently with respect to RMRs. To settle this question, we must fix a synchronization problem and a set of synchronization primitives (e.g., atomic reads and writes) that are available for accessing memory. Consider first the mutual exclusion (ME) problem [9], where processes contend for a shared resource and must coordinate with each

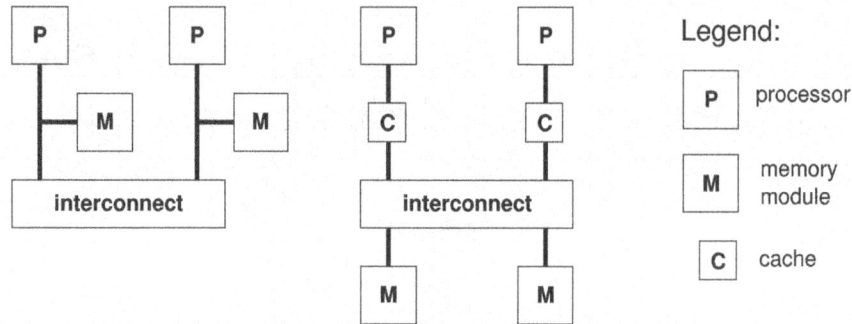

Figure 1: Models of shared memory architecture—DSM (left) and CC (right).

other to ensure that at most one process has access to the resource at any given time. Tight bounds for RMR complexity of N-process mutual exclusion are known for popular combinations of primitives, and do not show evidence that the CC model is more powerful than the DSM model, or vice-versa [3, 10, 5]. That is, although the RMR complexity may depend on the combination of primitives, for each combination studied, the tight bound is the same for the CC model as for the DSM model.

Surprisingly, Hadzilacos and Danek [8] discovered a separation between the CC model and DSM model by looking at the RMR complexity of solving *group mutual exclusion* (GME). This problem generalizes ordinary mutual exclusion by annotating each request for the shared resource with a *session* ID, and allowing multiple processes to access the resource concurrently provided that they request the same session. For a certain combination of primitives, it turns out that the RMR complexity of two-session N-process GME is less in the CC model than in the DSM model, by a factor of $\Theta(N/\log N)$.

Although we know that in one case the CC model is more powerful than the DSM model with respect to RMR complexity of a synchronization problem, the relative power of these two models is not well understood in the broader sense. For example, we do not know whether the CC model is at least as powerful as the DSM model for all problems, or whether perhaps the two models are incomparable because for some problem DSM is more powerful than CC. We also do not know how the two models compare under other notions of power, particularly the power to solve problems efficiently with respect to amortized (as opposed to worst-case) RMR complexity.

Answers to the above questions have interesting implications regarding the possibility of an *RMR-preserving simulation* of one model using another other. Such a simulation, if it exists, could be used to transform an algorithm that solves a given problem in one model to an algorithm that solves the same problem in another model, with at most a constant-factor increase in RMR complexity. A simulation of the CC model using the DSM model would be particularly interesting for both software and hardware designers because the CC model is arguably easier to program in, whereas the DSM model is easier to implement in hardware. Known results show only that such a simulation cannot exist if we define RMR complexity in the worst-case sense, leaving open the possibility that a simulation could at least preserve amortized RMR complexity.

Another open question is whether it is possible to show a separation in the RMR complexity of a problem between the CC and DSM models without leaning on *wait-freedom*—the requirement that a process must make progress in a bounded number of its own steps [16]. The complexity separation shown in [8] depends crucially on a restricted form of wait-freedom in the specification of the GME problem, which makes it more difficult to synchronize when one process releases the shared resource and allows a subset of other processes to emerge from busy-wait loops and make progress. This aspect of the problem specification tends to favor the CC model, where the problem can be solved by having the former process signal the others through a single spin variable. In contrast, in the DSM model spin variables cannot be shared by processes (or else RMR complexity becomes unbounded), and so more elaborate synchronization mechanisms must be used. Wait-freedom restricts the possible mechanisms that can be used, and in that sense penalizes the DSM model. Consequently, we wonder whether removing wait-freedom from the problem specification might create a more level playing field within which to judge the power of the CC and DSM models.

Summary of contributions.

The key contribution of this paper is the proof of a separation between the DSM and CC models in terms of the amortized RMR complexity of solving a simple synchronization problem. The "direction" of the separation is consistent with the one discovered by Hadzilacos and Danek [8]; the problem under consideration is solved more efficiently in the CC model than in the DSM model. However, our result is stronger in two ways. First, it applies to amortized RMR complexity and not only worst-case RMR complexity. Second, it is insensitive to progress properties in the sense that it holds for both the wait-free version of the synchronization problem and the version that allows busy-waiting.

Our result implies that the CC model cannot be simulated using the DSM model without introducing more than a constant-factor overhead in terms of the total number of RMRs performed by all processes executing an algorithm.

Road map.

We give the model and definitions in Section 2. We then survey related work in Section 3. In Section 4, we specify a simple synchronization problem, called the *signaling problem*. In Section 5 we give a simple algorithm that solves this problem in the CC model using very few RMRs. Section 6 presents a lower bound for the DSM model, which establishes a complexity separation from the CC model. We then discuss the complexity of variations on the signaling problem in Section 7. Finally, we consider the practical implications of our main result in Section 8, and conclude the paper in Section 9.

2. MODEL

There are N asynchronous processors that communicate by accessing shared memory using the following atomic primitives: reads, writes, Compare-And-Swap (CAS) and Load-Linked/Store-Conditional (LL/SC). (For definitions of CAS and LL/SC see [17].)

Processes and steps.

There are up to N *processes* running on the processors, at most one process per processor. The set of processes is denoted $\mathcal{P} = \{p_1, p_2, ..., p_N\}$, and we say that p_i has *ID i*. Each process is a sequential thread of control that repeatedly applies *steps*, where each step entails a memory access and some local computation. A step may cause a process to *terminate*, meaning that it stops performing steps. Processes can be modeled formally as input/output automata [27], but here we adopt a more informal approach by describing their possible behaviors through a shared memory algorithm. The algorithm is expressed through pseudo-code for each process, which is a collection of procedures that a process may call, one at a time. A procedure may accept some input arguments and may return some response to the caller. We specify a process by defining the possible sequences of procedure calls a process may make before terminating. We say that a process *crashes* if it terminates while performing a procedure call.

Histories.

A *history* is a finite or infinite sequence of steps that describes an execution of the multiprocessor from well-defined initial conditions. Process steps can be scheduled arbitrarily, and there is no bound on the number of steps that can be interleaved between two steps of the same process. A process *participates* in a history if it takes at least one step in that history. A history is *fair* if every process that participates either takes infinitely many steps, or terminates eventually.

Progress properties.

We will analyze the algorithms presented in this paper with respect to two progress properties: *wait-free* and *terminating*. An algorithm is wait-free if there is an upper bound B such that for any history H of the algorithm, each (partially or fully completed) call to a procedure in H incurs at most B steps. An algorithm is terminating if, for any fair history H of the algorithm where no process crashes, each (partially or fully completed) call to a procedure in H incurs a finite number of steps. (That is, in H each process that participates either terminates after completing a finite number of procedure calls, or else it makes infinitely many procedure calls.)

Remote Memory References.

RMRs were introduced in Section 1. In the DSM model, a memory access is an RMR if and only if the address accessed by the processor maps to a memory module tied to another processor. In the CC model, the definition of an RMR is more complex; it depends on the state of each processor's cache, as well as the type of coherence protocol used to maintain consistency among caches. For our purposes, we need only a loose definition of RMRs in the CC model that makes it possible to establish upper bounds on RMR complexity. To that end, we assume that if a process reads some memory location several times, then this entire sequence of reads incurs only one RMR in total provided that between the first and last of these reads there is no nontrivial operation performed by another process on that memory location. (A nontrivial operation overwrites a memory location, possibly with the same value as before.)

3. RELATED WORK

A number of interesting complexity results have appeared in literature on algorithms for asynchronous shared memory multiprocessors. Many of these pertain to mutual exclusion (ME) [9, 25], the problem of ensuring exclusive access to a shared resource among competing processes. RMRs were originally motivated in this context as an alternative to traditional step complexity. (In an asynchronous model, ME cannot be solved with bounded step complexity per process.) The key result in RMR complexity of ME is a separation between the complexity (per passage through the critical section) of two classes of algorithms characterized by the set of primitives used. For the class based on reads and writes, the tight bound is $\Theta(\log N)$ RMRs per process in the worst case [30, 22, 10, 5]. In contrast, for the class that uses reads, writes, and Fetch-And-Increment or Fetch-And-Store, the tight bound is $O(1)$ RMRs [4, 14]. Analogous bounds hold for first-come-first-served (FCFS) ME [24, 3, 7].

RMR complexity bounds for the class of algorithms that use reads and writes only can be generalized to the class that in addition uses comparison primitives (e.g., Compare-And-Swap) [3]. For ME, the reason is that comparison primitives can be simulated efficiently using reads and writes. For example, any comparison primitive can be implemented using reads and writes with only $O(1)$ RMRs per operation in the CC and DSM models [13, 12]. Note that in such implementations *every* operation incurs RMRs, in contrast to a comparison primitive implemented in hardware, which can sometimes be applied locally. *Locally-accessible* implementations address this issue and can be used to transform any algorithm that uses reads, writes, and comparison primitives into one that uses reads and write only, and has the same RMR complexity asymptotically [12, 11]. Note that because this transformation necessarily introduces busy-waiting ([16]), it can break certain correctness properties of the algorithm, such as bounded exit in ME, and bounded doorway in FCFS ME [3]. (This is precisely why the transformation was not used in [7].)

For ME and FCFS ME, the same RMR complexity bounds hold in the CC model as in the DSM model, with the exception of so-called Local-Failed Comparison with write-Update (LFCU) systems [1]. An LFCU system is a type of cache-coherent machine that is almost never implemented in practice. In such systems, ME can be solved using reads, writes and Test-And-Set in $O(1)$ RMRs, which beats the $\Theta(\log N)$ tight bound for the DSM model. The complexity results presented in this paper for the CC model hold just as well for LFCU systems as for the more standard write-through and write-back systems [29].

Mutual exclusion has been studied not only asynchronous systems, but also in semi-synchronous systems, where consecutive steps by the same process occur at most Δ time units apart for some Δ [3]. In one class of such systems, every process knows Δ, and processes have the ability to delay their own execution by at least Δ time units in order to force others to make progress. Given reads, writes and comparison primitives, ME can be solved in such systems using $O(1)$ RMRs in the DSM model, but in the CC model $\Omega(\log \log N)$ RMRs are needed in the worst case [23]. To our knowledge, this is the first result that separates the CC and DSM models in terms of RMR complexity for solving a fundamental synchronization problem. (In this context we ignore complexity bounds for LFCU systems because they are not representative of the more common variants of the CC model.)

An interesting complexity separation has also been shown for the group mutual exclusion (GME) problem [19] in asynchronous systems. GME is a generalization of ME where requests for the shared resource are annotated with session IDs, and two processes can access the shared resource concurrently provided that they request the same session. Several specifications for this problem have been proposed, differing in fairness and progress properties [19, 20, 15, 18, 6]. Upper bounds for RMR complexity of GME in asynchronous systems range from $O(\log N)$ to $O(N)$ depending on the particular specification, and are subject to any lower bound known for ME. Some algorithms use only atomic reads and writes, while others rely also on CAS and/or Fetch-And-Add primitives. To our knowledge, the only known lower bound on RMRs for GME, except those for ME, is the $\Omega(N)$ bound by Hadzilacos and Danek for the DSM model [8], which applies to the version of GME defined by Hadzilacos [15] and holds even when there are only two sessions. This result separates the DSM model from the CC model, in which the two-session case can be solved using only $O(\log N)$ RMRs [8]. The "direction" of the separation is opposite to the one for ME in semi-synchronous systems.

Another line of research related to this paper pertains to transforming an algorithm that solves some synchronization problem in one shared memory model into an algorithm that solves the same problem in another model, with the same RMR complexity up to a constant factor. A few transformations have been proposed for mapping mutual exclusion algorithms from the CC model to the DSM model [26, 2]. (In [2], see footnote 7.) These transformations work only for a restricted class of ME algorithms, and to our knowledge no general transformation exists for ME or any other widely studied synchronization problem.

4. PROBLEM SPECIFICATION

In this section we specify the *signaling problem*, for which we establish RMR complexity bounds in the remainder of the paper. The problem belongs to the family of problems where two types of processes, called *signalers* and *waiters*, must exchange information regarding some event (e.g., a shared resource has been released). That is, the signalers must ensure that the waiters are aware that the event has occurred. There are several important dimensions within which the safety properties for the signaling problem problem can be pinned down: Is there one signaler/waiter or are there many? Are the IDs of the signalers/waiters fixed in

advance or decided arbitrarily at runtime? How do waiters learn about the signal?

We also consider two ways to specify the semantics of the signaling problem. With *polling semantics*, a solution to the problem consists of two procedures, called `Signal()` and `Poll()`. A signaler issues the signal by calling `Signal()`, which has no return value. A waiter learns about the signal by calling `Poll()`, which returns a Boolean indicating whether the signal has been issued. A process may call the two procedures arbitrarily many times, in any order. (Alternately, we can require that waiters and signalers be distinct. This has no effect on the complexity bounds presented in this paper.) The safety properties for the procedures `Signal()` and `Poll()` are stated formally below in Definition 4.1.

SPECIFICATION 4.1. *For any history where each process makes zero or more calls to* `Signal()` *and zero or more calls to* `Poll()`, *in any order, the following hold:*

- *If some call to* `Poll()` *returns* true, *then some call to* `Signal()` *has already begun.*
- *If some call to* `Poll()` *returns* false, *then no call to* `Signal()` *completed before this call to* `Poll()` *began.*

With *blocking semantics*, a solution to the problem consists of procedures `Signal()` and `Wait()`. Procedure `Signal()` is specified as for polling semantics. A waiter learns about the signal by calling `Wait()`, which returns (with a trivial response) only after some call to `Signal()` has begun. If the signal is never issued, then `Wait()` never returns. As before, a process may call the two procedures arbitrarily many times, in any order.

To derive a complexity separation between the CC and DSM models, we consider one of the most difficult variations of the signaling problem: there is one signaler and there are many waiters, whose IDs are not fixed in advance; polling semantics are used; and waiters can terminate after a finite number of calls to `Poll()` even if no such call returned true—a key point exploited in our lower bound proof.

Orthogonal to the above safety properties are the progress properties a solution may satisfy. Terminating solutions are certainly possible, and with polling semantics wait-free solutions can also be considered. Note that in terminating solutions, one process may busy-wait for another during a call to `Poll()` regardless of the values returned by such calls. However, if the signal has not yet been issued, each call to `Poll()` must eventually terminate provided that the history is fair.

5. UPPER BOUND FOR CC MODEL

We are interested in solutions to the signaling problem that are efficient with respect to RMRs. More precisely, we would like to minimize the total number of RMRs a process incurs across all the procedure calls it makes in a given history. In the CC model, a very simple and RMR-efficient solution is obtained using a single Boolean shared variable, call it B, set to false initially. With polling semantics, procedure `Signal()` assigns $B := $ true, and `Poll()` reads and returns the value of B. With blocking semantics, `Signal()` also assigns $B := $ true, and `Wait()` busy-waits until $B = $ true holds before returning.

The solution described above is wait-free, has $O(1)$ RMR complexity per process in the CC model, and uses only atomic reads and writes. As we show next in Section 6, such a solution cannot be obtained in the DSM model, even if we care only about terminating solutions, settle for $O(1)$ amortized RMR complexity, and allow additional synchronization primitives. We then discuss additional upper bounds for variations of signaling problem in Section 7.

6. LOWER BOUND FOR DSM MODEL

Our main result, to which we devote the remainder of this section, is captured in Theorem 6.2 below. (In this section, "signaling problem" refers to the particular variation described at the end of Section 4.)

DEFINITION 6.1. *For any algorithm $\mathcal{A}$ that solves the signaling problem with polling semantics, let $\mathcal{H}_{\mathcal{A}}$ denote the set of histories (and all their finite prefixes) where each process makes zero or more calls to* Poll() *and zero or more calls to* Signal(), *in arbitrary order, and then terminates.*

THEOREM 6.2. *For any deterministic terminating algorithm $\mathcal{A}$ that solves the signaling problem (with polling semantics) using atomic reads and writes, and for any constant $c \in \mathbb{Z}^+$, there exists a constant $k \in \mathbb{Z}^+$ and a history $H \in \mathcal{H}_{\mathcal{A}}$ where k processes participate and incur more than ck RMRs in total in the DSM model.*

At the end of this section (see Corollary 6.14), we generalize the above result to algorithms that use compare-and-swap (CAS) or load-linked/store-conditional (LL/SC) in addition to reads and writes.

6.1 Overview of proof

To establish Theorem 6.2, we apply a two-part proof whose first part is very similar to Kim and Anderson's construction for proving a lower bound on the RMR complexity of adaptive mutual exclusion [21]. The key idea we borrow from them is to construct inductively a history where communication among processes is minimized using the strategies of erasing and rolling forward. (Eventually there are no more processes to erase or roll forward, and the construction halts.) The main difference between their construction and ours is the end goal. Whereas Kim and Anderson apply the maximum possible number of rounds in order to trigger many RMRs, our goal is to apply just enough rounds so that waiters "stabilize," meaning that they stop performing RMRs and start busy-waiting on local memory. In fact, for our purposes it helps to use as few rounds as possible, as that maximizes the number of waiters remaining. Part two of our proof then shows how to extend this construction so that a signaler executes many (i.e., more than ck) RMRs communicating with the waiters.

In the inductive construction, we begin with all N processes participating as waiters, making repeated calls to Poll(). The strategies for erasing and rolling forward are analogous to Kim and Anderson's. In our context, rolling forward means that a waiter is allowed to complete any ongoing call to Poll() it may have, and terminate. After applying the inductive construction for only a constant number of rounds, there are a few processes that have been rolled forward, and many more "invisible" processes that have not communicated with each other. Next, we proceed to part two. Here we show that many of the invisible processes created in part one have stabilized, and that if a judiciously

chosen process calls Signal(), then it can be forced into an expensive (in terms of RMRs) "wild goose chase." Since the signaler does not know who the waiters are, it must discover them by performing RMRs, but in that case we intervene and erase the waiter (if it is invisible) just before the RMR.

In the remainder of this section, we describe in more detail our two-part proof. We proceed by contradiction, supposing that Theorem 6.2 is false. That is, we suppose that some deterministic terminating algorithm $\mathcal{A}$ (consisting of subroutines Poll() and Signal() for each process) exists that solves the signaling problem using atomic reads and writes with $O(1)$ amortized RMR complexity. Then there is a constant $c \in \mathbb{Z}^+$ such that for any $H \in \mathcal{H}_{\mathcal{A}}$ (see Definition 6.1), if k processes participate in H then the total number of RMRs incurred by these processes in the DSM model is at most ck.

6.2 Proof—Part 1

We first give some definitions based on those of [21]. These definitions are specialized for the DSM model, which makes them different from Kim and Anderson's more elaborate definitions that deal with the CC and DSM models simultaneously.

DEFINITION 6.3. *For any $H \in \mathcal{H}_{\mathcal{A}}$, let $Par(H)$ denote the set of processes that participate in H. The set of finished processes in H, denoted $Fin(H)$, is the subset of $Par(H)$ consisting of processes that have terminated by the end of H. The set of active processes in H, denoted $Act(H)$, is defined as $Par(H) \setminus Fin(H)$ (i.e., participating processes that have not yet terminated).*

DEFINITION 6.4. *For any $H \in \mathcal{H}_{\mathcal{A}}$ and any $p, q \in Par(H)$, we say that p sees q in H if and only if p reads a variable that was last written by q.*

DEFINITION 6.5. *For any $H \in \mathcal{H}_{\mathcal{A}}$ and any $p, q \in Par(H)$, we say that p touches q in H if and only if p accesses a variable local to q.*

DEFINITION 6.6. *For any $H \in \mathcal{H}_{\mathcal{A}}$, we say that H is regular if and only if all of the following conditions hold:*

1. *For any distinct $p, q \in Par(H)$, if p sees q in H then $q \in Fin(H)$.*

2. *For any distinct $p, q \in Par(H)$, if p touches q in H then $q \in Fin(H)$.*

3. *For any variable v written in H, if v is written by more than one process and the last write is by $p \in Par(H)$, then $p \in Fin(H)$.*

LEMMA 6.7. *For any $H \in \mathcal{H}_{\mathcal{A}}$ and any $p \in Act(H)$, if no $q \in Par(H)$ sees p in H, then the history H' obtained by erasing all steps of p from H is also an element of $\mathcal{H}_{\mathcal{A}}$.*

We will use Lemma 6.7 implicitly in the proof sketches that follow whenever we need to erase an active process from a history.

At this point we depart from Kim and Anderson's definitions [21] and introduce a few of our own.

DEFINITION 6.8. *For any regular $H \in \mathcal{H}_{\mathcal{A}}$ and any $p \in Act(H)$, p is stable if and only if for any extension H' of H where p runs solo and continues calling Poll() repeatedly, p incurs zero RMRs in H' after the prefix H. Otherwise p is unstable.*

Our end goal in this part of the proof is to show that $\mathcal{H}_\mathcal{A}$ contains a regular history such that $Act(H)$ contains many more stable processes than $Fin(H)$. To that end, we will construct inductively a sequence of regular computations H_1, H_2, H_3, ..., H_c and prove the following invariant in the case when N is large enough (with respect to c):

DEFINITION 6.9. *For any i, $0 \le i \le c$, let $S(i)$ denote the statement that $\mathcal{H}_\mathcal{A}$ contains a regular history H_i satisfying all of the following properties:*

1. *$|Fin(H_i)| \le i$*

2. *$|Act(H_i)| \ge N^{1/3^i}$*

3. *Each $p \in Act(H_i)$ incurs at most i RMRs.*

4. *Each unstable $p \in Act(H_i)$ incurs exactly i RMRs.*

5. *Each $p \in Fin(H_i)$ incurs at most ci RMRs.*

LEMMA 6.10. *If N is large enough then for any i, $0 \le i \le c$, $S(i)$ holds.*

PROOF SKETCH: The analysis is similar to that of [21] at a high level, with some technical differences. We proceed by induction. For $S(0)$, note that in H_0 there N active processes and no finished processes, and no process has performed an RMR. Now for any $0 \le i < c$ suppose that $S(i)$ holds. We must prove $S(i+1)$. To that end, we will construct H_{i+1} from H_i. If there are no unstable processes in $Act(H_i)$, we simply let each active process take one more step, which is necessarily local step.

Otherwise, we let each unstable process in $Act(H_i)$ take steps until it is about to perform an RMR, and determine for each such process its next RMR. We will refer to these as the "next RMRs" of the unstable processes. Allowing each such process to apply its next RMR may yield a history H_i' that is not regular because it violates one of the properties in Definition 6.6. As in Kim and Anderson's proof, properties 1 and 2 of Definition 6.9 are dealt with easily by erasing at most a constant fraction of active processes. To that end, we construct a "conflict graph" where vertices represent active processes and an edge $\{p, q\}$ exists if and only if p sees or touches $q \ne p$ in its next RMR (or vice versa). Since a process can see or touch at most one other process by performing an RMR, the conflict graph has average degree $d \le 4$. (For each process we add at most two edges, and each edge contributes to the degree of two vertices.) By Turán's theorem, the conflict graph contains an independent set containing at least $\frac{1}{d+1} = \frac{1}{5}$ of the active processes. Keeping these and erasing the remaining active processes resolves all the conflicts. Once this is done, we apply any next RMRs that perform a read, and consider the remaining RMRs for property 3 of Definition 6.9. We consider two cases as in Kim and Anderson's proof – one dealt with by rolling forward, the other by erasing. Let X denote the number of unstable processes remaining after properties 1–2 of Definition 6.6 are dealt with.

Roll-forward case.

If at least $\lfloor\sqrt{X}\rfloor$ unstable processes are about to access the same shared variable v in their next RMRs, we erase all other unstable processes, and allow the ones remaining to apply their next RMRs on v in some arbitrary order. The last process to write v, call it r, is then rolled forward. As we roll forward r, it may see or touch other processes. If r

sees or touches an active process p, then this is an RMR for r and we erase p. (It follows from H_i being regular that r cannot see p via a local access prior to r's next RMR.) If r executes more than $c(i+1)$ RMRs in total as a result of being rolled forward, then we obtain a contradiction easily: Erasing all other active processes we obtain a history where there are at most $i+1$ finished processes, namely i from H_i (by property 1 of Definition 6.9) plus r, and no other processes. The total number of RMRs in this history is more than $c(i+1)$, which contradicts our definition of $\mathcal{A}$. Thus, by rolling forward r we erase at most $c(i+1) \le c^2 + c$ active processes. The number of active processes remaining is at least $\lfloor\sqrt{X}\rfloor - (c^2 + c + 1)$.

Erasing case.

If there is no single variable that is about to be accessed by at least $\lfloor\sqrt{X}\rfloor$ unstable processes in their next RMRs, then these RMRs collectively access at least $\lfloor\sqrt{X}\rfloor$ distinct variables. For each such variable, we choose arbitrarily an unstable process that will access it, and we erase all the other unstable processes. This leaves at least $\lfloor\sqrt{X}\rfloor$ active processes. It is possible that some of the next RMRs of these remaining processes are about to write registers that have already been written by active processes. We can eliminate this problem by erasing some of the active processes. To that end, we construct a conflict graph where each vertex is an active process and an edge $\{p, q\}$ exists if and only if p writes in its next RMR a variable previously written by $q \ne p$. Since each active process has at most one next RMR, the conflict graph has average degree $d \le 2$. (For each process we add at most one edge, and each edge contributes to the degree of two vertices.) By Turán's theorem, the conflict graph contains an independent set containing at least $\frac{1}{d+1} = \frac{1}{3}$ of the active processes. Keeping these and erasing the remaining active processes resolves all the conflicts, leaving $\lceil\lfloor\sqrt{X}\rfloor \times \frac{1}{3}\rceil$ active processes.

Let H_{i+1} denote the history obtained from H_i by our construction. It follows from our construction that H_{i+1} is regular, and so it remains to show that it satisfies properties 1–5 of $S(i+1)$ given that $S(i)$ holds. Property 1 holds because $|Fin(H_{i+1})| \le |Fin(H_i)| + 1 \le i$. Property 2 holds because $|Act(H_{i+1})| \ge |Act(H_i)|^{1/3} \ge N^{1/3^{(i+1)}}$ for N large enough. Properties 3 and 4 follow from $S(i)$ and the application of the next RMRs round $i+1$ of the construction. Property 5 follows from $S(i)$ and the fact that any process being rolled forward in round $i+1$ incurs at most $c(i+1)$ RMRs in H_{i+1} under our original supposition that Theorem 6.2 is false. Thus, $S(i+1)$ holds. $\square$

6.3 Proof—Part 2

LEMMA 6.11. *In the history H_c referred to by Lemma 6.10 there are at least $\lfloor N^{1/3^c}/2\rfloor$ stable processes.*

PROOF SKETCH: Recall that, by Lemma 6.10, the following hold: $|Fin(H_c)| \le c$, $|Act(H_c)| \ge N^{1/3^c}$, and that each unstable process in $Act(H_c)$ has performed exactly c RMRs in H_c. Now suppose for contradiction that fewer than $\lfloor N^{1/3^c}/2\rfloor$ of the active processes are stable. Then at least $\lfloor N^{1/3^c}/2\rfloor$ are unstable, and moreover each one has performed exactly c RMRs in H_c. Let H_c' be the history obtained from H_c by erasing all active processes except for exactly $\lfloor N^{1/3^c}/2 \rfloor$ unstable ones, and then letting each unstable process make one more RMR (in any order). This history satisfies the following: $|Fin(H'_c)| = |Fin(H_c)| \leq c$, $|Act(H'_c)| = \lfloor N^{1/3^c}/2 \rfloor$, and each process in $Act(H'_c)$ has incurred $c+1$ RMRs. Consequently, $|Par(H'_c)| \leq c + \lfloor N^{1/3^c}/2 \rfloor$, and the total number of RMRs incurred in H'_c is at least $(c+1)\lfloor N^{1/3^c}/2 \rfloor = c\lfloor N^{1/3^c}/2 \rfloor + \lfloor N^{1/3^c}/2 \rfloor$, which is greater than c times $|Par(H'_c)|$ when N is large enough. This contradicts the RMR complexity of $\mathcal{A}$. $\square$

LEMMA 6.12. *There exists a regular history $H \in \mathcal{H}_\mathcal{A}$ in which there are exactly $\lfloor N^{1/3^c}/2 \rfloor$ stable active processes, at most c finished processes, and no other processes participating. Furthermore, in H, each process that participates incurs at most c^2 RMRs in the DSM model.*

PROOF SKETCH: By Lemma 6.11, the history H_c referred to by Lemma 6.10 contains at least $\lfloor N^{1/3^c}/2 \rfloor$ stable processes. It also contains at most c finished processes by Lemma 6.10. To construct H, take H_c and erase all active processes except $\lfloor N^{1/3^c}/2 \rfloor$ unstable ones. The remaining processes incur the same number of RMRs in H as in H_c, which is bounded in Lemma 6.10: each active process in H_c incurs at most c RMRs, and each finished process incurs at most c^2 RMRs. Thus, each process incurs at most c^2 RMRs, as wanted. $\square$

We now describe how to use the history H referred to by Lemma 6.12 to derive a contradiction.

LEMMA 6.13. *For large enough N, there exists a history $H' \in \mathcal{H}_\mathcal{A}$ and a constant $k \in \mathbb{Z}^+$, such that at most k processes participate in H and yet the total number of RMRs incurred in H is more than ck.*

PROOF SKETCH: Let H be the history referred to by Lemma 6.12. In this history, each process that participates incurs at most c^2 RMRs, and at most $c+\lfloor N^{1/3^c}/2 \rfloor$ processes participate. Thus, in total the participating processes write to at most $(c + \lfloor N^{1/3^c}/2 \rfloor)(1 + c^2)$ distinct memory modules. (Each process may write its own module, and at most c^2 remote ones.) For N large enough, this means there is some process s whose memory module is not written in H.

Now construct H' from H as follows. First, let each stable process run solo, one by one, completing any pending call to Poll() that it may have. Since each process is stable, by Definition 6.8, it will not incur any RMRs doing so. Now let s run solo and make a call to Signal(), which must eventually terminate. As s performs this call, each time s is about to see a process p that is active in H, or is about to write memory local to p, erase p and then allow s to take its step. Note that this step by s must be an RMR because $s \neq p$, and because by our choice of s, process p has never written memory local to s. It follows that s performs one such RMR for each stable process $p \in Act(H)$, otherwise after s completes its call to Signal() there is some p that remains stable and whose local memory is in the same state as at the end of H. Consequently, if p now calls Poll(), then its call returns the same response as p's last call, namely false, contradicting the specification of the signaling problem (see Definition 4.1). Thus, s performs at least $\lfloor N^{1/3^c}/2 \rfloor$ RMRs. Finally, erase any active process that remains, which leaves only s and at most c finished processes participating in the history. Let H' denote this history. Note that at most $k = c+1$ processes participate in H', and yet s incurs at

least $\lfloor N^{1/3^c}/2 \rfloor$ RMRs in H' in the DSM model. For large enough N, this means that the number of RMRs is more than $ck = c(c+1)$, as wanted. $\square$

PROOF OF THEOREM 6.2: Lemma 6.13 contradicts our assumption on the RMR complexity of $\mathcal{A}$. Thus, $\mathcal{A}$ does not exist and Theorem 6.2 holds. $\square$

COROLLARY 6.14. *For any deterministic algorithm $\mathcal{A}$ that solves the signaling problem (with polling semantics) using atomic reads and writes, and either CAS or LL/SC, and for any constant $c \in \mathbb{Z}^+$, there exists a constant $k \in \mathbb{Z}^+$ and a history $H \in \mathcal{H}_\mathcal{A}$ where k processes participate and incur more than ck RMRs in total in the DSM model.*

PROOF. Suppose for contradiction that Corollary 6.14 is false, namely that some deterministic terminating algorithm $\mathcal{A}$ exists that solves signaling problem using the stated set of base object types, and there is a constant $c \in \mathbb{Z}^+$ such that for any $H \in \mathcal{H}_\mathcal{A}$ the total number of RMRs incurred in the DSM model in H is at most c times the number of processes participating. Replacing the variables accessed via CAS or LL/SC in $\mathcal{A}$ with the locally-accessible $O(1)$-RMR implementations of these primitives presented in [11, 12], we obtain another terminating algorithm $\mathcal{A}'$ that solves the signaling problem using only atomic reads and writes, and there exists a constant $c' \in \mathbb{Z}^+$ such that for any $H \in \mathcal{H}_{\mathcal{A}'}$ the total number of RMRs incurred in the DSM model in H is at most c' times the number of processes participating. The existence of $\mathcal{A}'$ contradicts Theorem 6.2. $\square$

7. ADDITIONAL COMPLEXITY BOUNDS

In this section we discuss solutions to variations of the signaling problem defined in Section 4. Recall that there are two flavors of the problem: with polling semantics, waiters repeatedly call Poll() to determine if the signal has been issued; with blocking semantics, waiters instead call Wait(), which does not return until the signal has been issued. Both flavors of the signaling problem are solved easily in the CC model using $O(1)$ RMRs per process worst-case. The solution is presented in Section 5.

As one might suspect, in light of our lower bound result, the solution space for variations of the signaling problem in the DSM model is somewhat more complex. The solutions proposed for the CC model do not work "out of the box" in the DSM model in the sense that they have unbounded RMR complexity. Nevertheless, RMR-efficient algorithms for the DSM model can be devised using more elaborate synchronization techniques. We explore such solutions in detail in the remainder of this section. For each problem variation we consider, we will describe the polling solution, from which blocking solution can be achieved easily by implementing Wait() via repeated execution of the code for Poll(). In some cases, a more efficient solution is possible for blocking semantics, as we indicate below.

Single waiter.

If there is at most a single waiter, and its ID is not necessarily fixed in advance, the problem can be solved using two global variables, say W (process ID, initially NIL) and S (Boolean, initially false), as well as an array $V[1..N]$ of Boolean variables (initially false), where $V[i]$ is local to process p_i. The first call to Poll() writes the waiter's ID to W, and then reads and returns the value of S. On subsequent invocations by process p_i, Poll() reads and returns $V[i]$ instead. Signal() sets S to true, and then reads W. If NIL is read, Signal() returns immediately. If a non-NIL value is read, it must be the waiter's ID, say p_j, in which case the signaler writes true to $V[j]$. This algorithm has $O(1)$ RMR complexity per process in the worst case, matching the upper bound for the CC model.

Many waiters, fixed in advance.

In this formulation of the problem, the signaler knows in advance the IDs of the waiters that will participate eventually (i.e., if the history is extended by sufficiently many steps). A simple solution in this case is to use an array of Boolean variables $V[1..N]$, initially all false, $V[i]$ local to process p_i. A call to Poll() by p_i reads and returns $V[i]$, and Signal() sets $V[j]$ for each waiter p_j whose ID is fixed in advance. Letting W denote the number of waiters, this solution has $O(W)$ RMR complexity per process worst-case. However, amortized RMR complexity may be more than $O(1)$ RMRs if the signaler performs W RMRs but only $o(W)$ waiters participate so far in the history. (This is possible if the history is not yet long enough for every fixed waiter to begin participating.)

For terminating solutions, it is easy to reduce the amortized RMR complexity to $O(1)$ in all histories. The signaler can simply wait for each waiter to participate, using another array of Boolean flags, before writing any element of V. With blocking semantics, the worst-case RMR complexity per process can also be reduced to $O(1)$ using the work sharing techniques described in [13].

For wait-free solutions using reads, writes and comparison primitives, $O(1)$ amortized RMR complexity is impossible to achieve for all histories when W is large enough (e.g., $W \in \Theta(N)$). This result follows by a lower bound proof similar to the one given in Section 6. (Although the signaler knows which waiters will participate eventually, it does not know which waiters participate at the time when it calls Signal(), which must return in a bounded number of steps.)

For terminating solutions with polling semantics, it is also possible to show that in the worst case the signaler must perform $\Omega(W)$ RMRs if all W waiters participate by the time Signal() is called. This follows by a simplified version of the lower bound proof from Section 6. (This simplified proof is similar in spirit to the lower bound proof of Hadzilacos and Danek [8], but does not rely on any form of wait-freedom.) The main idea is as follows: First, W waiters call Poll() repeatedly until they are all stable (i.e., accessing only local memory). We then allow each waiter to complete any ongoing call to Poll() it may have. Next, a signaler makes a call to Signal(), which must terminate in a finite number of steps because the signaler is running solo starting from a state where each waiter is not required to take any more steps (i.e., it is "in between" calls to Poll()). Furthermore, before this call to Signal() terminates, the signaler must write remotely to the local memory of each waiter, except possibly itself, which incurs $\Omega(W)$ RMRs. To see this, suppose that the signaler neglects to write p_i's memory for some waiter p_i different from itself. In that case, after the call to Signal() completes, p_i may make another call to Poll() that will incorrectly return the same value as p_i's previous call (i.e., false).

Many waiters not fixed in advance, one signaler fixed in advance.

The solution is similar to the case with fixed waiters, with a few additional steps. Upon calling Poll() for the first time, a waiter "registers" with the signaler by setting a dedicated Boolean flag in the signaler's local memory. The signaler, upon calling Signal(), checks for each i whether p_i has registered, and if so, performs a remote write to $V[i]$. In addition, we must handle correctly the race condition when waiters register while the signaler is calling Signal(). To that end, it suffices to use an additional global variable analogous to S from the single waiter case. The signaler writes S at the beginning of Signal(), and waiters check S at the end of their first call to Poll() (i.e., after registering).

A terminating algorithm for this version of the problem appears in [12]. It uses using atomic reads and writes only and incurs $O(1)$ RMRs per process in the worst case.

Many waiters not fixed in advance, one signaler not fixed in advance.

With polling semantics the problem is subject to the lower bound from Section 6. That is, if only reads, writes and CAS or LL/SC are used, the problem can be solved more efficiently in the CC model than in the DSM model with respect to amortized RMR complexity. It is possible to close this gap by using stronger primitives. Recall from Section 3 that if Fetch-And-Increment or Fetch-And-Add are available in addition to reads and writes, then it is possible to solve mutual exclusion using $O(1)$ RMRs per process, which can be used to construct a shared queue with the same RMR complexity. Waiters and signalers can leverage such a queue as follows: During its first call to Poll(), a waiter adds itself to the queue, and also checks a global flag to see if a signaler has started a call to Signal(). During subsequent calls to Poll(), a waiter only checks a dedicated flag in its own local memory. During a call to Signal(), the signaler sets the global flag, then retrieves the set of all waiters from the shared queue, and writes the dedicated flag for each waiter found in the queue. The worst-case RMR complexity per process of this solution is $O(1)$ for waiters, and $O(k)$ for the signaler when there are k waiters participating. Thus, amortized RMR complexity is $O(1)$.

With blocking semantics, the problem can be reduced to the single-waiter case by having the waiters elect a leader, which learns about the signal and then ensures that the signal is propagated to the remaining waiters. Using the synchronization techniques described in [12], such a solution is possible with $O(1)$ RMR complexity per process worst-case, using only atomic reads and writes. (The leader election algorithm must tell each waiter the ID of the leader rather than merely telling each waiter whether it is the leader.)

Many waiters not fixed in advance, many signalers.

One possibility is to reduce this case to "one signaler not fixed in advance" by having signalers elect a leader that will signal the waiters. Leader election can be solved in $O(1)$ RMRs per process worst-case using atomic reads and writes by a terminating algorithm [13], or in one step per process using virtually any read-modify-write primitive (e.g., Test-And-Set or Fetch-And-Store).

8. RMRS VS. OBSERVED PERFORMANCE

In this section, we discuss the relationship between RMR complexity and observed performance in real world multiprocessors, and comment on the practical interpretation of our complexity separation result.

The RMR complexity measure attempts to quantify interprocess communication by counting memory accesses that engage the interconnect joining processors and memory (see Figure 1). Since the interconnect is slow relative to processor speed, observed performance tends to degrade as communication over the interconnect increases. This effect has been demonstrated in the context of mutual exclusion algorithms on the Sequent Symmetry (a CC machine) and the BBN Butterfly (a DSM machine) [4, 14, 28, 30]. The key lesson from this body of literature is that algorithms with bounded RMR complexity (i.e., so-called *local-spin* algorithms) outperform algorithms that have unbounded RMR complexity by a significant margin under worst-case conditions (i.e., maximum concurrency).

Although the benefits of local-spin algorithms are well understood, it is important to note that RMR complexity is not a very precise tool for predicting real world performance, especially for cache-coherent machines. For example, to derive our upper bound in Section 5, we made the simplifying assumption that a cache behaves "ideally," meaning that it never drops data spuriously (see Section 2). Since this assumption does not hold in a preemptive multitasking environment, especially under high load, theoretical RMR complexity bounds are prone to underestimate the actual number of RMRs. An even more important concern is the imprecise relationship between RMRs and communication. We focus on the latter issue in more detail in the remainder of this section.

Consider the simplified example of a cache-coherent system where processes communicate using read and write operations, and coherence is ensured by a *write-through* protocol [29]. In such a system, a read operation on a shared object O either finds a cached copy of O locally, or else it fetches O from main memory and creates a copy of O in the local cache. A write operation on O applies the new value for O to main memory, creates (or updates) a copy of O in the local cache, and invalidates (i.e., destroys) all copies of O in remote caches. Thus, while an RMR on read generates a fixed amount of communication, an RMR on write may trigger multiple "invalidation messages." This is in contrast to the DSM model where, in the absence of a coherence protocol, any RMR generates a fixed amount of communication.

The above example illustrates that RMRs in the CC model and RMRs in the DSM model are very different "currencies" for describing the cost of an algorithm. Consequently, a meaningful comparison between them requires that we define the "exchange rate." To that end, we must fix a particular cache-coherent architecture and coherence protocol. The simplest scenario occurs when the interconnect joining processors and memory is a shared bus, and any message generated by the coherence protocol is broadcast to all processors. In that case, a single message suffices to invalidate all remote copies of an object on write, and so RMRs in this type of system are "at par" with RMRs in the DSM model.

Since a shared bus offers limited communication bandwidth, realistic large-scale cache-coherent systems use more elaborate interconnects. In such systems, an RMR on write may generate multiple invalidation messages, the exact number depending on the topology of the interconnect and the state information maintained by the coherence protocol. Consequently, RMR complexity per process can underestimate vastly the amount of communication triggered by a process. But what about amortized RMR complexity, which is the focus of this paper?

A key observation is that in any cache-coherent system, a cached copy of a shared object can be invalidated at most once, because invalidation destroys it. Since an RMR is necessary to create a cached copy in the first place, this means that the total number of *invalidations* (i.e., events where a cached copy of an object is destroyed) is bounded from above by the number of RMRs. The implications of this on message complexity depend on how the number of invalidations relates to the number of invalidation messages that trigger them.

Ideally, the cache coherence protocol would maintain sufficient information so that an invalidation message for a particular shared object O is only sent to remote caches that actually hold a copy of O. This is an unrealistic assumption because in an N-processor system, it requires roughly N bits of state for each cached object! However, it does ensure that at most one invalidation message is generated for each invalidation that actually occurs. In that case, amortized RMR complexity corresponds well to amortized message complexity.

In realistic large-scale cache-coherent systems, the coherence protocol maintains far less state than in an ideal system, and so RMRs may trigger superfluous invalidation messages (i.e., ones that do not actually cause an invalidation). In such systems, amortized RMR complexity may be lower asymptotically than amortized message complexity, and so our RMR complexity separation does not imply that in practice a large-scale cache-coherent machine could solve the signaling problem more efficiently than a DSM machine with the same number of processors.

9. CONCLUSION

In this paper, we showed that the signaling problem can be solved in a wait-free manner using only atomic reads and writes, with $O(1)$ RMRs per process in the CC model, and $O(1)$ space. We then showed that the same problem cannot be solved in the DSM model with the same parameters, even if we weaken these parameters in all of the following ways simultaneously: (1) we allow only one signaler instead of many, (2) we settle for $O(1)$ RMRs complexity in the amortized sense rather than in the worst case, (3) we allow unbounded space, (4) we weaken the progress condition from wait-free to terminating, and (5) we allow use of Compare-And-Swap or Load-Linked/Store-Conditional in addition to reads and writes. Thus, we separate the CC and DSM models in terms of their power for solving the signaling problem efficiently with respect to amortized RMR complexity.

Acknowledgments.

Sincere thanks to Prof. Philipp Woelfel at the University of Calgary for stimulating discussions on the subject of RMRs and the relative power of the CC and DSM models for solving synchronization problems efficiently with respect to amortized RMR complexity. We are grateful to the anonymous referees for their insightful comments and suggestions. Special thanks to Dr. Mark Tuttle at Intel for his perspective on the performance of CC systems in the real world and the shortcomings of the RMR complexity measure. Thanks also to Dr. Ram Swaminathan at HP Labs and Dr. Robert Danek at Oanda for their careful proofreading of this work.

10. REFERENCES

[1] J. Anderson and Y.-J. Kim. An improved lower bound for the time complexity of mutual exclusion. *Distributed Computing*, 15(4):221–253, 2002.

[2] J. Anderson and Y.-J. Kim. A generic local-spin fetch-and-phi-based mutual exclusion algorithm. *Journal of Parallel and Computing*, 67(5):551–580, 2007.

[3] J. Anderson, Y.-J. Kim, and T. Herman. Shared-memory mutual exclusion: Major research trends since 1986. *Distributed Computing*, 16(2-3):75–110, 2003.

[4] T. Anderson. The performance of spin lock alternatives for shared-memory multiprocessors. *IEEE Transactions on Parallel and Distributed Systems*, 1(1):6–16, 1990.

[5] H. Attiya, D. Hendler, and P. Woelfel. Tight RMR lower bounds for mutual exclusion and other problems. In *Proc. of the 40th Annual ACM Symposium on Theory of Computing*, pages 217–226, 2008.

[6] V. Bhatt and C.-C. Huang. Group mutual exclusion in $O(\log n)$ RMR. In *Proc. of the 29th ACM symposium on Principles of Distributed Computing*, pages 45–54, 2010.

[7] R. Danek and W. Golab. Closing the complexity gap between FCFS mutual exclusion and mutual exclusion. *Distributed Computing*, 23(2):93–108, 2010.

[8] R. Danek and V. Hadzilacos. Local-spin group mutual exclusion algorithms. In *Proc. of the eighteenth annual ACM symposium on Principles of distributed computing*, pages 71–85, 2004.

[9] E. W. Dijkstra. Solution of a problem in concurrent programming control. *Communications of the ACM*, 8(9):569, 1965.

[10] R. Fan and N. Lynch. An $\Omega(n \log n)$ lower bound on the cost of mutual exclusion. In *Proc. of the 25th annual ACM symposium on Principles of distributed computing*, pages 275–284, 2006.

[11] W. Golab. *Constant-RMR Implementations of CAS and Other Synchronization Primitives Using Read and Write Operations*. PhD thesis, University of Toronto, 2010.

[12] W. Golab, V. Hadzilacos, D. Hendler, and P. Woelfel. Constant-RMR implementations of CAS and other synchronization primitives using read and write operations. In *Proc. of the 26th annual ACM symposium on Principles of distributed computing*, 2007.

[13] W. Golab, D. Hendler, and P. Woelfel. An O(1) RMRs leader election algorithm. In *Proc. of the 25th annual ACM symposium on Principles of distributed computing*, pages 238–247, 2006.

[14] G. Graunke and S. Thakkar. Synchronization algorithms for shared-memory multiprocessors. *IEEE Computer*, 23:60–69, 1990.

[15] V. Hadzilacos. A note on group mutual exclusion. In *Proc. of the twentieth annual ACM symposium on Principles of distributed computing*, pages 100–106, 2001.

[16] M. Herlihy. Wait-free synchronization. *ACM TOPLAS*, 13(1), 1991.

[17] P. Jayanti. A complete and constant time wait-free implementation of CAS from LL/SC and vice versa. In *Proc. of the 12th International Symposium on Distributed Computing*, pages 216–230, 1998.

[18] P. Jayanti, S. Petrovic, and K. Tan. Fair group mutual exclusion. In *Proc. of the 22nd ACM symposium on Principles of Distributed Computing*, pages 275–284, 2003.

[19] Y.-J. Joung. Asynchronous group mutual exclusion. *Distributed Computing*, 13(4):189–206, 2000.

[20] P. Keane and M. Moir. A simple local-spin group mutual exclusion algorithm. *IEEE Trans. Parallel Distrib. Syst.*, 7(12):673–685, 2001.

[21] Y.-J. Kim and J. Anderson. A time complexity bound for adaptive mutual exclusion. In *Proc. of the 15th International Conference on Distributed Computing*, pages 1–15, 2001.

[22] Y.-J. Kim and J. Anderson. A space- and time-efficient local-spin spin lock. *Information Processing Letters*, 84(1):47–55, 2002.

[23] Y.-J. Kim and J. Anderson. Timing-based mutual exclusion with local spinning. In *Proc. of the 17th International Symposium on Distributed Computing Systems*, pages 30–44, 2003.

[24] L. Lamport. A new solution of dijkstra's concurrent programming problem. *Communications of the ACM*, 17(8):453–455, 1974.

[25] L. Lamport. The mutual exclusion problem: part II – statement and solutions. *J. ACM*, 33(2):327–348, 1986.

[26] H. Lee. Transformations of mutual exclusion algorithms from the cache-coherent model to the distributed shared memory model. In *Proc. of the 25th IEEE International Conference on Distributed Computing Systems (ICDCS'05)*, pages 261–270, 2005.

[27] N. Lynch and M. Tuttle. An introduction to input/output automata. *CWI-Quarterly*, 2(3):219–246, 1989.

[28] J. Mellor-Crummey and M. Scott. Algorithms for scalable synchronization on shared-memory multiprocessors. *ACM Trans. Comput. Syst.*, 9(1):21–65, 1991.

[29] D. Patterson and J. Hennessy. *Computer Organization and Design: The Hardware/Software Interface*. Morgan Kaufmann Publishers, second edition, 1997.

[30] J.-H. Yang and J. Anderson. A fast, scalable mutual exclusion algorithm. *Distributed Computing*, 9(1):51–60, 1995.

From Bounded to Unbounded Concurrency Objects and Back

Yehuda Afek
afek@post.tau.ac.il

Adam Morrison
adamx@post.tau.ac.il

Guy Wertheim
vgvertex@gmail.com

School of Computer Science
Tel Aviv University

ABSTRACT

We consider the power of objects in the unbounded concurrency shared memory model, where there is an infinite set of processes and the number of processes active concurrently may increase without bound. By studying this model we obtain new results and observations that are relevant and meaningful to the standard bounded concurrency model.

First we resolve an open problem from 2006 and provide, contrary to what was conjectured, an unbounded concurrency wait-free implementation of a `swap` object from 2-consensus objects. This construction resolves another puzzle that has eluded us for a long time, that of considerably simplifying a 16 year old complicated bounded concurrency `swap` construction.

A further insight to the traditional bounded concurrency model that we obtain by studying the unbounded concurrency model, is a refinement of the top level of the wait-free hierarchy, the class of infinite-consensus number objects. First we resolve an open question of Merritt and Taubenfeld from 2003, showing that having n-consensus objects for all n does *not* imply consensus under unbounded concurrency. I.e., consensus alone, treated as a black box, *cannot* be "boosted" in this way. We continue to show an infinite-number consensus object that while able to perform consensus for any n-bounded concurrency (n unknown in advance) cannot solve consensus in the face of unbounded concurrency. This divides the infinite-consensus class of objects into two, those that can solve consensus for unbounded concurrency, and those that cannot.

Categories and Subject Descriptors

C.2.4 [**Computer-Communication Networks**]: Distributed Systems; F.1.2 [**Computation by Abstract Devices**]: Modes of Computation—*parallelism and concurrency*

General Terms

Algorithms, Theory

Keywords

Common2, Consensus, Swap, Unbounded concurrency, Wait-free

1. INTRODUCTION

We consider the power of objects in the wait-free unbounded concurrency model [10,18] that consists of a shared memory system with an infinite set of processes in which the number of concurrently active processes may increase without a bound. In addition to broadening our understanding of the limits of distributed computation, our unbounded concurrency results lead to new insights on the traditional bounded concurrency shared memory model. Our motivation is to improve the understanding of shared objects' wait-free computational power beyond what is possible with the classic characterization based on an object's *consensus number* [13,15], since it lumps together all objects with the *same* consensus number, providing little insight on the relationship between such objects. Here we use unbounded concurrency to provide some distinction between the objects with infinite consensus number.

In [2], Common2, the class of objects wait-free constructible from 2-consensus objects, was extended to the unbounded concurrency model. It was shown there that all previously known Common2 objects are also in unbounded concurrency Common2 with one exception: the `swap` object, which was conjectured in [2] to be impossible to implement in unbounded concurrency — hinting that `swap` is inherently more difficult to implement than, say, `fetch-and-add`. Here we show this is not the case, presenting an unbounded concurrency wait-free implementation of `swap` from 2-consensus objects, thus refuting the conjecture of [2]. This indicates that bounded concurrency Common2 and unbounded Common2 are possibly the same. Interestingly, despite the harder requirements, our unbounded concurrency `swap` implementation is *considerably simpler* than the previous (16-year old) n-process (bounded concurrency) algorithm [3, 21]. This demonstrates an appealing property of the unbounded concurrency model, which is part of the motivation for studying this model in the first place: it provides constructions that deal with the essence of the problem, and not with the artifacts of n, the *a priori* bound on the number of active processes. This yields simpler and cleaner algorithms and proofs.

A further insight we obtain on the traditional model concerns the nature of infinite-consensus number objects. We embark by resolving an open problem of Merritt and Taubenfeld from [19], showing that having n-consensus objects for all n does not imply consensus under unbounded concurrency. Next, we consider a natural extension of the Common2 question to the top level of the wait-free hierarchy: Does an infinite-consensus number object, which can solve consensus for any n, necessarily also solve consensus in the face of unbounded concurrency (i.e., $n = \infty$)? We show that there is an infinite-consensus object that while able to perform consensus for any n-bounded concurrency (even if n is unknown in advance) cannot solve consensus in the face of unbounded concurrency. This divides the infinite-consensus class of objects into two, those that can solve consensus for unbounded concurrency, and those that cannot, showing that consensus number alone is not sufficient to fully characterize object power.

2. RELATED WORK

Power of objects. The possibility that consensus power alone may not completely characterize the relation between shared objects was already raised by Herlihy with the introduction of the wait-free hierarchy [13]. This was proved for atomic registers by Herlihy, who showed a nondeterministic consensus power 1 object that cannot be implemented in a wait-free manner from registers for 2 processes [12]. Jayanti has considered whether an object hierarchy is *robust*, i.e., whether combining different "weak" objects enables implementations of stronger objects [15]. The exploration of consensus power 2 objects was initiated by Afek, Weisberger and Weisman in [3], where they defined the Common2 class of objects. Subsequently Common2 was shown to contain the stack object [2], various restricted versions of the FIFO queue [6–8,16,17], and the blurred history object [7]. In [3] Afek, Weisberger and Weisman sketched a wait-free `swap` implementation from 2-consensus objects, and the full construction appears in [21]. Gafni and Rajsbaum recently demonstrated a simple *recursive* `swap` implementation from 2-consensus [11], however it is not linearizable and is wait-free only under bounded concurrency.

Unbounded concurrency. The unbounded concurrency model was introduced by Merritt and Taubenfeld in [18], which focused on models with objects stronger than registers but not on wait-free computation. In [10], Gafni, Merritt and Taubenfeld explored unbounded concurrency wait-free computation using only read/write registers. They showed that increasing the allowed concurrency level leads to a weaker read/write computational model. Unbounded concurrency is the weakest level in this *concurrency hierarchy*, yet still many problems (such as snapshot and renaming) are solvable in this model. In [19], Merritt and Taubenfeld investigated consensus in the unbounded concurrency model. They focused on models where consensus is available as a base object, however it is constrained in the number of processes allowed to access it or the number of faults tolerated. Common2 was extended to the unbounded concurrency model in [2], where it was shown that except for the `swap` object all previously known Common2 objects had unbounded concurrency implementations from 2-consensus. Additional work on the unbounded concurrency model includes Aspnes, Shah and Shah's randomized unbounded concurrency consensus algorithms from registers [4] and Chockler and Malkhi's active disk paxos protocol for infinitely many processes [5].

3. PRELIMINARIES

System model. The system consists of a set of sequential processes and a set of atomic base objects that the processes use to implement high-level objects.

Objects. An *object* is defined by its *sequential specification*, which is a state machine consisting of a set of possible *states*, a set of *operations* used to transition between the states, and the possible *transitions* between the states. For every pair (s, op) of state and operation, there is a transition $T(s, op) = (s', r)$, such that invoking operation op when the object is in state s elicits the response r, and moves the object to state s'.

Implementations. An *implementation* of a high-level object O is a protocol specifying the base object operations that each process needs to perform when invoking the high-level operations of O in order to complete and return a response. The system's *state* consists of the state of all processes and base objects. An *execution* of the system is a (possibly infinite) sequence of *events*. Each event consists of a process invoking an operation on a base object and immediately receiving a response (since the base object is atomic), thereby moving the system to a new state.

Concurrency levels. As in [10,18], we assume the number of processes in the system is infinite. However, the *concurrency level* can be bounded: In an *n-bounded* model, at most n processes may be active concurrently. (This is essentially the standard n-process model where processes repeatedly arrive to invoke new operations [13]; we think of each new invocation as coming from a new process.) In a *bounded concurrency* model, the concurrency in every execution has some finite limit, however it is not known *a priori* and can differ between executions. Finally, in an *unbounded concurrency* model the concurrency may increase without bound as more and more processes join the execution.

Correctness. We require implementations to be wait-free and linearizable [14]. In a *wait-free* implementation the protocol guarantees that a process completes any operation in a finite number of its own steps, regardless of how other processes are scheduled in the execution. An implementation is *linearizable* if the high-level operations appear to take effect atomically during the invoking process' execution.

Object specifications. *Consensus* objects support a single `propose`(v) operation satisfying two properties: all `propose`() invocations return the same response (*agreement*), and this value is the input of some invocation (*validity*). We consider *binary consensus*, where only 0 or 1 can be proposed. A *c-consensus* object is a consensus object that can be accessed by at most c processes. A *swap* object holds a value (initially $\perp$) as its state, and supports a `swap`(v) operation. In state x, a `swap`(y) changes the state to y and returns x. A *test-and-set* (T&S) object supports a single T&S operation. Its state is a bit, initially TRUE. The T&S operation sets the bit to FALSE and returns the previous value of the bit. The first process to invoke T&S therefore receives the response TRUE and is said to *win* the T&S. All other T&S invocations *lose* and receive a response of FALSE. A *fetch-and-add* (F&A) object holds a natural number. A F&A operation takes a natural number x as input and adds x to the number stored in the F&A object, returning the original value in the response. A *fetch-and-inc* object is a F&A that is only used for increments and reads (by adding zero). An (unbounded concurrency) *snapshot* object [1, 10] holds an infinite array of registers. It supports two types of operations: $update_i(v)$, which writes v to cell i of the array, and $scan()$, which returns the (finite) prefix of the array written to before the $scan()$. That is, if the highest cell updated before a $scan()$ is cell i, the $scan()$ will return the sequence with the contents of cells $1, \ldots, i$.

4. SWAP IMPLEMENTATION

To gain some intuition on the difficulty of implementing swap from 2-consensus (even in the standard n-bounded model), consider that a process returning from a swap must know who is immediately before it in the linearization order so it can return its input. Yet the implementation must be such that the process cannot apply this knowledge transitively, or it would be able to determine the first process in the linearization order and solve consensus for arbitrary n. Obtaining this balance without compromising wait-freedom is not trivial. To demonstrate this, we sketch a natural idea for implementing swap that is flawed even in the n-bounded model. We then explain our new ideas for fixing the flaws in a way that is independent of the concurrency level.

Straw man algorithm. We use an array of **test-and-set** objects and a **fetch-and-inc** object. An arriving process obtains a unique array index using the F&I and then tries to *capture* that cell in the array. If it succeeds, it works its way backwards looking for another captured cell whose value it can return. Otherwise, it obtains another cell to compete in using the F&I and tries again. The linearization order is thus established based on the order in the array: the process that captures cell i is linearized after any process that captures a cell $j < i$. To avoid having two processes return the same value, process P_i must *block* any other process from capturing a cell in the range between cap_i (the cell P_i captures) and $ret_i = cap_j$ (the cell whose value P_i eventually returns). To do this, P_i searches for ret_i by competing in each cell $< cap_i$ in descending order until it loses some T&S (or falls off the bottom and returns $\perp$). Losing the T&S at cell c means that $c = cap_j$ for some P_j and P_i can return P_j's input, after it has ensured that no process can capture any cell between cap_j and cap_i.

Unfortunately, this straw man algorithm is not wait free. A process Q can *starve*: each time Q tries to capture some cell c, a new arriving process might capture a cell $c' > c$ and proceed to block c during its descent. Q must then try to capture a new cell larger than c', and this scenario may repeat forever[1]. To avoid this starvation, we would like to guarantee that only a finite number of competing processes can cause Q to lose at a cell and move to another one. This can be achieved if, beyond some point in the execution of an existing process Q, newly arriving processes will "move out of Q's way" and only try to capture cells *smaller* than the cell that Q is trying to capture. As a result, a newly arriving process P_i will never block Q while it descends from cap_i to ret_i, and so Q could lose only to the finite set of already active processes, achieving wait-freedom. To allow this our data structure must support ordering an *unbounded* number of cells between each two cells. This is because during the interval between Q failing to capture cell c_0 and competing in another cell c_1, an unbounded number of new processes may arrive with each one returning from a distinct cell c such that $c_0 < c < c_1$.

---

[1]This is possible with only two concurrent processes, so this problem is not unique to the unbounded concurrency setting.

Such a data structure was constructed in [3, 21] for the n-bounded model. The construction is a complicated infinite tree with unbounded node degree that guarantees wait-freedom only by inherently relying on having a fixed concurrency bound, n. In our new swap implementation we obtain a considerably simpler infinite tree structure that allows ordering an unbounded number of nodes between any two nodes. We exploit the structure of an *infinite binary tree* (Figure 1), where the **in-order** order on the nodes defines exactly the desired structure: each node is larger than its left subtree and smaller than its right subtree, so there is an unbounded number of nodes that can be ordered between any two nodes. Figure 1 depicts an example of this.

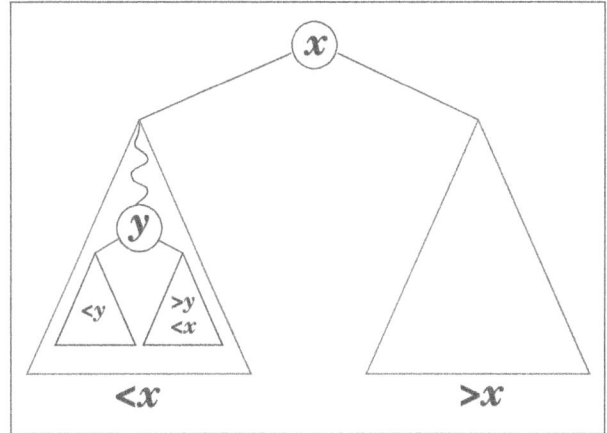

Figure 1: Infinite binary tree: Each triangle is an infinite binary tree. For each z in y's (infinite) right subtree, $y < z < x$.

Our algorithm (like the straw man algorithm) consists of a *capturing phase* and a *returning phase*. A process P_i initially obtains a unique depth (distance from the root) $depth_i$ using a **fetch-and-inc** object. It then enters the capturing phase, where it loops trying to capture the smallest node at $depth_i$ that is larger than any previously accessed node. P_i determines which nodes in the tree have been accessed by scanning a snapshot object in which each process announces the nodes it has accessed. Thus, after trying to capture some node v, P_i announces that it has accessed v in the snapshot. Once P_i captures a node, cap_i, it enters the returning phase, in which it looks for the largest captured node smaller than cap_i whose value it can return. Where can this node be? New processes observe that cap_i has been accessed and therefore move to the right in the tree and compete in nodes larger than cap_i. The only uncertainty is about existing processes: have they observed cap_i accessed and moved on to larger nodes, or are they about to capture some cell $< cap_i$? P_i must therefore *block* all nodes where another process might still be active. To do this, P_i reads the **fetch-and-inc** object and obtains $maxdepth_i$, the maximum possible depth a process in the capturing phase may still be in. It then iterates over all nodes with depth $\leq maxdepth_i$ and that are $< cap_i$ in descending order, attempting to block each one, until it loses some T&S (or wins them all and returns $\perp$). Notice that the number of nodes with depth $\leq maxdepth_i$ and that are $< cap_i$ is bounded (they are all contained in a finite binary tree). Figure 2 depicts an example execution.

121

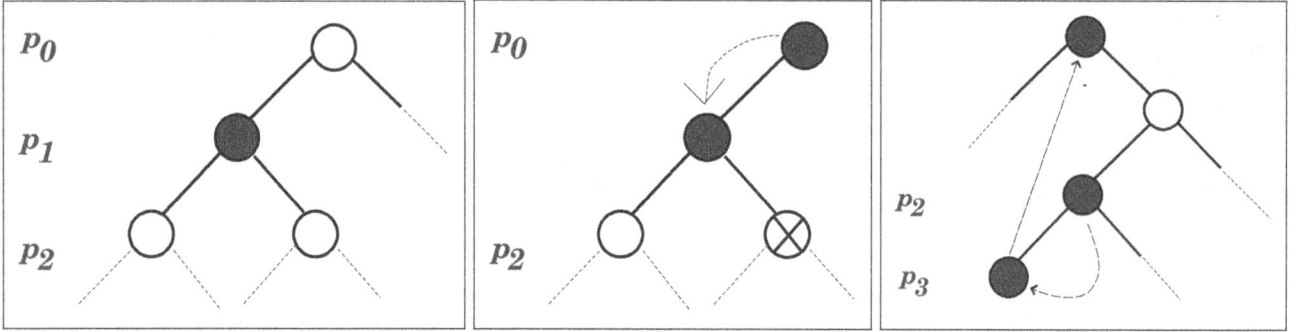

(a) P_0, P_1 and P_2 arrive. P_1 captures its node and returns $\perp$.

(b) P_0 captures its node, blocks P_2 and returns P_1.

(c) P_2 moves to root's right subtree. New process P_3 enters this subtree and captures its node. The node P_3 captures is the smallest accessed node in the right subtree, so P_3 returns P_0. P_2 captures its node and returns P_3.

Figure 2: Example execution of Algorithm 1. Black nodes are captured. Crossed nodes are blocked.

To see how wait-freedom is obtained, consider process P_0 that obtained $depth = 0$. As long as P_0 is delayed and does not access the root, the root node will not appear in the snapshot. Every other process will therefore only "play" in the root's left subtree T_L. This is because such a process tries to capture the *smallest* node at its depth that is larger than any previously accessed node, and nodes in the left subtree are smaller than those in the right subtree. In addition, a process capturing a node in T_L never attempts to block the root node, since it only tries to block nodes smaller than its captured node. It is therefore guaranteed that once P_0 moves it captures the root node and announces the root has been accessed in the snapshot. From this point, T_L becomes "closed" to new arriving processes who all go into the root's right subtree T_R, since they need to capture a node larger than the root. Furthermore, a process Q that captures a node in T_R will never try to block a node in T_L. Because Q attempts to block nodes in descending order, it will always try the root and stop there before going into T_L. Thus, only P_0 and processes that already captured a node in T_L can block the nodes in T_L — this is a finite number of processes. Working recursively, similar intuition applies to P_1 with $depth = 1$. The only difference is that P_1 might fail to capture its first node if it is slower than P_0. In this case P_1 moves to T_R, where all other processes are "playing" in P_1's *left subtree*, T_{R_L}, and cannot block P_1. In general, a process P_i can lose a competition on a node only to a process with depth $< depth_i$, of which there is only a finite number, thus achieving wait-freedom. We capture this intuition more formally in Section 4.2.

4.1 Detailed algorithm description

We now explain our unbounded concurrency swap implementation (Algorithm 1) in detail. Each node in the infinite binary tree has two fields: a read/write register, reg, and a test-and-set object, tst. (We prove later in Lemma 3 that these test-and-set objects can be accessed by at most two processes, and can therefore simply be 2-consensus objects.) An unbounded concurrency snapshot object [10], called $accessed$, is used to record all the nodes that the processes try to capture. A process trying to capture nodes at depth i of the tree posts the largest node it has accessed to

---

Algorithm 1 Wait-free, linearizable, unbounded concurrency swap

Shared variables:
    max_depth: unbounded concurrency fetch-and-add
        object initialized to 1
    $tree$: infinite binary tree, each node with the fields:
        reg: atomic register
        tst: test-and-set object
    $accessed$: unbounded concurrency snapshot object

procedure Swap($value$)
1:    depth := F&A(max_depth, 1)   // Capture phase
    repeat
2:        cap := NextUnaccessedNodeAtDepth(depth)
3:        cap.reg := $value$
4:        win := T&S(cap.tst)
5:        update$_{depth}$($accessed$, cap)
6:    **until** win
7:    max_depth := F&A(max_depth, 0) // Return phase
8:    ret := cap
    repeat
9:        ret := GetPrevNodeMaxDepth(ret, max_depth)
10:     **if** ret = $\perp$ **then return** $\perp$
11:    **until** !T&S(ret.tst)
12:    **return** ret.reg
end Swap

procedure NextUnaccessedNodeAtDepth($depth$)
    S := $\{v \mid v \in tree$ with depth $depth$ such that
        $v > a\ \forall a \in$ scan($accessed$)$\}$
    return the smallest node from S
end NextUnaccessedNodeAtDepth

procedure GetPrevNodeMaxDepth(cur, max_depth)
    S := $\{v \mid v \in tree$ with depth $\leq max\_depth$ and
        $v < cur\}$
    if $S = \phi$ **then return** $\perp$
    return the largest node from S
end GetPrevNodeMaxDepth

cell i of the snapshot. Finally, an unbounded concurrency `fetch-and-inc` (`F&I`) object [2], max_depth, maintains the maximum depth accessed thus far. We use this `F&I` to simplify the presentation of the algorithm. Later we describe how to do without it.

Performing a `swap(value)` operation consists of two phases. The invoking process, P_i, begins the *capturing phase* (Lines 1-6) by obtaining a unique depth, $depth_i$, in which it tries to capture a node (Line 1). P_i then snapshots *accessed* and uses it to compute *cap*, the smallest node at $depth_i$ that is larger (in the in-order order) than all previously accessed nodes (Line 2). Then P tries to capture *cap* by writing *value* into its *reg* field and trying to win its *tst* field (Lines 3-4). Regardless of the outcome, P_i then marks *cap* as accessed in the *accessed* snapshot object (Line 5). This repeats until P_i captures some node denoted cap_i.

Once the capturing phase is over, P_i enters the *returning phase*. Here P_i first reads the `F&I` object max_depth to obtain $maxdepth_i$, the maximum depth accessible in the tree at this time (Line 7). From this point P_i tries to return from each of the accessible nodes starting from cap_i (Line 8). In each iteration P_i computes the next largest accessed node of depth $\leq depth_i$ that is smaller than cap_i (Line 9) and tries to return from it (or block it) by performing a `test-and-set` at that node (Line 11-12). If P_i wins all these `T&S`es then P_i is the first process in the linearization order and returns $\perp$ (Line 10).

Reducing reliance on Common2 objects. To gain insight on where the ability to perform consensus is crucial for implementing unbounded concurrency `swap`, we now show that the `F&I` object max_depth can be removed from Algorithm 1. The max_depth object serves two purposes: to obtain a unique depth for capturing nodes at the beginning of the capture phase, and to bound the maximum depth that an old process may try to capture a node in during the return phase. We can therefore replace it with a combination of a snapshot and the unbounded concurrency $(2k-1)$-renaming algorithm of [10] as follows. Each process starts its capture phase by writing its id into a new *ids* snapshot. It then renames itself and proceeds to use the new id as its unique depth (i.e., $depth_i$ is P_i's new name). In the returning phase, the process first scans the *ids* snapshot. The number of ids written in the snapshot cannot be smaller than the number of processes that completed the renaming. Hence, the maximum depth accessible to such processes (i.e., $maxdepth_i$) can be bounded by $2|ids|-1$.

4.2 Wait-freedom proof

We proceed to prove that Algorithm 1 is wait-free. We denote by cap_i the node captured by process P_i (i.e., the value held by `cap` when winning the `T&S` in Line 4). We use ret_i to denote the node from which process P_i returns a value, or $\perp$ if P_i returns $\perp$. Finally, $depth_i$ and $maxdepth_i$ denote the values obtained by P_i from max_depth in Line 1 and Line 7 respectively.

The return phase of the algorithm is clearly wait-free, since during it a process P_i accesses a finite number of nodes with depth $\leq maxdepth_i$. The core of the wait-freedom proof is thus showing that the *capturing* phase is wait-free, i.e., that given enough steps a process always manages to capture a node. To show this we require the following:

LEMMA 1. *A process in the capturing phase cannot try to capture nodes in the right subtree of a node v before v itself has been recorded in* accessed.

PROOF. Consider towards a contradiction an execution of Algorithm 1 violating the lemma, and let the capture attempt of node v_r by some process P_i be the first such violating access. That is, v_r is in the right subtree of some node v at depth d, but an $\text{update}_d(v)$ has not been executed by the time P_i tries to capture v_r. Denote by v_l the largest node in v's left subtree at the same depth as v_r (i.e., $depth_i$). Figure 3 depicts this scenario.

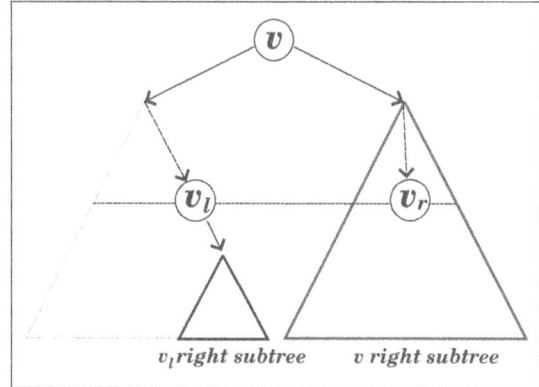

Figure 3: State of tree violating Lemma 1: P_i tries to capture v_r without v being written to *accessed* beforehand.

There are two cases to consider. Suppose P_i fails to capture v_l. Then some process P_j blocked v_l. Thus $cap_j > v_l$. In addition, since P_i eventually accesses v_r it follows that $cap_j < v_r$. Otherwise, because P_j (who tries to return from cells $< cap_j$ in descending order) reaches v_l it must block v_r first. But then after failing to capture v_l, P_i would observe cap_j in *accessed* (since P_j does no further updates to *accessed* after capturing a cell) and P_i would therefore not try to capture v_r at all, a contradiction. Therefore, $v_l < cap_j < v_r$. We now proceed to show that cap_j itself is captured before v_l is first written to *accessed*. By Lemma 3 below, only P_i can write v_l to *accessed*. This occurs after P_i fails to capture v_l. Thus, P_j is the first to access v_l, and P_j captures cap_j before that.

The remaining case is that P_i does not try to capture v_l. Thus P must observe some node $u \in$ *accessed* such that $v_l < u < v_r$ causing P to skip v_l, i.e. some process tried to capture u before v_l is written to *accessed*.

Either way, we find there is a node u that is accessed before both v and v_l are written to *accessed*, and satisfies $v_l < u < v_r$. Because v_l is the largest node in v's left subtree at depth $depth_i$, u must either be in v's right subtree or v_l's right subtree. This means the access to u violates the lemma, contradicting the assumption that the access to v_r is the first such event. □

Lemma 1 implies wait-freedom of the capturing phase. This holds because a process can fail its capturing phase either due to losing at v, the right-most node of its level, or because it cannot find a node to access (i.e., it finds v smaller than some node in *accessed*). In any case this implies that some node in v's right subtree was accessed prior to v being accessed, contradicting Lemma 1. It remains to prove Lemma 3, which is implied by the following:

LEMMA 2. *If $cap_i > cap_j$ then $maxdepth_i > depth_j$.*

PROOF. Suppose this is false. Then P_i obtains $maxdepth_i$ from max_depth before P_j performs its initial F&I in its capture phase. Thus P_j in its capture phase observes cap_i in *accessed* and always tries to capture cells $> cap_i$, a contradiction. □

LEMMA 3. *For any node v, at most one process tries to capture it and at most one process tries to return from it.*

PROOF. By the code, it is clear that each process captures a node in a unique depth. Let us assume to the contrary that two processes, P_i and P_j, try to return the same node v. Say $cap_i > cap_j$. If $v > cap_j$, P_j will not try to return from it, a contradiction. Thus $v < cap_j < cap_i$. By Lemma 2, $maxdepth_i > depth_j$, and so, since P_i tries to return from v and P_i tries to return from cells in descending order, it must have tried to return from cap_j before that. As cap_j is captured by P_j, P_i must lose the test-and-set at cap_j, implying that P_i returns from cap_j and never accesses v, a contradiction. □

4.3 Linearizability proof

Here we prove that Algorithm 1 yields linearizable swap executions. This amounts to showing two things. First, that the swap specification is not violated. In other words, that the processes can be ordered so that the first process returns $\perp$, and subsequent processes each return the input value of the previous process. We refer to this as establishing a *chain* relation between the processes. The second task is showing that the chain relation respects the real-time ordering of processes: if P_i arrives after P_j returns, then P_i must be ordered after P_j.

We begin by proving the chain relationship. Given that Algorithm 1 is wait-free we consider only *finite* executions in which all of the processes finish their operations. This implies the theorem for unbounded concurrency as well, since any counter-example to linearizability occurs at a finite point in time, where our proof applies.

Definition 1. The relation $\leadsto$ is defined as follows: $P_i \leadsto P_j$ if P_i returns the value of P_j.

To show that the chain is well-formed we need the following lemmas:

LEMMA 4. *There is precisely one process that returns $\perp$.*

PROOF. Consider a process, P_{small} who captures the smallest node cap_{small}. This process will not be able to lose in any node and will return $\perp$ (Line 10). Now suppose two processes, P_i and P_j, both return $\perp$. Say $cap_i > cap_j$. From Lemma 2 we have $maxdepth_i > depth_j$ and so P_i must try and succeed to return from cap_j, otherwise P_j fails to capture it. This contradicts P_i returning $\perp$. Since P_j is able to capture that node, P_i is able to return cap_j and thus does not return $\perp$. □

LEMMA 5. *In a finite executions in which all of the processes finish their operations, there is exactly one process whose input is not returned by any process.*

PROOF. P_{big} will be the process who captured the largest node, cap_{big}. By the code, $\forall i \; ret_i < cap_i$. By definition of P_{big}, $\forall i \; cap_i \leq cap_{big}$. Therefore no process can return P_{big}'s value. □

LEMMA 6. *Each process returns precisely one value.*

LEMMA 7. *Each process's value can be returned by at most one process.*

PROOF. Process P_i can store its value in several nodes. However, in every node v but the last one it fails to capture the node, implying that another process P_v wins the the test-and-set at v. By Lemma 3, P_v must be a process trying to return from v who will not not return from v (because it won the test-and-set). By Lemma 3, no process but P_v will try to return from v. Finally, for the final node that P_i captures, only one process can try to return that value (again by Lemma 3). □

Combining the above, we obtain:

LEMMA 8. *The relation $\leadsto$ is acyclic.*

PROOF. We know that $P_i \leadsto P_j$ implies that $ret_i = cap_j$ and $cap_i > ret_i$. From this we know that $P_i \leadsto P_j \Rightarrow cap_i > cap_j$. Thus a cycle $P_i \leadsto P_j \leadsto \cdots \leadsto P_k \leadsto P_i$ implies $cap_i > cap_j > \cdots > cap_k > cap_i$, which is impossible. □

We are now ready to prove:

THEOREM 9. *Algorithm 1 is linearizable.*

PROOF. Combing Lemmas 4-8 we have that the $\leadsto$ relation constructs a chain between the processes. We can now proceed to linearize the processes based on the total order established by the transitive closure of $\leadsto$. It remains only to show that this order respects the real-time order of process execution. Suppose this is not the case and some P_i that returns before P_j starts is ordered before P_j. Then $P_i \leadsto P_1 \leadsto P_2 \leadsto \cdots \leadsto P_j$. Therefore $cap_i > cap_j$. But if P_i terminates before P_j starts then when P_j starts its capture phase, cap_i is written to *accessed*, so P_j always tries to capture nodes $> cap_i$. This contradicts the assumption that $cap_i > cap_j$. □

5. UNBOUNDED CONCURRENCY APPLIED TO INFINITE CONSENSUS

In this section we explore consensus in the unbounded concurrency model. We first consider systems that have n-consensus base objects for all n (i.e., the number of processes allowed to access each consensus base object is finite). This model was first explored by Merritt and Taubenfeld in [19] and they showed that a system with n-consensus objects for all $n \geq 2$ can solve consensus in the face of *bounded concurrency*, where there are infinitely many processes, but the concurrency in every execution has some finite limit that is not known *a priori* and can differ between executions. Their consensus implementation fundamentally relies on the fact that *some* finite concurrency bound exists. Our first result in this section (Theorem 10 below) is that this is a fundamental limitation. Base objects capable of solving finite consensus for any finite set *cannot* solve unbounded concurrency consensus.

THEOREM 10. *There is no unbounded concurrency wait-free implementation of consensus from read/write registers and n-consensus objects for all n.*

PROOF. Assume that such an implementation exists. We construct an execution of the algorithm in which processes take an infinite number of steps but do not reach a decision, thereby contradicting wait-freedom. We say a state s of the system is P-*bivalent* for a set of processes P, if s can be extended with steps of processes in P to yield different decision values. Otherwise s is called P-*univalent*. A state is P-*critical* if it is P-bivalent and the next step of any process from P moves the system to a P-univalent state.

Our inductive construction follows. In each step we move the system from a P-critical state to a P'-critical state, for some $P' \supset P$. During this move all processes of P take a step. Thus, continuing this forever leads to an execution in which processes take an infinite number of steps without deciding and contradicts wait-freedom. The base case of the construction is simple: pick two processes p_1, p_2 with distinct inputs and execute them until a $\{p_1, p_2\}$-critical state is reached [9, 13].

Now assume we have a P-critical state s for some finite set P of size k. The standard FLP valency arguments applied to the k processes of P [9, 13] show that in s all processes of P are poised to access the same c-consensus object O for some $c \geq k$. However, consider what happens if we next schedule a process *not* from P (this would be the first step for such a process). While the next step of each process from P moves the system to a univalent state, we will show that there exists a new process whose next step from s will move the system to another bivalent state. Specifically, consider the set $P' = P \cup \{p_{k+1}, \ldots, p_c, p_{c+1}\}$ of size $c + 1$, that is P with $c - k + 1$ new processes added. Because $P \subset P'$, s is P'-bivalent. It cannot, however, be P'-critical as there can be at most c processes from P' poised to access O, leaving at least one process about to access a different object, which is impossible [9, 13]. The standard valency arguments show that from s there is an execution α, consisting of steps by processes from P', that leads to a P'-critical state s'. As before, in this state all processes from P' are poised to access a c'-consensus object O' for some $c' \geq c + 1$. Hence all processes from P took a step in α (in s they were about to access a different object O). $\square$

This result implies that consensus is not interesting as a base object in the unbounded concurrency model: solving unbounded concurrency consensus cannot be done using n-consensus objects (for all n), so we would need a consensus object accessible to an unbounded number of processes, making the solution vacuous. Therefore, what can we say about *infinite power consensus objects*, those that can solve consensus for any n? Do all of them admit unbounded concurrency consensus implementations? Some infinite power consensus objects (such as `compare-and-swap` or Plotkin's `sticky-bit` [20]) have consensus algorithms that do not depend on the concurrency bound and work even in the face of unbounded concurrency. However, for other objects — like Jayanti's `weak-sticky` object [15] — the implementation depends on a known concurrency bound n. It is thus plausible that the unbounded concurrency model exposes a gap in the strength of infinite power consensus objects: some may not be strong enough to solve consensus in the unbounded concurrency model. Our main result in this section is that this is indeed the case.

THEOREM 11. *There exists an object O with infinite consensus number that cannot solve consensus in a wait-free manner in the unbounded concurrency model.*

In the following we prove Theorem 11. Section 5.1 introduces a new infinite power consensus object, the *iterator stack*. In Section 5.2 we show the iterator stack can solve consensus for any concurrency bound n, even if n is not known in advance. Yet it cannot solve unbounded concurrency consensus (Section 5.3).

5.1 The iterator stack

A state of the *iterator stack* consists of two (unbounded) sequences: V, a sequence of values that functions as a write-only stack (initially empty), and I, a sequence of non-negative integers called *iterators* (initially, I is all zeroes). The iterator stack provides two operations, `write()` and `read()`. A `write`(v) has two effects: (1) the value v is prepended to V (shifting previous values one place to the right), and (2) the first iterator with value 0 is set to 1 and its index is returned. The effect of a `read`(i) operation depends on whether iterator i points to an element of V. If $0 < I[i] \leq |V|$, then $V[I[i]]$ (the value iterator i points to) is returned. Otherwise, if iterator i is *uninitialized* ($I[i] = 0$) or is *invalid* ($I[i] > |V|$), then $\perp$ is returned. In any case, if $I[i] > 0$ then $I[i]$ is incremented (reading an invalid iterator does not stop it from being incremented). Figure 4 shows an example of an iterator's stack execution. Notice that an initialized iterator i can switch from returning $\perp$ to returning values from V if enough writes are performed in between the reads, increasing the size of V to the point where i is valid again.

Iterator stack examples	
Each row consists of an operation applied to a given state, leading the object to the the state in the next row.	
State	**Operation leading to next state**
$\langle V = [v_2, v_1], I = [3, 4, 0, 0, \ldots] \rangle$	`read`(3) **returns** $\perp$ (iterator 3 is uninitialized)
$\langle V = [v_2, v_1], I = [3, 4, 0, 0, \ldots] \rangle$	`read`(1) **returns** $\perp$ (iterator 1 is invalid)
$\langle V = [v_2, v_1], I = [4, 4, 0, 0, \ldots] \rangle$	`write`(x) **returns** 3
$\langle V = [x, v_2, v_1], I = [4, 4, 1, 0, \ldots] \rangle$	`write`(y) **returns** 4
$\langle V = [y, x, v_2, v_1], I = [4, 4, 1, 1, \ldots] \rangle$	`read`(1) **returns** v_1

Figure 4: Example state transitions of the iterator stack.

5.2 Iterator stack implements bounded concurrency consensus

Here we present Algorithm 2, a bounded concurrency consensus algorithm from registers and a single iterator stack. This shows that the iterator's stack consensus number is infinite. The idea behind Algorithm 2 is that participating processes write to the iterator stack, with the first process to write *winning* and its value becoming the *decision value*. To discover the decision value, a process traverses the iterator stack using the iterator it received when writing. When it reads the value $\perp$, it knows the previous read value was the first to be written, hence it is the decision value. However, notice that new processes can keep arriving and writing new values to the iterator stack, causing an iterating process to never reach the end of the sequence. This is due to the fact that while the *concurrency* is bounded, *arrivals* are not — so processes may continuously leave and enter the algorithm. To avoid such starvation, a process that determines the winner announces the winner in a *result* register. A new process will only write to the iterator stack if *result* is empty, adopting the value in *result* otherwise. This ensures the iterator stack is only written to a finite number of times.

Algorithm 2 Iterator stack bounded concurrency consensus protocol

> **Shared variables:**
>> *result* : atomic register, initialized to ⊥
>> *IteratorStack* : `iterator stack` object
> **Local variables:**
>> last, itr, cur : atomic registers, initialized to ⊥
>
> **procedure** propose(value)
> 1:   **if** *result* ≠⊥ **then return** *result*
> 2:   itr := *IteratorStack*.write(value)
>   **repeat**
> 3:   last := cur
> 4:   cur := *IteratorStack*.read(itr)
>   **until** cur = ⊥
> 5:   *result* := last
> 6:   **return** *result*
>   **end** propose

THEOREM 12. *Algorithm 2 is a wait-free bounded concurrency consensus implementation.*

PROOF. Validity is immediate. Similarly, we show agreement by proving that all writes to *result* write the same value. To see this, note that when a process first reads ⊥, then the last value it read is the first value written to the iterator stack, and this is the value it writes to *result*. Wait-freedom follows from the fact that before *result* is written, only a finite number of processes can participate, due to the bound on concurrency. Therefore only a finite number of values can be written to the iterator stack, and so all iterations must terminate. □

5.3   Iterator stack cannot implement unbounded concurrency consensus

In this section we show that the iterator stack object is too weak to solve unbounded concurrency consensus. We assume towards a contradiction that such a consensus algorithm **A** exists. We derive the contradiction by adapting Fischer, Lynch and Paterson's *valency* argument [9] to the unbounded concurrency model. We call a state s of **A** *bivalent* if s can be extended to yield different decision values. Otherwise s is called *univalent*. All executions continuing from a univalent state s return the same value v, which is called s's *valency*. We also say that s is v-valent.

If we were in the n-bounded model, we could start with a bivalent state and execute each process until just before it moves the algorithm to a univalent state, ultimately reaching a bivalent state from which *any* next step leads to a univalent state. From this *bounded critical* state a contradiction can be derived by showing the different univalent states reachable

from it are indistinguishable. However, this fails in the face of unbounded concurrency. There may always be a *new* process leading to a bivalent state, so we could end up with an execution in which infinitely many processes each take a single step, not violating wait-freedom. Instead, our notion of a *critical state* (below) is weaker, requiring two steps of certain processes to reach states with distinct valency.

Definition 2. A state s is *critical* if and only if s is bivalent, and there exist two processes, P and Q, such that: (1) from s, a single step of P leads to a p-valent state, (2) from s, a single step of Q followed by a single step of P leads to a q-valent state, (3) $p \neq q$.

LEMMA 13. *A critical state of **A** exists.*

PROOF. We construct an execution E leading to a critical state s_{crit}. We start with a bivalent state s_0. We let process P run solo from s_0 until the system reaches a state s_1, from which P's next step takes the system to a p-valent state. The state s_1 satisfies the following: (1) it is bivalent, (2) P moving at s_1 leads to a univalent state. Since s_1 is bivalent, there is an execution L_1 from s_1 that brings the system to a q-valent state, $q \neq p$. Notice that each step in L_1 but the last keeps the system in a bivalent state.

We now execute L_1 one step at a time until it is no longer the case that if P takes the next step, then the system moves to a p-valent state. This eventually happens, since the last step of L_1 leads to a q-valent state. When P's next step does not lead to a p-valent state, one of the following must hold: either (1) if P performs the next step the system moves to a bivalent state, or (2) if P performs the next step the system moves to a q-valent state. Note that condition (2) holds when L_1 ends at a q-valent state.

If (1) is the first condition to occur, we switch back to running P solo until we reach a state s_2 where, if P takes the next step, the system moves to some p_2-valent state (it could be that $p_2 \neq p$). The state s_2 satisfies the same two properties as s_1: both are bivalent and in both states P's next step brings the system to a univalent state. This means we can repeat the same procedure as done on s_1, executing a different extension L_2 leading from s_2 to a q_2-valent state ($q_2 \neq p_2$) one step at a time, until P's next step no longer leads to a p_2-valent state. If at this point P's next step moves the system to a bivalent state we run P solo again until its next step will take the system to a p_3-valent state, at which point we start scheduling an execution L_3, and so on. Eventually, during the execution of some L_i we must reach a state x where condition (2) holds, i.e., scheduling P next moves the system to a q_i-valent state. Otherwise, we would keep scheduling P forever without it completing, contradicting wait-freedom.

We denote each scheduling step of L_i by $l_1, \ldots, l_k$, so x is the state after the execution of $l_1, \ldots, l_k$. We claim the state s after the execution of $l_1, \ldots, l_{k-1}$ is a critical state. By construction, the next step of P at s moves the system to a p_i-valent state, for $p_i \neq q_i$. Therefore, the process Q performing the step leading from s to x cannot be P, since x is not p_i-valent. As condition (2) is true at x, P's next move from x leads to a q_i-valent state, and so a single step of Q at s (leading to x) followed by a single step of P leads to a q_i-valent state. The state s is thus indeed a critical state. □

We have established the existence of a critical state, s_{crit}. Let P be the process whose next step, o_P, at s_{crit} leads to a univalent state p-valent state, and Q the process whose next step, o_Q, at s_{crit}, followed by o_P, leads to a q-valent state, $q \neq p$. Let s_P be the p-valent state resulting from o_P, o_Q being scheduled at s_{crit}, and s_Q be the q-valent state reached by scheduling o_Q, o_P. We proceed to derive a contradiction by examining the different operations o_P and o_Q might be and ruling out each one. Due to our weaker definition of a critical state, s_P and s_Q will turn out to be distinguishable, differing in the state of an iterator stack object O. We will therefore prevent some *victim* process R from observing this difference by constantly adding new processes that write to O, preventing R from observing the difference in O's state. In doing so, these processes may themselves distinguish between s_P and s_Q and hence we do not allow them to perform any further operations on the shared memory. Here we use the unbounded concurrency requirement — we need an endless supply of new processes to induce an infinite execution of process R.

Let us first consider the types of operation o_P and o_Q can be (i.e., atomic register **read** or **write**, or iterator stack **read** or **write**). It is easy to see that o_P and o_Q may not *commute* since then s_P and s_Q would be indistinguishable states — all objects would have the same state in both. Therefore, o_P and o_Q must be operations on the same object O, and O cannot be an atomic register. To see this, recall that scheduling o_P at s_{crit} leads to a p-valent state, s_u. Thus o_P must be a write [13]. But then, s_Q and s_u would be indistinguishable to P, but with different valency — a contradiction. Additionally, o_P and o_Q cannot both be **read** operations on an iterator stack. This is because the only state change such a **read** affects is an increment of an iterator, a commutative operation. We now show that both operations must be iterator stack **write**s.

LEMMA 14. *Both o_P and o_Q are* **write**s *to the same iterator stack O.*

PROOF. Assume, w.l.o.g., that o_P is a **write** and o_Q is a read of iterator j. Let O's state at s_{crit} be

$$\langle V = [v_m, \ldots, v_1], I = [i_1, i_2, \ldots, i_m, 0, 0, \ldots] \rangle.$$

o_P and o_Q commute in their effect on the shared memory state unless $j = m + 1$, i.e., j is the iterator that the next **write** to O receives as a response. In this case, when scheduling o_Q first, iterator $m+1$ is uninitialized and so O's state does not change. Scheduling the **write** o_P after o_Q thus causes $I[m+1]$ to take the value 1. In contrast, scheduling o_Q after P's **write** causes an increment of $I[m+1]$ from 1 to 2. Thus, states s_P and s_Q differ only in the value of iterator $m+1$. Consider the solo executions of a new process R starting at each of these states, e_P and e_Q. Since s_P and s_Q are of different valency, R must distinguish between them by applying an operation that returns a different response in e_P than in e_Q. This can only be a **read** of O with iterator $m + 1$. In e_Q (where $I[m+1]$ is initially 1) we stop R immediately after its first **read** of O with iterator $m + 1$ (causing $I[m + 1]$ to become 2). In e_P (where $I[m + 1]$ is initially 1) we stop R immediately before its first such **read** of O. The state of all objects after these executions is identical, yet these are states with different valency, a contradiction. □

We are left only with the possibility that both o_P and o_Q are **write**s to the iterator stack O. To conclude the proof, we rule this out as well, reaching a contradiction.

LEMMA 15. *Both o_P and o_Q cannot be* **write**s *to the same iterator stack O.*

PROOF. Assume $o_P = \texttt{write}(v_P)$ and $o_P = \texttt{write}(v_Q)$. Let O's state at s_{crit} be

$$\langle V = [v_m, \ldots, v_1], I = [i_1, i_2, \ldots, i_m, 0, 0, \ldots] \rangle.$$

Then in s_P, $V = [v_Q, v_P, v_m, \ldots, v_1]$ and in s_Q it is $[v_P, v_Q, v_m, \ldots, v_1]$. The state of I is identical. We introduce a new *victim* process R, which must be able to distinguish between s_P and s_Q, and construct executions in which R takes infinitely many steps without completing, contradicting wait-freedom of **A**. Consider two executions, e_P and e_Q, starting at s_P and s_Q respectively. We run R until it is about to perform a **read** of O using iterator i which will return v_P or v_Q, i.e., $I[i] = k$ and $V[k] = v_P$ or $V[k] = v_Q$. (Note the executions are identical up to these points.) Let T be the set of initialized iterators in O at this point. Note that, assuming no new value is written to O from here on, each $i \in T$ can be read only a finite number of times (perhaps 0) before it can no longer return v_P or v_Q. We thus repeat the following: introduce a new process and execute it until either (1) it **read**s from O using an iterator $i \in T$, or (2) it is about to **write** to O. No process can distinguish e_P from e_Q without applying an operation to O, so either (1) or (2) must occur. If only (1) occurs, then eventually all iterators in T become invalid and so any further **read** of O returns the same response in both executions, resulting in a contradiction. Thus we must eventually have two processes poised to **write** to O. We let each of them execute their **write** — this "shifts" V down two place, making $V[k]$ not point to v_P or v_Q. Notice that by construction, the writing processes cannot distinguish between e_P and e_Q since they did not read from O using an iterator from T, and so the values they write to O are the same in both executions. Finally, we schedule R's **read** of O using i, which returns the value in $V[k]$. Therefore in both e_P and e_Q this read returns the same value. We can indefinitely repeat the above process: go back to running R solo until it is about to read v_P or v_Q from O, then prevent it from doing this by using new processes. □

6. CONCLUSION

We have used unbounded concurrency to distinguish between different infinite power consensus objects. This extends Gafni, Merritt and Taubenfeld's work that used unbounded concurrency to present a hierarchy of concurrency levels within the class of read/write objects [10]. They show that there are read/write solvable problems that are solvable with a certain concurrency level but not with higher concurrency. Thus we have shown that also in the higher levels, the unbounded wait-free hierarchy does not look the same as the bounded wait-free hierarchy. Few of the remaining open questions are: Can these results be extended to sub-consensus objects? Can we provide a clean and simple characterization of unbounded concurrency infinite consensus objects?

Acknowledgments. We thank Eli Gafni and Gadi Taubenfeld for helpful discussions, and the anonymous referees for their comments.

7. REFERENCES

[1] Yehuda Afek, Hagit Attiya, Danny Dolev, Eli Gafni, Michael Merritt, and Nir Shavit. Atomic snapshots of shared memory. *Journal of the ACM*, 40:873–890, September 1993.

[2] Yehuda Afek, Eli Gafni, and Adam Morrison. Common2 extended to stacks and unbounded concurrency. In *Proceedings of the 25th Annual ACM Symposium on Principles of Distributed Computing*, PODC '06, pages 218–227, New York, NY, USA, 2006. ACM.

[3] Yehuda Afek, Eytan Weisberger, and Hanan Weisman. A completeness theorem for a class of synchronization objects. In *Proceedings of the 12th Annual ACM Symposium on Principles of Distributed Computing*, PODC '93, pages 159–170, New York, NY, USA, 1993. ACM.

[4] James Aspnes, Gauri Shah, and Jatin Shah. Wait-free consensus with infinite arrivals. In *Proceedings of the 34th Annual ACM Symposium on Theory of Computing*, STOC '02, pages 524–533, New York, NY, USA, 2002. ACM.

[5] Gregory Chockler and Dahlia Malkhi. Active disk paxos with infinitely many processes. *Distributed Computing*, 18:73–84, July 2005.

[6] Matei David. A single-enqueuer wait-free queue implementation. In *Proceedings of the 18th International Symposium on Distributed Computing (DISC'04)*, volume 3274 of *LNCS*, pages 132–143. Springer-Verlag, Jan 2004.

[7] Matei David, Alex Brodsky, and Faith Ellen Fich. Restricted stack implementations. In *Proceedings of the 19th International Symposium on Distributed Computing (DISC'05)*, volume 3724 of *LNCS*, pages 137–151. Springer-Verlag, Oct 2005.

[8] David Eisenstat. A two-enqueuer queue. arXiv:0805.0444v2 [cs.DC], 2009.

[9] Michael J. Fischer, Nancy A. Lynch, and Michael S. Paterson. Impossibility of distributed consensus with one faulty process. *Journal of the ACM*, 32:374–382, April 1985.

[10] Eli Gafni, Michael Merritt, and Gadi Taubenfeld. The concurrency hierarchy, and algorithms for unbounded concurrency. In *Proceedings of the 20th Annual ACM Symposium on Principles of Distributed Computing*, PODC '01, pages 161–169, New York, NY, USA, 2001. ACM.

[11] Eli Gafni and Sergio Rajsbaum. Recursion in distributed computing. In Shlomi Dolev, Jorge Cobb, Michael Fischer, and Moti Yung, editors, *Stabilization, Safety, and Security of Distributed Systems (SSS 2010)*, volume 6366 of *Lecture Notes in Computer Science*, pages 362–376. Springer Berlin / Heidelberg, 2010.

[12] Maurice Herlihy. Impossibility results for asynchronous pram (extended abstract). In *Proceedings of the 3rd Annual ACM Symposium on Parallel Algorithms and Architectures*, SPAA '91, pages 327–336, New York, NY, USA, 1991. ACM.

[13] Maurice Herlihy. Wait-free synchronization. *ACM Transactions on Programming Languages and Systems (TOPLAS)*, 13:124–149, January 1991.

[14] Maurice P. Herlihy and Jeannette M. Wing. Linearizability: a correctness condition for concurrent objects. *ACM Transactions on Programming Languages and Systems (TOPLAS)*, 12:463–492, July 1990.

[15] Prasad Jayanti. Robust wait-free hierarchies. *Journal of the ACM*, 44:592–614, July 1997.

[16] Zongpeng Li. Non-blocking implementations of queues in asynchronous distributed shared-memory systems. Master's thesis, University of Toronto, 2001.

[17] D. Scott McCrickard. A study of wait-free hierarchies in concurrent systems. Technical Report GIT-CC-94-04, Georgia Institute of Technology, 1994.

[18] Michael Merritt and Gadi Taubenfeld. Computing with infinitely many processes. In *Proceedings of the 14th International Symposium on Distributed Computing (DISC'00)*, volume 1914 of *LNCS*, pages 164–178. Springer-Verlag, Oct 2000.

[19] Michael Merritt and Gadi Taubenfeld. Resilient consensus for infinitely many processes. In *Proceedings of the 17th International Symposium on Distributed Computing (DISC'03)*, volume 2848 of *LNCS*, pages 1–15. Springer-Verlag, Oct 2003.

[20] Serge A. Plotkin. Sticky bits and universality of consensus. In *Proceedings of the 8th Annual ACM Symposium on Principles of Distributed Computing*, PODC '89, pages 159–175, New York, NY, USA, 1989. ACM.

[21] Hanan Weisman. Implementing shared memory overwriting objects. Master's thesis, Tel Aviv University, 1994.

Distributed Deterministic Edge Coloring using Bounded Neighborhood Independence

Leonid Barenboim[*]
Department of Computer Science,
Ben-Gurion University of the Negev,
Beer-Sheva, Israel.
leonidba@cs.bgu.ac.il

Michael Elkin[**]
Department of Computer Science,
Ben-Gurion University of the Negev,
Beer-Sheva, Israel.
elkinm@cs.bgu.ac.il

ABSTRACT

We study the *edge-coloring* problem in the message-passing model of distributed computing. This is one of the most fundamental problems in this area. Currently, the best-known deterministic algorithms for $(2\Delta - 1)$-edge-coloring requires $O(\Delta) + \log^* n$ time [23], where Δ is the maximum degree of the input graph. Also, recent results of [5] for vertex-coloring imply that one can get an $O(\Delta)$-edge-coloring in $O(\Delta^\epsilon \cdot \log n)$ time, and an $O(\Delta^{1+\epsilon})$-edge-coloring in $O(\log \Delta \log n)$ time, for an arbitrarily small constant $\epsilon > 0$.

In this paper we devise a significantly faster deterministic edge-coloring algorithm. Specifically, our algorithm computes an $O(\Delta)$-edge-coloring in $O(\Delta^\epsilon) + \log^* n$ time, and an $O(\Delta^{1+\epsilon})$-edge-coloring in $O(\log \Delta) + \log^* n$ time. This result improves the state-of-the-art running time for deterministic edge-coloring with this number of colors in almost the entire range of maximum degree Δ. Moreover, it improves it exponentially in a wide range of Δ, specifically, for $2^{\Omega(\log^* n)} \leq \Delta \leq polylog(n)$. In addition, for small values of Δ (up to $\log^{1-\delta} n$, for some fixed $\delta > 0$) our deterministic algorithm outperforms all the existing *randomized* algorithms for this problem.

On our way to these results we study the *vertex-coloring* problem on graphs with bounded *neighborhood independence*. This is a large family of graphs, which strictly includes line graphs of r-hypergraphs (i.e., hypergraphs in which each hyperedge contains r or less vertices) for $r = O(1)$, and graphs of bounded growth. We devise a very fast deterministic algorithm for vertex-coloring graphs with bounded neighborhood independence. This algorithm directly gives rise to our edge-coloring algorithms, which apply to *general* graphs.

Our main technical contribution is a subroutine that computes an $O(\Delta/p)$-defective p-vertex coloring of graphs with bounded neighborhood independence in $O(p^2) + \log^* n$ time, for a parameter p, $1 \leq p \leq \Delta$. In all previous efficient distributed routines for m-defective p-coloring the product $m \cdot p$ is super-linear in Δ. In our routine this product is *linear* in Δ, and this enables us to speed up the coloring drastically.

Categories and Subject Descriptors

F.2.2 [**Nonnumerical Algorithms and Problems**]: Computations on Discrete Structures; G.2.2 [**Graph Theory**]: Network Problems

General Terms

Algorithms

Keywords

Legal-Coloring, Defective-Coloring, Line-Graphs

1. INTRODUCTION

1.1 Edge-Coloring

We study the *edge-coloring* problem in the *message passing model* of distributed computing. Specifically, we are given an n-vertex undirected unweighted graph $G = (V, E)$, with each vertex hosting an autonomous processor. The processors have distinct identity numbers (henceforth, Ids) from the range $\{1, 2, ..., n\}$. They communicate with each other over the edges of E. The communication occurs in discrete rounds. In each round each vertex can send a message to each of its neighbors, and these messages arrive to their destinations before the next round starts. The running time of an algorithm in this model is the number of rounds of communication that are required for the algorithm to terminate.

A legal *edge-coloring* φ of $G = (V, E)$ is a function $\varphi : E \to N$ that satisfies that for any pair of edges $e, e' \in E$ that share an endpoint (henceforth, *incident*), it holds that $\varphi(e) \neq \varphi(e')$. Denote by $\Delta = \Delta(G)$ the maximum degree of the graph G. A classical theorem of Vizing [29] shows that for any graph G, its edges can be legally colored in $(\Delta + 1)$ colors. Obviously, at least Δ colors are required.

The edge coloring problem is one of the most fundamental problems in Graph Theory and Graph Algorithms. It also has numerous applications in Computer Science, including job-shop scheduling, packet-routing, and resource allocation [16, 12]. This problem was also extensively studied in the message-passing model [10, 11, 12, 14, 23, 25]. Panconesi and Rizzi [23] showed that a $(2\Delta - 1)$-edge-coloring can be computed deterministically in $O(\Delta) + \log^* n$ time. Panconesi and Srinivasan [25] devised a randomized $(1.6\Delta +$

[*]Supported by the Adams Fellowship Program of the Israel Academy of Sciences and Humanities.
[**] Supported by the Binational Science Foundation, grant No. 2008390. Additional funding was provided by the Lynn and William Frankel Center for Computer Sciences.

$O(\log^{1+\epsilon} n)$)-edge coloring algorithm that runs in polylogarithmic time, where $\epsilon > 0$ is an arbitrarily small constant. Dubhashi et. al. [11] used the Rödl nibble method to improve this to a randomized $(1 + \epsilon)\Delta$-edge-coloring in time $O(\log n)$, as long as $\Delta = \omega(\log n)$. Grable and Panconesi [14] showed that if for every edge $e = (u, w)$, the degree of either u or w is sufficiently large (at least $2^{\Omega(\frac{\log n}{\log \log n})}$), then a $(1 + \epsilon)\Delta$-edge-coloring, for an arbitrarily small constant $\epsilon > 0$, can be computed in $O(\log \log n)$ time by a randomized algorithm. Czygrinow et. al. [10] devised a deterministic $O(\Delta \log n)$-edge-coloring that requires $O(\log^4 n)$ time.

A more general approach to the edge-coloring and many other related problems was taken in [1, 22, 24]. These papers presented algorithms that compute a *network decomposition*, i.e., a partition of the input graph into regions of small diameter. This partition admits also additional helpful properties. This partition can then be used to compute edge-coloring, vertex-coloring, maximal independent set, and other related structures. In particular, by this technique one can get a deterministic $(2\Delta - 1)$-edge-coloring algorithm that requires $2^{O(\sqrt{\log n})}$ time [24, 1].

A (legal) vertex coloring ψ of $G = (V, E)$ is a function $\psi : V \to N$ that satisfies that for any edge $e = (u, w) \in E$, $\psi(u) \neq \psi(w)$. We refer to $\psi(u)$ as the ψ-*color of u*. By considering the line graph $L(G) = (E, \mathcal{E} = \{(e, e') \mid e \cap e' \neq \emptyset\})$, it is easy to see that any vertex-coloring algorithm that employs $f(\Delta)$ colors, for a function $f()$, translates into an edge-coloring algorithm that employs $f(2\Delta)$ colors, with essentially the same running time [1]. This observation enables one to harness many of the recent advances in vertex-coloring for obtaining significantly faster edge-coloring algorithms as well. Most relevant in this context are the results of [18, 28, 5]. Kothapalli et. al. [18] showed that an $O(\Delta)$-vertex-coloring (and, consequently, $O(\Delta)$-edge-coloring as well) can be computed in $O(\sqrt{\log n})$ rounds, by a randomized algorithm. Recently Schneider and Wattenhofer [28] devised a randomized algorithm that computes (1) a $(\Delta+1)$-vertex-(and edge-) coloring in $O(\log \Delta + \sqrt{\log n})$ time; (2) an $O(\Delta + \log n)$-coloring in $O(\log \log n)$ time; and (3) an $O(\Delta \log^{(k)} n + \log^{1+1/k} n)$-coloring in $f(k) = O(1)$ time, for some fixed function $f()$ and any positive integer k. In [5] the authors of the current paper devised a deterministic algorithm that, for an arbitrarily small constant $\epsilon > 0$, computes (1) an $O(\Delta^{1+\epsilon})$-coloring in $O(\log \Delta \log n)$ time; and (2) an $O(\Delta)$-coloring in $\Delta^\epsilon \log n$ time.

In the current paper we show that in the case of edge-coloring the factor $\log n$ can be eliminated. Specifically, we devise a deterministic algorithm that for an arbitrarily small constant $\epsilon > 0$, computes (1) an $O(\Delta^{1+\epsilon})$-edge-coloring in $O(\log \Delta) + \log^* n$ time; (2) an $O(\Delta)$-edge-coloring in $O(\Delta^\epsilon) + \log^* n$ time. In addition we have a tradeoff curve with a number of results along it, in which the number of colors is larger than $\Omega(\Delta)$, but smaller than $\Delta^{1+\epsilon}$.

These results compare very favorably to the state-of-the-art. We start with comparing them to deterministic algorithms. For Δ in the range $\omega(\log^* n) \leq \Delta \leq O(\log n \log \log n)$ the fastest currently known algorithm for edge-coloring with $O(\Delta^{1+\epsilon})$ or less colors is due to Panconesi and Rizzi [23]. Its running time is $O(\Delta) + \log^* n$. Our algorithm runs *exponentially* faster, in time $O(\log \Delta) + \log^* n$, but it employs more

colors ($O(\Delta^{1+\epsilon})$ instead of $(2\Delta - 1)$). In addition, another variant of our algorithm employs only $O(\Delta)$ colors, and has a significantly better running time than that of the algorithm of [23], specifically, $O(\Delta^\epsilon) + \log^* n$. We stress that this result holds in particular for the range $\Delta = o(\log n)$. In this range, all previously known deterministic algorithms for $O(\Delta)$-edge-coloring and $O(\Delta)$-vertex-coloring on general graphs have running time $\Omega(\Delta)$. Therefore, our algorithm is the first to compute an $O(\Delta)$-edge-coloring in sublinear in Δ time on general graphs.

For $\Delta = \Omega(\log n \log \log n)$ the fastest known algorithm for edge-coloring with $O(\Delta^{1+\epsilon})$ colors is due to [5]. Its running time is $O(\log \Delta \log n)$, instead of $O(\log \Delta) + \log^* n$ for our new algorithm. Note that as long as Δ is at most polylogarithmic in n, the new running time is $O(\log \log n)$ instead of $O(\log n \log \log n)$ of [5], i.e., our improvement in this range is exponential as well. To summarize, our algorithm improves the state-of-the-art running time for deterministic algorithms in almost the entire range of the maximum degree Δ, i.e., for $\Delta = \omega(\log^* n)$, and it improves it exponentially for $2^{\Omega(\log^* n)} \leq \Delta \leq O(\log^k n)$, for an arbitrarily large constant k. We remark that even when Δ is greater than polylogarithmic in n, the running time $O(\log \Delta + \log^* n)$ of our $O(\Delta^{1+\epsilon})$-coloring algorithm is at least *quadratically* smaller than the previous state-of-the-art $O(\log \Delta \log n)$ due to [5]. In other words, the factor of $\log n$ is a huge factor in this context, and eliminating it results in major improvements. See Table 1 below for a concise comparison of previous and new deterministic results.

Next, we compare the running time and the number of colors of our *deterministic* algorithm with the state-of-the-art with respect to *randomized* algorithms. For $\Delta = \Omega(\log n)$ the recent randomized algorithm of Schneider and Wattenhofer [28] outperforms our algorithm. However, for $\Delta \leq \log^{1-\delta} n$, for an arbitrarily small constant $\delta > 0$, the algorithm of [28] either employs $\Omega(\log n)$ colors (i.e., more than $\Delta^{1+\epsilon}$ for an arbitrarily small $\epsilon > 0$), or its running time is $\Omega(\sqrt{\log n})$. (Note, however, that the randomized algorithm of [28] solves a generally harder vertex-coloring problem, rather than edge-coloring.) Hence in the range $\omega(\log^* n) \leq \Delta \leq \log^{1-\delta} n$, for some fixed constant $\delta > 0$, our deterministic algorithm outperforms all previous algorithms, deterministic and randomized. Moreover, in the range $2^{\Omega(\log^* n)} \leq \Delta \leq \log^{1-\delta} n$ our algorithm is *exponentially faster* than the previous ones. Indeed, for $\Delta \leq \sqrt{\log n}$ the best previous algorithm that achieves $O(\Delta^{1+\epsilon})$ or less colors is due to [23], whose running time is $O(\Delta) + \log^* n$. On the other hand, the running time of our algorithm is $O(\log \Delta) + \log^* n$. For $\sqrt{\log n} \leq \Delta \leq \log^{1-\delta} n$ the best previous algorithms that achieve that many colors are due to [28, 18], and their running time is $O(\sqrt{\log n})$. Our algorithm requires in this range just $O(\log \Delta) + \log^* n = O(\log \log n)$ time. (On the other hand, the variant of the algorithm of [28] that runs in $O(\sqrt{\log n})$ time employs just $(2\Delta - 1)$ colors, as opposed to $\Delta^{1+\epsilon}$ colors that are employed by our algorithm. The algorithm of [23] also employs only $(2\Delta - 1)$ colors.) See Table 2 below for a concise comparison.

Observe also that the $\log^* n$ term in the running time of our algorithms is optimal up to a factor of 2, in view of the lower bounds of [21]. Specifically, Linial's lower bound [21] implies that $f(\Delta)$-edge-coloring, for any fixed function $f()$, requires at least $\frac{1}{2} \log^* n$ time. Moreover, there is a variant of our algorithm that achieves the precisely optimal

---

[1] As long as one allows arbitrarily large messages.

Range of Δ	$\omega(\log^* n) = \Delta = o(\log n \log \log n)$	$\Omega(\log n \log \log n) = \Delta$
Previous	$(2\Delta - 1)$ colors, $O(\Delta) + \log^* n$ time [23]	$O(\Delta)$ colors, $O(\Delta^\epsilon \log n)$-time [5]
		$O(\Delta^{1+\epsilon})$ colors, $O(\log \Delta \log n)$-time [5]
New	$O(\Delta)$ colors, $O(\Delta^\epsilon) + \log^* n$ time	$O(\Delta)$ colors, $O(\Delta^\epsilon) + \log^* n$ time
	$O(\Delta^{1+\epsilon})$ colors, $O(\log \Delta) + \log^* n$ time	$O(\Delta^{1+\epsilon})$ colors, $O(\log \Delta) + \log^* n$ time

Table 1: *A concise comparison of previous state-of-the-art edge-coloring deterministic algorithms with our new algorithms.*

Range of Δ	$\omega(\log^* n) = \Delta = O(\sqrt{\log n})$	$\Omega(\sqrt{\log n}) = \Delta \le \log^{1-\delta} n$
Previous	$(2\Delta - 1)$ colors, $O(\Delta) + \log^* n$ time [23]	$(2\Delta - 1)$ colors, $O(\sqrt{\log n})$ time [28]
New (Deter.)	$O(\Delta^{1+\epsilon})$ colors, $O(\log \Delta) + \log^* n$ time	$O(\Delta^{1+\epsilon})$ colors, $O(\log \log n)$ time

Table 2: *A concise comparison of previous state-of-the-art edge-coloring randomized and deterministic algorithms with our new deterministic algorithm. The algorithm of [23] is deterministic. The algorithm of [28] is randomized.*

additive term of $\frac{1}{2}\log^* n$, while achieving almost the same dependence on Δ. By "almost" the same dependence on Δ we mean that it achieves (for an arbitrarily small constant $\epsilon > 0$), (1) an $O(\Delta)$-edge-coloring in $O(\Delta^\epsilon) + \frac{1}{2}\log^* n$ time, and (2) an $O(\Delta^{1+\epsilon})$-edge-coloring in $O(\log \Delta \cdot \frac{\log^* \Delta}{\log(\log^* \Delta)}) + \frac{1}{2}\log^* n$ time. In other words, item (1) is the same as that cited above, except that $\log^* n$ is replaced by $\frac{1}{2}\log^* n$, and in item (2) there is also a tiny slack factor of $\frac{\log^* \Delta}{\log(\log^* \Delta)}$.

1.2 Bounded Neighborhood Independence

Our results for edge-coloring follow from far more general results that we describe below. *Neighborhood independence* $I(G)$ of a graph $G = (V, E)$ is the maximum number of independent [1] neighbors of a single vertex $v \in V$. The family of graphs with constant neighborhood independence (henceforth, *bounded neighborhood independence*) is a very general family of graphs. Indeed, for any graph G, the neighborhood independence of its line graph $L(G)$ is at most 2. Moreover, for an r-hypergraph $\mathcal{H}$ (i.e., a hypergraph in which every hyperedge contains at most r vertices), $I(L(\mathcal{H})) \le r$.

Another important family of graphs which is subsumed by the family of graphs with bounded neighborhood independence is the family of graphs of *bounded growth*. A graph $G = (V, E)$ is said to be of bounded growth if there exists a function $f()$ such that for any $r = 1, 2, ...$, the number of independent vertices at distance at most r from any given vertex is at most $f(r)$. Distributed algorithms for vertex-coloring and computing a maximal independent set on graphs from this family is a subject of intensive recent research [17, 13, 27]. The crowning result of this effort is the deterministic algorithm of [27] that computes a maximal independent set and a $(\Delta + 1)$-vertex-coloring for graphs from this family in optimal time $O(\log^* n)$. Note, however, that a graph G with a constant neighborhood independence may contain an arbitrarily large independent set U whose all vertices are at distance at most 2 from some given vertex v in G. Thus, graphs with bounded neighborhood independence may have unbounded growth. (Consider, for example, a graph H that is obtained by connecting each vertex of an $n/2$-vertex clique with a distinct isolated vertex. Each vertex in H has at most 2 independent neighbors. However,

each vertex v in the clique has at least $n/2 = \Omega(\Delta)$ independent vertices in $\Gamma_2(v)$, and so the graph H is not a graph of bounded growth.)

Yet another family of graphs which is subsumed by the family of graphs of bounded independence is the family of *claw-free* graphs. A graph is *claw-free* if it excludes $K_{1,3}$ as an induced subgraph. (In fact, for any $r = 2, 3, ...$, the family of graphs with independence at most r is precisely the family of graphs that exclude induced $K_{1,r+1}$.) The family of claw-free graphs attracted enormous attention in Structural Graph Theory. See, e.g., the series of papers by Chudnovsky and Seymour, starting with [7].

In this paper we devise a vertex-coloring algorithm for graphs of bounded neighborhood independence that computes (for an arbitrarily small constant $\epsilon > 0$) (1) an $O(\Delta)$-vertex-coloring in $O(\Delta^\epsilon) + \frac{1}{2}\log^* n$ time, and (2) an $O(\Delta^{1+\epsilon})$-vertex-coloring in $O(\log \Delta \cdot \frac{\log^* \Delta}{\log(\log^* \Delta)}) + \frac{1}{2}\log^* n$ time. Modulo some subtleties, these results imply our main results about edge-coloring described in Section 1.1. In addition, they apply to line graphs of r-hypergraphs for any constant r, to claw-free graphs, to graphs of bounded growth, and to many other graphs.

1.3 Our Techniques

In the heart of our algorithms lie improved algorithms for computing *defective colorings*. For a non-negative integer m and positive integer χ, an *m-defective χ-vertex-coloring* φ of a graph $G = (V, E)$ is a function $\varphi : V \to \{1, 2, ..., \chi\}$ that satisfies that for every vertex $v \in V$, it has at most m neighbors colored by $\varphi(v)$. The parameter m is called the *defect* of the coloring. Defective coloring was introduced by Cowen et. al [8] and by Harary and Jones [15]. It was extensively studied from a graph-theoretic perspective [2, 9]. Recently defective coloring was discovered to be very useful in the context of distributed graph coloring [4, 19]. Specifically, the state-of-the-art $(\Delta + 1)$-vertex-coloring algorithms for general graphs [4, 19] are based on subroutines for computing defective coloring. For a parameter p, these subroutines compute an $O(\Delta/p)$-defective p^2-coloring. (In [4] the running time of such a subroutine is $O(p^2) + \frac{1}{2}\log^* n$, and in [19] it is $O(\log^* \Delta) + \frac{1}{2}\log^* n$.) It was observed in [4] that one could have devised significantly faster coloring algorithms if there were an efficient (distributed) routine for computing an

---

[1] Two vertices u, w are *independent* in G if $(u, w) \notin E$.

m-defective χ-coloring with a *linear* in Δ product of m and χ. (The current state-of-the-art [4, 19], has $m = O(\Delta/p)$, $\chi = p^2$, i.e., $m \cdot \chi = O(\Delta \cdot p)$ instead of the desired $O(\Delta)$.)

In this paper we show that if one restricts his attention to the family of bounded neighborhood independence graphs, then this goal can be achieved. Specifically, we devise an algorithm that computes an $O(\Delta/p)$-defective p-vertex-coloring of a given graph of bounded neighborhood independence in $O(p^2) + \frac{1}{2}\log^* n$ time. As a result we obtain a bunch of drastically faster algorithms for vertex-coloring these graphs, and, consequently, for edge-coloring general graphs.

Whether it is possible to devise an efficient $O(\Delta/p)$-defective p-vertex-coloring algorithm for general graphs remains a challenging open question. Recently in [5] the authors of the current paper were able to circumvent this question by the means of *arbdefective coloring*. Note that an $O(\Delta/p)$-defective p-vertex-coloring can be seen as a partition of the vertex set into p subsets, each inducing a subgraph of maximum degree at most $O(\Delta/p)$. In [5] the authors showed that the vertex set of a graph of arboricity [1] a can be efficiently partitioned into p subsets, each inducing a subgraph of arboricity $O(a/p)$. This partition is then employed in [5] to devise a suite of efficient algorithms for vertex-coloring general graphs. In particular, using this technique [5] devised an $O(\Delta^{1+\epsilon})$-vertex coloring algorithm in $O(\log \Delta \log n)$ time, for an arbitrarily small constant $\epsilon > 0$.

Note, however, that the factor of $\log n$ in the running time of the algorithms of [5] is inherent, because these algorithms rely heavily on the notion of arboricity, and more specifically, on the machinery of forest-decompositions developed in [3] for working with graphs of bounded arboricity. On the other hand, a lower bound shown in [3] stipulates that computing a forests-decomposition requires $\Omega(\frac{\log n}{\log a})$ time, where a is the arboricity. Consequently, the factor of $\log n$ in the running time is unavoidable [2] using the approach of [5]. In the current paper we pursue a different line of attack. Specifically, we devise improved algorithms for *defective* coloring, rather than circumventing it and going through *arbdefective* coloring.

1.4 Structure of the Paper
In Section 2 we describe the definitions and notation employed in our algorithms. In Section 3 we devise defective vertex-coloring algorithms for graphs with bounded neighborhood independence. In Section 4 we devise legal vertex-coloring algorithms for this family of graphs. In Section 5 we devise legal edge-coloring algorithms for general graphs.

2. PRELIMINARIES

Unless the base value is specified, all logarithms in this paper are of base 2. For a non-negative integer i, the *iterative log-function* $\log^{(i)}(\cdot)$ is defined as follows. For an integer $n > 0$, $\log^{(0)} n = n$, and $\log^{(i+1)} n = \log(\log^{(i)} n)$, for every $i = 0, 1, 2, \ldots$. Also, $\log^* n$ is defined by: $\log^* n = \min\{i \mid \log^{(i)} n \le 2\}$.

---

[1] The *arboricity* of a graph $G = (V,E)$ is $a(G) = \max\{\left\lceil \frac{|E(U)|}{|U|-1} \right\rceil : U \subseteq V, |U| \ge 2\}$.

[2] In fact, the algorithm of [5] computes an $O(a^{1+\epsilon})$-coloring in time $O(\log a \log n)$ for graphs of arboricity a. An $O(\Delta^{1+\epsilon})$-coloring in $O(\log \Delta \log n)$ time is a direct corollary of this result. On the other hand, it is known [3] that $O(a^{1+\epsilon})$-coloring requires $\Omega(\frac{\log n}{\log a})$ time.

The *degree* of a vertex v in a graph $G = (V,E)$, denoted $\deg(v) = \deg_G(v)$, is the number of edges incident to v. A vertex u such that $(u,v) \in E$ is called a *neighbor* of v in G. The *neighborhood* $\Gamma(v) = \Gamma_G(v)$ of v is the set of neighbors of v. The maximum degree of a vertex in G, denoted $\Delta(G)$, is defined by $\Delta = \Delta(G) = \max_{v \in V} \deg(v)$. The graph $G' = (V', E')$ is a *subgraph* of $G = (V,E)$, denoted $G' \subseteq G$, if $V' \subseteq V$ and $E' \subseteq E$. The notation $V(G')$ and $E(G')$ is used to denote the vertex set V' of G', and the edge set E' of G', respectively.

The *line graph* $L(G) = (V'', E'')$ of a graph $G = (V,E)$ is a graph in which V'' contains a vertex v_e for each edge $e \in E$, and an edge $(v_e, w_{e'})$ if and only if the edges e and e' of E share a common endpoint. We say that a vertex $v_e \in V''$ and an edge $e \in E$ *correspond* to each other.

The *out-degree* of a vertex v in a directed graph $\hat{G}$ is the number of edges incident to v that are oriented outwards of v. An *orientation* σ of (the edge set of) a graph is an assignment of direction to each edge $(u,v) \in E$, either towards u or towards v. An edge (u,v) that is oriented towards v is denoted by $\langle u, v \rangle$. The *out-degree* of an orientation σ of a graph G is the maximum out-degree of a vertex in G with respect to σ. In a given orientation, each neighbor u of v that is connected to v by an edge oriented towards u is called a *parent* of v. In this case we say that v is a *child* of u.

For a graph $G = (V,E)$, a set of vertices $U \subseteq V$ is called an *independent set* if for every pair of vertices $v, w \in U$ it holds that $(v,w) \notin E$.

The minimum number of colors that can be used in a legal vertex-coloring of a graph G is called *the chromatic number* of G, denoted $\chi(G)$.

Next, we state a number of known results that will be used in our algorithms.

Lemma 2.1. *(1) [21] A legal $O(\Delta^2)$-vertex-coloring can be computed in $\log^* n$ time.*
(2) [4, 19] A legal $(\Delta + 1)$-vertex-coloring can be computed in $O(\Delta) + \log^* n$ time.
(3) [19] A $\lfloor \Delta/p \rfloor$-defective $O(p^2)$-vertex-coloring can be computed in $O(\log^* n)$ time.

3. DEFECTIVE COLORING

In this section we present a defective vertex coloring algorithm for graphs with bounded neighborhood independence. We begin with a formal definition of this family of graphs.

Definition 3.1. Graphs with neighborhood independence bounded by c.
For a graph $G = (V,E)$ and a vertex $v \in V$, the neighborhood independence of v, denoted $I(v)$, is the size of maximum-size independent subset $U \subseteq \Gamma(v)$.
The neighborhood independence of a graph G is defined as $I(G) = \max_{v \in V}\{I(v)\}$. For a positive parameter c, a graph $G = (V,E)$ is said to have neighborhood independence bounded by c if $I(G) \le c$.

Let c be a fixed positive constant, and p be a parameter such that $1 \le p \le \Delta$. We devise a procedure, called *Procedure Defective-Color*, that computes an $O(\Delta/p)$-defective p-coloring on graphs with neighborhood independence bounded by c. This coloring is achieved by first computing a defective $O(p^2)$-coloring, and then reducing the number of colors to p, using special properties of graphs with bounded neighborhood independence. Procedure Defective-Color receives as input a graph G with neighborhood independence bounded by c, a positive parameter b, and the parameter Λ which serves as an upper bound on the maximum degree of the input graph. The parameter b satisfies that $b \geq 1$, $b \cdot p \leq \Lambda$. This parameter controls the tradeoff between the defect of the resulting coloring and the running time of the procedure. Specifically, the defect behaves as $\frac{\Lambda}{p}(1 + O(1/b))$, and the running time is at most $O(b^2 \cdot p^2 + \log^* n)$. We assume that all vertices know the value of c before the computation starts.

The procedure starts with computing a $\lfloor \Lambda/(b \cdot p) \rfloor$-defective $O((b \cdot p)^2)$-coloring φ of G using Lemma 2.1(3). The coloring φ is employed for computing another defective coloring ψ of the vertices of G. The recoloring step spends one round for each φ-color class. Specifically, each vertex $v \in V$ computes $\psi(v)$ as follows. The vertex v waits for each neighbor u of v with $\varphi(u) < \varphi(v)$ to select a color $\psi(u)$. Once v receives a message from each such neighbor u with its color $\psi(u)$, it sets $\psi(v)$ to be a value from the range $\{1, 2, .., p\}$ that is used by the minimum number of neighbors u with $\varphi(u) < \varphi(v)$. Once v selects its color $\psi(v)$, it sends it to all its neighbors. This completes the description of the algorithm.

We need the following piece of notation. For a vertex v and an index $k \in \{1, 2, ..., p\}$, let $N_v(k) = |\{u \in \Gamma(v) \mid \psi(u) = k, \varphi(u) < \varphi(v)\}|$ denote the number of neighbors u of v that have smaller φ-color than v has, and whose ψ-color was set to k. Next, we provide the pseudocode of Procedure Defective-Color.

Algorithm 1 Procedure Defective-Color(G, b, p, Λ)

An algorithm for each vertex $v \in V$

1: $\varphi(v) :=$ compute $\lfloor \Lambda/(b \cdot p) \rfloor$-defective $O((b \cdot p)^2)$-coloring using Lemma 2.1(3)
2: send $\varphi(v)$ to all neighbors
3: $\psi(v) := 0$
4: **while** $\psi(v) = 0$, in each round **do**
5:    **if** v received $\psi(u)$ for each neighbor u of v with $\varphi(u) < \varphi(v)$ **then**
6:      $m := \min\{N_v(k) \mid k \in \{1, 2, ..., p\}\}$
7:      $\psi(v) :=$ a color $k \in \{1, 2, ..., p\}$ such that $N_v(k) = m$
8:      send $\psi(v)$ to all neighbors
9:    **end if**
10: **end while**

Observe that a vertex v waits only for neighbors with smaller φ-color before selecting $\psi(v)$. Consequently, it selects the color $\psi(v)$ after at most $\varphi(v)$ rounds from the time when step 2 of Algorithm 1 was executed. This fact is stated in the following lemma.

Lemma 3.2. *Let φ be the coloring computed in the first step of Algorithm 1. Let R be the round in which step 2 is executed. A vertex v selects a color $\psi(v) \neq 0$ in round $R + \varphi(v)$ or earlier.*

PROOF. Let $\ell = O((b \cdot p)^2)$ be the number of colors employed by φ. The lemma is proved by induction on the number of rounds. We prove that once a round $i = R + 1, R + 2, \ldots, R + \ell$ is completed, all vertices v with $\varphi(v) \leq i$ have already selected the color $\psi(v)$. For the base case, observe that the vertices v with $\varphi(v) = 1$ have no neighbors with smaller φ-color. Therefore they select a ψ-color

in round $R + 1$, immediately after receiving the φ-colors of their neighbors in round R. For the induction step, suppose that in round $i - 1$ all vertices v with $\varphi(v) \leq i - 1$ have already selected the color $\psi(v)$. Hence, each vertex u with $\varphi(u) \leq i$ receives the color ψ for each neighbor with smaller φ-color before round i. Consequently, the vertices u select a ψ-color in round i or earlier. $\square$

Since the coloring φ employs $\ell = O((b \cdot p)^2)$ colors, it follows that all vertices select a ψ-color at most ℓ rounds after the computation of the defective coloring in step 1 of Algorithm 1. By Lemma 2.1(3), step 1 requires $O(\log^* n)$ rounds. The overall running time of Algorithm 1 is given in the following corollary.

Corollary 3.3. *The running time of Procedure Defective-Color is $O((b \cdot p)^2 + \log^* n)$.*

In what follows we prove the correctness of Procedure Defective-Color. By the Pigeonhole principle, the number of neighbors u of a vertex v such that $\varphi(u) < \varphi(v)$ and $\psi(u) = \psi(v)$ is at most Λ/p. (Otherwise, there are more than (Λ/p) neighbors of v that are colored by a ψ-color i, for each $i = 1, 2, ..., p$. Hence, v has more than Λ neighbors, a contradiction.) In addition, since φ is a $\lfloor \Lambda/(b \cdot p) \rfloor$-defective coloring, there are at most $\lfloor \Lambda/(b \cdot p) \rfloor$ neighbors u of v that have the same φ-color as v has, i.e., satisfy $\varphi(u) = \varphi(v)$. These neighbors may also end up selecting the same ψ-color that v selects. Hence the number of neighbors u of v that satisfy $\varphi(u) \leq \varphi(v)$ and $\psi(u) = \psi(v)$ is at most $\Lambda/p + \Lambda/(b \cdot p)$. In order to prove that ψ is an $O(\Lambda/p)$-defective coloring we also prove a somewhat surprising claim regarding the other neighbors of v. Specifically, we prove that the number of neighbors u of a vertex v such that $\varphi(u) > \varphi(v)$ and $\psi(u) = \psi(v)$ is $O(\Lambda/p)$ as well. Consequently, ψ is an $O(\Lambda/p)$-defective p-coloring.

For $i = 1, 2, ..., p$, let G_i be the subgraph induced by the ψ-color class i, i.e., by the vertex set $\{v \in V \mid \psi(v) = i\}$. As a first step we show that the chromatic number $\chi(G_i)$ of G_i is at most $(\Lambda/(b \cdot p) + \Lambda/p) + 1$. (See Lemma 3.5.) We prove this claim by presenting an acyclic orientation of G_i with out-degree at most $(\Lambda/(b \cdot p) + \Lambda/p)$. Since a graph with acyclic orientation with out-degree d is legally $(d + 1)$-colorable (see Lemma 3.4), the claim follows. Then we show that bounded chromatic number in conjunction with bounded neighborhood independence imply a bounded degree.

Lemma 3.4. *A graph G with an acyclic orientation μ with out-degree d satisfies that $\chi(G) \leq d + 1$.*

Lemma 3.4 is widely known. Its correctness follows from the fact that if a graph G has an acyclic orientation with out-degree d, then the degeneracy [1] of G is at most d. Therefore, it is $(d + 1)$-colorable.

Lemma 3.5. *For $i = 1, 2, ..., p$, it holds that $\chi(G_i) \leq (\Lambda/(b \cdot p) + \Lambda/p) + 1$.*

PROOF. Let μ_i be the following orientation of G_i. For each edge $e = (u, v) \in E(G_i)$, orient the edge towards the endpoint that is colored by a smaller φ-color. If $\varphi(u) = \varphi(v)$, then orient e towards the endpoint with smaller Id among u, v. Each vertex v in G_i has at most Λ/p neighbors u in

---

[1] A graph G has *degeneracy* at most d if any subgraph of G contains a vertex with degree at most d.

G_i with smaller φ-colors. (This is because $\psi(u) = \psi(v)$ and $\varphi(u) < \varphi(v)$.) In addition, each vertex v in G_i has at most $\Lambda/(b \cdot p)$ neighbors u in G_i with $\varphi(v) = \varphi(u)$. Consequently, μ_i has out-degree at most $(\Lambda/(b \cdot p) + \Lambda/p)$.

Next, we prove that the orientation μ_i is acyclic. Let C be a cycle of G_i. Let v be a vertex on the cycle C with the largest φ-color. If there are several vertices that satisfy this condition, let v be the vertex with the greatest Id. Let u and w be the neighbors of v in C. Since $\varphi(u) < \varphi(v)$ or $(\varphi(u) = \varphi(v)$ and $Id(u) < Id(v))$, the edge (v, u) is oriented by μ_i towards u. Similarly, the edge (v, w) is oriented towards w. Therefore, C is not an oriented cycle. Consequently, μ_i is acyclic. Since the out-degree of μ_i is at most $(\Lambda/(b \cdot p) + \Lambda/p)$, Lemma 3.4 implies that $\chi(G_i) \leq (\Lambda/(b \cdot p) + \Lambda/p) + 1$. $\square$

The next lemma shows that the family of graphs with bounded neighborhood independence is closed under taking vertex-induced subgraphs.

Lemma 3.6. *For a positive integer c, let $G = (V, E)$ be a graph with neighborhood independence at most c. The subgraph induced by a subset $U \subseteq V$ also has neighborhood independence at most by c.*

PROOF. Let $\mathcal{G} = G(U)$ be the subgraph induced by U. For a vertex $u \in U$, $\Gamma_{\mathcal{G}}(u)$ is the neighborhood of u in $\mathcal{G}$, and $\Gamma_G(u)$ is the neighborhood of u in G. Suppose for contradiction that there exists a vertex $u \in U$ such that there is an independent set $W \subseteq \Gamma_{\mathcal{G}}(u)$ with cardinality $|W| > c$. For a pair of vertices $v, w \in W$, it holds that $(v, w) \notin E$. In addition, $\Gamma_{\mathcal{G}}(u) \subseteq \Gamma_G(u)$. Therefore, $W \subseteq \Gamma_G(u)$ is an independent set with more than c vertices, and it is contained in the neighborhood $\Gamma_G(u)$ of the vertex u. This is a contradiction. $\square$

We employ Lemmas 3.4 - 3.6 to prove the correctness of Procedure Defective-Color.

Theorem 3.7. *Suppose that Procedure Defective-Color is invoked on a graph G with maximum degree Δ and with neighborhood independence bounded by a positive constant c. Suppose also that it receives as input three integer parameters $b \geq 1, p \geq 1, \Lambda \geq 1$, such that $b \cdot p \leq \Lambda$, and $\Lambda \geq \Delta$. Then Procedure Defective-Color computes a $((\Lambda/(b \cdot p) + \Lambda/p) \cdot c + c)$-defective p-coloring.*

PROOF. Recall that G_i is the graph induced by vertices with ψ-color i returned by Procedure Defective-Color, for $i = 1, 2, ..., p$. By Lemma 3.6, since G_i is a subgraph of G, the neighborhood independence of G_i is bounded by c. We prove that the maximum degree of G_i, for $i = 1, 2, ..., p$, is at most $(\Lambda/(b \cdot p) + \Lambda/p) \cdot c + c$. Suppose for contradiction that there is a vertex $v \in G_i$ such that $\deg_{G_i}(v) > (\Lambda/(b \cdot p) + \Lambda/p) \cdot c + c$. Let φ' be a legal coloring of G_i that employs the minimum number of colors. Each color class of φ' is an independent set. Therefore, for a positive integer q, the number of neighbors u of v such that $\varphi'(u) = q$ is at most c. Consequently, the number of different colors employed for coloring the set $\Gamma_{G_i}(v)$ of neighbors of v in G_i is at least $\lceil \deg_{G_i}(v)/c \rceil > (\Lambda/(b \cdot p) + \Lambda/p) + 1$. However, by Lemma 3.5, $\chi(G_i) \leq (\Lambda/(b \cdot p) + \Lambda/p) + 1$, contradiction. $\square$

We summarize this section with the following corollary.

Corollary 3.8. *For an integer parameter p, $1 \leq p \leq \Lambda$, $\Lambda \geq \Delta$, and a constant $\epsilon > 0$, a $((c + \epsilon) \cdot \frac{\Lambda}{p} + c)$-defective*

p-coloring of a graph G with $I(G) \leq c$ can be computed in $O(p^2 + \log^* n)$ time.

PROOF. Set $b < \frac{1}{\epsilon}$. Now the corollary follows from Corollary 3.3 and Theorem 3.7. $\square$

Observe that for graphs with bounded neighborhood independence, the product of the defect $O(\Delta/p)$ and the number of colors p in the coloring produced by Corollary 3.8 is $O(\Delta)$. This is in sharp contrast to the current state-of-the-art for distributed defective coloring in *general* graphs [4, 19], which is $O(\Delta/p)$-defective p^2-coloring. On the other hand, the latter coloring can be computed faster, specifically, within $O(\log^* n)$ time [19].

4. LEGAL COLORING GRAPHS WITH BOUNDED NEIGHBORHOOD INDEPENDENCE

In this section we employ the defective coloring algorithm from the previous section for legal vertex coloring of graphs with neighborhood independence at most $c = O(1)$. Fix an arbitrarily small constant $\epsilon > 0$. Once a $(c + \epsilon) \cdot \frac{\Delta}{p} + c = O(\Delta/p)$-defective p-coloring ψ of a graph G is computed, it constitutes a vertex partition $V_1, V_2, ..., V_p$, in which V_i is the set of vertices with ψ-color i, for $i = 1, 2, ..., p$. In other words, $V = \bigcup_{i=1}^n V_i$, and for a pair of distinct indices $i, j \in \{1, 2, ..., p\}$, $i \neq j$, $V_i \cap V_j = \emptyset$. The subgraph G_i induced by V_i has maximum degree $O(\Delta/p)$, since each vertex in G has at most $O(\Delta/p)$ neighbors with the same ψ-color. Therefore, one can legally color the subgraphs $G_1, G_2, ..., G_p$ employing $O(\Delta/p)$ colors for each subgraph, using Lemma 2.1(2). These colorings, denoted $\varphi_1, \varphi_2, ..., \varphi_p$, are computed in parallel on the subgraphs $G_1, G_2, ..., G_p$. Let $m = O(\Delta/p)$ denote the maximum number of colors employed by φ_i, for $i = 1, 2, .., p$. Next, the colorings are combined into a unified legal coloring φ of G as follows. Observe that each vertex $v \in V$ belongs exactly to one subgraph G_j among $G_1, G_2, ..., G_p$. We set $\varphi(v) = \varphi_j(v) + (j - 1) \cdot m$. (The color $\varphi(v)$ can also be thought of as a pair $(j, \varphi_j(v))$, where $v \in V_j$.)

The coloring φ is a legal coloring of G, since for any pair of vertices $u, v \in G$, if they belong to the same subgraph G_i, $i \in \{1, 2, ..., p\}$, then $\varphi_i(v) \neq \varphi_i(u)$, and, therefore, $\varphi(v) \neq \varphi(u)$. Otherwise, u belongs to G_i, and v belong to G_j, for some $1 \leq i \neq j \leq p$. Since $|(j - 1) \cdot m - (i - 1) \cdot m| \geq m$, and $|\varphi_j(u) - \varphi_i(v)| \leq m - 1$, in this case also it holds that $\varphi(v) \neq \varphi(u)$.

The running time required for computing φ is the running time of computing a legal coloring of a graph with degree $\lfloor (c + \epsilon) \cdot \frac{\Delta}{p} + c \rfloor = O(\Delta/p)$. Hence, by Lemma 2.1(2), the running time of computing φ from a given $O(\Delta/p)$-defective p-coloring ψ is $O(\Delta/p + \log^* n)$. By Corollary 3.8, the running time of computing ψ is $O(p^2 + \log^* n)$. Therefore, the overall running time of computing φ from scratch is $O(\Delta/p + p^2 + \log^* n)$. This running time is optimized by setting $p = \lfloor \Delta^{1/3} \rfloor$, resulting in overall $O(\Delta^{2/3} + \log^* n)$ time. The number of colors employed by the resulting legal coloring is at most $((c + \epsilon) \cdot \frac{\Delta}{p} + c + 1) \cdot p \leq (c + \epsilon') \cdot \Delta$, for any constant ϵ', $\epsilon' > \epsilon$. (Note that $c = O(1)$ and $\Delta/p = \omega(1)$.) We summarize this result in the following lemma.

Lemma 4.1. *For any constant $\epsilon' > 0$, a legal $((c + \epsilon') \cdot \Delta)$-coloring of graphs with neighborhood independence at most c can be computed in $O(\Delta^{2/3} + \log^* n)$ time.*

Next, we present a significantly faster $O(\Delta)$-coloring procedure for the family of graphs with neighborhood independence bounded by c, for a positive constant c. The procedure is called *Procedure Legal-Color*. During its execution defective colorings are computed several times. In the first phase of the procedure a defective coloring of the input graph is computed. This coloring forms a partition of the original graph into vertex-disjoint subgraphs, each with maximum degree smaller than Δ. Then the procedure is invoked recursively on these subgraphs in parallel. This invocation partitions each subgraph into more subgraphs with yet smaller maximum degrees. This process repeats itself until the maximum degrees of all subgraphs are sufficiently small. Then, legal colorings of these subgraphs are computed in parallel, and merged into a unified legal coloring of the input graph. Even though Procedure Defective-Color is invoked many times by Procedure Legal-Color, the running time of Procedure Legal-Color is much smaller than the time given in Lemma 4.1. The improvement in time is achieved by selecting different parameters in the defective colorings computations, making the invocations significantly faster than a single invocation with the parameter $p = \lfloor \Delta^{1/3} \rfloor$.

In particular, in the algorithm that was described above we partitioned the vertex set of the graph into p disjoint subsets with maximum degree $\Delta' \leq (c + \epsilon')\frac{\Delta}{p}$ each. In each of the p subgraphs one can invoke recursively the algorithm from Lemma 4.1. It will produce a $((c + \epsilon')^2 \cdot \frac{\Delta}{p})$-coloring of each of the subgraphs, i.e., a $((c + \epsilon')^2 \cdot \Delta)$-coloring of the original graph. The running time becomes $O((\frac{\Delta}{p})^{2/3} + p^2 + \log^* n)$. By setting $p = \Delta^{1/4}$, we achieve the running time $O(\Delta^{1/2} + \log^* n)$. Generally, suppose for a constant $i = 1, 2, \dots$ that we have a $((c + \epsilon')^i \cdot \Delta)$-coloring algorithm with running time $O(\Delta^{\frac{2}{2+i}} + \log^* n)$. Then the above argument converts it into a $((c + \epsilon')^{i+1} \cdot \Delta)$-coloring algorithm with running time $O(\Delta^{\frac{2}{2+(i+1)}} + \log^* n)$. To summarize:

Theorem 4.2. *For any constant $i = 1, 2, \dots$, and any arbitrarily small constant $\eta > 0$, a $((c^i + \eta) \cdot \Delta)$-coloring of a graph G with maximum degree Δ and neighborhood independence at most c can be computed in $O(\Delta^{\frac{2}{2+i}} + \log^* n)$ time.*

In what follows we extend this argument to the case of superconstant i. Procedure Legal-Color receives as input a graph G, positive integer parameters b, p such that $p > 4c$, $1 \leq b \cdot p \leq \Delta$, a parameter λ such that $2c < \lambda \leq \Delta$, and a parameter Λ. The parameter Λ represents an upper bound on the maximum degree of the input graph. Initially, Λ is set to Δ. Later as the procedure is invoked recursively, this parameter is set to smaller values, and it keeps decreasing as the recursion proceeds. The threshold parameter λ determines the termination condition of the recursion. Specifically, if $\Lambda \leq \lambda$ then a legal $(\Lambda + 1)$-coloring of G is computed directly using Lemma 2.1(2). Otherwise, an $O(\Delta/p)$-defective p-coloring ψ of G is computed, producing the subgraphs $G_1, G_2, \dots, G_p$ induced by the ψ-color classes $1, 2, \dots, p$, respectively. Let $\lambda' = O(\Delta/p)$ denote the defect of the coloring ψ. Next, Procedure Legal-Color is invoked on each of these subgraphs recursively, with the degree parameter λ'. All other parameters, that is, b, p, and λ, do not change throughout the recursion.

For technical convenience, Procedure Legal-Color returns not only the resulting coloring φ, but also an upper bound ϑ on the number of colors that this coloring employs. On the bottom level of the recursion, i.e., when $\Lambda \leq \lambda$, the number of colors that is used by φ is at most $\Lambda + 1$. In this case the algorithm (see line 3) sets $\vartheta = \Lambda + 1$. In the more general case when Λ is greater than the threshold value λ, the algorithm invokes itself recursively on each of the subgraphs $G_1, G_2, \dots, G_p$. These recursive invocations return the pairs $(\varphi_1, \vartheta_1), (\varphi_2, \vartheta_2), \dots, (\varphi_p, \vartheta_p)$, where for each $i = 1, 2, \dots, p$, φ_i is a ϑ_i-coloring of G_i. These colorings are merged into a unified ϑ-coloring φ of the entire graph G, with $\vartheta = \Sigma_{i=1}^p \vartheta_i$. It will be shown later that, in fact, $\vartheta_i = \vartheta_j$ for every $i, j \in \{1, 2, \dots, p\}$. (In other words, the *upper bound* on the number of colors employed by the coloring φ_i that the algorithm returns is equal to the *upper bound* that it returns for the coloring φ_j. This does not necessarily mean that the two coloring use exactly the same number of colors.) This implies that one can actually set $\vartheta = \vartheta' \cdot p$, where $\vartheta' = \vartheta_i$ for some $i \in \{1, 2, \dots, p\}$, as the algorithm indeed does in line 11.

Moreover, to obtain the unified legal coloring φ the algorithm just adds to the color $\varphi_i(v)$ of a vertex $v \in V_i = V(G_i)$ the value $(i - 1) \cdot \vartheta_i$. Since $\vartheta_i = \vartheta'$ for every $i \in \{1, 2, \dots, p\}$, it follows that this way vertices of V_i end up being φ-colored by a color from the palette $\{(i-1)\vartheta'+1, (i-1)\vartheta'+2, \dots, i \cdot \vartheta'\}$. Consequently, for two vertices u, w, $u \in V_i$, $w \in V_j$, $i \neq j$, their φ-colors belong to disjoint palettes, and are, thus, different. Below we provide the pseudocode of Procedure Legal-Color.

Algorithm 2 Procedure Legal-Color$(G, b, p, \lambda, \Lambda)$

An algorithm for each vertex $v \in V$.

1: **if** $(\Lambda \leq \lambda)$ **then**
2:     $\varphi :=$ a legal $(\Lambda + 1)$-coloring of G using Lemma 2.1(2)
3:     $\vartheta := \Lambda + 1$ /* number of colors employed by φ */
4: **else**
5:     $\psi :=$ Defective-Color(G, b, p, Λ)
    /* for $i = 1, 2, \dots, p$, let G_i be the graph induced by vertices of ψ-color i */
6:     $\Lambda' := \lfloor (\Lambda/(b \cdot p) + \Lambda/p) \cdot c + c \rfloor$ /* defect parameter of ψ */
7:     **for** $i = 1, 2, \dots, p$, in parallel **do**
8:         $(\varphi_i, \vartheta') :=$ Legal-Color$(G_i, b, p, \lambda, \Lambda')$
        /* recursive invocation that computes ϑ'-coloring φ_i of G_i */
9:         **if** $v \in V(G_i)$ **then**
10:             $\varphi(v) := \varphi_i(v) + (i - 1) \cdot \vartheta'$
11:             $\vartheta := \vartheta' \cdot p$
12:         **end if**
13:     **end for**
14: **end if**
15: **return** (φ, ϑ) /* return the legal coloring and the number of employed colors */

Let ϵ be an arbitrarily small positive constant. We execute Procedure Legal-Color on the input graph G of maximum degree Δ and neighborhood independence bounded by c, with the parameters $b = \lceil \Delta^{\epsilon/6} \rceil$, $p = \lceil \Delta^{\epsilon/3} \rceil$, $\lambda = \lceil \Delta^{\epsilon} \rceil$, $\Lambda = \Delta$. The running time analysis and the correctness proof of this invocation are provided in the next Lemmas.

Lemma 4.3. *Procedure Legal-Color invoked with the parameters* $b = \left\lceil \Delta^{\epsilon/6} \right\rceil, p = \left\lceil \Delta^{\epsilon/3} \right\rceil, \lambda = \lceil \Delta^{\epsilon} \rceil, \Lambda = \Delta$ *terminates in* $O(\Delta^{\epsilon} + \log^* n)$ *time.*

PROOF. In each recursion level it holds that

$$\Lambda' = \lfloor (\Lambda/(b \cdot p) + \Lambda/p) \cdot c + c \rfloor \leq$$

$$(\Lambda/\Delta^{\epsilon/2} + \Lambda/\Delta^{\epsilon/3}) \cdot c + c \leq 3 \cdot c \cdot \Lambda/\Delta^{\epsilon/3}. \quad (1)$$

Therefore, for a sufficiently large Δ, the number of recursion levels r satisfies

$$r \leq \log_{\Delta^{\epsilon/3}/3c} \Delta = \frac{\log \Delta}{\log(\Delta^{\epsilon/3}/3c)} = O(1). \quad (2)$$

(Recall that both ϵ and c are constants.)

By Lemma 3.3, each recursion level, except for the last one, requires $O(\Delta^{\epsilon} + \log^* n)$ time. (This running time is dominated by the time required for executing Procedure Defective-Color in line 5 of Algorithm 2.) By Lemma 2.1(2), the last recursion level, in which $\Lambda \leq \lambda$, requires $O(\lambda + \log^* n) = O(\Delta^{\epsilon} + \log^* n)$ time. Therefore, the overall running time is also $O(\Delta^{\epsilon} + \log^* n)$. $\square$

We remark that equation (1) in the proof of Lemma 4.3 holds for any (not necessarily constant) ϵ, $0 < \epsilon < 1$. On the other hand, for constant $\epsilon > 0$ this equation can be refined.

Lemma 4.4. *For any constant $\eta > 0$, for a sufficiently large Δ it holds that $\Lambda' \leq c \cdot (1 + \eta) \cdot \Lambda/\Delta^{\epsilon/3}$.*

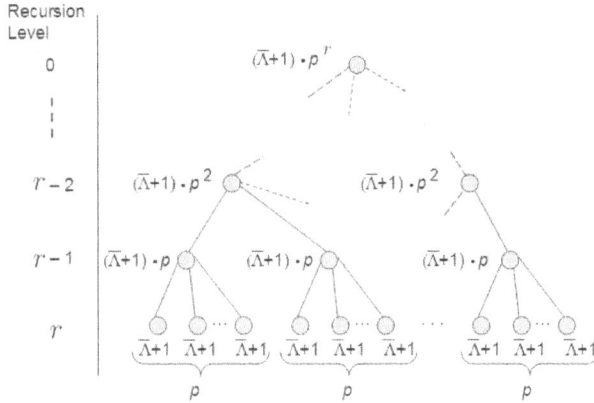

Fig. 1. *The recursion tree. For each node α, the value that appears near α in the figure represents the number of colors that are employed by the recursive invocation that corresponds to α.*

Lemma 4.5. *Procedure Legal-Color invoked with the parameters $b = \left\lceil \Delta^{\epsilon/6} \right\rceil, p = \left\lceil \Delta^{\epsilon/3} \right\rceil, \lambda = \lceil \Delta^{\epsilon} \rceil, \Lambda = \Delta$ computes a legal $O(\Delta)$-coloring.*

PROOF. Consider the recursion tree τ of Procedure Legal-Color invoked with the parameters $(G, b, p, \lambda, \Lambda)$, set as above. (See Figure 1.) With each node α of τ we associate the value Λ_α of the parameter Λ in the recursive invocation corresponding to α. By induction on the level i in the tree τ it can be shown that all nodes α of τ that have level i have the same value $\Lambda_\alpha = \Lambda^{(i)}$. The choice of parameters also

guarantees that $\Lambda = \Lambda^{(0)} > \Lambda^{(1)} > \Lambda^{(2)} > \ldots$. Let r be the smallest index such that $\Lambda^{(r)} \leq \lambda$. Denote $\Lambda^{(r)} = \hat{\Lambda}$. Observe that nodes α of level r in τ are the leaves of τ, and every leaf of τ has level r. Hence all leaves of τ have the same level. Moreover, it follows that in each of theses leaf-invocations α of τ, the corresponding subgraph $G[\alpha]$ is colored with at most $\Lambda^{(r)} + 1$ colors, and that each of these invocations returns $\vartheta^{(r)} = \Lambda^{(r)} + 1$. Hence, by induction on j, $j = 1, 2, \ldots, r$, for any two invocations α and β of the j'th level in the recursion tree τ, these two invocations return the same values of ϑ. (The induction base is the case $j = r$, and in the step we proceed from $j + 1$ to j, for $j \in \{2, 3, \ldots, r\}$.)

For $j \in \{1, 2, \ldots, r\}$, denote by $\vartheta^{(j)}$ the parameter ϑ returned by some invocation α of level j. Next, we argue, again by the induction on i with the base case $j = r$, that the ϑ-coloring φ returned by the invocation α is legal. The base case follows from Lemma 2.1(2). For the induction step let $G[\alpha]$ denote the subgraph of G on which the invocation of Procedure Legal-Color that corresponds to the node α is invoked. Also, denote by $G_1[\alpha], G_2[\alpha], \ldots, G_p[\alpha]$ the p subgraphs of $G[\alpha]$ that correspond to the p children of α. We remark that, in general, line 5 of Procedure Legal-Color may partition the graph $G[\alpha]$ into less than p subgraphs. In this case, however, the routine leaves $\vartheta^{(j+1)}$ empty color classes for each of the "missing" subgraphs. It does so by setting $\vartheta^{(j)} = p \cdot \vartheta^{(j+1)}$, even though it really needs a smaller palette. These redundant colors help to maintain uniform bounds on the number of colors used to color subgraphs of the same recursion level.

For each $i \in \{1, 2, \ldots, p\}$, vertices of $G_i[\alpha]$ are colored by colors from the palette $\{(i - 1) \cdot \vartheta^{(j+1)} + 1, (i - 1) \cdot \vartheta^{(j+1)} + 2, i \cdot \vartheta^{(j+1)}\}$. Thus, for a pair of vertices u, w, $u \in G_i[\alpha]$, $w \in G_{i'}[\alpha]$, $i \neq i'$, $i, i' \in \{1, 2, \ldots, p\}$, the invocation α colors them by distinct colors. (Denote these colors by $\varphi[\alpha](u)$ and $\varphi[\alpha](w)$, respectively. Then $\varphi[\alpha](u) \neq \varphi[\alpha](w)$.) Consider also the case that $u, w \in G_i[\alpha]$ belong to the same subgraph $G_i[\alpha]$ of G_i, and $(u, w) \in E$. By the induction hypothesis, the coloring $\varphi_i[\alpha]$ of $G_i[\alpha]$ returned by the i'th child invocation of α is legal. Hence $\varphi_i[\alpha](u) \neq \varphi_i[\alpha](w)$. Recall that $\varphi[\alpha](u) = \varphi_i[\alpha](u) + (i - 1) \cdot \vartheta^{(i+1)}$ and $\varphi[\alpha](w) = \varphi_i[\alpha](w) + (i - 1) \cdot \vartheta^{(i+1)}$, and so $\varphi[\alpha](u) \neq \varphi[\alpha](w)$, as required.

Finally, we provide an estimate on the number of colors $\vartheta = \vartheta^{(0)}$ employed by the coloring φ returned by the root invocation Legal-Color$(G, b, p, \lambda, \Lambda)$ of the recursion tree τ. We have already shown that $\vartheta^{(r)} = \Lambda^{(r)} = \hat{\Lambda} + 1$. Also, for any level j, $0 \leq j \leq r - 1$, $\vartheta^{(j)} = p \cdot \vartheta^{(j+1)}$. Hence the overall number of colors satisfies $\vartheta^{(0)} \leq \vartheta^{(r)} \cdot p^r = (\hat{\Lambda} + 1) \cdot p^r$. By equation (2) in proof of Lemma 4.3, it holds that
$r \leq \log(\Delta/\hat{\Lambda}) / \log(\Delta^{\epsilon/3}/3c) = O(1)$. (This is true for a constant $\epsilon > 0$.) Finally, for a sufficiently large Δ,

$$(\hat{\Lambda} + 1) \cdot p^r$$

$$\leq (\hat{\Lambda} + 1) \cdot \left\lceil \Delta^{\epsilon/3} \right\rceil^r \leq (\hat{\Lambda} + 1) \cdot (3c + 1)^r \cdot (\frac{\Delta^{\epsilon/3}}{3c})^r$$

$$\leq (\hat{\Lambda} + 1) \cdot (3c + 1)^r \cdot (\frac{\Delta^{\epsilon/3}}{3c})^{\frac{\log(\Delta/\hat{\Lambda})}{\log(\Delta^{\epsilon/3}/3c)}}$$

$$= (3c + 1)^r \cdot (\hat{\Lambda} + 1) \cdot (\Delta/\hat{\Lambda}) = O(\Delta),$$

since $c, r = O(1)$, and $\frac{\hat{\Lambda}+1}{\hat{\Lambda}} \leq 2$. Hence $\vartheta^{(0)} = O(\Delta)$, completing the proof. $\square$

It follows that for any constant $\epsilon > 0$, our algorithm computes an $O(\Delta)$-coloring of graphs with bounded neighborhood independence in time $O(\Delta^\epsilon + \log^* n)$. See also Theorem 4.2. Next, we show that one can compute a legal coloring of G much faster, at the expense of increasing the number of employed colors. To this end, one needs only to select different parameters for the invocation of Procedure Legal-Color.

Theorem 4.6. *For an arbitrarily small positive constant η, our algorithm computes an $O(\Delta^{1+\eta})$-coloring of graphs with bounded neighborhood independence, in time $O(\log \Delta \log^* n)$.*

PROOF. Let $t > 2$ be an arbitrarily large constant. Set $\lambda = (3c+1)^{6t}, b = \lambda^{1/3} = (3c+1)^{2t}, p = \lambda^{1/6} = (3c+1)^t, \Lambda = \Delta$. In each recursion level it holds that

$$\Lambda' = \lfloor (\Lambda/(b \cdot p) + \Lambda/p) \cdot c + c \rfloor$$

$$\leq (\Lambda/(3c+1)^{3t} + \Lambda/(3c+1)^t) \cdot c + c \leq 3 \cdot c \cdot \Lambda/(3c+1)^t.$$

Therefore, the number of recursion levels in this case is at most $r = \log_{(3c+1)^{t-1}} \Delta$. By Corollary 3.3, invoking Procedure Defective-Color on each level requires $O((3c+1)^{6t} + \log^* n) = O(\log^* n)$ time. Other steps of Algorithm 2, except for the recursive invocation step, are executed locally, and require zero time. Hence each recursion level (except for the bottom level) requires $O(\log^* n)$ time. On the bottom level of the recursion we invoke a $(\Lambda + 1)$-coloring algorithm from [4] on subgraphs of maximum degree at most Λ. (See Lemma 2.1(2).) This algorithm requires $O(\Lambda + \log^* n)$ time. Note that at the bottom line of the recursion $\Lambda \leq \lambda$, and $\lambda = (3c+1)^t = O(1)$ is a constant. Hence this running time is $O(\log^* n)$ as well. We conclude that the overall running time is $O(\log_{(3c+1)^{t-1}} \Delta \cdot \log^* n) = O(\log \Delta \log^* n)$.

The inductive proof of Lemma 4.5 is applicable as is also for the new selection of parameters. Hence, the produced coloring is legal. The number of colors in this case is at most

$$(\lambda + 1) \cdot p^r = ((3c+1)^{6t} + 1) \cdot (3c+1)^{(t-1) \cdot r} \cdot (3c+1)^r$$

$$\leq ((3c+1)^{6t} + 1) \cdot \Delta \cdot \Delta^{1/(t-1)} = O(\Delta^{1+1/(t-1)}).$$

Given a constant $\eta > 0$, set t to be sufficiently large so that $\frac{1}{t-1} < \eta$. Hence the number of colors is $O(\Delta^{1+\eta})$. $\square$

We remark that our algorithms can be modified to guarantee running time of $O(\log \Delta \cdot \frac{\log^* \Delta}{\log(\log^* \Delta)}) + \frac{1}{2} \log^* n$, while maintaining the same bound of $O(\Delta^{1+\epsilon})$ on the number of colors. Also, a $\Delta^{1+o(1)}$-coloring can be computed in $O((\log \Delta)^{1+\epsilon}) + \frac{1}{2} \log^* n$ time. See the full version of this paper [6]. Consequently, we achieve the following results.

Theorem 4.7. *For any constant $\epsilon > 0$, and a graph G with bounded neighborhood independence: (1) an $O(\Delta)$-coloring of G can be computed in $O(\Delta^\epsilon) + \frac{1}{2} \log^* n$ time,*
***(2)** an $O(\Delta^{1+\epsilon})$-coloring of G can be computed in $O(\log \Delta \frac{\log^* \Delta}{\log(\log^* \Delta)}) + \frac{1}{2} \log^* n$ time,*
***(3)** a $\Delta^{1+o(1)}$-coloring of G can be computed in $O((\log \Delta)^{1+\epsilon}) + \frac{1}{2} \log^* n$ time.*

5. LEGAL EDGE COLORING IN GENERAL GRAPHS

In this section we show that the techniques described in Sections 3 and 4 can be used to devise very efficient edge coloring algorithms for *general* graphs. First, observe that every line graph is claw-free, hence its neighborhood independence is at most 2

Lemma 5.1. *For a graph $G = (V, E)$, the line graph $L(G)$ has neighborhood independence bounded by 2.*

Observe also that Lemma 5.1 extends directly to line graphs of general r-hypergraphs. Specifically, for any hypergraph $\mathcal{H}$, the neighborhood independence of the line graph $L(\mathcal{H})$ is at most r. It follows that our results for graphs of bounded neighborhood independence (Theorem 4.7) apply to line graphs of r-hypergraphs, for any constant positive integer r.

Observe that, by definition, for any graph G and positive integer k, a legal k-coloring of *vertices* of $L(G)$ is a legal k-coloring of *edges* of G, and vice versa. Note also that for an edge $e = (u, w)$ in G, the number of edges incident to it is $(\deg(u) - 1) + (\deg(w) - 1)$. Hence the maximum degree $\Delta(L(G))$ of the line graph $L(G)$ satisfies $\Delta(L(G)) \leq 2(\Delta - 1)$, where $\Delta = \Delta(G)$. Consequently, if we are given a line graph $L(G)$ of a graph G with $\Delta(G) = \Delta$, our algorithm can compute an $O(\Delta(L(G))) = O(\Delta)$-vertex-coloring of $L(G)$ in $O(\Delta^\epsilon) + \frac{1}{2} \log^* n$ time, for any constant $\epsilon > 0$. Similarly, one can also compute $O(\Delta^{1+\eta})$-vertex-coloring (respectively, $\Delta^{1+o(1)}$-vertex-coloring) of $L(G)$ in $O(\log \Delta \frac{\log^* \Delta}{\log(\log^* \Delta)}) + \frac{1}{2} \log^* n$ (resp., $(\log \Delta)^{1+\zeta} + \frac{1}{2} \log^* n$) time, for $\eta, \zeta > 0$ being arbitrarily small positive constants. These vertex colorings give rise directly to edge coloring of G with the same number of colors.

On the other hand, in the distributed edge-coloring problem we are given as input the graph G, rather than its line graph $L(G)$. Nevertheless, one can simulate the distributed computation of an algorithm on $L(G)$ using the network $G = (V, E)$. To this end, each vertex of $L(G)$ is simulated by one endpoint of an appropriate edge in G. Consequently, a message sent over an edge of $L(G)$, will be sent over at most two (adjacent) edges in the simulation on G.

Lemma 5.2. *Any algorithm with running time T for the line graph $L(G)$ of the input graph G, can be simulated by G, and requires at most $2T + O(1)$ time.*

We apply Lemma 5.2 in conjunction with our results for vertex-coloring of $L(G)$, and obtain the following theorem.

Theorem 5.3. *For a graph $G = (V, E)$ with maximum degree Δ, and positive arbitrarily small constants $\epsilon, \eta, \zeta > 0$, our algorithm computes: (1) $O(\Delta)$-edge-coloring of G in $O(\Delta^\epsilon) + \frac{1}{2} \log^* n$ time,*
***(2)** $O(\Delta^{1+\eta})$-edge-coloring of G in $O(\log \Delta \frac{\log^* \Delta}{\log(\log^* \Delta)}) + \frac{1}{2} \log^* n$ time,*
***(3)** $\Delta^{1+o(1)}$-edge-coloring of G in $O((\log \Delta)^{1+\zeta}) + \frac{1}{2} \log^* n$ time.*

We remark that the simulation of a vertex-coloring algorithm on a line graph increases the size of messages by a factor of Δ. In the full version of this paper [6] we address this issue, and show that the result stated in Theorem 5.3 can be achieved with messages of size $O(\log n)$.

By Theorem 4.2 (using $c = 2$) we also get the following corollary.

Corollary 5.4. *For any constant $i = 1, 2, ...,$ and any arbitrarily small $\epsilon > 0$, a $((2^i + \epsilon) \cdot \Delta)$-edge-coloring of a graph with maximum degree Δ can be computed in $O(\Delta^{\frac{2}{2+i}} + \log^* n)$ time.*

6. CONCLUSION AND OPEN QUESTIONS

We showed that an $O(\Delta)$-edge-coloring can be computed in $O(\Delta^\epsilon + \log^* n)$ time, for an arbitrarily small $\epsilon > 0$. Specifically, a $((4 + \epsilon)\Delta)$-edge-coloring can be computed in $O(\Delta^{2/3} + \log^* n)$ time, a $((8 + \epsilon)\Delta)$-edge-coloring can be computed in $O(\Delta^{1/2} + \log^* n)$ time, etc'. Improving this tradeoff is an interesting open problem. Another challenging problem is to obtain an $O(\Delta)$-edge-coloring algorithm that requires polylogarithmic time. Our algorithm constructs a $\Delta^{1+o(1)}$-edge-coloring in polylogarithmic time.

Acknowledgements

The authors thank Alessandro Panconesi for sending them several papers and addressing their questions.

7. REFERENCES

[1] B. Awerbuch, A. V. Goldberg, M. Luby, and S. Plotkin. Network decomposition and locality in distributed computation. In *Proc. of the 30th Symposium on Foundations of Computer Science*, pages 364–369, 1989.

[2] J. Andrews, and M. Jacobson. On a generalization of a chromatic number. *Congressus Numer*, 47:33-48, 1985.

[3] L. Barenboim, and M. Elkin. Sublogarithmic distributed MIS algorithm for sparse graphs using Nash-Williams decomposition. In *Proc. of the 27th ACM Symp. on Principles of Distributed Computing*, pages 25–34, 2008.

[4] L. Barenboim, and M. Elkin. Distributed $(\Delta + 1)$-coloring in linear (in Δ) time. In *Proc. of the 41th ACM Symp. on Theory of Computing*, pages 111-120, 2009.

[5] L. Barenboim, and M. Elkin. Deterministic distributed vertex coloring in polylogarithmic time. In *Proc. of the 29th ACM Symp. on Principles of Distributed Computing*, pages 410-419, 2010.

[6] L. Barenboim, and M. Elkin. Distributed deterministic edge coloring using bounded neighborhood independence. *http://arXiv.org/abs/1010.2454*, 2010.

[7] M. Chudnovsky, and P. Seymour. The structure of claw-free graphs. *Surveys in Combinatorics 2005, London Math Soc. Lecture Note Series*, 327:153-171, 2005.

[8] L. Cowen, R. Cowen, and D. Woodall. Defective colorings of graphs in surfaces: partitions into subgraphs of bounded valence. *Journal of Grah Theory*, 10:187–195, 1986.

[9] L. Cowen, W. Goddard, and C. Jesurum. Coloring with defect. In *Proc. of the 8th ACM-SIAM Symp. on Discrete Algorithms, New Orleans, Louisiana, USA*, pages 548–557, January 1997.

[10] A. Czygrinow, M. Hanckowiak, and M. Karonski. Distributed $O(\Delta \log n)$-edge-coloring algorithm. In *Proc. of the 9th Annual European Symposium on Algorithms*, pages 345-355, 2001.

[11] D. Dubhashi, D. Grable, and A. Panconesi. Nearly-optimal, distributed edge-colouring via the nibble method. *Theoretical Computer Science*, 203:225–251, 1998.

[12] D. Durand, R. Jain, and D. Tseytlin. Applying randomized edge coloring algorithms to distributed communication: an experimental study. In *Proc. of the 7th Annual ACM Symposium on Parallel Algorithms and Architectures*, pages 264–274, 1995.

[13] B. Gfeller, and E. Vicari. A randomized distributed algorithm for the maximal independent set problem in growth-bounded graphs. In *Proc. of the 26th ACM Symp. on Principles of Distributed Computing*, pages 53–60, 2007.

[14] D. Grable, and A. Panconesi. Nearly optimal distributed edge coloring in $O(\log \log n)$ rounds *Random Structures and Algorithms*, 10(3):385–405, 1998.

[15] F. Harary, and K. Jones. Conditional colorability II: Bipartite variations. *Congressus Numer*, 50:205-218, 1985.

[16] R. Jain, K. Somalwar, J. Werth, and J. C. Browne. Scheduling parallel I/O operations in multiple bus systems. *ELSEVIER Journal of Parallel and Distributed Computing*, 16(4):352-362, 1992.

[17] F. Kuhn, T. Moscibroda, and R. Wattenhofer. On the Locality of Bounded Growth. In *Proc. of the 24rd ACM Symp. on Principles of Distributed Computing*, pages 60–68, 2005.

[18] K. Kothapalli, C. Scheideler, M. Onus, and C. Schindelhauer. Distributed coloring in $\tilde{O}(\sqrt{\log n})$ bit rounds. In *Proc. of the 20th International Parallel and Distributed Processing Symposium*, 2006.

[19] F. Kuhn. Weak graph colorings: distributed algorithms and applications. In *proc. of the 21st ACM Symposium on Parallel Algorithms and Architectures*, pages 138–144, 2009.

[20] F. Kuhn, and R. Wattenhofer. On the complexity of distributed graph coloring. In *Proc. of the 25th ACM Symp. on Principles of Distributed Computing*, pages 7–15, 2006.

[21] N. Linial. Locality in distributed graph algorithms. *SIAM Journal on Computing*, 21(1):193–201, 1992.

[22] N. Linial and M. Saks. Low diameter graph decomposition. *Combinatorica* 13: 441 - 454, 1993.

[23] A. Panconesi, and R. Rizzi. Some simple distributed algorithms for sparse networks. *Distributed computing*, 14(2):97–100, 2001.

[24] A. Panconesi, and A. Srinivasan. On the complexity of distributed network decomposition. *Journal of Algorithms*, 20(2):581-Ü592, 1995.

[25] A. Panconesi, and A. Srinivasan. Distributed edge coloring via an extension of the Chernoff-Hoeffding bounds. *SIAM J. on Computing*, 26(2):350–368, 1997.

[26] M. Szegedy, and S. Vishwanathan. Locality based graph coloring. In *Proc. 25th ACM Symposium on Theory of Computing*, pages 201-207, 1993.

[27] J. Schneider, and R. Wattenhofer. A log-star distributed Maximal Independent Set algorithm for Growth Bounded Graphs. In *Proc. of the 27th ACM Symp. on Principles of Distributed Computing*, pages 35–44, 2008.

[28] J. Schneider, and R. Wattenhofer. A new technique for distributed symmetry breaking. To appear in *Proc. of the 29th ACM Symp. on Principles of Distributed Computing*, 2010.

[29] V. G. Vizing. On an estimate of the chromatic class of a p-graph. *Diskret Analiz*, 3:25–30, 1964.

The Space Complexity of Long-lived and One-Shot Timestamp Implementations

[Extended Abstract]

Maryam Helmi
Dept. of Computer Science
University of Calgary
Calgary, T2N1N4 Alberta, Canada
mhelmikh@ucalgary.ca

Lisa Higham[*]
Dept. of Computer Science
University of Calgary
Calgary, T2N1N4 Alberta,
Canada
higham@ucalgary.ca

Eduardo Pacheco
Universidad Nacional
Autónoma de México
04510, México D.F.
pacheco_e@
uxmcc2.iimas.unam.mx

Philipp Woelfel[*]
Dept. of Computer Science
University of Calgary
Calgary, T2N1N4 Alberta,
Canada
woelfel@ucalgary.ca

ABSTRACT

This paper is concerned with the problem of implementing an unbounded timestamp object from multi-writer atomic registers, in an asynchronous distributed system of n processors with distinct identifiers where timestamps are taken from an arbitrary universe. Ellen, Fatourou and Ruppert [7] showed that $\sqrt{n}/2 - O(1)$ registers are required for any obstruction-free implementation of long-lived timestamp systems from atomic registers (meaning processors can repeatedly get timestamps).

We improve this existing lower bound in two ways. First we establish a lower bound of $n/6 - O(1)$ registers for the obstruction-free long-lived timestamp problem. Previous such linear lower bounds were only known for constrained versions of the timestamp problem. This bound is asymptotically tight; Ellen, Fatourou and Ruppert [7] constructed a wait-free algorithm that uses $n-1$ registers. Second we show that $\sqrt{n} - O(1)$ registers are required for any obstruction-free implementation of one-shot timestamp systems (meaning each processor can get a timestamp at most once). We show that this bound is also asymptotically tight by providing a wait-free one-shot timestamp system that uses fewer than $2\sqrt{n}$ registers, thus establishing a space complexity gap between one-shot and long-lived timestamp systems.

---

[*]Supported by Discovery Grants from the Natural Sciences and Research Council of Canada (NSERC)

Categories and Subject Descriptors

F.2.2 [**Analysis of Algorithms and Problem Complexity**]: Nonnumerical Algorithms and Problems; D.1.3 [**Programming Techniques**]: Concurrent Programming—*Distributed programming*

General Terms

Algorithms, Theory

Keywords

Timestamps, Solo-termination, Wait-free, Space Complexity, Shared Memory

1. INTRODUCTION

In asynchronous multiprocessor algorithms, processes have no information about the real-time order of events that are incurred by other processes. In order to solve distributed problems effectively, such as ensuring first-come-first-served fairness, or constructing synchronization primitives, it is often necessary that some reliable information about the relative order of these events can be gained.

Timestamp objects provide a means for processes to label events and then later compare those labels in order to gain information about the real-time order in which the corresponding events have occurred. Such timestamping mechanisms have been used to solve numerous problems associated with asynchrony in distributed shared memory and message passing algorithms. Examples of applications include mutual and k-exclusion algorithms [17, 21, 10, 2], consensus algorithms [1], register constructions [13, 19, 23], or adaptive renaming algorithms [3].

In 1978, Lamport [18] defined the "happens before" relation on events occurring in message passing systems to reflect the causal relationship of events. The happens before relation is a partial order, where, informally, an event e_1 happens before event e_2, if there is a causal relation that forces event e_1 to precede e_2. Lamport further devised a *logical clock* that assigns an integer value $C(e)$, called a timestamp, to each event e such that $C(e_1) < C(e_2)$ if event e_1 happens before event e_2. Lamport's logical clock system based on integers was extended to clocks based on vectors (e.g., Fidge [9] and Mattern [20]) and matrices (Wuu and Bernstein [24] and Sarin and Lynch [22]).

In shared memory systems, events correspond to method invocations and responses. The happens before relation orders time intervals associated with method calls. Method call m_1 happens before method call m_2, if the response of m_1 precedes the invocation of m_2. Timestamp objects provide a mechanism to label events with timestamps from a *timestamp universe* $\mathcal{T}$ through getTS() (sometimes called timestamping or label) method calls. If $\mathcal{T}$ is finite, then the timestamp object is said to be *bounded*, otherwise it is *unbounded*.

Often, $\mathcal{T}$ is a partially ordered set, and all timestamps returned by getTS() method calls during an execution preserve the happens before relation of these method calls. Such timestamp objects are called *static*. Non-static timestamp objects can take the current system state into account when comparing the order of two timestamps. Thus, different executions can lead to different partial orders of the set $\mathcal{T}$. Sometimes, in particular when $\mathcal{T}$ is bounded, the happens before relation is only preserved for a subset of *valid* timestamps in $\mathcal{T}$, e.g., the set of the last timestamps obtained by each process. In this case, timestamp objects often provide a scan method that returns an ordered list of all valid timestamps. The literature contains several examples of constructions of bounded and unbounded timestamp objects [17, 11, 16, 15, 5, 6, 13, 3, 12, 7].

Ellen, Fatourou, and Rupert [7] studied the number of atomic registers needed to implement timestamp objects. In order to prove strong lower bounds, the authors considered a very weak definition of an unbounded non-static timestamp object, that, in addition to getTS() provides a method compare(t_1, t_2) for two timestamps $t_1, t_2 \in \mathcal{T}$. The only requirement is that if a getTS() method g_1 that returns t_1 happens before another getTS() method g_2 that returns t_2 then any later compare(t_1, t_2) must return true and any later compare(t_2, t_1) must return false.

As their main result, Ellen etal. showed that any implementation that satisfies non-deterministic solo-termination (a progress condition weaker than wait-freedom or obstruction freedom, and that is defined in Section 2) requires at least $\frac{1}{2}\sqrt{n-1}$ registers, where n is the number of processes in the system. Despite the weak requirements, the best known algorithm (also in [7]) needs $n-1$ registers, leaving a large gap between the best known lower and upper bounds. However, for two stronger versions of the problem, Ellen etal. obtain tight lower bounds, showing that n registers are necessary, first, for static algorithms, where $\mathcal{T}$ is *nowhere dense* (i.e., any two elements $x, y \in \mathcal{T}$ satisfy $|\{z \in \mathcal{T} | x < z < y\}| < \infty$), and, second, for anonymous algorithms.

Our Contributions

We distinguish between *one-shot* timestamp objects, where each process is allowed to call getTS() at most once, and *long-lived* ones, where each process can call getTS() arbitrarily many times. (In either case, the number of compare methods calls is not restricted.) We first improve the $\Omega(\sqrt{n})$

lower bound of [7] for long-lived timestamp objects to an asymptotically tight one:

THEOREM 1.1. *Any long-lived unbounded timestamp object that satisfies non-deterministic solo-termination uses at least $n/6 - 1$ registers.*

Therefore, even under very weak assumptions, at least linear register space is necessary. Since it is not possible to implement general timestamp objects using sublinear space, it makes sense to look at restricted solutions.

Several methods have solutions that are simpler than the general case, if each process is allowed to execute it only once. Examples are renaming and mutual exclusion algorithms, splitter or snapshot objects, or agreement problems. Other problems, such as consensus or non-resettable test and set objects are inherently "one-time". It is conceivable that if an implementation of such an algorithm uses timestamp objects, then in the "one-shot" version of that algorithm each process needs to obtain a timestamp only once. Therefore, we study the space complexity of one-shot timestamp objects:

THEOREM 1.2. *There is a wait-free implementation of one-shot timestamp objects that uses $2\sqrt{n}$ registers, and any one-shot unbounded timestamp object that satisfies non-deterministic solo-termination uses at least $\sqrt{n} - O(1)$ registers.*

This lower bound is a factor of 2 larger than the previous best known lower bound for the long-lived case [7], and holds for historyless objects as well as registers as explained later.

Our proofs are based on covering arguments (as introduced by Burns and Lynch [4]), where one constructs an execution in which processes are poised to write to some registers (the processes are said to *cover* these registers). We rely heavily on a lemma by Ellen etal. [7] that shows how in a situation where some processes cover a set R of registers, other processes can be forced to write outside of R. In order to obtain our improved lower bound for the long-lived case, we look at very long executions in which "similar" coverings are obtained over and over again. Our lower bound proof for the one-shot case is inspired by a geometric interpretation of the covering structure of configurations. The one-shot timestamps upper bound exploits the structure exposed by the lower bound.

2. PRELIMINARIES

We consider an asynchronous shared memory system with a set $\mathcal{P} = \{p_1, \ldots, p_n\}$ of n processes and a set $\mathcal{R} = \{r_1, \ldots, r_m\}$ of m registers that support atomic read and write operations. Processes can only communicate via those operations on shared registers. We assume that processes can make arbitrary non-deterministic decisions, but we require that the result of any execution is correct, i.e., that the responses from method calls match the specification of timestamp objects.

A *configuration* C is a tuple $(s_1, \ldots, s_n, v_1, \ldots, v_m)$, denoting that process p_i, $1 \le i \le n$, is in state s_i, and register r_j, $1 \le j \le m$, has value v_j. Configurations will be denoted by capital letters, and the initial configuration is denoted C^*.

An implementation of a method satisfies *non-deterministic solo-termination*, if for any configuration

C and any process p_i, $1 \leq i \leq n$, there is an execution in which no process other than p_i takes any steps, and p_i finishes its method call within a finite number of steps [8]. Hence, a process is guaranteed to finish its method call with positive probability, whenever there is no interference from other processes. For deterministic algorithms, non-deterministic solo-termination is the same as obstruction freedom and weaker than wait-freedom. Both our lower bound results hold for timestamp objects that satisfy this progress condition, our algorithm, however, satisfies the stronger wait-free progress property.

A *schedule* σ is a (possibly infinite) sequence of process indices. We denote the empty schedule by ε. An *execution* $(C; \sigma)$ is a sequence of steps beginning in configuration C and moving through successive configurations one at a time. At each step, the next process p_i indicated in the schedule σ, takes the next step in its program. Since our computation model is non-deterministic, we fix the non-deterministic decision made by p_i in our lower bound proofs. We use an arbitrary (but fixed) one that guarantees that p_i terminates within a bounded number of steps in a solo execution. If σ is a finite schedule, the final configuration of the execution $(C; \sigma)$ is denoted $\sigma(C)$.

A configuration, C, is *reachable* if there exists a finite schedule, σ, such that $\sigma(C^*) = C$. If σ and π are finite schedules then $\sigma\pi$ denotes the concatenation of σ and π. Let P be a set of processes, and σ a schedule. We say σ is P-*only* if only indices of processes in P appear in σ.

Any execution $(C; \sigma)$ defines a partial *happens before* order "$\rightarrow$" on the method calls that occur during $(C; \sigma)$. A method call m_1 happens before m_2, denoted $m_1 \rightarrow m_2$, if the response of m_1 occurs before the invocation of m_2.

An unbounded timestamp object supports two methods, `getTS()` and `compare()`. The first one outputs a *timestamp* without receiving any input; the `compare` method receives any two timestamps as inputs, and returns true or false. If two `getTS()` instances g_1 and g_2 return t_1 and t_2, respectively, and $g_1 \rightarrow g_2$, then `compare`(t_1, t_2) returns true and `compare`(t_2, t_1) returns false.

A timestamp object is *long-lived*, if each process is allowed to invoke `getTS()` multiple times, and it is *one-shot* when each process is allowed to invoke `getTS()` only once.

Our lower bounds are based on covering arguments. We will construct executions, at the end of which processes are poised to write, i.e., they *cover* several registers. If other process are scheduled after this and if they write only to the same set of registers, their trace can be eliminated. More precisely, we say process p_i *covers* register r_j in a configuration C, if there is a non-deterministic decision δ, such that the one step execution $(C; (i))$ is a write to register r_j. A set of processes P covers a set of registers R if for every register $r \in R$ there is a process $p \in P$ such that p covers r.

For a process set P, let π_P denote an arbitrary (but fixed) permutation of P (for example the one that orders processes by their ID). If the process set P covers the register set R in configuration C, the information held in the registers in R can be overwritten by letting all processes in P execute exactly one step. Such an execution by the processes in P is called a *block-write*. More precisely, a *block-write* by P to R is an execution $(C; \pi_P)$.

Two configurations $C_1 = (s_1, \ldots, s_n, r_1, \ldots, r_m)$ and $C_2 = (s'_1, \ldots, s'_n, r'_1, \ldots, r'_m)$ are *indistinguishable* to process p_i if $s_i = s'_i$ and $r_j = r'_j$ for $1 \leq j \leq n$.

Both our lower bounds use a core lemma, due to Ellen, Fatourou, and Rupert [7], which is based on the following observation. Suppose in configuration C there are three disjoint sets of processes B_0, B_1, B_2, each covering a set R of registers, and p_0 and p_1 are processes not in $B_0 \cup B_1 \cup B_2$. Let σ_i, $i \in \{0, 1\}$, denote an arbitrarily long $\{p_i\}$-only schedule. If, for $i \in \{0, 1\}$, in the execution $(C; \pi_{B_i} p_i)$, p_i does not write outside R, then the configurations $\pi_{B_i} p_i(C)$ and $\pi_{B_{i-1}} p_{i-1} \pi_{B_i} p_i(C)$ are indistiguishable to p_i. Furthermore, after a subseqent third block write by B_2 all trace left inside of R can also be obliterated. Thus, the configurations $C_0 = \pi_{B_0} \sigma_0 \pi_{B_1} \sigma_1 \pi_{B_2}(C)$ and $C_1 = \pi_{B_1} \sigma_1 \pi_{B_0} \sigma_0 \pi_{B_2}(C)$ are indistinguishable to all processes, unless either p_0 or p_1 writes outside R in one of these executions. If, however, the solo executions by p_0 and p_1 both contain complete `getTS()` calls, then one happens after the other and so processes have to be able to distinguish between C_0 and C_1. Hence, either p_0 or p_1 writes outside R in one of the executions.

The same idea works if we replace p_0 and p_1 with disjoint sets of processes. This observation leads to the main lemma [7], which we restate here using the form and notation of this paper.

LEMMA 2.1 ([7]). *Consider any timestamp implementation from registers that satisfies non-deterministic solo-termination and let C be a reachable configuration. Let B_0, B_1, B_2, U_0, U_1 be disjoint sets of processes, where in C each of B_0, B_1, and B_2 cover a set R of registers. Then there exists $i \in \{0, 1\}$ such that every U_i-only execution starting from $C_i = \pi_{B_i}(C)$ that contains a complete* `getTS()` *method writes to some register not in R.*

3. A SPACE LOWER BOUND FOR LONG-LIVED TIMESTAMPS

We assume that a timestamp object is used in an algorithm where each process calls `getTS()` infinitely many times. Actually, the number of `getTS()` calls can be bounded (by a function growing exponentially in n), but for convenience we pass on computing this bound. Ellen etal. used their core lemma in order to inductively construct executions at the end of which k registers are covered by $\Omega(\sqrt{n} - k)$ processes, where k is bounded by $O(\sqrt{n})$. The lemma is used in the inductive step to show that in some execution following a block-write, many of the non-covering processes can be forced to write outside the set of covered registers. By the pigeon hole principle, one additional (previously not covered) register can then be covered with many processes. With this idea, however, the number of processes covering one register is reduced by one in each inductive step, and thus it is not hard to see that the technique cannot lead to a lower bound beyond $\Omega(\sqrt{n})$.

In our proof, rather than requiring that many processes cover the same register, we limit the number of processes covering the same register to three. In particular, we define a $(3, k)$-configuration to be one where k processes are covering registers, but no register is covered by more than three of them. We argue that if there is an execution that leads to some $(3, k)$-configuration, we can find a (much longer) execution, during which at least two $(3, k)$-configurations C_1 and C_2 are encountered that are similar in the sense that in both configurations each register is covered by the same number of processes. In addition, the execution $(C_1; \sigma)$ that leads from C_1 to C_2 starts with three block-writes to the registers that are covered by three processes, each. We then apply Lemma 2.1 to see that we can insert a p-only execution for some unused process p into the schedule σ after one of the block-writes, such that at the end of this new execution $(C_1; \sigma')$ process p is poised to write outside of the registers that are 3-covered in C_1. Since the other two block-writes are overwriting p's trace in σ', no process (other than p) can distinguish between $\sigma'(C_1)$ and $\sigma(C_1) = C_2$. It follows that in $\sigma'(C_1)$ process p covers a register that is covered by at most 2 other processes. Hence, we have obtained a $(3, k+1)$-configuration. We can do this for $k \leq n/2$, so in the end we obtain a $(3, \lfloor n/2 \rfloor)$-configuration. Clearly, this means that the number of registers is at least $\lfloor n/6 \rfloor$.

The signature of a configuration C, denoted $\text{sig}(C)$, is a tuple $(c_1, c_2, \ldots, c_m)$ where every c_i is the number of processes covering the i-th register in C. The set of registers whose corresponding entry in $\text{sig}(C)$ is equal to 3 is denoted $\mathcal{R}_3(C)$. (In terms of signatures, a configuration C is a $(3, k)$-configuration if $\text{sig}(C) = (c_1, c_2, \ldots, c_m)$ satisfies $\sum_{i=1}^{m} c_i = k$ and $c_i \leq 3$ for every $1 \leq i \leq m$.) Notice that in any $(3, k)$-configuration there are at least $\lceil k/3 \rceil$ registers covered. Configuration C is *quiescent* if in C no process has started but not finished executing a `getTS()` or `compare()` call.

LEMMA 3.1. *Let P be an arbitrary set of processes. Suppose for every reachable quiescent configuration D there exists a P-only schedule σ such that $\sigma(D)$ is a $(3, k)$-configuration. Then for any quiescent configuration D, there are two $(3, k)$-configurations C_0 and C_1, and P-only schedules γ_0, γ_1, and η such that:*

(a) $\gamma_0(D) = C_0$,   (b) $\gamma_1(C_0) = C_1$,   (c) $\text{sig}(C_0) = \text{sig}(C_1)$, and

(d) $\gamma_1 = \pi_{B_0} \pi_{B_1} \pi_{B_2} \eta$, where B_0, B_1 and B_2 are disjoint sets of processes each covering $\mathcal{R}_3(C_0)$.

PROOF. We inductively define an infinite sequence of schedules $\lambda_0, \delta_0, \lambda_1, \delta_1, \ldots, \lambda_i, \delta_i, \ldots$ and reachable $(3, k)$-configurations $E_0, E_1, E_2, \ldots$, where $E_{i+1} = \lambda_i \delta_i(E_i)$, as follows. E_0 is the $(3, k)$-configuration $\sigma(D)$ guaranteed by the hypothesis of the lemma. Let $B_{0,i}, B_{1,i}$ and $B_{2,i}$ be disjoint sets of processes each covering $\mathcal{R}_3(E_i)$. Execution $(E_i; \pi_{B_{0,i}} \pi_{B_{1,i}} \pi_{B_{2,i}})$ consists of three consecutive block-writes to $\mathcal{R}_3(E_i)$ by the processes in $B_{0,i}$, $B_{1,i}$, and $B_{2,i}$, respectively. Schedule λ_i is the concatenation of the sequence of permutations $\pi_{B_{0,i}} \pi_{B_{1,i}} \pi_{B_{2,i}}$ and some P-only schedule r_i in which every process in P with a pending operation, finishes that pending operation. Thus, configuration $\lambda_i(E_i) = \pi_{B_{0,i}} \pi_{B_{1,i}} \pi_{B_{2,i}} r_i(E_i)$ is quiescent. So by the hypothesis there exists a schedule δ_i such that $E_{i+1} = \lambda_i \delta_i(E_i)$ is again a $(3, k)$-configuration.

Since the set of signatures is finite, there are two indices $j < k$, such that $\text{sig}(E_j) = \text{sig}(E_k)$. Fix two such indices j and k. Let $\gamma_0 = \sigma \lambda_0 \delta_0 \lambda_1 \delta_1 \lambda_2 \delta_2 \ldots \lambda_{j-1} \delta_{j-1}$ and $\gamma_1 = \lambda_j \delta$ where $\delta = \delta_j \lambda_{j+1} \delta_{j+1} \ldots \lambda_{k-1} \delta_{k-1}$. Furthermore, let $C_0 = \gamma_0(D)$ and $C_1 = \gamma_1(C_0)$. By definition, the configurations C_0 and C_1 satisfy (a) and (b). Moreover, by construction $C_0 = E_j$ and $C_1 = E_k$ and since $\text{sig}(E_j) = \text{sig}(E_k)$, (c) is satisfied. Finally, let $\eta = r_j \delta$. Then, $\gamma_1 = \pi_{B_{0,j}} \pi_{B_{1,j}} \pi_{B_{2,j}} \eta$, where $B_{0,j}, B_{1,j}, B_{2,j}$ are disjoint sets of processes each covering $\mathcal{R}_3(E_j) = \mathcal{R}_3(C_0)$. This proves (d). $\square$

Let $\mathcal{P}_k$ denote the set $\{p_1, \ldots, p_k\}$ and P_0 denote the emptyset of processes.

LEMMA 3.2. *For every $0 \leq k \leq \lceil (n-1)/2 \rceil$ and for every reachable quiescent configuration D, there exists a $\mathcal{P}_{2k}$-only schedule σ_k such that $\sigma_k(D)$ is a $(3, k)$-configuration.*

PROOF. The proof is by induction on k. For $k = 0$ the claim is immediate by choosing σ_0 to be the empty schedule.

Let $k \geq 1$, and let D be an arbitrary reachable quiescent configuration. By the induction hypothesis, for every reachable quiescent configuration C, there exists a $\mathcal{P}_{2k-2}$-only schedule σ_{k-1}, such that $\sigma_{k-1}(C)$ is a $(3, k-1)$-configuration. Hence, by Lemma 3.1 with $P = \mathcal{P}_{2k-2}$ there are two reachable configurations C_0 and C_1, and $\mathcal{P}_{2k-2}$-only schedules γ_0, γ_1, and η, such that $\gamma_0(D) = C_0$, $\gamma_1(C_0) = C_1$, $\text{sig}(C_0) = \text{sig}(C_1)$, and $\gamma_1 = \pi_{B_0} \pi_{B_1} \pi_{B_2} \eta$, where B_0, B_1 and B_2 are disjoint sets of processes, each covering $\mathcal{R}_3(C_0)$.

Consider the two processes p_{2k-1} and p_{2k}. For $i \in \{0, 1\}$, let α_i be a $\{p_{2k-i}\}$-only schedule starting in $\pi_{B_i}(C_0)$, in which p_{2k-i} performs a complete `getTS()` instance. According to Lemma 2.1, there exists $i \in \{0, 1\}$, such that p_{2k-i} writes to some register not in $\mathcal{R}_3(C_0)$ during its p_{2k-i}-only execution $(\pi_{B_i}(C_0); \alpha_i)$. (Note that whether $i = 0$ or $i = 1$ depends on C_0.) Let r be the first register not in $\mathcal{R}_3(C_0)$ to which p_{2k-i} writes to in $(\pi_{B_i}(C_0); \alpha_i)$. Since $\text{sig}(C_0) = \text{sig}(C_1)$, we have $r \notin \mathcal{R}_3(C_1)$, and thus r is covered by at most two processes in C_0 as well as in C_1.

Let λ be the shortest prefix of α_i such that p_{2k-i} is about to write to r in $\pi_{B_i} \lambda(C_0)$. Since p_{2k-i} does not participate in schedule $\pi_{B_{1-i}} \pi_{B_2} \eta$, it is also covering r in the configuration $\pi_{B_i} \lambda \pi_{B_{1-i}} \pi_{B_2} \eta(C_0)$. Configurations $\pi_{B_i} \pi_{B_{1-i}} \pi_{B_2}(C_0)$ and $\pi_{B_{1-i}} \pi_{B_i} \pi_{B_2}(C_0)$ are indistinguishable to all processes; therefore, $\pi_{B_i} \pi_{B_{1-i}} \pi_{B_2} \eta(C_0) = C_1$. Moreover, since $C_1 = \pi_{B_0} \pi_{B_1} \pi_{B_2} \eta(C_0)$ is indistinguishable from $\pi_{B_i} \lambda \pi_{B_{1-i}} \pi_{B_2} \eta(C_0)$ to every process except p_{2k-i}, all processes other than p_{2k-i} cover the same registers in C_1 as in $\pi_{B_i} \lambda \pi_{B_{1-i}} \pi_{B_2} \eta(C_0)$. Since p_{2k-i} covers r in this configuration, and r is covered by at most 2 other processes, $\pi_{B_i} \lambda \pi_{B_{1-i}} \pi_{B_j} \eta(C_0)$ is a $(3, k)$-configuration. $\square$

Lemma 3.2 shows that in any long-lived unbounded timestamp implementation that satisfies non-deterministic solo-termination there exists a reachable $(3, \lceil (n-1)/2 \rceil)$-configuration. Clearly, at least $\lceil (n-1)/6 \rceil = n/6 - O(1)$ registers are covered in this configuration. This proves Theorem 1.1.

4. THE SPACE COMPLEXITY OF ONE-SHOT TIMESTAMPS

It seems natural to imagine that n registers would be required to construct a timestamp system for n processes. But this is not the case for some restricted versions of the problem. For example, if the timestamps are not required to come from a nowhere dense set, then, as shown by Ellen, Fatourou and Ruppert [7], $n-1$ registers suffice. Another instance is when each process is restricted to at most one call to the `getTS()` method. In this case $\Theta(\sqrt{n})$ registers are necessary and sufficient, as we establish below. We first prove the lower bound, and then, in Section 4.2, the (asymptotically) matching upper bound.

4.1 Lower Bound

Let $\ell = \lfloor \sqrt{n} \rfloor - 1$. We show that any one-shot timestamp system that satisfies non-deterministic solo-termination requires at least $\ell - 1$ shared registers. We assume w.l.o.g. that

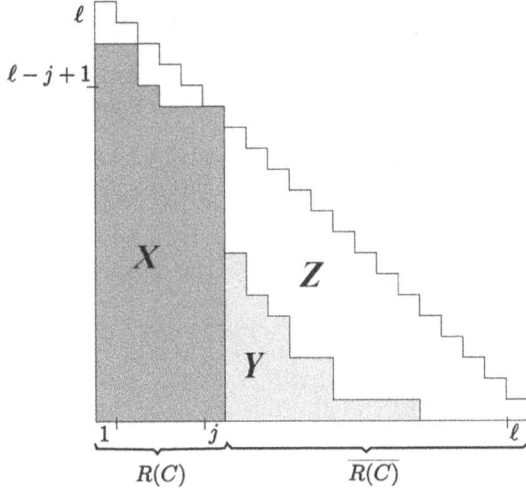

Figure 1: A constrained full configuration C, **with** $\text{fullpt}(C) = j$. **Area** Y **represents the processes poised on** $\overline{R(C)}$ **and Area** $Y \cup Z$ **is the target area of** C.

the distributed system provides a at least ℓ registers. Then for an arbitrary one-shot timestamp algorithm, we construct an execution at the end of which a configuration C_{last} is reached in which $\ell - 1$ shared registers are covered by processes.

We begin with some definitions concerning configurations. The *ordered-signature of a configuration* C, denoted $\text{ordSig}(C)$, is the ℓ-tuple $(c_1, c_2, \ldots, c_\ell)$ where $c_i \geq c_{i+1}$, and there is a permutation α of $\{1, \ldots, \ell\}$ such that for $1 \leq i \leq \ell$, c_i processes are covering the $\alpha(i)$-th register. Notice that the ordered-signature of a configuration is just its signature with the entries of the ℓ-tuple reordered so that they are non-increasing. For configuration C with $\text{ordSig}(C) = (c_1, \ldots, c_\ell)$, C is *constrained* if $c_i \leq \ell - i + 1$ for every $1 \leq i \leq \ell$. C is a *full configuration* if there is a j, $1 \leq j \leq \ell$, satisfying $c_j = \ell - j + 1$. The largest such j is called the *full-point* of C and is denoted $\text{fullpt}(C)$. If C is not full, then we define $\text{fullpt}(C) = 0$. If $\text{fullpt}(C) = j$, then there are j registers each covered by at least $\ell - j + 1$ processes. Denote this set of registers by $R(C)$, the set $\mathcal{R} - R(C)$ by $\overline{R(C)}$, and the value $\ell - j + 1$ by $\text{blockHeight}(C)$. Thus,

$$\text{blockHeight}(C) = |\overline{R(C)}| + 1. \tag{1}$$

Define $\text{targetSize}(C) = \sum_{i=1}^{\ell - \text{fullpt}(C)} i = (\ell - \text{fullpt}(C) + 1)(\ell - \text{fullpt}(C))/2$. For this proof, each configuration C that we use will be reached at the end of some unique execution $E_C = (C^*, \gamma_C)$ for some schedule γ_C that we construct below. We use $\text{avail}(C)$ to denote the set of *available* processes which contains just those processes that have not yet initiated a $\texttt{getTS()}$ method in the execution E_C. For a set of registers $R \subseteq \mathcal{R}$, $\text{poised}(C, R)$ denotes the number of processes in configuration C that are covering some register in R.

Intuition for these definitions and for our proof is aided by a geometric interpretation of constrained and full configurations. Let $\text{ordSig}(C) = (c_1, \ldots c_\ell)$. C is represented on a triangular grid of cells with a total of $\sum_{i=1}^{\ell} i = \ell(\ell+1)/2 < n/2 - \lfloor \sqrt{n/2} \rfloor$ cells, as in Figure 1.

For each $1 \leq j \leq \ell$, the lower c_j cells in column j are

shaded, to represent the processes that are covering the corresponding register. Since C is constrained, all shaded cells are within the triangular grid. If C is constrained and full with $\text{fullpt}(C) = j$, then the shaded cells reach to the boundary of the grid at column j and the shaded cells in all columns up to and including position j have height at least $\text{blockHeight}(C) = \ell - j + 1$ (Area X) and for all columns at position $k > j$ (Area $Y \cup Z$) have height at most $\ell - k$. The value $\text{targetSize}(C)$ is the number of cells in the triangular grid that are in columns with indices greater than $\text{fullpt}(C)$. Call this collection of cells (Area $Y \cup Z$) the *target area* of C. The value $\text{poised}(C, \overline{R(C)})$ is the number of shaded cells in the triangular grid that are in columns with indices greater than $\text{fullpt}(C)$ (Area Y). (For the rest of this proof, parenthetical remarks are used to describe interpretation of the construction and proof using the grid diagram.)

The proof proceeds by inductively constructing a sequence of constrained full configurations $(C_1, C_2, \ldots, C_{\text{last}})$ where $\text{fullpt}(C_i) < \text{fullpt}(C_{i+1})$ for $1 \leq i < \text{last}$, C_1 is reachable from the initial configuration, $C_0 := C^*$, and each subsequent configuration is reachable from its predecessor.

To move from C_0 to C_1, we repeatedly select one process from $\text{avail}(C_0)$, run it until it covers some shared register and then pause it. This is repeated until a full configuration is reached for the first time. For any reachable configuration C such that there are at least two processes $p, p' \in \text{avail}(C)$, one of p and p' must write to some shared register if it executes a complete $\texttt{getTS()}$ in a solo execution starting from C. This is immediate from Lemma 2.1 for $B_0 = B_1 = B_2 = \emptyset$ and $U_0 = \{p\}$ and $U_1 = \{p'\}$. So a full configuration is assured because $\text{targetSize}(C_0) < n - 1$. (The area of the grid is less than $n - 1$.) Since we stop at the first full configuration, C_1 is also constrained.

To move from constrained full configuration C_i to a new constrained full configuration C_{i+1} with a larger full-point, for $i \geq 1$, we invoke Lemma 2.1. This lemma guarantees that if each register in $R(C_i)$ is covered by at least 3 processes, there is a block-write to $R(C_i)$ such that up to half of the processes in $\text{avail}(C_i)$ can be made to begin executing $\texttt{getTS()}$ methods and can be manipulated to cover registers in $\overline{R(C_i)}$. Therefore, provided $\text{blockHeight}(C_i) \geq 3$, partition $\text{avail}(C_i)$ into two sets with sizes differing by at most 1, and choose a block write schedule, say β_i, and one of the two partitions of $\text{avail}(C_i)$, say $A(C_i)$, that are guaranteed by Lemma 2.1. Starting from configuration $\beta_i(C_i)$, run each process in $A(C_i)$ one after another pausing each when it first covers a register in $\overline{R(C_i)}$. (In terms of the grid diagram, processes in $A(C_i)$ move one at a time out of $\text{avail}(C_i)$ onto an unshaded cell in the target area and causing it to become shaded.) Let γ_i be such a schedule. Define σ_i to be the shortest prefix of γ_i such that $\beta_i \sigma_i(C_i)$ is full, if such a prefix exists. If there is no such prefix of γ_i or $\text{blockHeight}(C_i) \leq 2$, then the construction is terminated and we let $\text{last} = i$ (and in particular $C_{\text{last}} = C_i$). If $\text{blockHeight}(C_i) \geq 3$ and σ_i exists, we define $C_{i+1} = \beta_i \sigma_i(C_i)$, and repeat the inductive construction for C_{i+1}.

Since C_i is constrained and full, each register in $R(C_i)$ is covered by at least $\text{blockHeight}(C_i)$ processes, and each register in $\overline{R(C_i)}$ is covered by at most $\text{blockHeight}(C_i) - 2$ processes. Because of the block write β_i, in configuration $\beta_i(C_i)$ registers in $R(C_i)$ are covered by at least $\text{blockHeight}(C_i) - 1$ processes. Hence, $\beta_i(C_i)$ is not full. Provided blockHeight$(C_i) \geq 3$, the execution $E_i = (\beta_i(C_i), \gamma_i)$ is constructed in such a way that in configuration $C'_i := \beta_i \gamma_i(C_i)$, no new process covers any register in $R(C_i)$. Hence, if a full configuration C_{i+1} is reached during E_i, then in C_{i+1} all registers in $R(C_i)$ are still covered with at least blockHeight$(C_i) - 1$ processes. That is, in this case $R(C_i) \subsetneq R(C_{i+1})$ and so fullpt$(C_{i+1}) >$ fullpt(C_i).

We will show by induction that

$$\lfloor |\text{avail}(C_i)|/2 \rfloor + \text{poised}(C_i, \overline{R(C_i)}) \geq \text{targetSize}(C_i). \quad (2)$$

Given (2), we can see that the execution E_i must pass through a full configuration as follows. During the execution E_i, $|A(C_i)|$ processes are removed from avail(C_i) and become poised on registers in $\overline{R(C_i)}$, i.e., poised$(\beta_i \gamma_i(C_i), \overline{R(C_i)}) = \text{poised}(C_i, \overline{R(C_i)}) + |A(C_i)|$. Recall that $|A(C_i)| \in \{\lfloor |\text{avail}(C_i)|/2 \rfloor, \lfloor |\text{avail}(C_i)|/2 \rfloor + 1\}$. Thus, inequality (2) implies poised$(\beta_i \gamma_i(C_i), \overline{R(C_i)}) \geq$ targetSize(C_i). So it follows that there is a prefix σ_i of γ_i such that $\beta_i \sigma_i(C_i)$ is a constrained full configuration. (Enough new processes moved to the target area to ensure that some column must become shaded up to the grid boundary.)

So it only remains to confirm inequality (2). First, for the initial configuration $C_0 = C^*$, avail(C_0) contains all n processes, $\overline{R(C_0)} = \mathcal{R}$, poised$(C_0, \overline{R(C_0)}) = 0$, and targetSize$(C_0) = \ell(\ell+1)/2 < n/2 - \sqrt{n}/2$. (The grid representation of C_0 is completely unshaded, and there are n available processes, which in more than twice the number of grid cells.) Thus $\lfloor |\text{avail}(C_0)|/2 \rfloor + \text{poised}(C_0, \overline{R(C_0)}) = \lfloor n/2 \rfloor + 0 \geq$ targetSize(C_0), and so inequality (2) holds for $i = 0$.

Suppose inequality (2) holds for full configuration C_i with fullpt$(C_i) = j$, and consider configuration $C_{i+1} = \beta_i \sigma_i(C_i)$ with fullpt$(C_{i+1}) = k > j$. Let s be the number of processes that participate in schedule σ_i. Then, $|\text{avail}(C_{i+1})| = |\text{avail}(C_i)| - s$. In C_{i+1} all these s processes cover registers in $\overline{R(C_i)}$, so we have poised$(C_{i+1}, \overline{R(C_i)}) = \text{poised}(C_i, \overline{R(C_i)}) + s$. Also, since fullpt$(C_i) <$ fullpt(C_{i+1}), we have targetSize$(C_i) >$ targetSize(C_{i+1}). So using $s \geq 1$ and the induction hypothesis, we obtain

$$\left\lfloor \frac{|\text{avail}(C_{i+1})|}{2} \right\rfloor + \text{poised}(C_{i+1}, \overline{R(C_{i+1})})$$

$$= \left\lfloor \frac{|\text{avail}(C_i)| - s}{2} \right\rfloor + \text{poised}(C_i, \overline{R(C_i)}) + s$$

$$\geq \left\lfloor \frac{|\text{avail}(C_i)|}{2} \right\rfloor + \text{poised}(C_i, \overline{R(C_i)}) + (s-1)/2$$

$$\geq \left\lfloor \frac{|\text{avail}(C_i)|}{2} \right\rfloor + \text{poised}(C_i, \overline{R(C_i)})$$

$$\overset{I.H.}{\geq} \text{targetSize}(C_i) > \text{targetSize}(C_{i+1}).$$

This proves inequality (2).

The inductive construction can be repeated until we reach a configuration C_{last} where blockHeight$(C_{\text{last}}) \leq 2$. But then by (1), $|\overline{R(C_{\text{last}})}| \leq 1$. Hence in C_{last} at least $\ell - 1$ registers are covered. This completes the proof of the lower bound of Theorem 1.2.

4.2 Upper Bound

We now present a wait-free one-shot timestamp algorithm (see Figure 2), which uses at most $m : m(n) := \lceil 2\sqrt{n} \rceil$ regis-

ters. This establishes the upper bound of Theorem 1.2. The algorithm can easily be modified to work in systems with arbitrarily many processes each of which can call getTS() any number of times, as long as the total number of getTS() calls is at most n.

Timestamps are ordered pairs $(rnd, turn) \in \mathbb{N} \times (\mathbb{N} \cup \{0\})$, which are compared lexicographically (see Algorithm 1 in Figure 2).

The shared data structure used in the getTS() method is an array of atomic read-write registers. The content of each register is either $\perp$ (the initial value) or an ordered pair $\langle seq, rnd \rangle$ where, seq is a sequence of at most m process IDs, and rnd is a positive integer. The j-th element of seq is denoted $seq[j]$, and $last(R[j].seq)$ is the last element of the sequence $R[j].seq$. The algorithm will maintain the invariant that for some integer $k \geq 0$ the first k registers are non-$\perp$ and all other registers are $\perp$. Moreover, the sequence $R[j].seq$ for $j \leq k$ has either length 1 or j. In the following, x_p denotes process p's local variable that is identified by x in the code in Figure 2.

The algorithm uses an obstruction free method scan, which returns the sequence of values of the registers $R[1], \ldots, R[m]$ at some point t during the execution of scan (t is the linearization point of the scan). To scan, process p reads each register $R[1], \ldots, R[m]$ (the process of reading all register once is called a *collect*) and stores the resulting *view* locally. Then it continues until two contiguous views are the same. The linearization point is an arbitrary point in time between the last two collects performed by p. Although scan is not wait-free, our algorithm is, because in any execution, each process performs at most m writes, so each scan operation will be successful after a finite number of collects.

4.2.1 Idea of the Algorithm

A complete execution can be partitioned into phases. Roughly speaking, at the end of the $(k-1)$-th phase exactly the registers $R[1], \ldots, R[k-1]$ have non-$\perp$ values. Register $R[k-1].seq$ stores a sequence $(r_1, \ldots, r_{k-2})$ of values such that $last(R[i].seq) \neq r_i$ for all $1 \leq i \leq k-2$. In this situation, some process q will perform a scan during its getTS() call, and that scan returns the view $(r_1, \ldots, r_{k-1}, \perp, \ldots, \perp)$. (The k-th phase starts precisely at the point when this scan linearizes.) Process q then writes the sequence $(\ell_1, \ldots, \ell_{k-1})$ to $R[k].seq$, where $\ell_i = last(r_i.seq)$ for $1 \leq i \leq k-1$. Thus, shortly after the beginning of the k-th phase, the last entry stored in $R[i].seq$ equals the i-th entry ℓ_i stored in $R[k].seq$. In this situation, all registers are *valid*. From then on, processes that get timestamps will try to *invalidate* registers $R[1], \ldots, R[k-1]$ in this order – the i-th register gets invalidated when the next process writes to $R[i]$ and as a consequence $last(R[i].seq)$ is not equal to the i-th entry stored in $R[k].seq$. The idea is that a process that calls getTS() finds the first index i such that $R[i]$ has not yet been invalidated (i.e., $last(R[i].seq)$ is still equal to the i-th entry it previously read from $R[k]$), and then writes to it. It then returns the timestamp (k, i). Once all registers $R[1], \ldots, R[k-1]$ have been invalidated, phase $k + 1$ starts. We see that the algorithm works correctly if all getTS() calls are sequential: the j-th getTS() call during the k-th phase invalidates $R[j]$ and returns (k, j).

The main problem with concurrent getTS() executions is the following. At the end of phase $k - 1$, two differ-

Algorithm 1: compare($(rnd_1, turn_1), (rnd_2, turn_2)$)
1 **return**
$(rnd_1 < rnd_2) \vee ((rnd_1 = rnd_2) \wedge (turn_1 < turn_2))$

Algorithm 2: getTS()
/* Throughout, $m = \lceil 2\sqrt{n} \rceil$ and ID is the identifier of the process executing the code.   */
Shared:
$R[1 \dots m]$: array of multi-writer multi-reader registers, initialized to $\perp$
Local:
$r[1 \dots m]$ initialized to $\perp$
j initialized to 1
$myrnd$

```
1  while R[j] ≠ ⊥ do
2   │  r[j] = R[j]
3   │  j = j + 1
4  myrnd = j − 1
5  for j = 1 ... myrnd − 1 do
6   │  if R[myrnd + 1] == ⊥ then
7   │   │  if r[myrnd].seq[j] == last(R[j].seq) then
8   │   │   │  R[j] = ⟨(ID), myrnd⟩
9   │   │   │  return (myrnd, j)
10  │   │  else if R[j].rnd < myrnd then
11  │   │   │  R[j] = ⟨(ID), myrnd⟩
    │   │
    │  else
12  │   │  return (myrnd + 1, 0)
13  r[1 ... m] = scan(R[1], ..., R[m])
14  if r[myrnd + 1] == ⊥ then
15  │  R[myrnd + 1] =
    │  ⟨(last(r[1].seq), ..., last(r[myrnd].seq), ID),
    │                                   myrnd + 1⟩
16  return (myrnd + 1, 0)
```

Figure 2: A one-shot timestamp system for n processes, using $m = \lceil 2\sqrt{n} \rceil$ registers

ent processes, p and q, might be poised to execute a scan and then write the result into $R[k]$. However, the results of their scans might be different, because after p scans and before q scans, some "old" writes happen, say to registers $R[1], \dots, R[j]$. Thus, in this situation q's view matches all register values, but p's view matches only the contents of $R[j+1], \dots, R[k-1]$. Then, both, p and q proceed to a point where they are poised to write the result computed from their scan return values to $R[k]$. Suppose p writes to register $R[k]$ first. Then after that write, registers $R[1], \dots, R[j]$ are already invalidated, and a process a that starts its getTS() at this point invalidates $R[j+1]$ and thus gets timestamp $(k, j+1)$. If after that, q writes to $R[k]$, the first j registers are not invalid, and a process b that calls getTS() gets timestamp $(k, 1)$, which is less than a's timestamp. The walk-trough of the algorithm that follows explains how this potential problem is remedied.

4.2.2 Line-By-Line Description of the Algorithm

Each process p proceeds as follows to get a timestamp (see Figure 2). In the first while-loop, p reads regis-

ters $R[1], R[2], \dots$ into local variables $r[1], r[2], \dots$, until p finds the first index j such that $R[j] = \perp$. It then sets $myrnd = j - 1$ (line 4). As a consequence, at the point when p read register $R[myrnd]$, this register was the last one with a non-$\perp$ value. Hence, $r[myrnd].seq$ contains a sequence $(\ell_1, \dots, \ell_{myrnd-1})$ that was obtained from registers $R[1], \dots, R[myrnd-1]$ by a scan at the beginning of phase $myrnd$.

In the following for-loop, p tries to find a register to invalidate. In order to do so, p reads registers $R[1], R[2], \dots, R[myrnd - 1]$ again. But before p reads register j, it checks (in line 6), whether $R[myrnd + 1]$ still has value $\perp$. If not, then a new phase has already started, and so p can simply return the timestamp $(myrnd + 1, 0)$ (line 13). Otherwise, p compares $last(R[j].seq)$ with ℓ_j to determine whether the register has already been invalidated. If both values are equal, then p invalidates $R[j]$ by writing a 1-element sequence consisting only of p's ID to $R[j].seq$ and the value $myrnd$ to $R[j].rnd$ (line 8), and then returns the timestamp $(myrnd, j)$. If $last(R[j].seq) \neq \ell_j$, then $R[j]$ has already been invalidated. In this case, p reads $R[j].rnd$ in line 10. If that value is less than $myrnd$, then $R[j]$ has been invalidated by an "old" write, so p has to overwrite $R[j]$ again (line 11), and then continue with the iteration of the for-loop.

If p does not return a timestamp during the execution of its for-loop, then all registers $R[1], \dots, R[myrnd - 1]$ had already been invalidated at the points when p read them during the for-loop. In this case, p tries to start a new phase by first scanning all registers into local variables $r[1], \dots, r[m]$ (line 14). If $r[myrnd + 1] \neq \perp$, then some other process has already written a view to $R[myrnd + 1]$, so p can simply return the timestamp $(myrnd + 1, 0)$. Otherwise, before returning this timestamp, p writes the view $(last(r[1].seq), \dots, last(r[myrnd.seq])$ to $R[myrnd + 1].seq$ and $myrnd + 1$ to $R[myrnd + 1].rnd$ (line 16).

4.2.3 Proof of Correctness

The proof of correctness consists of two parts. We show that m registers are enough, i.e., no process attempts to access a shared array entry $R[j]$ for $j > m$.

LEMMA 4.1. *The algorithm in Figure 2 accesses no shared registers other than $R[1], \dots, R[m]$.*

For that we have to prove that there are at most m phases, i.e., each process' $myrnd$ value is bounded $m - 1$. The proof of this lemma is provided in Section 4.2.5 below. Given this result, we obtain that two timestamps returned by non-concurrent getTS() calls are ordered properly.

LEMMA 4.2. *Let p and q be two processes whose getTS() calls return $(rnd_p, turn_p)$ and $(rnd_q, turn_q)$, respectively. If p's getTS() call terminates before q calls getTS(), then compare($(rnd_p, turn_p), (rnd_q, turn_q)$) returns true.*

This lemma is proved in Section 4.2.4.

We now argue that compare() and getTS() are wait-free. Given that and Lemmas 4.1 and 4.2, Theorem 1.2 follows immediately from our choice of m.

Clearly, compare is wait-free, so it remains to show that getTS() is wait-free, too. All operations of that algorithm, except the scan, are wait-free, and it follows from Lemma 4.1 that the while-loop and the for-loop terminate. Hence, it remains to show that all calls of scan terminate within a bounded number of steps. It is immediate from the code that processes write to each register at most once, and thus by Lemma 4.1, each process writes at most m times. Thus, after a finite number of reads during the **scan**, the scanning process does not detect any changes and the **scan** terminates.

The rest of this paper is devoted to the proofs of Lemmas 4.1 and 4.2. We prove Lemma 4.2 first. Due to space restrictions we omit the proofs of some technical claims; complete arguments can be found in the preliminary technical report [14].

4.2.4 Proof of Lemma 4.2

Since the method **scan** is linearizable, for the rest of the discussion we will assume w.l.o.g. that **scan** is an atomic operation. We start with some simple properties of the algorithm. All of these properties are not hard to verify by looking at the code; a full proof is provided in [14].

CLAIM 4.3.

(a) If the content of a shared register changes from $\perp$ to some value that is not $\perp$, then it will never change back to $\perp$.

(b) If process p's **getTS()** call returns $(rnd, turn)$, then at that point $R[rnd] \neq \perp$.

(c) Suppose at time t_0 a sequence $(v_1, \ldots, v_k)$ is stored in $R[i].seq$. If and only if $last(R[i].seq) \neq v_k$ at time $t \geq t_0$, then some process writes to $R[i]$ during the time interval $[t_0, t]$.

(d) If process p writes to register $R[i]$ at a point when $R[i] = \perp$ or $R[i+1] = \perp$, then that write occurs in line 16.

(e) If $R[j] \neq \perp$ at a point in time t, then $\forall j' \leq j$, $R[j'] \neq \perp$ at any time $t' \geq t$.

We say a process *fails* iteration j, if it executes line 7 and the if-statement in that line evaluates to false. Only if a process fails iteration j, its **getTS()** call does not return during that iteration. The following claim gives a sufficient condition that process q fails an iteration. The proof can be found in the full version of the paper.

CLAIM 4.4. Let p and q be two processes executing **getTS()**, and $myrnd_p \geq myrnd_q$. If q's i-th iteration of the for-loop starts after p has written $R[i]$, then q fails iteration i.

We are now ready to show that the returned timestamps are correct.

PROOF OF LEMMA 4.2. By Claim 4.3(b), $R[rnd_p] \neq \perp$ at the time when p's **getTS()** completes. Then by Claim 4.3(e) $R[1], \ldots, R[rnd_p] \neq \perp$ throughout q's **getTS()** call, and thus by the semantics of the while-loop, $myrnd_q \geq rnd_p$. From the return statements in the algorithm, $rnd_q \geq myrnd_q \geq rnd_p$. If $rnd_q > rnd_p$, then **compare**$((rnd_p, turn_p), (rnd_q, turn_q))$ returns true.

Hence, for the purpose of a contradiction assume $rnd_q = rnd_p$ and $turn_q \leq turn_p$. Then, $myrnd_q = rnd_q = rnd_p$ and thus q's **getTS()** call returns in line 9. Thus, $turn_q > 0$, and so p's **getTS()** call also returns in line 9 because otherwise $turn_p = 0 < turn_q$.

If $turn_p = turn_q$, then p and q both succeed line 7 in iteration $j = turn_p = turn_q$. Thus, p writes to $R[j]$ in line 8 and by Claim 4.4, q must fail iteration j—a contradiction. If $turn_p > turn_q$, then q succeeds in line 7 for iteration $j = turn_q$, and p fails this iteration. Hence, p executes line 10 for $j = turn_q$ and possibly line 11. If p executes line 11, then it writes to $R[j]$. If it doesn't, then $R[j].rnd \geq myrnd_p = myrnd_q$ when p executes line 10, and thus some process p' with $myrnd_{p'} \geq myrnd_q$ has already written to $R[j]$. In either case, Claim 4.4 applies (using either p or p' in place of p), and thus q must fail line 7 in iteration $j = turn_q$—a contradiction. $\square$

4.2.5 Proof of Lemma 4.1

We show that the algorithm in Figure 2 accesses only register $R[1], \ldots, R[\lceil 2\sqrt{n} \rceil]$. Fix an arbitrary execution $E = (C^*, \sigma)$. We partition E into several *phases*. Phase 0 starts at the beginning of E. Phase $\varphi \geq 1$ starts at the point of a **scan** (line 14) by some process p, for which $myrnd_p = \varphi - 1$. We say that phase φ completes during E, if phase $\varphi + 1$ starts during E.

For each phase, the first write to register $R[j]$ during that phase is called an *invalidation write*. Let W be the set of all writes, and let $I \subseteq W$ be the set of all invalidation writes during execution E. Then $I_\varphi \subseteq I$ denotes the set of invalidation writes in phase φ. We will show that during phase φ, exactly φ invalidation writes happen. Moreover, we charge each invalidation write w to some other write operation, $f(w)$, such that

- each write operation is charged only for at most one invalidation write (i.e. f is injective), and

- each process executes at most two writes that are charged for some invalidation write (i.e. $|f(I)| \leq 2n$).

Therefore, the total number of invalidation writes is bounded by $2n$, and thus the number of phases, Φ, satisfies: $\sum_{\varphi=1}^{\Phi} \varphi \leq 2n$.

Hence, we conclude that $\Phi < 2 \cdot \sqrt{n}$. Since, as we show below, in phase φ only registers $R[1], \ldots, R[\varphi]$ are accessed, Lemma 4.1 follows.

The function $f : I \to W \cup \{\perp\}$ that maps each invalidation write w to $\perp$ or the operation $f(w)$ which we charge for the invalidation write is defined as follows. For each invalidation write $w \in I$ to register $R[j]$, executed by process p:

(i) If w is the last write or the first invalidation write by p, then $f(w) = w$.

(ii) Otherwise, $f(w) = w^*$, where w^* is the write that precedes p's last read of $R[j]$, if such a write exists, and otherwise $w^* = \perp$. (We will prove later that $f(w) \neq \perp$ for all $w \in I$.)

In the following, we show that during phase φ exactly the registers $R[1], \ldots, R[\varphi]$ get written, i.e., exactly φ invalidation writes occur during that phase.

We start with two technical statements (Claims 4.5 and 4.6) that relate the phase number φ to the value of a process' variable $myrnd$ and the time at which that process writes to certain registers.

CLAIM 4.5.

(a) Process p executes line 15 during some phase $\varphi \geq myrnd_p + 1$.

(b) Process p executes line 4 during some phase $\varphi' \geq myrnd_p$.

PROOF. When p executes line 15, it has already executed its scan in line 14. Thus, some process q with $myrnd_q = myrnd_p$ has already executed the scan in line 14, and so execution phase $myrnd_p + 1$ has already started. This proves part (a).

Now suppose p executes line 4. At the end of p's while-loop, $R[myrnd_p] \neq \bot$, and thus, at some earlier point in time $R[myrnd_p]$ had changed from $\bot$ to non-$\bot$. By Claim 4.3 (d), this change must have happened when some process r with $myrnd_r = myrnd_p - 1$ executed line 16. By part (a), r's write in line 16 happens after phase $myrnd_p$ has started. Thus, p executes line 4 during some phase $\varphi' \geq myrnd_p$. $\square$

CLAIM 4.6. If during phase $myrnd_p$, process p fails iteration i, then at that point a write to register $R[i]$ and a write to $R[myrnd_p]$ have already happened in the same phase.

PROOF. Let $v := (v_1, \ldots, v_k)$ be the value of the sequence stored in $R[myrnd_p].seq$ when p reads that register in line 2. At this point in time, $R[myrnd_p] \neq \bot$ and $R[myrnd_p + 1] = \bot$, as otherwise p's while-loop would not have terminated for $j = myrnd_p + 1$. (Recall that by Claim 4.3 (a), if $R[myrnd_p] \neq \bot$ at some point, that $R[myrnd_p]$ will never equal $\bot$ at a later point.) Let b be the process which previously has written the sequence v to $R[myrnd_p].seq$. Hence, $R[myrnd_p + 1] = \bot$ when b wrote h to $R[myrnd_p]$. Therefore, by Claim 4.3 (d), process b wrote to $R[myrnd_p]$ in line 16 and thus $myrnd_b = myrnd_p - 1$. By Claim 4.5 (a), b's write to $R[myrnd_p]$ happens during phase $\varphi \geq myrnd_p$. Since b's write to $R[myrnd_p]$ happens before p reads $R[i]$ in line 7 during phase $myrnd_p$, b's write to $R[myrnd_p]$ occurs in phase $myrnd_p$.

It remains to show that a write to $R[i]$ occurs in phase $myrnd_p$ before p fails iteration i. Before executing line 16, b executed a scan in line 14, and the value $last(R[i].seq)$ that b obtained during its scan is v_i. Let a be the process that started phase $myrnd_p$ and let v'_i be the value $last(R[i].seq)$ that a obtained during its own scan in line 14. By definition of phases, a is the first process with $myrnd_a = myrnd_b = myrnd_p - 1$ to execute the scan in line 14, and thus either $a = b$ or the scan by a must have happened before the scan by b.

By the assumption that process p fails iteration i, $v_i \neq last(R[i].seq)$ at the point t, when p reads $R[i]$ in line 7. If $v'_i = v_i$, then between a's scan and point t, $R[i]$ must be written. If $v'_i \neq v_i$, $R[i]$ must be written between a's scan and b's scan, which also happens before t. In either case, a write to $R[i]$ occurs after a's scan (and thus the start of phase $myrnd_p$) and before t. $\square$

We are now ready to show that during a phase φ that completes, exactly the registers $R[1], \ldots, R[\varphi]$ get written:

LEMMA 4.7. Throughout phase φ, no register $R[i]$, $i > \varphi$ is written, and if φ completes during E, then all registers $R[1], \ldots, R[\varphi]$ are written during that phase, and in particular $|I_\varphi| = \varphi$.

PROOF. Until the first process has executed line 16, and thus phase 1 has started, no process writes to any register. Hence, the lemma is true for $\varphi = 0$. Now let $\varphi \geq 1$.

First, we show that if process q writes to register $R[i]$ during phase φ, then $i \leq \varphi$. If q writes to $R[i]$ in lines 8 or 11, then by Claim 4.5 (a), $\varphi \geq myrnd_q$, and by the semantics of the for-loop, $i < myrnd_q$. If q writes to $R[i]$ in line 16, then $i = myrnd_q + 1$ and by Claim 4.5 (b), $\varphi \geq myrnd_q + 1$. Hence, in either case $i \leq \varphi$.

Now suppose that phase φ completes during E, and let $1 \leq i' \leq \varphi$. We show that some process writes to $R[i']$ during phase φ. Let p be the process that starts phase $\varphi + 1$. Then by definition of phases $myrnd_p = \varphi$. Since p executes line 14, its getTS() call does not return during the for-loop. Therefore, p fails iteration i', or else p's getTS() call would return in line 9. Thus, by Claim 4.6, a write to register $R[i']$, happens in phase φ. $\square$

We now prove that f has the desired properties, i.e., that f is injective and $|f(I)| \leq 2n$. We need a technical claim whose proof can be found in the full version of the paper.

CLAIM 4.8. For any invalidation write w by process p, if $f(w) = w^* \neq w$, then

(a) w^* is the last write of some process (and thus $w^* \neq \bot$),

(b) w^* is not an invalidation write,

(c) w^* occurs in phase $myrnd_p$, and

(d) w occurs during phase $myrnd_p + 1$.

Using this result, it is now easy to show that the function f has the desired properties.

LEMMA 4.9. $|f(I)| \leq 2n$ and f is injective.

PROOF. To see that $|f(I)| \leq 2n$, it suffices to show for any $w \in I$ that $f(w)$ is the first invalidation write or the last write by some process. If $f(w) = w$, then this is immediate from the definition of f Otherwise, by Claim 4.8 (a), $f(w)$ is a last write by some process.

It remains to show that f is injective. Let $w, w' \in I$ be write operations by processes p and p' respectively, s.t. $w \neq w'$. If $f(w) = w$ and $f(w') = w'$, then $f(w) \neq f(w')$. Hence, suppose $f(w) \neq w$ or $f(w') \neq w'$. W.l.o.g. assume $w^* := f(w) \neq w$.

For the purpose of a contradiction assume $f(w) = f(w') = w^*$. If $f(w') = w'$, then $f(w') \in I$, and thus $f(w) \in I$. But by Claim 4.8 (b), since $f(w) \neq w$, we know that $f(w) \notin I$. Therefore, $f(w') \neq w'$. By Claim 4.8 (c),(d), w^* occurs in phase $\varphi := myrnd_p = myrnd_{p'}$ and w and w' both occur in phase $\varphi + 1$. By definition of f, w, w', and w^* are writes to the same register. But then w and w' are both writes to the same register during the same phase $\varphi + 1$, and so one of them cannot be an invalidation write—a contradiction. $\square$

Lemma 4.1 now follows almost immediately from Lemmas 4.7 and 4.9:

PROOF OF LEMMA 4.1. Suppose there are $\Phi + 1$ phases $0, \ldots, \Phi$ during execution E. From Lemma 4.7, only registers $R[1], \ldots, R[\Phi]$ are written during E. For any process p, by Claim 4.5, $myrnd_p \leq \Phi$. Hence, only registers $R[1], \ldots, R[\Phi + 1]$ are accessed throughout E. Therefore, it suffices to show that $\Phi < 2\sqrt{n}$.

From Lemma 4.9, $|I| = |f(I)| \leq 2n$. By Lemma 4.7, the number of invalidation writes is $|I| = \sum_{\varphi=0}^{\Phi} \varphi = \frac{\Phi \cdot (\Phi + 1)}{2} \leq 2n$. Hence, $\Phi < 2\sqrt{n}$. $\square$

5. FURTHER REMARKS

The lower and upper bounds for long-lived and one-shot timestamps compare and contrast in several ways. In the execution constructed in the lower bound for one-shot timestamps, each process that participates in a block write, takes no further steps in the computation. As a consequence, the proof actually applies without change if each register is replaced by any historyless object. The asymptotically matching upper bound is, however, achieved using registers. In contrast, our proof of the lower bound for long-lived timestamps does not extend to historyless objects. So it remains an open question whether there is an implementation of long-lived timestamps from a sub-linear number of historyless objects. Both the long-lived and the one-shot lower bounds apply even to non-deterministic solo-terminating algorithms, while the asymptotically matching algorithms are wait-free.

The upper bound for one-shot timestamps applies for any bounded number of getTS() method invocations. The covering argument in the proof of the lower bound, however, prevents any similar generalization: it depends on each process invoking at most one getTS() method. The wait-free property of the one-shot algorithm is really just a consequence of bounding the number of allowed getTS() invocations. The one-shot algorithm generalizes even to the situation where the number of getTS() method invocations is not bounded, provided that the system could acquire additional registers as needed. In this case however, progress would be non-blocking only instead of wait-free.

Acknowledgments

The authors thank Faith Ellen for valuable comments on an earlier draft of the paper.

6. REFERENCES

[1] K. R. Abrahamson. On achieving consensus using a shared memory. In *Proceedings of the 7th Annual ACM Symposium on Principles of Distributed Computing (PODC)*, pages 291–302, 1988.

[2] Y. Afek, D. Dolev, E. Gafni, M. Merritt, and N. Shavit. A bounded first-in, first-enabled solution to the *l*-exclusion problem. *ACM Transactions on Programming Languages and Systems*, 16(3):939–953, 1994.

[3] H. Attiya and A. Fouren. Algorithms adapting to point contention. *Journal of the ACM*, 50(4):444–468, 2003.

[4] J. E. Burns and N. A. Lynch. Bounds on shared memory for mutual exclusion. *Information and Computation*, 107(2):171–184, 1993.

[5] D. Dolev and N. Shavit. Bounded concurrent time-stamping. *SIAM Journal on Computing*, 26(2):418–455, 1997.

[6] C. Dwork and O. Waarts. Simple and efficient bounded concurrent timestamping and the traceable use abstraction. *Journal of the ACM*, 46(5):633–666, 1999.

[7] F. Ellen, P. Fatourou, and E. Ruppert. The space complexity of unbounded timestamps. *Distributed Computing*, 21(2):103–115, 2008.

[8] F. E. Fich, M. P. Herlihy, and N. Shavit. On the space complexity of randomized synchronization. *Journal of the ACM*, 45(5):843–862, 1998.

[9] C. J. Fidge. Timestamps in message-passing systems that preserve the partial ordering. In *11th Australian Computer Science Conference (ACSC'88)*, pages 56–66, 1988.

[10] M. J. Fischer, N. A. Lynch, J. E. Burns, and A. Borodin. Distributed fifo allocation of identical resources using small shared space. *ACM Transactions on Programming Languages and Systems*, 11(1):90–114, 1989.

[11] R. Gawlick, N. A. Lynch, and N. Shavit. Concurrent timestamping made simple. In *1st Israel Symposium on Theory of Computing Systems (ISTCS)*, pages 171–183, 1992.

[12] R. Guerraoui and E. Ruppert. Anonymous and fault-tolerant shared-memory computing. *Distributed Computing*, 20(3):165–177, 2007.

[13] S. Haldar and P. M. B. Vitányi. Bounded concurrent timestamp systems using vector clocks. *Journal of the ACM*, 49(1):101–126, 2002.

[14] M. Helmi, L. Higham, E. Pacheco, and P. Woelfel. The space complexity of long-lived and one-shot timestamp implementations. 2011, arXiv:1103.5794 [cs.DC].

[15] A. Israeli and M. Li. Bounded time-stamps. *Distributed Computing*, 6(4):205–209, 1993.

[16] A. Israeli and M. Pinhasov. A concurrent time-stamp scheme which is linear in time and space. In *Distributed Algorithms, 6th International Workshop (WDAG)*, pages 95–109, 1992.

[17] L. Lamport. A new solution of dijkstra's concurrent programming problem. *Communications of the ACM*, 17(8):453–455, 1974.

[18] L. Lamport. Time, clocks, and the ordering of events in a distributed system. *Communications of the ACM*, 21(7):558–565, 1978.

[19] M. Li, J. Tromp, and P. M. B. Vitányi. How to share concurrent wait-free variables. *Journal of the ACM*, 43(4):723–746, 1996.

[20] F. Mattern. Virtual time and global states of distributed systems. In *Proceedings of the International Workshop on Parallel and Distributed Algorithms*, pages 215–226, 1989.

[21] G. Ricart and A. K. Agrawala. An optimal algorithm for mutual exclusion in computer networks. *Communications of the ACM*, 24(1):9–17, 1981.

[22] S. K. Sarin and N. A. Lynch. Discarding obsolete information in a replicated database system. *IEEE Transactions on Software Engineering*, 13(1):39–47, 1987.

[23] P. M. B. Vitányi and B. Awerbuch. Atomic shared register access by asynchronous hardware. In *27th Annual Symposium on Foundations of Computer Science (FOCS)*, pages 233–243, 1986.

[24] G. T. J. Wuu and A. J. Bernstein. Efficient solutions to the replicated log and dictionary problems. *Operating Systems Review*, 20(1):57–66, 1986.

Compact Policy Routing

Gábor Rétvári, András Gulyás, Zalán Heszberger, Márton Csernai, and József J. Bíró
Department of Telecommunications and Media Informatics
Budapest University of Technology and Economics
1117 Budapest, Magyar tudósok körútja 2. Hungary
{retvari,gulyas,heszberger,csernai,biro}@tmit.bme.hu

ABSTRACT

This paper takes a first step towards generalizing compact routing to arbitrary routing policies that favor a broader set of path attributes beyond path length. Using the formalism of routing algebras we identify the algebraic requirements for a routing policy to be realizable with sublinear size routing tables and we show that a wealth of practical policies can be classified by our results. By generalizing the notion of stretch, we also discover the algebraic validity of compact routing schemes considered so far and we show that there are routing policies for which one cannot expect sublinear scaling even if permitting arbitrary constant stretch.

Categories and Subject Descriptors

C.2.1 [**Computer-Communication Networks**]: Network Architecture and Design—*Packet-switching networks Store and forward networks*; F.2.2 [**Analysis of Algorithms and Problem Complexity**]: Nonnumerical Algorithms and Problems—*Routing and layout*; G.2.2 [**Discrete Mathematics**]: Graph Theory—*Trees, Graph labeling*

General Terms

Algorithms, Theory

Keywords

compact routing, policy routing, routing algebras

1. INTRODUCTION

Compact routing theory is the research field aimed at identifying the fundamental scaling limits of shortest path routing and constructing algorithms that meet these limits [1–7]. Shortest path routing is a key ingredient in many modern network architectures, as it generally ensures low transmission delay while also minimizes the effort needed

G. Rétvári was supported by the Janos Bolyai Fellowship of the Hungarian Academy of Sciences.

to transmit one unit of information from the source to the destination. To what extent shortest path routing can scale to large networks, in terms of the memory requirements of implementing the local forwarding functionality at network nodes, has for a long time been researched. It turns out that in general it is impossible to implement shortest path routing with routing tables whose size in all network topologies grows slower than linear with the increase of the network size [1, 2]. To answer this challenge, compact routing research seeks algorithms to decrease routing table sizes at the price of letting packets to flow along suboptimal paths. In this context, suboptimal means that the forwarding paths are allowed to be longer than the shortest ones, but length increase is bounded by a constant stretch factor. By now, the research community has built a strong theoretical foundation for compact shortest path routing, fully characterizing its pinnacles and pitfalls on a broad catalog of network topologies including hypercubes, trees, scale-free networks, and planar graphs [4, 5, 8–10], while having defined efficient compact routing algorithms for the generic case as well [3, 4].

In order to ensure an expedient flow of information through the network, one often needs to provision routes taking into consideration a broader set of attributes beyond mere path length, such as path reliability and resilience constraints [11], bandwidth and perceived congestion [12–14], business relations and service level agreements between ISPs [15, 16], etc. These path selection strategies are usually described under the umbrella of policy routing. Practically speaking, a *routing policy* is a function that selects a preferred transmission route from the set of all forwarding paths available between two endpoints, according to predefined requirements. Indeed, a significant portion of the Internet today runs over policy routing [11, 12, 15, 17, 18]. Unfortunately, at the moment no theory is available to characterize the inherent scaling properties of these policy routing architectures, leaving a considerable gap in our understanding of their long term sustainability.

In this paper, we take the first steps towards filling this gap. We build on the recent work of Sobrinho and Griffin [19–22], who lay the theoretical foundations for describing disparate routing policy structures in a single theoretical framework using the notion of routing algebras, abstracting away their syntactic and semantic diversity and letting us to study them in a general, abstract sense. Using this framework, we give an algebraic characterization of the scalability of policy routing. As the main contribution of the paper, we determine the algebraic requirements for a policy to be implementable with sublinear routing tables and we give a comprehensive characterization of many practically important routing policies in networking. By generalizing the notion of stretch, we also explore the algebraic conditions under which the well-known shortest-path-based compact routing schemes [3,4] generalize to policy routing and we show that introducing stretch cannot always eventuate sublinear scaling.

The rest of this paper is structured as follows. In Section 2, we introduce the basic notations and models used throughout the paper. Next, in Section 3 we characterize the local memory requirements for implementing an important subset of routing algebras, called regular algebras, and we apply the results to real-world routing policies. In Section 4 we deal with an algebraic interpretation of stretch and we generalize compact routing algorithms to regular algebras. Then, in Section 5 we discuss some practical considerations and finally Section 6 concludes the paper.

2. AN ALGEBRAIC MODEL FOR POLICY ROUTING

Let the communications network be modeled by a finite, connected, simple, undirected graph $G(V, E)$, let $|V| = n$ and let $|E| = m$. Communication between nodes is carried out by sending packets: neighboring nodes exchange packets directly, while remote nodes communicate through intermediate hops. We assume that nodes v (edges e) are uniquely identified by a natural number $ID(v)$ ($ID(e)$). We often write simply v (e) in place of $ID(v)$ ($ID(e)$). Let $\deg(v)$ denote the degree of $v \in V$ and let $d = \max_{v \in V} \deg(v)$. An $s-t$ walk is a sequence of nodes $p = (s = v_1, v_2, \ldots, v_k = t)$, where k is the length of the walk and $(v_i, v_{i+1}) \in E : \forall i = 1, \ldots, k-1$, a cycle is a walk with $s = t$, and a path is a walk that visits a node at most once.

2.1 Routing algebras

Generally speaking, a routing policy can be considered as a function $p_{st}^* = \mathrm{Pol}(\mathcal{P}_{st})$ that selects from the set of available $s-t$ paths $\mathcal{P}_{st}$ a single preferred path p_{st}^* according to some predefined rules. This definition is broad enough to contain basically every conceivable policy, including extreme cases like choosing a random path as well as traditional ones like shortest path routing.

To be more specific, we choose the abstract notion of routing algebras from Sobrinho and Griffin to describe routing policies within this paper [19–24]. This allows us to infer generic properties instead of having to define particular routing policies one by one and building piecemeal compact routing frameworks. In addition, it has been shown that basically all practically important routing policies possess an algebraic representation [21]. Thus, we shall use the terms routing policy and routing algebra interchangeably in this paper.

A routing algebra abstracts away the most important concepts of shortest path routing, namely weight composition (the method of constructing the weight of a path from the weights of its constituent edges) and weight comparison (expressing the preference between edges or paths). In this paper, a routing algebra $\mathcal{A}$ is defined as a totally ordered semigroup with a compatible infinity element: $\mathcal{A} = (W, \phi, \oplus, \preceq)$, where W is the set of (abstract) weights that can be assigned to edges, ϕ ($\phi \notin W$) is a special infinity weight meaning that

an edge/path is not traversable, $\oplus$ is a composition operator for weights, and $\preceq$ is weight comparison.

More formally, the following properties are presumed:

- $(W, \oplus)$ is a commutative semigroup
  - Closure: $w_1 \oplus w_2 \in W$ for all $w_1, w_2 \in W$
  - Associativity: $(w_1 \oplus w_2) \oplus w_3 = w_1 \oplus (w_2 \oplus w_3)$ for all $w_1, w_2, w_3 \in W$
  - Commutativity: $w_1 \oplus w_2 = w_2 \oplus w_1$ for all $w_1, w_2 \in W$

- $\preceq$ is a total order on W
  - Reflexivity: $w \preceq w$ for any $w \in W$
  - Anti-symmetry: if $w_1 \preceq w_2$ and $w_2 \preceq w_1$, then $w_2 = w_1$ for any $w_1, w_2 \in W$
  - Transitivity: if $w_1 \preceq w_2$ and $w_2 \preceq w_3$, then $w_1 \preceq w_3$ for any $w_1, w_2, w_3 \in W$
  - Totality: for all $w_1, w_2 \in W$ either $w_1 \preceq w_2$ or $w_2 \preceq w_1$

- ϕ is compatible with $(W, \oplus)$ according to $\preceq$
  - Absorptivity: $w \oplus \phi = \phi$ for all $w \in W$
  - Maximality: $w \prec \phi$ for all $w \in W$

Given a path $p = (v_1, v_2, \ldots, v_k)$ we obtain the weight $w(p)$ of p by combining the weight of its constituent edges: $w(p) = \bigoplus_{i=1}^{k-1} w(v_i, v_{i+1})$. Then a preferred path in the algebra $\mathcal{A}$ between two nodes is simply one with the smallest weight according to $\preceq$:

$$\mathrm{Pol}(\mathcal{P}_{st}) = p^* : w(p^*) \preceq w(p), \forall p \in \mathcal{P}_{st} .$$

Now, one easily checks that shortest path routing corresponds to the algebra $(\mathbb{R}^+, \infty, +, \leq)$, while widest-path routing, where preferred paths are those with the largest bottleneck capacity, is simply $(\mathbb{R}^+, 0, \min, \geq)$. See further examples later in Section 3.1 and Section 5.

A special family of routing algebras, called regular routing algebras, will play an essential role in this paper.

DEFINITION 1. A routing algebra $\mathcal{A}$ is said to be regular, if it satisfies the following properties[1]:

- Monotonicity (M): $w_1 \preceq w_2 \oplus w_1$ for all $w_1, w_2 \in W$

- Isotonicity (I): $w_1 \preceq w_2 \Rightarrow w_3 \oplus w_1 \preceq w_3 \oplus w_2$ for all $w_1, w_2, w_3 \in W$

Monotonicity (M) means that prepending an edge (or path) of weight w_1 with another edge (or path) of w_2 can only make it less preferred: $w_2 \oplus w_1 \succeq w_1$. By commutativity, the same applies to appending edges/paths: $w_1 \oplus w_2 \succeq w_1$. Isotonicity (I), on the other hand, requires $\preceq$ to be compatible with the semigroup $(W, \oplus)$ in the following sense: if an edge/path is preferred over some other one, then prepending or suffixing both with a common edge or path maintains this relation.

Below are some further algebraic properties we shall often use to characterize routing policies [22].

---

[1] In this paper, we use the definitions of Sobrinho [19] with the understanding that other authors may adopt different terminology. For instance, what will be called isotonicity here is called monotonicity in conventional order theory. The reason is that this terminology seems to be widely adopted in the literature.

- Delimited (D): $w_1 \oplus w_2 \neq \phi$ for all $\forall w_1, w_2 \in W$

- Strictly monotone (SM): $w_1 \prec w_2 \oplus w_1$ for all $w_1, w_2 \in W$.

- Selective (S): $w_1 \oplus w_2 \in \{w_1, w_2\}$ for each $w_1, w_2 \in W$.

- Cancellative (N): $w_1 \oplus w_2 = w_1 \oplus w_3 \Rightarrow w_2 = w_3$ for each $w_1, w_2, w_3 \in W$.

- Condensed (C): $w_1 \oplus w_2 = w_1 \oplus w_3$ for each $w_1, w_2, w_3 \in W$.

From the above, perhaps only delimitedness deserves more explanation. This property ensures that edges can be combined in an arbitrary sequence without the danger of obtaining an untraversable path. Intra-domain routing policies, like shortest path routing or widest path routing, are usually delimited, while inter-domain BGP routing policies are not.

2.2 Composite algebras

An attractive feature of routing algebras is that surprisingly complex and expressive policy constructions can be built using only an elemental set of primitive algebras by applying simple algebra composition and decomposition operators appropriately [21]. Two of these operators have particular importance in this paper, namely the lexicographic product operator [22] and subalgebras.

Given two routing algebras $\mathcal{A} = (W_\mathcal{A}, \phi_\mathcal{A}, \oplus_\mathcal{A}, \preceq_\mathcal{A})$ and $\mathcal{B} = (W_\mathcal{B}, \phi_\mathcal{B}, \oplus_\mathcal{B}, \preceq_\mathcal{B})$, the *lexicographic product* of $\mathcal{A}$ and $\mathcal{B}$ is a routing algebra $\mathcal{A} \times \mathcal{B} = (W, \phi, \oplus, \preceq)$ where

- $W = W_\mathcal{A} \times W_\mathcal{B}$, $\phi = (\phi_\mathcal{A}, \phi_\mathcal{B})$

- $(w_1, v_1) \oplus (w_2, v_2) = (w_1 \oplus_\mathcal{A} w_2, v_1 \oplus_\mathcal{B} v_2)$ for all $w_1, w_2 \in W_\mathcal{A}$ and $v_1, v_2 \in W_\mathcal{B}$

- $(w_1, v_1) \preceq (w_2, v_2) = \begin{cases} v_1 \preceq_\mathcal{B} v_2 & \text{if } w_1 =_\mathcal{A} w_2 \\ w_1 \preceq_\mathcal{A} w_2 & \text{otherwise} \end{cases}$

Note that ϕ is well-defined if $\mathcal{A}$ and $\mathcal{B}$ are delimited. In other cases, defining ϕ needs more attention.

PROPOSITION 1. *The lexicographic product operator transforms the properties of the constituent algebras according to the following rules [22]:*

- $M(\mathcal{A} \times \mathcal{B}) \Leftrightarrow SM(\mathcal{A}) \vee (M(\mathcal{A}) \wedge M(\mathcal{B}))$

- $I(\mathcal{A} \times \mathcal{B}) \Leftrightarrow I(\mathcal{A}) \wedge I(\mathcal{B}) \wedge (N(\mathcal{A}) \vee C(\mathcal{B}))$

- $SM(\mathcal{A} \times \mathcal{B}) \Leftrightarrow SM(\mathcal{A}) \vee (M(\mathcal{A}) \wedge SM(\mathcal{B}))$

The second algebra composition operator we consider in this paper is subalgebras. Given a routing algebra $\mathcal{A} = (W, \phi, \oplus, \preceq)$ and a weight set $W' \subseteq W$, the restriction of $\mathcal{A}$ to W': $(W', \phi, \oplus, \preceq)$ is a subalgebra of $\mathcal{A}$ if and only if W' is closed for $\oplus$. Subalgebras inherit the properties of the root algebra, but new ones may also emerge. For instance, the subalgebra $(\mathbb{R}^+, \infty, +, \leq)$ of the weakly monotone algebra $(\mathbb{R}^+ \cup \{0\}, \infty, +, \leq)$ is also strictly monotone.

2.3 Routing model

In order to describe the complex process of policy routing and forwarding, we generalize the model of *routing functions* from [1, 2]. In this model, a packet contains a payload plus a header[2] with routing related information. Now, given a routing policy $\mathcal{A}$ and a graph G, a *policy routing function* is a mapping $R : \mathbb{N} \times \mathbb{N} \mapsto \mathbb{N} \times \mathbb{N}$ together with a labeling of the nodes $L_V : V \mapsto \mathbb{N}$ and a labeling of the edges $L_E : E \mapsto \mathbb{N}$ with the following property: for every node pair s, t, the successive application of R

$$(h_{i+1}, l_{i+1}) = R(v_i, h_i), \quad \forall i = 1, \ldots, k-1$$

yields a preferred path $p_{st}^* = (s = v_1, \ldots, v_i, \ldots, v_k = t)$ according to $\mathcal{A}$ and corresponding edge labels $l_{i+1} = (v_i, v_{i+1})$, where h_1 is some appropriate initial header. We shall say that R implements $\mathcal{A}$ on G for indicating that R produces preferred paths according to $\mathcal{A}$ on G.

Similarly to [1, 2], we assume that node labels (or addresses) can be encoded on $c \log n$ bits[3] for some c constant. We further assume that for each node $v_i \in V$ the edges emanating from v_i are labeled locally: $L_E(v_i, v_j) \in \{1, \ldots, \deg(v_i)\}$. Additionally, the edge label l_{i+1} is understood as coming from the local label space $L_E(v_i)$ of v_i. These limitations are to ensure that no extra routing information can be encoded into the labels besides pure identification. No such limitation exists, however, on the header size.

Now, routing according to the policy routing function R occurs as follows. Upon receiving a packet with header h, a node u simply evaluates its *local routing function* $R_u(h) = R(u, h)$ to obtain a new header h' and an outgoing port at edge l. Then, u sets the packet's header to h' and forwards it on l. In general, this routing model is suitable to represent oblivious routing architectures, i.e., ones in which the route of a packet depends only on the contents of the packet itself and some static forwarding information. Yet, it is broad enough to capture basically any practically relevant forwarding scheme, like traditional destination-based and source-destination-based forwarding, label swapping, etc. For further details, consult [1, 2].

Introducing routing functions makes it comfortable to characterize the local memory needed at network nodes to implement a routing policy.

DEFINITION 2. *The local memory requirement $M_\mathcal{A}$ of implementing the routing policy $\mathcal{A}$ is defined as:*

$$M_\mathcal{A} = \max_{G \in \mathcal{G}_n} \min_{R \in \mathcal{R}} \max_{u \in V} M_\mathcal{A}(R, u) ,$$

where $M_\mathcal{A}(R, u)$ is the minimum number of bits needed to encode the local routing function R_u, $\mathcal{R}$ is the set of all policy routing functions implementing $\mathcal{A}$ on some graph G, and $\mathcal{G}_n$ is the set of all graphs of size n.

A routing policy is said to be *incompressible*, if $M_\mathcal{A}$ is $\Omega(n)$. Otherwise $\mathcal{A}$ is *compressible*. Easily, an incompressible routing policy does not scale well, as the memory needed to store the local routing process of some node increases with the number of nodes in at least one graph. On the other hand, compressible routing policies scale well.

---

[2]Without loss of generality, headers can be represented by natural numbers.

[3]Logarithms are of base 2.

2.4 Algebraic compact routing

At this point, we have all the definitions in place to focus on our main concern what we call algebraic compact routing: given a routing algebra describing a particular routing policy, *(i)* identify the theoretical bounds on the memory requirements needed to implement that algebra and *(ii)* examine the local storage vs. path optimality trade-off, that is, design compact routing schemes that implement the algebra with sublinear local storage at the price of letting traffic to flow along non-preferred paths, whose suboptimality is upper bounded by some suitably defined stretch.

From the standpoint of routing, regular algebras manifest the "well-behaved cases" [19, 20, 23]. Monotonicity and isotonicity on the one hand guarantee that the preferred paths themselves can be obtained in polynomial time using a generalization of Dijkstra's algorithm. On the other hand, in a regular algebra preferred paths emanating from a node always make up a tree, allowing for a single routing entry to be maintained with respect to each node and forwarding packets based on the destination address only. This allows us to store local routing information on at most $\tilde{O}(n)$ bits local memory. We formulate these ideas as follows.

For some graph G and algebra $\mathcal{A}$, define a *destination-based routing function* $\hat{R}$ for implementing $\mathcal{A}$ on G as follows. Let the packet header consist of the identifier of the packet's destination and let node u forward a packet destined to some v on the first edge l_v along the preferred path p_{uv}^*: $\hat{R}_u(v) = (v, l_v)$. Sobrinho makes the following observation [20]:

PROPOSITION 2. *$\mathcal{A}$ can be implemented by a destination-based routing function on any graph, if and only if $\mathcal{A}$ is regular.*

One easily sees that $\hat{R}$ basically corresponds to destination-oriented routing tables, storing a single entry for each destination node. This leads to the following observation.

OBSERVATION 1. *If $\mathcal{A}$ is regular, then it can be implemented using $O(n \log d)$ bits local information.*

A key question in compact routing research is whether this trivial routing function is optimal in the sense that it requires the minimum possible local memory to encode preferred paths, or there are better algorithms using less local space. For shortest path routing in particular, Fraigniaud and Gavoille present the following negative result [1, 2].

PROPOSITION 3. *The shortest path routing algebra $\mathcal{A} = (\mathbb{R}^+, \infty, +, \leq)$ is incompressible.*

For shortest path routing at least, routing tables are optimal. For other routing policies, no such results exist. Therefore, in the next section we give an algebraic characterization of the memory requirements of policy routing.

3. LOCAL MEMORY REQUIREMENTS OF POLICY ROUTING

In what follows, we discuss the algebraic requirements for a routing policy to be implementable with sublinear local storage and we also give negative results indicating incompressibility of some practically important routing policies.

THEOREM 1. *If $\mathcal{A}$ is selective and monotone, then it is compressible.*

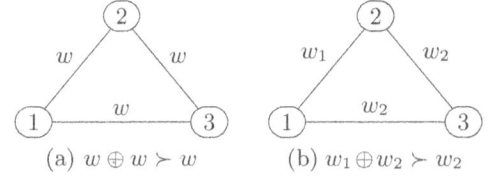

(a) $w \oplus w \succ w$ (b) $w_1 \oplus w_2 \succ w_2$

Figure 1: Counter-examples for different violations of selectivity.

In fact, we shall prove a bit more. We shall show that if a routing policy is selective, then a "preferred" spanning tree always exists, that is, for any $s, t \in V$ the only path p_{st} contained in the tree is a preferred path. We say that algebra $\mathcal{A}$ *maps to a tree*, if for any connected graph and any weighing of the edges one can always find such a "preferred" spanning tree. Then, compressibility follows as routing over a tree is possible with $\log n$ bits local memory.

LEMMA 1. *$\mathcal{A}$ maps to a tree, if and only if $\mathcal{A}$ is selective and monotone.*

PROOF. To prove sufficiency, we construct an optimal spanning tree assuming that the algebra is selective and monotone. Take the edges in order of non-decreasing weight according to $\preceq$, add an edge to the spanning tree T if no cycle arises and terminate when T spans G. We show that the only in-tree path p_{st}^T between any two nodes s and t is a preferred path over $\mathcal{A}$. To see this, take any other $s - t$ path p_{st} in G. Obviously, there is at least one edge (u, v) in p_{st} so that $w(u, v) \succeq w(i, j)$ for all (i, j) in p_{st}^T. Then, due to selectivity $w(p_{st}^T) \in \{w(i, j) : (i, j) \text{ in } p_{st}^T\}$, and by monotonicity $w(p_{st}^T) \preceq w(u, v) \preceq w(p_{st})$, therefore p_{st}^T is a preferred $s - t$ path. This proves sufficiency.

Next, we prove that if $\mathcal{A}$ maps to a tree then $\mathcal{A}$ is monotone and selective. Easily, $\mathcal{A}$ is monotone, otherwise preferred paths might contain loops. Next, we show that if $\mathcal{A}$ is non-selective, then in some graphs preferred paths do not reside in a tree. Obviously, a monotone non-selective algebra $\mathcal{A}$ either contains a weight $w \in W$, so that $w \oplus w \succ w$ (auto-selectivity), or $\mathcal{A}$ contains two weights $w_1, w_2 \in W, w_1 \prec w_2$, so that $w_1 \oplus w_2 \succ w_2$. For both of these cases, Fig. 1 gives counter-examples in which the preferred paths are always through the direct edges, and so preferred paths do not make up a tree. Thus, for any non-selective algebra there is a graph in which preferred paths are not in a tree, which concludes the proof. $\square$

A special case of this result for minimum- and maximum-type of weight composition operators appeared in [25], and [24] gives similar results for special routing algebras called *dioids*.

Theorem 1 suggests that routing policies characterized by selective algebras can be implemented using tree routing schemes, needing only logarithmic sized local storage [4, 10]. In contrast to selective algebras however, many routing policies can only be implemented using at least $\Omega(n)$ bits local memory as the next result shows.

THEOREM 2. *If $\mathcal{A}$ is strictly monotone, then it is incompressible.*

We shall prove a deeper, more general claim, of which the above is a simple corollary.

LEMMA 2. *If $\mathcal{A}$ contains a delimited, strictly monotone subalgebra, then $\mathcal{A}$ is incompressible.*

Table 1: Local memory requirements of various routing policies.

Algebra	Definition	Properties	Local memory
Shortest path	$\mathcal{S} = (\mathbb{R}^+, \infty, +, \leq)$	SM, I	$\Theta(n)$
Widest path	$\mathcal{W} = (\mathbb{R}^+, 0, \min, \geq)$	S, I, M	$\Theta(\log n)$
Most reliable path	$\mathcal{R} = ((0,1], 0, *, \geq)$	SM, I	$\Theta(n)$
Usable path	$\mathcal{U} = (\{1\}, 0, *, \geq)$	S, I, M	$\Theta(\log n)$
Widest-shortest path	$\mathcal{WS} = \mathcal{S} \times \mathcal{W}$	SM, I	$\Theta(n)$
Shortest-widest path	$\mathcal{SW} = \mathcal{W} \times \mathcal{S}$	SM, $\neg I$	$\Omega(n)$

PROOF. We trace back incompressibility to the incompressibility of shortest path routing (Proposition 3), by showing that a delimited, strictly monotone algebra has subalgebras possessing the same structure as shortest path routing. We use the following basic facts from semigroup theory [26]. Every element $w \in W$ of a semigroup $(W, \oplus)$ generates a subsemigroup, the so called cyclic semigroup, $(W_w, \oplus) : W_w = \{w, w^2, w^3, \ldots\}$ through the power operation:

$$\forall n \in \mathbb{N}: \quad w^n = \begin{cases} w & \text{if } n = 1 \\ w \oplus w^{n-1} & \text{otherwise} \end{cases}$$

If the ordered semigroup $(W, \oplus, \preceq)$ is delimited and strictly monotone, then any of its cyclic subsemigroups $(W_w, \oplus)$ is of infinite order, in which case it is isomorphic to the semigroup $(\mathbb{N}, +)$ of natural numbers under addition through the mapping $f : \mathbb{N} \leftrightarrow W_w$, $f(n) = w^n$. In addition, f is also an order preserving isomorphism between the shortest path routing algebra $S = (\mathbb{N}, \infty, +, \leq)$ and $(W_w, \phi, \oplus, \preceq)$ in this case, as $i < j \Leftrightarrow w^i \prec w^j$ due to strict monotonicity. One easily checks this by observing that for any $i < j : w^i \prec w^i \oplus w = w^{i+1} \preceq w^j$. Thus, if $\mathcal{A} = (W, \phi, \oplus, \preceq)$ has a strictly monotone subalgebra, then for any graph G and any labeling of the edges of G by natural numbers as weights, we can construct a labeling using weights from W so that a path is a shortest path in the algebra $\mathcal{S} = (\mathbb{N}, \infty, +, \leq)$ if and only if it is a preferred path in $\mathcal{A}$. This implies that routing in $\mathcal{A}$ requires at least as much local memory as shortest path routing (i.e., $\Omega(n)$ by Proposition 3), which completes the proof. □

3.1 Examples

In Table 1, we list the intra-domain routing policies studied most extensively in the literature, together with their algebraic definition, basic properties, and the local memory requirements as indicated by our results. Note that all the listed algebras are delimited and regular except the last one. Here, $\mathcal{S}$ is the well-known shortest path routing algebra, for which Proposition 3 provides an adequate incompressibility characterization. Easily, Theorem 2 gives the same characterization.

$\mathcal{W}$ denotes the widest path routing policy [12]. Here, the weight of an edge is its capacity, the end-to-end capacity of a path equals the bandwidth of its bottleneck edge (the one with the smallest capacity) and the higher the capacity along a path the more preferred. Easily, this corresponds to the selective algebra $(\mathbb{R}^+, 0, \min, \geq)$, and so $\mathcal{W}$ is compressible by Theorem 1. In particular, under the tree routing scheme due to Fraigniaud and Gavoille [10] widest path routing can be implemented using $5 \log n$ bit addresses and $3 \log n$ bits local memory, or $\log^2 n$ bits using the scheme of Thorup and Zwick [4]. Similar is the case for the usable path rout-

ing strategy ($\mathcal{U}$), applied extensively in Ethernet switching[4]. However, the rest of the routing policies listed in the table are incompressible.

Most reliable path routing ($\mathcal{R}$) denotes the policy when edges are assigned a reliability metric denoting the possibility that a packet will be transmitted successfully over the edge and the path with the highest probability of success is favored. Easily, $\mathcal{R}$ contains a strictly monotone subalgebra. Widest-shortest path ($\mathcal{WS}$) routing prefers from the set of shortest paths the one with the highest free capacity [13], and shortest-widest path ($\mathcal{SW}$, [12, 14]), just contrarily, prefers the shortest one out of the set of widest paths. These algebras can be expressed as lexicographic products of the $\mathcal{S}$ and $\mathcal{W}$ algebras and, by Proposition 1, strictly monotone [22]. Hence, for $\mathcal{R}$ and $\mathcal{WS}$, which are isotone, Theorem 2 supplies the local memory requirement of $\Omega(n)$. This characterization is tight apart from a logarithmic factor, as simple table-based destination-oriented routing requires $\tilde{O}(n)$ bits by Observation 1. On the other hand, $\mathcal{SW}$ is not isotone. Theorem 2 holds for non-isotone algebras as well, which supplies a $\Omega(n)$ bits local memory requirement for $\mathcal{SW}$ too. At the moment, it is an open question whether this characterization is tight, as the only trivial routing function for $\mathcal{SW}$ stores a separate routing table entry for each source-destination pair, which needs $O(n^2 \log d)$ bits per router.

4. COMPACT POLICY ROUTING

As has been shown in the previous section, many practically relevant routing policies are impossible to implement with sublinear size routing tables. In the case of shortest path routing, a standard way to improve scalability is to define *compact routing schemes*. In these schemes, paths are allowed to be longer than the shortest one, but path increase is upper bounded by a *multiplicative stretch factor k*, meaning that the paths yielded by the compact routing scheme are at most k times as long as the shortest one. In the followings, we characterize the routing policies that admit similar compact implementations, at least for a sufficient abstract notion of stretch. Consider the following definition:

DEFINITION 3. *A routing scheme is of stretch k over algebra $\mathcal{A}$, if for any path p_{st} selected by the scheme: $w(p_{st}) \preceq (w(p_{st}^*))^k$, where p_{st}^* is some preferred $s - t$ path in $\mathcal{A}$.*

Note that $(w(p_{st}^*))^k = \underbrace{w(p_{st}^*) \oplus w(p_{st}^*) \cdots \oplus w(p_{st}^*)}_{k \text{ times}}$, which implies that the above definition indeed generalizes the notion of multiplicative stretch originally defined for shortest path routing.

---

[4] The fact that Ethernet runs over what is called the Spanning Tree Protocol shows the expressiveness of Lemma 1.

4.1 Algebraic requirements of compact policy routing

First, we ask which routing algebras lend themselves to be implemented by a compact routing scheme of finite stretch.

THEOREM 3. *If a routing algebra $\mathcal{A}$ is regular, then there is a stretch-3 compact routing scheme for $\mathcal{A}$.*

We show that the stretch-3 shortest path routing scheme due to Cowen [3] readily generalizes to regular algebras. Below, we briefly reproduce that scheme. For further details, see [3] and [4].

For each $u \in V$, choose some node set $L \subseteq V$ and with each $u \in V$ associate a *landmark* l_u as the node closest (according to $\mathcal{A}$) to u in the set L. Additionally, for each $u \in V$ define a *ball* $B(u) : \{v \in V : w(p^*_{u,v}) \preceq w(p^*_{u,l_u})\}$, where $p^*_{s,t}$ refers to the preferred $s-t$ path for any s and t. Finally, let the *cluster* of u be $C(u) = \{v \in V : u \in B(v)\}$. When $\mathcal{A}$ is regular, one can use the lexicographic lightest path algorithms in [19, 20] to obtain unique connected clusters for each u.

The routing scheme is a hop-by-hop technique. The label of node v consists of the triplet $(v, l_v, \text{port}_{l_v,v})$, where v is the identifier of the node, l_v is the identifier of its corresponding landmark, and $\text{port}_{l_v,v}$ is the local port at l_v to the first hop on the preferred path from l_v to v. The packet header is the label of the target node. The routing table at node $u \notin L$ consists of $(v, \text{port}_{u,v})$ tuples with respect to each $v \in C(u) \cup L$, where $\text{port}_{u,v}$ is again the local port label of the first edge along the preferred $u - v$ path.

Packet forwarding *inside* a cluster occurs along preferred paths using the entries in the local routing tables. To route a packet to a node v *outside* the cluster, node u first forwards the packet to v's landmark, from where it arrives to v using again a direct route. In particular, when a packet with target v arrives to a node $u \neq v$, u checks whether v is contained in its local routing table. If not, then l_v, the landmark of v is extracted from the header. If $u = l_v$, then appropriate port label is also extracted from the header, otherwise it is looked up in the local routing table. Forwarding terminates when $u = v$.

From Proposition 2, we know that if $\mathcal{A}$ is regular, then standard destination-based hop-by-hop routing is correct. To show that the above scheme is also correct, the following crucial fact is enough (observed for shortest path routing by Cowen in [3]).

LEMMA 3. *Suppose that $\mathcal{A}$ is monotone. Now, if u stores an entry in its local routing table towards some t, then the next hop v along the preferred p^*_{ut} path also stores an entry to t.*

PROOF. Easily, by monotonicity $p^*_{vt} \preceq p^*_{ut} \preceq p^*_{l_t,t}$ so v also stores an entry for t. $\square$

Next, we show that the scheme is stretch-3 on $\mathcal{A}$. As forwarding inside clusters occurs along preferred paths, we only need to prove stretch-3 for indirect forwarding via landmarks.

LEMMA 4. *If $\mathcal{A}$ is regular, then for any $u, v \in V$ with $v \notin C(u) : w(p^*_{u,l_v}) \oplus w(p^*_{l_v,v}) \preceq (w(p^*_{u,v}))^3$.*

PROOF. *(i)* by assumption, $w(p^*_{l_v,v}) \preceq w(p^*_{u,v})$; *(ii)* using the triangle inequality, $w(p^*_{u,l_v}) \preceq w(p^*_{u,v}) \oplus w(p^*_{v,l_v}) = $

$w(p^*_{u,v}) \oplus w(p^*_{l_v,v})$ (the latter equality comes by commutativity); *(iii)* by isotonicity, from *(i)* and *(ii)* we have $w(p^*_{u,l_v}) \preceq w(p^*_{u,v}) \oplus w(p^*_{u,v})$. Combining *(i)* and *(iii)* by isotonicity we obtain $w(p^*_{u,l_v}) \oplus w(p^*_{l_v,v}) \preceq w(p^*_{u,v}) \oplus w(p^*_{u,v}) \oplus w(p^*_{u,v})$. $\square$

Finally, we show that the local information is indeed sublinear. Obviously, addresses can be encoded on $3 \log n$ bits. The size of the local routing table at node u is $O(|C(u)| + |L|)$. Using the landmark selection technique given by Cowen one obtains a local memory requirement of $O(n^{2/3})$ [3], which is improved by Thorup and Zwick to $\tilde{O}(n^{1/2})$ in [4].

An extremely interesting case is when the policy is the widest-path routing algebra $\mathcal{W}$. In this case, for any $n \in \mathbb{N}$ and any $w \in W : w^n = w$. Hence, stretch-3 paths are exactly the preferred paths in this case. The same applies to any selective and monotone algebra. Thus, Theorem 3 in fact gives an alternative proof to the claim that monotone and selective algebras are compressible.

We argued in Section 2.4 that regular algebras are the "well behaved" cases from the aspect of distributed routing, as they can be implemented by destination-based routing tables. Our results so far indicate that regular algebras are "well-behaved" from the standpoint compact routing as well: not just that we could give a general result characterizing the memory requirements for implementing regular algebras, but we also found that even when a regular algebra turns out incompressible a stretch-3 compact routing scheme is guaranteed to exist. In the next section, we show that if regularity fails, then finite stretch compact routing becomes significantly more difficult.

4.2 Compact routing when isotonicity fails

We have shown that regularity of a routing algebra is sufficient to define a stretch-3 compact routing scheme. It is an intriguing question whether it is necessary as well. At the moment, we do not have an answer to this question. What we can show, however, is that when isotonicity fails in a very intricate way, then no stretch-k routing exists for any k constant.

THEOREM 4. *Let $k \geq 1$ and let $\mathcal{A} = (W, \phi, \oplus, \preceq)$ be a monotone algebra with the property that for any $p \geq 2$, $\exists \{w_1, w_2, \ldots, w_p\} \subseteq W$ so that $\forall i, j \in \{1, \ldots, p\}, i \neq j$:*

$$w_i \oplus w_j \succ w_i^{2k} \text{ and } w_i \oplus w_j \succ w_j^{2k} . \quad (1)$$

Then, there is no stretch-k routing scheme with sublinear memory requirement at all nodes.

PROOF. Borrowing the idea from [1], we present a family of graphs on which any stretch-k implementation of $\mathcal{A}$ requires $\Omega(n)$ bits at some nodes. Start with a set of nodes $c_i \in C$, $|C| = p \geq 2$. To each $c_i \in C$, add $\delta \geq 2$ neighbors $z_{ij}, i \in \{1, \ldots, p\}, j \in \{1, \ldots, \delta\}$ and label the edges by w_i. Finally, add δ^p nodes $t \in T$ and connect these to the z_{ij} nodes according to the following rule: for each $t \in T$ take the alphabet consisting of the symbols $(1, \ldots, \delta)$, construct a word of length p from this alphabet and add an edge from z_{ij} to t if the ith symbol in the word is exactly j. Label any (z_{ij}, t) edge by w_i. Fig. 2 gives an example.

By monotonicity and (1), the preferred path $p^*_{c_i,t}$ from any $c_i \in C$ to any $t \in T$ is the min-hop path, so $w(p^*_{c_i,t}) = w_i \oplus w_i = w_i^2$. Fraigniaud and Gavoille in [1] show that encoding these paths in the above family of graphs requires $\Omega(n \log \delta)$ bits of storage space at the nodes in C. Intuitively

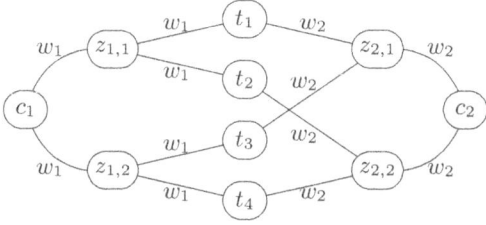

Figure 2: A sample graph for $p = 2$, $\delta = 2$ if the words for the target nodes are $[1,1]$, $[1,2]$, $[2,1]$ and $[2,2]$.

speaking, the idea is that there is an astronomical number of different graphs in this graph family, and to encode the min-hop paths the routing algorithm needs to be able to differentiate amongst them, which requires huge storage space.

Unfortunately, any stretch-k compact routing scheme for k finite needs to encode the exact same min-hop paths. By construction, any non-preferred path $p_{c_i,t}$ goes through at least two edges of weight w_j for some $j \in \{1,\ldots,p\}, j \neq i$, and hence is at least of stretch k: $w(p_{c_i,t}) \succeq w_i \oplus w_i \oplus w_j \oplus w_j \stackrel{(i)}{=} (w_i \oplus w_j) \oplus (w_i \oplus w_j) \stackrel{(ii)}{\succeq} w_i \oplus w_j \stackrel{(iii)}{\succ} (w_i^2)^k = w(p_{c_i,t}^*)$, where (i) is by associativity and commutativity, (ii) is by monotonicity, and (iii) is by (1). $\square$

A key to the above result is the weight set with the special structure (1), an extreme form of strict monotonicity. For $k \geq 2$, (1) violates isotonicity, therefore the theorem does not apply to regular algebras. But to many non-regular algebras it does. For the shortest-widest path policy in particular, one easily generates the weights w_i with the required properties. Let $w_i = (b_i, c_i)$, where b_i denotes the capacity and c_i a positive cost, and for each $i = 1, \ldots, p$ choose $b_i = i$ and let $c_i = (2k)^{i-1}$. One easily checks that this construction satisfies (1), since if $i < j$ then $b_i < b_j$ implies $(b_i, c_i) + (b_j, c_j) = (b_j, c_i + c_j) > (b_j, c_j)^{2k}$, while from $c_i < 2kc_i \leq c_j$ we get $(b_j, c_i + c_j) > (b_i, c_i)^{2k}$. This then implies that the shortest-widest path policy does not admit a compact implementation by Theorem 4.

5. PRACTICAL IMPLICATIONS

We have seen that regular algebras are the easy cases for compact policy routing. However, many real-world routing policies do not lead to regular algebras (or commutative, or associative algebras, for that matter). The most prominent of these is the routing policies used by the Border Gateway Protocol (BGP), the inter-domain routing mechanism that glues the Internet together [27, 28]. Below, we very briefly discuss to what extent the above algebraic treatment can be applied to BGP policy routing algebras.

BGP policy routing can be described at various levels of depth. At the first, elemental level, BGP policy routing corresponds to the *valley-free routing* policy: each edge is labeled as *customer* (c), *peer* (r) or *provider* (p), and the only rule is that no path can contain a $c - p$, $c - r$, $r - p$, or a $r - r$ subpath [29]. This policy can be described by the algebra $\mathcal{B}_1 = (\{p, r, c\}, \phi, \oplus, \preceq)$, where $\oplus$ given in Table 2 and all permitted paths (i.e., ones whose weight is not ϕ) have the same preference [20, 21]. To correctly represent the valley-free routing policy, the underlying graph is supposed to be a digraph in which the opposite arc of a p (r) arc is always labeled as c (r, respectively). Furthermore, $\oplus$ is

Table 2: Weight composition in valley-free routing.

$\oplus$	c	r	p
c	c	ϕ	ϕ
r	r	ϕ	ϕ
p	p	p	p

right-associative. In line with what we see in the Internet, it is usually assumed that every node has a valley-free route to every other node and the network contains no provider-loops (directed p-cycles). Even though this setting violates basically every assumption in terms of which we stated our previous results, the basic ideas are still applicable as illustrated below.

THEOREM 5. $\mathcal{B}_1$ *is compressible.*

PROOF (SKETCH). By temporarily neglecting peer arcs, split the graph to *strongly connected valley-free components* (SVFC) with the property that in each component any pair of nodes u, v can be bidirectionally connected by a valley-free path using customer-provider arcs only. In each SVFC, valley-free routing reduces to the selective and monotone subalgebra $\mathcal{B}_1' = (\{p\}, \phi, \oplus, \preceq)$ with $p \oplus p = p$. As the graph contains no provider loops, every SVFC has a single node, call this the root node, that possesses no outgoing provider link. Then, a straightforward extension of Lemma 1 yields that routing inside a SVFC according to $\mathcal{B}_1'$ equals routing on an arborescence, which is possible with $O(\log n)$ local memory. Furthermore, roots are connected in a full-mesh due to global reachability, routing on which can be done using $O(\log n)$ local memory by a special port labeling [30]. The combination of these two routing schemes yields an $O(\log n)$ routing scheme for valley free routing. $\square$

At the second level, BGP classifies paths according to the *local preference* rules. A minimalistic rule contained in basically every local preference setting is that customer paths are favored over peer and provider paths. This can be described by the algebra $\mathcal{B}_2 = (\{p, r, c\}, \phi, \oplus, \preceq)$, where $\oplus$ again is as in Table 2 and $c \prec r \preceq p$.

THEOREM 6. $\mathcal{B}_2$ *is incompressible. Additionally, there is no stretch-k compact routing scheme for $\mathcal{B}_2$ for any finite $k \geq 2$.*

PROOF (SKETCH). We show a weight set satisfying (1), from which Theorem 4 gives the required result. Simply, let $w_i = c$. As customer arcs are exactly provider arcs in the reverse direction, we have that the weight of any non-preferred path is at least $c \oplus p = \phi \succ c^k$ for any $k \geq 1$. $\square$

BGP policy routing is, naturally, substantially richer than $\mathcal{B}_1$ or $\mathcal{B}_2$. At the third level, for instance, usually path length is taken into account, leading to the algebra $\mathcal{B}_3 = \mathcal{B}_2 \times \mathcal{S}$. Using the foregoing argumentation, one easily checks that $\mathcal{B}_3$ is also incompressible.

6. CONCLUSIONS AND OPEN QUESTIONS

Thanks to the tenacious research efforts in the field of compact routing, we now have a remarkable insight into the theoretical scalability of shortest path routing. Motivated by the fact that many routing applications adopt a significantly more complex way to classify paths than pure shortest path routing (for instance, BGP places path length only at the third place when fixing path preference), in this paper we proposed an algebraic approach towards generalizing the theory of compact routing to policy routing. Our contribution is twofold: first, we presented some "landmark" theorems, which can be used as guidelines to roughly classify routing policies based on their algebraic properties, and second we identified some algebraic requirements for effectively trading between path preference and memory. As an important message, we identified regularity as the cornerstone of compact policy routing, allowing for a generic compressibility theory to be formulated as well as defining a finite stretch compact routing scheme. The fact that regular algebras are exactly the ones that can be efficiently implemented in a distributed way [19–22] makes these algebras highly attractive for designing future routing policies [31].

Besides answering the most elemental questions, this paper perhaps leaves more issues open than it answers. We have seen that selectivity is sufficient for a routing algebra to be compressible, and strict monotonicity is sufficient for incompressibility. However, it is not clear which are the corresponding necessary conditions. Easily, strict monotonicity is not necessary for incompressibility as evidenced by the non-monotone $\mathcal{B}_2$ algebra. Finding a minimal algebra that eventuates incompressibility is therefore an interesting open issue. On the other hand, by requiring selectivity for compressibility we seem to be on the safe side, since selectivity not only guarantees compressibility but also a very appealing memory requirement of $O(\log n)$. Whether there are compressible algebras with $\Omega(\log n)$ local memory requirement is also an intriguing problem. As pointed out in the paper, it is also an open question whether the $\Omega(n)$ characterization for non-isotone algebras is tight, as the only trivial routing function needs $O(n^2 \log d)$ bits per router.

We have shown some real-world routing policies whose memory requirement cannot be relaxed, even by allowing arbitrary finite stretch. Unfortunately, the widely applied BGP policy qualifies for this property. Therefore, perhaps the most compelling question raised in this paper is "what can we do if stretch doesn't help?"

Acknowledgements

This work was performed in the High Speed Networks Laboratory at BME-TMIT. This work is connected to the scientific program of the "Development of quality-oriented and cooperative R+D+I strategy and functional model at BME" project. This project is supported by the New Hungary Development Plan (Project ID: TÁMOP-4.2.1/B-09/1/KMR-2010-0002).

7. REFERENCES

[1] P. Fraigniaud and C. Gavoille. Memory requirement for universal routing schemes. In *Proceedings of the fourteenth annual ACM symposium on Principles of distributed computing*, PODC '95, pages 223–230, 1995.

[2] C. Gavoille and S. Pérennès. Memory requirement for routing in distributed networks. In *Proceedings of the fifteenth annual ACM symposium on Principles of distributed computing*, PODC '96, pages 125–133, 1996.

[3] L. Cowen. Compact routing with minimum stretch. In *ACM-SIAM SODA'99*, pages 255–260, 1999.

[4] M. Thorup and U. Zwick. Compact routing schemes. In *ACM SPAA'01*, pages 1–10, 2001.

[5] C. Gavoille. Routing in distributed networks: Overview and open problems. *ACM SIGACT News*, 32(1):52, 2001.

[6] D. Krioukov, kc claffy, K. Fall, and A. Brady. On compact routing for the Internet. *ACM Comp. Comm. Review*, 37(3):41–52, 2007.

[7] C. Gavoille. An overview on compact routing. In *Workshop on Peer-to-Peer, Routing in Complex Graphs, and Network Coding*, 2007.

[8] G.N. Frederickson and R. Janardan. Designing networks with compact routing tables. *Algorithmica*, 3(1):171–190, 1988.

[9] D. Krioukov, K. Fall, and X. Yang. Compact routing on Internet-like graphs. In *INFOCOM 2004, the Twenty-third Annual Joint Conference of the IEEE Computer and Communications Societies*, volume 1, 2004.

[10] P. Fraigniaud and C. Gavoille. Routing in trees. In *ICALP '01*, pages 757–772, 2001.

[11] O. Younis and S. Fahmy. Constraint-based routing in the Internet: Basic principles and recent research. *IEEE Communications Surveys and Tutorials*, 5(1), 2004.

[12] Zheng Wang and Jon Crowcroft. Quality-of-service routing for supporting multimedia applications. *IEEE Journal of Selected Areas in Communications*, 14(7):1228–1234, 1996.

[13] G. Apostolopoulos, R. Guerin, S. Kamat, and S. K. Tripathi. Quality of service based routing: A performance perspective. In *SIGCOMM*, pages 17–28, 1998.

[14] Qingming Ma and P. Steenkiste. On path selection for traffic with bandwidth guarantees. In *Proceedings of the 1997 International Conference on Network Protocols (ICNP '97)*, page 191, 1997.

[15] M. Caesar and J. Rexford. BGP routing policies in ISP networks. Technical Report UCB/CSD-05-1377, EECS Department, University of California, Berkeley, 2005.

[16] G. Apostolopoulos, R. Guerin, S. Kamat, A. Orda, and S. K. Tripathi. Intra-domain QoS routing in IP networks: A feasibility and cost/benefit analysis. *IEEE Network*, 13:42–54, 1999.

[17] D. Awduche. MPLS and traffic engineering in IP networks. *IEEE Communications Magazine*, 37(12):42–47, Dec 1999.

[18] W. Lee, M. Hluchyi, and P. Humblet. Routing subject to quality of service constraints in integrated communication networks. *IEEE Network Magazine*, 9(4):46–55, July-August 1999.

[19] J. Sobrinho. Algebra and algorithms for QoS path computation and hop-by-hop routing in the Internet. *IEEE/ACM Trans. Netw.*, 10:541–550, August 2002.

[20] J. Sobrinho. Network routing with path vector protocols: theory and applications. In *SIGCOMM '03*, pages 49–60, 2003.

[21] T. Griffin and J. Sobrinho. Metarouting. In *SIGCOMM '05*, pages 1–12, 2005.

[22] A. Gurney and T. Griffin. Lexicographic products in

metarouting. In *Network Protocols, IEEE International Conference on*, pages 113–122, 2007.

[23] C.-K. Chau, R. Gibbens, and T. G. Griffin. Towards a unified theory of policy-based routing. In *INFOCOM 2006, the 25th IEEE International Conference on Computer Communications. Proceedings*, pages 1–12, 2006.

[24] M. Gondran and M. Minoux. *Graphs, Dioids and Semirings: New Models and Algorithms*. Springer Publishing Company, Incorporated, 1 edition, 2008.

[25] B. Awerbuch and Y. Shavitt. Topology aggregation for directed graphs. *IEEE/ACM Trans. Netw.*, 9:82–90, February 2001.

[26] A. H. Clifford and G. B. Preston. *The Algebraic Theory of Semigroups, Volume I*. Number 7 in Mathematical Surveys. American Mathematical Society, 1961.

[27] G. Huston. Interconnection, peering, and settlements. In *Proceedings of the INET*, 1999.

[28] F. Wang and L. Gao. On inferring and characterizing Internet routing policies. In *Proceedings of the 3rd ACM SIGCOMM conference on Internet measurement*, pages 15–26, 2003.

[29] L. Gao. On inferring autonomous system relationships in the Internet. *IEEE/ACM Trans. on Networking*, 9:733–745, 2000.

[30] Pierre Fraigniaud and Cyril Gavoille. Local memory requirement of universal routing schemes. Technical Report 96-01, École Normale Supérieure de Lyon, 69364 Lyon Cedex 07, 1996.

[31] A. Seehra, J. Naous, M. Walfish, D. Mazieres, A. Nicolosi, and S. Shenker. A policy framework for the future Internet. *HotNets-VIII*, 2009.

Locally Checkable Proofs

Mika Göös
mika.goos@cs.helsinki.fi

Jukka Suomela
jukka.suomela@cs.helsinki.fi

Helsinki Institute for Information Technology HIIT, University of Helsinki
P.O. Box 68, FI-00014 University of Helsinki, Finland

ABSTRACT

This work studies *decision problems* from the perspective of *nondeterministic distributed algorithms*. For a *yes*-instance there must exist a *proof* that can be verified with a distributed algorithm: all nodes must accept a valid proof, and at least one node must reject an invalid proof. We focus on *locally checkable proofs* that can be verified with a constant-time distributed algorithm.

For example, it is easy to prove that a graph is bipartite: the locally checkable proof gives a 2-colouring of the graph, which only takes 1 bit per node. However, it is more difficult to prove that a graph is *not* bipartite—it turns out that any locally checkable proof requires $\Omega(\log n)$ bits per node.

In this work we classify graph problems according to their local proof complexity, i.e., how many bits per node are needed in a locally checkable proof. We establish tight or near-tight results for classical graph properties such as the chromatic number. We show that the proof complexities form a natural hierarchy of complexity classes: for many classical graph problems, the proof complexity is either 0, $\Theta(1)$, $\Theta(\log n)$, or $\mathsf{poly}(n)$ bits per node. Among the most difficult graph properties are symmetric graphs, which require $\Omega(n^2)$ bits per node, and non-3-colourable graphs, which require $\Omega(n^2/\log n)$ bits per node—any pure graph property admits a trivial proof of size $O(n^2)$.

Categories and Subject Descriptors

C.2.4 [**Computer-Communication Networks**]: Distributed Systems; F.1.3 [**Computation by Abstract Devices**]: Complexity Measures and Classes

General Terms

Algorithms, Theory

1. INTRODUCTION

This work studies *decision problems* from the perspective of distributed algorithms. As argued by Fraigniaud in his

PODC 2010 keynote talk [8], the appropriate model for yes–no tasks is the following:

- For a *yes*-instance, all nodes must output 1.
- For a *no*-instance, at least one node must output 0.

Intuitively, if we have an acceptable input, all nodes will be happy, and if we have an invalid input, at least one node has to raise an alarm.

1.1 Locally Checkable Properties

Our focus is on decision tasks that can be solved *locally*, by using a constant-time distributed algorithm [18, 23]. That is, each node must make its decision based on its constant-radius neighbourhood in the communication graph; equivalently, we run the distributed algorithm for $O(1)$ rounds and after that all nodes must stop and announce their outputs.

A trivial example of a decision problem that can be solved locally is determining if a given connected graph is Eulerian: it is sufficient that each node outputs 1 if its degree is even, and 0 otherwise. Such graph properties are called *locally checkable properties*—there exists a local algorithm, called *verifier*, that accepts all Eulerian graphs and rejects all non-Eulerian graphs.

Another example of locally checkable properties is deciding if a given graph is a line graph. If the nodes have unique identifiers, a constant-time verifier can check that the graph does not contain any of the nine forbidden subgraphs in Beineke's [3] characterisation of line graphs.

1.2 Locally Checkable Proofs

Local checkability as such does not seem to lead to an interesting complexity theory—there are very few locally checkable properties. The key insight of Korman et al. [14–17] is to study locally checkable *proofs*.

To illustrate the idea, consider the problem of deciding if a given graph is bipartite. This is not a locally checkable property—indeed, if we consider odd vs. even cycles, we can see that any verifier that solves the problem must have the running time $\Omega(n)$. However, if we want to convince a distributed algorithm that the graph is indeed bipartite, we can augment the graph with a *locally checkable proof*. In this case, it is sufficient to give 1 bit of proof per node: if the graph is bipartite, we can give a 2-colouring of the graph as the proof, and a local verifier can check that the proof is correct. Conversely, if the graph is not bipartite, no matter what proof bits we choose, at least one node will detect that the proof is invalid. Hence we say the property of bipartiteness is in the class $\mathsf{LCP}(1)$: for any bipartite graph, there is a locally checkable proof of size 1 bit per node (refer to Section 2 for a precise definition).

The concepts of locally checkable proofs and locally checkable properties are analogous to, e.g., the familiar pair of complexity classes NP and P. If a problem is in NP, then *yes*-instances have a concise proof that can be verified in P. Similarly, if the problem is in LCP(f), then *yes*-instances have a concise proof with at most $f(n)$ bits per node and the proof itself is checkable with a local algorithm. Equivalently, we can interpret locally checkable proofs as *nondeterministic* local algorithms: in the algorithm, each node can nondeterministically guess $f(n)$ bits.

1.3 Contributions

In this work, we define the class LCP(f) that consists of graph problems that admit locally checkable proofs of size $f(n)$ bits per node. The model is similar to that studied by Korman et al. [14–17], but strictly stronger.

We catalogue problems according to their local proof complexities, and we show that the LCP(f) classes form a natural hierarchy of decision problems. In particular, there are natural graph problems that separate the following levels of the hierarchy: LCP(0), LCP($O(1)$), LCP($O(\log n)$), and LCP(poly(n)); see Table 1.

We argue that LogLCP = LCP($O(\log n)$) is a particularly good candidate for a complexity class of independent interest. The class is robust to variations in the exact definition of the LCP hierarchy (see Section 7.1). Many central graph problems are contained in LogLCP, and they are not contained in LCP($o(\log n)$).

We present proof techniques that can be used to derive tight and near-tight lower bounds for the local proof complexity. We show how to apply tools from other fields of computer science and mathematics: results in extremal graph theory, fooling set arguments from the field of communication complexity, and gadgets that are typical in NP-hardness proofs. The same techniques can be applied to derive lower bounds for many other problems in addition to those mentioned in this work.

2. DEFINITIONS AND EXAMPLES

In what follows, $\mathcal{F}$ is a family of simple, undirected graphs. For a graph $\mathcal{G} \in \mathcal{F}$, we write $V(\mathcal{G})$ for the set of nodes, $E(\mathcal{G})$ for the set of edges, and $n(\mathcal{G}) = |V(\mathcal{G})|$ for the number of nodes in $\mathcal{G}$. If graph $\mathcal{G}$ is clear from the context, we simply use the symbols V, E, and n. We assume that the nodes of any $\mathcal{G} \in \mathcal{F}$ are identified with small natural numbers with $O(\log n)$ bits, that is, $V(\mathcal{G}) \subseteq \{1, 2, \ldots, \text{poly}(n(\mathcal{G}))\}$. Depending on the problem that we study, nodes and edges may also be associated with weights, colours, labels, etc.

2.1 Proofs and Verifiers

A *proof* P for $\mathcal{G}$ is a function $P\colon V(\mathcal{G}) \to \{0,1\}^{*}$ that associates a binary string to each node of $\mathcal{G}$. The size $|P|$ of proof P is the maximum number of bits in any string $P(v)$. We write ϵ for an empty proof of size 0.

A *verifier* $\mathcal{A}$ is a computable function that maps each triple $(\mathcal{G}, P, v)$ to a binary output 0 or 1. Here $\mathcal{G} \in \mathcal{F}$ is a graph, $P\colon V(\mathcal{G}) \to \{0,1\}^{*}$ is a proof, and $v \in V(\mathcal{G})$ is a node of $\mathcal{G}$. Intuitively, $\mathcal{A}(\mathcal{G}, P, v)$ is the *output* of node v if we run the distributed algorithm $\mathcal{A}$ in graph $\mathcal{G}$ and each node $u \in V(\mathcal{G})$ is provided with *input* $P(u)$.

Table 1: Local Proof Complexities

(a) The local proof complexity of verifying graph property $\mathcal{P}$, assuming that the input graph is in graph family $\mathcal{F}$. Constant k is a natural number. In reachability problems, nodes s and t are labelled; otherwise the graphs are unlabelled (i.e., the focus is on pure graph properties).

Proof size s	Graph property $\mathcal{P}$	Family $\mathcal{F}$	Ref.
LCP(0):			
0	Eulerian graph	conn.	§1.1
0	line graph	general	§1.1
LCP($O(1)$):			
$\Theta(1)$	s–t reachability	undir.	§4.1
$\Theta(1)$	s–t unreachability	undir.	§4.1
$\Theta(1)$	s–t unreachability	directed	§4.1
$\Theta(1)$	s–t connectivity $= k$	planar	§4.2
$\Theta(1)$	bipartite graph	general	§1.2
$\Theta(1)$	even $n(\mathcal{G})$	cycles	
LCP($O(\log k)$):			
$O(\log k)$	s–t connectivity $= k$	general	§4.2
$O(\log k)$	chromatic number $\leq k$	general	§2.2
LogLCP:			
$O(\log n)$	coLCP(0) properties	conn.	§7.3
$O(\log n)$	monadic Σ_1^1 properties	conn.	§7.5
$\Theta(\log n)$	odd $n(\mathcal{G})$	cycles	§5
$\Theta(\log n)$	chromatic number > 2	conn.	§5
LCP(poly(n)):			
$\Theta(n)$	fixpoint-free symmetry	trees	§6.2
$\Theta(n^2)$	symmetric graphs	conn.	§6.1
$\Omega(n^2/\log n)$	chromatic number > 3	conn.	§6.3
$O(n^2)$	computable properties	conn.	§6
—	connected graph	general	

(b) The local proof complexity of verifying a solution of graph problem $\mathcal{P}$, assuming that the input graph is in graph family $\mathcal{F}$. Here W is the maximum weight of an edge.

Proof size s	Graph problem $\mathcal{P}$	Family $\mathcal{F}$	Ref.
LCP(0):			
0	maximal matching	general	§2.3
0	LCL problems	general	§3, [18]
0	LD problems	conn.	§3, [10]
LCP($O(1)$):			
$\Theta(1)$	maximum matching	bipartite	§2.3
LCP($O(\log W)$):			
$O(\log W)$	max-weight matching	bipartite	§2.3
LogLCP:			
$O(\log n)$	coLCP(0) problems	conn.	§7.3
$\Theta(\log n)$	leader election	conn.	§5, [16]
$\Theta(\log n)$	spanning tree	conn.	§5, [16]
$\Theta(\log n)$	maximum matching	cycles	§5
$\Theta(\log n)$	Hamiltonian cycle	conn.	§5
LCP(∞):			
unlimited	NLD problems	conn.	§3, [10]
unlimited	NLD$^{\#n}$ problems	conn.	§3, [10]

For a natural number $r \in \mathbb{N}$ and a node $v \in V(\mathcal{G})$, let $V[v, r] \subseteq V(\mathcal{G})$ be the set of nodes that are within distance r from v (the shortest path from v to any node in $V[v, r]$ has at most r edges). Let $\mathcal{G}[v, r]$ be the subgraph of $\mathcal{G}$ induced by $V[v, r]$, and let $P[v, r] \colon V[v, r] \to \{0, 1\}^\star$ be the restriction of a proof $P \colon V(\mathcal{G}) \to \{0, 1\}^\star$ to $V[v, r]$.

A verifier $\mathcal{A}$ is a *local verifier* if there exists a constant $r \in \mathbb{N}$ such that

$$\mathcal{A}(\mathcal{G}, P, v) = \mathcal{A}(\mathcal{G}[v, r], P[v, r], v) \text{ for all } \mathcal{G}, P, v.$$

That is, the output of a node v only depends on the input in its radius-r neighbourhood. Constant r is the *local horizon* of $\mathcal{A}$.

Local verifiers are local algorithms [18, 23]. If we consider Peleg's [19] *local* model, a local verifier is a constant-time distributed algorithm: a local verifier with horizon r can be implemented as a distributed algorithm that completes in r synchronous communication rounds.

2.2 Locally Checkable Proofs

A *graph property* $\mathcal{P} \subseteq \mathcal{F}$ is a subset of graphs that is closed under re-assigning the identifiers of the nodes. Put otherwise, if $\mathcal{G}$ and $\mathcal{G}'$ are isomorphic (they have the same structure but possibly different node identifiers), then $\mathcal{G}' \in \mathcal{P}$ if and only if $\mathcal{G} \in \mathcal{P}$. Examples of graph properties include Hamiltonian graphs, Eulerian graphs, bipartite graphs, connected graphs, line graphs, trees, and cycles.

A graph property $\mathcal{P} \subseteq \mathcal{F}$ admits *locally checkable proofs* of size $s \colon \mathbb{N} \to \mathbb{N}$ on family $\mathcal{F}$ if there is a local verifier $\mathcal{A}$ such that for every $\mathcal{G} \in \mathcal{F}$:

(i) If $\mathcal{G} \in \mathcal{P}$ then there exists a proof $P \colon V(\mathcal{G}) \to \{0, 1\}^\star$ with $|P| \le s(n(\mathcal{G}))$ such that $\mathcal{A}(\mathcal{G}, P, v) = 1$ for each node $v \in V(\mathcal{G})$.

(ii) If $\mathcal{G} \notin \mathcal{P}$ then for any proof $P \colon V(\mathcal{G}) \to \{0, 1\}^\star$ there is at least one node $v \in V(\mathcal{G})$ such that $\mathcal{A}(\mathcal{G}, P, v) = 0$.

That is, *yes*-instances have a valid proof that is accepted by all nodes, *no*-instances do not have valid proofs, and at least one node detects an invalid proof. If f is a function that associates a valid proof $P = f(\mathcal{G})$ with each $\mathcal{G} \in \mathcal{P}$, we say that the pair $(f, \mathcal{A})$ is a *proof labelling scheme*.

If a property $\mathcal{P}$ admits locally checkable proofs of size s, we write $\mathcal{P} \in \mathsf{LCP}(s)$. We use $\mathsf{coLCP}(s)$ to denote the class of graph properties whose complement is in $\mathsf{LCP}(s)$; that is, if $\mathcal{F} \setminus \mathcal{P} \in \mathsf{LCP}(s)$, we write $\mathcal{P} \in \mathsf{coLCP}(s)$. The class LogLCP consists of properties that are in $\mathsf{LCP}(s)$ for $s = O(\log n)$; see Section 7.1 for an equivalent, alternative characterisation.

As we observed in Section 1, Eulerian graphs and line graphs can be verified without a proof, and hence they are in $\mathsf{LCP}(0)$. Bipartite graphs are not in $\mathsf{LCP}(0)$ but they are contained in $\mathsf{LCP}(1)$, as they can be verified with one bit of input per node. More generally, if a graph has chromatic number at most k, we can prove it with $O(\log k)$ bits per node: simply give a proper k-colouring as the proof.

2.3 Extension: Solutions of Graph Problems

If we consider graphs with labelled nodes, we can also define graph properties such as independent sets (*"nodes with label 1 form an independent set"*) or spanning trees (*"edges with label 1 induce a spanning tree"*). That is, we can extend the definitions of locally checkable proofs to the verification of the solutions of graph problems (see Section 7.2 for two variants of the theme).

For example, maximal matchings can be verified without any proofs, and hence we say that this problem is in $\mathsf{LCP}(0)$. On the other hand, verifying a maximum matching (*"edges with label 1 form a maximum-cardinality matching"*) requires some auxiliary information. The general case is non-trivial, but in the case of bipartite graphs we can use König's theorem [5, p. 35] to construct a constant-size proof P: take any minimum vertex cover $C \subseteq V(\mathcal{G})$, and set $P(v) = 1$ iff $v \in C$. Now a local verifier can check that the node labelling encodes a valid matching M, the set C encoded in the proof forms a vertex cover, and each edge of M has exactly one endpoint in C; hence $|C| = |M|$, C is a minimum vertex cover, and M must be a maximum matching. Therefore maximum matchings in bipartite graphs are in $\mathsf{LCP}(1)$, as the size of P is 1.

More generally, we can use linear-programming duality to prove that in an edge-weighted bipartite graph $\mathcal{G}$, a subset of edges $M \subseteq E(\mathcal{G})$ is a maximum-weight matching. Associate a variable $x_e \ge 0$ with each edge $e \in E$, and a dual variable $y_v \ge 0$ with each node $v \in V$. Let $w_e \in \mathbb{N}$ be the weight of edge e, and let A be the incidence matrix of graph $\mathcal{G}$. Recall that matrix A and its transpose $A^\top$ are totally unimodular, and hence there are integral vectors x and y that maximise $\sum_e w_e x_e$ subject to $Ax \le 1$ (primal LP) and minimise $\sum_v y_v$ subject to $A^\top y \ge w$ (dual LP). Each maximum-weight matching M corresponds to an optimal integral solution x of the primal LP, and we can use an optimal dual solution y as a proof; for each node $v \in V$, the proof consists of a binary encoding of the value y_v. To verify the proof, it is sufficient to check that x and y satisfy the complementary slackness conditions. If the weights are integers from $0, 1, \ldots, W$, then we can find an optimal dual solution such that $y_v \in \{0, 1, \ldots, W\}$ for each node v. Hence the size of the proof is $O(\log W)$ bits.

3. RELATED WORK

Our definition of the LCP hierarchy is an extension of the concept of *locally checkable labellings* introduced by Naor and Stockmeyer [18] in their seminal work. Naor and Stockmeyer focus on bounded-degree graphs and constant-size labels, but if we generalise the class LCL defined by Naor and Stockmeyer in a straightforward manner, we arrive at the class $\mathsf{LCP}(0)$.

Our classes $\mathsf{LCP}(f)$ with $f > 0$ thus extend the classical concept of locally checkable labellings by providing $f(n)$ bits of additional information per node. Similar extensions have been studied in prior work, from two complementary perspectives: local computation with advice and locally checkable proofs.

3.1 Local Computation with Advice

Gavoille and Peleg [11] survey *informative localised labelling schemes* that can be used in the context of distributed algorithms. The idea is to provide each node with a piece of *advice*—a short bit string that helps with local algorithms that solve graph problems. For example, Fraigniaud et al. [9] have recently investigated the following question: how long strings of advice are needed in order to solve classical graph problems such as graph colouring by using local or almost-local algorithms.

The main difference between advice strings and locally checkable proofs is that the advice strings are *assumed* to be correct, while the correctness of a proof can be *verified*. Put otherwise, localised labelling schemes are only applicable in a friendly and fault-free environment, while a local verifier cannot be fooled even by an adversarial entity.

3.2 Locally Checkable Proofs

The definition of LCP is inspired by the notion of *proof labelling schemes* of Korman et al. [14–17]. While the concepts are closely related to each other, there are subtle differences: In the model of Korman et al., the output of a single node must be determined on the basis of its own identifier, own input label, own proof label and the proof labels of the neighbouring nodes. In this model, some trivial problems that are in LCL become unsolvable without proof labels of nonzero size; one example is the *agreement problem* of checking whether all nodes in a connected graph are assigned the same input label [16, Lemma 2.1]. Hence the notion of proof labelling schemes is not a straightforward generalisation of the LCL model—something our LCP model strives to be. The positive results by Korman et al. translate directly to the LCP model, but their lower-bound results do not directly apply, as their model is strictly weaker.

Very recently, Fraigniaud et al. [10] have also studied distributed decision problems. Their focus is on connected graphs; to clarify the relation to our work, let us define that $LCP'(f)$ is equal to $LCP(f)$ restricted to computable properties of connected graphs. With this notation, the class LD of local decision problems defined by Fraigniaud et al. is equal to $LCP'(0)$. Fraigniaud et al. have also studied two nondeterministic versions of this class, called NLD and $NLD^{\#n}$; in the latter class each node knows the total number of nodes in the graph. While NLD resembles the class $LCP'(\infty)$ in our work, there is a major difference: proofs in the NLD model cannot refer to the node identifiers. It turns out that our class $LCP'(\infty)$ is equal to $NLD^{\#n}$: both classes contain all computable properties of connected graphs. Hence using the separation results of Fraigniaud et al. we have $LCP'(0) = LD \subsetneq NLD \subsetneq NLD^{\#n} = LCP'(\infty)$. While Fraigniaud et al. place one class between the extreme ends of $LCP'(0)$ and $LCP'(\infty)$, our work introduces an entire hierarchy of $LCP(f)$ classes.

4. PROBLEMS IN LCP(O(1))

As a warm-up, this section gives examples of graph properties and graph problems that admit locally checkable proofs of size $O(1)$ but for which there is no locally checkable proof of size 0. We will see that many fundamental problems related to graph connectivity are in this class.

To ask meaningful questions about connectivity in the LCP model, we require that two nodes s and t are always distinguished in the input graph $\mathcal{G}$; that is, we have the promise that there is exactly one node with label s and exactly one node with label t. It is easy to see that in LCP(0) we cannot decide whether there is a path from s to t in $\mathcal{G}$. However, many questions related to reachability and connectivity are in LCP(O(1)).

4.1 Reachability

Let us first consider the *s–t reachability* problem in an undirected graph $\mathcal{G}$, i.e., proving that there is a path from s to t. This problem admits a locally checkable proof of size 1: we find a shortest path from s to t in $\mathcal{G}$, define that $U \subseteq V$ consists of all nodes on the shortest path, and set $P(v) = 1$ iff $v \in U$. A verifier can locally check that: (i) $s, t \in U$;

(ii) s and t have unique neighbours in U; and (iii) every $u \in U \setminus \{s, t\}$ has exactly two neighbours in U [13, p. 130].

Interestingly, the above method breaks down in directed graphs because of back-edges. In graphs of maximum degree Δ, one can still give an easy upper bound of $O(\log \Delta)$ by using edge pointers in the proof labelling to describe a path from s to t, but it is an open problem whether directed s–t reachability is in LCP(O(1)) for general graphs (see also Ajtai and Fagin [1]).

However, it is easy to show that the complement of the above problem, *s–t unreachability*, is in LCP(O(1)) both for undirected and directed graphs. We find a partition $S \cup T$ of V such that $s \in S$, $t \in T$, and there is no (directed) edge from S to T. Such a partition can be encoded with 1 bit per node, and it can be verified locally.

4.2 Connectivity

As a natural generalisation of reachability, we can study the *s–t connectivity* of undirected graphs; throughout this text, we focus on the *vertex connectivity*. By extending the techniques of Korman et al. [16] we can show that graphs with s–t connectivity equal to k admit locally checkable proofs of size $O(\log k)$. Here we assume that k is given as input to all nodes (or, equivalently, that k is a global constant).

If and only if the vertex connectivity is exactly k, then by Menger's theorem we can find (i) a partition $S \cup C \cup T$ of V such that $s \in S$, $t \in T$, and $|C| = k$, and (ii) k vertex-disjoint s–t paths $p_1, p_2, \ldots, p_k$ such that $|C \cap p_i| = 1$. W.l.o.g., we can assume that each p_i is locally minimal in the sense that it can not be made shorter without colliding with the other paths p_j, $j \neq i$.

The proof label $P(v)$ encodes whether $v \in S$, $v \in C$, or $v \in T$. Moreover, in the proof label $P(v)$ of a vertex $v \in p_i \setminus \{s, t\}$, we include the path index i (in binary) and also the distance of v from s modulo 3: this allows us to store the orientation on the path p_i. The local verifier can verify that:

(i) Nodes s and t have exactly k neighbours labelled with path indices $1, 2, \ldots, k$.

(ii) Each $v \in p_i \setminus \{s, t\}$ has exactly one predecessor and one successor along p_i.

(iii) We have $s \in S$, $t \in T$, and there is no edge between S and T.

(iv) Each $v \in C$ is on a path p_i, its predecessor along p_i is in S and its successor is in T.

If the above checks go through, the structure encoded by the proof P contains exactly k disjoint s–t paths. It may contain some oriented cycles inside S or inside T as well, but this is sufficient to convince the verifier that the connectivity of s and t is at least k. Moreover, if a path crosses C, its colour changes from S to T; its colour cannot change back to S, and it cannot disappear without reaching t. Hence the above checks are also sufficient to convince the verifier that the size of the s–t separator C is at most k. In summary, s–t-connectivity has to be equal to k.

Finally, we note that the sole source for the $O(\log k)$ label size was the need to store the path indices. However, on planar graphs, only 3 path indices suffice to tell adjacent paths from one another; an adaptation of the above method gives a constant size proof in the case of planar graphs.

5. PROBLEMS IN LogLCP

In this section we give examples of graph properties and graph problems that admit locally checkable proofs of size $O(\log n)$ but for which there is no locally checkable proof of size $o(\log n)$. That is, these problems are in LogLCP but not in any lower level of the LCP hierarchy.

We begin with positive results that directly build on prior work—a key ingredient is the observation that spanning trees in connected graphs are in LogLCP. After that, we give our new lower-bound results.

5.1 Positive Results

A spanning tree is not locally checkable, but Korman et al. [16] show that any spanning tree T can be equipped with a proof of size $O(\log n)$ that, for each vertex v, consists of (i) the identity of a particular vertex a, *the root*, and (ii) the distance from v to a in T. Such a proof can be locally verified by checking that the root-distance at a is 0, and that for each vertex v (i) all neighbours of v agree on the identity of the root, and (ii) the root-distance decreases at exactly one neighbour of v in T and increases at other neighbours.

A locally checkable, rooted spanning tree is a versatile tool. For example, it solves the leader election problem in a connected graph: the root of the tree is the leader. Spanning trees can be used to prove that the graph is acyclic: we simply show that each component is a tree. Hamiltonian cycles and Hamiltonian paths can be verified by using the same technique: a Hamiltonian path can be interpreted as a spanning tree.

With spanning trees, we can also gather global information about the input graph. For instance, every node can be convinced of the value of $n(\mathcal{G})$ on a connected graph $\mathcal{G}$ with the aid of a spanning tree with node counters along the paths towards the root. Hence graph properties such as having an odd number of nodes are also in LogLCP.

In LogLCP, we can also show that the chromatic number of a connected graph is larger than 2 (i.e., the graph is not bipartite). To construct a proof, first find an odd cycle in the graph—such a cycle exists if and only if the graph is non-bipartite. Then select one of the nodes of the cycle as the leader a. Construct a spanning tree rooted at a; this way the verifier can check that there exists exactly one leader. Then propagate a node counter along the cycle, starting and ending at a; this way the leader node can be convinced that it is indeed part of an odd cycle.

5.2 Negative Results: Overview

In what follows, we will show that the following graph properties and graph problems do not admit locally checkable proofs of size $o(\log n)$: graphs with an odd number of nodes, non-bipartite graphs, spanning trees, and leader election. Hence these are examples of problems whose containment in LogLCP is tight: their local proof complexity is exactly $\Theta(\log n)$.

The negative results build on the same basic idea. We will focus on cycles. We will assume that there is a proof labelling scheme $(f, \mathcal{A})$ with $o(\log n)$-bit proofs. We will take several *yes*-instances—each of them is a short cycle—and inspect the encoding produced by f. Then we will use extremal results to show that some of the *yes*-instances are necessarily *compatible with each other* in the following sense: we can take several short cycles and *glue them together* to form a longer cycle; the unique identifiers and the proof labels are

inherited from the short cycles, and each node of the long cycle will be locally indistinguishable from a node of a short cycle. Hence the verifier will accept the long cycle, as it has to accept all short cycles.

However, even though the short cycles are *yes*-instances, we will show that the long cycle is a *no*-instance. For example, in the case of non-bipartiteness, each short cycle has an odd number of nodes, but the long cycles is composed of an even number of short cycles, and is therefore a *no*-instance. In the case of leader election, each short cycle has one leader node, while the long cycle will contain multiple leaders, and is therefore an invalid solution. Similar ideas can be applied to many other lower bounds.

5.3 Gluing Cycles Together

Let $\mathcal{F}$ be a family of graphs that contains (at least) all cycles. In each graph $\mathcal{G} \in \mathcal{F}$, we may have a constant number of bits of auxiliary information per node (colours, labels, etc.). Let $\mathcal{P} \subseteq \mathcal{F}$ be a graph property.

Assume that $(f, \mathcal{A})$ is a proof labelling scheme for property $\mathcal{P}$ that uses $o(\log n)$-bit proofs. Fix an integer constant $k \geq 2$. Let n be a sufficiently large positive integer. We will assume that n-cycles (with appropriate auxiliary information) are in $\mathcal{P}$.

Our plan is to show that we can always find k *yes*-instances, each of which is an n-cycle, and we can glue them together to form a kn-cycle that inherits the proof labels (and auxiliary information, if any) from the *yes*-instances. Verifier $\mathcal{A}$ will accept each n-cycle, and therefore it will also accept the kn-cycle. For an example, see Figure 1.

Let us first construct the *yes*-instances. Let $n_1 = \lfloor n/2 \rfloor$ and $n_2 = \lceil n/2 \rceil$; that is, $n_1 + n_2 = n$. Let $A = \{1, 2, \dots, n\}$ and $B = \{n+1, n+2, \dots, 2n\}$. For each $a \in A$ and $b \in B$, let $\mathcal{C}(a, b)$ be the n-cycle that contains the following nodes in this order:

$$a, a+4n, a+6n, a+8n, \dots, a+2nn_1,$$
$$b+2nn_2, \dots, b+8n, b+6n, b+4n, b.$$

Note that $V(\mathcal{C}(a, b))$ and $V(\mathcal{C}(a', b'))$ are disjoint if $a \neq a'$ and $b \neq b'$.

For each a and b, augment $\mathcal{C}(a, b)$ with auxiliary information such that $\mathcal{C}(a, b)$ is in $\mathcal{P}$, if necessary; let $L_{ab}(v) \in \{0, 1\}^*$ be the bit string associated with node $v \in V(\mathcal{C}(a, b))$. For example, if we focus on the leader election problem, label exactly one node in each $\mathcal{C}(a, b)$ as the leader: select a node $u \in V(\mathcal{C}(a, b))$ and set $L_{ab}(u) = 1$ and $L_{ab}(v) = 0$ for all $v \neq u$. We can consider either best-case or worst-case choice of the leader, thus covering both weak and strong proof labelling schemes (see Section 7.2).

Then we apply f to $\mathcal{C}(a, b)$ to construct a locally checkable proof P_{ab} of size $o(\log n)$. For each node $v \in V(\mathcal{C}(a, b))$, let $P'_{ab}(v) = (L_{ab}(v), P_{ab}(v))$. Finally, define

$$c(a, b) = \big(P'_{ab}(a + 2n \cdot (2r+1)), P'_{ab}(a + 2n \cdot 2r), \dots,$$
$$P'_{ab}(a + 2n \cdot 2), P'_{ab}(a), P'_{ab}(b), P'_{ab}(b + 2n \cdot 2),$$
$$P'_{ab}(b + 2n \cdot 4), \dots, P'_{ab}(b + 2n \cdot (2r+1)) \big).$$

That is, $c(a, b)$ consists of all auxiliary information and all proof bits that are available within distance $2r+1$ from the node a or b in $\mathcal{C}(a, b)$. By assumption, we have $o(r \log n)$ bits of information in $c(a, b)$.

Now let $K_{n,n} = (A \cup B, E)$ be the complete bipartite graph with $E = \{\{a, b\} : a \in A, b \in B\}$. We define an edge

Monochromatic 2k-cycle in $K_{n,n}$:

$(n = 10, r = 1, k = 2)$

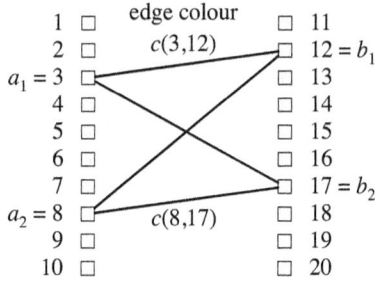

Constructing the kn-cycle C by gluing together two compatible n-cycles:

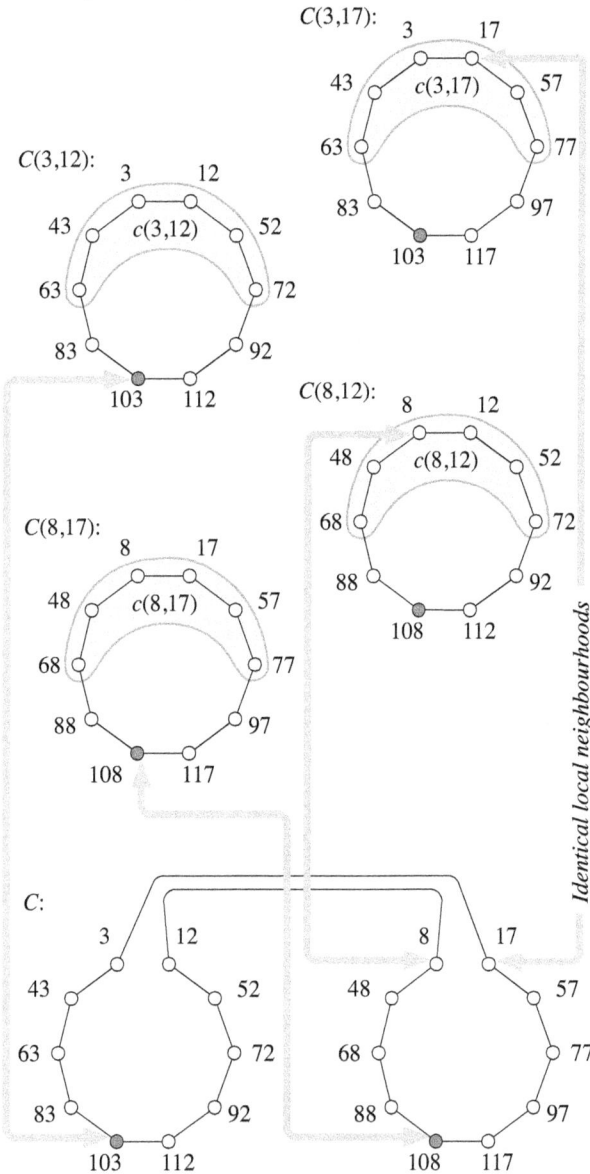

Figure 1: Gluing cycles together.

colouring of $K_{n,n}$ as follows: the colour of the edge $\{a, b\} \in E$ is $c(a, b)$.

For a sufficiently large n, the number of bits of information in $c(a, b)$ is smaller than $\log(n)/3$, and the number of distinct colours in $K_{n,n}$ is therefore smaller than $\sqrt[3]{n}$. Hence there is a subset of edges $H \subseteq E$ such that $|H| > |E|/\sqrt[3]{n} = n^{5/3}$ and all edges of H have the same colour.

Now we can apply a result due to Bondy and Simonovits [4]: for any $k \geq 2$ and for a sufficiently large n, the subgraph $(A \cup B, H)$ necessarily contains a $2k$-cycle. Let the nodes of the cycle be $a_1, b_1, a_2, b_2, \ldots, a_k, b_k$ in this order, such that $a_i \in A$ and $b_i \in B$ for each i. As all edges of the cycle have the same colour, we have $c(a_1, b_1) = c(a_2, b_2) = \cdots = c(a_k, b_k) = c(a_1, b_k) = c(a_2, b_1) = \cdots = c(a_k, b_{k-1})$. For convenience, define $b_0 = b_k$ and $a_{k+1} = a_1$.

Now we construct a kn-cycle C by gluing together n-cycles $\mathcal{C}(a_1, b_1), \mathcal{C}(a_2, b_2), \ldots, \mathcal{C}(a_k, b_k)$. That is, we take the node-disjoint graphs $\mathcal{C}(a_i, b_i)$, remove the edges $\{a_i, b_i\}$ for each i, and add $\{b_{i-1}, a_i\}$ for each $i > 1$. For each node $v \in V(\mathcal{C})$, we inherit the auxiliary information $L(v)$ and the proof bits $P(v)$ from the cycles $\mathcal{C}(a_i, b_i)$.

It remains to argue that the computation of $\mathcal{A}$ on C with the labels L and proof P is accepting. To see this, pick a vertex $v \in V(\mathcal{C})$. Then there is an i such that $v \in V(\mathcal{C}(a_i, b_i))$. If v is far from a_i and b_i, then the local neighbourhood of v looks identical in $\mathcal{C}$ and $\mathcal{C}(a_i, b_i)$; as $\mathcal{C}(a_i, b_i)$ is a yes-instance, v accepts the input. If v is near b_i, then the local neighbourhood of v looks identical in $\mathcal{C}$ and $\mathcal{C}(a_{i+1}, b_i)$, which is another yes-instance. Similarly, if v is near a_i, then its local neighbourhood looks identical in $\mathcal{C}$ and $\mathcal{C}(a_i, b_{i-1})$, which is also a yes-instance. In all cases, v accepts the input.

Thus the kn-cycle C is accepted by all nodes. If $C \notin \mathcal{P}$, we have a contradiction, and we can conclude that the graph property $\mathcal{P}$ does not admit locally checkable proofs of size $o(\log n)$.

5.4 Implications

Now we can give concrete examples of graph properties and graph problems $\mathcal{P}$ for which $C \notin \mathcal{P}$, provided that we choose the parameters k and n properly:

- Non-bipartite graphs: We can select an odd n and $k = 2$.

- Leader election: It is sufficient to choose $k = 2$. Then each $\mathcal{C}(a, b)$ contains exactly one node labelled as a leader and $\mathcal{C}$ contains two nodes.

- Spanning trees: Again, we can choose $k = 2$. The spanning tree in each $\mathcal{C}(a, b)$ contains all edges of $E(\mathcal{C}(a, b))$ except one, i.e., it is a spanning path. The solution encoded in C consists of two disjoint paths, and is therefore not a spanning tree.

We can also apply the same construction to counting problems: to give a simple example, if we choose an odd n and an even k, then $n(\mathcal{C}(a, b))$ is odd while $n(\mathcal{C})$ is even.

We can also prove lower bounds for optimisation problems. Consider, for example, the problem of finding a maximum matching in a cycle. If n is odd, then each $\mathcal{C}(a, b)$ has necessarily one unmatched node. The solution inherited from $\mathcal{C}(a, b)$ to C has therefore k unmatched nodes, and cannot be optimal.

Hence all of these problems require proofs of size $\Omega(\log n)$, and the lower bound is tight.

6. PROBLEMS IN LCP(poly(n))

In the previous sections, we have seen problems that admit locally checkable proofs of size $O(\log(n))$. Now we turn our attention to the problems that require much larger proofs.

If the nodes can have arbitrary labels (e.g., weights), it is easy to come up with artificial problems that require arbitrarily large proofs. However, in this section we will focus on *pure graph properties*: we do not have any additional information besides the structure of the graph $\mathcal{G}$ and the unique node identifiers.

In connected graphs, *any* computable pure graph property admits locally checkable proofs of size $O(n^2)$. We can encode the structure of $\mathcal{G}$ and the unique node identifiers in $O(n^2)$ bits; the nodes can verify that their neighbours agree on the structure of $\mathcal{G}$, and then they can solve the problem by brute force.

In this section, we will show that there are pure graph properties that require $\Omega(n^2)$-bit proofs. Such problems are the most difficult problems from the LCP perspective—we can only save a constant factor in comparison with the brute-force solution.

6.1 Symmetric Graphs

We will focus on the family $\mathcal{F}$ of connected graphs. In what follows, we say that a graph $\mathcal{G}$ is *symmetric* if it has a non-trivial automorphism, that is, there is an automorphism $g\colon V \to V$ that is not the identity function; otherwise it is *asymmetric*.

Let $\mathcal{P} \subset \mathcal{F}$ consist of symmetric graphs. We will show that property $\mathcal{P}$ does not admit locally checkable proof of size $o(n^2)$. That is, a proof with $o(n^2)$ bits per node is not sufficient to convince a local verifier that a given connected graph is symmetric. To reach a contradiction, assume that there exists a proof labelling scheme $(f, \mathcal{A})$ with $o(n^2)$-bit proofs.

To facilitate the proof, we will use *canonical forms* of graphs. We associate a canonical form $C(\mathcal{G})$ with any graph $\mathcal{G}$. Graphs $\mathcal{G}$ and $C(\mathcal{G})$ are isomorphic; moreover, whenever $\mathcal{G}$ and $\mathcal{H}$ are isomorphic, their canonical forms $C(\mathcal{G})$ and $C(\mathcal{H})$ are equal. We assume that the node identifiers of a canonical form are $V(C(\mathcal{G})) = \{1, 2, \ldots, n(\mathcal{G})\}$. We also define a graph with *shifted identifiers* as follows: for an integer i, graph $C(\mathcal{G}, i)$ has

$$V(C(\mathcal{G}, i)) = \{i+1, i+2, \ldots, i+n(\mathcal{G})\}$$

as the set of node identifiers. Moreover, we assume that $g\colon v \mapsto i + v$ is an isomorphism from $C(\mathcal{G})$ to $C(\mathcal{G}, i)$. In particular, $C(\mathcal{G}, 0) = C(\mathcal{G})$.

Now we are ready to give the lower-bound construction. Given connected graphs $\mathcal{G}_1$ and $\mathcal{G}_2$ with $n(\mathcal{G}_1) = n(\mathcal{G}_2) = k$, we construct a graph $\mathcal{G} = \mathcal{G}_1 \odot \mathcal{G}_2$ with $V(\mathcal{G}) = \{1, 2, \ldots, 3k\}$ as follows: $\mathcal{G}$ consists of a copy of $C(\mathcal{G}_1, k)$, a copy of $C(\mathcal{G}_2, 2k)$, and the path $(k+1, 1, 2, \ldots, k, 2k+1)$. That is, $\mathcal{G}$ consists of a path that joins graphs that are isomorphic to $\mathcal{G}_1$ and $\mathcal{G}_2$.

Assume that $\mathcal{G}_1$ and $\mathcal{G}_2$ are asymmetric. If $\mathcal{G}_1$ and $\mathcal{G}_2$ are isomorphic, then by construction $\mathcal{G} = \mathcal{G}_1 \odot \mathcal{G}_2$ is symmetric: there is a non-trivial automorphism that maps, e.g., $1 \mapsto k$ and $k+1 \mapsto 2k+1$. Conversely, if $\mathcal{G}_1$ and $\mathcal{G}_2$ are not isomorphic, then $\mathcal{G}$ must be asymmetric.

Let $\mathcal{F}_k$ be a family containing a representative from each isomorphism class of asymmetric connected graphs with k nodes. For any $\mathcal{G}_1 \in \mathcal{F}_k$, the local verifier $\mathcal{A}$ has to accept

$\mathcal{G}_1 \odot \mathcal{G}_1$, as it is symmetric. Since almost all graphs are connected [5, Cor. 11.3.3] and asymmetric [6], we have

$$|\mathcal{F}_k| = (1 - o(1))2^{\binom{k}{2}}/k! \quad \text{and} \quad \log|\mathcal{F}_k| = \Theta(k^2).$$

Now assume that $k \geq 2r + 1$, and consider the proof labels of the nodes in $U = \{1, 2, \ldots, 2r + 1\}$. There are only $o(rn^2)$ proof bits in U. As $r = O(1)$ and $n = 3k$, we have only $o(k^2)$ proof bits in U; for sufficiently large k this is less than $\log|\mathcal{F}_k|$. Hence we must have two different graphs $\mathcal{G}_1, \mathcal{G}_2 \in \mathcal{F}_k$ such that the labelling scheme assigns the same proof bits to the nodes $1, 2, \ldots, 2r + 1$ in both $\mathcal{G}_1 \odot \mathcal{G}_1$ and $\mathcal{G}_2 \odot \mathcal{G}_2$.

Now we can construct the asymmetric graph $\mathcal{G} = \mathcal{G}_1 \odot \mathcal{G}_2$. For the nodes $k+1, k+2, \ldots, 2k$ we inherit the proof labels from $f(\mathcal{G}_1 \odot \mathcal{G}_1)$, and for the nodes $2r+2, 2r+3, \ldots, k, 2k+1, 2k+2, \ldots, 3k$ we inherit the proof labels from $f(\mathcal{G}_2 \odot \mathcal{G}_2)$. For the nodes $1, 2, \ldots, 2r+1$ we use the common labelling of $f(\mathcal{G}_1 \odot \mathcal{G}_1)$ and $f(\mathcal{G}_2 \odot \mathcal{G}_2)$. Now the radius-$r$ neighbourhood of any node in $\mathcal{G}$ looks identical to the neighbourhood of a node in $\mathcal{G}_1 \odot \mathcal{G}_1$ or $\mathcal{G}_2 \odot \mathcal{G}_2$. Hence all nodes will accept the input even though $\mathcal{G}$ is not symmetric, a contradiction.

In conclusion, in order to verify that a given connected graph is symmetric, we need proofs of size $\Theta(n^2)$.

6.2 Fixpoint-Free Symmetry on Trees

Let us now focus on the family $\mathcal{F}$ of connected trees. Then any pure graph property $\mathcal{P} \subseteq \mathcal{F}$ admits a locally checkable proof of size $O(n)$: for each node v of the tree $\mathcal{G} \in \mathcal{P}$, we encode the structure of $\mathcal{G}$ and an index that identifies which node of $\mathcal{G}$ is v; the structure of a tree can be encoded in $\Theta(n)$ bits, and the index requires $\Theta(\log n)$ bits.

Now we will show that there are pure graph properties that require $\Theta(n)$-bit proofs. We will use the following (artificial) problem as an example. We say that a graph $\mathcal{G}$ has a *fixpoint-free symmetry* if there is an automorphism that fixes no nodes, i.e., there is an automorphism $g\colon V(\mathcal{G}) \to V(\mathcal{G})$ such that $g(v) \neq v$ for all $v \in V(\mathcal{G})$.

Let $\mathcal{P} \subset \mathcal{F}$ consists of those connected trees that have a fixpoint-free symmetry. We will show that $\mathcal{P}$ does not admit proofs of size $o(n)$, and is therefore among the most difficult properties of trees.

The proof is analogous to the case of symmetric graphs. The only difference is that we let $\mathcal{F}_k$ consist of rooted trees with k nodes; if $\mathcal{G}_1, \mathcal{G}_2 \in \mathcal{F}_k$ and k is even, then $\mathcal{G}_1 \odot \mathcal{G}_2$ has a fixpoint-free symmetry if and only if $\mathcal{G}_1 = \mathcal{G}_2$. We have $\log|\mathcal{F}_k| = \Theta(k)$ [22, Seq. A000081]; hence a proof of size $o(n)$ bits leads to a contradiction. We conclude that trees with a fixpoint-free symmetry require locally checkable proofs of size $\Theta(n)$.

6.3 Non-3-Colourability

Now we turn our attention to the classical problem of graph colouring. In Section 5 we have already seen that in the case of 2-colourability, the complement of the problem is strictly more difficult: to show that a graph can be coloured with 2 colours a $\Theta(1)$-bit proof is sufficient, but to show that a graph cannot be coloured with 2 colours we need $\Theta(\log n)$-bit proofs.

In the case of 3-colourings, the difference between the problem and its complement is even more dramatic. Again, constant-size proofs are enough to show that a graph can be coloured with 3 colours, as we can give a 3-colouring as a proof. However, to prove that a graph cannot be coloured with 3 colours, we need very large proofs, with polynomially many bits per node.

More specifically, let us again focus on the family $\mathcal{F}$ of connected graphs, and let $\mathcal{P} \subset \mathcal{F}$ consist of graphs that have chromatic number larger than 3. We will show that property $\mathcal{P}$ does not admit locally checkable proofs of size $o(n^2/\log n)$. Recall that any pure graph property admits proofs of size $O(n^2)$; hence the result is almost tight, and shows that non-3-colourability does not have a proof labelling scheme that is substantially better than the brute-force approach.

Let k be a positive integer. Define $I = \{0, 1, \ldots, 2^k - 1\}$. Given a set $A \subseteq I \times I$, we construct a graph $\mathcal{G}_A$, with the following properties:

(i) The total number of nodes in $\mathcal{G}_A$ is $\Theta(2^k)$.

(ii) The set of nodes $V(\mathcal{G}_A)$ contains the following nodes: $T, F, N, x_0, x_1, \ldots, x_{k-1}$, and $y_0, y_1, \ldots, y_{k-1}$.

Moreover, valid 3-colourings of $\mathcal{G}_A$ have the following properties:

(iii) The nodes T, F, and N have three different colours. The nodes with the same colour as T are said to be *true*, those with the same colour as F are *false*, and others are *neutral*.

(iv) Each of x_i and y_i has to be true or false. Hence we can interpret the colouring of the nodes x_i as a binary encoding of an integer $x \in \{0, 1, \ldots, 2^k - 1\}$; similarly the colouring of the nodes y_i is a binary encoding of an integer y.

(v) In any 3-colouring, we must have $(x, y) \in A$. Conversely, we can find a valid 3-colouring that encodes any $(x, y) \in A$.

Such graphs exist; for an explicit construction of $\mathcal{G}_A$ as well as additional illustrations, see the extended version of this work [12].

We denote by $\mathcal{G}'_A$ an isomorphic copy of $\mathcal{G}_A$; we use the primed symbols T', F', N', x'_i, and y'_i to refer to the nodes of $\mathcal{G}'_A$.

In addition to graphs $\mathcal{G}_A$ and $\mathcal{G}'_A$, we will need *wires* that propagate colours. A wire w consists of $9r$ nodes, labelled $w(i, j)$ for $i = 1, 2, \ldots, 3r$ and $j = 1, 2, 3$. For each i, the nodes $w(i, 1)$, $w(i, 2)$, and $w(i, 3)$ form a triangle. For each $i < 3r$ and $j \neq j'$, the nodes $w(i, j)$ and $w(i + 1, j')$ are connected with an edge. It follows that in any 3-colouring of a wire, the nodes $w(i, 1)$, $w(i, 2)$ and $w(i, 3)$ must have different colours, and $w(i, j)$ must have the same colour as $w(i + 1, j)$.

Given two sets $A, B \subseteq I \times I$, we construct a graph $\mathcal{G} = \mathcal{G}_{A,B}$ that consists of $\mathcal{G}_A$ and $\mathcal{G}'_B$ that are connected to each other by $2k + 1$ wires. The wires are labelled with $w_T, w^x_1, w^x_2, \ldots, w^x_k$, and $w^y_1, w^y_2, \ldots, w^y_k$. The endpoints of the wires are identified with the nodes of the subgraphs $\mathcal{G}_A$ and $\mathcal{G}'_B$ as follows:

$$w(1, 1) = N \quad \text{and} \quad w(3r, 1) = N' \quad \forall \text{ wire } w,$$

$$w_T(1, 2) = T \quad \text{and} \quad w_T(3r, 2) = T',$$

$$w^x_i(1, 2) = x_i \text{ and } w^x_i(3r, 2) = x'_i \quad \forall \, i = 0, 1, \ldots, k-1,$$

$$w^y_i(1, 2) = y_i \text{ and } w^y_i(3r, 2) = y'_i \quad \forall \, i = 0, 1, \ldots, k-1.$$

We make the following observations of $\mathcal{G}$:

(i) The total number of nodes in $\mathcal{G}$ is $n = \Theta(2^k)$.

(ii) Let $W \subset V(\mathcal{G})$ consist of the nodes that are not in $\mathcal{G}_A$ or $\mathcal{G}'_B$; these are internal nodes of the wires. The number of nodes in W is $\Theta(rk) = \Theta(r \log n)$.

(iii) The shortest path from a node of $\mathcal{G}_A$ to a node of $\mathcal{G}'_B$ has length at least $3r - 1$. In particular, for sufficiently large r, the local neighbourhood of any node is a subset of $W \cup V(\mathcal{G}_A)$ or a subset of $W \cup V(\mathcal{G}'_B)$.

Moreover, 3-colourings of $\mathcal{G}$ have the following properties:

(iv) Nodes N and N' have the same colour, nodes T and T' have the same colour, and nodes F and F' have the same colour. Hence the concepts of true, false, and neutral nodes are well-defined in $\mathcal{G}$.

(v) Nodes x_i and x'_i have the same colour for each i, and nodes y_i and y'_i have the same colour for each i. In particular, both $\mathcal{G}_A$ and $\mathcal{G}'_B$ agree on the encoding of the same pair (x, y), and we must have $(x, y) \in A \cap B$.

It follows that $\mathcal{G}_{A,B}$ has a 3-colouring if and only if $A \cap B \neq \emptyset$.

Let $A \subseteq I \times I$ and let $\bar{A}$ be its complement. Now $A \cap \bar{A} = \emptyset$ and $\mathcal{G}_{A,\bar{A}}$ does not have a 3-colouring; hence it is in $\mathcal{P}$. If we had locally checkable proofs of size $o(n^2/\log n)$, the total number of proof bits in W would be $o(rn^2)$; on the other hand, there are $\Theta(n^2)$ elements in $I \times I$. Hence for sufficiently large n there are two different sets $A, B \subseteq I \times I$ such that we have the same proof bits in W for both $\mathcal{G}_{A,\bar{A}}$ and $\mathcal{G}_{B,\bar{B}}$.

Now we are ready to apply a fooling set argument. As $A \neq B$, we have $A \cap \bar{B} \neq \emptyset$ or $\bar{A} \cap B \neq \emptyset$ (or both). W.l.o.g., assume that $A \cap \bar{B} \neq \emptyset$. Hence $\mathcal{G}_{A,\bar{B}}$ admits a 3-colouring, and it is therefore not in $\mathcal{P}$. But we can construct a proof as follows: the proof bits of $\mathcal{G}_A$ are inherited from the proof of $\mathcal{G}_{A,\bar{A}}$, the proof bits of $\mathcal{G}'_{\bar{B}}$ are inherited from the proof of $\mathcal{G}_{B,\bar{B}}$, and the proof bits of wires are the same as in $\mathcal{G}_{A,\bar{A}}$ and $\mathcal{G}_{B,\bar{B}}$. Hence each node of $\mathcal{G}_{A,\bar{B}}$ has a local neighbourhood that looks identical to a node of $\mathcal{G}_{A,\bar{A}}$ or $\mathcal{G}_{B,\bar{B}}$. As $\mathcal{G}_{A,\bar{A}}$ and $\mathcal{G}_{B,\bar{B}}$ are *yes*-instances, all nodes will accept $\mathcal{G}_{A,\bar{B}}$, a contradiction.

We conclude that non-3-colourability requires proofs of size $\Omega(n^2/\log n)$, and proofs of size $O(n^2)$ are trivially sufficient.

7. DISCUSSION

We conclude this work by discussing alternative definitions and extensions of the LCP hierarchy, and by relating the LCP classes to each other as well as other complexity classes.

7.1 Alternative Characterisations of LogLCP

Throughout this work, we use the assumption that the local verifier can access the unique identifiers of the nodes, and our definition of the class LogLCP builds on this assumption as well. However, we can use spanning trees to show that the definition of LogLCP is robust in the sense that we can change our underlying model of distributed computation and yet arrive at exactly the same class of graph properties. For the sake of simplicity, we will focus on connected graphs.

Let us consider two different models of distributed computation, M_1 and M_2. Model M_1 has *unique identifiers*, while model M_2 has a *port numbering* and a *leader*. In more detail, model M_1 is the one defined in Section 2: each node has a unique identifier of size $O(\log n)$ bits. Model M_2 is defined as follows: The nodes do not have unique identifiers. There is only port numbering [2] available in the network, i.e., a node of degree d can refer to its neighbours by integers $1, 2, \ldots, d$. In addition to the port numbering, we know that there is exactly one node $a \in V(\mathcal{G})$ that is designated as a leader.

From the perspective of properties that can be verified without auxiliary information, the two models are very different. To give an example, in M_1 it is easy to verify that the graph is triangle-free, while this is not solvable in M_2. However, it turns out that the class of properties that can be verified with $O(\log n)$ bits in M_1 is equal to the class of properties that can be verified with $O(\log n)$ bits in M_2.

To see this, assume that $(f_2, \mathcal{A}_2)$ is a proof labelling scheme for a graph property $\mathcal{P}$ in model M_2. Then we can construct a scheme $(f_1, \mathcal{A}_1)$ for model M_1 as follows: Consider a graph $\mathcal{G} \in \mathcal{P}$ with an arbitrary choice of unique identifiers. We assign the port numbers as follows: for each node the neighbour number i is the neighbour with the ith smallest unique identifiers. We choose an arbitrary leader node $a \in \mathcal{G}$ and an arbitrary spanning tree T rooted at a. Now f_1 constructs a proof that consists of $f_2(\mathcal{G})$ and an encoding of the spanning tree (T, a). Then $\mathcal{A}_1$ can first verify the encoding of (T, a), and then simulate $\mathcal{A}_2$.

Conversely, if $(f_1, \mathcal{A}_1)$ is a proof labelling scheme for $\mathcal{P}$ in model M_1, we can construct a scheme $(f_2, \mathcal{A}_2)$ for M_2 as follows: Consider a graph $\mathcal{G} \in \mathcal{P}$ with an arbitrary port numbering and a leader a. Let T be an arbitrary spanning tree rooted at a. Generate unique identifiers for $V(\mathcal{G})$ by doing a depth-first traversal on T starting at a and recording, for every node v, its discovery time $x(v)$ and finishing time $y(v)$; the unique identifier of a node v is an encoding of the pair $(x(v), y(v))$. Now f_2 constructs a proof that consists of $f_1(\mathcal{G})$, an encoding of (T, a), and the unique identifier of each node. Then $\mathcal{A}_2$ can first verify the encoding of (T, a), and it can check that the pairs $(x(v), y(v))$ are locally consistent with a depth-first traversal on the rooted spanning tree—it follows that the node identifiers must be globally unique. Finally, $\mathcal{A}_2$ can simulate $\mathcal{A}_1$ using the unique identifiers that were encoded in the proof.

In essence, we can use a locally checkable spanning tree [16] and a simple *ancestor labelling scheme* [11] to translate proof labelling schemes between models M_1 and M_2 with only $O(\log n)$ overhead. Hence the class LogLCP can be defined equally well using either of these models.

7.2 Weak and Strong Schemes

For graph problems, we can consider two variants of proof labelling schemes:

- *Strong* proof labelling schemes: in any graph $\mathcal{G}$, for any feasible solution X, there is a proof that shows that X is a correct solution.

- *Weak* proof labelling schemes: in any graph $\mathcal{G}$, there is at least one feasible solution X, such that we can prove that X is a correct solution.

Put otherwise, in a strong proof labelling scheme, an adversary can choose both the input and the solution, and we must come up with a locally checkable proof. However, in a weak proof labelling scheme, an adversary chooses the input but we can choose a solution.

Intuitively, solving the weak version of the problem might be easier, and a weak proof labelling scheme could admit smaller proofs. For example, in the leader election problem, we could focus on convenient solutions: perhaps we could select the node with the smallest identifier as the leader, and come up with a small locally checkable proof for such a selection.

However, for many natural problems studied in this work, the proof complexities of strong and weak proof labelling schemes are within a constant factor of each other. In Section 5 we saw that problems such as leader election and spanning trees admit locally checkable proofs of size $O(\log n)$. All of these results are *strong* proof labelling schemes: for example, we can take *any* spanning tree and augment it with a proof of size $O(\log n)$. We also saw that these problems do not admit locally checkable proofs of size $o(\log n)$. The lower-bound result precludes not only the existence of strong proof labelling schemes, but it also shows that there is no weak proof labelling scheme.

7.3 Complement of LCP(0)

On connected graphs, one can employ spanning trees to reverse the decision made by an LCP(0) verifier $\mathcal{A}$ as follows. Let $\mathcal{P}$ be a graph property in LCP(0). If we have a *no*-instance $\mathcal{G} \notin \mathcal{P}$, then we can construct a proof P of size $O(\log n)$ that convinces a local verifier $\bar{\mathcal{A}}$ of $\mathcal{G} \notin \mathcal{P}$.

To construct the proof P, select a root node a with $\mathcal{A}(\mathcal{G}, \epsilon, a) = 0$, i.e., a is a node that rejects the input $\mathcal{G}$. Then choose an arbitrary spanning tree T rooted at a. Let P consist of an encoding of (T, a) and a proof of its correctness. Then a local verifier $\bar{\mathcal{A}}$ can verify that T is valid spanning tree rooted at a; in particular, there is a finite path from any $v \in V(\mathcal{G})$ to a. Moreover, at the root node, $\bar{\mathcal{A}}$ can simulate $\mathcal{A}$ and verify that $\mathcal{A}(\mathcal{G}, \epsilon, a) = 0$. We conclude that coLCP(0) $\subseteq$ LogLCP on connected graphs.

7.4 Containment in NP and NP/poly

Comparing classes such as LogLCP and NP is not straightforward. To define the LCP hierarchy, we have used the *local* model, which allows unlimited local computation. Hence if we have unbounded node degrees in $\mathcal{G}$ (or unbounded amount of additional information per node in the form of colours or weights), we can easily come up with artificial problems that are in LCP(0) but not in NP.

However, the situation becomes much more interesting if we focus on bounded-degree graphs; moreover, we will focus on pure graph properties, i.e., there is no additional information besides the node identifiers and the topology of the graph.

In this restricted case, we can still show that there are problems in LogLCP that are not contained in NP. Once again, we can resort to spanning tree methods: w.l.o.g., we can assume that a LogLCP verifier has access to $n(\mathcal{G})$ in any connected graph $\mathcal{G}$. Hence the verifier can solve arbitrarily hard computable problems concerning the integer $n(\mathcal{G})$, including those that are not in NP.

However, if $\mathcal{P} \in$ LogLCP is a pure graph property related to bounded-degree graphs, we *can* show that $\mathcal{P}$ is in NP$_{/\text{poly}}$, i.e., NP with a polynomial-size non-uniform advice. In a bounded-degree graph, the number of nodes inside the local horizon is bounded by a constant, and hence a LogLCP verifier $\mathcal{A}$ uses only $O(\log n)$ bits of input in total. Thus verifier $\mathcal{A}$ can be encoded as a lookup table of size $2^{O(\log n)}$, which is polynomial in n. We can provide the entire lookup table as the advice string S to an NP$_{/\text{poly}}$ machine M. Then M merely guesses the $O(n \log n)$-bit proof $P \colon V(\mathcal{G}) \to \{0, 1\}^\star$, and uses the advice string S to verify the guess.

7.5 Connections to Descriptive Complexity

A central result in descriptive complexity theory and one that began the field is Fagin's [7], [13, Ch. 7] characterization of the class NP as graph problems expressible by *existential second-order formulas* (Σ_1^1). Some NP-complete graph properties are even expressible by *monadic* Σ_1^1 formulas that only quantify over *unary* relation symbols [1, 20]. In this section, we make observations of a connection between the LogLCP class and the class of graph properties that are expressible by monadic Σ_1^1 formulas.

In the study of *first-order* expressibility, locality is a thematic subject; this is illustrated by Hanf's theorem and the work of Gaifman [13, Ch. 6]. Building on this work, Schwentick and Barthelmann [21] have shown that on connected graphs, every monadic Σ_1^1 formula is equivalent to a formula of the form

$$\vartheta = \exists X_1 \exists X_2 \ldots \exists X_k \exists x \forall y : \varphi(X_1, \ldots, X_k, x, y),$$

where φ is first-order and *local around* y. Here, a formula φ is local around y if there is a constant r so that for all graphs $\mathcal{G}$ and all interpretations of $X_1, X_2, \ldots, X_k, x, y$ it can be determined whether $\mathcal{G} \models \phi(X_1, X_2, \ldots, X_k, x, y)$ on the basis of the r-radius neighbourhood of y in $\mathcal{G}$. More specifically, the quantifications in φ are always of the form $\exists z : (\mathrm{dist}(z, y) \leq r \wedge \psi)$ or $\forall z : (\mathrm{dist}(z, y) \leq r \rightarrow \psi)$.

Let us focus on the family $\mathcal{F}$ of connected graphs. If and only if a graph $\mathcal{G} \in \mathcal{F}$ has property ϑ, there are monadic relations $A_1, A_2, \ldots, A_k$ and a node $a \in V$ such that $\mathcal{G} \models \forall y : \varphi(A_1, A_2, \ldots, A_k, a, y)$. For each node v and each relation A_i, encoding $A_i(v)$ takes 1 bit. To prove the existence of the node a, we can use a spanning tree rooted at a; a locally checkable spanning tree requires $O(\log n)$ bits per node (recall Section 5). To check the proof, the verifier $\mathcal{A}$ first checks the spanning tree, and then evaluates $\varphi(A_1, A_2, \ldots, A_k, a, y)$ for each node y. As φ is local around y, the verifier $\mathcal{A}$ is a local algorithm.

Hence in connected graphs, any monadic Σ_1^1 graph property $\mathcal{P}$ admits locally checkable proofs of size $O(\log n)$, i.e., $\mathcal{P} \in$ LogLCP.

8. ACKNOWLEDGEMENTS

This work was supported in part by the Academy of Finland, Grant 132380, the Finnish Cultural Foundation, and the Research Funds of the University of Helsinki.

9. REFERENCES

[1] Miklos Ajtai and Ronald Fagin. Reachability is harder for directed than for undirected finite graphs. *The Journal of Symbolic Logic*, 55(1):113–150, 1990.

[2] Dana Angluin. Local and global properties in networks of processors. In *Proc. 12th Symposium on Theory of Computing (STOC 1980)*, pages 82–93. ACM Press, 1980.

[3] Lowell W. Beineke. Characterizations of derived graphs. *Journal of Combinatorial Theory*, 9(2):129–135, 1970.

[4] John A. Bondy and Miklós Simonovits. Cycles of even length in graphs. *Journal of Combinatorial Theory, Series B*, 16(2):97–105, 1974.

[5] Reinhard Diestel. *Graph Theory*. Springer, 3rd edition, 2005.

[6] Paul Erdős and Alfréd Rényi. Asymmetric graphs. *Acta Mathematica Hungarica*, 14:295–315, 1963.

[7] Ronald Fagin. Generalized first-order spectra and polynomial-time recognizable sets. In R. Karp, editor, *Complexity of Computation*, volume 7, pages 43–73. 1974.

[8] Pierre Fraigniaud. Distributed computational complexities: are you Volvo-addicted or NASCAR-obsessed? In *Proc. 29th Symposium on Principles of Distributed Computing (PODC 2010)*, pages 171–172. ACM Press, 2010.

[9] Pierre Fraigniaud, Cyril Gavoille, David Ilcinkas, and Andrzej Pelc. Distributed computing with advice: Information sensitivity of graph coloring. In *Proc. 34th International Colloquium on Automata, Languages and Programming (ICALP 2007)*, volume 4596 of *LNCS*, pages 231–242. Springer, 2007.

[10] Pierre Fraigniaud, Amos Korman, and David Peleg. Local distributed decision, 2010. Manuscript, arXiv:1011.2152 [cs.DC].

[11] Cyril Gavoille and David Peleg. Compact and localized distributed data structures. *Distributed Computing*, 16(2–3):111–120, 2003.

[12] Mika Göös and Jukka Suomela. Locally checkable proofs. http://www.iki.fi/jukka.suomela/lcp, 2011. Manuscript.

[13] Neil Immerman. *Descriptive Complexity*. Springer, 1999.

[14] Amos Korman and Shay Kutten. On distributed verification. In *Proc. 8th International Conference on Distributed Computing and Networking (ICDCN 2006)*, volume 4308 of *LNCS*, pages 100–114. Springer, 2006.

[15] Amos Korman and Shay Kutten. Distributed verification of minimum spanning trees. *Distributed Computing*, 20(4):253–266, 2007.

[16] Amos Korman, Shay Kutten, and David Peleg. Proof labeling schemes. In *Proc. 24th Symposium on Principles of Distributed Computing (PODC 2005)*, pages 9–18. ACM Press, 2005.

[17] Amos Korman, David Peleg, and Yoav Rodeh. Constructing labeling schemes through universal matrices. *Algorithmica*, 57(4):641–652, 2010.

[18] Moni Naor and Larry Stockmeyer. What can be computed locally? *SIAM Journal on Computing*, 24(6):1259–1277, 1995.

[19] David Peleg. *Distributed Computing – A Locality-Sensitive Approach*. SIAM, 2000.

[20] Thomas Schwentick. Graph connectivity and monadic NP. In *Proc. 35th Symposium on Foundations of Computer Science (FOCS 1994)*, pages 614–622. IEEE, 1994.

[21] Thomas Schwentick and Klaus Barthelmann. Local normal forms for first-order logic with applications to games and automata. *Discrete Mathematics and Theoretical Computer Science*, 3:109–124, 1999.

[22] N. J. A. Sloane. The on-line encyclopedia of integer sequences. http://oeis.org, 2010.

[23] Jukka Suomela. Survey of local algorithms. http://www.iki.fi/jukka.suomela/local-survey, 2011. Manuscript submitted for publication.

Fault-Tolerant Spanners: Better and Simpler[*]

Michael Dinitz
Weizmann Institute of Science
Rehovot, Israel
michael.dinitz@weizmann.ac.il

Robert Krauthgamer
Weizmann Institute of Science
Rehovot, Israel
robert.krauthgamer@weizmann.ac.il

ABSTRACT

A natural requirement for many distributed structures is *fault-tolerance*: after some failures in the underlying network, whatever remains from the structure should still be effective for whatever remains from the network. In this paper we examine spanners of general graphs that are tolerant to vertex failures, and significantly improve their dependence on the number of faults r for all stretch bounds.

For stretch $k \geq 3$ we design a simple transformation that converts *every* k-spanner construction with at most $f(n)$ edges into an r-fault-tolerant k-spanner construction with at most $O(r^3 \log n) \cdot f(2n/r)$ edges. Applying this to standard greedy spanner constructions gives r-fault tolerant k-spanners with $\tilde{O}(r^2 n^{1+\frac{2}{k+1}})$ edges. The previous construction by Chechik, Langberg, Peleg, and Roddity [CLPR09] depends similarly on n but *exponentially* on r (approximately like k^r).

For the case of $k = 2$ and unit edge-lengths, an $O(r \log n)$-approximation is known from recent work of Dinitz and Krauthgamer [DK11], in which several spanner results are obtained using a common approach of rounding a natural flow-based linear programming relaxation. Here we use a different (stronger) LP relaxation and improve the approximation ratio to $O(\log n)$, which is, notably, *independent* of the number of faults r. We further strengthen this bound in terms of the maximum degree by using the Lovász Local Lemma.

Finally, we show that most of our constructions are inherently local by designing equivalent distributed algorithms in the $\mathcal{LOCAL}$ model of distributed computation.

Categories and Subject Descriptors

G.2.2 [**Discrete Mathematics**]: Graph Theory—*Graph Algorithms*

[*]A full version appears at http://arxiv.org/abs/1101.5753. Work supported in part by The Israel Science Foundation (grant #452/08), and by a Minerva grant.

General Terms

Algorithms, Theory

Keywords

Approximation Algorithms, Fault Tolerance, Spanners

1. INTRODUCTION

Let $G = (V, E)$ be a graph, possibly with edge-lengths $\ell : E \to \mathbb{R}_{\geq 0}$. A *$k$-spanner* of G, for $k \geq 1$, is a subgraph $G' = (V, E')$ that preserves all pairwise distances within factor k, i.e. for all $u, v \in V$,

$$d_{G'}(u, v) \leq k \cdot d_G(u, v). \tag{1}$$

Here and throughout, d_H denotes the shortest-path distance in a graph H, and $n = |V|$. The distance preservation factor k is called the *stretch* of the spanner. It is easy to see that requiring (1) only for edges $\{u, v\} \in E$ suffices. This definition also extends naturally to *directed* graphs. Obviously G is a 1-spanner of itself, so usually the goal is to compute a "small" spanner. One traditional notion of "small" is the number of edges in G', called the *size* of G'.

This notion of graph spanners, first introduced by Peleg and Schäffer [PS89] and Peleg and Ullman [PU89], has been studied extensively, with applications ranging from routing in networks (e.g. [AP95, TZ05]) to solving linear systems (e.g. [ST04, EEST08]). Many of these applications, especially in distributed computing, arise by modeling computer networks or distributed systems as graphs. But one aspect of distributed systems that is not captured by the above spanner definition is the possibility of *failure*. We would like our spanner to be robust to failures, so that even if some nodes fail we still have a spanner of what remains. More formally, G' is an *r-fault tolerant k-spanner* of G if for every set $F \subseteq V$ with $|F| \leq r$, the spanner condition holds for $G \setminus F$, i.e. for all $u, v \in V \setminus F$ we have $d_{G' \setminus F}(u, v) \leq k \cdot d_{G \setminus F}(u, v)$.

This notion of fault-tolerant spanners was first introduced by Levcopoulos, Narasimhan, and Smid [LNS98] in the context of geometric spanners (the special case when the vertices are in Euclidean space and the distance between two points is the Euclidean distance). They provided both size and weight bounds for $(1 + \epsilon)$-spanners, which were later improved by Lukovski [Luk99] and Czumaj and Zhao [CZ03]. The first result on fault-tolerant spanners for general graphs, by Chechik, Langberg, Peleg, and Roditty [CLPR09], constructs r-fault tolerant $(2k-1)$-spanners with size $O(r^2 k^{r+1} \cdot n^{1+1/k} \log^{1-1/k} n)$, for any integer $k \geq 1$. Since it has long been known how to construct $(2k-1)$-spanners with size

$O(n^{1+1/k})$ (see e.g [ADD+93]), this means that the extra cost of r-fault tolerance is $O(r^2 k^{r+1})$. While this is independent of n, it grows rapidly as the number of faults r gets large. We address an important question left open in [CLPR09] of improving this dependence on r from exponential to polynomial.

Nontrivial absolute bounds on the size of a k-spanner are possible only when the stretch $k \geq 3$. For $k = 2$, there are graphs with $\Omega(n^2)$ edges for which every edge must be included in the spanner (e.g. a complete bipartite graph). So the common approach is to provide relative bounds, namely, design approximation algorithms for the problem of computing a minimum size r-fault tolerant 2-spanner. In this context one typically assumes that all edges have unit length. Without fault tolerance, the problem is reasonably well understood: there are algorithms that provide an $O(\log n)$-approximation [KP94, EP01] (or, with some extra effort, an $O(\log(|E|/|V|))$-approximation), and the problem is NP-hard to approximate better than $\Omega(\log n)$ [Kor01]. For the r-fault tolerant 2-spanner problem, the first nontrivial approximation was recently given by Dinitz and Krauthgamer [DK11], who designed an $O(r \log n)$ approximation. However, they did not provide evidence that this loss of r was necessary, an issue that we address in this paper.

1.1 Results and Techniques

Stretch bounds $k \geq 3$.

Our main result for general $k \geq 3$ is a new r-fault tolerant k-spanner with size that depends only polynomially on r, thereby improving over the exponential dependence by Chechik et al. [CLPR09].

THEOREM 1.1. *For every graph $G = (V, E)$ with positive edge-lengths and odd $k \geq 3$, there is an r-fault tolerant k-spanner with size $O(r^{2-\frac{2}{k+1}} n^{1+\frac{2}{k+1}} \log n)$.*

In fact, we prove something slightly stronger: a general conversion theorem that turns any algorithm for constructing k-spanners with size $f(n)$ into an algorithm for constructing r-fault tolerant k-spanners with size $O(r^3 \log n \cdot f(2n/r))$. Applying this conversion to the well-known greedy spanner algorithm (see e.g. [ADD+93]) immediately yields Theorem 1.1.

At a high level, Chechik et al. [CLPR09] apply the spanner construction of Thorup and Zwick [TZ05] to every possible fault set, eventually taking the union of all of these spanners. They show, through a rather involved analysis that relies on specific properties of the Thorup-Zwick construction, that taking a union over as many as $O(n^r)$ spanners increases the size bound only by an $O(r^2 k^r)$ factor. Our conversion technique, on the other hand, is extremely general. Inspired by the *color-coding* technique of Alon, Yuster, and Zwick [AYZ95] and its recent incarnation in designing data structures and oracles (e.g. [WY10]), we randomly sample nodes to act as a fault set, and then apply a generic spanner algorithm on what remains. Our sampling dramatically oversamples nodes — instead of fault sets of size r, we end up with sampled fault sets of size approximately $(1 - \frac{1}{r})n$. This allows us to satisfy many fault sets of size r with a single iteration of the generic algorithm. The size bound follows almost immediately.

Stretch $k = 2$ (and assuming unit edge-lengths).

Here, our main result is an approximation algorithm with ratio that is *independent* of r. Our algorithm actually works in an even more general setting, where the graph is directed and edges have arbitrary nonnegative *costs* $c_e : E \to \mathbb{R}_{\geq 0}$. The goal is to find an r-fault tolerant 2-spanner of minimum total cost. We refer to this problem as MINIMUM COST r-FAULT TOLERANT 2-SPANNER. Since our algorithms are randomized, we will say that they provide an α-approximation if, with probability at least 2/3, they return a valid r-fault 2-spanner of cost at most α times the minimum cost r-fault tolerant 2-spanner. Our algorithms will in fact be a little stronger: they return a valid r-fault tolerant 2-spanner with high probability, and this spanner will be an α-approximation with probability at least 3/4.

THEOREM 1.2. *There is a (randomized) $O(\log n)$ approximation algorithm for MINIMUM COST r-FAULT TOLERANT 2-SPANNER for all $r \leq n$ (even on directed graphs).*

This removes the dependence on r from the previously known $O(r \log n)$-approximation [DK11]. Similarly to this previous approximation [DK11], we design a flow-based linear programming (LP) relaxation of the problem and then apply a rounding scheme that uses randomization at the vertices, rather than naively at the edges. However, the relaxation used by [DK11] is not strong enough to achieve approximation factor independent of r; even simple graphs (such as the complete graph with unit costs) have integrality gaps of $\Omega(r)$. We thus design a different relaxation, and add to it a large family of constraints that are essentially the *knapsack-cover inequalities* of Carr, Fleischer, Leung, and Phillips [CFLP00], adapted to our context. With these additional constraints, we are able to show that the simple rounding scheme devised in [DK11] now achieves an $O(\log n)$-approximation.

We further show that in the special case where all edge costs are unit the integrality gap is at most $O(\log \Delta)$, where Δ is the maximum degree of the graph. Note that this bound is at least as good as the $O(\log n)$ bound (and possibly better). We prove this by a more careful analysis of essentially the same randomized rounding scheme using the Lovász Local Lemma. By using constructive versions of the LLL [MT10] we can achieve this gap algorithmically, giving a better approximation algorithm.

Distributed versions of our algorithms.

Finally, one feature that is shared by both the $k = 2$ and the $k \geq 3$ case is that the algorithms are *local* (assuming that the generic algorithm used by the conversion theorem is itself local). To show this formally, we provide distributed versions of the algorithm in the $\mathcal{LOCAL}$ model of distributed computation. The $\mathcal{LOCAL}$ model is a standard message-passing model in which in each round, every node is allowed to send an unbounded-size message to each of its neighbors [Pel00]. While the unbounded message-size assumption may not be realistic, this model captures locality in the sense that in t rounds, each node has knowledge of, and is influenced by, only the nodes that are within hop-distance t of it.

Assuming that the underlying generic spanner algorithm is distributed in this sense, our general conversion theorem trivially provides a distributed algorithm since the failure sampling is done independently by every node. Designing a distributed version of the r-fault tolerant 2-spanner algorithm is not quite as simple, since our centralized algorithm uses the Ellipsoid method to solve a linear program that has an exponential number of constraints. While there is a significant amount of literature on solving linear programs in a distributed manner, much of the time strong assumptions are made about the structure of the linear program. In particular, it is common to assume that the LP is a *positive* (i.e. a packing/covering) LP. Unfortunately the LP relaxation that we use is not positive, even for $r = 0$, so we cannot simply use an off-the-shelf distributed LP solver. Instead, we leverage the fact that the LP itself is "mostly" local — we partition the graph into clusters, solve the LP separately on each cluster, and then repeat this process several times, eventually taking the average values. This technique is quite similar to the work of Kuhn, Moscibroda, and Wattenhofer [KMW06], who showed how to approximately solve positive LPs using the graph decompositions of Linial and Saks [LS93]. We construct padded decompositions using a variant of the methods developed by Bartal [Bar96] and by Linial and Saks [LS93]. Combining this distributed methodology for solving the LP relaxation together with the obvious distributed implementation of the aforementioned rounding scheme, we obtain a distributed $O(\log n)$-approximation. While the approximation works on directed graphs, we need to assume that communication along edges is bidirectional.

THEOREM 1.3. *There is a distributed randomized algorithm in the $\mathcal{LOCAL}$ model that takes $O(\log^2 n)$ rounds and is an $O(\log n)$-approximation for* MINIMUM COST r-FAULT TOLERANT 2-SPANNER *(even on directed graphs).*

2. GENERAL STRETCH k

In this section we give our construction of r-vertex-tolerant k-spanners (with arbitrary edge-lengths). For each $F \subseteq V$ with $|F| \leq r$, we let E_F denote the edges of $G \setminus F$, i.e. $E_F = \{\{u, v\} \in E : u, v \notin F\}$. We first give a general conversion theorem that turns any k-spanner construction into an r-fault tolerant k-spanner construction at an extra cost of at most $poly(r) \cdot \log n$. This conversion actually works fine even when the underlying spanner construction is randomized, but since good deterministic constructions exist we will assume for simplicity that the underlying construction is deterministic. We say that an event happens with high probability if it happens with probability at least $1 - \frac{1}{n^C}$ for constant C that can be made arbitrarily large (at the cost of increasing the constants hidden by $O(\cdot)$ notation).

THEOREM 2.1. *If there is an algorithm A that on every graph builds a k-spanner of size $f(n)$, then there is an algorithm that on any graph builds with high probability an r-fault tolerant k-spanner of size $O(r^3 \log n \cdot f(\frac{2n}{r}))$.*

PROOF. Our algorithm is simple: in each iteration, we independently add each vertex to a set J with probability $p = 1 - 1/r$, and then use the given algorithm A to build a k-spanner on the remaining graph $G \setminus J$. If $r = 1$ then we can set $p = 1/2$, which will just affect the constants in the $O(\cdot)$. We do this for $\alpha = \Theta(r^3 \log n)$ iterations, each independent of the others. Let H be the graph obtained by taking the union of the iterations.

We first bound the size of H. Without loss of generality we can assume that $r \leq n^{2/3}$, since when $r > n^{2/3}$ the claimed size bound is larger than $r^3 \geq n^2$, and it is trivially

true that H has at most $O(n^2)$ edges since H is a graph on n vertices. In each iteration, the expected number of vertices in $G \setminus J$ is n/r. By a simple Chernoff bound, the probability that a given iteration has more than $2n/r$ vertices in $G \setminus J$ is at most $e^{-(1/3)n/r} \leq e^{-(1/3)n^{1/3}}$. Since there are only $\alpha = O(r^3 \log n)$ iterations, we can take a union bound over the iterations and get that with high probability the number of vertices in $G \setminus J$ is at most $2n/r$ in *every* iteration. Thus the total size of H is at most $O(\alpha \cdot f(\frac{2n}{r}))$. Now we just need to prove that this algorithm results in a valid r-fault tolerant k-spanner for $\alpha = O(r^3 \log n)$.

For each $F \subseteq V$ with $|F| \leq r$, let E'_F be the edges in E_F for which the shortest path in $G \setminus F$ between the endpoints is just the edge. More formally, $E'_F = \{\{u, v\} \in E_F : d_{G \setminus F}(u, v) = \ell(\{u, v\})\}$. It is easy to see that it is sufficient for there to be a path of length at most $k \cdot \ell(\{u, v\})$ between u and v in $G \setminus F$ for every $F \subseteq V$ with $|F| \leq r$ and $\{u, v\} \in E'_F$. To show this, consider some fault set F and some $u, v \notin F$. Let $P \subseteq E_F$ be the shortest path from u to v in $G \setminus F$. Since this is a shortest path, every edge in P is actually in E'_F. Thus for every edge $\{x, y\} \in P$ there is a path of length at most $k \cdot \ell(\{x, y\})$ in $G \setminus F$, so by concatenating these paths together we get a path from u to v in $G \setminus F$ of length at most $k \cdot \sum_{e \in P} \ell(e) = k \cdot d_{G \setminus F}(u, v)$.

So we consider a particular such F and $\{u, v\}$ and upper bound the probability that there is no stretch-k path between u and v in $G \setminus F$. Suppose that in some iteration neither u nor v is in J, but all of F is in J. Then since $\{u, v\} \in E'_F$, the spanner that we build on $G \setminus J$ contains a path between u and v of length at most $k \cdot d_{G \setminus J}(u, v) = k \cdot \ell(\{u, v\}) = k \cdot d_{G \setminus F}(u, v)$. Obviously this path also exists in $G \setminus F$, since $F \subseteq J$. So if this happens then H is valid for $\{u, v\}$ and F. The probability that this happens in a particular iteration is clearly $(1 - p)^2 \cdot p^r$, which is at least $1/(4r^2)$ as long as $r \geq 2$ (if $r = 1$ then this probability it $1/8$, which does not significantly affect the results). Thus the probability that this never happens in any iteration is at most $(1 - \frac{1}{4r^2})^\alpha \leq e^{-\alpha/4r^2}$, so if we set $\alpha = \Theta(r^3 \log n)$ this becomes less than $1/n^{C(r+2)}$ for arbitrarily large constant C. Now taking a union bound over all $\{u, v\}$ and F gives the theorem, since there are less than $O(n^r)$ fault sets and at most n^2 edges. $\square$

COROLLARY 2.2. *For every graph $G = (V, E)$ with nonnegative edge lengths $\ell : E \to \mathbb{R}_{\geq 0}$ and every odd $k \geq 1$, there is a polynomial time algorithm that with high probability constructs an r-vertex-tolerant k-spanner with at most $O(r^{2 - \frac{2}{k+1}} n^{1 + \frac{2}{k+1}} \log n)$ edges.*

PROOF. Althöfer et al. [ADD+93] showed that the simple greedy spanner construction has size at most $O(n^{1 + \frac{2}{k+1}})$. Applying Theorem 2.1 to this construction completes the proof. $\square$

Since Theorem 2.1 applies to any k-spanner construction, we can apply it to *distributed* spanner constructions:

THEOREM 2.3. *If there is a distributed algorithm A that on every graph builds a k-spanner of size $f(n)$ in $t(n)$ rounds, then there is a distributed algorithm that on any graph builds with high probability an r-fault tolerant k-spanner of size $O(r^3 \log n \cdot f(2n/r))$ in $O(r^3 \log n \cdot t(n))$ rounds.*

PROOF. The algorithm is simple: $O(r^3 \log n)$ times, each node independently decides whether or not to join J with probability $1-1/r$, and then A is run on the remainder. This obviously takes at most $O(r^3 \log n \cdot t(n))$ rounds, and the analysis of Theorem 2.1 proves the desired size bound. $\square$

COROLLARY 2.4. *There is a distributed algorithm in the $\mathcal{LOCAL}$ model that in $O(kr^3 \log n)$ rounds constructs with high probability an r-fault tolerant k-spanner with at most $O(kr^{2-\frac{2}{k+1}} n^{1+\frac{2}{k+1}} \log n)$ edges.*

PROOF. Apply Theorem 2.3 to the distributed deterministic spanner construction of Derbel, Gavoille, Peleg, and Viennot [DGPV08], which has size $O(kn^{1+\frac{2}{k+1}})$ and runs in $O(k)$ rounds. $\square$

3. UNIT-LENGTH r-FAULT TOLERANT 2-SPANNER

We now move from general k to the specific case of $k = 2$. It is easy to see (and has long been known) that no non-trivial absolute bounds on the size of a 2-spanner are possible, so following previous work, we instead consider the approximation version. In this section we will mostly work in the directed setting in which every edge e has an arbitrary cost $c_e \geq 0$. This is more general in some ways than the setting in Section 2 (which is undirected and has unit edge costs), but in other ways it is much less general (we now assume that $k = 2$ and edge lengths are unit). Recent work of Dinitz and Krauthgamer [DK11] achieves approximation ratio $O(r \log n)$ for MINIMUM-COST r-FAULT TOLERANT 2-SPANNER, and an $O(r \log \Delta)$ ratio when all edge costs are 1 (where Δ is the maximum degree). Here we improve these results to $O(\log n)$ and $O(\log \Delta)$ (for all r) via a different LP relaxation, and also provide a distributed implementation.

3.1 The Previous LP Relaxation

The relaxation in [DK11] uses, at a high level, a characterization of r-fault tolerant 2-spanners based on flows where for every set of r faults, it is possible to send one unit of (integral) flow from u to v along paths of length at most 2 for any edge (u, v) still present in the graph once the faults have been removed. More formally, for each $(u, v) \in E$ let $\mathcal{P}_{u,v}$ denote the paths of length *exactly* two from u to v, so $\mathcal{P}_{u,v} \cup \{(u,v)\}$ is the set of all paths of length at most 2. Let $\mathcal{F} = \{F \subseteq V : |F| \leq r\}$ be the set of possible fault sets, and as in Section 2, for any possible fault set $F \in \mathcal{F}$ let E_F be the set of edges in E with neither endpoint in F. Let $\mathcal{P}_{u,v}^F$ be the subset of $\mathcal{P}_{u,v} \cup \{(u,v)\}$ that still survives in E_F. The integer program (IP) used by Dinitz and Krauthgamer [DK11] is presented below as IP (2).

$$
\begin{aligned}
\min \quad & \sum_{e \in E} c_e x_e \\
\text{s.t.} \quad & \sum_{P \in \mathcal{P}_{u,v}^F : e \in P} f_P^F \leq x_e && \forall F \in \mathcal{F}, \ \forall (u,v) \in E_F, \\
& && \forall e \in E_F \\
& \sum_{P \in \mathcal{P}_{u,v}^F} f_P^F \geq 1 && \forall F \in \mathcal{F}, \ \forall (u,v) \in E_F \\
& x_e \in \{0, 1\} && \forall e \in E \\
& f_P^F \in \{0, 1\} && \forall F \in \mathcal{F}, \ \forall (u,v) \in E_F, \\
& && \forall P \in \mathcal{P}_{u,v}^F
\end{aligned}
$$
(2)

This formulation has capacity variables x_e for every edge e, flow variables f_P^F for every possible fault set F and every path $P \in \mathcal{P}_{u,v}^F$ (for every $(u,v) \in E$), and constraints that require flows to obey the capacities and still send one unit of flow for every possible fault set. Even though there are an exponential number of both constraints and variables, it can be solved in polynomial time [DK11].

While IP (2) is the obvious integer programming formulation, its straightforward relaxation to a linear program is not strong enough to give an approximation that is independent of r (despite having an exponential number of both constraints and variables). An easy way to see this is by considering the complete graph. On the complete graph, every vertex obviously needs at least r incoming and outgoing edges, or else it could be isolated with less than r faults. So on K_n the optimum spanner has size at least rn. On the other hand, when we relax the integrality constraints we can set the capacity of every edge to $1/(n-r-2)$ and still have enough capacity to send one unit of flow from any vertex to any other even after r of them have failed. So the linear program has cost of only $n^2/(n-r-2)$, which is $O(n)$ as long as $r < cn$ for some constant $c < 1$. Thus the integrality gap of the relaxation is $\Omega(r)$ for an extremely wide range of r.

3.2 A New LP Relaxation

To get around this problem, we will use a different relaxation based on *weighted* flow. Before we give our formulation, we first prove a simple and useful characterization of r-fault-tolerant 2-spanners:

LEMMA 3.1. *For every (directed) graph $G = (V, E)$, a subgraph $H = (V, E')$ is an r-fault tolerant 2-spanner if and only if for every (u, v) in E either $(u, v) \in E'$ or there are at least $r + 1$ paths of length 2 from u to v in E'*

PROOF. Let H be an r-fault tolerant 2-spanner of G, and for the sake of contradiction assume that there is some $(u, v) \in E$ that is not in E' and for which there are at most r paths of length 2 from u to v. Let $W \subseteq V$ be the vertices that are the midpoints of these paths. Then if we let our fault set F be W, in the remaining graph $H \setminus W$ there is no $u-v$ path, while in $G \setminus W$ the edge (u, v) still exists. Thus H is not an r-fault tolerant 2-spanner, giving the contradiction.

For the other direction, suppose that for every $(u, v) \in E$ either $(u, v) \in E'$ or there are at least $r+1$ paths of length 2 from u to v. Let $F \subseteq V$ with $|F| \leq r$ be some fault set. We need to show that H is a valid 2-spanner for $G \setminus F$. As usual, it will suffice for us to show that $d_{H \setminus F}(u, v) \leq 2 \cdot d_{G \setminus F}(u, v)$ for all $(u, v) \in E_F$, so since we are assuming unit lengths we just need to show that $d_{H \setminus F}(u, v) \leq 2$ for all $(u, v) \in E_F$. Let $(u, v) \in E_F$ be an arbitrary edge in $G \setminus F$. If $(u, v) \in E'$ then obviously $d_{H \setminus F}(u, v) = 1$, and if $(u, v) \notin E'$ then by assumption there are at least $r + 1$ paths from u to v of length 2 in H. At most r of the intermediate vertices on those paths can be in F, so in $H \setminus F$ there is at least one such path remaining and thus $d_{H \setminus F}(u, v) \leq 2$, as required. $\square$

With this lemma in hand, it is easy to see that the following integer program is an exact formulation of the r-fault tolerant 2-spanner problem. It simply forces the conditions of Lemma 3.1 to be true, i.e. every edge e is either included (has x_e value of 1) or there are $r + 1$ paths of length 2 that are included.

$$\begin{aligned}
\min \quad & \sum_{e \in E} c_e x_e \\
\text{s.t.} \quad & \sum_{P \in \mathcal{P}_{u,v}:e \in P} f_P \leq x_e && \forall (u,v) \in E, \\
& && \forall e \in E \\
& (r+1)x_{(u,v)} + \sum_{P \in \mathcal{P}_{u,v}} f_P \geq r+1 && \forall (u,v) \in E \\
& x_e \in \{0,1\} && \forall e \in E \\
& f_P \in \{0,1\} && \forall (u,v) \in E, \\
& && \forall P \in \mathcal{P}_{u,v}
\end{aligned}$$
(3)

So now we have a different IP formulation than the one that was used in [DK11] to get an $O(r \log n)$-approximation. Unfortunately, it is still not strong enough to yield an approximation ratio independent of r; there are still simple examples that give an integrality gap of $\Omega(r)$. For example, consider a graph with nodes u and v and an edge of cost M from u to v (for some arbitrarily large M), together with r nodes $w_1, \ldots, w_r$ and an edge of cost 1 from u to w_i and from w_i to v for all $i \in [r]$. The set of all w_i nodes is a valid fault set, so the optimum spanner needs to include the (u,v) edge in order to still be valid. So the optimum spanner has cost at least M. On the other hand, the LP can set x_e to 1 for all edges e incident on some w_i, and set $x_{(u,v)} = 1/(r+1)$. This has cost of only $M/(r+1) + 2r$. By setting M large enough, we get a gap of $\Omega(r)$.

We will strengthen the relaxation by adding a set of valid inequalities that are essentially the *knapsack-cover inequalities* of Carr et al. [CFLP00] applied to this IP. Let $(u,v) \in E$, and let $\mathcal{W}_{u,v} = \{W \subseteq P_{u,v} : |W| \leq r\}$. Consider some arbitrary subset $W \in \mathcal{W}_{u,v}$. If $x_{(u,v)} = 0$, then the covering inequality for (u,v) implies that $\sum_{P \in \mathcal{P}_{u,v}} f_P \geq r+1$, and thus $\sum_{P \in \mathcal{P}_{u,v} \setminus W} f_P \geq r+1 - |W|$. On the other hand, if $x_{(u,v)} = 1$ then clearly $(r+1-|W|)x_{(u,v)} \geq r+1-|W|$. So for all $(u,v) \in E$ and all $W \subseteq \mathcal{P}_{u,v}$ with $|W| \leq r$, we can add the constraint

$$(r+1-|W|)x_{(u,v)} + \sum_{P \in \mathcal{P}_{u,v} \setminus W} f_P \geq r+1-|W|.$$

To simplify notation, for any such W let $r_W = r+1-|W|$. These are the knapsack-cover inequalities, and when we add them to our IP formulation and relax the integrality constraints we get the following LP relaxation:

$$\begin{aligned}
\min \quad & \sum_{e \in E} c_e x_e \\
\text{s.t.} \quad & \sum_{P \in \mathcal{P}_{u,v}:e \in P} f_P \leq x_e && \forall (u,v) \in E, \\
& && \forall e \in E \\
& r_W x_{(u,v)} + \sum_{P \in \mathcal{P}_{u,v} \setminus W} f_P \geq r_W && \forall (u,v) \in E, \\
& && \forall W \in \mathcal{W}_{u,v} \\
& 0 \leq x_e \leq 1 && \forall e \in E \\
& f_P \geq 0 && \forall (u,v) \in E, \\
& && \forall P \in \mathcal{P}_{u,v}
\end{aligned}$$
(4)

We refer to the first type of constraints as *capacity* constraints, the second type as *knapsack-cover* constraints (or

inequalities), and the third as *multiplicity* constraints. This relaxation has a polynomial number of variables but a possibly exponential number of constraints, so we first need to show that we can solve it. To do this we construct a separation oracle, which allows us to solve it in polynomial time by using the Ellipsoid algorithm.

LEMMA 3.2. *There is a polynomial time algorithm that solves LP (4).*

PROOF. We want to construct a separation oracle. Note that there are only a polynomial number of capacity constraints and multiplicity constraints, so we can check them all in polynomial time. To find a violated knapsack-cover inequality, note that if there is some $(u,v) \in E$ and some $W \subseteq \mathcal{P}_{u,v}$ that violates the inequality, then the set W' which consists of the $|W|$ paths in $\mathcal{P}_{u,v}$ with the largest f_P value also violates the inequality. So for every $(u,v) \in E$, for every $i \in [0,r]$, it suffices to check the constraint for (u,v) and the i paths in $\mathcal{P}_{u,v}$ with largest flow. Since $r \leq n$, this takes only polynomial time. $\square$

3.3 O(log n)-approximation

We now give the main result of this section.

THEOREM 3.3. *There is a randomized $O(\log n)$ approximation for MINIMUM COST r-FAULT TOLERANT 2-SPANNER on directed graphs that works for all r.*

PROOF. The first step of the algorithm is to solve LP (4) using Lemma 3.2. We then round the solution using Algorithm 1 below. (This rounding algorithm was designed in [DK11] but was used to round a different relaxation, hence they were forced to set $\alpha = \Theta(r \log n)$ and the analysis therein is not applicable here.)

Algorithm 1: Rounding algorithm for r-fault tolerant 2-spanner.

Input: Graph $G = (V, E)$, fractional solution $\langle x, f \rangle$ to LP (4)

1 Set $\alpha = C \ln n$ (for a large enough constant C).
2 For every $v \in V$ choose independently a random threshold $T_v \in [0,1]$.
3 Output $E' = \{(u,v) \in E : \min\{T_u, T_v\} \leq \alpha \cdot x_{(u,v)}\}$.

We first show that the cost of the solution is likely to be at most 6α times the LP value. The probability that some edge e is selected to be in E' is at most $2\alpha x_e$, so the expected cost of the solution E' is $\sum_{e \in E} c_e \cdot 2\alpha x_e = 2\alpha \sum_e c_e x_e$. By Markov's inequality, the cost of the solution E' exceeds $8\alpha \sum_e c_e x_e$ with probability at most $1/4$.

We now argue that this algorithm returns a valid r-fault tolerant 2-spanner with high probability. We say that E' *satisfies* an edge (u,v) if either $(u,v) \in E'$ or E' contains at least $r+1$ length 2 paths from u to v. By Lemma 3.1, if E' satisfies all edges then it is a valid r-fault tolerant 2-spanner. Consider some edge $(u,v) \in E$. Order the paths in $\mathcal{P}_{u,v}$ in nonincreasing order by their flow values in the LP solution, so P_i is the path with the ith largest flow. Let $W_i = \{P_1, P_2, \ldots, P_i\}$, and let $i^* = \max\{i : f_{P_i} \geq 1/\alpha\}$. If $i^* > r$ then $r+1$ paths have flow value at least $1/\alpha$, so both of the edges in each path have x value at least $1/\alpha$, so they are included in E' with probability 1. Thus (u,v) is satisfied with probability 1.

On the other hand, suppose that $i^* \leq r$. Let us denote $r' = r + 1 - i^* \geq 1$. By the knapsack-cover constraint for (u,v) and W_{i^*}, we know that

$$r' x_{(u,v)} + \sum_{P \in \mathcal{P}_{u,v} \setminus W_{i^*}} f_P \geq r'.$$

If $r' x_{(u,v)} \geq r'/2$ then $x_{(u,v)} \geq 1/2$ and thus (u,v) is included in E' with probability 1, satisfying (u,v). Otherwise it must be the case that $\sum_{P \in \mathcal{P}_{u,v} \setminus W_{i^*}} f_P \geq r'/2$. For $P \in \mathcal{P}_{u,v}$, let I_P be an indicator for the event that the T value of the middle vertex is at most α times the flow value f_P (formally, if $P = (u,z,v)$ then $I_P = 1_{\{T_z \leq \alpha f_P\}}$), and observe that this event implies that both edges of P are included in E' (because then we have $T_z \leq \alpha \cdot \min\{x_{(u,z)}, x_{(z,v)}\}$). Note that for $P \in W_{i^*}$, we have $I_P = 1$ with probability 1. For $P \in \mathcal{P}_{u,v} \setminus W_{i^*}$, we have $I_P = 1$ with probability at least $\alpha f_P \in [0,1]$. The number of paths from $\mathcal{P}_{u,v} \setminus W_{i^*}$ included in E' is clearly at least $\sum_{P \in \mathcal{P}_{u,v} \setminus W_{i^*}} I_P$, and we can bound that last quantity (which is a sum of independent indicators) by a Chernoff bound (see e.g. [MR95, DP09]). Its expectation is

$$\mathbb{E}\Big[\sum_{P \in \mathcal{P}_{u,v} \setminus W_{i^*}} I_P\Big] \geq \sum_{P \in \mathcal{P}_{u,v} \setminus W_{i^*}} \alpha f_P \geq \alpha r'/2,$$

so by our choice of $\alpha = C \log n$ for a large enough C,

$$\Pr\Big[\sum_{P \in \mathcal{P}_{u,v} \setminus W_{i^*}} I_P \leq \alpha r'/4\Big] \leq e^{-\Omega(\alpha r')} \leq 1/n^{\Omega(C)} \leq 1/n^3.$$
(5)

Thus with high probability the total number of length 2 paths between u and v included in E' is at least $i^* + \alpha r'/4 \geq r+1$, and so (u,v) is satisfied. The theorem follows by taking a union bound over these events for all edges (u,v), and the aforementioned event that the solution's cost exceeds 6α times the LP value. $\square$

3.4 Bounded-Degree Graphs

When the maximum degree of the graph is bounded by Δ and the edge costs c_e are all 1, we can improve Theorem 3.3 slightly and give an $O(\log \Delta)$-approximation. We simply change the inflation parameter α in Algorithm 1 to be $O(\log \Delta)$ instead of $O(\log n)$. We then need a more careful analysis, using an algorithmic version of the Lovász Local Lemma.

THEOREM 3.4. *There is a randomized $O(\log \Delta)$ approximation for* MINIMUM COST r-FAULT TOLERANT 2-SPANNER *on directed graphs in which $c_e = 1$ for all $e \in E$ and the maximum (in and out) degree is at most $\Delta \geq 2$.*

We shall use the following constructive version of the symmetric Lovász Local Lemma, which is an immediate corollary of the nonsymmetric version proved by Moser and Tardos [MT10].

LEMMA 3.5 (MOSER AND TARDOS [MT10]). *Let $\mathcal{P}$ be a finite set of mutually independent random variables in a probability space. Let $\mathcal{A}$ be a finite set of events determined by the variables in $\mathcal{P}$. Suppose that each $A \in \mathcal{A}$ is mutually independent of all but at most d other events in $\mathcal{A}$, and suppose that $\Pr[A] \leq p$ for all $A \in \mathcal{A}$. If $ep(d+1) \leq 1$ then there exists an assignment of values to the variables $\mathcal{P}$*

such that no event $A \in \mathcal{A}$ occurs. Moreover, there is a randomized algorithm that finds such an assignment in expected time $O(|\mathcal{P}| + |\mathcal{A}| \cdot |\mathcal{P}|/d)$.

PROOF OF THEOREM 3.4. Consider a directed graph G with unit edge costs $c_e = 1$ and vertex degrees bounded by Δ. Consider a solution to the LP relaxation (4), and apply Algorithm 1 to it but with inflation factor $\alpha = C \log \Delta$ instead of $C \log n$.

For an edge $(u,v) \in E$, let $A_{u,v}$ be the event that E' does not satisfy this edge, i.e. $(u,v) \notin E'$ and the graph $G' = (V, E')$ has less than $r+1$ paths of length 2 from u to v. The analysis of Theorem 3.3 shows (after modifying (5) with our new value of α), that

$$\Pr[A_{u,v}] \leq e^{-\Omega(\alpha)} \leq 1/\Delta^{\Omega(C)}.$$

Furthermore, note that $A_{u,v}$ depends only on the random variables T_z for $z \in (N^+(u) \cap N^-(v)) \cup \{u,v\}$. Here and throughout, $N^+(u)$ and $N^-(u)$ denote the out-neighbors and in-neighbors respectively of $u \in V$. Observe that $A_{u,v}$ is independent of all but Δ^3 other events $A_{u',v'}$, simply because there are at most Δ choices for each of z, u', and v'.

We could now apply Lemma 3.5 to these events. The underlying mutually independent random variables $\mathcal{P}$ would be the T_u variables, and the "bad events" $\mathcal{A}$ would be the events $A_{u,v}$. This would give us an algorithm that in polynomial time returned a valid r-fault tolerant k-spanner, but we also need a bound on the cost of this spanner. The analysis via Markov's inequality in Theorem 3.3 is too weak now, because when we apply the algorithm of Lemma 3.5 we change the overall distribution in a way that might destroy the cost bound. We need to integrate the cost analysis into the events that Lemma 3.5 is applied to, so at a high level we employ a more local approach where the cost of E' is split among the vertices and events bounding the cost are added to the $A_{u,v}$ events. More specifically, we shall create many events, each of which controls how the cost of E' compares *locally* with the cost of the LP, and then apply the Local Lemma to the new events together with the $\{A_{u,v}\}$ events. A formal argument follows.

For each vertex $u \in V$, let the random variable Z_u^+ be the number of outgoing edges (u,v) for which $T_v \leq \alpha \cdot x_{(u,v)}$, and let Z_u^- be the number of incoming edges (v,u) for which $T_v \leq \alpha \cdot x_{(u,v)}$. Informally, $Z_u^+ + Z_u^-$ is the number of edges incident to u whose inclusion in E' can be charged to their other endpoint. The algorithm's cost is $|E'| \leq \sum_{u \in V}(Z_u^+ + Z_u^-)$, since every edge (u,v) included in E' adds 1 to either Z_u^+ or Z_v^- (or both).

For each vertex $v \in V$, let B_u be the event that $Z_u^+ + Z_u^- > 4\alpha(\sum_{(u,v) \in E} x_{(u,v)} + \sum_{(v,u) \in E} x_{(v,u)})$. We would like to show that this event happens only with small probability. Note that $\mathbb{E}[Z_u^+] = \sum_{(u,v) \in E} \min\{\alpha x_{(u,v)}, 1\} \leq \alpha \sum_{(u,v) \in E} x_{(u,v)}$, so by a Chernoff bound (see e.g. [MR95, DP09]) we get

$$\Pr\Big[Z_u^+ > 2\alpha \sum_{(u,v) \in E} x_{(u,v)}\Big] \leq e^{-(1/3)(C \ln \Delta) \sum_{(u,v) \in E} x_{(u,v)}}$$

$$\leq \Delta^{-C/3},$$

where in the final inequality we assume there is at least one outgoing edge from u and thus $\sum_{(u,v) \in E} x_{(u,v)} \geq 1$ (since otherwise $Z_u^+ = 0$ with probability 1). We can use a similar

174

argument to get the same bound for Z_u^-, and by combining them we get that

$$\Pr[B_u] \leq \Pr\left[Z_u^+ > 2\alpha \sum_{(u,v) \in E} x_{(u,v)}\right]$$
$$+ \Pr\left[Z_u^- > 2\alpha \sum_{(v,u) \in E} x_{(v,u)}\right]$$
$$\leq 2\Delta^{-C/3}.$$

We now apply Lemma 3.5 to the events $A_{u,v}$ and B_u. Note that B_u depends only on the random variables T_z for $z \in N^+(u) \cup N^-(u)$, and recall that $A_{u,v}$ depends only on T_z for $z \in N^+(u) \cap N^-(v)$. Thus each event is mutually independent of all but $O(\Delta^3)$ other events — for an event $A_{u,v}$ we exclude at most Δ^3 events $A_{u',v'}$ and at most $2\Delta^2$ events $B_{u'}$; for an event B_u we exclude at most $4\Delta^2$ events $B_{u'}$ and at most $2\Delta^3$ events $A_{u',v'}$. We can thus apply Lemma 3.5 with dependency parameter $d = O(\Delta^3)$, because by setting sufficiently large C, the probability of each event is at most a suitable $p = \Delta^{-\Omega(C)} < 1/e(d+1)$. Since the number of events is at most $O(n^2)$ and the number of underlying variables is only n, we conclude that there is a polynomial time algorithm to find the underlying variables T_u so that none of the events $A_{u,v}$ and B_u occur. This implies that $G' = (V, E')$ is an r-fault tolerant 2-spanner of G of cost

$$|E'| \leq \sum_{u \in V}\left(Z_u^+ + Z_u^-\right) \leq 8\alpha \sum_{(u,v) \in E} c_{u,v} x_{(u,v)}$$
$$\leq O(\log \Delta) \cdot \mathrm{LP},$$

which proves Theorem 3.4. □

3.5 Distributed Construction

We now show how to adapt and use the $O(\log n)$ approximation that we designed in Section 3.3 to give a distributed $O(\log n)$-approximation. We will assume that communication along an edge is bidirectional, even if the graph is directed. The main problem that we run into when trying to design a distributed algorithm based on Algorithm 1 is solving the linear program. If we had a solution, and every vertex knew the x_e value of its incident edges, then we would be done; the rounding scheme in Algorithm 1 is entirely local, so every vertex $v \in V$ would just locally pick its threshold T_v and include the appropriate edges. If we want both endpoints of an edge to know that it has been included in the spanner, we can then just have every vertex tell all of its neighbors (in a single round) which edges it bought based on its threshold.

In order to (approximately) solve the LP we partition the graph into clusters, solve the LP separately on each cluster, and then repeat this process several times, eventually taking the average. This technique is quite similar to the work of Kuhn, Moscibroda, and Wattenhofer [KMW06], who showed how to approximately solve *positive* LPs using the graph decompositions of Linial and Saks [LS93].

The fundamental tool that we will use is the ability to quickly compute a good *padded decomposition*, which is a basic tool in metric embeddings that has found numerous applications in approximation and online algorithms (e.g. for network design problems). This notion is essentially a version of low-diameter decompositions, such as a sparse covers [AP90]. This specific version was (probably) introduced by Rao [Rao99], who observed that it can be derived from

an earlier construction of Klein, Plotkin and Rao [KPR93]. An explicit formulation of padded decompositions appeared only later, in [KL03, GKL03], and used a construction of Bartal [Bar96]. The definition given below is actually a special case of the usual notion, where the so-called padding requirement is a unit radius around each vertex, i.e. just the vertex's neighborhood.

Let $\mathcal{T} = \mathcal{T}(V)$ denote the set of all partitions of V (irrespective of the graph structure). For a partition $P \in \mathcal{T}$, we call each set $C \in P$ a *cluster*. Let G' be the *undirected* graph corresponding to G, and define the diameter of C to be $\mathrm{diam}(C) = \max_{u,v \in C} d_{G'}(u,v)$ (this is usually called weak diameter, because it corresponds to the shortest $u - v$ path in G', possibly going out of C along the way). Finally, for $x \in V$ and a partition $P \in \mathcal{T}$, we let $P(x)$ denote the cluster of P that contains x. Since G' is undirected, we let $N(x)$ denote the set of all neighbors of x in G'

DEFINITION 3.6. *A padded decomposition of G is a probability measure μ on $\mathcal{T}$ that satisfies the following two conditions:*

1. *For every $P \in \mathrm{supp}(\mu)$ and every $C \in P$ we have $\mathrm{diam}(C) \leq O(\log n)$.*

2. *For every $x \in V$ we have $\Pr_{P \sim \mu}[N(x) \subseteq P(x)] \geq 1/2$.*

It is known that every metric space admits such a padded decomposition, and there are polynomial-time randomized algorithms to sample from such a decomposition [Bar96, FRT04]. It is convenient to assign to each cluster a vertex, called the *cluster center*. One could always choose an arbitrary vertex in the cluster (e.g. one whose identifier is the smallest), but in many constructions there is a natural center point. The next lemma is a straightforward adaptation of the construction of Bartal [Bar96] to the distributed context; it can also be viewed as a slight modification of the graph decompositions of Linial and Saks [LS93].

LEMMA 3.7. *There is a distributed algorithm that runs in $O(\log n)$ rounds and with high probability samples from a padded decomposition, so that every vertex knows the cluster containing it, meaning all other vertices in the same cluster. Every cluster C also has a cluster center $v \in V$ (which is not necessarily in the cluster) with the property that $\mathrm{diam}(C \cup \{v\}) \leq O(\log n)$.*

PROOF. The construction of Bartal [Bar96] is simple, and is usually described iteratively. (As mentioned above, the padding property is not formally proved there, but it can be derived from the analysis therein, see also [KL03, GKL03].) Working in the metric completion of G' (so removing vertices does not change distances), repeat the following procedure until every vertex has been assigned to some cluster: Pick an arbitrary vertex u from those that have not yet been assigned a cluster. Randomly pick a radius r_u from the geometric distribution with some constant parameter $p > 0$. Create a new cluster consisting of u and all unclustered vertices that are within distance r_u of u.

While this procedure is phrased iteratively, it quite obviously can be made distributed with only minor changes. First, every vertex $u \in V$ locally chooses a value r_u from the geometric distribution with parameter p. Then every node u simultaneously sends a message containing the ID of u to all nodes within distance $\min\{r_u, O(\log n)\}$ of u. Note that this take only $O(\log n)$ rounds, and with high probability $\max_u\{r_u\} \le O(\log n)$ (the analysis of [KL03] shows that this truncation at $O(\log n)$ does not significantly affect the padding probability). Now every node chooses as a cluster center the sender with the smallest ID (i.e. the sender that comes earliest in the lexicographic ordering) of the vertices whose messages it received. The only difference between the output of this algorithm and Bartal's algorithm is that in Bartal's algorithm only unclustered nodes can be the center of a new cluster, while in our variation every vertex (in lexicographic order) gets the chance to create a cluster (which it might not be a member of itself). It is well known (see e.g. [KL03, GKL03]) that this change does not affect anything in the analysis.

We remark that the construction above has a natural choice of cluster centers. Under this choice, a cluster C might not contain its center $v \in V$, but $\mathrm{diam}(C \cup \{v\}) \le O(\log n)$, which is sufficient for our purposes. $\square$

Now that we can construct padded decompositions, we want to use them to decompose LP (4) into "local" parts. Let P be a partition sampled from μ. For each cluster $C \in P$, let $N(C)$ denote the set of vertices in $V \setminus C$ that are adjacent (in G') to at least one vertex in C, let $\delta(C) \subseteq E$ be all edges with one endpoint in C and one endpoint not in C, and let $E(C) \subseteq E$ be the set of edges with both endpoints in C. Let $G(C)$ be the subgraph of G induced by $C \cup N(C)$. We define $\mathrm{LP}(C)$ to be LP (4) for $G(C)$, but where edges in $\delta(C)$ are modified to have cost 0.

Let LP^* be the value of an optimal solution to LP (4), and let $\mathrm{LP}^*(C)$ be the value of an optimal solution to $\mathrm{LP}(C)$.

LEMMA 3.8. $\sum_{C \in P} \mathrm{LP}^*(C) \le \mathrm{LP}^*$ for every partition $P \in \mathcal{T}$.

PROOF. Let $\langle x, f \rangle$ be an optimal fractional solution to LP (4). We want to use this solution to build fractional solutions to $\mathrm{LP}(C)$ for all $C \in P$ whose total cost is at most LP^*. For each cluster $C \in P$, define a solution $\langle x^C, f^C \rangle$ for $\mathrm{LP}(C)$ as follows: Let $x_e^C = x_e$ if $e \in E(C)$ and let $x_e^C = 1$ if $e \in \delta(C)$. Note that this already satisfies all of the knapsack-cover constraints for edges in $\delta(C)$. For edges $(u,v) \in E(C)$, note that every path in $\mathcal{P}_{u,v}$ appears in $G(C)$, so we can set $f_P^C = f_P$ for these paths. Since these flows satisfy the knapsack-cover constraints in LP (4), they also satisfy all of the knapsack-cover constraints in $\mathrm{LP}(C)$. All other flows f_P^C (e.g. between vertices in $N(C)$) are set to 0. Obviously the capacity constraints are satisfied, and thus $\langle x^C, f^C \rangle$ is a feasible solution to $\mathrm{LP}(C)$.

Since in $\mathrm{LP}(C)$ the edges in $\delta(C)$ have cost 0, and every edge of E is in $E(C)$ for at most one cluster C,

$$\sum_{C \in P} \mathrm{LP}^*(C) = \sum_{C \in P} \sum_{e \in E(C)} c_e x_e^C \le \sum_{e \in E} c_e x_e = \mathrm{LP}^*,$$

which proves the lemma. $\square$

With this lemma in hand, we can now design a distributed approximation algorithm and prove the main theorem of this section.

THEOREM 3.9. There is a distributed algorithm that terminates in $O(\log^2 n)$ rounds and is an $O(\log n)$ approximation to MINIMUM COST r-FAULT TOLERANT 2-SPANNER.

Algorithm 2: Distributed algorithm for r-fault tolerant 2-spanner.

---

1 **for** $i \leftarrow 1$ **to** $t = O(\log n)$ **do**
2 $\quad$ Sample a partition P_i from μ using Lemma 3.7
$\quad$ // we assume the center of each cluster
$\qquad$ $C \in P_i$ knows $G(C)$
3 $\quad$ The center of each cluster $C \in P_i$ solves $\mathrm{LP}(C)$
$\quad$ using Lemma 3.2, and sends the solution $\langle x^{C,i}, f^{C,i} \rangle$
$\quad$ to all vertices in C
4 For each edge $(u,v) \in E$, let $\mathcal{I}_{(u,v)} = \{i : P_i(u) = P_i(v)\}$
$\quad$ // these are the iterations in which both
$\qquad$ endpoints are in same cluster
5 $\tilde{x}_e \leftarrow \min\{1, \frac{4}{t} \sum_{i \in \mathcal{I}_e} x_e^{P_i(e),i}\}$
$\quad$ // $P_i(e)$ is the cluster of P_i containing both
$\qquad$ endpoints of e
6 Round $\tilde{x}_e$ using Algorithm 1
$\quad$ // each edge is rounded by its endpoints

PROOF. Our algorithm is show as Algorithm 2. We first prove the time bound. Lemma 3.7 implies that sampling from μ takes only $O(\log n)$ rounds, and since the diameter of every cluster is at most $O(\log n)$ the other two steps of the loop also take only $O(\log n)$ rounds. Since we execute the loop $O(\log n)$ times, the number of rounds needed to complete the loop is at most $O(\log^2 n)$. After the loop, each vertex can compute x_e for all incident edges e without any extra communication (since each endpoint of an edge e knows $\mathcal{I}_e$ and the LP values for that iteration). Finally, as already pointed out, the rounding of Algorithm 1 can be done locally, with one extra round used to make sure that both endpoints of an edge know if the edge was included by the rounding. Thus the total number of rounds is $O(\log^2 n)$, as claimed.

To prove that this algorithm returns an $O(\log n)$ approximation, we will show that with high probability the $\tilde{x}_e$ values it computes form a feasible solution to LP (4) (when appropriate flow values $\tilde{f}_P$ are chosen) of cost at most $O(\mathrm{LP}^*)$. Once we have this, the analysis of Theorem 3.3 implies that the rounding step outputs an r-fault tolerant 2-spanner $G' = (V, E')$ whose cost is $O(\log n) \sum_e c_e \tilde{x}_e \le O(\log n) \cdot \mathrm{LP}^*$ with probability at least $2/3$. To bound the cost, note that the $\tilde{x}_e/4$ values are just the averages of the $\mathrm{LP}(C)$ values for all rounds in which the edge e does not have cost 0. In other words, $\sum_e c_e \tilde{x}_e \le \frac{4}{t} \sum_{i=1}^{t} \sum_{C \in P_i} \mathrm{LP}^*(C) \le 4\,\mathrm{LP}^*$, where the final inequality is from Lemma 3.8. So it just remains to show that the $\tilde{x}_e$'s form a feasible solution to LP (4).

To prove this, consider an edge $e = (u,v)$, and let $\mathcal{I}_e' \subseteq \mathcal{I}_e$ be the set of iterations i in which $N(u) \cup \{u\}$ is all in the same cluster of P_i. By the second property of padded decompositions, the probability that $N(u) \cup \{u\}$ is all in the same cluster is at least $1/2$. The iterations are independent, so a straightforward Chernoff bound implies that $\Pr[|\mathcal{I}_e'| \ge t/4] \ge 1 - 1/n^3$. For a path $P \in \mathcal{P}_{u,v}$, set $\tilde{f}_P = \frac{1}{|\mathcal{I}_{(u,v)}'|} \sum_{i \in \mathcal{I}_{(u,v)}'} f_P^{P_i(u,v),i}$. In other words, the flow along a path from u to v is equal to the average flow along it in the LP solutions that were computed in iterations when $N(u) \cup \{u\}$ were all in the same cluster.

The capacity constraints are obviously satisfied, since each iteration satisfies the capacity constraints, and the edge capacities are scaled by $4/t$ while flows are scaled by $1/|\mathcal{I}_{u,v}'| \le$

$4/t$. Note that here we depend on the fact that *all* of $N(u)$ is in the same cluster as u; if some vertex $z \in N(u)$ were in a different cluster, then in the LP solution for the cluster containing u and v there could be flow sent from u to v through z. This flow would not have the corresponding capacity added to the $\tilde{x}_e$ variables, which would be a problem.

Similarly, consider the knapsack-cover constraint for some $(u,v) \in E$ and some $W \in \mathcal{W}_{u,v}$. Then since we could send enough flow in each iteration in $\mathcal{I}'_{(u,v)}$, when we take the average we can still send enough flow, i.e.

$$r_W \tilde{x}_{(u,v)} + \sum_{P \in \mathcal{P}_{u,v} \setminus W} \tilde{f}_P$$
$$\geq \sum_{i \in \mathcal{I}'_{(u,v)}} \left(\frac{4}{t} r_W x^i_{u,v} + \sum_{P \in \mathcal{P}_{u,v} \setminus W} \frac{1}{|\mathcal{I}'_{(u,v)}|} f_P^{P_i(u,v),i} \right)$$
$$\geq \frac{1}{|\mathcal{I}'_{(u,v)}|} \sum_{i \in \mathcal{I}'_{(u,v)}} \left(r_W x^i_{u,v} + \sum_{P \in \mathcal{P}_{u,v} \setminus W} f_P^{P_i(u,v),i} \right)$$
$$= r_W,$$

where the last inequality is by the knapsack-cover constraint for the cluster $P_i(u,v)$. Thus we have a valid LP solution, so rounding using Algorithm 1 gives an $O(\log n)$ approximation. $\square$

Remark.

While for our purposes it was enough to solve the LP to within a constant factor (since we lose an $O(\log n)$ factor in the rounding anyway), it is easy to see that we could in fact solve the LP to within a $(1+\epsilon)$ factor. First, we could change the padded decomposition to have the padding property (u and $N(u)$ are all in the same cluster) hold with probability at least $1-\epsilon$, which would require increasing the diameter of the clusters, and thus the number of rounds it takes to solve the LP, by an $O(1/\epsilon)$ factor. Second, when we apply the Chernoff bound, instead of asking the number of times the padding event occurs to be at least $t/4$, we could ask that it is at least $(1-\epsilon)^2 t$. By increasing t by an $O(1/\epsilon^2)$ factor, we still get the right probabilities. Overall, the number of rounds would now be $O(\varepsilon^{-3} \log n)$.

4. CONCLUSIONS AND FUTURE WORK

This paper considers the problem of constructing r-fault tolerant spanners and gives two basic constructions. For general stretch bounds $k \geq 3$, we show how to construct r-fault tolerant k-spanners whose size is at most polynomially (in r) larger than spanners without fault tolerance, improving over the previous exponential dependency (on r) of [CLPR09]. Our main technique is oversampling failure sets, in order to handle many of them in one iteration. An interesting open question is to provide nontrivial lower bounds on the size of the best r-fault tolerant k-spanner; to the best of our knowledge, no such bounds are known other than the trivial bound of $\Omega(rn)$ and those that apply even when $r = 0$.

For $k = 2$ and unit edge lengths we design an $O(\log n)$-approximation algorithm (for all r), improving over the previous $O(r \log n)$ factor of [DK11] and showing that the approximation ratio can be independent of the desired amount of fault tolerance r. Our main technique here is to design a new linear programming relaxation that includes the exponentially many knapsack-cover inequalities of [CFLP00].

We also provided a distributed version of the algorithm, and showed that when all edge costs are 1 the approximation can be improved to $O(\log \Delta)$. An interesting open question is to improve this ratio to $O(\log(|E|/|V|))$, which would match the approximation known for the non-fault tolerant version.

5. REFERENCES

[ADD+93] I. Althöfer, G. Das, D. Dobkin, D. Joseph, and J. Soares. On sparse spanners of weighted graphs. *Discrete Comput. Geom.*, 9(1):81–100, 1993.

[AP90] B. Awerbuch and D. Peleg. Sparse partitions. In *31st Annual IEEE Symposium on Foundations of Computer Science*, pages 503–513, 1990.

[AP95] B. Awerbuch and D. Peleg. Online tracking of mobile users. *J. ACM*, 42(5):1021–1058, 1995.

[AYZ95] N. Alon, R. Yuster, and U. Zwick. Color-coding. *J. ACM*, 42(4):844–856, 1995.

[Bar96] Y. Bartal. Probabilistic approximation of metric spaces and its algorithmic applications. In *37th Annual Symposium on Foundations of Computer Science*, pages 184–193. IEEE, 1996.

[CFLP00] R. D. Carr, L. K. Fleischer, V. J. Leung, and C. A. Phillips. Strengthening integrality gaps for capacitated network design and covering problems. In *11th Annual ACM-SIAM Symposium on Discrete Algorithms*, pages 106–115. SIAM, 2000.

[CLPR09] S. Chechik, M. Langberg, D. Peleg, and L. Roditty. Fault-tolerant spanners for general graphs. In *41st Annual ACM Symposium on Theory of Computing*, pages 435–444. ACM, 2009.

[CZ03] A. Czumaj and H. Zhao. Fault-tolerant geometric spanners. In *Proceedings of the 19th Annual Symposium on Computational Geometry*, pages 1–10. ACM, 2003.

[DGPV08] B. Derbel, C. Gavoille, D. Peleg, and L. Viennot. On the locality of distributed sparse spanner construction. In *27th Annual ACM Symposium on Principles of Distributed Computing*, pages 273–282. ACM, 2008.

[DK11] M. Dinitz and R. Krauthgamer. Directed spanners via flow-based linear programs. In *STOC*, 2011. To appear.

[DP09] D. Dubhashi and A. Panconesi. *Concentration of Measure for the Analysis of Randomized Algorithms*. Cambridge University Press, New York, NY, USA, 2009.

[EEST08] M. Elkin, Y. Emek, D. A. Spielman, and S.-H. Teng. Lower-stretch spanning trees. *SIAM J. Comput.*, 38(2):608–628, 2008.

[EP01] M. Elkin and D. Peleg. The client-server 2-spanner problem with applications to network design. In *8th International Colloquium on Structural Information and Communication Complexity (SIROCCO)*, pages 117–132, 2001.

[FRT04] J. Fakcharoenphol, S. Rao, and K. Talwar. A tight bound on approximating arbitrary metrics by tree metrics. *J. Comput. Syst. Sci.*, 69(3):485–497, 2004.

[GKL03]   A. Gupta, R. Krauthgamer, and J. R. Lee. Bounded geometries, fractals, and low-distortion embeddings. In *44th Annual IEEE Symposium on Foundations of Computer Science*, pages 534–543, October 2003.

[KL03]   R. Krauthgamer and J. R. Lee. The intrinsic dimensionality of graphs. In *Proceedings of the 35th ACM Symposium on Theory of Computing*, pages 438–447, June 2003.

[KMW06]   F. Kuhn, T. Moscibroda, and R. Wattenhofer. The price of being near-sighted. In *27th Annual ACM-SIAM symposium on Discrete Algorithm*, pages 980–989. ACM, 2006.

[Kor01]   G. Kortsarz. On the hardness of approximating spanners. *Algorithmica*, 30(3):432–450, 2001.

[KP94]   G. Kortsarz and D. Peleg. Generating sparse 2-spanners. *J. Algorithms*, 17(2):222–236, 1994.

[KPR93]   P. Klein, S. A. Plotkin, and S. Rao. Excluded minors, network decomposition, and multicommodity flow. In *25th Annual ACM Symposium on Theory of Computing*, pages 682–690, May 1993.

[LNS98]   C. Levcopoulos, G. Narasimhan, and M. Smid. Efficient algorithms for constructing fault-tolerant geometric spanners. In *30th ACM Symposium on Theory of Computing*, pages 186–195. ACM, 1998.

[LS93]   N. Linial and M. Saks. Low diameter graph decompositions. *Combinatorica*, 13(4):441–454, 1993.

[Luk99]   T. Lukovszki. New results on fault tolerant geometric spanners. In *Proceedings of the 6th International Workshop on Algorithms and Data Structures*, WADS '99, pages 193–204, London, UK, 1999. Springer-Verlag.

[MR95]   R. Motwani and P. Raghavan. *Randomized Algorithms*. Cambridge University Press, 1995.

[MT10]   R. A. Moser and G. Tardos. A constructive proof of the general Lovász Local Lemma. *J. ACM*, 57:11:1–11:15, February 2010.

[Pel00]   D. Peleg. *Distributed computing: a locality-sensitive approach*. SIAM, 2000.

[PS89]   D. Peleg and A. A. Schäffer. Graph spanners. *J. Graph Theory*, 13(1):99–116, 1989.

[PU89]   D. Peleg and J. D. Ullman. An optimal synchronizer for the hypercube. *SIAM J. Comput.*, 18:740–747, August 1989.

[Rao99]   S. Rao. Small distortion and volume preserving embeddings for planar and Euclidean metrics. In *Proceedings of the 15th Annual Symposium on Computational Geometry*, pages 300–306. ACM, 1999.

[ST04]   D. A. Spielman and S.-H. Teng. Nearly-linear time algorithms for graph partitioning, graph sparsification, and solving linear systems. In *36th Annual ACM Symposium on Theory of Computing*, pages 81–90. ACM, 2004.

[TZ05]   M. Thorup and U. Zwick. Approximate distance oracles. *J. ACM*, 52(1):1–24, 2005.

[WY10]   O. Weimann and R. Yuster. Replacement paths via fast matrix multiplication. In *51st Annual IEEE Symposium on Foundations of Computer Science*, pages 655 –662, 2010.

Adaptively Secure Broadcast, Revisited

Juan A. Garay
AT&T Labs – Research
garay@research.att.com

Jonathan Katz[*]
University of Maryland
jkatz@cs.umd.edu

Ranjit Kumaresan
University of Maryland
ranjit@cs.umd.edu

Hong-Sheng Zhou
University of Maryland
hszhou@cs.umd.edu

ABSTRACT

We consider the classical problem of synchronous broadcast with dishonest majority, when a public-key infrastructure and digital signatures are available. In a surprising result, Hirt and Zikas (Eurocrypt 2010) recently observed that all existing protocols for this task are insecure against an *adaptive* adversary who can choose which parties to corrupt as the protocol progresses. Moreover, they prove an impossibility result for adaptively secure broadcast in their setting.

We argue that the communication model adopted by Hirt and Zikas is unrealistically pessimistic. We revisit the problem of adaptively secure broadcast in a more natural synchronous model (with rushing), and show that broadcast *is* possible in this setting for an arbitrary number of corruptions. Our positive result holds under a strong, simulation-based definition in the universal-composability framework.

We also study the impact of adaptive attacks on protocols for secure multi-party computation where broadcast is used as a sub-routine.

Categories and Subject Descriptors

C.2.1 [**Computer-Communication Networks**]: Network Architecture and Design—*Distributed networks*

General Terms

Security, Theory

Keywords

Broadcast, fault-tolerant distributed computing, adaptive security, cryptographic protocols

---

[*]Supported by the US DoD/ARO MURI program, and the US Army Research Laboratory and the UK Ministry of Defence under agreement number W911NF-06-3-0001.

1. INTRODUCTION

Broadcast [14, 12] is a fundamental primitive in fault-tolerant distributed computing. It also serves as an important subcomponent of most multi-party cryptographic protocols. Indeed, cryptographic protocols are typically designed and analyzed under the assumption that a broadcast channel is available, but in almost any real-world scenario the broadcast channel needs to be realized using a broadcast protocol. Fortunately, known composition results (including, most powerfully, those within the *universal composability* (UC) framework [3]) imply that this approach is *sound*: namely, given a protocol Π proven secure under the assumption that a broadcast channel exists, and then instantiating the broadcast channel using a secure broadcast protocol bc, the composed protocol Π^{bc} is guaranteed to be secure when run over a point-to-point network.

The construction of broadcast protocols has a long history, starting from the seminal work of Pease, Shostak, and Lamport [14, 12] who showed that broadcast (and the closely related primitive known as consensus or Byzantine agreement) is possible if and only if the number of corrupted parties t is strictly less than $1/3$ of the total number of parties n. (Here and throughout the paper, we assume a synchronous model of communication.) This holds in the "plain model" with no additional setup, but it is known that the bound on the tolerable number of corrupted parties can be exceeded if a public-key infrastructure (PKI) and digital signatures are available to the parties. In this setting, it is possible to construct broadcast protocols resilient to a computationally bounded adversary corrupting $t < n$ of the parties [9].[1] In what follows, we always have in mind this setting when we speak of protocols tolerating $t \geq n/3$ corrupted parties.

As far as questions of feasibility are concerned, broadcast had appeared to be a solved problem. A recent result by Hirt and Zikas [11] therefore came as quite a surprise. They studied the problem of designing broadcast protocols with security against *adaptive* adversaries who can choose which parties to corrupt during the course of the protocol (cf. [5]). Hirt and Zikas showed explicit attacks against all existing broadcast protocols when $t \geq n/3$ and, moreover, proved the *impossibility* of realizing adaptively secure broadcast with corruption threshold $t > n/2$. (They gave constructions of adaptively secure protocols for the regime $n/3 \leq t \leq n/2$.) Their work calls into question the feasibil-

---

[1]With a different sort of initial setup, broadcast resilient to an unbounded adversary corrupting $t < n$ of the parties is also possible [16].

ity of realizing adaptively secure multi-party computation (MPC) for $t > n/2$ in point-to-point networks.

A closer look at the Hirt-Zikas result shows that they make a very strong assumption regarding the adversary (or, alternately, a very weak assumption regarding the communication network): namely, they assume the adversary has the ability to corrupt parties *in the middle of a round*, in between sending messages to two other parties in the network. Specifically, their impossibility result crucially relies on the fact that the following sequence of events can occur when an honest party P sends its messages in some round:

1. The adversary (who has already corrupted some of the other players) receives the message(s) sent to it by P.

2. Based on this, the adversary then decides whether to corrupt P.

3. If the adversary corrupts P, it can then send messages of its choice (on behalf of P) to the remaining parties in the same round.

While the above is consistent with theoretical models for *asynchronous* cryptographic protocols, as well as some previous treatments of adaptive security in the synchronous setting (e.g., [3]), allowing such adversarial behavior seems unrealistically pessimistic: in the real world, implementing such an attack would require either an exceedingly fast adversary or an extremely slow network. A more realistic model of synchronous communication (see, e.g., [2]) is one in which messages sent by honest parties within any given round are delivered *atomically* to all other parties.[2]

Importantly, however, the attacks that were demonstrated by Hirt and Zikas [11] on existing broadcast protocols remain valid even if we assume atomic message delivery. Consider, for example, the authenticated broadcast protocol of Dolev and Strong [9] where, at a high level, in the first round the sender digitally signs and sends his message to all the other parties, while in subsequent rounds parties append their signatures and forward the result. Roughly, if any party ever observes valid signatures of the sender on two *different* messages then that party forwards both signatures to all other parties and disqualifies the sender (and all parties output some default message). The Hirt-Zikas attack against this protocol works as follows: a corrupted party P in the network waits to receive the initial message from the (uncorrupted) sender. If P likes the message sent by the sender then P runs the protocol honestly. If P does not like the message sent by the sender then P adaptively corrupts the sender, uses the sender's signing key to generate a valid signature on another message (in the next round), and thus ensures that the sender will be disqualified and the default message used.

While this outcome might be acceptable with respect to a *property-based* definition (since the sender is corrupted by the end of the protocol in the second case), the outcome is not something that should be possible with respect to a *simulation-based* definition (since corruption of the sender depends on the sender's initial input). Realizing the latter,

stronger definition is a natural goal; moreover, a simulation-based definition is especially critical for broadcast which is typically used as a sub-protocol within some larger protocol.

Given that the Hirt-Zikas attack applies even when atomic message delivery is assumed, one might wonder whether their impossibility result holds in that model as well. Alternately, one may be willing to give up on "full" broadcast and hope that some weaker form of broadcast might be sufficient to achieve secure MPC for $t > n/2$. (Indeed, in the presence of a dishonest majority the standard definitions of secure MPC give up on guaranteed output delivery, so in particular secure MPC for $t > n/2$ does not imply broadcast for $t > n/2$.) These are the questions with which we concern ourselves in this paper.

1.1 Our Results

As our main result, we show that the Hirt-Zikas impossibility result does *not* apply in the synchronous model with atomic message delivery. That is, we show a construction of an adaptively secure broadcast protocol tolerating an arbitrary number of corruptions in this communication model. We prove security of our protocol within the UC framework [3], under the usual assumptions that a PKI and digital signatures are available. We stress that we require only a standard PKI where each party chooses their public key and all other parties know it; in particular, we do not require the stronger "registered public key" model considered in [1].

The main idea for avoiding the Hirt-Zikas attack is to design a protocol where the adversary does not learn the (honest) sender's message until agreement has already been reached; that way, the adversary must make its decision as to whether or not to corrupt the sender independently of the sender's input. This suggests the following two-stage approach: First, the signer broadcasts a *commitment* to its message; once agreement is reached, the signer then decommits. While this does prevent the above attack, it also introduces a new problem when we try to prove security, since the simulator must commit to the sender's message before knowing what the sender's message is! (Since the sender might still get corrupted in the middle of the protocol, it also does not work for the simulator to obtain the output of the broadcast functionality before starting the simulation.) This could be handled by using a universally composable commitment scheme (e.g., [6]), which satisfies even stronger properties, but we would prefer to avoid the stronger setup assumptions that are required for constructing universally composable commitments [6].

Instead, we show that a very weak form of commitment suffices to make the approach sound. Specifically, we use commitment schemes that (informally) are hiding and binding for an *honest* sender, but where binding can be (easily) violated by a *dishonest* sender. To see why this works, note that the only time binding is needed is when the adversary corrupts the sender *after* the sender has already committed to its message. Since the sender in that case was honest at the time the commitment was generated, the binding property holds and the adversary will not be able to change the committed value. On the other hand, the simulator can behave as a dishonest sender and generate a commitment that it can later open to any desired value, and in particular to the sender's true input in case the sender remains uncorrupted until the end of the protocol. We show that commitment schemes with the desired properties can be constructed from

---

[2]We still allow *rushing*, meaning that corrupted parties may receive their messages in some round before having to send any of their own. This reflects the fact that corrupted parties can choose to delay their own communication. However, it seems unrealistic to assume that honest parties would delay sending any of their own messages.

one-way functions (which are, in turn, implied by digital signature schemes); thus, in summary, we obtain an adaptively secure, universally-composable broadcast protocol assuming a PKI and digital signatures.

We also study the impact of adaptive attacks on secure multi-party computation protocols (where broadcast is commonly used as a subcomponent), and establish the variants of broadcast that are needed in this setting. Interestingly, we show that the full functionality of broadcast is not needed in order to obtain secure MPC for $t \geq n/2$; instead, a weaker form of broadcast — which can be realized even in the Hirt-Zikas communication model — suffices.

1.2 Organization of the Paper

In Section 2 we present our network model and elaborate on simulation-based definitions of security. Section 3 defines various notions of broadcast, and contains our construction of adaptively secure broadcast. We discuss the consequences for adaptively secure multi-party computation in Section 4.

2. PRELIMINARIES

2.1 Network Model

We consider a network with synchronous communication, where there is a set of n players (probabilistic polynomial-time Turing machines) $\mathcal{P} = \{P_1, P_2, \cdots, P_n\}$ connected by point-to-point authenticated channels. Each round of the protocol proceeds as follows. The honest parties send their messages for that round, and these messages are received by all parties (both honest and corrupted). The adversary may then choose to corrupt additional players, and then it sends messages on behalf of the parties who were corrupted at the beginning of that round. (This models a *rushing* adversary.) When it is done, the adversary must then "advance the clock" to the next round. We allow the adversary to corrupt any $t < n$ of the parties, and to behave in an arbitrary ("Byzantine") manner.

We stress that our model is different from that considered by Hirt and Zikas [11], where in each round the honest parties' messages are first delivered *to the corrupted parties only* and then the adversary is allowed to corrupt additional parties and decide what messages to send on behalf of those parties to other honest players. In contrast, we assume that honest parties' messages are delivered "atomically", which is equivalent to assuming that adversarial corruption cannot occur in the time interval between when a message is sent and when it is received. We sometimes refer to our model as "atomic", and to the Hirt-Zikas model as "non-atomic".

2.2 Simulation-Based Security

We use a simulation-based definition of security, which is in line with work in the area of cryptographic-protocol design but which differs from most of the classical work on Byzantine agreement and broadcast. Simulation-based definition are formulated by defining an "ideal" version of some desired functionality that is implemented by a trusted third-party; a protocol is secure if the protocol "emulates" this ideal world no matter what the adversary does. One advantage of a simulation-based approach is that it simultaneously captures *all* the properties that are guaranteed by the ideal world, without having to enumerate some list of desired properties. Simulation-based definitions are also useful

for applying *composition theorems* that enable proving security of protocols that use other protocols as sub-routines.

We formulate our simulation-based definitions by presenting appropriate functionalities within the UC framework. We give a brief introduction to this model, and refer readers elsewhere for more details [3]. The basic entities involved are players $P_1, \ldots, P_n$, an adversary $\mathcal{A}$, and an "environment" $\mathcal{Z}$. The environment $\mathcal{Z}$ gives inputs to and receives outputs from all the players; it also interacts with $\mathcal{A}$ in an arbitrary way throughout its execution. In the ideal world, the parties and $\mathcal{Z}$ all interact via an ideal functionality $\mathcal{F}$: the parties send their inputs to (with corrupted parties sending anything they like) and receive outputs from $\mathcal{F}$, and $\mathcal{A}$ interacts with $\mathcal{F}$ as specified by $\mathcal{F}$ itself. We let $\text{IDEAL}_{\mathcal{F},\mathcal{A},\mathcal{Z}}(n)$ denote the output of $\mathcal{Z}$ in this case. In the real world, the parties run some protocol π with the corrupted parties behaving arbitrarily as directed by $\mathcal{A}$. We let $\text{REAL}_{\pi,\mathcal{A},\mathcal{Z}}(n)$ denote the output of $\mathcal{Z}$ in that case. A protocol π *securely realizes the functionality* $\mathcal{F}$ if for any probabilistic polynomial-time (PPT) real-world adversary $\mathcal{A}$ there exists a PPT ideal-world adversary $\mathcal{S}$ (often called a *simulator*) such that for all PPT environments $\mathcal{Z}$ the following is negligible:

$$\left| \Pr[\text{REAL}_{\pi,\mathcal{A},\mathcal{Z}}(n) = 1] - \Pr[\text{IDEAL}_{\mathcal{F},\mathcal{S},\mathcal{Z}}(n) = 1] \right|.$$

Say we want to design a protocol for some functionality $\mathcal{F}$. It is often helpful to design and reason about this in a *hybrid world* where the parties can run a protocol π while at the same time having access to some ideal functionality $\mathcal{G}$. We let $\text{HYBRID}^{\mathcal{G}}_{\pi,\mathcal{A},\mathcal{Z}}(n)$ denote the output of $\mathcal{Z}$ in that case, and say that π *securely realizes $\mathcal{F}$ in the $\mathcal{G}$-hybrid model* if for any PPT hybrid-world adversary $\mathcal{A}$ there exists a PPT ideal-world adversary $\mathcal{S}$ such that for all PPT environments $\mathcal{Z}$ we have $\left| \Pr[\text{HYBRID}^{\mathcal{G}}_{\pi,\mathcal{A},\mathcal{Z}}(n) = 1] - \Pr[\text{IDEAL}_{\mathcal{F},\mathcal{S},\mathcal{Z}}(n) = 1] \right|$. In the UC framework, the following useful composition result holds: if π securely realizes $\mathcal{F}$ in the $\mathcal{G}$-hybrid model, and ρ is any protocol that securely realizes $\mathcal{G}$, then the composed protocol π^ρ securely realizes $\mathcal{F}$ (in the real world).

3. ADAPTIVELY SECURE BROADCAST

In Section 3.1 we propose two definitions of broadcast: a "strong" definition that corresponds to the intuitive notion of broadcast, and a "relaxed" definition that corresponds to the type of broadcast shown to be possible in the non-atomic communication model considered by Hirt and Zikas. (Recall that the stronger notion of broadcast was shown to be impossible in the non-atomic setting.) In Section 3.2 we introduce a special type of commitment scheme, and we show how to construct such schemes in Section 3.2.1. In Section 3.3 we show how to use such commitments to realize adaptively secure broadcast in the atomic communication model.

3.1 Definitions

Classical results show that broadcast (or even relaxed broadcast) cannot be realized for $t \geq n/3$ corrupted parties in a "plain model", and so some setup must be considered if we wish to go beyond this bound. As stated in the Introduction, we will assume a PKI and digital signatures. Within the UC framework, this is modeled by the certificate functionality $\mathcal{F}_{\text{CERT}}$ introduced in [4]. This functionality provides both message-signing capability as well as binding between a signature and a party in the network, and thus simultaneously captures both the presence of a PKI and the ability to issue signatures.

```
┌─────────────────────────────────────────────────┐
│            Functionality 𝓕_BC                     │
│                                                   │
│  The functionality interacts with an adversary 𝒮  │
│  and a set 𝒫 = {P₁, . . . , Pₙ} of parties.      │
│                                                   │
│   • Upon receiving (Bcast, sid, m) from Pᵢ, send  │
│     (Bcast, sid, Pᵢ, m) to all parties in 𝒫 and to 𝒮.│
└─────────────────────────────────────────────────┘
```

Figure 1: The broadcast functionality.

Our definitions of broadcast are induced by ideal functionalities in the UC framework. Namely, we say a protocol π achieves (strong) *broadcast* if it securely realizes the functionality $\mathcal{F}_{\mathrm{BC}}$ shown in Figure 1; it achieves *relaxed broadcast* if it securely realizes the functionality $\mathcal{F}_{\mathrm{RBC}}$ given in Figure 2. Our definition of broadcast is essentially standard, though one can also consider a definition where the sender's message m is not revealed to $\mathcal{S}$. (I.e., our definition does not guarantee secrecy for m; note that this only makes a difference when $\mathcal{S}$ corrupts no parties.) Our definition of relaxed broadcast is from [11].

It is instructive to examine the two functionalities in light of the Hirt-Zikas attack. Observe that $\mathcal{F}_{\mathrm{BC}}$ does not allow their attack (and so any protocol securely realizing $\mathcal{F}_{\mathrm{BC}}$ must not be susceptible to the attack) since the adversary cannot change the sender's message m unless the adversary corrupts the sender P_i in advance, before it learns m. On the other hand, $\mathcal{F}_{\mathrm{RBC}}$ allows their attack: this is so because the adversary can first learn m (in step 1) and then decide whether to corrupt the sender P_i based on that information; if the adversary decides to corrupt P_1 then the adversary is allowed change the message that will be received by all the other parties in step 2.

The following result was proved in [11]:

LEMMA 3.1. *The Dolev-Strong protocol [9] securely realizes $\mathcal{F}_{\mathrm{RBC}}$ in the $\mathcal{F}_{\mathrm{CERT}}$-hybrid model against an adaptive adversary corrupting any $t < n$ parties.*

In fact, the above result holds even in the non-atomic communication model.

It is also possible to define a stronger variant of $\mathcal{F}_{\mathrm{RBC}}$, called $\mathcal{F}_{\mathrm{RBC}}^{+}$, that more closely corresponds to what is actually accomplished by the Hirt-Zikas attack. The difference between $\mathcal{F}_{\mathrm{RBC}}$ and $\mathcal{F}_{\mathrm{RBC}}^{+}$ is that the latter only allows the adversary to have $m' = \perp$. That is, the adversary is allowed to adaptively corrupt the sender (based on the sender's original message) and thereby cause agreement on an error, but is unable to cause agreement on some other valid message. $\mathcal{F}_{\mathrm{RBC}}^{+}$ can be realized fairly easily in the $\mathcal{F}_{\mathrm{RBC}}$-hybrid model using the commitment scheme defined in the following section. Alternately, it can be realized directly in the $\mathcal{F}_{\mathrm{CERT}}$-hybrid model using an appropriate variant of the Dolev-Strong protocol. We omit the details.

3.2 Honest-Binding Commitment Schemes

Commitment schemes are a standard cryptographic tool. Roughly, a commitment scheme allows a sender S to generate a commitment com to a message m in such a way that (1) the sender can later open the commitment to the original value m (*correctness*); (2) the sender cannot generate a commitment that can be opened to two different values (*binding*); and (3) the commitment reveals nothing about

```
┌─────────────────────────────────────────────────┐
│            Functionality 𝓕_RBC                    │
│                                                   │
│  The functionality interacts with an adversary 𝒮  │
│  and a set 𝒫 = {P₁, . . . , Pₙ} of parties.      │
│                                                   │
│   1. Upon receiving (Bcast, sid, m) from Pᵢ, send │
│      (Bcast, sid, Pᵢ, m) to 𝒮.                    │
│                                                   │
│   2. Upon receiving m′ from 𝒮, do:                │
│                                                   │
│       • If Pᵢ is corrupted, send (Bcast, sid, Pᵢ, │
│         m′) to all parties in 𝒫;                  │
│                                                   │
│       • If Pᵢ is not corrupted, send (Bcast, sid, │
│         Pᵢ, m) to all parties in 𝒫.               │
└─────────────────────────────────────────────────┘
```

Figure 2: The relaxed broadcast functionality.

the sender's value m until it is opened (*hiding*). For our application, we need a variant of standard commitments that guarantees binding when the sender is honest but ensures that binding can be violated if the sender is dishonest. (In the latter case, we need some additional properties as well; these will become clear in what follows.) Looking ahead, we will use such commitment schemes to construct a broadcast protocol in the following way: the sender will first generate and send a *commitment* to its message, and then send the decommitment information needed to open the commitment. In the simulation for the case when the sender P_i starts out uncorrupted, we will have the simulator $\mathcal{S}$ generate a commitment *dishonestly*. This will give $\mathcal{S}$ the flexibility to break binding and open the commitment to any desired message (if needed), while also being able to ensure binding (when desired) by claiming that it generated the commitment honestly. We defer the details to the next section.

We consider only non-interactive commitment schemes. For simplicity, we define our schemes in such a way that the decommitment information consists of the sender's random coins ω that it used when generating the commitment.

Definition 1. A (non-interactive) *commitment scheme* for message space $\{\mathcal{M}_k\}$ is a pair of PPT algorithms S, R such that for all $k \in \mathbb{N}$, all messages $m \in \mathcal{M}_k$, and all random coins ω it holds that $R(m, S(1^k, m; \omega), \omega) = 1$.

A commitment scheme for message space $\{\mathcal{M}_k\}$ is *honest-binding* if it satisfies the following:

Binding (for an honest sender) For all PPT algorithms $\mathcal{A}$ (that maintain state throughout their execution), the following is negligible in k:

$$\Pr\left[\begin{array}{l} m \leftarrow \mathcal{A}(1^k); \\ \omega \leftarrow \{0,1\}^*; \mathsf{com} \leftarrow S(1^k, m; \omega); \\ (m', \omega') \leftarrow \mathcal{A}(\mathsf{com}, \omega) : \\ \quad R(m', \mathsf{com}, \omega') = 1 \bigwedge m' \neq m \end{array}\right]$$

Equivocation There is an algorithm $\tilde{S} = (\tilde{S}_1, \tilde{S}_2)$ such that for all PPT $\mathcal{A}$ (that maintain state throughout their execution) the following is negligible:

$$\left| \Pr\left[\begin{array}{l} m \leftarrow \mathcal{A}(1^k); \\ \omega \leftarrow \{0,1\}^*; \mathsf{com} \leftarrow S(1^k, m; \omega) : \\ \quad \mathcal{A}(1^k, \mathsf{com}, \omega) = 1 \end{array}\right] \right.$$

$$\left. - \Pr\left[\begin{array}{l} (\mathsf{com}, \mathsf{st}) \leftarrow \tilde{S}_1(1^k); \\ m \leftarrow \mathcal{A}(1^k); \omega \leftarrow \tilde{S}_2(\mathsf{st}, m) : \\ \quad \mathcal{A}(1^k, \mathsf{com}, \omega) = 1 \end{array}\right] \right|$$

Equivocation implies the standard hiding property, namely, that for all PPT algorithms $\mathcal{A}$ (that maintain state throughout their execution) the following is negligible:

$$\left| \Pr \left[\begin{array}{c} (m_0, m_1) \leftarrow \mathcal{A}(1^k); \; b \leftarrow \{0,1\}; \\ \mathsf{com} \leftarrow S(1^k, m_b): \\ \mathcal{A}(\mathsf{com}) = b \end{array} \right] - \frac{1}{2} \right|.$$

We also observe that if (com, ω) are generated by $(\tilde{S}_1, \tilde{S}_2)$ for some message m as in the definition above, then binding still holds: namely, no PPT adversary can find (m', ω') with $m' \neq m$ such that $R(m', \mathsf{com}, \omega') = 1$.

3.2.1 Constructing Honest-Binding Commitment

We show two constructions of honest-binding commitment schemes. The proofs that these schemes satisfy Definition 1 are relatively straightforward, and are therefore omitted.

The first construction, based on the commitment scheme of Naor [13], relies on the minimal assumption that one-way functions exist. We describe the scheme for committing single-bit messages, though it could be extended to arbitrary length messages in the obvious way. In the following, G is a length-tripling pseudorandom generator.

$S(1^k, m; \omega)$	$R(m, (\mathsf{crs}, c), \omega)$
parse ω as $\mathsf{crs} \| r$, with $|\mathsf{crs}| = 3k$ and $|r| = k$;	parse ω as $\mathsf{crs} \| r$, with $|\mathsf{crs}| = 3k$ and $|r| = k$;
$c := G(r) \oplus (\mathsf{crs} \cdot m)$;	if $c \overset{?}{=} G(r) \oplus (\mathsf{crs} \cdot m)$
$\mathsf{com} := (\mathsf{crs}, c)$;	return 1;
return com;	else return 0;

$\tilde{S}_1(1^k)$	$\tilde{S}_2(\mathsf{st}, m)$
$r_0, r_1 \leftarrow \{0,1\}^k$;	parse st as (r_0, r_1, com);
$\mathsf{crs} := G(r_0) \oplus G(r_1)$;	parse com as (crs, c);
$c := G(r_0)$;	if $m \overset{?}{=} 0$
$\mathsf{com} := (\mathsf{crs}, c)$;	$\omega := \mathsf{crs} \| r_0$;
$\mathsf{st} := (r_0, r_1, \mathsf{com})$;	else
return $(\mathsf{com}, \mathsf{st})$;	$\omega := \mathsf{crs} \| r_1$;
	return ω;

Next, we show an efficient scheme that allows for direct committments to strings. This construction, based on the Pedersen commitment scheme [15], relies on the discrete-logarithm assumption. In the following, we let $\mathbb{G}$ be a cyclic group of order q, with generator $g \in \mathbb{G}$. (For simplicity, we view $(\mathbb{G}, q, g)$ as public parameters, though they could just as well be generated by the sender.)

$S(1^k, m; \omega)$	$R(m, \mathsf{com}, \omega)$
Parse ω as $h \| x$, with $h \in \mathbb{G}$ and $x \in \mathbb{Z}_q$;	Parse ω as $h \| x$, with $h \in \mathbb{G}$ and $x \in \mathbb{Z}_q$;
return $\mathsf{com} := (h, g^m h^x)$;	if $\mathsf{com} \overset{?}{=} (h, g^m h^x)$
	return 1;
	else return 0;

$\tilde{S}_1(1^k)$	$\tilde{S}_2((r, y), m)$
$r, y \leftarrow \mathbb{Z}_q$;	if $r \overset{?}{=} 0$ return $\perp$;
$\mathsf{com} := (g^r, g^y)$	$x := (y - m) \cdot r^{-1} \bmod q$;
return $(\mathsf{com}, (r, y))$;	return $\omega := g^r \| x$;

3.3 An Adaptively Secure Broadcast Protocol

In this section we show a protocol that securely realizes $\mathcal{F}_{\mathrm{BC}}$ in the $\mathcal{F}_{\mathrm{CERT}}$-hybrid model, in the presence of $t < n$ adaptive corruptions. The challenge of realizing $\mathcal{F}_{\mathrm{BC}}$, and the property that is exactly exploited in the Hirt-Zikas attack on existing protocols, is that when the sender is uncorrupted then the adversary should not learn the sender's message unless all honest parties will (eventually) *agree* on that message (cf. Figure 1). In [11], the authors construct a broadcast protocol for $t < n/2$ by having the sender use verifiable secret sharing (VSS) to "commit" to its message before revealing it. (For $t = n/2$ they use a slight variant of this idea.) This approach works even in the non-atomic communication setting; however, it requires at least half of the parties to be honest.

Our approach is to use computationally secure commitment schemes in place of VSS. That is, we first have the sender announce a *commitment* to its message; once agreement on this commitment is reached, the sender then decommits. (We add an additional stage in which the sender's decommitment is "echoed" by all parties; this prevents a dishonest sender from sending valid decommitment information to some honest parties but not others.) In order to simulate this protocol, we have the sender use honest-binding commitments as introduced in the previous section.

The details of our protocol π_{BC} are presented in Figure 3. We describe our protocol in the $\mathcal{F}_{\mathrm{RBC}}$-hybrid model. Since $\mathcal{F}_{\mathrm{RBC}}$ can be securely realized in the $\mathcal{F}_{\mathrm{CERT}}$-hybrid model (cf. Lemma 3.1), this implies that $\mathcal{F}_{\mathrm{BC}}$ can be securely realized in the $\mathcal{F}_{\mathrm{CERT}}$-hybrid model as well.

THEOREM 3.2. *Let (S, R) be an honest-binding commitment scheme. Then protocol π_{BC} securely realizes $\mathcal{F}_{\mathrm{BC}}$ in the $\mathcal{F}_{\mathrm{RBC}}$-hybrid model against an adaptive adversary corrupting any $t < n$ of the parties.*

The above theorem holds only in the atomic communication model considered in this paper; protocol π_{BC} does *not* securely realize $\mathcal{F}_{\mathrm{BC}}$ in the non-atomic communication model of [11]. (Indeed, by the impossibility result proven in [11], it cannot.) Atomic communication is used crucially in the second stage of our protocol when the sender transmits decommitment information to all the parties. (Observe this is the only step in our protocol in which parties communication directly, rather than via the ideal functionality $\mathcal{F}_{\mathrm{RBC}}$.) If non-atomic communication were assumed, then the adversary could learn the decommitment information (and thus the sender's message) first, and then decide to corrupt the sender and *not* transmit the decommitment information to any of honest parties.

PROOF. Let $\mathcal{A}$ be an active, adaptive adversary that interacts with players running the above protocol in the $\mathcal{F}_{\mathrm{RBC}}$-hybrid model. We construct an adversary (simulator) $\mathcal{S}$ running in the ideal world with access to functionality $\mathcal{F}_{\mathrm{BC}}$, such that no PPT environment $\mathcal{Z}$ can distinguish whether it is interacting with $\mathcal{A}$ and parties running π_{BC} in the $\mathcal{F}_{\mathrm{RBC}}$-hybrid model, or whether it is interacting with $\mathcal{S}$ and (dummy) parties communicating directly with $\mathcal{F}_{\mathrm{BC}}$. The simulator $\mathcal{S}$ starts by internally invoking the adversary $\mathcal{A}$, and forwarding all messages between $\mathcal{A}$ and $\mathcal{Z}$ in the usual way. The simulator will simulate both the ideal functionality $\mathcal{F}_{\mathrm{RBC}}$ for $\mathcal{A}$, as well as an execution of protocol π_{BC}.

In our description of $\mathcal{S}$, we distinguish two cases depend-

---

Protocol π_{BC}

The protocol is carried out among a set $\mathcal{P} = \{P_1, \ldots, P_n\}$ of parties. For notational convenience, we let P_i denote the sender (though in fact any party can act as sender). We let (S, R) be a non-interactive commitment scheme.

- **Stage 1:** Upon receiving input $(\mathsf{Bcast}, \mathsf{sid}, m)$ from the environment $\mathcal{Z}$, the sender P_i chooses random $\omega \leftarrow \{0, 1\}^*$, computes $\mathsf{com} := S(1^k, m; \omega)$, and sends $(\mathsf{Bcast}, \mathsf{sid}, \mathsf{com})$ to $\mathcal{F}_{\mathrm{RBC}}$. Let com^* denote the value received by the honest parties in this stage (note that this value is the same for all honest parties).

- **Stage 2:** Upon receiving $(\mathsf{Bcast}, \mathsf{sid}, P_i, \mathsf{com})$ from $\mathcal{F}_{\mathrm{RBC}}$, the sender P_i sends (m, ω) to every other party over point-to-point channels.

- **Stage 3:** The following is done by each party $P_j \in \mathcal{P}$: Let (m_j, ω_j) denote the value that P_j received from P_i in stage 2. (If P_j receives nothing, it takes (m_j, ω_j) as some default values.) P_j sends $(\mathsf{Bcast}, \mathsf{sid}, (m_j, \omega_j))$ to $\mathcal{F}_{\mathrm{RBC}}$.

- **Stage 4:** Each party P_j receives messages $\{(\mathsf{Bcast}, \mathsf{sid}, P_k, (m_k, \omega_k))\}_{P_k \in \mathcal{P}}$ from $\mathcal{F}_{\mathrm{RBC}}$, taking (m_k, ω_k) as some default values if nothing is received (note that the (m_k, ω_k) values are the same for all honest parties). Each party P_j then decides on its output as follows: Let $\mathsf{valid} = \{k \in \{1, \ldots, n\} \mid R(m_k, \mathsf{com}^*, \omega_k) = 1\}$. If valid is empty, then output some default value. Otherwise, let k^* be the smallest value in valid and output m_{k^*}.

Figure 3: A protocol realizing $\mathcal{F}_{\mathrm{BC}}$ in the $\mathcal{F}_{\mathrm{RBC}}$-hybrid model.

ing on whether or not the sender P_i is corrupted at the outset.

Case 1: We first treat the easier case where P_i is corrupted at the outset. Here, $\mathcal{A}$ requests to corrupt P_i (in the hybrid world) and so $\mathcal{S}$ corrupts P_i (in the ideal world). Any additional corruptions that $\mathcal{A}$ requests throughout its execution can be easily simulated by $\mathcal{S}$, so we do not mention them.

When $\mathcal{Z}$ provides input to P_i, this input is read by $\mathcal{S}$ who forwards it to $\mathcal{A}$. Then $\mathcal{A}$ begins running the first stage of π_{BC} (on behalf of the corrupted P_i) by specifying some message $(\mathsf{Bcast}, \mathsf{sid}, \mathsf{com}^*)$ to send to $\mathcal{F}_{\mathrm{RBC}}$. The simulator $\mathcal{S}$ stores com^*, and simulates the response of $\mathcal{F}_{\mathrm{RBC}}$ by giving $(\mathsf{Bcast}, \mathsf{sid}, P_i, \mathsf{com}^*)$ to $\mathcal{A}$ (and all corrupted parties). Next, $\mathcal{A}$ (now executing the second stage of π_{BC}) decides on messages (m_j, ω_j) to send to each honest party P_j on behalf of P_i. In response, $\mathcal{S}$ simulates the third stage of π_{BC} by giving $(\mathsf{Bcast}, \mathsf{sid}, P_j, (m_j, \omega_j))$ to $\mathcal{A}$ for every honest party P_j. For each such P_j, the adversary $\mathcal{A}$ may then choose to (corrupt P_j and) replace (m_j, ω_j) by some other message (m'_j, ω'_j). Once $\mathcal{A}$ has sent some (m'_j, ω'_j) to the appropriate instance of $\mathcal{F}_{\mathrm{RBC}}$ for all P_j, the simulator simulates the output of $\mathcal{F}_{\mathrm{RBC}}$ for all corrupted parties in the obvious way. Finally, $\mathcal{A}$, executing the third stage of π_{BC} on behalf of the remaining corrupted parties, specifies messages $(\mathsf{Bcast}, \mathsf{sid}, (m'_j, \omega'_j))$ that each such party P_j should send to $\mathcal{F}_{\mathrm{RBC}}$.

$\mathcal{S}$ now has values (m_k, ω_k) for every $P_k \in \mathcal{P}$, defined by the output of each appropriate (simulated) instance of $\mathcal{F}_{\mathrm{RBC}}$ in the (simulated) third stage of the protocol. $\mathcal{S}$ defines a set valid and determines k^*, m_{k^*} as prescribed by the protocol. It then sends $(\mathsf{Bcast}, \mathsf{sid}, m_{k^*})$ (on behalf of P_i) to its own ideal functionality $\mathcal{F}_{\mathrm{BC}}$.

It is not hard to see that $\mathcal{S}$ provides a perfect simulation. The view of $\mathcal{A}$ is clearly identical whether it is running in the $\mathcal{F}_{\mathrm{RBC}}$-hybrid model or whether it is being run as a subroutine by $\mathcal{S}$ in the ideal world with access to $\mathcal{F}_{\mathrm{BC}}$. As for the outputs of the honest parties (i.e., those that are honest by the end of the protocol execution), note that if $\mathcal{A}$ were

running in the $\mathcal{F}_{\mathrm{RBC}}$-hybrid model then every honest party P_j would receive com^* in the first stage and $\{(m_k, \omega_k)\}_{P_k \in \mathcal{P}}$ in the third stage, and would thus decide on output m_{k^*} exactly as $\mathcal{S}$ does. Since $\mathcal{S}$ sends m_{k^*} to $\mathcal{F}_{\mathrm{BC}}$, the output of each honest party in the ideal world is also m_{k^*}. We remark that the fact that the commitment scheme is not binding (for a malicious sender) is irrelevant here.

Case 2: We now turn to the more difficult case where P_i is not corrupted at the outset. As before, adaptive corruptions of parties other than P_i can be handled easily, so we do not mention it. Corruption of P_i will, however, be explicitly mentioned.

$\mathcal{S}$ begins by computing $(\mathsf{com}, \mathsf{st}) \leftarrow \tilde{S}_1(1^k)$. It then simulates the first stage of π_{BC} (on behalf of the honest P_i) by giving to $\mathcal{A}$ the message $(\mathsf{Bcast}, \mathsf{sid}, P_i, \mathsf{com})$ on behalf of $\mathcal{F}_{\mathrm{RBC}}$. At this point, $\mathcal{A}$ can choose whether to corrupt P_i or not, and we further divide our description of $\mathcal{S}$ depending on which is the case.

If $\mathcal{A}$ requests to corrupt P_i, then $\mathcal{S}$ corrupts P_i and waits until it receives input $(\mathsf{Bcast}, \mathsf{sid}, m)$ from $\mathcal{Z}$. At that point, $\mathcal{S}$ computes $\omega \leftarrow \tilde{S}_2(\mathsf{st}, m)$ and gives m and ω to $\mathcal{A}$ as the state of P_i. The remainder of the simulation then proceeds exactly as in the case when P_i was corrupted at the outset. (Note in particular that $\mathcal{A}$ may choose to change com to some other value com^*.)

If $\mathcal{A}$ does not corrupt P_i, then $\mathcal{S}$ waits until it receives a message $(\mathsf{Bcast}, \mathsf{sid}, P_i, m)$ from its ideal functionality $\mathcal{F}_{\mathrm{BC}}$. (Note that at this point, the output of every honest party in the ideal world is m.) $\mathcal{S}$ then computes $\omega \leftarrow \tilde{S}_2(\mathsf{st}, m)$, and simulates the second phase of the protocol by sending (m, ω) to every corrupted party. The remainder of the protocol is simulated in the obvious way, essentially the same as before (with the only difference being that it provides state m, ω to $\mathcal{A}$ if P_i is ever corrupted).

In this case, $\mathcal{S}$ provides a computationally indistinguishable simulation for $\mathcal{Z}$. The only difference between the view of $\mathcal{A}$ in the above simulation and the view of $\mathcal{A}$ when it is running in the $\mathcal{F}_{\mathrm{RBC}}$-hybrid model is with regard to

(com, ω): in the former case these are produced using $(\tilde{S}_1, \tilde{S}_2)$, whereas in the latter case these are produced using the honest sender algorithm. Definition 1 guarantees that these distributions are computationally indistinguishable. As for the outputs of the honest parties, if P_i is corrupted during stage 1 then the argument is as given previously. If P_i is not corrupted during stage 1, then we need to argue that with all but negligible probability every honest party would output m in that case in the $\mathcal{F}_{\mathrm{RBC}}$-hybrid world (since, as noted above, every honest party outputs m in that case in the ideal world). This follows from the honest-binding property of Definition 1. $\square$

4. ADAPTIVELY SECURE MPC

In the previous section we showed a protocol (call it bc) that securely realizes the broadcast functionality $\mathcal{F}_{\mathrm{BC}}$ in the presence of an adaptive adversary corrupting any number of parties. Given any protocol π (e.g., the one of [7]) for securely computing some function f in the presence of an adaptive adversary corrupting any number of parties in the $\mathcal{F}_{\mathrm{BC}}$-hybrid model (i.e., protocol π assumes an ideal broadcast channel), the composed protocol π^{bc} securely computes f in the presence of an adaptive adversary corrupting any number of parties in the $\mathcal{F}_{\mathrm{CERT}}$-hybrid model, using point-to-point communication only. The above is stated in the UC framework, but an analogous composition theorem could be stated with respect to "stand-alone" notions of security as well [2]. (We refer the reader to [10] for a detailed treatment of security notions for MPC with dishonest majority.)

Even given the above, it is interesting to explore whether adaptively secure MPC can be achieved in the weaker $\mathcal{F}_{\mathrm{RBC}}$-hybrid model, for at least two reasons:

- If we take as our communication model the non-atomic, point-to-point model of Hirt-Zikas, it is impossible to realize $\mathcal{F}_{\mathrm{BC}}$ when $t > n/2$. Thus, if we want to realize adaptively secure MPC for $t > n/2$ in this communication model, some other approach is needed.

- Even in the atomic communication model, one may prefer to base adaptively secure MPC on relaxed broadcast rather than broadcast since protocols for the former may be more efficient than protocols for the latter.

Note that, in the case of dishonest majority, adaptively secure MPC does not imply adaptively secure broadcast because the usual notions of security for MPC do not guarantee output delivery or fairness (see [10] for a more extensive treatment) — these properties are, in general, not achievable [8] — whereas definitions of security for broadcast do require guaranteed output delivery. In particular, the Hirt-Zikas impossibility result for adaptively secure broadcast in the non-atomic communication model says nothing about the feasibility of adaptively secure MPC in that setting.

Although we cannot claim that all adaptively secure MPC protocols using broadcast remain secure when broadcast is replaced with relaxed broadcast, it turns out that specific protocols from the literature do remain secure in that case. Once again, we focus on protocols proven secure in the UC framework, though we expect these results would extend to protocols analyzed in the "stand-alone" setting as well.

Specifically, consider the adaptively secure MPC protocol π of Canetti, Lindell, Ostrovsky, and Sahai [7], which relies on a broadcast channel. We first observe that the protocol remains secure even in the non-atomic communication model. In either communication model, the protocol also remains secure if the broadcast channel is replaced with relaxed broadcast. At a high level, the reason is that the messages that are broadcast are always commitments to some values, except in the last round where the broadcast messages reveal the output. The ability to corrupt a sender based on the message being broadcast is "useless" in the former case; in the latter case such an attack corresponds to preventing output delivery/violating fairness, something which is permitted by the definitions of security when there is a dishonest majority. We remark that the advantage of using relaxed broadcast as opposed to the "echo broadcast" protocol from [10] is that the former ensures agreement on abort.

Even given the above, there are several reasons to securely realize $\mathcal{F}_{\mathrm{BC}}$ rather than be contended with $\mathcal{F}_{\mathrm{RBC}}$. First, one may be interested in broadcast itself, rather than as a sub-protocol for some larger task. Furthermore, there is an advantage to working with $\mathcal{F}_{\mathrm{BC}}$ in that it can be safely used to instantiate the broadcast channel in *arbitrary* protocols, so one can avoid having to examine protocols on a case-by-case basis to determine whether $\mathcal{F}_{\mathrm{RBC}}$ suffices.

Note: The views and conclusions contained in this document are those of the authors and should not be interpreted as representing the official policies, either expressed or implied, of the US Army Research Laboratory, the US Government, the UK Ministry of Defence, or the UK Government. The US and UK Governments are authorized to reproduce and distribute reprints for Government purposes, notwithstanding any copyright notation herein.

5. REFERENCES

[1] B. Barak, R. Canetti, J. B. Nielsen, and R. Pass. Universally composable protocols with relaxed set-up assumptions. In *45th Annual Symposium on Foundations of Computer Science (FOCS)*, pages 186–195. IEEE, 2004.

[2] R. Canetti. Security and composition of multiparty cryptographic protocols. *Journal of Cryptology*, 13(1):143–202, 2000.

[3] R. Canetti. Universally composable security: A new paradigm for cryptographic protocols. In *42nd Annual Symposium on Foundations of Computer Science (FOCS)*, pages 136–145. IEEE, 2001. Full version at http://eprint.iacr.org/2000/067/.

[4] R. Canetti. Universally composable signature, certification, and authentication. In *17th IEEE Computer Security Foundations Workshop*, pages 219–235. IEEE Computer Society, 2004. Full version at http://eprint.iacr.org/2003/239/.

[5] R. Canetti, U. Feige, O. Goldreich, and M. Naor. Adaptively secure multi-party computation. In *28th Annual ACM Symposium on Theory of Computing (STOC)*, pages 639–648. ACM Press, May 1996.

[6] R. Canetti and M. Fischlin. Universally composable commitments. In *Advances in Cryptology — Crypto 2001*, volume 2139 of *LNCS*, pages 19–40. Springer, 2001.

[7] R. Canetti, Y. Lindell, R. Ostrovsky, and A. Sahai. Universally composable two-party and multi-party secure computation. In *34th Annual ACM Symposium*

on *Theory of Computing (STOC)*, pages 494–503. ACM Press, May 2002.

[8] R. Cleve. Limits on the security of coin flips when half the processors are faulty. In *18th Annual ACM Symposium on Theory of Computing (STOC)*, pages 364–369. ACM Press, 1986.

[9] D. Dolev and H. Strong. Authenticated algorithms for Byzantine agreement. *SIAM Journal on Computing*, 12(4):656–666, 1983.

[10] S. Goldwasser and Y. Lindell. Secure multi-party computation without agreement. *Journal of Cryptology*, 18(3):247–287, 2005.

[11] M. Hirt and V. Zikas. Adaptively secure broadcast. In *Advances in Cryptology — Eurocrypt 2010*, volume 6110 of *LNCS*, pages 466–485. Springer, 2010.

[12] L. Lamport, R. E. Shostak, and M. C. Pease. The Byzantine generals problem. *ACM Trans. Programming Language Systems*, 4(3):382–401, 1982.

[13] M. Naor. Bit commitment using pseudorandomness. *Journal of Cryptology*, 4(2):151–158, 1991.

[14] M. Pease, R. E. Shostak, and L. Lamport. Reaching agreement in the presence of faults. *J. ACM*, 27(2):228–234, 1980.

[15] T. P. Pedersen. Non-interactive and information-theoretic secure verifiable secret sharing. In *Advances in Cryptology — Crypto '91*, volume 576 of *LNCS*, pages 129–140. Springer, 1992.

[16] B. Pfitzmann and M. Waidner. Unconditional Byzantine agreement for any number of faulty processors. In *9th Annual Symposium on Theoretical Aspects of Computer Science (STACS)*, volume 577 of *LNCS*, pages 339–350. Springer, 1992.

Scalable Rational Secret Sharing

[Extended Abstract]

Varsha Dani
Dept. of Computer Science
University of New Mexico
varshadani@gmail.com

Mahnush Movahedi
Dept. of Computer Science
University of New Mexico
movahedi@cs.unm.edu

Yamel Rodriguez
Dept. of Computer Science
University of New Mexico
yamel@cs.unm.edu

Jared Saia[*]
Dept. of Computer Science
University of New Mexico
saia@cs.unm.edu

ABSTRACT

We consider the classical secret sharing problem in the case where all agents are selfish but rational. In recent work, Kol and Naor show that in the non-simultaneous communication model (i.e. when rushing is possible), there is no Nash equilibrium that ensures all agents learn the secret. However, they describe a mechanism for this problem that is an ϵ-Nash equilibrium, i.e. it is close to an equilibrium in the sense that no player can gain more than ϵ utility by deviating from it.

Unfortunately, the Kol and Naor mechanism, and, to the best of our knowledge, all previous mechanisms for this problem require each agent to send $O(n)$ messages in expectation, where n is the number of agents. This may be problematic for some applications of rational secret sharing such as secure multiparty computation and simulation of a mediator.

We address this issue by describing a mechanism for rational n-out-of-n secret sharing that is an ϵ-Nash equilibrium, and is *scalable* in the sense that it requires each agent to send only an expected $O(1)$ bits. Moreover, the latency of our mechanism is $O(\log n)$ in expectation, compared to $O(n)$ expected latency for the Kol and Naor result. We also design mechanisms for a relaxed variant of rational m-out-of-n secret sharing where $m = \Theta(n)$ that require each processor to send $O(\log n)$ bits and have $O(\log n)$ latency. Our mechanisms are non-cryptographic, and are not susceptible to backwards induction.

"Three can keep a secret if two of them are dead."
- Benjamin Franklin

[*]Movahedi, Rodriguez and Saia were partially supported by NSF CAREER Award 0644058, NSF CNS-1017509, and AFOSR MURI grant FA9550-07-1-0532.

Categories and Subject Descriptors

F.m [**Theory of Computation**]: Miscellaneous

General Terms

Theory

Keywords

Game Theory, Cryptography, Secret Sharing, Multiparty Computation

1. INTRODUCTION

Secret sharing is one of the most fundamental problems in security, and is an important primitive in many cryptographic protocols, including secure multiparty computation. Recently, there has been interest in solving *rational secret sharing* [8, 4, 5, 1, 11]. In this setting, there are n selfish but rational agents, and we want to distribute shares of a secret to each agent, and design a protocol for the agents ensures that: (1) if any group of m agents follow the protocol they will all learn the secret; and (2) knowledge of less than m of the shares reveals nothing about the secret. Moreover, we want our protocol to be a *Nash equilibrium* in the sense that no player can improve their utility by deviating from the protocol, given that all other players are following the protocol.

Unfortunately, all previous solutions to this problem require each agent to send $O(n)$ messages in expectation, and so do not scale to large networks. Rational secret sharing is a primitive for rational multiparty computation, which can be used to compute an arbitrary function in a completely decentralized manner, without a trusted external party. A typical application of rational multiparty computation might be to either run an auction, or to hold a lottery to assign resources in a network. It is easy to imagine such applications where the number of players is large, and where it is important to have algorithms whose bandwidth and latency costs scale well with the number of players. Moreover, in a game theoretic setting, standard tricks to circumvent scalability issues, like running the protocol only on a small subset of the players, may be undesirable since they could lead to increased likelihood of bribery attacks.

In this paper, we address this issue by designing scalable

mechanisms for rational secret sharing. Our main result is a protocol for rational n-out-of-n secret sharing that (1) requires each agent to send only an expected $O(1)$ bits; and (2) has $O(\log n)$ expected latency. We also design scalable mechanisms for a relaxed variant of m-out-of-n rational secret sharing in the case where m is $\Theta(n)$.

1.1 The Problem

We assume there are n rational but selfish players. The players' utility functions are such that they prefer to learn the secret, but also prefer that other players not learn the secret. Following previous work [8, 4, 5, 11], we assume all the players have the same utility function, which is specified by three constants U_+, U, and U_-. Here U_+ is the utility to a player if he alone learns the secret, U is the utility if he learns the secret but at least one other player learns it as well, and finally U_- is the utility when the player does not learn the secret. We further assume that $U_+ > U > U_-$, so that the players' preferences are strict. We note that, as in previous work, the utility function does not distinguish the cases where different numbers of other players may learn the secret.

We will assume that the secret is an arbitrary element of a large (fixed) finite set $\mathcal{S}$. The shares are provided to the players by a dealer, who is active only once, at the beginning of the game. The players must then communicate with each other in order to reconstruct the secret.

We assume that the communication between the players is *point-to-point* and through private channels. In other words, if player A sends a message to player B, then a third player C is not privy to the message that was sent, or indeed even to the fact of a message having been sent. We assume communication is synchronous in that there is an upperbound known on the maximum amount of time required to send a message from one player to another. However, we assume *non-simultaneous* communication, and thus allow for the possibility of *rushing*, where a player may receive messages from other players in a round before sending out its own messages.

Our goal is to provide protocols for the dealer and rational players such that the players following the protocol can reconstruct the secret. Moreover, we want a protocol that is *scalable* in the sense that the amount of communication and the latency of the protocol should be a slow growing function of the number of players.

We are also concerned with the problem of rational multiparty computation, which is an important application of n-out-of-n rational secret sharing. In the problem of rational multiparty computation, there are n rational agents, and each agent i has an input x_i to a function f of n variables. Each player prefers to learn the output of f, but also prefers that other players do not. In particular, the utility functions are the same as for the secret sharing problem. The goal is to design a protocol for rational players that will ensure that all players learn the output of f. As described in [5], the algorithm from [3] can be used to solve the problem of rational multiparty computation provided one has a solution to n-out-of-n rational secret sharing.

1.2 Our Results

In their recent work, Kol and Naor [8] show that in the non-simultaneous broadcast model (i.e. when rushing is possible), there is no Nash equilibrium that ensures all agents learn the secret. They thus consider the case of designing an ϵ-*Nash equilibrium* for the problem in this communication model, where an ϵ-Nash equilibrium is close to an equilibrium in the sense that no player can gain more than ϵ utility by deviating from it. In addition, their protocol is Monte Carlo, succeeding with probability $1-\delta$ for any fixed positive δ.

Our main result is a scalable, Monte Carlo protocol for n-out-of-n rational secret sharing that is also an ϵ-Nash equilibrium. This result is summarized in the following theorem.

THEOREM 1.1. *For any fixed positive ϵ, δ there exists a protocol for rational n-out-of-n secret sharing that with probability $1 - \delta$ has the following properties:*

- *The protocol is an ϵ-Nash equilibrium*

- *All players learn the secret*

- *The protocol, in expectation, requires each player to send $O(1)$ bits, and has latency $O(\log n)$*

As discussed above, the n-out-of-n case for rational secret sharing is a critical component of rational multiparty computation. Our result for n-out-of-n rational secret sharing enables a protocol for rational multiparty computation that is an ϵ-Nash equilibrium in the point-to-point, synchronous, non-simultaneous communication model. Moreover, it reduces worst case bandwidth by a multiplicative factor of n, and latency by a multiplicative factor of $\Theta(n/\log n)$ over the rational multiparty protocol in this communication model from [8].

In this paper, we also consider the problem of m-out-of-n rational secret sharing for the case where $m < n$. Designing scalable algorithms for this problem is challenging because of the tension between reduced communication, and the need to ensure that *any* active set of m players can reconstruct the secret. For example, consider the case where each player sends $O(\log n)$ messages. If $m = o(n/\log n)$, even if the set of active players is chosen *randomly*, it is likely that there will be some active player that will never receive a message from any other active player. Moreover, even if $m = \Theta(n)$, if the set of active players is chosen in a worst case manner, it is easy to see that a small subset of the active players can easily be isolated so that they never receive messages from the other active players, and are thus unable to reconstruct the secret.

Despite the difficulty of the problem, scalable rational secret sharing for the m-out-of-n case may still be of interest for applications like the Vanish peer-to-peer system [2]. To determine what might at least be possible, we consider a significantly relaxed variant of the problem. In particular, we require $m = \Theta(n)$ and that the set of m active players be chosen independently of the random bits of the dealer. Our result is given in the following theorem, whose sketch is given in Section 4.

THEOREM 1.2. *For any fixed positive $\epsilon, \delta, , \lambda$, and threshold τ, there exists a protocol for rational secret sharing with absent players, which with probability $1 - \delta$ has the following properties, provided that the subset of m active players is chosen independently of the random bits of the dealer:*

- *The protocol is an ϵ-Nash equilibrium.*

- *The protocol ensures that if at least a $(\tau + \lambda)$ fraction of the players are active, (i.e. $m/n \geq \tau + \lambda$) then all active players will learn the secret; and if less than a $(\tau - \lambda)$ fraction of the players are active, (i.e. $m/n \leq \tau - \lambda$) then the secret can not be recovered*

- *The protocol requires each player to send $O(\log n)$ bits, and has latency $O(\log n)$*

1.3 Our Approach

Our protocol shares many similarities with the approach of Kol and Naor in [8]. Following are the techniques we use from their protocol. First, each player i receives a set of lists from the dealer, and the j-th element of each list is used in round j. Second, we make use of two lists from [8]: (1) the list L_i that contains potential secrets, for some value t^*, the t^*-th element in each of these lists is the true secret; and (2) the list S_i that contains shares of an indicator sequence, for each round j, that reveals whether or not the j-th round is the t^*-th round. Finally, we make use of a clever technique from [8] to avoid backwards induction. In particular, one player, chosen uniformly at random by the dealer, is designated the *short* player and the remaining players are designated the *long* players. The length of the short player's lists is determined by geometric distributions, and the length of the long players' lists exceeds the length of the short player's list by an amount that is geometrically distributed. This scheme protects against backwards induction by making it difficult for any player to know exactly how many rounds the protocol will last.[1]

.Following are the novel techniques in our approach. First, we restrict communication in our protocol to a certain type of complete binary tree; this is critical for ensuring that the total number of messages sent by each player is scalable. Second, we make use of an iterated secret sharing scheme over this tree to divide up shares of secrets among the players. This scheme is similar to that used in recent work by King and Saia [7] on the problem of scalable Byzantine agreement, and suggests deeper connections between the two problems. Finally, we make use of an iterated tag and hash scheme [13, 12] to enable checking of secrets and iterated shares of secrets. Tag and hash schemes were used previously in [8], but applying them in our setting, where communication is severely curtailed, is technically challenging.

1.4 Related Work

Since its introduction by Halpern and Teague in [5], there has been significant work on the problem of rational secret sharing, including results of Halpern and Teague [5], Gordon and Katz [4], Abraham et al. [1], Lysyanskaya and Triandopoulos [11] and Kol and Naor [8]. All of this related work except for [8], assumes the existence of simultaneous communication, either by broadcast or private channels. Several of the protocols proposed [4, 1, 11] make use of cryptographic assumptions and achieve equilibria under the assumption that the players are computationally bounded. The protocol from [1] is robust to coalitions; and the protocol from [11]

works in the situation where players may be either rational or adversarial.

The work of Kol and Naor [8] is closest to our own work in that they do not assume simultaneous communication, and do not make cryptographic assumptions. As we have already discussed, our protocols make use of several clever ideas from their result.

Additional work by Lepinski et al. [10, 9] and Izmalkov et al. [6] describe protocols for rational secure multiparty computation that are fair and robust to coalitions. However, their results rely on the physical assumption of "secure envelopes" [10], which seem difficult to implement for participants that are physically distant.

2. RATIONAL SECRET SHARING WHEN ALL PLAYERS ARE PRESENT

We now describe our mechanism for n-out-of-n secret sharing. We give an informal description of the dealer's and players' protocols in Sections 2.1 and 2.2. The formal descriptions of these protocols appears in Algorithm 1 and Algorithm 4.

2.1 Dealer's Protocol

The dealer is active only once at the beginning of the game, and during this phase of the game the players' inputs are prepared.

Communication between the players in our protocol will be restricted to sending messages to their neighbors in a complete binary tree.[2] First the players are assigned to nodes of a complete binary tree with n leaves. Each player is assigned to one leaf. Next the layer of internal nodes just above the leaves is assigned to players. This is done in such a way as to ensure that the player assigned to the parent node of two leaves is one of the two players assigned to those leaves. Then the remaining internal nodes are assigned arbitrarily to players who have not yet been assigned an internal node. Since there are $n - 1$ internal nodes in a tree with n leaf nodes, we can ensure that no player is assigned to more than one internal node. One of the players will not be assigned to an internal node, and this will not matter.

Next, the dealer will select a player uniformly at random to be the "short player". The rest of the players will be "long players". It is important that the players *not be told* which player is the short player. This is necessary to avoid backwards induction as is discussed in Section 3.2.

Now the dealer independently samples three random variables X, Y and Z from a geometric distribution with parameter β. X will be the definitive iteration, or the round of the game in which the true secret is revealed. Y will be the amount of padding on the short player's input. Z will be the amount of additional padding on the long players' input. Thus, the short player will receive enough input to last for $X + Y$ rounds of the game, while the long players will receive enough input to last for $X + Y + Z$ rounds of the game.

The players' input will consist of several lists, with one list element for each round of the game. Thus the lists sent

---

[1]It is also what makes their protocol and ours Monte Carlo, since with some small but constant probability, all the geometric random variables may be so small that it is better for each player to randomly try to guess the secret from the elements in their L_i list than to follow the protocol.

[2]Recall that a complete binary tree is a binary tree in which all the internal nodes have two descendants; all the leaves are at the two deepest levels; and the leaves on the deepest level are as far left as possible.

Algorithm 1 *Dealer's Protocol*

n players, $\mathcal{S}$: set of potential secrets, $\mathbb{F}_q$: field of size q. $\beta \in (0,1)$: geometric distribution parameter.

1. Create a complete binary tree with n leaf nodes. Assign players to leaf nodes from left to right. Assign players to parents of leaf nodes by choosing the player assigned to one of the children of the node. Assign all other internal nodes to players who have not yet been assigned to an internal node, top down and left to right. Thus each player is assigned to a distinct leaf node, and each player except one, is assigned to a distinct internal node.

2. Choose X, Y, and Z independently from a geometric distribution with parameter β.

3. Create the following lists for each player i:

   - List L_i for potential secrets
   - List S_i for shares of the indicator sequence.
   - For each node w with which i is associated, list T_i^w for tags.
   - For each node w with which i is associated and each neighbor w' of w, list $H_i^{(w,w')}$ for verification functions.

4. (Populate the lists) For each round $t \leq X + Y + Z$:

   (a) if $t = X$, $\sigma \leftarrow$ true secret.
   else $\sigma \leftarrow$ random element from $\mathcal{S}$
   Add σ to all the lists L_i at position t.

   (b) if $t = X$, $h_t \leftarrow 0$
   else $h_t \leftarrow$ random non-zero element from $\mathbb{F}_q$.

   (c) For each node w of the tree, create a 'share' v_t^w (to be set by *RecursiveShares*, subroutine 2)

   (d) Call *RecursiveShares*(root, h_t)

   (e) For each leaf w add v_t^w to the shares list S_i of corresponding player i at position t.

   (f) For each node w in the binary tree choose $(g_t^w, \bar{g}_t^w)$ uniformly at random from $\mathbb{F}_q^2$ and add it to T^w at position t

   (g) For node each w in the binary tree:

       i. if w has a parent $p(w)$:
       $V_p \leftarrow VerificationFunction(h_t, g_t^{p(w)})$
       Add V_p to list $H^{w,p(w)}$ at position t.

       ii. if w has a left child $\ell(w)$:
       $V_\ell \leftarrow VerificationFunction(v_t^{\ell(w)}, \bar{g}_t^{\ell(w)})$
       Add V_ℓ to list $H^{w,\ell(w)}$ at position t.

       iii. if w has a right child $r(w)$:
       $V_r \leftarrow VerificationFunction(v_t^{r(w)}, \bar{g}_t^{r(w)})$
       Add V_r to list $H^{w,r(w)}$ at position t.

5. Choose a player i uniformly at random to be the short player. Truncate each list (L_i S_i, and multiple tag and hash lists) associated with player i to be length $X + Y$ *i.e.* delete the last Z elements of each such list. (All other players' lists remain of length $X + Y + Z$.)

6. Send the data to the appropriate players

Algorithm 2 *RecursiveShares* (node w, integer y):

1. $v_t^w \leftarrow y$.

2. If w has children $\ell(w)$ and $r(w)$:

   (a) Choose random slope μ.
   (b) Let f be the line with slope μ and y-intercept y.
   (c) *RecursiveShares*($\ell(w), f(-1)$).
   (d) *RecursiveShares*($r(w), f(1)$).

Algorithm 3 *VerificationFunction* ($\mathbb{F}_q$-element v, $\mathbb{F}_q$-element g): // v is the message, g is the tag

1. Choose a and b uniformly at random $\mathbb{F}_q^* = \mathbb{F}_q \setminus \{0\}$

2. $c = a * v + b * g$.

3. return (a, b, c).

Algorithm 4 *Player's Protocol* for Player i

On round t:

Up-Stage:

1. Send $(S_i[t], \bar{g}_t^i)$ to parent in the tree.

2. If player i is also internal node w, then:

   (a) Receive $(v_t^{\ell(w)}, \bar{g}_t^{\ell(w)})$ from left child and check using verification function $H_t^{w,\ell(w)}$. If no message is received or message does not satisfy verification function, output $L_i[t]$ and QUIT. Otherwise set $f(-1) \leftarrow v_t^{\ell(w)}$.

   (b) Receive $(v_t^{r(w)}, \bar{g}_t^{r(w)})$ from left child and check using verification function $H_t^{w,r(w)}$. If no message is received or message does not satisfy verification function, output $L_i[t]$ and QUIT. Otherwise set $f(1) \leftarrow v_t^{r(w)}$.

   (c) Reconstruct a degree 1 polynomial f from $(-1, f(-1))$ and $(1, f(1))$.

   (d) if w is not the root, $v_t^w \leftarrow f(0)$
   Send $(v_t^w, \bar{g}_t^w)$ to parent in the tree.

   (e) Else if w is the root $h_t \leftarrow f(0)$.

Down-Stage:

1. If player i is the root: send (h_t, g^{root_t}) to left and right children.

2. Else if i is node w (including leaves):

   (a) Receive $(h_t, g_t^{p(w)})$ from parent $p(w)$. If no message received output $L_i[t]$ and QUIT.

   (b) Use verification function $H^{(w,p(w))}[t]$ to check validity of message. If message does not satisfy verification function, output $L_i[t]$ and QUIT.

   (c) If w is an internal node, then send indicator (h_t, g_t^w) to left and right children.

   (d) If $h_t = 0$, output $L_i[t]$ and QUIT.

3. $t \leftarrow t + 1$

to the short player will be of length $X + Y$ and those sent to long players will be of length $X + Y + Z$. Each player i will receive the following four lists:

- A list L_i consisting of elements of $\mathcal{S}$, or potential secrets. The true secret will be at index X of the list.

- A list S_i containing the shares of the indicator sequence for player i (in his role as a leaf of the tree.)

- For each node w (including leaves) with which i is associated, player i will receive a list T_i^w of pairs of tags (one for the *Up-Stage*, one for the *Down-Stage*) which will be used in the tag and hash scheme described below.

- For each node w with which i is associated, for each neighbor w' of w, player i will receive a list $H_i^{w,w'}$ with verification functions to check the authenticity of messages from w'.

The dealer's next task is to populate these lists. For simplicity of exposition, we assume that all the lists are created to be of length $X + Y + Z$, and that the short player's lists are truncated to length $X + Y$ later, before being sent to him. The dealer will fill the potential secret-lists L_i with elements chosen independently and uniformly at random from the set $\mathcal{S}$. These lists have the property that the true secret is in position X of the list.

Let q be a (fixed) large prime. The indicator sequence and tags will all be elements of the field $\mathbb{F}_q$ and all of the algebraic operations described hereafter will be over $\mathbb{F}_q$.

Next, to populate the shares-lists S_i, for each round $t \neq X$, the dealer will set h_t to be a uniformly random non-zero element of $\mathbb{F}_q$. h_X will be set to 0. Then for each t the dealer will create *iterated shares* of h_t as follows. First, the value h_t is assigned to the root of the tree. Next, for each node w of the tree for which a value v_t^w has been assigned, if w is a leaf, assign the value v_t^w to be the share of the corresponding player for round t. Otherwise, pick a random slope $\mu \neq 0$ and let f be the line with slope μ and y-intercept v_t^w (so that $f(0) = v_t^w$). Assign values $f(-1)$ and $f(1)$ to the left and right children of w, and recurse. The formal algorithm for this process is given in Algorithm 2, and an example run of this algorithm is illustrated in Figure 1.

The dealer's remaining task is to populate lists that implement the tag and hash verification scheme that will be used by the players. For each round t and each internal node w of the tree, the dealer generates tags g_t^w and $\bar{g}_t^w$ which are elements chosen independently and uniformly at random from $\mathbb{F}_q$. These elements are put into the appropriate lists T^w. The tag g_t^w will be used on the *Down-Stage* of the protocol for the players that is described in Section 2.2, and $\bar{g}_t^w$ will be used in the *Up-Stage* of this protocol.

Now, for each round t and each node w, let $p(w)$ denote the parent of w, and let $\ell(w)$ and $r(w)$ be the left and right children of w if any. The dealer samples uniformly random non-zero elements a_t^w and b_t^w from $\mathbb{F}_q$ and sets

$$c_t^w = a_t^w * h_t + b_t^w * g_t^{p(w)}$$

The triple (a_t^w, b_t^w, c_t^w) consists of the verification function for the *Down-Stage* round of t for the node w. Similarly, the dealer generates such verification triples (a, b, c) to check the validity of the messages $(v_t^{\ell(w)}, \bar{g}_t^{\ell(w)})$ and $(v_t^{r(w)}, \bar{g}_t^{r(w)})$ that

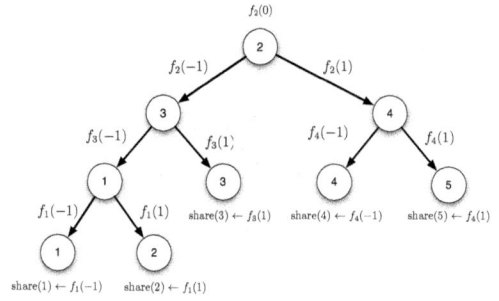

Figure 1: **Example run of the dealer's protocol for a fixed round** t. **The function** f_i **is defined as** $f_i(x) = a_i x + b_i$ **where** a_i **and** b_i **are elements chosen independently and uniformly at random from the field** $\mathbb{F}_q$. **When** $t = t^*$, b_2 **is fixed at 0 and** a_i **is chosen uniformly at random; this ensures that** $f_2(0)$ **will be 0. When** $t \neq t^*$, b_2 **is chosen uniformly at random from** $\mathbb{F}_q - 0$, **which ensures that** $f_2(0) \neq 0$.

are to be received by w in the *Up-Stage*. These verification function triples are put into the appropriate lists H^w. (See Algorithm 3.) Note that for any triple $(a, b, c) \in \mathbb{F}_q^3$ with $a, b \neq 0$ there are q pairs $(x, y) \in \mathbb{F}_q^2$ which satisfy $ax + by = c$, so the values of the message and tag cannot be guessed from the verification function, except with probability $1/q$.

The dealer's task is now almost done. All that remains is to truncate the short player's lists and communicate the input to the players. The formal description of the entire protocol for the dealer is given in Algorithm 1.

2.2 Player's Protocol

The players' protocol consists of two stages: the *Up-Stage* and the *Down-Stage*. In the *Up-Stage* for round t each player i will send his share $S_i[t]$ along with the tag $\bar{g}_t^i$ up the tree to the parent node of the leaf with which player i is associated. Each internal node w receives two shares and tags from its two children and after checking their validity with the provided verification function ($H_t^{w,\ell(w)}$), uses these to reconstruct a line f, where the non-tag part of the messages received from the left and right children respectively represent $f(-1)$ and $f(1)$. Once f is reconstructed, w will send his "share", $f(0)$ along with his tag $\bar{g}_t^w$ to his parent, up the tree, who will recursively do the same thing. This procedure continues up the tree until the root is reached. At the root, the function f, reconstructed from the shares of the two children, when evaluated at 0 will yield the indicator for the current round. In particular, the root sets $h_t = f_{\text{root}}(0)$. We next move into the *Down-Stage*.

In the *Down-Stage* for round t the root will send h_t (determined by the end of the *Up-Stage*) and its tag g_t^{root} to both of its children. Now each child node w, receiving from its parent $p(w)$ the pair $(h_t, g_t^{p(w)})$, will first check this message for consistency using its verification function (a_t^w, b_t^w, c_t^w). Once the message is verified, w, if it is itself an internal node, will recursively append its own tag to h_t and send the pair (h_t, g_t^w) to its children. If w is a leaf, then if $h_t = 0$ then $t = X$ and the player associated with w will output the secret for the current round as the true secret, and quit the protocol. Otherwise the next round begins.

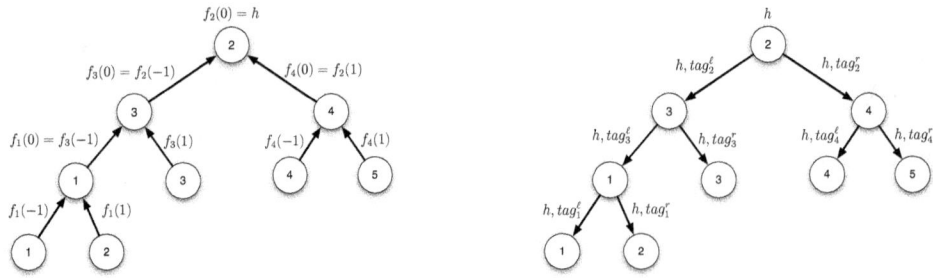

Figure 2: On the left is the up stage of the algorithm; on the right is the down stage.

If at any time in the protocol, a player detects deviation from the protocol by another player, then the player immediately outputs the potential secret for the current round as the true secret and quits the protocol. This detection of deviation could be in the form of no message being received when a message was supposed to be sent, or in the form of messages received that do not satisfy the verification function. Note that detection of cheating propagates to all the players, since once a player detecting cheating quits the protocol, everyone who was expecting messages from him will also fail to get these messages. The formal description of the protocol for the players is given in Algorithm 4, and an example run of this algorithm is illustrated in Figure 2.

3. ANALYSIS OF OUR PROTOCOL

There are two ways in which a player may try to deviate from the protocol. First, he may try to remain in the protocol and send messages not specified by the protocol, or "fake" messages, in order to confuse other players. Second, he may simply output a value for the secret and leave the protocol early. As the following proposition shows, the tag-and-hash verification scheme used in the protocol makes it hard for a player to successfully fool other players by sending fake messages.

PROPOSITION 3.1. *The probability that a faked message will satisfy the verification function is* $\frac{1}{q-1}$

PROOF. Suppose a player A is to send a message v with tag g to player B who has a verification triple (a, b, c) such that $av + bg = c$. Suppose further that A wants to send a fake message instead. Note that A has no information about the verification function except that the message he is supposed to send satisfies it. In fact, recall that the verification function was created by the dealer by randomly selecting a and b and setting c to the appropriate value. Consider the following two cases.

Case 1: A wants to send a particular fake message v'. In this case, there is a unique $g' = (c - av')/b$ such that the pair (v', g') satisfies the verification function. With no knowledge of a or b, A's chance of correctly guessing g' is $\frac{1}{q-1}$.

Case 2: A just wants to send a fake message, but does not care what it is. In this case, there are exactly q pairs (v', g') which satisfy the verification function; one of these is (v, g). Thus only $q - 1$ fake pairs work. On the other hand, there are $(q-1)^2$ pairs of elements in $\mathbb{F}_q^2$ which are not of the form $(v, *)$ or $(*, g)$. So again, with no information about a or b, A's chance of guessing a pair that works is $\frac{1}{q-1}$. □

We will next consider the second type of deviation from

the protocol, where a player deviates by leaving the protocol early. A player may consider deviating in this way if he either knows the secret with certainty, or with sufficiently high probability. The former only happens partway through the definitive iteration, when some of the players have learned this fact, but have not yet communicated it to the others. However, if a player decides not to transmit the fact that $h_t = 0$ to players lower in the tree, he does not gain anything by doing so. This is because the players who do not get the messages they are expecting will, in accordance with the protocol, output the secret for the current round, which is the correct secret. Thus, the only situation we still need to consider is whether a player can guess the position of the secret, with sufficiently high probability, before the definitive iteration. We deal with this situation in the next few lemmas.

LEMMA 3.2. *A player deviating from the protocol cannot increase his expected payoff by more than* ϵ *unless his probability of successfully learning the secret by deviating is at least* $\frac{U - U_- + \epsilon}{U_+ - U_-}$

PROOF. Let p be the threshold success probability required to make deviating worthwhile, ie to increase one's payoff by ϵ. Since the game ends when a player is caught deviating from the protocol (and certainly if the player stops sending messages, this *will* be detected by the other players), a failed attempt at cheating means that the player does not learn the secret. Thus a player's expected utility from cheating while everyone else follows the protocol is $pU_+ + (1-p)U_-$. On the other hand, following the protocol results in everyone learning the secret, with a utility of U. Thus, at the threshold for making cheating worthwhile, we have

$$pU_+ + (1-p)U_- = U + \epsilon$$

Solving this for p gives the desired result. □

We will now compute the probability of a player successfully guessing the secret before it is actually revealed during the protocol.

LEMMA 3.3. *A player who initially received a list of length* α *has at most* $\frac{3}{\alpha - t}$ *chance of (correctly) guessing the position of the secret on round* t *if it has not already been revealed.*

PROOF. For $j \geq t$ let $P(\alpha, t, j)$ denote the probability that the secret is in the jth position in the list of potential secrets, given that the player initially received a list of length α, and $t - 1$ rounds of the protocol have ended without the secret being revealed.

Let $|L_i|$ be the length of the list of potential secrets received by player i. Recall that X, Y and Z are geometric random variables with parameter β, corresponding to the position of the secret, the amount of padding on the short player's list, and the amount of additional padding on the long players' lists respectively. Then $|L_i| = X + Y$ if i is the short player, and $|L_i| = X + Y + Z$ if i is a long player. Let ξ be the event that the player was chosen as the short player; its complement $\bar{\xi}$ is the event that the player was chosen as a long player. Now

$$P(\alpha, t, j) = \Pr(X = j | X \geq t, |L_i| = \alpha)$$

By the law of total probability, this equals

$$\Pr(X = j | X \geq t, |L_i| = \alpha, \xi) \Pr(\xi | X \geq t, |L_i| = \alpha)$$
$$+ \Pr(X = j | X \geq t, |L_i| = \alpha, \bar{\xi}) \Pr(\bar{\xi} | X \geq t, |L_i| = \alpha)$$

Bounding both conditional probabilities by 1 and observing that the event $|L_i| = \alpha \wedge \xi$ is the same as $X + Y = \alpha$ while the event $|L_i| = \alpha \wedge \bar{\xi}$ is the same as $X + Y + Z$, we see that

$$P(\alpha, t, j) \leq \Pr(X = j | X \geq t, X + Y = \alpha)$$
$$+ \Pr(X = j | X \geq t, X + Y + Z = \alpha)$$

so it suffices to bound these two conditional probabilities. Let $P_{short}(\alpha, t, j)$ and $P_{long}(\alpha, t, j)$ respectively be the two summands on the right side above; we will now compute these.

$$\begin{aligned}
P_{short}(\alpha, t, j) &= \Pr(X = j | X \geq t, X + Y = \alpha) \\
&= \frac{\Pr(X = j, X \geq t, X + Y = \alpha)}{\Pr(X \geq t, X + Y = \alpha)} \\
&= \frac{\Pr(X = j, Y = \alpha - j)}{\sum_{x=t}^{\alpha-1} \Pr(X = x, Y = \alpha - x)} \\
&= \frac{\Pr(X = j) \Pr(Y = \alpha - j)}{\sum_{x=t}^{\alpha-1} \Pr(X = x) \Pr(Y = \alpha - x)} \\
&= \frac{(1-\beta)^{j-1}\beta(1-\beta)^{\alpha-j-1}\beta}{\sum_{x=t}^{\alpha-1}(1-\beta)^{x-1}\beta(1-\beta)^{\alpha-x-1}\beta} \\
&= \frac{(1-\beta)^{\alpha-2}\beta^2}{(\alpha-t)(1-\beta)^{\alpha-2}\beta^2} \\
&= \frac{1}{\alpha-t}
\end{aligned}$$

Also

$$\begin{aligned}
P_{long}(\alpha, t, j) &= \Pr(X = j | X \geq t, X + Y + Z = \alpha) \\
&= \frac{\Pr(X = j, X \geq t, X + Y + Z = \alpha)}{\Pr(X \geq t, X + Y + Z = \alpha)} \\
&= \frac{\Pr(X = j, Y + Z = \alpha - j)}{\sum_{x=t}^{\alpha-2} \Pr(X = x, Y + Z = \alpha - x)} \\
&= \frac{\Pr(X = j) \Pr(Y + Z = \alpha - j)}{\sum_{k=1}^{\alpha-t-1} \Pr(X = \alpha - k - 1, Y + Z = k + 1)}
\end{aligned}$$

where the last equality is via the change of variables $k = \alpha - x - 1$. Since $\Pr(Y + Z = a) = (a-1)(1-\beta)^{a-2}\beta^2$ we

have

$$\begin{aligned}
P_{long}(\alpha, t, j) &= \frac{(1-\beta)^{j-1}\beta(\alpha-j-1)(1-\beta)^{\alpha-j-2}\beta^2}{\sum_{k=1}^{\alpha-t-1}(1-\beta)^{\alpha-k-2}\beta k(1-\beta)^{k-1}\beta^2} \\
&= \frac{(\alpha-j-1)}{\sum_{k=1}^{\alpha-t-1} k} \\
&= \frac{2(\alpha-j-1)}{(\alpha-t)(\alpha-t-1)}
\end{aligned}$$

Since $j \geq t$, $(\alpha - j - 1)/(\alpha - t - 1) \leq 1$ and from above $P_{long}(\alpha, t, j) \leq \frac{2}{\alpha-t}$. It follows that

$$P(\alpha, t, j) \leq \frac{3}{\alpha-t}$$

as asserted. $\square$

We make the observation that if player i received a list of length α at the beginning, and $t - 1$ rounds of the protocol did not reveal the secret, then if player i guesses that the true secret is in position j, $P(\alpha, t, j)$ represents the probability that this guess is correct. For $j \geq t + 1$ this also represents the probability that player can succesfully cheat by outputting the potential secret at position j and dropping out of the protocol. The situation is slightly different for $j = t$ because if the player is caught cheating on round t, all other players following the protocol will output the secret at position j so if that is correct, player i will gain no advantage from having guessed it. Thus, on round t the best probability of a successful cheat is obtained by guessing that the secret is in position $t + 1$. As we have just seen, the probability of success is at most $3/(\alpha - t)$.

3.1 Proof of Theorem 1.1

We are now ready to present the proof of Theorem 1.1

PROOF. By Proposition 3.1 and Lemma 3.2, if $q > 1 + \frac{U_+ - U_-}{(U - U_- + \epsilon)}$ then no player can gain ϵ or more by faking messages in the protocol.

By Lemma 3.3 and Lemma 3.2, to prevent cheating by guessing the secret and prematurely exiting the protocol, it suffices if

$$\frac{3}{\alpha-t} < \frac{U - U_- + \epsilon}{U_+ - U_-}$$

Now, we know that $t < X$ and $\alpha - t$ is at least the short player's padding, and thus $\alpha - t > Y$. Thus it suffices to have $Y > \frac{U_+ - U_-}{3(U - U_- + \epsilon)}$. But Y is a geometric random variable with parameter β, so we require that

$$\Pr\left(Y > \frac{U_+ - U_-}{3(U - U_- + \epsilon)}\right) = (1-\beta)^{\frac{U_+ - U_-}{3(U - U_- + \epsilon)}} \tag{1}$$

Now, if we set

$$\beta = 1 - (1-\delta)^{\frac{3(U - U_- + \epsilon)}{U_+ - U_-}}$$

then $\Pr(Y > \frac{U_+ - U_-}{2(U - U_- + \epsilon)}) = 1 - \delta$ so that by Lemma 3.2, Lemma 3.3 and equation 1, with probability at least $1 - \delta$ no player can gain more than ϵ in expectation by guessing the position of the secret before the definitive iteration. It follows that with probability at least $1 - \delta$ the protocol is an ϵ-Nash equilibrium.

We now analyze the resource costs of our protocol. The communication tree has $2n-1$ nodes. Each player is mapped to one leaf and at most one internal node. Players only communicate with their neighbors in the tree. So on each round, in the *Up-Stage* player i acting as a leaf, sends two field elements (a share and a tag) up to his parent, and then two more acting as an internal node. In the *Down-Stage*, acting as an internal node he sends two field elements each to his left and right child. Thus each player sends at most eight field elements per round, and thus the expected number of messages sent is $O(1)$ and the expected number of bits sent is $O(\log q)$ which does not depend on n. Since the expected number of rounds is constant and the tree has $O(\log n)$ height, it follows that the expected latency is $O(\log n)$. $\square$

3.2 A Note on Backwards Induction

The *backwards induction* problem arises when a multi-round protocol has a last round number that is known to all players. In particular, if it is globally known that the last round of the protocol is ℓ, then on the ℓ-th round, there is no longer any fear or reprisal to persuade a player to follow the protocol. But then if no player follows the protocol in the ℓ-th round, then in the $(\ell-1)$-th round, there is no reason for any player to follow the protocol. This same logic continues backwards to the very first round.

The backwards induction problem can occur with protocols that make cryptographic assumptions, since there will always be some round number, ℓ, in which enough time has passed so that even a computationally bounded player can break the cryptography. Even though ℓ may be far off in the future, it is globally known that the protocol will end at round ℓ, and so by backwards induction, even in the first round, there is no incentive for a player to follow the protocol.

As in [8], we protect against backwards induction by having both long and short players. As the above analysis shows, if β is chosen sufficiently small, we can ensure that Y will be large enough so that the probability of making a correct guess as to when the protocol ends is too small to enable profitable cheating for any player. Thus, even when a player gets to the second to the last element in all its lists, it can not be very sure that the protocol will end in the next round. All players are aware of these probabilities at the beginning of the protocol, and thus each player knows that no other player will be able to accurately guess when the protocol ends.

4. SCALABLE RATIONAL SECRET SHARING WITH ABSENT PLAYERS

In this section we discuss m-out-of-n secret sharing where $m < n$. Here we want a subset of m or more of the players to be able to reconstruct the secret even when the remaining players are absent. However, fewer than m players should *not* be able to reconstruct the secret on their own. As discussed previously, it does not seem possible to design *scalable* algorithms for secret sharing in the case when either m is much smaller than n or the subset of size m of active players may be chosen in a completely arbitrary manner. We now describe the situation where (1) $m < n$, but $m = \Theta(n)$; and (2) the subset of active players does not depend on the random bits of the dealer. More precisely, we will present

an algorithm with parameters τ and λ (in addition to the parameters of our n-out-of-n algorithm) such that when the number of active players $m > (\tau + \lambda)n$ then with high probability the algorithm is an ϵ-Nash equilibrium for the active players and all the active players learn the secret. On the other hand, if the number of active players $m < (\tau - \lambda)n$, then with high probability the active players cannot reconstruct the secret.

We will assume, as in previous work, that the set of active players is known to all the active players, before the start of the algorithm. This set may be arbitrary or randomly chosen but it does not depend on the random communication tree created by the algorithm.

Here we present a sketch of the algorithm and analysis. Details will appear in the full version of the paper.

Since the algorithm is a variant of the n-out-of-n scheme, for conciseness, we describe here only the places where the two algorithms differ. Let c be a large constant (which we will specify later.) First, the dealer partitions the players into $\frac{n}{c \log n}$ mutually disjoint groups of $c \log n$ players each.[3] This is done using a random permutation of the players. (The first $c \log n$ players in the permutation are the first group, the next $c \log n$ are the second group and so on.) The next step is to create a communication tree as illustrated in Figure 3. The tree is a complete binary tree with $\frac{n}{c \log n}$ leaves (*i.e.* it has $\frac{2n}{c \log n} - 1$ nodes in all.) All of the nodes are *supernodes*, in that they correspond to groups of $c \log n$ players instead of single players. Each group is assigned to a distinct leaf node. Then all but one of the groups are additionally assigned to distinct internal nodes, as in the n-out-of-n algorithm.

Dealer's Protocol: In order to create the sharelist S_i for each player i, the dealer once again creates iterated shares starting with the value h_t (the indicator for round t) at the root of the tree, and creating 2-out-of-2 Shamir shares of the value at a node, as values for its children. Then at each leaf node, $\tau c \log n$-out-of-$c \log n$ Shamir shares are created for the value at the leaf node. These shares are added to the players' sharelists, one for each of the $c \log n$ players assigned to the leaf. Note that this means that $\tau c \log n$ or more of the $c \log n$ players at a leaf can reconstruct the value at the leaf, but fewer than $\tau c \log n$ of them cannot. The algorithm for populating the other lists (L_i, T_i^w, and $H_i^{w,w'}$) is similar to that used for the n-out-of-n algorithm.

Player's Protocol: The protocol for the players consists of an upward and downward phase. In the upward phase, the active players at each leaf node first send their iterated shares to all the other players at the same leaf, in a clique. Assuming that $\tau c \log n$ players are active at the leaf, they can now reconstruct the value at the leaf. This value is sent by all the active players to all the players at the parent supernode. The players in these supernodes use the shares received from the two children to reassemble the appropriate value for that supernode, check this value with the hash and tag scheme and then send the value up to the players in the supernode above them. This continues until the root node is reached, at which point, the value h_t for the current round is reconstructed.

---

[3]It is convenient to assume that $c \log n$ is an integer and divides n. In fact, for arbitrary n, there will be $\left\lfloor \frac{n}{\lceil c \log n \rceil} \right\rfloor$ groups, each with either $\lceil c \log n \rceil$ or $\lceil c \log n \rceil + 1$ players.

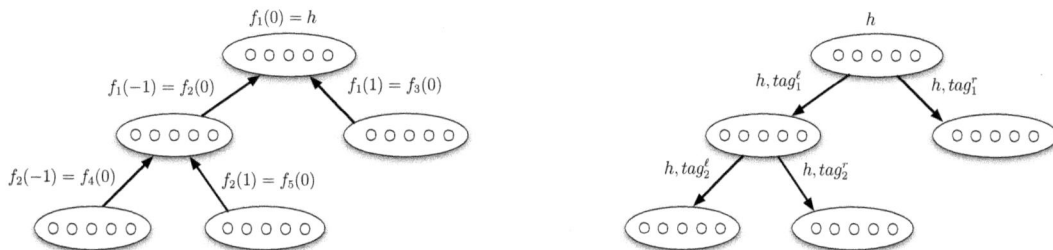

Figure 3: Illustration of the scalable m-out-of-n secret sharing algorithm. The supernodes each consist of $c \log n$ players, selected as described in Section 4. The players in each leaf supernode are connected in a clique. For any parent and child supernodes, the players in the child and the players in the parent are connected in a full bipartite graph. On the left is the up stage of the algorithm; on the right is the down stage.

In the downward phase, h_t is sent down the tree from each parent supernode to its children, using all-to-all communication among the players in the supernodes, until at the bottom, all players learn the value of h_t for that round. The players now act on the information they receive (or do not receive) exactly as they do in the n-out-of-n algorithm.

Analysis Sketch: In order to show correctness of the algorithm, we need to make two arguments. The first argument is that the active players are well distributed in the tree, so that at any stage of the players' protocol sufficiently many shares are available to do the desired reconstruction. The second argument is that is is an ϵ-Nash equilibrium for the active players to follow the protocol. The proof of this part is essentially identical to the proof that the n-out-of-n protocol was an ϵ-Nash equilibrium for all the players, and we omit it here. In the remainder of this section, we sketch why reconstruction is possible with high probability, despite absent players.

We note that for the value at an internal node to be reconstructed it is necessary that the values of both of its children be received. Therefore, it is necessary that there is at least one active player at each internal node. Since no other reconstruction is to be done at internal nodes, this is also sufficient. However, note that the group of $c \log n$ players assigned to an internal node is the same group as those assigned to some leaf. Hence if there are no active players at some internal node, then there is a leaf at which there are also no active players. Since at the leaves we will have a more stringent requirement for how many players need to be active, it is sufficient to consider the failure of the algorithm at the leaves.

Now, the value at a leaf is distributed as $\tau c \log n$-out-of-$c \log n$ Shamir shares to the $c \log n$ players associated with that leaf. Thus, this value can be reconstructed if and only if there are at least $\tau c \log n$ active players at the leaf. Moreover, in order for the protocol to succeed, the values at all the leaves must be reconstructable.

Recall that the players are assigned to leaves of the tree by the following random process: first choose a random permutation of the n players, then partition into $\frac{n}{c \log n}$ mutually disjoint groups by choosing successive contiguous blocks of length $c \log n$. Moreover, the choice of which players are active is made *independently* of the above process. It turns out that in this case, the number of active players in a fixed block is tightly concentrated around its mean. A more precise statement is in the following lemma, whose proof is an

application of the Azuma-Hoeffding inequality. We omit the details here.

LEMMA 4.1. *Let $b_1, b_2, \ldots, b_n$ be n bits such that exactly m of them are 1 and $n - m$ of them are 0. Let $\sigma \in S_n$ be a random permutation of n symbols and $b_{\sigma(1)}, b_{\sigma(2)}, \ldots, b_{\sigma(n)}$ be the induced permutation on bits. Then for any contiguous block $b_{\sigma(i+1)}, b_{\sigma(i+2)}, \ldots, b_{\sigma(i+c \log n)}$ of length $c \log n$, the number U of bits in the block which are 1 has expectation $\frac{mc \log n}{n}$ and satisfies*

$$\Pr\left(U - \frac{mc \log n}{n} > \lambda c \log n\right) \le e^{-(\lambda^2 c \log n)/2}$$

and

$$\Pr\left(U - \frac{mc \log n}{n} < -\lambda c \log n\right) \le e^{-(\lambda^2 c \log n)/2}$$

We can now prove

THEOREM 4.2. *Our m-out-of-n secret sharing algorithm is correct with high probability.*

PROOF. Imagine the permutation of players is a bit string such that every bit corresponds to one player. If a bit is 1 it means the corresponding player is active and if a bit is 0 the corresponding player is inactive.

Case (1) $m \ge (\tau + \lambda)n$. Consider a particular leaf node ℓ and let U_ℓ denote the number of active players at ℓ. By Lemma 4.1,

$$\Pr(U_\ell < \tau c \log n) = \Pr\left(U_\ell - \frac{mc \log n}{n} < \left(\tau - \frac{m}{n}\right) c \log n\right)$$

$$\le \Pr\left(U_\ell - \frac{mc \log n}{n} < -\lambda c \log n\right)$$

$$\le e^{-(\lambda^2 c \log n)/2}$$

Thus the reconstruction fails at ℓ with probability at most $e^{-(\lambda^2 c \log n)/2}$. Taking a union bound over all the $\frac{n}{c \log n}$ leaves we see that the probability that the algorithm fails (which happens only when the reconstruction fails at *some* leaf) is at most $ne^{-(\lambda^2 c \log n)/2} = n^{1 - \lambda^2 c/2}$. Setting $c = \frac{2(k+1)}{\lambda^2}$ we see that the probability that the algorithm fails is at most $1/n^k$.

Case (2) $m \le (\tau - \lambda)n$. Once again consider a particular leaf node ℓ, and let U_ℓ be the number of active players at ℓ.

By Lemma 4.1,

$$\Pr(U_\ell > \tau c \log n) = \Pr\left(U_\ell - \frac{mc\log n}{n} > \left(\tau - \frac{m}{n}\right)c\log n\right)$$
$$\leq \Pr\left(U_\ell - \frac{mc\log n}{n} > \lambda c\log n\right)$$
$$\leq e^{-(\lambda^2 c\log n)/2}$$

Therefore with probability at least $1 - e^{-(\lambda^2 c\log n)/2} = 1 - 1/n^{k+1}$ reconstruction fails at ℓ. Since the failure of the reconstruction at a single leaf is sufficient to break the protocol completely (since no reconstruction is possible at any node along the path from that leaf to the root) it follows that with probability at least $1 - 1/n^{k+1}$ the algorithm fails in this case. $\square$

5. CONCLUSIONS AND FUTURE WORK

We have presented *scalable* mechanisms for rational secret sharing problems. Our algorithms are scalable in the sense that the number of bits sent by each player is $O(1)$ and the latency is at most logarithmic in the number of players. For the n-out-of-n rational secret sharing, we give a scalable algorithm that is an ϵ-Nash equilibrium to solve this problem. For m-out-of-n rational secret sharing where (1) $m = \Theta(n)$; and (2) the set of active players is chosen independently of the random bits of the dealer, we give a scalable algorithm with threshold parameter τ that is an ϵ-Nash equilibrium and ensures that for any fixed, positive λ that if (1) at least a $m/n > \tau + \lambda$ fraction of the players are active, all players will learn the secret; and (2) if fewer than a $\tau - \lambda$ fraction of the players are active, then the secret can not be recovered.

Several open problems remain. First, while our algorithms lead to a $\Theta(n)$ multiplicative reduction in communication costs for rational secure multiparty computation (SMPC), the overall bandwidth for this problem is still very high. It is known that there are certain functions, for which rational SMPC can not be performed in a scalable manner (for example, the parity function). However, we ask: Can we find classes of well-motivated functions for which scalable SMPC is possible? This is related to our second open problem which is: Can we design scalable algorithms for simulating a class of well-motivated mediators? In some sense, this problem may be harder than the SMPC problem, since some types of mediators offer different advice to different players. In other ways, the problem is easier: a simple global coin toss is an effective mediator for many games. A final important problem is: Can we design coalition-resistant scalable algorithms for rational secret sharing?

6. ACKNOWLEDGMENTS

We are grateful to Tom Hayes and Jonathan Katz for useful discussions.

7. REFERENCES

[1] I. Abraham, D. Dolev, R. Gonen, and J. Halpern. Distributed computing meets game theory: robust mechanisms for rational secret sharing and multiparty computation. In *Proceedings of the twenty-fifth annual ACM symposium on Principles of distributed computing*, pages 53–62. ACM, 2006.

[2] R. Geambasu, T. Kohno, A. Levy, and H. Levy. Vanish: Increasing data privacy with self-destructing data. In *Proceedings of the 18th conference on USENIX security symposium*, pages 299–316. USENIX Association, 2009.

[3] O. Goldreich, S. Micali, and A. Wigderson. How to play any mental game. In *Proceedings of the nineteenth annual ACM symposium on Theory of computing*, pages 218–229. ACM, 1987.

[4] S. Gordon and J. Katz. Rational secret sharing, revisited. *Security and Cryptography for Networks*, pages 229–241, 2006.

[5] J. Halpern and V. Teague. Rational secret sharing and multiparty computation: extended abstract. In *Proceedings of the thirty-sixth annual ACM symposium on Theory of computing*, page 632. ACM, 2004.

[6] S. Izmalkov, S. Micali, and M. Lepinski. Rational secure computation and ideal mechanism design. In *Foundations of Computer Science, 2005. FOCS 2005. 46th Annual IEEE Symposium on*, pages 585–594. IEEE, 2005.

[7] V. King and J. Saia. Breaking the O (n 2) bit barrier: scalable byzantine agreement with an adaptive adversary. In *Proceeding of the 29th ACM SIGACT-SIGOPS symposium on Principles of distributed computing*, pages 420–429. ACM, 2010.

[8] G. Kol and M. Naor. Games for exchanging information. In *Proceedings of the 40th annual ACM symposium on Theory of computing*, pages 423–432. ACM, 2008.

[9] M. Lepinksi, S. Micali, and A. Shelat. Collusion-free protocols. In *ANNUAL ACM SYMPOSIUM ON THEORY OF COMPUTING*, volume 37, page 543. Citeseer, 2005.

[10] M. Lepinski, S. Micali, C. Peikert, and A. Shelat. Completely fair SFE and coalition-safe cheap talk. In *Proceedings of the twenty-third annual ACM symposium on Principles of distributed computing*, pages 1–10. ACM, 2004.

[11] A. Lysyanskaya and N. Triandopoulos. Rationality and adversarial behavior in multi-party computation. *Advances in Cryptology-CRYPTO 2006*, pages 180–197, 2006.

[12] T. Rabin and M. Ben-Or. Verifiable secret sharing and multiparty protocols with honest majority. In *Proceedings of the twenty-first annual ACM symposium on Theory of computing*, pages 73–85. ACM, 1989.

[13] M. Wegman and J. Carter. New hash functions and their use in authentication and set equality. *Journal of computer and system sciences*, 22(3):265–279, 1981.

Analyzing Consistency Properties for Fun and Profit

Wojciech Golab
Hewlett-Packard Labs
Palo Alto, California, USA
wojciech.golab@hp.com

Xiaozhou (Steve) Li
Hewlett-Packard Labs
Palo Alto, California, USA
xiaozhou.li@hp.com

Mehul A. Shah
Hewlett-Packard Labs
Palo Alto, California, USA
mehul.shah@hp.com

ABSTRACT

Motivated by the increasing popularity of eventually consistent key-value stores as a commercial service, we address two important problems related to the consistency properties in a history of operations on a read/write register (i.e., the start time, finish time, argument, and response of every operation). First, we consider how to detect a consistency violation as soon as one happens. To this end, we formulate a specification for online verification algorithms, and we present such algorithms for several well-known consistency properties. Second, we consider how to quantify the severity of the violations, if a history is found to contain consistency violations. We investigate two quantities: one is the staleness of the reads, and the other is the commonality of violations. For staleness, we further consider time-based staleness and operation-count-based staleness. We present efficient algorithms that compute these quantities. We believe that addressing these problems helps both key-value store providers and users adopt data consistency as an important aspect of key-value store offerings.

Categories and Subject Descriptors: C.2.4 [Computer Systems Organization]: Computer-Communication Networks, *Distributed Systems.*

General Terms: Algorithms, verification, theory.

Keywords: Consistency, atomicity, key-value store.

1. INTRODUCTION

In recent years, large-scale key-value stores such as Amazon's S3 [2] have become commercially popular. A key-value store provides a simple get(key) and put(key,value) interface to the user. Providing strong consistency properties for these operations has become an increasingly important goal [8, 16, 30]. However, the implementations of many key-value stores are proprietary and, as such, opaque to the users. Consequently, the users cannot reason about the implementations so as to be confident about their correctness. Instead, they can only test the system empirically, and analyze the test results (e.g., traces of operations) to see if it is delivering the promised level of consistency. To be useful, such consistency analysis should address two important problems. One,

the analysis should reveal consistency violations as soon as they happen so that corrective actions can be taken (e.g., tuning the consistency level for future operations [3]). Two, the analysis should quantify the severity of violations. If consistency is part of the Service Level Agreement (SLA), and the severity of violations can be quantified in some way, then some proportional compensation, monetary or otherwise, may be negotiated between the user and the service provider (hence the title of the paper).

We model a key-value store by a collection of read/write registers where each key identifies a register and the get/put requests translate into read/write operations on the appropriate register. Given a history of operations (i.e., the start time, finish time, argument, and response of every operation) on a read/write register, how do we determine whether the history satisfies certain consistency properties such as atomicity (i.e., linearizability) [18, 22]? The basic decision problem, which seeks only a yes/no answer, has been addressed in the literature [5, 14, 23]. In this paper, we are interested in two questions beyond the decision problem. First, how to detect a consistency violation as soon as it happens, rather than analyze the entire history potentially long after the fact? Second, if the history is found to violate the desired consistency property, how to quantify the severity of the violations? To our knowledge, these problems have not been addressed in literature, mainly because (1) storage as a service is new, and (2) traditionally, stores avoid inconsistency altogether rather than briefly sacrifice consistency for better availability.

In this paper, after laying out the model and definitions (Section 2), we present online consistency verification algorithms for several well-known consistency properties, namely safety, regularity, atomicity, and sequential consistency (Section 3). The distinctive feature of these algorithms is that they operate not by processing the entire history at once, but rather by processing a history incrementally as events (i.e., start or finish of an operation) occur, and reporting violations as they are detected. We note that our online algorithms do not control what or when operations are to be issued: they merely analyze the histories passively and report violations according to formal consistency property definitions.

We then propose several ways to quantify the severity of atomicity violations in a history (Sections 4 and 5). The first quantity we consider is the maximum staleness of all the reads (Section 4). Staleness attempts to capture how much older the value read is compared to the latest value written. We propose two definitions of "older than" in this context. One is based on the passage of time. The second is based on the number of intervening writes, a notion that coincides precisely with the k-atomicity concept proposed by Aiyer et al. [1]. We present algorithms that compute the maximum time-based staleness and, for special cases, operation-count-based staleness.

The second quantity for evaluating the severity of violations is the commonality of violations. Defining this concept precisely is nontrivial as violations are not easily attributed to individual operations. Instead, we define commonality as the minimum "proportion" of the history that must be removed in order to make the history atomic (Section 5). To simplify the problem computationally, we do not consider the removal of individual operations but rather of entire *clusters*—groups of operations that read or write the same value. We give two formulations. In the unweighted formulation, we treat all clusters equally and try to remove the smallest subset of clusters. We solve this problem using a greedy algorithm (Section 5.1). In the weighted formulation, we weigh clusters according to their size (i.e., number of operations in the cluster), and we try to remove a subset of clusters with minimum total weight. We solve this problem using a dynamic programming algorithm (Section 5.2). Finally, we survey related work (Section 6) and conclude the paper with a discussion of some open problems (Section 7). Due to space limitations, we defer all proofs of correctness to the companion technical report [15].

2. MODEL

A collection of client machines interact with a key-value store via two interfaces: get(key) and put(key,value), where key and value are uninterpreted strings. In order to determine whether the key-value store provides certain consistency properties, a client machine can timestamp when it sends out a get/put request and when it receives a response, and can record the value read or written. Since different client machines can access the same key, the individual client histories are sent to a centralized *monitor* where the individual histories are merged. Furthermore, since accesses to different keys are independent of each other, the monitor groups operations by key and then examines whether each group satisfies the desired consistency properties. We further assume that all client machines have well-synchronized clocks (often accomplished by time synchronization protocols such as NTP), or have access to a global clock, so that client timestamps can be considered to represent real time. See the technical report [15] for additional discussions on this scenario and our assumptions.

We model a key-value store as a collection of read/write registers, each identified by a unique key. We consider a collection of operations on such a register. Each operation, either a read or a write, has a start time, finish time, and value. The value of a write is the value written to the register and the value of a read is the value obtained by the read. Note that the value of a write is known at the start of the write, but the value of a read is known only at the finish of the read. This distinction is important for online verification of consistency properties (Section 3). We assume that all writes assign a distinct value. We make this assumption for two reasons. First, in our particular application, all writes can be tagged with a globally unique identifier, typically consisting of the local time of the client issuing the write followed by the client's identifier. Therefore, this assumption does not incur any loss of generality. Second, when the values written are not unique, the decision problem of verifying consistency properties is NP-complete for several well-known properties, in particular atomicity and sequential consistency [7, 14, 27].

We next define some terminology and notations. An *event* is the start or finish of a read or write operation. We assume that the system has the ability to pair up start/finish events for the same operation. We denote the start and finish events of an operation op by $|op$ and $op|$ respectively, and the start and finish times of op by $op.s$ and $op.f$ respectively. The start of a read whose return value is not yet known is denoted by $|r(?)$. We assume that all

start and finish times are unique. We say that operation op *time-precedes* (or simply precedes) operation op', written as $op < op'$, if $op.f < op'.s$. We say that op *time-succeeds* (or simply succeeds) op' iff op' time-precedes op. If neither $op < op'$ nor $op' < op$, then we say op and op' are *concurrent* with each other. A *history* is a collection of events that describes a collection of operations, some of which may not have finished. Without loss of generality, we assume that a history begins with an artificial pair of start/finish events for a write that assigns the initial value of the register. For a read, its *dictating write* is the (unique) write that assigns the value obtained by the read. Typically, every read in a history has a dictating write, otherwise either the history contains incomplete information or the system is buggy. For a write, the set of reads that obtain the value written is called the *dictated reads* of the write. A write can have any number of dictated reads (including zero). The time-precedence relation defines a partial order on the operations in a history H. A total order of the operations in H is called *valid* if it conforms to the time-precedence partial order.

3. ONLINE VERIFICATION OF CONSISTENCY PROPERTIES

Determining whether a given history satisfies certain consistency properties such as atomicity has been addressed in the literature [5, 14, 23]. However, known solutions are *offline* algorithms in the sense that they analyze the entire history at once, even though a violation may occur in some short prefix of the history. In this section, we investigate how to detect a violation as soon as one happens, and we present efficient algorithms that achieve this goal for three well-known consistency properties: safety, regularity, and atomicity. We also discuss the complications associated with verifying sequential consistency in an online manner.

3.1 Specifying online verification algorithms

Online verification algorithms work by inspecting the start event and finish event of each operation one by one, in time order, and determine on-the-fly whether a violation has happened. In contrast to an offline algorithm, which simply indicates whether a history satisfies some consistency property, we would like an online algorithm to output more fine-grained information. For example, if a history initially satisfies the consistency property and then fails to satisfy it (after some long-enough prefix), then the output from the online algorithm should be different from the case where violations occur from the beginning. From a theoretical perspective, another attractive feature for an online algorithm is the ability to report meaningful information for infinitely long histories—a property that an offline algorithm cannot satisfy because its output summarizes upon termination the entire input history in one yes/no answer.

To meet the requirements discussed above, we define an online algorithm as one whose input is a sequence of events $H = \langle e_1, \ldots, e_n \rangle$, and whose output is a sequence $\Gamma = \langle \gamma_1, \ldots, \gamma_n \rangle$, where $\gamma_i \in \{good, bad\}$. The output value γ_i provides information about the prefix $\langle e_1, \ldots, e_i \rangle$ of H, which we denote by H_i. For a given history H, we call H *good* with respect to a consistency property P (which is external to our specification) if H satisfies P, and *bad* with respect to P otherwise. Intuitively, $\gamma_i = bad$ indicates that H_i is bad, and furthermore the consistency violation can be attributed in some way to the last event e_i. An output value $\gamma_i = good$ indicates that e_i does not introduce any additional consistency violations, but does not say whether H_i is good or bad. This is because it is possible that a violation has occurred in some short prefix of H_i, and no other violations have occurred since then. The above intuitive notion is captured by the following

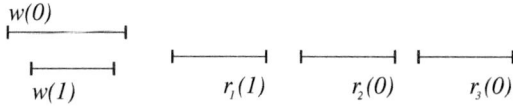

Figure 1: Online verification of a non-atomic history.

formal specification for how a correct online verification algorithm should behave:

SPECIFICATION 3.1. *Let $H = \langle e_1, \ldots, e_n \rangle$ be an input history for an online verification algorithm for some consistency property P. Let $\Gamma = \langle \gamma_1, \ldots, \gamma_n \rangle$ be the sequence of good/bad output values produced by the algorithm, one for each event in H. For any i, let $\tilde{H}_i$ denote the history obtained by taking H_i and removing every event e_j, where $1 \leq j < i$, such that $\gamma_j = $ bad, along with its matching start/finish event. Then for any i such that $1 \leq i \leq n$, $\gamma_i = $ good iff $\tilde{H}_i$ is good with respect to P.*

It is easy to show that, for safety, regularity, atomicity, and sequential consistency, $\gamma_i = $ *bad* only if e_i is the finish event for a read. This is not because write operations cannot participate in violations, but rather because only reads can reveal such violations, namely through their return values. For this reason we adopt the convention in this section that violations are attributed to reads only. We also think of an online algorithm as deciding for each read whether it has caused a violation with respect to the consistency property under consideration. If so, the algorithm outputs *bad* when it processes the read's finish event, and subsequently continues as if the offending read did not happen at all. We remark that this way of counting violations, informally speaking, does not necessarily report the smallest possible set of violations. For example, consider the history depicted in Figure 1, which is not atomic. An online verification algorithm greedily considers $r_1(1)$ valid, and classifies $r_2(0)$ and $r_3(0)$ as violations. We could instead suppose that $w(1)$ takes effect before $w(0)$, and attribute the violation to $r_1(1)$. Deciding which option is better at the time when $r_1(1)$ finishes would require seeing into the future. Thus, we cannot expect an online verification algorithm to make the best decision on-the-fly.

For the properties of safety, regularity and atomicity, it is also straightforward to show that any online verification algorithm ALG satisfying Specification 3.1 also has the following properties: (1) Validity: For any good history H, the output vector Γ of ALG on H contains all *good*. (2) Completeness: For any bad history H, the output vector Γ of ALG on H contains at least one *bad*. The same is not true for sequential consistency (i.e., validity does not hold), and we comment on that in more detail in Section 3.6.

3.2 Efficiency of online verification algorithms

A straightforward approach to devising an online verification algorithm is to simply apply an offline algorithm repeatedly on successively longer prefixes of the history. Assuming that the online algorithm discards all reads that cause violations, it is correct in the sense of satisfying Specification 3.1, provided of course that the offline algorithm is correct. However, this approach may be inefficient. For example, consider the atomicity verification algorithm of Gibbons and Korach [14] (simply referred to as the GK algorithm henceforth), which runs in $O(n \log n)$ time on an n-operation history. If we use the GK algorithm for online checking, then each stage of checking takes $O(n' \log n')$ time, where n' is the length of the prefix, and altogether the algorithm takes $O(n^2 \log n)$ time.

The key to efficient online verification lies in managing the bookkeeping information in various data structures (e.g., zones [14], a value graph [23], or an operation graph [5]). Instead of throwing away and reconstructing these data structures each time the history grows by one event, we modify the data structures and try to perform computation on them incrementally. Furthermore, to reduce the time and space complexity of the computation we try to discard any information that is no longer needed. For example, suppose that we are checking for atomicity. Consider two successive writes $w(0)w(1)$. Upon the finish of $w(1)$, we observe that reads starting after that time cannot return the value 0 without causing a violation. (Recall our assumption that each write assigns a unique value.) Therefore, $w(0)$ can be "wiped from the books" once $w(1)$ ends, if there are no ongoing reads at that time. This makes any future read returning 0 appear as though it lacks a dictating write, causing the algorithm to report a violation for that read. Another observation is that a finished read can always be discarded, as long as the constraints that the read places on the order of writes are properly recorded. These ideas are explained in detail in the sections below.

3.3 Verifying safety

Safety is one of the weakest consistency properties. A history is *safe* iff there exists a valid total order on the operations such that (1) a read not concurrent with any writes returns the value of the latest write before it in the total order, and (2) a read concurrent with one or more writes may return an arbitrary value.

The online safety verification algorithm is presented in Algorithm 1. We use shorthands such as "$e_i = \lfloor w(a) \rfloor$" to mean "event e_i is the start of a write of value a" (line 3). The algorithm maintains a set of values. These values are those that may be obtained by ongoing or future reads, and we call these values *allowable values*. For each allowable value a, the algorithm maintains a variable $w[a]$ that keeps track of the start time and finish time of $w(a)$ (line 8). As a slight abuse of notation, we use square brackets to denote variables and braces to denote operations; this convention is adopted throughout the rest of the paper. We use "$w[b] < w[a]$" to mean the write of b precedes that of a (line 9). The algorithm maintains some additional data structures: (1) I: the set of reads that can be ignored (because they are concurrent with some writes), (2) R: the set of pending reads, and (3) nw: the number of pending writes. The algorithm creates new allowable values as new writes are seen. However, the algorithm also discards old values (line 18) as soon as those values are determined to be not allowable. The algorithm outputs *bad* when a read obtains a value that is not in the set of allowable values (line 19).

3.4 Verifying atomicity

We say that a history is *atomic* iff there exists a valid total order on the operations such that every read returns the value of the latest write before it in the total order. Offline verification of atomicity has been addressed in the literature before [5, 14, 23]. The online algorithm presented in this section uses core ideas from an offline algorithm, and some additional ideas on discarding obsolete values. Fundamentally, it does not matter which offline algorithm we begin with, but in what follows, we adopt the GK algorithm [14]. This is because the GK algorithm lends itself most conveniently to incremental computation. More discussion on offline algorithms can be found in the related work section (Section 6).

The GK algorithm works as follows. For a history, the set of operations that take the same value is called a *cluster*. Let $C(a)$ denote the cluster for value a. Let $\bar{s}(a)$ be the maximum start time of all the operations in $C(a)$, that is, $\bar{s}(a) = \max\{op.s : op \in$

Algorithm 1: Online safety verification

Input: sequence of events $\langle e_1, e_2, \ldots \rangle$
Output: sequence of *good/bad* values $\langle \gamma_1, \gamma_2, \ldots \rangle$
Init: $I = R = \emptyset$, $nw = 0$

1 **upon** event e_i **do**
2      $\gamma_i := good$;
3   **if** $e_i = |w(a)$ **then**
4          $nw := nw + 1$;
5          $I := I \cup R$
6   **else if** $e_i = w(a)|$ **then**
7          $nw := nw - 1$;
8   create $w[a]$; $w[a].(s,f) := w(a).(s,f)$;
9   **foreach** $(b : w[b] < w[a])$ **do** discard $w[b]$ **end**
10   **else if** $e_i = |r(?)$ **then**
11   add $r(?)$ to R;
12   **if** $nw > 0$ **then** add $r(?)$ to I **end**
13   **else if** $e_i = r(a)|$ **then**
14   remove $r(a)$ from R;
15   **if** $r \in I$ **then**
16   remove $r(a)$ from I
17   **else**
18   **if** $\exists w[a]$ **then** $\forall b, b \neq a$: discard $w[b]$
19   **else** $\gamma_i := bad$
20   **end**
21   **end**
22   **end**;
23   **output** γ_i
24 **end**

Figure 2: When to discard bookkeeping information.

$C(a)\}$. Let $\underline{f}(a)$ be the minimum finish time of all the operations in $C(a)$, that is, $\underline{f}(a) = \min\{op.f : op \in C(a)\}$. The *zone* for a value a, denoted by $Z(a)$, is the closed interval of time between $\underline{f}(a)$ and $\bar{s}(a)$. If $\underline{f}(a) < \bar{s}(a)$, this zone is called a *forward zone* and spans from $\underline{f}(a)$ to $\bar{s}(a)$. Otherwise, the zone is called a *backward zone* and spans from $\bar{s}(a)$ to $\underline{f}(a)$. We use $Z.l$ and $Z.r$ to denote the left endpoint and right endpoint of zone Z. In other words, if $Z(a)$ is a forward zone, then $Z(a).l = \underline{f}(a)$ and $Z(a).r = \bar{s}(a)$. If $Z(a)$ is a backward zone, then $Z(a).l = \bar{s}(a)$ and $Z(a).r = \underline{f}(a)$. We write $Z_1 < Z_2$ iff $Z_1.r < Z_2.l$. We use $\overrightarrow{Z}$ to denote a forward zone and $\overleftarrow{Z}$ to denote a backward zone.

We say that two zones Z_1 and Z_2 *conflict* with each other, denoted by $Z_1 \not\sim Z_2$, iff they are both forward zones and they overlap, or one is a forward zone and the other is a backward zone contained entirely in the former forward zone. Two zones are *compatible* with each other, written as $Z_1 \sim Z_2$, iff they do not conflict. According to this definition, two backward zones never conflict. Gibbons and Korach [14] show that a history is atomic iff (1) every read has a dictating write, (2) no read precedes its dictating write, and (3) all pairs of zones are compatible.

Our online algorithm is based on the GK algorithm, and has the ability to discard obsolete information. The technique for identifying such information is based on the following observation, illustrated in Figure 2. Consider a write $w(a)$, which is succeeded by another write $w(b)$. Let R be the set of ongoing reads when $w(b)$ finishes. We observe that at the time when all the reads in R have finished, no ongoing or future reads can obtain the value a without causing a violation. To see this, let t be $w(b)$'s finish time and t' be the largest finish time of all the reads in R. Consider an ongoing read r at t'. This read does not belong to R because at t', all reads in R have finished. Therefore, r starts after time t, yet at time t,

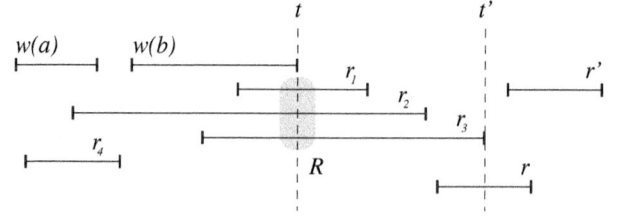

value a has been superseded by value b. Thus, r should not return a. Next, consider a read r' that starts after t'. Since $t < t'$, by the same argument, r' should not return value a either. In other words, at time t', we can discard all information related to value a, and if subsequently a read returns a, we can immediately report a violation. Based on this observation, we define the α *set of value* a, denoted by $\alpha(a)$, to be the set of ongoing reads at the earliest finish time of all the writes that succeed $w(a)$. For the example in Figure 2, $\alpha(a) = \{r_1, r_2, r_3\}$. In an online algorithm, we can use a variable $\alpha[a]$ to keep track of which reads in $\alpha(a)$ are still ongoing, and once this set becomes empty, value a can be discarded. Due to the nature of online algorithms, $\alpha(a)$ is initially undefined (because the algorithm has not seen any writes that succeed $w(a)$); for that period of time the $\alpha[a]$ variable is nil (not $\emptyset$).

Clearly, how much space can be saved depends on the history. However, we observe that new writes cause new variables to be created, but in the meantime, they increase the chances that old variables can be discarded. Therefore, we expect that in long histories, space saving in practice is substantial.

Algorithm 2 implements the above ideas. The finish event of a read is determined to be *bad* under two circumstances: (1) when a read obtains a value not allowable (line 19), and (2) when an updated zone conflicts with an existing, fully formed zone (line 24). In the latter case the algorithm undoes the update to the zone so that it can "pretend" that this bad event didn't happen. In both cases, the present read is removed from R and α-sets (lines 28 to 32), so the effect of the matching start event is also eliminated (recall Specification 3.1). The rest of the algorithm mainly adds and removes the bookkeeping information as new events arrive, following the ideas described above. For example, upon the start of a write (line 3), the algorithm creates the corresponding data structures, leaving $\underline{f}$ of the new zone to be ∞ (i.e., "undefined") as no finish event for that zone has been seen. As other events are seen, the algorithm initializes (line 12) and updates (line 30) the α-sets accordingly so that old values can be discarded in a timely manner.

3.5 Verifying regularity

We say that a history is *regular* iff there exists a valid total order of the operations such that a read returns the value of the latest write before it in the total order, except that a read concurrent with one or more writes may return the value of one of the writes concurrent with the read. Online verification of regularity is similar to verification of atomicity, except that we discard immediately any read that returns the value of some write concurrent with the read. We omit the details due to space limitations.

3.6 Verifying sequential consistency

We say that a history is *sequentially consistent* iff there exists a total order on the operations such that (1) the total order is consistent with process order (i.e., operations by the same process are placed in the same order as they are issued), and (2) a read returns the value of the latest write before it in the total order. The total

Algorithm 2: Online atomicity verification

Input: sequence of events $\langle e_1, e_2, \ldots \rangle$
Output: sequence of $good/bad$ values $\langle \gamma_1, \gamma_2, \ldots \rangle$
Init: $R = \emptyset$; no $w[\cdot], Z[\cdot],$ or $\alpha[\cdot]$ variables

```
1  upon event e_i do
2  |   γ_i := good;
3  |   if e_i = |w(a) then
4  |   |   create w[a], Z[a], α[a];
5  |   |   w[a].(s, f) := (w(a).s, ∞);
6  |   |   Z[a].(f, s̄) := (∞, w(a).s);
7  |   |   α[a] := nil
8  |   else if e_i = w(a)| then
9  |   |   w[a].f := w(a).f;
10 |   |   Z[a].f := min(Z[a].f, w(a).f);
11 |   |   foreach (b : w[b] < w[a] ∧ α[b] = nil) do
12 |   |   |   α[b] := R ;
13 |   |   |   if α[b] = ∅ then discard w[b], Z[b], α[b] end
14 |   |   end
15 |   else if e_i = |r(?) then
16 |   |   add r(?) to R
17 |   else if e_i = r(a)| then
18 |   |   if ∄ w[a] then
19 |   |   |   γ_i := bad
20 |   |   else
21 |   |   |   Z[a].s̄ := max(Z[a].s̄, r(a).s);
22 |   |   |   Z[a].f := min(Z[a].f, r(a).f);
23 |   |   |   if (∃b : Z[b].f ≠ ∞ ∧ Z[a] ⊀ Z[b]) then
24 |   |   |   |   γ_i := bad ;
25 |   |   |   |   undo updates to Z[a] for e_i
26 |   |   |   end
27 |   |   end;
28 |   |   remove r(a) from R ;
29 |   |   foreach (b : r(a) ∈ α[b]) do
30 |   |   |   remove r(a) from α[b] ;
31 |   |   |   if α[b] = ∅ then discard w[b], Z[b], α[b] end
32 |   |   end
33 |   end;
34 |   output γ_i
35 end
```

order need not be valid (i.e., conform to the real-time partial order) as long as property (1) holds. In order to define process order, we assume that each process issues one operation at a time.

Note that to verify sequential consistency, we need to know which process issues which operation in the history, in contrast to the previous three consistency properties. In this section, we assume that the history includes such information, and that we know in advance the full set of processes that may issue operations. Both assumptions can be realized easily in practice.

Offline verification of sequential consistency is NP-complete if writes can assign duplicate values [14, 27], but admits straightforward solutions if we assume that each write assigns a unique value. For example, we can use an operation graph approach [5]. In particular, we can model each operation as a vertex in a directed graph. We add edges to this graph in the following three steps: (1) $op \rightarrow op'$ if op and op' are from the same process and op precedes op', (2) $w(a) \rightarrow r(a)$ for all values a, and (3) $w(a) \rightarrow w(b)$ if $w(a) \rightarrow r(b)$, for all values a and b. It is easy to show that the history is sequentially consistent iff each read has a dictating write and the resulting graph is a DAG.

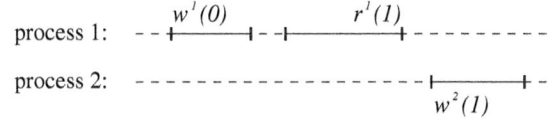

Figure 3: A sequentially consistent history that is not safe.

Online verification of sequential consistency poses unique challenges owing to weaker constraints on the total order of operations, which need not conform to the real-time partial order. The fundamental problem is illustrated by the history depicted in Figure 3. This history violates safety, regularity, and atomicity because the real-time partial order of operations forces $r^1(1)$ before $w^2(1)$ in any total ordering, meaning that $r^1(1)$ precedes its dictating write (the superscripts denote the processes issuing the operations). On the other hand, the history is sequentially consistent, and so in online verification we would like the algorithm to output a sequence of $good$ values for this particular input. (See the "Validity" property defined in Section 3.1.) This is problematic because when the online algorithm sees the prefix $w^1(0)r^1(1)$, there is no dictating write for $r^1(1)$ and so Specification 3.1 stipulates $\gamma_4 = bad$.

We work around this problem by making the following simplifying assumption: in the real-time partial order of operations, a read never precedes its dictating write. In practical terms, a key-value store can break this assumption only if there is a software bug causing reads to return values that have not yet been written, or if there is significant clock skew among servers, making a read appear to precede its dictating write when events are collected at a centralized monitor. We ignore these possibilities as they are orthogonal to the core problem of determining what consistency property a key-value store actually provides when it is designed (correctly) to provide some weaker property such as eventual consistency.

Even with our simplifying assumption, we still face the problem that in online verification of sequential consistency, timing information cannot be used to determine which operations can be discarded. Instead, the following rule can be used to discard obsolete operations: As soon as there is an operation $op(a)$ such that each process has executed some operation that is downstream of op in the DAG (possibly $op(a)$ itself), then any operation upstream of $op(a)$'s dictating write (which can be $op(a)$ itself if $op(a)$ is a write) can be discarded from the graph. This rule is correct because no ongoing or future reads can return a or any value whose dictating write is upstream of $op(a)$'s dictating write. To see this, suppose otherwise, and let b be the value returned by the read such that b's dictating write is upstream of a's. Then from the above rules for adding edges, it is easy to construct a cycle involving $w(b)$ and $w(a)$, indicating a violation of sequential consistency. The verification algorithm for sequential consistency that implements this rule under our simplifying assumption is straightforward, and we omit the details due to space limitations.

4. QUANTIFYING STALENESS

What can we do if we discover that a history contains consistency violations? We can try to quantify the severity of the violations. In this paper we consider two quantities: staleness of reads and commonality of violations. This section addresses the former, and the next section addresses the latter. Informally, the *staleness of a read* quantifies the "distance" between the write operation that assigns the value returned by the read, and the operation that writes the latest value (in some valid total order of the operations). We can then define the *staleness of a history* as the maximum staleness over all the reads in the history. In this paper we consider two natural ways to formalize the notion of "distance": (1) by measuring the passage of time, and (2) by counting the number of intervening writes. We elaborate on these two approaches in the subsections that follow. (Note: From here on, the algorithms that we consider are no longer online algorithms.)

4.1 Time-based staleness

In this section, we discuss Δ-*atomicity*, a consistency property that we feel is appropriate for reasoning about eventually consistent read/write storage systems. This property is a generalization of atomicity, and is defined for any non-negative real number Δ. Informally, Δ-atomicity allows a read to return either the value of the latest write preceding it, or the value of the latest write as of "Δ time units ago." Thus, if $\Delta > 0$, Δ-atomicity is strictly weaker than atomicity [22], and if $\Delta = 0$, it is identical to atomicity. We now give a more precise definition.

We first observe that some histories may contain the following "bad" reads: (1) a read obtains a value that has never been written, and (2) a read precedes its own dictating write. We call a history *simple* iff it contains neither anomaly. For non-simple histories, we define their staleness to be ∞. It is straightforward to check if a history is simple, and so in what follows we only consider simple histories.

For a simple history H, let H_Δ be the history obtained from H by decreasing the start time of each read by Δ time units. We say that H is Δ-*atomic* iff H_Δ is atomic. Therefore, given a history H and Δ, checking if H is Δ-atomic is reduced to computing H_Δ from H and checking if H_Δ is atomic. (For $\Delta = 0$, the reduction is trivial.) The following captures some useful properties of Δ-atomicity.

FACT 4.1. *(1) Two compatible zones remain compatible if we decrease the start times of the reads in these zones by arbitrary amounts. (2) For any simple history H, there exists a $\Delta \geq 0$ such that H is Δ-atomic. (3) For any simple history H and $0 \leq \Delta \leq \Delta'$, if H is Δ-atomic then it is also Δ'-atomic.*

We state in the following lemma an alternative (and somewhat more intuitive) definition of Δ-atomicity:

LEMMA 4.2. *A simple history H is Δ-atomic iff there exists an assignment of a unique timestamp to each operation such that: each timestamp is within the operation's time interval, and a read with timestamp t obtains the value of the write with the greatest timestamp $t' < t - \delta_t$ for some δ_t such that $0 \leq \delta_t \leq \Delta$.*

For the remainder of this section, we focus on the problem of computing for any simple history H the smallest $\Delta \geq 0$ that makes H Δ-atomic, and hence makes H_Δ atomic. Since shifting the start times of read operations (by increasing Δ) may break the assumption that start and finish times are unique (see Section 2), we must carefully handle corner cases where two zones share an endpoint. To that end, we adopt the convention that two forward zones are compatible if they overlap at exactly one point, and a forward zone is compatible with any backward zone that shares one or both endpoints with the forward zone.

To compute the optimal Δ, we propose a solution based on the GK algorithm for verifying atomicity [14] (see Section 3.4). Given a simple history H, we first compute the set of zones $\mathcal{Z}$. For each pair of distinct zones $Z_1, Z_2 \in \mathcal{Z}$, we assign a score $\chi(Z_1, Z_2) \geq 0$, which quantifies the severity of the conflict between Z_1 and Z_2, and has the property that $\chi(Z_1, Z_2) = \chi(Z_2, Z_1)$. Intuitively, $\chi(Z_1, Z_2)$ is the minimum value of Δ that eliminates any conflict between Z_1 and Z_2.

To understand how χ is computed, consider first the effect of decreasing the starting times of all reads in H by Δ. For a zone that does not contain any reads, there is no effect. For a forward zone, which necessarily contains at least one read, the right endpoint of the zone shifts to the left, up to the limit where the forward zone collapses into a single point. Once this limit is reached, the zone becomes a backward zone and behaves as we describe next. For any backward zone containing at least one read, the left endpoint of the zone shifts to the left, up to the limit where the left endpoint coincides with the start of the dictating write. Beyond this limit there is no effect. Thus, for large enough Δ, all zones become backward zones, and there are no conflicts.

The score function $\chi(Z_1, Z_2)$ is defined precisely as follows. Let $Z_1 \cap Z_2$ denote the time interval corresponding to the intersection of Z_1 and Z_2, and let $|Z_1 \cap Z_2|$ denote length of this intersection interval.

- If $Z_1 \sim Z_2$, then $\chi(Z_1, Z_2) = 0$.

- If Z_1, Z_2 are conflicting forward zones, then $\chi(Z_1, Z_2) = |Z_1 \cap Z_2|$. (Intuitively, to resolve the conflict we shift the right endpoint of the zone that finishes earliest to the left, until either this zone becomes a backward zone, or its right endpoint meets the left endpoint of the other zone.)

- If Z_1 is a forward zone and Z_2 is a conflicting backward zone that contains at least one read and whose dictating write begins before $Z_1.l$, then

$$\chi(Z_1, Z_2) = \min\left(Z_1.r - Z_2.r, Z_2.l - Z_1.l\right).$$

(Intuitively, to resolve the conflict we shift $Z_1.r$ and $Z_2.l$ to the left by the smallest amount ensuring that Z_1 no longer contains Z_2.)

- If Z_1 is a forward zone and Z_2 is a conflicting backward zone of any other kind, then $\chi(Z_1, Z_2) = Z_1.r - Z_2.r$. (Intuitively, to resolve the conflict we shift $Z_1.r$ to the left until Z_1 no longer contains Z_2. Shifting $Z_2.l$ does not help.)

It follows from the discussion above that increasing Δ can only eliminate existing conflicts, and never creates new ones. Consequently, choosing $\Delta = \max\{\chi(Z_1, Z_2) : Z_1, Z_2 \in \mathcal{Z}\}$ eliminates simultaneously all conflicts among the zones in H_Δ, and ensures that H_Δ is atomic. Furthermore, no smaller Δ has the latter property. These results are captured in Theorem 4.3 below.

THEOREM 4.3. *Let H be a simple history and $\mathcal{Z}$ be the set of zones corresponding to the clusters in H (see Section 3.4). Define $\Delta_{opt} = \max\{\chi(Z_1, Z_2) : Z_1, Z_2 \in \mathcal{Z}\}$. Then $H_{\Delta_{opt}}$ is atomic. Furthermore, $\Delta_{opt} = \min\{\Delta : H_\Delta \text{ is atomic}\}$.*

Computing Δ_{opt} is a straightforward exercise of tabulating the scores for all pairs of distinct zones and taking the maximum of the scores.

4.2 Operation-count-based staleness

A different way to quantify the staleness of a read is to count how many writes intervene between the read and its dictating write. For this purpose, Aiyer et al. [1] have defined the notion of k-*atomicity*. A history is called k-*atomic* iff there exists a valid total order of the operations such that every read obtains the value of one of the k latest writes before it in the total order. By this definition, ordinary atomicity is identical to 1-atomicity. We are not aware of any algorithm, online or offline, that verifies whether a history is k-atomic,

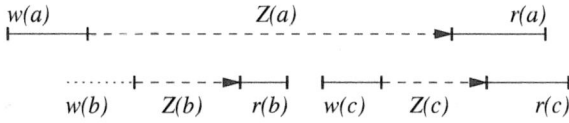

Figure 4: A history that may or may not be 2-atomic.

for $k > 1$. In this section, we present the first 2-atomicity verification algorithm (an offline algorithm), albeit it only works for a special class of histories.

Our first attempt is to extend existing 1-atomicity verification algorithms to $k > 1$, but it is not obvious to us how to do that. For example, consider the GK algorithm [14]. When $k = 2$, it is no longer sufficient to just look at the zones as in the GK algorithm. To see this, consider the history depicted in Figure 4, where the start time of $w(b)$ is left unspecified. By the GK algorithm, this history is not atomic (because there are overlapping forward zones), but whether or not it is 2-atomic depends on the start time of $w(b)$. If $w(b)$ starts after $w(a)$ finishes, then the history is not 2-atomic, because $w(a)$ is separated from $r(a)$ by $w(b)$ and $w(c)$. However, if $w(b)$ starts before $w(a)$ finishes, then the history is 2-atomic, in which case the total order would be $w(b)w(a)r(b)w(c)r(a)r(c)$.

In what follows, we present an offline 2-atomicity verification algorithm for nice histories. We call a history *nice* if (1) it is simple (see Section 4.1), (2) each write has at least one dictated read, and (3) each read succeeds its dictating write. We first observe that, for these histories, we can assume without loss of generality that each write has exactly one dictated read, because otherwise, we can condense the history by keeping, for each write, the dictated read that starts last and remove the other dictated reads. If we can construct a k-atomic total order for the condensed history, then we can add back the removed reads to the total order (by adding back the removed read somewhere between its dictated write and that write's surviving dictated read) while preserving k-atomicity. On the other hand, if the condensed history is not 2-atomic, then neither is the original history. Therefore, it suffices to consider nice histories where each write has exactly one dictated read.

Given a nice history, the algorithm's overall strategy is to construct a total order by laying out the writes from right to left in the total order, generally in the order of decreasing finish times, but in the meantime being mindful about the additional constraints imposed by previously placed writes. The full algorithm is presented in Algorithm 3.

All operations start as "unpicked," and the algorithm picks the operations from the history and puts them into the total order, which is initially empty. When the algorithm starts, it picks a write $w(a)$ with the largest finish time as the rightmost write in the total order. Once it picks $w(a)$, it computes the set S, the set of unpicked reads that succeed $w(a)$ in the history. Note that those reads in S have to follow $w(a)$ in the total order, given that $w(a)$ is the next write to be laid out. The algorithm then prepends $w(a)$ and S to the total order such that all the reads in S follow $w(a)$ in the total order. Let $R = S \setminus \{r(a)\}$. If R is not empty, then it imposes additional constraints on what the next write should be, because of the 2-atomicity requirement. In particular, if $|R| > 1$, then it means that, in order to keep the 2-atomicity requirement, we have to lay out multiple writes at the next step, an obviously impossible task. Hence, the algorithm outputs *bad*. If $|R| = 1$, then the algorithm is obliged to lay out the dictating write for the lone read in R: there is no other choice. If $|R| = 0$, then the algorithm is free to pick any unpicked write and it picks the one with the largest finish time. The intuition of picking such a write is that, compared to other

---

Algorithm 3: Offline 2-atomicity verification

Input: condensed nice history H
Output: whether or not H is 2-atomic
Init: $R = S = \emptyset$; none of the operations are picked

1 **while** $\exists$ unpicked writes **do**
2   **if** $|R| > 1$ **then output** *bad*
3   **else**
4   **if** $|R| = 1$ **then**
5           $w(a) :=$ dictating write for the lone $r(a) \in R$
6   **else**
7           $w(a) :=$ unpicked write with largest finish time
8   **end**
9   **if** $\exists$ unpicked $w(b) : w(a) < w(b)$ **then**
10   **output** *bad*
11   **end**
12        $S :=$ {unpicked reads $r : w(a) < r$};
13   // $r(a)$ may or may not be in S
14   pick $w(a)$ and S, prepend them to the total order;
15   // order of reads in S is unimportant
16        $R := S \setminus \{r(a)\}$
17   **end**
18 **end**;
19 **output** *good*

---

choices, such a write forces the fewest number of reads that have to be included in S, which in turn makes the algorithm more likely to continue. The algorithm continues until all operations are picked.

5. QUANTIFYING COMMONALITY

In some sense, the staleness notion that we consider in the previous section focuses on the worst violation in a history. In this section, we consider how common violations are in a history. To this end, our first attempt is to partition the operations in a history into two classes, "good" and "bad," such that the removal of bad operations makes the remaining sub-history atomic. Then we can compute the smallest subset of bad operations and treat its size as the number of atomicity violations. However, classifying operations as good or bad is problematic because atomicity violations are not easily attributed to specific operations. Consider for example the history $w(a)w(b)r(a)$. On the one hand, $r(a)$ is bad because it returns a value other than the one most recently written. On the other hand, we can also blame $w(b)$, which completes before $r(a)$ but does not appear to take effect. Thus, of the three operations that exhibit the atomicity violation, there are two that, if removed individually, make the remaining sub-history atomic.

This example motivates a method of classifying operations as good or bad other than the one based on individual operations. To that end, we propose to group operations by their values. In the terminology of the GK algorithm [14], the set of operations that take the same value (i.e., a write plus zero or more reads) is called a *cluster*. We propose to classify entire clusters as good or bad, and compute an optimal subset of clusters whose removal makes the remaining sub-history atomic. There are two ways to define "optimal" in this context. In the unweighted formulation, each cluster is counted equally, and we try to maximize the number of clusters leftover. In the weighted formulation, we use the number of operations as the weight of a cluster, and we try to maximize the total weight of the clusters leftover. In what follows, we present a greedy algorithm for the former problem, and a dynamic programming algorithm for the latter. We note that these algorithms are not online algorithms.

Algorithm 4: Max subset of compatible clusters

Input: simple history H
Output: maximum size subset of compatible clusters in H
1   $\mathcal{C}$:= set of clusters for operations in H;
2   $\mathcal{Z}$:= set of zones corresponding to $\mathcal{C}$;
3   R := subset of clusters in $\mathcal{C}$ with backward zones;
4   **foreach** $\overrightarrow{Z(a)} \in \mathcal{Z} : (\exists \overleftarrow{Z(b)} \in \mathcal{Z} : Z(a) \not\prec Z(b))$ **do**
5 | remove $C(a)$ from $\mathcal{C}$
6   **end**;
7   R' := max compatible subset of $\mathcal{C}$ with forward zones;
8   // a standard greedy algorithm can compute R'
9   $R := R \cup R'$;
10   **output** R

Our algorithms operate on simple histories, which are defined in Section 3. Given an arbitrary history, a preprocessing stage is used to obtain simple history—any cluster containing one or more reads but no dictating write is removed, and any cluster where a read precedes its dictating write is removed. These steps are necessary in the context of algorithms that select or discard entire clusters, and they are done identically for the two algorithms we present.

5.1 The unweighted formulation

Let H be a simple history, and let $\mathcal{Z}_H$ be the set of zones corresponding to the clusters of operations in H. We call a set of zones *compatible* if no two zones in this set conflict with each other. Conflicts between pairs of zones are defined as in the GK algorithm [14], which is explained in Section 3.4. Our goal is to find a maximum-size compatible subset of $\mathcal{Z}_H$, which yields an atomic sub-history with the largest possible number of clusters. Our algorithm first picks all the backward zones, and discards any forward zones that conflict with any of the backward zones. The algorithm then selects a maximum compatible subset of the remaining forward zones. The latter sub-problem can be solved optimally using another greedy algorithm [17], which works as follows. It first sorts the remaining forward zones in increasing order of their right endpoints. It then picks the first unpicked forward zone, removes any forward zones that conflict with the forward zone just picked, and repeats until there are no more unpicked forward zones. The running time is dominated by the time needed to sort the operations and zones, and hence the algorithm can run in $O(n \log n)$ time on an n-operation history. The full algorithm is shown in Algorithm 4. The correctness of this algorithm is stated in Theorem 5.1.

THEOREM 5.1. *Given a history H, Algorithm 4 outputs a maximum size subset of clusters that form an atomic sub-history of H.*

5.2 The weighted formulation

Keeping a cluster containing only one operation sounds very different from keeping a cluster containing a hundred operations, and yet in the previous section we do not favor one choice over the other. To account for this disparity, we present a dynamic programming algorithm that identifies a subset of clusters to keep that has the maximum total number of operations. Informally, this approach approximates a solution to the more general problem of finding the smallest subset of operations that must be removed in order to make a history atomic.

Suppose there are m zones in the given history H. Define the *weight* of a zone Z, denoted by $\pi(Z)$, to be the number of operations in that zone. We order these zones in increasing order of their right endpoints and denote them by Z_1 to Z_m. (These endpoints are unique as we assume that start/finish times are unique.) Let $\Pi(i)$, where $1 \le i \le m$, denote the maximum total weight of any compatible subset of $\{Z_1, ..., Z_i\}$. We make the following observation about the connection between $\Pi(i)$ and $\Pi(i-1)$. If Z_i is a backward zone, then it is always better to keep Z_i than to discard it, because by the ordering of the zones, Z_i does not conflict with any zones in $\{Z_1, ..., Z_{i-1}\}$. Therefore, $\Pi(i) = \Pi(i-1) + \pi(Z_i)$. If Z_i is a forward zone, then the algorithm has to consider whether it is better to keep Z_i or to discard it. If the algorithm discards Z_i, then $\Pi(i) = \Pi(i-1)$. However, if the algorithm keeps Z_i, then the analysis is slightly more involved.

For any i, let $f(i)$, where $1 \le f(i) < i$, be the largest index such that $Z_{f(i)}$ precedes (hence does not conflict with) Z_i, or 0 if all zones $\{Z_1, ..., Z_{i-1}\}$ overlap with Z_i. Also let $L(i) = \{\ell : f(i) < \ell < i$ and Z_ℓ is a backward zone that does not conflict with $Z_i\}$. We observe that, if the algorithm keeps forward zone Z_i, then

$$\Pi(i) = \Pi(f(i)) + \pi(Z_i) + \sum_{\ell \in L(i)} \pi(Z_\ell).$$

Therefore, for a forward zone Z_i, the algorithm picks the max of the above quantity and $\Pi(i-1)$. The complete idea is presented in Algorithm 5. The correctness of the algorithm is stated in Theorem 5.2.

THEOREM 5.2. *Given a history H, Algorithm 5 outputs a subset of clusters with maximum total weight that form an atomic sub-history of H.*

In terms of efficiency, extracting the zones takes $O(n \log n)$ time (assuming that the operation endpoints are initially unsorted), sorting the zones takes $O(m \log m)$ time, finding $f(i)$ takes $O(\log m)$ time, and computing $L(i)$ takes $O(m)$ time. Therefore, this algorithm runs in $O(n \log n + m^2)$ time.

6. RELATED WORK

Many consistency properties have been proposed before, and we focus on a few well-known ones in this paper. Misra [23] is the first to consider what axioms a read/write register should abide by in order to provide atomic behavior, although the term atomic is not coined there. Lamport [22] first coins the term atomic; the same paper proposes safety and regularity. Herlihy and Wing [18] extend the notion to general data types and define the concept of linearizability. For read/write registers, atomicity and linearizability are equivalent definitions. Lamport [21] proposes sequential consistency.

In the literature, several notions have been proposed to allow an operation or transaction to violate stringent consistency properties, up to a certain limit [1, 20, 26, 28]. The Δ-atomicity property considered in this paper is different from those proposed before, and is motivated by the desire to have a simple number that relates a non-atomic history to a similar atomic one. Yu and Vahdat [32] propose a continuous consistency model that includes a time-based staleness concept similar in spirit to ours, but defined with respect to database replicas rather than individual operations.

To the best of our knowledge, all existing consistency verification algorithms [5, 14, 23] are offline algorithms. Misra [23] presents an elegant algorithm for verifying whether a history is atomic. Given a history, Misra's algorithm defines a "before" relation on the values (of the operations) that appear in the history as follows: (1) a before a if $r(a) < w(a)$ (i.e., a read precedes its dictating write) or there is a $r(a)$ but not $w(a)$, (2) a before b if there

Algorithm 5: Compatible clusters with max total weight

Input: simple history H
Output: subset of compatible clusters in H with maximum total number of operations

```
1  Π[0] := 0;
2  R[0] := ∅;
3  Z_{1:m} := zones in H sorted by increasing right endpoints;
4  C_{1:m} := clusters corresponding to Z_{1:m};
5  for i := 1 to m do
6  │   if Z⃗_i then
7  │   │   if (∃j : 1 ≤ j < i ∧ Z_j < Z_i) then
8  │   │   │   f := max of such j
9  │   │   else
10 │   │   │   f := 0
11 │   │   end;
12 │   │   L := {ℓ : f < ℓ < i ∧ Z⃖_ℓ ∧ Z_ℓ ∼ Z_i};
13 │   │   Π[i] := max{Π[i−1], Π[f] + π(Z_i) + Σ_{ℓ∈L} π(Z_ℓ)};
14 │   │   if Π[i] = Π[i−1] then
15 │   │   │   R[i] := R[i−1]
16 │   │   else
17 │   │   │   R[i] := R[f] ∪ {C_i} ∪ {C_l : l ∈ L}
18 │   │   end
19 │   else
20 │   │   Π[i] := Π[i−1] + π(Z_i);
21 │   │   R[i] := R[i−1] ∪ {C_i}
22 │   end
23 end;
24 output R
```

exist two operations $op(a), op'(b)$ such that $op(a) < op'(b)$, and (3) a before c if a before b and b before c. A history is atomic iff the "before" relation is irreflexive, anti-symmetric, and transitive. Misra's algorithm can also be viewed as constructing a directed graph called the *value graph*, where each vertex represents a value, and an edge $a \rightarrow b$ exists iff a at some point appears before b (i.e., there exist $op(a), op(b)$ such that $op(a) < op(b)$). Then a history is atomic iff (1) it is simple, and (2) its value graph is a DAG.

Despite the apparent dissimilarity, Misra's algorithm and the GK algorithm have an inherent connection. It is not hard to show that, in Misra's algorithm, for simple histories, if the value graph contains a cycle, then the smallest cycle is of length 2 (i.e., there exist two values a, b such that $a \rightarrow b$ and $b \rightarrow a$). Therefore, it suffices to examine, for each pair of values a, b, whether there are operations that take these two values that appear before each other. And this interpretation translates directly into the GK algorithm's approach of inspecting zone pairs (see Section 3.4). However, similar to the GK algorithm, for verifying 2-atomicity, it is insufficient to examine the value graph in Misra algorithm: it is not hard to construct two histories, one 2-atomic but the other not, that share the same value graph.

Anderson et al. [5] propose offline verification algorithms for safety, regularity, and atomicity, and test the Pahoehoe key-value store [4] using a benchmark similar to YCSB [9]. It is found that consistency violations increase with the contention of accesses to the same key, and that for benign workloads, Pahoehoe provides atomicity most of the time.

The complexity of verification has been investigated for several consistency properties [7, 14, 27]. Taylor [27] shows that verifying sequential consistency is NP-Complete. Gibbons and Korach [14] show that, in general, verifying sequential consistency

(VSC) and verifying linearizability (VL) are both NP-Complete problems. They also consider several variants of the problem and show that, for most variants, VSC remains NP-Complete yet VL admits efficient algorithms for some variants. Cantin et al. [7] show that verifying memory coherence, which is equivalent to VSC for one memory location, is still NP-Complete. However, as we discussed in Section 3.6, if write values are unique, then VSC on a single memory location is solvable easily in polynomial time.

In recent years, key-value stores such as Amazon's S3 [2] have become popular storage choices for large-scale Internet applications. According to Brewer's CAP principle [6], among consistency, availability, and partition-tolerance, only two of these three properties can be attained simultaneously. Since partition-tolerance is a must for modern Internet applications, most key-value stores favor availability over consistency. For example, Amazon's S3 [2] and Dynamo [10] only promise eventual consistency [29]. However, more recently, data consistency is becoming a more important consideration, and various key-value stores have proposed ways to provide consistency properties stronger than just eventual consistency [8, 16, 30]. Finally, sometimes data consistency is indispensable, even when an application favors availability. For example, the creation of a bucket in Amazon's S3 [2] is an atomic operation so that no two users can create two buckets of the same name. For such an operation, data consistency is critical and hence in Amazon, availability can be sacrificed if need be. Consequently, many cloud systems are starting to provide atomic primitives that applications can use to implement strong consistency.

Wada et al. [31] investigate the consistency properties provided by commercial storage systems and made several useful observations. However, the consistency properties they investigated are the client-centric properties such as read-your-write or monotonic-read, which are easy to check. In contrast, the consistency properties we consider in this paper are the data-centric ones and are stronger and harder to verify. Fekete et al. [11] investigate how often integrity violations are produced by varying degrees of isolation in database systems, but those violations are easy to verify.

On the surface, the k-atomicity verification problem is somewhat similar to the graph bandwidth problem (problem GT40 of Garey and Johnson [13]). For general graphs, if k is part of the input, then the problem is NP-Complete [12, 24], but if k is fixed, then the problem admits a polynomial-time solution [25]. However, for interval graphs, even if k is part of the input, the problem is polynomial-time solvable [19]: the 2-atomicity algorithm presented in Section 4.2 is similar in spirit to the algorithm therein.

7. CONCLUDING REMARKS

In this paper, we have addressed several problems related to the verification of consistency properties in histories of read/write register operations. In particular, we have considered how to perform consistency verification in an online manner. In addition, we have proposed several ways to quantify the severity of violations in case a history is found to contain consistency violations. We have also presented algorithms for computing those quantities. In practice, the online verification algorithms enable systems to monitor the consistency provided in real time so that corrective actions can be taken as soon as violations are detected. Quantifying the severity of violations enables customers and service providers to negotiate compensations proportional to the severity of violations. On the other hand, we have not addressed several problems in their full generality, such as the k-atomicity verification problem. We hope to address them in future work.

Acknowledgments

We are thankful to the anonymous referees for their feedback, and to Dr. Ram Swaminathan of HP Labs for his careful proofreading of this paper.

8. REFERENCES

[1] A. Aiyer, L. Alvisi, and R. A. Bazzi. One the availability of non-strict quorum systems. In *Proceedings of the 19th International Symposium on Distributed Computing (DISC)*, pages 48–62, September 2005.

[2] Amazon's Simple Storage Service. Available at http://aws.amazon.com/s3.

[3] Amazon's SimpleDB. Available at http://aws.amazon.com/simpledb.

[4] E. Anderson, X. Li, A. Merchant, M. A. Shah, K. Smathers, J. Tucek, M. Uysal, and J. J. Wylie. Efficient eventual consistency in Pahoehoe, an erasure-coded key-blob archive. In *Proceedings of the 2010 IEEE/IFIP International Conference on Dependable Systems and Networks (DSN)*, pages 181–190, January 2010.

[5] E. Anderson, X. Li, M. A. Shah, J. Tucek, and J. Wylie. What consistency does your key-value store actually provide? In *Proceedings of the Sixth Workshop on Hot Topics in System Dependability (HotDep)*, October 2010.

[6] E. Brewer. Towards robust distributed systems, 2000. Available at http://www.cs.berkeley.edu/~brewer/cs262b-2004/PODC-keynote.pdf.

[7] J. F. Cantin, M. H. Lipasti, and J. E. Smith. The complexity of verifying memory coherence and consistency. *IEEE Transactions on Parallel and Distributed Systems*, 16(7):663–671, July 2005.

[8] Cassandra. Available at http://incubator.apache.org/cassandra/.

[9] B. F. Cooper, A. Silberstein, E. Tam, R. Ramakrishnan, and R. Sears. Benchmarking cloud serving systems with YCSB. In *ACM Symposium on Cloud Computing (SoCC)*, pages 143–154, June 2010.

[10] G. DeCandia, D. Hastorun, M. Jampani, G. Kakulapati, A. Lakshman, A. Pilchin, S. Sivasubramanian, P. Vosshall, and W. Vogels. Dynamo: Amazon's highly available key-value store. In *Proceedings of the 21st ACM Symposium on Operating System Principles (SOSP)*, pages 205–220, October 2007.

[11] A. Fekete, S. N. Goldrei, and J. P. Asejo. Quantifying isolation anomalies. In *Proceedings of the 35th International Conference on Very Large Data Bases (VLDB)*, pages 467–478, August 2009.

[12] M. R. Garey, R. L. Graham, D. S. Johnson, and D. E. Knuth. Complexity results for bandwidth minimization. *SIAM Journal on Applied Mathematics*, 34(3):477–495, May 1978.

[13] M. R. Garey and D. S. Johnson. *Computers and Intractability: A Guide to the Theory of NP-Completeness*. Freeman, NY, 1979.

[14] P. Gibbons and E. Korach. Testing shared memories. *SIAM Journal on Computing*, 26:1208–1244, August 1997.

[15] W. Golab, X. Li, and M. A. Shah. Analyzing consistency properties for fun and profit. Technical Report HPL-2011-6, Hewlett-Packard Laboratories, 2011. Available at http://www.hpl.hp.com/techreports/2011/HPL-2011-6.pdf.

[16] Google Storage for Developers. Available at http://code.google.com/apis/storage.

[17] U. I. Gupta, D. T. Lee, and J. Y.-T. Leung. Efficient algorithms for interval graphs and circular-arc graphs. *Networks*, 12:459–467, Winter 1982.

[18] M. Herlihy and J. M. Wing. Linearizability: A correctness condition for concurrent objects. *ACM Transactions on Programming Languages and Systems*, 12(3):463–492, July 1990.

[19] D. J. Kleitman and R. V. Vohra. Computing the bandwidth of interval graphs. *SIAM Journal on Discrete Mathematics*, 3(3):373–375, August 1990.

[20] N. Krishnakumar and A. J. Bernstein. Bounded ignorance in replicated systems. In *Proceedings of the Tenth ACM Symposium on Principles of Database Systems (PODS)*, pages 63–74, May 1991.

[21] L. Lamport. How to make a multiprocessor computer that correctly executes multiprocess programs. *IEEE Transactions on Computers*, C-28(9):690–691, September 1979.

[22] L. Lamport. On interprocess communication, Part I: Basic formalism and Part II: Algorithms. *Distributed Computing*, 1(2):77–101, June 1986.

[23] J. Misra. Axioms for memory access in asynchronous hardware systems. *ACM Transactions on Programming Languages and Systems*, 8(1):142–153, January 1986.

[24] C. H. Papadimitriou. The NP-completeness of the bandwidth minimization problem. *Computing*, 16(3):263–270, September 1976.

[25] J. Saxe. Dynamic-programming algorithms for recognizing small-bandwidth graphs in polynomial time. *SIAM Journal on Algebraic and Discrete Methods*, 1(4):363–369, December 1980.

[26] A. Singla, U. Ramachandran, and J. Hodgins. Temporal notions of synchronization and consistency in Beehive. In *Proceedings of the Ninth ACM Symposium on Parallel Algorithms and Architectures (SPAA)*, pages 211–220, June 1997.

[27] R. N. Taylor. Complexity of analyzing the synchronization structure of concurrent progreams. *Acta Informatica*, 19(1):57–84, April 1983.

[28] F. J. Torres-Rojas, M. Ahamad, and M. Raynal. Timed consistency for shared distributed objects. In *Proceedings of the 18th ACM Symposium on Principles of Distributed Computing (PODC)*, pages 163–172, May 1999.

[29] W. Vogels. Eventually consistent. *Communications of the ACM*, 52(1):40–44, January 2009.

[30] Voldemort. Available at http://project-voldemort.com/.

[31] H. Wada, A. Fekete, L. Zhao, K. Lee, and A. Liu. Data consistency properties and the trade-offs in commercial cloud storages: the consumers' perspective. In *Proceedings of the Fifth Biennial Conference on Innovative Data Systems Research (CIDR)*, January 2011.

[32] H. Yu and A. Vahdat. Design and evaluation of a conit-based continuous consistency model for replicated services. *ACM Transactions on Computer Systems*, 20(3):239–282, August 2002.

Brief Announcement: Distributed k–Core Decomposition[*]

Alberto Montresor
DISI - University of Trento
via Sommarive 14
IT – 38123
Povo, Trento, Italy
alberto.montresor@unitn.it

Francesco De Pellegrini
CREATE-NET
via Alla Cascata 56/D
IT – 38123
Povo, Trento, Italy
fdepellegrini@create-net.org

Daniele Miorandi
CREATE-NET
via Alla Cascata 56/D
IT – 38123
Povo, Trento, Italy
dmiorandi@create-net.org

Categories and Subject Descriptors

C.2.4 [**Computer-Communication Networks**]: Distributed Systems; F.2.2 [**Analysis of Algorithms and Problem Complexity**]: Nonnumerical Algorithms and Problems

General Terms

Algorithms, Design

Introduction

In the last few years, a number of metrics and methods have been introduced for studying the relative "importance" of nodes within complex network structures [6]. Among these metrics, k-core decomposition is a well-established method for identifying particular subsets of the graph called k-cores, or k-shells [7]. Informally, a k-core is obtained by recursively removing all nodes of degree smaller than k, until the degree of all remaining vertices is larger than or equal to k. Nodes are said to have coreness k (or, equivalently, to belong to the k-shell) if they belong to the k-core but not to the $(k + 1)$-core. We consider an undirected graph $G = (V, E)$ with $N = |V|$ nodes and $M = |E|$ edges. We denote by $d_G(u)$ the degree of node u within G, and by $k(u)$ its coreness index.

DEFINITION 1. *A subgraph $G(C)$ induced by the set $C \subseteq V$ is a k-core if and only if $\forall u \in C : d_{G(C)}(u) \geq k$, and $G(C)$ is the maximum subgraph with this property.*

k-core decomposition has found a number of applications; for example, it has been used to characterize social networks [7], to help in the visualization of complex graphs [1], to determine the role of proteins in complex proteinomic networks [2], and finally to identify nodes with good "spreading" properties in epidemiological studies [4].

Efficient centralized algorithms for the k-core decomposition already exist [3]. Here, we consider the distributed version of this problem, motivated by the following scenarios. *One Host, one Node Scenario*: The graph to be analyzed could be a "live" distributed system, such as a P2P overlay, that needs to inspect itself; *one* host is also *one* node in the graph, and connections among hosts are the edges. This information could be used at run-time to optimize the

[*]This work is supported by the Autonomous Security project, financed by MIUR Programme PRIN 2008.

diffusion of messages in epidemic protocols [4].

One Host, Multiple Nodes Scenario: The graph could be so large to not fit into a single host, due to memory restrictions; or its description could be inherently distributed over a collection of hosts, making it inconvenient to move each portion to a central site. So, *one* host stores *many* nodes and their edges.

The two scenarios turn out to be related: the former can be seen as a special case of the "inherent distribution" of the latter taken to its extreme consequences, with each host storing only one node and its edges.

Main Results

The main result of our work is the definition of a distributed algorithm able to efficiently compute the coreness index for the *one host, one node* and *one host, multiple nodes* cases.

Our distributed algorithm is based on the property of locality of the k-core decomposition: due to the maximality of cores, the coreness of node u is the largest value k such that u has at least k neighbors that belong to a k-core or a larger core. More formally,

THEOREM 1 (LOCALITY). *For each $u \in V$, $k(u) = k$ iff*

(i) *there exist a subset V_k of the neighbours of u such that $|V_k| = k$ and $\forall v \in V_k : k(v) \geq k$;*

(ii) *there is no subset V_{k+1} of the neighbours of u such that $|V_{k+1}| = k + 1$ and $\forall v \in V_{k+1} : k(v) \geq k + 1$.*

The locality property tells us that the information about the coreness of the neighbors of a node is sufficient to compute its own coreness. Our algorithm works as follows. Each node produces an *estimate* of its own coreness and communicates it to its neighbors. The initial estimate is set equal to the node degree. Each nodes receives estimates from its neighbors and uses them to recompute its own estimate. In the case of a change, the new value is sent to the neighbors and the process goes on until convergence. The complete algorithm, together with optimizations, is reported in [5].

The procedure can be easily generalized to the case where a host x is responsible for a collection of nodes $V(x)$. In this case, x runs the algorithm on behalf of its nodes, storing the estimates for all of them and sending messages to the hosts that are responsible for their neighbors. The algorithm can be optimized by having each node x, upon reception of a message for a node $u \in V(x)$, to "internally emulate" the estimation update protocol. The estimates received from outside can indeed generate new estimates for some of the

Name	$|V|$	$|E|$	⌀	d_{max}	k_{max}	k_{avg}	t_{avg}	t_{min}	t_{max}	m_{avg}	m_{max}
1) CA-AstroPh	18 772	198 110	14	504	56	12.62	19.55	18	21	47.21	807
2) CA-CondMat	23 133	93 497	15	280	25	4.90	15.65	14	17	13.97	410
3) p2p-Gnutella31	62 590	147 895	11	95	6	2.52	27.45	25	30	9.30	131
4) soc-sign-Slashdot090221	82 145	500 485	11	2 553	54	6.22	25.10	24	26	29.32	3 192
5) soc-Slashdot0902	82 173	582 537	12	2 548	56	7.22	21.15	20	22	31.35	3 319
6) Amazon0601	403 399	2 443 412	21	2 752	10	7.22	55.65	53	59	24.91	2 900
7) web-BerkStan	685 235	6 649 474	669	84 230	201	11.11	306.15	294	322	29.04	86 293
8) roadNet-TX	1 379 922	1 921 664	1049	12	3	1.79	98.60	94	103	4.45	19
9) wiki-Talk	2 394 390	4 659 569	9	100 029	131	1.96	31.60	30	33	5.89	103 895

Table 1: Results with the one-to-one algorithm. Name of the data set, number of nodes, number of edges, diameter, maximum degree, maximum coreness, average coreness, average-minimum-maximum number of cycles to complete, average/maximum number of messages sent per node.

nodes in $V(x)$; in turn, these can generate other estimates, again in $V(x)$; and so on, until no new internal estimate is generated and the nodes in $V(x)$ become quiescent. At that point, all the new estimates that have been produced by this process are sent to the neighboring hosts, where they can ignite these cascading changes all over again. Such an optimization proved to reduce consistently the number of messages sent. The algorithm can be proved to be correct and to eventually terminate [5].

THEOREM 2 (SAFETY). *During the execution, the local estimate of coreness index at each node is always larger or equal than the real coreness index.*

By induction, we can prove that the algorithm eventually converges to the exact value.

THEOREM 3 (LIVENESS). *There is a time after which the local estimate of the coreness index is always equal to the real coreness index.*

Both centralized termination mechanisms as well as distributed ones can be introduced. As shown in [5], most of real-world graphs can be completed in a very small number of rounds (few tens); if an approximate k-core decomposition could be sufficient, running the protocol for a fixed number of rounds is also an option. The next results provide bounds on the execution time, i.e., the time it takes for the distributed algorithm to converge to the exact value and become quiescent. The proofs are again in [5].

THEOREM 4. *Given a graph $G = (V, E)$, the execution time is bounded by* $1 + \sum_{u \in V} [d(u) - k(u)]$.

A bound on the execution time that depends only on the graph size (and not on the knowledge of the actual coreness index of nodes) can be introduced.

THEOREM 5. *The execution time is not larger than N.*

The result can be slightly improved as:

COROLLARY 1. *Let K be the number of nodes with minimal degree in G. Then the execution time on G is not larger than $N - K + 1$ rounds.*

While one may intuitively associate the execution time of the algorithm to the diameter of the network, this turns out not to be always the case. In [5] we identified a class of graphs with constant diameter 3 having execution time equal to $N - 1$.

We have also analysed the message complexity of the proposed algorithm, leading to the following result:

COROLLARY 2. *Given a graph $G = (V, E)$, the message complexity is bounded by $\left[\sum_{v \in V(G)} d^2(v) \right] - 2M$, where Δ is the largest degree of nodes in the graph.*

Based on such result, the message complexity of the distributed k-core computation results $O(\Delta \cdot M)$.

Outlook

The *one host, one node* scenario is relevant for optimizing diffusion of messages in unstructured P2P systems. The *one host, multiple nodes* scenario may lend itself to a number of applications related to the analysis of massive-scale networks. The next step is the implementation and optimization of the proposed techniques in frameworks like Hadoop [8].

References

[1] ALVAREZ-HAMELIN, J. I., BARRAT, A., AND VESPIGNANI, A. Large scale networks fingerprinting and visualization using the k-core decomposition. In *Proc. of NIPS* (2005), vol. 18, MIT Press, pp. 41–50.

[2] BADER, G., AND HOGUE, C. Analyzing yeast protein–protein interaction data obtained from different sources. *Nature biotechnology 20*, 10 (2002), 991–997.

[3] BATAGELJ, V., AND ZAVERSNIK, M. An $O(m)$ algorithm for cores decomposition of networks. *CoRR cs.DS/0310049* (2003). http://arxiv.org/abs/cs.DS/0310049.

[4] KITSAK, M., GALLOS, L. K., HAVLIN, S., LILJEROS, F., MUCHNIK, L., STANLEY, H. E., AND MAKSE, H. A. Identification of influential spreaders in complex networks. *Nature Physics 6* (Nov. 2010), 888–893.

[5] MONTRESOR, A., DE PELLEGRINI, F., AND MIORANDI, D. Distributed k-core decomposition. *CoRR cs.OH/1103.5320* (2011). http://arxiv.org/pdf/1103.5320v2.

[6] NEWMAN, M. The structure and function of complex networks. *SIAM Review 45* (2003), 167–256.

[7] SEIDMAN, S. Network structure and minimum degree. *Social Networks 5*, 3 (1983), 269–287.

[8] WHITE, T. *Hadoop: The definitive guide (2nd ed.).* Yahoo Press, 2010.

Brief Announcement:
Fork-Consistent Constructions From Registers*

Matthias Majuntke, Dan Dobre, and Neeraj Suri
Technische Universität Darmstadt, DEEDS Group
Hochschulstraße 10
64289 Darmstadt, Germany
{majuntke,dan,suri}@cs.tu-darmstadt.de

ABSTRACT

So far, all implementations providing fork-consistent semantics are based on objects with read-modify-write capabilities (also termed *servers*). We propose constructions of fork-consistent shared objects from single-writer multiple-reader (SWMR) read/write base *registers*, that are strictly weaker than servers. Our shared object constructions provide linearizability if all base registers behave correctly, and gracefully degrade to either fork-linearizability or weak fork-linearizability if any number of registers fails Byzantine. We make the following contributions: (a) A fork-linearizable construction of a universal type where operations are allowed to abort under concurrency, and (b) a weak fork-linearizable implementation of a shared memory that ensures wait-freedom when the registers are correct.

Categories and Subject Descriptors

H.3.4 [**Information Systems**]: Information Storage and Retrieval—*Systems and Software*; C.2.4 [**Computer Systems Organization**]: Computer-Communication Networks—*Distributed Systems*

General Terms

Theory

1. INTRODUCTION

In the context of storage and services "in the cloud", fork-consistency is a key property to ensure that the only harm an untrusted, maliciously behaving service provider can do is to *fork* the views of the clients to the system. Intuitively, fork-consistency guarantees that after the views of two clients are forked, they will subsequently never see each other's updates to the system — hence, the malicious behavior becomes easily detectable for the clients.

Currently, all existing fork-consistent solutions are implemented on top of servers (i.e. universal read-modify-write objects) even if implementing only weaker read/write semantics [7, 2]. In this paper we raise the question if fork-consistent protocols can be constructed only from *registers*

---

*Research funded in part by DFG GRK 1362 (TUD GKmM) and LOEWE CASED.

providing the same properties as their counterparts implemented using *servers*. This question can be answered in the affirmative which is surprising given that servers are strictly stronger than registers according to Herlihy's hierarchy [4].

Our constructions guarantee linearizability [5] in the fault-free case, and *gracefully degrade* to either fork-linearizability or weak fork-linearizability in the presence of faults: *Fork-linearizability* [7, 2] is the strongest fork-consistent property, ensuring linearizability of the history seen by each client and that two clients, once forked will never again see any operation of the other one (i.e. they share the same history prefix up to the forking point). It has been found [2] that while providing fork-linearizability, it is not possible to ensure wait-free operations — the strongest possible liveness condition — in case the service is correct. Consequently, in all solutions implementing fork-linearizability client operations either block [7, 2] or are abortable (obstruction-free) [6]. As a first contribution, we propose a fork-linearizable construction of a universal object only from registers, where operations of the universal object are allowed to *abort* under concurrency. Note that a wait-free, register-based construction of a universal object is impossible in an asynchronous system. As the strongest existing universal type construction from registers allows *abortable* operations [1], our results imply that extending such a construction by fork-linearizability can be achieved without additional assumptions.

Weak fork-linearizability is the strongest fork-consistent property that allows wait-free operations. It weakens fork-linearizability in two ways: the last operation of each client is allowed to violate the real-time order of operations (weak real-time order), and two clients after being forked may see a single operation of each other (at-most-one-join property). As our second contribution, we show how to built a weak fork-linearizable shared memory from registers where operations are wait-free when the base registers behave correctly. Our construction demonstrates that for this task registers instead of servers are sufficient.

2. FORK-CONSISTENT TYPES

2.1 Fork-linearizable Universal Type

In this section we present our first contribution of the process to implement a shared object of universal type from atomic registers. The shared object ensures fork-linearizability in the presence of any number of faulty base registers. The high-level operations of the implemented object are *abortable* [1], i.e. under concurrency, an operation may return the special response ABORT.

Intuitively, our approach combines the INC&READ counter object from the abortable universal type construction of Aguilera *et al.* [1] with the mechanisms that ensure fork-consistency in the bare-bones protocol of Mazières and Shasha [7]. This INC& READ counter C provides the operations INC&READ(C) and READ(C). A call to INC&READ(C) advances the counter object C and returns a value which is higher than any value returned before the invocation of INC&READ(C). An invocation to READ(C) returns the current value of the counter object. To implement a universal type, we use n SWMR registers to store the states of the universal object. To implement high-level operations, the client reads from the register which holds the most current state, then it applies the according state transformation, and finally writes the new state into its private register.

We allow operations to abort under concurrency for two reasons: there is no wait-free construction of a universal type from registers [4], and no fork-linearizable protocol can be wait-free in all executions [2]. The latter impossibility stems from the fact that a READ[1] operation may not distinguish whether it cannot read a value v because v is concurrently written, or because v has been previously written and is hidden by the malicious registers. Thus, our protocol implements a concurrency detection mechanism using the INC&READ counter, and if concurrency is detected, the corresponding operation is aborted. At the invocation of a high-level operation op, INC&READ(C) is called; at the end of op, READ(C) is executed and the returned timestamps are compared: If it was changed, another operation op' was invoked during op, and op is aborted.

Our algorithm uses timestamp vectors, called *versions*, whose order reflects causality and the real-time order in which operations are applied to the shared object. The idea is that each operation reads the most recent version from the storage, increments its own entry and writes the new version back to the storage. Thereby, each operation checks, if the version it reads, causally depends on the version of its own last successful operation, i.e. one which was not aborted. If the last successful operation of client C_i is hidden from C_j (as the registers may be Byzantine), then C_i does not accept operations of C_j as they do *not* causally depend on the last successful operation of C_i. This ensures that the views of the clients after a successful forking attack are not rejoined and the forking can be detected.

2.2 Weak Fork-Linearizable Shared Memory

This section describes our second contribution of a wait-free construction implementing a shared memory object from atomic registers. The presented construction satisfies weak fork-linearizability in the presence of any number of faulty base objects. The implemented shared memory object provides n atomic registers, such that each client can write to one dedicated register exclusively and may read from all. Our algorithm makes use of an atomic single-writer snapshot object S with n components [3], implemented only from registers, that provides two atomic operations: UPDATE(d, S, i), that changes the state of component i of S to d, and SCAN(S) that returns vector $(d_1, \ldots, d_n)$ such that d_i is the state of component i of S, $i = 1 \ldots, n$.

Each client locally maintains a timestamp that respects causality as well as real-time order of its own operations. The basic idea for both high-level READ and WRITE opera-

tions is that (1) a timestamp (timestamp plus value respectively) is written, and (2) the timestamps of other operations are read. Thereby, READ operations use the UPDATE primitive of the snapshot object S to write their current timestamp while WRITE operations read timestamps using operation SCAN.

Whenever high-level READ operation r of C_i and WRITE(v) operation w of C_j appear in an execution of the algorithm such that operation r does not read v but an earlier value, then, by the properties of atomic registers, $w.write$[2] cannot precede $r.read$. This means, that $r.read$ is invoked *before* $w.write$ finishes. Consequently, r.UPDATE precedes w.SCAN, i.e. if r does not "see" w, then w "sees" r. Thus, we can require that client C_j writes this information with its next WRITE such that C_i may check in the future whether operation w actually has seen operation r. More concrete, during a READ operation a client performs the following check: if READ r has seen WRITE w then, WRITE $w + 1$ must have seen READ operation r or a newer one. Else, the base objects are corrupted.

3. CONCLUSIONS

We have shown, as a first known result, that fork-consistent semantics can be implemented using registers only. So far, all existing implementations are based on servers (read-modify-write objects). Our first protocol implies that fork-linearizability may be "added" to universal type constructions from registers without making additional assumptions. Our second protocol implements a shared memory object that ensures *weak* fork-linearizability and where operations are wait-free as long as the base registers behave correctly. Weak fork-linearizability is the strongest known fork-consistency property that may be implemented in a wait-free manner. Although it weakens fork-linearizability it is of practical relevance. Moreover, our second algorithm shows for the first time that registers are sufficient to implement a fork-consistent shared memory.

4. REFERENCES

[1] M. K. Aguilera, S. Frolund, V. Hadzilacos, S. L. Horn, and S. Toueg. Abortable and Query-Abortable Objects and Their Efficient Implementation. In *PODC*, New York, NY, USA, 2007. ACM.

[2] C. Cachin, A. Shelat, and A. Shraer. Efficient Fork-Linearizable Access to Untrusted Shared Memory. In *PODC*, New York, NY, USA, 2007. ACM.

[3] F. E. Fich. How Hard Is It to Take a Snapshot? In *SOFSEM*, Berlin, Heidelberg, 2005. Springer-Verlag.

[4] M. Herlihy. Wait-Free Synchronization. *ACM Trans. Program. Lang. Syst.*, 13(1), 1991.

[5] M. P. Herlihy and J. M. Wing. Linearizability: A Correctness Condition for Concurrent Objects. *ACM Trans. Program. Lang. Syst.*, 12(3), 1990.

[6] M. Majuntke, D. Dobre, M. Serafini, and N. Suri. Abortable Fork-Linearizable Storage. In *OPODIS*, Berlin, Heidelberg, 2009. Springer-Verlag.

[7] D. Mazières and D. Shasha. Building Secure File Systems out of Byzantine Storage. In *PODC*, New York, NY, USA, 2002. ACM.

---

[1]We type high-level operations in CAPITALS.

[2]The notation $x.y$ denotes the call of low-level operation y during high-level operation x.

Brief Announcement: Unbounded Contention Resolution in Multiple-Access Channels *

Antonio Fernández Anta
Institute IMDEA Networks
Madrid, Spain
antonio.fernandez@imdea.org

Miguel A. Mosteiro
Dept. of Computer Science,
Rutgers University
Piscataway, NJ, USA
and LADyR, GSyC,
Universidad Rey Juan Carlos
Madrid, Spain
mosteiro@cs.rutgers.edu

Jorge R. Muñoz
LADyR, GSyC, Universidad
Rey Juan Carlos
Madrid, Spain
jorge.ramon@madrimasd.net

ABSTRACT

Recent work on shared-resource contention resolution has yielded fruitful results for local area networks and radio networks, although either the solution is suboptimal [2] or a (possibly loose) upper bound on the number of users needs to be known [5]. In this work, we present the first (two) protocols for contention resolution in radio networks that are asymptotically optimal (with high probability), work without collision detection, and do not require information about the number of contenders. In addition to the theoretical analysis, the protocols are evaluated and contrasted with the previous work by extensive simulations.

ACM Classification Keywords: C.2.1 [Network Architecture and Design] : Wireless communication.

General Terms: Algorithms, Theory.

Keywords: Radio Networks, Contention Resolution, Selection.

1. INTRODUCTION

The topic of this work is the resolution of contention in settings where an unknown number of users must access a single shared resource, but multiple simultaneous accesses are not feasible. The scope of interest in this problem is wide, ranging from radio and local area networks to databases and transactional memory. (See [2] and the references therein.)

A common theme in protocols used for this problem is the adaptive adjustment of some user variable that reflects its eagerness in trying to access the shared resource. Examples of such variable are the probability of transmitting a message in a radio network or the frequency of packet transmission in a local area network. When such adjustment reduces (resp. increases) the contention, the technique is called *back-off* (resp. *back-on*). Combination of both methods are called *back-on/back-off*. Protocols used may be further characterized by the rate of adjustment. E.g., *exponential back-off*, *polynomial back-on*, etc. In particular, exponential back-off is widely used and it has proven to be efficient in practi-

cal applications where statistical arrival of contenders is expected. Nevertheless, worst case arrival patterns, such as bursty or *batched* arrivals, are frequent [7,9].

A technique called *loglog-iterated back-off (LLIBO)* was shown to be within a sublogarithmic factor from optimal with high probability in [2]. The protocol was presented in the context of packet contention resolution in local area networks for batched arrivals. Later on, also for batched arrivals, we presented a back-on/back-off protocol in [5], instantiated in the *k*-selection problem in Radio Networks. The latter protocol, named here *log-fails adaptive (LFA)*, is asymptotically optimal for any significant probability of error, but additionally requires that some upper bound (possibly loose) on the number of contenders is known. In the present work, we remove such requirement. In particular, we present and analyze two protocols, both of interest, that we call *one-fail adaptive (OFA)* and *exponential back-off/back-on (EBOBO)* for *k*-selection in Radio Networks. These protocols resolve contention among an unknown and unbounded number of contenders with high probability in optimal time up to constants. Additionally, by means of simulations, we evaluate and contrast the average performance of all four protocols. The simulations show that the complexity bounds obtained in the analysis (with high probability) for the protocols presented are rather tight. Additionally, they show that they are faster that LLIBO and more predictable for all network sizes than LFA.

The Model: We consider a Radio Network comprised of *n* stations called *nodes*. Each node is assumed to be potentially reachable from any other node in one communication step, hence, the network is characterized as *single-hop* or *one-hop* indistinctively. Before running the protocol, nodes have no information, not even the number of nodes *n* or their own label. Time is supposed to be slotted in *communication steps*. Assuming that the computation time-cost is negligible in comparison with the communication time-cost, time efficiency is studied in terms of communication steps only. The piece of information assigned to a node in order to deliver it to other nodes is called a *message*. The assignment of a message is due to an external agent and such an event is called a *message arrival*. Communication among nodes is carried out by means of radio broadcast on a shared channel. If exactly one node transmits at a communication step, such a transmission is called *successful* or *non-colliding*, we say that the message was *delivered*, and all other nodes *receive*

---

*A full version of this work is available at [6]. This research was partially supported by Spanish MICINN grant no. TIN2008-06735-C02-01, Comunidad de Madrid grant no. S2009TIC-1692, and NSF grant no. 0937829.

such a message. If more than one message is transmitted at the same time, a *collision* occurs, the messages are garbled, and nodes only receive *interference noise*. If no message is transmitted in a communication step, nodes receive only *background noise*. In this work, nodes can not distinguish between interference noise and background noise, thus, the channel is called *without collision detection*. Each node is in one of two states, *active* if it holds a message to deliver, or *idle* otherwise. As in [1,2,8], we assume that a node becomes idle upon delivering its message. For settings where the channel does not provide such functionality (e.g., a base station acknowledgement), such as Sensor Networks, a hierarchical infrastructure may be predefined to achieve it [4].

The Problem: One of the problems that require contention resolution in Radio Networks is the problem known in the literature as *all-broadcast* [3], or *k-selection* [8]. In k-selection, a set of k out of n network nodes have to access a unique shared channel of communication, each of them at least once. As in [2,8], in this work we study k-selection when all messages arrive simultaneously, or in a *batch*. Under this assumption the k-selection problem is called *static*. A *dynamic* counterpart where messages arrive at different times was also studied [8].

Related Work: A randomized adaptive protocol for static k-selection in a one-hop Radio Network without collision detection was presented in [5]. The protocol is shown to solve the problem in $(e + 1 + \xi)k + O(\log^2(1/\varepsilon))$ steps with probability at least $1 - 2\varepsilon$, where $\xi > 0$ is an arbitrarily small constant and $0 < \varepsilon \leq 1/(n+1)$. Modulo a constant factor, the protocol is optimal if $\varepsilon \in \Omega(2^{-\sqrt{n}})$. However, the algorithm makes use of the value of ε, which must be upper bounded as above in order to guarantee the running time. Therefore, knowledge of n is required. Monotonic back-off strategies for contention resolution of batched arrivals of k packets on simple multiple access channels, a problem that can be seen as static k-selection, have been analyzed in [2]. In that paper, it is shown that *r-exponential back-off*, a monotonic technique used widely that has proven to be efficient for many practical applications is in $\Theta(k \log^{\log_2 r} k)$ for batched arrivals. The best strategy shown in the same paper is the so-called *loglog-iterated back-off* with a makespan in $\Theta(k \log \log k / \log \log \log k)$ with probability at least $1 - 1/k^c, c > 0$, which does not use any knowledge of k or n.

2. CONTRIBUTIONS

In this work, we present the first randomized protocols for static k-selection in a one-hop Radio Network that are asymptotically optimal (with high probability), work without collision detection, and do not require information about the number of contenders. As mentioned, these protocols are called EBOBO and OFA. EBOBO is shown to solve static k-selection within $4(1 + 1/\delta)k$ steps with probability at least $1 - 1/k^c$ for some constant $c > 0$, $0 < \delta < 1/e$, and big enough k. On the other hand, it is proved that OFA solves static k-selection within $2(\delta + 1)k + O(\log^2 k)$ steps, with probability at least $1 - 2/(1 + k)$, for $e < \delta \leq \sum_{j=1}^{5}(5/6)^j$. Given that k is a lower bound for this problem, both protocols are optimal (modulo a small constant factor). Protocol EBOBO is simpler, but OFA achieves a better multiplicative factor, although the constant in the sublinear additive factor may be big for small values of k.

Additionally, results of the evaluation by simulation of the average behavior of OFA and EBOBO and a comparison with LFA and LLIBO are presented. Both algorithms OFA and EBOBO run faster than LLIBO on average, even for small values of k. Although LLIBO has higher asymptotic complexity, one may have expected that it may run fast for small networks. On the other hand, the knowledge on a bound of k assumed by LFA seems to provide an edge with respect to OFA and EBOBO for large values of k. However, LFA has a much worse behavior than the proposed protocols for small to moderate network sizes ($k \leq 10^5$). In any case, for all values of k simulated, OFA and EBOBO have a very stable and efficient behavior.

EBOBO is a non-adaptive protocol based on contention windows. The size of those windows is (iteratively and multiplicatively) increased in each round and decreased in each sub-round. On the other hand, OFA is an adaptive protocol where the probability of transmission of each node is adjusted in each step according to the success in achieving communication by any other node in the previous step. Further details of the protocols, the analysis, and the simulations can be found in [6]. The stability of monotonic strategies, such as exponential back-off, has been studied in [2]. In light of the improvements obtained in the present work for batched arrivals, the application of non-monotonic strategies to the dynamic problem is promising and left for future work.

3. REFERENCES

[1] Ali Balador, Ali Movaghar, and Sam Jabbehdari. History based contention window control in ieee 802.11 mac protocol in error prone channel. *Journal of Computer Science*, 6:205–209, 2010.

[2] Michael A. Bender, Martín Farach-Colton, Simai He, Bradley C. Kuszmaul, and Charles E. Leiserson. Adversarial contention resolution for simple channels. In *17th Ann. ACM Symp. on Parallel Algorithms and Architectures*, pages 325–332, 2005.

[3] B. S. Chlebus. Randomized communication in radio networks. In P. M. Pardalos, S. Rajasekaran, J. H. Reif, and J. D. P. Rolim, editors, *Handbook on Randomized Computing*, volume 1, pages 401–456. Kluwer Academic Publishers, 2001.

[4] M. Farach-Colton and M. A. Mosteiro. Sensor network gossiping or how to break the broadcast lower bound. In *Proc. of the 18th Intl. Symp. on Algorithms and Computation*, volume 4835 of *Lecture Notes in Computer Science*, pages 232–243, 2007.

[5] A. Fernández Anta and M. A. Mosteiro. Contention resolution in multiple-access channels: k-selection in radio networks. *Discrete Mathematics, Algorithms and Applications*, 2(4):445–456, 2010.

[6] Antonio Fernández Anta, Miguel A. Mosteiro, and Jorge Ramón Muñoz. Unbounded contention resolution in multiple-access channels. Technical Report TR-IMDEA-Networks-2011-1, Institute IMDEA Networks, March 2011.

[7] R. Gusella. A measurement study of diskless workstation traffic on an ethernet. *IEEE Transactions on Communications*, 38(9):1557 –1568, 1990.

[8] D. R. Kowalski. On selection problem in radio networks. In *Proc. 24th Ann. ACM Symp. on Principles of Distributed Computing*, pages 158–166, 2005.

[9] Will E. Leland, Murad S. Taqqu, Walter Willinger, and Daniel V. Wilson. On the self-similar nature of ethernet traffic (extended version). *IEEE/ACM Transactions on Networking*, 2:1–15, 1994.

Brief Announcement: Tracking Distributed Aggregates over Time-based Sliding Windows

Graham Cormode
AT&T Labs–Research
Florham Park, NJ, USA
graham@research.att.com

Ke Yi
Hong Kong University of Science and Technology
Hong Kong, PRC
yike@cse.ust.hk

ABSTRACT

The area of distributed monitoring requires tracking the value of a function of distributed data as new observations are made. An important case is when attention is restricted to only a recent time period, such as the last hour of readings—the sliding window case. In this announcement, we outline a novel paradigm for handling such monitoring problems, which we dub the "forward/backward" approach. This provides clean solutions for several fundamental problems, such as counting, tracking frequent items, and maintaining order statistics. We obtain efficient protocols for these problems that improve on previous work, and are easy to implement. Specifically, we obtain optimal $O(\frac{k}{\varepsilon} \log(\varepsilon n/k))$ communication per window of n updates for tracking counts and heavy hitters with accuracy ε across k sites; and near-optimal communication of $O(\frac{k}{\varepsilon} \log^2(1/\varepsilon) \log(n/k))$ for quantiles.

Categories and Subject Descriptors

F.2.2 [**Analysis of algorithms and problem complexity**]: Nonnumerical algorithms and problems

General Terms

Algorithms

Keywords

Data streams, sliding windows

1. INTRODUCTION

Problems of distributed tracking involve trying to compute various aggregates over data that is distributed across multiple observing sites. Each site observes a stream of information, and aims to collaborate with the other sites to continuously track a function over the union of the streams. For example, a number of routers in a network might try to collaborate to track the most popular destinations. The goal is to allow a single distinguished entity, known as the "coordinator", to track the desired function. Within such settings, it is natural to only want to capture the recent behavior—say, the most popular destinations within the last 24 hours. Thus, attention is limited to a "time-based sliding window".

For these problems, the primary goal is to analyze the (total) communication required to achieve accurate tracking. This should be much smaller than the trivial solution of simply centralizing all the observations at the coordinator site. In this area, prior work has tended to be network topology agnostic, and measures just the total number of bytes transmitted by the protocols. Secondary goals include minimizing the space required at each site to run the protocol, and the time to process each new observation. These quantities are functions of k, the number of distributed sites, n, the total size of the input data, and ε, an approximation parameter to tolerate some imprecision in the computed answer.

Within this context, there has been much work on the "infinite window" case, where all historic data is included. Results have been shown for monitoring functions such as counts, distinct counts, order statistics, join sizes, entropy, and others [1, 3, 5, 6, 8, 10, 13]. Lately, there has been interest in only tracking a window of recent observations, defined by all those elements which arrived within the most recent w time units. Results in this model have been shown for tracking counts and frequent items [3], and for sampling [7].

Our results are most directly related to the recent work of Chan et al. [3]. The approach taken in [3] is somewhat complicated: the analysis of the proposed protocols is quite lengthy, and requires detailed analysis of multiple cases. They consider three problems: basic counting, which is to maintain the count of items observed within the window; heavy hitters, which is to maintain all items whose frequency (within the window) is more than a given fraction; and to maintain the quantiles of the distribution. Each problem tolerates an error of ε, and is parameterized by k, the number of sites participating in the computation, and n, the number of items arriving in a window. [3] shows (per window) communication costs of $O(\frac{k}{\varepsilon} \log \frac{\varepsilon n}{k})$ bits for basic counting, $O(\frac{k}{\varepsilon} \log \frac{n}{k})$ words for frequent items and $O(\frac{k}{\varepsilon^2} \log \frac{n}{k})$ words for quantiles. Our main contributions are simple algorithms with straightforward analysis which meet and in some cases improve on these bounds. To do this, we outline a conceptually simple approach for decomposing sliding windows, which also extends naturally to other problems in this setting. We call this the "forward/backward" framework. This can be applied to tracking counts, heavy hitters and quantiles to obtain optimal or near optimal communication bounds. It also extends to other functions, such as distinct counts and geometric properties.

Problem definitions and our results. Figure 1 shows the model: k sites each observe a stream S_i of item arrivals, and communicate with a single distinguished coordinator node to continuously compute some function of the union of the update streams.

The *basic counting* problem is to track (approximately) the number of items which have arrived across all sites within the last w time units. More precisely, let the stream of items observed at site i be S_i, a set of $(x, t(x))$ pairs, which indicates that an item x arrives at time $t(x)$. Then the exact basic count at time t is given by

$$C(t) = \sum_{1 \le i \le k} |\{(x, t(x)) \in S_i \mid t - t(x) \le w\}|.$$

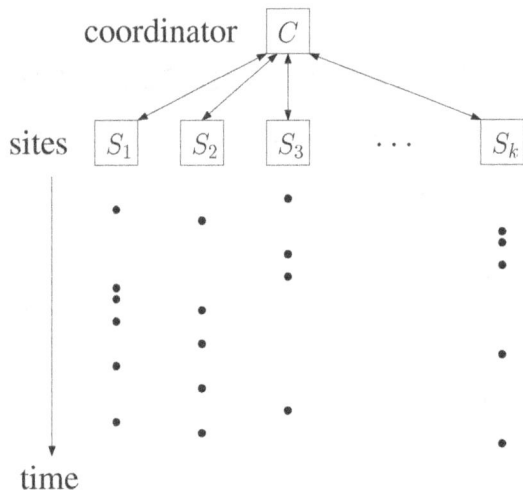

Figure 1: Schematic of the distribute streaming model

Problem	Communication Cost	Space Cost
Basic Counting	$O(\frac{k}{\varepsilon}\log(\varepsilon n/k))$ bits	$O(\frac{1}{\varepsilon}\log \varepsilon n)$
Heavy Hitters	$O(\frac{k}{\varepsilon}\log(\varepsilon n/k))$	$O(\frac{1}{\varepsilon}\log \varepsilon n)$
Quantiles	$O(\frac{k}{\varepsilon}\log^2(1/\varepsilon)\log(n/k))$	$O(\frac{1}{\varepsilon}\log^2(1/\varepsilon)\log n)$

Figure 2: Summary of Results. All bounds are in terms of words unless specified otherwise.

many functions of interest, implies monotonic behavior of the desired output also. Consequently, we obtain monitoring algorithms for these problems which are based on running simple protocols assuming an unbounded window for the "forward" (arriving) part of the data, and building data structures which allow approximate computations of the desired function on the "backward" (departing) part of the data.

A summary of our results appears in Figure 2. Here, the communication cost is measured as the total amount of communication between all k sites and the central coordinator site, as a function of n, the number of observations in each window, and ε, the approximation parameter. We also list the space required local to each site to run the protocol.

2. REFERENCES

[1] C. Arackaparambil, J. Brody, and A. Chakrabarti. Functional monitoring without monotonicity. In *ICALP*, 2009.

[2] C. Busch, S. Tirthapura, and B. Xu. Sketching asycnhronous streams over sliding windows. In *ACM PODC*, 2006.

[3] H.-L. Chan, T.-W. Lam, L.-K. Lee, and H.-F. Ting. Continuous monitoring of distributed data streams over a time-based sliding window. In *STACS*, 2010.

[4] G. Cormode and M. Garofalakis. Sketching streams through the net: Distributed approximate query tracking. In *VLDB*, 2005.

[5] G. Cormode, M. Garofalakis, S. Muthukrishnan, and R. Rastogi. Holistic aggregates in a networked world: Distributed tracking of approximate quantiles. In *ACM SIGMOD*, 2005.

[6] G. Cormode, S. Muthukrishnan, and K. Yi. Algorithms for distributed, functional monitoring. In *ACM-SIAM SODA*, 2008.

[7] G. Cormode, S. Muthukrishnan, K. Yi, and Q. Zhang. Optimal sampling from distributed streams. In *ACM PODS*, 2010.

[8] Y. Emek and A. Korman. Efficient threshold detection in a distributed environment. In *ACM PODC*, 2010.

[9] P. Gibbons and S. Tirthapura. Distributed streams algorithms for sliding windows. In *ACM SPAA*, 2002.

[10] R. Keralapura, G. Cormode, and J. Ramamirtham. Communication-efficient distributed monitoring of thresholded counts. In *ACM SIGMOD*, 2006.

[11] F. Kuhn, T. Locher, and S. Schmid. Distributed computation of the mode. In *ACM PODC*, 2008.

[12] B. Patt-Shamir. A note on efficient aggregate queries in sensor networks. In *ACM PODC*, 2004.

[13] I. Sharfman, A. Schuster, and D. Keren. A geometric approach to monitoring threshold functions over distributed data streams. In *ACM SIGMOD*, 2006.

[14] K. Yi and Q. Zhang. Optimal tracking of distributed heavy hitters and quantiles. In *ACM PODS*, 2009.

Tracking $C(t)$ exactly requires alerting the coordinator every time an item arrives or expires, so the goal is to track $C(t)$ approximately within an ε-error, i.e., the coordinator should maintain a $\tilde{C}(t)$ such that $(1-\varepsilon)C(t) \leq \tilde{C}(t) \leq (1+\varepsilon)C(t)$ at all times t.

The *heavy hitters* problem extends the basic counting problem, and generalizes the concept of finding the mode [11]. In the basic counting problem we count the total number of all items, while here we count the frequency of every distinct item x, i.e., the coordinator tracks the approximate value of

$$n_x(t) = \sum_{1 \leq i \leq k} |(x, t(x)) \in S_i \mid t - t(x) \leq w\}|.$$

Since it is possible that many $n_x(t)$ are small, say 0 or 1 for all x, requiring a multiplicative approximation for all x would require reporting all items to the coordinator. Consequently, the commonly adopted approximation guarantee for heavy hitters is to maintain a $\tilde{n}_x(t)$ that has an additive error of at most $\varepsilon C(t)$, where $C(t)$ is the total count of all items. This essentially makes sure that the "heavy" items are counted accurately while compromising on the accuracy for the less frequent items. In particular, all items x with $n_x(t) \leq \varepsilon C(t)$ can be ignored altogether as 0 is considered a good approximation for their counts. This way, at most $1/\varepsilon$ distinct items will have nonzero approximated counts.

The *quantiles* problem is to continuously maintain approximate order statistics on the distribution of the items. That is, the items are drawn from a total order, and we wish to retain a set of items $q_1, \ldots, q_{1/\varepsilon}$ such that the rank of q_i (number of input items within the sliding window that are less than q_i) is between $(i-1)\varepsilon C(t)$ and $(i+1)\varepsilon C(t)$ [12]. It is known that this is equivalent to the "prefix-count" problem, where the goal is to maintain a data structure on the sliding window such that for any given x, the number of items smaller than x can be counted within an additive error of at most $\varepsilon C(t)$.

The key insight of the forward-backward approach is that we can partition time into fixed intervals of length w, the desired window size. Now at any time, our sliding window of interests intersects two of these fixed partitions. In one of these partitions, new items are arriving only; in the other, old items are expiring only. We can consider these two windows independently, and combine approximations of each to obtain overall guarantees over the whole data. This simplifies the problem dramatically, since we now have to deal only with monotonic behavior (arrivals or departures), which, for

Brief Announcement: Accurate Byzantine Agreement with Feedback

Vijay K. Garg,[*] John Bridgman and Bharath Balasubramanian
Department of Electrical and Computer Engineering
The University of Texas at Austin
Austin, TX 78712-1084, USA
garg@ece.utexas.edu, johnfb@mail.utexas.edu, balasubr@ece.utexas.edu

ABSTRACT

The Byzantine Agreement (BA) problem requires non-faulty processes to agree on a common value. In many applications, it is important that the processes agree on the *correct* value. In this paper, we present a problem called Accurate Byzantine Agreement with Feedback (ABAF) in which all processes receive common feedback from the environment indicating if the value they agreed upon was correct or not (accuracy). We present an algorithm that solves the ABAF problem based on a standard solution to the BA problem and a multiplicative method to maintain and update process weights indicative of how often they are correct. We make guarantees on the accuracy of the algorithm based on assumptions on the accuracy of the processes and the proportion of faulty and non-faulty processes in the system. For each iteration, if the weight of accurate processes is at least $3/4^{th}$ the weight of the non-faulty processes, the algorithm always decides on the correct value. When the non-faulty processes are accurate with probability greater than $1/2$, the algorithm decides on the correct value with very high probability after some initial number of mistakes. In fact, among n processes, if there exists even *one* process which is accurate for all iterations, the algorithm is wrong only $O(\log n)$ times for any large number of iterations of the algorithm.

Categories and Subject Descriptors

H.3.4 [**Systems and Software**]: Distributed Systems

General Terms

Algorithms, Reliability, Security

Keywords

Byzantine Agreement, Multiplicative Weight Update

1. INTRODUCTION

In real-world applications, processes in a distributed system may be compromised, leading to malicious or unpredictable behavior. The Byzantine Agreement (BA) problem

[*]This research was supported in part by the NSF Grants CNS-0718990, CNS-0509024, Texas Education Board Grant 781, SRC Grant 2006-TJ-1426, and Cullen Trust for Higher Education Endowed Professorship.

[9, 7, 6, 3] requires all non-faulty processes to agree on a common value given that some of the processes may show arbitrary faulty or Byzantine behavior. In many applications, it is better for the system to agree on the correct value among the two binary values as specified by environmental feedback. We refer to this version of the BA problem as Accurate Byzantine Agreement with Feedback (ABAF). For example, suppose in a distributed control system a coordinated action needs to be taken (such as opening or closing a valve) depending upon the observations made by possibly faulty distributed processes. Depending upon the outcome of the action, the environment can provide feedback on whether the action taken was correct or not. In this paper, we give an algorithm, referred to as the ABAF algorithm that incorporates the external feedback for subsequent iterations of the algorithm. Our algorithm is based on two key components: a standard solution to the BA problem and a multiplicative weight update method. The concept of weighted majority and multiplicative weight update is used in many disciplines such as learning theory, game theory and linear programming [5, 8]. Typically, there are a set of experts and based on their views or predictions, a binary value needs to be chosen (such as the decision to buy or sell stocks in a stock market). Weights are assigned over some common distribution to these experts and a value is chosen according to the weighted majority. To improve predictions over time, the weight of each wrong expert is decreased by some constant proportion of its previous weight after every iteration. In this paper, we assume the presence of malicious Byzantine experts and apply this method to BA. We summarize our contributions in the following sections. The complete version of this paper can be found in [4].

2. ABAF PROBLEM

We consider a distributed system of processes with a completely connected topology. We assume a reliable, FIFO communication system in which there is a strict upper bound on message delivery (synchronous system). The processes may undergo Byzantine failures, i.e., fail in an arbitrary fashion; in particular, they may lie and collude with other failed processes to foil any algorithm. In the standard BA problem, all non-faulty processes must agree on a common value. The only requirement on the decided value is that it must be proposed by a non-faulty process (validity). We define the ABAF problem by replacing validity with the notion of accuracy.

Definition 1. (Accurate Byzantine Agreement with Feedback) Assume n processes, among which at most f Byzantine faults can occur such that $n \geq 3f + 1$. Each of the non-faulty processes propose either 0 or 1. An algorithm that solves the Accurate Byzantine Agreement with Feedback (ABAF) problem, must satisfy these properties:

- Agreement: All non-faulty processes decide on the same value.

- Accuracy: All non-faulty processes decide on a value that is deemed correct by the environmental feedback.

- Termination: The algorithm terminates in a finite number of rounds.

3. ABAF ALGORITHM

We propose an algorithm for the ABAF problem based on maintaining a common weight vector at all processes and updating this vector based on the feedback for each iteration. Initially, the weight of each process is a non-negative value proportional to the trust of the system on that process. If there is no prior information available, then the weights can simply be initialized to $1/n$. The algorithm has four steps. In step 1, the processes propose a value and exchange this value with each other to populate a vector V of all inputs. In step 2, a standard BA algorithm [1, 2] is used to ensure that each non-faulty process agrees on all the values in V. In step 3, processes determine the sum of weights of all processes that support value 0 or 1 in V. The value with the weighted majority is decided upon. Finally, in step 4, processes receive the common feedback from the environment to determine the correct value. If the value decided was incorrect, then the weights of the processes that proposed an incorrect value is reduced by a constant proportion ϵ ($0 < \epsilon < 1$) of its previous weight (multiplicative update). We show in [4] that this algorithm guarantees agreement and termination. We summarize the accuracy results in the following section.

4. ACCURACY GUARANTEES

We make guarantees on the accuracy of the ABAF algorithm based on the accuracy of the processes in the system and the proportion of faulty and non-faulty processes. A process is called accurate for an iteration if it proposes the correct value for that particular iteration of the ABAF algorithm. We define fault ratio (r), to be the ratio of the total weight of the faulty processes to that of the non-faulty processes.

THEOREM 1. *(Deterministic Accuracy) For each iteration, if the total weight of the accurate processes is greater than $(1/2 + d)$ times the total weight of the non-faulty processes, and if the initial fault ratio of the system is less than $2d$, i.e., ($r_0 < 2d$), then the ABAF algorithm guarantees accuracy.*

THEOREM 2. *(Probabilistic Accuracy) For each iteration, if the probability with which a non-faulty process proposes the correct value is greater than $1/2 + d$ $(0 < d < 1/2)$, and if the fault ratio of the system is less than $2d$, i.e., ($r < 2d$), then the ABAF algorithm guarantees accuracy with probability greater than $(1 - e^{-\mu\delta^2/2})$, where $\mu = p(1/2 + d)$ and $\delta = (2d - r)/(2d + 1)$.*

THEOREM 3. *(At-Least-One Accuracy) If there exists at least one process such that it is inaccurate at most b out of j iterations of the ABAF algorithm, then the algorithm is inaccurate at most $2(1 + \epsilon)b + (2/\epsilon)\log n$ times.*

5. EXPERIMENTAL EVALUATION

The experimental evaluation compares three different update methods: "update-on-inaccuracy" (model used in the ABAF algorithm), in which the weights are updated only when the decided value is incorrect, "always-update", in which the weights are updated after every iteration, and "never-update", in which the weights are never updated. The last option reduces to standard Byzantine agreement. Our simulation uses two models for faulty processes. Model 1 uses a Byzantine process that will always propose the incorrect value. Model 2 uses a Byzantine process that proposes the correct value based on the percentage of its own weight to the weight of all processes. We compare the performance of the three update methods for all three accuracy models (deterministic, probabilistic, at-least-one). The results of all three experiments show that always-update performs very well with model 1 and very badly with model 2, never-update performs vice-versa, but update-on-inaccuracy, the model used in this paper, offers the best compromise for both models.

6. REFERENCES

[1] P. Berman, J. Garay, and K. Perry. Towards optimal distributed consensus. *Foundations of Computer Science, Annual IEEE Symposium on*, 0:410–415, 1989.

[2] P. Berman and J. A. Garay. Asymptotically optimal distributed consensus (extended abstract). In *Proceedings of the 16th International Colloquium on Automata, Languages and Programming*, pages 80–94, London, UK, 1989. Springer-Verlag.

[3] A. Clement, M. Marchetti, E. Wong, L. Alvisi, and M. Dahlin. Making byzantine fault tolerant systems tolerate byzantine faults. In *6th USENIX Symposium on Networked Systems Design and Implementation (NSDI)*, Apr. 2009.

[4] V. K. Garg, J. Bridgman, and B. Balasubramanian. A report on accurate byzantine agreement with feedback. Technical Report TR-PDS-2011-001 http://maple.ece.utexas.edu/TechReports/2011/TR-PDS-2011-001.pdf, Parallel and Distributed Systems Laboratory, ECE Dept. University of Texas at Austin, 2011.

[5] S. Kale. *Efficient algorithms using the multiplicative weights update method*. PhD thesis, Princeton, NJ, USA, 2007. AAI3286120.

[6] V. King and J. Saia. Breaking the $O(n^2)$ bit barrier: scalable byzantine agreement with an adaptive adversary. In *Proceeding of the 29th ACM SIGACT-SIGOPS symposium on Principles of distributed computing*, PODC '10, pages 420–429, New York, NY, USA, 2010. ACM.

[7] L. Lamport, R. Shostak, and M. Pease. The byzantine generals problem. *ACM Trans. Program. Lang. Syst.*, 4:382–401, July 1982.

[8] N. Littlestone and M. K. Warmuth. The weighted majority algorithm. *Inf. Comput.*, 108:212–261, February 1994.

[9] M. Pease, R. Shostak, and L. Lamport. Reaching agreements in the presence of faults. *Journal of the ACM*, 27(2):228–234, Apr. 1980.

Brief Announcement: B-Neck – A Distributed and Quiescent Max-min Fair Algorithm

Alberto Mozo
Dpto. Arquitectura y
Tecnología de Computadores
U. Politécnica de Madrid
Madrid, Spain
amozo@eui.upm.es

Jose Luis López-Presa
DIATEL
U. Politécnica de Madrid
Madrid, Spain
jllopez@diatel.upm.es

Antonio Fernández Anta
Institute IMDEA Networks
Madrid, Spain
antonio.fernandez@imdea.org

ABSTRACT

In this brief announcement we propose B-Neck, a max-min fair distributed algorithm that is also quiescent. As far as we know, B-Neck is the first max-min fair distributed algorithm that does not require a continuous injection of control traffic to compute the rates. When changes occur, affected sessions are asynchronously informed, so they can start the process of computing their new rate (i.e., sessions do not need to poll the network for changes). The correctness of B-Neck is formally proved, and extensive simulations are conducted. In them it is shown that B-Neck converges relatively fast and behaves nicely in presence of sessions arriving and departing.

Categories and Subject Descriptors

C.2.2 [**Computer-Communication Networks**]: Network Protocols

General Terms

Algorithms, Experimentation, Performance, Theory

Keywords

Max-min fairness, quiescence, distributed algorithms

1. INTRODUCTION

The fair distribution of network resources among a set of sessions is a recurring problem. In this problem, each session connects via a single communication path a source node and a destination node in the network, with the objective of maximizing the transmission rate (i.e., throughput) between them. Since the links of the network have limited capacity, the solution of the problem must use some criterion to fairly distribute the network resources among the sessions.

A popular fairness criterion to share the available network capacity among a set of sessions without incurring in link overload is the, so called, *max-min fairness* [3]. The basic idea behind the max-min fairness criterion is to first allocate equal bandwidth to all contending sessions at each link, and

*This research was supported in part by Comunidad de Madrid grant S2009TIC-1692 and Spanish MICINN grant TIN2008–06735-C02-01.

if a session can not utilize its bandwidth because of constraints elsewhere in its path, then the residual bandwidth is distributed among the other sessions. Thus, no session is penalized, and a certain minimum quality of service is guaranteed to all sessions. More precisely, max-min fairness takes into account the path of each session and the capacity of each link. Then, each session i is allocated a transmission rate λ_i so that no link is overloaded, and a session can only increase its rate at the expense of a session with the same or smaller rate.

2. RELATED WORK

We are interested in computing the max-min fair rate allocation for single path sessions. The max-min fair rates of the sessions can be efficiently computed in a centralized way with the Water-Filling algorithm [3]. Max-min fairness has usually been chosen as the target fairness criterion implemented by congestion control protocols to allocate the bandwidth of network links among the sessions that cross them. From a taxonomic point of view, centralized and distributed algorithms have been proposed. The latter have typically been implemented as congestion control protocols.

To our knowledge, the proposals of Gallager [7] and Katevenis [11] were the first to apply max-min fairness to share bandwidth among sessions in a packet switched network. Later on, when ATM networks appeared, several distributed algorithms were proposed to calculate virtual circuit max-min fair rates in the Available Bit Rate (ABR) traffic mode [1, 2, 4, 8, 12]. Charny et al. [4] seem to have been the first to analytically prove the correctness of their proposed algorithm. Hou et al. [8] generalized the Charny algorithm to extend the max-min fairness criterion with minimum rate requests and peak rate constraints. A problem of the algorithm in [4] (when pseudo-saturated links appear) was identified and documented by Tsai and Kim [12]. While the distributed algorithms mentioned need per-session state information at the routers of the network, distributed algorithms that only use constant state information in each router have also been proposed [1, 5].

Recent research trends in explicit congestion control protocols (XCP [10], RCP [6], PIQI-RCP [9]) implement efficient congestion controllers in routers, without the need to store and process state information for each session (in the case of RCP, even with a low per packet computational overhead), and guarantee that the max-min fair rate assignments are achieved when controllers are in steady state. These papers analyze the stability of these protocols, but the experimental evaluations are done on simple topologies composed by a small number of links and sessions (far from real scenarios of large networks with transient dynamics).

None of the distributed algorithms mentioned above is quiescent, and so, traffic must be injected continuously in to the network in order to keep the system stable. It is not straightforward to transform any of these algorithms to achieve quiescence since they do not have mechanisms to detect convergence to the max-min fair rate.

3. CONTRIBUTIONS

In this brief announcement we propose B-Neck, a max-min fair distributed algorithm that is also quiescent. As far as we know, B-Neck is the first such algorithm. Instead of requiring a continuous injection of traffic to compute the max-min fair rates, B-Neck uses a limited number of control packets. In addition, each node only requires information of the sessions that traverse it. When changes occur, affected sessions are asynchronously informed, so they can start the process of computing their new rate (i.e., sessions do not need to poll the network for changes). Quiescence is a key design concept of B-Neck, because B-Neck routers are capable to detect by themselves changes in the convergence conditions (from instability to stability and vice-versa) of max-min fair session rates, and to notify them to the affected sessions. Additionally, affected sessions collaborate with routers to propagate atomically these changes to the rest of the routers in their paths. This behavior is not present by design in any of the non-quiescent published algorithms, and so, as mentioned, the transformation of any of these algorithms to a quiescent one is not a trivial problem.

We have formalized the interaction between the (applications that create and use the) sessions and B-Neck, with a set of primitives. Then, primitives to start and end sessions have been defined (namely, *API.Join* and *API.Leave*). A primitive that B-Neck uses to notify a session of a change in its rate is also defined (namely, *API.Rate*). Finally, the interface allows a session to fix the maximum rate that it requires both at the time it is created (with *API.Join*) and by using a fourth primitive, defined to change the requested maximum rate (namely, *API.Change*).

The properties of B-Neck are formally proved. This proof has two parts. Firstly, we show its *correctness*, i.e., if sessions do not change (for a time period large enough) B-Neck correctly finds the max-min fair rates of all the sessions, and notifies these rates to them. Secondly, we show *quiescence*, i.e., after computing the rates, eventually B-Neck stops injecting traffic into the network. We want to note that, once B-Neck is quiescent, changes in the sessions (new arrivals, departures, or changes in the requested maximum rates) reactivate it, so that, once the changes end, the new appropriate rates are found and notified, and eventually B-Neck becomes quiescent again.

The properties of B-Neck have been tested with extensive simulations. In them, we have used networks of several sizes (with up to hundreds of thousands of nodes), with LAN and WAN characteristics, and with a wide range of session cardinalities (up to hundreds of thousands of sessions). To guarantee the correctness of our implementation of B-Neck, the max-min fair rates obtained have been compared with rates computed with a centralized algorithm (similar to the Water-Filling algorithm [3]). B-Neck has always converged to the right set of max-min fair rates. Our simulations have

shown that B-Neck converges very quickly (30% faster than [2] in our simulations), even in the presence of many interacting sessions. We have also stressed the algorithm by, once quiescent, causing large number of simultaneous departures and rate changes. In all cases B-Neck has shown to be robust and efficient, reaching convergence and quiescence again quickly. The control traffic caused in the network by the algorithm is also shown to be limited, and only for highly dynamic systems with many sessions has more than a few packets per session. Finally, we have observed that, during transient behavior, B-Neck assigns temporal rate values to the sessions that are smaller than the max-min fair rates. Hence, it is expected that the network links will not suffer from packet overloading before convergence, due to these conservative temporal rate assignments.

4. REFERENCES

[1] Y. Afek, Y. Mansour, and Z. Ostfeld. Phantom: a simple and effective flow control scheme. *Computer Networks*, 32(3):277–305, 2000.

[2] Y. Bartal, M. Farach-Colton, S. Yooseph, and L. Zhang. Fast, fair and frugal bandwidth allocation in atm networks. *Algorithmica*, 33(3):272–286, 2002.

[3] D. Bertsekas and R. G. Gallager. *Data Networks (2nd Edition)*. Prentice Hall, 1992.

[4] A. Charny, D. Clark, and R. Jain. Congestion control with explicit rate indication. In *International Conference on Communications, ICC'95, vol. 3*, pages 1954 – 1963, 1995.

[5] J. A. Cobb and M. G. Gouda. Stabilization of max-min fair networks without per-flow state. In S. S. Kulkarni and A. Schiper, editors, *SSS*, volume 5340 of *Lecture Notes in Computer Science*, pages 156–172. Springer, 2008.

[6] N. Dukkipati, M. Kobayashi, R. Zhang-Shen, and N. McKeown. Processor sharing flows in the internet. In H. de Meer and N. T. Bhatti, editors, *IWQoS*, volume 3552 of *Lecture Notes in Computer Science*, pages 271–285. Springer, 2005.

[7] E. L. Hahne and R. G. Gallager. Round robin scheduling for fair flow control in data communication networks. In *IEEE International Conference in Communications, ICC'86*, pages 103–107, 1986.

[8] Y. T. Hou, H. H.-Y. Tzeng, and S. S. Panwar. A generalized max-min rate allocation policy and its distributed implementation using abr flow control mechanism. In *INFOCOM*, pages 1366–1375, 1998.

[9] S. Jain and D. Loguinov. Piqi-rcp: Design and analysis of rate-based explicit congestion control. In *Fifteenth IEEE International Workshop on Quality of Service, IWQoS 2007*, pages 10 –20, June 2007.

[10] D. Katabi, M. Handley, and C. E. Rohrs. Congestion control for high bandwidth-delay product networks. In *SIGCOMM*, pages 89–102. ACM, 2002.

[11] M. Katevenis. Fast switching and fair control of congested flow in broadband networks. *IEEE Journal on Selected Areas in Communications*, SAC-5(8):1315–1326, 1987.

[12] W. K. Tsai and Y. Kim. Re-examining maxmin protocols: A fundamental study on convergence, complexity, variations, and performance. In *INFOCOM*, pages 811–818, 1999.

Brief Announcement: Information Dissemination on Multiple Channels

Stephan Holzer[1], Yvonne-Anne Pignolet[2], Jasmin Smula[1], Roger Wattenhofer[1]
[1]Computer Eng. and Networks Laboratory (TIK), ETH Zurich, Switzerland
[2]ABB Corporate Research, Dättwil,Switzerland
{stholzer,smulaj,wattenhofer}@tik.ee.ethz.ch, yvonne-anne.pignolet@ch.abb.com

ABSTRACT

This article presents an algorithm for detecting and disseminating information in a single-hop multi-channel wireless network: k arbitrary nodes have information they want to share with the entire network. Neither the nodes that have information nor the number k of these nodes are known initially. This communication primitive lies between the two other fundamental primitives regarding information dissemination: broadcasting (one-to-all communication) and gossiping (total information exchange). The time complexity of the algorithm is linear in the number of information items and thus asymptotically optimal with respect to time. The algorithm does not require collision detection and thanks to using several channels the lower bound of $\Omega(k + \log n)$ established for single-channel communication can be broken.

Categories and Subject Descriptors

F.2.2 [**Nonnumerical Algorithms and Problems**]: Computations on discrete structures; C.2.4 [**Distributed Systems**]

General Terms

Algorithms, Theory

1. INTRODUCTION

In this paper we study a basic communication primitive for wireless networks without collision detection.

PROBLEM 1.1 (INFORMATION EXCHANGE).
Consider a network of n nodes with an arbitrary subset of $k \leq n$ nodes where each of these k nodes (called reporters*) is given a distinct piece of information. The* Information Exchange Problem *consists of disseminating these k information items to every node in the network. The subset of the nodes with information items is not known to the network.*

We restrict ourselves to the simplest possible network topology, the single-hop network, where every node can communicate directly with each other node, with multiple communication channels available. I.e., we generalize the *Information Exchange Problem* [3] (also known as *k-Selection* [4] and *Many-to-All Communication* [2]) for networks with several communication channels. We study a static case where a worst-case adversary inserts k information items at the beginning of the first time slot and no more items are inserted later.

Let the network consist of a set of n nodes, each node v with a built-in unique ID id_v known to all other nodes. We assume time to be divided into synchronized time slots and each message can only contain a constant number of information items. In each time slot a node v chooses a channel c and performs one of the actions *transmit* (v broadcasts on channel c) or *receive* (v monitors channel c). A transmission is successful, if exactly one node is transmitting on channel c at a time, and all nodes monitoring this channel receive the message sent. If more than one node transmits on channel c simultaneously, listening nodes can neither receive any message due to interference (called a *collision*) nor do they recognize any communication on the channel (the nodes have *no collision detection* mechanism).

As bandwidth is typically fixed (i.e., a constant number of information items fit into one message), a lower bound on the time complexity for the Information Exchange problem is $\Omega(k)$: at any point in time the message from at most one node can be received successfully on one channel. Furthermore we assume that each node can only monitor one channel at a time and needs to receive all k items. In this paper we propose an algorithm that solves the problem in asymptotically optimal time complexity for any k with high probability in n.[1] In addition we construct an algorithm that solves the Information Exchange problem even if k is unknown.

It turned out that just estimating the number of nodes with information items k (e.g. using [1]) and then let all these nodes send with probability $1/k$ will solve the task in time $O(k)$ whp$_{2^k}$. As long as $k \in o(\log n)$ this is not whp$_n$. Thus a more sophisticated method is necessary to tackle this problem efficiently and have a high success probability for all values of k.

---

[1]An event $\mathcal{E}$ occurs with high probability in x (whp$_x$), if $\Pr[\mathcal{E}] \geq 1 - \frac{1}{x^\alpha}$ for any fixed constant $\alpha \geq 1$. By choosing α, this probability can be made arbitrarily low. Usually one is interested in whp in n.

2. ALGORITHMS

In a first step we assume the number of information items k to be known up to a constant, i.e., we assume that the algorithm knows a number $\tilde{k} \in \mathbb{N}$ satisfying $\tilde{k}/2 \leq k \leq 2\tilde{k}$. Later we show that this bound is not necessary.

Depending on the value of $\tilde{k}$, different strategies are applied to guarantee a timely detection and distribution of information items whp_n. More precisely, we devise three algorithms, each suitable for a different range of k: Algorithms $\mathcal{A}_{tiny}$, $\mathcal{A}_{small}$ and $\mathcal{A}_{tree}$. All algorithms run in time $O(\tilde{k})$ and run correctly whp_n. The constant β influences the success probability.

THEOREM 2.1. *For $\tilde{k} < \sqrt{\log n}$, Algorithm $\mathcal{A}_{tiny}$ distributes all information items in $\Theta(\tilde{k})$ time slots whp_n, for $\sqrt{\log n} \leq \tilde{k} < \frac{\log n - 3}{\beta}$, Algorithm $\mathcal{A}_{small}$ achieves the same (constant β defined later). The deterministic Algorithm $\mathcal{A}_{tree}$ completes in $\Theta(\tilde{k} + \log n)$ time slots.*

The above algorithms can be combined to solve the selection problem for unknown k even without needing given bounds on k like $\tilde{k}/2 \leq k \leq 2\tilde{k}$. For this task we can extend the randomized algorithms to detect if k is too large, i.e., if $k > 2\tilde{k}$ and the algorithm is not able to work correctly whp_n (see full version). With these extensions we can construct Algorithm $\mathcal{A}$ for unknown k. We start with estimating $\tilde{k}$ to be $\tilde{k} = 2$ and double $\tilde{k}$ until the testing procedure of the algorithms presented confirms that $\tilde{k}$ is in the right order of magnitude.

THEOREM 2.2. *Algorithm $\mathcal{A}$ completes in $\Theta(k)$ time slots after which all information items have been detected and distributed whp_n even if k is unknown and no bounds on k are given.*

The number of channels our randomized algorithms need is large in order to guarantee high success probability ($\Theta(\sqrt{n})$ channels). The deterministic algorithm presented requires even more channels for a timely distribution. Such large numbers of channels are rarely available in practice. Thus we mainly view our work as a first step to generalizing the information exchange problem to multiple channels and as a proof that time-optimal distribution is possible. Reducing the number of channels necessary is left as an open problem for future research.

2.1 Deterministic Tree Dissemination $\mathcal{A}_{tree}$

We can use a balanced binary tree of depth $\log n$ and n channels (one for each node) to disseminate information deterministically in time $O(\tilde{k} + \log n)$. The IDs of the nodes determine their position in the tree as well as the channel assignment and a schedule specifying when each node transmits its message on its own channel or listens to its children or parent nodes on their channel. Once the root of the tree has obtained all information items, it broadcasts them on channel 1 and all other nodes listen. $\mathcal{A}_{tree}$ distributes all information items within $O(\tilde{k} + \log n)$ time slots without collisions.

2.2 $\mathcal{A}_{tiny}$ for $\tilde{k} < \sqrt{\log n}$

Each reporter selects a random channel from a set of $K := n^{1/(2\tilde{k})}$ channels, such that at least half of the reporters choose a unique channel. We call a transmission of a reporter that chooses a unique channel a "successful transmission" since in this case no collision occurs. The number K is selected in such a way that it is small enough to ensure that for each of the $\sum_{i=0}^{\tilde{k}} \binom{K}{i}$ possible subsets of at most $\tilde{k}$ channels with a successful transmission there is a non-reporter node in the network that can be assigned to listen to that subset. Each such listener then listens on all channels from the assigned subset one after another. We argue that there is a exactly one node (called the "boss") that listens exactly on those channels on which the information items were transmitted successfully. Thus this boss collects the information of all successful reporters (at least half of all reporters transmitted successfully) and broadcasts it subsequently. Since the boss is unique it can successfully transmit the gathered information to the network and the number of reporters is cut in half in time $O(\tilde{k})$. Repeating this procedure until no reporters are left takes time $O(\tilde{k})/2^0 + O(\tilde{k})/2^1 + O(\tilde{k})/2^2 + \cdots + O(\tilde{k})/2^{\log O(\tilde{k})} = O(\tilde{k})$.

2.3 $\mathcal{A}_{small}$ for $\sqrt{\log n} \leq \tilde{k} < \frac{\log n - 3}{\beta}$

$\mathcal{A}_{small}$ consists of four steps. In step 1, the nodes determine which role they are going to play during the execution (there are k reporters, $2^{\beta \tilde{k}/2}$ listeners and $n - k - 2^{\beta \tilde{k}/2}$ others). In step 2, each of the k reporters tries to tell a randomly picked listener its information item (a balls-into-bins-style procedure: each listener node listens on a unique channel—these are the bins, each reporter chooses a random channel to send its information item, i.e., it throws ball into a random bin, repeated $\tilde{k}$ times). In step 3, the listeners send all collected information items to the boss with the tree dissemination algorithm $\mathcal{A}_{tree}$. In step 4, the boss broadcasts the collected information items.

We can show that each step completes in $O(\tilde{k})$ time slots and all reporters are successful at least once during step 2 whp_n for k in the range considered. Furthermore, no collisions occur in step 3 and 4 and $\mathcal{A}_{small}$ achieves its goal.

3. REFERENCES

[1] I. Caragiannis, C. Galdi, and C. Kaklamanis. Basic computations in wireless networks. In *ISAAC 05*, volume 3827, page 533, 2005.

[2] B.S. Chlebus, D.R. Kowalski, and T. Radzik. Many-to-Many Communication in Radio Networks. *Algorithmica*, 2009.

[3] S. Gilbert and D. Kowalski. Trusted Computing for Fault-Prone Wireless Networks. *Distributed Computing*, pages 359–373, 2010.

[4] D.R. Kowalski. On selection problem in radio networks. In *PODC*, 2005.

Brief Announcement: Robust Data Sharing with Key-Value Stores

Cristina Basescu
Vrije Universiteit Amsterdam
1081 HV Amsterdam
Netherlands
cristina.basescu@
gmail.com

Christian Cachin
IBM Research - Zurich
CH-8803 Rüschlikon
Switzerland
cca@zurich.ibm.com

Ittay Eyal
Technion — Israel Institute of
Technology
Haifa 32000, Israel
ittay@tx.technion.ac.il

Robert Haas
IBM Research - Zurich
CH-8803 Rüschlikon
Switzerland
rha@zurich.ibm.com

Marko Vukolić
Eurécom
F-06904 Sophia Antipolis
France
vukolic@eurecom.fr

ABSTRACT

A key-value store (KVS) offers functions for storing and retrieving values associated with unique keys. KVSs have become widely used as shared storage solutions for Internet-
scale distributed applications.

We present a fault-tolerant wait-free efficient algorithm
that emulates a multi-reader multi-writer register from a
set of KVS replicas in an asynchronous environment. Our
implementation serves an unbounded number of clients that
use the storage. It tolerates crashes of a minority of the
KVSs and crashes of any number of clients. We provide
two variants of our algorithm: one implementing an atomic
register and one implementing a regular register; the latter
does not require read operations to store data at the underlying KVSs. We note that applying state-of-the-art reliable
storage solutions to this scenario is either impossible or prohibitively inefficient.

Categories and Subject Descriptors

C.2.4 [**Distributed Systems**]: Distributed Applications

General Terms

Algorithms, Theory

Keywords

Distributed Storage, Cloud Storage

1. INTRODUCTION

Recent years have seen an explosion of Internet-scale applications, ranging from web search to social networks. These
applications are typically implemented with many machines
running in multiple data centers. In order to coordinate
their operation, these machines access some shared storage.

In this context, a prominent storage model is the *key-value
store* (*KVS*). A KVS offers a range of simple functions for

manipulation of unstructured data objects (called *values*),
each one identified by a unique *key*. KVSs are used as storage services directly [2, 5] or indirectly, as non-relational
(NoSQL) databases [15, 4]. While different services and
systems offer various extensions to the KVS interface, the
common denominator of existing KVS services implements
an associative array: A client may *store* a value by associating the value with a key, *retrieve* a value associated with a
key, *list* the keys that are currently associated, and *remove*
a value associated with a key.

Storage services provide reliability using replication and
tolerate the failure of individual data replicas. However,
when all data replicas are managed by the same entity,
there are naturally common system components, and therefore failure modes common to all replicas. A failure of these
components may lead to data becoming not available or even
being lost, as recently witnessed during an Amazon S3 outage [1] and Google's temporary loss of email data [3]. Therefore, a client can increase data reliability by replicating it
among several storage services using the guarantees offered
by *robust* distributed storage algorithms [13, 7]. Such an algorithm uses multiple storage providers, called *base objects*
here, and emulates a single, more reliable shared storage
abstraction, which we model as a *read/write register*. The
register tolerates asynchrony, concurrency, and faults among
the clients and the base objects.

Many well-known robust distributed storage algorithms
exist [7, 10, 9]. Perhaps surprisingly, none of them dire-
cly exploits key-value stores as base objects. The problem
arises because existing solutions are either (1) unsuitable for
KVSs since they rely on storage nodes that perform custom
computation, which a KVS cannot do, or (2) prohibitively
expensive, in the sense that they require as many base objects as there are clients [12, 6].

In the following, we describe the challenges behind running robust storage algorithms over a set of KVS base objects.

2. CHALLENGES

Many existing robust register emulations are based on ver-
sioning, in the sense that they associate each stored value

with a *version* (also called a timestamp) that increases over time. Consider the classical multi-writer emulation of a fault-tolerant register [13, 7]. A writer determines first the largest version from some majority of the base objects, derives a larger version, and then stores the new value together with the larger version at a majority of base objects. The base object then performs *computation* and actually stores the new value only if it comes with a larger version than the one it stores locally. However, a KVS does not offer such an operation.

Similar to existing emulations, we want the robust storage solution to be *wait-free* [14], such that every correct client may proceed independently of the speed or failure of other clients (or more precisely, every operation invoked by a correct client eventually completes).

If a classical algorithm is cast blindly into the KVS context without adjustment, all values are stored with the same key. This may cause a larger version and an associated, recently written value to be overwritten by a smaller version and an outdated value. We call this the *old-new overwrite* problem.

Another equally naïve solution is to store each version under a separate key; such a KVS accumulates all versions that have ever been stored and takes up unbounded space. As remedy for this, one could remove small versions from a KVS after a value with a larger version has been stored. But this might, in turn, jeopardize wait-freedom. Consider a read operation that lists the existing keys and then retrieves the value with the largest version. If this version is removed between the time when the KVS executes the list operation and the time when the client retrieves it from the KVS, the read operation will fail. We refer to this as the *garbage-collection race* problem.

3. CONTRIBUTION

We provide two robust, asynchronous, and efficient emulations of a register over a set of fault-prone KVS replicas. Both emulations are designed for an unbounded number of clients, which may all read from and write to the register (i.e., the emulations implement a multi-writer multi-reader register). This makes the algorithms appropriate for Internet-scale systems. Both emulations are *wait-free* and *optimally resilient*. The latter property means that the algorithm tolerates crash-stop failures of any minority of the KVS replicas and of any number of clients.

The two emulations differ in their consistency semantics. The first one emulates a multi-writer *regular* register [17][1] and it does not require read operations to write to KVSs (that is, to change the state of a KVS by storing a value). Precluding readers from storing values is practically appealing, since the clients may belong to different domains and not all of them should be permitted to write to the shared memory. But this poses a problem because of the garbage-collection race problem described previously. Our solution instructs a write operation to store the same value *twice*, under different keys: Once under an *eternal* key, which is never removed by garbage collection but vulnerable to an old-new overwrite, and a second time under a *temporary* key, named according to the version. Outdated temporary keys are garbage-collected periodically, for instance by write

operations, which exposes them to garbage-collection races. Taken together, however, the eternal and temporary copies complement each other and guarantee a wait-free emulation with regular semantics.

The second algorithm emulates an *atomic* or *linearizable* register [16], where all read and write operations appear to execute at a single point in time between their invocation and response. This emulation requires read operations to store values at the underlying KVS replicas, but this cannot be avoided [16, 11]. We derive our atomic emulation from the regular emulation, by instructing the readers to write back the value they are about to return [7]. Details appear in the full version [8].

4. REFERENCES

[1] Amazon S3 availability event: July 20, 2008. http://status.aws.amazon.com/s3-20080720.html.
[2] Amazon Simple Storage Service. http://aws.amazon.com/s3/.
[3] Gmail back soon for everyone. http://gmailblog.blogspot.com/2011/02/gmail-back-soon-for-everyone.html.
[4] Project Voldemort: A distributed database. http://project-voldemort.com/.
[5] Windows Azure Storage. http://www.microsoft.com/windowsazure/storage/.
[6] I. Abraham, G. Chockler, I. Keidar, and D. Malkhi. Byzantine disk Paxos: Optimal resilience with Byzantine shared memory. *Distributed Computing*, 18(5):387–408, 2006.
[7] H. Attiya, A. Bar-Noy, and D. Dolev. Sharing memory robustly in message-passing systems. *J. ACM*, 42(1):124–142, 1995.
[8] C. Basescu, C. Cachin, I. Eyal, R. Haas, and M. Vukolić. Robust data sharing with key-value stores. Research Report RZ 3802, IBM Research, 2011.
[9] C. Cachin, R. Guerraoui, and L. Rodrigues. *Introduction to Reliable and Secure Distributed Programming (Second Edition)*. Springer, 2011.
[10] G. Chockler and D. Malkhi. Active disk Paxos with infinitely many processes. *Distributed Computing*, 18:73–84, 2005. 10.1007/s00446-005-0123-x.
[11] R. Fan and N. A. Lynch. Efficient replication of large data objects. In *Distributed Computing (DISC)*, pages 75–91, 2003.
[12] E. Gafni and L. Lamport. Disk Paxos. *Distributed Computing*, 16(1):1–20, 2003.
[13] D. K. Gifford. Weighted voting for replicated data. In *Symposium on Operating System Principles (SOSP)*, pages 150–162, 1979.
[14] M. P. Herlihy and J. M. Wing. Linearizability: a correctness condition for concurrent objects. *ACM Trans. Program. Lang. Syst.*, 12:463–492, July 1990.
[15] A. Lakshman and P. Malik. Cassandra: A decentralized structured storage system. *SIGOPS Oper. Syst. Rev.*, 44:35–40, 2010.
[16] L. Lamport. On interprocess communication. *Distributed Computing*, 1(2):77–101, 1986.
[17] C. Shao, E. Pierce, and J. L. Welch. Multi-writer consistency conditions for shared memory objects. In *Distributed Computing (DISC)*, pages 106–120, 2003.

---

[1]Roughly, a regular read may return a value written by the latest write that precedes it or one of the concurrently written values [16, 17].

Brief Announcement: Network Synchronization and Localization Based on Stolen Signals

Christian Schindelhauer
Dept. of Computer Science
University of Freiburg, D
schindel@
informatik.uni-freiburg.de

Zvi Lotker
Dept. of Communication
Systems Engineering
Ben-Gurion University, IL
zvilo@bgu.ac.il

Johannes Wendeberg
Dept. of Computer Science
University of Freiburg, D
wendeber@
informatik.uni-freiburg.de

ABSTRACT

We consider an anchor-free, relative localization and synchronization problem where a set of n receiver nodes and m wireless signal sources are independently, uniformly, and randomly distributed in a disk in the plane. The signals can be distinguished and their capture times can be measured. At the beginning neither the positions of the signal sources and receivers are known nor the sending moments of the signals. Now each receiver captures each signal after its constant speed journey over the unknown distance between signal source and receiver position. Given these nm capture times the task is to compute the relative distances between all synchronized receivers. In a more generalized setting the receiver nodes have no synchronized clocks and need to be synchronized from the capture times of the stolen signals.

Categories and Subject Descriptors: G.1.2 Approximation: Nonlinear approximation

General Terms: Algorithms, Measurement

Keywords: TDOA, localization, synchronization

1. INTRODUCTION

Localization and synchronization are fundamental and well researched problems. In this paper we take a fresh look at this problem. We use the time difference of arrival of abundantly available, distinguishable signal sources of unknown location and timing, which can be received at a set of receivers. Assuming that the senders and receivers are on the plane the task is to find the locations of all receivers.

We assume a uniform distribution in a disk of the same or larger size. After collecting all the time information from all receivers we want to compute the time offsets and positions of all nodes without knowing where or when the random signals are produced. We only assume that we can distinguish the signals and that they reach all nodes of our network.

The survey in [1] describes a selection of range-based approaches. Also of interest is the analysis of the uniqueness of ranged networks [2]. The term *time differences of arrival* (TDOA) describes the reception of an unknown signal without any given range information. Close to our problem is the setting in [3] where only TDOA information is used to locate wireless sensor nodes. An elegant solution for a fixed number of 10 microphones is shown in [4]. However, it does not scale for large numbers of microphones.

In [5] we present a technique for robust distance estimation between microphones by evaluating the timing information of sharp sound signals. We assume synchronized receivers and signals originating from a far distance, but we have no further information about their location.

2. ESTIMATING DISTANCES

Our distance estimation approach begins with only two receivers. As we have pointed out in [5] it is possible to estimate the distance between two receiver nodes if the signals are uniformly distributed on a circle around the receivers at a large distance. Here, we show that this method also results in a reasonable estimation if the signals are distributed in the same disk where the receivers lie.

Max-Min-Technique.

Given two vertices i, j $(1 \leq i < j \leq n)$ and the relative time differences of the stolen signals: $t_{r_i,s_k} - t_{r_j,s_k}$ for all stolen signals $s_1, \ldots, s_m$, we compute the *estimated distance* $d_{i,j}$ between i and j as

- $d_{i,j} := \max_k\{|t_{r_i,s_k} - t_{r_j,s_k}|\}$ if the receivers are synchronized and as

- $d_{i,j} := \frac{1}{2}\left(\max_k\{t_{r_i,s_k} - t_{r_j,s_k}\} - \min_k\{t_{r_i,s_k} - t_{r_j,s_k}\}\right)$ if the receivers are not synchronized. The estimated relative time offset will be computed using the time signal $k^* := \arg\max_k\{t_{r_i,s_k} - t_{r_j,s_k}\}$. Then, $t_{r_i,s_{k*}} - t_{r_j,s_{k*}} - d_{i,j}$ yields the approximation of the correction for the clocks at i and j.

First, note that in both cases the estimation is always upper-bounded by the real distance: $\|r_i - r_j\| \geq d_{i,j}$. We now describe a sufficient condition for the accuracy of the estimator. For this we define the ϵ-critical area.

Definition 1 *The ϵ-critical area of two nodes (u, v) is the set of points p in the plane where*

$$\|u - v\| - (\|p - v\| - \|p - u\|) \leq \epsilon .$$

This convex area is bounded by a hyperbola containing the point u. If in this critical area signals are produced, then the distance estimation is accurate up to an absolute error of ϵ.

Lemma 1 *If in both of the ϵ-critical areas of (u, v) and (v, u) signals are produced, then the Max-Min distance estimation $d_{u,v}$ is in the interval $d_{u,v} \in [\|u-v\| - 2\epsilon, \|u-v\|]$.*

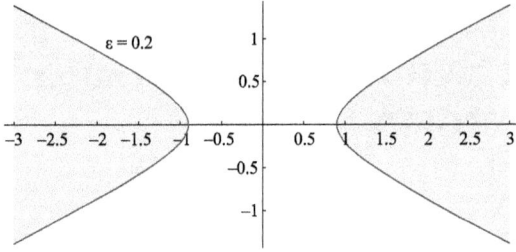

Figure 1: The 0.2-critical areas of two nodes at $(-1,0)$ and $(1,0)$ are on the left and right side of the hyperbolas.

The time offset between the clocks of u and v can be computed up to an absolute error margin of 2ϵ.

If at least in one of the ϵ-critical areas of (u,v) and (v,u) a signal is produced, then for synchronized receivers the Max-Min distance estimation $d_{u,v}$ is in the interval $d_{u,v} \in [\|u - v\| - \epsilon, \|u - v\|]$. These signals can be found in time $\mathcal{O}(m)$.

PROOF. The proof of the accuracy of the distance estimators follows from the definition of the critical areas. For the accuracy of the time offset consider that one clock u is assumed to be correct, then the other node's clock offset is chosen such that the signal arrives later at time $d_{u,v}$ if the signal was detected at the ϵ-critical area of u.

The best signals can be found by computing the minimum or maximum of the differences of the time points at the receivers u and v. □

Lemma 2 *For two receivers u, v with $\ell := \|u - v\|$ the intersection of the ϵ-critical area (v,u) of a disk with center $\frac{1}{2}(u + v)$ and radius r has*

- *at least an area of $\min\{\pi\ell^2, \frac{1}{2}\epsilon^2\}$ if $r = \ell$ and*

- *at least an area of $\min\{\pi r^2, (r - \ell)^2 \sqrt{\epsilon/\ell}\}$ if $r > \ell$.*

Since the critical areas are rather large there is a good chance that a signal could be found in one of these areas.

Theorem 1 *For m stolen signals the Max-Min distance estimator for two receiver nodes u, v with distance $\ell := \|u - v\|$ within the disk with center $(0,0)$ and radius 1 outputs a result $d_{u,v}$ with $d_{u,v} \in [\|u - v\| - \epsilon, \|u - v\|]$ with probability $1 - p$, where for ϵ and p we have:*

1. *If u and v are unsynchronized and the m signal sources are uniformly distributed in the unit disk we have $\epsilon = \mathcal{O}\left(\sqrt{\frac{\log m}{m}}\right)$ and $p = \frac{1}{m^c}$ for any $c > 1$.*

2. *If u and v are unsynchronized, u and v are not close to the unit disk boundary, i.e. $|u| < 1 - k$ and $|v| < 1 - k$ for some constant $k > 0$, and the m signal sources are uniformly distributed in the unit disk we have $\epsilon = \mathcal{O}\left(\frac{\log^2 m}{m^2}\right)$ and $p = \frac{1}{m^{ck^2}}$ for any $c > 1$.*

Theorem 2 *For unsynchronized receivers we can compute in time $\mathcal{O}(nm)$ an approximation of the positions and the clock offset within an absolute error of $\mathcal{O}\left(\sqrt{\frac{\log m}{m}}\right)$ with probability $1 - m^{-c} - e^{-c'n}$ (for any $c \in \mathcal{O}(1)$ and some $c' > 0$).*

Theorem 3 *For synchronized receivers we can compute in time $\mathcal{O}(nm)$ an approximation of the correct relative positions within an absolute error margin of $\mathcal{O}\left(\frac{\log^2 m}{m^2}\right)$ with probability $1 - m^{-c} - e^{-c'n}$. This error bound holds also for unsynchronized receivers if we consider a normal distribution of the sound signals, or if the sound signals are randomly distributed in a surrounding larger disk.*

In an ad hoc network a distributed algorithm can approximate the positions and clock offsets for the network within an absolute error of $\mathcal{O}\left(\sqrt{\frac{\log m}{m}}\right)$ with probability $1 - n^{-c}$ if $m > n$ using $\mathcal{O}(nm \log n)$ messages.

3. OUTLOOK

From now on, we will use the distance estimation information and compute the locations of the receiver nodes. While our focus is the localization and synchronization of the receivers, it is straight-forward to determine the time and position of the signals using the receivers as anchor points.

Anchor-free localization based on TDOA signals faces the characteristic problems of possible ambiguous solutions and an incoherent solution set. Combined with the non-linear, non-convex nature of this optimization problem (which can be expressed as a set of nm polynomial equations of quadratic degree) one may expect an ill-posed problem. In this paper we overcome this problem with an efficient approximation algorithm. Moreover, we can prove the quality of the result for a random input set with high probability.

The output of our algorithm can be used as the initial starting point of standard non-linear optimization methods like gradient-based search or Newton's method. Our algorithm computes the start position in time $\mathcal{O}(mn)$, i.e. in linear time with respect to the problem size. So, computing such a starting point amounts for the same time as a constant number of iterations for these problems. Whether the success rate of optimization algorithms improves with such an input set is part of further research.

4. REFERENCES

[1] K. Langendoen and N. Reijers. Distributed localization in wireless sensor networks: a quantitative comparison. *Computer Networks*, 43(4):499–518, 2003.

[2] T. Eren, D. K. Goldenberg, W. Whiteley, Y. R. Yang, A. S. Morse, B. D. O. Anderson, and P. N. Belhumeur. Rigidity, Computation, and Randomization in Network Localization. In *INFOCOM 2004. Twenty-third annual Joint Conference of the IEEE Computer and Communications Societies*, volume 4, pages 2673–2684. IEEE, 2004.

[3] R. Biswas and S. Thrun. A Passive Approach to Sensor Network Localization. In *2004 IEEE/RSJ International Conference on Intelligent Robots and Systems, 2004. (IROS 2004). Proceedings.*, volume 2, pages 1544–1549, 2004.

[4] M. Pollefeys and D. Nister. Direct computation of sound and microphone locations from time-difference-of-arrival data. In *IEEE International Conference on Acoustics, Speech and Signal Processing, 2008. ICASSP 2008.*, pages 2445–2448. IEEE, 2008.

[5] T. Janson, C. Schindelhauer, and J. Wendeberg. Self-Localization Application for iPhone using only Ambient Sound Signals. In *Proceedings of the 2010 International Conference on Indoor Positioning and Indoor Navigation (IPIN)*, pages 259–268, Nov. 2010.

Brief Announcement: Validity Bound of Regular Registers with Churn and Byzantine Processes [*]

Roberto Baldoni Silvia Bonomi Amir Soltani Nezhad
Dipartimento di Informatica e Sistemistica "Antonio Ruberti"
Università degli Studi di Roma "La Sapienza"
Via Ariosto 25, I-00185 Roma, Italy
baldoni,bonomi,amir@dis.uniroma1.it

ABSTRACT

This paper studies the problem of building a byzantine fault tolerant storage service in a distributed system affected by servers join and leave (i.e., servers churn). We show a bound for ensuring both validity of read operations and the persistence of a value written by a write operation. This bound correlates the churn rate, the number of faulty processes and the time taken by register operations (i.e., join, read and write operations).

Categories and Subject Descriptors

H.3.4 [**Information Storage and Retrieval**]: System and Software—*distributed systems*; D.4.2 [**Operating Systems**]: Storage Management—*distributed memories*; D.4.5 [**Operating Systems**]: Reliability—*fault-tolerance*

General Terms

Reliability, Theory

Keywords

Regular Register, Dynamic Distributed Systems, Byzantine failure, Churn.

1. INTRODUCTION

Building a storage able to tolerate arbitrary failures is a central component in any mission-critical system that has to ensure both correct and highly-available operation executions despite software and accidental errors as well as malicious operations. Protocols that can tolerate such failures are said to be Byzantine Fault-Tolerant (BFT) [5]. In the recent years, BFT storage has become a first class abstraction in large scale distributed systems to implement services such as directory services, sequencer services, namespaces, key management etc. These services are usually implemented by dozens of servers geographycally deployed over large scale settings (e.g. interconnected datacenters) that notoriously have to withstand various types, patterns, degrees and rates of churn. In such environments, churn creates unpredictable patterns of servers that leave and join a computation and no

[*]This work is partially supported by the European STREP project SM4All

assumption can be done on the duration of the churn period and on the distance in time between two successive churn periods (i.e., churn is non-quiescent). Thus, churn adds a new complexity dimension to the implementation of BFT storage, and it must be handled to avoid the storage to become unavailable.

To the best of our knowledge, this is the first paper analyzing implications of building a BFT storage under churn. Implementations of registers resilient to crash failures have been provided indeed on the top of a distributed system prone to quiescent and non-quiescent churn respectively.

2. SYSTEM MODEL

The distributed system is composed of a *universe of clients* U_c (i.e. clients system) and of a disjoint *universe of servers* U_s (i.e. servers system). The clients system is composed of a finite arbitrary number of processes, while the servers system is dynamic, i.e. processes may join and leave the system at their will. A server enters the server system by executing the join_System procedure. Such an operation aims at connecting the new process to both clients and servers that already belonged to the system. A server leaves the system by means of the leave_System operation. In order to model processes continuously arriving to and departing from the system, we assume the infinite arrival model. The set of processes that can participate in the servers system, i.e. the server system *population*, is composed of a potentially infinite set of processes $U_s = \{ \ldots s_i, s_j, s_k \ldots \}$, each one having a unique identifier (i.e. its index). However, the servers system is composed, at each time, of a finite subset of the population. Clients and servers can communicate only by exchanging messages through reliable and authenticated channels. We assume the existence of a protocol managing the arrival and the departure of servers from the distributed system; such a protocol is also responsible for the connectivity maintenance among processes of the system.

Distributed Computation. At time t_0, when the server system is set up, n servers belong to the servers computation. A server s_i, belonging to the servers system, that wants to join the distributed computation has to execute the join_Server() operation. Such an operation, invoked at some time t, is not instantaneous and takes time to be executed; how much this time is, depends on the specific implementation provided for the join_Server() operation. However, from time t, the server s_i can receive and process messages sent by any other processes participating in the computation. When a server s_j participating in the distributed computation wishes to leave the computation, it executes the leave_Server() operation. We model the leave_Server() operation as an implicit operation, i.e., when a process p_i leaves the computation, it just stops to send and process messages related to the register computation. Moreover, we assume that if a server leaves the computation and later wishes to re-join, it executes again the join_Server() operation with a new identity. We assume at most $f \leq n/3$ servers can deviate from their specifications during the whole life of the computation. The remaining servers are *correct*.

Non-Quiescent Churn. The computation alternates periods of churn (T_c) and periods of stability (T_s). More specifically, there exist some periods T_c, T_c', T_c'' etc. in which servers join and leave the computation, and between two churn periods T_c and T_c', there exists a period T_s where the computation becomes stable and no join or leave operations occur. However, no assumption is made about how long T_c and T_s are. During the churn periods, we assume that the churn refreshes a fraction of the computation participants at each time unit. More precisely, we define as *churn rate*, denoted c, the percentage of processes that are "refreshed" at every time unit ($c \in [0,1]$). This means that while the number of servers remains constant (equal to n), in every time unit in T_c, $c \times n$ processes leave the computation and the same number of processes invok the join_Server() operation.

3. REGULAR REGISTER

A register is a shared variable accessed by a set of processes, i.e. clients, through two operations, namely read() and write(). We consider a regular register specified as follows:
Termination: If a correct process participating in the computation invokes an operation and does not leave the system, it eventually returns from that operation.
Validity: A read operation returns the last value written before its invocation, or a value written by a write operation concurrent with it.

Due to the presence of churn, we add one more property, namely *write persistency*, that an algorithm has to satisfy:

WritePersistency: Servers maintain the last value written by a write operation despite server departures.

Protocol Model. A protocol $\mathcal{P}_{reg}$ implementing a regular register is a collection of distributed algorithms, one for each operation (i.e. $\mathcal{P}_{reg} = \{\mathcal{A}_{JS}, \mathcal{A}_R, \mathcal{A}_W\}$ where $\mathcal{A}_{JS}, \mathcal{A}_R, \mathcal{A}_W$ are respectively the distributed algorithms implementing the join_Server(), the read() and the write() operations). Each algorithm is composed of a sequence of computation steps and communication steps. A computation step is represented by the computation executed locally to each process while a communication step is represented by the sending and the delivering events of a message.
A register is maintaied by a set of servers (possibly a subset of the ones belonging to the computation). No agreement abstraction is assumed to be available at a server. Clients do not maintain any register information; they can just trigger operations and interact with servers through message exchanges. Moreover, we assume that each server has the same role in the distributed computation (i.e. there is no special server acting as a coordinator).
For the sake of simplicity, we assume a single register replicated at each server belonging to the computation.

4. VALIDITY BOUND

Consider a generic protocol $\mathcal{P}_{reg}$ implementing a regular register such that (i) every operation terminates and that (ii) there exists a period of churn longer than the longest operation issued on the register. Starting form the lower bound of $3f + 1$ processes needed to tolerate f failures [7], in [3] we prove the following Theorem.

THEOREM 1. *Let $\mathcal{A}_{JS}$, $\mathcal{A}_R$ and $\mathcal{A}_W$ be the algorithms implementing respectively join_Server(), read() and write() operations. Let Δt_j, Δt_r and Δt_w be the maximum time intervals needed by $\mathcal{A}_{JS}$ to terminate an operation. If $c \geq min\{\frac{n-3f}{n \times \Delta t_r}, \frac{n-3f}{n \times (\Delta t_j + \Delta t_w)}\}$, then it is not possible to ensure both the write-persistency and the read-validity.*

Interestingly, the bound is affected by the time taken by the operations to be executed, which depends on the algorithm implementing the operations and on the synchrony assumptions of the underlying distributed systems. In the case of a synchronous distributed system, the values of Δt_j, Δt_r and Δt_w are finite and thus, the value of c can be calculated exactly. Moving towards an asynchronous system, the values of Δt_j, Δt_r and Δt_w can only be estimated; thus, there is no more a deterministic guarantee that the system works, but it is still possible to provide an estimation of the churn rate that can be tolerated by the system. This result confirms the impossibility result found in [2] that is no algorithm can implement a regular register in the presence of non quiescent churn on the top of a fully asynchronous distributed system.

5. FUTURE WORK

This paper has established a bound for ensuring validity of read operations issued on a regular register which is able to resist arbitrary failures and non-quiescent churn. Future work will study if register storage is weaker than consensus not only in distributed systems prone to both crash failures and quiescent churn (as shown in [1]) but also in a setting including byzantine failures.

6. REFERENCES

[1] Aguilera M. K., Keidar I., Malkhi D., Shraer A., Dynamic atomic storage without consensus, *in Proceedings of 28th Annual ACM Symposium on Principles of Distributed Computing (PODC) 2009*, 17-25
[2] Baldoni R., Bonomi S., Kermarrec A.M., Raynal M., Implementing a Register in a Dynamic Distributed System, *in Proceedings of the 29th IEEE International Conference on Distributed Computing Systems (ICDCS'09)*, IEEE Computer Society Press, Montreal (Canada), June 2009.
[3] Baldoni R., Bonomi S., Soltani Nezhad A. Regular Registers in Dynamic Distributed Systems with Byzantine Processes: Bounds and Performance Analysis, Technical report - MIDLAB 3/11 - 2011
http://www.dis.uniroma1.it/~midlab/articoli/
[4] Lamport. L., On Interprocess Communication, Part 1: Models, Part 2: Algorirhms, *Distributed Computing*, 1(2):77-101, 1986.
[5] Lamport L., Shostak R. E., Pease M. C., The Byzantine Generals Problem, *ACM Transactions on Programming Languages and Systems (TOPLAS)* 4(3), 382-401, 1982.
[6] Malkhi D., Reiter M. K. Byzantine Quorum Systems, *Distributed Computing* 11(4): 203-213, 1998
[7] Martin J., Alvisi L., Dahlin M.. Minimal Byzantine Storage, *in Proceedings of the 16th International Symposium on Distributed Computing (DISC 2002)*, pp. 311-325, 2002.

Brief Announcement: Easy Impossibility Proofs for k-Set Agreement in Message Passing Systems[*]

Martin Biely
Embedded Computing
Systems Group (E182/2)
Technische Universität Wien,
Treitlstrasse
1040 Vienna, Austria
martin.biely@epfl.ch

Peter Robinson
Nanyang Technological
University
Division of Mathematical
Sciences
Singapore 637371
peter.robinson@ntu.edu.sg

Ulrich Schmid
Embedded Computing
Systems Group (E182/2)
Technische Universität Wien,
Treitlstrasse
1040 Vienna, Austria
s@ecs.tuwien.ac.at

Categories and Subject Descriptors: C.4 [Computer Systems Organization]: Performance of Systems — *Fault Tolerance*

General Terms: Algorithms,Reliability,Theory.

1. INTRODUCTION

We study distributed algorithms that solve agreement problems, namely, k-set agreement. Their purpose is to compute and irrevocably set the output y_p of process p to some decision value, based on the proposal values $x_q \in V$, for $1 \leqslant q \leqslant n$ and $|V| \geqslant n$,[1] such that every correct process eventually decides on a value proposed by some process and the set of all decision values contains at most k values.

Despite of being quite similar agreement problems, consensus (= 1-set agreement) and general k-set agreement require surprisingly different techniques for proving the impossibility in asynchronous systems with crash failures: Rather than relatively simple bivalence arguments as in the impossibility proof for consensus in the presence of a single crash failure ($f = k = 1$), known proofs for the impossibility of k-set agreement in systems with $f \geqslant k > 1$ crash failures use algebraic topology or a variant of Sperner's Lemma.

In this paper, we present a generic theorem for proving the impossibility of k-set agreement in various message passing settings, which is based on a simple reduction to the consensus impossibility in a certain subsystem.

2. RESTRICTIONS OF ALGORITHMS AND INDISTINGUISHABILITY OF RUNS

We will occasionally use a subsystem $\mathcal{M}'$ that is a *restriction* of a model $\mathcal{M}$, in the sense that it consists of a subset of processes in Π, while using the same mode of computation (atomicity of computing steps, time-driven vs. message-driven, etc.) as $\mathcal{M}$. We make this explicit by using the notation $\mathcal{M} = \langle \Pi \rangle$ and $\mathcal{M}' = \langle D \rangle$, for some set of processes

[*]This work has been supported by the Austrian Science Foundation (FWF) project P20529.

Peter Robinson has also been supported by Nanyang Technological University grant M58110000.

[1]The assumption $|V| \geqslant n$ allows runs where all processes start with different propose values.

PODC'11, June 6–8, 2011, San Jose, California, USA.
ACM 978-1-4503-0719-2/11/06.

$D \subseteq \Pi$. Note that this definition does not imply anything about the synchrony assumptions which hold in $\mathcal{M}'$. All that is required is that $\mathcal{M}'$ is computationally compatible with $\mathcal{M}$: Any algorithm designed for $\mathcal{M}$ can also be run in $\mathcal{M}'$, albeit on a smaller set of processes.

Let A be an algorithm that works in system $\mathcal{M} = \langle \Pi \rangle$ and let $D \subseteq \Pi$ be a nonempty set of processes. Consider a restricted system $\mathcal{M}' = \langle D \rangle$. The *restricted algorithm* $A_{|D}$ for system $\mathcal{M}'$ is constructed by dropping all messages sent to processes outside D in the message sending function of A, obtaining the message sending function of $A_{|D}$.

Note that we do not change the actual code of algorithm A in any way. In particular, the restricted algorithm still uses the value of $|\Pi|$ for the size of the system, even though the real size of D might be much smaller.

We will use a concept of similarity/indistinguishability of runs that is slightly weaker than the usual notion [2, Page 21], as we require the same states only *until* a decision state is reached. This makes a difference for algorithms where p can help others in reaching their decision after p has decided, for example, by forwarding messages.

Two runs α *and* β *are indistinguishable (until decision) for a process* p, if p has the same sequence of states in α and β until p decides. By $\alpha \overset{D}{\sim} \beta$ we denote the fact that α and β are indistinguishable (until decision) for every $p \in D$.

Let $\mathcal{R}$ and $\mathcal{R}'$ be sets of runs. We say that *runs* $\mathcal{R}'$ *are compatible with runs* $\mathcal{R}$ *for processes in* D, denoted by $\mathcal{R}' \preccurlyeq_D \mathcal{R}$, if $\forall \alpha \in \mathcal{R}' \; \exists \beta \in \mathcal{R} : \alpha \overset{D}{\sim} \beta$.

3. THE IMPOSSIBILITY THEOREM

In this section, we will present our general k-set agreement impossibility theorem. Due to its very broad applicability, the theorem itself is stated in a highly generic and somewhat abstract way. It captures a reasonably simple idea, however, which boils down to extracting a consensus algorithm for a certain subsystem where consensus is unsolvable: Suppose that a given k-set agreement algorithm A for some system model $\mathcal{M}$ has runs, where processes start with distinct values and k partitions $D_1, \ldots, D_{k-1}$ and $\overline{D}$ can be formed: Processes in the $k - 1$ partitions D_i decide on (at least) $k - 1$ different values, and no process in partition $\overline{D}$ ever hears from any process in D_i before it decides. Note carefully that processes in $\overline{D}$ can communicate arbitrarily within $\overline{D}$. Then, the ability of A to solve k-set agreement would imply that the restricted algorithm $A_{|\overline{D}}$ can solve consensus in the restricted model $\mathcal{M}' = \langle \overline{D} \rangle$. However, if the synchrony and failure assumptions of $\mathcal{M}$ are such that consensus cannot be solved in $\mathcal{M}'$, this is a contradiction.

THEOREM 1 (k-SET AGREEMENT IMPOSSIBILITY). *Let* $\mathcal{M} = \langle \Pi \rangle$ *be a system model and consider the runs* $\mathcal{M}_A$ *that are generated by some fixed k-set agreement algorithm A in* $\mathcal{M}$, *where every process starts with a distinct input value. Fix some nonempty disjoint sets of processes* $D_1, \ldots, D_{k-1}$, *and a set of distinct decision values* $\{v_1, \ldots, v_{k-1}\}$. *Moreover, let* $D = \bigcup_{1 \leqslant i < k} D_i$ *and* $\overline{D} = \Pi \setminus D$. *Consider the following two properties:*

(dec-D) *For every set D_i, value v_i was proposed by some process in D, and there is some process in D_i that decides on v_i.*

(dec-$\overline{D}$) *If $p_j \in \overline{D}$ then p_j receives no messages from any process in D until after every process in $\overline{D}$ has decided.*

Let $\mathcal{R}_{(\overline{D})} \subseteq \mathcal{M}_A$ *and* $\mathcal{R}_{(D, \overline{D})} \subseteq \mathcal{M}_A$ *be the sets of runs of A where (dec-$\overline{D}$) respectively both, (dec-D) and (dec-$\overline{D}$), hold. Suppose that the following conditions are satisfied:*

(A) $\mathcal{R}_{(\overline{D})}$ *is nonempty.*

(B) $\mathcal{R}_{(\overline{D})} \preccurlyeq_{\overline{D}} \mathcal{R}_{(D, \overline{D})}$.

In addition, consider a restricted model $\mathcal{M}' = \langle \overline{D} \rangle$ such that the following hold:

(C) *There is no algorithm that solves consensus in $\mathcal{M}'$.*

(D) $\mathcal{M}'_{A_{|\overline{D}}} \preccurlyeq_{\overline{D}} \mathcal{M}_A$.

Then, A does not solve k-set agreement in $\mathcal{M}$.

PROOF. For the sake of a contradiction, assume that there is a k-set agreement algorithm A for model $\mathcal{M}$, sets of runs $\mathcal{R}_{(\overline{D})}$ and $\mathcal{R}_{(D, \overline{D})}$ and some sets of processes $D_1, \ldots, D_{k-1}$ such that conditions (A)–(D) hold. Due to (A) we have $\mathcal{R}_{(\overline{D})} \neq \emptyset$; then, (B) implies that $\mathcal{R}_{(D, \overline{D})}$ is nonempty too. Observe that (dec-D) ensures that there are $\geqslant k-1$ distinct decision values among the processes in D, in every run in $\mathcal{R}_{(D, \overline{D})}$. Since algorithm A satisfies k-agreement, the compatibility requirement (B) between runs $\mathcal{R}_{(\overline{D})}$ and $\mathcal{R}_{(D, \overline{D})}$ for processes in $\overline{D}$ implies the following constraint:

(Fact 1) *In each run in $\mathcal{R}_{(\overline{D})}$, all processes in $\overline{D}$ must decide on a common value.*

We will now show that this fact yields a contradiction. Starting from $\mathcal{M}'_{A_{|\overline{D}}}$, i.e., the set of runs of the restricted algorithm in model $\mathcal{M}'$, we know by (D) that for each $\rho' \in \mathcal{M}'_{A_{|\overline{D}}}$, there exists a run $\rho \in \mathcal{M}_A$ such that $\rho' \overset{\overline{D}}{\sim} \rho$. Obviously, no process $p \in \overline{D}$ receives messages from a process $q \in D$ in ρ' before p's decision, as such a process q does not exist in the restricted model $\mathcal{M}'$. Clearly, the same is true for the indistinguishable run ρ (even though such a process q does exist in model $\mathcal{M}$). Therefore, we have that, in fact, $\rho \in \mathcal{R}_{(\overline{D})}$, and due to (Fact 1), we know that in each run $\rho' \in \mathcal{M}'_{A_{|\overline{D}}}$ all processes decide on the same value. This, however, means that we could employ $A_{|\overline{D}}$ to solve consensus in $\mathcal{M}'$, which is a contradiction to (C). $\square$

The proof of Theorem 1 neither restricts the types of failures that can occur in $\mathcal{M}$ nor the underlying synchrony assumptions of $\mathcal{M}$ in any way. Moreover, our impossibility argument uses a 2-partitioning argument but does *not* require the system to (temporarily or permanently) decompose into $k+1$ partitions. In particular, there is no further restriction on the communication among processes within D and within $\overline{D}$. Despite its main purpose of showing impossibilities, our theorem is also useful when developing new algorithms for achieving k-set agreement. For example, suppose that we are given some unproven but seemingly promising new algorithm A for a model close to asynchrony. Then, checking whether the runs of A are such that the conditions of Theorem 1 are satisfied will allow us to determine already at an early stage (i.e., before developing a detailed correctness analysis) whether it is worthwhile to explore A further. In particular, if (dec-D) can be satisfied in some runs, i.e., (A) holds, the algorithms is very likely flawed, as the remaining conditions are typically easy to construct in sufficiently asynchronous systems.

4. DERIVED RESULTS

In the full paper [1], we have used our result to derive impossibility results both for partially synchronous systems and for asynchronous systems augmented with failure detectors:

THEOREM 2. *There is no algorithm that solves k-set agreement in a system $\mathcal{M}$ of n processes where*

- *processes are synchronous,*
- *communication is asynchronous,*
- *a process can broadcast a message in an atomic step, and*
- *receiving and sending are part of the same atomic step,*

for any

$$k \leqslant \frac{n-1}{n-f}, \qquad (1)$$

even if, of the f possibly faulty processes, $f-1$ can fail by crashing initially and only one process can crash during the execution.

THEOREM 3. *There is no $(n-1)$-resilient algorithm that solves k-set agreement in an asynchronous system with failure detector (Σ_k, Ω_k), for all $2 \leqslant k \leqslant n-2$.*

5. CONCLUSION

The main advantage of our approach is that we are independent of a specific system model, since Theorem 1 neither makes assumptions on the available amount of synchrony, nor on the power of computing steps and communication primitives available to the processes. This genericity allows to apply our theorem in very different contexts.

6. REFERENCES

[1] Martin Biely, Peter Robinson, and Ulrich Schmid, *Easy impossibility proofs for k-set agreement in message passing systems*, Research Report 2/2011, Technische Universität Wien, Institut für Technische Informatik, Treitlstr. 1-3/182-1, 1040 Vienna, Austria, 2011, available at ArXiv http://arxiv.org/abs/1103.3671.

[2] Nancy Lynch, *Distributed algorithms*, Morgan Kaufman Publishers, Inc., San Francisco, USA, 1996.

Brief Announcement: Solving the At-Most-Once Problem with Nearly Optimal Effectiveness

[Extended Abstract]

Sotirios Kentros[*]
Computer Science and Engineering
University of Connecticut, Storrs, USA
skentros@engr.uconn.edu

Aggelos Kiayias[†]
Computer Science and Engineering
University of Connecticut, Storrs, USA
aggelos@kiayias.com

ABSTRACT

We present and analyze a wait-free deterministic algorithm for solving the at-most-once problem: how m fail-prone processes perform asynchronously n tasks at most once using shared memory. Our algorithmic strategy provides for the first time nearly optimal effectiveness, which is a measure that expresses the total number of tasks completed in the worst case. Our algorithm's effectiveness equals $n - 2m + 2$. This is up to an additive factor of m close to the known effectiveness lower bound $n - m + 1$ and improves on the previously best known deterministic solutions that have effectiveness only $n - \log m \cdot o(n)$. We also present a work and space complexity analysis for suitable ranges of the algorithm parameters and demonstrate further that (i) we can achieve work $O(nm \log n \log m)$ and simultaneously effectiveness of $n - 3m^2 - m + 2$, which is asymptotically optimal for any $m = o(\sqrt{n})$, (ii) we can achieve optimal work up to logarithmic factors $\tilde{O}(n)$ and asymptotically optimal effectiveness whenever $m = o(\sqrt[3]{n})$.

Categories and Subject Descriptors

F.1.2 [**Computation by Abstract Devices**]: Models of Computation—*Parallelism and concurrency*
; F.2.m [**Analysis of Algorithms and Problem Complexity**]: Miscellaneous

General Terms

Algorithms,Reliability,Theory

Keywords

Shared Memory, At-Most-Once Semantics

1. INTRODUCTION

The *at-most-once problem* for asynchronous shared memory systems was introduced by Kentros et al. [3] as the problem of performing a set of n jobs by m fail-prone processes while maintaining at-most-once semantics. The *at-most-once* semantic for object invocation ensures that an

---

[*]Research supported in part by the State Scholarships Foundation of Greece.
[†]Research supported in part by NSF awards 0447808, 0831304, 0831306.

operation accessing and altering the state of an object is performed no more than once and it provides important means for reasoning about the safety of critical applications. Uniprocessor systems may trivially provide solutions for at-most-once semantics by using central scheduling. The problem becomes very challenging for autonomous processes in a system with concurrent invocations on multiple objects.

Perhaps the most important question in this area is devising algorithms for the at-most-once problem with good *effectiveness*. The complexity measure of effectiveness [3] describes the number of jobs completed (at-most-once) by an implementation, as a function of the overall number of jobs n, the number of processes m, and the number of crashes f. The only deterministic solutions known [3] exhibit very low effectiveness $\left(n^{\frac{1}{\log m}} - 1\right)^{\log m}$ which for most choices of the parameters is very far from optimal (unless $m = O(1)$ and $n \to \infty$). Contrary to this, the present work presents the first deterministic algorithm for at-most-once which is optimal up to additive factors of m. Specifically our effectiveness is $n - (2m - 2)$ which comes close to an additive factor of m to the lower bound for effectiveness $n - m + 1$.
Contributions: In this paper we present and analyze the algorithm KK_β that solves the at-most-once problem. The algorithm is parametrized by $\beta \geq m$ and has effectiveness $n - \beta - m + 2$. For $\beta = m$ the algorithm has optimal effectiveness of $n - 2m + 2$ up to an additive factor of m. Note that the bound for the effectiveness of any algorithm is $n - f$ [3], where $f \leq m - 1$ is the number of failures in the system. We further prove that for $\beta \geq 3m^2$ the algorithm has work complexity $O(nm \log n \log m)$, while it has asymptotically optimal effectiveness for any $m = o(\sqrt{n})$. This is better compared to the algorithm presented in [3] which is asymptotically optimal only if $m = O(1)$. If work is the main concern, for $n > 3m^3 \log m$ we can use KK_β as the base for an implementation that solves the at most once problem with optimal up to a logarithmic factor work complexity $\tilde{O}(n)$ and asymptotically optimal effectiveness for $m = o(\sqrt[3]{n})$. We note that our solutions are deterministic and assume worst-case behavior. In the probabilistic setting Hillel [2] shows that optimal effectiveness can be achieved with expected work complexity $O(nm^2 \log m)$.

2. MODEL, PROBLEMS, DEFINITIONS

We consider a system of m asynchronous, shared-memory processors in the presence of crashes. We use the *Input/Output Automata* formalism, and specifically the *asynchro-*

nous *shared memory automaton* that consists of a set of *processes* that interact by means of a collection of *shared variables* that support atomic read/write operations [4]. The adversary controls the asynchrony and the crashes, causing up to $f < m$ crashes.

We consider algorithms whose purpose is to perform a set of tasks or activities that we call *jobs*. Let A be an algorithm specified for m processes with ids from set $\mathcal{P} = [1 \ldots m]$, and with jobs with unique ids from set $\mathcal{J} = [1 \ldots n]$. We assume that there are at least as many jobs as there are processes, i.e., $n \geq m$. A job is *performed* in an execution α of A by process p if α includes action $\mathsf{do}_{p,j}$. For an sequence κ, we let $len(\kappa)$ denote its length, and we let $\kappa|_\pi$ denote the sequence of elements π occurring in κ. Then for an execution α, $len\left(\alpha|_{\mathsf{do}_{p,j}}\right)$ is the number of times process p performs job j. Let the set of performed jobs in execution α be denoted by $J_\alpha = \{j \mid \mathsf{do}_{p,j} \text{ occurs in } \alpha\}$. The total number of jobs performed in α is $Do(\alpha) = |J_\alpha|$. We next define the *at-most-once* problem, the measures of performance for at-most-once algorithms and repeat the lower bound on effectiveness. Note here that we are borrowing the definitions and bound from Kentros et al. [3].

Definition 1. Algorithm A solves the At-Most-Once problem if for each execution α of A we have:

$$\forall j \in \mathcal{J} : \sum_{p \in \mathcal{P}} len\left(\alpha|_{\mathsf{do}_{p,j}}\right) \leq 1.$$

Effectiveness counts the number of jobs performed by an algorithm in the worst case.

Definition 2. The **effectiveness** of algorithm A is defined as $E_A(n, m, f) = \min\{Do(\alpha)\}$ where α is any fair execution of A with m processes, n jobs, and at most f crashes.

We also assess efficiency of our algorithms in terms of work and space complexity. **Work complexity** measures the worst case total number of bits read from or written to the shared memory by an algorithm. **Space complexity** measures the total number of bits in shared and internal variables used by an algorithm.

THEOREM 1. *from Kentros et al. [3]*
For all algorithms A that solve the at-most-once problem with m processes and $n \geq m$ jobs in the presence of $f < m$ crashes it holds that $E_A(n, m, f) \leq n - f$.

3. ALGORITHM KK_β

We present and analyse algorithm KK_β, that solves the at-most-once problem. Parameter $\beta \in \mathbb{N}$ is the termination parameter of the algorithm. Algorithm KK_β is defined for all $\beta \geq m$. If $\beta = m$, algorithm KK_β has optimal up to an additive factor of m effectiveness.

The idea behind the algorithm KK_β is quite intuitive and is based on an algorithm for renaming processes presented by Attiya *et al.* [1]. Each process p, picks a job i to perform, announces (by writing in shared memory) that it is about to perform the job and then checks if it is safe to perform it (by reading the announcements other processes made in the shared memory, and the jobs other processes announced they have performed). If it is safe to perform the job i, process p will perform job i and then mark the job completed. If it is not safe to perform i, p will release the job. In either case, p picks a new job to perform. In order to pick a new job, p reads from the shared memory and gathers information

on which jobs are safe to perform. This again is done by reading the announcements that other processes made in the shared memory concerning the jobs they are about to perform, and the jobs other processes announced they have already performed. Assuming that those jobs are ordered, p splits the set of "free" jobs in m intervals and picks the first job of the interval with rank equal to p's rank. Since the information needed in order to decide whether it is safe to perform a specific job and in order to pick the next job to perform is the same, these steps are combined in the algorithm.

We prove that the algorithm solves the at-most-once problem. Moreover we prove that for $\beta \geq m$ the algorithm is wait-free and has effectiveness $n - (\beta + m - 2)$. For $\beta = O(m)$ the effectiveness is asymptotically optimal for any $m = o(n)$. We also prove that for $\beta \geq 3 \cdot m^2$ the algorithm has work complexity $O(mn \log n \log m)$.

By partitioning the jobs in sets of $m \log m$ jobs, we can use KK_β with $\beta \geq 3m^2$ on the $\frac{n}{m \log m}$ sets, where performing a job i will be performing all the $m \log m$ jobs of set i. This results in $O(n \log n)$ work complexity and $n - 3m^3 \log m - m^2 \log m + 3m \log m$ effectiveness. This implementation gives optimal to a logarithmic factor work complexity of $\tilde{O}(n)$ and asymptotically optimal effectiveness of $n - o(n)$ for $m = o(\sqrt[3]{n})$. Finally we prove that the algorithm has space complexity $O(nm \log n)$.

4. CONCLUSIONS

We devised and analyzed a deterministic algorithm called KK_β which for $\beta = m$ has effectiveness $n - 2m + 2$ which is asymptotically optimal for any $m = o(n)$ and close to the effectiveness bound $n - m + 1$ by an additive factor of m. This is a significant improvement over the previous best known deterministic algorithm [3], that achieves asymptotically optimal effectiveness only for the case $m = O(1)$. With respect to work complexity, for any $m = o(\sqrt[3]{n})$ we can use KK_β to achieve optimal work up to logarithmic factors $\tilde{O}(n)$ with asymptotically optimal effectiveness $n - o(n)$.

In terms of open questions there exists still an effectiveness gap between the shown effectiveness of $n - 2m + 2$ of algorithm KK_β and the known effectiveness bound of $n - m + 1$ if $f = m - 1$. It would be interesting to see if this can be bridged for deterministic algorithms. Moreover, there is a lack of an upper bound on work complexity, when the effectiveness of an algorithm becomes very close to the effectiveness bound. Finally it would be interesting to study the existence and performance of algorithms that try to implement at-most-once semantics in systems with different means of communication, such as message-passing systems.

5. REFERENCES

[1] H. Attiya, A. Bar-Noy, D. Dolev, D. Peleg, and R. Reischuk. Renaming in an asynchronous environment. *J. ACM*, 37(3):524–548, 1990.
[2] K. C. Hillel. Multi-sided shared coins and randomized set-agreement. In *Proc. of the 22nd ACM Symp. on Parallel Algorithms and Architectures (SPAA'10)*, pages 60–68, 2010.
[3] S. Kentros, A. Kiayias, N. C. Nicolaou, and A. A. Shvartsman. At-most-once semantics in asynchronous shared memory. In *DISC*, pages 258–273, 2009.
[4] N. A. Lynch. *Distributed Algorithms*. Morgan Kaufmann Publishers, 1996.

Transforming Worst-case Optimal Solutions for Simultaneous Tasks into All-case Optimal Solutions

Maurice P. Herlihy
Brown University
mph@cs.brown.edu

Yoram Moses
Technion
moses@ee.technion.ac.il

Mark R. Tuttle
Intel
tuttle@acm.org

ABSTRACT

Decision tasks require that nonfaulty processes make decisions based on their input values. Simultaneous decision tasks require that nonfaulty processes decide in the same round. Most decision tasks have known worst-case lower bounds. Most also have known *worst-case* optimal protocols that halt in the number of rounds given by the worst-case lower bound, and some have *early-stopping* protocols that can halt earlier than the worst-case lower bound (sometimes in as early as two rounds). We consider what might be called *earliest-possible* protocols for simultaneous decision tasks. We present a new technique that converts *worst-case optimal* decision protocols into *all-case optimal* simultaneous decision protocols: For every behavior of the adversary, the all-case optimal protocol decides as soon as *any* protocol can decide in a run with the same adversarial behavior. Examples to which this can be applied include set consensus, condition-based consensus, renaming and order-preserving renaming. Some of these tasks can be solved significantly faster than the classical simultaneous consensus task. A byproduct of the analysis is a proof that improving on the worst-case bound for any simultaneous task by even a single round is as hard as reaching simultaneous consensus.

Categories and Subject Descriptors

C.2.4 [**Computer-Communication Networks**]: Distributed Systems—*Distributed applications*; D.4.5 [**Operating Systems**]: Reliability—*Fault-tolerance*; D.4.7 [**Operating Systems**]: Organization and Design—*Distributed systems*

General Terms

Theory, Algorithms, Reliability

Keywords

Synchronous message passing model, crash failure model, consensus, k-set agreement, condition-based consensus, renaming, common knowledge, topology.

1. INTRODUCTION

Decision tasks are fundamental problems in distributed computation. Each nonfaulty process begins with an input value and chooses an output value (decides), subject to conditions given by the task, even if t of the n processes fail by crashing. Some famous examples of decision tasks are

- *consensus* [PSL80, LSP82, FL81, DS82, FLP85]
- *k-set agreement* [HS99, BG93, SZ00, CHLT00]
- *condition-based consensus* [MRR03, MRR06]
- *renaming* [ABND+90, HS99, AR02, HT90]

Simultaneous decision tasks [DM90, MT88, MM08] are decision tasks in which all nonfaulty processes decide in the same round. Simultaneity is important when processes must coordinate their behavior in time. Such coordination may be needed, for example, to cleanly end the execution of one protocol or one protocol phase and begin the next. Indeed, in many protocols the behavior of processes is a function of the round number, which depends on a simultaneous start.

Most decision tasks have known worst-case lower bounds, and most have known optimal protocols matching these lower bounds. Some protocols are *worst-case optimal* in the sense that every execution halts in the number of rounds given by the worst-case lower bound. Some are *early stopping* in the sense that they may occasionally halt earlier than this worst-case lower bound, sometimes as early as two rounds. Some are *all-case optimal* in the sense that, in every execution (and not just the worst-case execution), no protocol stops faster: For every behavior of the adversary (controlling input values and process failures), the all-case optimal protocol halts as early as any other protocol would in an execution with the same adversarial behavior.

Among our results, two stand out. Given a decision task P with a tight worst-case lower bound L,

1. Any worst-case optimal protocol for P can be transformed into an all-case optimal protocol for the simultaneous version of P.

2. Beating the worst-case lower bound is as hard as solving consensus: For every behavior of the adversary, if some simultaneous solution to P decides at time $k < L$ in this behavior, then simultaneous consensus can be obtained at time k in this behavior as well. In fact, the key to deciding early is agreeing that the adversary did not behave in the worst-case manner.

The novelty of our work is, after a decade of distillation, an elegant, almost too-simple combination of known results from knowledge and topology yielding powerful results and new insights.

With topology, we have an extremely powerful tool for proving lower bounds for decision tasks. In this approach, a protocol is modeled as a combinatorial structure called a *simplical complex* that describes the final states of the protocol and how much any two final states have in common (that is, which processes find the two states indistinguishable). A task, too, is modeled as a simplical complex, and a protocol solves a task if and only if a certain map exists from the protocol complex to the task complex. Lower bounds can be derived by comparing these complexes' degrees of *connectivity*, the dimensions below which their "surfaces" have no "holes." Nearly every lower bound proof for a decision task can be understood in terms of topology. In fact, for set agreement and renaming, the only lower bound proofs known to date are either based on or inspired by topological arguments.

With knowledge, we have the dominant tool for reasoning about simultaneity. A process *knows* that a predicate φ holds if φ holds in every global state compatible with the local state of the process. *Common knowledge* of φ occurs when each process knows φ, each process knows that each process knows φ, and so on. In this approach, lower bounds can be derived by observing that certain tasks require attaining common knowledge of particular facts [HM90, FHMV95], and protocol design can reduce to implementing tests for common knowledge. For simultaneous consensus, for example, Moses and Dwork [DM90] show that the optimal simultaneous consensus protocol takes time $t + 1 - W$, where W, the *waste* of the execution, is a measure of how far the execution deviates from the worst-case failure pattern (defined below).

As Moses and Raynal observed [MR08], simultaneous decision tasks require that processes agree on two things:

- on mutually-compatible decision values, and
- on a common decision round.

They started with two known results: that simultaneous consensus is solvable in $t+1-W$ rounds; and that *condition-based consensus*, which restricts the set of input vectors to those satisfying a condition involving d, is solvable in $t+1-d$ rounds. The question that they considered was whether it is possible to compound the savings—one based on the input structure and the other (the waste) stemming from the failure pattern. They showed that there is no "double discount"—that it is possible to solve simultaneous condition-based consensus in the minimum of $t+1-W$ and $t+1-d$ rounds, but no earlier. Moreover, the protocol that achieves this is all-case optimal: for every behavior of the adversary, determining the inputs and the failure pattern, no other simultaneous-decision protocol can decide earlier than their protocol does. This all-case optimality property is the same as that of the simultaneous consensus protocol of Dwork and Moses, which decides in $t + 1 - W$ rounds when the inputs are unconstrained.

Our work was inspired by [MR08], and shows that it is a particular case of a general phenomenon. A large class of simultaneous tasks can be solved in an all-case optimal fashion. Indeed, given a protocol that solves a simultaneous task in time that matches the worst-case lower bound L, we show how to use this protocol in order to obtain one that is all-case optimal, by executing it concurrently with a

continuous consensus protocol, and deciding at the earlier of the *a priori* worst-case bound L and time $t + 1 - W$.

Returning to simultaneous decision tasks, common knowledge has the property that a fact about the initial state (that is, about the input values) becomes common knowledge to all processes at the same time. A decision task can usually be solved simultaneously once some fact (enough facts) about the initial state become common knowledge. On the other hand, many decision tasks are much easier than testing for common knowledge. It may take as many as $t + 1$ rounds for any fact about the initial state to become common knowledge in the worst case, but the renaming task can be solved in $\log n$ rounds in the worst case. Of course, worst-case executions are the longest executions, and it is usually possible to decide much earlier in other executions. In this paper we show that, for any decision task, deciding simultaneously at any point before the decision task's worst-case lower bound—a bound typically proven using topology—reduces to testing for common knowledge, and we show that running a protocol matching the topological lower bound in parallel with a knowledge-theoretic protocol results in a protocol that is optimal in every execution (and not just the worst-case execution).

More precisely, our main results are the following:

- We show that a protocol for *continuous consensus* called CONCON [MM08], derived by knowledge-theoretic means, can be adapted to solve any decision task simultaneously in $t+1-W$ rounds, which is the time required to solve simultaneous consensus.

- We show that any protocol for a decision task can be transformed into a simultaneous protocol, and that running it in parallel with CONCON yields a simultaneous protocol that decides in time that is the minimum of original protocol's worst-case execution time and CONCON's $t + 1 - W$.

- We show that — for problems with tight worst-case bounds — running CONCON in parallel with a protocol that is optimal in the worst-case execution yields a protocol that is *all-case* optimal: For every behavior of an adversarial scheduler, our protocol halts at least as early as any other protocol for the problem would in the context of this behavior.

Interestingly, beating the worst-case bound of a simultaneous decision task is as hard as simultaneous consensus: while some simultaneous decision tasks are easy and some are hard, the cost of beating a problem's worst-case lower bound is the same $t + 1 - W$ for all problems, easy or hard.

This paper is organized as follows. Section 2 presents the synchronous model and the class of simultaneous decision tasks. It then reviews material about continuous consensus and the CONCON protocol. Section 3 considers how protocols solving a given simultaneous decision task can be composed. Section 4 presents our main theorem, showing how CONCON can be used to obtain simultaneous solutions that are optimal in all runs. Applications of this theorem are presented and discussed in Section 5. Finally, in Section 6 we discuss the results, focusing on the interaction between combinatorial topology and common knowledge that they demonstrate.

2. MODEL AND PRELIMINARIES

2.1 Synchronous computation

Our model of computation is a synchronous, message-passing model with crash failures. A system has $n \geq 2$ processes denoted by $\mathcal{P} = \{p_1, p_2, \ldots, p_n\}$. Each pair of processes is connected by a two-way communication link, and each message is tagged with the identity of the sender. They share a discrete global clock that starts out at time 0 and advances by increments of one. Communication in the system proceeds in a sequence of *rounds*, with round $k + 1$ taking place between time k and time $k + 1$. Each process starts in some *initial state* at time 0, usually with an *input value* of some kind. In every round, each process first sends a set of messages to other processes, then receives messages sent to it by other processes during the same round, and then performs some local computation based on the messages it has received.

A faulty process fails by *crashing* in some round $k \geq 1$. It behaves correctly in the first $k - 1$ rounds and sends no messages from round $k + 1$ on. During its crashing round k, the process may succeed in sending messages on an arbitrary subset of its links. We assume that at most $t \leq n - 1$ processes fail in any given execution.

A *failure pattern* describes how processes fail in an execution. It is a graph where a vertex is a process-time pair $\langle p, k \rangle$ denoting process p and time k, and an edge is of the form $(\langle p, k-1 \rangle, \langle q, k \rangle)$ denoting the fact that p succeeded in sending a message to q during round k. We write $\mathsf{Fails}(t)$ to denote the set of failure patterns in which at most t processes fail.

An *input vector* describes what input the processes receive in an execution. It is a vector $(i_1, \ldots, i_n)$ where i_k is the input to p_k.

A *run* is a description of an infinite behavior of the system. Given a run r and a time k, we write $r(k)$ to denote the global state at time k in r, and $r_p(k)$ to denote the local state of process p at time k in r.

A *protocol* describes what messages a process sends and how a process changes state during a round as a function of its local state at the start of a round and the messages received during a round. We assume that a protocol A has access to the values of n and t, typically passed to A as parameters. A run r of a protocol is uniquely determined by the protocol A, the input vector $\vec{\imath}$, and the failure pattern F, and we write $r = A[\vec{\imath}, F]$.

2.2 Decision tasks

A *decision task* is given by a relation from input vectors to output vectors. We think of each process as having an input and output register, and we think of a process as deciding on a value when it writes the value to its output register. Let I_i and O_i be sets of input values and output values for process p_i for each $i = 1, \ldots, n$. Let $\mathcal{I}$ be a subset of input vectors $I_1 \times \cdots \times I_n$,[1] and let $\mathcal{O}$ be the set of output vectors $O_1 \times \cdots \times O_n$. A *decision task* P over $\mathcal{I}$ and $\mathcal{O}$ is specified by a relation on $\mathcal{I} \times \mathcal{O}$ whose projection on the first component coincides with $\mathcal{I}$. The interpretation is that if $(\vec{\imath}, \vec{o}) \in P$ and processes begin with input values in $\vec{\imath}$, then processes

are allowed to decide on output values in $\vec{o}$. Formally, a protocol A solves a decision task P if every run r of A in which at most t of n processes fail satisfies the following conditions:

- *Completeness*: Every nonfaulty process decides on some output value.

- *Correctness*: The set of deciding processes choose correct values: If $\vec{\imath} \in \mathcal{I}$ is the vector of input values in the run r, then there is an output vector $\vec{o} \in \mathcal{O}$ such that $(\vec{\imath}, \vec{o}) \in P$ and each process p_j that decides in r decides on the value o_j given by $\vec{o}$.

Well-known examples of decision tasks are consensus, k-set agreement, condition-based consensus, renaming, and order-preserving renaming. We note that the values n and t are known to processes following a decision protocol in the sense that they are parameters to the protocol, and the sets $\mathcal{I}$ and $\mathcal{O}$ are known in the sense that a protocol is written with a specific family of sets (whose definitions probably depend in part on n and t) in mind.

For every decision task P, there is an associated *simultaneous decision task* denoted by $\mathrm{SIM}(P)$. The protocol A solves $\mathrm{SIM}(P)$ if, in addition to completeness and correctness, every run r of A also satisfies

- *Simultaneity*: All processes that decide in r do so in the same round.

2.3 Continuous Consensus

A central tool in our study will be the CONCON protocol [MM08], which is an efficient implementation of a *continuous consensus* service. We briefly describe continuous consensus, and then present the protocol.

In continuous consensus, every process maintains a copy of a "core" of information, with all copies guaranteed to be identical at all times. Moreover, this core should ultimately contain as many of the facts of interest in a given application as possible. The set of facts being "monitored" in the cores are a parameter of the service. They can involve various events such as input values, information about external events or about communication or process failures. For the purposes of this paper we focus on the case where the monitored facts are simply pairs of the form (p_j, v_j) denoting that processes p_j had input value v_j. We define a continuous consensus (CC) service with respect to initial input values to be a distributed protocol that at all times $k \geq 0$ provides each process i with a (possibly empty) core $M_i[k]$ of input values. In every run of this protocol the following properties are required to hold for all nonfaulty processes p_i and p_j:

- *Accuracy*: All values $M_i[k]$ occurred in the run.

- *Consistency*: $M_i[k] = M_j[k]$ at all times k.

- *Completeness*: If a nonfaulty process p_j has input value v_j, then $(p_j, v_j) \in M_i[k]$ must hold for some time k.

The consistency property allows for simultaneous actions that depend on input values to be consistently performed simultaneously at all times. Completeness is a liveness condition, guaranteeing that the core will contain relevant information eventually. Notice that a CC protocol can be easily used to solve simultaneous consensus, for example. If processes decide on the first input value that enters the core

---

[1] Most decision tasks in the literature are exhaustive, in the sense that $\mathcal{I} = I_1 \times \cdots \times I_n$. When not exhaustive, the set $\mathcal{I}$ is often called a *condition* restricting the input vectors [MRR03, MRR06].

(and on the minimal value, in case a number of input values enter in the same round), the conditions of simultaneous consensus are all satisfied. As we shall see, a CC protocol is a useful tool for solving simultaneous decision tasks in general. In a precise sense, continuous consensus is closely related to the notion of *common knowledge*. Indeed, all of the facts in the CC core are guaranteed to be common knowledge. (We defer a more detailed definition of common knowledge and the connection to Section 4.)

Mizrahi and Moses [MM08] introduced continuous consensus and gave an efficient implementation called CONCON for the crash and sending omissions failure models. In addition to sending linear-sized messages per round, the CONCON protocol has a number of useful properties in the crash failure model:

- $M_i[k] = M_j[k]$ for all processes that are still active at time k, for all $k \geq 0$.

- There is a property W (standing for *waste*) of the particular failure pattern in a given execution, such that (i) $M_i[t + 1 - W]$ contains the input values of all active processes, and possibly of the failed processes, and (ii) $M_i[k] = \emptyset$ for all $k < t + 1 - W$.

- CONCON maintains the maximal core of all possible CC protocols: For every behavior of the adversary (determining the vector of inputs and every failure pattern), the core $M_i[k]$ at time k in CONCON is a superset of the core at time k in any other CC protocol, under the same adversary.

3. FAST PROTOCOLS

In this section, we show that CONCON yields fast protocols for simultaneous decision tasks.

There is a simple construction that transforms a decision protocol into a simultaneous decision protocol for the same problem with the same worst-case execution time. Let P be any decision task, and let A be any protocol that solves P. For any given time k, the protocol DELAY(A, k) is obtained from A simply by having processes delay decisions until time k. Thus, processes send exactly the same messages in A and DELAY(A, k). The only change is that whenever A specifies that a process should decide before time k, the process keeps track of its decision value and writes the value to its output registers only at time k. (Decisions after time k in A are performed unchanged.) Since processes communicate with each other via messages and not output registers, a process can change the time it writes to its output register without changing the views of other processes.

LEMMA 1. *If protocol A solves decision task P, and $\hat{k}$ is an upper bound on the worst-case execution time of A, then* DELAY$(A, \hat{k})$ *solves* SIM(P) *with execution time exactly $\hat{k}$.*

PROOF. Completeness is satisfied since the nonfaulty processes will survive until time $\hat{k}$ and write to their output registers. Correctness is satisfied since the values chosen in a run of DELAY$(A, \hat{k})$ are a subset of those chosen in A: every run r' of DELAY$(A, \hat{k})$ maps to a run r of A where processes do not delay their decisions as they do in r', so there is a pair $(\vec{i}, \vec{o}) \in P$ such that $\vec{i}$ is the input vector for r (and hence r') and such that every process p_i that decides in r (and hence every process p_i that decides in r') chooses the value o_i in $\vec{o}$. Simultaneity is satisfied since all processes decide at time $\hat{k}$. □

There is a simple construction based on CONCON that transforms any decision protocol A into a simultaneous decision protocol CONCON(A) for the same problem with execution time $t + 1 - W$. Let P be a decision task, and let A be a protocol that solves P. In the protocol CONCON(A), each process $p_j \in \mathcal{P}$ follows the protocol CONCON until the core becomes nonempty. It then simulates an execution of A in which all processes whose initial values are in the core starts with these values and are fault-free, while all remaining processes are crashed and silent from the outset. The process then decides in CONCON(A) on the value it should decide on in the simulated run.

THEOREM 2. *If protocol A solves the decision task P, then* CONCON(A) *solves* SIM(P). *In a run with failure pattern F, it decides at time $t + 1 - W(F)$.*

PROOF. It follows from the discussion in Section 2.3 that CONCON satisfies several important properties: the core becomes nonempty for the first time at time $t + 1 - W$, all processes surviving to the end of round $t + 1 - W$ compute the same core at time $t + 1 - W$, and the initial states of all nonfaulty processes are in the core. Notice that the nonfaulty processes are nonfaulty in the simulated run of A, since the initial states of all nonfaulty processes are in the core, and hence at most t processes fail in the run of A and the remaining processes decide in this run of A. Completeness is satisfied since all nonfaulty processes are nonfaulty in the simulated run of A and decide. Simultaneity is satisfied since all processes learn that the core is nonempty for the first time at time $t + 1 - W$. Correctness is satisfied since all processes learn the same core at time $t + 1 - W$, and hence simulate the same run of A, and hence choose output values consistent with the input values according to the problem specification P. □

Given two solutions for a simultaneous decision task SIM(P) that run in time $\hat{k}$ and $t + 1 - W$, respectively, we can compose them and run them in parallel to get a solution that decides simultaneously at the time which is the minimum of $\hat{k}$ and $t + 1 - W$. Moses and Raynal [MR08] define parallel composition as follows. Suppose that A and B are two protocols for a simultaneous decision task SIM(P). Define A else B to be the protocol that runs A and B in parallel, but gives preference to A over B when choosing output values: In the composed protocol, process $p \in \mathcal{P}$ executes both protocols in parallel until the first round k at the end of which one of A and B has p decide. At that point, if only one protocol has p decide, then p decides on the value determined by that protocol; and if both protocols have p decide, then p decides on the value determined by A.

THEOREM 3. *Let $\hat{k}$ be an upper bound on the worst-case running time of a protocol A. If A solves P, then*

$$\text{DELAY}(A, \hat{k}) \text{ else } \text{CONCON}(A)$$

solves SIM(P) *with execution time* $\min\{\hat{k}, t + 1 - W\}$.

PROOF. First we prove that if A and B are simultaneous decision protocols, then in any run of A else B either all deciding processes choose according to A or all choose according to B. Suppose that p decides at time k_p and q

decides at time k_q. Further assume (without loss of generality) that $k_p \leq k_q$. Whichever simultaneous protocol (A or B) caused p to decide at time k_p would also have caused q to decide at time k_p. So $k_q \leq k_p$ and it follows that $k_p = k_q$. Suppose that (without loss of generality) p decides at time k, and does so according to $X \in \{A, B\}$. If $X = A$ then A has q decide at time k as well, and so p and q both decide according to A in the composition. If $X = B$ then p does *not* decide before round k in either protocol, and does not decide according to A at time k. By the simultaneity of A and B, the same is true for q. Thus, q decides on the value determined by B in the composed protocol. It follows that in every run of $\text{DELAY}(A, \hat{k})$ else $\text{CONCON}(A)$, either all deciding processes decide according to $\text{DELAY}(A, \hat{k})$ or all decide according to $\text{CONCON}(A)$. Thus, (i) every run of the composition satisfies completeness, correctness, and simultaneity, and (ii) every run of the composition has processes decide at the earlier of $\hat{k}$ and $t + 1 - W$. □

4. OPTIMAL PROTOCOLS

In this section, we prove that the protocol

$$\text{Opt}(A, \hat{k}) \;=\; \text{DELAY}(A, \hat{k}) \text{ else } \text{CONCON}(A)$$

for a decision task $\text{SIM}(P)$ is not only fast, it is all-case optimal when $\hat{k}$ is the worst-case lower bound for P and A is a protocol that solves P in $\hat{k}$ rounds. To say that $\text{Opt}(A, \hat{k})$ is *all-case optimal* means that for any input vector and failure pattern, $\text{Opt}(A, \hat{k})$ decides as soon as any other protocol for $\text{SIM}(P)$ would decide with the same input and failure pattern.

This generalizes a result by Moses and Raynal [MR08], shown for the particular decision task of condition-based consensus, where the condition (the set of possible input vectors) is assumed to satisfy a property called d-tightness. As in their case, we will use knowledge theory and known results about the structure of common knowledge to prove our claim. However, while proving optimality in [MR08] required a tailor-made lower bound argument, we present a novel proof technique that allows proving the claim at once for *all* decision problems. Before presenting the proof, we review just enough material from knowledge theory to support our proof.

Our lower bound is based on a well-known connection between simultaneous actions and common knowledge [DM90, MT88, MM08]. Rather than develop the logic of knowledge in detail here, we will employ a simple graph-theoretic interpretation of common knowledge that applies in our setting. For the rest of this section, fix a set $\mathcal{I}$ of input vectors, a number n of processes, and a bound $t \leq n-1$ on the number of failures. Define the *runs of A* to be the set of all runs of the form $A[\vec{\imath}, F]$ for all input vectors $\vec{\imath} \in \mathcal{I}$ and all failure patterns $F \in \text{Fails}(t)$.

Similarity graph.

Given a protocol A, we say that two runs r and r' of A are *indistinguishable* to a process p at time k if process p survives round k in both runs and has the same local state at the end of round k in both runs. We define the *similarity graph* for A at time k to be the undirected graph where the vertices are the runs of A and the edges are all pairs $\{r, r'\}$ such that r and r' are indistinguishable to some process p at time k. We say that two runs r and r' of A are *connected* at time k if they are in the same connected component of the similarity graph for A at time k, which we denote by $r \overset{k}{\sim} r'$.

Common knowledge.

One way to define common knowledge is in terms of the connected components of the similarity graph [DM90]. Given a protocol A, a fact φ is *common knowledge* at time k in a run r of A if φ holds at time k in all runs r' of A satisfying $r' \overset{k}{\sim} r$. One can prove that if A solves $\text{SIM}(P)$ and if processes decide at time k in a run r of A, then it is common knowledge at time k in r that processes are deciding at time k. Formulating this observation in terms of similarity, we have

LEMMA 4. *Let P be a decision task and A be a protocol that solves P simultaneously. If the nonfaulty processes decide at time k in a run r of A, then they decide at time k in every run r' of A satisfying $r' \overset{k}{\sim} r$.*

PROOF. It is enough to prove the result for the case of a single edge from r to r' in the similarity graph at time k, and the result will follow by induction since $r \overset{k}{\sim} r'$ means there is a finite path of edges from r to r'. Since there is an edge from r to r', there is a process p that survives round k in both runs and has the same local state at the end of round k in both runs. Since the nonfaulty processes decide at time k in r and p has not failed, process p must decide at time k in r. Since p has the same local state at time k in both runs, it must decide at time k in r' as well. Since decisions are simultaneous in runs of A, all nonfaulty processes must decide at time k in r', and we are done. □

Waste.

It is known that an adversarial scheduler can keep a fact from becoming common knowledge by failing processes that know this fact, and the best strategy for the adversary is to fail one process per round to keep a fact from becoming common knowledge until the end of round $t+1$. To fail more than one process per round is a waste. Following [DM90], we capture this intuition as follows. Given a failure pattern F, we say that the failure of a process p is *exposed* in round k if the round k edge from p to q is missing in F for some process q that survives round k in F. Let $E(F, k)$ be the number of processes whose failure is exposed in round k or earlier. Observe that $E(F, 0) = 0$ for all $F \in \text{Fails}(t)$. Let $W(F)$ denote the *waste* inherent in F defined by

$$W(F) = \max_{k \geq 0} \{E(F, k) - k\}.$$

Notice that $0 \leq W(F) \leq t - 1$ for all $F \in \text{Fails}(t)$. In the language of [MR09], we say that round k is *premature* in a run $r = A[\vec{\imath}, F]$ if $k < t+1-W(F)$, since we shall see that no nontrivial fact can be be common knowledge at the end of a premature round. Specifically, the analysis of connectivity in the similarity graph performed in [DM90] showed the following. We say that the set $\mathcal{I}$ of input vectors is *complete* if it is equal to a Cartesian product $I_1 \times \cdots \times I_n$, meaning that process input values can be chosen independently.

LEMMA 5. [DM90, MR08] *Suppose the set $\mathcal{I}$ of input vectors is complete. If round k is premature in two runs r and r' of A, then $r \overset{k}{\sim} r'$.*

We now have the combinatorial machinery that we need to prove our main result:

THEOREM 6   (ALL-CASE OPTIMALITY). *Let P be a decision task with worst-case lower bound $\hat{k}$ and let A be a protocol that solves P in time $\hat{k}$. If P's set of input vectors is complete, then*

$$\mathsf{Opt}(A, \hat{k}) = \mathrm{Delay}(A, \hat{k}) \text{ else } \mathrm{ConCon}(A)$$

is a protocol for $\mathrm{SIM}(P)$ that is all-case optimal.

PROOF. Since A solves P in time $\hat{k}$, Theorem 3 implies that $\mathsf{Opt}(A, \hat{k})$ solves $\mathrm{SIM}(P)$ in time $\min\{\hat{k}, t + 1 - W(F)\}$, where F is the failure pattern.

Suppose that the theorem is false: that $\mathsf{Opt}(A, \hat{k})$ is not all-case optimal. This means there is a protocol B solving $\mathrm{SIM}(P)$ and an input vector $\vec{\imath} \in \mathcal{I}$ and a failure pattern $F \in \mathsf{Fails}(t)$ such that processes decide at time $k_0 < \min\{\hat{k}, t + 1 - W(F)\}$ in the run $r = B[\vec{\imath}, F]$. Let $\hat{B} = \mathsf{Opt}(B, k_0)$. Notice that in the run $\hat{r} = \hat{B}[\vec{\imath}, F]$ corresponding to r, processes decide according to B at time k_0 since $k_0 < t + 1 - W(F)$ is premature in $\hat{r}$. We now prove that $\hat{B}$ solves $\mathrm{SIM}(P)$ within at most $k_0 < \hat{k}$ rounds, contradicting the assumption that $\hat{k}$ is a worst-case lower bound for P.

Since B solves $\mathrm{SIM}(P)$ by assumption and $\mathrm{ConCon}(B)$ solves $\mathrm{SIM}(P)$ by Theorem 2, any decision by $\mathrm{Delay}(B, k_0)$ or $\mathrm{ConCon}(B)$ is correct and simultaneous, and hence any decision by $\hat{B}$ is correct and simultaneous. We need only prove that one of $\mathrm{Delay}(B, k_0)$ or $\mathrm{ConCon}(B)$ actually makes a decision at or before time k_0 in every run, and hence that $\hat{B}$ does so as well. Let $\hat{r}' = \hat{B}[\vec{\jmath}, F']$ be any run of $\hat{B}$. Let $k_1 = t + 1 - W(F')$ and consider two cases:

- Suppose that $k_1 \leq k_0$. Theorem 2 says $\mathrm{ConCon}(B)$ decides at time $k_1 = t + 1 - W(F')$ in $\hat{r}' = \hat{B}[\vec{\jmath}, F']$, so $\hat{B}$ can decide at time $k_1 \leq k_0$ in $\hat{r}'$.

- Suppose that $k_1 > k_0$. In this case, k_0 is premature in both $\hat{r}$ and $\hat{r}'$, and thus $\hat{r} \overset{k_0}{\sim} \hat{r}'$ by Lemma 5. Since processes decide at k_0 in $\hat{r}$, they decide at k_0 in $\hat{r}'$ by Lemma 4. □

The proof shows that beating the worst-case lower bound is as hard as solving consensus. In particular, if $\mathrm{Delay}(A, \hat{k})$ solves $\mathrm{SIM}(P)$ at time $k < \hat{k}$, then $k \geq t + 1 - W$ at which time consensus can be solved.

Coverability.

Theorem 6 requires that the set of input vectors is complete, meaning that is a Cartesian product, which is typically true of most decision tasks. We can generalize this theorem using an inherently topological notion of coverability. A set $\mathcal{I}$ of input vectors is *c-coverable* if for every pair of input vectors $\vec{\imath}$ and $\vec{\jmath}$ in $\mathcal{I}$ there is a finite sequence of input vectors $\vec{\imath} = \vec{\imath}_0, \vec{\imath}_1, \ldots, \vec{\imath}_h = \vec{\jmath}$ in $\mathcal{I}$ with the property that adjacent vectors $\vec{\imath}_\ell$ and $\vec{\imath}_{\ell+1}$ differ on the inputs of at most c processes. Note that if $\mathcal{I}$ is complete (a Cartesian product), then $\mathcal{I}$ is 1-coverable. We can generalize Lemma 5 from complete to *c*-coverable sets of input vectors:

LEMMA 7. [MR08] *Suppose the set $\mathcal{I}$ of input vectors is c-coverable. If $k \leq t + 1 - c$ and round k is premature in two runs r and r' of A, then $r \overset{k}{\sim} r'$.*

We can generalize Theorem 6 from complete to *c*-coverable sets of input vectors:

THEOREM 8   (ALL-CASE OPTIMALITY). *Let P be a decision task with worst-case lower bound $\hat{k}$ and let A be a protocol that solves P in time $\hat{k}$. If P's set of input vectors is c-coverable and $\hat{k} \leq t + 2 - c$, then*

$$\mathsf{Opt}(A, \hat{k}) = \mathrm{Delay}(A, \hat{k}) \text{ else } \mathrm{ConCon}(A)$$

is a protocol for $\mathrm{SIM}(P)$ that is all-case optimal.

PROOF. Simply use Lemma 7 in place of Lemma 5 in the proof of Theorem 6. The only tricky observation is that Lemma 5 is applied with $k = k_0 < \hat{k} \leq t + 2 - c$ which implies the hypothesis $k \leq t + 1 - c$ required by the lemma. □

5.   APPLICATIONS

The construction of Theorem 6 yields simultaneous protocols that are all-case optimal for some of the most famous problems in distributed computation.

5.1   Set agreement and consensus

The k-set agreement problem [Cha90] is a well-known generalization of consensus [PSL80, LSP82]. Given a set V of at least $k + 1$ values, processes start with inputs from V and must choose outputs from V subject to three requirements:

- *Termination*: Every nonfaulty process chooses an output value.

- *Validity*: Every process's output value is some process's input value.

- *Agreement*: The set of output values chosen must contain at most k distinct values.

The sets $\mathcal{I}$ and $\mathcal{O}$ of input and output vectors are $V \times \cdots \times V$ (n copies of V). Consensus is k-set agreement with $k = 1$.

Set agreement is most famous for a trio of papers [HS99, BG93, SZ00] proving that set agreement is impossible in asynchronous systems, generalizing the impossibility result for consensus [FLP85]. One paper [CHLT00], however, proves that $\lfloor t/k \rfloor + 1$ is a tight worst-case bound on the number of rounds required for k-set agreement in the synchronous model. This matches and generalizes the tight bound of $t + 1$ rounds for consensus [FL81, DS82]. Let SA be a k-set agreement protocol that halts in $\lfloor t/k \rfloor + 1$ rounds. Theorem 6 implies:

COROLLARY 9. $\mathsf{Opt}(\text{SA}, \lfloor t/k \rfloor + 1)$ *is a protocol for k-set agreement that is all-case optimal. It halts in time*

$$\min\{\lfloor t/k \rfloor + 1, t + 1 - W\}.$$

5.2   Condition-based consensus

Consensus and k-set agreement are decision tasks whose set $\mathcal{I} = V \times \cdots \times V$ of input vectors allows any process to start with any value in V. Condition-based consensus was defined [MRR03] as a way of circumventing the impossibility of consensus in asynchronous models [FLP85] by restricting the set $\mathcal{I}$ of input vectors to a subset of $V \times \cdots \times V$. The intuition is that consensus is easier to solve when fewer input vectors are possible. A protocol solves condition-based consensus for a given condition $\mathcal{I}$ if all of its executions satisfy the termination, agreement, and validity conditions for 1-set agreement (consensus).

Every subset $\mathcal{I}$ of $V \times \cdots \times V$ defines a condition, and hence defines an instance of condition-base consensus. A property of conditions called d-*legality* was defined in [MRR06], and a protocol was presented that solves condition-based consensus for all d-legal conditions in $t + 1 - d$ rounds. However, not all d-legal conditions require $t + 1 - d$ rounds in the worst case. A stronger property called d-*tightness* was defined in [MR08] to mean both d-legal and $(d + 1)$-coverable. An example of a d-tight condition is the set M_t^d of all vectors such that the largest value appearing in the vector appears there more than d times.

The results of [MR08] imply that for every d-tight condition $\mathcal{I}_d$, there is a worst-case lower bound of $t + 1 - d$ rounds for decision in condition-based consensus. The results of [MRR06] imply there is a condition-based consensus protocol that halts in $t + 1 - d$ rounds on d-legal (and hence on d-tight) conditions. Let CBC(d) be any such condition-based consensus protocol. Theorem 8 implies:

COROLLARY 10. Opt(CBC(d), $t + 1 - d$) *is a protocol for condition-based consensus that is all-case optimal on d-tight conditions. It halts in time*

$$\min\{t + 1 - d, t + 1 - W\}.$$

PROOF. Apply Theorem 8 with $c = d + 1$ and $\hat{k} = t + 1 - d$. The input vectors are c-coverable because they are d-tight and thus $(d + 1)$-coverable. The bound $\hat{k} \leq t + 2 - c$ holds because $\hat{k} = t + 1 - d$. □

We note that Corollary 10 is the central result of Moses and Raynal in [MR08]. While their proof required a careful and nontrivial explicit lower bound proof for condition-based consensus, ours is obtained in a more uniform manner.

5.3 Renaming

The renaming and strong renaming problems were first defined in the asynchronous model [ABND$^+$90]. In the renaming problem, processes start with distinct names from a large namespace and are required to choose distinct names from a small namespace, a namespace of size roughly equal to the number of processes participating in the protocol. In the strong renaming problem, processes are required to preserve the order of names: if p and q start with names $i_p < i_q$, then they are required to choose names $o_p < o_q$. In both problems, given sets I and O of initial and final names, the set $\mathcal{I}$ is the subset of $I \times \cdots \times I$ consisting of vectors of distinct names, and the set $\mathcal{O}$ is the set $O \times \cdots \times O$.

The first paper to consider strong renaming in the synchronous model was [HT90]. They proved a tight $\log c$ worst-case bound for strong renaming, where c is the number of processes concurrently participating in the protocol. Since c depends on the execution, their results imply a worst-case bound of $\log n$. Let SR be a strong renaming protocol that halts in $\log n$ rounds. Since the input vectors are 1-coverable, Theorem 8 implies:

COROLLARY 11. Opt(SR, $\log n$) *is a protocol for strong renaming that is all-case optimal assuming $\log n \leq t + 1$. It halts in time*

$$\min\{\log n, t + 1 - W\}.$$

PROOF. Apply Theorem 8 with $c = 1$ and $\hat{k} = \log n$. The input vectors are 1-coverable. The bound $\hat{k} \leq t + 2 - c$ holds because $\hat{k} = \log n \leq t + 1$. □

A few comments on Opt(SR, $\log n$) are in order. While the original protocol SR of [HT90] allows a subset of the non-faulty processes not to participate in the execution, the optimal protocol Opt(SR, $\log n$) does not. This may be justified by the intuition that a protocol that must be optimally fast under all conditions cannot be expected to allow some of the processes be dormant, unless their identity is built into the protocol.

6. CONCLUSIONS

This work shows how knowledge and topology can be used together to attain interesting results about distributed computation, and begins what we hope will be a fruitful approach to reasoning about distributed computation. While the proofs we presented in this paper are combinatorial, the definitions and results used in the paper all come from or are inspired by knowledge and topology.

Our technical results concern the construction of simultaneous protocols for decision tasks. We have demonstrated that the protocol CONCON derived by knowledge-theoretic means can be used to solve any decision task simultaneously, and running it in parallel with a protocol A solving the decision task can solve the task faster than A or CONCON alone, and that if A matches the worst-case bound, the parallel composition yields an all-case optimal solution to the task.

Our primary insights, however, come from the proofs of the technical results:

- *Stopping early requires attaining common knowledge of a nontrivial fact.* Every protocol has a worst-case run $\hat{r}$ in which processes decide at a time $\hat{k}$ late in the run. Consider any other run r in which processes decide earlier time k. Lemma 4 says that processes decide at time k in every run r' connected to r. It follows that $\hat{r}$ cannot be connected to r since processes do not decide at time $k < \hat{k}$ in $\hat{r}$. So it is common knowledge at time k in the run r that the current run is not connected to $\hat{r}$, a nontrivial fact.

- *Stopping early means consensus can be solved.* Stopping early implies a nontrivial fact has become common knowledge. The CONCON protocol computes a core that characterizes all nontrivial facts that are common knowledge. Stopping early means the core has become nonempty, and it is known that consensus can be solve once the core becomes nonempty.

Notice that the conclusion of the first point—common knowledge that the current run is not connected to the worst-case run—is inherently a statement about knowledge of topology (connectivity). We hope the combination of knowledge and topology will yield many more insights in the years to come.

Acknowledgments

We thank our anonymous referees for their helpful comments and advice.

7. REFERENCES

[ABND+90] H. Attiya, A. Bar-Noy, D. Dolev, D. Peleg, and R. Reischuk. Renaming in an asynchronous environment. *Journal of the ACM*, 37(3):524–548, 1990.

[AR02] H. Attiya and S. Rajsbaum. The combinatorial structure of wait-free solvable tasks. *SIAM Journal on Computing*, 31(4):1286–1313, 2002.

[BG93] E. Borowsky and E. Gafni. Generalized FLP impossibility result for t-resilient asynchronous computations. In *Proc. 25th ACM Symp. on Theory of Computing*, pages 91–100, 1993.

[Cha90] S. Chaudhuri. Agreement is harder than consensus: Set consensus problems in totally asynchronous systems. In *Proc. 9th ACM Symp. on Principles of Distributed Computing*, pages 311–324, 1990.

[CHLT00] S. Chaudhuri, M. Herlihy, N. A. Lynch, and M. R. Tuttle. Tight bounds for k-set agreement. *Journal of the ACM*, 47(5):912–943, 2000.

[DM90] C. Dwork and Y. Moses. Knowledge and common knowledge in a Byzantine environment: Crash failures. *Information and Computation*, 88(2):156–186, 1990.

[DS82] D. Dolev and H. R. Strong. Polynomial algorithms for multiple processor agreement. In *Proc. 14th ACM Symp. on Theory of Computing*, pages 401–407, 1982.

[FHMV95] R. Fagin, J. Y. Halpern, Y. Moses, and M. Y. Vardi. *Reasoning about Knowledge*. MIT Press, Cambridge, MA, 1995.

[FL81] M. J. Fischer and N. A. Lynch. A lower bound for the time to assure interactive consistency. *Information Processing Letters*, 14:183–186, 1981.

[FLP85] M. J. Fischer, N. A. Lynch, and M. S. Paterson. Impossibility of distributed consensus with one faulty processor. *Journal of the ACM*, 32(2):374–382, 1985.

[HM90] J. Y. Halpern and Y. Moses. Knowledge and common knowledge in a distributed environment. *Journal of the ACM*, 37(3):549–587, 1990.

[HS99] M. Herlihy and N. Shavit. The topological structure of asynchronous computability. *Journal of the ACM*, 46(6):858–923, 1999.

[HT90] M. Herlihy and M. R. Tuttle. Wait-free computation in message-passing systems. In *Proc. 9th ACM Symp. on Principles of Distributed Computing*, pages 347–362, August 1990.

[LSP82] L. Lamport, R. Shostak, and M. Pease. The Byzantine generals problem. *ACM Trans. on Programming Languages and Systems*, 4(3):382–401, 1982.

[MM08] T. Mizrahi and Y. Moses. Continuous consensus via common knowledge. *Distributed Computing*, 20(5):305–321, 2008.

[MR08] Y. Moses and M. Raynal. No double discount: Condition-based simultaneity yields limited gain. In *Proc. 22nd Int. Symp. on Distributed Computing*, pages 423–437, September 2008.

[MR09] Y. Moses and M. Raynal. Revisiting simultaneous consensus with crash failures. *Journal of Parallel and Distributed Computing*, 69(4):400–409, 2009.

[MRR03] A. Mostefaoui, S. Rajsbaum, and M. Raynal. Conditions on input vectors for consensus solvability in asynchronous distributed systems. *Journal of the ACM*, 50(6):922–954, 2003.

[MRR06] A. Mostéfaoui, S. Rajsbaum, and M. Raynal. Synchronous condition-based consensus. *Distributed Computing*, 18(5):325–343, April 2006.

[MT88] Y. Moses and M. R. Tuttle. Programming simultaneous actions using common knowledge. *Algorithmica*, 3:121–169, 1988.

[PSL80] M. Pease, R. Shostak, and L. Lamport. Reaching agreement in the presence of faults. *Journal of the ACM*, 27(2):228–234, 1980.

[SZ00] M. Saks and F. Zaharoglou. Wait-free k-set agreement is impossible: The topology of public knowledge. *SIAM Journal on Computing*, 29(5):1449–1483, 2000.

Optimal-Time Adaptive Strong Renaming, with Applications to Counting

[Extended Abstract]

Dan Alistarh *
EPFL

James Aspnes †
Yale University

Keren Censor-Hillel ‡
MIT

Seth Gilbert§
NUS

Morteza Zadimoghaddam
MIT

ABSTRACT

We give two new randomized algorithms for strong renaming, both of which work against an adaptive adversary in asynchronous shared memory. The first uses repeated sampling over a sequence of arrays of decreasing size to assign unique names to each of n processes with step complexity $O(\log^3 n)$. The second transforms any sorting network into a strong adaptive renaming protocol, with an expected cost equal to the depth of the sorting network. Using an AKS sorting network, this gives a strong adaptive renaming algorithm with step complexity $O(\log k)$, where k is the contention in the current execution. We show this to be optimal based on a classic lower bound of Jayanti. We also show that any such strong renaming protocol can be used to build a monotone-consistent counter with logarithmic step complexity (at the cost of adding a max register) or a linearizable fetch-and-increment register (at the cost of increasing the step complexity by a logarithmic factor).

Categories and Subject Descriptors

D.1.3 [**Software**]: Programming Techniques—*Concurrent programming*; E.1 [**Data**]: Data Structures; F.2 [**Theory of Computation**]: Analysis of Algorithms and Problem Complexity—*Nonnumerical Algorithms and Problems*

General Terms

Algorithms, Theory

Keywords

distributed computing, shared memory, renaming, adaptive algorithms, sorting networks, lower bounds

*Supported by the SNF MICS Project.
†Supported in part by NSF grant CCF-0916389.
‡Supported by the Simons Postdoctoral Fellows Program.
§Supported in part by NUS (FRC) R-252-000-443-133

1. INTRODUCTION

The availability of unique names, or identifiers, is a fundamental prerequisite for efficiently solving a variety of problems in distributed systems. In some settings unique names are available, but come from a very large, practically unbounded namespace, which reduces their usefulness. Thus, the renaming problem, in which a set of processes are assigned distinct names from a small namespace, is one of the fundamental problems in distributed computing, and a significant amount of research, e.g. [1–7], studied its solvability and complexity in fault-prone distributed systems.

Renaming deterministically in the presence of crash faults can be expensive, and there are inherent limitations on the size of the achievable namespace. In particular, tight deterministic renaming, where the size of the namespace is exactly n, the size of the set of processes, is known to be impossible [1–3], and even the best known *loose* renaming algorithms, which relax the tight namespace requirement, have total step complexity at least $\Theta(n^2)$ [8,9].

On the other hand, randomized solutions to renaming, e.g. [10–12], are known to be able to circumvent these limitations. The general strategy behind these algorithms is the following: we start from a list of randomized test-and-set objects, implemented using e.g. [10,12,13], and associate each test-and-set object with a unique name, which is usually its index in the list. By winning a certain test-and-set, a process acquires the associated name. In the simplest such algorithm [4,11], a process starts at the head of the list and competes in test-and-set objects of increasing index, until it acquires a name. This simple strategy ensures a tight namespace, and is also *adaptive*, in that the size of the resulting namespace depends on the number of participants k, not on the maximum number of processes n. However, this algorithm has linear step complexity[1] in the number of participating processes.

Other, more complex strategies have been used, e.g. [10, 12], however the existence of a renaming algorithm that achieves a tight adaptive namespace using step complexity less than linear has remained an open problem. One of the challenges in building such algorithms is that each process has to acquire a unique name without probing linearly through the namespace, even though a large portion of the identifiers may be already taken. Moreover, the algorithm has to work in spite of a strong adversary, which may adjust

---

[1]In the following, by step complexity we always mean *local*, per process, step complexity.

concurrency and failures dynamically. Even worse, in the case of *adaptive* algorithms, the size of the namespace is not known initially, and has to be adjusted to match exactly the size of the set of participants.

Contribution. In this paper, we present two new randomized algorithms for strong renaming, both of which work against a strong adaptive adversary, and have polylogarithmic step complexity, with high probability.

Our first algorithm, called BitBatching, is a strong renaming algorithm that allows process to find a single available test-and-set among n such objects using $O(\log^2 n)$ random probes, with high probability. To accomplish this, we start from a vector of n randomized test-and-set objects, which we partition into segments of decreasing size $n/2$, $n/4$, etc., down to $\Theta(\log n)$. Each process attempts to grab $\Theta(\log n)$ randomly chosen test-and-set objects in each segment sequentially; if it fails to win one of these objects, it proceeds to the next segment. We prove that if a process makes it through all $O(\log n)$ segments without finding a free test-and-set, then, with high probability, all n objects have been acquired by the $n-1$ other processes, which is impossible. The proof is based on a backward induction argument: we show that if a segment is full, then the previous segment must also be full with high probability. The algorithm is presented in Section 4.

Our second algorithm is the first to achieve a namespace that is both tight *and* adaptive in sub-linear time. The approach is different from those presented so far: we start from a sorting network [14] where the comparators are replaced with two-process test-and-set objects, which we call a *renaming network*, and prove that it solves strong adaptive renaming. The mechanism is that each process is assigned a distinct input port corresponding to its unique initial name, and follows a path through the network determined by leaving each comparator on its lower output wire if it wins the test-and-set, and on the upper output wire otherwise; the output name is the index of the output port it reaches. The expected step complexity of the algorithm is equal to the depth of the sorting network.

The procedure described above has the disadvantage that its complexity depends on the size of the initial namespace, since each process needs a distinct input port. We eliminate this limitation in Section 6, where we present a construction with unboundedly many ports, which maintains the properties of a sorting network when truncated to a finite number of input and output ports. In particular, when using an optimal AKS sorting network [15] as the basis for our renaming network construction, we obtain an adaptive strong renaming algorithm whose step complexity is $O(\log k)$, in expectation, and $O(\log^2 k)$, with high probability.

We show that this algorithm is optimal in terms of time complexity in Section 7 by adapting a lower bound of Jayanti on the wakeup problem [16]. We prove that, for any c, any adaptive strong renaming algorithm that terminates with probability c has worst-case step complexity $\Omega(c \log k)$. The lower bound holds even if test-and-set objects with unit cost are available.

We find that being able to assign unique consecutive identifiers with logarithmic cost also has applications to counting. In Section 8.1, the strong adaptive algorithm is used to implement a monotone-consistent counter with $O(\log k)$ step complexity. To increment, a process requests a new name, and then writes it to a max-register, implemented in

logarithmic time using the construction from [17]. To read the counter, a process simply returns the value of the max-register. Our counter implementation is more efficient by a logarithmic factor than the best previously known [17], but only guarantees monotone consistency, not linearizability.

We also show how to implement a linearizable fetch-and-increment object from any strong adaptive renaming protocol. In Section 8.2, we obtain a linearizable m-valued fetch-and-increment with $O(\log k \log m)$ cost, which can be shown to be optimal within a logarithmic factor by the same lower bound technique. The lower bound in Section 7 shows that this implementation is optimal within a logarithmic factor.

Discussion. Our results reveal a connection between sorting networks, adaptive strong renaming, and distributed counting, and provide tight bounds for adaptive tight randomized renaming.

The impossibility of wait-free strong renaming [1–3] is circumvented since we use randomization. There exist infinite length executions, in which the algorithms do not terminate, however these occur with probability 0.

The renaming network construction, the counter and fetch-and-increment implementations can be made deterministic with no loss in terms of step complexity if two-process test-and-set or compare-and-swap objects with unit cost are available in hardware.

The efficient counting upper bounds require renaming implementations that are tight and locally efficient, so they cannot be obtained from previous renaming upper bounds. Also, note that our adaptive tight algorithm supersedes the BitBatching algorithm since it is adaptive and has better step complexity; however, the latter is superior in terms of space complexity.

We use AKS sorting networks [15] as the basis of our renaming networks in order to achieve optimal time complexity; however, these networks are known to be impractical [14]. Since our results hold for any sorting networks, an alternative would be to use constructible networks such as bitonic networks [14]; this trades constructibility for a logarithmic increase in running time.

Our renaming algorithms also show a separation in terms of step complexity between randomized renaming and randomized consensus. The results in [18] imply a lower bound of $\Omega(n)$ on the step complexity of randomized consensus, while we achieve randomized renaming in $O(\log n)$ steps per process, i.e. exponentially faster.

Due to space limitations, we only present proof sketches for some of our results, and some proofs are omitted. A full version of the paper with complete proofs can be found in [19].

2. MODEL AND PROBLEM STATEMENT

Model. We assume an asynchronous shared memory model with n processes, $t < n$ of which may fail by crashing. Let M be the size of the space of initial identifiers that processes in the system may have, which may be arbitrarily large. In the case of adaptive algorithms, we consider k to denote total *contention*, i.e. the total number of processes that take steps during a certain execution. We assume that processes know n, but do not know k. Processes communicate through multiple-writer-multiple-reader atomic registers. Our algorithms are randomized, i.e. the processes' actions may depend on random local coin flips. We assume that the process failures and the scheduling are controlled by a strong adaptive adversary. In particular, the adversary knows the results of the random coin flips that the processes make, and can adjust the schedule and the failure pattern accordingly.

Problem Statement. The *renaming problem* [1] requires that each correct process should eventually return a name, and that the names returned should be unique. The size of the resulting namespace should only depend on n and on t. In the case of the *adaptive* renaming problem, the size of the namespace should depend on k, the contention in the current execution. The *tight* renaming problem requires that the size of the namespace be exactly n, while the *adaptive tight* renaming problem requires that the resulting namespace be of size exactly k. The complexity of our solutions is measured in terms of process steps (reads and writes, including random coin flips; we count all coin flips between two shared memory operations as one step). Therefore, by *step complexity* we mean the number of steps a given process takes during an execution. *Total* step complexity is the total number of steps that all processes take in an execution. Since atomic test-and-set operations are available on most modern machines, we state some of the complexity upper bounds also counting test-and-set operations as having unit cost.

Preliminaries. In the following, we say that an event happens "with high probability" (w.h.p.) if it occurs with probability $\geq 1 - 1/n^c$, with $c \geq 1$ constant. In the case of the adaptive algorithms, the probability bound is at least $\geq 1 - 1/k^c$, with $c \geq 1$. Note that the failure probability in the adaptive case may be tuned to depend on n, at the cost of increased complexity (i.e., a $\log n$ factor).
In our algorithms, we use probabilistic implementations of test-and-set objects. It is known that such objects are implementable in asynchronous shared memory using randomization [13]. The implementation we use for n-process test-and-set is that of [12], which is adaptive to total contention; more precisely, the number of steps per process required by a test-and-set operation is $O(\log^2 k)$ w.h.p., where k is the number of participating processes. For 2-process test-and-set, we use the algorithm by Tromp and Vitányi [20], which has expected step complexity $O(1)$, and $O(\log n)$ step complexity with probability at least $1 - 1/n^c$ for $c > 1$ constant. We say that a process *wins* a test-and-set if it returns 1 from the object; otherwise, the process *loses* the test-and-set. A test-and-set is *acquired* if it has been won by a process.

3. RELATED WORK

The renaming problem was introduced in [1] by Attiya et al., where the authors also introduce a wait-free solution using $(2n - 1)$ names in an asynchronous message-passing system, and show that at least $(n + 1)$ names are required in the wait-free case. The lower bound on the size of the namespace for deterministic solutions was improved to $(2n - 2)$ in a landmark paper by Herlihy and Shavit [2], later improved by Rajsbaum and Castañeda [3]. Adaptive renaming has been shown to be related to the set agreement task by Gafni et al. [21].
Considerable research has analyzed the complexity of deterministic implementations, e.g. [7,9,22–24]. For a detailed description of the deterministic results, we refer the reader to [12,24]. Note that the deterministic lower bound on the

namespace size does not apply in the case of our protocols since the "bad" executions in the lower bound occur with a probability that goes to 0 as the protocol takes more steps.
The first paper to analyze randomized renaming in an asynchronous system is by Panconesi et al. [10]. The authors present a non-adaptive solution ensuring a namespace of size $(1+\epsilon)n$, for $\epsilon > 0$ constant, with expected $O(M \log^2 n)$ total step complexity, where M is the size of the initial namespace. Their strategy is to introduce a new test-and-set implementation, and to assign names to processes based on the index of the test-and-set object they acquire. Along the same vein, Eberly et al. [11] obtained *tight* non-adaptive randomized renaming based on the test-and-set by Afek et al. [13]. Their implementation has $O(n \log n)$ amortized step complexity per process, under a given cost measure. The average-case total step complexity of their algorithm is $\Omega(n^3)$.
A recent paper by Alistarh et al. [12] introduced an *adaptive* test-and-set implementation with logarithmic step complexity called RatRace. They use this object to obtain a non-adaptive tight algorithm with $O(n \operatorname{polylog} n)$ total step complexity, and an adaptive loose algorithm with polylogarithmic step complexity. Our strong adaptive algorithm uses the randomized splitter tree idea to reduce the size of the namespace to polynomial in k. This procedure has first been analyzed in [25] in the context of collect algorithms.
Compared to previous work, our algorithms achieve a tight namespace using only logarithmic step complexity.
We derive an $\Omega(\log k)$ lower bound on the time complexity of adaptive randomized renaming using the lower bound on the wakeup problem by Jayanti [16]. To the best of our knowledge, this is the first non-trivial lower bound on the time complexity of randomized renaming.
Monotone consistency has been introduced in reference [17], where the authors also present max-register and counter implementations with sub-linear time complexity. Their counter is deterministic and linearizable, and has $O(\log^2 n)$ complexity for polynomially many increments. Our counter implementation has complexity $O(\log n)$ in expectation, but is only monotone-consistent, and not linearizable.
Counting networks, introduced in [26], are other shared objects related to sorting networks. However, since their aim is to balance the number of processes exiting on the output ports, their applications and structure are in general different than those of renaming networks. The fact that any sorting network can be used as a counting network when only one process enters on each wire was observed by Attiya et al. [27] to follow from earlier results of Aspnes et al. [26]; this is equivalent to our use of sorting networks for non-adaptive renaming in Section 5.

4. A NON-ADAPTIVE ALGORITHM

In this section, we present an algorithm that renames into n names, using polylogarithmic operations per process, with high probability. The algorithm assigns unique names to processes by repeatedly sampling over batches of test-and-set bits of decreasing size.

Description. The n processes share a vector of n test-and-set objects, each implemented using the RatRace algorithm [12]. For simplicity, we will assume that $n = 2^\kappa$, for an integer κ. We partition the vector of n test-and-set objects in *batches* as follows. Let $\ell = \lfloor \log(n/\log n) \rfloor$. For $1 \leq i < \ell$, batch B_i consists of vector positions from

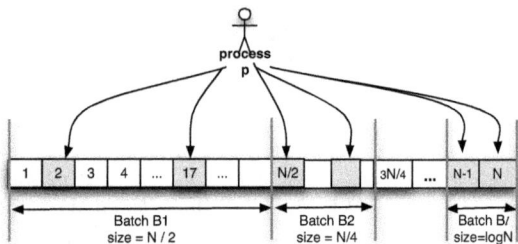

Figure 1: The BitBatching algorithm. The process makes $\Theta(\log n)$ random trials in each batch, until it first wins a test-and-set object.

$n(2^{i-1} - 1)/2^{i-1} + 1$ to $n(2^i - 1)/2^i$. In particular, batch B_1 consists of the first half of the vector (from left to right), batch B_2 consists of the next quarter, and so on. Batch B_ℓ, which does not follow the above formula, consists of positions from $n(2^{\ell-1} - 1)/2^{\ell-1} + 1$ to position n. For $1 \le i < \ell$, the length of batch B_i is $n/2^i$. Batch B_ℓ has length between $\log n$ and $2\log n$ (see Figure 1 for an illustration).

Given this partitioning of the vector, processes (sequentially) compete in $O(\log n)$ test-and-set objects in each batch, starting from batch number 1 up to batch ℓ, and stopping when they first win a test-and-set object. More precisely, we define two *stages* in the algorithm. In the first stage, for every $1 \le i < \ell$, each process p (sequentially) competes in $3\log n$ *randomly chosen* test-and-set objects from every batch B_i. If it did not stop before entering batch B_ℓ, the process competes in *every* test-and-set object in this batch. If the process finishes competing in batch B_ℓ and still did not win a test-and-set, then it enters the second stage, where it competes in all test-and-set objects from 1 to n, in sequence, from left to right. In the following, we will show that, with high probability, every process wins a test-and-set while in the first stage.

Analysis. The termination property holds with probability 1, by the properties of test-and-set, and by the structure of the algorithm. The name uniqueness property follows since no two processes may win the same test-and-set. In the following, we prove upper bounds on the step complexity of the algorithm.

The first lemma shows that, with high probability, every process gets a name while doing the first pass through the test-and-set vector.

LEMMA 1 (LOCAL TRIALS). *With high probability, every process terminates while executing the first stage, i.e. it returns a name after competing in $O(\log^2 n)$ test-and-set objects.*

PROOF (SKETCH). Consider a process p that competes in test-and-set objects in all batches $(B_i)_{i \in \{1, \ldots, \ell\}}$ without winning any test-and-set objects. In particular, this implies that p has competed in all the test-and-set objects in batch B_ℓ. Since p did not win any test-and-set in this batch, it follows that this batch is already "full," i.e. there are at least $\log n$ distinct processes that won each of the test-and-set objects in this batch[2]. Let S_ℓ be this set of processes.

It follows that each of the processes in S_ℓ has performed $3\log n$ random trials in the batch $B_{\ell-1}$, and did not succeed

---

[2] We consider the linearization order at each of these objects.

in acquiring a name in this batch. By a standard coupon-collector analysis [28], we obtain that, for each batch index $i \ge 1$, if at least $|B_i|/2$ processes perform $3\log n$ random trials each in batch B_i, then the batch is "full" with high probability, i.e. there exists a set of processes F_i that each won a distinct test-and-set in batch B_i, with $S_\ell \cap F_i = \emptyset$. In particular, we obtain that batch $B_{\ell-1}$ is full with high probability. The processes occupying batches B_ℓ and $B_{\ell-1}$ have tried for $3\log n$ times each in batch $B_{\ell-2}$, without success. In this case, the previous argument implies that batch $B_{\ell-2}$ is full w.h.p. By backward induction over the batch number, we obtain that all batches $(B_i)_{i \in \{\ell, \ldots, 1\}}$ are full w.h.p.

By the union bound, it follows that the vector is full with high probability if process p executes stage two of the algorithm. Assuming the vector is full, then, since the algorithm guarantees that a process may win a single test-and-set object, it follows that there are at least $n + 1$ participating processes in this execution, which is impossible. Therefore the event that process p terminates while in stage one occurs with high probability. □

Using this bound on the number of trials, we obtain bounds on the local and total step complexity of our algorithm, by carefully bounding the maximum number of processes that access a test-and-set object.

COROLLARY 1. *With high probability, every process returns after $O(\log^3 n \log \log n)$ local steps. The expected step complexity is $O(\log^2 n \log \log n)$.*

COROLLARY 2. *With high probability, the total step complexity of the algorithm is $O(n \log^2 n \log \log n)$. The expected total step complexity is $O(n \log n \log \log n)$. The total number of test-and-set operations performed in an execution is $O(n \log n)$ with high probability.*

5. RENAMING USING A SORTING NETWORK

In this section, we present a solution for adaptive strong renaming using a sorting network. For simplicity, we first describe the solution when the bound on the size of the initial namespace, M, is finite and known. We circumvent this limitation in Section 6.

Description. We start from an arbitrary sorting network of size M, in which we replace the comparator modules with two-process test-and-set objects to obtain a *renaming network*. We use the renaming network to solve adaptive strong renaming as follows. Each participating process enters the execution on the input wire in the sorting network corresponding to its unique initial value. The process competes in two-process test-and-set instances as follows: if the process *wins* a two-process test-and-set, then it moves "up" in the network; otherwise it moves "down." The process continues until it reaches an output port. The process returns the index of the output port as its output value.

Analysis. In the following, we show that the renaming network construction solves adaptive strong renaming, i.e. that processes return values between 1 and k, the total contention in the execution, as long as the size of the initial namespace is bounded by M. In particular, if we use the optimal AKS sorting network [15] as the basis for the renaming network, then we solve strong renaming using expected $O(\log M)$ step complexity. In Section 6.1, we show how to use this idea to obtain an adaptive strong renaming algorithm with $O(\log k)$ step complexity, which is optimal, as per Section 7.

THEOREM 1. *The renaming network construction solves strong adaptive renaming with probability 1.*

PROOF (SKETCH). Termination with probability 1 follows from the structure of the sorting network and from the termination property of the two-process test-and-set implementation [20].

We prove name uniqueness and namespace tightness in the following. The proof is based on a simulation argument from an execution of a renaming network to an execution of a sorting network. We start from an arbitrary execution $\mathcal{E}$ of the renaming network, and we build a valid execution of a sorting network. The structure of the outputs in the sorting network execution will imply that the tightness and uniqueness properties hold in the renaming network execution.

Let P be the set of processes that have taken at least one step in $\mathcal{E}$. Each of these processes has assigned a unique input port i of the renaming network. Let I denote the set of input ports on which there is a process present. We then introduce a new set of "ghost" processes G, each assigned to one of the input ports not in I.

The next step in the transformation is to assign input values to these processes. We assign input value 0 to processes in P (and correspondingly to their input ports), and input value 1 to processes in G.

Note that, in execution $\mathcal{E}$, not all test-and-set objects in the renaming network may have been accessed by processes (e.g., the test-and-set objects corresponding to processes in G), and not all processes have reached an output port (e.g., crashed processes and ghost processes). The next step is to simulate the output of these processes by extending the current renaming network execution. The rules for deciding the outputs of test-and-set objects for these processes are the following: if the current test-and-set already has a winner, i.e. a (distinct) process that goes "up", then the current process automatically goes "down" at this test-and-set. Otherwise, if the winner has not yet been decided, then we decide the test-and-set according to the input value corresponding to the two processes: the process with the smaller input value goes "up," while the other process goes "down." Test-and-set objects where both processes have the same corresponding value are decided arbitrarily.

In this way, we obtain an execution of a renaming network in which M processes participate, and each test-and-set object has a winner and a loser. Notice that we can re-order these test-and-set operations into *stages*, such that all test-and-set operations that may be performed in parallel are assigned to the same stage. The final step in this transformation is to replace every test-and-set operation with a comparator between the binary values corresponding to the two processes that participate in the test-and-set. Thus, we obtain a sequence of comparator operations ordered in stages, in which each stage contains only comparison operations that may be performed in parallel. The key observation now is that all these test-and-set operations obey the comparison property of the comparators in a sorting network, applied to the values we assigned to the corresponding processes. In particular, when input values are different, the lower value (corresponding to participating processes) always goes "up," while the higher value always goes "down."

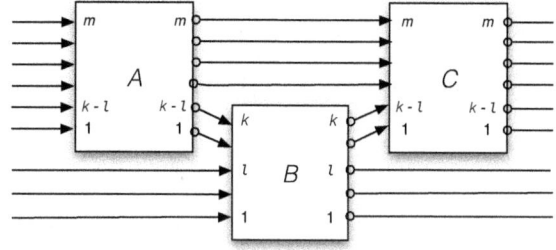

Figure 2: One stage in the construction of the adaptive sorting network. The original network B is "sandwiched" between the larger networks A and C.

Thus, the execution resulting from the last transformation step is in fact a valid execution of the sorting network from which the renaming network has been obtained. Recall that we have associated each process that took a step to a 0 input value, and each ghost process to a 1 input value to the network. Since no two input values may be sorted to the same output port, we first obtain that the output port values the processes in P return are unique. For namespace tightness, recall that we have obtained an execution of a sorting network with M input values, $M - k$ of which are 1. By the sorting property of the network, it follows that the lower $M - k$ output ports of the sorting network are occupied by 1 values. Therefore the $M - k$ processes that have not taken a step in $\mathcal{E}$ must be associated with the lower $M - k$ output ports of the sorting network. Conversely, processes that have returned a value in the execution $\mathcal{E}$ must have returned a value between 1 and k. $\square$

We can then obtain an upper bound on the step complexity of the protocol when starting from an AKS sorting network [15]. The key observation is that that the number of test-and-set objects a process enters is bounded by the depth of the original sorting network.

COROLLARY 3. *The renaming network obtained from an AKS sorting network [15] with M inputs solves the strong adaptive renaming problem with M initial names. It guarantees termination with probability 1 and name uniqueness in all executions, using expected $O(\log M)$ local steps. The step complexity is $O(\log M \log n)$ w.h.p., and the total step complexity is $O(k \log M)$ w.h.p. for $M = \Theta(n)$, where k is the contention in the execution.*

6. STRONG ADAPTIVE RENAMING

In this section, we present an algorithm for adaptive strong renaming based on an adaptive sorting network construction. In particular, the algorithm works irrespective of the size of the initial namespace.

6.1 An Adaptive Sorting Network

We present a recursive construction of a sorting network of arbitrary size. We will guarantee that the resulting construction ensures the properties of a sorting network whenever truncated to a finite number of input (and output) ports. The sorting network is adaptive, in the sense that any value entering on wire n and leaving on wire m traverses at most $O(\log \max(n, m))$ comparators.

The basic observation is that we can extend a small sorting network B to a wider range by inserting it between two much larger sorting networks A and C. The resulting network is non-uniform—different paths through the network have different lengths, with the lowest part of the sorting network having the same width as B.

Formally, let us suppose we have sorting networks A, B, and C, where A and C have width m and B has width k. Label the inputs of A as $A_1, A_2, \ldots, A_m$ and the outputs as $A'_1, A'_2, \ldots, A'_m$, where $i < j$ means that A'_i receives a value less than or equal to A'_j. Similarly, label the inputs and outputs of B and C. Fix $\ell \le k/2$ and construct a new sorting network ABC with inputs $B_1, B_2, \ldots B_\ell, A_1, \ldots A_m$ and outputs $B'_1, B'_2, \ldots B'_m, A'_1, A'_2, \ldots A'_m$. Internally, insert B between A and C by connecting outputs $A'_1, \ldots, A'_{k-\ell}$ to inputs $B_{\ell+1}, \ldots, B_k$; and outputs $B'_{\ell+1}, \ldots B'_k$ to inputs $C'_1, \ldots C'_{k-\ell}$. The remaining outputs of A are wired directly across to the corresponding inputs of C: outputs $A'_{k-\ell+1}, \ldots, A'_m$ are wired to inputs $C_{k-\ell+1}, \ldots, C_m$ (see Figure 2). We now show that the resulting construction is a sorting network.

LEMMA 2. *The network ABC constructed as described above is a sorting network.*

PROOF. The proof uses the well-known Zero-One Principle [14]: we show that the network correctly sorts all input sequence of zeros and ones, and deduce from this fact that it correctly sorts all input sequences.

Given a particular 0-1 input sequence, let z_B and z_A be the number of zeros in the input that are sent to inputs $B_1 \ldots B_\ell$ and $A_1 \ldots A_m$. Because A sorts all of its incoming zeros to its lowest outputs, B gets a total of $z_B + \max(k - \ell, z_A)$ zeros on it inputs, and sorts those zeros to outputs $B'_1 \ldots B'_{z_B + \max(k-\ell, z_A)}$. An additional $z_A - \max(k - \ell, z_A)$ zeros propagate directly from A to C. We consider two cases, depending on the value of the max:

Case 1: $z_A \le k - \ell$. Then B gets $z_B + z_A$ zeros (all of them), sorts them to its lowest outputs, and those that reach outputs $B'_{\ell+1}$ and above are not moved by C. The sorting network works in this case.

Case 2: $z_A > k - \ell$. Then B gets $z_B + k - \ell$ zeros, while $z_A - (k - \ell)$ zeros are propagated directly from A to C. Because $\ell \le k/2$, $z_B + k - \ell \ge k/2 \ge \ell$, and B sends ℓ zeros out its direct outputs $B'_1 \ldots B'_\ell$. All remaining zeros are fed into C, which sorts them to the next $z_A + z_B - \ell$ positions. Again the sorting network works. □

When building the adaptive network, it will be useful to constrain which parts of the network particular values traverse. The key tool is given by the following lemma, whose proof is immediate from the construction and Lemma 2.

LEMMA 3. *If a value v is supplied to one of the inputs B_1 through B_ℓ in the network ABC, and is one of the ℓ smallest values supplied on all inputs, then v never leaves B.*

Now let us show how to recursively construct a large sorting network with polylog N depth when truncated to the first N positions. We assume that we are using a construction of a sorting network that requires at most $a \log^c n$ depth to sort n values, where a and c are constants. For the AKS sorting network [15], we have $c = 1$; for constructible networks (e.g., the bitonic sorting network [14]), we have $c = 2$.

Start with a sorting network S_0 of width 2. In general, we will let w_k be the width of S_k; so we have $w_0 = 2$. We also write d_k for the depth of S_k (the number of comparators on the longest path through the network).

Given S_k, construct S_{k+1} by appending two sorting networks A_{k+1} and C_{k+1} with width $w_k^2 - w_k/2$, and attach them to the top half of S_k as in Lemma 2, setting $\ell = w_k/2$.

Observe that $w_{k+1} = w_k^2$ and $d_{k+1} = 2a \log^c(w_k^2 - w_k/2) + d_k \le 4a \log^c w_k + d_k$. Solving these recurrences gives $w_k = 2^{2^k}$ and $d_k = \sum_{i=0}^k 2^{c(i+2)} a = O(2^{ck})$.

If we set $N = 2^{2^k}$, then $k = \lg \lg N$, and $d_k = O(2^{c \lg \lg N}) = O(\log^c N)$. This gives us polylogarithmic depth for a network with N lines, and a total number of comparators of $O(N \log^c N)$.

But we can in fact state something stronger:

THEOREM 2. *Each of the networks S_k constructed above is a sorting network, with the property that any value that enters on the n-th input and leaves on the m-th output traverses $O(\log^c \max(n, m))$ comparators.*

PROOF. That S_k is a sorting network follows from induction on k using Lemma 2. For the second property, let $S_{k'}$ be the smallest stage in the construction of S_k to which input n and output m are directly connected. Then $w_{k'-1}/2 < \max(n, m) \le w_{k'}/2$, which we can rewrite as $2^{2^{k'-1}} < 2 \max(n, m) \le 2^{2^{k'}}$ or $k' - 1 < \lg \lg \max(n, m) \le k'$, implying $k' = \lceil \lg \lg \max(n, m) \rceil$. By Lemma 3, the given value stays in $S_{k'}$, meaning it traverses at most $d_{k'} = O\left(2^{ck'}\right) = O\left(2^{c \lceil \lg \lg \max(n,m) \rceil}\right) = O\left(\lg^c \max(n, m)\right)$ comparators. □

6.2 Strong Adaptive Renaming Algorithm

We show how to apply the adaptive sorting network construction to solve strong adaptive renaming when the size of the initial namespace, M, is unknown, and may be arbitrarily large.

Description. Our algorithm is composed of two stages. In the first stage, each process obtains a unique temporary name in a namespace of size polynomial in k, with high probability. The algorithm, which we call TempName, is as follows. We allocate a binary tree of randomized splitters (as previously defined in [25]), of unbounded height. (In brief, a randomized splitter is a component such that at most one process may "win" the splitter; losing processes go left or right with probability $1/2$.) Each process starts the protocol at the root splitter in the tree; if it does not stop at the current splitter, it goes either left or right, each with probability $1/2$, until it manages to acquire a splitter. Notice that, by the properties of the splitter, the process will stop at height at most k in the tree. Once it stops at a splitter, the process adopts a temporary name corresponding to the index of the splitter in a breadth-first search labeling of the tree nodes. Variants of this algorithm have been previously analyzed in [12, 25].

In the second stage, we consider a renaming network as defined in Section 5, instantiated using the adaptive sorting network of Section 6.1. Let R be the resulting renaming network. Each process uses the temporary name it has acquired in the first stage as the index of its input port to the renaming network R. The process then executes the renaming network R starting at the given input port, and returns the index of its output port as its name.

Wait-freedom. Notice that, technically, our algorithm may not be wait-free if k is unbounded. In particular, if the number of processes k participating in an execution is *infinite*, then it is possible that a process either fails to acquire a temporary name during the first stage, or it continually fails to reach an output port by always losing the test-and-set objects it participates in. Therefore, in the following, we assume that k is finite, and present bounds on step complexity that depend on k.

Analysis. Before we proceed with the proof of the main theorem, please recall that the TempName algorithm has the following properties: (1) given k participating processes, it assigns names from 1 to k^c with probability $1 - 1/k^{c-1}$, where $c > 1$ is a constant; (2) its step complexity is $O(\log k)$ with high probability in k. The proof can be found in [12,25]. We now prove the following.

THEOREM 3. *For any finite $k > 0$, the adaptive renaming network construction based on the AKS sorting network solves adaptive strong renaming for k processes. The local time complexity of the protocol is $O(\log^2 k)$ with high probability, and $O(\log k)$ in expectation.*

PROOF. We first prove that the resulting construction solves adaptive strong renaming for any $k > 0$. First, we know that the temporary names obtained in stage one are between 1 and k^c, with high probability, for a constant $c \geq 1$. Therefore we will assume that, during the current execution, each process enters an input port of the renaming network between 1 and k^c. We will truncate the renaming network after the first k^c input ports. By Theorem 2, we obtain that the original comparison network truncated after the first k^c input ports is in fact a sorting network. From Theorem 1, we obtain that the second stage of the construction implements adaptive strong renaming for at most k^c processes. The first claim follows.

For the complexity bound, first recall that any process takes $O(\log k)$ steps during the first stage, with high probability. Second, from Theorem 2 we obtain that the number of test-and-sets a process competes in during an execution of the renaming network is $O(\log \max(\ell, m))$, where ℓ is the number of the input port for the process, and m is the number of the output port for the process. Notice that $\ell \leq k^c$, with high probability, and $m \leq k$, by the adaptive tight property of the renaming network.

Therefore a process competes in $O(\log k)$ test-and-set instances in the second stage. By the properties of the two-process test-and-set, we obtain that a process takes expected $O(\log k)$ steps in an execution, and at most $O(\log^2 k)$ steps, with high probability in k. $\square$

7. LOWER BOUND

We prove that our adaptive renaming algorithm is optimal in terms of local time complexity starting from a lower bound for the wakeup problem. Recall that the *wakeup problem* for n processes [16] is specified as follows: (1) Every process terminates in a finite number of its steps, returning either 0 or 1, (2) In every run in which all processes terminate, at least one process returns 1, and (3) In every run in which one or more processes return 1, every process takes at least one step before any process returns 1. We start by re-stating the lower bound result by Jayanti.

THEOREM 4 (JAYANTI, [16]). *Consider any algorithm for the n-process wakeup problem in shared memory where only LL, SC, validate, move, and swap operations may be used. If the algorithm terminates with probability c, then its worst-case expected shared-access time complexity is at least $c \log n$.*

Based on this, we prove the following lower bound on adaptive strong renaming. Note that the lower bound holds even when test-and-set operations are available, and are assumed to have unit cost. Also, since shared-access time complexity as used in [16] is a lower bound on the (local) step complexity of the algorithm, we claim our lower bound for expected step complexity.

THEOREM 5 (LOWER BOUND). *Consider a randomized algorithm for adaptive strong renaming in shared memory augmented with test-and-set operations, which terminates with probability c. Then the algorithm has worst-case expected step complexity $\Omega(c \log k)$, where k is the number of participating processes.*

PROOF (SKETCH). We assume for contradiction that there exists an algorithm A that solves adaptive strong renaming and terminates with probability c, which has worst-case expected time complexity $o(c \log k)$, for any k.

We first transform algorithm A from an algorithm using read, write, and test-and-set operations, to an algorithm that uses only LL, SC and move operations. (Recall that the move operation takes as arguments a register R and a value v, and changes the value of R to v atomically. It is essentially the same as a write operation in read-write shared memory. For a precise definition of the LL/SC and move operations, please see [16]). We first replace all registers and test-and-set bits with registers supporting LL/SC and move, initialized to $\perp$. Any read operation on a register is replaced with a LL operation on the corresponding register. Any write(v) operation on a register R is replaced with a move(R, v) operation on that register. Any test-and-set operation is replaced with a LL operation followed by a SC operation with value 1 on the same register. Clearly, this transforms algorithm A into an algorithm A' that uses only LL/SC and move operations, with a constant increase in time complexity.

We now consider the algorithm A' in a system where k, the number of participating processes, is fixed and known. We can use the algorithm A' to solve the wakeup problem as follows: if a process receives name k from A', then it returns 1. Otherwise, it returns 0. We now check that this solves the wakeup problem.

First, if every process terminates, then, by the strong adaptivity of the namespace, there has to exist a process that obtains name k and returns 1 in the wakeup problem. On the other hand, if a process p returns 1, then it has obtained name k, therefore, by the strong adaptivity of the namespace, there have to exist $k - 1$ other processes that took at least one step in this execution. (Otherwise, by indistinguishability, process p would have to return name $k-1$ or smaller.) Hence, this algorithm solves the wakeup problem in a system with k processes.

Termination is ensured with the same probability c, and the time complexity of the protocol is $o(c \log k)$. Therefore, we obtain that the wakeup problem can be solved in a system with k processes using $o(c \log k)$ local steps by an algorithm which terminates with probability c, contradicting Theorem 4. $\square$

Based on the same rationale, we can obtain a lower bound for linearizable fetch-and-increment objects.

8. APPLICATIONS TO COUNTING

8.1 A Monotone-Consistent Counter

We now build a monotone-consistent counter algorithm with logarithmic step complexity, based on the strong adaptive renaming algorithm.

Description. The processes share an adaptive renaming object implemented using the construction from Section 6.2, and a linearizable max register, implemented using the logarithmic construction from [17]. For the increment operation, a process acquires a new name from the adaptive renaming object. It then writes the newly obtained name to the max register and returns. For the read operation, the process simply reads the value of the max register and returns it.

Analysis. We now prove the properties of the counter.

LEMMA 4 (COUNTER PROPERTIES). *The counter implementation is monotone-consistent, and has expected step complexity $O(\log v)$ per increment, where v is the number of* increment *operations started before the operation returns. A* read *operation has cost $O(\min(\log v, O(n)))$.*

PROOF. Termination with probability 1 for finite v follows from the properties of the objects we use. For monotone consistency, we need to prove the following.
(1) There exists a total ordering $<$ on the read operations such that if an operation $R1$ finishes before some operation $R2$ starts, then $R1 < R2$, and if $R1 < R2$, then the value returned by $R1$ is less than or equal to the value returned by $R2$. For this, we order the read operations by their linearization points when reading the max register object. This ordering clearly has the required properties.
(2) The value v returned by a read is always $\geq$ the number of completed increment operations. Let y be the number of completed increment operations. Notice that each completed operation obtains a unique name, and writes it to the max registers (this holds also if a single process performs multiple increment operations). It then follows that the value in the max register at the time of the read is at least y.
(3) The value v returned by a read is always $\leq$ the number of started increment operations. Let z be the number of started increment operations. Assume for contradiction that a process returns a value v which is larger than z. In this case, there must exist a process that returned a name which is strictly larger than the number of name requests on the adaptive renaming object. This contradicts the *adaptive* property of the object.

Therefore the counter object is monotone-consistent. For the complexity bound on the increment operation, notice that the complexity of the first stage of the adaptive renaming protocol is $O(\log v)$, and the number of temporary names is $O(\text{poly } v)$ with high probability. It then follows that the complexity of the adaptive renaming object is $O(\log v)$ in expectation, and $O(\log^2 v)$ with high probability in v. By the properties of the max register, it follows that that the complexity of an increment operation is $O(\log v)$. The complexity of the read operation is the same as the complexity of the max register. □

```
Shared: boolean doorway, initially open;

procedure ℓ-test-and-set();
if O.doorway = closed then
 │ return false
else
 │  name ← tight-renaming();
 │  if name ≤ ℓ then  return true
 │  else
 │   │  O.doorway ← closed
 │   │  return false
```

Algorithm 1: The ℓ-test-and-set implementation.

```
Shared: test, an ℓ/2-test-and-set object;
left, an ℓ/2-valued f&inc object;
right, an ℓ/2-valued f&inc object;

procedure ℓ-fetch-and-increment();
 │  if ℓ = 0 then  return  0;
 │  if ℓ/2-test-and-set(O.test) then
 │   │  return fetch-and-increment(O.left)
 │  else
 │   │  return ℓ/2 + fetch-and-increment(O.right)
```

Algorithm 2: The ℓ-fetch-and-increment object.

Linearizability. We show a non-linearizable execution of our counter implementation. Consider three processes p_1, p_2, and p_3. Process p_2 obtains name 2 and writes it to the max register. After p_2's operation terminates, p_1 starts its increment operation and obtains name 1 from the renaming network and writes it to the max register (this is possible in a renaming network). We insert a read operation R_1 between the end point of p_2's operation and the start point of p_1's operation. We insert a second read operation R_2 between the end point of p_1's operation and before p_3 writes to the max register. Both read operations have to return value 2 for the counter. Notice that, in this case, p_1's operation cannot be properly linearized, since it is located between two read operations returning the same value.

8.2 Linearizable Bounded-Value Fetch-and-Increment

In this section, we show how to use an adaptive strong renaming protocol to construct a linearizable m-valued fetch-and-increment object, i.e. a fetch-and-increment object that supports only values up to m. The sequential specification of the object is the same as that of fetch-and-increment, except that the object keeps returning $m - 1$ once it has reached the threshold value m.

Description. We first use the strong adaptive renaming protocol to build a linearizable ℓ-test-and-set object, which generalizes a standard test-and-set object by providing ℓ winners instead of a single one. We implement such an object by having processes run the adaptive strong renaming algorithm and return *true* if and only if their acquired name is at most ℓ. To ensure this is linearizable, we protect the renaming protocol with a doorway bit, which guarantees that processes arriving after some process returns *false* cannot prevent a process that already started the operation earlier from winning. Algorithm 1 presents the pseudocode.

The second part of the m-valued fetch-and-increment construction is based on a recursive tree construction, whose pseudocode is presented in Algorithm 2. For simplicity, we present the construction when m is a power of two. (The construction for general m can be easily obtained from the construction for the smallest power of two larger than m, by returning $m-1$ instead of any value larger than $m-1$.) For $\ell \geq 1$, we build an ℓ-fetch-and-increment object out of (a) one $\ell/2$-test-and-set object, and (b) two $\ell/2$-fetch-and-increment objects (the left child, and the right child of the current node, respectively). If a process wins in the $\ell/2$-test-and-set object, then it calls the left $\ell/2$-valued fetch-and-increment object; otherwise it calls the right object. The two children of a 1-fetch-and-increment are two 0-fetch-and-increment objects. We implement such an object with an empty data structure on which the fetch-and-increment operation always returns 0.

The construction starts at level m and unfolds to a tree, whose leaves are 0-valued fetch-and-increment objects. For each level ℓ at which it accesses the right fetch-and-increment child, the process adds the value $\ell/2$ in a local variable, and returns the final value of this variable.

Analysis. We start by precisely defining the ℓ-test-and-set object.

DEFINITION 1. *An ℓ-test-and-set object O supports one type of operation which returns either* true *or* false. *The sequential specification of the object is that the first ℓ invocations of the operation return* true *and the rest return* false.

We now show the correctness of our ℓ-test-and-set implementation. Intuitively, we show that exactly ℓ processes may get *true*, by the adaptivity and tightness of the namespace; any operation that starts later sees the doorway closed, and must therefore must return *false*.

LEMMA 5 (ℓ-TEST-AND-SET). *The ℓ-test-and-set procedure presented in Algorithm 1 implements a linearizable ℓ-test-and-set object with expected step complexity $O(\log k)$.*

PROOF. By the correctness of the adaptive strong renaming algorithm, ℓ processes obtain a name whose value is at most m, and therefore exactly ℓ processes return *true*. For linearizability, we partition the operations into two disjoint categories, C_{true} and C_{false}, according to their return values. We order all operations in C_{true} before the time that the doorway is set to *closed*, and all operations in C_{false} afterwards. Within each category we order the operations according to the order of non-overlapping operations. It is clear that this order satisfies the sequential specification of the ℓ-test-and-set object, since all operations that return *true* are linearized before those that return *false*, and there are exactly ℓ of those.

To show that this procedure preserves the order of non-overlapping operations, we only need to argue about non-overlapping operations in different categories, since this order is preserved within each category by construction. Let op_1 be an operation that returns *true* and op_2 be an operation that returns *false* and assume, towards a contradiction, that op_2 finishes before op_1 starts. Then op_2 must set the doorway to *closed*, implying that after op_1 reads the doorway it returns *false*. This contradiction concludes the proof that the above implements a linearizable ℓ-test-and-set object. □

We conclude with a proof of correctness of the fetch-and-increment implementation. The basic idea is that the linearizability of the $\ell/2$-test-and-set object allows us to linearize any operation incrementing to value v before any operation incrementing to value $v' > v$. The complexity bound follows from the construction.

THEOREM 6 (m-FETCH-AND-INCREMENT). *The m-fetch-and-increment implementation in Algorithm 2 is linearizable, and has step complexity $O(\log k \log m)$ in expectation, and $O(\log^2 k \log m)$ with high probability.*

PROOF. Since $O.left$ and $O.right$ are linearizable, we can associate each access to them with its linearization point. We partition the operations into two disjoint categories, C_{left} and C_{right}, according to the $\ell/2$-fetch-and-increment object they access. We linearize operations in C_{left} before those in C_{right}.

Within each category, we linearize the operations according to the order of their linearization points with respect to the $\ell/2$-fetch-and-increment object they access ($O.left$ for C_{left}, and $O.right$ for C_{right}). By correctness of the $\ell/2$-test-and-set object, exactly $\ell/2$ processes return *true* and the rest return *false*. Hence, this ordering preserves the sequential specification of an ℓ-fetch-and-increment, given the assumption that $O.left$ and $O.right$ are linearizable $\ell/2$-fetch-and-increment objects. To show this preserves the order of non-overlapping operations, we need to argue only about non-overlapping operations in different categories, since this order is preserved within each category by the assumption on the linearizability of $O.left$ and $O.right$.

Let op_1 be an operation in C_{left} and op_2 be an operation in C_{right} and assume, towards a contradiction, that op_2 finishes before op_1 starts. Since op_2 is in C_{right} then its return value of the $\ell/2$-test-and-set object is *false*. Since op_1 starts after op_2 finishes it must also return *false* by correctness of the $\ell/2$-test-and-set object, and therefore op_1 must be in C_{right} as well. This contradicts the assumption that op_1 is in C_{left}, which completes the proof. □

9. CONCLUSIONS AND FUTURE WORK

In this paper, we introduce new randomized algorithms for adaptive strong renaming which work against a strong adaptive adversary. Our upper bound in the strong adaptive case is time-optimal, and shows a connection between sorting networks, renaming, and distributed counting. In particular, it can be used to obtain a monotone-consistent counter implementation with logarithmic complexity, and a linearizable fetch-and-increment implementation with polylogarithmic complexity.

The renaming network technique and the resulting counter implementations can be made deterministic with no loss in terms of step complexity if two-process test-and-set or compare-and-swap objects are available in hardware, which is common on modern machines.

One immediate direction of future work is to see if our techniques can be used to obtain a *linearizable* counter implementation with optimal logarithmic cost. A more general direction would be to see whether we can use the connection between counting, renaming and sorting to obtain lower bounds for counting or renaming from sorting lower bounds. A third direction would be to try to apply our techniques to other problems, such as *long-lived* renaming [24], resource allocation, or mutual exclusion.

10. ACKNOWLEDGEMENTS

We would like to thank Hagit Attiya, Rachid Guerraoui and Prasad Jayanti for useful discussions and support. We would also like to thank the anonymous reviewers for many useful comments.

11. REFERENCES

[1] H. Attiya, A. Bar-Noy, D. Dolev, D. Peleg, and R. Reischuk, "Renaming in an asynchronous environment," *Journal of the ACM*, vol. 37, no. 3, pp. 524–548, 1990.

[2] M. Herlihy and N. Shavit, "The topological structure of asynchronous computability," *J. ACM*, vol. 46, no. 2, pp. 858–923, 1999.

[3] A. Castañeda and S. Rajsbaum, "New combinatorial topology upper and lower bounds for renaming," in *PODC '08: Proceedings of the twenty-seventh ACM symposium on Principles of distributed computing*, (New York, NY, USA), pp. 295–304, ACM, 2008.

[4] J. H. Anderson and M. Moir, "Using local-spin k-exclusion algorithms to improve wait-free object implementations," *Distrib. Comput.*, vol. 11, no. 1, pp. 1–20, 1997.

[5] M. Moir and J. H. Anderson, "Fast, long-lived renaming (extended abstract)," in *WDAG '94: Proceedings of the 8th International Workshop on Distributed Algorithms*, (London, UK), pp. 141–155, Springer-Verlag, 1994.

[6] M. Moir and J. A. Garay, "Fast, long-lived renaming improved and simplified," in *WDAG '96: Proceedings of the 10th International Workshop on Distributed Algorithms*, (London, UK), pp. 287–303, Springer-Verlag, 1996.

[7] M. Moir and J. A. Garay, "Fast, long-lived renaming improved and simplified," in *PODC '96: Proceedings of the fifteenth annual ACM symposium on Principles of distributed computing*, (New York, NY, USA), p. 152, ACM, 1996.

[8] B. S. Chlebus and D. R. Kowalski, "Asynchronous exclusive selection," in *PODC '08: Proceedings of the twenty-seventh ACM symposium on Principles of distributed computing*, (New York, NY, USA), pp. 375–384, ACM, 2008.

[9] H. Attiya and A. Fouren, "Adaptive and efficient algorithms for lattice agreement and renaming," *SIAM J. Comput.*, vol. 31, no. 2, pp. 642–664, 2001.

[10] A. Panconesi, M. Papatriantafilou, P. Tsigas, and P. M. B. Vitányi, "Randomized naming using wait-free shared variables," *Distributed Computing*, vol. 11, no. 3, pp. 113–124, 1998.

[11] W. Eberly, L. Higham, and J. Warpechowska-Gruca, "Long-lived, fast, waitfree renaming with optimal name space and high throughput," in *DISC*, pp. 149–160, 1998.

[12] D. Alistarh, H. Attiya, S. Gilbert, A. Giurgiu, and R. Guerraoui, "Fast randomized test-and-set and renaming," in *DISC*, pp. 94–108, 2010.

[13] Y. Afek, E. Gafni, J. Tromp, and P. M. B. Vitányi, "Wait-free test-and-set (extended abstract)," in *WDAG '92: Proceedings of the 6th International Workshop on Distributed Algorithms*, (London, UK), pp. 85–94, Springer-Verlag, 1992.

[14] D. E. Knuth, *The art of computer programming, volume 3: (2nd ed.) sorting and searching*. Redwood City, CA, USA: Addison Wesley Longman Publishing Co., Inc., 1998.

[15] M. Ajtai, J. Komlós, and E. Szemerédi, "An O(n log n) sorting network," in *STOC '83: Proceedings of the fifteenth annual ACM symposium on Theory of computing*, (New York, NY, USA), pp. 1–9, ACM, 1983.

[16] P. Jayanti, "A time complexity lower bound for randomized implementations of some shared objects," in *Proceedings of the Seventeenth Annual ACM Symposium on Principles of Distributed Computing*, PODC '98, (New York, NY, USA), pp. 201–210, ACM, 1998.

[17] J. Aspnes, H. Attiya, and K. Censor, "Max registers, counters, and monotone circuits," in *PODC*, pp. 36–45, 2009.

[18] H. Attiya and K. Censor, "Tight bounds for asynchronous randomized consensus," *J. ACM*, vol. 55, no. 5, pp. 1–26, 2008.

[19] D. Alistarh, J. Aspnes, K. Censor-Hillel, S. Gilbert, and M. Zadimoghaddam, "Optimal-time adaptive tight renaming, with applications to counting." EPFL Technical Report, Jan. 2011.

[20] J. Tromp and P. Vitányi, "Randomized two-process wait-free test-and-set," *Distrib. Comput.*, vol. 15, no. 3, pp. 127–135, 2002.

[21] E. Gafni, A. Mostéfaoui, M. Raynal, and C. Travers, "From adaptive renaming to set agreement," *Theor. Comput. Sci.*, vol. 410, pp. 1328–1335, March 2009.

[22] J. E. Burns and G. L. Peterson, "The ambiguity of choosing," in *PODC '89: Proceedings of the eighth annual ACM Symposium on Principles of distributed computing*, (New York, NY, USA), pp. 145–157, ACM, 1989.

[23] E. Borowsky and E. Gafni, "Immediate atomic snapshots and fast renaming," in *PODC '93: Proceedings of the twelfth annual ACM symposium on Principles of distributed computing*, (New York, NY, USA), pp. 41–51, ACM, 1993.

[24] A. Brodsky, F. Ellen, and P. Woelfel, "Fully-adaptive algorithms for long-lived renaming," in *DISC*, pp. 413–427, 2006.

[25] H. Attiya, F. Kuhn, C. G. Plaxton, M. Wattenhofer, and R. Wattenhofer, "Efficient adaptive collect using randomization," *Distrib. Comput.*, vol. 18, no. 3, pp. 179–188, 2006.

[26] J. Aspnes, M. Herlihy, and N. Shavit, "Counting networks," *J. ACM*, vol. 41, pp. 1020–1048, Sept. 1994.

[27] H. Attiya, M. Herlihy, and O. Rachman, "Efficient atomic snapshots using lattice agreement (extended abstract)," in *Proceedings of the 6th International Workshop on Distributed Algorithms*, WDAG '92, (London, UK), pp. 35–53, Springer-Verlag, 1992.

[28] M. Mitzenmacher and E. Upfal, *Probability and Computing: Randomized Algorithms and Probabilistic Analysis*. New York, NY, USA: Cambridge University Press, 2005.

The Round Complexity of Distributed Sorting

[Extended Abstract]

Boaz Patt-Shamir*
School of Electrical Engineering
Tel Aviv University
boaz@eng.tau.ac.il

Marat Teplitsky
School of Electrical Engineering
Tel Aviv University
marattep@tau.ac.il

ABSTRACT

We consider the model of fully connected networks, where in each round each node can send an $O(\log n)$-bit message to each other node (this is the CONGEST model with diameter 1). It is known that in this model, min-weight spanning trees can be found in $O(\log \log n)$ rounds. In this paper we show that distributed sorting, where each node has at most n items, can be done in time $O(\log \log n)$ as well. It is also shown that selection can be done in $O(1)$ time. (Using a concurrent result by Lenzen and Wattenhofer, the complexity of sorting is further reduced to constant.) Our algorithms are randomized, and the stated complexity bounds hold with high probability.

Categories and Subject Descriptors

C.2.4 [**Computer-Communication Networks**]: Distributed Systems; F.2.2 [**Analysis of Algorithms and Problem Complexity**]: Nonnumerical Algorithms and Problems

General Terms

Theory, Algorithms

Keywords

network algorithms, communication complexity, distributed sorting, CONGEST model

1. INTRODUCTION

The round complexity of network algorithms can measure either the *locality* of information required for decision making (when the critical restriction is that messages progress

*Supported in part by the Israel Science Foundation (grant 1372/09) and by Israel Ministry of Science and Technology. Research done in part while visiting MIT CSAIL.

at the maximal rate of one hop per round), or it can also measure the *quantity of information* required to solve the given problem—when the throughput of communication link is also restricted. The former model is called the LOCAL model, and the latter is called the CONGEST model [18]. In the LOCAL model, all problems (functions) can be solved in D rounds, where D is the diameter of the network. This is because in D rounds, all input values can be made available in all processors, allowing for local computation of all outputs. In the CONGEST model, on the other hand, it is known that there are problems (such as minimum-weight spanning tree [8, 15, 17] and stable marriage [10]) with classes of instances whose graphs have small diameter but whose worst-case round complexity is high. For example, finding the minimum-weight spanning tree (abbreviated MST) of graphs of diameter 3 graphs takes roughly $\Omega(n^{1/3})$ communication rounds in the worst case, where n is the number of nodes in the network.[1]

One special case of the CONGEST model is particularly intriguing: The fully connected graph (a.k.a. clique), where the diameter is 1. The point is that any piece of information is within easy reach (at most one hop away), so locality is not an issue. However, getting *all* input into a single node (which allows any question to be answered at that node) takes $\Omega(N/n)$ rounds, where N denotes the number input items. It therefore seems that the fully-connected CONGEST model allows one to investigate the *complexity of congestion*, in a model almost completely divorced from locality. Unfortunately, the exact power of the fully-connected CONGEST model is unknown, except the fact that it admits an ultra-fast algorithms in a few cases. In fact, the only pertinent result in this model is by Lotker et al. [14], where it was shown that MST can be computed in this case in $O(\log \log n)$ rounds.

In this paper we do not resolve the mystery of the communication complexity of the fully-connected CONGEST model. Rather, we continue the exploration of this curious model, and show that the basic task of *sorting* can also be accomplished by an ultra-fast algorithm, whose time complexity is $O(\log \log n)$ rounds (with high probability). To achieve this time complexity, we need to carefully balance the work

---

[1] More precisely, the lower bound is $\Omega((n/B)^{1/3})$ rounds, where B is the maximal number of bits in a message. Following the convention, we assume that $B = O(\log n)$ bits.

load over the nodes (and communication load over links). We hope that the techniques developed in this paper will be helpful in the next steps of understanding this model.

Related Work. Sorting is a classical computational problem, possibly one of the best studied ones, with many algorithms and analyzes. Knuth [11] covers classical algorithms in depth. Below we give a very brief summary of a few highlights in parallel sorting.

Multi-processor sorting was also the target of much research, starting with Batcher's odd-even sorting network [3]. There is an $O(\log n)$ time algorithms for sorting in an $O(n)$-processor PRAM due to Cole [5], and the celebrated AKS $O(\log n)$-depth sorting network [2] (extended in a non-uniform way by Chvátal [4]). Valiant proved that finding the maximum of n items using n parallel comparisons in a round requires $\Theta(\log \log n)$ rounds [19].

PRAM abstract data access completely (every read and every write may use the shared memory in a single computational cycle). This critical drawback is addressed by later models, such as the BSP model [20] and the LogP model [6]. In the BSP model, each processor can send and receive at most h messages in each communication round (this model abstracts away a major difficulty of our model, in that it allows a processor to send h distinct messages to another processor in a single round). It is known [9] that sorting can be done in the BSP model in $O(\frac{\log N}{\log(h+1)})$ communication rounds for the case of N keys, n processors and $h = \Theta\left(\frac{N}{n}\right)$. Recently, Lenzen and Wattenhofer [12] considered a similar model, where in each communication round, each node can send and receive $O(n^\epsilon)$ bits, for a constant $\epsilon > 0$. They show that any algorithm that runs in T rounds, using less than n^ϵ bits of memory, over networks of polylogarithmic maximal degree in the LOCAL model, can be emulated in the globally restricted model in time $O(\log T + T(\log \log n / \log n))$, which means that any problem with a log-time algorithm in the polylog-bounded-degree CONGEST model has an $O(\log \log n)$ time algorithm in the globally-restricted model. (We note that our a part of algorithm can be used to emulate this model: see Section 5).

Our Results. In this paper we give a randomized algorithm that sorts n^2 items in $O(\log \log n)$ rounds over a fully-connected n-node graph, where each link can carry $O(\log n)$ bits in each round. We also show how to solve the selection (and median finding) problem in this model, in constant number of rounds.

Paper Organization. The remainder of this paper is organized as follows. In Section 2 we formalize the computational model and the problem statement. In Section 3 we describe our algorithm, and we analyze it in Section 4. Some extensions are outlined in Section 5, and we conclude in Section 7.

Remark: Later developments. After the initial submission of this work, we have learned that concurrently and independently, Lenzen and Wattenhofer [13] have showed that in the same model, N messages can be routed to their destinations in time $O(\frac{s+r}{n})$ w.h.p., where s is the maximal number of messages originating at any node, and r is the maximal number of messages destined to any node. A direct consequence of the result of [13] is that sorting n^2 items can be performed in $O(1)$ rounds in this model, as we explain in Section 6.

2. MODEL AND PROBLEM STATEMENT

In this section we define the main problem we study. In a nutshell, we use the fully-connected network topology under the CONGEST model [18], and we assume that in each processor there are n input values, called keys, that need to be globally sorted. A full specification is given below.

We are given a set of n *processors*, where each processor is a randomized state machine. We refer to processors also as *nodes* and denote them as $V = \{v_1, \ldots, v_n\}$. Each processor has some *input* registers and corresponding *output* registers. The value of the input registers may be an integer or a special symbol signifying "no input." The values of the input registers are initially set by the environment (users). Upon termination of the computation, the output registers in each processor indicate the *ranks* of the input values, i.e., the output register corresponding to the largest value should be "1," the output register corresponding to the second largest value should be "2" and so on.

To compute this input, the processors execute a *protocol* that proceeds in synchronous *rounds*: in each round each processor may send $O(\log n)$ bits to each other processor.[2] Formally, each round consists of three steps:
(1) Receive messages from the previous round. There may be at most $n - 1$ such messages: one from every processor.
(2) Perform local computation. This step may read from a tape (sequence) of random bits.
(3) Send messages to other processors. Each other processor may be sent an $O(\log n)$ bits message.

Execution starts when input is injected to the processors: We assume that n or less input values called *keys* are placed in the input registers of each processor (this may be viewed as receiving messages from round 0). We assume that all input values are encoded using $O(\log n)$ bits. The execution terminates when all processors enter a special *halting* state. The *round complexity* of the protocol is the number of rounds until the protocol terminates. We say that the protocol solves the problem *with high probability* in time T if with probability $1 - n^{-\Omega(1)}$, for any input values, after T rounds the protocol has terminated with the correct values in its output registers (probability is taken over the space of random bit tapes).

We assume that processors are numbered 1 through n. This assumption does not restrict generality when speaking of computations that succeed with high probability, because

---

[2] The choice of $\log n$ as the number of bits in a message is motivated similarly to the choice of $\log n$ to be the number of bits in a computer word: the idea is that values polynomial in the input length can be stored in a single unit. In the context of network algorithms, the essential assumption is that a message may contain a constant number of node and link IDs, counters, and input items.

in our model each processor can choose an ID of $O(\log n)$ bits and broadcast it to all its neighbors in the first round, and then take the rank of its ID to be their number. This little pre-processing procedure adds just one round to the time complexity, and a term of $n^{-\Omega(1)}$ to the probability of failure.

3. THE ALGORITHM

In this section we describe the algorithm for the sorting problem described in Section 2. Analysis is provided in Section 4.

Overview. The basic idea underlying the algorithm is to partition the input keys into n disjoint ranges, gather all keys of each range in a distinct node, and sort them locally. It turns out that the bottleneck in this approach is the "gathering" step: it may be the case that a node needs to send multiple keys to another node, something that cannot be implemented by the primitive send operation in a single round. We therefore develop a simple "scatter-gather" procedure that allows any single sender to send n items to any set of receivers, using intermediate nodes. However, since there are n parallel senders, the link between an intermediate node and a destination node might also get congested. To overcome this difficulty we employ a simple but subtle control mechanism, that first takes care of the less loaded destinations, and then of the heavily loaded ones.

Pseudo-code of the high-level algorithm is given in Algorithm 1. We now elaborate on the way it is implemented.

Assigning keys to nodes. The idea is as follows. Let a_i be the number of keys at node v_i, and let $N \overset{\text{def}}{=} \sum_{i=1}^{n} a_i$ be the total number of keys. We first order all keys in an arbitrary order (not necessarily sorted) as follows. Locally, each node v_i orders its a_i keys arbitrarily $k_{i_1}, \ldots, k_{i_{a_i}}$. This induces a global order, obtained by concatenating the local node orders in the natural way: the key k_{i_j} indexed locally at node i is the key whose global index is $\sum_{l=1}^{i-1} a_l + k_{i_j}$. From this global indexation, $n-1$ keys $k_{r_2}, \ldots, k_{r_n}$ are chosen independently and uniformly at random from $\{1, \ldots, N\}$ (Step 1). These keys serve as "range delimiters," in the sense that all keys in the range $[k_{r_i}, k_{r_{i+1}} - 1]$ are associated with node v_i for $1 \leq i \leq n$, where $k_{r_1} = -\infty$ and $k_{r_{n+1}} = \infty$ by convention (Step 2).

The implementation is as follows. Each node v_i broadcasts to all other nodes the number a_i of keys it has. This allows each node to compute the global index of each of its keys as explained above. Node v_1, which will be the designated "leader" for the remainder of the algorithm, chooses $n-1$ indices $r_2, \ldots, r_n$ uniformly at random from $\{1, \ldots, N\}$, and for each $2 \leq i \leq n$, v_1 sends r_i to node v_i. Node v_i then broadcasts r_i to all other nodes. This way, after 3 rounds, all nodes know all r_i values. Using the known global ranking, each node that holds k_{r_i} sends it to node i (a node may send more than a single value, but to different destinations). Finally, each node i broadcasts to all the value of k_{r_i}, and, as a result, all nodes know, for each key k, what is $d(k)$, i.e., which node is the destination of each key.

Next, we route each key k to its destination $d(k)$ in two

Algorithm 1 SORT

(1) Choose $n-1$ keys $k_{r_2}, \ldots, k_{r_n}$ uniformly at random.
    // delimiter keys

(2) Define, for $1 \leq i \leq n$, *range i* $R_i \overset{\text{def}}{=} [k_{r_i}, k_{r_{i+1}} - 1]$, where $k_{r_1} \overset{\text{def}}{=} -\infty$ and $k_{r_{n+1}} \overset{\text{def}}{=} \infty$.
    Define, for each key k, $d(k) = i$ if $k_{r_i} \in R_i$.
    // key k needs to get to node $d(k)$

(3) Let $c(i) = |\{k : d(k) = i\}|$. A node i is called *active destination* only if $c(i) < 2n \ln \ln n$. A key k is *active* only if $d(k)$ is an active destination.

(4) **repeat**

   (4a) Each node picks a random intermediate destination $m(k)$ for each active key k it has.

   (4b) At each node i: For $j = 1, \ldots, n$, let $P_i(j) = \{k \mid k$ is active and $m(k) = j\}$; If $P_i(j) \neq \emptyset$, pick a random $k \in P_i(j)$ and send k to j.   *// source to intermediate*

   (4c) At each node j: For $l = 1, \ldots, n$, let $Q_j(l) = \{k \mid m(k) = j$ and $d(k) = l\}$. If $Q_j(l) \neq \emptyset$, pick a random $k \in Q_j(l)$ and send it to l. Mark k *inactive*. All other keys are sent back to their sources.   *// intermediate to destination*

   until all active keys have reached their destination.

(5) **Cleanup stage:** Repeat Steps 1–4 only with keys that did not reach their destinations.

(6) Each node sorts all keys associated with it, and determines their global rank.

(7) Ranks are routed back by reversing the routes taken by the keys.

stages as follows. In the first stage, only keys whose destination is the destination of at most $2n \ln \ln n$ keys are routed (Step 3). To implement this distinction, each node v_i sends to each other node v_j the number of keys v_i whose destination is v_j. Each node v_j thus finds the total number of keys destined to it, and v_j broadcast this number to all. (We note that the size of all ranges is recorded by all nodes, so that local ranking of the keys in a range can be translated to the global ranking later in Step 6.)

Routing the keys. In Step 4, we solve the following problem. We have n nodes, each with n or less keys, where each key has a destination in $\{v_1, \ldots, v_n\}$ so that no node is the destination of more than $2n \log \log n$ keys. The difficulty stems from the fact that each link can carry at most one key in each round, while the number of keys that initially reside at the same node and share the same destination node may be $\Omega(n)$. We solve this problem using the Valiant an Brebner paradigm of random intermediate destination [21] as follows. We run a sequence of phases (phases are iterations of the loop in Step 4). In each phase, each node first selects a random intermediate destination for each of its remaining undelivered keys. Then the node selects a random single key for each possible intermediate destination, i.e., congestion conflicts in source-to-intermediate links are resolved at the source nodes. After resolving the conflicts, the keys are sent to their intermediate destination in a single round. Next, each node (now playing as an intermediate destination) picks one key for each final destination and sends it over, i.e., congestion conflicts on the intermediate-to-destination links are resolved at the intermediate node. In the following round, keys that were not sent to their final destination (due to congestion in the intermediate-to-destination link) are sent back to their origin, where they are ready for the next phase. We shall show that with high probability, all keys arrive at their destination within $O(\log \log n)$ phases.

We are then left with the keys associated with large ranges (and were therefore not routed in the first routing stage). This case is in fact easier to handle than the original instance because, as we show, only about a $\frac{1}{\log n}$ fraction of the keys remain, and applying Steps 1–4 again will deliver all of them to their destinations in $O(\log \log n)$ additional rounds, because now, w.h.p., all ranges have size only $O(n)$.

Finally, when we know the rank of each key in its range, the global ranks can be computed as the size (and ordering) of all ranges is known from Step 3. To comply with the problem requirement, these computed ranks are routed back to the source nodes, using the reverse of routing schedule that brought the keys in.

4. ANALYSIS

In this section we analyze the algorithm specified in Section 3. We start by analyzing the partition into ranges, and then analyze the routing procedure.

4.1 Partition Into Ranges

Partition into ranges (Steps 1–2) is done twice during the execution of the algorithm. We analyze them in order.

4.1.1 The First Stage

We first analyze the partition of the key set into ranges in the first stage. We start with a technical lemma, that analyzes the following scenario. Order the N keys by value, and partition them into $\lceil n/\ln \ln n \rceil$ segments of about the same size $(N/n)\ln \ln n$ (rounded up and down as necessary; we'll ignore rounding for simplicity of exposition). Now, call a segment *selected* if one of the keys it contains was selected in Step 1 (of the first stage) as a delimiter. Then the following holds true.[3]

LEMMA 4.1. *With high probability, the number of non-selected segments is at most $\frac{2n}{\ln n \ln \ln n}$.*

Proof: Let Y_i to be binary indicator variable, taking the value 1 if segment i is *not* selected and 0 otherwise. Then

$$\Pr[Y_i = 1] = \left(1 - \frac{\ln \ln n}{n}\right)^n \leq e^{-\ln \ln n} = \frac{1}{\ln n} ,$$

and therefore, $E[\sum Y_i] \leq \frac{n}{\ln n \ln \ln n}$. Now, it is easy to see that the vector of Y_i random variables is *negatively associ-*

---
[3]We note that the constants in Lemma 4.2 can be improved; we make no attempt to optimize them here.

ated ([7], and see also [16]). Therefore we may apply the Chernoff-Hoeffding bound and conclude that

$$\Pr\left[\sum Y_i > \frac{2n}{\ln n \ln \ln n}\right] < e^{\frac{-n}{3 \ln n \ln \ln n}} < n^{-\Omega(1)}$$

for all $n > 1$. ∎

We can now deduce the following.

LEMMA 4.2. *Suppose that the number of keys is at most n^2. Then, with high probability, the number of ranges with more than $2n \ln \ln n$ keys is at most $2n/(\ln n \cdot \ln \ln n)$.*

Proof: First, note that since $N \leq n^2$ by assumption, segment size is at most $n \ln \ln n$ keys. Therefore, a range with $2n \ln \ln n$ keys or more must contain a complete segment that is not *selected*. It follows that the number of non-selected segments is an upper bound on the number of ranges of size at least $2n \ln \ln n$, and by Lemma 4.1 this number is, with high probability, bounded by $\frac{2n}{\ln n \ln \ln n}$. ∎

4.1.2 Cleanup Stage

We need to show that one more iteration of steps 1–3 is enough to sort all remaining keys. To this end, we apply Lemma 4.1 once again as follows.

LEMMA 4.3. *W.h.p, the number of keys remaining to the cleanup at most $\frac{4n^2}{\ln n}$.*

Proof: Since each range that is deferred to the cleanup stage contains at least $2n \ln \ln n$ keys, each such range must contain a run of non-selected segments. It follows that the total number of keys in ranges that are deferred to the cleanup stage is at most $2n \ln \ln n$ times the number of non-selected ranges. Applying Lemma 4.1 once again, we conclude that w.h.p., the number of keys in the cleanup stage is at most

$$2n \ln \ln n \cdot \frac{2n}{\ln n \cdot \ln \ln n} = \frac{4n^2}{\ln n} .$$ ∎

Lemma 4.3 implies the following.

LEMMA 4.4. *In the cleanup stage, with high probability, all ranges are of size $O(n)$.*

Proof: By Lemma 4.3, the number of remaining keys is at most $4n^2/\ln n$. Similarly to the analysis of the range selection in the first stage, we partition the keys in segments of length $12n$ (say). The probability that a particular segment is unselected is at most $(1 - 3\ln n/n)^n \leq n^{-3}$, and hence the probability that all segments are selected (implying that the size of all ranges is bounded by $24n$) is at least $1 - \frac{2\ln n}{n^2}$. ∎

4.2 Analysis of Routing

Routing keys to their destination nodes is done in both stages by Step 4. It is immediate from the code that each iteration takes $O(1)$ rounds; it remains to analyze the number of iterations taken in Step 4.

We distinguish between two cases: "heavily loaded" destinations and "lightly loaded" ones. For the first case, we have the following lemma.

LEMMA 4.5. *Suppose that there are $m \geq n$ active keys with destination v_i at the beginning of an iteration of Step 4. Then with high probability, at least $n/9$ keys will be delivered at v_i in that iteration.*

Proof: It may be helpful to note that we have a classical balls-and-bins type of situation here, where keys are balls and intermediate destinations are bins. So, keeping this intuition in mind, consider first the choice of intermediate destinations at the source nodes.

The probability that an intermediate destination is unique at a source node (i.e., was chosen for exactly one key at that source) is at least $1/e$, because there are at most n keys at the source, and there are exactly n intermediate random choices for each. It therefore follows from standard balls-and-bins results (see [7]) that with high probability, at least $n/3$ (say) nodes will receive, as intermediate destinations, keys whose final destination is v_i.

Next, consider the situation at an intermediate destination v^*: if there is any key at v^* whose final destination is v_i, then v_i will receive *some* key from v^* in the next round. Applying [7] once again, we may conclude that with high probability, if there are $m \geq n$ keys destined to v_i, then at least $n/9$ of them (say) will be delivered at v_i. ∎

To analyze the lightly-loaded destination case, we use a fundamental fact proven in [1]. Consider the following iterative balls-and-bins process. There are n balls at start, and in each round, all remaining balls are thrown (independently, randomly) into n bins. In each round, each bin accepts only one of the balls thrown into (if any), and all other balls are thrown again in the next round, until all balls are placed in bins.

LEMMA 4.6. *Suppose that there are at most n active keys with destination v_i. Then with high probability, all keys are delivered in $O(\log \log n)$ iterations.*

Proof: Follows from the fact that Step 4 is implemented like the algorithm THRESHOLD(1) in [1], wherein it is shown that in $O(\log \log n)$ rounds suffice with probability $1 - n^{-\Omega(1)}$. ∎

4.3 Summary

THEOREM 4.7. *With high probability, Algorithm SORT solves the sorting problem and terminates in $O(\log \log n)$ communication rounds.*

Proof: Correctness is immediate from the Union Bound: all statements hold with high probability, and there is only a polynomial number of times a failure may occur. Consider now the round complexity. Steps 1–3 take $O(1)$ rounds. Regarding Step 4, in the first stage, all destinations have at most $O(n \log \log n)$ keys routed to them. By Lemma 4.5, w.h.p., after $O(\log \log n)$ rounds, for each destination there are at most n keys that are still undelivered, and therefore, by Lemma 4.6, after $O(\log \log n)$ additional rounds, the first stage is over. In the cleanup stage, there are at most

$O(n)$ keys to be routed to each destination, and therefore, by Lemmas 4.5 and 4.6, in $O(\log \log n)$ additional rounds, the cleanup stage is over as well. Step 6 is communication-free, and Step 7 just doubles the overall complexity. ∎

5. EXTENSIONS AND APPLICATIONS

In this section we outline two simple extensions of the algorithm. One is for a small number of input keys, and the other is for the median problem. But let us first point out an application to models with global restriction on the communication that can be delivered in a round.

Application: global restriction on communication. We note that the routing step of our algorithm can be used to emulate the model used by Lenzen and Wattenhofer in [12]. Specifically, the model considered in [12] allows for the global exchange of $O(n^\epsilon)$ bits in each round (for some constant parameter $0 < \epsilon \leq 1$), without any other restriction on communication. Let us call this model $G(\epsilon)$. In our fully-connected CONGEST model, we only restrict the number of bits exchanged by any pair of nodes in a round to be $O(\log n)$ (but the total number of bits moving in a round can be as high as $O(n^2 \log n)$). Clearly, algorithms for the $G(\epsilon)$ model cannot be run directly on the fully connected CONGEST model, because in the $G(\epsilon)$ model, it may be the case that n^ϵ bits may need to move from one node to another in a single round. However, our analysis implies that any algorithm running in time T on the $G(\epsilon)$ model can be emulated (w.h.p.) on our model in time $O(T)$ for any $\epsilon \leq 1$. This can be done in a round-by-round emulation as follows. First, we break the model $G(\epsilon)$ messages to packets of size $O(\log n)$ bits. Then we run Step 4 of the algorithm, using the actual destinations of the packets instead of ranges. Since by assumption all node are the destination of at most $O(n^\epsilon)$ bits, Lemma 5.2 ensures (w.h.p.) that all $O(n/\log n)$ packets will be delivered in $O(1)$ time.

A small number of input items. The algorithm specified in Section 3 works when the number of input keys is at most the square of the number of processors, i.e., $N \leq n^2$. It should be noted that if the number of keys is smaller than $n^2/\log^2 n$, then the time complexity drops to $O(1)$: this follows from the following facts.

LEMMA 5.1. *Suppose we have $K \leq (n/\log n)^2$ ordered elements, and we choose uniformly at random n elements. Then with high probability, the longest gap between two consecutive chosen elements is $O(n/\log n)$.*

Proof: As in the proof of Lemma 4.1, we partition the elements into n segments of length $n/\log^2 n$ each (up to rounding). The probability that a segment remains unselected (i.e., no delimiter is contained in it) after Step 1 is $(1 - \frac{1}{n})^n < e^{-1}$, and thus the probability that $\log n$ segments or more are unselected is $n^{-\Omega(1)}$. The claim follows from the fact that a gap of $n/\log n$ is possible only if there are $\log n - 1$ unselected segments. ∎

LEMMA 5.2. *If $n/\log n$ balls are thrown into n bins, the maximal number of balls in a bin is $O(1)$ with high probability.*

Proof: Follows from the Chernoff Bound. ∎

COROLLARY 5.3. *If the number of keys is $N = O(n^2/\log^2 n)$ then sorting on the fully connected n-clique can be done in $O(1)$ rounds.*

Proof: Algorithm 1 works. Lemma 5.1 implies that w.h.p., all nodes are active, and Lemma 5.2 implies that the routing can be done in $O(1)$ rounds. ∎

Finding the median (and general selection). In the selection problem, we are asked to output the kth largest key, where k is part of the input. The median problem is a special case of selection, where $k = N/2$ (N is the number of input keys). It turns out that a minor modification in Algorithm 1 yields a simple $O(1)$ selection algorithm. First, we run Steps 1–3 to figure out what is exactly the range the contains the kth largest key. This is easy because after Step 3 each node knows what is the number of keys in each range. We then apply the sorting algorithm with input that consists of the keys of this range *only* (this is also easy because after Step 2 each key knows what is its range). When the algorithm terminates, we can identify exactly what is the kth largest requested key. To analyze the time complexity, we need the following straightforward fact.

LEMMA 5.4. *With high probability, no range defined by the delimiters chosen in Step 1 contains more than $O(n \log n)$ keys.*

Now, the following holds with high probability. First, Steps 1–3 take $O(1)$ rounds. Also, by Lemma 5.4, the invocation of Algorithm SORT has only $O(n \log n)$ keys as input, and therefore Corollary 5.3 ensures that SORT will terminate in $O(1)$ rounds as well. We therefore have the following.

COROLLARY 5.5. *The Selection problem can be solved in the fully-connected CONGEST model in $O(1)$ rounds, with high probability.*

6. POSTSCRIPT: SORTING IN $O(1)$ ROUNDS

Concurrently to our work, Lenzen and Wattenhofer proved the following result.

THEOREM 6.1. **[13]** *Suppose there are $O(n)$ messages in each node, and that the number of messages destined to each node is $O(n)$. Then routing all messages to their destinations can be done in $O(1)$ rounds with probability $1 - n^{-\Omega(1)}$.*

Using this result, we propose the following algorithm for sorting.

(1) Select each key with probability $\frac{1}{\log^2 n}$. Let S denote the set of selected keys.

(2) Apply Algorithm 1 to S. For an integer $1 \le i \le |S|$, let $k_S(i)$ denote the key ranked i in S.

(3) Define delimiters $l(0), \ldots, l(n)$ by
$$l(i) = \begin{cases} -\infty & \text{if } i = 0 \\ k_s(\lceil |S| \frac{i}{n} \rceil) & \text{if } 0 < i \le n, \end{cases}$$
and set the destination of each key k to be $d(k) \stackrel{\text{def}}{=} i$ if $l(i-1) < k \le l(i)$.

(4) Send each key k to destination $d(k)$ using the routing implied by Theorem 6.1.

(5) Locally sort all received keys and send back their ranks.

To see why this procedure works, we first note that by the Chernoff Bound, the set S selected at Step 1 has size $O(n/\log^2 n)$ w.h.p., and therefore, by Corollary 5.3, Step 2 ends in $O(1)$ rounds. Finding the delimiters takes $O(1)$ time. The key to the success of the algorithm is that with high probability, for all $1 \le i \le n$, the number of keys in the range $[l_{i-1}+1, l_i]$ (which are all destined to node i) is bounded from above by $O(n)$. This fact can be shown to follow from the Chernoff bound as well. We can therefore conclude with the following theorem.

THEOREM 6.2. *The sorting problem can be solved in $O(1)$ communication rounds with high probability.*

7. CONCLUSION

In this paper we have given more evidence that the fully-connected CONGEST model allows for ultra-fast algorithms for basic problems. Specifically, it turns out that sorting can be solved in constant time with high probability. Many very interesting problems remain open for this problem and this model. Regarding sorting, it may be the case that good deterministic algorithms exist. Regarding the model, we see two main directions that complement each other: One is to come up with a non-trivial lower bound for some natural problem in this model, and the other is to come up with ultra-fast algorithms for key problems in this model (e.g., weighted matching).

Acknowledgment

We thank the anonymous referees, and Christoph Lenzen and Roger Wattenhofer for providing us with a preprint and an explanation of [13].

8. REFERENCES

[1] Micah Adler, Soumen Chakrabarti, Michael Mitzenmacher, and Lars Rasmussen. Parallel randomized load balancing. In *Proceedings of the twenty-seventh annual ACM symposium on Theory of computing*, STOC '95, pages 238–247, New York, NY, USA, 1995. ACM.

[2] M. Ajtai, J. Komlós, and E. Szemerédi. An $O(n \log n)$ sorting network. In *Proc. 15th Ann. ACM Symp. on Theory of Computing (STOC)*, pages 1–9. ACM Press, May 1983.

[3] K. E. Batcher. Sorting networks and their applications. In *Proc. 1968 Spring Joint Computer Conference*, pages 307–314, Reston, VA, 1968. AFIPS Press.

[4] V. Chvátal. Lecture notes on the new AKS sorting network. Technical Report DCS-TR-294, Computer Science Department, Rutgers University, 1992.

[5] Richard Cole. Parallel merge sort. In *Proc. 27th Ann. Symp. on Foundations of Computer Science*, pages 511–516, October 1986.

[6] David E. Culler, Richard M. Karp, David Patterson, Abhijit Sahay, Eunice E. Santos, Klaus Erik Schauser, Ramesh Subramonian, and Thorsten von Eicken. LogP: A practical model of parallel computation. *Comm. ACM*, 39:78–85, November 1996.

[7] Devdatt Dubhashi and Desh Ranjan. Balls and bins: a study in negative dependence. *Random Struct. Algorithms*, 13:99–124, September 1998.

[8] Micheal Elkin. An unconditional lower bound on the time-approximation tradeoff for the minimum spanning tree problem. *SIAM Journal on Computing*, 36(2):463–501, 2006.

[9] Michael T. Goodrich. Communication-efficient parallel sorting (preliminary version). In *Proc. 28th Ann. ACM Symp. on Theory of Computing (STOC)*, pages 247–256, New York, NY, USA, 1996. ACM.

[10] Alex Kipnis and Boaz Patt-Shamir. A note on distributed stable matching. In *Proc. 29th International Conf. on Distributed Computing Systems (ICDCS)*, June 2009.

[11] Donald E. Knuth. *Sorting and Searching*, volume 3 of *The Art of Computer Programming*. Addison-Wesley, 2nd edition, 1998.

[12] Christoph Lenzen and Roger Wattenhofer. Brief announcement: Exponential speed-up of local algorithms using non-local communication. In *Proc. 29th ACM Symp. On Principles of Distributed Computing (PODC)*, pages 295–296, 2010.

[13] Christoph Lenzen and Roger Wattenhofer. Tight Bounds for Parallel Randomized Load Balancing. In *Proc. 43rd ACM Symposium on Theory of Computing (STOC)*, 2011. To appear.

[14] Zvi Lotker, Boaz Patt-Shamir, Elan Pavlov, and David Peleg. Minimum-weight spanning tree construction in O(log log n) communication rounds. *SIAM Journal on Computing*, 35(1):120–131, 2005.

[15] Zvi Lotker, Boaz Patt-Shamir, and David Peleg. Distributed MST for constant diameter graphs. *Distributed Computation*, 18(6):453–460, 2006.

[16] Colin McDiarmid. On the method of bounded differences. In *Surveys in Combinatorics*, pages 148–188. Cambridge University Press, Cambridge, UK, 1989.

[17] D. Peleg and V. Rubinovich. Near-tight lower bound on the time complexity of distributed MST construction. *SIAM Journal on Computing*, 30:1427–1442, 2000.

[18] David Peleg. *Distributed Computing: A Locality-Sensitive Approach*. Society for Industrial and Applied Mathematics, Philadelphia, PA, USA, 2000.

[19] Leslie G. Valiant. Parallelism in comparison problems. *SIAM Journal on Computing*, 4(3):348–355, 1975.

[20] Leslie G. Valiant. A bridging model for parallel computation. *Commun. ACM*, 33:103–111, August 1990.

[21] Leslie G. Valiant and G. J. Brebner. Universal schemes for parallel communication. In *Proceedings of the 13th Annual ACM Symposium on Theory of Computing (STOC)*, pages 263–277, Milwaukee, WI, May 1981.

A Tight Unconditional Lower Bound on Distributed Random Walk Computation [*]

Danupon Nanongkai
University of Vienna & Georgia
Institute of Technology
Austria & USA
danupon@gmail.com

Atish Das Sarma
Google Research
Mountain View, USA.
dassarma@google.com

Gopal Pandurangan[†]
Nanyang Technological
University & Brown University
Singapore & USA
gopalpandurangan@gmail.com

ABSTRACT

We consider the problem of performing a random walk in a distributed network. Given bandwidth constraints, the goal of the problem is to minimize the number of rounds required to obtain a random walk sample. Das Sarma et al. [PODC'10] show that a random walk of length ℓ on a network of diameter D can be performed in $\tilde{O}(\sqrt{\ell D} + D)$ time. A major question left open is whether there exists a faster algorithm, especially whether the multiplication of $\sqrt{\ell}$ and $\sqrt{D}$ is necessary.

In this paper, we show a tight unconditional lower bound on the time complexity of distributed random walk computation. Specifically, we show that for any n, D, and $D \leq \ell \leq (n/(D^3 \log n))^{1/4}$, performing a random walk of length $\Theta(\ell)$ on an n-node network of diameter D requires $\Omega(\sqrt{\ell D} + D)$ time. This bound is *unconditional*, i.e., it holds for any (possibly randomized) algorithm. To the best of our knowledge, this is the first lower bound that the diameter plays a role of multiplicative factor. Our bound shows that the algorithm of Das Sarma et al. is time optimal.

Our proof technique introduces a new connection between *bounded-round* communication complexity and distributed algorithm lower bounds with D as a trade-off parameter, strengthening the previous study by Das Sarma et al. [STOC'11]. In particular, we make use of the bounded-round communication complexity of the pointer chasing problem. Our technique can be of independent interest and may be useful in showing non-trivial lower bounds on the complexity of other fundamental distributed computing problems.

---

[*]A full version of this paper is available as [28] at `http://arxiv.org/abs/1102.2906`

[†]Supported in part by the following grants: Nanyang Technological University grant M58110000, NSF grant CCF-1023166, and by a grant from the United States-Israel Binational Science Foundation (BSF).

Categories and Subject Descriptors

C.2.4 [**Computer Systems Organization**]: Computer-Communication Networks—*Distributed Systems*; F.0 [**Theory of Computation**]: General; G.2.2 [**Mathematics of Computing**]: Discrete Mathematic—*Graph Theory*

General Terms

Algorithms, Theory

Keywords

Distributed Algorithms, Random Walk, Lower Bound, Time Complexity, Communication Complexity

1. INTRODUCTION

The random walk plays a central role in computer science, spanning a wide range of areas in both theory and practice. The focus of this paper is on performing a random walk in distributed networks, in particular, decentralized algorithms for performing a random walk in arbitrary networks. The random walk is used as an integral subroutine in a wide variety of network applications ranging from token management [19, 4, 8], small-world routing [21], search [32, 1, 7, 18, 27], information propagation and gathering [5, 20], network topology construction [18, 24, 25], expander testing [12], constructing random spanning trees [6, 3, 2], distributed construction of expander networks [24], and peer-to-peer membership management [16, 33]. For more applications of random walks to distributed networks, see e.g. [11]. Motivated by the wide applicability of the random walk, [10, 11] consider the running time of performing a random walk on the synchronous distributed model. We now explain the model and problems before describing previous work and our results.

1.1 Distributed Computing Model

Consider a synchronous network of processors with unbounded computational power. The network is modeled by an undirected connected n-node multi-graph, where nodes model the processors and edges model the links between the processors. The processors (henceforth, nodes) communicate by exchanging messages via the links (henceforth, edges). The nodes have limited global knowledge, in particular, each of them has its own local perspective of the network (a.k.a graph), which is confined to its immediate neighborhood.

There are several measures to analyze the performance of algorithms on this model, a fundamental one being the running time, defined as the worst-case number of *rounds* of distributed communication. This measure naturally gives rise to a complexity measure of problems, called the *time complexity*. On each round at most $O(\log n)$ bits can be sent through each edge in each direction. This is a standard model of distributed computation known as the $\mathcal{CONGEST}$ model [30] and has been attracting a lot of research attention during last two decades (e.g., see [30] and the references therein). We note that our result also holds on the $\mathcal{CONGEST}(B)$ model, where on each round at most B bits can be sent through each edge in each direction (see the remark after Theorem 1.1). We ignore this parameter to make the proofs and theorem statements simpler.

1.2 Problems

The basic problem is *computing a random walk where destination outputs source*, defined as follows. We are given a network $G = (V, E)$ and a source node $s \in V$. The goal is to devise a distributed algorithm such that, in the end, some node v outputs the ID of s, where v is a destination node picked according to the probability that it is the destination of a random walk of length ℓ starting at s. We assume the standard random walk where, in each step, an edge is taken from the current node v with probability proportional to $1/d(v)$ where $d(v)$ is the degree of v. Our goal is to output a true random sample from the ℓ-walk distribution starting from s.

For clarity, observe that the following naive algorithm solves the above problem in $O(\ell)$ rounds. The walk of length ℓ is performed by sending a token for ℓ steps, picking a random neighbor in each step. Then, the destination node v of this walk outputs the ID of s. The main objective of distributed random walk problem is to perform such sampling with significantly less number of rounds, i.e., in time that is sublinear in ℓ. On the other hand, we note that it can take too much time (as much as $\Theta(|E| + D)$ time) in the $\mathcal{CONGEST}$ model to collect all the topological information at the source node (and then computing the walk locally).

The following variations were also previously considered.

1. *Computing a random walk where source outputs destination*: The problem is almost the same as above except that, in the end, the source has to output the ID of the destination. This version is useful in nodes learning the topology of their surrounding networks and related applications such as a decentralized algorithm for estimating the mixing time [11].

2. *Computing a random walk where nodes know their positions*: Instead of outputting the ID of source or destination, we want each node to know its position(s) in the random walk. That is, if $v_1, v_2, ..., v_\ell$ (where $v_1 = s$) is the result random walk starting at s, we want each node v_j in the walk to know the number j at the end of the process. This version is used to construct a random spanning tree in [11].

1.3 Previous work and our result

A key purpose of the random walk in many network applications is to perform node sampling. While the sampling requirements in different applications vary, whenever a true sample is required from a random walk of certain steps, typ-

ically all applications perform the walk naively — by simply passing a token from one node to its neighbor: thus to perform a random walk of length ℓ takes time linear in ℓ. Das Sarma et al. [10] showed this is not a time-optimal strategy and the running time can be made sublinear in ℓ, i.e., performing a random walk of length ℓ on an n-node network of diameter D can be done in $\tilde{O}(\ell^{2/3} D^{1/3})$ time where $\tilde{O}$ hides polylog n. Subsequently, Das Sarma et al. [11] improved this bound to $\tilde{O}(\sqrt{\ell D} + D)$ which holds for all three versions of the problem.

There are two key motivations for obtaining sublinear time bounds. The first is that in many algorithmic applications, walks of length significantly greater than the network diameter are needed. For example, this is necessary in two applications presented in [11], namely distributed computation of a random spanning tree (RST) and computation of mixing time. More generally, many real-world communication networks (e.g., ad hoc networks and peer-to-peer networks) have relatively small diameter, and random walks of length at least the diameter are usually performed for many sampling applications, i.e., $\ell >> D$.

The second motivation is understanding the time complexity of distributed random walks. Random walk is essentially a global problem which requires the algorithm to "traverse" the entire network. Classical "global" problems include the minimum spanning tree, shortest path etc. Network diameter is an inherent lower bound for such problems. Problems of this type raise the basic question whether n (or ℓ as the case here) time is essential or is the network diameter D, the inherent parameter. As pointed out in the seminal work of [17], in the latter case, it would be desirable to design algorithms that have a better complexity for graphs with low diameter. While both upper and lower bounds of time complexity of many "global" problems are known (see, e.g., [9]), the status of the random walk problem is still wide open.

A preliminary attempt to show a random walk lower bound is presented in [11]. They consider a restricted class of algorithms, where each message sent between nodes must be in the form of an interval of numbers. Moreover, a node is allowed to send a number or an interval containing it only after it receives such number. For this very restricted class of algorithms, a lower bound of $\Omega(\sqrt{\ell} + D)$ is shown [11] for the version where every node must know their positions in the end of the computation. While this lower bound shows a potential limitation of random walk algorithms, it has many weaknesses. First, it does not employ an information theoretic argument and thus does not hold for all types of algorithm. Instead, it assumes that the algorithms must send messages as intervals and thus holds only for a small class of algorithms, which does not even cover all deterministic algorithms. Second, the lower bound holds only for the version where nodes know their position(s), thereby leaving lower bounds for the other two random walk versions completely open. More importantly, there is still a gap of $\sqrt{D}$ between lower and upper bounds, leaving a question whether there is a faster algorithm.

Motivated by these applications, past results, and open problems, we consider the problem of finding lower bounds for random walk computation. In this work, we show an *unconditional* lower bound of $\Omega(\sqrt{\ell D} + D)$ for all three versions of the random walk computation problem. This means that the algorithm in [11] is optimal for all three variations. In particular, we show the following theorem.

Theorem 1.1 *For any n, D and ℓ such that $D \leq \ell \leq (n/(D^3 \log n))^{1/4}$, there exists a family of n-node networks of diameter D such that performing a random walk (any of the three versions) of length $\Theta(\ell)$ on these networks requires $\Omega(\sqrt{\ell D} + D)$ rounds.*

We note that our lower bound of $\Omega(\sqrt{\ell D} + D)$ also holds for the general $\mathcal{CONGEST}(B)$ model, where each edge has bandwidth B instead of $O(\log n)$, as long as $\ell \leq (n/(D^3 B))^{1/4}$. Moreover, one can also show a lower bound on simple graphs by subdividing edges in the network used in the proof and double the value of ℓ.

1.4 Techniques and proof overview

Our main approach relies on enhancing the connection between communication complexity and distributed algorithm lower bounds first studied in [9]. It has been shown in [9] that a fast distributed algorithm for computing a function can be converted into a two-party communication protocol with small message complexity to compute the same function. In other words, the communication complexity lower bounds implies the time complexity lower bounds of distributed algorithms. This result is then used to prove lower bounds on many *verification problems*. (In the verification problems, we are given H, a subgraph of the network G, where each vertex of G knows which edges incident on it are in H. We would like to verify whether H has some properties, e.g., if it is a tree or if it is connected.) The lower bounds of verification problems are then used to prove lower bounds of approximation algorithms for many graph problems. Their work, however, does not make progress on achieving *any* unconditional lower bound on the random walk problem.

Further, while this approach has been successfully used to show lower bounds for several problems in terms of network size (i.e., n), it is not clear how to apply them to random walk computation. All the lower bounds previously shown are for *optimization* problems for well-defined metrics - for e.g. computing a minimum spanning tree. Random walk computation, on the other hand, is not deterministic; the input requires parameters such as the length of the walk ℓ and even if the source node and ℓ are fixed, the *solution* (i.e. the walk) is not uniquely determined. While even other problems, such as MST, can have multiple solutions, for optimization problems, *verification* is well-defined. It is not clear what it even means to verify whether a random walk is *correct*. For this reason, proving a lower bound of random walk computation through verification problems seems impossible.

Additionally, in terms of the theoretical bound we obtain, a key difficulty in our result is to introduce the graph parameter diameter (i.e., D) into the lower bound multiplied by ℓ. A crucial shortcoming in extending previous work in this regard is that the relationship between communication complexity and distributed computing shown in [9] does not depend on the network diameter D at all. In fact, such a relationship might not exist since the result in [9] is tight for some functions.

To overcome these obstacles, we consider a variation of communication complexity called *r-round two-party com-*

munication complexity, which has been successfully used in, e.g., circuit complexity and data stream computation (see, e.g., [15, 29]). We obtain a new connection showing that a fast distributed algorithm for computing a function can be converted to a two-party communication protocol with a small message complexity *and number of rounds* to compute the same function. Moreover, the larger the network diameter is, the smaller the number of rounds will be. To obtain this result one need to deal with a more involved proof; for example, the new proof does not seem to work for the networks previously considered [9, 14, 22, 26, 31] and thus we need to introduce a new network called $G(\Gamma, \kappa, \Lambda)$ (which is essentially an extension of the network F_m^2 in [31]). This result and related definitions are stated and proved in Section 2.

A particular communication complexity result that we will use is that of Nisan and Wigderson [29] for the *r-round pointer chasing problem*. Using the connection established in Section 2, we derive a lower bound of any distributed algorithms for solving the pointer chasing problem on a distributed network. This result is in Section 3.

Finally, we prove Theorem 1.1 from the lower bound result in Section 3. The main idea, which was also used in [11], is to construct a network that has the same structure as $G(\Gamma, \kappa, \Lambda)$ (thus has the same diameter and number of nodes) but different edge capacities (depending on the input) so that a random walk follows a desired path (which is unknown) with high probability. This proof is in Section 4.

2. FROM BOUNDED-ROUND COMMUNI-CATION COMPLEXITY TO DISTRIBU-TED ALGORITHM LOWER BOUNDS

Consider the following problem. There are two parties that have unbounded computational power. Each party receives a b-bit string, for some integer $b \geq 1$, denoted by $\bar{x}$ and $\bar{y}$ in $\{0,1\}^b$. They both want to together compute $f(\bar{x}, \bar{y})$ for some function $f : \{0,1\}^b \times \{0,1\}^b \to \mathbb{R}$. At the end of the computation, the party receiving $\bar{y}$ has to output the value of $f(\bar{x}, \bar{y})$. We consider two models of communication.

- *r-round direct communication:* This is a variant of the standard model in communication complexity (see [29] and references therein). Two parties can communicate via a bidirectional edge of unlimited bandwidth. We call the party receiving $\bar{x}$ *Alice*, and the other party *Bob*. Two parties communicate in *rounds* where each round Alice sends a message (of any size) to Bob followed by Bob sending a message to Alice.

- *Communication through network $G(\Gamma, \kappa, \Lambda)$:* Two parties are distinct nodes in a distributed network $G(\Gamma, \kappa, \Lambda)$, for some integers Γ and Λ and real κ; all networks in $G(\Gamma, \kappa, \Lambda)$ have $\Theta(\kappa\Gamma\Lambda^\kappa)$ nodes and a diameter of $\Theta(\kappa\Lambda)$. (This network is described below.) We denote the nodes receiving $\bar{x}$ and $\bar{y}$ by s and t, respectively.

We consider the *public coin randomized algorithms* under both models. In particular, we assume that all parties (Alice and Bob in the first model and all nodes in $G(\Gamma, \kappa, \Lambda)$ in the second model) share a random bit string of infinite length. For any $\epsilon \geq 0$, we say that a randomized algorithm $\mathcal{A}$ is ϵ-*error* if for any input, it outputs the correct answer with probability at least $1 - \epsilon$, where the probability is over all possible random bit strings. In the first model, we focus on the message complexity, i.e., the total number of bits exchanged between Alice and Bob, denoted by $R_\epsilon^{r-cc-pub}(f)$. In the second model, we focus on the running time, denoted by $R_\epsilon^{G(\Gamma,\kappa,\Lambda),s,t}(f)$.

Before we describe $G(\Gamma,\kappa,\Lambda)$ in detail, we note the following characteristics which will be used in later sections. An essential part of $G(\Gamma,\kappa,\Lambda)$ consists of Γ *paths*, denoted by $\mathcal{P}^1,\ldots,\mathcal{P}^\Gamma$ and nodes s and t (see Fig. 2). Every edge induced by this subgraph has infinitely many copies (in other words, infinite capacity). (We let some edges to have infinitely many copies so that we will have a freedom to specify the number of copies later on when we prove Theorem 1.1 in Section 4. The leftmost and rightmost nodes of each path are adjacent to s and t respectively. Ending nodes on the same side of the path (i.e., leftmost or rightmost nodes) are adjacent to each other. The following properties of $G(\Gamma,\kappa,\Lambda)$ follow from the construction of $G(\Gamma,\kappa,\Lambda)$ described in Section 2.2.

Lemma 2.1 *For any $\Gamma \geq 1$, $\kappa \geq 1$ and $\Lambda \geq 2$, network $G(\Gamma,\kappa,\Lambda)$ has $\Theta(\Gamma\kappa\Lambda^\kappa)$ nodes. Each of its path $\mathcal{P}^i$ has $\Theta(\kappa\Lambda^\kappa)$ nodes. Its diameter is $\Theta(\kappa\Lambda)$.*

PROOF. It follows from the construction of $G(\Gamma,\kappa,\Lambda)$ in Section 2.2 that the number of nodes in each path $\mathcal{P}^i$ is $\sum_{j=-\lceil\kappa\rceil\Lambda^{\lfloor\kappa\rfloor}}^{\lceil\kappa\rceil\Lambda^{\lfloor\kappa\rfloor}} \phi'_j = \Theta(\kappa\Lambda^\kappa)$ (cf. Eq. (3)). Since there are Γ paths, the number of nodes in all paths is $\Theta(\Gamma\kappa\Lambda^\kappa)$. Each highway $\mathcal{H}^i$ has $2\lceil\kappa\rceil\Lambda^i + 1$ nodes. Therefore, there are $\sum_{i=1}^{\lfloor\kappa\rfloor}(2\lceil\kappa\rceil\Lambda^i + 1)$ nodes in the highways. For $\Lambda \geq 2$, the last quantity is $\Theta(\lceil\kappa\rceil\Lambda^{\lfloor\kappa\rfloor})$. Hence, the total number of nodes is $\Theta(\Gamma\kappa\Lambda^\kappa)$.

To analyze the diameter of $G(\Gamma,\kappa,\Lambda)$, observe that each node on any path $\mathcal{P}^i$ can reach a node in highway $\mathcal{H}^{\lfloor\kappa\rfloor}$ by traveling through $O(\kappa\Lambda)$ nodes in $\mathcal{P}^i$. Moreover, any node in highway $\mathcal{H}^i$ can reach a node in highway $\mathcal{H}^{i-1}$ by traveling trough $O(\Lambda)$ nodes in $\mathcal{H}^i$. Finally, there are $O(\kappa\Lambda)$ nodes in $\mathcal{H}^1$. Therefore, every node can reach any other node in $O(\kappa\Lambda)$ steps by traveling through $\mathcal{H}^1$. Note that this upper bound is tight since the distance between s and t is $\Omega(\kappa\Lambda)$. $\square$

The rest of this section is devoted to prove Theorem 2.3 which strengthens Theorem 3.1 in [9]. Recall that Theorem 3.1 in [9] states that if there is a fast ϵ-error algorithm for computing function f on any network $G(\Gamma,\kappa,\Lambda)$, then there is a fast ϵ-error algorithm for Alice and Bob to compute f, as follows[1].

Theorem 2.2 (Theorem 3.1 in [9]) *Consider any integers $\Gamma \geq 1$, $\Lambda \geq 2$, real $\kappa \geq 1$ and function $f : \{0,1\}^b \times \{0,1\}^b \to \mathbb{R}$. Let $r = R_\epsilon^{G(\Gamma,\kappa,\Lambda),s,t}(f)$. For any b, if $r \leq \kappa\Lambda^\kappa$ then f can be computed by a direct communication protocol using at most $(2\kappa\log n)r$ communication bits in total. In other words,*

$$R_\epsilon^{\infty-cc-pub}(f) \leq (2\kappa\log n)R_\epsilon^{G(\Gamma,\kappa,\Lambda),s,t}(f).$$

The theorem above does not try to optimize number of rounds used by direct communication protocols. In fact,

---

[1]Note that Theorem 3.1 in [9] is in fact stated on a graph different from $G(\Gamma,\kappa,\Lambda)$ but its proof can be easily adapted to prove Theorem 2.2.

a closer look into the proof of Theorem 3.1 in [9] reveals that $\tilde\Theta((2\kappa\log n)R_\epsilon^{G(\Gamma,\kappa,\Lambda),s,t}(f))$ rounds of communication are used.

Theorem 2.3 stated below strengthens the above theorem by making sure that the number of rounds needed in the direct communication is small. In particular, it says that if there is a fast ϵ-error algorithm for computing function f on any network $G(\Gamma,\kappa,\Lambda)$, then there is a fast *bounded-round* ϵ-error algorithm for Alice and Bob to compute f. More importantly, the number of rounds depends on the diameter of $G(\Gamma,\kappa,\Lambda)$ (which is $\Theta(\kappa\Lambda)$), i.e., the larger the network diameter, the smaller the number of rounds.

Theorem 2.3 *Consider any integers $\Gamma \geq 1$, $\Lambda \geq 2$, real $\kappa \geq 1$ and function $f : \{0,1\}^b \times \{0,1\}^b \to \mathbb{R}$. Let $r = R_\epsilon^{G(\Gamma,\kappa,\Lambda),s,t}(f)$. For any b, if $r \leq \kappa\Lambda^\kappa$ then f can be computed by a $\frac{8r}{\kappa\Lambda}$-round direct communication protocol using at most $(2\kappa\log n)r$ communication bits in total. In other words,*

$$R_\epsilon^{\frac{8R_\epsilon^{G(\Gamma,\kappa,\Lambda),s,t}(f)}{\kappa\Lambda}-cc-pub}(f) \leq (2\kappa\log n)R_\epsilon^{G(\Gamma,\kappa,\Lambda),s,t}(f).$$

2.1 Preliminary: the network $F(\Gamma,\kappa,\Lambda)$

Before we describe the construction of $G(\Gamma,\kappa,\Lambda)$, we first describe a network called $F(\Gamma,\kappa,\Lambda)$ which is a slight modification of the network F_m^K introduced in [31]. In the next section, we show how we modify $F(\Gamma,\kappa,\Lambda)$ to obtain $G(\Gamma,\kappa,\Lambda)$.

$G(\Gamma,\kappa,\Lambda)$ has three parameters, a real $\kappa \geq 1$ and two integers $\Gamma \geq 1$ and $\Lambda \geq 2$.[2] The two basic units in the construction of $F(\Gamma,\kappa,\Lambda)$ are *highways* and *paths*.

Highways. There are $\lfloor\kappa\rfloor$ highways, denoted by $\mathcal{H}^1$, $\mathcal{H}^2$, ..., $\mathcal{H}^{\lfloor\kappa\rfloor}$. The highway $\mathcal{H}^i$ is a path of $2\lceil\kappa\rceil\Lambda^i + 1$ nodes, i.e.,

$$V(\mathcal{H}^i) = \{h_0^i, h_{\pm\Lambda^{\lfloor\kappa\rfloor-i}}^i, h_{\pm2\Lambda^{\lfloor\kappa\rfloor-i}}^i, h_{\pm3\Lambda^{\lfloor\kappa\rfloor-i}}^i,$$
$$\ldots, h_{\pm\lceil\kappa\rceil\Lambda^i\Lambda^{\lfloor\kappa\rfloor-i}}^i\}$$
$$E(\mathcal{H}^i) = \{(h_{-(j+1)\Lambda^{\lfloor\kappa\rfloor-i}}^i, h_{-j\Lambda^{\lfloor\kappa\rfloor-i}}^i), (h_{j\Lambda^{\lfloor\kappa\rfloor-i}}^i, h_{(j+1)\Lambda^{\lfloor\kappa\rfloor-i}}^i)$$
$$| 0 \leq j < \lceil\kappa\rceil\Lambda^i\}.$$

We connect the highways by adding edges between nodes of the same subscripts, i.e., for any $0 < i \leq \lfloor\kappa\rfloor$ and $-\lceil\kappa\rceil\Lambda^i \leq j \leq \lceil\kappa\rceil\Lambda^i$, there is an edge between $h_{j\Lambda^{\lfloor\kappa\rfloor-i}}^i$ and $h_{j\Lambda^{\lfloor\kappa\rfloor-i}}^{i+1}$.

For any $j \neq 0$, let

$$\phi_j = 1 \text{ if } j = 0, \text{ and } \phi'_j = \Lambda \text{ otherwise.} \quad (1)$$

We use ϕ'_j to specify the number of nodes in the paths (defined next), i.e., each path will have $\sum_{j=-\lceil\kappa\rceil\Lambda^{\lfloor\kappa\rfloor}}^{\lceil\kappa\rceil\Lambda^{\lfloor\kappa\rfloor}} \phi'_j$ nodes. Note that

$$\sum_{j=-\lceil\kappa\rceil\Lambda^{\lfloor\kappa\rfloor}}^{\lceil\kappa\rceil\Lambda^{\lfloor\kappa\rfloor}} \phi'_j = (2\lceil\kappa\rceil\Lambda^{\lfloor\kappa\rfloor} + 1)\Lambda = \Theta(\kappa\Lambda^{\lfloor\kappa\rfloor+1}). \quad (2)$$

Paths. There are Γ paths, denoted by $\mathcal{P}^1, \mathcal{P}^2, \ldots, \mathcal{P}^\Gamma$. To construct each path, we first construct its subpaths as follows. For each node $h_j^{\lfloor\kappa\rfloor}$ in $\mathcal{H}^{\lfloor\kappa\rfloor}$ and any $0 < i \leq \Gamma$, we

---

[2]Note that we could restrict κ to be an integer here since $F(\Gamma,\kappa,\Lambda) = F(\Gamma,\kappa',\Lambda)$ for any Λ, Γ, κ and κ' such that $\lfloor\kappa\rfloor = \lfloor\kappa'\rfloor$. However, we will need κ to be a real when we define $G(\Gamma,\kappa,\Lambda)$ so we allow it to be a real here as well to avoid confusion.

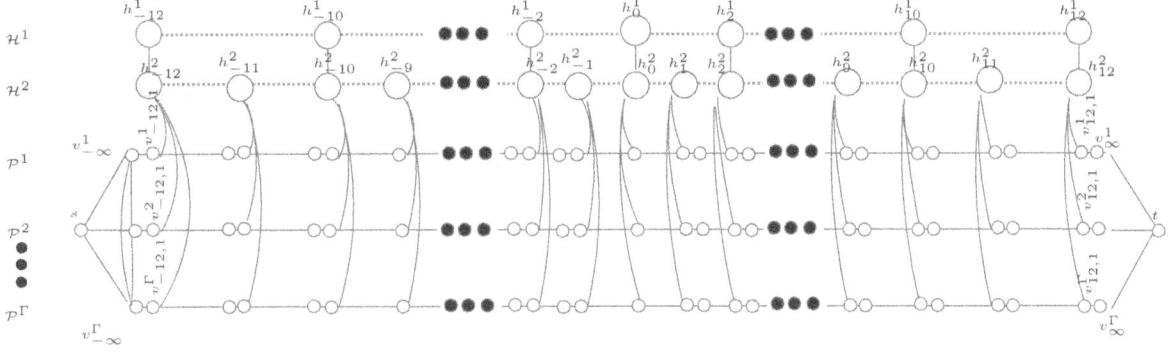

Figure 1: An example of $F(\Gamma, \kappa, \Lambda)$ where $\Lambda = 2$ and $2 \leq \kappa < 3$.

create a subpath of $\mathcal{P}^i$, denoted by $\mathcal{P}^i_j$, having ϕ'_j nodes. Denote nodes in $\mathcal{P}^i_j$ in order by $v^i_{j,1}, v^i_{j,2}, \ldots, v^i_{j,\phi'_j}$. We connect these paths together to form $\mathcal{P}^i_j$, i.e., for any $j \geq 0$, we create edges $(v^i_{j,\phi'_j}, v^i_{j+1,1})$ and $(v^i_{-j,\phi'_{-j}}, v^i_{-(j+1),1})$. Let

$$v^i_{-\infty} = v^i_{-\lceil\kappa\rceil\Lambda^{\lfloor\kappa\rfloor}, \phi'_{-\lceil\kappa\rceil\Lambda^{\lfloor\kappa\rfloor}}} \quad \text{and} \quad v^i_{\infty} = v^i_{\lceil\kappa\rceil\Lambda^{\lfloor\kappa\rfloor}, \phi'_{\lceil\kappa\rceil\Lambda^{\lfloor\kappa\rfloor}}}.$$

These two nodes can be thought of as the leftmost and rightmost nodes of path $\mathcal{P}^i$. We connect the paths together by adding edges between the leftmost (rightmost, respectively) nodes in the paths, i.e., for any i and i', we add edges $(v^i_{-\infty}, v^{i'}_{-\infty})$ $((v^i_{\infty}, v^{i'}_{\infty})$, respectively).

We connect the highways and paths by adding an edge from each node $h^{\lfloor\kappa\rfloor}_j$ to $v^i_{j,1}$. We also create nodes s and t and connect s (t, respectively) to all nodes $v^i_{-\infty}$ (v^i_{∞}, respectively). See Fig. 1 for an example.

2.2 Description of $G(\Gamma, \kappa, \Lambda)$

We now modify $F(\Gamma, \kappa, \Lambda)$ to obtain $G(\Gamma, \kappa, \Lambda)$. Again, $G(\Gamma, \kappa, \Lambda)$ has three parameters, a real $\kappa \geq 1$ and two integers $\Gamma \geq 1$ and $\Lambda \geq 2$. The two basic units in the construction of $G(\Gamma, \kappa, \Lambda)$ are *highways* and *paths*. The highways are defined in exactly the same way as before. The main modification is the definition of ϕ' (cf. Eq. (1)) which affects the number of nodes in the subpaths $\mathcal{P}^i_j$ of each path $\mathcal{P}^i$.

Definition of ϕ'. First, for a technical reason in the proof of Theorem 2.3, we need ϕ'_j to be small when $|j|$ is small. Thus, we define the following notation ϕ. For any j, define

$$\phi_j = \left\lfloor \frac{|j|}{\Lambda^{\lfloor\kappa\rfloor-1}} \right\rfloor + 1.$$

Note that ϕ_j can be viewed as the number of nodes in $\mathcal{H}_1$ with subscripts between 0 and j, i.e.,

$$\phi_j = \begin{cases} |\{h^1_{j'} \mid 0 \leq j' \leq j\}| & \text{if } j \geq 0 \\ |\{h^1_{j'} \mid j \leq j' \leq 0\}| & \text{if } j < 0. \end{cases}$$

We now define ϕ' as follows. For any $j \geq 0$, let

$$\phi'_j = \phi'_{-j} = \min\left\{ \phi_j, \max\left(1, \left\lceil\lceil\kappa\rceil\Lambda^{\kappa}\right\rceil - \sum_{j'>j} \phi_{j'}\right) \right\}.$$

The reason we define ϕ' this way is that we use it to specify the number of nodes in the paths (as described in the previous section) and we want to be able to control this number

precisely. In particular, while each path $\mathcal{P}^i$ in $F(\Gamma, \kappa, \Lambda)$ has $\Theta(\kappa\Lambda^{\lfloor\kappa\rfloor+1})$ nodes (cf. Eq. (2)), the number of nodes in each path in $G(\Gamma, \kappa, \Lambda)$ is

$$\sum_{j=-\lceil\kappa\rceil\Lambda^{\lfloor\kappa\rfloor}}^{\lceil\kappa\rceil\Lambda^{\lfloor\kappa\rfloor}} \phi'_j = \Theta(\kappa\Lambda^{\kappa}). \tag{3}$$

We need this precision so that we can deal with any value of ℓ when we prove Theorem 1.1 in Section 4.

Finally, we make infinite copies of every edge except highway edges, i.e., those in $\cup_{i=1}^{\lfloor\kappa\rfloor} E(\mathcal{H}^i)$. (In other words, we make them have infinite capacity). As mentioned earlier, we do this so that we will have a freedom to specify the number of copies later on when we prove Theorem 1.1 in Section 4. Observe that if Theorem 2.3 then it also holds when we set the numbers of edge copies in $G(\Gamma, \kappa, \Lambda)$ to some specific numbers. Fig. 2 shows an example of $G(\Gamma, \kappa, \Lambda)$.

2.3 Terminologies

For any numbers i, j, i', and j', we say that $(i', j') \geq (i, j)$ if $i' > i$ or ($i' = i$ and $j' \geq j$). For any $-\lceil\kappa\rceil\Lambda^{\lfloor\kappa\rfloor} \leq i \leq \lceil\kappa\rceil\Lambda^{\lfloor\kappa\rfloor}$ and $1 \leq j \leq \phi'_i$, define the (i, j)-*set* as

$$S_{i,j} = \begin{cases} \{h^x_{i'} \mid 1 \leq x \leq \kappa, \ i' \leq i\} \\ \quad \cup \ \{v^x_{i',j'} \mid 1 \leq x \leq \Gamma, \ (i,j) \geq (i',j')\} \cup \{s\} \\ \quad \text{if } i \geq 0 \\ \{h^x_{i'} \mid 1 \leq x \leq \kappa, \ i' \geq i\} \\ \quad \cup \ \{v^x_{i',j'} \mid 1 \leq x \leq \Gamma, \ (-i,j) \geq (-i',j')\} \cup \{r\} \\ \quad \text{if } i < 0. \end{cases}$$

See Fig. 3 for an example. For convenience, for any $i > 0$, let $S_{i,0} = S_{i-1,\phi'_{i-1}}$ and $S_{-i,0} = S_{-(i-1),\phi'_{-(i-1)}}$, and, for any j, let $S_{\lceil\kappa\rceil\Lambda^{\lfloor\kappa\rfloor}+1,j} = S_{\lceil\kappa\rceil\Lambda^{\lfloor\kappa\rfloor},\phi'_{\lceil\kappa\rceil\Lambda^{\lfloor\kappa\rfloor}}}$ and $S_{-\lceil\kappa\rceil\Lambda^{\lfloor\kappa\rfloor}-1,j} = S_{-\lceil\kappa\rceil\Lambda^{\lfloor\kappa\rfloor},\phi'_{-\lceil\kappa\rceil\Lambda^{\lfloor\kappa\rfloor}}}$.

Let $\mathcal{A}$ be any *deterministic* distributed algorithm run on $G(\Gamma, \kappa, \Lambda)$ for computing a function f. Fix any input strings $\bar{x}$ and $\bar{y}$ given to s and t respectively. Let $\varphi_{\mathcal{A}}(\bar{x}, \bar{y})$ denote the execution of $\mathcal{A}$ on $\bar{x}$ and $\bar{y}$. Denote the *state* of the node v at the end of time τ during the execution $\varphi_{\mathcal{A}}(\bar{x}, \bar{y})$ by $\sigma_{\mathcal{A}}(v, \tau, \bar{x}, \bar{y})$. Let $\sigma_{\mathcal{A}}(v, 0, \bar{x}, \bar{y})$ be the state of the node v before the execution $\varphi_{\mathcal{A}}(\bar{x}, \bar{y})$ begins. Note that $\sigma_{\mathcal{A}}(v, 0, \bar{x}, \bar{y})$ is independent of the input if $v \notin \{s, t\}$, depends only on $\bar{x}$ if $v = s$ and depends only on $\bar{y}$ if $v = t$. Moreover, in two different executions $\varphi_{\mathcal{A}}(\bar{x}, \bar{y})$ and $\varphi_{\mathcal{A}}(\bar{x}', \bar{y}')$, a node reaches

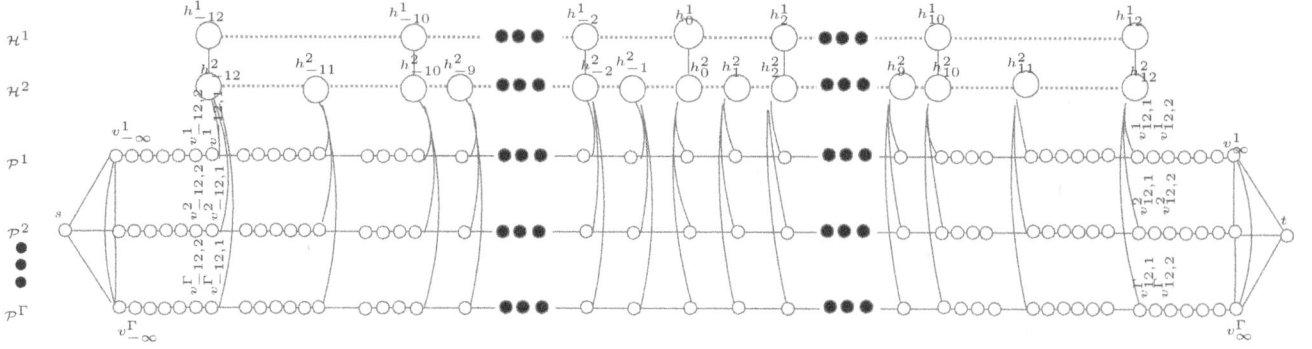

Figure 2: An example of $G(\Gamma, \kappa, \Lambda)$ where $\kappa = 2.5$ and $\Lambda = 2$. The dashed edges (in red) have one copy while other edges have infinitely many copies. Note that $\phi'_{10} = 4$ and thus there are 4 nodes in each subpath $\mathcal{P}^i_{10}$, for all i. Note also that ϕ'_{10} is less than ϕ_{10} which is 6.

the same state at time τ (i.e., $\sigma_\mathcal{A}(v, \tau, \bar{x}, \bar{y}) = \sigma_\mathcal{A}(v, \tau, \bar{x}', \bar{y}')$) if and only if it receives the same sequence of messages on each of its incoming links.

For a given set of nodes $U = \{v_1, \ldots, v_\ell\} \subseteq V$, a *configuration*

$$C_\mathcal{A}(U, \tau, \bar{x}, \bar{y}) = <\sigma_\mathcal{A}(v_1, \tau, \bar{x}, \bar{y}), \ldots, \sigma_\mathcal{A}(v_\ell, \tau, \bar{x}, \bar{y})>$$

is a vector of the states of the nodes of U at the end of time τ of the execution $\varphi_\mathcal{A}(\bar{x}, \bar{y})$. From now on, to simplify notations, when $\mathcal{A}$, $\bar{x}$ and $\bar{y}$ are clear from the context, we use $C^\tau_{i,j}$ to denote $C_\mathcal{A}(S_{i,j}, \tau, \bar{x}, \bar{y})$.

2.4 Proof of Theorem 2.3

Let $G = G(\Gamma, \kappa, \Lambda)$. Let f be the function in the theorem statement. Let $\mathcal{A}_\epsilon$ be any ϵ-error distributed algorithm for computing f on G. Fix a random string $\bar{r}$ used by $\mathcal{A}_\epsilon$ (shared by all nodes in G) and consider the *deterministic* algorithm $\mathcal{A}$ run on the input of $\mathcal{A}_\epsilon$ and the fixed random string $\bar{r}$. Let $T_\mathcal{A}$ be the worst case running time of algorithm $\mathcal{A}$ (over all inputs). We only consider $T_\mathcal{A} \leq \kappa \Lambda^\kappa$, as assumed in the theorem statement. We show that Alice and Bob, when given $\bar{r}$ as the public random string, can simulate $\mathcal{A}$ using $(2\kappa \log n)T_\mathcal{A}$ communication bits in $8T_\mathcal{A}/(\kappa\Lambda)$ rounds, as follows. (We provide an example in the end of this section.)

Rounds, Phases, and Iterations. For convenience, we will name the rounds backward, i.e., Alice and Bob start at round $\lceil \kappa \rceil \Lambda^{\lfloor \kappa \rfloor}$ and proceed to round $\lceil \kappa \rceil \Lambda^{\lfloor \kappa \rfloor} - 1$, $\lceil \kappa \rceil \Lambda^{\lfloor \kappa \rfloor} - 2$, and so on. Each round is divided into two *phases*, i.e., when Alice sends messages and Bob sends messages (recall that Alice sends messages first in each iteration). Each phase of round r is divided into ϕ'_r *iterations*. Each iteration simulates one round of algorithm $\mathcal{A}$. We call the ith iteration of round r when Alice (Bob, respectively) sends messages the *iteration* $I_{r,A,i}$ ($I_{r,B,i}$, respectively). Therefore, in each round r we have the following order of iterations: $I_{r,A,1}$, $I_{r,A,2}$, $\ldots$, I_{r,A,ϕ'_r}, $I_{r,B,1}$, $\ldots$, I_{r,B,ϕ'_r}. For convenience, we refer to the time before communication begins as round $\lceil \kappa \rceil \Lambda^{\lfloor \kappa \rfloor} + 1$ and let $I_{r,A,0} = I_{r+1,A,\phi'_{r+1}}$ and $I_{r,B,0} = I_{r+1,B,\phi'_{r+1}}$.

Our goal is to simulate one round of algorithm $\mathcal{A}$ per iteration. That is, after iteration $I_{r,B,i}$ finishes, we will finish the $(\sum_{r'=r+1}^{\lceil \kappa \rceil \Lambda^{\lfloor \kappa \rfloor}} \phi'_{r'} + i)^{th}$ round of algorithm $\mathcal{A}$. Specifically,

we let

$$t_r = \sum_{r'=r+1}^{\lceil \kappa \rceil \Lambda^{\lfloor \kappa \rfloor}} \phi'_{r'}$$

and our goal is to construct a protocol with properties as in the following lemma.

Lemma 2.4 *There exists a protocol such that there are at most $\kappa \log n$ bits sent in each iteration and satisfies the following properties. For any $r \geq 0$ and $0 \leq i \leq \phi'_r$,*

1. *after $I_{r,A,i}$ finishes, Alice and Bob know $C^{t_r+i}_{r-i\Lambda^{\lfloor \kappa \rfloor}-1,1}$ and $C^{t_r+i}_{-r,\phi'_{-r}-i}$, respectively, and*

2. *after $I_{r,B,i}$ finishes, Alice and Bob know $C^{t_r+i}_{r,\phi'_r-i}$ and $C^{t_r+i}_{-r+i\Lambda^{\lfloor \kappa \rfloor}-1,1}$, respectively.*

PROOF. We first argue that the properties hold for iteration $I_{\lceil \kappa \rceil \Lambda^{\lfloor \kappa \rfloor}+1,A,0}$, i.e., before Alice and Bob starts communicating. After round $r = \lceil \kappa \rceil \Lambda^{\lfloor \kappa \rfloor}$ starts, Alice can compute $C^0_{r+1,0} = C^0_{r+1,1} = C^0_{r,\phi'_r}$ which contains the states of all nodes in $G(\Gamma, \kappa, \Lambda)$ except t. She can do this because every node except s and t has the same state regardless of the input and the state of s depends only on her input string $\bar{x}$. Similarly, Bob can compute $C^0_{-(r+1),0} = C^0_{-(r+1),1} = C^0_{r,\phi'_r}$ which depends only on his input $\bar{y}$.

Now we show that, if the lemma holds for any iteration $I_{r,A,i-1}$ then it also holds for iteration $I_{r,A,i}$ as well. Specifically, we show that if Alice and Bob know $C^{t_r+i-1}_{r-(i-1)\Lambda^{\lfloor \kappa \rfloor}-1,1}$ and $C^{t_r+i-1}_{-r,\phi'_{-r}-(i-1)}$, respectively, then they will know $C^{t_r+i}_{r-i\Lambda^{\lfloor \kappa \rfloor}-1,1}$ and $C^{t_r+i}_{-r,\phi'_{-r}-i}$, respectively, after Alice sends at most $\kappa \log n$ messages.

First we show that Alice can compute $C^{t_r+i}_{r-i\Lambda^{\lfloor \kappa \rfloor}-1,1}$ without receiving any message from Bob. Recall that Alice can compute $C^{t_r+i}_{r-i\Lambda^{\lfloor \kappa \rfloor}-1,1}$ if she knows

- $C^{t_r+i-1}_{r-i\Lambda^{\lfloor \kappa \rfloor}-1,1}$, and

- all messages sent to all nodes in $S_{r-i\Lambda^{\lfloor \kappa \rfloor}-1,1}$ at time $t_r + i$ of algorithm $\mathcal{A}$.

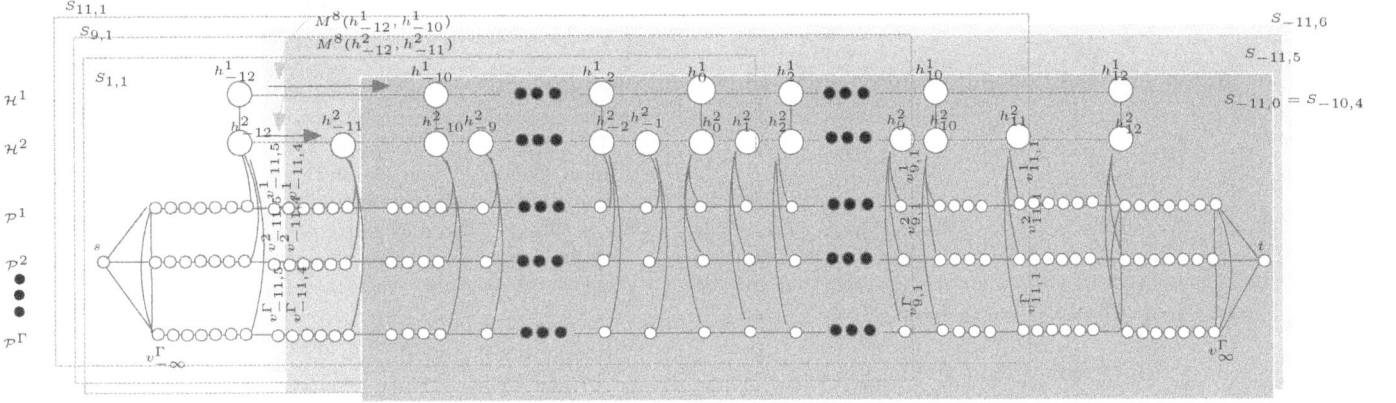

Figure 3: An example of round 11 in the proof of Theorem 2.3 (see detail in Example 2.6).

By assumption, Alice knows $C^{t_r+i-1}_{r-(i-1)\Lambda^{\lfloor\kappa\rfloor-1},1}$ which implies that she knows $C^{t_r+i-1}_{r-i\Lambda^{\lfloor\kappa\rfloor-1},1}$ since

$$S_{r-i\Lambda^{\lfloor\kappa\rfloor-1},1} \subseteq S_{r-(i-1)\Lambda^{\lfloor\kappa\rfloor-1},1}.$$

Moreover, observe that all neighbors of all nodes in $S_{r-i\Lambda^{\lfloor\kappa\rfloor-1},1}$ are in $S_{r-(i-1)\Lambda^{\lfloor\kappa\rfloor-1},1}$. Thus, Alice can compute all messages sent to all nodes in $S_{r-i\Lambda^{\lfloor\kappa\rfloor-1},1}$ at time t_r+i of algorithm $\mathcal{A}$. Therefore, Alice can compute $C^{t_r+i}_{r+i\Lambda^{\lfloor\kappa\rfloor-1},1}$ without receiving any message from Bob.

Now we show that Bob can compute $C^{t_r+i}_{-r,\phi'_{-r}-i}$ by receiving at most $\kappa\log n$ bits from Alice and use the knowledge of $C^{t_r+i-1}_{-r,\phi'_{-r}-i+1}$. Note that Bob can compute $C^{t_r+i}_{-r,\phi'_{-r}-i}$ if he knows

- $C^{t_r+i-1}_{-r,\phi'_{-r}-i}$, and

- all messages sent to all nodes in $S_{-r,\phi'_{-r}-i}$ at time t_r+i of algorithm $\mathcal{A}$.

By assumption, Bob knows $C^{t_r+i-1}_{-r,\phi'_{-r}-i+1}$ which implies that he knows $C^{t_r+i-1}_{-r,\phi'_{-r}-i}$ since $S_{-r,\phi'_{-r}-i} \subseteq S_{-r,\phi'_{-r}-i+1}$. Moreover, observe that all neighbors of all nodes in $S_{-r,\phi'_{-r}-i}$ are in $S_{-r,\phi'_{-r}-i+1}$, except

$$h^{\lfloor\kappa\rfloor}_{-(r+1)}, h^{\lfloor\kappa\rfloor-1}_{-(\lfloor r/\Lambda\rfloor+1)}, \dots, h^{\lfloor\kappa\rfloor-i}_{-(\lfloor r/\Lambda^i\rfloor+1)}, \dots, h^{1}_{-(\lfloor r/\Lambda^{\lfloor\kappa\rfloor-1}\rfloor+1)}.$$

In other words, Bob can compute all messages sent to all nodes in $S_{-r,\phi'_{-r}-i}$ at time t_r+i except

$$M^{t_r+i}(h^{\lfloor\kappa\rfloor}_{-(r+1)}, h^{\lfloor\kappa\rfloor}_{-r}), \dots, M^{t_r+i}(h^{\lfloor\kappa\rfloor-i}_{-(\lfloor r/\Lambda^i\rfloor+1)}, h^{\lfloor\kappa\rfloor-i}_{-\lfloor r/\Lambda^i\rfloor}),$$
$$\dots, M^{t_r+i}(h^{1}_{-(\lfloor r/\Lambda^{\lfloor\kappa\rfloor-1}\rfloor+1)}, h^{1}_{-(\lfloor r/\Lambda^{\lfloor\kappa\rfloor-1}\rfloor)})$$

where $M^{t_r+i}(u,v)$ is the message sent from u to v at time t_r+i of algorithm $\mathcal{A}$. Observe further that Alice can compute these messages because she knows $C^{t_r+i-1}_{r-(i-1)\Lambda^{\lfloor\kappa\rfloor-1},1}$ which contains the states of

$$h^{\lfloor\kappa\rfloor}_{-(r+1)}, \dots, h^{\lfloor\kappa\rfloor-i}_{-(\lfloor r/\Lambda^i\rfloor+1)}, \dots, \quad h^{1}_{-(\lfloor r/\Lambda^{\lfloor\kappa\rfloor-1}\rfloor+1)}$$

at time t_r+i-1. (In particular, $C^{t_r+i-1}_{r-(i-1)\Lambda^{\lfloor\kappa\rfloor-1},1}$ is a superset of $C^{t_r+i-1}_{0,1}$ which contains the states of $h^{\lfloor\kappa\rfloor}_{-(r+1)}, \dots,$

$h^{1}_{-(\lfloor r/\Lambda^{\lfloor\kappa\rfloor-1}\rfloor+1)}$.) So, Alice can send these messages to Bob and Bob can compute $C^{t_r+i}_{-r,\phi'_{-r}-i}$ at the end of the iteration. Each of these messages contains at most $\log n$ bits since each of them corresponds to a message sent on one edge. Therefore, Alice sends at most $\kappa\log n$ bits to Bob in total. This shows the first property.

After Alice finishes sending messages, the two parties will switch their roles and a similar protocol can be used to show that the second property, i.e., if the lemma holds for any iteration $I_{r,B,i-1}$ then it also holds for iteration $I_{r,B,i}$ as well. That is, if Alice and Bob know $C^{t_r+i-1}_{r,\phi'_{-r}-(i-1)}$ and $C^{t_r+i-1}_{-r+(i-1)\Lambda^{\lfloor\kappa\rfloor-1},1}$, respectively, then Bob can send $\kappa\log n$ bits to Alice so that they can compute $C^{t_r+i}_{r,\phi'_{-r}-i}$ and $C^{t_r+i}_{-r+i\Lambda^{\lfloor\kappa\rfloor-1},1}$, respectively. $\square$

Let P be the protocol as in Lemma 2.4. Alice and Bob will run protocol P until round r', where r' is the largest number such that $t_{r'}+\phi'_{r'} \geq T_{\mathcal{A}}$. Lemma 2.4 implies that after iteration $I_{r',B,T_{\mathcal{A}}-t_{r'}}$, Bob knows

$$C^{t_{-r'}+T_{\mathcal{A}}-t_{r'}}_{-r',\phi'_{-r'}-T_{\mathcal{A}}+t_{r'}} = C^{T_{\mathcal{A}}}_{-r',\phi'_{-r'}-T_{\mathcal{A}}+t_{r'}}$$

(note that $\phi'_{-r'} - T_{\mathcal{A}} + t_{r'} \geq 0$). In particular, Bob knows the state of node t at time $T_{\mathcal{A}}$, i.e., he knows $\sigma_{\mathcal{A}}(t, T_{\mathcal{A}}, \bar{x}, \bar{y})$. Thus, Bob can output the output of $\mathcal{A}$ which is output from t.

Since $\mathcal{A}_\epsilon$ is ϵ-error, the probability (over all possible shared random strings) that $\mathcal{A}$ outputs the correct value of $f(\bar{x}, \bar{y})$ is at least $1-\epsilon$. Therefore, the communication protocol run by Alice and Bob is ϵ-error as well. The number of rounds is bounded as in the following claim.

Claim 2.5 *If algorithm $\mathcal{A}$ finishes in time $T_{\mathcal{A}} \leq \lceil\kappa\rceil\Lambda^\kappa$ then $r' > \lceil\kappa\rceil\Lambda^\kappa - 8T_{\mathcal{A}}/(\lceil\kappa\rceil\Lambda)$. In other words, the number of rounds Alice and Bob need to simulate $\mathcal{A}$ is $8T_{\mathcal{A}}/(\lceil\kappa\rceil\Lambda)$*

PROOF. Let $R^* = 8T_{\mathcal{A}}/(\lceil\kappa\rceil\Lambda)$ and let $r^* = \Lambda^{\lfloor\kappa\rfloor} - R^* + 1$. Assume for the sake of contradiction that Alice and Bob need more than R^* rounds. This means that $r' < r^*$. Alice and Bob requiring more than R^* rounds implies that

$$\sum_{r=r^*}^{\lceil\kappa\rceil\Lambda^{\lfloor\kappa\rfloor}} \phi'_r = t_{r^*} + \phi'_{r^*} < T_{\mathcal{A}} \leq \lceil\kappa\rceil\Lambda^\kappa. \tag{4}$$

263

It follows that for any $r \geq r^*$,

$$\phi_r' = \min\left(\phi(h_r^{k'}), \max(1, \lceil \lceil \kappa \rceil \Lambda^\kappa \rceil - \sum_{r' > r} \phi_{r'})\right) \quad (5)$$

$$= \phi_r \quad (6)$$

$$= \left\lfloor \frac{r}{\Lambda^{\lfloor \kappa \rfloor - 1}} \right\rfloor + 1 \quad (7)$$

where Eq. (5) follows from the definition of ϕ_r', Eq. (6) is because $\sum_{r \geq r^*} \phi_r' < \lceil \kappa \rceil \Lambda^\kappa$, and Eq. (7) is by the definition of ϕ_r. Therefore, the total number of steps that can be simulated by Alice and Bob up to round r^* is

$$\sum_{r=r^*}^{\lceil \kappa \rceil \Lambda^{\lfloor \kappa \rfloor}} \phi_r' = \sum_{r=r^*}^{\lceil \kappa \rceil \Lambda^{\lfloor \kappa \rfloor}} \left(\left\lfloor \frac{r}{\Lambda^{\lfloor \kappa \rfloor - 1}} \right\rfloor + 1\right)$$

$$\geq \Lambda^{\lfloor \kappa \rfloor - 1} \sum_{i=1}^{\lfloor R^*/\Lambda^{\lfloor \kappa \rfloor - 1} \rfloor} (\lceil \kappa \rceil \Lambda - i)$$

$$\geq \Lambda^{\lfloor \kappa \rfloor - 1} \cdot \frac{\lfloor R^*/\Lambda^{\lfloor \kappa \rfloor - 1} \rfloor (\lceil \kappa \rceil \Lambda - 1)}{2}$$

$$\geq \frac{R^* \lceil \kappa \rceil \Lambda}{8}$$

$$\geq T_\mathcal{A}$$

contradicting Eq. (4). $\quad \square$

Since there are at most $\kappa \log n$ bits sent in each iteration and Alice and Bob runs P for $T_\mathcal{A}$ iterations, the total number of bits exchanged is at most $(2\kappa \log n) T_\mathcal{A}$. This completes the proof of Theorem 2.3.

Example 2.6 *Fig. 3 shows an example of the protocol we use above. Before iteration $I_{11,A,1}$ begins, Alice and Bob know $C_{11,1}^7$ and $C_{-11,5}^7$, respectively (since Alice and Bob already simulated $\mathcal{A}$ for $\phi_{12}' = 7$ steps in round 12). Then, Alice computes and sends $M^8(h_{-12}^2, h_{-11}^2)$ and $M^8(h_{-12}^1, h_{-10}^1)$ to Bob. Alice and Bob then compute $C_{11,1}^8$ and $C_{-11,6}^8$, respectively, at the end of iteration $I_{11,A,1}$. After they repeat this process for five more times, i.e. Alice sends*

$$M^9(h_{-12}^2, h_{-11}^2), M^{10}(h_{-12}^2, h_{-11}^2), \ldots, M^{13}(h_{-12}^2, h_{-11}^2), \quad and$$

$$M^9(h_{-12}^1, h_{-10}^1), M^{10}(h_{-12}^1, h_{-10}^1), \ldots, M^{13}(h_{-12}^1, h_{-10}^1),$$

Bob will be able to compute $C_{-11,0}^{13} = C_{-10,4}^{13}$. Note that Alice is able to compute $C_{9,1}^8$, $C_{7,1}^9$, ..., $C_{1,1}^{12}$ without receiving any messages from Bob so she can compute and send the previously mentioned messages to Bob.

3. THE POINTER CHASING PROBLEM

In this section, we define the pointer chasing problem and prove its lower bound (Lemma 3.2) which will be used to prove Theorem 1.1 in the next section.

Informally, the r-round pointer chasing problem has parameters r and m and there are two players, which could be Alice and Bob or nodes s and t, who receive functions $f_A : [m] \to [m]$ and $f_B : [m] \to [m]$, respectively. The goal is to compute a function starting from 1 and alternatively applying f_A and f_B for r times each, i.e., compute $f_B(\ldots f_A(f_B(f_A)))$ where f_A and f_B appear r times each. To be precise, let $\mathcal{F}_m$ be the set of functions $f : [m] \to [m]$. For any $i \geq 0$ define $g^i : \mathcal{F}_m \times \mathcal{F}_m \to [m]$ inductively as

$$g^0(f_A, f_B) = 1 \quad \text{and}$$

$$g^i(f_A, f_B) \begin{cases} f_A(g^{i-1}(f_A, f_B)) & \text{if } i > 0 \text{ and } i \text{ is odd,} \\ f_B(g^{i-1}(f_A, f_B)) & \text{if } i > 0 \text{ and } i \text{ is even.} \end{cases}$$

Also define function $\text{PC}^{i,m}(f_A, f_B) = g^{2i}(f_A, f_B)$. The goal of the r-round pointer chasing problem is to compute $\text{PC}^{r,m}(f_A, f_B)$.

Observe that if Alice and Bob can communicate for r rounds then they can compute $\text{PC}^{r,m}$ naively by exchanging $O(r \log m)$ bits. Interestingly, Nisan and Wigderson [29] show that if Alice and Bob are allowed only $r - 1$ rounds then they essentially cannot do anything better than having Alice sent everything she knows to Bob.[3]

Theorem 3.1 *[29] $R_{1/3}^{(r-1)-cc-pub}(\text{PC}^{r,m}) = \Omega(m/r^2 - r \log m)$.*

The pointer chasing problem on $G(\Gamma, \kappa, \Lambda)$. We now consider the pointer chasing problem on network $G(\Gamma, \kappa, \Lambda)$ where s and t receive f_A and f_B respectively. The following lemma follows from Theorem 2.3 and 3.1.

Lemma 3.2 *For any $\kappa, \Gamma, \Lambda \geq 2$, $m \geq \kappa^2 \Lambda^{4\kappa} \log n$, $16\Lambda^{\kappa-1} \geq r > 8\Lambda^{\kappa-1}$, $R_{1/3}^{G(\Gamma,\kappa,\Lambda),s,t}(\text{PC}^{r,m}) = \Omega(\kappa \Lambda^\kappa)$.*

PROOF. Let $r = R_{1/3}^{G(\Gamma,\kappa,\Lambda),s,t}(\text{PC}^{r,m})$. If $r > \kappa \Lambda^\kappa$ then we are done so we assume that $r \leq \kappa \Lambda^\kappa$. Thus,

$$r \geq \frac{R_{1/3}^{\frac{sR_{1/3}^{G(\Gamma,\kappa,\Lambda),s,t}(\text{PC}^{r,m})}{\kappa\Lambda} - cc-pub}(\text{PC}^{r,m})}{(2\kappa \log n)} \quad (8)$$

$$\geq \frac{R_{1/3}^{\frac{8\kappa\Lambda^\kappa}{\kappa\Lambda} - cc-pub}(\text{PC}^{r,m})}{(2\kappa \log n)} \quad (9)$$

$$= \Omega\left(\frac{(m(8\Lambda^{\kappa-1})^{-2} - 8\Lambda^{\kappa-1} \log m)}{(\kappa \log n)}\right) \quad (10)$$

$$= \Omega(\kappa \Lambda^\kappa) \quad (11)$$

where Eq. (8) is by Theorem 2.3 and the fact that $r \leq \kappa \Lambda^\kappa$, Eq. (9) uses the fact that the communication does not increase when we allow more rounds and $R_{1/3}^{G(\Gamma,\kappa,\Lambda),s,t}(\text{PC}^{r,m}) \leq \kappa \Lambda^\kappa$, Eq. (10) follows from Theorem 3.1 with the fact that $16\Lambda^{\kappa-1} \geq r > 8\Lambda^{\kappa-1}$ and Eq. (11) is because $m \geq \kappa^2 \Lambda^{4\kappa} \log n$. $\quad \square$

4. PROOF OF THE MAIN THEOREM

In this section, we prove Theorem 1.1. An $\Omega(D)$ lower bound has already been shown (and is fairly straightforward) in [10]; so we focus on showing the $\Omega(\sqrt{\ell D})$ lower bound. Moreover, we will prove the theorem only for the version where destination outputs source. This is because we can convert algorithms for the other two version to solve this version by adding $O(D)$ rounds. To see this, observe that once the source outputs the ID of the destination, we can take additional $O(D)$ rounds to send the ID of the source to the destination. Similarly, if nodes know their positions, the node with position ℓ can output the source's ID by taking additional $O(D)$ rounds to request for the source's ID. Theorem 1.1, for the case where destination outputs source, follows from the following lemma.

---

[3] In fact this holds even when Alice and Bob are allowed r rounds but Alice cannot send a message in the first round.

Lemma 4.1 *For any real $\kappa \geq 1$ and integers $\Lambda \geq 2$, and $\Gamma \geq 32\kappa^2\Lambda^{6\kappa-1}\log n$, there exists a family of networks $\mathcal{H}$ such that any network $H \in \mathcal{H}$ has $\Theta(\kappa\Gamma\Lambda^\kappa)$ nodes and diameter $D = \Theta(\kappa\Lambda)$, and any algorithm for computing the destination of a random walk of length $\ell = \Theta(\Lambda^{2\kappa-1})$ requires $\Omega(\sqrt{\ell D})$ time on some network $H \in \mathcal{H}$.*

PROOF. We show how to compute $\mathrm{PC}^{r,m}$ on $G = G(\Gamma, \kappa, \Lambda)$ by reducing the problem to the problem of sampling a random walk destination in some network H_{f_A, f_B}, obtained by restrict the number of copies of some edges in G, depending on input functions f_A and f_B. We let $\mathcal{H}$ be the family of network H_{f_A, f_B} over all input functions. Note that for any input functions, an algorithm on H_{f_A, f_B} can be run on G with the same running time since every edge in G has more capacity than its counterpart in H_{f_A, f_B}.

Let $r = 16\Lambda^{\kappa-1}$ and $m = \kappa^2\Lambda^{5\kappa}\log n$. Note that $2rm \leq \Gamma$. For any $i \leq r$ and $j \leq m$, let

$$S^{i,j} = \mathcal{P}^{2(i-1)m+j} \quad \text{and} \quad T^{i,j} = \mathcal{P}^{2(i-1)m+m+j}.$$

That is, $S^{1,1} = \mathcal{P}^1$, ..., $S^{1,m} = \mathcal{P}^m$, $T^{1,1} = \mathcal{P}^{m+1}$, ..., $T^{1,m} = \mathcal{P}^{2m}$, $S^{2,1} = \mathcal{P}^{2m+1}$, ..., $T^{r,m} = \mathcal{P}^{2rm}$. Let L be the number of nodes in each path. Note that $L = \Theta(\kappa\Lambda^\kappa)$ by Lemma 2.1. Denote the nodes in $S^{i,j}$ from *left to right* by $s_1^{i,j}, \ldots, s_L^{i,j}$. (Thus, $s_1^{i,j} = v_{-\infty}^{2(i-1)m+j}$ and $s_L^{i,j} = v_\infty^{2(i-1)m+j}$.) Also denote the nodes in $T^{i,j}$ from *right to left* by $t_1^{i,j}, \ldots, t_L^{i,j}$. (Thus, $t_1^{i,j} = v_\infty^{2(i-1)m+m+j}$ and $t_L^{i,j} = v_{-\infty}^{2(i-1)m+m+j}$.) Note that for any i and j, $s_1^{i,j}$ and $t_L^{i,j}$ are adjacent to s while $s_L^{i,j}$ and $t_1^{i,j}$ are adjacent to t.

Now we construct H_{f_A, f_B}. For simplicity, we fix input functions f_A and f_B and denote H_{f_A, f_B} simply by H. To get H we let every edge in G have one copy (thus with capacity $O(\log n)$), except the following edges. For any $i \leq r$, $j \leq m$, and $x < L$, we have $(6\Gamma\ell)^{2(i-1)L+x}$ copies of edges between nodes $s_x^{i,j}$ and $s_{x+1}^{i,j}$ and $(6\Gamma\ell)^{2(i-1)L+L+x}$ copies of edges between nodes $t_x^{i,j}$ and $t_{x+1}^{i,j}$. Note that these numbers of copies of edges are always the same, regardless of the input f_A and f_B.

Additionally, we have the following numbers of edges which depend on the input functions. First, s specifies the following number of edges between its neighbors. For any $i \leq r$, $j \leq m$, we have $(6\Gamma\ell)^{2(i-1)L+L}$ copies of edges between nodes $t_L^{i,j}$ and $s_1^{i,f_A(j)}$. These numbers of edges can be specified in one round since both $s_1^{i,j}$ and $t_L^{i,f_A(j)}$ are adjacent to s. Similarly, we have $(6\Gamma\ell)^{2(i-1)L+2L}$ copies of edges between nodes $t_1^{i,j}$ and $s_L^{i+1,f_B(j)}$ which can be done in one round since both $t_1^{i,j}$ and $s_L^{i+1,f_B(j)}$ are adjacent to t. This completes the description of H.

Now we use any random walk algorithm to compute the destination of a walk of length $\ell = 2rL - 1 = \Theta(\Lambda^{2\kappa-1})$ on H by starting a random walk at $s_1^{1,f(A)}$. If the random walk destination is $t_L^{r,j}$ for some j, then node t outputs the number j; otherwise node t outputs an arbitrary number.

Now observe the following claim.

Claim 4.2 *Node t outputs $\mathrm{PC}^{r,m}(f_A, f_B)$ with probability at least $2/3$.*

PROOF. Let P^* be the path consisting of nodes $s_1^{1,f_A(1)}$, ..., $s_L^{1,f_A(1)}$, $t_1^{1,f_B(f_A(1))}$, ..., $t_L^{1,f_B(f_A(1))}$, $s_1^{1,f_A(f_B(f_A(1)))}$, ...,

$s_L^{i,g^{2i-1}(f_A,f_B)}$, $t_1^{i,g^{2i}(f_A,f_B)}$, ..., $t_L^{r,g^{2r}(f_A,f_B)}$. We claim that the random walk will follow path P^* with probability at least $2/3$. The node of distance $(2rL-1)$ from $s_1^{1,f_A(1)}$ in this path is $t_L^{i,g^{2r}(f_A,f_B)} = t_L^{r,\mathrm{PC}^{r,m}(1)}$ and thus the algorithm described above will output $\mathrm{PC}^{r,m}(1)$ with probability at least $2/3$.

To prove the above claim, consider any node u in path P^*. Let u' and u'' be the node before and after u in P^*, respectively. Let m' and m'' be the number of multiedges (u, u') and (u, u''), respectively. Observe that $m'' \geq 6\Gamma\ell m'$. Moreover, observe that there are at most Γ edges between u and other nodes. Thus, if a random walk is at u, it will continue to u'' with probability at least $1 - \frac{1}{3\ell}$. By union bound, the probability that a random walk will follow P^* is at least $1 - \frac{1}{3}$, as claimed. $\square$

Thus, if there is any random walk algorithm with running time $O(T)$ on all networks in $\mathcal{H}$ then we can use such algorithm to solve $\mathrm{PC}^{r,m}$ (with error probability $1/3$) in time $O(T)$. Using the lower bound of computing solving $\mathrm{PC}^{r,m}$ in Lemma 3.2, the random walk computation also has a lower bound of $\Omega(\kappa\Lambda^\kappa) = \Omega(\sqrt{\ell D})$ as claimed. $\square$

To prove Theorem 1.1 with the given parameters n, D and ℓ, we simply set Λ and κ so that $\kappa\Lambda = D$ and $\Lambda^{2\kappa-1} = \Theta(\ell)$. This choice of Λ and κ exists since $\ell \geq D$. Setting Γ large enough so that $\Gamma \geq 32\kappa^2\Lambda^{6\kappa-1}\log n$ while $\Gamma = \Theta(n)$. (This choice of Γ exists since $\ell \leq (n/(D^3\log n))^{1/4}$.) By applying the above lemma, Theorem 1.1 follows.

5. CONCLUSION

In this paper we prove a tight unconditional lower bound on the time complexity of distributed random walk computation, implying that the algorithm in [11] is time optimal. To the best of our knowledge, this is the first lower bound that the diameter plays a role of multiplicative factor. Our proof technique comes from strengthening the connection between communication complexity and distributed algorithm lower bounds initially studied in [9] by associating *rounds* in communication complexity to the distributed algorithm running time, with network diameter as a trade-off factor.

There are many open problems left for random walk computation. One interesting open problem is showing a lower bound of performing a long walk. We conjecture that the same lower bound of $\tilde{\Omega}(\sqrt{\ell D})$ holds for any $\ell = O(n)$. However, it is not clear whether this will hold for longer walks. For example, one can generate a *random spanning tree* by computing a walk of length equals the cover time (using the version where every node knows their positions) which is $O(mD)$ where m is the number of edges in the network (see detail in [11]). It is interesting to see if performing such a walk can be done faster. Additionally, the upper and lower bounds of the problem of generating a random spanning tree itself is very interesting since its current upper bound of $\tilde{O}(\sqrt{m}D)$ [11] simply follows as an application of random walk computation [11] while no lower bound is known. Another interesting open problem prove the lower bound of $\tilde{\Omega}(\sqrt{K\ell D})$ for some value of ℓ for the problem of performing K walks of length ℓ.

In light of the success in proving distributed algorithm lower bounds from communication complexity in this and the previous work [9], it is also interesting to explore further applications of this technique. One interesting approach is to show a connection between distributed algorithm lower bounds and other models of communication complexity, such as multiparty and asymmetric communication complexity (see, e.g., [23]). One particular interesting research topic is applying this technique to distance-related problems such as shortest s-t path, single-source distance computation, and all-pairs shortest path. The lower bound of $\Omega(\sqrt{n})$ are shown in [9] for these types of problems. It is interesting to see if there is an $O(\sqrt{n})$-time algorithm for these problems (or any sub-linear time algorithm) or a time lower bound of $\omega(\sqrt{n})$ exists. The special cases of these problems on complete graphs (as noted in [13]) are particularly interesting. Besides these problems, there are still some gaps between upper and lower bounds of problems considered in [9] such as the minimum cut and generalized Steiner forest.

6. REFERENCES

[1] L. A. Adamic, R. M. Lukose, A. R. Puniyani, and B. A. Huberman. Search in power-law networks. *Physical Review*, 64, 2001.

[2] H. Baala, O. Flauzac, J. Gaber, M. Bui, and T. El-Ghazawi. A self-stabilizing distributed algorithm for spanning tree construction in wireless ad hoc networks. *J. Parallel Distrib. Comput.*, 63(1):97–104, 2003.

[3] J. Bar-Ilan and D. Zernik. Random leaders and random spanning trees. In *Proceedings of the 3rd International Workshop on Distributed Algorithms*, pages 1–12, London, UK, 1989. Springer-Verlag.

[4] T. Bernard, A. Bui, and O. Flauzac. Random distributed self-stabilizing structures maintenance. In *ISSADS*, pages 231–240, 2004.

[5] A. R. Bharambe, M. Agrawal, and S. Seshan. Mercury: supporting scalable multi-attribute range queries. In *SIGCOMM*, pages 353–366, 2004.

[6] A. Z. Broder. Generating random spanning trees. In *FOCS*, pages 442–447, 1989.

[7] B. F. Cooper. Quickly routing searches without having to move content. In *IPTPS*, pages 163–172, 2005.

[8] D. Coppersmith, P. Tetali, and P. Winkler. Collisions among random walks on a graph. *SIAM J. Discret. Math.*, 6(3):363–374, 1993.

[9] A. Das Sarma, S. Holzer, L. Kor, A. Korman, D. Nanongkai, G. Pandurangan, D. Peleg, and R. Wattenhofer. Distributed Verification and Hardness of Distributed Approximation. In *STOC*, 2011.

[10] A. Das Sarma, D. Nanongkai, and G. Pandurangan. Fast distributed random walks. In *PODC*, pages 161–170, 2009.

[11] A. Das Sarma, D. Nanongkai, G. Pandurangan, and P. Tetali. Efficient distributed random walks with applications. In *PODC*, pages 201–210, 2010.

[12] S. Dolev and N. Tzachar. Spanders: distributed spanning expanders. In *SAC*, pages 1309–1314, 2010.

[13] M. Elkin. Distributed approximation: a survey. *SIGACT News*, 35(4):40–57, 2004.

[14] M. Elkin. An Unconditional Lower Bound on the Time-Approximation Trade-off for the Distributed Minimum Spanning Tree Problem. *SIAM J. Comput.*, 36(2):433–456, 2006. Also in STOC'04.

[15] J. Feigenbaum, S. Kannan, A. McGregor, S. Suri, and J. Z. 0004. Graph Distances in the Data-Stream

[16] Model. *SIAM J. Comput.*, 38(5):1709–1727, 2008. Also in SODA'05.

[16] A. J. Ganesh, A.-M. Kermarrec, and L. Massoulié. Peer-to-peer membership management for gossip-based protocols. *IEEE Trans. Comput.*, 52(2):139–149, 2003.

[17] J. A. Garay, S. Kutten, and D. Peleg. A Sublinear Time Distributed Algorithm for Minimum-Weight Spanning Trees. *SIAM J. Comput.*, 27(1):302–316, 1998. Also in FOCS '93.

[18] C. Gkantsidis, M. Mihail, and A. Saberi. Hybrid search schemes for unstructured peer-to-peer networks. In *INFOCOM*, pages 1526–1537, 2005.

[19] A. Israeli and M. Jalfon. Token management schemes and random walks yield self-stabilizing mutual exclusion. In *PODC*, pages 119–131, 1990.

[20] D. Kempe, J. M. Kleinberg, and A. J. Demers. Spatial gossip and resource location protocols. In *STOC*, pages 163–172, 2001.

[21] J. M. Kleinberg. The small-world phenomenon: an algorithmic perspective. In *STOC*, pages 163–170, 2000.

[22] L. Kor, A. Korman, and D. Peleg. Tight bounds for distributed mst verification. In *STACS*, pages 69–80, 2011.

[23] E. Kushilevitz and N. Nisan. *Communication complexity*. Cambridge University Press, New York, NY, USA, 1997.

[24] C. Law and K.-Y. Siu. Distributed construction of random expander networks. In *INFOCOM*, 2003.

[25] D. Loguinov, A. Kumar, V. Rai, and S. Ganesh. Graph-theoretic analysis of structured peer-to-peer systems: routing distances and fault resilience. In *SIGCOMM*, pages 395–406, 2003.

[26] Z. Lotker, B. Patt-Shamir, and D. Peleg. Distributed MST for constant diameter graphs. *Distributed Computing*, 18(6):453–460, 2006. Also in PODC'01.

[27] Q. Lv, P. Cao, E. Cohen, K. Li, and S. Shenker. Search and replication in unstructured peer-to-peer networks. In *ICS*, pages 84–95, 2002.

[28] D. Nanongkai, A. Das Sarma, and G. Pandurangan. A tight lower bound on distributed random walk computation. *CoRR*, abs/1102.2906, 2011.

[29] N. Nisan and A. Wigderson. Rounds in communication complexity revisited. *SIAM J. Comput.*, 22(1):211–219, 1993. Also in STOC'91.

[30] D. Peleg. *Distributed computing: a locality-sensitive approach*. Society for Industrial and Applied Mathematics, Philadelphia, PA, USA, 2000.

[31] D. Peleg and V. Rubinovich. A Near-Tight Lower Bound on the Time Complexity of Distributed Minimum-Weight Spanning Tree Construction. *SIAM J. Comput.*, 30(5):1427–1442, 2000. Also in FOCS'99.

[32] M. Zhong and K. Shen. Random walk based node sampling in self-organizing networks. *Operating Systems Review*, 40(3):49–55, 2006.

[33] M. Zhong, K. Shen, and J. I. Seiferas. Non-uniform random membership management in peer-to-peer networks. In *INFOCOM*, pages 1151–1161, 2005.

Minimum Congestion Mapping in a Cloud*

Nikhil Bansal, Kang-Won Lee, Viswanath Nagarajan, and Murtaza Zafer
IBM T.J. Watson Research Center
{nikhil, kangwon, viswanath, mzafer}@us.ibm.com

ABSTRACT

We study a basic resource allocation problem that arises in cloud computing environments. The physical network of the cloud is represented as a graph with vertices denoting servers and edges corresponding to communication links. A workload is a set of processes with processing requirements and mutual communication requirements. The workloads arrive and depart over time, and the resource allocator must map each workload upon arrival to the physical network. We consider the objective of minimizing the *congestion*.

We show that solving a subproblem (SingleMap) about mapping a *single workload* to the physical graph essentially suffices to solve the general problem. In particular, an α-approximation for SingleMap gives an $O(\alpha \log nD)$ competitive algorithm for the general problem, where n is the number of nodes in the physical network and D is the maximum to minimum workload duration ratio.

We also show how to solve SingleMap for two natural class of workloads, namely *depth-d trees* and *complete-graph* workloads. For depth-d tree, we give an $n^{O(d)}$ time $O(d^2 \log(nd))$-approximation based on a strong LP relaxation inspired by the *Sherali-Adams* hierarchy.

Categories and Subject Descriptors

F.2.2 [**Theory of Computation**]: Analysis of Algorithms and Problem Complexity; C.2.5 [**Computer Systems Organization**]: Computer-Communication Networks

General Terms

Algorithms, Theory

Keywords

Cloud Computing, Graph Mapping, Congestion Minimization, Approximation Algorithms

1. INTRODUCTION

In cloud computing, the underlying resource is a physical network (also called the *substrate*) consisting of servers that are inter-connected via communication links. Each server has a processing capacity[1] and each communication link has a bandwidth capacity. *Workloads* are service demands made to the cloud, modeled as a graph with a set of processes with communication requirements between them. Each workload must be assigned/mapped to some physical resources. The goal of the cloud service provider is to allocate resources to workloads in the best possible way.

The allocation of a workload to the substrate can be viewed as mapping one graph into another. This consists of two aspects: (a) *node-mapping*, the assignment of processes to servers, and (b) *path-mapping*, the assignment of each communication request (i.e. edge between two processes) to a path in the substrate between the respective servers. The load on a substrate node (resp. edge) is the total demand using that node (resp. edge). Ideally, one would like that the mapping should not cause the load on any node or edge to exceed it capacity. However if this constraint is enforced strictly, the problem can be shown hard to approximate to within any reasonable factor. This holds even for simple workloads such as stars for trivial reasons (in particular, due to NP-hardness of the Partition problem). So, we relax this requirement and consider the natural and well-studied objective of minimizing the maximum node and edge congestion, where the congestion of node or edge is defined as the ratio of its load to capacity.

We will refer to our problem as GraphMap and the objective as *network congestion*. There are two natural variants of

---

* Research was sponsored in part by the U.S. Army Research Laboratory and the U.K. Ministry of Defense and was accomplished under Agreement Number W911NF-06-3-0001. The views and conclusions contained in this document are those of the author(s) and should not be interpreted as representing the official policies, either expressed or implied, of the U.S. Army Research Laboratory, the U.S. Government, the U.K. Ministry of Defence or the U.K. Government. The U.S. and U.K. Governments are authorized to reproduce and distribute reprints for Government purposes notwithstanding any copyright notation hereon. The research is also supported through participation in the Measurement Science for Cloud Computing sponsored by the National Institute of Standards and Technology (NIST) under Agreement Number 60NANB10D003.

---

[1]Our results extend easily to settings with multiple resources such as CPU, memory, disk etc. However, for notational clarity, we only consider the single resource case here, and defer the generalization to the full version of this paper.

GraphMap: In the offline case, the workloads are all known in advance. In the (harder) online case, the workloads arrive and depart over time, and the existence of a workload is unknown until it arrives. Here we seek an online algorithm that assigns each workload (immediately upon its arrival) to the substrate such that the worst case network congestion over time is minimized. Many previous papers [24, 23, 11, 18] have proposed heuristics to solve such mapping problems, but without any performance guarantees. In this paper we design algorithms with provable guarantees.

Interestingly, even the (seemingly simple) problem of mapping a single workload to the substrate is quite hard in general. For example, several classic and well-studied problems are simple special cases of mapping a single workload:

- *Balanced Separator.* The substrate is a single edge with each node having capacity $n/2$. This reduces to partitioning the vertices of the workload H into near-balanced parts such that the resulting cut is minimized. This is an extensively studied graph partitioning problem, and the best known approximation ratio is $O(\sqrt{\log n})$ [2].

- *Cut-width:* The substrate is a line on n vertices with equal capacity edges. This reduces to finding an ordering $v_1, \ldots, v_n$ of the vertices in the workload H such that $\max_{i=1}^n \delta_H(v_1, \ldots, v_i)$ is minimized. The best known approximation ratio is $O(\log^{3/2} n)$ [16].

- *Min-max k-partitioning:* The substrate is a star with k leaves and equal capacity edges; the node capacity of the center is zero and each leaf has capacity n/k. This reduces to partitioning the vertices of the workload H into k nearly balanced parts $V_1, \ldots, V_k$ such that $\max_{i=1}^k \delta_H(V_i)$ is minimized, a basic problem in distributed computing.

One of our main results will be that the problem of mapping a *single workload* to the substrate essentially captures the hardness of the online GraphMap problem. More precisely, a cost-aware variant of the single workload mapping problem, that we call SingleMap, suffices to solve both the offline and online GraphMap problem. In addition to this connection, clearly SingleMap is a natural assignment problem on graphs, applicable in a wider context.

As the SingleMap problem (and hence GraphMap) appears very challenging in full generality, we obtain results for the following natural subclasses of workloads that seem to arise most often in practice:

- *Constant depth trees.*
- *Complete graphs* with uniform demands.

Tree-shaped workloads arise commonly as they corresponding to processes arranged hierarchically. The constant depth corresponds to having a small number of hierarchies. The complete graph workloads represent a clique of processes all of them communicating with each other. We require that the processing requirements be identical and also the communication requirement be identical for every pair of processes[2].

---

[2]Such a restriction is necessary, as any arbitrary workload H can be modeled as a complete graph with zero requirement for edges not in H.

1.1 Model

The General Mapping Problem: The substrate is a graph $G = (V, E)$ with edge-capacities $c : E \to \mathbb{R}_+$ and node-capacities $u : V \to \mathbb{R}_+$. There is a set of workloads that need to be mapped into the substrate. Each workload is a virtual graph $H = (W, F)$ with processing demands $g : W \to \mathbb{R}_+$ and traffic demands $b : F \to \mathbb{R}_+$. A *mapping* of H to the substrate G is specified by a tuple $\langle \pi, \sigma \rangle$, where:

- $\pi : W \to V$ assigns each process $w \in W$ to some node $\pi(w) \in V$ in the substrate G.

- $\sigma : F \to 2^E$ maps each edge $f = (w_1, w_2) \in F$ to a *path* $\sigma(f)$ in G between nodes $\pi(w_1)$ and $\pi(w_2)$; the $b(f)$ units of traffic between processes w_1 and w_2 are routed along $\sigma(f)$. This is an *unsplittable routing* model. An alternate model is splittable routing, where $\sigma(f)$ can be a flow of $b(f)$ units between $\pi(w_1)$ and $\pi(w_2)$.

For each edge $e \in E$ in the physical network let L_e denote the total traffic (from all workloads) routed through edge e; then the congestion of edge e is L_e/c_e. Similarly, for a node $v \in V$ let N_v denote the total processing demands assigned to v; and congestion of v is N_v/u_v. We define the *network-congestion* to be the maximum of the edge and node congestions.

Given a set of workloads and the substrate graph, the objective in the GraphMap problem is to map all workloads so as to minimize the network-congestion. We give algorithms for both offline and online settings. In the offline setting, the algorithm knows all the workloads in advance before computing the mapping. The more realistic online setting is when workloads arrive (and depart) over time, and the algorithm has to make irrevocable assignments to the workloads upon their arrival. We consider the model of known durations (see eg. [4]), i.e. each workload specifies upon arrival the time it will spend in the cloud.

Single Workload Mapping: This is an important subroutine that is useful in obtaining algorithms for both the offline and online mapping problems. The input to SingleMap consists of the following:

- A workload represented by an undirected graph $H = (W, F)$ with demands $g : W \to \mathbb{R}_+$ and $b : F \to \mathbb{R}_+$.
- Substrate $G = (V, E)$ with edge-capacities $c : E \to \mathbb{R}_+$ and node-capacities $u : V \to \mathbb{R}_+$.
- Cost functions $\alpha : E \to \mathbb{R}_+$ and $\beta : V \to \mathbb{R}_+$.

A mapping of H into G assigns vertices W to V and each edge in F to a path in G between the respective end-points (as in the definition of GraphMap). The mapping is called *valid* if it respects all edge and node capacities, i.e. $L_e \leq c_e \ \forall e \in E$ and $N_v \leq u_v \ \forall v \in V$. The goal is to find a valid mapping of H into G that minimizes the total cost $\sum_{e \in E} \alpha_e \cdot L_e + \sum_{v \in V} \beta_v \cdot N_v$.

An algorithm for SingleMap is said to be a (ρ_1, ρ_2) *bicriteria approximation* algorithm if: (1) it produces a solution of cost at most ρ_1 times the optimum, and (2) such that all edge and node capacities are satisfied within a ρ_2 factor.

We note that the objective in SingleMap is not congestion (as in GraphMap), but the cost of the mapping.

1.2 Our Results and Techniques

First, we describe the general frameworks for designing both offline and online algorithms of GraphMap, assuming a (ρ_1, ρ_2) bicriteria approximation algorithm for SingleMap. In particular,

- For offline GraphMap (where all workloads are given upfront) we show an $O\left((\rho_1 + \rho_2) \cdot (\log n / \log \log n)\right)$ approximation algorithm. To obtain this result, we formulate a configuration LP relaxation for GraphMap, and solve it approximately using SingleMap as the dual separation routine. The final solution is obtained by applying randomized rounding to the approximate LP solution.

- For online GraphMap we give an $O\left((\rho_1 + \rho_2) \cdot \log(nD)\right)$-competitive algorithm, where D is the ratio of maximum to minimum durations. This result uses multiplicative updates and builds upon the ideas developed previously in the context of online virtual circuit routing [3].

These results appear in Section 2 and Section 3 respectively. An immediate consequence of this framework is that there is a logarithmic approximation for GraphMap on constant-sized workloads. This follows as the SingleMap problem can be (trivially) solved optimally by enumerating all possibilities for such workloads.

Next, we consider SingleMap for arbitrary sized workloads for the cases of constant depth trees and uniform complete graphs. The following theorem is proved in Section 4.

THEOREM 1.1. *There is a randomized $\left(2, O(d^2 \cdot \log nd)\right)$ bicriteria approximation algorithm for SingleMap on d-depth tree workloads, that runs in time $n^{O(d)}$. Here n is the number of vertices in the substrate.*

This implies a polynomial time $O(\log n)$-approximation algorithm for SingleMap when $d = O(1)$, and a quasipolynomial, poly-logarithmic approximation when d is polylogarithmic in n. This result is based on a strong LP relaxation, which is inspired by the *Sherali-Adams* lift-and-project procedure. It is easy to show that direct LP relaxations [11, 18] with just assignment variables have very large integrality gaps even when the workload is a single edge. The main idea in our LP is to use joint assignment variables with d-tuples and 'conditional congestion' constraints. The rounding algorithm uses the tree structure of the workload and proceeds in d iterations, each time assigning vertices of a new level via randomized rounding.

For complete graph workloads, the idea is to solve the problem on a tree substrate and then use Räcke decomposition [20, 14]. However some more care is required in this reduction since the Räcke tree only provides a splittable routing, and we finally want an unsplittable routing.

THEOREM 1.2. *For GraphMap under uniform complete-graph workloads there is:*
- *An offline $O(\log^3 n)$-approximation algorithm.*
- *An $O(\log^2 n \log \log n \log(nR))$-competitive randomized online algorithm.*

Here n is the number of vertices in the substrate and R is the time horizon of the online algorithm.

1.3 Related Work

Our graph mapping problem (GraphMap) has two aspects. First, how the vertices of the workload H should be mapped. Second, given a mapping of the vertices of H, how to map

the edges. Both these issues have been studied separately in previous works. In particular, the Quadratic Assignment problem [8] is related to the first issue and the goal there is to find mapping *nodes* of one graph into another such that a certain quadratic objective is minimized [15] or maximized [19, 17]. On the other hand, the virtual circuit routing problem [3] deals with the second issue (although only for single edge workloads). Here, the mapping of the endpoints of the workload edge are given, and the goal is to map the edge to a path in the substrate graph to minimize edge congestion.

Another related problem is minimizing congestion for quorum placement on networks [13], for which a poly-logarithmic approximation is known. This also involves mapping nodes and paths simultaneously (here routing is splittable). However all paths are between one vertex that is fixed (called client) and another (called quorum) that is mapped. In contrast, both end points of a path in SingleMap are mapped vertices. Moreover, the demand between clients and quorums has a "product multicommodity" structure, whereas demands in SingleMap are arbitrary.

The online framework we present for GraphMap uses ideas from the online virtual circuit routing algorithm [3]. In [3] costs on edges are maintained using multiplicative updates and each request is routed along a shortest-path from its source to destination. Our framework is a generalization of this result, where requests have more complicated mappings (instead of just a path). Consequently, the subproblem (SingleMap) that we need to solve is also harder, as opposed to shortest-path in [3].

A natural approach to mapping nodes in SingleMap is to consider an LP relaxation similar to ones used for quadratic assignment [1, 17]. However, as we show in Section 4, such LPs have a large integrality gap for SingleMap. Instead, our result for d-depth tree workloads uses substantially stronger LPs based on the *Sherali-Adams* hierarchy [22]. We are not aware of a more direct approach that yields a poly-logarithmic approximation for this problem. This adds to a small list of problems for which lift-and-project LP hierarchies have proved useful in obtaining algorithms. Some other examples are graph coloring [9], independent set in 3-uniform hypergraphs [10], dense-k-subgraph [6], and max-min degree arborescence [5].

If we consider *splittable routing* in the GraphMap problem then one can assume (at the loss of a poly-logarithmic approximation factor) that the substrate is always a tree [20, 14]. Although we are interested in unsplittable routing, this connection is useful in our algorithm for complete-graph workloads.

2. OFFLINE FRAMEWORK

We show the following result.

THEOREM 2.1. *For any $\rho_1, \rho_2 \geq 1$, a (ρ_1, ρ_2) bicriteria approximation algorithm for the SingleMap problem can be used to obtain an $O\left((\rho_1 + \rho_2) \cdot \frac{\log n}{\log \log n}\right)$ approximation algorithm for the offline GraphMap problem.*

The main idea is to solve a *configuration LP* relaxation for GraphMap, and then apply randomized rounding. The separation oracle for this LP will be the SingleMap problem.

Let $H_1, \ldots, H_k$ denote the workloads to be mapped into substrate $G = (V, E)$ with edge capacities c_e and node capacities u_v. Without loss of generality we assume that the optimum congestion is 1 (the algorithm can do a binary search on the value of the optimum congestion, and scale the capacities accordingly). For each $i \in [k]$ let $\mathcal{F}_i$ denote the set of all possible valid mappings of H_i into G, such that the load on each edge e (resp. vertex v) is at most c_e (resp. u_v). We define a variable $x_i(\tau)$ for each possible map $\tau \in \mathcal{F}_i$ for H_i. As the optimal solution must use some map from $\mathcal{F}_i$ for each H_i and has overall congestion 1, the following LP is a valid relaxation of GraphMap and has a feasible solution.

$$
\begin{aligned}
\min \quad & 0 \\
s.t. \quad & \sum_{\tau \in \mathcal{F}_i} x_i(\tau) \geq 1 && \forall i \in [k] \\
& \sum_{i=1}^{k} \sum_{\tau \in \mathcal{F}_i} \ell(e, \tau) \cdot x_i(\tau) \leq c_e && \forall e \in E \\
& \sum_{i=1}^{k} \sum_{\tau \in \mathcal{F}_i} \ell(v, \tau) \cdot x_i(\tau) \leq u_v && \forall v \in V \\
& x_i(\tau) \geq 0 && \forall \tau \in \mathcal{F}_i, \forall i \in [k].
\end{aligned}
$$

Here, for any $i \in [k]$ and $\tau \in \mathcal{F}_i$, $\ell(e, \tau)$ denotes the load on edge $e \in E$ under mapping τ; similarly $\ell(v, \tau)$ denotes the load on vertex $v \in V$.

This LP has an exponential number of variables but only polynomially many constraints, so we consider its dual:

$$
\begin{aligned}
\max \quad & \sum_{i=1}^{k} z_i - \sum_{e \in E} c_e \cdot \alpha_e - \sum_{v \in V} u_v \cdot \beta_v \\
s.t. \quad & \sum_e \ell(e, \tau) \cdot \alpha_e + \sum_v \ell(v, \tau) \cdot \beta_v \geq z_i, \quad \forall \tau \in \mathcal{F}_i, i \in [k] \\
& z_i, \alpha_e, \beta_v \geq 0 \quad \forall i \in [k], e \in E, v \in V
\end{aligned}
$$

Observe that given values for (z, α, β) the dual separation problem is precisely SingleMap for each of $\{H_i\}_{i=1}^{k}$ with capacities c, u and costs α, β. Since we have a (ρ_1, ρ_2) bicriteria approximation algorithm for SingleMap, we can solve the dual LP approximately using the Ellipsoid algorithm. By standard LP duality arguments, this gives a primal solution $\{y_i(\tau) : i \in [k], \tau \in \widetilde{\mathcal{F}}_i\}$ where:

- For each map in $\widetilde{\mathcal{F}}_i$, the load on each edge e (resp. vertex v) is at most $\rho_2 \cdot c_e$ (resp. $\rho_2 \cdot u_v$).
- For all $e \in E$, $\sum_{i=1}^{k} \sum_{\tau \in \mathcal{F}_i} \ell(e, \tau) \cdot y_i(\tau) \leq \rho_1 \cdot c_e$.
- For all $v \in V$, $\sum_{i=1}^{k} \sum_{\tau \in \mathcal{F}_i} \ell(v, \tau) \cdot y_i(\tau) \leq \rho_1 \cdot u_v$.
- Each $\widetilde{\mathcal{F}}_i$ has polynomial size.

Given a primal solution with these properties, the algorithm now chooses a mapping for each workload H_i by picking $\tau \in \widetilde{\mathcal{F}}_i$ independently with probability $y_i(\tau)$. Using standard probabilistic tail bounds (as in [21]), it follows that the total load on any edge or vertex is $O((\rho_1 + \rho_2) \cdot (\log n / \log \log n))$ times its capacity with high probability, which implies the result.

3. ONLINE FRAMEWORK

In this section we show the following result:

THEOREM 3.1. *Given a (ρ_1, ρ_2) bicriteria approximation algorithm for SingleMap, There is an $O((\rho_2 + \rho_1)\log(nD))$-competitive online algorithm for GraphMap with known durations. Here n is the number of vertices in the substrate graph and D is the maximum duration of any workload.*

Using standard arguments the term D above can be replaced with the ratio of maximum to minimum durations, however we defer this technicality to the full version of the paper.

The algorithm is similar to the online algorithm for virtual circuit routing [3, 4, 7]. The idea is that at each time,

the algorithm maintains a cost on the edges that is an exponentially increasing function of their load. Upon the arrival of a workload, the solution of an SingleMap instance with these costs determines where this workload will be placed. Since the highly loaded edges are severely penalized, the SingleMap solution will prefer edges with low load.

Notation: Let $H_1, H_2, \ldots, H_k$ denote the workloads in the order in which they arrive; we use i to index the workloads. Each H_i appears at time s_i with a specified duration t_i, which means that H_i stays in the cloud from time s_i to $s_i + t_i$. We assume that the duration t_i becomes known when H_i arrives at s_i. Note that the s_is are non-decreasing. We assume that all times and durations are integral and $\max_i t_i \leq D$. Also, given SingleMap algorithm as a black-box, our algorithm for GraphMap will treat edges and vertices identically, and hence we will use the term element to refer to either an edge or a vertex of G. The set of elements will be denoted by U and c_e will denote the capacity of $e \in U$. For each workload H_i, the algorithm finds a map $\tau_i \in \mathcal{F}_i$ and H_i is assigned to G using this map during the interval $[s_i, s_i + t_i]$. The network congestion is the maximum congestion over all elements $e \in U$ and over all times h, i.e.

$$
\max_{e \in U} \quad \max_{h \geq 0} \quad \frac{\sum_{i: s_i \leq h \leq s_i + t_i} \tau_i(e)}{c_e}
$$

where $\tau_i(e)$ is the load on e due to map τ_i for workload H_i.

The SingleMap problem can be restated in the above notation: given workload H_i, costs $\alpha : U \to \mathbb{R}_+$ and capacities $\bar{c} : U \to \mathbb{R}_+$, find a feasible map $\tau \in \mathcal{F}_i$ minimizing $\sum_{e \in U} \alpha_e \cdot \tau(e)$ such that $\tau(e) \leq \bar{c}_e$ for all $e \in U$. As previously, we assume a (ρ_1, ρ_2) bicriteria approximation algorithm for SingleMap.

3.1 Algorithm

In the description below we assume that optimum solution has congestion at most 1. This assumption can be removed by standard doubling techniques (see eg. Theorem 12.5 [7]), where the online maintains an upper bound Λ on the optimal congestion thus far.

Let $\gamma \in (0, 1)$ be a constant to be fixed later. Also let $B := \rho_2$. For any $i \geq 1$, let $\ell_i(e, h)$ denote the load of element e at time h, induced by requests $H_1, \ldots, H_{i-1}$. Formally,

$$
\ell_i(e, h) = \sum_{j=1}^{i-1} \tau_j(e) \cdot \mathbb{I}(h \in [s_j, s_j + t_j])
$$

where $\mathbb{I}(h \in [s_j, s_j + t_j])$ is an indicator 0-1 variable representing whether $s_j \leq h \leq s_j + t_j$.

Upon the arrival of workload H_i at time s_i, the algorithm does the following:

1. Set costs $\alpha_e := \frac{\gamma}{B\, c_e} \cdot \sum_{h=s_i}^{s_i + t_i} \exp(\frac{\gamma \ell_i(e, h)}{B \cdot c_e})$ for all $e \in U$.

2. Run the (ρ_1, ρ_2) bicriteria approximation algorithm for SingleMap on instance $\langle H_i, \alpha, c \rangle$ to obtain $\tau_i \in \mathcal{F}_i$ and assign workload H_i according to τ_i during the time interval $[s_i, s_i + t_i]$.

3. Update $\ell_{i+1}(e, h) \leftarrow \ell_i(e, h) + \tau_i(e)$ for all $e \in U$ and $s_i \leq h \leq s_i + t_i$.

Note that the above updates to the variables ℓ are consistent with their definition.

3.2 Analysis

We will show that this algorithm is $O((\rho_1+\rho_2)\log(D|U|))$-competitive. We begin with a simple claim.

CLAIM 3.1. *For any $\tau \in \mathcal{F}_i$ with $\tau(e) \leq B \cdot c_e$ for all $e \in U$, we have:*

$$\sum_{e\in U}\sum_{h=s_i}^{s_i+t_i}\exp\left(\frac{\gamma\cdot\ell_i(e,h)}{Bc_e}\right)\left[\exp\left(\frac{\gamma\cdot\tau(e)}{Bc_e}\right)-1\right]$$

lies in the range $\left[\sum_{e\in U}\alpha_e\cdot\tau(e),\ 2\sum_{e\in U}\alpha_e\cdot\tau(e)\right]$.

Proof: For all $x \in [0,1]$ and $\gamma \in (0,1)$ we have $\exp(\gamma x)-1 \in [\gamma x, 2\gamma x]$. Consider any $e \in U$. As $\tau(e) \in [0, B\cdot c_e]$, setting $x = \tau(e)/(Bc_e)$ above,

$$\exp\left(\frac{\gamma\cdot\tau(e)}{Bc_e}\right)-1 \in \left[\frac{\gamma\cdot\tau(e)}{Bc_e}, 2\frac{\gamma\cdot\tau(e)}{Bc_e}\right].$$

The claim now follows by the definition of costs $\alpha_e = \frac{\gamma}{B\,c_e} \cdot \sum_{h=s_i}^{s_i+t_i}\exp(\gamma\cdot\ell_i(e,h)/B\cdot c_e)$, and summing over e. ∎

For each $e \in U$ and time $h \geq 0$, let $\bar{\ell}(e,h) = \max_i \ell_i(e,h)$ denote the observed load on element e at time h. Observe that for any index i with $s_i > h$, we have $\ell_i(e,h) = \bar{\ell}(e,h)$. Clearly, the objective value of the online algorithm is $\max_{e\in U}\max_{h\geq 0}\bar{\ell}(e,h)/c_e$, that we wish to bound. To this end, for any integer $j \geq 1$ define:

$$L_j = \sum_{e\in U}\sum_{h=(j-1)\cdot D}^{j\cdot D}\exp\left(\frac{\gamma\cdot\bar{\ell}(e,h)}{B\,c_e}\right)$$

We will show that,

LEMMA 3.1. *Setting $\gamma := \min\{\frac{\rho_2}{6\rho_1}, 1\}$, for each $j \geq 1$, we have $L_j \leq 6\cdot D\,|U|$.*

Before we prove Lemma 3.1, we note that this already implies our main result, Theorem 3.1. In particular, for all $e \in U$ and $h \geq 0$, taking logarithms,

$$\bar{\ell}(e,h) \leq \frac{1}{\gamma}\ln(6D|U|)\cdot Bc_e \leq \frac{\rho_2\ln(6D|U|)}{\gamma}\cdot c_e$$
$$\leq \max\{\rho_2, 6\rho_1\}\ln(6D|U|)c_e$$

by the definition of γ.

Proof:(Lemma 3.1) The proof is by induction on j. Define $L_0 = 0$ for the base case. Consider now any $j \geq 1$, assuming inductively that $L_{j-1} \leq 6\cdot D\,|U|$. Let $R = \{r, r+1, \ldots, t\}$ denote the indices of workloads that are released in the interval $[(j-2)D, jD]$. For any index $i \in R$, define

$$A_i = \sum_{e\in U}\sum_{h=(j-2)D}^{(j+1)D}\exp\left(\gamma\cdot\frac{\ell_i(e,h)}{B\,c_e}\right).$$

CLAIM 3.2. $A_r \leq 2D\,|U| + L_{j-1}$.

Proof: By the choice of R, $s_{r-1} < (j-2)D$. As D is the maximum duration, $s_{r-1} + t_{r-1} < (j-1)D$ and hence $\ell_r(e,h) = 0$ for all $e \in U$ and $h \geq (j-1)D$. Thus,

$$A_r = \sum_{e\in U}\left(\sum_{h=(j-2)D}^{(j-1)D}\exp\left(\frac{\gamma\cdot\ell_r(e,h)}{B\,c_e}\right) + \sum_{h=(j-1)D}^{(j+1)D}\exp(0)\right)$$

$$\leq \sum_{e\in U}\left(\sum_{h=(j-2)D}^{(j-1)D}\exp\left(\frac{\gamma\cdot\bar{\ell}(e,h)}{B\,c_e}\right)+2D\right)$$
$$= L_{j-1} + 2D\,|U|$$
∎

For convenience, for any $i \in R$, $e \in U$ and $h \geq 0$, let us define $\tau_i^*(e,h) = \tau_i^*(e)$ if $s_i \leq h \leq s_i + t_i$, and 0 otherwise. Also define $\tau_i(e,h)$ similarly.

CLAIM 3.3. *For any $i \in R$, we have*

$$A_{i+1}-A_i \leq 2\rho_1\gamma\cdot\sum_{e\in U}\sum_{h=(j-2)D}^{(j+1)D}\exp\left(\frac{\gamma\cdot\bar{\ell}(e,h)}{B\,c_e}\right)\cdot\frac{\tau_i^*(e,h)}{B\,c_e}.$$

Proof: By definition, $A_{i+1}-A_i$

$$= \sum_{e\in U}\sum_{h=(j-2)D}^{(j+1)D}\exp\left(\frac{\gamma\cdot\ell_i(e,h)}{B\,c_e}\right)\left[\exp\left(\frac{\gamma\cdot\tau_i(e,h)}{B\,c_e}\right)-1\right].$$

Since $\tau_i(e,h) \leq \tau_i(e) \leq B\cdot c_e$, we can use (see Claim 3.1) $\exp\left(\gamma\frac{\tau_i(e,h)}{B\,c_e}\right)-1 \leq 2\gamma\cdot\frac{\tau_i(e,h)}{B\,c_e}$, and hence $A_{i+1}-A_i$ is at most:

$$\sum_{e\in U}\sum_{h=(j-2)D}^{(j+1)D}\exp\left(\frac{\gamma\cdot\ell_i(e,h)}{B\,c_e}\right)\cdot\frac{2\gamma\cdot\tau_i(e,h)}{B\,c_e}$$
$$= \sum_{e\in U}\sum_{h=s_i}^{s_i+t_i}\exp\left(\frac{\gamma\cdot\ell_i(e,h)}{B\,c_e}\right)\cdot\frac{2\gamma\cdot\tau_i(e)}{B\,c_e}$$
$$= 2\sum_{e\in U}\alpha_e\cdot\tau_i(e) \qquad (1)$$

The first equality is by definition of $\tau_i(e,h)$ and the second is by the definition of α_es. Now, recall the algorithm for mapping workload H_i that solves **SingleMap** instance $\langle H_i, \alpha, c\rangle$. As τ_i^* is also a candidate feasible solution to this instance and τ_i is a (ρ_1, ρ_2)-approximate solution to this **SingleMap** instance, we have:

$$\sum_{e\in U}\alpha_e\cdot\tau_i(e) \leq \rho_1\cdot\sum_{e\in U}\alpha_e\cdot\tau_i^*(e). \qquad (2)$$

Moreover, since $\ell_i(e,h) \leq \bar{\ell}(e,h)$ and $(j-2)D \leq s_i \leq s_i + t_i \leq (j+1)D$, we have:

$$\alpha_e \leq \frac{\gamma}{B\,c_e}\cdot\sum_{h=(j-2)D}^{(j+1)D}\exp\left(\frac{\gamma\cdot\bar{\ell}(e,h)}{B\,c_e}\right), \quad \forall e \in U$$

Combined with (1) and (2), we obtain $A_{i+1}-A_i$,

$$\leq 2\rho_1\gamma\cdot\sum_{e\in U}\sum_{h=(j-2)D}^{(j+1)D}\exp\left(\frac{\gamma\cdot\bar{\ell}(e,h)}{B\,c_e}\right)\cdot\frac{\tau_i^*(e,h)}{B\,c_e}.$$

which proves the claim. ∎

Summing the inequality in Claim 3.3 over all $i \in R$, we can upper bound $A_{t+1}-A_r$ as:

$$\leq 2\rho_1\gamma\cdot\sum_{e\in U}\sum_{h=(j-2)D}^{(j+1)D}\exp\left(\frac{\gamma\cdot\bar{\ell}(e,h)}{B\,c_e}\right)\cdot\left(\sum_{i\in R}\frac{\tau_i^*(e,h)}{B\,c_e}\right)$$

$$\leq \frac{2\rho_1\gamma}{\rho_2}\cdot\sum_{e\in U}\sum_{h=(j-2)D}^{(j+1)D}\exp\left(\frac{\gamma\cdot\bar{\ell}(e,h)}{B\,c_e}\right).$$

271

The second inequality uses $B = \rho_2$ and our assumption that the optimum congestion is at most 1, i.e. $\sum_i \tau_i^*(e,h) \le c_e$.

As $\gamma := \min\{\frac{\rho_2}{6\rho_1}, 1\}$, this gives that

$$A_{t+1} - A_r \le \frac{2\rho_1\gamma}{\rho_2} \cdot A_{t+1} \le \frac{1}{3} A_{t+1},$$

which implies that $A_{t+1} \le 1.5 \cdot A_r$. Together with Claim 3.2, this implies that

$$A_{t+1} \le 3D\,|U| + 1.5\,L_{j-1}.$$

On the other hand, $A_{t+1} \ge L_{j-1} + L_j$. This follows because, by definition of R, workload $t+1$ arrives after time jD, i.e. $s_{t+1} > jD$, and so for all $e \in U$ and $h \le jD$, we have $\ell_{t+1}(e,h) = \bar{\ell}(e,h)$. Thus, $L_{j-1} + L_j \le A_{t+1} \le 3D\,|U| + 1.5 \cdot L_{j-1}$, and hence

$$L_j \le 3D\,|U| + \frac{L_{j-1}}{2}.$$

As $L_{j-1} \le 6D\,|U|$ by the inductive hypothesis, this proves Lemma 3.1. ∎

4. SINGLE WORKLOAD MAPPING ON D-DEPTH TREE WORKLOADS

In this section we prove Theorem 1.1. As mentioned previously, our result in based on an LP formulation inspired by the Sherali-Adams Hierarchy. It is instructive to see why simpler approaches do not seem to work. Clearly, an LP formulation based on assignment variables $x_{p,v}$ which indicate that node p in mapped to vertex v, is very weak, as it cannot capture the pairwise traffic constraints. However, it turns out that even a quadratic assignment type LP with variables x_{p_i,v_i,p_j,v_j} (representing whether p_i mapped to v_i and p_j mapped to v_j) is also very weak, unless strengthened by additional Sherali-Adams type constraints.

In particular, consider a star workload with center r and n leaves $\ell_1, \ldots, \ell_n$ with unit traffic and processing demands. The substrate consists of n disjoint edges $\{(a_i, b_i)\}_{i=1}^n$ each of capacity one; each vertex also has capacity one. All costs are zero; so this is a feasibility question.

Clearly, any integral mapping must violate the capacity of some edge by a factor of n. However, it turns out that is a feasible solution for Quadratic Assignment LPs [1], that satisfies all the capacities. We set,

$$y(r, v) = \begin{cases} \frac{1}{n} & \text{if } v \in \{a_i\}_{i=1}^n \\ 0 & \text{otherwise} \end{cases}$$

For each $i, j \in [n]$ we have

$$y(r, a_i, \ell_j, v) = \begin{cases} \frac{1}{n} & \text{if } v = b_i \\ 0 & \text{otherwise} \end{cases}$$

Basically this solution is a convex combination of the n integral solutions, where for each $i \in [n]$, r maps to a_i and all the leaves $\{\ell_j\}_{j=1}^n$ map to b_i. This LP solution is feasible as the total usage of each edge $\{(a_i, b_i)\}_{i=1}^n$ is one; so edge capacities are satisfied. Similarly the total usage of each vertex is also at most one.

The trouble with this LP is that it fails to capture the fact that when the center is mapped to some vertex s, the traffic from all leaves must come to s. To get around this problem, we will add additional constraints that we call *conditional congestion constraints*. Roughly speaking, they ensure that conditional on the center being mapped to some vertex s,

the total congestion induced by all edges remains at most one. These are formally described later.

Before describing our LP based algorithm for d-level tree workloads, we describe a simpler combinatorial algorithm for star workloads with uniform demands. This is useful as such workloads are likely to appear frequently in practice and combinatorial algorithms are simpler to implement that LP based approaches. Also, this algorithm explicitly illustrates the problem with the LP described above, and motivates the Sherali-Adams approach better. Interestingly, we do not know how to extend this combinatorial algorithm to trees with depth two or more.

4.1 Uniform Star Workload

Let ℓ denote the number of edges in the star workload and $b \in \mathbb{R}_+$ the demand on each edge.

The Algorithm: For each vertex $s \in V$, we do the the following: Define a flow network N_s on G with s as source and a new sink vertex t that is connected to all vertices V. Set the capacity of each edge $e \in E$ to be $\lfloor c_e/b \rfloor$; the capacity of each edge (v,t) to be u_v (for $v \in V \setminus \{s\}$) and capacity of (s,t) to $u_s - 1$. There is a cost of α_e on each edge $e \in E$, and cost of β_v for each edge (v,t).

The network flow instance on N_s involves computing the *minimum cost flow* of ℓ units from s to t, which can be done efficiently [12]. Observe that there is a one-to-one correspondence between feasible solutions to this flow instance N_s and valid mappings of the star-workload where the center is mapped to s. Note that having fixed the center at s, the flow instance N_s captures both node and path mappings. Thus the minimum cost optimum amongst instances $\{N_s : s \in V\}$ yields an optimal solution to SingleMap on uniform star workloads.

The main idea in the above algorithm was to enumerate over the mapping of the center (s), which enabled a reduction to single commodity flow. This approach can be extended to workloads with a constant number of non-leaf vertices, since we can again enumerate over all non-leafs and reduce to single commodity flow. However extending this idea to even a 2-level tree workload appears problematic since we can no longer perform such an enumeration (there may be super-logarithmic number of non-leaf vertices).

4.2 Depth d-tree Workload

Notation. We fix some notation relevant to this section. We use $H = (W, F)$ to denote the workload which is a tree of depth d rooted at some node r. The *level* of a vertex $v \in W$ is the number of edges on the path from v to root r, so the root has level zero. We use $[d] := \{0, 1, \ldots, d\}$. For any $i \in [d]$, we use p_i to refer to some node at level i (p_0 is always the root r). An edge (p_i, p_{i+1}) has demand $b(p_i, p_{i+1})$, and a node p has processing demand $g(p)$. The substrate is a graph $G(V, E)$ with edge and vertex capacities c_e and u_v. The costs of the edges and vertices are $\{\alpha_e\}_{e \in E}$ and $\{\beta_v\}_{v \in V}$. For any $i \in [d]$, we use $(p_0, \ldots, p_i)$ to denote a path in H from the root p_0 that contains exactly one vertex in each level $0, 1, \ldots, i$.

The LP relaxation We describe here the LP relaxation. First, we describe the variables we use. There will be two types of variables, that we call assignment variables, and flow variables.

Assignment Variables: For every index $i \in [d]$, and path $(p_0, p_1, \ldots, p_i)$ in H, and vertices $v_0, \ldots, v_i \in V$, we introduce a variable $y(p_0, v_0, \ldots, p_i, v_i) \in \{0, 1\}$ which we relax to take values in the range $[0, 1]$. In the integral solution, this variable is intended to be 1, if each p_j in the path is mapped to v_j for each $j \in \{0, \ldots, i\}$, and is 0 otherwise. It is convenient to view this variable as the probability of the event $\bigwedge_{j=0}^{i} (p_j$ is mapped to $v_j)$. Also, we only allow variables where each p is mapped v such that $g(p) \leq u_v$ (we set the y variable to 0 otherwise).

Flow Variables: For every path $(p_0, p_1, \ldots, p_i)$ in H with $i \geq 1$ and collection of vertices $v_0, \ldots, v_i \in V$, we will define a network flow instance. This instance will be denoted by $\mathcal{F}(p_0, v_0, \ldots, p_{i-1}, v_{i-1}, p_i, v_i)$ and is supposed to correspond to the mapping of edge (p_{i-1}, p_i) under the event that "p_j is mapped to v_j for each $j \in \{0, \ldots, i\}$. We will denote the variables in this flow instance by $\mathcal{F}_e(p_0, v_0, \ldots, p_i, v_i)$

The underlying network $N(p_{i-1}, v_{i-1}, p_i, v_i)$ in this flow instance is the substrate graph G restricted to edges of capacity at least $b(p_{i-1}, p_i)$, the source-vertex is v_{i-1} and sink is v_i. There are flow-variables $\mathcal{F}_e(p_0, v_0, \ldots, p_{i-1}, v_{i-1}, p_i, v_i)$ for each edge $e \in G$. The flow on edges $G \backslash N(p_{i-1}, v_{i-1}, p_i, v_i)$ are *fixed to zero*; i.e. only edges $N(p_{i-1}, v_{i-1}, p_i, v_i)$ participate in this flow. The variables satisfy flow-conservation constraints and send

$$y(p_0, v_0, \ldots, p_{i-1}, v_{i-1}, p_i, v_i) \cdot b(p_{i-1}, p_i) \quad (3)$$

units of flow from v_{i-1} to v_i. One can view $\left\{ \frac{\mathcal{F}_e(p_0, v_0, \ldots, p_i, v_i)}{y(p_0, v_0, \ldots, p_i, v_i)} \right\}_e$ as defining $b(p_{i-1}, p_i)$ units of flow conditioned upon p_j being mapped to v_j for each $j \in \{0, \ldots, i\}$. We note that the network $N(p_{i-1}, v_{i-1}, p_i, v_i)$ itself is independent of where $p_0, \ldots, p_{i-2}$ are mapped.

We impose three types of constraints.

Consistency Constraints: Since we intend the y variables to model probabilities, we impose the following natural consistency constraints.

1. For all paths $(p_0, p_1, \ldots, p_i)$ in H and $v_0, \ldots, v_{i-1} \in V$,

$$\sum_{v_i \in V} y(p_0, v_0, \ldots, p_i, v_i) = y(p_0, v_0, \ldots, p_{i-1}, v_{i-1}).$$
$$(4)$$

This can be viewed as saying that

$$\frac{y(p_0, v_0, \ldots, p_{i-1}, v_{i-1}, p_i, v_i)}{y(p_0, v_0, \ldots, p_{i-1}, v_{i-1})}$$

defines valid probability distribution for mapping p_i to v_i conditional upon $p_0, \ldots, p_{i-1}$ being mapped to $v_0, \ldots, v_{i-1}$.

2. As the root must be assigned somewhere, we have:

$$\sum_{v_0 \in V} y(p_0, v_0) = 1. \quad (5)$$

Together (4) and (5) imply that every path $(p_0, p_1, \ldots, p_i)$ in H is mapped somewhere, i.e.

$$\sum_{v_0 \ldots v_i \in V} y(p_0, v_0, \ldots, p_i, v_i) = 1.$$

Global Congestion Constraints: These ensure that the load of any each edge or vertex in G is at most its capacity.

For each edge $e \in E$, we have

$$\sum_{(p_{i-1}, p_i) \in F} \sum_{v_0, \ldots, v_i} \mathcal{F}_e(p_0, v_0, \ldots, p_{i-1}, v_{i-1}, p_i, v_i) \leq c_e. \quad (6)$$

Note that the left hand side is precisely the total fractional load on edge e due to pairs (p_{i-1}, p_i) in the workload.

Similarly, for each vertex $v \in V$, we have

$$\sum g(p_i) \cdot y(p_0, v_0, \ldots, p_{i-1}, v_{i-1}, p_i, v) \leq u_v, \quad (7)$$

where the summation is over all indices $i \geq 0$, and paths $(p_0, \ldots, p_i) \in H$ and vertices $v_0, \ldots, v_{i-1} \in V$.

Conditional Congestion Constraints: These final types of constraints are perhaps the least natural, but these are critical to strengthening the LP.

For each index $i \geq 0$, and each path $(p_0, \ldots, p_i)$ and each possible choice of vertices $v_0, \ldots, v_i \in V$, and edge $e \in E$, we add the constraint:

$$\sum_{j \geq i} \sum_{p_{i+1}, v_{i+1}, \ldots, p_j, v_j} \mathcal{F}_e(p_0, v_0, \ldots, p_i, v_i, \ldots p_j, v_j)$$
$$\leq c_e \cdot y(p_0, v_0, \ldots, p_i, v_i). \quad (8)$$

This constraint is similar to global edge congestion constraint, except that we condition on event that $p_0, \ldots, p_i$ are mapped to $v_0, \ldots, v_i$ respectively. That is, conditional on $p_0, \ldots, p_i$ being mapped to $v_0, \ldots, v_i$, the total load on e due to mapping edges in subtree rooted at p_i must be no more than c_e. Note that if $y(p_0, v_0, \ldots, p_i, v_i) \in \{0, 1\}$, then this is a valid constraint, and hence the above relaxation is valid.

Similarly, for each vertex $v \in V$, index $i \geq 0$, each path $(p_0, \ldots, p_i)$ and vertices $v_0, \ldots, v_i \in V$, we add:

$$\sum_{j \geq i} \sum_{p_{i+1}, v_{i+1}, \ldots, p_j} g(p_j) \cdot y(p_0, v_0, \ldots, p_i, v_i, \ldots p_j, v)$$
$$\leq u_v \cdot y(p_0, v_0, \ldots, p_i, v_i). \quad (9)$$

That is, conditional on $p_0, \ldots, p_i$ being mapped to $v_0, \ldots, v_i$, the load on v due to nodes in subtree rooted at p_i must be no more than u_v.

Objective: The objective is to minimize:

$$\sum_{e \in E} \alpha_e \cdot \sum \mathcal{F}_e(p_0, v_0, \ldots, p_{i-1}, v_{i-1}, p_i, v_i) \quad (10)$$
$$+ \sum_{v \in V} \beta_v \cdot \sum g(p_i) \cdot y(p_0, v_0, \ldots, p_{i-1}, v_{i-1}, p_i, v).$$

Here, the first summation (over edges) is over all indices $i \geq 1$, all paths $(p_0, \ldots, p_i)$ in H and all vertices $v_0, \ldots, v_i \in V$, and the second summation (for vertices) is over all indices $i \geq 0$, all paths $(p_0, \ldots, p_i)$ and all vertices $v_0, \ldots, v_{i-1} \in V$.

This completes the description of the linear program. Observe that the total number of variables and constraints is $n^{O(d)}$ which is polynomial for constant d. Hence this LP can be solved exactly in $n^{O(d)}$ time. Moreover, as argued above, this LP is a valid relaxation of the SingleMap problem with d-depth tree workloads.

4.3 The Rounding Algorithm

We round the optimal LP solution in d phases, where in the ith phase we fix the mapping of all level-i vertices in H.

Vertex Mapping: The algorithm incrementally constructs a mapping $\tau : W \to V$ as follows.

1. Set $\tau(p_0) \leftarrow v$ with probability $y(p_0, v)$. This fixes the mapping of the root.

2. For each $i \in \{1, \ldots, d\}$ do:

   For each vertex p_i at level-i:

   - Let $(p_0, \ldots, p_{i-1}, p_i)$ denote the path from the root to p_i.
   - Set $\tau(p_i) \leftarrow v$ independently with probability:

   $$\frac{y(p_0, \tau(p_0), \ldots, p_{i-1}, \tau(p_{i-1}), p_i, v)}{y(p_0, \tau(p_0), \ldots, p_{i-1}, \tau(p_{i-1}))} \quad (11)$$

Note that the algorithm is well-defined as at any iteration i, the map τ is already known for all vertices at levels up to $i-1$. Also, (11) defines a valid (conditional) probability distribution for mapping p_i, due to LP constraint (4).

Edge Mapping: Having obtained the vertex mapping τ above, the map σ from edges of H to paths in G is constructed by randomized rounding. For each edge (p_{i-1}, p_i) in H do:

- Obtain a flow-path decomposition of

$$\frac{\mathcal{F}(p_0, \tau(p_0), \ldots, p_{i-1}, \tau(p_{i-1}), p_i, \tau(p_i))}{b(p_{i-1}, p_i) \cdot y(p_0, \tau(p_0), \ldots, p_{i-1}, \tau(p_{i-1}), p_i, \tau(p_i))}.$$

  By (3) this gives a probability distribution on $\tau(p_{i-1})$ to $\tau(p_i)$ paths.

- Assign edge (p_{i-1}, p_i) to a random $\tau(p_{i-1})$ to $\tau(p_i)$ path chosen according to the above distribution; call this path $\sigma(p_{i-1}, p_i)$ and send $b(p_{i-1}, p_i)$ units of flow along $\sigma(p_{i-1}, p_i)$.

Two simple properties: This completes the description of the rounding procedure. We note here two useful properties of this procedure.

1. For any path $(p_0, \ldots, p_i) \in H$, vertices $v_0, \ldots, v_i \in V$,

$$\Pr[\tau(p_0) = v_0, \ldots, \tau(p_i) = v_i] = y(p_0, v_0, \ldots, p_i, v_i).$$

2. Similarly, for any edge $e \in E$, edge $(p_{i-1}, p_i) \in F$ with $(p_0, \ldots, p_i)$ being its path from r and $v_0, \ldots, v_i \in V$,

$$\Pr[e \in \sigma(p_{i-1}, p_i) \mid \tau(p_0) = v_0, \ldots, \tau(p_i) = v_i]$$
$$= \frac{\mathcal{F}_e(p_0, v_0, \ldots, p_{i-1}, v_{i-1}, p_i, v_i)}{b(p_{i-1}, p_i) \cdot y(p_0, v_0, \ldots, p_{i-1}, v_{i-1}, p_i, v_i)} \quad (12)$$

4.4 The Analysis

We need to show two things. First, the cost of the mapping is close to optimum. Second, the edge and node congestions are not too high.

CLAIM 4.1. *The expected cost of the algorithm's mapping $\langle \tau, \sigma \rangle$ equals the optimal LP objective.*

This claim along with Markov inequality implies that with probability at least half, the cost of $\langle \tau, \sigma \rangle$ is at most twice the LP optimum.

Proof:(Claim 4.1) The cost of any mapping $\langle \tau, \sigma \rangle$ is

$$\sum_{p \in W} \beta_{\tau(p)} \cdot g(p) + \sum_{(p,q) \in F} \sum_{e \in \sigma(p,q)} \alpha_e \cdot b(p,q),$$

given by the total of node costs and edge costs.

For any level i node p_i with $(p_0, \ldots, p_{i-1}, p_i)$ as its path from the root, and vertices $v_0, \ldots, v_i \in V$, recall that our rounding procedure satisfies

$$\Pr[\tau(p_0) = v_0, \ldots, \tau(p_i) = v_i] = y(p_0, v_0, \ldots, p_i, v_i).$$

So, $\Pr[\tau(p_i) = v] = \sum_{v_0, \ldots, v_{i-1}} y(p_0, v_0, \ldots, p_{i-1}, v_{i-1}, p_i, v)$ and hence the expected node-cost of mapping $\langle \tau, \sigma \rangle$:

$$\sum_{p_i \in W} \sum_v \beta_v \cdot g(p_i) \cdot \Pr[\tau(p_i) = v] =$$
$$\sum_v \beta_v \sum_{p_i \in W} g(p_i) \sum_{v_0, \ldots, v_{i-1}} y(p_0, v_0, \ldots, p_{i-1}, v_{i-1}, p_i, v).$$

which is exactly the second term in the LP objective (10).

We now compute the expected edge-cost. Consider any edge $(p_{i-1}, p_i) \in F$. By (12), and unconditioning over the events $\tau(p_0) = v_0, \ldots, \tau(p_{i-1}) = v_{i-1}, \tau(p_i) = v_i$,

$$\Pr[\sigma(p_{i-1}, p_i) \ni e] = \sum_{v_0, \ldots, v_i} \frac{\mathcal{F}_e(p_0, v_0, \ldots, p_{i-1}, v_{i-1}, p_i, v_i)}{b(p_{i-1}, p_i)}.$$

So the expected edge-cost is:

$$\sum_{(p_{i-1}, p_i) \in F} b(p_{i-1}, p_i) \cdot \sum_{e \in E} \alpha_e \cdot \Pr[\sigma(p_{i-1}, p_i) \ni e] =$$
$$\sum_{e \in E} \alpha_e \sum_{(p_{i-1}, p_i) \in F} \sum_{v_0, \ldots, v_i} \mathcal{F}_e(p_0, v_0, \ldots, p_{i-1}, v_{i-1}, p_i, v_i)$$

which is exactly the first term in the LP objective (10). This implies the claim. ∎

Bounding edge and node congestion: We now bound the edge and node congestion of the mapping produced by our algorithm.

THEOREM 4.1. *With probability at least $1 - 1/n^2$, the maximum node or edge congestion is at most $O(d^2 \log(nd))$.*

We describe here the analysis for edge congestion, the analysis for node congestion is essentially identical.

Fix an edge $e \in E$ in the substrate. For each level i edge $(p_{i-1}, p_i) \in F$ in the workload, the load assigned by the LP solution to e is

$$\sum_{v_0, \ldots, v_i} \mathcal{F}_e(p_0, v_0, \ldots, p_{i-1}, v_{i-1}, p_i, v_i).$$

We will be interested in how this load evolves as the rounding proceeds on each level of nodes in W.

For $\ell \in [d]$, let $\tau^{(\ell)}$ denote some mapping of the first $\ell - 1$ levels of nodes in W. So, $\tau^{(0)}$ denotes the empty mapping and $\tau^{(d+1)}$ denote a mapping of all the vertices. Let us define, $L_e(\tau^{(\ell)}, p_{i-1}, p_i)$ as the load on e due to edge (p_{i-1}, p_i) based on the mapping $\tau^{(\ell)}$ thus far. Formally, we define $L_e(\tau^{(\ell)}, p_{i-1}, p_i)$ as follows: if $\ell \geq i + 1$ then

$$\frac{\mathcal{F}_e(p_0, \tau^{(\ell)}(p_0), \ldots, p_{i-1}, \tau^{(\ell)}(p_{i-1}), p_i, \tau^{(\ell)}(p_i))}{y(p_0, \tau^{(\ell)}(p_0), \ldots, p_i, \tau^{(\ell)}(p_i))},$$

and otherwise (i.e. $\ell \leq i$),

$$\sum_{v_\ell, \ldots, v_i} \frac{\mathcal{F}_e(p_0, \tau^{(\ell)}(p_0), \ldots, p_{\ell-1}, \tau^{(\ell)}(p_{\ell-1}), p_\ell, v_\ell, \ldots, p_i, v_i)}{y(p_0, \tau^{((\ell)}p_0), \ldots, p_{\ell-1}, \tau^{(\ell)}(p_{\ell-1}))}.$$

We note that by conditional congestion constraints (8), $L_e(\tau^{(\ell)}, p_{i-1}, p_i)$ is well-defined and always bounded by c_e.

A crucial observation is the following.

LEMMA 4.1. *Let $\tau^{(\ell)}$ be any arbitrary mapping on the first $\ell - 1$ levels. Let $\tau^{(\ell+1)}$ be obtained from $\tau^{(\ell)}$ by applying our rounding procedure to level ℓ nodes. Then, For any substrate edge $e \in E$ and workload edge $(p_{i-1}, p_i) \in F$,*

$$\mathbb{E}[L_e(\tau^{(\ell+1)}, p_{i-1}, p_i)] = L_e(\tau^{(\ell)}, p_{i-1}, p_i)$$

where expectation is taken over the randomness in the rounding procedure applied to level ℓ nodes.

Proof: Firstly, if $\ell > i$, then the mapping of p_{i-1} and p_i are already fixed in $\tau^{(\ell)}$ and the lemma is trivially true, so we assume that $\ell \leq i$.

Let p_ℓ denote the level-ℓ node on the path from p_0 to p_i. By the rounding procedure, the probability that p_ℓ is mapped to v conditioned on the mapping $\tau^{(\ell)}$ until level $\ell - 1$, is $\Pr[\tau^{(\ell+1)}(p_\ell) = v \mid \tau^{(\ell)}]$

$$= \frac{y(p_0, \tau^{(\ell)}(0), \ldots, p_{\ell-1}, \tau^{(\ell)}(p_{\ell-1}), p_\ell, v)}{y(p_0, \tau^{(\ell)}(0), \ldots, p_{\ell-1}, \tau^{(\ell)}(p_{\ell-1}))} \quad (13)$$

Thus,

$$\mathbb{E}[L_e(\tau^{(\ell+1)}, p_{i-1}, p_i)]$$
$$= \sum_{v_\ell} \Pr[\tau^{(\ell+1)}(p_\ell) = v_\ell \mid \tau^{(\ell)}] \cdot L_e(\tau^{(\ell+1)}, p_{i-1}, p_i)$$
$$= L_e(\tau^{(\ell)}, p_{i-1}, p_i)$$

where the equality in the last step follows by (13) and the definition of L_e (in the regime $\ell \leq i$). ∎

Given a partial mapping $\tau^{(\ell)}$ (of nodes on first $\ell - 1$ levels), let $L_e(\tau^{(\ell)}) = \sum_{(p_{i-1}, p_i) \in F} L_e(\tau^{(\ell)}, p_{i-1}, p_i)$ denote total load on edge $e \in E$ due to all edges in F. Call $\tau^{(\ell)}$ *good* if $L_e \leq 16d(\ell+1)c_e \log nd$. Clearly, the empty mapping $\tau^{(0)}$ is good, since

$$L_e(\tau^{(0)}) = \sum_{(p_{i-1}, p_i) \in F} \sum_{v_0, \ldots, v_i} \mathcal{F}_e(p_0, v_0, \ldots, p_i, v_i)$$

which by the global congestion constraint in the LP (6) is at most c_e.

LEMMA 4.2. *For any $\ell \in [d]$,*

$$\Pr[\tau^{(\ell+1)} \text{ is good} \mid \tau^{(\ell)} \text{ is good}] \geq 1 - 1/(dn)^4.$$

Proof: Let E'' denote the edges of H induced on the vertices of the first $\ell - 1$ levels. For any vertex p_ℓ in level ℓ (with $p_0, \ldots, p_{\ell-1}, p_\ell$ being its path from the root), let $E'(p_\ell)$ denote the set of edges in the subtree rooted at p_ℓ plus the edge $(p_{\ell-1}, p_\ell)$. For any subset S of edges, define $L_e(\tau^{(\ell)}, S) = \sum_{(p_{i-1}, p_i) \in S} L_e(\tau^{(\ell)}, p_{i-1}, p_i)$; and $L_e(\tau^{(\ell+1)}, S)$ is defined similarly. Since E'' and $\{E'(p_\ell)\}$ partition edges of H,

$$L_e(\tau^{(\ell)}) = L_e(\tau^{(\ell)}, E'') + \sum_{p_\ell} L_e(\tau^{(\ell+1)}, E'(p_\ell))$$

and a similar equality holds for $L_e(\tau^{(\ell+1)})$. Recall that $\tau^{(\ell)}$ is a fixed mapping for levels until $\ell-1$. The randomness is in the choice of mapping for level-ℓ vertices, which gives $\tau^{(\ell+1)}$. So $L_e(\tau^{(\ell+1)}, E'') = L_e(\tau^{(\ell)}, E'')$ is a deterministic quantity. Note also that each $L_e(\tau^{(\ell+1)}, E'(p_\ell))$ depends only on the choice $\tau^{(\ell+1)}(p_\ell)$, i.e. $L_e(\tau^{(\ell+1)}, E'(p_\ell))$s are independent random variables. Moreover, by Lemma 4.1, the expectation $\mathbb{E}[L_e(\tau^{(\ell+1)}, E'(p_\ell))] = L_e(\tau^{(\ell+1)}, E'(p_\ell))$ over the random

choice of $\tau^{(\ell+1)}(p_\ell)$ as in (13). Finally, by the conditional congestion LP constraints (8), it holds that for any choice of $\tau^{(\ell+1)}(p_\ell)$, $L_e(\tau^{(\ell+1)}, E'(p_\ell)) \leq c_e$.

Thus $L_e(\tau^{(\ell+1)}) - L_e(\tau^{(\ell+1)}, E'')$ is the sum of independent $[0, c_e]$ random variables having mean:

$$L_e(\tau^{(\ell)}) - L_e(\tau^{(\ell)}, E'') \leq 16d(\ell+1)\log nd \cdot c_e - L_e(\tau^{(\ell)}, E'')$$

The inequality uses the fact that $\tau^{(\ell)}$ is good. By a Chernoff Bound (recall that $L_e(\tau^{(\ell+1)}, E'')$ is fixed),

$$\Pr[L_e(\tau^{(\ell+1)}) > 16d(\ell+2)\log nd \cdot c_e] \leq \frac{1}{(dn)^4}$$

this uses the fact that $\ell \leq d$. ∎

Applying lemma 4.2 inductively, it follows that the final mapping $\tau^{(d+1)}$ is good for edge e with probability at least $1 - (d+1)/(nd)^4 > 1 - 1/n^4$. Taking union bound over the possible n^2 edges implies Theorem 1.1.

5. COMPLETE GRAPH WORKLOADS

In this section we consider the GraphMap problem when the workloads are complete graphs with uniform processing and traffic demands, and the substrate is a general graph. We first present an algorithm for SingleMap where the substrate is a tree and the workload is a uniform complete graph. Later we show that the Räcke decomposition tree can be used to obtain results on general substrates. If only splittable routing is needed, the Räcke decomposition can be used directly; however we show that we can also obtain unsplittable routings with some more care. Using our general framework, this gives poly-logarithmic ratio offline and online algorithms for GraphMap. However, as Räcke decomposition is an intermediate step, we need some more care in the reduction to SingleMap. Due to lack of space we defer details of the online algorithm to the full version.

SingleMap on trees. By scaling edge capacities in the substrate graph, we can assume that the workload H is a complete graph K_r with unit demand between every pair of vertices. The substrate graph is a tree $T = (V', E)$ with leaves $V \subseteq V'$, where processes can be mapped only to leaves. There are capacities $c : E \to \mathbb{R}_+$ on edges and $u : V \to \mathbb{R}_+$ on leaves. In addition there are cost functions $\alpha : E \to \mathbb{R}_+$ and $\beta : V \to \mathbb{R}_+$. Since the substrate is a tree, a mapping is already determined by an assignment of H-vertices to V. The goal is to find such an assignment satisfying node and edge capacities with minimum cost. We show now how this problem can be solved exactly by dynamic programming.

Since the workload is a complete graph with unit demands, the load on any edge $e \in T$ is determined by the number of H-vertices assigned to either side of e in the tree: if the two components in $T \setminus \{e\}$ contain ℓ and $r - \ell$ vertices from H then the load on e equals $\ell \cdot (r - \ell)$.

Root the tree T at an arbitrary non-leaf vertex $s \in V' \setminus V$. By splitting high-degree vertices (introducing dummy vertices connected by edges of infinite capacity and zero cost), we can assume that each non-leaf vertex in T has at most two children (this makes the dynamic program simpler). For any $v \in V'$ let T_v denote the subtree of T rooted at vertex v. Define the following recurrence. For all leaves $v \in V$ and $0 \leq \ell \leq r$, set

$$D[v, \ell] = \begin{cases} \beta_v \cdot \ell & \text{if } \ell \leq u_v \\ \infty & \text{otherwise} \end{cases}$$

For any non-leaf vertex $v \in V'$ with children v_1 and v_2, and $0 \le \ell \le r$, set

$$D[v, \ell] = \min \quad D[v_1, \ell_1] + D[v_2, \ell_2] + \alpha_{(v,v_1)} \cdot \ell_1(r - \ell_1)$$
$$+ \alpha_{(v,v_2)} \cdot \ell_2(r - \ell_2)$$

where the minimum is over all $0 \le \ell_1, \ell_2 \le r$ such that $\ell_1 + \ell_2 = \ell$ and $\ell_1(r - \ell_1) \le c_{(v,v_1)}$ and $\ell_2(r - \ell_2) \le c_{(v,v_2)}$.

Above ℓ_1, ℓ_2 are the numbers of H-vertices in the subtrees T_{v_1} and T_{v_2}. $D[v, \ell]$ is obtained by enumerating over all possibilities (at most r many) for ℓ_1 and ℓ_2. The constraints on ℓ_1 and ℓ_2 ensure that the loads on edges (v, v_1) and (v, v_2) do not exceed their capacity. If there is no feasible solution $\{\ell_1, \ell_2\}$ then set $D[v, \ell] = \infty$. It is clear that using this recurrence, the value $D[s, r]$ at the root equals the optimum of the SingleMap instance.

Offline Algorithm. Here the substrate G is general, and workloads are complete graphs with unit demands.

The algorithm guesses value $\Lambda \in [\mathsf{Opt}, 2\mathsf{Opt}]$ where Opt is the optimal value– we can try all possibilities. Then we apply the procedure of [14] to substrate G *restricted to edges of capacity at least $1/\Lambda$*, to obtain a Räcke decomposition tree $T(\Lambda)$. Note that the optimal solution uses only edges of capacity at least $1/\Lambda$ in G since $\mathsf{Opt} \le \Lambda$. The idea behind restricting edges is to ensure that the mapping obtained from the tree only uses high capacity edges of G. Now we consider the offline GraphMap instance on substrate $T(\Lambda)$, for which there is an $O(\frac{\log n}{\log \log n})$-approximation algorithm using the SingleMap algorithm above within the offline framework (Appendix 2). By the property of Räcke tree $T(\Lambda)$ [3] and guess Λ, the optimal value of this tree instance is at most Λ. So we obtain a mapping on $T(\Lambda)$ having congestion $O(\frac{\log n}{\log \log n}) \cdot \Lambda$. Using the flow template [14] on $T(\Lambda)$, this yields a splittable-routing solution in G, where:

- The node congestion is $O(\frac{\log n}{\log \log n}) \cdot \Lambda$.
- The edge congestion is $O(\log^2 n \log \log n) \cdot O(\frac{\log n}{\log \log n}) \cdot \Lambda = O(\log^3 n) \cdot \Lambda$.
- Every edge used in this solution has capacity $\ge \frac{1}{\Lambda}$, by definition of $T(\Lambda)$.

Note that in this solution, each demand edge e is mapped to a unit flow $\mathcal{F}_e$ between its end-points. The total usage of each edge $e' \in G$ is at most $O(\log^3 n) \Lambda \cdot c_{e'}$. Finally each demand edge e chooses one path between its end-points independently according to a flow-path decomposition of $\mathcal{F}_e$. By a Chernoff bound[4], it follows that the final congestion is $O(\log^3 n) \cdot \Lambda$ with high probability.

6. REFERENCES

[1] W. P. Adams and T. A. Johnson. Improved linear programming-based lower bounds for the quadratic assignment problem. In *DIMACS Series in Discrete Mathematics and Theoretical Computer Science*, volume 16, pages 43–77, 1994.

[2] Sanjeev Arora, Satish Rao, and Umesh V. Vazirani. Expander flows, geometric embeddings and graph partitioning. *J. ACM*, 56(2), 2009.

[3] James Aspnes, Yossi Azar, Amos Fiat, Serge A. Plotkin, and Orli Waarts. On-line routing of virtual circuits with applications to load balancing and machine scheduling. *J. ACM*, 44(3):486–504, 1997.

[4] Yossi Azar, Bala Kalyanasundaram, Serge A. Plotkin, Kirk Pruhs, and Orli Waarts. Online load balancing of temporary tasks. In *WADS*, pages 119–130, 1993.

[5] MohammadHossein Bateni, Moses Charikar, and Venkatesan Guruswami. Maxmin allocation via degree lower-bounded arborescences. In *STOC*, pages 543–552, 2009.

[6] Aditya Bhaskara, Moses Charikar, Eden Chlamtac, Uriel Feige, and Aravindan Vijayaraghavan. Detecting high log-densities: an $n^{1/4}$ approximation for densest k-subgraph. In *STOC*, pages 201–210, 2010.

[7] A. Borodin and R. El-Yaniv. *Online Computation and Competitive Analysis*. Cambridge University Press, 1998.

[8] Eranda Cela. *The Quadratic Assignment Problem: Theory and Algorithms*. Springer, 1998.

[9] Eden Chlamtac. Approximation algorithms using hierarchies of semidefinite programming relaxations. In *FOCS*, pages 691–701, 2007.

[10] Eden Chlamtac and Gyanit Singh. Improved approximation guarantees through higher levels of sdp hierarchies. In *APPROX-RANDOM*, 2008.

[11] N. Chowdhury, M. Rahman, and R. Boutaba. Virtual network embedding with coordianted node and link mapping. In *INFOCOM*, 2009.

[12] W.J. Cook, W.H. Cunningham, W.R. Pulleyblank, and A. Schrijver. *Combinatorial Optimization*. John Wiley and Sons, 1998.

[13] Daniel Golovin, Anupam Gupta, Bruce M. Maggs, Florian Oprea, and Michael K. Reiter. Quorum placement in networks: minimizing network congestion. In *PODC*, pages 16–25, 2006.

[14] Chris Harrelson, Kirsten Hildrum, and Satish Rao. A polynomial-time tree decomposition to minimize congestion. In *SPAA*, pages 34–43, 2003.

[15] Refael Hassin, Asaf Levin, and Maxim Sviridenko. Approximating the minimum quadratic assignment problems. *ACM TALG*, 6(1), 2009.

[16] Frank Thomson Leighton and Satish Rao. Multicommodity max-flow min-cut theorems and their use in designing approximation algorithms. *J. ACM*, 46(6):787–832, 1999.

[17] Konstantin Makarychev, Rajsekar Manokaran, and Maxim Sviridenko. Maximum quadratic assignment problem: Reduction from maximum label cover and lp-based approximation algorithm. In *ICALP (1)*, pages 594–604, 2010.

[18] X. Meng, V. Pappas, and L. Zhang. Impact of Data Center Network Architecture on Virtual Machine Placement. In *INFOCOM*, 2010.

[19] Viswanath Nagarajan and Maxim Sviridenko. On the maximum quadratic assignment problem. *Math. Oper. Res.*, 34(4):859–868, 2009.

[20] Harald Räcke. Minimizing congestion in general networks. In *FOCS*, pages 43–52, 2002.

[21] Prabhakar Raghavan and Clark D. Thompson. Randomized rounding: a technique for provably good algorithms and algorithmic proofs. *Combinatorica*, 7(4):365–374, 1987.

[22] Hanif D. Sherali and Warren P. Adams. A hierarchy of relaxations between the continuous and convex hull representations for zero-one programming problems. *SIAM J. Discrete Math.*, 3(3):411–430, 1990.

[23] M. Yu, Y. Yi, J. Rexford, and M. Chiang. Rethinking virtual network embedding: substrate support for path splitting and migration. *ACM SIGCOMM CCR*, 38(2):17–29, 2008.

[24] Y. Zhu and M. Ammar. Algorithms for assigning substrate network resources to virtual network components. In *INFOCOM*, 2006.

---

[3] Every cut in $T(\Lambda)$ has capacity larger than the corresponding cut in G.

[4] This uses the fact that the splittable-routing was restricted to high capacity edges.

Conflict on a Communication Channel

[Extended Abstract]

Valerie King[*]
University of Victoria,
Department of Computer
Science
Victoria, BC, Canada
val@cs.uvic.ca

Jared Saia[†]
University of New Mexico,
Department of Computer
Science
Albuquerque, NM, USA
saia@cs.unm.edu

Maxwell Young[‡]
University of Waterloo, David
R. Cheriton School of
Computer Science
Waterloo, ON, Canada
m22young@cs.uwaterloo.ca

ABSTRACT

Imagine that Alice wants to send a message m to Bob, and that Carol wants to prevent this. Assume there is a communication channel between Alice and Bob, but that Carol is capable of blocking this channel. Furthermore, there is a cost of S dollars to send on the channel, L dollars to listen on the channel and J to block the channel. How much will Alice and Bob need to spend in order to guarantee transmission of m?

This problem abstracts many types of conflict in information networks including: jamming attacks in wireless networks and distributed denial-of-service (DDoS) attacks on the Internet, where the costs to Alice, Bob and Carol represent an expenditure of energy or network resources. The problem allows us to quantitatively analyze the economics of information exchange in an adversarial setting and ask: Is communication cheaper than censorship?

We answer this question in the affirmative by showing that it is significantly more costly for Carol to block communication of m than for Alice to communicate it to Bob. Specifically, if S, L and J are fixed constants, and Carol spends a total of B dollars trying to block m, then Alice and Bob must spend only $O(B^{\varphi-1} + 1) = O(B^{.62} + 1)$ dollars in expectation to transmit m, where $\varphi = (1 + \sqrt{5})/2$ is the golden ratio. Surprisingly, this result holds even if (1) B is *unknown* to both Alice and Bob; (2) Carol knows the algorithms of Alice and Bob, but not their random bits; and (3) Carol has total knowledge of past actions of both players.

Finally, we apply our work to two problems: (1) DoS attacks in wireless sensor networks and (2) application-level DDoS attacks in a wired client-server scenario. Our applications show how our results can provide an additional tool in mitigating such attacks.

[*]This research was supported by NSERC.

[†]This research was partially supported by NSF CAREER Award 0644058, NSF CCR-0313160, NSF CNS-1017509, and AFOSR MURI grant FA9550-07-1-0532.

[‡] This research was partially supported by a NSERC Postgraduate Scholarship and an Ontario Graduate Scholarship.

Categories and Subject Descriptors

C.2.1 [**Computer Communications Networks**]: Network Architecture and Design—*Wireless communication*; F.2.2 [**Analysis of Algorithms and Problem Complexity**]: Nonnumerical Algorithms and Problems—*Routing and layout*

General Terms

Algorithms, Reliability, Security

Keywords

Byzantine fault tolerance, distributed denial-of-service attacks, energy efficiency, jamming attacks, wireless sensor networks

1. INTRODUCTION

In November of 2010, several web hosting and banking companies, including Amazon.com, Visa, Mastercard, and PayPal, severed ties with the website Wikileaks [1]. In retaliation, the Anonymous group of Internet activists launched distributed denial-of- service (DDoS) attacks against these companies [1]. Surprisingly, the web pages of both Wikileaks, and all the companies that were attacked by Anonymous emerged relatively unscathed despite the fact that Wikileaks suffered a significant attack on its financial and computational resources, and all parties suffered prolonged and sophisticated DDoS attacks. Some interesting questions arise in light of this incident: Is it fundamentally easier to communicate in large-scale networks than it is to block communication? Is it harder to block communication on the Internet compared with wireless networks where denial-of-service (DoS) attacks are easily launched via disruption of the communication medium [32]? When altercations arise on modern networks, what are the most effective strategies for both sides?

To consider these questions from an algorithmic perspective, we define the following simple problem, which we call the *3-Player Scenario*: Alice wishes to guarantee transmission of a message m directly to Bob over a single communication channel. However, there exists an adversary Carol who aims to prevent communication by blocking transmissions over the channel. We consider two cases: (Case 1) when Carol may spoof or even control Bob, which allows her to manipulate an unwitting Alice into incurring excessive sending costs; and (Case 2) where Bob is both correct, unspoofable, and his communications cannot be blocked. Here, "cost" corresponds to a network resource, such as energy in wireless sensor networks (WSNs) or bandwidth in wired networks.

In the 3-Player Scenario, we show that communication is fundamentally cheaper than censorship. Specifically, we describe a protocol that guarantees correct transmission of m, and given that Carol incurs a cost of B, has the following properties. In Case 1, the expected cost to both Alice and Bob is $O(B^{\varphi-1} + 1)$ where φ is the golden ratio. In Case 2, the expected cost to both Alice and Bob is $O(B^{0.5} + 1)$. In both cases, Carol's cost asymptotically exceeds the expected cost of either correct player.

In the remainder of this section, we describe our model setup, state our main results and summarize related work. Section 2 includes our full proofs for the 3-Player Scenario. Section 3 addresses jamming adversaries in WSNs and applies our results to the problems of single-hop local broadcast and multi-hop reliable broadcast. Section 4 shows how our results can be employed to mitigate application-level DDoS attacks. We conclude with a discussion of open problems in Section 5.

1.1 Model Specification & Assumptions

We describe the model parameters of the 3-Player Scenario.

Las Vegas Property: Communication of m from Alice to (a correct) Bob must be guaranteed with probability 1; that is, we require a Las Vegas protocol for solving the 3-Player Scenario. An obvious motivation for this Las Vegas property is a critical application, such as an early warning detection system or the dessimination of a crucial security update, where minimizing the probability of failure is paramount. The Las Vegas property has additional merit in multi-hop WSNs for the following reason. Let n be the number of devices within transmitting distance of a device, and let N be the total number of devices in the network. Monte Carlo protocols that succeed with high probability in n are possible. However, typically, $n \ll N$ and messages will traverse multiple hops; consider $\Omega(N)$ hops. *Even if the failure probability for each hop is $O(n^{-c})$ for some constant $c > 0$, or even $O(2^{-n})$, then communication fails along the chain with constant probability.* Alternatively, we might achieve protocols that succeed with high probability in N. However, in large networks, N may not be known *a priori*. Furthermore, a high probability guarantee in N typically involves $\Omega(\log N)$ operations which, for large N, may be too costly. Therefore, by devising Las Vegas protocols, we avoid problematic assumptions when $n \ll N$.

Channel Utilization: Sending or listening on the communication channel by Alice and Bob is measured in discrete units called *slots*. For example, in WSNs, a slot may correspond to an actual time slot in a time division multiple access (TDMA) type access control protocol. The cost for sending or listening is S or L per slot, respectively. When Carol blocks a slot, she disrupts the channel such that no communication is possible; blocking costs J per slot. If a slot contains traffic or is blocked, this is detectable by a player who is *listening* at the *receiving end* of the channel, but not by the originator of the transmission. For example, a transmission (blocked or otherwise) from Bob to Alice is detectable only by Alice; likewise, a transmission (blocked or otherwise) from Alice to Bob is detectable only by Bob. A player cannot discern whether a blocked slot has disrupted a legitimate message; only the disruption is detectable. For example, high energy noise is detectable over the wireless channel in WSNs, but a receiving device cannot tell if this results from a message collision or a device deliberately disrupting the channel. We let B be the total amount Carol will spend over the course of the algorithm; this value is *unknown* to either Alice or Bob. Finally, we say that any player is *active* in a slot if that player is sending, listening or blocking in that slot.

Correct & Faulty Players: If Alice is faulty, there is clearly no hope of communicating m; therefore, Alice is assumed to be correct. Regarding the correctness of Bob, in Case 1, Carol may spoof or control Bob; in Case 2, communications from Bob are always

trustworthy. We emphasize that, in Case 1, Alice is uncertain about whether to trust Bob since he may be faulty. This uncertainty corresponds to scenarios where a trusted dealer attempts to dessiminate content to its neighbors, some of whom may be faulty and attempt to consume resources by requesting numerous retransmissions. Case 2 corresponds to situations where communications sent by Bob are never disrupted and can be trusted; here, the blocking of m is the only obstacle.

Types of Adversary: Carol has full knowledge of past actions by Alice and Bob. This allows for *adaptive attacks* whereby Carol may alter her behavior based on observations collected over time. Furthermore, under conditions discussed in Section 2.2, Carol can also be *reactive*: in any slot, she may detect a transmission and then disrupt the communication (however, she cannot detect when a player is listening). This is pertinent to WSNs where the effectivess of a reactive adversary has been shown experimentally.

1.2 Fair & Favorable Protocols

We analyze the cost of our algorithms as a function of B. In this way, we obtain a notion of cost incurred by a player that is *relative to the cost incurred by Carol*. In devising our algorithms, we seek to achieve two properties with regards to relative cost.

First, our protocol should be *fair*; that is, Alice and Bob should incur the same *worst case asymptotic cost*. When network devices have similar resource constraints, such as in WSNs where devices are typically battery powered, this is critical. Alternatively, in networks where a collection of resource-scarce devices (i.e. client machines represented by Alice) occupy one side of the communication channel and a single well-provisioned device (i.e. a server represented by Bob) occupies the other side, the *aggregate* cost to Alice's side should be roughly equal to that of Bob.

Second, we desire *favorable* protocols; that is, for B sufficiently large, Alice and Bob both incur asymptotically less expected cost than Carol. DoS attacks are effective because a correct device is *always* forced to incur a higher cost relative to an attacker. However, if the correct players incur asymptotically less cost than Carol, then Alice and Bob enjoy the advantage, and Carol is faced with the problem of having her resources consumed disproportionately in her attempt to censor communication.

1.3 Our Main Contributions

Throughout, let $\varphi = (1 + \sqrt{5})/2$ denote the golden ratio. We assume that S, L, and J are fixed constants. Our main analytical contributions are listed below.

THEOREM 1. *Assume Carol is an adaptive adversary and that she is active for B slots. There exists a fair and favorable algorithm for the 3-Player Scenario with the following properties:*

- *In Case 1, the expected cost to each correct player is $O(B^{\varphi-1} + 1) = O(B^{0.62} + 1)$. In Case 2, the expected cost to each correct player is $O(B^{0.5} + 1)$.*

- *If Bob is correct, then transmission of m is guaranteed and each correct player terminates within $O(B^{\varphi})$ slots in expectation.*

In networks with sufficient traffic, Theorem 1 still holds when Carol is also reactive (Section 2.2). We also prove that any protocol which achieves $o(B^{0.5})$ expected cost for Bob requires more than $2B$ slots to terminate (Section 2.3); this lower bound has bearing on the worst-case $\omega(B)$ slots required by our protocol.

Our next Theorems 2 & 3 are applications of Case 1 of Theorem 1 to WSNs. We consider a more general setting where Alice wishes to locally (single-hop) broadcast to n neighboring receivers of which any number are spoofed or controlled by Carol. Unfortunately, a naive solution of having each receiver execute a separate instance of our 3-Player Scenario protocol fails to be fair. Thus, we need a different algorithm to achieve the following result.

THEOREM 2. *There exists a fair (up to small polylogarithmic factors in n) and favorable algorithm for achieving local broadcast with the following properties:*

- *If Carol's receivers are active for a total of B slots, then the expected cost to Alice is $O(B^{\varphi-1}\ln n + \ln^\varphi n)$ and the expected cost to any correct receiver is $O(B^{\varphi-1} + \ln n)$.*

- *Transmission of m is guaranteed and all correct players terminate within $O((B + \ln^{\varphi-1} n)^{\varphi+1})$ slots (not in expectation). For $B \geq \ln^{\varphi-1} n$, this is within an $O(B^\varphi)$-factor of the optimal latency.*

Reliable broadcast in *multi-hop* WSNs deals with conveying m from one node to all other nodes in the network. We make the standard assumptions that any node p can be heard by the set of neighboring nodes in the topology, $N(p)$ and that, for any p, at most t nodes in $N(p)$ suffer a fault (t-bounded fault model) [5, 6, 19]. We analyze the grid model using the result of Bhandari & Vaidya [6], and general graphs using the Certified Propagation Protocol (CPA) protocol of Pelc & Peleg [24].

THEOREM 3. *For each correct node p, assume the t nodes in $N(p)$ are Byzantine and can be used by Carol to disrupt p's communications for $\beta \leq B_0$ time slots. Then, using the local broadcast protocol of Theorem 2, fair and favorable reliable broadcast is possible under the following topologies:*

- *In the grid with the optimal fault tolerance.*

- *In any graph, assuming that (a) t is appropriately bounded such that CPA achieves reliable broadcast and (b) the topology and location of the dealer is known to all nodes.*

To the best of our knowledge, all previous reliable broadcast protocols require correct nodes to spend more energy in communication attempts than that spent by adversarial nodes. Our results are the first favorable protocols and, importantly, we also address the *cost of listening* to the wireless channel.

Finally, Theorem 4 is an application of Case 2 of Theorem 1 to a client-server scenario where Carol represents malicious clients engaging in a DDoS attack on a server.

THEOREM 4. *Assume Carol commits her DDoS attack using bandwidth R. Service is guaranteed given that the expected aggregate bandwidth (upstream or downstream bits per second) of both the clients and the server is $O(R^{0.5})$.*

Therefore, against a server defended by our protocol, Carol must incur additional monetary costs in order to procure the number of machines necessary for sustaining the level of attack she would otherwise achieve.

1.4 Related Work

Jamming Attacks in WSNs: Several works addressing applied security considerations show that devices in a WSN are vulnerable to adversarial jamming [33]. A number of defenses have been proposed (see [32]). There are a number of theoretical results on jamming adversaries [34]; however, none explicitly account for listening costs and there is no notion of favorability. A number of

game-theoretic approaches are present in the literature (see [21]). Gilbert *et al.* [15] examine the duration for which communication between two players can be disrupted in a model with collision detection in a time-slotted network against an adversary who interferes with an unknown number of transmissions. As we do, the authors assume channel traffic is always detectable at the receiving end (i.e. silence cannot be "forged"). Pelc and Peleg [25] examine an adversary that randomly corrupts messages; we do not require the adversary to behave randomly. Awerbuch *et al.* [3] give a jamming-resistant MAC protocol in a single-hop network with an adaptive, but non-reactive, adversary. Richa *et al* [28] significantly extend this work to multi-hop networks. Dolev *et al.* [10] address a variant of the gossiping problem when multiple channels are jammed. Gilbert *et al.* [14] derive bounds on the time required for information exchange when a reactive adversary jams multiple channels. Meier *et al.* [22] examine the delay introduced by a jamming adversary for the problem of node discovery, again in a multi-channel setting. Dolev *et al.* [11] address secure communication using multiple channels with a non-reactive adversary. Recently, Dolev *et al.* [9] consider wireless synchronization in the presence of a jamming adversary.

Reliable Broadcast: Reliable broadcast has been extensively studied in the grid model [4, 7, 8, 18, 19, 30]. Listening costs are accounted for by King *et al.* [18, 30] but jamming adversaries are not considered; however, the authors introduce the *Bad Santa* problem which we use to achieve a lower bound result in Section 2.3. With a reactive jamming adversary, Bhandhari *et al.* [8] give a reliable broadcast protocol when the amount of jamming is bounded and known *a priori*; however, correct nodes must expend more energy than the adversary. Progress towards fewer broadcasts is made by Bertier *et al.* [4]; however, each node spends significant time in the costly listening state. Alistarh *et al.* [2] assume collision detection and achieve non-cryptographic authenticated reliable broadcast. They apply their result to the grid model with a reactive jamming adversary; however, nodes incur considerable listening costs.

Wired DDoS Attacks: Proposals for dealing with DDoS attacks include over-provisioning, throttling techniques, currency schemes, and others (see [31] and references therein). In currency schemes, the server provides service only to a client who pays in some form of currency. In [31], bandwidth is used as currency and, if the clients' aggregate bandwidth exceeds that of the attackers, then clients capture server resources. Our work is complementary in that it delineates bounds on the expected bandwidth required in order to guarantee that the correct clients avoid zero throughput.

2. SOLVING THE 3-PLAYER SCENARIO

Figure 1 gives the pseudocode for our 3-PLAYER SCENARIO PROTOCOL (3PSP). Each round $i \geq 2$ consists of 2 phases and the constant c is determined later. We summarize a round i:

- *Send Phase:* In each of the 2^{ci} slots: Alice sends m with probability $\frac{2}{2^i}$ for an expected total of $2^{(c-1)i+1}$ slots and Bob listens with probability $\frac{2}{2^{(c-1)i}}$ for an expected total of 2^{i+1} slots.
- *Ack Phase:* If Bob has not received m, then Bob sends a request for retransmission, req, for all 2^i slots. Alice listens in each slot with probability $4/2^i$ (note $i \geq 2$) for an expected total 4 slots.

We note that Bob need not obey 3PSP if he is controlled by Carol.

Termination Conditions: Termination conditions are important because Carol cannot be allowed to keep the players active in perpetuity while simultaneously forcing them to incur a *higher* cost. Bob terminates the protocol upon receiving m. Since Alice is not spoofed, as discussed in Section 1.1, this termination condition suf-

---

```
3-PLAYER SCENARIO PROTOCOL for round i ≥ 2

Send Phase: For each of the 2^{ci} slots do
  • Alice sends m with probability 2/2^i.
  • Bob listens with probability 2/2^{(c-1)i}.
If Bob received the message, then Bob terminates.

Ack Phase: For each of the 2^i slots do
  • Bob sends a req message.
  • Alice listens with probability 4/2^i.
If Alice listened to a slot in the Ack Phase where no req mes-
sage or blocking was detected, she terminates.
```

Figure 1: Pseudocode for 3-PLAYER SCENARIO PROTOCOL.

fices. Alice terminates if she listens to a slot in the Ack Phase which is not blocked and does not contain req message; since blocked slots are detectable by Alice (who is on the receiving end of a req message) while listening (Section 1.1), this condition suffices. In other words, Alice continues into the next round if and only if (1) Alice listens to zero slots or (2) all slots listened to by Alice in the Ack Phase contain a blocked slot or req. We highlight the two situations where this condition is met:

• *Send Failure:* Bob is correct and has not received m.

• *Ack Failure:* Bob is faulty and sends reqs, *or* Bob is correct and terminated and Carol either spoofs reqs or blocks slots to trick Alice into thinking a valid req was indeed sent and/or blocked.

Ack Failures and Cases 1 & 2: Note that an "acknowledgement" occurs via silence in at least one slot in the Ack Phase. We say an *Ack Failure* occurs when Carol blocks for all slots in the Ack Phase.

In Case 1, an Ack Failure corresponds to a critical attack that can be employed in Ack Phase after the delivery of m. Carol can avoid the listening costs in the Send Phase, and then drain Alice's energy by making it appear that Bob repeatedly did not receive m and is requesting a retransmission in the Ack Phase. This attack affects Alice only. Note that if Bob is actually correct, the attack is only effective once m is received since, if a correct Bob has not received m, a req will be issued anyway.

In Case 2, no blocking occurs in the Ack Phase and, therefore, no Ack Failure can occur. In fact, in Case 2, the Ack Phase can be shortened to a single slot where Bob sends his req and Alice listens; however, this does not change our cost analysis and our current presentation is more general.

2.1 Analysis of the 3-Party Scenario Protocol

For a given round, we say it is a *send-blocking* round if Carol blocks at least half of the slots in the Send Phase; otherwise, it is a *non-send-blocking* round. Similarly, a *ack-blocking* round is a round where Carol blocks or spoofs req messages from Bob in at least half the slots in the Ack Phase; otherwise, it is *non-ack-blocking*. Throughout, assume ceilings on the number of active slots of a player if it is not an integer.

Bounds on c: Clearly, $c > 1$ or Bob's listening probability in the Send Phase is nonsensical. For Case 1, note that if $c \geq 2$, then the expected cost to Alice is at least as much as the expected cost to a potentially faulty/spoofed Bob. If Bob happens to be faulty/spoofed, then the cost to him for an Ack Failure is less than the expected cost to Alice since a faulty/spoofed Bob will simply not listen in the Send Phase; as discussed above, we must avoid this since it admits a draining attack against Alice. Therefore, we have $1 < c < 2$. For Case 2, since Bob is guaranteed to be correct, the acceptable range is $1 < c \leq 2$.

LEMMA 1. *Consider a non-send-blocking round of* 3-PLAYER SCENARIO PROTOCOL. *The probability that Bob does not receive the message from Alice is less than* e^{-2}.

PROOF. Let $s = 2^{ci}$ be the number of slots in the Send Phase. Let p_A be the probability that Alice sends in a particular slot. Let p_B be the probability that Bob listens in a particular slot. Let $X_j = 1$ if the message is not delivered from Alice to Bob in the jth slot. Then $Pr[m$ is not delivered in the Send Phase$]=Pr[X_1 X_2 \cdots X_s = 1]=Pr[X_s = 1 \mid X_1 X_2 \cdots X_{s-1} = 1] \cdot \prod_{i=1}^{s-1} Pr[X_i = 1]$. Let $q_j = 1$ if Carol does not block in slot j; otherwise, let $q_j = 0$. The value of q_j can be selected arbitrarily by Carol. Then $Pr[X_i = 1 \mid X_1 X_2 \cdots X_{i-1} = 1] = 1 - p_A p_B q_j$ and substituting for each conditional probability, we have $Pr[X_1 X_2 \cdots X_s = 1] = (1 - p_A p_B q_1) \cdots (1 - p_A p_B q_s) = \prod_{j=1}^{s} (1 - p_A p_B q_j) \leq e^{-p_A p_B \sum_{j=1}^{s} q_j} < e^{-2}$ since $p_A p_B \sum_{j=1}^{s} q_j > (2/2^i)(2/2^{(c-1)i})$ $(s/2) = (2/2^i)(2/2^{(c-1)i})(2^{ci}/2) = 2$ since the round is not send-blocking and so Carol blocks less than $s/2$ slots. □

Note that Lemma 1 handles adaptive (but not reactive) adversaries. A simple but critical feature of tolerating adaptive adversaries is: the probability that a player is active in one slot is independent from the probability that the player is active in another slot. Therefore, knowing that a player was active for k slots in the past conveys no information about future activity. For reactive adversaries, we need only modify Lemma 1 as we do later.

LEMMA 2. *Assume that Bob is correct and there are no send-blocking rounds and no ack-blocking rounds. Then, the expected cost of each player is* $O(S + L) = O(1)$.

PROOF. Using Lemma 1, the expected cost to Alice is at most $\sum_{i=2}^{\infty} e^{-2(i-2)} \cdot (2 \cdot 2^{(c-1)i} \cdot S + 4 \cdot L) \leq \sum_{i=2}^{\infty} (e^{5-i} \cdot S + e^{2-2i} \cdot 4 \cdot L) = (e^5 \cdot S \cdot \sum_{i=2}^{\infty} e^{-i}) + (e^2 \cdot 4 \cdot L \cdot \sum_{i=2}^{\infty} e^{-2i}) = O(S+L) = O(1)$. Similarly, the expected cost to Bob is at most $\sum_{i=2}^{\infty} e^{-2(i-2)} \cdot (2^{i+1} \cdot L + 2^i \cdot S) \leq \sum_{i=2}^{\infty} (e^{5-i} \cdot L + e^{4-i} \cdot S) = O(S + L) = O(1)$ since S and L are constants. □

Now consider when attacks may occur in the Ack Phase:

LEMMA 3. *Assume that Bob has received m by round i and that round i is non-ack-blocking. Then the probability that Alice retransmits m in round $i + 1$ is less than* e^{-2}.

PROOF. Let $s = 2^i$ be the number of slots in the Ack Phase and let $p = 4/2^i$ be the probability that Alice listens in a slot. For slot j, define X_j such that $X_j = 1$ if Alice does not terminate. Then $Pr[$ Alice retransmits m in round $i+1] = Pr[X_1 X_2 \cdots X_s = 1]$. Let $q_j = 1$ if Carol does not block in slot j; otherwise, let $q_j = 0$. The q_j values are determined arbitrarily by Carol. Since Alice terminates if and only if she listens and does not detect any activity, then $Pr[X_j = 1] = (1 - pq_j)$. Therefore, $Pr[X_1 X_2 \cdots X_s = 1] \leq e^{-p \sum_{j=1}^{s} q_j} < e^{-2}$. □

LEMMA 4. *Assume there is at least one send-blocking round. Then, the expected cost to Alice is* $O(B^{(c-1)/c} + B^{(c-1)})$ *and the expected cost to a correct Bob is* $O(B^{\frac{1}{c}})$.

PROOF. We consider Case 1 and Case 2 with regards to Bob, discussed in Section 1.1. Let $i \geq 2$ be the last round which is send-blocking. Let $j \geq i$ be the last round which is ack-blocking; if no such ack-blocking round exists, then assume $j = 0$. In Case 1, the total cost to Carol is $B = \Omega(2^{ci} + 2^j)$ since J is a constant. In Case 2, only send-blocking occurs and so $B = \Omega(2^{ci} \cdot J) = \Omega(2^{ci})$.

Alice: We first calculate the expected cost to Alice prior to successfully transmitting m. In round i, Carol blocks the channel for at least $2^{ci}/2$ slots. Using Lemma 1, the expected cost to Alice prior to m being delivered is $O(2^{(c-1)i} \cdot S + 4 \cdot L) + \sum_{k=1}^{\infty} e^{-2(k-1)} \cdot (2 \cdot 2^{(c-1)(i+k)} \cdot S + 4 \cdot L) = O(2^{(c-1)i} \cdot S + L) = O(2^{(c-1)i})$

by the bounds on c and given that S and L are constants; note, this is the total cost to Alice for Case 2.

Now, using Lemma 3, we calculate the expected cost to Alice after delivery; this addresses ack-blocking rounds possible only in Case 1. By assumption, the last ack-blocking round occurs in round j and therefore Alice's expected cost is $O(2^{(c-1)j} \cdot S + 4 \cdot L) + \sum_{k=1}^{\infty} e^{-2(k-1)} \cdot (2 \cdot 2^{(c-1)(j+k)} \cdot S + 4 \cdot L) = O(2^{(c-1)j} \cdot S + L)$ by the bounds on c. Therefore, the total expected cost to Alice is $O(2^{(c-1)i} \cdot S + 2^{(c-1)j} \cdot S + L) = O(2^{(c-1)i} + 2^{(c-1)j})$. Since $B = \Omega(2^{ci} + 2^j)$, this cost as a function of B is $O(B^{(c-1)/c} + B^{(c-1)})$.

Bob: Finally, assume Bob is correct. Using Lemma 1, his expected cost prior to receiving m is $O(2^{i+1} \cdot L + 2^i \cdot S) + \sum_{k=1}^{\infty} e^{-2(k-1)} \cdot (2 \cdot 2^{i+k} \cdot L + 2^{i+k} \cdot S) = O(2^i \cdot L + 2^i \cdot S) = O(2^i)$ since S and L are constants. Thus, the expected cost for Bob as a function of B is $O(B^{1/c})$. $\square$

We now give the proof for Theorem 1 stated in Section 1.3:

Proof of Theorem 1: In Case 1, Lemma 4 tells us that the expected cost to Alice and Bob in terms of B is $O(B^{(c-1)/c} + B^{(c-1)})$ and $O(B^{1/c})$, respectively. Therefore, the exponents of interest which control the cost to each player are $(c-1)/c, c-1$, and $1/c$. The value of c that should be chosen must minimize $\max\{(c-1)/c, c-1, 1/c\}$ since we are interested in fair protocols. Given that $1 < c < 2$, we have $1/c > (c-1)/c$. Therefore, we solve for c in $c - 1 = 1/c$, this gives $c = (1 + \sqrt{5})/2$ which is the golden ratio. By Lemma 2 and the above argument, the expected cost to each player is $O(B^{\varphi-1} + 1)$. In Case 2, Lemma 4 tells us that Alice's expected cost in terms of B is $O(B^{(c-1)/c})$ the exponents of interest are simply $(c-1)/c$ and $1/c$; minimizing them yields $c = 2$. Therefore, the cost to each player is $O(B^{1/2} + 1)$.

Finally, define latency to be the number of slots prior that occur to termination by both correct players. Consider how many non-send-blocking or non-ack-blocking rounds *either* player may endure before terminating successfully; let X denote the random variable for this number of rounds. Then, $E[X] \leq 1/(1 - e^{-2}) = O(1)$ which translates into $O(1)$ time slots consumed by non-send or non-ack-blocking rounds. Now consider the send- or ack-blocking rounds; note that Carol is limited to at most $\lg(B) + O(1)$ such rounds which translates to $O(B^{\varphi})$ time slots. Therefore, regardless of how Carol blocks, the expected number of time slots prior to successful termination is $O(B^{\varphi})$. $\square$

2.2 Tolerating a Reactive Adversary

Consider a reactive adversary Carol who can detect channel activity without cost, and then block; this ability is possible in WSNs (see Section 3.1). Carol can now detect that m is sent in the Send Phase and block it without fail. To address this powerful adversary, we consider the case where critical data, m, and more often, non-critical data m', is sent over the channel by other participants in addition to Alice and Bob. Carol can detect the traffic; however, she cannot discern whether it is m or m' without listening to a portion of the communication (such as packet header information).

In a slot where channel activity is detected, even if Carol listens for a portion of the message, she incurs a substantial cost. Therefore, the cost to Carol is proportional to the number of messages to which she listens. Importantly, in the presence of m', Carol's ability to detect traffic for free is unhelpful since m' provides "camouflage" for m. Certainly Carol may block *all active slots* to prevent transmission of m; however, this is no different than blocking *all slots* in our original 3-Player Scenario.

This setting corresponds to situations where communication occurs steadily between many participants or via several distributed applications, and Carol wishes to target only a critical few. If m

and m' are sent over the channel in the same slot, the two messages collide and Bob receives neither. Define a slot as *active* if either m or m' is sent in that slot. For this result only, redefine a send-blocking round as one where Carol listens or blocks for at least a $1/3$-fraction of the *active* slots; otherwise, it is a *non-send-blocking round*. We provide a result analagous to Lemma 1.

LEMMA 5. *Let Carol be an adaptive and reactive adversary. Then, in a non-send-blocking round of the* 3-PLAYER SCENARIO PROTOCOL, *the probability that Bob does not receive m from Alice is at most e^{-2}.*

PROOF. Let $x = 2^{ci}$ be the number of slots in the Send Phase. Consider the set of slots used by all participants other than Alice. We assume these participants pick their slots at random to send, so that for any slot the probability is $2/3$ that the slot is chosen by at least one of them. Since we assume these messages m' are sent independently at random, then Chernoff bounds imply that w.h.p., i.e., $1 - 1/x^{c'}$ for a constants c', ϵ and sufficiently large x, the number of slots y during which m' is sent is greater than $(2x/3)(1 - \epsilon)$ where x is the total number of slots in a phase. In the same way, assume the number of slots in which Alice sends is at least $a = (1 - \delta)xp_A = (1 - \delta)2^{(c-1)i+1}$ with probability $1 - 1/x^{c''}$ for a constant δ, c'' and sufficiently large x. The number of active slots sent by Alice or other participants is at least y.

By definition of a non-send-blocking round, Carol listens to or blocks less than $x/3$ (active) slots. As Carol has no information about the source of a message sent in an active slot until she listens to it, her choice is independent of the source of the message. Given a slot that Alice sends on, there is at least a $1 - (x/3)/y$ chance it will not be listened to or blocked by Carol. The probability that this slot will not be used by another participant is $1/3$ and the probability that Bob will listen to the slot is p_B. Hence the probability of a successful transmission from Alice to Bob on a slot which Alice sends on is at least $(1 - x/(3y))(1/3)p_B = (1 - 1/(2(1-\epsilon)))(1/3)p_B \geq (1/6)p_B$ when $y > (1-\epsilon)(2x/3)$. The probability that all messages that Alice sends fail to be delivered is at most $(1 - p_B/6)^a - 2/x^{c''}$ where the last term is the probability that y or a is small and $c'' > 0$ is a constant. Redefine $p_B = 6/((1-\delta)2^{(c-1)i})$; note that this constant factor increase in the listening probability does not change our asymptotic results and our analysis in Section 2.1 proceeds almost identically. Therefore, we then have $(1 - p_B/6)^a - 2/x^{c''} \leq e^{-2}$. $\square$

The 3-PLAYER SCENARIO PROTOCOL can be modified so that the initial value of i is large enough to render the error arising from the use of Chernoff bounds sufficiently small; we omit these details. Also, the required level of channel traffic detected by Carol is flexible and different values can be accomodated if the players' probabilities for sending/listening are modified appropriately in the 3-PLAYER SCENARIO PROTOCOL; our results hold asymptotically.

We emphasize that Lemma 3 does not require modification. Carol cannot decide to block only when Alice is listening since detecting when a node is listening is impossible. Alternately, Carol cannot silence a `req` through (reactive) blocking since this is still interpreted as a retransmission request. Using Lemma 5, Theorem 1 follows as before. Finally, we note that the conclusion of our argument aligns with claims put forth in empirical results on reactive jamming in WSNs; that is, such behavior does not necessarily result in a more energy-efficient attack because the adversary must still be listening to the channel for broadcasts prior to committing itself to their disruption [33].

2.3 On Latency & Lower Bounds

King *et al.* [18, 30] introduced the *Bad Santa* problem which is described as follows. A child is presented with K boxes, one after another. When presented with each box, the child must immediately decide whether or not to open it. If the child does not to open a box, it can never be revisited. Half the boxes have presents in them, but the decision as to which boxes have presents is made by an adversarial Santa who wants the child to open as many empty boxes as possible. The goal is for the child to obtain a present *with probability 1*, while opening the smallest expected number of boxes. In [18, 30], the authors prove a lower bound of $\Omega(K^{0.5})$ on the expected number of opened boxes.

THEOREM 5. *Any algorithm that solves the 3-Player Scenario with $o(B^{0.5})$ cost to Bob must have a latency exceeding $2B$.*

PROOF. A lower bound for the 3-Player Scenario is complicated by the possibility that the strategies of Alice and Bob may adapt over time; for example, they may change depending on how Carol blocks. To address this, we assume a more powerful Bob. Specifically, assume that communication of m occurs if Bob is able to find an unblocked time slot in which to listen *or* to send. Furthermore, assume Bob can tell when he has found such a slot once he listens or sends in that slot. Therefore, such a Bob is at least as powerful as the Bob in the 3-Player Scenario.

Now, if Carol has a budget of size B, we ask: Does Bob have a strategy with $o(B^{0.5})$ expected active slots such that, with probability 1, he finds at least one unblocked slot within $2B$ slots? Assume that such a strategy exists and consider the Bad Santa problem on $2B$ boxes. Using Bob's strategy, the child is guaranteed to obtain a present with probability 1 while opening $o(B^{0.5})$ boxes in expectation. However, this contradicts the $\Omega(B^{0.5})$ lower bound result in [18] and the result follows. □

This result illustrates a relationship between the Bad Santa problem and the 3-Player Scenario, and it provides some insight into why our protocol has a worst case latency of $\omega(B)$ slots.

3. JAMMING RESISTANCE IN WSNs

The shared wireless medium of sensor networks renders them vulnerable to jamming attacks. A jamming attack occurs when an attacker transmits noise at high energy, possibly concurrently with a (legitimate) transmission, such that communication is disrupted within the area of interference. Consequently, this behavior threatens the availability of sensor networks.

3.1 Rationale for the 3-Player Scenario

Wireless network cards offer states such as *sleep, receive (or listen)* and *transmit (or send)*. While the sleep state requires negligible power, the cost of the send and listen states are roughly equivalent and dominate the operating cost of a device. For example, the send and listen costs for the Telos motes are 38mW and 35mW, respectively (note $S \approx L$) and the sleep state cost is 15μW [26]; therefore, the cost of the send/listen state is more than a factor of 2000 greater and the sleep state cost is negligible. Disruption may not require jamming an entire slot so we set $J < S$ and assume a small m such that J and S are within a constant factor of each other; larger messages can be sent piecewise. In our protocols, we account for both send and receive costs. Throughout, when a node is not active, we assume it is in the energy-efficient sleep state.

Slots: There is a single channel and a time division multiple access (TDMA)-like medium access control (MAC) protocol; that is, a time-slotted network. For example, the well-known LEACH [16]

protocol is TDMA-based. For simplicity, a *global* broadcast schedule is assumed; however, this is likely avoidable if nodes maintain multiple schedules. Even then, global scheduling has been demonstrated by experimental work in [20].

A blocked slot occurs when Carol jams. Clear channel assessment (CCA), which subsumes carrier sensing, is a common feature on devices for detecting such events [27]. Collisions are only detectable by the receiver. When a collision occurs, a correct node discards any received data. The absence of channel activity cannot be forged; this aligns with the empirical work by Niculescu [23] who shows that channel interference increases linearly with the combined rate of the sources. Finally, we also note that several theoretical models feature collision detection (see [2, 3, 8, 15, 28]).

On Reactive Adversaries: CCA is performed via the radio chip using the *received signal strength indicator* (RSSI). If the RSSI value is below a clear channel threshold, then the channel is assumed to be clear. Such detection consumes on the order of 10^{-6} W which is three orders of magnitude smaller than the send/listen costs; therefore, Carol can detect activity (but not message content) at essentially zero-cost. Listening to even a small portion of a message costs on the order of milliwatts and our argument from Section 2.2 now applies.

Cryptographic Authentication: We assume that messages can be authenticated. Therefore, Carol cannot spoof Alice; however, Bob's req can essentially be spoofed by an Ack-Failure (as discussed in Section 2) which, along with jamming, makes the problem non-trivial. Several results show how light-weight cryptographic authentication can be implemented in sensor networks(see [12]); therefore, it is important to consider its impact as we do here. However, the adversary may capture a limited number of players (such as Bob in the 3-Player Scenario); these players are said to suffer a Byzantine fault and are controlled by the adversary. Given this attack, we emphasize that, while we assume a shared key to achieve authentication, attempts to share a secret send/listen schedule between Alice and Bob allows Carol to manipulate players in ways that are problematic.

3.2 Local Broadcast & Guaranteed Latency

Our protocol LOCAL BROADCAST handles the general single-hop broadcast situation where Alice sends m to n neighboring receivers within her transmission range. At first glance, this seems achievable by having each receiver execute an instance of 3PSP with Alice. However, the expected active time for Alice is an $\Omega(n)$-factor larger than any correct receiver; thus, this is unfair. Furthermore, this protocol has poor latency. Here, we give a fast protocol that is both fair and favorable up to small polylogarithmic factors.

Our pseudocode is given in Figure 2. The probabilities for sending and listening are modified and there are two more phases (the Deterministic Send and Deterministic Ack Phases) where players act deterministically. Note that req messages can collide in the Probabilistic Ack Phase and will certainly collide in the Deterministic Ack Phase. This is correct as such a collision is due to either jamming or multiple receivers (correct or faulty) requesting a retransmission; this is fine and Alice will resend. LOCAL BROADCAST takes in as arguments the message m, the sender (Alice) and the set of receivers R_{Alice}. If the adversary jams, then none of the correct receivers receive m in that slot.

An important property of LOCAL BROADCAST is that there is a guaranteed bound on the latency. This is useful for achieving reliable broadcast in multi-hop networks in the next section.

LEMMA 6. *Alice and all correct receivers terminate* LOCAL BROADCAST *in $25 \cdot (B + \ln^{\varphi-1} n)^{\varphi}$ time slots.*

Figure 2: Pseudocode for LOCAL BROADCAST.

PROOF. The deterministic phases play a key role in establishing the bound on latency. If the adversary is not active for all slots in the deterministic Send Phase, then all correct receivers obtain m. Once all correct receivers terminate, the adversary must be active in all slots of the deterministic Ack Phase in order to prevent Alice from terminating. Therefore, prior to successful termination of all correct players (including Alice), the adversary is active for at least $2^{(\varphi-1)i+1}$ slots per round i in Epochs 2 & 4. For $d = \lg(4 \ln n)$, we seek the number of rounds ρ such that $\sum_{i=d}^{\rho} 2^{(\varphi-1)i+1} \geq B$ which yields that $\rho \geq \varphi \lg(B + 2^{\varphi-1} \ln^{\varphi-1} n)$ rounds suffices to exhaust the adversary (we are not being exact). Each round i has at most $4 \cdot 2^{\varphi \cdot i+1}$ slots so $\rho \leq 25 \cdot (B + \ln^{\varphi-1} n)^{\varphi+1}$ slots. $\square$

LEMMA 7. *Assume that Carol's receivers are active for a total of B slots. Then, LOCAL BROADCAST guarantees communication of m to all correct nodes and has the following properties:*

- *The expected cost to Alice is $O(B^{\varphi-1} \ln n + \ln^{\varphi} n)$. Therefore, for $B = \omega(\ln^{\varphi+1} n)$, Alice spends asymptotically less than Carol.*

- *The expected cost to any correct receiver is $O(B^{\varphi-1} + \ln n)$. Therefore, for $B = \omega(\ln n)$, Bob spends asymptotically less than Carol.*

The value n is the number of devices within the broadcast range of Alice. For a determined adversary, we expect $B > n$; that is, for an adversary intent on preventing communication, the number of time slots jammed will likely exceed the number of neighbors. Therefore, $B \gg \ln^{\varphi+1} n$. In this case (actually for $B \geq \ln^{\varphi-1} n$), the latency is $O(B^{\varphi+1})$ and, noting that Carol can prevent transmission for at least B slots, this is within an $O(B^{\varphi})$-factor of the optimal latency. By this and Lemmas 6 & 7, Theorem 2 follows.

3.3 Mitigating Unfavorable Listening Costs

Reliable broadcast has been extensively studied in the multi-hop grid model [5–7, 19, 30], particularly with a jamming adversary [2,4,8]. Reliable broadcast is possible when t Byzantine nodes can each corrupt at most n_c transmissions [8]. Unfortunately, the protocol of [8], and the improvement by [4], requires that *correct nodes possess much more energy than the Byzantine nodes*. In particular, while the sending costs are improved in [4], both [4,8] allow

the adversary to force a correct node to *listen* for $\Omega(t \cdot n_c)$ slots (listening costs in [2] are similar). In contrast, each Byzantine node is active for n_c. This $\Omega(t)$-factor advantage affords the adversary a DDoS attack since these previous protocols are unfavorable.

Setup: Here, each node $p(x, y)$ is situated at (x, y) in a grid. The dealer d is located at $(0, 0)$ and seeks to propagate m to all correct nodes in the network. When a node p sends a message, all listening nodes in $N(p)$ receive the message (analogous results will hold for the Euclidean metric [6]). There are $t < (r/2)(2r + 1)$ Byzantine nodes in any neighborhood. For any correct node p, the adversary can use its t Byzantine nodes in $N(p)$ to jam for up to $B_0 = t \cdot n_c$ slots total. There is a global schedule (obeyed by the correct nodes) that assigns each node a slot for broadcasting.

Unlike the single-hop case, here the amount of jamming in a neighborhood is upper bounded by B_0 and known. This is required in [4,8] and a similar assumption is made in [3,28]. B_0 represents the number of times a Byzantine node can deviate from the global schedule within some time frame before being identified and subjected to defensive techniques (see [32]). Not exceeding B_0 in each time frame allows the adversary to attack throughout the lifetime of the network and we pessimistically assume that B_0 is large so that the adversary may inflict sustained attacks.

We incorporate LOCAL BROADCAST into the protocol of Bhandari & Vaidya [6] to achieve the first favorable reliable broadcast protocol. The hard latency bound of LOCAL BROADCAST is crucial for establishing when nodes send and listen in order to propagate m. Due to space constraints, we defer our protocol to a complete version of the paper; however, we can show the following:

LEMMA 8. *Assume for each node p, $t < (r/2)(2r + 1)$ nodes in $N(p)$ are Byzantine and used by Carol to disrupt p's communications for $\beta \leq B_0$ time slots. Let $C = \{$Nodes q at (x, y) s.t. $(-r \leq x \leq r) \wedge (y \geq 0)\}$ be a corridor in the grid. There is a protocol for reliable broadcast in C with the following properties:*

- *If $\beta = O(r^2 \ln^{\varphi+1} r)$, then the expected cost to each each correct node is $O(r^2 \ln^{\varphi+2} r)$.*

- *If $\beta = \omega(r^2 \ln^{\varphi+1} r)$, then the protocol is fair and the expected cost to each correct node is $O(r^{2(2-\varphi)} \beta^{\varphi-1} \ln r + r^2 \ln^{\varphi} r) = o(\beta)$; that is, the expected cost to each correct node is asymptotically less than that incurred by Carol.*

For ease of exposition, our result applies to a single corridor; however, this is sufficient to prove reliable broadcast in the *entire network* since the grid can be covered piecewise by such corridors.

3.3.1 Reliable Broadcast for General Topologies

In this section, we apply our results to reliable broadcast in an arbitrary graph $G = (V, E)$. Pelc & Peleg [24] examine the broadcast protocol of Koo [19], which the authors call the *Certified Propagation Algorithm* (CPA), with the aim of establishing conditions for which it achieves reliable broadcast on general graphs. Again, CPA addresses the case where all nodes obey a global broadcast schedule (i.e. there is no jamming adversary). The authors define $X(p, d)$ to be the number of nodes in p's neighborhood $N(p)$ that are closer to d than p and then introduce the parameter $X(G) = \min\{X(p, d) \mid p, d \in V, (p, d) \notin E\}$. One of their main results is that, for *any* graph G with dealer d such that $t < X(G)/2$, CPA achieves reliable broadcast; although, it does not always achieve optimal fault tolerance. For example, CPA cannot tolerate the optimal number of faults in the grid; however, we address CPA because its generality is powerful.

283

Figure 3: Pseudocode for FCPA.

3.3.2 A Favorable Protocol in General Topologies

For each node p, define $X(p)$ to be those $X(p, d)$ nodes closer to the dealer than p. We assume each node knows the full network topology and the location of the dealer (i.e. preprogrammed before deployment, or learned robustly after deployment). Call a single iteration of the global broadcast schedule a *cycle*. Time is measured from when the dealer first broadcasts m in cycle 1. Under CPA, regardless of the worst case delay imposed by the adversary, there is a cycle where p must have received at least $t + 1$ copies of m from distinct correct nodes in $X(p)$ allowing p to commit to m; denote this cycle by s_p. In any execution of reliable broadcast, p may actually be able to commit prior to s_p, but s_p is the maximum cycle by which p is guaranteed the information it needs to commit to m regardless of how the adversarial nodes behave.

Each node p can calculate s_p. This is done by simulating the propagation of m using CPA. In this simulation, each node p has the maximum $t = X(G)/2 - 1$ Byzantine nodes in $X(p)$ and these Byzantine nodes send their faulty messages prior to the $t + 1$ correct responses in order delay propagation of m for as long as possible. By assuming that every $X(p)$ has the maximum number of Byzantine nodes, the actual placement of the Byzantine nodes in G does not affect the worst case broadcast time s_p. In tracing this propagation, any node can calculate s_p for any node p.

Consider the following minor modifications to CPA: each correct node p (1) only listens to $q \in X(p)$ in cycle $s_q + 1$, and (2) only sends its commit message in cycle $s_p + 1$. In all other slots, p is sleeping; call this protocol CPA_0. These minor changes synchronize the sending/listening and allow nodes to otherwise sleep instead of perpetually listening. The following lemma is clear:

LEMMA 9. *If CPA achieves reliable broadcast, then CPA_0 achieves reliable broadcast.*

Each node requires knowledge of the full network topology and the location of the dealer. Clearly, it is possible to identify $X(p)$. In Figure 3, we provide pseudocode for a fair and favorable reliable broadcast algorithm FAVORABLE CPA, abbreviated FCPA, that tolerates the jamming adversary described in Theorem 3; here, $D = 25 \cdot (B_0 + \ln^{\varphi-1} n)^\varphi$.

LEMMA 10. *Assume CPA achieves reliable broadcast on a graph G. Then, FCPA guarantees reliable broadcast on G.*

PROOF. Using FCPA, we claim that every correct node can commit by cycle $s_p \cdot D$. To prove this, assume the opposite: that some node p does not commit to the correct message m by cycle $s_p \cdot D$. Then, there is some correct node $q \in X(p)$ that: (1) could not commit to m by time slot $s_q \cdot D$ (and could not send p a committment message), or (2) committed to a wrong message (and sent a wrong message to p). The time for any node u to send its commit message to v is at most D cycles by Lemma 6. Therefore, if q cannot commit by cycle $s_q \cdot D$ in FCPA, then q cannot commit by cycle s_q in CPA_0; therefore, CPA_0 fails to achieve reliable broadcast. Similarly, if q commits to the wrong message in FCPA, then it would also commit to the wrong message in CPA_0, and so CPA_0 fails. However, if CPA_0 fails to achieve reliable broadcast, then by the contrapositive of Lemma 9, this contradicts the assumption that CPA achieves reliable broadcast. $\square$

Combining Lemma 10 with the cost analysis below yields the results stated in Theorem 3 for general graphs.

Theorem 3 – Cost Analysis: In both of our protocols, each correct node p partakes in an execution of LOCAL BROADCAST $O(t)$ times as a sender and receiver; let k denote the total number of such executions. For the ith such execution, let τ_i be the number of slots for which the adversary is active for $i = 1, ..., k$. Denote Carol's total active time by $\beta = \sum_{i=1}^{k} \tau_i \le B_0$. Consider two cases:

Case I: Assume $\beta = \sum_{i=1}^{k} \tau_i = O(t \ln^{\varphi+1} t)$ slots over all k executions of LOCAL BROADCAST involving p. For each execution, p incurs $O(\tau_i^{\varphi-1} \ln t + \ln^\varphi t)$ cost in expectation by Theorem 2. Therefore, over $k = O(t)$ executions, p's expected total cost is $O((\sum_i^k \tau_i^{\varphi-1}) \ln t + t \ln^\varphi t) = O((\sum_i^k \tau_i) \ln t + t \ln^\varphi t) = O(\beta \ln t + t \ln^\varphi t)) = O(t \ln^{\varphi+2} t)$.

Case II: Otherwise, $\beta = \sum_{i=1}^{k} \tau_i = \omega(t \ln^{\varphi+1} t)$. By a corollary of Jensen's inequality for concave functions, for a concave function f, $f(\frac{1}{k} \sum_{i=1}^{k} \tau_i) \ge \frac{1}{k} \sum_{i=1}^{k} f(\tau_i)$. Since $f(\tau) = \tau^{\varphi-1}$ is concave, it follows that $\sum_{i=1}^{k} \tau_i^{\varphi-1} \le k(\frac{1}{k} \sum_{i=1}^{k} \tau_i)^{\varphi-1} = k^{2-\varphi} (\sum_{i=1}^{k} \tau_i)^{\varphi-1}$. Therefore, the total expected cost to p over $k = O(t)$ executions is $O((\sum_{i=1}^{k} \tau_i^{\varphi-1}) \ln t) + O(t \ln^\varphi t) = O(t^{2-\varphi}(\sum_{i=1}^{k} \tau_i)^{\varphi-1} \ln t) + O(t \ln^\varphi t) = O(t^{(2-\varphi)} \beta^{\varphi-1} \ln t + t \ln^\varphi t) = o(\beta)$. Therefore, p's expected cost is less than Carol's. Substituting $t = O(r^2)$ into the above analysis yields the favorability result above in Lemma 8 and, together, gives our result for the grid model in Theorem 3. $\square$

4. APPLICATION-LEVEL DDoS ATTACKS

Typically in application-level DDoS attacks, a number of compromised clients, known collectively as a *botnet*, are employed to overwhelm a server with requests. These botnets have become commercialized with botmasters renting out time to individuals for the purposes of launching attacks. We assume a model of botnet attacks similar to that described by Walfish *et al.* [31]. Here, a request is cheap for a client to issue, expensive for the server to service, and all requests incur the same computational cost. There is a high-capacity communication channel and the crucial bottleneck is the server's inability to process a heavy request load.

The client rate is g requests per second. The aggregate botnet rate is R requests per second and this is assumed to be both relatively constant and the botnet's maximum possible rate. If the server is overloaded, it randomly drops excess requests. In this case, the good clients only receive a fraction $g/(g + R)$ of the servers resources; it is assumed that $R \gg g$ so that $g/(g + R)$ is very small.

Walfish *et al.* [31] propose a protocol SPEAK-UP for resisting DDoS attacks by having clients increase their sending rate such that their aggregate bandwidth G is on the same order as that of R. Since botnet machines are assumed to have already "maxed-out" their available bandwidth in attacking, SPEAK-UP greatly increases the chance that the server processes a legitimate request since $G/(G + R) \gg g/(g + R)$. A crucial component of SPEAK-UP is a front-end to the server called the "thinner" which controls which requests are seen by the server and asks a client to retry her request if it was previously dropped.

4.1 Our Speak-Up-*Like* Protocol

We employ Case 2 of our 3-Player Scenario to achieve a SPEAK-UP-*like* algorithm with provable guarantees. Bandwidth (upstream and downstream rates in bits per second) is our measure of cost and our results should be interpreted as quantifying the expected upstream bandwidth required by the client and the expected downstream bandwidth with which the server should be provisioned.

The client plays the role of Alice where the message is a request; the server plays the role of Bob. This application falls into Case 2 of Theorem 1: a DDoS attack targets the server while communications from the server to the clients are not disrupted. The client and server are assumed to be synchronized such that they always agree on the current round and a maximum round number is set *a priori*. Such synchronization is possible over Internet-connected machines and the maximum round value should be set to account for the level of DDoS resistance the participants wish to have; for most attacks, R is in the low hundreds of Mbits/second [29]. We give an overview of our protocol.

Send Phase: Each Send Phase occurs over a uniform and fixed duration Δ; for simplicity, we set $\Delta = 1$ second, and the slot length changes in each round appropriately. The client sends in each slot with probability $2/2^i$ with an expected 2^i upstream bits per second. The server listens in each slot with probability $2/2^i$ for an expected 2^i downstream bits per second. If the received traffic substantially exceeds 2^i, requests are dropped; probabilistic listening and traffic measurement on the server side can be performed by the thinner.

Note that in each round, the client increases her sending rate in the Send Phase to "speak up". A correct client that reaches its bandwidth limit remains at this limit for the remainder of the protocol. When the maximum round number is reached, the clients maintain their sending rate until the thinner informs them that the attack has ended. We define a blocked slot as one where Carol overwhelms the server with requests and the client's request is dropped in that slot. Define a send-blocked phase as one where Carol blocks at least $2^{2i}/2$ slots; therefore, Carol uses an upstream bandwidth of *at least* $2^{2i}/2$ bits per second. As in [31], if the thinner drops a request, it immediately asks the client to retry in the next round.

Ack Phase: The server does not increase its sending rate per round (only the client speaks up) since there are no attacks in the Ack Phase for Case 2. This simplifies the Ack Phase as mentioned in Section 2 in our discussion of Ack Failures; the server simply returns the requested data to the client at some reasonable rate.

The constants $S = J$ and L correspond to the rate of 1 bit per second. We assume upstream and downstream bandwidth are capped; this is true of residential Internet packages, as well as hosted services. In the case of residential service, upstream bandwidth is scarcer than downstream bandwidth, while servers are generally well-provisioned for both; this can be reflected in our cost constants. By Case 2 of Theorem 1 we have:

COROLLARY 1. *If Carol uses bandwidth R to attack, then the client's request is serviced, and the expected bandwidth (upstream and downstream) used by the client and the server is $O(R^{0.5})$.*

Bob can represent multiple good clients. Again, synchronization with the server is assumed; clients joining at different times are informed by the thinner of the current round. In order to be guaranteed *some* of the server's resources, the clients' expected aggregate

bandwidth is $G = \Omega(R^{0.5})$. Therefore, our result quantifies the minimum expected aggregate upstream bandwidth for clients and the expected downstream bandwidth for the server required to ensure that total censorship is averted; in contrast, SPEAK-UP cannot make such a guarantee. This is useful for applications where a critical update or warning must be dessiminated, and delivery to even a handful of clients is sufficient since they may share it with others (via multicast, peer-to-peer distribution, etc.).

As with SPEAK-UP, the probability of a legitimate request being serviced is still $G/(G + R)$. In addition to admitting an analysis, our iterative approach of geometrically increasing the aggregrate bandwidth should mitigate attempts by Carol at launching short duration DDoS attacks in order to provoke a steep and disruptive traffic increase from correct clients. Our protocol is fair as described in Section 1.2 – the *aggregate* requirement of the bandwidth constrained clients is asymptotically equal to that of the well-provisioned server. Restating our result above in the context of multiple clients yields Theorem 4.

Finally, in order to achieve the same level of denial-of-service against a server that is defended by our protocol, Carol must procure a much larger botnet in order to obtain the necessary bandwidth; however, this comes at a cost. For example, one study found the cost of a single bot to be between $2 and $25 [13]. Therefore, since Carol's bandwidth requirements increase quadratically, her monetary costs increase significantly with the use of our protocol.

5. CONCLUSION

We have examined an abstract model of conflict over a communication channel. In the 3-Player Scenario, we remark that there is an $O(1)$ up-front cost per execution of our protocol when there are no send- or ack-blocking attacks. Similarly, there are small up-front costs for our other favorable protocols. This is the (tolerable) price for communication in the presence of a powerful adversary, even if that adversary is not necessarily very active. The golden ratio arises naturally from our analysis, and its appearance in this adversarial setting is interesting; an important open question is whether $\Omega(B^{\varphi-1} + 1)$ cost is necessary.

Also of interest is determining whether there are fair and favorable algorithms for other types of problems. An interesting starting point would be the problem of conflict over dissemination of an idea in a social network, using the models of Kempe *et al.* [17].

Acknowledgements: We thank Martin Karsten, Srinivasan Keshav, and James Horey for their valuable comments.

6. REFERENCES

[1] E. Addley and J. Halliday. WikiLeaks Supporters Disrupt Visa and MasterCard Sites in 'Operation Payback'. www.guardian.co.uk/world/2010/dec/08/wikileaks-visa-mastercard-operation-payback, 2010.

[2] D. Alistarh, S. Gilbert, R. Guerraoui, Z. Milosevic, and C. Newport. Securing Your Every Bit: Reliable Broadcast in Byzantine Wireless Networks. In *Proceedings of the Symposium on Parallelism in Algorithms and Architectures (SPAA)*, pages 50–59, 2010.

[3] B. Awerbuch, A. Richa, and C. Scheideler. A Jamming - Resistant MAC Protocol for Single-Hop Wireless Networks. In *Proceedings of the 27th ACM Symposium on Principles of Distributed Computing (PODC)*, pages 45–54, 2008.

[4] M. Bertier, A.-M. Kermarrec, and G. Tan. Message-Efficient Byzantine Fault-Tolerant Broadcast in a Multi-Hop Wireless Sensor Network. In *Proceedings of the International*

Conference on Distributed Computing Systems (ICDCS), pages 408–417, 2010.

[5] V. Bhandari and N. H. Vaidya. On Reliable Broadcast in a Radio Network. In *Proceedings of the ACM Symposium on Principles of Distributed Computing (PODC)*, pages 138–147, 2005.

[6] V. Bhandari and N. H. Vaidya. On Reliable Broadcast in a Radio Network: A Simplified Characterization. Technical report, CSL, UIUC, May 2005.

[7] V. Bhandari and N. H. Vaidya. Reliable Broadcast in Wireless Networks with Probabilistic Failures. In *INFOCOM*, pages 715–723, 2007.

[8] V. Bhandhari, J. Katz, C.-Y. Koo, and N. Vaidya. Reliable Broadcast in Radio Networks: The Bounded Collision Case. In *Proceedings of the ACM Symposium on Principles of Distributed Computing (PODC)*, pages 258 – 264, 2006.

[9] S. Dolev, S. Gilbert, R. Guerraoui, F. Kuhn, and C. Newport. The Wireless Synchronization Problem. In *Proceedings of the 28th ACM Symposium on Principles of Distributed Computing (PODC)*, pages 190–199, 2009.

[10] S. Dolev, S. Gilbert, R. Guerraoui, and C. Newport. Gossiping in a Multi-channel Radio Network: An Oblivious Approach to Coping with Malicious Interference. In *Proceedings of the International Symposium on Distributed Computing (DISC)*, pages 208–222, 2007.

[11] S. Dolev, S. Gilbert, R. Guerraoui, and C. Newport. Secure communication over radio channels. In *Proceedings of the Symposium on Principles of Distributed Computing (PODC)*, pages 105–114, 2008.

[12] T. Eisenbarth, S. Kumar, C. Paar, A. Poschmann, and L. Uhsadel. A Survey of Lightweight-Cryptography Implementations. *IEEE Design & Test of Computers*, 24:522–533, 2007.

[13] J. Franklin, V. Paxson, A. Perrig, and S. Savage. An Inquiry into the Nature and Causes of the Wealth of Internet Miscreants. In 14th *ACM Conference on Computer and Communications Security*, pages 375–388, 2007.

[14] S. Gilbert, R. Guerraoui, D. Kowalski, and C. Newport. Interference-resilient information exchange. In *INFOCOM*, pages 2249–2257, 2009.

[15] S. Gilbert, R. Guerraoui, and C. C. Newport. Of Malicious Motes and Suspicious Sensors: On the Efficiency of Malicious Interference in Wireless Networks. In *International Conference On Principles Of Distributed Systems (OPODIS)*, pages 215–229, 2006.

[16] W. R. Heinzelman, A. Chandrakasan, and H. Balakrishnan. Energy-Efficient Communication Protocol for Wireless Microsensor Networks. In *HICSS*, pages 3005–3014, 2000.

[17] D. Kempe, J. Kleinberg, and É. Tardos. Maximizing the spread of influence through a social network. In *Proceedings of the 9th ACM SIGKDD International Conference on Knowledge Discovery and Data Mining*, pages 137–146. ACM, 2003.

[18] V. King, C. Phillips, J. Saia, and M. Young. Sleeping on the Job: Energy-Efficient and Robust Broadcast for Radio Networks. In *Proceedings of the ACM Symposium on Principles of Distributed Computing (PODC)*, pages 243–252, 2008.

[19] C.-Y. Koo. Broadcast in Radio Networks Tolerating Byzantine Adversarial Behavior. In *Proceedings of the ACM Symposium on Principles of Distributed Computing (PODC)*, pages 275–282, 2004.

[20] Y. Li, W. Ye, and J. Heidemann. Energy and Latency Control in Low Duty Cycle MAC Protocols. In *Proceedings of the IEEE Wireless Communications and Networking Conference (WCNC)*, pages 676–682, 2005.

[21] M. H. Manshaei, Q. Zhu, T. Alpcan, T. Başar, and J.-P. Hubaux. Game Theory Meets Network Security and Privacy. Technical report, Ecole Polytechnique Fédérale de Lausanne (EPFL), September 2010.

[22] D. Meier, Y. A. Pignolet, S. Schmid, and R. Wattenhofer. Speed Dating Despite Jammers. In *Proceedings of the International Conference on Distributed Computing in Sensor Systems (DCOSS)*, pages 1–14, 2009.

[23] D. Niculescu. Interference Map for 802.11 Networks. In *Proceedings of the Internet Measurement Conference (IMC)*, pages 339–350, 2007.

[24] A. Pelc and D. Peleg. Broadcasting with Locally Bounded Byzantine Faults. *Information Processing Letters*, 93(3):109–115, 2005.

[25] A. Pelc and D. Peleg. Feasibility and Complexity of Broadcasting with Random Transmission Failures. In *Proceedings of the ACM Symposium on Principles of Distributed Computing (PODC)*, pages 334–341, 2005.

[26] J. Polastre, R. Szewczyk, and D. Culler. Telos: Enabling Ultra-Low Power Wireless Research. In *IPSN*, 2005.

[27] I. Ramachandran and S. Roy. Clear Channel Assessment in Energy-Constrained Wideband Wireless Networks. *IEEE Wireless Communications*, 14(3):70–78, 2007.

[28] A. Richa, C. Scheideler, S. Schmid, and J. Zhang. A Jamming-Resistant MAC Protocol for Multi-Hop Wireless Networks. In *Proceedings of the International Symposium on Distributed Computing (DISC)*, pages 179–193, 2010.

[29] V. Sekar and J. V. D. Merwe. LADS: Large-Scale Automated DDoS Detection System. In *Proceedings of the USENIX ATC*, pages 171–184, 2006.

[30] Valerie King and Cynthia Phillips and Jared Saia and Maxwell Young. Sleeping on the Job: Energy-Efficient and Robust Broadcast for Radio Networks. *Accepted to Algorithmica*, 2010.

[31] M. Walfish, M. Vutukuru, H. Balakrishnan, D. Karger, and S. Shenker. DDoS Defense by Offense. In *Proceedings of the 2006 Conference on Applications, Technologies, Architectures, and Protocols for Computer Communications (SIGCOMM)*, pages 303–314, 2006.

[32] A. D. Wood and J. A. Stankovic. Denial of Service in Sensor Networks. *Computer*, 35(10):54–62, 2002.

[33] W. Xu, W. Trappe, Y. Zhang, and T. Wood. The Feasibility of Launching and Detecting Jamming Attacks in Wireless Networks. In *MobiHoc*, pages 46–57, 2005.

[34] M. Young and R. Boutaba. Overcoming Adversaries in Sensor Networks: A Survey of Theoretical Models and Algorithmic Approaches for Tolerating Malicious Interference. Accepted to *IEEE Communications Surveys & Tutorials*, 2011.

Brief Announcement:
The Universe of Symmetry Breaking Tasks

Damien Imbs
IRISA
Campus de Beaulieu
35042 Rennes Cedex, France
damien.imbs@irisa.fr

Sergio Rajsbaum
Instituto de Matemáticas
UNAM
Mexico City, Mexico
rajsbaum@math.unam.mx

Michel Raynal
IRISA
Campus de Beaulieu
35042 Rennes Cedex, France
raynal@irisa.fr

ABSTRACT

This brief announcement introduces the family of *generalized symmetry breaking* (GSB) tasks, that includes election, renaming and many other symmetry breaking tasks. Differently from agreement tasks, a GSB task is "inputless", in the sense that processes do not propose values; the task specifies only the symmetry breaking requirement, independently of the system's initial state (where processes differ only on their identifiers). Among various results characterizing the family of GSB tasks, it is shown that (non adaptive) perfect renaming is universal for all GSB tasks.

Categories and Subject Descriptors

C.2.4 [**Computer-Communication Network**]: Distributed Systems—*distributed applications, network operating systems*; D.4.1 [**Operating Systems**]: Process Management—*concurrency, multiprocessing, synchronization*; D.4.5 [**Operating Systems**]: Reliability—*fault-tolerance*; F.1.1 [**Computation by Abstract Devices**]: Models of Computation—*Computability theory*

General terms: Theory.

Keywords: Agreement, Coordination, Decision task, Disagreement, Distributed computability, Election, Symmetry breaking, Renaming, Universal construction, Wait-freedom.

1. DECISION TASKS

The processes of a distributed system need to coordinate through a communication medium (shared memory or message-passing subsystem) in order to solve various forms of agreement problems. If no coordination is ever needed in the computation, then we have a set of centralized, independent programs rather than a global distributed computation. Agreement coordination is one of the main issues of distributed computing. As an example, consensus is a very strong form of agreement where processes have to agree on the input of some process. It is a fundamental problem in distributed computing, and the cornerstone when one has to implement a replicated state machine, e.g. [3, 11, 13].

Considering a shared memory asynchronous system where processes may fail by crashing, we are interested here in *tasks* [12], defined by an input/output relation Δ, and where

processes start with private input values forming an *input vector I* and, after communication, individually decide on output values forming an *output vector O*, satisfying the specification of the considered task, i.e., $O \in \Delta(I)$. Several specific agreement tasks have been studied in detail, such as consensus [6] and set agreement [4]. Indeed, the importance of agreement is such that it has been studied deeply, from a more general perspective, defining families of agreement tasks, such as loop agreement [8], approximate agreement [5] and convergence [7].

Motivation.

An important form of coordination is when processes need to *disagree*. This form of coordination is needed to "break symmetry" among the processes that are initially in the same state. Indeed, specific forms of symmetry breaking have been studied, most notably election, mutual exclusion and renaming. And it is easy to come up with more natural situations related to symmetry breaking. As a simple example, let us consider n persons (processes) such that each one is required to participate in exactly one of m distinct committees (process groups). Each committee has predefined lower and upper bounds on the number of its members. The goal is to design a distributed algorithm that allows these persons (processes) to choose their committees in spite of asynchrony and failures.

2. GSB TASKS

While the theory of agreement tasks is pretty well developed, it seems that the same substantial research effort has not yet been devoted to understanding symmetry breaking in general. The full paper [10] introduces *generalized symmetry breaking* (GSB) tasks, a family of tasks that includes election [14], renaming [2], weak symmetry breaking (called *reduced renaming* in [9]), and many other symmetry breaking tasks. A GSB task for n processes is defined by a set of possible output values, and for each value v, a lower bound and an upper bound (resp., ℓ_v and u_v) on the number of processes that have to decide this value. When these bounds can vary from value to value, we say it is an *asymmetric* GSB task, otherwise we simply say it is a GSB task. For example, we can define the *election* asymmetric GSB task by requiring that exactly one process outputs 1 and exactly $n-1$ processes output 2. In the symmetric case, we use the notation $\langle n, m, \ell, u \rangle$-GSB to denote the task on n processes, for m possible output values, $[1..m]$, where each value has to be decided at least ℓ and at most u times. In the m-renaming task, the processes have to decide new distinct names in the set $[1..m]$. Thus, m-renaming is nothing else than the $\langle n, m, 0, 1 \rangle$-GSB task.

Symmetry breaking tasks seem more difficult to study than agreement tasks, because in a symmetry breaking task we need to find a solution given an initial situation that looks essentially the same to all processes. For example, lower bound proofs (and algorithms) for renaming are substantially more complex than for set agreement (e.g., [9]). At the same time, if processes are completely identical, it has been known for a long time that symmetry breaking is impossible [1] (even in failure-free models). Thus, as in previous papers, we assume that processes can be identified by initial names given to them, which are taken from some large space of possible identities (but otherwise they are initially identical). Thus, in an algorithm that solves a GSB task, the outputs of the processes can depend only on their initial identities and on the interleaving of the execution.

When combined with another "output-independence" feature, the symmetry of the initial state of a system differentiates fundamentally GSB tasks from agreement tasks. Namely, the specification of a symmetry breaking task is given simply by a set of legal output vectors, $\mathcal{O}$, that the processes can produce: in any execution, any of these output vectors can be produced for any input vector I (we stress that an input vector defines only the identities of the processes), i.e., $\forall I$ we have $\Delta(I) = \mathcal{O}$. For example, for the election GSB task, $\mathcal{O}$ consists of all binary output vectors with exactly one entry equal to 1 and $n-1$ equal to 2. In contrast, an agreement task typically needs to relate inputs and outputs, where processes should not only agree on closely related values, but in addition the agreed upon values have to be somehow related to the input values given to the processes. Notice that the $\langle n, m, 0, 1 \rangle$-GSB renaming task is different from the *adaptive* renaming task, where the size of the new name space depends on the number of processes that participate. Similarly, the classic test-and-set task looks similar to the election GSB task: in both cases exactly one process outputs 1. But test-and-set is adaptive: there is the additional requirement that in every execution, even if less than n processes participate (i.e., take steps), at least one process outputs 1. That is, election GSB is a non-adaptive form of test-and-set.

3. CONTRIBUTIONS

The full paper [10] investigates the family of GSB tasks in a wait-free setting (where any number of processes can crash). Its main contributions are:

- The introduction of the family of GSB tasks, and a formal setting to study them. It is shown that several tasks that were previously considered separately belong actually to the same family and can consequently be compared and analyzed within a single conceptual framework. Thus, it is shown that several properties that were known for specific GSB tasks, actually hold for all of them. Moreover, new GSB tasks are introduced that are interesting in themselves, notably the *k-slot* GSB task, the election GSB task and the k-weak symmetry breaking task.

- The structure of the GSB family of tasks is characterized, identifying when two GSB tasks are actually the same task, and giving a unique representation for each one.

- Computability and complexity properties associated with the GSB task family are studied. First it is noticed that (non-adaptive) renaming is a GSB task. It is then shown that perfect renaming (i.e., when the n processes have to rename in the set $[1..n]$) is a universal GSB task. This means that any GSB task can be solved given a solution to perfect renaming. In the other extreme, $(2n-1)$-renaming is trivially solved, without communication. WSB and election are in between these two tasks: they are not solvable without communication. Moreover, election is strictly stronger than weak symmetry breaking.

- As far as the k-slot task is concerned, a simple algorithm is presented that solves the $(n+1)$-renaming task from the $(n-1)$-slot GSB task. There is also a simple algorithm that solves the $(2n-2)$-renaming task from the 2-slot GSB task.

The reader is referred to [10] for more technical details and many interesting questions that remain open.

4. REFERENCES

[1] Angluin D., Local and Global Properties in Networks of Processors. *Proc. 12th ACM Symposium on Theory of Computing (STOC'80)*, ACM Press, pp. 82-93, 1980.

[2] Attiya H., Bar-Noy A., Dolev D., Peleg D. and Reischuk R., Renaming in an Asynchronous Environment. *Journal of the ACM*, 37(3):524-548, 1990.

[3] Chandra T. and Toueg S., Unreliable Failure Detectors for Reliable Distributed Systems. *Journal of the ACM*, 43(2):225-267, 1996.

[4] Chaudhuri S., More Choices Allow More Faults: Set Consensus Problems in Totally Asynchronous Systems. *Information and Computation*, 105(1):132-158, 1993.

[5] Dolev D., Lynch N., Pinter S., Stark E. and Weihl W. Reaching Approximate Agreement in the Presence of Faults. *Journal of the ACM*, 33(3):499–516, 1986.

[6] Fischer M.J., Lynch N.A. and Paterson M.S., Impossibility of Distributed Consensus with One Faulty Process. *Journal of the ACM*, 32(2):374-382, 1985.

[7] Herlihy M. and Rajsbaum S. The Decidability of Distributed Decision Tasks. *Proc. 29th ACM Symposium on Theory of Computing (STOC'97)*, ACM Press, pp. 589-598, 1997.

[8] Herlihy M. and Rajsbaum S. A Classification of Wait-Free Loop Agreement Tasks. *Theoretical Computer Science*, 291(1):55-77, 2003.

[9] Herlihy M.P. and Shavit N., The Topological Structure of Asynchronous Computability. *Journal of the ACM*, 46(6):858-923,, 1999.

[10] Imbs D., Rajsbaum S. and Raynal M., The Universe of Symmetry Breaking Tasks. *Tech Report #1965*, IRISA, Univ. de Rennes 1, France, January 2011.

[11] Lamport. L., The Part-time Parliament. *ACM Transactions on Computer Systems*, 16(2):133-169, 1998.

[12] Moran, S., and Wolfsthal, Y., An extended Impossibility Result for Asynchronous Complete Networks. *Information Processing Letters* 26:141-151, 1987.

[13] Raynal M., Communication and Agreement Abstractions for Fault-Tolerant Asynchronous Distributed Systems. *Morgan & Claypool Publishers*, 251 pages, 2010 (ISBN 978-1-60845-293-4).

[14] Styer, E., and Peterson, G. L., Tight Bounds for Shared Memory Symmetric Mutual Exclusion Problems. *Proc. 8th ACM Symposium on Principles of Distributed Computing (PODC'89)*, ACM Press, pp. 177-192, 1989.

Brief Announcement: Rationality Authority for Provable Rational Behavior *

Shlomi Dolev
Ben-Gurion Univ. of the
Negev, Israel
dolev@cs.bgu.ac.il

Panagiota N.
Panagopoulou
Research Academic Computer
Tech. Inst., Greece.
panagopp@cti.gr

Mikaël Rabie
Ben-Gurion Univ. of the
Negev, Israel
rabie@cs.bgu.ac.il

Elad M. Schiller
Chalmers Univ. Tech., Sweden
elad@chalmers.se

Paul G. Spirakis
Research Academic Computer
Tech. Inst., Greece.
spirakis@cti.gr

Categories and Subject Descriptors

F.1.1 [**Models of Computation**]: Bounded-action devices

General Terms

Algorithms; Economics; Security; Theory;, Verification

Keywords

Game Theory; Privacy; Game Authority; Rationality Authority

Game theory is based on the assumption that (at least, some) *agents* play rationally. This assumption is questionable in the face of the sophistication for obtaining the best strategy in (even simple) games. Thus, the application of game theory in real life is limited by the degree in which the agents (who are rarely mathematicians, economic experts, or computer scientists) can understand the meaning of the game rules and the way to act. One famous example is auctions where every variant of an auction introduces the need for a new proof that, say, reconfirms that the second price auction is the best to use. We have in mind a framework that will let the ordinary and inexperienced Joe and Jane safely figure their best-reply

Distributed computer systems can implement the *rationality authority* framework that in turn, can enable rational behavior, without sacrificing the agents' privacy, e.g., keeping the individual preferences private. [1] The framework (Fig. 1) includes:

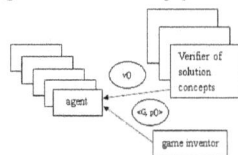

Inventors advice the agents about actions and their optimality proof via $\langle G, p() \rangle$ (game and proof). Verifiers $v()$ sends to the agents verification procedures for $p()$.

Figure 1: Framework

• The *game inventor*, which may possibly gain revenues from the game. We consider inventors that create games for which they could predict and prove optimal best-replies.

• The agents participate in the game and receive verifiable advices on action optimality.

• The *verifiers* are trustable service providers that profit from

selling general purpose *verification procedures*, $v()$, using formal methods, and therefore aim at having long-lasting reputation on being honest in checking proofs. Verifiers use libraries for specifying and informing about solution concepts. [2]

Separation principles. We propose a rationality authority for separating the interest, benefit and goals of the parties (inventors, verifiers and agents) and enabling agents to take rational actions. The separation also disjoins inventors from game revenues and the verifiers from selling reliable verification procedures.

All agents are aware of the existence of the rationality authority as common knowledge. Since it communicates with agents before they choose their actions, one might view the authority as synchronization mechanisms that are used in correlated equilibria or as moderators that are used in multi-party computation. However, the rationality authority is *not* trusted, where as synchronization mechanisms are. Vis., the inventors must demonstrate their trustworthiness and have only the (trusted) verifiers at their disposal. [3]

We focus on case studies in which the authority privately consults the agents using knowledge that only they have (perhaps only as a collective) and yet offers proof for its advices.

Interactive theorem provers for verifying pure Nash equilibria. As a first case study, we generalize Vickrey auctions and detail how the agents can verify this variation. Our generalization resembles Google's approach in which the highest bidder gets the auctioned object but pays "the second-highest bid, plus perhaps a penny".

General 2-agent game with privacy guarantees. We present an equilibrium verification method that does not reveal the agent pref-

---

*Partially supported by EU's ICT-2008-215270 (FRONTS). An extended version of this paper appears as a technical report [2].

[1] Revealing private preferences could jeopardize the action success. Moreover, even when such preferences are known to a trusted third party, security concerns and privacy restrictions limit the use of such information, e.g., taxation authorities.

[2] Ron (the rational) and Norton (the irrational) walked in a far away road in the middle of a rainy night. At some point they decide to sleep. Ron chooses to sleep on the road's muddy side, in order to avoid cars that drive in the road's paved part. Norton decides to sleep on the more convenient paved part. A car arrives, the driver sees Norton at the last minute, and turns to the road's side, exactly where Ron decided to sleep... Later, Norton claims that he could not predict the influence of his irrational action on Ron. Rationality authority can suggest the way to act and produce checkable optimality proof of the suggestion. This eliminates the possible validity of Norton's excuse and may be used (after auditing Norton's actions) to blame Norton for not complying with rationality.

[3] The verifier reputations can be updated according to the (majority of their) results. Once the rationality authority requirements are satisfied, a *game authority* [1] can guarantee that all agents take rational and honest actions; actions that follow the game rules. Moreover, actions of dishonest inventors, agents, and verifiers can exclude the participant from acting in games and can be reported to a *reputation system* that audits their actions.

P_1: Provide each agent the agents' supports, i.e., strategy profiled played with non-zero probabilities.
Row agent i verifier: Let the support S_2 of the other agent (the column agent) be $\{j_1, \ldots j_k\}$. Let $y_{j_1}, \ldots y_{j_k}$ be the Nash probabilities of the column agent. Let S_1 be the support of the row agent and $S_1 = \{i_1, \ldots i_\ell\}$. The verifier solves the linear system (1) and verifies that $\forall t \in \{j_1, \ldots j_k\}: 0 \le y_t \le 1$ and $\forall i \notin S_1$, the expected gain $y_{j_1} A(i, j_1) + \cdots y_{j_k} A(i, j_k) < \lambda_1$.

$$\lambda_1 = y_{j_1} A(i_1, j_1) + \cdots y_{j_k} A(i_1, j_k) \qquad (1)$$

$$\vdots$$

$$\lambda_1 = y_{j_\ell} A(i_\ell, j_1) + \cdots y_{j_k} A(i_\ell, j_k)$$

$$y_{i_1} + \cdots + y_{j_k} = 1$$

P_2: Send to each agent its support and λ_1, λ_2.
Row agent i verifier: Agent $i \in \{1, 2\}$ asks the prover for two random indices j_1, j_2. Honest provers return ($j_1 \in S_2 \wedge j_2 \in S_2$). Then the verifier computes the *other agents' expected gain* for the indices $\lambda_2(j_1), \lambda_2(j_2)$. The verifier then checks
∘ "both j's in S_2", i.e., $\lambda_2(j_1) = \lambda_2(j_2) = \lambda_2$.
∘ "1-in/1-out", say j_1 is in, i.e., $\lambda_2(j_1) = \lambda_2 \ge \lambda_2(j_2)$.
The test is inconclusive for both $j_1, j_2 \notin S_2$ but at least one will be in with probability at least $1/n$. Thus, on average, $O(n)$ random verifier queries need for a play.

Figure 2: Interactive provers P_1 and its extension P_2.

erences, and by that, preserves user privacy and secures action success when acting upon the advised equilibria. Consider a 2-agent game, defined by the $n \times m$ matrices A, B of the payoffs of the two agents (row and column agents whose pure strategies are the n rows, and m columns, respectively). Broadly speaking, the equilibrium is hard to compute. However, the interactive provers P_1 and P_2 (Fig. 2) lead to a polynomial-time verification. P_1 reveals the agent supports, but does not need to send them explicitly and its extension, P_2, still has a polynomial time, and yet does not reveal to any agent the other agent support!

Equilibrium Consultant with Provable Advices. We present the *Participation* game in which c is the auction participation fee and no gain is offered to the solo participant. The game's equilibrium is hard to compute without the rationality authority's advice. We explain how the agent can use the advice for computing the game equilibrium and verify the advice. Consider n firms that are eligible to participate in an auction. The auction rules are:
• Firm f gets a value $v > 0$ if at least $k = 2$ firms choose to participate and f chooses *not* to.
• Firm f gets a value $v - c > 0$ when at least $k = 2$ firms participate and f is one of them.
• If nobody participates, then each firm gains zero.
• If firm f participates but the total number of participants is less than k, then f *pays* $c > 0$.
Provers provide each firm with the equilibrium value of p and the verifier asserts Eq. (2).

$$(v - c) \cdot A_k + (-c) \cdot B_k = v \cdot C_k + 0 \cdot D_k, \text{ where}$$

$$A_k = \Pr\{\text{at least } k \text{ firms participate} \mid f \text{ participates}\}$$
$$B_k = \Pr\{\text{at most } k - 1 \text{ firms participate} \mid f \text{ participates}\}$$
$$C_k = \Pr\{\text{at least } k \text{ firms participate} \mid f \text{ does not}\}$$
$$D_k = \Pr\{\text{at most } k - 1 \text{ firms participate} \mid f \text{ does not}\}$$

Computing p is hard but, once it is given, computing A_k, B_k, and C_k and verifying the equilibrium is easy. I.e., firms *expect to get the same* by using p to decide whether to play. The agents can cross-check that the prover has sent the *same* p to all, because we might have several symmetric equilibria.

On-line Network Congestion Games. We study competitive on-line games in which each agent joins the game at a different time. Each agent, upon arrival, has to choose a strategy. With probability

p, the agent follows the inventor's suggested strategy. With probability $(1 - p)$, it chooses a strategy based on its knowledge about the strategic (off-line) version of the game. The inventor (network operator) chooses agent strategies based on statistics and provides to the agent (endusers) a formal proof that can be checked by the verifier. We show that, in the network of m parallel links, a greedy strategy guarantees a total link load of $(2 - \frac{1}{m})$ times the optimal maximum machine load.

Let $N = (V, E, (d_e)_{e \in E})$ be a communication network, where $d_e : \mathbb{R}_+ \to \mathbb{R}_+$ is a non-decreasing load function for each $e \in E$, indicating the delay on arc e as a function of its congestion. Initially, the set of agents is unknown to the inventor, but number of agents, n, is known. Agent i, joins the network at time τ_i and

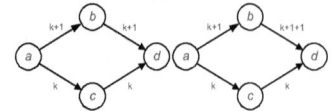

Consider unit loads, and agent $2k+1$ that chooses a path from a to d. Each edge has congestion k. Agent $2k+1$ best-reply is $a \to b \to d$ (shortest path). Suppose that the next agent to enter the network, agent $2k + 2$, has to choose a path from b to d. Its only option is the path $b \to d$. Therefore, at time τ_{2k+2}, the delay experienced by agent $2k + 1$ is $2k + 3$, while its best-reply would be path $a \to c \to d$ with a total delay of $2k + 2$.

Figure 3: Edge delay $d_e(x) = x$

chooses a path π_i from a source $s_i \in V$ to sink $t_i \in V$ to route its load $w_i \in \mathbb{R}_+$. The decision is irrevocable. Let $[i] = \{1, \ldots, i\}$. The network *configuration* at time τ_i (right after agent i joins) is $\pi(i) = (\pi_j)_{j \in [i]}$. Given a configuration $\pi(k)$, let $W_e(\pi(k)) = \sum_{j \in [k]: e \in \pi_j} w_j$ denote the total load on $e \in E$. At time τ_k, agent i's total delay experienced is $\lambda_i(\pi(k)) = \sum_{e \in \pi_i} d_e(\pi(k))$.

The inventor goal is to minimize total congestion $\Lambda(\pi(n)) = \sum_{e \in E} d_e(\pi(n))$. Agent i's goal is to choose a path, π_i, that minimizes $\lambda_i(\pi(n))$ without knowing the final configuration $\pi(n)$. At time τ_i, its best-reply is to choose a shortest path, but this path cannot remain a best-reply for i at time τ_n when the game ends (see Fig. 3). How should an agent choose its path? Agent i can either to choose a shortest path given $\pi(i - 1)$, or to follow the inventor's advice. What is the statistical information that the inventor maintains? We consider two cases: In the first case, the inventor has *prior* knowledge about the agent loads, e.g., they are drawn from some particular probability distribution. In the second case, the inventor dynamically updates its information, i.e., at time τ_i, assuming that the total number of agents n is known, the inventor knows that loads $w_1, \ldots, w_i$ have appeared, and expects for example $(n - i)$ loads of expected value $\frac{\sum_{k=1}^{i} w_k}{i}$.

Greedy strategies for parallel links. Consider a network of parallel links $[m] = \{1, \ldots m\}$. What is i's best-reply for load w_i? It is not necessarily the least loaded link, because i expect $n - i$ loads to arrive and knows the total link congestion by time τ_i and its own load w_i. We compare the greedy strategy (each agent on arrival chooses the least loaded link) to inventor advised strategy. For agent i, the inventor computes the average load $\overline{w_i}$ that has appeared so far. Given the congestion on the links by time τ_i, agents i computes a Nash equilibrium assignment of its own load w_i and of $n - i$ loads $\overline{w_i}$. Namely, each load is assigned to the least loaded link, greatest load first. Then the inventor suggests that i chooses the link that is suggested by that assignment. In [2], we show that the greedy strategy is outperformed by the inventor advices (a factor of $(2 - \frac{1}{m})$).

1. REFERENCES

[1] S. Dolev et al. Robust and scalable middleware for selfish-computer systems. *C.S. Review*, 5(1):69 – 84, 2011.
[2] S. Dolev et al. Rationality Authority for Provable Rational Behavior. *CSE Department, Chalmers Univ. Tech*, 2011:03.

Brief Announcement: Secure Data Structures based on Multi-Party Computation

Tomas Toft
Dept. of CS, Aarhus University
Åbogade 34, DK-8200
Aarhus N, Denmark
ttoft@cs.au.dk

ABSTRACT

This work considers data structures based on multi-party computation (MPC) primitives: structuring secret (e.g. secret shared and potentially unknown) data such that it can both be queried and updated efficiently. Implementing an oblivious RAM (ORAM) using MPC allows any existing data structure to be realized using MPC primitives, however, by focusing on a specific example – a priority queue – it is shown that it is possible to achieve much better results than the generic solutions can provide. Moreover, the techniques differ significantly from existing ORAM constructions. Indeed it has recently been shown that any information theoretically secure ORAM with n memory locations requires at least $\log n$ random bits per read/write to hide the access pattern. In contrast, the present construction achieves security with a completely deterministic access pattern.

Categories and Subject Descriptors

E.1 [**Data Structures**]: Distributed data structures; F [**Theory of Computation**]: Miscellaneous—*secure computation*

General Terms

Security, Algorithms

Keywords

Reactive functionalities, secure multi-party computation

1. MULTI-PARTY COMPUTATION

Multi-party computation (MPC) proposed by Yao [15] considers the problem of evaluating a function f on data held in a distributed manner, i.e. on $(x_1, \ldots, x_N)$ where x_i is held by party P_i. The core goal is *privacy*: to have the parties learn $f(x_1, \ldots, x_N)$, but do so without revealing any additional information about the x_i. The concept can be generalized to consider reactive tasks: MPC protocols may consist of multiple sequential function evaluations, where each evaluation depends on and potentially updates a secret state.[1] Classic results show that any function can be computed securely

---

[1]The secret state can be stored, e.g. in secret shared form.

with a polynomial overhead, [8, 2, 4]. This is true even when a subset of the parties collude and deviate arbitrarily.

Specialized protocols for well-motivated problems such as auctions are often considered for efficiency reasons. Though the solutions may be reactive, this is rarely the case for the tasks considered despite such tasks being common in practice. E.g. databases structure data to allow efficient queries, while updates simply restructure the data. Put differently, the topic of data structures based on MPC primitives has received surprisingly little attention.

2. THE MODEL AND GOAL

The underlying protocols are modelled as an ideal functionality, the arithmetic black-box (ABB) $\mathcal{F}_{ABB}$ of Damgård and Nielsen [7], augmented with comparison (greater than). The latter can be constructed in the ABB, e.g. using the protocol of Nishide and Ohta [10]. This approach abstracts away the details of the underlying protocols leaving only the desired properties. The ABB can be viewed as an trusted third party providing secure storage and computation:

- **Input:** When the (honest) parties agree, $\mathcal{F}_{ABB}$ will receive and store an input in $\mathbb{Z}_M$ from a specified party.

- **Output:** When the (honest) parties agree, $\mathcal{F}_{ABB}$ will send a stored value to all parties.

- **Arithmetic:** When the (honest) parties agree, $\mathcal{F}_{ABB}$ will compute the sum or product (in $\mathbb{Z}_M$) of two stored values and store the result.

- **Comparison:** When the (honest) parties agree, $\mathcal{F}_{ABB}$ will determine which of two stored values is bigger and store the result, either 0 or 1.

Input and output can be viewed as secret sharing and reconstruction. With this intuition in mind, if input/output consists of Shamir sharing [13], the protocols of Ben-Or et al. [2] may be used to perform the arithmetic operations. Using the real/ideal paradigm it can be formally proved that these protocols realize $\mathcal{F}_{ABB}$. It is noted that other realizations are possible, e.g. based on Paillier encryption [11, 5].

Though $\mathcal{F}_{ABB}$ can be viewed as a trusted third party, it cannot perform branching on stored values. This is obvious when considering the actual protocols: the parties cannot branch depending on a secret (i.e. unknown) value. Any construction must therefore be a simple straightline program. However, multiple operations may be executed in parallel; this represents multiple concurrent protocol invocations. Overall complexity (computation and communication) is the overall number of operations performed, while round complexity is the number of sequential operations.[2]

The desired goal may now be presented as additional operations of $\mathcal{F}_{ABB}$. In addition to the above, $\mathcal{F}_{ABB}$ will contain a priority queue (PQ), i.e. store a set S of pairs of values, priority and data (p, x), and allow the element with minimal priority to be extracted (and stored within $\mathcal{F}_{ABB}$).

- INSERT(p, x): When the (honest) parties agree, $\mathcal{F}_{ABB}$ will insert the values stored as p and x into S.

- GETMIN(): When the (honest) parties agree, $\mathcal{F}_{ABB}$ will determine the pair with smallest priority p, remove (p, x) from S, and store x as min.

To the author's knowledge, this work contains the first specific data structure based on MPC primitives. Note that when viewing these as reactive MPC tasks only the state is updated; the output to the parties is empty.

3. THE OBLIVIOUS RAM

The closest related work is the *Oblivious RAM* (ORAM) proposed by Goldreich and Ostrovky [9]. This allows a CPU with a small, private memory to execute some program residing in main memory, without leaking information to an adversary observing the memory access pattern. Implementing the CPU using MPC primitives allows array indexing; through "pointers" this allows data structures, [9, 6]. In other words: The ORAM provides a completeness theorem; any data structure can be implemented with poly-logarithmic overhead.

Oblivious RAMs hide the access pattern by randomizing it. [9] achieved this using a random oracle, instantiated by a one-way function. This was recently improved by Pinkas and Reinman, [12], who brought the computational overhead down to $O(\log^2 n)$ and the memory overhead to $O(1)$. Due to the use of one-way functions, this approach cannot provide security against computationally unbounded adversaries. Independently, Ajtai [1], and Damgård et al. [6] have proposed information theoretic (i.t.) ORAMs. Though the solutions are different, in both cases, both the computation and memory overhead are poly-logarithmic.

4. THE SECURE PRIORITY QUEUE

The present PQ is the first specific data structure based on MPC primitives. The construction is a variation of the bucket heap of Brodal et al. [3]. Performing n operations on an initially empty queue requires $O(n \log^2 n)$ $\mathcal{F}_{ABB}$ operations – i.e. amortized cost for each operation is $O(\log^2 n)$. Further, only a constant number of rounds are required on average. The main idea is to store the queue as a sorted list. However, elements are not inserted directly, but travel along the list in buffers until they reach their position. These buffers are processed when the cost can be paid for by previous operations. For details see the full version [14].

The construction improves over the ORAM-based solutions, where *every memory access* requires $\Omega(\log^2 n)$ arithmetic operations.[3] Moreover, the sequential nature of the ORAM implies that implementing e.g. a heap ($\log n$ memory

---

[2]All operations are realizable in $O(1)$ rounds.
[3]The exact complexity depends on the ORAM solution used.

accesses) will require $\Omega(\log n)$ rounds. Finally, both unconditionally secure ORAMs have a poly-logarithmic memory overhead, thus, the present work contains the *only* i.t. secure data structure with constant memory overhead.

The techniques used to construct the PQ differ radically from those of the ORAMs and may be of independent interest. The ORAM constructions randomize the access pattern. Indeed it was recently shown that *any* unconditionally secure realization of the ORAM requires at least $\log n$ bits of randomness per operation, where n is the overall size of the memory, [6]. In contrast to this, the present PQ is *completely deterministic*: no ABB operation depends on the inputs or any randomness, only on the order of the PQ operations.

5. ACKNOWLEDGMENTS

The author would like to thank Gerth Brodal, Ivan Damgård, Sigurd Meldgaard, Jesper Buus Nielsen, and Berry Schoenmakers for discussions underway.

6. REFERENCES

[1] M. Ajtai. Oblivious rams without cryptogrpahic assumptions. In *STOC*, 2010.

[2] M. Ben-Or, S. Goldwasser, and A. Wigderson. Completeness theorems for noncryptographic fault-tolerant distributed computations. In *STOC*, 1988.

[3] G. Brodal, R. Fagerberg, U. Meyer, and N. Zeh. Cache-oblivious data structures and algorithms for undirected breadth-first search and shortest paths. In *SWAT*, 2004.

[4] D. Chaum, C. Crépeau, and I. Damgård. Multiparty unconditionally secure protocols. In *STOC*, 1988.

[5] R. Cramer, I. Damgård, and J. Nielsen. Multiparty computation from threshold homomorphic encryption. In *Eurocrypt*, 2001.

[6] I. Damgård, S. Meldgaard, and J. B. Nielsen. Perfectly secure oblivious ram without random oracles. In *Theory of Cryptography*, 2011.

[7] I. Damgård and J. Nielsen. Universally composable efficient multiparty computation from threshold homomorphic encryption. In *Crypto*, 2003.

[8] O. Goldreich, S. Micali, and A. Wigderson. How to play any mental game. In *STOC*, 1987.

[9] O. Goldreich and R. Ostrovsky. Software protection and simulation on oblivious rams. *J. ACM*, 43(3):431–473, 1996.

[10] T. Nishide and K. Ohta. Multiparty computation for interval, equality, and comparison without bit-decomposition protocol. In *PKC*, 2007.

[11] P. Paillier. Public-key cryptosystems based on composite degree residuosity classes. In *Eurocrypt*, 1999.

[12] B. Pinkas and T. Reinman. Oblivious RAM revisited. In *Crypto*, 2010.

[13] A. Shamir. How to share a secret. *Communications of the ACM*, 22(11):612–613, 1979.

[14] T. Toft. Secure datastructures based on multiparty computation. Cryptology ePrint Archive, Report 2011/081, 2011. http://eprint.iacr.org/.

[15] A. Yao. Protocols for secure computations (extended abstract). In *FOCS*, 1982.

Brief Announcement:
Robust Network Supercomputing
Without Centralized Control*

Seda Davtyan
Dept. of Computer Science &
Engineering
University of Connecticut
seda@engr.uconn.edu

Kishori M. Konwar
Dept. of Immunology and
Microbiology
University of British Columbia
kishori@interchange.ubc.ca

Alexander A. Shvartsman
Dept. of Computer Science &
Engineering
University of Connecticut
aas@cse.uconn.edu

ABSTRACT

Traditional approaches to network supercomputing employ a master process and a large number of potentially undependable worker processes that must perform a collection of tasks on behalf of the master. In such a centralized scheme, the master process is a performance bottleneck and a single point of failure. This work develops an original approach that eliminates the master and instead uses a decentralized algorithm, where each worker is able to determine locally that all tasks have been performed, and to collect locally the results of all tasks. The failure model assumes that the *average* probability of a worker returning a wrong result is inferior to $1/2$. A randomized synchronous algorithm for n processes and n tasks is presented. The algorithm terminates in $\Theta(\log n)$ rounds, and it is proved that upon termination the workers know the results of all tasks with high probability, and that these results are correct with high probability. The message complexity of the algorithm is $\Theta(n \log n)$, and the bit complexity is $O(n^2 \log^3 n)$.

Categories and Subject Descriptors: F.2.0 [Theory of Computation]: ANALYSIS OF ALGORITHMS AND PROBLEM COMPLEXITY – *General*

General Terms: Algorithms, Reliability

Keywords: Distributed Algorithms, Fault-Tolerance, Randomized Algorithms, Internet Supercomputing

1. OVERVIEW

Internet Supercomputing comes at a cost substantially lower than acquiring a supercomputer, or building a cluster of powerful machines, however with it come the challenges of marshaling distributed resources and dealing with failures. Several Internet supercomputers are in existence today [1, 2, 3]. A phenomenon of increasing concern is that workers may return incorrect results. This may happen due to unintended failures caused, e.g., by over-clocked processes, or workers may claim to have performed assigned work so as to obtain incentives associated with earning a high rank in the system.

One apparent drawback of this approach is the assumption of the existence of a reliable master process. Indeed, in the

*This work is supported in part by the NSF award 1017232.

traditional centralized network supercomputing the master process itself is a performance bottleneck and a single point of failure. The master is further assumed to be able to keep up with the results returned by a large number of workers, making such systems poorly scalable.

We aim to remove the assumption of an infallible and bandwidth-unlimited master process. Instead we target a fully decentralized computing architecture consisting of just workers, some of whom can behave erratically.

Related Work. Several schemes have been proposed to improve the quality of the results obtained from untrusted workers. Fernandez, Georgiou, Lopez, and Santos [5] and Konwar, Rajasekaran, and Shvartsman [7] consider a distributed system consisting of a reliable master process and a collection of worker processes that can perform tasks on behalf of the master, where the workers may act maliciously by deliberately returning wrong results. Works [5, 6, 7] focus on designing algorithms that help the master determine the correct result with high probability and at the least possible cost in terms of the total number of tasks performed. The failure models assume that some fraction of processes can exhibit faulty behavior.

Contributions. We consider the problem of performing n tasks in a distributed system of n workers. The tasks are independent, they admit at-least-once execution semantics, and each task can be performed by any worker in constant time. We assume that the workers can obtain the tasks from some repository (equivalently we can assume that the tasks are initially known to all processes).

The fully-connected message-passing system is synchronous and the workers communicate using authenticated messages (to prevent malicious workers from impersonating other workers). We deal with failure models where workers can return incorrect results and ultimately crash. The system is fully decentralized in the sense that it does not contain any distinguished participants (e.g., a master). We present an original randomized decentralized algorithm that terminates in the number of rounds proportional to $\log n$. In each round each worker sends only one message to one other process, thus the message complexity of the algorithm is $\Theta(n \log n)$. We consider several other failure models that specialize the initial model by making additional assumptions about the fraction of possibly faulty workers and the failure probabilities. We assess the performance of our algorithm under these different failure models. In more detail our contributions are as follows.

We define a general failure model $\mathcal{F}$, where each worker i, for $i \in [n]$, independently returns incorrect result with probability p_i each time it performs a task. The average such probability is inferior to $\frac{1}{2}$, more formally, $\frac{1}{n}\sum_i p_i < \frac{1}{2} - \varepsilon$ for some $\varepsilon > 0$. We present a randomized algorithm and analyze its complexity under model $\mathcal{F}$.

We show that failure model $\mathcal{F}$ can be extended to incorporate process crashes in the way that does not require any changes to our algorithm. We also present three additional failure models that specialize model $\mathcal{F}$ in natural ways. In model $\mathcal{F}_a$ each worker returns faulty results for a task with probability $p < \frac{1}{2}$ independently of other workers. In model $\mathcal{F}_b$ some fixed fraction f of the workers returns faulty results for any task with probability p, such that $fp < \frac{1}{2}$. In model $\mathcal{F}_c$ some fixed fraction f of the workers can return faulty results, for any task, such that $f < \frac{1}{2}$. Since each model is a formal specialization of model $\mathcal{F}$, the same algorithm works in each of the models with the same (at least) efficiency.

We developed a simulation of the algorithm to contrast its simulated behavior with the theoretical findings. The empirical data shows that after $\Theta(\log n)$ rounds the correct results of every task are known to all workers with very few exceptions.

2. THE ALGORITHM

We present a new randomized algorithm solving our distributed cooperation problem for n workers and n tasks. Each worker process i maintains two arrays of size linear in n. Array $R_i(1..n)$ is used to accumulate knowledge gathered from different processes. Each element $R_i(j)$ is a set of results for task j, containing triples $\langle v_j, i, r \rangle$ representing the result v_j computed for task j by process i during round r. Such triples are used to eliminate repeated inclusions of the results for the same task, in the same round, and by the same process. The second array, $Results_i(1..n)$, stores the final results of the task executions.

The algorithm works in synchronous rounds. In every round a process performs a random task and communicates its cumulative knowledge to one other randomly chosen process. The number of rounds performed by the algorithm is an external (compile-time) parameter K (we prove that $K = 2L$ rounds are sufficient to obtain the high probability guarantee, for a certain L that is shown to be $\Theta(\log n)$).

The algorithm consists of four stages, viz., *Initialization*, *Receive*, *Compute*, and *Send*. We use the term *round* to describe a single iteration of the algorithm through the stages *Receive*, *Compute*, and *Send*.

***Initialization*:** In this stage each process i sets $R_i(j) \leftarrow \emptyset$ and initializes the round number $r \leftarrow 0$.

***Receive*:** At the beginning of each round each process i executes *Receive* stage, during which the process receives the messages sent to it by other processes (including possibly itself) during the previous round. The messages consist of the sender's collection of the results for different tasks including the ID of each process that carried out the computation. Upon receiving the messages a process updates its own local copy of the sets by taking a union (this excludes duplicated triples).

***Compute*:** In this stage each process i checks whether the required number of rounds K ($= 2L$) have passed and either completes its computation or continues.

If $r = K$ then it goes over the result set of every task and computes the result that corresponds to the plurality of the results (in the analysis we prove that in fact a majority exists). The process halts.

Else, if the number of rounds r is less than L, then process i randomly selects a task j from the list of tasks, computes the result v_j for task j and adds the triple $\langle v_j, i, r \rangle$ to the array of cumulative results $Results_i$.

***Send*:** In this stage a target process k is chosen randomly from the set $[n]$ of all processes. The sets of results $R_i(j)$ for every task j are sent in a message to process k. The algorithm then increments r and repeats the stages starting with *Receive*.

When the algorithm halts after K ($= 2L$) rounds, the results of the tasks are available in array $Results_i(1..n)$ of each process i; thus the results for all tasks are available at every worker locally.

3. ALGORITHM ANALYSIS

We prove that in $\Theta(\log n)$ rounds *w.h.p.* every task is performed $\Theta(\log n)$ times, possibly by different workers. Moreover, we prove that if a task has been performed $\Theta(\log n)$ times then *w.h.p.* in $\Theta(\log n)$ rounds of the algorithm each worker will acquire the results for every task.

The following theorem summarizes our main result.

THEOREM 1. *The algorithm computes all n tasks correctly at every process in $\Theta(\log n)$ rounds w.h.p.*

We further show that the *message complexity* of the algorithm is $\Theta(n \log n)$ and the *bit complexity* is $O(n^2 \log^3 n)$. The *space complexity* of the algorithm is $\Theta(n^2 \log^2 n)$.

Additionally we show that our algorithm can perform all n tasks correctly *w.h.p.* even when f-fraction, $0 < f < 1$ of workers crash as long as the *average* probability of a worker returning a wrong result remains inferior to $1/2$.

For additional details we refer the reader to [4]. Lastly, the authors thank Alex Russell for several technical discussions.

4. REFERENCES

[1] Distributed.net. http://www.distributed.net/.
[2] Internet primenet server.
    http://mersenne.org/ips/stats.html.
[3] Seti@home. http://setiathome.ssl.berkeley.edu/.
[4] S. Davtyan, K. M. Konwar, and A. A. Shvartsman. Robust network supercomputing without centralized control. Technical report, 2011. http://engr.uconn.edu/~sad06005/TR/DKS11.pdf.
[5] A. Fernandez, Ch. Georgiou, L. Lopez, and A Santos. Reliably executing tasks in the presence of untrusted entities. In *Proc. of the 25th IEEE Symposium on Reliable Distributed Systems*, pages 39–50, 2006.
[6] A. Fernández, Ch. Georgiou, and M. Mosteiro. Algorithmic mechanisms for internet-based master-worker computing with untrusted and selfish workers. In *Proc. 24th IEEE Int'l Symp. on Parallel and Distributed Processing*, pages 1–11, 2010.
[7] K. M. Konwar, S. Rajasekaran, and A. A. Shvartsman. Robust network supercomputing with malicious processes. In *Proc. of the 17th Int'l Symposium on Distributed Computing*, pages 474–488, 2006.

Brief Announcement: On the Hardness and Approximation of Minimum Topic-Connected Overlay[*]

Monika Steinová
Department of Computer Science
ETH Zurich, Switzerland
monika.steinova@inf.ethz.ch

ABSTRACT

The design of a scalable overlay network to support decentralized topic-based publish/subscribe communication is nowadays a problem of a great importance. We investigate here special instances of one such design problem called Minimum Topic-Connected Overlay. Given a collection of users together with the lists of topics they are interested in, the aim is to connect these users to a network by a minimum number of edges such that every graph induced by users interested in a common topic is connected. We investigate instances where in addition the number of users interested in a particular topic is bounded by a constant $d > 2$. It is known that the general Topic-Connected Overlay is $\Omega(\log n)$ hard to approximate and approximable by a logarithmic factor. For our special instances, we design a one-to-one reduction to special instances of the hitting set problem. This allows us to present the first constant approximation algorithm, the first kernelization and the first nontrivial exact algorithm for the special instances discussed.

Categories and Subject Descriptors

C.2.1 [**Computer-Communication Networks**]: Network Architecture and Design—*Network topology*; G.2.2 [**Discrete Mathematics**]: Graph Theory—*Network problems*

General Terms

Algorithms, Theory

1. INTRODUCTION

Nowadays, many internet applications support many-to-many communication based on sharing content: publishers publish information through a logical channel that is consumed by subscribed users. The situation is often modeled by publish/subscribe (pub/sub) systems. These sys-

[*]The research was partially funded by SNF grant 200021-132510/1.

tems can be classified into two categories. In the *content-based* pub/sub systems, the channels are associated with a collection of attributes and the messages are delivered to a subscriber only if their attributes match user-defined constraints. Each channel in the *topic-based* pub/sub systems is associated with a single topic. Here the messages are distributed to the users via channels by his/her topic selection.

In our paper, we focus on the topic-based peer-to-peer pub/sub systems. In such a system, subscribers interested in a particular topic have to be connected without the use of intermediate agents (such as servers). Many aspects of such a system can be studied (see [3, 8]). One may be interested in achieving a small diameter of the overlay network to minimize the total time in which a message is distributed to all the subscribers. If an (average) degree of nodes in the network is minimized, the subscribers need to maintain (in average) a smaller number of connections. Here, we consider the minimization of the number of all the connections in the system, i.e., the minimum number of edges the overlay network needs to have to satisfy the demands of the subscribers. A small number of edges may decrease the maintenance requirements as the network needs only a small number of connections. All messages sent via one edge of the network may be aggregated to a single message and thus amortize the head count of otherwise small messages.

We investigate here special instances of *Minimum Topic-Connected Overlay* which was studied under various scenarios ([2, 3, 5, 6]). In this problem, we are given a collection of vertices (subscribers) V, a set of topics T and a vertex interest assignment F (i.e., function $F : V \to 2^T$), we want to connect vertices in an overlay network G such that all vertices interested in a common topic are connected and the overall number of edges in G is minimal. The problem is $\Omega(\log n)$ hard to approximate ([2]) and approximable by a logarithmic factor ([3]). We focus here on the special case (called Min-d-TCO) where, for each topic, there are at most $d > 2$ users interested in it. We believe that Min-d-TCO has wide practical applications such as when a publisher has a limited number of slots for users.

We refer to special instances of the famous minimum hitting set problem. In the d-hitting set problem (d-HS), we are given a set of elements X and a finite family of sets $\mathcal{S} = \{S_1, \ldots, S_m\}$, $S_i \subseteq X$ such that $|S_i| \leq d$. Our goal is to find a set $H \subseteq X$ such that $S_i \cap H \neq \emptyset$ and the number of elements in H is minimal. The general hitting set problem does not bound the size of the sets of the family $\mathcal{S}$. There is a well known d-approximation algorithm for d-HS, it is not approximable within a factor better than d unless the unique game conjecture fails ([4]).

We design a one-to-one reduction of the instances of Min-d-TCO to d^2-HS. As these special instances of the hitting set problem are constantly approximable, we obtain the first constant approximation algorithm for Min-d-TCO. Furthermore, our one-to-one reduction allows us to use the known results to give the first bound on kernel size and design the first nontrivial exact algorithm for Min-d-TCO.

Note that Min-2-TCO is in $\mathcal{P}$, and when $v, u \in V$ and $F(v) \subseteq F(u)$, we can connect $\{u, v\}$ by a direct edge and remove the vertex v from the graph. Thus, in the following we assume that, for any two vertices u and v, the sets $F(u)$ and $F(v)$ are incomparable. Moreover, we assume that, for all $t \in T$, $|\{v \in V \mid t \in F(v)\}| > 2$. Otherwise, the two vertices interested in a topic t have to be connected in any overlay. Therefore, they can be contracted to a single vertex and then the problem can be solved on the smaller instance.

2. A CONSTANT APPROXIMATION ALGORITHM FOR Min-d-TCO

In this section, we present a reduction from Min-d-TCO to $O(d^2)$-HS, thus showing that there exists a constant approximation algorithm for Min-d-TCO as d-HS is constantly approximable.

Definition 1. Let $V = \{v_1, \ldots, v_n\}$ be a set of vertices. Let $\mathcal{S} = \{E_1, \ldots, E_m\}$ be a system of all sets of edges on $\{\{u, v\} \mid u, v \in V \wedge u \neq v\}$ such that the set $F_i = \{\{u, v\} \mid u, v \in V \wedge u \neq v\} \setminus E_i$ is maximal and the graph (V, F_i) is not connected (for all i, $1 \leq i \leq m$). We call the system $\mathcal{S}$ a *characteristic system* of edges on vertices V.

Lemma 1. Let $\mathcal{S} = \{E_1, \ldots, E_m\}$ be a characteristic system of edges on set V of n vertices. Then

1. $m = 2^{n-1} - 1$.

2. $|E_j| \leq \lfloor n/2 \rfloor \cdot \lceil n/2 \rceil$, for all j, $1 \leq j \leq m$.

3. Any two sets E_i and E_j differ in at least $n-1$ elements $(1 \leq i < j \leq m)$.

4. $H \subseteq \{\{u, v\} \mid u, v \in V \wedge u \neq v\}$ is a hitting set of $(\{\{u, v\} \mid u, v \in V \wedge u \neq v\}, \mathcal{S})$ if and only if graph (V, H) is connected.

5. The size of $\mathcal{S}$ is minimal such that property 4 holds.

Now we are ready to present a simple one-to-one reduction of Min-d-TCO to $O(d^2)$-HS. The core concept is to construct a system of sets that has to be hit in $O(d^2)$-HS as a union over all the topics of the characteristic systems of edges on the vertices interested in the topic.

Theorem 1. There exists a one-to-one reduction of instances of Min-d-TCO to instances of $O(d^2)$-HS.

Proof. Let $I_{\text{TCO}} = (V, T, F)$ be an instance of Min-d-TCO. For each topic $t \in T$, we define $\mathcal{S}_t$ to be the characteristic system of edges on vertices in $\{v \in V \mid t \in F(v)\}$. Note that the size of this set is at most d and thus Lemma 1 holds for each $\mathcal{S}_t$ with $n := d$. We construct a $O(d^2)$-HS instance $I_{\text{HS}} = (X, \mathcal{S})$ as follows:

$$X = \{\{u, v\} \mid u, v \in V \wedge u \neq v\}$$
$$\mathcal{S} = \bigcup_{t \in T} \mathcal{S}_t.$$

The size of the instance and its construction time is polynomial in size of I_{TCO}. It can be easily shown that a feasible solution of I_{TCO} corresponds to a feasible solution of I_{HS} and vice versa. $\square$

Theorem 2. There exists a polynomial-time approximation algorithm for Min-d-TCO with ratio $(\lfloor d/2 \rfloor \cdot \lceil d/2 \rceil)$.

3. Min-d-TCO AND PARAMETRIZED COMPLEXITY THEORY

We parametrize Min-d-TCO by the size k of its solution to a parametrized problem Min-d-TCO(k). Similarly we can define parametrized problem d-HS(k).

In this section, we shortly summarize the consequences of our reduction from Theorem 1 for the parametrized complexity. We transform the given instance of Min-d-TCO into an instance of $O(d^2)$-HS as in Theorem 1 and then we apply the kernelization from [1] to obtain a kernel of Min-d-TCO(k) or the exact algorithm from [7] to obtain the first nontrivial exact algorithm for solving Min-d-TCO(k).

Theorem 3. Min-d-TCO(k) has a kernel of size $(2c-1) \cdot k^{c-1}$ with $c = \lfloor d/2 \rfloor \cdot \lceil d/2 \rceil$.

Theorem 4. Min-d-TCO(k) on n vertices can be solved in time $O(c^k + n^2)$ with $c = \lfloor d/2 \rfloor \cdot \lceil d/2 \rceil - 1 + O(d^{-2})$.

4. ACKNOWLEDGEMENTS

The author is grateful to Koichi Wada and Juraj Hromkovič for introducing the topic and Hans-Joachim Böckenhauer for helping to improve the presentation of this brief announcement.

5. REFERENCES

[1] F. N. Abu-Khzam. Kernelization algorithms for d-hitting set problems. In *Proc. of the 10th International Workshop on Algorithms and Data Structures (WADS 2007)*, volume 4619 of LNCS, pages 434–445. Springer-Verlag, 2007.

[2] D. Angluin, J. Aspnes, and L. Reyzin. Inferring social networks from outbreaks. In *Proc. of the 21st International Conference on Algorithmic Learning Theory (ALT 2010)*, pages 104–118, 2010.

[3] G. Chockler, R. Melamed, Y. Tock, and R. Vitenberg. Constructing scalable overlays for pub-sub with many topics. In *Proc. of the 26th Annual ACM Symposium on Principles of Distributed Computing (PODC 2007)*, pages 109–118. ACM, 2007.

[4] S. Khot and O. Regev. Vertex cover might be hard to approximate to within 2-epsilon. *Journal of Computer and System Sciences*, 74(3):335–349, 2008.

[5] E. Korach and M. Stern. The clustering matroid and the optimal clustering tree. *Mathematical Programming*, 98(1-3):385–414, 2003.

[6] E. Korach and M. Stern. The complete optimal stars-clustering-tree problem. *Discrete Applied Mathematics*, 156(4):444–450, 2008.

[7] R. Niedermeier and P. Rossmanith. On efficient fixed-parameter algorithms for weighted vertex cover. *Journal of Algorithms*, 47(2):63–77, 2003.

[8] M. Onus and A. W. Richa. Minimum maximum degree publish-subscribe overlay network design. In *Proc. of IEEE INFOCOM 2009*, pages 882–890. IEEE, 2009.

Brief Announcement: A Generalization of Multiple Choice Balls-into-Bins

Gahyun Park
The State University of New York at Geneseo
1 College Circle
Geneseo, New York
park@geneseo.edu

ABSTRACT

In the multiple choice balls into bins problem, each ball is placed into the least loaded one out of d bins chosen independently and uniformly at random ($i.u.r.$). It is known that the maximum load after n balls are placed into n bins is $\ln \ln n / \ln d + O(1)$.

In this paper, we consider a variation of the standard multiple choice process. For $k < d$, we place k balls at a time into k least loaded bins among d possible locations chosen $i.u.r.$ We provide the maximum load in terms of k, d and n. The maximum load in the standard multiple choice problem can be derived from our general formulation as a special case with $k = 1$. More interestingly, our result indicates that, for any $d \leq (\ln n)^{\Theta(1)}$ and $k < d$, the maximum load is still $O(\ln \ln n)$. Our allocation scheme can be employed as optimal file replication and data partition policies in distributed file systems and databases. When a new file is created, k copies/fragments of the file are stored into k least loaded among d randomly chosen servers, where k is a tunable parameter that may depend on the level of load balance, file availability, fault tolerance, and popularity or size of a file.

Categories and Subject Descriptors

F.2.2 [**Analysis of Algorithms and Problem Complexity**]: Nonnumerical Algorithms and Problems; G.3 [**Probability and Statistics**]: Stochastic Processes

General Terms

Algorithms, Theory

1. INTRODUCTION

In the classic single choice balls-into-bins problem, n balls are sequentially placed into n bins by putting each ball into a bin chosen independently and uniformly at random ($i.u.r.$). It is well known that the maximum load is $(1 + o(1)) \ln n / \ln \ln n$ with high probability. Azar $et\ al.$ [1] showed that the maximum load is reduced to $\ln \ln n / \ln d + O(1)$ in the d-choice process where each ball is placed into the least loaded among d bins chosen $i.u.r.$ Since the multiple choice paradigm was introduced in 1990's, a number of variants of the load balancing process have been studied [8, 5, 7, 2, 4].

In this paper, we consider the following questions. If we place 2 balls at a time into 2 least loaded out of 3 destination bins chosen $i.u.r.$, is the system still balanced? More generally, if we place $k < d$ balls into k least loaded bins among d possible destinations at a time, what is the maximum load of any bin? The problem we address here is not only interesting in its own right but also has applications to large scale distributed file systems.

Without loss of generality, we assume that n is a multiple of k and use n_k to denote n/k. Our allocation process, denoted by $\mathcal{A}(k,d,n)$, consists of n_k rounds, in each of which $k < d$ balls are placed into k least loaded bins among d bins chosen $i.u.r.$ and ties are broken randomly.

1.1 Main Results

THEOREM 1. *Let $M(k,d,n)$ be the maximum load after n balls are placed into n bins using $\mathcal{A}(k,d,n)$ with $1 \leq k < d$. The following holds with probability $1 - o(1/n)$.*
i) For any $1 \leq k < d$,

$$M(k,d,n) \leq \frac{\ln \ln n}{\ln(d-k+1)} + O\left(\frac{d}{d-k}\right). \quad (1)$$

ii) In particular, when $d \to \infty$ as $n \to \infty$ and $d - k \ll d$ then

$$M(k,d,n) \leq \frac{\ln \ln n}{\ln(d-k+1)} + \frac{\ln \frac{d}{d-k}}{\ln \ln \frac{d}{d-k}} (1 + o(1)). \quad (2)$$

If $k = 1$, the maximum load resulting from (1) is $\ln \ln n / \ln d + O(1)$ which coincides with the well-known maximum load in the standard d-choice process. If $d/(d - k) = O(1)$, then M(k,d,n) is $\ln \ln / \ln(d - k + 1) + O(1)$, same bound obtained from the standard $(d - k + 1)$-choice process. Observe that, even when $k = \Omega(\ln n)$, a constant maximum load is achieved as long as $d - k \geq \alpha d$ for some constant $\alpha > 0$. A more interesting result is obtained from (2) with $d = (\ln n)^{\Theta(1)}$ and $k = d - 1$, in which the maximum load is still on $O(\ln \ln n)$. In other words, if we place $d - 1$ balls into d randomly chosen bins except the fullest one in each round, the maximum load is only $O(\ln \ln n)$ whp.

1.2 Applications

In many distributed file systems, data replication and partition have been widely used to provide reliability, availability, scalability, and load balancing. An important design consideration for such storage systems is to decide how many replicas/blocks of each file should be created and where to place them in the system.

The $\mathcal{A}(k,d,n)$ allocation scheme can be naturally applied to storage systems using consistent hashing such as Amazon's Dynamo [3] and Facebook's Cassandra [6]. When a

PODC'11, June 6–8, 2011, San Jose, California, USA.
ACM 978-1-4503-0719-2/11/06.

new file is created, k copies (or blocks) of the file are placed into k least loaded among d servers chosen by d hash values. Parameter k can be determined considering the popularity or size of a file, fault tolerance, and file availability.

The $\mathcal{A}(k, d, n)$ process achieves load balance in a more effective way than the standard multiple choice allocation in terms of the cost of data insertion and search operations. Assume that d is suitably large (e.g., $d = \ln n$) and $k = \alpha d$ with constant $\alpha > 0$, the maximum load is $\ln \ln n / \ln(d - k + 1) + O(1)$ as stated in Theorem 1. In order to achieve the same level of load balance, the standard multiple choice strategy requires $d - k + 1$ choices. In each round, $\mathcal{A}(k, d, n)$ needs to probe $O(d)$ servers to decide k least loaded servers. Thus the total insertion cost is $O(dn/k) = O(n)$. The standard $(d - k + 1)$-choice process requires $O(d - k + 1) = O(d)$ probing per replica, resulting in $O(dn)$ insertion cost in total. In order to retrieve data in $\mathcal{A}(k, d, n)$, any of its k copies will suffice and hence the search cost is $O(d/k) = O(1)$ on average, where as the average search cost incurred in the corresponding $(d-k+1)$-choice process is $(d - k + 1)/2$ on average.

2. ANALYSIS

We use $\nu_{\geq i}(r)$ to denote the number of bins loaded with at least i balls immediately after the r-th round is finished. As in [1], we use induction to construct values β_i such that, with high probability, $\nu_{\geq i}(n_k) \leq \beta_i$. Due to space limitations, we sketch the proof of Theorem 1 and discuss the main differences from [1]. First, k balls are placed at once in $\mathcal{A}(k, d, n)$, we need to deal with the dependencies among random variables that take values in the range $\{0, 1, ..., k\}$. Existing Chernoff-Hoeffding type bounds for bounded random variables, however, are no longer be sufficiently useful in our case. The following lemma provides a Chernoff-like bound which allows us to treat bounded random variables as binary $(0/1)$ random variables when a certain condition is met.

LEMMA 1. *Let Y_r be independent random variables with $p_j = \Pr(Y_r = j)$ and $\sum_{j=0}^{k} p_j = 1$. Suppose that there exists $\eta > 1$ for which $p_1 \geq p_j \eta^{j-1}$ holds for each $j = 2, \ldots, k$. Then the following tail probability bounds hold.*
i) For $\delta > 0$, we have

$$\Pr(\sum_{r=1}^{m} Y_r \geq (1 + \delta)p_1 m) \leq \left(\frac{e^\delta}{(\eta(1 + \delta)/(\eta + 1 + \delta))^{1+\delta}} \right)^{p_1 m}.$$

ii) If $\eta > e$, then

$$\Pr\left(\sum_{r=1}^{m} Y_r \geq \frac{\eta e}{\eta - e} p_1 m \right) \leq e^{-p_1 m}.$$

For a fixed value i and any $r \leq n_k$, define $X_{r,i}$ as the number of balls placed into bins with load at least i in the rth round when $\nu_{\geq i}(r - 1) \leq \beta_i$. Then we can bound the probability distribution for $X_{r,i}$ as follows.

$$\Pr(X_{r,i} = j \mid X_{1,i}, \ldots, X_{r-1,i}) \leq \binom{d}{d - k + j} \left(\frac{\beta_i}{n} \right)^{d-k+j}.$$

Let $p_{j,i} = \binom{d}{d-k+j} \left(\frac{\beta_i}{n} \right)^{d-k+j}$ for $j = 1, \ldots, k$ and let $p_{0,i} = 1 - \sum_{j=1}^{k} p_{j,i}$. Let $Y_{r,i}$ represent an independent random variable with $p_{0,i}, \ldots, p_{k,i}$ as its probability distribution.

Another challenge in extending the analysis [1] to our case is that when d is large and k is close d, the sequence of β_i decreases very slowly for large range of i values. We determine i_* such that, for all $i > i_*$, $p_{1,i} \geq p_{j,i}(2e)^{j-1}$ holds for $j = 2, ..., k$, and a sequence of $\{\beta_i\}_{i \geq i_*}$ decreases doubly exponentially. Let $\mathcal{E}_i$ be the event that $\nu_{\geq i}(n_k) \leq \beta_i$. Using Lemma 1, we obtain

$$\Pr(\nu_{\geq i+1}(n_k) \geq 2ep_{1,i}n_k \mid \mathcal{E}_i) \leq \frac{\Pr\left(\sum_{r=1}^{n_k} X_{r,i} \geq 2ep_1 n_k\right)}{\Pr(\mathcal{E}_i)}$$

$$\leq \frac{\Pr\left(\sum_{r=1}^{n_k} Y_{r,i} \geq 2ep_1 n_k\right)}{\Pr(\mathcal{E}_i)}$$

$$\leq \frac{e^{-p_{1,i}n_k}}{\Pr(\mathcal{E}_i)}.$$

Now we can construct β_{i+1} from β_i as

$$\beta_{i+1} = 2e \binom{d}{d - k + 1} \left(\frac{\beta_i}{n} \right)^{d-k+1} n_k,$$

and obtain

$$\beta_{i+i_*} \leq \left(\frac{\beta_{i_*}}{n/g_{k,d}} \right)^{(d-k+1)^i} n,$$

where $g_{k,d} = \left(\frac{2e}{k} \binom{d}{d-k+1} \right)^{\frac{1}{d-k}} = O(d/(d-k))$. Thus we choose i_* to be the smallest i such that $\beta_i \leq \frac{n}{2g_{k,d}}$ in order to guarantee that $\beta_{i+i_*} \leq \frac{n}{2^{(d-k+1)^i}}$, for any $i > 0$. Since $\mathcal{A}(k, d, n)$ is *majorized* by the single choice process, β_i is bounded above by $\Theta(n/i!)$. Thus we set i_* to $\frac{\ln(d/(d-k))}{\ln\ln(d/(d-k))}(1 + o(1))$.

3. REFERENCES

[1] Y. Azar, A. Z. Broder, A. R. Karlin, and E. Upfal. Balanced allocations. *SIAM Journal on Computing*, 29(1):180–200, September 1999.

[2] P. Berenbrink, A. Czumaj, A. Steger, and B. Vöcking. Balanced allocations: the heavily loaded case. In *STOC*, pages 745–754, 2000.

[3] G. DeCandia, D. Hastorun, M. Jampani, G. Kakulapati, A. Lakshman, A. Pilchin, S. Sivasubramanian, P. Vosshall, and W. Vogels. Dynamo: amazon's highly available key-value store. In *SIGOPS*, pages 205–220, 2007.

[4] L. Devroye, G. Lugosi, G. Park, and W. Szpankowski. Multiple choice tries and distributed hash tables. In *SODA*, pages 891–899, 2007.

[5] P. B. Godfrey. Balls and bins with structure: balanced allocations on hypergraphs. In *SODA*, pages 511–517, 2008.

[6] A. Lakshman and P. Malik. Cassandra: a decentralized structured storage system. *SIGOPS Oper. Syst. Rev*, 44(2):35–40, April 2010.

[7] Y. Peres, K. Talwar, and U. Wieder. The $(1 + \beta)$-choice process and weighted balls into bins. In *SODA*, pages 1613–1619, 2010.

[8] B. Vöcking. How asymmetry helps load balancing. *Journal of ACM*, 50(4):568–589, July 2003.

Brief Announcement: A Theory of Goal-Oriented Communication[*]

Oded Goldreich
Weizmann Institute for
Science
Rehovot, Israel
oded.goldreich@weizmann.ac.il

Brendan Juba[†]
MIT CSAIL & Harvard SEAS
Cambridge, MA, USA
bjuba@alum.mit.edu

Madhu Sudan
Microsoft Research
Cambridge, MA, USA
madhu@mit.edu

ABSTRACT

We put forward a general theory of *goal-oriented communication*, where communication is not an end in itself, but rather a means to achieving some *goals* of the communicating parties. Focusing on goals provides a framework for addressing the problem of potential "misunderstanding" during communication, where the misunderstanding arises from lack of initial agreement on what protocol and/or language is being used in communication. Despite the enormous diversity among the goals of communication, we propose a simple model that captures *all* goals.

Categories and Subject Descriptors

F.0 [**Theory of Computation**]: General; E.4 [**Coding and Information Theory**]: Formal models of communication

General Terms

Theory

1. INTRODUCTION

Modern computer systems consist of pieces that are built at different times, by different groups, that make no special effort to coordinate with one another. Moreover, any "standards" employed by these parties change over time as the amount of data (and/or address spaces) grows and as new applications and features are introduced. Thus, there are no longer any guarantees that these pieces *interoperate*—and indeed, everyday experience shows that new components are often incompatible with the old. We therefore wish to understand when interoperability in the absence of fixed standards is possible and at what expense.

To our knowledge, though, all existing models of communication problems – building on the seminal work by Shannon [7] – implicitly assume that the communicating components are designed together, so the issues of (in)compatibility that we wish to study do not arise and cannot be captured in these models. This deficiency was pointed out in an earlier work by Juba and Sudan [3], who suggested that these

problems might be addressed by explicitly introducing the *goal of the communication*, and furthermore demonstrated that for one example goal – delegating computation of a function – *universal* interoperability can be guaranteed. In this work, we establish that the earlier suggestion of Juba and Sudan is essentially valid by introducing a mathematical model of generic goal-oriented communication and showing that for broad classes of goals in this model, we can design components (algorithms) with universal compatibility.

In particular, the main feature of our work is the level of generality: while the earlier work of Juba and Sudan relied on a computational imbalance between the components, and in particular only considered the delegation of a PSPACE-complete function by a polynomial-time bounded algorithm, our work addresses any case in which there is something to gain from the communication. For example, the problem of using a printer to produce a document – which cannot be cast as a problem of delegating computation in any reasonable sense – is captured naturally by the simple model introduced in the current work.

2. THE MODEL OF GOAL-ORIENTED COMMUNICATION

We focus primarily on the case of communication between a pair of entities, since this is sufficient to capture the essential issues of incompatibility that may arise. Moreover, we focus on an asymmetric setting of communication between parties that we refer to as a *user* – who represents "us" or "our point of view," and in any case, operates on our behalf – and a *server*, whose assistance towards achieving a *goal* we seek via communication.[1] In particular, we consider a synchronous model of communication in which the parties are described by *strategies* that take a *internal state* and an incoming message profile to a (distribution over) a new state and an outgoing message profile. Following the work of Juba and Sudan [3], the core of the problems of incompatibility that we consider are captured by considering, instead of a single server strategy, a *class* of possible server strategies: roughly, a user strategy is compatible with the entire class of servers if its goal of communication is achieved whenever the user is paired with any (adversarially selected) server in the class.

Note, however, that in our model as described thus far, neither the user strategy, nor the server strategy, and *cer-*

---

[*]The full version of this work is available on ECCC [1] and in adapted form in the second author's Ph.D. thesis [2].

[†]Supported by NSF Award CCF-0939370

---

[1]We remark that the full version [1] briefly considers a symmetric setting with more than two parties, but this primarily consists of a reduction to the two-party setting.

tainly not the contents of the communications channels they share should be specified (fixed) by the goal of communication. The goal is thus introduced by introducing a *third* entity to the model, capturing either a hypothetical "referee," "the rest of the system," or "the environment," which monitors the communication between the user and the server by communicating with them, that we refer to as the *world*. We postulate that the (user's) goal for the communication can be described in terms of the states of this third party's strategy. That is, to fix a goal of communication, we take the world's (non-deterministic[2]) strategy as fixed, and fix a set of acceptable sequences of world states (or equivalently, define a *referee* predicate on the set of all possible histories of world states). We say that "the goal is achieved" if the system produces a sequence of world states that is acceptable.

At this level of generality, clearly not every goal can be achieved by some user-server pair, and our focus is naturally on cases in which the only issue is compatibilty: that is, in which *some* reasonable (e.g., polynomial time) user strategy would achieve the goal with an adequate server. Actually, in order to simplify matters, we focus exclusively on *forgiving* goals in which every finite partial history can be extended to a successful history. Fixing such a forgiving goal, we say that a server strategy is *helpful* for the goal and a class of user strategies if there is some user strategy U such that when U is paired with the server, and the server and world are started from *any* initial state, the goal is achieved (i.e., the referee is satisfied). We then refer to a user strategy as *universal* for a goal (and a class of user strategies) if it achieves the goal with every server that is helpful for the goal (with respect to this class of user strategies).

3. NOTIONS AND RESULTS OF THE THEORY

As stated in the introduction, our second main contribution is that we are able to identify broad classes of goals of communication for which universal user strategies can be designed. These classes are described in terms of the feedback available to the user regarding its performance towards achieving the goal. Broadly speaking, we consider two families of goals, with different notions of feedback: one is *finite* goals, in which the user must halt at some point, and the referee is defined on these finite histories, and the other is *compact* goals in which the system runs for infinite time, and the referee's decision is determined by whether the number of "unacceptable" prefixes of the history is finite or infinite. In each of these two cases, we introduce notions of feedback that we call *sensing*, which formally are predicates of the history of the portion of the system visible to the user. In each case, we specify two properties, called viability and safety, that the Boolean indications produced by sensing should satisfy, in order to be useful as a source of feedback. Loosely speaking, for compact goals, *viability* means that the user only obtains positive indications whenever it is coupled with a server that leads to achieving the goal (i.e., producing an acceptable execution), whereas *safety* means that negative indications are obtained when the user strategy is coupled with a server that does not lead

to achieving the goal. For finite goals, *safety* roughly means that positive indications are only obtained on acceptable histories, and *viability* means that a positive indication would be obtained by *some* (unknown) user strategy with a given server strategy.

Our main result asserts that whenever feedback (captured by safe and viable sensing) is available for a goal and a class of servers, there exists a user strategy (i.e., a universal one) that achieves the goal whenever coupled with any server in the class.

THEOREM 1 (MAIN RESULT, LOOSELY STATED). *For any (compact or finite) goal and any class of server strategies for which there exists safe and viable sensing, there exists a universal user strategy.*

In particular, if sensing is safe and viable with all helpful server strategies, then the theorem guarantees that we can design a user strategy that is universal with respect to any helpful server; that is, this universal strategy achieves the goal when coupled with a server S *iff* there is *some* user strategy that achieves the goal when coupled with S.

Loosely speaking, in the compact case, Theorem 1 is proved by enumerating all relevant user strategies and switching from the current strategy to the next one when a negative indication is obtained from the sensing function; in the finite case, strategies are enumerated "in parallel" as in Levin's approach in [6], and sensing is used to decide when to stop. We mention that, in general, the overhead introduced by the enumeration is essentially necessary; that is, there exist natural cases in which any universal strategy must incur such an overhead. However, in special cases of interest, better performance may be possible. Indeed, we view our results as the first steps in a new direction, which motivate the search for algorithms that are compatible with broad classes (that may not include all helpful servers). We note that some examples of such algorithms have been subsequently identified by Juba and Sudan [4] and Juba and Vempala [5] (also described in [2]).

4. ACKNOWLEDGEMENTS

We thank Boaz Patt-Shamir for encouraging this announcement, and an anonymous reviewer for insightful comments.

5. REFERENCES

[1] O. Goldreich, B. Juba, and M. Sudan. A Theory of Goal-Oriented Communication. Technical Report TR09-075, ECCC, 2009.

[2] B. Juba. Universal Semantic Communication. PhD thesis, MIT, September 2010.

[3] B. Juba and M. Sudan. Universal Semantic Communication I. In *40th STOC*, pages 123–132, 2008.

[4] B. Juba and M. Sudan. Efficient Semantic Communication via Compatible Beliefs. In *2nd ICS*, pages 22–31, 2011.

[5] B. Juba and S. Vempala. Semantic Communication for Simple Goals is Equivalent to On-line Learning. Manuscript, 2011.

[6] L. A. Levin. Universal Search Problems. *Probl. Inform. Transm.*, 9:265–266, 1973.

[7] C. Shannon. A Mathematical Theory of Communication. *Bell System Technical Journal*, 27:379–423, 623–656, 1948.

---

[2]Precisely, we find it convenient to assume that the world makes a single non-deterministic choice of a standard probabilistic strategy.

Xheal: Localized Self-healing using Expanders

[Extended Abstract]

Gopal Pandurangan[*]
Division of Mathematical Sciences, Nanyang
Technological University, Singapore 637371
and
Department of Computer Science, Brown
University, Providence, RI 02912, USA.
gopalpandurangan@gmail.com

Amitabh Trehan[†]
Faculty of Industrial Engineering and
Management,
Technion - Israel Institute of Technology,
Haifa, Israel - 32000.
amitabh.trehaan@gmail.com

ABSTRACT

We consider the problem of self-healing in reconfigurable networks (e.g. peer-to-peer and wireless mesh networks) that are under repeated attack by an omniscient adversary and propose a fully distributed algorithm, *Xheal*, that maintains good expansion and spectral properties of the network, also keeping the network connected. Moreover, *Xheal* does this while allowing only low stretch and degree increase per node. The algorithm heals global properties like expansion and stretch while only doing local changes and using only local information. We use a model similar to that used in recent work on self-healing. In our model, over a sequence of rounds, an adversary either inserts a node with arbitrary connections or deletes an arbitrary node from the network. The network responds by quick "repairs," which consist of adding or deleting edges in an efficient localized manner.

These repairs preserve the edge expansion, spectral gap, and network stretch, after adversarial deletions, without increasing node degrees by too much, in the following sense. At any point in the algorithm, the expansion of the graph will be either 'better' than the expansion of the graph formed by considering only the adversarial insertions (not the adversarial deletions) or the expansion will be, at least, a constant. Also, the stretch i.e. the distance between any pair of nodes in the healed graph is no more than a $O(\log n)$ factor. Similarly, at any point, a node v whose degree would have been d in the graph with adversarial insertions only, will have degree at most $O(\kappa d)$ in the actual graph, for a small

[*]Supported in part by the following grants: Nanyang Technological University grant M58110000, US NSF grant CCF-1023166, and by a grant from the United States-Israel Binational Science Foundation (BSF).

[†]Work done partly at Brown University and University of Victoria. Supported in part at the Technion by a fellowship of the Israel Council for Higher Education.

parameter κ. We also provide bounds on the second smallest eigenvalue of the Laplacian which captures key properties such as mixing time, conductance, congestion in routing etc. Our distributed data structure has low amortized latency and bandwidth requirements. Our work improves over the self-healing algorithms *Forgiving tree* [PODC 2008] and *Forgiving graph* [PODC 2009] in that we are able to give guarantees on degree and stretch, while at the same time preserving the expansion and spectral properties of the network.

Categories and Subject Descriptors

C.2.1 [**Computer-Communication Networks**]: Network Architecture and Design;Distributed networks, Network communications, Network topology, Wireless communication; C.2.4 [**Computer-Communication Networks**]: Distributed Systems; C.4 [**Computer Systems Organization**]: Performance of SystemsFault tolerance, Reliability, availability and serviceability; E.1 [**Data Structures**]: Distributed data structures, Graphs and networks; G.2.2 [**Graph Theory**]: Graph algorithms; G.3 [**Probability and Statistics**]: Probabilistic algorithms; H.3.4 [**Systems and Software**]: Distributed systems, Information networks

General Terms

Algorithms, Design, Reliability, Security, Theory

Keywords

self-healing, reconfiguration, local, distributed, expansion, spectral properties, expanders, randomized

1. INTRODUCTION

Networks in the modern age have grown to such an extent that they have now begun to resemble self-governing living entities. Centralized control and management of resources has become increasingly untenable. Distributed and localized attainment of self-* properties is fast becoming the need of the hour.

As we have seen the baby Internet grow through its adolescence into a strapping teenager, we have experienced and are experiencing many of its growth pangs and tantrums. There have been recent disruption of services in networks such as Google, Twitter, Facebook and Skype. On August 15, 2007 the Skype network crashed for about 48 hours, disrupting service to approximately 200 million users [8, 21, 23, 28, 30]. Skype attributed this outage to failures in their "self-healing mechanisms" [2]. We believe that this outage is indicative of the unprecedented complexity of modern computer systems: we are approaching scales of billions of components. Unfortunately, current algorithms ensure robustness in computer networks through the increasingly unscalable approach of hardening individual components or, at best, adding lots of redundant components. Such designs are increasingly unviable. No living organism is designed such that no component of it ever fails: there are simply too many components. For example, skin can be cut and still heal. It is much more practical to design skin that can heal than a skin that is completely impervious to attack.

This paper adopts a *responsive* approach, in the sense that it responds to an attack (or component failure) by changing the topology of the network. This approach works irrespective of the initial state of the network, and is thus orthogonal and complementary to traditional non-responsive techniques. This approach requires the network to be *reconfigurable*, in the sense that the topology of the network can be changed. Many important networks are *reconfigurable*. Many of these we have designed e.g. peer-to-peer, wireless mesh and ad-hoc computer networks, and infrastructure networks, such as an airline's transportation network. Many have existed since long but we have only now closely scrutinized them e.g. social networks such as friendship networks on social networking sites, and biological networks, including the human brain. Most of them are also dynamic, due to the capacity of individual nodes to initiate new connections or drop existing connections.

In this setting, our paper seeks to address the important and challenging problem of efficiently and responsively maintaining global invariants in a localized, distributed manner. It is obvious that it is a significant challenge to come up with approaches to optimize various properties at the same time, especially with only local knowledge. For example, a star topology achieves the lowest distance between nodes, but the central node has the highest degree. If we were trying to give the lowest degrees to the nodes in a connected graph, they would be connected in a line/cycle giving the maximum possible diameter. Tree structures give a good compromise between degree increase and distances, but may lead to poor spectral properties (expansion) and poor load balancing. Our main contribution is a self-healing algorithm *Xheal* that maintains spectral properties (expansion), connectivity, and stretch in a distributed manner using only localized information and actions, while allowing only a small degree increase per node. Our main algorithm is described in Section 3.

Our Model: Our model, which is similar to the model introduced in [15, 31], is briefly described here. We assume that the network is initially a connected (undirected, simple) graph over n nodes. An adversary repeatedly attacks the network. This adversary knows the network topology and our algorithm, and it has the ability to delete arbitrary nodes from the network or insert a new node in the system which it can connect to any subset of nodes currently in the system. However, we assume the adversary is constrained in that in any time step it can only delete or insert a single node. (Our algorithm can be extended to handle multiple insertions/deletions.) The detailed model is described in Section 2.

Our Results: For a reconfigurable network (e.g., peer-to-peer, wireless mesh networks) that has both insertions and deletions, let G' be the graph consisting of the original nodes and inserted nodes without any changes due to deletions. Let n be the number of nodes in G', and G be the present (healed) graph. Our main result is a new algorithm *Xheal* that ensures (cf. Theorem 2 in Section 4): 1) *Spectral Properties:* If G' has expansion equal or better than a constant, *Xheal* achieves at least a constant expansion, else it maintains at least the same expansion as G'; Furthermore, we show bounds on the second smallest eigenvalue of the Laplacian of G, $\lambda(G)$ with respect to the corresponding $\lambda(G')$. An important special case of our result is that if G' is an (bounded degree) expander, then Xheal guarantees that G is also an (bounded degree) expander. We note that such a guarantee is not provided by the self-healing algorithms of [15, 14]. 2)*Stretch:* The distance between any two nodes of the actual network never increases by more than $O(\log n)$ times their distance in G'; and 3) the degree of any node never increases by more than κ times its degree in G', where κ is a small parameter (which is implementation dependent, can be chosen to be a constant — cf. Section 5).

Our algorithm is distributed, localized and resource efficient. We introduce the main algorithm separately (Section 3) and a distributed implementation (Section 5). The high-level idea behind our algorithm is to put a κ-regular expander between the deleted node and its neighbors. Since this expander has low degree and constant expansion, intuitively this helps in maintaining good expansion. However, a key complication in this intuitive approach is efficient implementation while maintaining bounds on degree and stretch. The κ parameter above is determined by the particular distributed implementation of an expander that we use. Our construction is randomized which guarantees efficient maintenance of an expander under insertion and deletion, albeit at the cost of a small probability that the graph may not be an expander. This aspect of our implementation can be improved if one can design efficient distributed constructions that yield expanders deterministically. (To the best of our knowledge no such construction is known). In our implementation, for a deletion, repair takes $O(\log n)$ rounds and has amortized complexity that is within $O(\kappa \log n)$ times the best possible. The formal statement and proof of these results are in Sections 4 and 5.

Related Work: The work most closely related to ours is [15, 31], which introduces a distributed data structure *Forgiving Graph* that, in a model similar to ours, maintains low stretch of a network with constant multiplicative degree increase per node. However, *Xheal* is more ambitious in that it not only maintains similar properties but also the spectral properties (expansion) with obvious benefits, and also uses different techniques. However, we pay with larger message sizes and amortized analysis of costs. The works of [15, 31] themselves use models or techniques from earlier work [31, 14, 29, 4]. They put in tree like structures of nodes in place of the deleted node. Methods which put in tree like sructures of nodes are likely to be bad for expansion. If the original network is a star of $n+1$ nodes and the central node gets deleted, the repair algorithm puts in a tree, pulling the expansion down from a constant to $O(1/n)$. Even the algorithms *Forgiving tree* [14] and *Forgiving graph* [15], which

302

put in a tree of virtual nodes (simulated by real nodes) in place of a deleted node don't improve the situation. In these algorithms, even though the real network is an isomorphism of the virtual network, the 'binary search' properties of the virtual trees ensure a poor cut involving the root of the trees.

The importance of spectral properties is well known [5, 18]. Many results are based on graphs having enough expansion or conductance, including recent results in distributed computing in information spreading etc. [16]. There are only a few papers showing distributed construction of expander graphs [20, 6, 11]; Law and Siu's construction gives expanders with high probability using Hamilton cycles which we use in our implementation.

Many papers have discussed strategies for adding additional capacity or rerouting in anticipation of failures [3, 7, 10, 19, 26, 32, 33]. Some other results are also responsive in some sense: [22, 1] or have enough built-in redundancy in separate components [12], but all of them have fixed network topologies. Our approach does not dictate routing paths or require initially placed redundant components. There is also some research in the physics community on preventing cascading failures which empirically works well but unfortunately performs very poorly under adversarial attack [17, 25, 24, 13].

1.1 Preliminaries

Edge Expansion: Let $G = (V, E)$ be an undirected graph and $S \subset V$ be a set of nodes. We denote $\overline{S} = V - S$. Let $|E|_{S,\overline{S}} = \{(u,v) \in E | u \in S, v \in \overline{S}\}$ be the number of edges crossing the cut $(S, \overline{S})$. We define the *volume* of S to be the sum of the degrees of the vertices in S as $vol(S) = \sum_{x \in S} degree(x)$. The edge expansion of the graph h_G is defined as, $h_G = \min_{|S| \leq |V|/2} \frac{|E|_{S,\overline{S}}}{|S|}$.

Cheeger constant: A related notion is the Cheeger constant ϕ_G of a graph (also called as *conductance*) defined as follows [5]: $\phi_G = \min_{|S|} \frac{|E|_{S,\overline{S}}}{min(vol(S), vol(\overline{S}))}$.

The Cheeger constant can be more appropriate for graphs which are very non-regular, since the denominator takes into account the sum of the degrees of vertices in S, rather than just the size of S. Note for $k-$regular graphs, the Cheeger constant is just the edge expansion divided by k, hence they are essentially equivalent for regular graphs. However, in general graphs, key properties such as mixing time, congestion in routing etc.are captured more accurately by the Cheeger constant, rather than edge expansion. For example, consider a constant degree expander of n nodes and partition the vertex set into two equal parts. Make each of the parts a clique. This graph has expansion at least a constant, but its conductance is $O(1/n)$. Thus while the expander has logarithmic mixing time, the modified graph has polynomial mixing time.

The Cheeger constant is closely related to the the second-smallest eigenvalue of the Laplacian matrix denoted by λ_G (also called the "algebraic connectivity" of the graph). Hence λ_G, like the Cheeger constant, captures many key "global" properties of the graph [5]. λ_G captures how "well-connected" the graph is and is strictly greater than 0 (which is always the smallest eigenvalue) if and only if the graph is connected. For an expander graph, it is a constant (bounded away from zero). The larger λ_G is, larger is the expansion.

THEOREM 1. CHEEGER INEQUALITY*[5]* $2\phi_G \geq \lambda_G > \phi_G^2/2$

Figure 1: The Node Insert, Delete and Network Repair Model – Distributed View.

Each node of G_0 is a processor.
Each processor starts with a list of its neighbors in G_0.
Pre-processing: Processors may send messages to and from their neighbors.
for $t := 1$ to T **do**
  Adversary deletes or inserts a node v_t from/into G_{t-1}, forming U_t.
  if node v_t is inserted **then**
    The new neighbors of v_t may update their information and send messages to and from their neighbors.
  if node v_t is deleted **then**
    All neighbors of v_t are informed of the deletion.
    Recovery phase:
    Nodes of U_t may communicate (synchronously, in parallel) with their immediate neighbors. These messages are never lost or corrupted, and may contain the names of other vertices.
    During this phase, each node may insert edges joining it to any other nodes as desired. Nodes may also drop edges from previous rounds if no longer required.
  At the end of this phase, we call the graph G_t.

Success metrics: Minimize the following "complexity" measures:

Consider the graph G'_t which is the graph, at timestep t, consisting solely of the original nodes (from G_0) and insertions without regard to deletions and healings.

1. **Degree increase.** $\max_{v \in G_t} \frac{degree(v, G_t)}{degree(v, G'_t)}$

2. **Edge expansion.** $h(G_t) \geq min(\alpha, \beta h(G'_t))$; for constants $\alpha, \beta > 0$

3. **Network stretch.** $\max_{x,y \in G_t} \frac{dist(x,y,G_t)}{dist(x,y,G'_t)}$, where, for a graph G and nodes x and y in G, $dist(x,y,G)$ is the length of the shortest path between x and y in G.

4. **Recovery time.** The maximum total time for a recovery round, assuming it takes a message no more than 1 time unit to traverse any edge and we have unlimited local computational power at each node. We assume the LOCAL message-passing model, i.e., there is no bound on the size of the message that can pass through an edge in a time step.

5. **Communication complexity.** Amortized number of messages used for recovery.

2. NODE INSERT, DELETE, AND NETWORK REPAIR MODEL

This model is based on the one introduced in [15, 31]. Somewhat similar models were also used in [14, 29]. We now describe the details. Let $G = G_0$ be an arbitrary graph on n nodes, which represent processors in a distributed network. In each step, the adversary either adds a node or deletes a node. After each deletion, the algorithm gets to add some new edges to the graph, as well as deleting old ones. At each insertion, the processors follow a protocol to update their information. The algorithm's goal is to maintain connectivity in the network, while maintaining good expansion properties and keeping the distance between the nodes small. At the same time, the algorithm wants to minimize the resources spent on this task, including keeping node degree small. We assume that although the adversary has full knowledge of the topology at every step and can add or delete any node it wants, it is oblivious to the random choices made by the self-healing algorithm as well as to the communication that takes place between the nodes (in other words, we assume private channels between nodes).

Initially, each processor only knows its neighbors in G_0, and is unaware of the structure of the rest of G_0. After each deletion or insertion, only the neighbors of the deleted or inserted vertex are informed that the deletion or insertion has occurred. After this, processors are allowed to communicate (synchronously) by sending a limited number of messages to their direct neighbors. We assume that these messages are always sent and received successfully. The processors may also request new edges be added to the graph. We assume that no other vertex is deleted or inserted until the end of this round of computation and communication has concluded.

We also allow a certain amount of pre-processing to be done before the first attack occurs. In particular, we assume that all nodes have access to some amount of local information. For example, we assume that all nodes know the address of all the neighbors of its neighbors (NoN). More generally, we assume the (synchronous) LOCAL computation model [27] for our analysis. This is a well studied distributed computing model and has been used to study numerous "local" problems such as coloring, dominating set, vertex cover etc. [27]. This model allows arbitrary sized messages to go through an edge per time step. In this model the NoN information can be exchanged in $O(1)$ rounds.

Our goal is to minimize the time (the number of rounds) and the (amortized) message complexity per deletion (insertion doesn't require any work from the self-healing algorithm). Our model is summarized in Figure 1.

3. THE ALGORITHM

We give a high-level view of the distributed algorithm deferring the distributed implementation details for now (these will be described later in Section 5). The algorithm is summarized in Algorithm 3. To describe the algorithm, we associate a color with each edge of the graph. We will assume that the original edges of G and those added by the adversary are all colored **black** initially. The algorithm can later recolor edges (i.e., to a color other than black — throughout when we say "colored" edge we mean a color other than black) as described below. If (u, v) is a black (colored) edge, we say that $v(u)$ is a black (colored) neighbor of $u(v)$. Let κ be a fixed parameter that is implementation dependent (cf. Section 5). For the purposes of this algorithm, we assume the existence of a κ-regular expander with edge expansion $\alpha > 2$.

At any time step, the adversary can add a node (with its incident edges) or delete a node (with its incident edges). Addition is straightforward, the algorithm takes no action. The added edges are colored black.

The self-healing algorithm is mainly concerned with what edges to add and/or delete when a node is deleted. The algorithm adds/deletes edges based on the colors of the edges deleted as well as on other factors as described below. Let v

be the deleted node and $NBR(v)$ be the neighbors of v in the network after the current deletion. We have the following cases:

Case 1: *All the deleted edges are black edges.* In this case, we construct a κ-regular expander among the neighbor nodes $NBR(v)$ of the deleted node. (If the number of neighbors is less than κ, then a clique (a complete graph) is constructed among these nodes.) All the edges of this expander are colored by a unique color, say C_v (e.g., the ID of the deleted node can be chosen as the color, assuming that every node gets a unique ID whenever it is inserted to the network). Note that the addition of the expander edges is such that multi-edges are not created. In other words, if (black) edge (u, v) is already present, and the expander construction mandates the addition of a (colored) edge between (u, v) then this done by simply re-coloring the edge to color C_v. Thus our algorithm does not add multi-edges.

We call the expander subgraph constructed in this case among the nodes in $NBR(v)$ as a *primary (expander) cloud* or simply *a primary cloud* and all the (colored) edges in the cloud are called primary edges. (The term "cloud" is used to capture the fact that the nodes involved are "closeby", i.e., local to each other.) To identify the primary cloud (as opposed to a secondary, described later) we assume that all primary colors are different shades of color **red**.

Case 2: *At least some of the deleted edges are colored edges.* In this case, we have two subcases.

Case 2.1: *All the deleted colored edges are primary edges.* Let the colored edges belong to the colors $C_1, C_2, \ldots, C_j$. This means that the deleted node v belonged to j primary clouds (see Figure 3). There will be κ edges of each color class deleted, since v would have degree κ in each of the primary expander clouds. In case v has black neighbors, then some black edges will also be deleted. Assume for sake of simplicity that there are no black neighbors for now. If they are present, they can be handled in the same manner as described later.

In this subcase, we do two operations. First, we fix each of the j primary clouds. Each of these clouds lost a node and so the cloud is no longer a κ-regular expander. We reconstruct a new κ-regular expander in each of the primary clouds (among the remaining nodes of each cloud). (This reconstruction is done in an incremental fashion for efficiency reasons — cf. Section 5.) The color of the edges of the respective primary clouds are retained. Second, we pick one *free* node, if available (free nodes are explained below), from each primary cloud (i.e., there will be j such nodes picked, one from each primary cloud) and these nodes will be connected together via a (new) κ-regular expander. (Again if the number of primary clouds involved are less than or equal $\kappa + 1$ i.e., $j \le \kappa + 1$, then a clique will be constructed.) The edges of this expander will have a new (unique) color of its own. We call the expander subgraph constructed in this case among the j nodes as a *secondary (expander) cloud* or simply a *secondary cloud* and all the (colored) edges in the cloud are called *secondary* edges. To identify a secondary cloud, we assume that all secondary colors are different shades of color **orange**.

If the deleted node v has black neighbors, then they are treated similarly, consider each of the neighbors as a singleton primary cloud and then proceed as above.

Free nodes and their choosing: The nodes of the primary clouds picked to form the secondary cloud are called

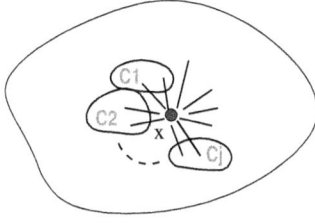

Figure 2: A node can be part of many primary clouds.

non-free nodes. Thus free nodes are nodes that belong to only primary clouds. We note that a free node can belong to more than one primary cloud (see e.g., Figure 3). In the above construction of the secondary cloud, we choose one unique free node from each cloud, i.e., if there are j clouds then we choose j different nodes and associate each with one unique primary cloud (if a free node belongs to two or more primary clouds, we associate it with only one of them) such that each primary cloud has exactly one free node associated with it. (How this is implemented is deferred to Section 5.) We call the free node associated with a particular primary cloud as the *bridge node* that "connects" the primary cloud with the secondary cloud. Note that our construction implies that any (bridge) node of a primary cloud can belong to at most one secondary cloud.

What if there are no free nodes associated with a primary cloud, say C? Then we pick a free node (say w) from another cloud among the j primary clouds (say C') and *share* the node with the cloud C. Sharing means adding w to C and forming a new κ-regular expander among the remaining nodes of C (including w). Thus w will be part of both C and C' clouds. w will be used as a free node associated with C for the subsequent repair. Note that this might render C' devoid of free nodes. To compensate for this, C' gets a free node (if available) from some other cloud (among the j primary clouds). Thus, in effect, every cloud will have its own free node associated with it, if there are at least j free nodes (totally) among the j clouds.

There is only one more possibility left to the discussed. If there are less than j free nodes among all the j clouds, then we *combine* all the j primary clouds into a *single* primary cloud, i.e., we construct a κ-regular expander among all the nodes of the j primary cloud (the previous edges belonging to the clouds are deleted). The edges of the new cloud will have a new (unique) color associated with it. Also all non-free nodes associated with the previous j clouds become free again in the combined cloud. We note that combining many primary clouds into one primary cloud is a costly operation (involves a lot of restructuring). We amortize this costly operation over many cheaper operations. This is the main intuition behind constructing a secondary expander and free nodes; constructing a secondary expander is cheaper than combining many primary expanders and this is not possible only if there are no free nodes (which happens only once in a while).

Case 2.2: *Some of the deleted edges are secondary edges.* In other words, the deleted node, say v, will be a bridge (non-free) node. Let the deleted edges belong to the primary clouds $C_1, C_2, \ldots, C_j$ and the secondary cloud F. (Our algorithm guarantees that a bridge node can belong to at most one secondary cloud.) We handle this deletion as fol-

1: **if** node v inserted with incident edges **then**
2:     The inserted edges are colored black.
3: **if** node v is deleted **then**
4:     **if** all deleted edges are black **then**
5:         MakeCloud($BlackNbrs(v), primary, Clr_{new}$)
6:     **else if** deleted colored edges are all primary **then**
7:         Let $C_1, \ldots, C_j$ be primary clouds that lost an edge
8:         FixPrimary($[C_1, \ldots, C_j]$)
9:         MakeSecondary($[C_1, \ldots, C_j] \cup BlackNbrs(v)$)
10:     **else**
11:         Let $[C_1, \ldots, C_j] \leftarrow$ primary clouds of v; $F \leftarrow$ secondary cloud of v; $[U] \leftarrow Clouds(F) \setminus [C_1, \ldots, C_j]$, $[C_1, \ldots, C_{j'}] \leftarrow F \cap [C_1, \ldots, C_j]$
12:         FixPrimary($[C_1, \ldots, C_j]$)
13:         FixSecondary(F, v)
14:         MakeSecondary($[C_{j'+1}, \ldots, C_j] \cup BlackNbrs(v)$)

Algorithm 3.1: XHEAL(G, κ)

lows. Let v be the bridge node associated with the primary cloud C_i (one among the j clouds). Without loss of generality, let the secondary cloud connect a strict subset, i.e., $j' < j$ primary clouds with possibly other (unaffected) primary clouds. This case is shown in Figure 3. As done in Case 2.1, we first fix all the j primary clouds by constructing a new κ-regular expander among the remaining nodes. We then fix the secondary cloud by finding another free node, say z, from C_i, and reconstructing a new κ-regular secondary cloud expander on z and other bridge nodes of other primary clouds of F. The edges retain the same color as their original. If there are no free nodes among all the primary clouds of F, then all primary clouds of F are combined into one new primary cloud as explained in Case 2.1 above (edges of F are deleted). The remaining $j - j'$ primary clouds are then repaired as in case 2.1 by constructing a secondary cloud between them.

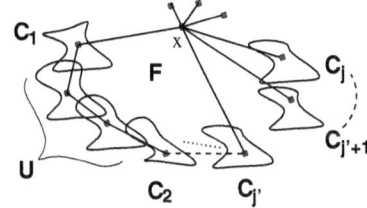

Figure 3: Case 2.2: Deleted node x part of secondary cloud F, and primary clouds

1: **if** $|V| \leq \kappa + 1$ **then**
2:     Make clique among $[V]$
3: **else**
4:     Make κ-reg expander among $[V]$ of edge $(Type, Clr)$

Algorithm 3.2: MakeCloud($[V], Type, Clr$)

1: **for** each cloud $C_i \in [C]$ **do**
2:     MakeCloud($C_i, primary, Color(C_i)$)

Algorithm 3.3: FixPrimary($[C]$)

```
1: for each cloud C_i ∈ [C] do
2:    if FrNode_i = PickFreeNode(C_i) == NULL then
3:       MakeCloud(Nodes([C]), primary, Clr_new)
4:       Return
5: MakeCloud(⋃ FrNode_i ∀C_i ∈ [C], secondary, Clr_new)
```

Algorithm 3.4: MakeSecondary([C])

```
1: if v is a bridge node of C_i in F then
2:    if FrNode_i = PickFreeNode(C_i) == NULL then
3:       MakeCloud(Nodes(F), primary, Clr_new)
4:    else
5:       MakeCloud(FrNode_i ∪ BridgeNode(C_j) ∀C_i ∈
         [C], secondary, Color(F))
```

Algorithm 3.5: FixSecondaryCloud(F, v)

```
1: Let a Free node be a primary node without secondary
   duties
2: if Free node in my cloud then
3:    Return Free node
4: else
5:    Ask neighbor clouds; if a free node found, return node,
      else return NULL
```

Algorithm 3.6: PickFreeNode()

4. ANALYSIS OF *XHEAL*

The following is our main theorem on the guarantees that *Xheal* provides on the topological properties of the healed graph. The theorem assumes that *Xheal* is able to construct a κ-regular expander (deterministically) of expansion $\alpha > 2$.

THEOREM 2. *For graph G_t (present graph) and graph G'_t (of only original and inserted edges), at any time t, where a timestep is an insertion or deletion followed by healing:*

1. *For all $x \in G_t$, $degree_{G_t}(x) \leq \kappa.degree_{G'_t}(y)$, for a fixed constant $\kappa > 0$.*

2. *For any two nodes $u, v \in G_t$, $\delta_{G_t}(u,v) \leq \delta_{G'_t}(u,v)O(\log n)$, where $\delta(u,v)$ is the shortest path between u and v, and n is the number of nodes in G_t.*

3. *$h(G_t) \geq min(\alpha, h(G'_t))$, for some fixed constant $\alpha \geq 1$.*

4. *$\lambda(G_t) \geq min\left(\Omega\left(\frac{\lambda(G'_t)^2 d_{min}(G'_t)}{(\kappa)^2(d_{max}(G'_t))^2}\right), \Omega\left(\frac{1}{(\kappa d_{max}(G'_t))^2}\right)\right)$, where $d_{min}(G'_t)$ and $d_{max}(G'_t)$ are the minimum and maximum degrees of G'_t.*

From the above theorem, we get an important corollary:

COROLLARY 1. *If G'_t is a (bounded degree) expander, then so is G_t. In other words, if the original graph and the inserted edges is an expander, then Xheal guarantees that the healed graph also is an expander.*

4.1 Expansion, Degree and Stretch

LEMMA 1. *Suppose at the first timestep (t=1), a deletion occurs. Then, after healing, $h(G_1) \geq min(c, h(G'_1))$, for a constant $c \geq 1$.*

PROOF. Observe that the initial graphs G_0 and G'_0 are identical. Suppose that node x is deleted at $t = 1$. For ease

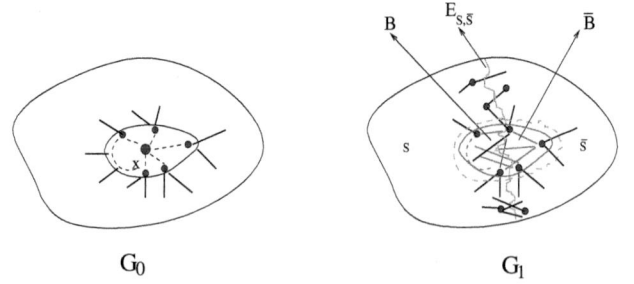

Figure 4: Healed graph after deletion of node x. The ball of x and its neighbors gets replaced by a κ-regular expander of its neighbors — Case 1 of the Algorithm.

of notation, refer to the graph G_0 as G and the healed graph G_1 as H. Notice that G'_1 is the same as G_0, since the graph G'_t does not change if the action at time t is a deletion. Consider the induced subgraph formed by x and its neighbors. Since all the deleted edges are black edges, Case 1 of the algorithm applies. Thus the healing algorithm will replace this subgraph by a new subgraph, a κ-regular expander over x's ex-neighbors. Let us call this new subgraph I. Note that this corresponds to **Case 1** of the Algorithm. We refer to Figure 4.1.

Consider a set $S(H)$ which defines the expansion in H i.e. $|S(H)| \leq n/2$ (where n is the number of nodes in G), and $S(H)$ has the minimum expansion over all the subsets of H. Call the cut induced by $S(H)$ as $E_{S,\bar{S}}(H)$ and its size as $|E|_{S,\bar{S}}(H)$. Also refer to the same set in G (without x if $S(H)$ included x) as $S(G)$, and the cut as $E_{S,\bar{S}}(G)$. The key idea of the proof is to directly bound the expansion of H, instead of looking at the change of expansion from of G. In particular, we have to handle the possibility that our self-healing algorithm may not add any new edges, because those edges may already be present. (Intuitively, this means that the prior expansion itself is good.)

We consider two cases depending on whether the healing may or may not have affected this cut.

1. $E_{S,\bar{S}}(H) \cap E(I) = \emptyset$:

   This implies that only the edges which were in G are involved in the cut $E_{S,\bar{S}}(H)$. Since expansion is defined as the minimum over all cuts, $|E|_{S,\bar{S}}(G) \geq h(G)|S(G)|$. Also, since $E_{S,\bar{S}}(H) = E_{S,\bar{S}}(G)$ and $S(H) \leq S(G)$, we have:

   $$h(H) = \frac{E_{S,\bar{S}}(H)}{S(H)} \geq \frac{E_{S,\bar{S}}(G)}{S(G)} \geq h(G).$$

2. $E_{S,\bar{S}}(H) \cap E(I) \neq \emptyset$: Notice that if there is any minimum expansion cut not intersecting $E(I)$, part 1 applies, and we are done.

   The healing algorithm tries to add enough new edges (if needed) into I so that I itself has an expansion of $\alpha > 2$ (cf. Algorithm in Section 3). Note that it may not succeed if $|I|$ is too small. However, in that case, the algorithm makes I a clique and achieves an expansion of c where $c \geq 1$. Thus, we have the following cases:

   (a) *I has an expansion of $\alpha > 2$:*
       Consider the nodes in I which are part of $S(H)$

i.e., $B = S(H) \cap I$. We want to calculate $h(H)$. Since expansion is defined over sets of size not more than half of the size of the graph, we can do so in two ways:

i. $B \leq I/2$: $S(H)$ expands at least as much as $h(G)$ except for the edges lost to x, and our algorithm ensures that I has expansion of at least $\alpha > 2$. Therefore, we have:

$$
\begin{aligned}
h(H) &= \frac{E_{S,\bar{S}}(H)}{S(H)} \\
&\geq \frac{(|S(H)| - |B|).h(G) - |B| + |B|.\alpha}{|S(H)|} \\
&= \frac{(|S(H)| - |B|).h(G) + |B|.(\alpha - 1)}{|S(H)|}
\end{aligned}
$$

In the numerator above, we have $(|S(H)| - |B|).h(G)$ which is a lower bound for the number of edges emanating from the set $S(H)$ (we minus $|B|$ from $|S(H)|$ to account for the edges that may be already present, note that Xheal does not add edges between two nodes if they are already present.) We subtract another $|B|$ or the edges lost to the deleted node and add $|B|\alpha$ edges due to the expansion gained.
The following cases arise: If $h(G) \geq \alpha - 1$, we have $h(H) \geq \frac{|S(H)|(\alpha-1)}{|S(H)|} \geq \alpha - 1 > 1$. Otherwise, if $h(G) \leq \alpha - 1$, we get: $h(H) \geq \frac{|S(H)|.h(G)}{|S(H)|} \geq h(G)$

ii. $\bar{B} \leq I/2$: By construction, nodes of $\bar{B}$ expand with expansion at least α in the subgraph I. Similar to above, we get, $h(H) \geq \frac{(|S(H)| - |\bar{B}|).h(G) + |\bar{B}|.(\alpha-1)}{|S(H)|}$. Thus, if $h(G) \geq \alpha - 1$, then $h(H) \geq \alpha - 1$, else $h(H) \geq h(G)$.

(b) I has an expansion of $c < \alpha$:
This happens in the case of the degree of x being smaller than k. In this case, the expander I is just a clique. Note that, even if degree of x is 2, the expansion is 1. (When the degree of x is 1, then the deleted node is just dropped, and it is easy to show that in this case, $h(H) \geq h(G)$.) The same analysis as the above applies, and we get $h(H) \geq min(c', h(G))$, for some constant $c' \geq 1$. Since G is G_1 and H is G_1', we get $h(G_1) \geq min(c', h(G_1'))$.

$\square$

COROLLARY 2. *Given a graph G, and a subgraph B of G, construct a new graph H as follows: Delete the edges of B and insert an expander of expansion $\alpha > 2$ among the nodes of B. Then $h(H) \geq \min(c, h(G))$, where c is a constant.*

The following lemmas have proofs defered to the complete version.

LEMMA 2. *At end of any timestep t, $h(G_t) \geq min(c', h(G_t'))$, where $c' \geq 1$ is a fixed constant.*

LEMMA 3. *For all $x \in G_t$, $degree_{G_t}(x) \leq O(\kappa.degree_{G_t'}(x))$, for a fixed parameter $\kappa > 0$.*

LEMMA 4. *For any two nodes $u, v \in G_t$, $\delta_{G_t}(u, v) \leq \delta_{G_t'}(u, v).O(\log n)$, where $\delta(u, v)$ is the shortest path between u and v, and n is the total number of nodes in G_t.*

4.2 Spectral Analysis

We derive bounds on the second smallest eigenvalue λ which is closely related to properties such as mixing time, conductance etc. While it is directly difficult to derive bounds on λ, we use our bounds on edge expansion and the Cheeger's inequality to do so.

We need the following simple inequality which relates the Cheeger constant $\phi(G)$ and the edge expansion $h(G)$ of a graph G which follows from their respective definitions. We use $d_{max}(G)$ and $d_{min}(G)$ to denote the maximum and minimum node degrees in G.

$$ \frac{h(G)}{d_{max}(G)} \leq \phi(G) \leq \frac{h(G)}{d_{min}(G)}. \tag{1} $$

LEMMA 5. *At the end of any timestep t,*
$\lambda(G_t) = min\left(\Omega\left(\lambda(G_t')^2 \frac{d_{min}(G_t')}{(\kappa)^2(d_{max}(G_t'))^2}\right), \Omega\left(\frac{1}{(\kappa d_{max}(G_t'))^2}\right)\right).$

PROOF. By Cheeger's inequality and by inequality 1 we have,

$$ \lambda(G_t) \geq \frac{\phi(G_t)^2}{2} \geq \frac{1}{2}\left(\frac{h(G_t)}{d_{max}(G_t)}\right)^2 $$

By Lemma 2, we have, $h(G_t) \geq min(c', h(G_t'))$, for some $c' \geq 1$.
So we have two cases:
Case 1: $h(G_t) \geq h(G_t')$. By using the other half of Cheeger's inequality, and inequality 1, and Lemma 3 we have:

$$
\begin{aligned}
\lambda(G_t) &\geq \frac{1}{2}\left(\frac{h(G_t')}{d_{max}(G_t)}\right)^2 \\
&\geq \frac{1}{2}\left(\frac{\lambda(G_t')d_{min}(G_t')}{2d_{max}(G_t)}\right)^2 \\
&\geq \frac{\lambda(G_t')^2}{8(\kappa)^2}\frac{d_{min}(G_t')}{(d_{max}(G_t'))^2} \\
&= \Omega\left(\lambda(G_t')^2\frac{d_{min}(G_t')}{(\kappa)^2(d_{max}(G_t'))^2}\right).
\end{aligned}
$$

Case 2: $h(G_t) \geq 1$:
This directly gives:

$$
\begin{aligned}
\lambda(G_t) &\geq \frac{1}{2}\left(\frac{1}{d_{max}(G_t)}\right)^2 \\
&\geq \Omega\left(\frac{1}{(d_{max}(G_t))^2}\right) \\
&\geq \Omega\left(\frac{1}{(\kappa d_{max}(G_t'))^2}\right).
\end{aligned}
$$

$\square$

5. DISTRIBUTED IMPLEMENTATION OF *XHEAL*: TIME AND MESSAGE COMPLEXITY ANALYSIS

We now discuss how to efficiently implement *Xheal*. A key task in *Xheal* involves the distributed construction and maintenance (under insertion and deletion) of a regular expander. We use a randomized construction of Law and Siu [20] that is described below. The expander graphs of [20] are formed by constructing a class of regular graphs called *H-graphs*. An H-graph is a $2d$-regular multigraph in which the set of edges is composed of d Hamilton cycles. A random graph from this class can be constructed (cf. Theorem below) by picking d Hamilton cycles independently and uniformly at random among all possible Hamilton cycles on the set of $z \geq 3$ vertices, and taking the union of these Hamilton cycles. This construction yields a random regular graph (henceforth called as a *random H-graph*) that that can be shown to be an expander with high probability (cf. Theorem 4). The construction can be accomplished incrementally as follows.

Let the neighbors of a node u be labeled as $nbr(u)_{-1}, nbr(u)_1, nbr(u)_{-2}, ..., nbr(u)_{-d}, nbr(u)_d$. For each i, $nbr(u)_{-i}$ and $nbr(u)_i$ denote a node's predecessor and successor on the ith Hamilton cycle (which will be referred to as the level-i cycle). We start with 3 nodes, because there is only one possible H-graph of size 3.

1.INSERT(u): A new node u will be inserted into cycle i between node v_i and node $nbr(v_i)_i$ for randomly chosen v_i, for $i = 1, \ldots, d$.

2. **DELETE(u):** An existing node u gets deleted by simply removing it and connecting $nbr(u)_i$ and $nbr(u)_{-i}$, for $i = 1, \ldots, d$.

Law and Siu prove the following theorem (modified here for our purposes) that is used in *Xheal* :

THEOREM 3 ([20]). *Let $H_0, H_1, H_2, \ldots$ be a sequence of H-graphs, each of size at least 3. Let H_0 be a random H-graph of size n and let H_{i+1} be formed from H_i by either INSERT or DELETE operation as above. Then H_i is a random H-graph for all $i \geq 0$.*

THEOREM 4 ([9, 20]). *A random n-node $2d$-regular H-graph is an expander (with edge expansion $\Omega(d)$) with probability at least $1 - O(n^{-p})$ where p depends on d.*

Note that in the above theorem, the probability guarantee can be made as close to 1 as possible, by making d large enough. Also it is known that λ, the second smallest eigenvalue, for these random graphs is close to the best possible [9]. Another point to note that although the above construction can yield a multigraph, it can be shown that similar high probabilistic guarantees hold in case we make the multi-edges simple, by making d large enough. Hence we will assume that the constructed expander graphs are simple.

We next show how *Xheal* algorithm is implemented and analyze the time and message complexity per node deletion. We note that insertion of a node by adversary involves almost no work from *Xheal* . The adversary simply inserts a node and its incident edges (to existing nodes). *Xheal* simply colors these inserted edges as black. Hence we focus on the steps taken by *Xheal* under deletion of a node by the adversary. First we state the following lower bound on the amortized message complexity for deletions which is easy to see in our model (cf. Section 2). Our algorithm's complexity will be within a logarithmic factor of this bound.

LEMMA 6. *In the worst case, any healing algorithm needs $\Theta(deg(v))$ messages to repair upon deletion of a node v,*

where $deg(v)$ is the degree of v in G'_t (i.e., the black-degree of v). Furthermore, if we there are p deletions, $v_1, v_2, \ldots, v_p$, then the amortized cost is $A(p) = (1/p)\sum_{i=1}^{p} \Theta(deg(v_i))$ which is the best possible.

THEOREM 5. *Xheal can be implemented to run in $O(\log n)$ rounds (per deletion). The amortized message complexity over p deletions is $O(\kappa \log n A(p))$ on average where n is the number of nodes in the network (at this timestep), κ is the degree of the expander used in the construction, and $A(p)$ is defined as in Lemma 6.*

PROOF. (Sketch) We first note that the healing operations will be initiated by the neighbors of the deleted node. We also note that primary and secondary expander clouds can be identified by the color of their edges (cf. Algorithm in Section3.)

Case 1: This involves constructing a (primary) expander cloud among the neighboring nodes $N(v)$ of the deleted node v. Note that $|N(v)| = deg(v)$, where $deg(v)$ is the black-degree of v. Since each node knows neighbor of neighbor's (NoN) addresses, it is akin to working on a complete graph over $N(v)$. We first elect a leader among $N(v)$: a *random* node (which is useful later) among $N(v)$ is chosen as a leader. This can be done, for example, by using the Nearest Neighbor Tree (NNT) algorithm of [?]. This takes $O(\log |N(v)|)$ time and $O(|N(v)| \log |N(v)|)$ messages. The leader then (locally) constructs a random κ-regular H-graph over $N(v)$ and informs each node in $N(v)$ (directly, since its address is known) of their respective edges. The total messages needed to inform the nodes is $O(\kappa |N(v)|)$, since that is the total number of edges. A neighbor of the leader in the expander graph is also elected as a vice-leader. This can be implemented in $O(1)$ time. Hence, overall this case takes $O(\log |N(v)|) = O(\log deg(v)) = O(\log n)$ time and $O(\kappa deg(v) \log deg(v))$ messages.

In particular, the following invariants will be maintained with respect to every expander (primary or secondary) cloud: (a) Every node in the cloud will have a leader (randomly chosen among the nodes) associated with it ; (b) every node in the cloud knows the address of the leader and can communicate with it directly (in constant time); and (c) the leader knows the addresses of all other nodes in the cloud; (d) one neighbor of the leader in the cloud will be designated vice-leader which will know everything the leader knows and will take action in case the leader is deleted. Note that this invariant is maintained in Case 1. We will show that it is also maintained in Case 2 below.

Case 2 (Cases 2.1 and 2.2 of Xheal): We have to implement three main operations in these cases. They are:
(a) Reconstructing an expander cloud (primary or secondary) on deletion of a node v: Let C be the primary (or secondary) cloud that loses v. The node is removed according to the DELETE operation of H-graph. This takes $O(1)$ time and $O(\kappa)$ messages. If v belongs to j primary clouds then the time is still $O(1)$ while the total message complexity is $O(j\kappa)$. For v to belong to j primary clouds its black degree should be at least j. Also v can belong to at most one secondary cloud. Hence the cost is at most $O(\kappa)$ times the black degree as needed. If the deleted node happens to be the leader of the (primary) cloud then a new *random* leader is chosen (by the vice-leader) and inform the rest of the nodes — this will take $O(|C|)$ messages and $O(1)$ time, where $|C|$ is the number of nodes in the cloud. Since

the adversary does not know the random choices made by the algorithm, the probability that it deletes a leader in a step is $1/|C|$ and thus the expected message complexity is $O((1/|C|)|C| = O(1)$. (Note that a new vice-leader, a neighbor of the new leader will be chosen if necessary.)

(b) Forming and fixing primary and secondary expander clouds (if there are enough free nodes): Let the deleted node belong to primary clouds $C_1, \ldots, C_j$ and possibly a secondary cloud F that connects a subset of these j clouds (and possibly other unaffected primary clouds). First, each of the clouds are reconstructed as in (a) above. This operation arises only if we have at least j free nodes, i.e., nodes that are not associated with any secondary cloud. We now mention how free nodes are found. To check if there are enough free nodes among the j clouds, we check the respective leaders. The leader always maintain a list of all free nodes in its cloud. Thus if a node becomes non-free during a repair it informs the leader (in constant time) which removes it from the list. Thus the neighbors of the deleted node can request the leaders of their respective clouds to find free nodes. Hence finding free nodes takes time $O(1)$ and needs $O(j)$ messages. The free nodes are then inserted to form the secondary cloud. We distinguish two situations with respect to formation of a secondary cloud: (i) The secondary cloud is formed for the first time (i.e., a new secondary cloud among the primary clouds). In this case, a leader of one of the associated primary cloud is elected to construct the secondary expander. This leader then gets the free nodes from the respective primary clouds, locally constructs a κ-regular expander and informs it to the respective free nodes of each primary cloud. This is similar to the construction of a primary cloud as in (a). The time and message complexity is also bounded as in (a).

(ii)The secondary cloud is already present, merely, a new free node is added. In this case, the new node is inserted to the secondary cloud by using the INSERT operation of H-graph. This takes $O(1)$ time and $O(1)$ messages, since INSERT can be implemented by querying the leader.

(c) Combining many primary expander clouds into one primary expander cloud (if there are not enough free nodes): This is a costly operation which we seek to amortize over many deletions. First, we compute the cost of combining clouds. Let $C_1, \ldots, C_j$ are the clouds that need to be combined into one cloud C. This is done by first electing a leader over all the nodes in the clouds $C_1, \ldots, C_j$. Note that the distance between any two nodes among these clouds is $O(\log n)$, since all the clouds had a common node (the deleted node) and each cloud is an expander (also note that the neighbors of the deleted nodes maintain connectivity during the leader election and subsequent repair process). A BFS tree is then constructed subsequently over the nodes of the j clouds with the leader as the root. The leader then collects all the addresses of all the nodes in the clouds (via the BFS tree) and locally constructs a H-graph and broadcasts it to all the other nodes in the cloud. The leader's address is also informed to all the other nodes in the cloud. Thus the invariant specified in Case 1 is maintained. The total time needed is $O(\log n)$ time and the total number of messages needed is $O(\kappa \sum_{i=1}^{j} |C_i|) \log n$, since each node (other than the leader) sends $O(1)$ number of messages over $O(\log n)$ hops, and the leader sends $O(\sum_{i=1}^{j} |C_i|) \log n$. However, note that the costly operation of combining is triggered by having less than j free nodes. This implies that there must

been at least $\Omega(\sum_{i=1}^{j} |C_i|)$ prior deletions that had enough free nodes and hence involved no combining. Thus, we can amortize the total cost of the combining cost over these "cheaper" prior deletions. Hence the amortized cost is

$$\frac{O(\kappa \sum_{i=1}^{j} |C_i|) \log n}{\Omega(\sum_{i=1}^{j} |C_i|)} = O(\kappa \log n).$$

Finally, we say how the probabilistic guarantee on the H-graph can be maintained. The implementation above uses a κ-regular random H-graph in the construction of an expander cloud. By theorem 4, κ can be chosen large enough to guarantee the probabilistic requirement needed. For example, choosing $\kappa = \Theta(\log n)$, then high probability (with respect to the size of the network) is guaranteed (this assumes that nodes know an upper bound on the size of the network). Furthermore, if there are f deletions, by union bound, the probability that it is not an expander increases by up to a factor of f. To address this, we reconstruct the H-graph after any cloud has lost half of its nodes; note that the cost of this reconstruction can be amortized over the deletions to obtain the same bounds as claimed. $\square$

6. CONCLUSION

We have presented an efficient, distributed algorithm that withstands repeated adversarial node insertions and deletions by adding a small number of new edges after each deletion. It maintains key global invariants of the network while doing only localized changes and using only local information. The global invariants it maintains are as follows. Firstly, assuming the initial network was connected, the network stays connected. Secondly, the (edge) expansion of the network is at least as good as the expansion would have been without any adversarial deletion, or is at least a constant. Thirdly, the distance between any pair of nodes never increases by more than a $O(\log n)$ multiplicative factor than what the distance would be without the adversarial deletions. Lastly, the above global invariants are achieved while not allowing the degree of any node to increase by more than a small multiplicative factor.

The work can be improved in several ways in similar models. Can we improve the present algorithm to allow smaller messages and lower congestion? Can we efficiently find new routes to replace the routes damaged by the deletions? Can we design self-healing algorithms that are also load balanced? Can we reach a theoretical characterization of what network properties are amenable to self-healing, especially, global properties which can be maintained by local changes? What about combinations of desired network invariants? We can also extend the work to different models and domains. We can look at designing algorithms for less flexible networks such as sensor networks, explore healing with non-local edges. We can also look beyond graphs to rewiring and self-healing circuits where it is gates that fail.

7. REFERENCES

[1] D. Andersen, H. Balakrishnan, F. Kaashoek, and R. Morris. Resilient overlay networks. *SIGOPS Oper. Syst. Rev.*, 35(5):131–145, 2001.

[2] V. Arak. What happened on August 16, August 2007. http://heartbeat.skype.com/2007/08/what-happened-on-august-16.html.

[3] B. Awerbuch, B. Patt-Shamir, D. Peleg, and M. Saks. Adapting to asynchronous dynamic networks (extended abstract). In *STOC '92: Proceedings of the twenty-fourth annual ACM symposium on Theory of computing*, pages 557–570, New York, NY, USA, 1992. ACM.

[4] I. Boman, J. Saia, C. T. Abdallah, and E. Schamiloglu. Brief announcement: Self-healing algorithms for reconfigurable networks. In *Symposium on Stabilization, Safety, and Security of Distributed Systems(SSS)*, 2006.

[5] F. Chung. *Spectral Graph Theory*. American Mathematical Society, 1997.

[6] S. Dolev and N. Tzachar. Spanders: distributed spanning expanders. In *SAC*, pages 1309–1314, 2010.

[7] R. D. Doverspike and B. Wilson. Comparison of capacity efficiency of dcs network restoration routing techniques. *J. Network Syst. Manage.*, 2(2), 1994.

[8] K. Fisher. Skype talks of "perfect storm" that caused outage, clarifies blame, August 2007. http://arstechnica.com/news.ars/post/20070821-skype-talks-of-perfect-storm.html.

[9] J. Friedman. On the second eigenvalue and random walks in random d-regular graphs. *Combinatorica*, 11:331-362, 1991.

[10] T. Frisanco. Optimal spare capacity design for various protection switching methods in ATM networks. In *Communications, 1997. ICC 97 Montreal, 'Towards the Knowledge Millennium'. 1997 IEEE International Conference on*, volume 1, pages 293–298, 1997.

[11] C. Gkantsidis, M. Mihail, and A. Saberi. Random walks in peer-to-peer networks: Algorithms and evaluation. *Performance Evaluation*, 63(3):241–263, 2006.

[12] S. Goel, S. Belardo, and L. Iwan. A resilient network that can operate under duress: To support communication between government agencies during crisis situations. *Proceedings of the 37th Hawaii International Conference on System Sciences*, 0-7695-2056-1/04:1–11, 2004.

[13] Y. Hayashi and T. Miyazaki. Emergent rewirings for cascades on correlated networks. cond-mat/0503615, 2005.

[14] T. Hayes, N. Rustagi, J. Saia, and A. Trehan. The forgiving tree: a self-healing distributed data structure. In *PODC '08: Proceedings of the twenty-seventh ACM symposium on Principles of distributed computing*, pages 203–212, New York, NY, USA, 2008. ACM.

[15] T. P. Hayes, J. Saia, and A. Trehan. The forgiving graph: a distributed data structure for low stretch under adversarial attack. In *PODC '09: Proceedings of the 28th ACM symposium on Principles of distributed computing*, pages 121–130, New York, NY, USA, 2009. ACM.

[16] K. C. Hillel and H. Shachnai. Partial information spreading with application to distributed maximum coverage. In *PODC '10: Proceedings of the 28th ACM symposium on Principles of distributed computing*, New York, NY, USA, 2010. ACM.

[17] P. Holme and B. J. Kim. Vertex overload breakdown in evolving networks. *Physical Review E*, 65:066109, 2002.

[18] S. Hoory, N. Linial, and A. Wigderson. Expander graphs and their applications. *Bulletin of the American Mathematical Society*, 43(04):439–562, August 2006.

[19] R. R. Iraschko, M. H. MacGregor, and W. D. Grover. Optimal capacity placement for path restoration in STM or ATM mesh-survivable networks. *IEEE/ACM Trans. Netw.*, 6(3):325–336, 1998.

[20] C. Law and K. Y. Siu. Distributed construction of random expander networks. In *INFOCOM 2003. Twenty-Second Annual Joint Conference of the IEEE Computer and Communications Societies. IEEE*, volume 3, pages 2133–2143 vol.3, 2003.

[21] O. Malik. Does Skype Outage Expose P2PÕs Limitations?, August 2007. http://gigaom.com/2007/08/16/skype-outage.

[22] M. Medard, S. G. Finn, and R. A. Barry. Redundant trees for preplanned recovery in arbitrary vertex-redundant or edge-redundant graphs. *IEEE/ACM Transactions on Networking*, 7(5):641–652, 1999.

[23] M. Moore. Skype's outage not a hang-up for user base, August 2007. http://www.usatoday.com/tech/wireless/phones/2007-08-24-skype-outage-effects-N.htm.

[24] A. E. Motter. Cascade control and defense in complex networks. *Physical Review Letters*, 93:098701, 2004.

[25] A. E. Motter and Y.-C. Lai. Cascade-based attacks on complex networks. *Physical Review E*, 66:065102, 2002.

[26] K. Murakami and H. S. Kim. Comparative study on restoration schemes of survivable ATM networks. In *INFOCOM*, pages 345–352, 1997.

[27] D. Peleg. *Distributed Computing: A Locality Sensitive Approach*. SIAM, 2000.

[28] B. Ray. Skype hangs up on users, August 2007. http://www.theregister.co.uk/2007/08/16/skype_down/.

[29] J. Saia and A. Trehan. Picking up the pieces: Self-healing in reconfigurable networks. In *IPDPS. 22nd IEEE International Symposium on Parallel and Distributed Processing.*, pages 1–12. IEEE, April 2008.

[30] B. Stone. Skype: Microsoft Update Took Us Down, August 2007. http://bits.blogs.nytimes.com/2007/08/20/skype-microsoft-update-took-us-down.

[31] A. Trehan. *Algorithms for self-healing networks*. Dissertation, University of New Mexico, 2010.

[32] B. van Caenegem, N. Wauters, and P. Demeester. Spare capacity assignment for different restoration strategies in mesh survivable networks. In *Communications, 1997. ICC 97 Montreal, 'Towards the Knowledge Millennium'. 1997 IEEE International Conference on*, volume 1, pages 288–292, 1997.

[33] Y. Xiong and L. G. Mason. Restoration strategies and spare capacity requirements in self-healing ATM networks. *IEEE/ACM Trans. Netw.*, 7(1):98–110, 1999.

Fast and Compact Self Stabilizing Verification, Computation, and Fault Detection of an MST

Amos Korman[*]
CNRS & U. Paris Diderot
Paris, France
Amos.Korman@liafa.jussieu.fr

Shay Kutten[†]
Faculty of IE&M, The Technion
Haifa, Israel
kutten@ie.technion.ac.il

Toshimitsu Masuzawa
IS&T Grad. Center, Osaka U.
Osaka, Japan
masuzawa@ist.osaka-u.ac.jp

ABSTRACT

This paper demonstrates the usefulness of distributed local verification of proofs, as a tool for the design of algorithms. In particular, it introduces a somewhat generalized notion of distributed local proofs, and utilizes it for improving the memory size complexity, while obtaining time efficiency too.

As a result, we show that optimizing the memory size carries at most a small cost in terms of time, in the context of Minimum Spanning Tree (MST). That is, we present algorithms that are both time and space efficient for constructing an MST, for verifying it, and for detecting the location of the faults. This involves several steps that may be considered contributions in themselves.

First, we generalize the notion of local proofs, trading off the locality (or, really, the time complexity) for memory efficiency. This adds a dimension to the study of distributed local proofs, that has been gaining attention recently.

Second, as opposed to previous studies that presented only the labels verification part of a proof labeling schemes, we present here also a space and time efficient distributed self stabilizing marker algorithm to generates those labels. This presents proof labeling schemes as an algorithmic tool.

Finally, we show how to enhance a known transformer that makes input/output algorithms self stabilizing. It now takes as input an efficient construction algorithm and an efficient self stabilizing proof labeling scheme, and produces an efficient self stabilizing algorithm.

When used for MST, the transformer produces a memory optimal (i.e., $O(\log n)$ bits per node) self stabilizing algorithm, whose time complexity, namely, $O(n)$, is significantly better even than that of previous algorithms that where not space optimal. (The time complexity of previous MST algorithms that used $\Omega(\log^2 n)$ memory bits per node was $O(n^2)$, and the time for optimal space algorithms was $O(n|E|)$.)

Our MST algorithm also has the important property that, if faults occur after the construction ended, then they are detected by some nodes within $O(\log^2 n)$ time in synchronous networks, or within $O(\triangle \log^2 n)$ time in asynchronous ones. This property is inherited from the specific proof labeling scheme we construct. It answers an open problem posed by Awerbuch and Varghese (FOCS 1991). We also show that $\Omega(\log n)$ time is necessary if the memory size is restricted to $O(\log n)$ bits, even in synchronous networks.

Another property is that if f faults occurred, then, within the required detection time above, they are detected by some node in the $O(f \log n)$ locality of each of the faults. We also show how to improve the above detection time and locality, at the expense of some increase in the memory.

Categories and Subject Descriptors

G.2.2 [**Discrete Mathematics**]: Graph Theory—*Graph algorithms, Graph labeling, Network problems*; E.1 [**Data Structures**]: *Distributed data structures*

General Terms

Algorithms

Keywords

Distributed algorithm, self stabilization, MST, distributed verification, local proof checking, fault detection, locality.

1. INTRODUCTION

In a non-distributed context, solving a problem is believed to be, sometimes, much harder than verifying it (e.g. for NP-Hard problems). Given a tree T, a task introduced by Tarjan [36] is to verify that T is indeed an MST. This non-distributed verification seems to be just slightly easier than the non-distributed computation of an MST. On the other hand, in the distributed context, the time complexity of an MST verification can be 1, when using $\Theta(\log^2 N)$ bits per node. In [29, 31], the MST was assumed to be represented distributively, such that each node stores a pointer to its parent. Similarly, the verification (termed a *proof labeling scheme*) assumed that each node stored some information, the node's *label*, to be used for verification. If the collection

[*]Supported in part by a France-Israel cooperation grant ("Mutli-Computing" project) from the French and Israeli Ministries of Science, by the ANR projects ALADDIN and PROSE, and by the INRIA project-team GANG.

[†]Supported in part by a France-Israel cooperation grant ("Mutli-Computing" project) from the French and the Israeli Ministries of Science, by a grant from the Israel Science Foundation, and by a grant from the Gordon Center at the Technion.

of these (node, parent) edges was not an MST, then at least one node *raised an alarm* in one time unit.

To make such a proof labeling scheme a useful algorithmic tool, one needs to present a *marker* algorithm for computing those labels. One of the contributions of the current paper is a time and memory efficient self stabilizing marker.

Every decidable graph property (not just an MST) can be verified in a short time given a large enough memory [31]. A second contribution is a generalization of such schemes to allow a reduction in the memory requirements, by trading off the locality (or the time). In the context of MST, yet another (third) contribution is a reduced space proof labeling scheme for MST. It uses just $O(\log n)$ bits of memory per node (the same as the amount needed for merely representing distributively the MST). This is below the lower bound of $\Omega(\log^2 n)$ of [29]. The reason this is possible is that the verification time is increased to $O(\log^2 n)$ in synchronous networks and to $O(\triangle \log^2 n)$ in asynchronous ones. Another important property of the new scheme is that any fault is detected rather close to the node where it happened.

Given a long enough time, one can verify T by recomputing the MST. An open problem posed by Awerbuch and Varghese [9] is to find an MST verification algorithm whose time complexity is smaller than the MST computation time, yet with a small memory. The above mentioned third contribution solves this open problem by showing a $Polylog(n)$ time penalty when using $O(\log n)$ memory size for the MST verification algorithm. In contrast, lower bounds which are polynomial in n for MST construction follow from [35, 34] (even for constant diameter graphs). Interestingly, it turns out that a logarithmic penalty is unavoidable. That is, we show that $\Omega(\log n)$ time for an MST verification scheme is necessary if the memory size is restricted to $O(\log n)$ bits, even in synchronous networks.

One known application of some methods of distributed verification is for general transformers, that transform non-stabilizing algorithms to produce self stabilizing ones. The fourth contribution of this paper is an adaptation of the transformer of [9] such that it can transform algorithms in our context (asynchronous network of unknown size and diameter, where the verification method is a proof labeling scheme whose verifier part is self stabilizing). Based on the strength of the original transformer of [9] (and that of its companion paper [8] it uses), our adaptation yields a result that is rather useful even without plugging in the new verification scheme. This is demonstrated by plugging in the proof labeling schemes of [31, 29], yielding an algorithm which already improves the time of previous $O(\log^2 n)$ memory self stabilizing MST construction algorithms, and also detects faults using 1 time and at distance f at most from the faults (if f faults occurred).

Finally, we obtain an optimal memory size, $O(n)$ time asynchronous self stabilizing MST construction algorithm. The state of the art time bound for such optimal memory algorithms was $O(n|E|)$ [10, 25]. In fact, our time bound improves significantly even the best time bound for algorithms using polylogarithmic memory, which was $O(n^2)$ [11].

Moreover, our self stabilizing MST algorithm inherits two important properties from our verification scheme, which are: (1) the time it takes to detect faults is small: $O(\log^2 n)$ time in a synchronous network, or $O(\triangle \log^2 n)$ in asynchronous ones; and (2) if some f faults occur, then each fault is detected within its $O(f \log n)$ neighborhood.

Outline: The MST verification and the MST construction algorithms are given in Sections 3 and 4. Throughout, to save space, many details and proofs are deferred to the full paper (some of which can be found also in [30]). This includes, for example, the logarithmic time lower bound.

The intuition behind the main technical problem: Informally, in [29, 31], each node v stores some $\log n$ "pieces" of information, each of size $\log n$. As explained later (Section 2), Node v uses its own pieces, as well as the pieces of its neighbors to verify the MST. In the current paper, each node has room for only a constant number of such pieces. One immediate idea is to store some of v's pieces in some other nodes. Whenever v needs a piece, some algorithm should move it for v. Moving pieces would cost time, hence, realizing some time versus memory size trade-off.

Unfortunately, the total (over all the nodes) number of pieces in the schemes of [31, 29] is $\Omega(n \log n)$. Any way one would assign these pieces to nodes would result in the memory of a single node needing to store $\Omega(\log^2 n)$ bits. Hence, our first technical step was to reduce the total number of pieces to $O(n)$, so that we could store at each node just a constant number of such pieces. However, each node still needs to use $\Omega(\log n)$ pieces. That is, each piece may be needed by many nodes. Next, we solve a combinatorial problem: locate each piece "close" to each of the nodes needing it, while storing only a constant number of pieces per node.

The solution of this combinatorial problem would have sufficed to construct the desired scheme in the local model. There, Node v can "see" the storage of nearby nodes [26]. However, in the congestion aware model, one actually needs to move pieces from node to node, while not violating the $O(\log n)$ memory per node constraint. This is difficult, since, at the same time v needs to see its own pieces, other nodes need to see their own ones.

Additional Related work: The distributed construction of an MST has yielded techniques and insights that were used in the study of many other problems of distributed network protocols. It has also become a standard to check a new paradigm in distributed algorithms theory. The first distributed algorithm was proposed by [15], its complexity was not analyzed. The seminal paper of Gallager, Humblet, and Spira presented a message optimal algorithm that used $O(n \log n)$ time, improved by Awerbuch to $O(n)$ time [21, 5], and later to $O(D + \sqrt{n} \log^* n)$ [22, 33]. This was coupled with an almost matching lower bound of $\Omega(\sqrt{n})$ [35].

Self stabilization [18] deals with algorithms that must cope with faults that are rather severe, though of a type that does occur in reality [27]. The faults may cause the states of different nodes to be inconsistent with each other. For example, the collection of marked edges may not be an MST.

Known transformers can transform any MST construction algorithms to be self stabilizing. The transformer of Katz and Perry [28] also assumes a leader whose memory must hold a snapshot of the whole network. The time of the resulting self stabilizing MST algorithm is $O(n)$ and the memory size is $O(|E|n)$. In [2], the first self stabilizing leader election algorithm was proposed in order to remove the assumptions of [28] that a leader and a spanning tree are given. (The algorithm of [4], presented independently, needed an extra assumption that a bound on n was known, and had a higher time complexity). The combination of [2] and [28]) implied a self stabilizing MST in $O(n^2)$ time. Using unbounded space, the time of self stabilizing leader election was later improved even to $O(D)$ (the actual diameter) [3, 17]. The bounded memory algorithms of [7] or [1, 16], together with [28] and [5], yield a self stabilizing MST algorithm using $O(n|E|\log n)$ bits per node and time $O(D\log n)$ or $O(n)$.

Gupta and Srimani [24] presented an $O(n\log n)$ bits algorithm. Higham and Lyan [25] improved the core memory requirement to $O(\log n)$, however, the time complexity went up again to $\Omega(n|E|)$. An algorithm with a similar time complexity and a similar memory per node was also presented by [10]. This algorithm assumes the existence of a unique leader in the network and exchanges less bits with neighbors than did the algorithm of [25]. The algorithm of [10] also maintains a tree at all times (after reaching an initial tree). The time complexity of the algorithm in [11] is $O(n^2)$ but the memory usage grows to $O(\log^2 n)$. This may be the first paper using labeling schemes for the design of a self stabilizing MST protocol, as well as the first paper implementing the algorithm by Gallager, Humblet, and Spira in a self stabilizing manner without using a general transformer.

2. PRELIMINARIES

Some General definitions: Since we use rather standard definitions, we allow ourselves to save on space by referring the reader to a more complete version [30] or to the model descriptions in the rich literature on these subjects. In particular, we use the rather standard definitions of self stabilization (including its definition of faults) and of an edge weighted graph $G = (V, E)$ to represent a network. (The weights are polynomial in $n = |V|$). Each node has a unique identity $\text{ID}(v)$ encoded using $O(\log n)$ bits. Moreover, the network can store an object such as an MST (Minimum Spanning Tree) by having each node store its *component* of the representation. A component includes a collection of pointers to neighbors, and the collection of the components induces a subgraph $H(G)$. Here, $H(G)$ is supposed to be an MST (and each component is one pointer).

The (rather common) ideal time complexity assumes that a node reads all of its neighbors in at most 1 time unit. See e.g. [10, 11]. Our results translate easily to an alternative, stricter, *contention* time complexity, where a node can access only one neighbor in one time unit. The time cost of such a translation is at most a multiplicative factor of $\triangle$, the (unknown) maximum degree of a node in the graph.

As is commonly assumed in the case of self stabilization, we also assume that each node has only some bounded number (here, $O(\log n)$) of memory bits available to be used. Without *some* bound, the adversary could have started the memory to any value, and the definition of the memory complexity would have become tricky. (Note that the upper bound on n that this memory bound implies is far from being a tight one – it can be any polynomial in n; our algorithms do not make use of this upper bound.)

Proof labeling schemes: This generalization of the schemes in [29, 31] is a framework for maintaining a distributed proof that the network satisfies some given predicate Ψ, e.g., that $H(G)$ is an MST. We are given a predicate Ψ and a graph family $\mathcal{F}$ (if Ψ and $\mathcal{F}$ are omitted, Ψ is MST and $\mathcal{F}$ is all connected undirected weighted graphs $\mathcal{F}(n)$). A *proof labeling scheme* includes the following two components.

- A *marker* algorithm $\mathcal{M}$ that generates a label $\mathcal{M}(v)$ for every node v in every graph $G \in \mathcal{F}$.

- A *verifier* distributed algorithm $\mathcal{V}$, initiated at each node of a *labeled* graph $G \in \mathcal{F}$, i.e., a graph whose nodes v have labels $L(v)$. The verifier at each node is initiated separately, and at an arbitrary time, and runs forever. The verifier may raise an alarm at some node v by outputting "no" at v.

Intuitively, if the verifier at v raises an alarm, then it detected a fault. That is, for any graph $G \in \mathcal{F}$,

- If G satisfies the predicate Ψ and if the label at each node v is $\mathcal{M}(v)$ (i.e., the label assigned to v by the marker algorithm $\mathcal{M}$) then no node raises an alarm. In this case, we say that the verifier *accepts* the labels.

- If G does not satisfy the predicate Ψ, then for *any* assignment of labels to the nodes of G, after some finite time t, there exists a node v that raises an alarm. In this case, we say that the verifier *rejects* the labels.

Note that the first property above concerns only the labels *produced by the marker algorithm* $\mathcal{M}$, while the second must hold even if the labels are assigned by some adversary.

We evaluate $(\mathcal{M}, \mathcal{V})$ by the following complexity measures.

- The *memory size*: the maximum number of bits stored in the memory of a single node v, taken over all the nodes v in all graphs $G \in \mathcal{F}(n)$ that satisfy the predicate Ψ (and over all the executions); this includes: (1) the bits used for encoding the identity $\text{ID}(v)$, (2) the marker memory: bits used for constructing and encoding the labels, and (3) the verifier memory: the bits used during the operation of the verifier.

- The (ideal) detection *time*: the maximum, taken over all the graphs $G \in \mathcal{F}(n)$ that do *not* satisfy the predicate Ψ and over all the labels given to nodes of G by adversaries (and over all the executions), of the time t required for some node to raise an alarm. (The time is counted from the *starting time*, when the verifier has been initiated at all the nodes).

- The *detection distance*: For a faulty node v, this is the (hop) distance to the closest node u raising an alarm within the detection time after the fault occurs. The detection distance of the scheme is the maximum, taken over all the graphs having at most f faults, and over all the faulty nodes v (and over all the executions), of the detection distance of v.

- The (ideal) *construction-time*: the maximum, taken over all the graphs $G \in \mathcal{F}(n)$ that satisfy the predicate Ψ (and over all the executions), of the time required for the marker $\mathcal{M}$ to assign labels to all nodes of G.

In our terms, the definitions of [29, 31] allowed only detection time complexity 1. Because of that, the verifier of [29, 31] at a node v, could only consult the neighbors of v. Whenever we use such a scheme, we refer to it as a 1-proof labeling scheme, to emphasis its running time. Also, in [29, 31], if f faults occurred, then the detection distance was f. Intuitively, a short detection distance and a small detection time may be helpful for the design of local correction and for fault containment algorithms [8, 23].

Generalizing the complexities to a computation: Above, we defined the memory size, detection time and the detection distance complexities of a *verification* algorithm. When considering a (self stabilizing) computation algorithm, we extend the notion of the memory size to include also the bits needed for encoding the component $c(v)$ at each node. (This was excluded from the definition of memory size for verification because, there, the designer of the verification scheme has no control over the nodes' components.)

The notions of detection time and the detection distance can be carried to the very common class of self stabilizing *computation* algorithms that use fault detection. Examples are algorithms that have silent stabilization [19]. Informally, algorithms in this class first compute an output. After that, all the nodes are required to stay in some *output state* where they (1) output the computation result forever (unless a fault occurs); and (2) check repeatedly until they discover a fault. In such a case, they recompute and enter an output state again. Here, informally, the detection time is the time from a fault (occurring after stabilization) until the detection. (There is a small delicate point, however; if, at this point, a node is not in the output state, this is considered a detection of a fault, since in the stabilized case, all the nodes are supposed to be and remain in an output state.) The detection distance is the distance from a node where a fault occurred to a node that detected a fault. A more formal definition appears in [30].

Trees, hierarchies and candidate functions: From now on, fix a spanning tree $T = (V(G), E(T))$ of a graph $G = (V(G), E(G))$, rooted at some node $r(T)$. Following [21], a *fragment* F is a subtree of T. Given a fragment F, an edge $(v, u) \in E(G)$ whose one endpoint v is in F, while the other endpoint u is not, is called *outgoing* from F. Such an edge of minimum weight is called a *minimum outgoing* edge from F. A fragment containing a single node is called *singleton*.

Below, we define a hierarchy and a candidate function, two notions that play a major role later. Hence, let us first explain them informally. The proof labeling scheme proves that T could have been computed by an algorithm that is similar to that of GHS, the algorithm of [21]. GHS starts when each node is a fragment by itself. Fragments merge over their minimum outgoing edges to form larger fragments. That is, each node belongs to one fragment F_1, then to a larger fragment F_2 that contains F_1, etc. This is repeated until one fragment spans the network. A tree constructed that way is an MST [21]. In GHS, each fragment has a *level*; in the case of v above, F_2's level is higher than that of F_1. The hierarchy $\mathcal{H}$ of fragments we define below follows that structure. Fragment F_1 is a descendant in $\mathcal{H}$ of F_2 if F_2 contains F_1. GHS managed to ensure that each node belongs to at most one fragment at each level, and that the number of levels is $O(\log n)$. Hence, $\mathcal{H}$ has a small depth.

The marker algorithm in the proof labeling scheme presented here performs, in some sense, a reverse operation. If T is an MST, the marker "slices" it back into fragments. Then, the proof labeling scheme gives each node v (1) the (unique) name of each of the fragments F_j that v belongs to, (2) the level of F_j, and (3) the weight of F_j's minimum outgoing edge. This (for $O(\log n)$ fragments) is really too much information to store in one node, so we shall see later how the scheme brings this information to the node without violating the memory size bound. For now, it suffices to know that given this information, the nodes can verify that T could have been constructed by an algorithm similar to GHS, and, hence, T is an MST. Finally, the "candidate" defined below for each fragment F_j is really what is supposed

to be F_j's minimum outgoing edge. We say a "candidate", and "supposed to be", to stress the point that this is, really, what the proof labeling scheme is supposed to check.

Formally, we define a *hierarchy* $\mathcal{H}$ for T as a collection of fragments of T satisfying the following: (1) $T \in \mathcal{H}$, and $\{v\} \in \mathcal{H}$ for every $v \in V(G)$, and (2) for any two fragments F and F' in $\mathcal{H}$, if $F \cap F' \neq \emptyset$ then either $F \subseteq F'$ or $F' \subseteq F$. (The collection of fragments is a laminar family).

For a fragment $F \in \mathcal{H}$, let $\mathcal{H}(F)$ denote the collection of fragments in $\mathcal{H}$ *strictly* contained in F. A child of a non-singleton fragment $F \in \mathcal{H}$ is a fragment $F' \in \mathcal{H}(F)$ such that no other fragment $F'' \in \mathcal{H}(F)$ satisfies $F'' \supset F'$. Note that the rooted tree induced by a hierarchy is unique (if the children are unordered). To avoid confusion with tree T, we refer to the tree induced by a hierarchy as a *fragment-tree*. We associate a *level* with each fragment $F \in \mathcal{H}$. It is defined as the height of the node corresponding to F in the fragment-tree induced by $\mathcal{H}$. In particular, the level of a singleton fragment is 1. The level of the fragment T is called the *height* of the hierarchy, and is denoted by ℓ.

Given a hierarchy $\mathcal{H}$ for T, a function $\chi : \mathcal{H} \backslash \{T\} \longrightarrow E(T)$ is called a *candidate function* of $\mathcal{H}$ if it satisfies $E(F) = \bigcup_{F' \in \mathcal{H}(F)} \chi(F')$ for every $F \in \mathcal{H}$, namely, F is precisely the union of candidates of all fragments of $\mathcal{H}$ strictly contained in it. The proof of the following lemma is similar, e.g., to the proof of [21]. See [30].

LEMMA 1. *Let T be a spanning tree of a graph G. If there exists a candidate function χ for a hierarchy $\mathcal{H}$ for T, such that for every $F \in \mathcal{H}$, $\chi(F)$ is a minimum outgoing edge from F, then T is an MST of G.*

3. FAST AND COMPACT PROOF SCHEME

In this section, we describe the labels used by the proof labeling scheme. The distributed implementation of the marker that actually *assigns* these labels to the nodes is deferred to the full paper. We begin with a few simplifying assumptions, called the *data structure assumptions*. The formal description of how to remove these assumptions is deferred to the full paper. (For the implementation and the removal, see also [30]). First, we assume that $H(G) \equiv T$ is a spanning tree of G rooted at some node r. Thus, our goal is to verify that T is in fact, minimal. Second, we assume that each node knows n. Third, we assume the existence of a hierarchy $\mathcal{H}$ for T of height $\ell \leqslant 1 + \lceil \log n \rceil$ and a candidate function χ for $\mathcal{H}$. which are represented distributively in the nodes of T as follows. Each node v is equipped with a data-structure marking exactly those levels $1 \leqslant j \leqslant \ell$ for which v belongs to a fragment $F_j(v)$ of level j in $\mathcal{H}$. For each such a level j, the data-structure at v also indicates (1) whether v is the root of $F_j(v)$ (in particular, whether v is the root r of T), and (2) whether v is an endpoint of the (unique) candidate edge of $F_j(v)$, and if so, which of the edges adjacent to v is the candidate edge. Furthermore, given the data-structures of two nodes u and v which are neighbors in G, one can find out whether they are neighbors in T as well, and if so: (1) whether u is v's child in T, and (2) for each $1 \leqslant j \leqslant \ell$, whether u belongs to $F_j(v)$.

Informally, to remove the third assumption, given an MST T, the marker $\mathcal{M}$ constructs a hierarchy, a candidate function, and data-structures as required by the above assumptions. We couple these constructions with a 1-proof labeling scheme that verifies that these are as required, using ideas similar to the ones described in [31]. The first two assumptions can be even more directly removed using simple known 1-proof labeling schemes from [31]. The resulted data-structure, together with the labels needed to verify it, can be constructed in $O(n)$ time using memory of at most $O(\log n)$ bits at each node. Hence, the removal of the assumptions does not violate the memory size nor the time requirements of the final proof labeling scheme.

Intuitively, the scheme below allows the nodes of each fragment F_j to detect whether the lowest weight edge connecting F_j to the rest of the graph is included in T. By Lemma 1, if this holds for every fragment, then T is an MST.

The pieces each node uses for verification (see the intuition paragraph, in the introduction): A crucial point in the scheme is letting each node v know, for each edge $(v, u) \in E$ and for each level j, whether u and v share the same level j fragment. (In the special case where u is also a neighbor of v in T, this information can be extracted by v using u's data-structure.) We assign each fragment a unique identifier, and v compares the identifier of its own level j fragment to the identifier of u's level j fragment.

Consider the number of bits required to represent the identifiers of all the fragments that a node v participates in. There exists a method to assign unique identifiers such that this total number is only $O(\log n)$ [20, 32]. Unfortunately, we did not manage to use that method here. Indeed, our marker can assign identifiers according to that method. However, we could not find a low space and short time method for the verifier to verify that given identifiers of the fragments where indeed assigned that way (in particular, we could not verify that the given identifiers are indeed unique).

Hence, we assign identifiers according to another method that appears more memory wasteful: the identifier of a fragment F is $\mathtt{ID}(F) = (\mathtt{ID}(r(F)), j_F)$, where $\mathtt{ID}(r(F))$ is the unique identity of the root $r(F)$ of F, and j_F is F's level. We also need each node v to know the weight $\omega(F)$ of the minimum outgoing edge of each fragments containing v. To summarize, the *piece of information* $\mathtt{I}(F)$ required in each node v per fragment F containing v is $\mathtt{ID}(F) \circ \omega(F)$. Thus, $\mathtt{I}(F)$ can be encoded using $O(\log n)$ bits. Since a node may participate in $\ell = O(\log n)$ fragments, the total number of bits used for storing all the $\mathtt{I}(F)$ for all fragments F containing v would thus be $\Theta(\log^2 n)$. Had no additional steps been taken, this would have violated the $O(\log n)$ memory constraint. To save on memory, our scheme distributes the above information, while guaranteeing that each node u holds $\mathtt{I}(F)$ for at most constant number of fragments F.

To allow some node v to check whether its neighbor u belongs to v's level j fragment $F_j(v)$ for some level j, the verifier at v needs first to reconstruct $\mathtt{I}(F_j(v))$. Intuitively, we had to distribute the information, so that $\mathtt{I}(F)$ is placed "not too far" from every node in F. To compare $\mathtt{I}(F_j(v))$ with a neighbor u, Node v must also obtain $\mathtt{I}(F_j(u))$ from u. This requires some mechanism to synchronize the reconstructions in neighboring nodes. Furthermore, the verifier must be able to overcome difficulties resulting from faults, that can corrupt the information stored, as well as the reconstruction and the synchronization mechanisms.

The above distribution of the $\mathtt{I}$'s is described in the next subsection. The distributed algorithm for the "fragment by fragment" reconstruction (and synchronization) is described in Subsection 3.2. The required verifications for validating

the $\mathtt{I}$'s and comparing the information of neighboring nodes are described in Subsection 3.3.

3.1 Distributing the information

At a very high level description, each node v stores permanently $\mathtt{I}(F)$ for a constant number of fragments F. Using that, $\mathtt{I}(F)$ is "rotated" so that each node in F "sees" $\mathtt{I}(F)$ in $O(\log n)$ time. We term the mechanism that performs this rotation a *train*. A first idea would have been to have a separate train for each fragment F that would "carry" the piece $\mathtt{I}(F)$ and would allow all nodes in F to see it. However, we did not manage to do that efficiently in terms of time and of space. That is, one train passing a node could delay the others. Since neighboring nodes may share only a subset of their fragments, it is not clear how to pipeline the trains. Hence, those delays could accumulate. Moreover, as detailed below, each train utilizes some (often more than constant) memory per node. Hence, a train per fragment would have prevented us from obtaining an $O(\log n)$ memory solution.

A more refined idea would have been to partition the tree into connected parts, such that each part P intersects $O(|P|)$ fragments. Had we managed such a partition, we could have allocated the $O(|P|)$ pieces (of these $O(|P|)$ fragments), so that each node of P would have been assigned only a constant number of such pieces, costing $O(\log n)$ bits per node. Moreover, just one train per part P could have sufficed to rotate those pieces among the nodes of P. Each node in P would have seen all the pieces $\mathtt{I}(F)$ for fragments F containing it in $O(|P|)$ time. Hence, this would have been time efficient too, had P been small.

Unfortunately, we did not manage to construct the above partition. However, we managed to obtain a similar construction: We constructed *two* partitions of T, called $\mathtt{Top}$ and $\mathtt{Bottom}$. We also partitioned the fragments into two kinds: "top" and "bottom" fragments. Now, each part P of Partition $\mathtt{Top}$ intersect with $O(|P|)$ "top" fragments. Each part P of Partition $\mathtt{Bottom}$ intersects with $O(|P|)$ "bottom" fragments. Hence, it is enough for each node to participate in two trains only, one for each partition.

The two partitions: The marker performs the partitioning in the preliminary stage, while assigning the labels using $O(\log n)$ memory and $O(n)$ time. This is deferred to the full paper (see also [30]). We now describe the desired partitions $\mathtt{Top}$ and $\mathtt{Bottom}$, and the classification of fragments to "top" and "bottom" ones. First, define the "top" fragments to be precisely those fragments which contain at least $\log n$ nodes. Observe that the "top" fragments correspond to a subtree $T_{\mathtt{Top}}$ of the hierarchy tree $\mathcal{H}$. Let us describe Partition $\mathtt{Top}$. A leaf fragment in subtree $T_{\mathtt{Top}}$ is colored red. A fragment not in $T_{\mathtt{Top}}$ which is a sibling in $\mathcal{H}_{\mathcal{M}}$ of a fragment in $T_{\mathtt{Top}}$ is colored blue. We say that a red fragment F_{red} and a blue fragment F_{blue} are *relatives* if F_{red} is a descendant of a sibling of F_{blue} in $\mathcal{H}$. Observe that the collection of red and blue fragments forms a partition $\mathcal{P}'$ of the nodes of T. Also, each fragment F_{large} that strictly contains blue fragments is composed of at least one red fragment F_{red} as well as one or more blue ones, and does not contain any additional nodes. Since F_{large} is connected, it is possible to partition F_{large} to connected components such that each component P'' contains precisely one red fragment and possibly several blue ones, and no additional *nodes*. (Of course, P'' may contain also the *edges* connecting the fragments P'' contains.)

The collection of such connected components P'' forms a

partition $\mathcal{P}''$ which is a coarsening of partition $\mathcal{P}'$. Since each part contains a red fragment, we get that each part is of size at least $\log n$. (This is the reason why we attach blue fragments to one of their relative red fragments, that is, a blue fragment cannot be a part by itself since it may not contain enough nodes to store all the pieces of information regarding all of its many ancestors.) Observe also that if $F_1, F_2, \cdots F_t$ are the ancestors of a blue fragment F in $\mathcal{H}$ then those $F_1, F_2, \cdots F_t$ fragments are also ancestors in $\mathcal{H}$ of each red fragment which is a relative of F. Hence, the "top" fragments intersecting a part P are precisely those fragments which are the ancestors in $\mathcal{H}$ of the red fragment in P. In particular, we get that each part $P \in \mathcal{P}''$ intersects at most one level j "top" fragment, for every j. (This is the reason for not putting more than one red fragment in a part.)

We would like to pass a train in each part P of $\mathcal{P}''$. Unfortunately, the diameter of P may be too large. In such a case, we partition P further to *neighborhoods*, such that each neighborhood is a subtree of T of size at least $\log n$ and of diameter $O(\log n)$, establishing the following lemma.

LEMMA 2. *There exists a partition* Top *of* $V(T)$ *such that* $\forall P \in$ Top, $|P| \geqslant \log n$ *and* $D(P) = O(\log n)$. *Moreover, P intersects at most one level j "top" fragment, for every j (in particular, it intersects at most $\log n$ "top" fragments).*

The "bottom" fragments are precisely those with less than $\log n$ nodes. The parts of the second partition Bottom are the following: (1) the blue fragments, and (2) the children in $\mathcal{H}_\mathcal{M}$ of the leaves of T_{Top}. Observe that each part of Bottom is a "bottom" fragment. Thus, the size, and hence the diameter, of each part P of Bottom is less than $\log n$. Observe also that P contains all of P's descendant fragments in $\mathcal{H}$ (recall, P is a fragment), and does not intersect other "bottom" fragments. Hence, P intersects at most $2|P| < 2\log n$ "bottom" fragments.

Consider either Partition Top or Bottom. The parts of the partition and their corresponding roots are represented using 1 bit at each node v. The bit indicates whether v is the root $r(P)$ of a part P (the highest node of P) or not. Thus, by consulting the data-structure of a tree neighbor u, Node v can detect whether u and v belong to the same part.

A delicate and interesting point is that the verifier does not need to verify directly that the partitions were constructed as explained here. This is explained in Section 3.3.

Initializing the trains: Given Partition Top (respectively, Bottom), we construct a train for each of its parts P. Recall that P is a subtree of T rooted at $r(P)$. Let $\{F_i\}_{i \in [1,k]}$ be the "top" (resp., "bottom") fragments intersecting P, for some integer k. Recall that $k \leqslant \min\{2|P|, 2\log n\}$. Assume w.l.o.g., that the indices are such that the level of F_i is at least the level of F_{i-1}, for each $1 < i \leqslant k$. Let $\mathtt{I}(P) = \mathtt{I}(F_1) \circ \mathtt{I}(F_2) \circ, \cdots, \circ \mathtt{I}(F_k)$. We break $\mathtt{I}(P)$ into $|P|$ pairs of pieces. Specifically, for $1 \leqslant i \leqslant \lceil k/2 \rceil$, the i'th pair, termed $\mathtt{PcP}(i)$, contains $\mathtt{I}(F_{2i-1}) \circ \mathtt{I}(F_{2i})$ (for odd k, $\mathtt{PcP}(\lceil k/2 \rceil) = \mathtt{I}(F_{2i-1})$). The subtree P stores distributively $\mathtt{I}(P)$, as follows. Consider a DFS traversal over P that starts at $r(P)$ and let $\mathtt{dfs}(i)$ denote the the i'th node visited in this traversal. For each i, $1 \leqslant i \leqslant \lceil k/2 \rceil$, $\mathtt{dfs}(i)$ stores permanently the i'th pair of $\mathtt{I}(P)$, i.e., $\mathtt{PcP}(i)$.

3.2 Viewing distributed informaion

Recall that $\mathtt{I}(F_j(v))$ should reside permanently in some node of a part P to which v belongs. To allow v to compare

$\mathtt{I}(F_j(v))$ to $\mathtt{I}(F_j(u))$ for a neighbor u, both these pieces must somehow be "brought" to v. The process handling this task contains several components. The first is called a "train" and is responsible for moving the pieces' pairs $\mathtt{PcP}(i)$ through P's nodes, such that each node does not hold more than $O(\log n)$ bits at a time, and such that in time $O(\log n)$, each node in P "sees" all pieces, and in their correct order. Unfortunately, this is not enough, since $\mathtt{I}(F_j(v))$ may arrive at v at a different time than $\mathtt{I}(F_j(u))$ arrives at u. Further complications arise from the fact that the neighbors of a node v may belong to different parts, so different trains pass there. Note that v may have many neighbors, and we would not want to synchronize so many trains. Moreover, had we delayed the train at v for synchronization, the delay would have accumulated, or even would have caused deadlocks. Hence, we do not delay these trains. Instead, v repeatedly samples a piece from its train, and synchronizes the comparison of this piece with pieces sampled by its neighbors, while both trains advance without waiting. Perhaps not surprisingly, this synchronization turns out to be easier in synchronous networks, than in asynchronous ones.

This process is presented below assuming that no fault occurs. The detection of faults is described later.

The trains: For simplicity, we split the task of a train into two subtasks, each performed repeatedly- the first, *convergecast*, moves the pieces one at a time *pipelined* from their permanent locations to $r(P)$ according to the DFS order. (Recall, $\mathtt{dfs}(i)$ stores permanently the i'th piece of $\mathtt{I}(P)$.) Call each consecutive delivery of the k pieces pair $\mathtt{PcP}(1), \mathtt{PcP}(2), \cdots, \mathtt{PcP}(k)$ to $r(P)$ a *cycle*. Since we are concerned with at most $k \leqslant 2\log n$ pieces's pairs, each cycle can be performed in $O(\log n)$ time. The second subtask, *broadcast*, broadcasts each piece from $r(P)$ to all other nodes in P (pipelined). This subtask can be performed in $D(P) = O(\log n)$ time, where $D(P)$ is the diameter of P. These two subtasks (and their stabilization) are rather straightforward, hence their description is omitted.

Consider now the case that a piece containing $\mathtt{I}(F)$ carried by the broadcast wave arrives at some node v. Abusing notations, we refer to this event by saying that Fragment F *arrives* at v. Recall that v does not have enough memory to remember the identifiers of all the fragments containing it. Thus, a mechanism for letting v know whether the arriving fragment F contains v must be employed. Note that the level j of F can be extracted from $\mathtt{I}(F)$, and recall that it is assumed that v knows whether it is contained in some level j fragment. Obviously, if v is not contained in a level j fragment then $v \notin F$. If $F_j(v)$ does exist, we now explain how to let v know whether $F = F_j(v)$.

Consider first a train in a part $P \in$ Top. Here, P intersects at most one level j "top" fragment, for each level j (see Lemma 2). Thus, this train carries at most one level j fragment F_j. Hence, $F_j = F_j(v)$ iff $F_j(v)$ exists.

Now consider a train in a part $P \in$ Bottom. Unfortunately, in this case, Part P may intersect several "bottom" fragments of the same level. To allow a node v to detect whether a fragment F_j arriving at v corresponds to Fragment $F_j(v)$, we refine the above mentioned train broadcast mechanism as follows. During the broadcast wave, we attach a flag to each $\mathtt{I}(F)$, which can be either "on" or "off", where initially, the flag is "off". Recall that $\mathtt{I}(F)$ contains the identity $\mathtt{ID}(r(F))$ of the root $r(F)$ of F. When the broadcast wave reaches this root $r(F)$ (or, when it starts in $r(F)$ in the case that

$r(F) = r(P))$, it changes the flag to "on". In contrast, before transmitting the broadcast wave from a leaf u of F to u's children in T (that do not belong to F), Node u sets the flag to "off". That way, a fragment F arriving at a node v contains v if and only if the corresponding flag is set to "on". (Recall that the data structure lets each node know whether it is a leaf of a level j fragment). Hence, node v can detect whether $F = F_j(v)$.

To avoid delaying the train beyond a constant time, each node multiplexes the two trains passing via it. That is, it passes one piece of one train, then one piece of the other.

Sampling and synchronizing: Node u maintains two variables: $\texttt{Show}(u)$ and $\texttt{Ask}(u)$, each for holding one piece $\texttt{I}(F)$. In $\texttt{Ask}(u)$, node u keeps $\texttt{I}((F_j(u))$ for some j, until u compares the piece $\texttt{I}(F_j(u))$ to the piece $\texttt{I}(F_j(v))$, for each of its neighbors v. Let $\mathcal{E}(u,v,j)$ denote the event that Node u holds $\texttt{I}(F_j(u))$ in $\texttt{Ask}(u)$ and sees $\texttt{I}(F_j(v))$ in $\texttt{Show}(v)$. (For simplicity of presentation, we consider here the case that both u and v *do* belong to some fragments of level j; otherwise, storing and comparing the information for a non-existing fragments is trivial.) For any point in time t, let $C(t)$ denote the minimal time interval $C(t) = [t, x(t)]$ in which every event of the type $\mathcal{E}(u,v,j)$ occurred. For the scheme to function, it is crucial that $C(t)$ exists for any time t. Moreover, to have a fast scheme, we must ensure that $\max_t |C(t)|$ is small.

Recall that the train brings the pieces $\texttt{I}(F)$ in a cyclic order. When u is done comparing $\texttt{I}((F_j(u))$ (to $\texttt{I}(F_j(v))$ for each of its neighbors v), node u waits until it receives (by the train) the first piece $\texttt{I}(F)$ following $\texttt{I}((F_j(u))$ in the cyclic order, such that F contains u (recall that u can identify this F). Let us denote the level of this next fragment F by j', i.e., $F = F_{j'}(u)$. Node u then removes $\texttt{I}(F_j(u))$ from $\texttt{Ask}(u)$ and stores $\texttt{I}(F_{j'}(u))$ there instead, and so forth.

Let us explain the comparing mechanism. Each node u also stores some piece $\texttt{I}(F_i(u))$ at $\texttt{Show}(u)$ to be seen by its neighbors. Fix a node v and one of its neighbors u. In a synchronous network, Node v sees $\texttt{Show}(u)$ in every pulse. Then, u waits until u receives (by the train) $\texttt{I}(F_{i'}(u))$, then u stores it in $\texttt{Show}(u)$, etc. Hence, if v waits some $O(\log n)$ time (while $\texttt{I}(F_j(v))$ is in $\texttt{Ask}(v)$), Node v sees $\texttt{I}(F_j(u))$ in $\texttt{Show}(u)$ and event $\mathcal{E}(v,u,j)$ occurs. The time for $\log n + 1$ such events to occur (one event per level j) is $O(\log^2 n)$.

The above result for synchronous networks is already enough to ensure that our asynchronous self stabilizing MST construction algorithm has $O(n)$ stabilization time. Intuitively, this is because the latter uses a self stabilizing synchronizer, see Section 4. However, since the synchronizer itself has stabilization time $O(n)$, the result is not enough to ensure a short detection time complexity of the self stabilizing MST construction. To ensure that, we also establish an upper bound of $O(\Delta \log^2 n)$ for the detection time of a verification algorithm in asynchronous networks. Because of lack of space, this is deferred to the full paper.

LEMMA 3. *If (1) two partitions are indeed represented, such that each part of each partition is of diameter $O(\log n)$, and the number of pieces in a part is $O(\log n)$, and (2) the trains have self stabilized, then the following holds.*

- *In a synchronous network, $\max_t |C(t)| = O(\log^2 n)$.*

- *In an asynchronous network, $\max_t |C(t)| = O(\Delta \log^2 n)$.*

3.3 Local verifications

In this section, we describe the measures taken in order to make the verifier self stabilizing. That is, the train process and also, the pieces of information carried by the train may be corrupted by an adversary. To stress this point and avoid confusion, a piece of information of the form $z \circ j \circ \omega$, carried by a train, is termed the *claimed* information $\hat{\texttt{I}}(F)$ of a fragment F whose root ID is z, whose level is j, and whose minimum outgoing edge is ω. Note that such a fragment F may not even exist, if the information is corrupted. Conversely, the adversary may also erase some (or even all) of such pieces corresponding to existing fragments. Finally, even correct pieces that correspond to existing fragments may not arrive at a node in the case that the adversary corrupted the partitions or the train mechanism. Below we explain how does the verifier detect such undesirable phenomenas, if they occur. Note that for a verifying, the ability to detect assuming any initial configuration means that the verifier is self stabilizing, since the sole purpose of the verifier is to detect. We show, in this section, that if an MST is not represented in the network, this is detected. (Since the detection time (the stabilization time) is sublinear, we still consider this detection as local, though some of the locality was traded for improving the memory size (when compared to the results of [31, 29]).

Verifying that *some* two partitions exist is easy, given the data structure assumptions (see the top of Section 3). It is sufficient to (1) let each node verify that its label contains the two bits corresponding to the two partitions; and (2) to have the root $r(T)$ of the tree verify that the value of each of its own two bits is 1. (Observe that if these two conditions hold then (1) $r(T)$ is a root of one part in each of the two partitions; and (2) for a node $v \neq r(T)$, if one of these two bits in v is zero, then v belongs to the same part in the corresponding partition as its parent.) Note that this module of the algorithm self stabilizes in constant time.

It is difficult to verify that the given partitions are as described in Section 3.1, rather than two arbitrary partitions generated by an adversary. Fortunately, this verification turns out to be unnecessary. First, after we verify that *some* partitions are indeed represented, it is a known art to self stabilize the train process, see, e.g. [12, 13]. After the trains stabilize, what we really want to ensure is (a) that the set of pieces stored in a part (and delivered by the train) includes all the (possibly corrupted) pieces of the form $\texttt{I}(F_j(v))$, for every v in the part and for every j such that v belongs to a level j fragment, and (b) that each node obtains all the the pieces it needs quickly, i.e., in $O(\log n)$ time.

Addressing (a) above, we shall show that the verifier at each node rejects if it does not obtain all the required pieces eventually, whether the partitions are correct or not. Informally, this is done as follows. Recall (the data structure assumptions) that each node v knows the set $J(v)$ of levels j for which there exists a fragment of level j containing it, namely, $F_j(v)$. Using a delimiter (stored at v), we partition $J(v)$ to $J_{\texttt{Top}}(v)$ and $J_{\texttt{Bottom}}(v)$; where $J_{\texttt{Top}}(v)$ (respectively, $J_{\texttt{Bottom}}(v)$) is the set of levels $j \in J(v)$ such that $F_j(v)$ is "top" (resp., "bottom"). Node v "expects" to receive the claimed information $\hat{\texttt{I}}(F_j(v))$ for $j \in J_{\texttt{Top}}(v)$ (respectively, $j \in J_{\texttt{Bottom}}(v)$) from the train of the part in $\texttt{Top}$ (respectively, $\texttt{Bottom}$) it belongs to. Let us now consider the part $P_{\texttt{Top}} \in \texttt{Top}$ containing v. In correct instances, by the way the train operate, it follows that the levels of fragments arriving at v should arrive in a strictly *increasing order* and in a *cyclical* manner, that is, $j_1 < j_2 < j_3 < \cdots < j_a, j_1 < j_2 < \cdots j_a, j_1 \cdots$ (observe that $j_a = \ell$). Consider the case that the verifier at v receives two consecutive pieces $z_1 \circ j_1 \circ \omega_1$ and $z_2 \circ j_2 \circ \omega_2$ such that $j_2 \leqslant j_1$. The verifier at v then "assumes" that the event S of the arrival of the second piece $z_2 \circ j_2 \circ \omega_2$ starts a new cycle of the train. Let the set of pieces arriving at v between two consecutive such S events be named a *cycle set*. To be "accepted" by the verifier, the set of levels of the fragments arriving at v in each cycle set must contain $J_{\text{Top}}(v)$. It is trivial to verify this in two cycles after the faults cease, given the fact that v knows $J_{\text{Top}}(v)$ (by the data structure assumptions) and the fact that the levels in each cycle set arrive in strictly increasing order. (The discussion above is based implicitly on the assumption that each node receives pieces infinitely often; this is guaranteed by the correctness of the train mechanism, assuming that at least one piece is indeed stored permanently in P_{Top}; Verifying this assumption is done easily by the root $r(P_{\text{Top}})$ of P_{Top}, simply by verifying that $r(P_{\text{Top}})$ itself does contain a piece.)

Verifying the reception of all the pieces in a part in **Bottom** is handled very similarly, and is thus omitted. This completes the informal description of how to guarantee (a) above.

We still need to show that the partitions are such that (b) above is also accomplished. It is a known art to show that the sub- tasks of the train stabilize in Given the $O(D(|P| + |\text{PcP}(P)|))$ where $|\text{PcP}(P)|$ is the number of pieces stored in the nodes of P, see [13, 12], as well as some more details in [30]. Hence, it is sufficient to verify that each part P of each of the two claimed partitions has diameter $D(P) = O(\log n)$, and that the number of pieces stored in each part is $O(\log n)$. Verifying this is done easily using a 1-proof labeling scheme that uses $O(\log n)$ bits, using the methods of [31] (see, also [30]). The stabilization time of (b) above is, thus, constant.

Hence, we can sum up the above discussion as follows: if the verifier accepts then each node v receives $\hat{\text{I}}(F_j(v))$, for every level $j \in J(v)$ (in the time stated in Lemma 3), and conversely, if a node does not receive $\hat{\text{I}}(F_j(v))$ (in the time stated in Lemma 3) then the verifier has rejects.

Let $p(v)$ denote the parent of v in T. In event $\mathcal{E}(v, p(v), j)$, Node v compares $\hat{\text{I}}(F_j(v))$ with $\hat{\text{I}}(F_j(p(v)))$. Consider the case that such a comparison finds these pieces are equal for every such pair of node $v, p(v)$ in a fragment. Intuitively, this means the nodes of the fragments agree (by transitivity) on the fragment's $\hat{\text{I}}$. Hence, in the full paper we show that the following is verified in in $O(\log n)$ time:

- The claimed identifiers of the fragments are compatible with the given hierarchy $\mathcal{H}$. (I.e., for every $F \in \mathcal{H}$, $\hat{\text{I}}(F)$ is of the form $z \circ j \circ \omega$, and we verify that the identifier of F's root is z.) In particular, this guarantees that the identifiers of fragments are indeed unique.

- For every $F \in \mathcal{H}$, all the nodes in F agree on the *claimed* weight of the minimum outgoing edge of Fragment F, denoted $\hat{\omega}(F)$.

So far, we have shown that each node does receive the necessary information needed for the verifier. Now, finally, we show how to use this information to detect whether this is an MST. Basically, we verify that $\hat{\omega}(F)$ is indeed the minimum outgoing edge $\omega(F)$ of F and that this minimum is indeed the candidate edge of F, for every $F \in \mathcal{H}$. Consider

a time when $\mathcal{E}(v, u, j)$ occurs. Node v proceeds and outputs "no" if any of the checks below is not valid.

- **C1:** If v is the endpoint of the candidate edge $e = (v, u)$ of $F_j(v)$ then v checks that u does not belong to $F_j(v)$, i.e., that $\hat{\text{ID}}(F_j(v)) \neq \hat{\text{ID}}(F_j(u))$, and that $\hat{\omega}(F_j(v)) = \omega(e)$ (recall, the data structure assumptions ensure that v knows whether it is an endpoint, and if so, which of its edges is the candidate);

- **C2:** If $\hat{\text{ID}}(F_j(v)) \neq \hat{\text{ID}}(F_j(u))$ then v verifies that $\hat{\text{ID}}(F_j(v)) \neq \hat{\text{ID}}(F_j(u)) \Rightarrow \hat{\omega}(F_j(v)) \leqslant \omega(v, u)$.

The following now follows from C1, C2 and Lemma 1.

LEMMA 4.
- *If by some time t, the events $\mathcal{E}(v, u, j)$ occurred for each node v and each neighbor u of v in G and for each level j, and the verifier did not reject, then T is an MST of G.*

- *If T is not an MST, then in the time stated in Lemma 3 after the fault cease, the verifier rejects.*

The following theorem now follows (the detection distance and more detailed analysis are deferred to the full; additional details also appears in [30]).

THEOREM 1. *The scheme described in this section is a correct proof labeling scheme for MST. Its memory complexity is $O(\log n)$ bits. Its detection time complexity is $O(\log^2 n)$ in synchronous networks and $O(\triangle \log^2 n)$ in asynchronous ones. Its detection distance is $O(f \log n)$ if f faults occurred. Its construction time is $O(n)$.*

4. THE SELF STABILIZING ALGORITHM

We use a transformer that inputs a non- stabilizing algorithm and outputs a self stabilizing one. For simplicity, we first explain how to use the transformer proposed in the seminal paper of [9] (which utilizes the transformer of its companion paper [8]) as a black box. This already yields an $O(n)$ time and $O(\log n)$ memory per node. Later, we refine that transformer somewhat to add the property that the verification time is of $O(\log^2 n)$ time in a synchronous network, or $O(\min\{\triangle \log^2 n, n\})$ in an asynchronous one. We then also establish the property that if f faults occur, then each fault is detected within its $O(f \log n)$ neighborhood.

The Resynchronizer of [9] gets as an input a non-stabilizing synchronous input/output algorithm Π whose running time and memory size are some T_Π and S_Π, respectively, and yields a self stabilizing version whose memory size is $O(S_\Pi + \log n)$ and whose time complexity is $O(T_\Pi + \hat{D})$ where $\hat{D}$ is an *upper bound* on the actual diameter D of the network. (An input/output algorithm is one whose correctness requirement can be specified as a relation between its input and its output). To have the Resynchronizer yield our desired result, we first need to come up with such a bound $\hat{D}$. Second, the result of the Resynchronizer is a synchronous algorithm, while we want an asynchronous one. Third, we need such a synchronous MST construction algorithm Π whose memory size is $O(\log n)$ bits per node and whose time complexity is $O(n)$. Let us describe briefly how we bridge these gaps. The detailed description is deferred to the full paper.

We use known self stabilizing protocols [1, 16] to compute (in $O(n)$ time, $O(\log n)$ bits) D, to be used as the desired

$\hat{D}$. Note that at the time that [9] was written, the only algorithm for computing a good bound on the diameter with a bounded memory had time complexity $\Theta(n^2)$ [2].

To bridge the second gap, of converting the resulting self stabilizing algorithm for an *asynchronous* network, we use a *self stabilizing synchronizer* that transforms synchronous algorithms to function correctly in asynchronous networks. Such a synchronizer was not known at the time of [9], but several are available now. The synchronizer of [6, 7] was first described as if it needs unbounded memory. However, as is stated in [7], this synchronizer is meant to be coupled with a reset protocol to bound the memory. To have a memory size of $O(\log n)$ and time $O(n)$, it is sufficient to use a reset protocol (such as the one of [8]) with these complexities. Similarly, this reset protocol of [8] is meant to be coupled with a self stabilizing spanning tree algorithm. The complexities of resulting protocol are dominated by those of the spanning tree construction. We plug in some self stabilizing spanning tree algorithm with the desired $O(\log n)$ and $O(n)$ memory size and time complexities in asynchronous networks (e.g. [1, 16]). (It is not hard to improve the time to $O(D)$ in synchronous networks). We, thus, obtain the desired reset protocol, and, hence, the desired synchronizer protocol. (An alternative synchronizer can be based on the one of [14], again, coupled with some additional known components, such as a module to compute n). Let us sum up the treatment of the first two gaps: thanks to some new modules developed after [9], one can now use the following version of the main result of [9].

THEOREM 2. **Enhanced Awerbuch-Varghese Theorem, (EAV):** *Assume we are given a distributed algorithm Π to compute an input/output relation R. Whether Π is synchronous or asynchronous, let T_Π and S_Π denote Π's time complexity and memory size, respectively, when executed in synchronous networks. The enhanced Resynchronizer compiler produces an asynchronous (respectively, synchronous) self stabilizing algorithm whose memory size is $O(S_\Pi + \log n)$ and whose time complexity is $O(T_\Pi + n)$ (resp., $O(T_\Pi + D)$).*

The EAV theorem differs from the result in [9] by (1) addressing also asynchronous algorithms, and (2) basing the time complexity on the actual values of n and D of the network rather than on an a-priori bound $\hat{D}$ that may be arbitrarily larger than D or n. Plugging in the algorithm of Awerbuch [5] as Π, the EAV theorem already yields a self stabilizing MST construction with $O(n)$ time and $O(\log^2 n)$ bits per node. This is faster than the best known result presented recently [11], with the same memory size complexity. Still, below, we improve that further to $O(n)$ time and $O(\log n)$ bits. This is obtained by plugging a different Π, with a better complexity, in the EAV theorem. It turns out that it is rather easy to implement the algorithm of [21] in a shared memory model such that it will use $O(\log n)$ bits per node, without increasing its time complexity T_{GHS}. However, T_{GHS} is somewhat too high, i.e., $\Theta(n \log n)$. Fortunately, it is easy to improve that time complexity to $O(n)$ provided that we implement that algorithm as a *synchronous algorithm*. (Recall that a synchronous algorithm suffices as an input for the Resynchronizer.) This $O(n)$ time implementation uses a very simplified version of the ideas of Awerbuch in [5]. (Awerbuch needed a more complex adaptation of the algorithms of [21] because he needed the algorithm to perform well in asynchronous networks). The description of Π is deferred to the full paper.

4.1 Obtaining fast verification

The Resynchronizer compiler performs iterations forever. Essentially, the first iteration is used to compute the result of Π, by executing Π (plus some additional staff needed for the self stabilization). Each of the later iterations is used to check that the above result is correct. For that, the Resynchronizer executes a checker. If the result is not correct, then the checker in at least one node "raises an alarm". This, in effect, signals that Resynchronizer to drop back to the first iteration. Let us term such a node a *detecting node*. Our refinement just replaces the checker, interfacing with the original Resynchronizer by supplying such a detection node.

We should mention that the original design in [9] is already modular in allowing such a replacement of a checker. In fact, two alternative such checkers are studied in [9]. The first kind of a checker is Π itself. That is, if Π is deterministic, then, if executed again, it must compute the same results again (this is adjusted later in [9] to accommodate randomized protocols). This checker functions by comparing the result computed by Π in each "non-first" iteration to the result it has computed before. If they differ, then a fault is detected. The second kind of a checker is a local checker of the kinds studied in [2, 8] or even one that can be derived from local proofs [31, 29]. That is, a checker whose time complexity is exactly 1. When using this kind of a checker, the Resynchronizer uses one iteration to execute Π, then the Resychronizer executes the checker repeatedly until a fault is detected. The door was left open in [9] for additional checkers. It was in this context that they posed the open problem whether MST has a checker which is faster than MST computation, and still uses small memory. (This paper answers the open problem in the affirmative).

We use a self stabilizing verifier (of a proof labeling scheme) as a checker. That is, if a fault occurs, then the checker detects it, at least in one node, regardless of the initial configuration. Such nodes where the fault is detected serve as the detecting nodes used above by the Resychronizer. The following theorem differs from the EAV theorem by stating that the final protocol (resulting from the transformation), also enjoys the good properties of the self stabilizing verifier. I.e., if the self stabilizing verifier has a good detection time and good detection distance, then, the detection time and distance of the resulting protocols are good too.

THEOREM 3. *Suppose we are given the following:*

- *A distributed algorithm Π to compute an input/output relation R. Whether Π is synchronous or asynchronous, let T_Π and S_Π denote Π's time complexity and memory size, when executed in* synchronous *networks.*

- *An asynchronous (respectively, synchronous) proof labeling scheme Π' for verifying R with memory size $S_{\Pi'}$, whose verifier self stabilizes with verification time and detection distance $t_{\Pi'}$ and $d_{\Pi'}$, and whose construction time (of the marker) is $T_{\Pi'}$.*

Then, the enhanced Resynchronizer produces an asynchronous (resp., synchronous) self stabilizing algorithm whose memory and time complexities are $O(S_\Pi + S_{\Pi'} + \log n)$ and $O(T_\Pi + T_{\Pi'} + t_{\Pi'} + n)$ (resp., $O(T_\Pi + T_{\Pi'} + t_{\Pi'} + D)$), and whose verification time and detection distance are $t_{\Pi'}$ and $d_{\Pi'}$.

To obtain the desired proof labeling scheme Π', we implemented two tasks. The first, is constructing a non-stabilizing distributed marker. The description is deferred to the full paper (See [30]). Note that the marker algorithm does not have to be self stabilizing, since it is transformed to be self stabilizing using the Resynchronizer compiler. (That is, the input of the Resynchronizer includes a combination of the marker and of the MST construction algorithm). Now, two possible checkers are the verifiers of the schemes of [29, 31]. Since their detection time is 1, they stabilize trivially. (Their distributed markers are simplified versions of the marker of the proof labeling scheme given of the current paper). Plugging either one of them (together with the above $O(n)$ time Π) yields the following.

COROLLARY 1. *There exists a self stabilizing MST algorithm with $O(\log^2 n)$ memory size and $O(n)$ time. Moreover, its detection time is 1 and its detection distance is $f + 1$.*

Finally, by plugging the self stabilizing verifier described in Section 3 in the Resychronizer, we obtain The following.

COROLLARY 2. *There exists a self stabilizing MST algorithm that uses optimal $O(\log n)$ memory size and $O(n)$ time. Moreover, its detection time complexity is $O(\log^2 n)$ in synchronous networks and $O(\triangle \log^2 n)$ in asynchronous ones. Furthermore, its detection distance is $O(f \log n)$.*

5. REFERENCES

[1] Y. Afek and A. Bremler-Barr. Self-Stabilizing Unidirectional Network Algorithms by Power Supply. Chicago J. Theor. Comput. Sci. 1998: (1998).

[2] Y. Afek, S. Kutten, and M. Yung. The Local Detection Paradigm and Its Application to Self-Stabilization. TCS 186(1-2): 199-229 (1997).

[3] S. Aggarwal and S. Kutten. Time Optimal Self Stabilizing Spanning Tree Algorithms. FSTTCS 1993.

[4] A. Arora, M. G. Gouda. Distributed Reset. IEEE Trans. Computers (TC) 43(9):1026-1038 (1994).

[5] B. Awerbuch. Optimal Distributed Algorithms for Minimum Weight Spanning Tree, Counting, Leader Election and Related Problems. STOC 1987: 230-240.

[6] B. Awerbuch, S. Kutten, Y. Mansour, B. Patt-Shamir, and G. Varghese. A Time-Optimal Self-Stabilizing Synchronizer Using A Phase Clock. IEEE Trans. Dependable Sec. Comput. 4(3): 180-190 (2007).

[7] B. Awerbuch, S. Kutten, Y. Mansour, B. Patt-Shamir, and G. Varghese. Time optimal self-stabilizing synchronization. STOC 1993: 652-661.

[8] B. Awerbuch, B. Patt-Shamir, and G. Varghese. Self-Stabilization By Local Checking and Correction. FOCS 1991, pp. 268-277.

[9] B. Awerbuch and G. Varghese. Distributed Program Checking: a Paradigm for Building Self-stabilizing Distributed Protocols. FOCS 1991: 258-267.

[10] L. Blin, M. Potop-Butucaru, S. Rovedakis and S. Tixeuil. A New Self-stabilizing minimum spanning tree construction with loop-Free property. DISC 2009.

[11] L. Blin, S. Dolev, M. Gradinariu Potop-Butucaru, and S. Rovedakis. Fast Self-Stabilizing Minimum Spanning Tree Construction. DISC 2010: 312-327.

[12] A. Bui, A. K. Datta, F. Petit, V. Villain. Space optimal PIF algorithm: self-stabilized with no extra space. IPCCC 1999:20-26.

[13] Z. Collin and S. Dolev. Self-stabilizing depth-first search. IPL, 49(6): 297-301 (1994).

[14] C. Boulinier, F. Petit, and V. Villain. When graph theory helps self-stabilization. PODC 2004.

[15] Y. K. Dalal. A Distributed Algorithm for Constructing Minimal Spanning Trees. IEEE Trans. Software Eng. 13(3): 398-405 (1987).

[16] A. K. Datta, L. L. Larmore, and P. Vemula. Self Stabilizing Leader Election in Optimal Space. SSS 2008: 109-123.

[17] A. K. Datta, L. L. Larmore, H. Piniganti. Self stabilizing Leader Election in Dynamic Networks. SSS 2010: 35-49.

[18] E. W. Dijkstra. Self-stabilizing systems in spite of distributed control. CACM, 17(11), 643–644, 1974.

[19] S. Dolev, M. Gouda, and M. Schneider. Requirements for silent stabilization. *Acta Informatica*, 36(6), 447-462, 1999.

[20] P. Fraigniaud and C. Gavoille. Routing in trees. ICALP 2001, pp. 757–772.

[21] R. G. Gallager, P. A. Humblet, and P. M. Spira. A Distributed Algorithm for Minimum-Weight Spanning Trees. ACM TOPLAS, 5(1): 66-77, 1983.

[22] J. Garay, S. Kutten, and D. Peleg. A sub-linear time distributed algorithm. FOCS, 1993.

[23] S. Ghosh, A. Gupta, T. Herman, and S. V. Pemmaraju. Fault-Containing Self-Stabilizing Algorithms. PODC 1996.

[24] S.K.S Gupta, P.K. Srimani. Self-stabilizing multicast protocols for ad hoc networks. JPDC, 63(1): 87-96.

[25] L. Higham, and Z. Liang. Self-stabilizing minimum spanning tree construction on message passing networks. DISC 2001: 194-208.

[26] D. Peleg. Distributed computing: a locality-sensitive approach. SIAM, 2000, ISBN:0-89871-464-8.

[27] G.M. Jayaram and G. Varghese. The fault span of crash failures. JACM, 47(2): 244-293 (2000).

[28] S. Katz, K. J. Perry. Self-Stabilizing Extensions for Message-Passing Systems. DC, 7(1): 17-26 (1993).

[29] A. Korman and S. Kutten. Distributed verification of minimum spanning trees. DC, 20(4):253-266 (2007).

[30] A. Korman, S. Kutten, and T. Masuzawa. Fast and Compact Self-Stabilizing Verification, Computation, and Fault Detection of an MST, an extended version of the PODC paper. http://iew3.technion.ac.il/~kutten/KKM2011-ext.pdf.

[31] A. Korman, S. Kutten, and D Peleg. Proof labeling schemes. DC, 22:215–233, 2010.

[32] A. Korman and D. Peleg. Compact Separator Decomposition for Dynamic Trees and Applications. DC, (2008), 21(2): 141-161.

[33] S. Kutten and D. Peleg. Fast Distributed Construction of k-Dominating Sets and Applications. PODC 1995.

[34] Z. Lotker, B. Patt-Shamir, and D. Peleg. Distributed MST for constant diameter graphs. DC, 18(6), 2006.

[35] D. Peleg, V. Rubinovich: A Near-Tight Lower Bound on the Time Complexity of Distributed Minimum Weight Spanning Tree Construction. SICOMP 30(5).

[36] R. E. Tarjan. Applications of path compression on balanced trees. *JACM* 26 (1979), pp. 690–715.

Stability of a Peer-to-Peer Communication System[*]

Ji Zhu
Coordinated Science Laboratory
University of Illinois at Urbana Champaign
1308 W Main Street
Urbana, IL 61801
jizhu1@illinois.edu

Bruce Hajek
Coordinated Science Laboratory
University of Illinois at Urbana Champaign
1308 W Main Street
Urbana, IL 61801
b-hajek@illinois.edu

ABSTRACT

Peer-to-peer (P2P) communication in networks for file distribution and other applications is a powerful multiplier of network utility, due to its ability to exploit parallelism in a distributed way. As new variations are engineered, to provide less impact on service providers and to provide better quality of service, it is important to have a theoretical underpinning, to weigh the effectiveness of various methods for enhancing the service. This paper focuses on the stationary portion of file download in an unstructured P2P network, which typically follows for many hours after a flash crowd initiation. The contribution of the paper is to identify how much help is needed from the seeds, either fixed seeds or peers dwelling in the system after obtaining the complete file, to stabilize the system. It is shown that dominant cause for instability is the missing piece syndrome, whereby one piece becomes very rare in the network. It is shown that very little dwell time is necessary–even if there is very little help from a fixed seed, peers need to dwell on average no longer than it takes to upload one additional piece, after they have obtained a complete collection.

Categories and Subject Descriptors

C.2.1 [**Computer-Communication Networks**]: Network Architecture and Design—*distributed networks, network topology*; H.1.1 [**Models and Principles**]: Systems and Information Theory—*general systems theory*

General Terms

Theory, Algorithms, Performance

Keywords

Peer to peer, missing piece syndrome, random peer contact, random useful piece upload, branching process, Foster-Lyapunov stability, Markov process

[*]This work was supported by the National Science Foundation under Grant NSF CCF 10-16959.

1. INTRODUCTION

Peer-to-peer communication has been enjoying great popularity in the Internet [5]. Second generation P2P networks such as *BitTorrent* [1], divide a file to be distributed into distinct pieces and enable clients (or peers) to share these pieces efficiently. BitTorrent, with its rarest first and choke algorithm, has been shown to scale well with the number of participating peers [7].

A P2P network under the BitTorrent protocol is of unstructured type, meaning there is no specific network topology to be formed by the participating peers. In such a network, a *fixed seed* refers to a server which holds the whole file; a *peer seed* refers to a peer which has collected the whole file but has not yet departed. The major difference between fixed seeds and peer seeds is that fixed seeds always stay in the network but peer seeds eventually depart.

One problem observed in an unstructured type P2P network is the *delay in endgame mode* [1] (or *last piece problem*). That is, when the last piece to be downloaded by a peer is rare in the network, or when the last piece is requested from a peer with small uploading capacity, it takes the peer a long time to finish downloading. If new peers keep arriving into the network and many of them suffer from the last piece problem, it may result a congestion of peers and affect the stability of the network.

We label as *missing piece syndrome*, which is related to the last piece problem, a specific abnormality in P2P networks [4, 11]. The missing piece syndrome happens when precisely one of the pieces becomes rare network wide and the upload rate of that piece from the seeds is not large enough. Once there are many peers in the system and most of them are missing that same piece, it is difficult for these peers to collect the last piece and depart. Peers lucky enough to get the missing piece can quickly collect the whole file so they have a short lifetime in the system. But, their ability to spread the missing piece is limited. As more and more new peers arrive, most of them cannot find peers with the missing piece, which enlarges the group of peers missing the piece. The result is that the P2P system becomes unstable.

The missing piece syndrome is evidenced in the work of Menasché et al. [10]. They point out that in their simulation studies, their "smooth download assumption" and "swarm sustainability" break down if the seed upload rate is not sufficiently large. There are different mechanisms for mitigating the missing piece syndrome. In the BitTorrent protocol, peers in endgame mode send requests for the last piece to all neighboring peers, searching for a suitable provider. Based on simulation, Gkantsidis [3] argues that the rarest first algorithm may not prevent the scarcity of some pieces and proposes a network coding solution. But Legout et al. [7] argue based on their simulation that the rarest first algorithm is efficient at mitigating the scarcity of the last piece. We show in this paper that requiring peer seeds to dwell in the network for only a short time is sufficient to prevent the missing piece syndrome.

Some theoretical works shown as follows are closely related to this paper. Qiu [12] and Yang [13] analyze the steady state performance by studying fluid models of P2P network. Massoulié [9] considers the fine structure of piece transferring in their open model of P2P file replication network, where continuous arrival of new peers is taken into consideration. Leskelä et al. [8] investigate stability conditions for a single piece file, or a two piece file when the pieces are obtained sequentially, when peers remain in the system for some time after obtaining the piece. Norros et al. [11] formulate a related model for the case that the file is divided into two pieces and prove some stability result.

Most works on P2P networks are based on simulation results or large testbeds. Theory-based works on P2P models, though few in number, are important complements for a better understanding of P2P networks. In this paper, we present a detailed analysis of the sensitivity of peer seeds dwell time to the stability of the network. The model discussed in this paper is a hybrid of related models in [9, 12, 13], which covers continuous arrival of new peers, a fixed seed, peer and piece selection, and limited upload link capacity. It is shown based on the model that there exists a threshold for the dwell time of peer seeds. The missing piece syndrome is avoided if the average dwell time of peer seeds is larger than the threshold. But the network is unstable if the average dwell time is less than the threshold. The threshold does not exceed the average transfer time of a single piece. It suggests that by requiring peer seeds to donate just one more piece instead of departing immediately, the missing piece syndrome can be avoided. That intuition can be applied in a realistic network, where the transfer time of one piece is usually small.

Outline. The structure of this paper is as follows. In Section 2 we formulate the model and state our main result. In Section 3 we describe three examples to provide intuition and to illustrate the model and result. A sketch of the proof is offered in Sections 4.1 and 4.2. Discussions and ideas for future work are given in Section 5.

2. MODEL AND RESULT

We consider a single fixed seed P2P network in this paper, where a large file is divided into $K, K \geq 1$ pieces, $1, 2, ...K$, which are stored in the fixed seed. Each peer in the system holds some subset of the K pieces. Define $\mathcal{F}$ to be the collection of all pieces: $\mathcal{F} := \{1, 2, ...K\}$. Define $\mathcal{C}$ to be the power set of $\mathcal{F}$. For any $C \in \mathcal{C}$, a peer holding the collection of pieces C is called a *type C peer*. In some real P2P network, peers can get some pieces from a tracker upon their arrival for initialization. To capture that case, we assume type C peers arrive into the system at times of a Poisson process with rate λ_C. Although we consider all possible values of $(\lambda_C, C \in \mathcal{C})$, typically in practice, λ_C is small or equal to zero when $|C| > 1$.

The fixed seed and all peers apply the *random peer contact* and *random useful piece upload* strategies at instants of Poisson processes. Define a *Poisson clock* with rate $x \geq 0$ to be

a clock which ticks at instants of a Poisson process with rate x, independent of all other processes in this paper. We suppose the fixed seed and each peer maintain internal Poisson clocks, with rate $U_s \geq 0$ and $\mu > 0$, respectively. Whenever the clock of the fixed seed ticks, the fixed seed contacts a peer, say peer A, which is selected uniformly from among all peers. According to the random useful piece upload strategy, the fixed seed checks to see if A needs any pieces, and uploads to A the copy of one piece uniformly chosen from among the pieces needed by A. If A does not need any pieces (because A is a peer seed), no piece is uploaded and the fixed seed remains silent between clock ticks. A peer similarly uploads pieces. When its rate μ Poisson clock ticks, it contacts a peer selected at random, and checks to see whether it has pieces needed by the contacted peer. If the answer is yes, it uploads to the contacted peer a copy of a piece uniformly chosen from among its pieces needed by the contacted peer; if the answer is no, no piece is uploaded and the peer does not upload pieces between clock ticks. The peer contacts and piece uploads of the fixed seed and peers are assumed to be instantaneous.

In a real P2P network, peers may upload two or more pieces to different peers at the same time, and peer selection, peer contact and piece upload are not instantaneous. For mathematical simplification, we consider a homogeneous network with the maximum number of upload links of each peer limited to one, with upload rate independent of the parallel downloads at the receiving side, and apply the waiting times of Poisson clocks to model the total time consumed for peer selection, contact, and piece upload. So $1/\mu$ and $1/U_s$ are approximately the average piece transmission time from peer to peer and from the fixed seed to peer in a real P2P network.

Assume that each peer seed dwells in the system for an exponentially distributed length of time with mean $1/\gamma$, with $0 < \gamma \leq \infty$. The case $\gamma = \infty$ is shorthand notation for the case that peers depart immediately after collecting all pieces, and if $\gamma = \infty$ without loss of generality we assume there are no arrivals of peer seeds: $\lambda_{\mathcal{F}} = 0$. Intuitively, smaller values of γ yield better system performance, because peer seeds can upload more pieces if they stay in the system longer. Our result identifies the smallest mean dwell time (i.e. largest γ) sufficient for a stable system. If the rate U_s of the fixed seed is sufficiently large, or if the rates λ_C are large enough for some nonempty C, the system can be stable even if peers do not become peer seeds (i.e. even if $\gamma = \infty$). The arrivals of new peers, the dwell times, and the ticking of Poisson clocks, are assumed to be mutually independent. The notation and assumptions of the model are summarized as follows:

- $\mathcal{C}$: Set of all subsets of $\mathcal{F} = \{1, \ldots, K\}$, where $K \geq 1$ is the number of pieces, and $\mathcal{F}$ is the collection of all pieces.

- Type C peer: A peer with set of pieces $C \in \mathcal{C}$ is a type C peer, which becomes a type $C \cup \{i\}$ peer if the seed or another peer uploads piece $i \notin C$ to it. A type $\mathcal{F}$ peer is also called a peer seed.

- Type C group: The set of type C peers in the system.

- Arrivals: Exogenous arrivals of type C peers form a rate $\lambda_C \in [0, \infty)$ Poisson process. To avoid triviality, assume the total arrival rate of peers — $\lambda_{total} =$

$\sum_{C:C \in \mathcal{C}} \lambda_C$ — is strictly positive. When $\gamma = \infty$, $\lambda_\mathcal{F}$ is assumed to be 0.

- Random peer contact: The fixed seed contacts a uniformly chosen peer at instants of a Poisson process with rate $U_s \in [0, \infty)$. Every peer contacts a uniformly chosen peer at instants of a Poisson process with rate $\mu \in (0, \infty)$.

- Random useful piece upload: When A contacts B, if B does not have all pieces that A has, A uploads to B a copy of one piece uniformly chosen from among the pieces A has but B does not have. Otherwise no piece is uploaded.

- Departures: If $\gamma \in (0, \infty)$, every peer becomes a peer seed after obtaining all K pieces, and subsequently remains in the system for an exponentially distributed length of time with mean $1/\gamma$ before departing. If $\gamma = \infty$, then $\lambda_\mathcal{F} = 0$ and peers depart immediately after obtaining all K pieces.

Under the assumptions above, the system is a Markov chain with state vector $\mathbf{n} = (n_C : C \in \mathcal{C}) \in \mathbb{N}^{|\mathcal{C}|}$ if $\gamma \in (0, \infty)$, and $\mathbf{n} = (n_C : C \in \mathcal{C} - \{\mathcal{F}\}) \in \mathbb{N}^{|\mathcal{C}|-1}$ if $\gamma = \infty$, where n_C is defined to be the number of type C peers, except we define $n_C = 0$ in the case $C = \mathcal{F}$ and $\gamma = \infty$. Define $\Gamma_{C,C'}$ for $C, C' \in \mathcal{C}$ as follows: If $C' = C \cup \{i\}$ with $i \in \mathcal{F} - C$ and $n \geq 1$,

$$\Gamma_{C,C'} := \frac{n_C}{n}\left(\frac{U_s}{K - |C|} + \mu \sum_{S:i \in S} \frac{n_S}{|S - C|}\right); \quad (1)$$

otherwise,

$$\Gamma_{C,C'} := 0, \quad (2)$$

where $n := \sum_{C:C \in \mathcal{C}} n_C$ is the total number of peers. In words, unless $C' = \mathcal{F}$ and $\gamma = \infty$, $\Gamma_{C,C'}$ is the aggregate rate of transition of peers from type C to type C'; If $C' = \mathcal{F}$ and $\gamma = \infty$, $\Gamma_{C,C'}$ is the aggregate rate of departures from the system of peers of type C.

Let $\mathbf{e}_C$ denote the vector with the same dimension as $\mathbf{n}$, with a one in position C and other coordinates equal to zero. The positive entries of the generator matrix $Q = (q(\mathbf{n}, \mathbf{n}'))$ are given by:

- if $\gamma \in (0, \infty)$, $\mathbf{n} = (n_{C'} : C' \in \mathcal{C})$, for all $C \in \mathcal{C}, i \in \mathcal{F} - C$,

$$q(\mathbf{n}, \mathbf{n} + \mathbf{e}_C) = \lambda_C$$
$$q(\mathbf{n}, \mathbf{n} - \mathbf{e}_\mathcal{F}) = \gamma n_\mathcal{F}$$
$$q(\mathbf{n}, \mathbf{n} - \mathbf{e}_C + \mathbf{e}_{C \cup \{i\}}) = \Gamma_{C,C \cup \{i\}}, \text{ if } |C| \leq K - 1$$

- if $\gamma = \infty$, $\mathbf{n} = (n_{C'} : C' \in \mathcal{C} - \{\mathcal{F}\})$, for all $C \in \mathcal{C} - \{\mathcal{F}\}, i \in \mathcal{F} - C$,

$$q(\mathbf{n}, \mathbf{n} + \mathbf{e}_C) = \lambda_C$$
$$q(\mathbf{n}, \mathbf{n} - \mathbf{e}_C + \mathbf{e}_{C \cup \{i\}}) = \Gamma_{C,C \cup \{i\}}, \text{ if } |C| \leq K - 2$$
$$q(\mathbf{n}, \mathbf{n} - \mathbf{e}_C) = \Gamma_{C,\mathcal{F}}, \text{ if } |C| = K - 1$$

The following theorem describes the stability region of the P2P system.

THEOREM 1. (a). Given $U_s \in [0, \infty)$, $\mu \in (0, \infty)$, $\gamma \in (0, \infty]$, $\{\lambda_C : C \in \mathcal{C}, \lambda_C \in [0, \infty)\}$ with $\lambda_\mathcal{F} = 0$ if $\gamma = \infty$, and $\lambda_{total} > 0$, the Markov process with generator matrix Q is transient if either of the following two conditions is true:

- $0 < \mu < \gamma \leq \infty$ and for some $k \in \mathcal{F}$,

$$\lambda_{total} > \left[U_s + \sum_{C:k \in C} \lambda_C(K + 1 - |C|)\right]\left(\frac{1}{1 - \mu/\gamma}\right) \quad (3)$$

- $0 < \gamma \leq \mu$ and for some piece $k \in \mathcal{F}$, no copies of piece k can enter the system.

(b). Conversely, the process is positive recurrent and $E[n] < \infty$ in equilibrium, if either of the following two conditions is true:

- $0 < \mu < \gamma \leq \infty$ and for any $k \in \mathcal{F}$,

$$\lambda_{total} < \left[U_s + \sum_{C:k \in C} \lambda_C(K + 1 - |C|)\right]\left(\frac{1}{1 - \mu/\gamma}\right) \quad (4)$$

- $0 < \gamma \leq \mu$ and for any $k \in \mathcal{F}$, it is possible for new copies of piece k to enter the system.

We remark that when we say new copies of piece k can enter the system, we mean $U_s > 0$ or $\lambda_C > 0$ for some $C \in \mathcal{C}$ such that $k \in C$. And we remark that condition (4) holding for all $k \in \mathcal{F}$ is equivalent to the following: for any $S \in \mathcal{C} - \{\mathcal{F}\}$, $\triangle_S < 0$, where $\triangle_S$ is defined as:

$$\triangle_S := \sum_{C:C \subseteq S} \lambda_C - \left(U_s + \sum_{C:C \not\subseteq S} \bar{\lambda}_C\right)\left(\frac{1}{1 - \mu/\gamma}\right), \quad (5)$$

where $\bar{\lambda}_C := \lambda_C(K - |C| + \mu/\gamma)$. In particular, (5) holds for all $S \in \mathcal{C} - \{\mathcal{F}\}$ if it holds for all $S' \in \{\mathcal{F} - \{k\} : k \in \mathcal{F}\}$.

From Theorem 1, we can generate the main result presented in our last paper about missing piece syndrome [4], as a corollary:

COROLLARY 2. If $\gamma = \infty$, $\lambda_C = 0$ for $C \neq \emptyset$ and $\mu > 0$, the Markov process with generator matrix Q is transient if $U_s < \lambda_\emptyset$, and it is positive recurrent if $U_s > \lambda_\emptyset$.

3. EXAMPLES

To illustrate Theorem 1, we examine three examples of specific P2P networks.

Example 1: This example is treated in [8]. As shown in Figure 1(a), the file is transferred as a single piece, that is, $K = 1$. New peers without any piece arrive into the system at the times of a Poisson process with rate λ_0. After obtaining the piece a peer becomes a peer seed. With rate U_s, the fixed seed contacts and uploads the piece to new peers, who become peer seeds after obtaining the piece. When peer seeds are in the system, they randomly contact and upload copies of the piece to new peers with rate μ, which creates more peer seeds. After staying for an exponentially distributed time period with mean $1/\gamma$, peer seeds depart from the system. This example illustrates our model with parameters $K = 1$, $U_s, \mu, \gamma, \lambda_\emptyset = \lambda_0 \in (0, \infty)$, and $\lambda_{\{1\}} = 0$.

The stability of a system is determined by its ability to recover from a heavy load. First consider the case that there are many peer seeds in the system. Because every peer seed departs at rate γ, in essence, the service rate $\gamma n_\mathcal{F}$ scales linearly with the number of peer seeds, $n_\mathcal{F}$, as in an infinite server system, so the system can recover however many peer seeds there are. Secondly consider the case that there are many type $\emptyset$ peers and few peer seeds. For a long time period, when the fixed seed or a peer seed randomly contacts

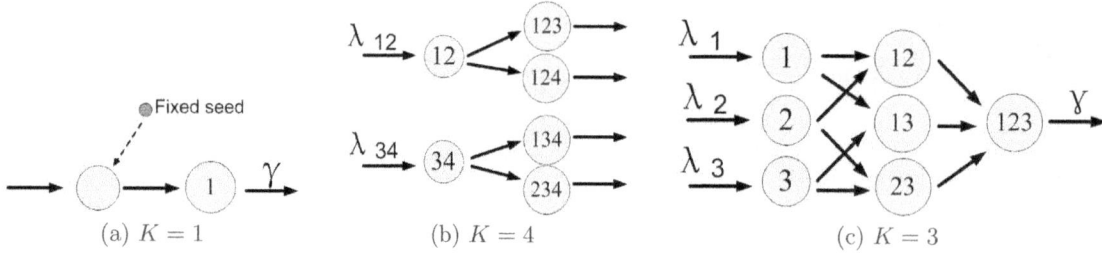

Figure 1: Examples

a peer to upload a piece, the probability they contact a type $\emptyset$ peer is close to one. So the group of type $\emptyset$ peers receives uploads from the fixed seed at rate almost U_s. Once a peer becomes a peer seed, it can upload more pieces to type $\emptyset$ peers, creating more peer seeds, which upload more pieces. So every peer seed can create a branching process [6] of departures from type $\emptyset$ group. The mean time for a peer seed to stay in the system is $1/\gamma$, and during this time it uploads pieces to type $\emptyset$ peers at rate close to μ. So on average every peer seed can upload to μ/γ type $\emptyset$ peers. By the theory of branching process, if $\mu/\gamma \geq 1$, the expected number of descendants of every peer seed is infinite, which stabilizes the process. If $\mu/\gamma < 1$, on average every peer seed has $\frac{\mu/\gamma}{1-\mu/\gamma}$ descendants. Hence, every upload of the piece by the fixed seed to a type $\emptyset$ peer causes, on average, to about $\frac{1}{1-\mu/\gamma}$ departures from the type $\emptyset$ group. Comparing to λ_0, the arrival rate of type $\emptyset$ peers, this suggests that the system is stable if either $\mu \geq \gamma$, or $\mu < \gamma$ and $\lambda_0 < U_s \frac{1}{1-\mu/\gamma}$. Conversely, if $\mu > \gamma$ and $\lambda_0 > U_s \frac{1}{1-\mu/\gamma}$, the arrival rate of type $\emptyset$ peers is larger than the average rate of departures from the type $\emptyset$ group, indicating that the system cannot recover from the heavy load of type $\emptyset$ group and so it is unstable. This conclusion is confirmed in [8] and by Theorem 1.

Example 2: As shown in Figure 1(b), the file is divided into four pieces, that is, $K = 4$. There are two types of new peers, type $\{1, 2\}$ and type $\{3, 4\}$, which arrive as two independent Poisson processes with respective rates λ_{12} and λ_{34}. There is no fixed seed in the system. Peers contact and upload pieces to each other so that they can depart. Peers depart immediately after obtaining all four pieces; there are no peer seeds in the system. This example illustrates our model with parameters $K = 4$, $U_s = 0$, $\gamma = \infty$, $\mu, \lambda_{\{1,2\}} = \lambda_{12}, \lambda_{\{3,4\}} = \lambda_{34} \in (0, \infty)$, $\lambda_C = 0$ for $C \neq \{1, 2\}, \{3, 4\}$.

Consider the ability of the system to recover from a heavy load. First, consider the network starting from a state such that all peers are type $\{1, 2, 4\}$ and there are so many type $\{1, 2, 4\}$ peers that the fraction of them among all peers is close to one for a long time. On one hand, most new type $\{1, 2\}$ peers download piece 4 from a type $\{1, 2, 4\}$ peer and join the type $\{1, 2, 4\}$ group, so the arrival rate of type $\{1, 2, 4\}$ peers is close to λ_{12}. On the other hand, most new type $\{3, 4\}$ peers download pieces 3 and 4 from type $\{1, 2, 4\}$ peers and then depart, with an expected lifetime in the system approximately $\frac{2}{\mu}$. During its lifetime, a type $\{3, 4\}$ peer uploads piece 3 to two type $\{1, 2, 4\}$ peers on average and induces two departures on average. So the medium term aggregate departure rate of type $\{1, 2, 4\}$ peers is close to $2\lambda_{34}$. Hence, if $\lambda_{12} < 2\lambda_{34}$, the system is able to recover from a

heavy load of type $\{1, 2, 4\}$ (or $\{1, 2, 3\}$) peers. Conversely, if the inequality goes the other way, that is, $\lambda_{12} > 2\lambda_{34}$, the arrival rate of type $\{1, 2, 4\}$ peers is larger than the aggregate departure rate of type $\{1, 2, 4\}$ peers. So the type $\{1, 2, 4\}$ group will keep growing. Thus if $\lambda_{12} > 2\lambda_{34}$ the system cannot recover from a heavy load of type $\{1, 2, 4\}$ (or $\{1, 2, 3\}$) peers. Similarly, if $\lambda_{34} < 2\lambda_{12}$ the system can recover from a heavy load of type $\{2, 3, 4\}$ (or $\{1, 3, 4\}$) peers. And the system cannot recover from the same heavy load if $\lambda_{34} > 2\lambda_{12}$.

The situation is similar if there is a heavy load of type $\{1, 2\}$ (or $\{3, 4\}$) peers, while the other groups are empty. The arrival rate of type $\{1, 2\}$ peers is λ_{12}. The aggregate departure rate of type $\{1, 2\}$ peers, from both the uploads from new arrived type $\{3, 4\}$ peers and from type $\{1, 2, x\}, x = 3, 4$ peers (which are formerly type $\{1, 2\}$ peers), is larger than $2\lambda_{34}$. So if $\lambda_{12} < 2\lambda_{34}$ the system is able to recover from the heavy load of type $\{1, 2\}$ peers.

Secondly, consider the case that there are heavy loads in groups of at least two types, e.g. type $\{1, 2\}$ and $\{1, 2, 3\}$. There is at least one type of peer that can upload to the other type of peer, e.g. type $\{1, 2, 3\}$ peers can upload to type $\{1, 2\}$ peers. There are many uploads from type $\{1, 2, 3\}$ peers to type $\{1, 2\}$ peers so that the departure rate from type $\{1, 2\}$ group is large, which stabilizes the system. This suggests that the system is stable if $\lambda_{12} < 2\lambda_{34}$ and $\lambda_{34} < 2\lambda_{12}$, and unstable if either $\lambda_{12} > 2\lambda_{34}$ or $\lambda_{34} > 2\lambda_{12}$. This conclusion is confirmed by Theorem 1.

Example 3: As shown in Figure 1(c), the file is divided into three pieces, that is, $K = 3$. New peers arrive at a total rate λ_{total}, and each peer arrives with one piece, having piece i with probability $\lambda_i/\lambda_{total}$. So there are three types of new peers, type $\{1\}$, type $\{2\}$, and type $\{3\}$, which arrive as three independent Poisson processes with rates λ_1, λ_2 and λ_3, respectively. There is no fixed seed in the system. With rate μ, peers randomly contact and upload pieces to each other. After collecting all three pieces, every peer stays in the system as a peer seed for an exponentially distributed time with mean $1/\gamma, \gamma > \mu$. This example illustrates our model with parameters $K = 3$, $U_s = 0$, $0 < \mu < \gamma \leq \infty$, $\lambda_{\{1\}} = \lambda_1, \lambda_{\{2\}} = \lambda_2, \lambda_{\{3\}} = \lambda_3 \in (0, \infty)$, $\lambda_C = 0$ for $|C| \neq 1$.

Consider whether the system can recover from a heavy load. First, consider the network starting from a state such that all peers are type $\{1, 2\}$ and there are so many type $\{1, 2\}$ peers that the fraction of them among all peers is close to one for a long time. By the reasoning of example two, almost every new type $\{1\}$ and type $\{2\}$ peer joins the type $\{1, 2\}$ group, so the arrival rate of the type $\{1, 2\}$ group is close to $\lambda_1 + \lambda_2$. Over the medium term, every new type

{3} peer has an expected lifetime approximately $\frac{2}{\mu} + \frac{1}{\gamma}$, with $\frac{2}{\mu}$ being the expected time for the type {3} peer to download two pieces from type {1, 2} peers, and with $\frac{1}{\gamma}$ being the expected time for the type {3} peer to be a peer seed. During its lifetime every type {3} peer uploads approximately $2 + \frac{\mu}{\gamma}$ pieces to type {1, 2} peers on average. By the reasoning of example one, every peer seed creates a branching process of departures of type {1, 2} peers, with the total number of new peer seeds (including the root) equal to $\frac{1}{1-\mu/\gamma}$. Thus, on average, every new type {3} peer induces $(2 + \frac{\mu}{\gamma})\frac{1}{1-\mu/\gamma}$ departures from type {1, 2} group, so the medium term aggregate departure rate of type {1, 2} peers is approximately $\lambda_3(2 + \frac{\mu}{\gamma})\frac{1}{1-\mu/\gamma}$. Hence if $\lambda_1 + \lambda_2 < \lambda_3(2 + \frac{\mu}{\gamma})\frac{1}{1-\mu/\gamma}$, the system is able to recover from a heavy load of type {1, 2} group. Conversely, if $\lambda_1 + \lambda_2 > \lambda_3(2 + \frac{\mu}{\gamma})\frac{1}{1-\mu/\gamma}$, type {1, 2} group will keep increasing and the system cannot recover from the heavy load. Similarly, if $\lambda_2 + \lambda_3 < \lambda_1(2 + \frac{\mu}{\gamma})\frac{1}{1-\mu/\gamma}$, or $\lambda_1 + \lambda_3 < \lambda_2(2 + \frac{\mu}{\gamma})\frac{1}{1-\mu/\gamma}$, the system is able to recover from a heavy load of type {2, 3}, or {1, 3} group. And if either of the two inequalities is reversed, the system cannot recover from a corresponding heavy load.

Secondly, through considerations similar to those in example one and two, we can see that the conditions of heavy load in other single-type group or heavy load in multiple-type groups can also be recovered from if the three inequalities above hold. This suggests that the system is stable if

$$\begin{cases} \lambda_1 + \lambda_2 < \lambda_3(2 + \frac{\mu}{\gamma})\frac{1}{1-\mu/\gamma} \\ \lambda_2 + \lambda_3 < \lambda_1(2 + \frac{\mu}{\gamma})\frac{1}{1-\mu/\gamma} \\ \lambda_1 + \lambda_3 < \lambda_2(2 + \frac{\mu}{\gamma})\frac{1}{1-\mu/\gamma} \end{cases}$$

If any one of the three inequalities is revised, it indicates the system is unstable. This is consistent with Theorem 1. If peers depart immediately after obtaining a complete collection (i.e. $\gamma = \infty$), we obtain a model analyzed in [9] using fluid limit analysis. The stability condition becomes

$$\begin{cases} \lambda_1 + \lambda_2 < 2\lambda_3 \\ \lambda_2 + \lambda_3 < 2\lambda_1 \\ \lambda_1 + \lambda_3 < 2\lambda_2 \end{cases}$$

If $\lambda_1, \lambda_2, \lambda_3$ are not all equal, at least one equality is reversed, so the system is unstable.

The analysis of the above three examples suggests that when we consider the system to be in heavy load, the worst distribution load is that nearly all peers have the same type C with $|C| = K - 1$. If the system is able to recover from that kind of heavy load, it can recover from other kinds of heavy load. With the intuition in mind, a sketch a proof of Theorem 1 is offered in next section.

4. A SKETCH OF PROOF

In this section, sketches of the proof of Theorem 1(a) and Theorem 1(b) are offered in Subsection 4.1 and Subsection 4.2, respectively.

4.1 Sketch of proof of Theorem 1(a)

We sketch the proof of Theorem 1(a) about transience when $0 < \mu < \gamma < \infty$. Without loss of generality, assume that (3) is true for $k = 1$, or equivalently, $\triangle_{\mathcal{F}-\{1\}} > 0$.

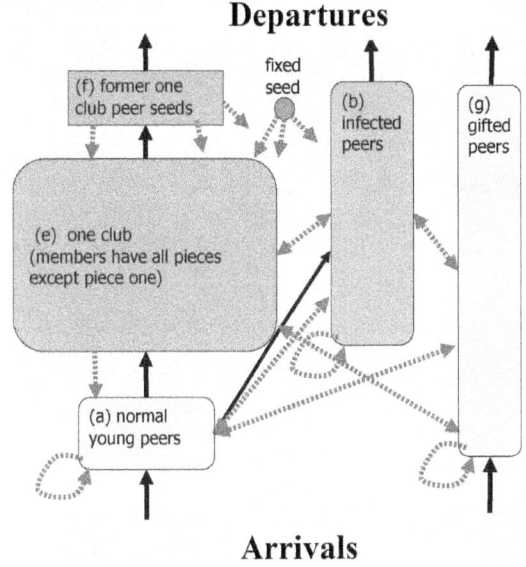

Figure 2: Solid lines show flow of peers and dashed lines show flow of pieces.

Consider the following partition of peers into five groups, as shown in Figure 2.

- *Normal young peer*: A normal young peer is a peer of type in $\{C \in \mathcal{C} : |C| \le K - 2, 1 \notin C\}$.

- *Infected peer*: An infected peer is a peer that obtained piece one after arriving, but before obtaining all the other pieces. Once a peer is infected, it remains infected until it leaves the system; it is considered to be infected even when it is a peer seed.

- *Gifted peer*: A gifted peer is a peer that arrived with piece one. A gifted peer is gifted for its entire time in the system; it is considered to be gifted even when it is a peer seed.

- *One-club peer*: A one-club peer is a peer that has all pieces except piece one. That is, the one-club is the group of peers of type $\{2, 3, ...K\}$.

- *Former one-club peer*: A former one-club peer is a peer in the system that is not a one-club peer but at some earlier time was a one-club peer. Note that a former one-club peer is a peer seed. The converse is not true, because infected peers and gifted peers can be peer seeds.

Consider the system starting from an initial state in which there are many peers in the system, and all of them are one-club peers. The system evolves as shown in Figure 2. Piece one can arrive into the system from outside the system in two ways: uploads by the fixed seed or arrivals of gifted peers. Ignore for a second the effect of normal young peers getting piece one (and becoming infected). Most of the uploads by the fixed seed are uploads of piece one to one-club peers. One such upload creates a new peer seed, which on average will upload piece one to about μ/γ more one-club peers, and each of those will upload piece one to about μ/γ more one-club peers, and so forth, in a branching process. Each upload of a piece by the fixed seed thus ultimately causes, on average, about $\frac{1}{1-\mu/\gamma}$ departures from the one-club. Each gifted peer, with type C on arrival, for some C with $1 \in C$, will directly upload to, on average, about $K - |C| + \mu/\gamma$ one-club peers, and those will become peer seeds who also could upload to about μ/γ more one-club peers, and so fourth, so that the total expected number of one-club departures caused by the type C gifted peer is $(K - |C| + \mu/\gamma)\frac{1}{1-\mu/\gamma}$. Summing these quantities and subtracting them from the arrival rate of peers without piece one gives $\triangle_{\mathcal{F}-\{1\}}$. So $\triangle_{\mathcal{F}-\{1\}} > 0$ indicates that the arrival rates of peers missing piece one is larger than the upload rate of piece one, causing the one-club size to grow linearly.

The above analysis neglects the possibility that normal young peers can also receive piece one, creating infected peers. An infected peer can upload to one club peers, creating former one-club peers, and to normal young peers, creating more infected peers. This results in a branching process comprised of infected peers and former one-club peers. By the theory of branching process, the expected number of infected offspring of a former one-club peer or an infected peer will converge to zero, as the fraction of one-club peers converges to one. Hence, when the one-club is large enough, the existence of infected peers is negligible; it will not affect the growth of the one-club. The detailed proof of transience is offered in a full version of this paper.

4.2 Sketch of proof of Theorem 1(b)

We sketch the proof of Theorem 1(b) about positive recurrence for the case $0 < \mu < \gamma \le \infty$ under the assumption that (5) is valid for all $S \in \mathcal{C} - \{\mathcal{F}\}$. The discussion in last subsection suggests that when $\triangle_{\mathcal{F}-\{1\}} < 0$, the departure rate of the one-club is larger than the arrival rate of peers missing piece one, therefore, the system has the ability to recover from a single heavy load in the one-club. Moreover, when $k = 2, 3, ...K$ and there is a single heavy load in type $\mathcal{F} - \{k\}$ group, similar reasoning suggests that the system can recover if $\triangle_{\mathcal{F}-\{k\}} < 0$. To get better idea of the proof, here we consider other distributions of heavy load.

- Suppose there is a single heavy load in some type S group with $|S| \le K - 2$. Uploads from the fixed seed (with rate U_s) and from new peers holding pieces not in S (with rate $\sum_{C:C\nsubseteq S} \lambda_C$) keep creating departures from the type S group. If we ignore the period of time from when a peer departs from the type S group until the same peer becomes a peer seed, we see that the average remaining lifetime of every peer who departs from the type S group is larger than $\frac{1}{\gamma}$. In this lifetime the peer uploads on average approximately μ/γ pieces to type S peers, which creates more departures from the type S group. Including the root, every departure from the type S group can ultimately cause at least $\frac{1}{1-\mu/\gamma}$ departures from the type S group, on average. Because every new type C peer with $C \nsubseteq S$ eventually uploads on average $K - |C| + \mu/\gamma$ pieces to type S peers, the departure rate of type S group is larger than $\left[U_s + \sum_{C:C\nsubseteq S} \lambda_C(K - |C| + \mu/\gamma) \right] \frac{1}{1-\mu/\gamma}$. Because peers mainly download pieces from type S peers, almost all new type C peers with $C \subseteq S$ ultimately join the type S group. So the near term arrival rate of type S group is less than but close to $\sum_{C:C\subseteq S} \lambda_C$, which is smaller than the aggregate departure rate of

type S peers by (5). So the system can recover from the heavy load.

- Suppose there is a single heavy load in the type $\mathcal{F}$ group, that is, the group of peer seed. The departure rate of peer seeds, $\gamma n_{\mathcal{F}}$, scales linearly with the number of peer seeds, $n_{\mathcal{F}}$, as in an infinite server system. So the system can recover however large the group of peer seeds is.

- Suppose there are heavy loads in at least two groups of different types, say types C_1 and C_2. In this condition, either $C_1 \nsubseteq C_2$ or $C_2 \nsubseteq C_1$ is true, so peers in at least one of the groups, say C_1, can upload pieces to peers in the other group, say C_2. The rate of peers departing from the type C_2 group is quite high, due to the large rate of uploads from type C_1 peers, so the system can quickly escape from that state space region of heavy load.

The above paragraphs summarize how the system can recover from all distributions of heavy load. To provide a proof of stability it must also be shown that the load cannot spiral up without bound through some oscillatory behavior. For that we use a Lyapunov function and apply the Foster-Lyapunov stability criterion [2]. A Lyapunov function is a nonnegative function on the state space that is a measure of load in the system. To prove stability it must be shown that if the system is in states with a large value of the Lyapunov function, then the drift of the function is negative.

We apply function $Q(*)$ to denote the drift of some nonnegative function: For any nonnegative function $F = F(\mathbf{n})$ on the state space of the system, the drift of F at state $\mathbf{n}$ is defined as

$$Q(F)(\mathbf{n}) := \sum_{\mathbf{n}':\mathbf{n}'\neq\mathbf{n}} q(\mathbf{n}, \mathbf{n}') \left[F(\mathbf{n}') - F(\mathbf{n}) \right] \qquad (6)$$

If, as usual, the diagonal elements $q(\mathbf{n}, \mathbf{n})$ of the matrix Q are chosen so that row sums are zero, $Q(F)$ is the product of the matrix Q and function F, viewed as a vector. For each $\mathbf{n}$, $q(\mathbf{n}, \mathbf{n}') \neq 0$ for only finitely many n', so $Q(F)$ is finite. In this paper, we apply the following lemma implied by the Foster-Lyapunov criterion [2]:

LEMMA 3. *The P2P Markov process is positive recurrent and $E[n] < +\infty$ in equilibrium, if there is a nonnegative function $W(\mathbf{n})$ on the state space of the process, with $\{\mathbf{n} : W(\mathbf{n}) \le c\}$ a finite set for any $c \ge 0$, such that there exists $n_0 \ge 0, \xi > 0$, whenever $n \ge n_0$, $QW \le -\xi n < 0$. We say W is a valid Lyapunov function.*

The particular Lyapunov function we use in case $0 < \mu < \gamma < \infty$, is:

$$W := \sum_{C:C\in\mathcal{C}} r^{|C|} T_C, \text{ with} \qquad (7)$$

$$T_C := \begin{cases} \frac{1}{2} E_C^2 + \alpha E_C \phi(H_C) & \text{if } C \neq \mathcal{F} \\ \frac{1}{2} n^2 & \text{if } C = \mathcal{F} \end{cases}$$

and in case $0 < \mu < \gamma = \infty$, is

$$W := \sum_{C:C\in\mathcal{C}-\{\mathcal{F}\}} r^{|C|} T_C, \qquad (8)$$

with the following notation:

- $r \in (0, \frac{1}{2}), d \in (1, \infty), \beta \in (0, \frac{1}{2}), \alpha \in (\frac{1}{2}, 1)$ are positive constants to be specified, with r and β small, d large, and α close to one.

- $\mathcal{E}_C := \{C' : C' \subseteq C\}$, which is the collection of types of peers which are or can become type C peers.

- $\mathcal{H}_C := \{C' : C' \in \mathcal{C}, C' \nsubseteq C\}$, which is the collection of types of peers which can help type C peers. Notice that $\mathcal{F} \in \mathcal{H}_C$ for any $C \in \mathcal{C} - \mathcal{F}$ and $\mathcal{H}_{\mathcal{F}} = \emptyset$.

- $E_C := \sum_{C':C' \in \mathcal{E}_C} n_{C'}$, $H_C := \frac{1}{1-\mu/\gamma} \sum_{C':C' \in \mathcal{H}_C} (K - |C'| + \mu/\gamma) n_{C'}$. e.g. $E_{\mathcal{F}} = n$ and $H_{\mathcal{F}} = 0$.

- ϕ is the function with parameters d, β, defined as

$$\phi(x) := \begin{cases} (2d + \frac{1}{2\beta} - x) & \text{if } 0 \leq x \leq 2d \\ \frac{\beta}{2}(x - 2d - \frac{1}{\beta})^2 & \text{if } 2d < x \leq 2d + \frac{1}{\beta} \\ 0 & \text{if } x > 2d + \frac{1}{\beta} \end{cases} \quad (9)$$

Thus $\phi'(x) = -1$ for $0 \leq x \leq 2d$, $\phi'(x) = 0$ for $x \geq 2d + 1/\beta$, and ϕ' increases linearly from -1 to 0 over the interval $[2d, 2d + 1/\beta]$. In particular, $-1 \leq \phi'(x) \leq 0$ for $x \geq 0$.

In this paper, we consider two (overlapping) classes of nonzero states of the P2P Markov process: *class I and class II*, with parameter $\epsilon \in (0, \frac{1}{2})$ to be selected, defined as:

Definition 1. Class I is the set of states $\mathbf{n}$ such that there exists $S \in \mathcal{C} - \{\mathcal{F}\}$, so that $n_S/n > 1 - \epsilon$; class II is the set of states $\mathbf{n}$ such that there exist $C_1, C_2 \in \mathcal{C}$, either C_1 and C_2 being distinct or both equal to $\mathcal{F}$, so that, $n_{C_1}/n > \epsilon/2^K$ and $n_{C_2}/n > \epsilon/2^K$.

If the process is in states of class I, there is a single heavy load aggregated in a type S group with $|S| \leq K - 1$; if the process is in states of class II, either there are many peer seeds, or there are many of at least two distinct types of peers. Any nonzero state is either in class I or class II, or both.

In the proof, we show that for an appropriate choice of $(r, d, \beta, \alpha, \epsilon)$, W is a valid Lyapunov function. The given parameters of the network, $K, U_s, \lambda = (\lambda_S : S \in \mathcal{C}), \gamma$ and μ, are treated as constants. The variables r, d, β, α and ϵ are applied in the proof, and functions on the state space are applied which may depend on these parameters. It is convenient to adopt the big theta notation $\Theta(*)$, with the understanding that it is uniform in these variables; this is summarized in the following definitions.

Definition 2. Given functions f and g on the state space, we say $f = \Theta(g)$ if there exist constants $k_1, k_2, n_0 > 0$, whose values do not depend on $(r, d, \beta, \alpha, \epsilon)$, such that $k_1|g(\mathbf{n})| \leq |f(\mathbf{n})| \leq k_2|g(\mathbf{n})|$ for all $\mathbf{n}$ such that $n > n_0$.

For example, $2 \in \Theta(1), \lambda_{total} n \in \Theta(n), d \notin \Theta(1), d \in \Theta(d)$. Similarly, we adopt notions of "small enough" and "large enough" that are uniform in $(r, d, \beta, \alpha, \epsilon)$:

Definition 3. The statement, "condition A is true if $x > 0$ is *small enough*", means there exists a constant $k > 0$, not depending on $(r, d, \beta, \alpha, \epsilon)$, such that A is true for any $x \in (0, k)$. Similarly, the statement, "condition A is true if $x > 0$ is *large enough*", means there exists a constant $k > 0$, not depending on $(r, d, \beta, \alpha, \epsilon)$, such that A is true for any $x \in (k, \infty)$.

Some additional notation is applied:

- $M_\phi := 3d + \frac{1}{\beta}$. We have $M_\phi > \max_x \phi(x)$ and $M_\phi > \min\{x : \phi(x) = 0\} + d > 1$.

- For any $\mathcal{X}, \mathcal{X}' \subseteq \mathcal{C}, \Gamma_{\mathcal{X}, \mathcal{X}'} := \sum_{C \in \mathcal{X}} \sum_{C':C' \in \mathcal{X}'} \Gamma_{C, C'}$, where $\Gamma_{C, C'}$ is defined in (1) and (2).

- D_C is defined by

$$D_C := \begin{cases} \sum_{i:i \in \mathcal{F}} \Gamma_{C, C \cup \{i\}} & \text{if } C \neq \mathcal{F}, \\ \gamma n_{\mathcal{F}} & \text{if } C = \mathcal{F}, \gamma < \infty, \\ 0 & \text{if } C = \mathcal{F}, \gamma = \infty. \end{cases}$$

Except in the case $C = \mathcal{F}$ and $\gamma = \infty$, D_C is the aggregate rate that peers leave the group of type C peers.

- For any $\mathcal{X} \subseteq \mathcal{C}, n_{\mathcal{X}} := \sum_{C:C \in \mathcal{X}} n_C, D_{\mathcal{X}} := \sum_{C:C \in \mathcal{X}} D_C$, $D_{total} := D_{\mathcal{C}}, \lambda_{\mathcal{X}} := \sum_{C:C \in \mathcal{X}} \lambda_C, \lambda_{\mathcal{X}}^* := \sum_{C:C \in \mathcal{X}} \lambda_C(K - |C| + \mu/\gamma)$.

Now we sketch the steps of showing (7) and (8) are valid Lyapunov functions. To begin, we identify a simple approximation to the drift of W. Notice that $Q(*)$ is linear, so if $0 < \mu < \gamma < \infty$,

$$Q(W) = \sum_{C:C \in \mathcal{C}} r^{|C|} Q(T_C), \text{ with}$$

$$Q(T_C) = \begin{cases} \frac{1}{2} Q(E_C^2) + \alpha Q(E_C \phi(H_C)) & \text{if } C \neq \mathcal{F} \\ \frac{1}{2} Q(n^2) & \text{if } C = \mathcal{F} \end{cases}$$

If $0 < \mu < \gamma = \infty$,

$$Q(W) = \sum_{C:C \in \mathcal{C} - \{\mathcal{F}\}} r^{|C|} Q(T_C)$$

Define LW, an approximation of $Q(W)$, as follows: If $0 < \mu < \gamma < \infty$,

$$LW := \sum_{C:C \in \mathcal{C}} r^{|C|} LT_C, \text{ with} \quad (10)$$

$$LT_C := \begin{cases} E_C Q(E_C) + \alpha E_C Q(\phi(H_C)) & \text{if } C \neq \mathcal{F} \\ n Q(n) & \text{if } C = \mathcal{F} \end{cases}$$

If $0 < \mu < \gamma = \infty$,

$$LW := \sum_{C:C \in \mathcal{C} - \{\mathcal{F}\}} r^{|C|} LT_C \quad (11)$$

The following lemmas are provided with the detailed proofs omitted here, but offered in the full version of this paper. These lemmas consider bounds on LW and the approximation error $|Q(W) - LW|$, thereby provide a bound of $Q(W)$.

LEMMA 4. $|Q(W) - LW| \leq M_\phi(D_{total} + 1)\Theta(1)$.

LEMMA 5. *If d is large enough, $Q(E_C) \leq \Theta(1), Q(\phi(H_C)) \leq M_\phi \Theta(1), LT_C \leq M_\phi \Theta(E_C) \leq M_\phi \Theta(n)$ for any $C \in \mathcal{C}$.*

LEMMA 6. *If d is large enough, $1 - \alpha, \epsilon M_\phi, \beta$ are small enough and $\beta \left(\frac{K + \mu/\gamma}{1 - \mu/\gamma}\right)^2 \leq \frac{1}{\alpha} - 1$, for any $S \in \mathcal{C} - \{\mathcal{F}\}$ and any nonzero state $\mathbf{n}$ such that $n_S/n > 1 - \epsilon$,*

$$LT_S \leq \frac{1}{2} \triangle_S E_S \quad (12)$$

REMARK: Instead of giving the proof of Lemma 6, we describe how the term $\alpha E_S Q(\phi(H_S))$ can help LT_S to be negative. It has been discussed that the worst distribution of heavy load is when the heavy load aggregates in a type with only one missing piece. Consider the case $|S| = K - 1$. Notice that $E_S Q(E_S) = E_S(\lambda_{\mathcal{E}_S} - \Gamma_{\mathcal{E}_S, \mathcal{H}_S})$ and $\Gamma_{\mathcal{E}_S, \mathcal{H}_S} \geq D_S \geq \frac{n_S}{n}[U_s + H_S \mu \frac{1-\mu/\gamma}{K+\mu/\gamma}]$. Here we assume $\frac{n_S}{n} \geq 1 - \epsilon$. So $\Gamma_{\mathcal{E}_S, \mathcal{H}_S}$ increases almost proportionally to H_S. When H_S is larger than d for d sufficiently large, $\Gamma_{\mathcal{E}_S, \mathcal{H}_S}$ is larger than $\lambda_{\mathcal{E}_S}$, so $E_S Q(E_S)$ is negative and is bounded above by $-\Theta(E_S) = -\Theta(n)$. But when H_S is smaller than d, $\Gamma_{\mathcal{E}_S, \mathcal{H}_S}$ can be smaller than $\lambda_{\mathcal{E}_S}$, so $E_S Q(E_S)$ is positive and is lower bounded by $\Theta(E_S) = \Theta(n)$, which has the wrong sign. The term $\alpha E_S \phi(H_S)$ is chosen so that $\alpha Q(\phi(H_S))$ can balance out the coefficient $\lambda_{\mathcal{E}_S} - \Gamma_{\mathcal{E}_S, \mathcal{H}_S}$ when H_S is small, so that LT_S is still negative and upper bounded by $-\Theta(E_S)$.

To see why the balance is possible, notice that $LT_S = E_S[Q(E_S) + \alpha Q(\phi(H_S))]$. The definition of H_S implies that, when n_S is close to n, H_S is the mean number of type S peers that will be helped by the helping peers, which are the ones in $\mathcal{H}_S$ (By saying a peer is helped, we mean a piece is uploaded to the peer). In other words, H_S is the stored potential for helping type S peers. As type S peers are helped by the helping peers, the potential decreases, with the magnitude of decrease equal to the number of type S peers which are helped. So if we only consider the piece transmissions involving one peer of type S and one peer of type in $\mathcal{H}_S$, the downward drift of H_S has magnitude less than or equal to the downward drift of E_S. If we only consider the external arrivals and the uploads from the fixed seed, the terms in the drift of H_S are $\frac{1}{1-\mu/\gamma}\left[\sum_{C:C \in \mathcal{H}_S}(K - |C| + \mu/\gamma)\lambda_C + U_S \mu/\gamma\right]$, and the terms in the drift of E_S are $\lambda_{\mathcal{E}_S} - U_s$, the former is larger than the latter because of (5). Finally, H_S has a bit more downward drift due to peers other than type S peers downloading from peers in $\mathcal{H}_S$, but that is small for ϵ sufficiently small. Combining the downward and the other drifts, we see that the drift of H_S is approximately the same as the drift of E_S, with the drift of H_S a little greater. The difference of the two drifts is $\triangle_S$, defined in (5). Also, when H_S is small, the function ϕ at H_S has derivative -1. Thus the coefficient of E_S in LT_S, which is $Q(E_S) + \alpha Q(\phi(H_S))$, is negative because α is close to 1, so LT_S is upper bounded by $-\Theta(E_S) = -\Theta(n)$.

In sum, the above explains the reason we included the term $E_S \phi(H_S)$ in the Lyapunov function; it balances out the positive drift of $\frac{1}{2}E_S^2$ when H_S is small. $\square$

Lemma 5 and 6 suggest the following lemma:

LEMMA 7. If d is large enough, $(1 - \alpha), \beta, r M_\phi, \epsilon M_\phi r^{-K}$ are small enough, and $\beta \left(\frac{K + \mu/\gamma}{1 - \mu/\gamma}\right)^2 \leq \frac{1}{\alpha} - 1$,

(a). On class I, $LW \leq -r^K \Theta(n)$;

(b). On class II, $LW \leq -r^K \epsilon^3 \Theta(n^2) + M_\phi \Theta(n)$.

With Lemmas 4 and 7, Theorem 1(b) at the case $0 < \mu < \gamma \leq \infty$ can be proved: On class I,

$$
\begin{aligned}
D_{total} &= D_S + \sum_{C:C \neq S} D_C \\
&\leq U_s + n_{\mathcal{H}_S} \mu + \sum_{C:C \neq S} \frac{n_C}{n}(U_s + n\mu) \\
&\leq 2(U_s + \epsilon n\mu) \in \Theta(1) + \epsilon \Theta(n)
\end{aligned}
$$

So Lemma 4 implies that on class I,

$$|Q(W) - LW| \leq \epsilon M_\phi \Theta(n) + M_\phi \Theta(1)$$

Combing with Lemma 7(a), implies that under the conditions of Lemma 7, on class I,

$$
\begin{aligned}
Q(W) &\leq LW + |Q(W) - LW| \\
&\leq -r^K \Theta(n) + \epsilon M_\phi \Theta(n) + M_\phi \Theta(1) \\
&\in -r^K \Theta(n) + M_\phi \Theta(1). \quad (13)
\end{aligned}
$$

if $\epsilon M_\phi r^{-K}$ is small enough.

On class II, $D_{total} \leq U_s + n\mu \in \Theta(n)$, so Lemma 4 implies that

$$|Q(W) - LW| \leq M_\phi \Theta(n)$$

Combining with Lemma 7(b), implies that under the conditions of Lemma 7, on class II,

$$
\begin{aligned}
Q(W) &\leq LW + |Q(W) - LW| \\
&\leq -r^K \epsilon^3 \Theta(n^2) + M_\phi \Theta(n) \quad (14)
\end{aligned}
$$

Equations (13) and (14) imply that if $(r, d, \beta, \alpha, \epsilon)$ satisfies the conditions of Lemma 7, there exists $\xi > 0$ sufficiently small such that $Q(W) \leq -\xi n$ for all n larger than some constant. For such ξ and such (r, d, β, α), W is a valid Lyapunov function, so by Lemma 3, Theorem 1(b) at the case $0 < \mu < \gamma \leq \infty$ is proved.

5. CONCLUSION

By focusing on the missing piece syndrome, which affects the performance of a P2P system, we have identified the minimum time peer seeds must dwell in order to stabilize the system. The model includes a fixed seed, peers arriving with pieces, and peers dwelling for a while as peer seeds after obtaining the complete file. It is a mathematical simplification of a P2P system during the period of several hours or days after a flash crowd initiation of a file transfer, when the arrival of new peers is relatively steady. Our result identifies the stability region under all possible rates of arrival, mean times between transfer attempts, and distribution of pieces brought in by new peers. A sketch of the proof is given here; the complete details are provided in the full version of this paper under preparation.

For tractability, we assumed that the times between upload attempts and the dwell times of seeds are exponentially distributed random variables. However, we conjecture the results hold for more general distributions; the instability half of our proof does not rely on the assumption of exponential distributions.

Issues for future investigation include considering different strategies of peer contact, different piece selection strategies that are biased more towards rare pieces, heterogeneous link speeds, network coding, etc. We believe similar conditions for stability can be found for those variations.

6. REFERENCES

[1] B. Cohen. Incentives build robustness in bittorrent. In *Workshop on Economics of Peer-to-Peer systems*, volume 6, pages 68–72, 2003.

[2] F. Foster. On the stochastic matrices associated with certain queuing processes. *The Annals of Mathematical Statistics*, 24(3):355–360, 1953.

[3] C. Gkantsidis and P. Rodriguez. Network coding for large scale content distribution. In *INFOCOM 2005*, volume 4, pages 2235–2245, 2005.

[4] B. Hajek and J. Zhu. The missing piece syndrome in peer-to-peer communication. In *Information Theory Proceedings (ISIT), 2010 IEEE International Symposium on*, pages 1748–1752, 2010.

[5] T. Karagiannis, A. Broido, N. Brownlee, K. Claffy, and M. Faloutsos. Is P2P dying or just hiding. In *IEEE Globecom*, volume 3, pages 1532–1538, 2004.

[6] V. Krishnan. *Probability and random processes*. John Wiley & Sons, 2006.

[7] A. Legout, G. Urvoy-Keller, and P. Michiardi. Rarest first and choke algorithms are enough. In *Proceedings of the 6th ACM SIGCOMM conference on Internet measurement*, pages 203–216, 2006.

[8] L. Leskelä, P. Robert, and F. Simatos. Interacting branching processes and linear file-sharing networks. *Advances in Applied Probability*, 42(3):834–854, 2010.

[9] L. Massoulié and M. Vojnovic. Coupon replication systems. *IEEE/ACM Transactions on Networking*, 16(3):603–616, 2008.

[10] D. Menasché, A. Rocha, E. de Souza e Silva, R. Leão, D. Towsley, and A. Venkataramani. Estimating self-sustainability in peer-to-peer swarming systems. *Performance Evaluation*, 2010.

[11] I. Norros, H. Reittu, and T. Eirola. On the stability of two-chunk file-sharing systems. *Queueing Systems*, pages 1–24, 2009.

[12] D. Qiu and R. Srikant. Modeling and performance analysis of BitTorrent-like peer-to-peer networks. *ACM SIGCOMM Computer Communication Review*, 34(4):367–378, 2004.

[13] X. Yang and G. de Veciana. Service capacity of peer to peer networks. In *INFOCOM 2004*, volume 4, pages 2242–2252, 2004.

Brief Announcement:
Scalability versus Semantics of Concurrent FIFO Queues∗

Christoph M. Kirsch, Hannes Payer, Harald Röck, and Ana Sokolova
Department of Computer Sciences
University of Salzburg, Austria
firstname.lastname@cs.uni-salzburg.at

ABSTRACT

Maintaining data structure semantics of concurrent queues such as first-in first-out (FIFO) ordering requires expensive synchronization mechanisms which limit scalability. However, deviating from the original semantics of a given data structure may allow for a higher degree of scalability and yet be tolerated by many concurrent applications. We introduce the notion of a k-FIFO queue which may be out of FIFO order up to a constant k (called semantical deviation). Implementations of k-FIFO queues may be distributed and therefore be accessed unsynchronized while still being starvation-free. We show that k-FIFO queues whose implementations are based on state-of-the-art FIFO queues, which typically do not scale under high contention, provide scalability. Moreover, probabilistic versions of k-FIFO queues improve scalability further but only bound semantical deviation with high probability.

Categories and Subject Descriptors

D.1.3 [**Software**]: Concurrent Programming

General Terms

Algorithms, Performance

1. INTRODUCTION

The scalability of applications is limited by Amdahl's Law, which states that the degree to which we can speed up an application on a multi-core system is limited by the amount of code that cannot be parallelized and must be executed sequentially. Since operations on shared data structures may not be fully parallelized there is an intrinsic concurrency bottleneck in many applications using shared data structures that gets increasingly problematic with an increasing number of cores.

Even basic concurrent data structures such as stacks and queues have negative scalability under high contention due to synchronization. However, maintaining data structure semantics may actually not be needed in some concurrent applications. Consider, for example, a webserver which stores incoming requests in a shared FIFO queue running on a server machine with possibly hundreds of cores. The requests are dequeued and handled by worker threads at a later

∗Supported by the EU ArtistDesign Network of Excellence on Embedded Systems Design, the National Research Network RiSE on Rigorous Systems Engineering (Austrian Science Fund S11404-N23), and an Elise Richter Fellowship (Austrian Science Fund V00125).

PODC'11, June 6–8, 2011, San Jose, California, USA.
ACM 978-1-4503-0719-2/11/06.

point in time. In such a scenario it may not be important to process the requests in perfect FIFO order. Instead, it may be sufficiently fair to handle the requests FIFO up to a constant that bounds the deviation from FIFO order. A detailed evaluation of the trade-off between scalability and semantical deviation of concurrent data structures can be found in [3]. A more recent survey exemplifies the trend towards scalable but semantically weaker concurrent data structures [5].

2. k-FIFO QUEUE

A k-FIFO queue provides an enqueue and a dequeue operation similar to a regular FIFO queue. Logically, a k-FIFO queue is a queue where an enqueue operation adds an element to the queue tail and a dequeue operation removes one of the $k - e$ oldest elements from the queue with e being the number of dequeue operations since the most recent dequeue operation that removed the oldest element from the queue, i.e., $e < k$ always holds. Thus, retrieving the oldest element from the queue may require up to k dequeue operations, which may not return any element younger than the k oldest elements in the queue and which may be interleaved with any number of enqueue operations. This implies that k-FIFO queues are starvation-free. Note that a 0-FIFO queue is equivalent to a regular FIFO queue.

We implement a k-FIFO queue using p versions of a regular FIFO queue, so-called partial FIFO queues, and a load balancer that distributes data structure operations among the p partial FIFO queues [3]. The value of p and the type of load balancer determine k (semantical deviation), as discussed below, as well as the scalability of the k-FIFO queue, i.e., how many data structure operations can potentially be performed concurrently and in parallel without causing contention. Note that p and the load balancer can be configured by the programmer at compile time or dynamically at runtime with the help of performance counters. For example, a load balancer may be chosen with $p = 1$ under low contention and with increasing p as contention increases.

A metric for the quality of the load balancer is the maximum imbalance of operations of a given operation type, which we define as the difference between the partial FIFO queue on which the most and the fewest operations of a given type have been performed at a given point in time. Starvation of elements in a k-FIFO queue is prevented if the maximum imbalance of operations for each operation type is bounded. In this case the semantical deviation of a k-FIFO queue from a regular FIFO queue is also bounded.

A load balancer that provides bounded semantical deviation for a k-FIFO queue can be implemented with two global counters indicating on which partial FIFO queue the last enqueue and the last dequeue operation was performed. We refer to it as perfect load balancer. The global counters are accessed and modified using atomic operations, which can cause cache conflicts when multiple threads try to modify the same memory locations concurrently. However, scalability may still be achieved under low concurrent load since the load balancer itself is simple and contention on the shared memory locations may rarely happen. It can be shown that if t threads perform concurrent data structure operations on a k-FIFO queue using the perfect load balancer the semantical deviation is $k \leq t \cdot (p-1)$.

A load balancer that randomly distributes operations over the partial FIFO queues bounds the semantical deviation probabilistically. This approach, also known as randomized load balancing [2], has been shown to provide good distribution quality if the random numbers are distributed independently and uniformly. However, generating such random numbers may be computationally expensive. Therefore, it is essential to find the right trade-off between quality and overhead of random number generation. Suppose that m enqueue operations and n dequeue operations have been performed on p partial FIFO queues using a random load balancer, then it can be shown that with high probability the semantical deviation is bounded by $k \leq \Theta\left(\sqrt{\frac{(m+n)\log p}{p}}\right) \cdot (p-1)$.

In order to improve the balancing quality of the random load balancer, d partial FIFO queues with $1 < d \leq p$ may be chosen randomly. Out of the d partial FIFO queues the queue that contributes most to a better balance is then selected. For example, an enqueue operation may be performed on the partial FIFO queue that contains the fewest elements. We refer to such a load balancer as d-random load balancer. The runtime overhead of the d-random load balancer increases linearly in d since the random number generator is called d times. It can be shown that a d-random load balancer bounds the semantical deviation with high probability to $k \leq 2 \cdot \Theta\left(\frac{\log\log p}{d}\right) \cdot (p-1)$.

3. EVALUATION

The experiments ran on a 24-core server machine (four 6-core 2.1GHz AMD Opteron processors). The benchmarks start with empty queues. Then, each thread enqueues and dequeues elements in alternating order. We use the number of operations performed by all threads per millisecond as our metric of throughput. Additionally, we compute from benchmark traces the average semantical deviation per operation of the different queues. We compare our k-FIFO queues with the lock-free Michael-Scott FIFO queue [4] (baseline) and a modified version of that FIFO queue called Random Dequeue Queue (RDQ) [1]. RDQ is semantically equivalent to a k-FIFO queue where k can be configured at compile time. The implementation of our k-FIFO queue uses the previously described load balancers and the Michael-Scott FIFO queue for the partial FIFO queues.

The throughput results are depicted in Figure 1(a). The throughput of the Michael-Scott baseline and RDQ decreases with an increasing number of threads. The k-FIFO queue with the perfect load balancer does not scale but performs better than the baseline. The k-FIFO queues with the random and the 2-random load balancers provide scalability.

The semantical deviation results are depicted in Figure 1(b). The average semantical deviation of the k-FIFO queue with the random load balancer is high. In comparison, the average semantical deviation of the k-FIFO queue with the 2-random load balancer is three orders of magnitude lower. The lowest average semantical deviation is achieved by RDQ and the k-FIFO queue with the perfect load balancer. Note that the semantical deviation of the Michael-Scott baseline is zero.

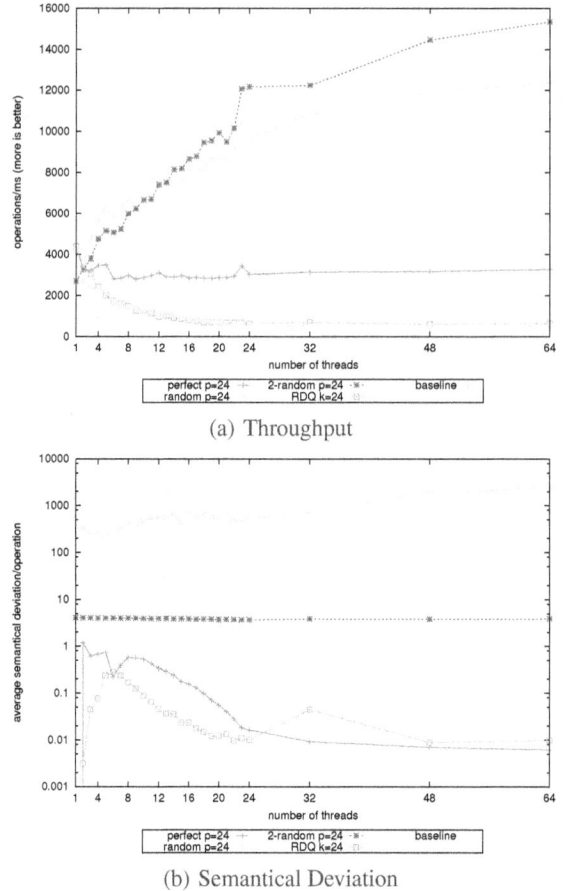

(a) Throughput

(b) Semantical Deviation

Figure 1: Increasing number of threads on a 24-core server machine

The k-FIFO queue with the 2-random load balancer provides the best compromise between scalability and semantical deviation for the presented workload. Depending on the workload a k-FIFO queue may be configured with the smallest p value and the most accurate load balancer to provide the best adherence to data structure semantics while still providing scalability. Interesting future work includes applying our implementation concept to other concurrent data structures and transaction-based systems such as software-transactional memory.

4. REFERENCES

[1] Y. Afek, G. Korland, and E. Yanovsky. Quasi-linearizability: Relaxed consistency for improved concurrency. In *Proc. Conference on Principles of Distributed Systems (OPODIS)*, pages 395–410. Springer, 2010.

[2] P. Berenbrink, A. Czumaj, A. Steger, and B. Vöcking. Balanced allocations: The heavily loaded case. *SIAM Journal on Computing*, 35(6):1350–1385, 2006.

[3] C. Kirsch, H. Payer, and H. Röck. Scal: Non-linearizable computing breaks the scalability barrier. Technical Report 2010-07, Department of Computer Sciences, University of Salzburg, November 2010.

[4] M. Michael and M. Scott. Simple, fast, and practical non-blocking and blocking concurrent queue algorithms. In *Proc. Symposium on Principles of Distributed Computing (PODC)*, pages 267–275. ACM, 1996.

[5] N. Shavit. Data structures in the multicore age. *Communications of the ACM*, 54:76–84, March 2011.

Brief Announcement:
Distributed Computing with Rules of Thumb

Aaron D. Jaggard[*]
Department of Computer
Science, Colgate University
Hamilton, NY USA
DIMACS, Rutgers University
New Brunswick, NJ USA
adj@dimacs.rutgers.edu

Michael Schapira
Department of Computer
Science
Princeton University
Princeton, NJ USA
ms7@cs.princeton.edu

Rebecca N. Wright[†]
Department of Computer
Science and DIMACS
Rutgers University
New Brunswick, NJ USA
rebecca.wright@rutgers.edu

ABSTRACT

We present our recent work (ICS 2011) on dynamic environments in which computational nodes, or decision makers, follow simple and unsophisticated rules of behavior (*e.g.*, repeatedly "best replying" to others' actions, and minimizing "regret") that have been extensively studied in game theory and economics. We aim to understand when convergence of the resulting dynamics to an equilibrium point is guaranteed if nodes' interaction is not synchronized (*e.g.*, as in Internet protocols and large-scale markets). We take the first steps of this research agenda. We exhibit a general non-convergence result and consider its implications across a wide variety of interesting and timely applications: routing, congestion control, game theory, social networks and circuit design. We also consider the relationship between classical nontermination results in distributed computing theory and our result, explore the impact of scheduling on convergence, study the computational and communication complexity of asynchronous dynamics and present some basic observations regarding the effects of asynchrony on no-regret dynamics.

Categories and Subject Descriptors

C.2.4 [**Computer-Communication Networks**]: Distributed Systems—*Distributed applications*; F.1.1 [**Computation by Abstract Devices**]: Models of Computation

General Terms

Economics, Reliability, Theory

Keywords

Adaptive heuristics, game dynamics, convergence, self stabilization

1. MOTIVATION

Dynamic environments where computational nodes or human decision makers repeatedly interact arise in a variety

[*]Supported in part by NSF grants 0751674 and 0753492.

[†]Supported in part by NSF grant 0753061.

of settings such as Internet protocols, large-scale markets, and multi-processor computer architectures. In many such settings, the behavior for the nodes is simple, natural and myopic—*i.e.*, they follow "rules of thumb" (or, in the language of Hart [5], "*adaptive heuristics*"). Often, this reflects the desire or necessity for nodes to provide quick responses and have a limited computational burden. Such behaviors, which include "repeated best response" and "regret minimization", have been extensively studied in game theory and economics.

In many interesting contexts, the resulting dynamics can, in the long run, move the global system in good directions and yield highly rational and sophisticated behavior, such as in game theory results demonstrating the convergence of best-response or no-regret dynamics to equilibrium points (see [5] and references therein). However, these positive results are based on the often unrealistic premise that nodes' actions are somehow synchronously coordinated.

It has long been known that asynchrony introduces substantial difficulties in distributed systems, as compared to synchrony [3], due to the "limitation imposed by local knowledge" [7]. There has been much work in distributed computing on identifying conditions that guarantee protocol termination in asynchronous computational environments. Over the past three decades, there have been many results regarding the possibility/impossibility borderline for failure-resilient computation (*e.g.*, [2, 7]). In these classical results, the risk of non-termination stems from the possibility of failures of nodes or other components. In contrast, in our setting the risk of non-convergence stems from limitations imposed by simplistic node behaviors.

We seek to bring together research in game theory and economics and research in distributed computing to form a new research agenda: "*distributed computing with adaptive heuristics*". Our aim is to investigate provable properties and possible worst-case system behavior of natural dynamics in asynchronous computational environments. We take the first steps of this research agenda in [6]. Here, we briefly describe the main contributions of [6]; we refer the reader to [6] for a more thorough exposition of our agenda, results, and directions for future research.

2. OUR CONTRIBUTIONS

We show that a large and natural class of dynamics fails to guarantee convergence to an equilibrium in an asynchronous setting, even if the nodes and communication channels are reliably failure-free. This has implications across a wide domain of applications, ranging from routing and congestion control on the Internet to the stabilization of asynchronous circuits. Conversely, we show that non-convergence is not inherent to simple behaviors, as some forms of regret minimization provably converge in asynchronous settings. We also explore the impact of scheduling on convergence guarantees and the computational and communication complexity of asynchronous dynamics. In more detail, we make the following contributions:

Model.

We state a formal model for use in analyzing the convergence of myopic dynamics to equilibria in asynchronous computational environments. Our modeling approach draws on ideas both from work on dynamics in game theory and economics [5] and from work on self stabilization in distributed computing [1] and on protocol stability in networking [4].

General non-convergence result.

Due to practical constraints, it is often desirable or necessary that computational nodes' behavior rely on limited memory and processing power. In such contexts, nodes' decisions are often based on *bounded recall*—i.e., dependent solely on recent history of interaction with others—and can even be *historyless*—i.e., nodes only react to other nodes' current actions. We exhibit a general impossibility result showing that a broad class of bounded-recall behaviors, in which each node's behavior is additionally *self-independent*—i.e., each node's choice of a new action is not allowed to depend on that node's previous actions—cannot always converge to a stable state. More specifically, we show that, for such behaviors, the existence of two "equilibrium points" implies that there is some execution that does not converge to any outcome even if all nodes and communication channels are guaranteed not to fail. We give evidence that our non-convergence result is essentially tight.

To prove our result we use a valency argument—a now-standard technique in distributed computing theory [2, 7], first introduced in the proof of the landmark non-termination result of Fischer, Lynch, and Paterson (FLP) for consensus protocols [3]. We point out that while the risk of protocol non-termination for consensus protocols in [3] and related work stems from the possibility of failures, the possibility of non-convergence in our framework stems from limitations on nodes' behaviors. Hence, there is no immediate translation from the FLP result to ours (and vice versa). We further discuss the link between consensus protocols and our framework in [6], where we also take an axiomatic approach and establish a non-termination result that holds for both contexts, thus unifying the treatment of these dynamic computational environments.

Implications across a wide variety of applications.

We apply our non-convergence result to a wide variety of interesting environments: (1) the Border Gateway Protocol (BGP), which handles Internet routing; (2) the Transmission Control Protocol (TCP), which handles congestion control on the Internet; (3) convergence of game dynamics to pure Nash equilibria; (4) stabilization of asynchronous circuits; and (5) diffusion of technologies in social networks.

Convergence, r-fairness, and randomness.

We study the effects on convergence to a stable state of natural restrictions on the order of nodes' activations (*i.e.*, the order in which nodes' have the opportunity to take steps) that have been extensively studied in distributed computing theory. We consider *r-fairness*, the guarantee that each node selects a new action at least once within every $r > 0$ consecutive time steps. Among other results, we show that there are systems that converge under all r-fair schedules, for some r that is exponential in the size of the system, but not for some $(r + 1)$-fair schedule.

Communication and computational complexity of asynchronous dynamics.

We study the tractability of determining whether convergence to a stable state is guaranteed (when such a guarantee is not precluded by our other results). We present two complementary hardness results establishing that, even for extremely restricted kinds of interactions, this task is hard: (1) an exponential communication complexity lower bound; and (2) a computational complexity PSPACE-completeness result that, alongside its computational implications, implies we cannot hope to have short witnesses of guaranteed asynchronous convergence (unless PSPACE = NP).

Asynchronous no-regret dynamics.

We present some basic observations about the convergence properties of no-regret dynamics in our framework, that establish that, in contrast to other simple behaviors, regret minimization is quite robust to asynchrony.

3. CONCLUSION

We believe that this work has but scratched the surface in the exploration of the behavior of natural dynamics in asynchronous computational environments. Many important questions remain wide open. In [6], we outline multiple general directions for future research.

4. REFERENCES

[1] S. Dolev. Self stabilization. *MIT Press*, 2000.
[2] F. Fich and E. Ruppert. Hundreds of impossibility results for distributed computing. *Distributed Computing*, 16(2–3):121–163, 2003.
[3] M. J. Fischer, N. A. Lynch, and M. S. Paterson. Impossibility of distributed consensus with one faulty process. *J. ACM*, 32(2):374–382, 1985.
[4] T. G. Griffin, F. B. Shepherd, and G. Wilfong. The stable paths problem and interdomain routing. *IEEE/ACM Trans. Netw.*, 10(2):232–243, 2002.
[5] S. Hart. Adaptive heuristics. *Econometrica*, 73:1401–1430, 2005.
[6] A. D. Jaggard, M. Schapira, and R. N. Wright. Distributed computing with adaptive heuristics. In *Proceedings of the Second Annual Symposium on Innovations in Computer Science*, pages 417–443, 2011.
[7] N. Lynch. A hundred impossibility proofs for distributed computing. In *Proceedings of the Eighth Annual ACM Symposium on Principles of Distributed Computing*, pages 1–28, 1989.

Brief Announcement:
Incentive-Compatible Distributed Greedy Protocols

Noam Nisan[*]
School of Engineering and
Computer Science
The Hebrew University
Jerusalem, Israel
noam@cs.huji.ac.il

Michael Schapira
Department of Computer
Science
Princeton University
Princeton, NJ USA
ms7@cs.princeton.edu

Gregory Valiant
Department of Computer
Science
UC Berkeley
Berkeley, CA USA
gvaliant@eecs.berkeley.edu

Aviv Zohar
Microsoft Research
Silicon Valley Lab
Mountain View, CA USA
avivz@microsoft.com

ABSTRACT

Under many distributed protocols, the prescribed behavior for participants is to behave greedily, *i.e.*, to repeatedly "best respond" to the others' actions. We present recent work (*Proc. ICS'11*) where we tackle the following general question: "*When is it best for a long-sighted participant to adhere to a distributed greedy protocol?*". We take a game-theoretic approach and exhibit a class of games where greedy behavior (*i.e.*, repeated best-response) is incentive compatible for all players. We identify several environments of interest that fall within this class, thus establishing the incentive compatibility of the natural distributed greedy protocol for each. These environments include models of the Border Gateway Protocol (BGP) [4], which handles routing on the Internet, and of the Transmission Control Protocol (TCP) [3], and also stable-roommates assignments [2] and cost-sharing [5], which have been extensively studied in economic theory.

Categories and Subject Descriptors

C.2.4 [**Computer-Communication Networks**]: Distributed Systems—*Distributed applications*

General Terms

Algorithms, Economics, Theory

Keywords

Game Theory, Greedy Protocols

1. WHEN IS IT BEST TO BE GREEDY?

The Internet has transformed computation from a largely local endeavor to one that frequently involves diverse collections of self-interested individuals and organizations. While

---

[*]Supported by a grant from the Israeli Science Foundation (ISF), and by the Google Inter-university center for Electronic Markets and Auctions.

in traditional cooperative networks non-faulty nodes are trusted to follow the protocol specification, in Internet environments we can no longer take for granted that nodes blindly and unquestioningly follow a prescribed behavior. To guarantee correct execution of a protocol we must hence ensure that the nodes have incentive to follow the protocol. Over the past decade, much research has been devoted to the design and analysis of incentive compatible computational protocols in both centralized [6] and distributed [1] settings.

Given the considerable size and volatility of the Internet, protocols that run on the Internet are often distributed across multiple computational nodes, whose actions rely on very limited processing power and memory, and on local information only. Often, under such protocols, nodes' prescribed behavior is simply to repeatedly "best respond" to each others' actions, *i.e.*, to behave in a greedy manner (*e.g.*, under the Border Gateway Protocol, which handles routing on the Internet, every router repeatedly selects the "best" route made available to it by its neighbors). We wish to understand when following such a distributed greedy protocol is *rational* from a computational node's perspective. We ask the following general question: "*When is it best, in the long run, for a participant to repeatedly best-respond to others' actions?*", that is, "*When can't a long-sighted participant improve over this repeated myopic optimization?*".

We take a game-theoretic approach to distributed greedy protocols. We now briefly and informally present our contributions. We refer the reader to [7] for a detailed exposition.

2. FRAMEWORK AND GENERAL RESULT

Our first contribution is a formal framework for reasoning about incentives for repeated best-response. We model the computational nodes as players in a partial-information game and their possible actions as strategies in this game. Each player aims to maximize a *private* utility function. We consider dynamic interactions where players take turns selecting strategies; at each (discrete) time step, some player (possibly more than one) selects and announces a strategy. The prescribed behavior for every player is to repeatedly choose his best-response (given his private utility function) to the most recently announced strategies of the others. We point out that there is nothing preventing a player from not following the prescribed behavior and from selecting strategies based on more complex computation that takes into account the entire history of interaction.

Intuitively, repeated best-response is incentive-compatible if, when all other players are repeatedly best-responding, a player has incentive to do the same, *i.e.*, no player can gain from unilaterally deviating from repeated best-response. In distributed protocol contexts, this translates to the desideratum that as long as other computational nodes execute the protocol, the best course of action for a node be to also adhere to the protocol. Defining incentive compatibility in our setting involves many intricacies. We opt to focus on a very general notion of incentive compatibility that, we believe, captures essentially any variant that the reader may desire.

Our main results are identifying a class of games for which repeated best-response is incentive compatible, and exhibiting several interesting environments that fall within this class. We formally present our class of games in [7]. Here, we settle for an intuitive exposition of this class of games. Games that belong to our class have the following property. When each player i considers the game after the other players have already iteratively eliminated "dominated strategies", *i.e.*, strategies that are inferior to other strategies and that can be eliminated regardless of what i does, he can already tell that he can do no better than the outcome that is reached via repeated best-response.

Our main, and quite easy to prove, general theorem is that in this class of games, for every starting state of the system and every (finite or infinite) order of player activations with "sufficiently many" rounds (where a round is a sequence of consecutive time steps in which each player gets to act at least once), repeated best-response is incentive compatible for every player. This result holds even when players are activated in an asynchronous manner and even when players' strategy announcements can be arbitrarily delayed.

3. APPLICATIONS

We prove that each of the four environments below can be formulated as a game that falls within our class of games. Thus, our general result above implies that repeated best-response is incentive compatible in all the contexts below.

Internet routing.

The Border Gateway Protocol (BGP) establishes routes between the smaller networks that make up the Internet. We abstract the results in [4] and prove that BGP is incentive compatible in realistic environments.

Congestion control.

The Transmission Control Protocol (TCP) handles congestion on the Internet. Building upon [3], which models key aspects of TCP, we consider TCP-like behavior: increase your attempted transmission rate until encountering congestion, and then decrease the transmission rate. We show that such behavior is in equilibrium, in the sense that no participant has incentive to deviate from it.

Stable-roommates.

In this classic setting [2], students must be paired for the purpose of sharing dorm rooms, and each student has a private order over possible roommates. The goal is to find a "stable matching" where no two students prefer each other to their assigned roommates. We show that a natural distributed protocol, in which a student repeatedly proposes to his most preferred roommate among those that would not immediately reject him, and immediately rejects all proposers except for his most preferred proposer, is incentive compatible and converges to a stable matching in well-studied environments (interns-hospitals, correlated markets).

Cost-sharing.

Cost-sharing arises in situations in which the cost of some public service (*e.g.*, building a bridge) must be distributed among self-interested users who can benefit from this service to different extents. We present a distributed protocol that achieves this goal in an incentive-compatible manner, and implements the outcome of the Moulin mechanism [5].

4. FUTURE RESEARCH

We view this work as a first step towards a more general research agenda. Natural dynamics, *e.g.*, repeated best-response, fictitious play and regret minimization, have been extensively studied in game theory and economics. Yet, little attention has been given to the question of when such dynamics are also rational to follow in the long run. We have tackled this question in the context of repeated best-response. However, we believe that the examination of other dynamics from the literature is an interesting direction for future research. Positive and negative results along these lines can help shed new light on the incentive structure of existing protocols (see our results for BGP and TCP and the results in [3, 4]), and provide new insights into the design of new incentive-compatible protocols.

In addition, our results establish *sufficient* conditions for distributed greedy protocols to be incentive compatible. We still lack a *characterization* of environments where distributed greedy protocols are incentive compatible.

5. REFERENCES

[1] Joan Feigenbaum, Michael Schapira, and Scott Shenker. *Distributed Algorithmic Mechanism Design.* "Algorithmic Game Theory", Chapter 14. Cambridge University Press, 2007.

[2] David Gale and Lloyd S. Shapley. College admissions and stability of marriage. *Amer. Math. Monthly*, (69):9–15, 1962.

[3] P. Brighten Godfrey, Michael Schapira, Aviv Zohar, and Scott Shenker. Incentive compatibility and dynamics of congestion control. *SIGMETRICS Perform. Eval. Rev.*, 38(1):95–106, 2010.

[4] Hagay Levin, Michael Schapira, and Aviv Zohar. Interdomain routing and games. In *STOC*, pages 57–66, 2008.

[5] Herve Moulin. Incremental cost sharing: Characterization by coalition strategy-proofness. *Social Choice and Welfare*, 16(2):279–320, 1999.

[6] Noam Nisan and Amir Ronen. Algorithmic mechanism design. *Games and Economic Behavior*, 35(1):166–196, 2001.

[7] Noam Nisan, Michael Schapira, Gregory Valiant, and Aviv Zohar. Best-response mechanisms. In *ICS '11: Proceedings of the 2nd symposium on Innovations in Computer Science*, 2011.

Brief Announcement: Sustaining Collaboration in Multicast despite Rational Collusion

Haifeng Yu
National Univ. of Singapore
Republic of Singapore
haifeng@comp.nus.edu.sg

Phillip B. Gibbons
Intel Labs Pittsburgh
USA
phillip.b.gibbons@intel.com

Chenwei Shi
National Univ. of Singapore
Republic of Singapore
shichen@comp.nus.edu.sg

ABSTRACT

This paper focuses on designing incentive mechanisms for overlay multicast systems. Existing proposals on the problem are no longer able to provide proper incentives when rational users collude or launch sybil attacks. To overcome this key limitation, we propose a novel decentralized DCast multicast protocol and prove that it offers a novel concept of safety-net guarantee: A user running the protocol will always obtain at least a reasonably good utility despite the deviation of any number of rational users that potentially collude or launch sybil attacks.

Categories and Subject Descriptors: C.2.4 [**Computer-Communication Networks**]: Distributed Systems – *distributed applications*

General Terms: Algorithms, Design, Security

1. INTRODUCTION

In *p2p multicast systems* (e.g., Adobe Flash Player 10.1 and PPLive online TV platform), rational/selfish peers are supposed to help forward/relay the multicast data to other peers. This paper focuses on a key challenge in these systems, namely, how to incentivize these peers and sustain the collaboration. Similar to Equicast [2] and BAR gossip [4], we will consider a simple gossiping paradigm for p2p multicast. Here the multicast *root* is the source of the multicast data. A *user* has one or more identities (i.e., we allow sybil attacks), and each identity is called a *peer*. The gossiping process proceeds in synchronous *rounds*. In each round, the root sends (new) *multicast blocks* to some small number of randomly selected peers, while each peer selects some other peer from whom to pull (existing) multicast blocks. Each multicast block contains some fixed number of *multicast bits*.

Peers are rational/selfish and aim to maximize their *utilities*. Receiving more multicast bits increases the utility, while sending more bits or receiving more non-multicast bits decreases the utility. We assume that there exists some constant $\sigma > 1$ such that for any peer, the benefit of receiving σ multicast bits exceeds the cost of sending one bit or receiving one non-multicast bit. The multicast system provides a *protocol* (i.e., a strategy) to the peers. A peer may choose to follow the protocol or choose to deviate from the protocol in arbitrary ways, based on the utility achievable. A rational peer is called a *non-deviator* if it chooses to follow the specified protocol, otherwise it is called a *deviator*.

[1]This work is partly supported by Academic Research Fund grant R-252-000-406-112.

Previous results. Researchers have proposed several interesting and practical p2p multicast protocols [2, 3, 4] that eliminate profitable *individual* deviation and thus form Nash equilibria. On the other hand, their guarantee no longer holds when rational users collude, launch sybil attacks, or launch whitewashing attacks where a user abandons her/his identity to evade punishment and then rejoins with a new identity. Notice that sybil/whitewashing attacks can be viewed as a special case of collusion. More recently, Tran et al. [5] aims to maintain collusion-resilient reputation scores for peers, but their final guarantee is rather weak and colluding peers can increase their reputation scores unboundedly as the number of colluding peers increases.

Challenges. The inability of these previous approaches to deal with collusion is related to the following two challenges. First, the key to incentivizing collaboration is always a punishment mechanism to punish or reward less those peers who fail to collaborate. The presence of collusion makes it challenging to punish. Evicting a peer (or refusing to send data to that peer) as in [2, 3, 4, 5] is no longer effective — the evicted peer may obtain multicast data from its colluding peers. Moreover, with sybil attacks and whitewashing attacks, eviction simply has no effect on the user.

Second, in some cases the colluding peers may be able to obtain the multicast data from each other more efficiently. For example, suppose the protocol provided by the multicast system is based on gossiping for better robustness against churn. If the colluding peers have low churn, then they can switch to using more efficient tree-based multicast among themselves. Such deviation is already profitable. Furthermore, the colluding peers can either continue to gossip with the non-deviators as usual, or they can participate in gossiping with the non-deviators less frequently. Detecting such deviation, from the non-deviators' perspective, is rather difficult if not impossible.

Our goal. Given such context, the goal of this work is to design a p2p multicast protocol that can properly sustain collaboration despite collusion and sybil/whitewashing attacks by rational users.

2. SAFETY-NET GUARANTEE

The natural way to capture rational collusion is to use the concept of various collusion-resistant Nash equilibria. However, our example earlier already hints that unless a protocol offers optimal performance (i.e., minimizing the overheads incurred by sending/receiving bits) for each possible subset of the peers (without knowing their specific properties such as low churn rate), some subset can *always* profit by switching to a more optimized protocol. Given such impossibility of preventing deviation, aiming to achieve collusion-resistant Nash equilibria would simply be futile. Fortunately, preventing deviation is not actually necessary to sustain collaboration. After all, deviation by itself is not harmful—it is the deviation's negative impact on other (non-deviating) peers that is harmful. This basic observation leads to to our novel concept of a *safety-net guarantee*, which formalizes the goal of this work.

We say that a protocol offers the *safety-net guarantee* if for any peer A that chooses to follow the protocol, A obtains at least a reasonably good utility (called the *safety-net utility*), despite *any* set of colluding peers deviating from the protocol using a *pareto-optimal strategy profile*. We require the collusion strategy to be pareto-optimal since the colluding peers are rational (see [6] for details). The safety-net guarantee is not concerned with protecting the utility of the deviators — if a deviator's utility is below the safety-net utility, it can always switch back to being a non-deviator. We emphasize that the safety-net guarantee does not prevent deviation. In the extreme, for a protocol offering the safety-net guarantee, it is possible for *all* peers to deviate from that protocol.

Our safety-net guarantee is related to the *price of collusion* [1], which quantifies the negative impact of collusion on the *overall* social utility in a congestion game. In comparison, the safety-net guarantee bounds the negative impact of collusion on the utility of *individual* non-deviators in a multicast game. Furthermore, we consider all pareto-optimal strategy profiles of the colluding peers, while the price of collusion focuses on one particular pareto-optimal strategy profile (i.e., the one maximizing the sum of the utilities).

3. DCAST PROTOCOL

Having introduced the safety-net guarantee, we now propose a novel and elegant *DCast* protocol, which is the first practical multicast protocol achieving such guarantee. This section focuses on the overview and intuition — see [6] for the detailed protocol, pseudocode, theorems, proofs, and implementation. We assume that the multicast session has an infinite number of rounds to avoid the well-known end-game effect in finite-horizon repeated games (see [6] for how this assumption can be weakened).

Overview of DCast. Section 1 described a simple pull-based gossiping paradigm for p2p multicast. In this paradigm, colluding peers can profitably deviate from the protocol in several ways. For example, a colluding peer A can pretend that it has no multicast blocks to offer when a non-deviator pulls from A. A can also pull from multiple non-deviators in each round. A user may further launch a sybil attack to attract more multicast blocks directly from the root. DCast builds proper incentives into such pull-based gossiping so that each such deviation *either* is non-profitable *or* will not bring down the utilities of the non-deviators below the safety-net utility. In designing the incentives, DCast addresses the two challenges discussed in Section 1 via the novel design of *debt-links* and *debt-coins* (or *doins* in short).

During the pull-based gossip in DCast, the propagation of a multicast block from one peer A to another peer B is always coupled with the propagation of a *doin* on an unoccupied *debt-link* from A to B. A *debt-link* from A to B is established by B sending $\sigma + 1$ *junk blocks* to A. A junk block contains only junk bits and is of the same size as a multicast block. Notice that establishing the debt-link hurts the utility of both A and B. A debt-link is *unoccupied* when first established. After propagating a doin via that debt-link, the debt-link becomes *occupied* until the corresponding doin is *paid*. A doin is a debt and can be *issued* by any peer. The current holder of a doin conceptually "owes" the issuer of the doin. Doins may circulate (i.e., be relayed) in the system and thus can be viewed as a special kind of bankless virtual currency. Doins will expire every fixed number of rounds, after which point new doins will be issued. A peer holding an expired doin will pay for that doin by sending the doin issuer σ multicast blocks.

Debt-links as *pairwise* entry fees. Fundamentally, the debt-links established by a peer in DCast are *pairwise entry fees* paid by that peer. In other words, the peer incurs some bandwidth consump-

tion to be allowed to interact with some specific peers (i.e., those peers from which the debt-links are established) in a limited form (i.e., the peer cannot borrow more multicast blocks than the number of unoccupied debt-links). This entry fee is pairwise instead of system-wide in the sense that the peer is not allowed to interact with all peers in the system. The pairwise nature prevents a colluding peer from giving other colluding peers interaction access to non-deviators.

The above entry fee serves as an effective punishment to a peer that fails to pay for a doin, since the cost of paying the doin is smaller than the entry fee itself. This is true even in the presence of collusion and sybil/whitewashing attacks. A colluding peer A may be able to obtain multicast blocks from other colluding peers. But if A does establish an incoming debt-link from another peer B, it indicates that A is not able to rely on other colluding peers only, and has to seek B's help. Given that doins are eventually paid, if A pulls from more than one non-deviator in a round, those non-deviators will get payment later and their utilities will be properly protected.

Making doin issuance/relay profitable. The implicit entry fee associated with debt-link establishment from A to B is in the form of junk blocks, which is necessary since a new peer B has no useful data to offer as entry fee. On the other hand, with this design A actually has disincentive to accept debt-link establishments. DCast solves this problem by setting the doin payment amount to be σ and by properly re-using debt-links. Under such payment amount, A makes some (constant) profit each time a doin is issued/relayed on a link and then paid. Even for colluding peers who may enjoy a more optimized (e.g., tree-based) protocol among themselves, we expect a σ of 2 or 3 will be sufficient to make them a profit. Re-using the debt-link a sufficient number of times during the multicast session will then enable the accumulated profit to exceed the initial setup cost of the debt-link. This in turn, incentivizes colluding peers to send multicast blocks when non-deviators pull from them.

Root sending blocks to peers. Finally, peers do not establish any debt-links from the root. Before the root sends a multicast block to a peer, the peer is required to send $\sigma + 2$ junk blocks to the root. This provides disincentive for a rational user to launch a sybil attack in order to attract more multicast blocks from the root.

Formal guarantees. We are able to prove [6] that DCast offers a safety-net guarantee under some reasonable conditions. Roughly speaking, the safety-net utility offered by DCast is such that with high probability, a non-deviator obtains all multicast data needed while sending $(\sigma + 2)(1 + \rho)$ bits for each multicast bit received. Here ρ is a constant describing the relative number of control bits in the protocol as compared to the number of multicast/junk bits.

4. REFERENCES

[1] A. Hayrapetyan, E. Tardos, and T. Wexler. The effect of collusion in congestion games. In *STOC*, 2006.

[2] I. Keidar, R. Melamed, and A. Orda. EquiCast: Scalable multicast with selfish users. In *PODC*, 2006.

[3] H. C. Li, A. Clement, M. Marchetti, M. Kapritsos, L. Robison, L. Alvisi, and M. Dahlin. Flightpath: Obedience vs. choice in cooperative services. In *OSDI*, 2008.

[4] H. C. Li, A. Clement, E. L. Wong, J. Napper, I. Roy, L. Alvisi, and M. Dahlin. BAR Gossip. In *OSDI*, 2006.

[5] N. Tran, J. Li, and L. Subramanian. Collusion-resilient Credit-based Reputations for Peer-to-peer Content Distribution. In *NetEcon*, 2010.

[6] H. Yu, P. B. Gibbons, and C. Shi. DCast: Sustaining Collaboration despite Rational Collusion. Technical Report TRA2/11, School of Computing, National University of Singapore, Feb 2011. Available at http://www.comp.nus.edu.sg/~yuhf/TRA2-11.pdf.

Brief Announcement: Reliable End-User Communication Under a Changing Packet Network Protocol*

Brendan Juba [†]
MIT CSAIL & Harvard SEAS
Cambridge, MA, USA
bjuba@alum.mit.edu

ABSTRACT

We present the first end-user protocol, guaranteeing the delivery of messages, that *automatically* adapts to any new packet format that is obtained by applying a short, efficient function to packets from an earlier protocol.

Categories and Subject Descriptors

C.2.2 [**Computer-Communication Networks**]: Network Protocols; C.4 [**Performance of Systems**]: Fault tolerance, Reliability, availability, and serviceability

General Terms

Theory, Reliability

1. INTRODUCTION

Although the general public tends to regard computational infrastructure as appliances, the rapid growth and change of computational infrastructures invalidates this conception: software needs to be kept up-to-date. As the Internet grows, it grows less feasible to expect that *all* of the devices could be modified to cope with *any* change in the underlying protocol. And yet, the address space of the original protocol (IPv4) is nearing exhaustion, necessitating just such a change. Although a replacement protocol, IPv6, was established as a standard over a decade ago, the adoption rate has been modest at best. Many end-users are unaware of the issue, and those who are aware are generally reluctant to upgrade until incompatibility presents a problem. Furthermore, conversely, the obstacles to adoption of a new standard naturally instill a sense of conservatism in the development of new standards: even if a redesign of the protocol would improve some aspect of the network from users' perspectives, it stands little chance of being deployed unless it is compatible with the existing protocol.

The bottom line is that due to the scale of the Internet and the expectations or lack of awareness of users, the current model for updating computer infrastructure is inadequate. Motivated by this, Juba and Sudan [6] considered whether or not it would be possible for computers to adapt to changes in protocols automatically. They suggested that,

---

*Adapted from the author's Ph.D. thesis [5, Chapter 9].

[†]Supported by NSF Award CCF-0939370

by focusing on the *goal* of the communication – i.e., the functionalities provided – it might be possible to design communication protocols that support broad compatibility. Subsequent work by Goldreich et al. [4] developed a framework for such problems, and established roughly that whenever correct functioning can be locally verified, broad compatibility can be guaranteed. Furthermore, they show that guaranteeing correct functioning while supporting broad compatibility *requires* local verifiability.

Returning to our motivating example of the internet-layer packet protocol, we note that this protocol is designed to support the functionality of a (unreliable) channel. Unfortunately, Juba and Sudan [6] observed that this *specific* goal for communication cannot be guaranteed for broad classes of protocols, due to the inability of end-users to distinguish between incompatible encodings of distinct messages (an inability to locally verify correctness). So, unfortunately, we can't hope to design such a packet protocol with broad compatibility. Nevertheless, the observation does not rule out the possibility that for some *specific* higher-level functionality, end-users might still be able to adapt to changes in the lower-level packet protocol—e.g., specifically for a transport-layer protocol similar to TCP [2] to adapt to changes in the supporting internet-layer protocol, as we consider here.

Our main result in this work is the construction of a modified version of TCP that achieves essentially the same ends – implements a reliable channel – and can automatically adapt to "sufficiently small" changes in the internet-layer protocol, with the caveat that either the users must know each others' addresses or else there can only be two users. The main contribution in this work is in showing how the higher-level protocol can be modified to provide the necessary feedback to the lower-level protocol to enable adaptive behavior. A secondary (related) contribution is the definition of an appropriate class of "sufficiently small" changes for which it is possible to prove that the protocol adapts to changes in a reasonable amount of time: an issue with the techniques in prior works [4, 6] is that the overhead of the adaptive protocol (in terms of the running time or number of errors, drops, etc.) tends to grow exponentially with the size (e.g., in bits) of the unknown protocol. In this case, we bound the overhead in terms of the size of the *modification* to an earlier protocol, which we hope to be much more reasonable.

2. PROBLEM AND SOLUTION CONCEPT

We use the framework introduced by Goldreich et al. [4] to model communication without a fixed protocol. Essentially, this means that we fix a "goal for communication" capturing the functionality we wish to support, and a class of (network) protocols with respect to which we wish to exhibit compatibility. In this work, we consider communication from the perspective of a pair of end-users. The goal for our end-users is to realize a channel using a network connecting them: that is, each end-user receives as input an infinite sequence of messages (of some bounded maximum length N) and the goal is achieved if the users respectively produce their partner's input sequence as output. The network, modeling the Internet, is assumed to have a packet format for each of the users such that when a packet in the respective users' formats is sent to the network, the network (probably, eventually) forwards the packet to that user. We allow the network to drop packets (randomly with some fixed probability δ) and delay and/or reorder the packets adversarially up to some known maximum delay bound D; if there are too many packets addressed to one of the users in a given period (e.g., if both users together attempt to send more than D packets to one user) then the network is also allowed to drop new packets addressed to that user.

Now, we suppose that the network is chosen adversarially from a class of networks using different packet formats that we describe below. The problem is for the end-users to achieve their goal with the unknown packet format. Our solution concept is an algorithm for the end-users such that they correctly receive each others' messages when communicating across this network, no matter which packet format (from the class to be specified) is chosen. Naturally, the larger this class of protocols is, the more flexible the end-users are, but there are limits to what we can hope for. In particular, Goldreich et al. [4] show that in general there is an exponential lower bound on the number of rounds needed to achieve a goal in terms of the length of a protocol. Therefore, in order to achieve reasonable performance, it is necessary to restrict the class of protocols somehow. Our choice of restriction here is to assume that some protocol is known to the end-users, and that the network protocol is a "small modification" of this known protocol. Specifically, we assume that packets encoded in the old format may be translated to valid packets in the new format by some function described by a program of some a priori bounded length ℓ. Thus, although we may pay an exponential price in terms of the lengths of these modifications, we may still be able to adapt to gradual changes to the protocol over time without paying too severe a price.

The specific class of protocols we consider are packet network protocols that moreover compute the packet encoding in a single pass over the message, while using at most b bits of state (i.e., 2^b distinct states). It is interesting to consider such a weak and restricted class of protocols since we merely wish to guarantee "compatibility" with some relatively broad, explicit class of modifications. Our class of protocols is powerful enough to attach headers and compute checksums, and is therefore powerful enough to compute the encodings of most real packet network protocols.

3. THE ADAPTIVE END-USER PROTOCOL

Prior work by Goldreich et al. [4] implies that the ability to verify correct functioning is necessary and sufficient to construct solutions to our compatibility problem. Thus, the main idea is that the end-users can attach a MAC (or signature, e.g., as proposed by Gilbert et al. [3]) to their messages prior to encoding so that the recipient can verify when the

message is decoded correctly; unconditional constructions of such MACs exist because the number of states b of the protocol is bounded, as is the size of the modification ℓ.[1] Thus, users can decode correctly (e.g., via trial-and-error). Given that the users can decode correctly, they can run a sliding-window scheme (following TCP [2]) so that they can confirm that a message was sent via an acknowledgement, and hence they can learn to encode messages as well.

The construction sketched above is sufficient to guarantee correctness, but because of the unreliability of the network, enumeration achieves poor performance—a protocol may fail due to a drop, and a naïve enumeration then cycles through the entire enumeration before returning to the "right" format. This performance issue can be circumvented by using an algorithm for the nonstochastic bandit problem [1] to select a candidate modification, rewarding the algorithm's choice whenever an acknowledgement is received, so the total reward received by the algorithm is a lower bound on the number of messages sent. (This *doesn't* reduce the initial overhead or improve the protocol search, but rather achieves a long-term transmission rate that approaches optimal.) The only difficulty is that the algorithm's choice needs to be evaluated before it makes a new choice, so the algorithm as stated can only handle a send window of size one. We circumvent this issue by using a number of copies of the algorithm equal to the (maximum) size of the send window, and invoking them in round-robin fashion. This increases the rate of failures due to bad choices by (only) the square root of the maximum size of the send window, which is independent of the total number of messages we attempt to send, so over time the algorithm's overall success rate still approaches the optimal rate of $1 - \delta$.[2]

4. REFERENCES

[1] P. Auer, N. Cesa-Bianchi, Y. Freund, and R. E. Schapire. The nonstochastic multiarmed bandit problem. *SIAM J. Comput.*, 32(1):48–77, 2003.

[2] V. G. Cerf and R. E. Kahn. A protocol for packet network intercommunication. *IEEE Trans. Comms.*, Com-22(5):637–648, 1974.

[3] E. N. Gilbert, F. J. MacWilliams, and N. J. A. Sloane. Codes which detect deception. *Bell Sys. Tech. J.*, 53:405–424, 1974.

[4] O. Goldreich, B. Juba, and M. Sudan. A theory of goal-oriented communication. Technical Report TR09-075, ECCC, 2009.

[5] B. Juba. *Universal Semantic Communication*. PhD thesis, MIT, 2010.

[6] B. Juba and M. Sudan. Universal semantic communication I. In *Proc. 40th STOC*, 2008.

[7] J. Kamp, A. Rao, S. Vadhan, and D. Zuckerman. Deterministic extractors for small-space sources. In *Proc. 38th STOC*, pages 691–700, 2006.

---

[1] Although we assume that the key for the MAC is known to both end-users, we can circumvent this assumption by using *deterministic extractors*, as constructed for the class of encodings we consider here by Kamp et al. [7], to exchange keys during a handshake (without knowing the encoding).

[2] Still, to allocate feedback correctly, we retransmit the messages one at a time. As long as the probability of a drop is sufficiently small relative to the size of the send window, though, this achieves reasonable performance.

Brief Announcement:
Securing Social Networks*

Michael Backes
Saarland University, Germany
MPI-SWS
backes@cs.uni-saarland.de

Matteo Maffei
Saarland University, Germany
maffei@cs.uni-saarland.de

Kim Pecina
Saarland University, Germany
pecina@cs.uni-saarland.de

ABSTRACT

We present a cryptographic framework to achieve access control, privacy of social relations, secrecy of resources, and anonymity of users in social networks. The main idea is to use pseudonyms to hide user identities, signatures on pseudonyms to establish social relations, and zero-knowledge proofs on these signatures to demonstrate the existence of the corresponding social relations without sacrificing user anonymity. Our framework is generally applicable and, in particular, constitutes an ideal plug-in for decentralized social networks.

We formally verified the aforementioned security properties using ProVerif, an automated theorem prover for cryptographic protocols. We also conducted an experimental evaluation to demonstrate the efficiency and the scalability of our framework.

Categories and Subject Descriptors

C.2.0 [**Computer-Communication Networks**]: Security and Protection

General Terms

Security, Verification

Keywords

Social network security, anonymity in distributed systems, cryptographic protocols, formal verification

1. INTRODUCTION

Over the last years, online social networks (OSNs) have become the natural means to get in touch with people and to engage in a number of social activities. As a matter of fact, the new dimensions of social interaction and the opportunities deriving from these novel functionalities tend to push to the background the impressive leakage of personal information and the consequent threats to users' privacy.

It is well-understood that proper *access control mechanisms* are indispensable. The threats to the privacy of users, however, go well beyond access control problems. For instance, OSNs are highly vulnerable to coercion attacks in which the coercer demands the user's password to access her profile and learn the list of friends together with their recent activities. These kinds of attacks have been reported in countries ruled by authoritarian governments [3, 5], where

people use social networks to organize protest activities and to publish dissident documents. In such settings, the *privacy of social relations* as well as *user anonymity* are fundamental properties. Combining anonymity with forms of access control is crucial to ensure that certain documents can only be read or posted by friends as opposed to hostile users.

Our contributions. We present a cryptographic framework to achieve a wide range of security properties in OSNs, including access control, privacy of social relations, secrecy of resources, and user anonymity. A principal may, for instance, post a comment on someone else's profile or download a picture proving to be a friend, but without disclosing her real identity. Our protocols do not involve any trusted third party, users retain the control over their own data, storing them on their own servers, and the privacy of the social relations is ensured even if these servers are compromised.

In a nutshell, the fundamental idea is to use pseudonyms to hide user identities, signatures on these pseudonyms to establish social relations, and non-interactive zero-knowledge proofs[1] to demonstrate the existence of social relations without revealing the corresponding signatures.

We developed a *prototypical implementation* of our cryptographic framework and conducted an *experimental evaluation* to demonstrate its efficiency. The zero-knowledge proofs, which dominate the communication and computational complexity of our protocols, are a few kilobytes in size and their generation and verification takes less than one second on average.

We formally verified the security of our protocols by formally defining the access control policies, secrecy requirements, and anonymity guarantees, and by making these definitions accessible to the cryptographic protocol verifier ProVerif [2]. For more details on our framework, we refer to the long version of this paper, which was presented at NDSS'11 [1].

2. OVERVIEW OF THE CRYPTOGRAPHIC FRAMEWORK

Pseudonyms. We use pseudonyms in place of plain names to protect user identities, while supporting fine-grained access control policies. Pseudonyms are self-generated: given a one-way function f,[2] a principal takes a random number r and let its pseudonym be $f(r)$. For using such a pseudonym,

*This work was partially supported by the initiative for excellence and the Emmy Noether program of the German federal government.

the owner has to prove the knowledge of r, without revealing it. This prevents impersonation attacks, since no other principle is capable of computing r, given f's one-wayness. In our protocols, we implement f as discrete exponentiation in a finite group, since there exist efficient zero-knowledge proofs to show the knowledge of discrete logarithms.

Establishing social relations. Signatures serve as witnesses to actual social relations. For establishing a social relation with A, B sends his pseudonym p_B to

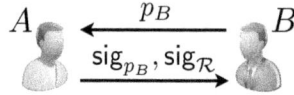

Figure 1: Registration

A (cf. Figure 2). A replies by sending B two signatures (in encrypted form): sig_{p_B} on B's pseudonym p_B and $\mathsf{sig}_{\mathcal{R}}$ on the social relation $\mathcal{R}$ (e.g., "friend"). Pseudonyms and social relations are used in the access control lists of the principals' resources. For instance, A may decide that a certain picture pic can be read only by users in relation $\mathcal{R}$ or that a certain video vid can be watched only by a specific set of users, individually addressed by their pseudonyms.

Sharing resources. For accessing pic, B uses a zero-knowledge proof to exhibit the knowledge of a signature issued by A on the social relation $\mathcal{R}$ (cf. Figure 2, values hidden by the proof are written as subscript). For accessing vid, B demon-

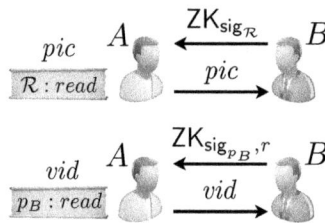

Figure 2: Obtain resources

strates the knowledge of a signature issued by A on the pseudonym p_B and, additionally, demonstrates the ownership of p_B, i.e., the knowledge of the corresponding discrete logarithm r. Notice that neither the signatures nor the discrete logarithm are revealed by these proofs.

Attacker model and privacy properties.
The attacker model comprises external observers eavesdropping the communication channel as well as attackers compromising the servers (e.g., by malware or coercion), reading the data stored thereon, and monitoring the subsequent incoming requests. The goal of our protocols is to preserve the privacy of social relations and to guarantee the anonymity of parties. Intuitively, external observers do not learn any meaningful information since all communication is encrypted. The only data revealing information about the social relations are the signatures used to witness social relations and these are kept secret. Since the verifier does not need them to verify a proof and the prover only needs them while requesting a specific resource, they do not have to be stored on the servers and may, instead, be stored on

---

a portable device and be hidden or destroyed in case of an attack. A principal B has two ways to authenticate with A: by revealing his pseudonym, in which case B implicitly reveals his identity to A, since she knows the link between pseudonyms and identities; or by revealing his social relation with A, in which case B obtains a form of k-anonymity in that his identity is hidden inside the group of people in the same social relation with A. Our system additionally provides a flavor of coercion-resistance: if a coercer asks a user for the links between pseudonyms and principal identities, the user can cheat and give fake associations since these cannot be verified by the coercer. Therefore, an attacker taking the control over the server of a principal does not gain any information about the social relations of that principal. We conducted a formal security analysis that is described in the long version [1].

3. EXPERIMENTAL EVALUATION

Although zero-knowledge proofs are the dominant factors in terms of computational costs and communication complexity, our experiments show that the proofs we deploy are very efficient and usable in practice. For 2048 bit RSA keys, both the proof generation and the proof verification take less than half a second and the proof size is roughly 20 kB. The proofs for pseudonymous authentication require slightly more computation time and are slightly larger because they additionally incorporate a proof of pseudonym ownership.

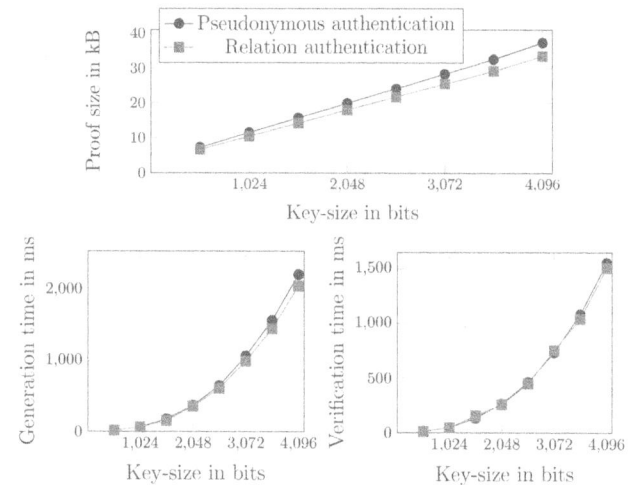

Figure 3: Experimental evaluation of the zero-knowledge proofs for various authentication methods.

4. REFERENCES

[1] M. Backes, M. Maffei, and K. Pecina. A security API for distributed social networks. In *NDSS'11*, pages 35–51. Internet Society, 2011.

[2] B. Blanchet. An efficient cryptographic protocol verifier based on Prolog rules. In *CSFW'01*, pages 82–96. IEEE Press, 2001.

[3] F. Fassihi. Iranian crackdown goes global. *The Wall Street Journal*, 2009. http://online.wsj.com/article/SB125978649644673331.html.

[4] O. Goldreich, S. Micali, and A. Wigderson. Proofs that yield nothing but their validity or all languages in NP have zero-knowledge proof systems. *Journal of the ACM*, 38(3):690–728, 1991.

[5] D. Wolman. Cairo activists use Facebook to rattle regime. *WIRED Magazine*, 2008. http://www.wired.com/techbiz/startups/magazine/16-11/ff_facebookegypt.

---

[1] A zero-knowledge proof combines two seemingly contradictory properties. First, it is a proof of a statement that cannot be forged, i.e., it is impossible, or at least computationally infeasible, to produce a zero-knowledge proof of a wrong statement. Second, a zero-knowledge proof does not reveal any information besides the bare fact that the statement is valid [4]. A non-interactive zero-knowledge proof is a zero-knowledge protocol consisting of one message sent by the prover to the verifier. A zero-knowledge proof of knowledge additionally ensures that the prover knows the witnesses to the given statement.

[2] Intuitively, a one-way function is easy to compute but hard to invert.

Brief Announcement: Parallel and Distributed Programming Extensions for Mainstream Languages Based on pi-Calculus

Patrick Viry

Ateji

73, rue Pascal

75013 Paris, France

patrick.viry@ateji.com

ABSTRACT

We describe an extension of the Java language with parallel programming primitives inspired by pi-calculus and outline the advantages compared to other parallel programming approaches.

Categories and Subject Descriptors

D.3.2 Concurrent, distributed, and parallel languages

D.3.3 Concurrent programming structures

General Terms

Languages

Keywords

Language extensions, parallelism

1. LANGUAGE EXTENSIONS

There are two major approaches for making parallel and distributed programming available to software developers:

- design parallel libraries for existing languages, or
- design new languages with native parallelism

The first approach is probably the most widespread at the moment, and exemplified by tools such as OS threading libraries [4], the Java concurrency library [7], Actor libraries [1], OpenMP [5] and MPI [16]. It does not require changes in the base language, but is strongly limited by the expressive power of libraries, is verbose, difficult to maintain and difficult to analyze for correctness [10].

The second approach avoids most of these problems, but faces an enormous adoption wall. It requires mastering a new language, installing and learning a whole set of new tools – when they exist – and drastically changing the development chain. Examples of languages dedicated to parallel programming include Occam [9], Erlang [6] and X10 [16].

We designed the Ateji PX language [13], an extension of the Java language, as a middle-term approach: it provides parallel primitives at the language level, but extends an already existing language rather than being a new one designed from scratch. The goal of our work is to make parallel programming more easily accessible and safer to use for a wide range of software developers with no specific expertise in parallelism:

- Learning is minimal for users familiar with the base language. Experience shows that Java developers can write, test and run their first parallel programs within half a day, starting from scratch.

- Learning of tools is also made minimal by providing an Eclipse IDE integration for the language

- The Ateji PX compiler is implemented as a source-to-source translator producing standard Java code, which makes it possible to reuse most of the existing tool chain of the Java ecosystem (the translation goes two-way, such that for instance errors and breakpoints always refer to the original source code).

Our choice of the Java platform and the Eclipse IDE was dictated by popularity only, in order to target a large community, rather than by any specific feature of the language or the tools. The same approach could indeed be applied to any other imperative language and its set of development tools.

2. PARALLELISM MODELS

Both Cilk [3] and OpenMP [5] can also be seen as providing language extensions. Cilk adds a handful of new keywords to the C/C++ language, while OpenMP makes a heavy use of the meta-programming facilities of the C/C++ preprocessor.

But the Ateji PX language implements a rather different model of parallel programming, based on process algebra [8]. Namely, it implements a complete set of parallel primitives inspired from pi-calculus [11], a specific process algebra providing a formal model for mobile distributed processes. The only attempt we know of a programming language based on process algebra is Occam [9], which had its moment of fame in the 80's when it was distributed by Inmos Ltd. as the system language for their Transputer chip. BPML [2], a modeling language for business processes, also used process algebra as its semantic basis.

Fortunately, Ateji PX users do not need to know about pi-calculus, because the parallel primitives have been integrated in the base language in a way that looks natural to Java developers. However, it is precisely the fact of being based on a strong and long studied mathematical foundation that makes parallelism simple and intuitive, as well as semantically clean, formally defined and thus amenable to automated analysis.

An essential aspect of process algebra as a parallel programming model is *compositionality*, which is dreadfully lacking in many widespread models such as threads [10] and all tools building upon threads. Compositionality is essential for building large systems (just compose) and for debugging (just decompose).

This approach also allows for efficient and scalable implementations, for example providing a 12.5x speedup on a 16-core server for the standard matrix multiplication algorithm [14].

In the rest of this abstract, we will show how a small number of parallel primitives inspired from pi-calculus make it possible to express a large family of parallel programming patterns, including data parallelism, task parallelism, data-flow and stream programming. These different patterns are typically provided by a combination of different languages, such as Cilk for task parallelism, OpenMP for data parallelism, Lustre for data-flow and IBM's Spade for stream programming.

2.1   Task parallelism

Statements or blocks of statements can be composed in parallel using the "||" operator inside a parallel block, introduced with square brackets:

```
[
    || a++;
    || b++;
]
```

Each parallel statement within the composition is called a *branch*. We purposely avoid using the terms "task" or "process" which mean very different things in different contexts.

2.2   Data parallelism

Branches in a parallel composition can be *quantified*. This is used for performing the same operation on all elements of an array or a collection:

```
[
    || (int i : N) array[i]++;
]
```

Quantification can introduce an arbitrary number of generators (iterators), filters and local variable declarations. Multiple quantified branches can be grouped in the same parallel block.

As a convenience, the case of a single quantified branch in a parallel block can also be written using the parallel-for syntax. This proves very useful for first time users who attempt to parallelize legacy Java applications. The code in the previous example is equivalent (up to some minor technical details) to the one below using the parallel-for notation:

```
for||(int i : N) array[i]++;
```

Parallel reductions form a special case of data parallelism. The term "reduction" is used in parallel programming with the meaning of "reducing" a collection of data into a single value, for instance computing the sum of all elements of an array. This is the parallel sum of all squares from 0 to N-1:

```
int sumOfSquares =
        `+ for||(int i : N) (i*i);
```

2.3   Sending and receiving messages

Ateji PX provides at the language level two syntactic constructs dedicated to message passing:

- Send a message over a channel:
  chan ! value

- Receive a message from a channel:
  chan ? value

Channels can be synchronous, efficiently implementing rendez-vous synchronization, or asynchronous (buffered). They can be mapped to I/O devices such as files and sockets.

In the following example, two parallel branches communicate through the channel chan:

```
    Chan<String> chan = new
Chan<String>();
    [
        || chan ! "Hello";
        || chan ? s;
System.out.println(s);
    ]
```

Explicit message passing forms the basis of data-flow and stream-based programs, including patterns such as the Actor model and MapReduce algorithms.

2.4   Compatibility with existing language features

Our integration of parallel programming features into Java goes rather deep (it is not limited to a couple of additional keywords), and has been designed to interact properly with all existing language features such as recursion, non-local exits (return, break, continue) and exceptions. Combining these language features with parallel primitives can lead to interesting results. Please refer to the language documentation [13,15] or the samples library downloadable from ateji.com for more details.

3.   REFERENCES

[1]   Agha et..al.. A Foundation for Actor Computation.. *J. Functional Programming*, vol 7, 1998.

[2]   BPMI.org. The BPML specification.

[3]   Blumofe et.al. Cilk: An Efficient Multithreaded Runtime System. *ACM PPoPP symposium*, 1995.

[4]   Butenhof. *Programming with POSIX Threads*, Addison-Wesley, ISBN 0-201-63392-2

[5]   Chandra et.al. *Parallel Programming in OpenMP*. Morgan Kaufmann, 2000. ISBN 1-55860-671-8

[6]   Erlang official website. http://www.erlang.org/

[7]   Goetz et.al.. *Java Concurrency in Practice*. Addison Wesley. ISBN 0-321-34960-1.

[8]   Hoare. *Communicating sequential processes*. CACM, August 1978.

[9]   INMOS. *Occam Programming Manual*. Prentice-Hall. ISBN 0-13-629296-8.

[10] Lee. The Problem with Threads. *IEEE Computer* 39(5):33-42, May 2006

[11] Milner et.al. A calculus of mobile processes. *Information and Computation*, 100.

[12] Snir et.al. *MPI: The Complete Reference*. MIT Press. ISBN 0-262-69215-5

[13] Viry. *The Ateji PX language manual*. Retrieved from http://www.ateji.com/px/1.0/manual/

[14] Viry. *The Ateji PX Matrix Multiplication White Paper*. Retrived from http://www.ateji.com/px/whitepapers/

[15] Viry. *The Ateji PX white-paper*. Retrieved from http://www.ateji.com/px/whitepapers

[16] X10 official home page. http://x10.codehaus.org/

Brief Announcement: A Nonblocking Set Optimized for Querying the Minimum Value

Yujie Liu and Michael Spear

Department of Computer Science and Engineering, Lehigh University

yul510@cse.lehigh.edu, spear@cse.lehigh.edu

Categories and Subject Descriptors

D.1.3 [**Parallel Techniques**]: Concurrent Programming—
Parallel Programming

General Terms

algorithms, experimentation, measurement, performance

Keywords

shared memory, lock-free data structures, linearizability

1. INTRODUCTION

Shared memory run-time systems, such as garbage collectors (GC) and transactional memory (TM) [2], often require global coordination. To keep costs low, designers of these systems identify a tradeoff that can prevent bottlenecks without affecting the common case, usually by optimizing the run time of one operation at the expense of other operations. The following variant is particularly interesting:

- There exists some set of states S, and a total order $<_t$ on the elements in S.
- There is a set of threads, T, and every thread $t_k \in T$ is always in exactly one state.
- $|S|$ is significantly larger than $|T|$, and multiple threads can be in the same state.
- The operation to optimize is a query that returns the minimum over all threads' states.

Among other examples, this characterization applies to recent problems encountered by Marathe et al. [5] and Koskinen et al. [4], where S is the set of possible start times for transactions in a TM system.

Our solution is inspired by the SNZI shared object [1]. The SNZI is a counter-like object, where queries indicate whether the value of the counter is zero or nonzero, but not the precise value of a nonzero counter. One of the innovations in SNZI is to represent the counter as a tree: an increment (or Arrive) operation can be initiated at any node in the tree, with a matching decrement (Depart) by the same thread initiating at the same node. In the common case, operations on a SNZI only interact with a thread-local subset of the nodes of the tree. This keeps costs low by limiting sharing of nodes among caches.

Though an unconventional characterization, we can think of the SNZI as tracking the minimum member in the set

$S = \{0, 1\}$ where $1 <_t 0$. In this setting, the logical act of incrementing the counter is equivalent to moving a thread to state 1, decrementing the counter is equivalent to moving a thread to state 0, and a SNZI query returns 1 if there exists any thread in state 1. This paper introduces the Mindicator, a tree-based datastructure optimized for the more general case where $|S|$ is large (i.e., $|S| \approx 2^{32} - 1$). A Mindicator takes $O(lg(T))$ time to register and deregister a thread's state, and $O(1)$ time to query the minimum over all thread states. The Mindicator is scalable and admits lock-free variants that are either linearizable [3] or quiesciently consistent.

2. ALGORITHM

Our lock-free Mindicator implementation is organized as a tree. In this tree, each thread is assigned a unique leaf node, and begins its `Arrive()` and `Depart()` operations at that node. `Arrive()` and `Depart()` operations propagate upward, transmitting values from children to their parents, until they reach a "turning point", after which the operations traverse downward to the leaf at which they originated. `Query()` operations access only the root node. Each leaf is read by several threads, but only modified by one thread. Mindicator nodes can have any number of children.

Figure 1 presents the lock-free Mindicator algorithm; $\infty = int\text{-}max$ is the default state, which is largest according to the $<_t$ relation. `Depart()` operations always reset a thread state to this value. The `childrenof` operator returns an empty set when applied to leaf nodes, and when X is the root node, a method invoked on `parentof(X)` will return immediately. In this simple variant, the set stored in the Mindicator can be found by reading the values of all leaf nodes. Intermediate nodes store the minimum values of their respective subtrees. The root stores the minimum value of the entire set.

The Mindicator tree is composed of Node objects, where each node contains a collection of child pointers, a parent pointer, and a 64-bit CAS object. The CAS object stores a tuple, consisting of an integer summary value (`min`), a state bit (`sta`), and a version number (`ver`). The `min` field summarizes the smallest summary value of all children of a Node. The `sta` bit indicates if that value is being propagated upward (in which case it is "tentative", not yet "steady"). The `ver` counter increments by one on every update to the Node, in order to prevent ABA problems and simplify the task of atomically summarizing the values of a node's children. All node objects are initialized to a steady value of ∞.

A `Query()` on a Node returns the `min` value of the node. Queries performed on the root of a Mindicator tree return the smallest value held in the Mindicator.

PODC'11, June 6–8, 2011, San Jose, California, USA.
ACM 978-1-4503-0719-2/11/06.

datatype NODE

sta	: $\mathbb{B}$	▷ *state bit*
min	: $\mathbb{N}$	▷ *minimum of children*
ver	: $\mathbb{N}$	▷ *version number*

initially NODE $(sta, min, ver) = (steady, \infty, 0)$

procedure $Arrive(X : \text{NODE}, n : \mathbb{N})$
```
 1: while true do
 2:     x ← Read(X)
 3:     if x.min > n or x.sta = tentative
 4:         break
 5:     if CAS(X, x, (steady, x.min, x.ver + 1))
 6:         return
 7: while true do
 8:     x ← Read(X)
 9:     if x.min ≤ n
10:         break
11:     if CAS(X, x, (tentative, n, x.ver + 1))
12:         x ← (tentative, n, x.ver + 1)
13:         break
14: if x.sta = tentative
15:     Arrive(parentof(X), n)
16:     if x.min = n
17:         CAS(X, x, (steady, n, x.ver + 1))
```

procedure $Depart(X : \text{NODE}, n : \mathbb{N})$
```
18: Revisit(X)
19: x ← Read(X)
20: if x.min < n and x.sta = steady
21:     return
22: Depart(parentof(X), n)
```

procedure $Revisit(X : \text{NODE})$
```
23: while true do
24:     x ← Read(X)
25:     min ← ∞
26:     if x.sta = tentative
27:         return
28:     for C in childrenof(X) do
29:         c ← Read(C)
30:         if c.min < min
31:             min ← c.min
32:     if min < x.min
33:         if CAS(X, x, (tentative, min, x.ver + 1))
34:             return
35:     elif CAS(X, x, (steady, min, x.ver + 1))
36:         return
```

function $Query(X : \text{NODE}) : \mathbb{N}$
```
37: return Read(X).min
```

Figure 1: The Lock-Free Mindicator Algorithm: Arrive() and Depart() should be initiated on leaves, while Query() should be executed on the root node.

Arrive() inserts a value into the set. It recursively climbs upward, starting at a leaf and ending at some "turning point." Then it regresses downward to the leaf at which it began. When climbing, the thread writes its value at nodes to lower their summary value, and marks those values as tentative. The turning point occurs either when the root is accessed, or when Arrive() reaches a node whose value is steady and $\leq$ the arriver's value. The thread then regresses, un-marking the tentative bits it marked in its climbing phase.

A Depart() begins at a leaf. It sets the leaf's min to the maximum value (e.g., ∞), and recurses upward. At each level, Depart() uses Revisit() to update a node by reading all of the node's children, and then setting the node's value to the minimum value of all children. As the operation

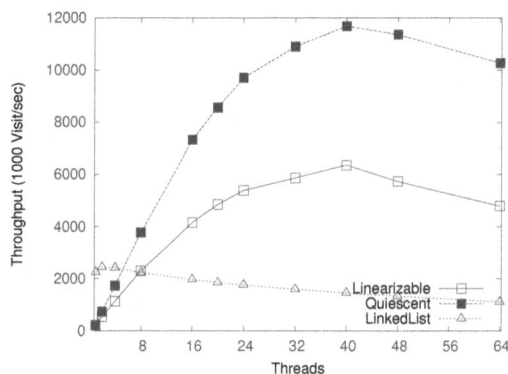

Figure 2: Preliminary Mindicator Performance.

already removed its own value from one of the children, this action serves to remove any copies of the departer's value from nodes in higher levels of the tree, but only when no peer also stores that value. A Depart() of value v propagates the removal of v until it reaches either the root, or some intermediate node that holds a steady value $v' \leq v$.

3. EVALUATION AND CONCLUSIONS

We have implemented Mindicators that are lock-based, quiescently consistent (QC), and lock-free (described above). We have also devised implementations that do not require Arrive() to begin at a leaf, and dynamically-resizing Mindicators. A proof of correctness is underway, and we have stress-tested our implementations extensively.

Figure 2 presents performance on a 64-thread Sun Niagara2 CPU. To maximize costs, all threads repeatedly Arrive() and Depart() from the Mindicator, with no Queries. Arrive() uses a random 10-bit value, instead of the monotonically increasing values expected in TM and GC workloads. Throughput is the average of five 5-second trials. We compare a locked doubly-linked list, a lock-free linearizable Mindicator, and a QC Mindicator. For all but the smallest thread counts, Mindicators outperform the list, and the QC algorithm, which is suitable for our target TM workloads, scales very well. We anticipate broad applicability of Mindicators to shared memory runtime systems, middleware, and operating systems.

4. REFERENCES
[1] F. Ellen, Y. Lev, V. Luchangco, and M. Moir. SNZI: Scalable NonZero Indicators. In *Proceedings of the Twenty-Sixth ACM Symposium on Principles of Distributed Computing*, Portland, OR, Aug. 2007.

[2] M. P. Herlihy and J. E. B. Moss. Transactional Memory: Architectural Support for Lock-Free Data Structures. In *Proceedings of the 20th International Symposium on Computer Architecture*, San Diego, CA, May 1993.

[3] M. P. Herlihy and J. M. Wing. Linearizability: a Correctness Condition for Concurrent Objects. *ACM Transactions on Programming Languages and Systems*, 12(3):463–492, 1990.

[4] E. Koskinen and M. Herlihy. Concurrent Non-commutative Boosted Transactions. In *Proceedings of the 4th ACM SIGPLAN Workshop on Transactional Computing*, Raleigh, NC, Feb. 2009.

[5] V. J. Marathe, M. F. Spear, and M. L. Scott. Scalable Techniques for Transparent Privatization in Software Transactional Memory. In *Proceedings of the 37th International Conference on Parallel Processing*, Portland, OR, Sept. 2008.

Brief Announcement: Time Bounds for Shared Objects in Partially Synchronous Systems[*]

Jiaqi Wang   Jennifer L. Welch   Hyunyoung Lee

Department of Computer Science and Engineering
Texas A&M University
E-mail: {ericaqi, welch, hlee}@cse.tamu.edu

Categories and Subject Descriptors

F.2 [**Theory of Computation**]: ANALYSIS OF ALGO-
RITHMS AND PROBLEM COMPLEXITY

General Terms

Algorithms, Theory

1. INTRODUCTION

Shared objects are a key component in today's ever growing distributed systems. Applications ranging from electronic commerce to social media on hand-held devices require shared data. Linearizability (or atomicity) is a popular and easy-to-use consistency condition for such shared
objects which gives the illusion of sequential execution of
operations. We focus on shared objects of arbitrary data
types (e.g., stacks, queues, sets, read-modify-write objects)
in addition to basic read/write registers.

These applications share data among a large number, n, of
geographically dispersed processes, which can communicate
only over a message passing system. We assume no process
failures and a reliable point-to-point message passing system. We also assume the system is partially synchronous
in that it provides bounded but uncertain message delays
and approximately synchronized clocks. More specifically,
the time for the delivery of any message between any two
processes falls in a certain range of $[d - u, d]$, where d is the
message delay upper bound and u is the message delay uncertainty. We assume that the time for local computation
is negligible compared to the message delays. The maximum clock skew between any two processes is denoted ϵ. It
has been shown that the optimal value of ϵ in this model is
$(1 - \frac{1}{n})u$ [3].

To guarantee the linearizability of an object of arbitrary
data type, a centralized mechanism can perform each operation with time at most $2d$ in the worst case, since the message from the invoking process to the control center takes
at most d and the response message also takes at most d.
Alternatively, one can use a total order broadcast primitive,
but this is not faster than the centralized scheme when taking into account the time overhead to implement the totally
ordered broadcast on top of a point-to-point message system [1]. Increasing pressure to speed up applications raises

the question whether operations can be executed faster than
$2d$.

Our goal is to find optimally fast implementations for linearizable shared objects of arbitrary data types. Inspired
by Weihl's work [5] using commutativity properties of operations for transaction processing, Kosa [2] characterized
operations by axioms on what operation sequences are legal
and proved a variety of upper and lower bounds in different
models. But there still exist gaps between the lower and
upper bounds for many commonly used data types. In this
work, we extend Kosa's approach as follows:

- We design an algorithm that uses the axiomatic properties of different operations to reduce the running time
  of each operation to below $2d$.

- We prove larger lower bounds on the time complexity of certain types of operations, by exploiting the
  message delay uncertainty and the presence of more
  processes in the system.

- As a result of the new upper and lower bounds, we have
  reduced the gap and in some cases have tight bounds.

- We also consider new classifications of operations based
  on new properties we found relevant to the lower bounds.

2. CONTRIBUTIONS

We seek tight time bounds for operations on objects of
arbitrary data type. We now describe our current work informally.

We have designed an algorithm to implement a linearizable shared object. The operations on the object are partitioned into three types: pure mutators, pure accessors, and
other operations. Informally, an *accessor* is an operation
that returns some information about the state of the object
and a *mutator* is an operation that changes the state of the
object. An operation that is an accessor but not a mutator
is a *pure* accessor, and an operation that is a mutator but
not an accessor is a *pure* mutator. Then given a parameter[1]
$X, 0 \leq X \leq d + \epsilon - u$, our algorithm guarantees that

- each operation that is a pure accessor takes at most
  $d + \epsilon - X$ time,

- each operation that is a pure mutator takes at most
  $\epsilon + X$ time, and

---

[1]The parameter value allows a tradeoff between the time for
pure mutators and the time for pure accessors and can be
set according to the relative frequency of the operations, as
in [4].

[*]Supported in part by NSF grant 0964696

- any other operation takes at most $d + \epsilon$ time.

We have the following lower bounds on the running time of operations in any algorithm:

1. Consider any operation for which there exist two instances (indicating choice of argument and return value) such that individually, each instance is legal but in sequence they are not (e.g., **read-modify-write** on a register, **dequeue** on a queue, and **pop** on a stack). Then the lower bound is $d + \min\{\epsilon, u, \frac{d}{3}\}$, which improves on the previous lower bound of d [2]. Pure mutators return no information about the object, thus instances of pure mutators are always legal, both individually and in sequence. Pure accessors do not change the state of the object, so the instances of the pure accessor should be legal in sequence as long as they are legal individually. Therefore, this type of operation cannot be a pure mutator or a pure accessor, indicating that in our algorithm it is of type "other" and takes time at most $d + \epsilon$. This bound is tight when ϵ is smaller than $\frac{d}{3}$ and smaller than u (which is the case when the clock skew has its optimal value of $(1 - \frac{1}{n})u$).

2. Consider any operation for which there exist $k \leq n$ instances such that each instance separately is legal and in any sequence they are legal, but the state of the object is different after different sequences (e.g., **write** on a register, **enqueue** on a queue, **push** on a stack, and **insert** or **delete** on a tree). Then the lower bound is $(1 - \frac{1}{k})u$, which improves on the previous lower bound of $\frac{u}{2}$ [2] when $k > 2$. One type of operations that fit this criterion are pure mutators. For these operations, our algorithm gives an upper bound of $\epsilon + X$, resulting in a tight bound when $k = n$, ϵ has its optimal value of $(1 - \frac{1}{n})u$, and $X = 0$.

3. Consider a pure mutator operation such that given a set of instances of the operation, the state of the object reflects the order in which the instances occur (e.g., **enqueue** on a queue, **push** on a stack, and **insert** or **delete** on a tree). Now consider a pure accessor operation with an instance that can detect whether or not an instance of the pure mutator occurred (e.g., **peek** on a queue, **peek** on a stack, and **find_depth** on a tree). Then the sum of the worst-case times for the pure mutator and the pure accessor (e.g., **enqueue+peek**, **push+peek**, **insert+find_depth**, and **delete+find_depth**) is at least $d + \min\{\epsilon, u, \frac{d}{3}\}$, which improves on the previous lower bound of d [2]. Our algorithm shows an upper bound on the combined time of $d + 2\epsilon$, leaving a gap of $2\epsilon - \min\{\epsilon, u, \frac{d}{3}\}$.

The lower bound on the sum of the time for a pair of operations mentioned in the third point above puts more restrictions on the pure mutator than does the corresponding result in [2], namely, it requires the state of the object to reflect the sequence in which instances of the pure mutator occurred.

Suppose this condition is dropped completely, so that the state of the object does not depend on the order in which the pure mutator instances are executed (e.g., **increment** and **decrement** on a counter, **insert** and **delete** on a set). Then the d lower bound in [2] holds for the sum of the times for the pure mutator and the pure accessor (e.g., **increment+read**

and **decrement+read** for a counter, and **insert+search** and **delete+search** for a set). We have another partially synchronous algorithm for a class of objects that includes set and counter, which shows the bound d for pure mutator+pure accessor is tight for objects in this class.

Now suppose the state of the object partially depends on the order in which the pure mutator instances are executed. For instance, given a sequence of **writes**, the state of the register depends only on which write is last, while the order of the preceding writes is irrelevant. Finding the tight time complexity on the sum of a pure mutator and a pure accessor in this case (e.g., **write+read**) is open; the d lower bound from [2] still holds, but we do not know of a partially synchronous algorithm that matches this bound.

The different time bounds resulting from the different properties of pure mutators indicate new classifications within the pure mutator group.

3. CONCLUSIONS

The contributions in this work are not limited to proving new time bounds for operations on linearizable shared objects. We also developed a new method for proving lower bounds for this problem and made new observations concerning properties of operations, which may be useful in future research.

Previous time lower bounds for partially synchronous systems have frequently used the method of "shifting" executions (e.g., [3]). The main idea is to ensure that every process in the system has the same local view in the shifted execution as in the original execution. We use a modification of the time shift method; our new method only ensures that the original and new executions are indistinguishable to certain processes during certain time intervals which are still large enough to suit our purposes. Since the guarantee is weaker, we are able to shift by larger amounts and thus prove larger lower bounds than before.

Unlike previous lower bounds which only involved operations invoked by a small number of processes (say two to four), we exploited the presence of an arbitrary number of processes to get larger lower bounds. In large-scale distributed systems, we expect there to be many processes that participate in shared object applications. Meanwhile, more concurrent operations bring forward more complicated relationships than commutativity, as well as more specific properties of operations.

4. REFERENCES

[1] H. Attiya and J.L. Welch. Sequential consistency versus linearizability. *ACM Trans. Comput. Syst.*, 12:91–122, May 1994.

[2] M.J. Kosa. Time bounds for strong and hybrid consistency for arbitrary abstract data types. *Chicago Journal of Theoretical Computer Science*, 1999.

[3] J. Lundelius and N. Lynch. An upper and lower bound for clock synchronization. *Information and Control*, 62(2-3):190–204, 1984.

[4] M. Mavronicolas and D. Roth. Linearizable read/write objects. *Theoretical Computer Science*, 220(1):267–319, June 1999.

[5] W.E. Weihl. Commutativity-based concurrency control for abstract data types. *IEEE Trans. Computers*, 37(12):1488–1505, 1988.

Brief Announcement: The Inherent Difficulty of Timely Primary-Backup Replication

Pramod Koppol
Bell Labs, Alcatel-Lucent
Murray Hill, NJ, USA
pramod.koppol@alcatel-lucent.com

Kedar S. Namjoshi
Bell Labs, Alcatel-Lucent
Murray Hill, NJ, USA
kedar@research.bell-labs.com

Thanos Stathopoulos
Bell Labs, Alcatel-Lucent
Murray Hill, NJ, USA
thanos.stathopoulos@alcatel-lucent.com

Gordon T. Wilfong
Bell Labs, Alcatel-Lucent
Murray Hill, NJ, USA
gtw@research.bell-labs.com

ABSTRACT

We show that existing methods for primary-backup replication may disrupt the timing behavior of an underlying service to the extent of making it unusable. We prove that the problem is inherent to the primary-backup model.

Categories and Subject Descriptors

D.4.5 [**Operating Systems**]: Reliability—*Fault-tolerance*

General Terms

Theory, Reliability

Keywords

Primary-backup, replication, fault-tolerance, knowledge

1. INTRODUCTION

The advent of cloud computing, with its remote compute and data centers, is changing the way in which computing services are offered. We are interested in the question of whether *telecommunications* services can be offered in a cloud environment. These services differ from the ones hosted currently on cloud platforms in that they have rather strict requirements on delay and jitter. The requirements may be regulatory, or imposed by human perception; large values for delay, jitter, or packet loss can seriously degrade audio quality in a phone conversation. In addition, such services are expected to be highly reliable.

Traditionally, telecommunications services have been protected against faults using special hardware, which also allows the software to meet timing constraints [9]. The environment offered by compute centers is quite different: hardware is standardized, a shared broadcast medium is generally not available, and communication and computation failures may be frequent [4]. This model is akin to that of a distributed computing system.

A natural and important question, therefore, is whether time-sensitive services can be run reliably under a distributed computing model, while also preserving timing constraints. We examine methods for fault tolerance which are based on primary-backup replication. We show that known methods can give rise to large jitter and unbounded delays under high load, *even under failure-free operation*. We further prove that *any* primary-backup method operating under this model must have similar impediments; these result from an unavoidable synchronization between primary and backup. The proof is based on a theorem of Chandy and Misra [2], which connects increases in process knowledge to the existence of causal chains of messages.

The most closely related work which we are aware of is an analysis of the effect of primary-backup synchronization on real-time scheduling [10]. That paper accounts for delays caused by primary-backup synchronization by adjusting the admission policy for real-time tasks, allowing fewer tasks to be admitted, which effectively reduces throughput. The real-time task model is different from our setting, which is the processing of message streams.

A paper by Budhiraja et al. [1] gives upper and lower bounds on the blocking time of primary-backup protocols. The system models considered there, however, are different from ours in crucial respects. In the most closely related crash+link model, a transmission failure is counted against the failure budget—i.e., a protocol with a budget of $f = 1$ failures trivially meets its specification after failures on two links—whereas we consider transmission failure to be normal. Therefore, the non-blocking protocol given in [1] for crash+link failures does not apply, as message acknowledgments are necessary in our model.

2. LIMITATIONS OF KNOWN METHODS

A primary-backup protocol allows the state of a server, which can be thought of as a state machine, to be recovered after a failure of the machine on which the server is executed. We consider protection for a single crash failure. In *active replication* [6, 8], all replicas receive the same messages in the same order. This suffices for fault-tolerance if message processing is deterministic. In *passive replication*, a checkpoint of the server state is taken periodically; after a primary failure, recovery proceeds with the backup server starting from the latest checkpoint state.

In both approaches, the root cause of timing disruptions is the synchronization between primary and backup. We examine more closely the source of the disruptions arising in Remus [3], which is a representative implementation of passive replication. An analysis of active replication results in similar conclusions. The essence of the Remus synchronization is as follows.

1. Primary and backup are synchronized at the start of an *epoch* (the period between checkpoints)

2. Primary receives and processes a sequence of input messages; generated output messages are buffered (Releasing output messages immediately can cause the environment and the backup to have inconsistent views of the primary state after a primary failure.)

3. Primary sends its current state to the backup and waits for an acknowledgment

4. Primary receives acknowledgment from backup; synchronization is complete

5. Primary sends the buffered output to the environment

Let T represent the round-trip time from the primary to the backup. Suppose that, without any synchronization, the primary is able to process input arriving at a constant rate $r > 1/T$. At rate r, at least one message arrives during synchronization (steps 3,4). As the primary is suspended at step 3, these messages must be processed in the next epoch (after step 4). If there is insufficient slack time during that epoch, some messages remain unprocessed. Repeating this sequence of events, unprocessed messages must accumulate beyond bound in input buffers, which results in an unbounded delay in processing input messages.

A possible resolution is to drop some input messages, but that may result in a service failure (e.g., for voice packets) or in lowered throughput. Moreover, releasing output all at once (step 5) can cause bursty traffic. In an experiment with Remus on a single audio stream, we observed that burstiness (caused by step 5) and delay due to checkpointing can seriously degrade audio quality. The processor was lightly loaded, so we did not observe an input queue buildup.

3. FORMAL ANALYSIS

We show that timing disruptions are inevitable for any primary-backup mechanism. The central claim is stated in the following theorem. The computing model is that of asynchronous computation, crash failures, and message-passing communication over (normally) lossy channels.

THEOREM 1. *For any generic primary-backup mechanism there exists a service and an environment for which timing disruption is inevitable during fault-free operation.*

A proof of this theorem is in [5]; we give a sketch of the key argument. The main difficulty for the proof is that it must quantify over *all* correct primary-backup mechanisms. This is done through an analysis of the *states of knowledge* of the relevant parties: the environment (E), the primary (P), the backup (B) and the service (S). Knowledge is represented by an assertion, "M *knows* b", which holds for

a process M and predicate b at a computation x if b holds at *all* computations y which agree with x on the history of events for M.

A key invariant is the following: for any computation x, and a predicate b on the state of S, if E knows b at x, then E *knows* (P *knows* (B *knows* b)) at x. From this, we show that any increase of knowledge by E (precisely, if $\neg b$ holds at x, and E *knows* b holds at an extension y of x) requires a causal chain of messages going through the processes in the order P; B; P; E in the interval (x, y). This follows from a beautiful theorem of Chandy and Misra [2] which connects knowledge gain to the existence of causal chains. The chain P; B; P is a round-trip synchronization between primary and backup, which must occur before a message to E increases its knowledge.

We choose a particular E and S with a computation which can be partitioned into infinitely many disjoint intervals, in each of which E gains new knowledge. By the previous result, a synchronizing process chain is required for each of those intervals. That induces the behavior analyzed in the previous section; hence, timing disruption is inevitable.

4. SUMMARY AND ONGOING WORK

We show that any primary-backup mechanism operating in a distributed environment must disrupt timing, even in the absence of faults. This holds for both active and passive replication strategies. We conjecture that some form of timing disruption is inevitable for all generic fault-tolerance mechanisms. If this conjecture holds, it may be necessary to create protection mechanisms which are specialized to each service and to the characteristics of its media traffic.

5. REFERENCES

[1] N. Budhiraja, K. Marzullo, F. B. Schneider, and S. Toueg. The Primary-Backup Approach. In Mullender [7].

[2] K. M. Chandy and J. Misra. How processes learn. *Distributed Computing*, 1(1):40–52, 1986.

[3] B. Cully, G. Lefebvre, D. T. Meyer, M. Feeley, N. C. Hutchinson, and A. Warfield. Remus: High availability via asynchronous virtual machine replication. In *NSDI*. USENIX, 2008.

[4] J. Dean. Software engineering advice from building large-scale distributed systems. http://research.google.com/people/jeff, 2007.

[5] P. Koppol, K. S. Namjoshi, T. Stathopoulos, and G. T. Wilfong. The Inherent Difficulty of Timely Primary-Backup Replication. Technical report, Bell Labs, 2011.

[6] L. Lamport. Time, clocks, and the ordering of events in a distributed system. *Commun. ACM*, 21(7):558–565, 1978.

[7] S. Mullender, editor. *Distributed Systems (Second Edition)*. Addison-Wesley, 1993.

[8] F. B. Schneider. Replication Management using the State-Machine Approach. In Mullender [7].

[9] D. P. Siewiorek and R. S. Swarz. *Reliable Computer Systems (Second Edition)*, chapter High Availability Systems. Digital Press, 1992.

[10] H. Zou and F. Jahanian. A real-time primary-backup replication service. *IEEE Trans. Parallel Distrib. Syst.*, 10(6):533–548, 1999.

Brief Announcement: Randomized Compact Routing in Decomposable Metrics

Goran Konjevod
Lawrence Livermore National
Laboratory, CA, USA
konjevod1@llnl.gov

Andréa W. Richa[*]
Arizona State University
Tempe, AZ, USA
aricha@asu.edu

Donglin Xia
Microsoft
Redmond, WA, USA
doxia@microsoft.com

Ling Zhou
Microsoft
Redmond, WA, USA
lizho@microsoft.com

ABSTRACT

We study the compact routing problem in networks whose shortest path metrics are decomposable. Decomposable metrics are more general than doubling metrics, growth-bounded metrics, and metrics induced by graphs excluding $K_{r,r}$ as a minor. In this work, we present both name-dependent and name-independent constant stretch compact routing schemes for bounded decomposable metrics with polylogarithmic storage requirements at each node and polylogarithmic packet headers. Our work is the first to design compact routing schemes with constant stretch for networks as general as decomposable metrics.

Categories and Subject Descriptors

C.2.2 [**Computer Communication Networks**]: Network Protocols - Routing protocols; E.1 [**Data Structures**]: Distributed data structures; F.2.2 [**Analysis of Algorithms and Problem Complexity**]: Nonnumerical Algorithms and Problems - Computations on discrete structures, Routing and Layout; G.2.2 [**Discrete Mathematics**]: Graph Theory - Graph algorithms, Graph labeling, Network problems

General Terms

Algorithms, Design

1. INTRODUCTION

Decomposable metrics have been used as a fundamental tool in the design of randomized algorithms on metric spaces in recent years. An *r-bounded δ-padded decomposition* of a metric (X, d) is a distribution over X's partitions such that (i) for each random-generated partition, all of its clusters have radius no more than r; and (ii) the probability that the distance from any node $x \in X$ to the "boundary" of the partition is no less than δr is no less than $1/2$. We say a

---
[*]This work was supported in part by NSF awards CCF-0830791 and CCF-0830704.

metric (X, d) is *α-decomposable*, if for all $r > 0$ there exists an r-bounded $1/\alpha$-padded decomposition.

A routing scheme is a distributed algorithm that deliver packets from any source to any destination node. Making the routing storage requirment scalable with the network size while minimizing the routing stretch is one of the fundamental trade-offs for routing scheme design, where the *stretch* is the maximum ratio of the routing path length to the shortest path length over all source destination pairs. We say a routing scheme is compact if its storage requirement at each node and for each packet header is polylogarithmic on the number of nodes. There are two variants of routing scheme design: (i) name-dependent (or labeled) routing and (ii) name-independent routing. Labeled routing allows the scheme designer to label the nodes with additional routing information. In name-independent routing, the scheme must use solely the (arbitrary) original naming.

In this paper, we present both labeled (name-dependent) and name-independent compact routing with polylogarithmic storage and constant stretch for networks with bounded decomposable metrics. Compact routing has been studied in various networks, such as growth-bounded networks [3], power-law networks [4], and doubling metrics [1, 9, 10]. It is known [7, 11] that a bound on the doubling dimension implies a bound on the padded decomposability. In [8, 12, 5], it is shown that every metric space X induced by an edge-weighted graph excluding $K_{r,r}$ as a minor is $O(r^2)$-decomposable. To the best of our knowledge, our work is the to provide randomized schemes for compact routing with constant stretch in networks as general as bounded decomposable metrics.

2. RANDOMIZED COMPACT ROUTING SCHEMES

Given an edge-weighted n-node Δ-diameter graph $G = (V, E)$ whose shortest path metric is α-decomposable, we present (i) a 4α-stretch labeled routing scheme w.h.p.[1] with $O(\log \Delta \log^3 n / \log \log n)$-bit routing labels, $O(\log^2 n / \log \log n)$-bit packet headers, and $O(\log \Delta \log^3 n / \log \log n)$-bit routing tables of size; and (ii) a 22α-stretch name-independent rout-

---
[1]With high probability, i.e., with probability at least $1 - 1/n^c$, where $c > 0$ is a constant.

ing scheme w.h.p. with $O(\log \Delta \log^5 n/(\log\log n)^2)$-bit routing labels, and $o(\log^2 n)$)-bit packet headers.

Since G is α-decomposable, there are a bundle of 2^i-bounded $1/\alpha$-padded decompositions, $\forall i \in [\log(\alpha\Delta)]$ [2]. For each $i \in [\log\alpha\Delta]$, we randomly pick up $\log n$ partitions from the 2^i-bounded $1/\alpha$-padded decomposition. The key observation is that, for any source-destination pair (u,v) with $d(u,v) \leq 2^i/\alpha$, the probability that u and v are contained in the same cluster for one of the $\log n$ random 2^i-bounded partitions is no less than $1-(1/2)^{\log n} = 1-1/n$. Thus with the help of local compact routing schemes at each cluster at each level, searching for the destination from lower to higher levels $i \in [\log\alpha\Delta]$ could result in constant stretch (depending on α) with high probability. In the following, we build upon this idea in our labeled and name-independent routing schemes.

2.1 Labeled Routing Scheme

Each cluster of all the $\log n$ random 2^i-bounded partitions, for each $i \in [\log\alpha\Delta]$, maintains a labeled routing scheme as in the following lemma on the shortest path tree of the cluster with its center as the root.

Lemma 2.1 ([6]) *For every weighted tree T on n nodes, there exists a labeled routing scheme that, given any destination label, routes optimally on T from any source to the destination. The storage per node, the label size, and header size are $O(\log^2 n/\log\log n)$ bits.*

The label of a node consists of its local routing labels given by Lemma 2.1 for all clusters containing the node over all partitions and all levels. Thus it has $O(\log \Delta \log^3 n/\log\log n)$ bits. Similarly, the total size of the routing table at each node is also $O(\log \Delta \log^3 n/\log\log n)$ bits.

The routing algorithm from u to v, $\forall u, v \in V$, is described as follows. Node u identifies the minimal $i \in [\log(\alpha\Delta)]$ such that u and v have the local labels from the same cluster of one of the $\log n$ random partitions P at level i. Then u uses the local tree labeled routing scheme on P to route to v by the local label of v.

Stretch Analysis.
W.l.o.g.[3], assume that $2^{i-1}/\alpha < d(u,v) \leq 2^i/\alpha$. Thus with probability $(1-1/n)$, nodes u and v are in the same cluster of one of the $\log n$ partition, i.e. node u could route the message to v with cost 2^{i+1}. Therefore, by $2^{i-1}/\alpha < d(u,v)$, we have that the routing stretch is at most 4α w.h.p..

2.2 Name-independent Routing Scheme

Each cluster of all the $\log n$ random 2^i-bounded partitions, for each $i \in [\log\alpha\Delta]$, maintains a name-independent tree routing scheme as in the following lemma on the shortest path tree of the cluster with its center as the root.

Lemma 2.2 ([2]) *Every weighted rooted tree with n nodes has a single-source name-independent routing scheme (in the designer port model) such that the distance traveled between the root r and a destination v is at most $d(r,v) + 2d(T)$, where $d(T)$ is the height of the tree, and the error-report to the root costs at most $4d(T)$ if the destination is not in the*

tree. *Moreover, only $O(\log^4 n/(\log\log n)^2)$ bits are needed per node and headers have size $o(\log^2 n)$.*

Since we pick up $\log n$ partitions, $\forall i \in [\log(\alpha\Delta)]$, the routing table at each node has size $O(\log \Delta \log^5 n/(\log\log n)^2)$ bits.

We now present the name-independent routing algorithm from any source node u to any destination v. For i from 0 to $\log(\alpha\Delta)$, node u repeatedly searches for the destination v using the single source name-indepement routing algorithm at the cluster containing u of one of the $\log n$ partitions at level i such that u is $2^i/\alpha$-padded in the partition, where the probability that such partition exists is $1 - 1/n$.

Stretch Analysis.
Note that for each iteration i, the cost of an error report is $d(u,c) + 4d(T) + d(c,u) \leq 6 \cdot 2^i$, where c is the center of the cluster with u and T is the shortest path tree rooted at c and spanning the cluster. For the last iteration where the destination is reached, the cost is $d(u,c) + 2d(c,v) + 2d(T) \leq 5 \cdot 2^i$. W.l.o.g., we assume that $2^{i-1}/\alpha < d(u,v) \leq 2^i/\alpha$. Thus with probability $(1-1/n)$, the routing cost is at most $\sum_{j=0}^{i-1} 6 \cdot 2^j + 5 \cdot 2^i < 11 \cdot 2^i$. Therefore, $2^{i-1}/\alpha < d(u,v)$, and thus the routing stretch is at most 22α w.h.p.

3. REFERENCES

[1] I. Abraham, C. Gavoille, A. V. Goldberg, and D. Malkhi. Routing in networks with low doubling dimension. In *Proc. 26th ICDCS*, page 75, 2006.

[2] I. Abraham, C. Gavoille, and D. Malkhi. Routing with improved communication-space trade-off. In *Proc. 18th DISC*, pages 305–319, 2004.

[3] I. Abraham and D. Malkhi. Name independent routing for growth bounded networks. In *Proc. 17th SPAA*, pages 49–55, 2005.

[4] W. Chen, C. Sommer, S.-H. Teng, and Y. Wang. Compact routing in power-law graphs. In *Proc. 23rd DISC*, pages 379–391, 2009.

[5] J. Fakcheroenphol and K. Talwar. An improved decomposition theorem for graphs excluding a fixed minor. In *APPROX*, pages 36–46, 2003.

[6] P. Fraigniaud and C. Gavoille. Routing in trees. In *Proc. 28th ICALP*, pages 757–772, 2001.

[7] A. Gupta, R. Krauthgamer, and J. R. Lee. Bounded geometries, fractals and low-distortion embeddings. In *Proc. 44th FOCS*, pages 534–543, 2003.

[8] P. Klein, S. A. Plotkin, and S. Rao. Excluded minors, network decomposition, and multicommodity flow. In *Proc. 25th STOC*, pages 682–690, 1993.

[9] G. Konjevod, A. W. Richa, and D. Xia. Optimal-stretch name-independent compact routing in doubling metrics. In *Proc. 25th PODC*, pages 198–207, 2006.

[10] G. Konjevod, A. W. Richa, and D. Xia. Optimal scale-free compact routing schemes in networks of low doubling dimension. In *Proc. 18th SODA*, pages 939–948, 2007.

[11] R. Krauthgamer, J. R. Lee, M. Mendel, and A. Naor. Measured descent: A new embedding method for finite metrics. In *Proc. 45th FOCS*, pages 434–443, 2004.

[12] S. Rao. Small distortion and volume preserving embeddings for planar and euclidean metrics. In *Proc. 15th SCG*, pages 300–306, 1999.

---

[2]For any integer $x > 0$, let $[x]$ denote the set $\{0, 1, \cdots, x-1\}$.
[3]Without loss of generality.

Brief Announcement: Partial Reversal Acyclicity *

Tsvetomira Radeva
MIT, Cambridge, MA
radeva@csail.mit.edu

Nancy Lynch
MIT, Cambridge, MA
lynch@csail.mit.edu

ABSTRACT

Partial Reversal (PR) is a link reversal algorithm which ensures that an initially directed acyclic graph (DAG) is eventually a destination-oriented DAG. While proofs exist to establish the acyclicity property of PR, they rely on assigning labels to either the nodes or the edges in the graph. In this work we show that such labeling is not necessary and outline a simpler direct proof of the acyclicity property.

Categories and Subject Descriptors

G.2 [**Discrete Mathematics**]: Graph Theory—*Graph algorithms*

General Terms

Algorithms, Theory

Keywords

Partial Reversal, Link Reversal, Graph Algorithms

1. INTRODUCTION

Link reversal algorithms were first introduced in [1] to provide an efficient graph structure for routing. The main goal of link reversal algorithms is to ensure that all the nodes in a directed acyclic graph (DAG) have paths to a destination node or nodes. These algorithms can also be used to solve problems such as leader election and mutual exclusion [4].

This work focuses on a specific link reversal algorithm: *partial reversal* (PR). In PR the initial graph is a DAG with a single destination node; however, some nodes may not have paths to the destination D. The goal is to ensure that all nodes have paths to D. In PR only the nodes, except for D, that become sinks (all their incident edges are incoming) take steps. Each node u maintains a list of the edges reversed by its neighbors since the last time u took a step. When u becomes a sink, it reverses only the edges which are *not* in the list, and then clears the list.

A key property of PR is that it does not create cycles in the graph. This has been proved in [1] and [4]. The proof in [1] assigns to each node an integer 3-tuple such that each edge is directed from a node with a lexicographically larger value of the 3-tuple to a node with a smaller value. The proof establishes the existence of such an assignment

*This work is supported in part by an Akamai Presidential Fellowship, AFOSR FA9550-08-1-0159, and NSF CCF-0726514. A full version of this paper is available in [3].

forming a total order on the nodes. Consequently, no cycles exist in the graph. In [4], PR is described as a special case of the Binary Link Labels (BLL) algorithm, which uses an assignment of binary labels to edges. The proof of acyclicity of PR in [4] follows from a specific such assignment.

Here, we outline a novel proof of the acyclicity property of PR that is agnostic to node and edge labels. First, we introduce a simpler version of PR and prove its acyclicity property without recourse to external or dynamic labeling. Next, we provide a simulation relation from the original algorithm to the new one, and consequently, our new acyclicity proof also applies to the original PR algorithm.

2. ORIGINAL ALGORITHM

We model the system as an undirected graph $G = (V, E)$ with a set of nodes V and a set of edges E. For each node u, $nbrs_u$ is the set of neighbors of u in G. Consider a directed version of G, denoted $G' = (V, E')$, such that for a given edge $\{u, v\} \in E$ either $(u, v) \in E'$ or $(v, u) \in E'$, but not both. Let G'_{init} be one such G' corresponding to the initial state. Let $in\text{-}nbrs_u$ and $out\text{-}nbrs_u$ be the sets of nodes corresponding to incoming and outgoing edges of a node u in G'_{init}. Note that the sets $in\text{-}nbrs_u$ and $out\text{-}nbrs_u$ are static and remain unchanged.

Next, we present the original PR algorithm [1], and express it as an I/O automaton (PR) (as described in [2]) with a single set of actions – $reverse(S)$. The set S represents all the nodes that are taking a step together. PR has a variable $list[u]$, for each node u, which consists of all neighbors of u that took a step since the last time u took a step. Additionally, PR has a $dir[u, v]$ variable for each ordered pair (u, v), which represents the direction of the edge between u and v.

Algorithm 1 PR automaton

Signature: $reverse(S)$, $S \subseteq V \setminus \{D\}$, $S \neq \emptyset$
States: for each u, v where $\{u, v\} \in E$:
  $dir[u, v] \in \{in, out\}$, initially in if $v \in in\text{-}nbrs_u$, else out
  $dir[v, u] \in \{in, out\}$, initially in if $u \in in\text{-}nbrs_v$, else out
for each u, $list[u]$, a set of nodes $W \subseteq nbrs_u$, initially empty
Transitions: $reverse(S)$
Precond: for each $u \in S$, for each $v \in nbrs_u$, $dir[u, v] = in$
Effect: for each $u \in S$
  if $list[u] \neq nbrs_u$ then for each $v \in nbrs_u \setminus list[u]$:
    $dir[u, v] := out$; $dir[v, u] := in$; $list[v] := list[v] \cup \{u\}$
  else for each $v \in nbrs_u$:
    $dir[u, v] := out$; $dir[v, u] := in$; $list[v] := list[v] \cup \{u\}$
  $list[u] := \emptyset$
Tasks: $\{reverse(S), S \subseteq V \setminus \{D\}, S \neq \emptyset\}$

The precondition for the $reverse(S)$ action is that all nodes in S are sinks. The effect of the reversal is that the edge between u and each neighbor of u *not* in $list[u]$ is reversed. However, if $list[u]$ contains all neighbors of u, then the edges to all neighbors are reversed. Also, each neighbor v of u that has its edge to u reversed, adds u to $list[v]$. Finally, after reversing the particular edges, u empties $list[u]$. The following corollaries establish the possible contents of $list[u]$ for any node u.

COROLLARY 1. *In all reachable states, for each node u, $list[u] \subseteq in\text{-}nbrs_u$ or $list[u] \subseteq out\text{-}nbrs_u$.*

COROLLARY 2. *In all reachable states, if u is a sink, then $list[u] = in\text{-}nbrs_u$ or $list[u] = out\text{-}nbrs_u$.*

3. NEW ALGORITHM

In *NewPR*, nodes use only the initial *in-nbrs* and *out-nbrs* sets to determine which edges to reverse in each step. Whenever a node is a sink, it reverses either its *in-nbrs* or *out-nbrs* set, alternating between the two. A history variable $count[u]$ keeps track of the number of steps u has taken so far, and a derived variable $parity[u]$ represents the parity of $count[u]$. The precondition for a node u to perform a $reverse(u)$ action is that it is a sink. The effect of the reversal is that, depending on the value of $parity[u]$, either the edges corresponding to $in\text{-}nbrs_u$ or $out\text{-}nbrs_u$ are reversed. Also, $count[u]$ is incremented.

Algorithm 2 *NewPR* automaton

Signature: $reverse(u)$, $u \in V$, $u \neq D$
States: for each u, v where $\{u, v\} \in E$:
  $dir[u, v] \in \{in, out\}$, initially in if $v \in in\text{-}nbrs_u$, else out
  $dir[v, u] \in \{in, out\}$, initially in if $u \in in\text{-}nbrs_v$, else out
for each node u, $count[u]$, integer, initially 0
Derived: for each node u, $parity[u] \in \{even, odd\}$,
  $even$ if $count[u]$ is even; else odd
Transitions: $reverse(u)$
Precond: for each $v \in nbrs_u$, $dir[u, v] = in$
Effect: if $parity[u] = even$ then
  for each $v \in in\text{-}nbrs_u$: $dir[u, v] := out$; $dir[v, u] := in$
else
  for each $v \in out\text{-}nbrs_u$: $dir[u, v] := out$; $dir[v, u] := in$
$count[u] := count[u] + 1$
Tasks: $\{reverse(u), u \in V, u \neq D\}$

Note that it is possible that a node u does not reverse any edges because either $in\text{-}nbrs_u = \emptyset$ or $out\text{-}nbrs_u = \emptyset$. This case occurs only if u is initially a sink or a source. When such an action is performed, u increments its step counter without reversing any edges. Therefore, u remains a sink but now the parity has the correct value, so u can reverse its incident edges in the next step.

A main difference between the two algorithms is that while PR keeps a dynamic list of nodes, $NewPR$ maintains two static lists of nodes to determine the edges to be reversed. The description of the algorithm in $NewPR$ is simpler and makes the algorithm easier to understand.

Since the input to the PR algorithm is a DAG, we can embed it in a plane, ensuring all edges are initially directed from left to right. Therefore, for each node u all nodes in $in\text{-}nbrs_u$ are to the left of u, and all nodes in $out\text{-}nbrs_u$ are to the right of u. The following invariants establish some properties of $NewPR$, and are combined into the main theorem concluding that PR maintains acyclicity.

INVARIANT 1. *In any reachable state, if u and v are neighbors, then:*
(a) *If $parity[u] = parity[v] = even$, then the edge $\{u, v\}$ is directed from left to right.*
(b) *If $parity[u] = parity[v] = odd$, then the edge $\{u, v\}$ is directed from right to left.*

INVARIANT 2. *In any reachable state, if u and v are neighbors, then:*
(a) *If $count[u] = n$, then $count[v] \in \{n - 1, n, n + 1\}$.*
(b) *If $count[u] = n$, where n is odd, and v is to the right of u, then $count[v] = n$.*
(c) *If $count[u] = n$, where n is even, and v is to the left of u, then $count[v] = n$.*
(d) *If $count[u] > count[v]$, then the edge $\{u, v\}$ is directed from u to v.*

THEOREM 1. *PR maintains acyclicity.*

PROOF. Suppose in contradiction that there exists a cycle in some reachable state s of the system. Therefore, there is a sequence of nodes: $u, v_1, \ldots, v_n, u$ such that the edges between these nodes are directed from u to v_1, from v_i to v_{i+1} for all $1 \leq i < n$, and from v_n to u. By Invariant 2 (d) the number of steps of the nodes in the sequence is non-increasing, and because the nodes form a cycle, $s.count[u] = s.count[v_1] = \ldots = s.count[v_n]$. Let v_{i-1}, v_i, v_{i+1} be a sequence on nodes where v_i is the rightmost node in the cycle. Assume the edge $\{v_{i-1}, v_i\}$ is directed from left to right, and the edge $\{v_i, v_{i+1}\}$ is directed from right to left. Since, $s.count[v_{i-1}] = s.count[v_i] = s.count[v_{i+1}]$, $s.parity[v_{i-1}] = s.parity[v_i] = s.parity[v_{i+1}] = p$. By Invariant 1 (b) applied to v_{i-1} and v_i, $p = even$. By Invariant 1 (a) applied to v_i and v_{i+1}, $p = odd$, a contradiction. $\square$

4. SIMULATION RELATION

We define a simulation relation R from states of PR to states of $NewPR$ which guarantees that the two algorithms preserve the same edge directions. Let s be a state of PR and t be a state of $NewPR$. We define $(s, t) \in R$ if:

1. $t.G' = s.G'$
2. For each u, if $t.parity[u] = even$, then $s.list[u] \subseteq out\text{-}nbrs_u$; else $s.list[u] \subseteq in\text{-}nbrs_u$.

THEOREM 2. *For each reachable state s of PR there exists a reachable state t of $NewPR$ such that $(s, t) \in R$.*

COROLLARY 3. *PR maintains acyclicity.*

The proof follows from Theorem 1, Theorem 2, and the fact that by part 1 of the simulation relation both algorithms produce the same directed versions of the graph.

5. REFERENCES

[1] E. Gafni and D. Bertsekas. Distributed algorithms for generating loop-free routes in networks with frequently changing topology. *IEEE Trans. on Comm.*, C-29(1):11–18, 1981.
[2] N. Lynch. *Distributed Algorithms*. Morgan Kaufmann Publishers, San Mateo, CA, 1996.
[3] T. Radeva and N. Lynch. Partial reversal acyclicity. Technical Report MIT-CSAIL-TR-2011-xxx, MIT CSAIL, Cambridge, MA.
[4] J. Welch and J. Walter. Link reversal algorithms. In *Synthesis Lectures on Distributed Computing Theory*. Morgan Claypool, (to appear).

Tight Bounds on Information Dissemination in Sparse Mobile Networks*

Alberto Pettarin
Department of Information
Engineering
University of Padova
Padova, 35131, Italy
pettarin@dei.unipd.it

Andrea Pietracaprina
Department of Information
Engineering
University of Padova
Padova, 35131, Italy
capri@dei.unipd.it

Geppino Pucci
Department of Information
Engineering
University of Padova
Padova, 35131, Italy
geppo@dei.unipd.it

Eli Upfal
Department of Computer
Science
Brown University
Providence, RI 02912, USA
eli@cs.brown.edu

ABSTRACT

Motivated by the growing interest in mobile systems, we study the dynamics of information dissemination between agents moving independently on a plane. Formally, we consider k mobile agents performing independent random walks on an n-node grid. At time 0, each agent is located at a random node of the grid and one agent has a rumor. The spread of the rumor is governed by a dynamic communication graph process $\{G_t(r) \mid t \geq 0\}$, where two agents are connected by an edge in $G_t(r)$ iff their distance at time t is within their transmission radius r. Modeling the physical reality that the speed of radio transmission is much faster than the motion of the agents, we assume that the rumor can travel throughout a connected component of G_t before the graph is altered by the motion. We study the *broadcast time* T_B of the system, which is the time it takes for all agents to know the rumor. We focus on the sparse case (below the percolation point $r_c \approx \sqrt{n/k}$) where, with high probability, no connected component in G_t has more than a logarithmic number of agents and the broadcast time is dominated by the time it takes for many independent random walks to meet one other. Quite surprisingly, we show that for a system below the percolation point, the broadcast time does not depend on the transmission radius. In fact,
we prove that $T_B = \tilde{\Theta}\left(n/\sqrt{k}\right)$ for any $0 \leq r < r_c$, even when the transmission range is significantly larger than the mobility range in one step, giving a tight characterization up to logarithmic factors. Our result complements a recent result of Peres et al. (SODA 2011) who showed that above the percolation point the broadcast time is polylogarithmic in k.

Categories and Subject Descriptors

G.3 [**Probability and Statistics**]: Probabilistic algorithms; F.2.m [**Analysis of Algorithms and Problem Complexity**]: Miscellaneous; G.2.2 [**Discrete Mathematics**]: Graph Theory—*network problems*

General Terms

Algorithms, Theory

Keywords

Information Dissemination, Mobile Networks, Multiple Random Walks, Broadcast

1. INTRODUCTION

The emergence of mobile computing devices has added a new intriguing component, *mobility*, to the study of distributed systems. In fully mobile systems, such as wireless mobile ad-hoc networks (MANETs), information is generated, transmitted and consumed within the mobile nodes, and communication is carried out without the support of static structures such as cell towers. These systems have been implemented in vehicular networks and sensor networks attached to soldiers on a battlefield or animals in a nature reserve [23, 14, 17, 26]. Characterizing the power and limitations of mobile networks requires new models and analytical tools that address the unique properties of these systems [15, 8], which include:

- *Small transmission radius*: the transmission range of individual agents is restricted by limitations on energy consumption and interference from other agents;

*Support for the first three authors was provided, in part, by MIUR of Italy under project AlgoDEEP, and by the University of Padova under the Strategic Project STPD08JA32 and Project CPDA099949/09. This work was done while the first author was visiting the Department of Computer Science of Brown University, partially supported by "Fondazione Ing. Aldo Gini", Padova, Italy.

- *Planarity*: agents reside, move and transmit on (subsets of) a plane. Low diameter graphs that are often used to model static communication networks are not useful here;

- *Dynamic communication graphs*: communication channels between agents are changing dynamically as mobile agents move in and out of the transmission radius of other agents;

- *Relative speeds*: transmission speed is significantly faster than the physical movement of the agents. A message can execute several hops before the network is altered by motion.

In this work we study the dynamics of information dissemination between agents moving independently on a plane. We consider a system of k mobile agents performing independent random walks on an n-node grid, starting at time 0 in a uniform distribution over the grid nodes. We focus on the fundamental communication primitive of broadcasting a rumor originating at one arbitrary agent to all other agents in the system. We characterize the *broadcast time* T_B of the system, which is the time it takes for all agents to receive the rumor.

We model the spreading of information in a mobile system by a dynamic communication graph process $\{G_t(r) \mid t \geq 0\}$, where the nodes of $G_t(r)$ are the mobile agents, and two agents are connected by an edge iff their distance at time t is within their transmission radius r. We are interested in *sparse systems* in which the transmission radius is below the percolation point $r_c \approx \sqrt{n/k}$ (i.e., the minimum radius which guarantees that $G_t(r_c)$ features a giant connected component), and where, with high probability, no connected component of $G_t(r_c)$ has more than a logarithmic number of agents [24, 25]. The broadcast time in sparse systems is dominated by the time it takes for many independent random walks to meet one another. Incorporating the fact that radio transmission is much faster than the motion of the agents, we assume that the rumor can travel throughout a connected component of G_t within one step, before the graph is altered by the motion.

Our main result is quite surprising: we show that below the percolation point the broadcast time does not depend on the transmission radius. We prove that $T_B = \tilde{\Theta}\left(n/\sqrt{k}\right)$ for any r below r_c, giving a tight characterization up to logarithmic factors[1]. Our bound holds both when the transmission radius is significantly larger than the mobility range (i.e., the distance an agent can travel in one step), and when, in contrast to previous work [7, 8], the transmission radius as well as the the mobility range are very small. Our work complements a recent result by Peres et al. [25] who proved an upper bound polylogarithmic in k for the broadcast time in a system of k mobile agents which follow independent Brownian motions in $\mathbb{R}^d$, with transmission radius above the percolation point.

Our analysis techniques are applicable to a number of interesting related problems such as covering the grid with many random walks and bounding the extinction time in random predator-prey systems.

---

[1]The tilde notation hides polylogarithmic factors, e.g. $\tilde{O}(f(n)) = O(f(n) \log^c n)$ for some constant c.

1.1 Related Work

Information dissemination has been extensively studied in the literature under a variety of scenarios and objectives. Here we restrict our attention to the results more directly related to our work.

A prolific line of research has addressed broadcasting and gossiping in static graphs, where the nodes of the graph represent active entities which exchange messages along incident edges according to specific protocols (e.g., *push*, *pull*, *push-pull*). The most recent results in this area relate the performance of the protocols to expansion properties of the underlying topology, with particular attention to the case of social networks, where broadcasting is often referred to as *rumor spreading* [6]. (For a relatively recent, comprehensive survey on this subject, see [16].) Unfortunately, mobile networks do not feature properties similar to those of social networks, mostly because of the physical limitations of both the movement and the radio transmission processes. Indeed, as noted in [20], the short range of communication attainable by low-power antennas enforces the same local dynamics typical of disease epidemics [11], which require physical proximity to propagate. Indeed, the analysis of opportunistic networks, where nodes relay messages as they come close to one another, employs models from the study of human mobility [5, 4].

Iin the theory community there has been growing interest in modeling and analyzing information dissemination in dynamic scenarios, where a number of agents move either in a continuous space or along the nodes of some underlying graph and exchange information when their positions satisfy a specified proximity constraint. In [7, 8] the authors study the time it takes to broadcast information from one of k mobile agents to all others. The agents move on a square grid of n nodes and in each time step an agent can (a) exchange information with all agents at distance at most r from it, and (b) move to any random node at distance at most ρ from its current position. The results in these papers only apply to a very dense scenario where the number of agents is linear in the number of grid nodes (i.e., $k = \Theta(n)$). They show that the broadcast time is $\Theta(\sqrt{n}/r)$ w.h.p., when $\rho = O(r)$ and $r = \Omega\left(\sqrt{\log n}\right)$ [7], and it is $O((\sqrt{n}/\rho) + \log n)$ w.h.p., when $\rho = \Omega\left(\max\{r, \sqrt{\log n}\}\right)$ [8]. These results crucially rely on $r + \rho = \Omega\left(\sqrt{\log n}\right)$, which implies that the range of agents' communications or movements at each step defines a connected graph.

In more realistic scenarios, like the one adopted in this paper, the number of agents is decoupled from the number of locations (i.e., the graph nodes) and a smoother dynamics is enforced by limiting agents to move only between neighboring nodes. A reasonable model consists of a set of multiple, simple random walks on a graph, one for each agent, with communication between two agents occurring when they are nodes whose distance is at most $r \geq 0$. One variant of this setting is the so-called *Frog Model*, where initially one of k agents is active (i.e., is performing a random walk), while the remaining agents do not move. Whenever an active agent hits an inactive one, the latter is activated and starts its own random walk. This model was mostly studied in the infinite grid focusing on the asymptotic (in time) shape of the set of vertices containing all active agents [3, 18].

A model similar to our scenario is often employed to represent the spreading of computer viruses in networks, and the spreading time is also referred to as *infection time*. Kesten and Sidoravicius [19] characterized the rate at which an infection spreads among particles performing continuous-time random walks with the same jump rate. In [10], the authors provide a general bound on the average infection time when k agents (one of them initially affected by the virus) move in an n-node graph. For general graphs, this bound is $O(t^* \log k)$, where t^* denotes the maximum average meeting time of two random walks on the graph, and the maximum is taken over all pairs of starting locations of the random walks. Also, in the paper tighter bounds are provided for the complete graph and for expanders. Observe that the $O(t^* \log k)$ bound specializes to $O(n \log n \log k)$ for the n-node grid by applying the known bound on t^* of [1]. A tight bound of $\Theta((n \log n \log k)/k)$ on the infection time on the grid is claimed in [28], based on a rather informal argument where some unwarranted independence assumptions are made. Our results show that this latter bound is incorrect.

Recent work by Peres et al. [25] studies a process in which agents follow independent Brownian motions in $\mathbb{R}^d$. They investigate several properties of the system, such as detection, coverage and percolation times, and characterize them as functions of the spatial density of the agents, which is assumed to be greater than the percolation point. Leveraging on these results, they show that the broadcast time of a message is polylogarithmic in the number of agents, under the assumption that a message spreads within a connected component of the communication graph instantaneously, before the graph is altered by agents' motion.

1.2 Organization of the Paper

The rest of the paper is organized as follows. In Section 2, we define the quantities of interest and establish some technical facts which are used in the analysis. Section 3 contains our main results: first, we prove the upper bound on the broadcast time in the most restricted case, that is, when the information exchange occurs through physical contact of the agents (i.e., $r = 0$), and then we provide a matching lower bound, which holds for every value of the transmission radius r below the percolation point. Finally, in Section 4 we briefly discuss the connection between our result and other interesting related problems and devise some future research directions.

2. PRELIMINARIES

We study the dynamics of information exchange among a set A of k agents performing independent random walks on an n-node 2-dimensional square grid $\mathcal{G}_n$, which is commonly adopted as a discrete model for the domain where agents wander. We assume that $n \geq 2k$, since sparse scenarios are the most interesting from the point of view of applications; however, our analysis can be easily extended to denser scenarios. We suppose that the agents are initially placed uniformly and independently at random on the grid nodes. Time is discrete and agent moves are synchronized. At each step, an agent residing on a node v with n_v neighbors ($n_v = 2, 3, 4$), moves to any such neighbor with probability $1/5$ and stays on v with probability $1 - n_v/5$. With these probabilities it is easy to see that at any time step the agents are placed uniformly and independently at random on the grid nodes. The following two lemmas con-

tain important properties of random walks on $\mathcal{G}_n$, which will be employed for deriving our results[2].

LEMMA 1. *Consider a random walk on $\mathcal{G}_n$, starting at time $t = 0$ at node v_0. There exists a positive constant c_1 such that for any node $v \neq v_0$, the probability $p(v, v_0)$ that v is visited within $(\|v - v_0\|)^2$ steps is*

$$p(v, v_0) \geq \frac{c_1}{\max\{1, \log(\|v - v_0\|)\}}.$$

PROOF. The Lemma is proved in [3, Theorem 2.2] for the infinite grid $\mathbb{Z}^2$. By the "Reflection Principle" [13, Page 72], for each walk in $\mathbb{Z}^2$ that started in $\mathcal{G}_n$, crossed a boundary and then crossed the boundary back to $\mathcal{G}_n$, there is a walk with the same probability that does not cross the boundary and visits all the nodes in $\mathcal{G}_n$ that were visited by the first walk. Thus, restricting the walks to $\mathcal{G}_n$ can only change the bound by a constant factor. □

LEMMA 2. *Consider the first ℓ steps of a random walk in $\mathcal{G}_n$ which was at node v_0 at time 0.*

1. *The probability that at any given step $1 \leq i \leq \ell$ the random walk is at distance at least $\geq \lambda\sqrt{\ell}$ from v_0 is at most $2e^{-\lambda^2/2}$.*

2. *There is a constant c_2 such that, with probability greater than $1/2$, by time ℓ the walk has visited at least $c_2\ell/\log \ell$ distinct nodes in $\mathcal{G}_n$.*

PROOF. We observe that the distance from v_0 in each coordinate defines a martingale with bounded difference 1. Then, the first property follows from the Azuma-Hoeffding Inequality [22, Theorem 2.6]. As for the second property, let R_ℓ be the set of nodes reached by the walk in ℓ steps. By Lemma 1, $E[R_\ell] = \Omega(\ell/\log \ell)$ (even when v_0 is near a boundary), while $\text{Var}(R_\ell) = \Theta(\ell^2/\log^4 \ell)$ (see [27]). The result follows by applying Chebyshev's inequality. □

Let M be a set of messages, which will be referred to as *rumors* henceforth, such that for each $m \in M$ there is (at least) one agent *informed* of m at time $t = 0$. W.l.o.g., we can assume that the number of distinct rumors is at most equal to the number of agent. We denote by $M_a(t)$ the set of rumors that agent $a \in A$ is informed of at time t, for any $t \geq 0$; possibly, $M_a(0) = \emptyset$. We assume that each agent is equipped with a *transmission radius* $r \in \mathbb{N}$, representing the maximum distance at which the agent can send information in a single time step.

The spread of rumors can be represented by a dynamic communication graph process $\{G_t(r) \mid t \geq 0\}$, where $G_t(r)$, the *visibility graph at time t*, is a graph with vertex set A and such that there is an edge between two vertices iff the corresponding agents are within distance r at time t. Following a common assumption justified by the physical reality that the speed of radio transmission is much faster than the motion of the agents [25], we suppose that rumors can travel throughout a connected component of $G_t(r)$ before the graph is altered by the motion. We assume that within the same connected component agents exchange all rumors they are informed of. Formally, let C be a connected component of $G_t(r)$: for all $a \in C$, $M_a(t) = \bigcup_{a' \in C} M_{a'}(t - 1)$.

---

[2]Throughout the paper, the distance between two grid nodes u and v, denoted by $\|u - v\|$, is defined to be the Manhattan distance. Also, all logarithms are taken to the base two.

Note that the sets $M_a(t)$ can only grow over time, that is, agents do not "forget" rumors. The following quantities will be studied in this paper.

DEFINITION 1 (BROADCAST TIME, GOSSIP TIME). *The* broadcast time T_B^m *of a rumor* $m \in M$ *is the first time at which every agent is informed of* m, *that is, for all* $t \geq T_B^m$ *and* $a \in A$, $m \in M_a(t)$. *The* gossip time T_G *of the system is the first time at which every agent is informed of every rumor, that is, for any* $t \geq T_G$ *and* $a \in A$, $M_a(t) = M$.

Note that both T_B^m and T_G depend on the transmission radius r, but we will omit this dependence to simplify the notation. We will also write T_B instead of T_B^m when the message m is clearly identified by the context.

3. BROADCASTING BELOW THE PERCOLATION POINT

In this section we give bounds to the broadcast time T_B of a rumor when the transmission radius is below the percolation point $r_c \approx \sqrt{n/k}$, that is, when all the connected components of $G_t(r)$ comprise at most a logarithmic number of agents. In this regime, we show that quite surprisingly T_B does not depend on the transmission radius, the reason being that the broadcast time is dominated by the time it takes for many independent random walks to intersect one another. In Subsection 3.1 we prove an upper bound on the broadcast time T_B in the extreme case $r = 0$, that is, when agents can exchange information only when they meet on a grid node. The same upper bound clearly holds for any other $r > 0$. Then, in Subsection 3.2 we show that the upper bound is tight, within logarithmic factors, for all values of the transmission radius below the percolation point. We also argue that the bounds on T_B easily extend to gossip time T_G.

3.1 Upper Bound on the Broadcast Time

The main technical ingredient of the analysis carried out in this subsection is the following lower bound on the probability that two random walks $\bar{a}, \bar{b}$ on the grid meet within a given time interval and not too far from their starting positions, which is a result of independent interest.

LEMMA 3. *Consider two independent simple random walks on the grid* $\bar{a} = \langle a_0, a_1, \ldots \rangle$, *and* $\bar{b} = \langle b_0, b_1, \ldots \rangle$, *where* a_t *and* b_t *denote the locations of the walks at time* $t \geq 0$. *Let* $d = ||a_0 - b_0|| \geq 1$ *and define* D *to be the set of nodes at distance at most* d *from both* a_0 *and* b_0. *For* $T = d^2$, *there exists a constant* $c_3 > 0$ *such that*

$$P_{\bar{a},\bar{b}}(T) \triangleq \Pr\left(\exists t \leq T \text{ such that } a_t = b_t \in D\right)$$
$$\geq c_3/\max\{1, \log d\}.$$

PROOF. The case $d = 1$ is immediate. Consider now the case $d > 1$. Let $P_t(w, x)$ denote the probability that a walk that started at node w at time 0 is at node x at time t, and let $R(w, u, D, s)$ be the expected number of times that two walks which started at nodes w and u at time 0 meet at nodes of D during the time interval $[0, s]$, then

$$R(w, u, D, s) = \sum_{t=0}^{s} \sum_{x \in D} P_t(w, x) P_t(u, x).$$

Let $\tau(a, b)$ be the first meeting time of the walks $\bar{a}$ and $\bar{b}$ at a node of D. Then

$$R(a_0, b_0, D, T) = \sum_{t=0}^{T} \Pr\left(\tau(a, b) = t\right) R(a_t, a_t, D, T - t)$$
$$\leq P_{\bar{a},\bar{b}}(T) \max_x R(x, x, D, T).$$

Thus,

$$P_{\bar{a},\bar{b}}(T) \geq \frac{R(a_0, b_0, D, T)}{\max_x R(x, x, D, T)}.$$

It is easy to verify that $|D| \geq d^2/4$. Applying Theorem 1.2.1 in [21] we have:

$$R(a_0, b_0, D, T) \geq \sum_{t=0}^{T} \sum_{x \in D} P_t(a_0, x) P_t(b_0, x)$$
$$\geq \sum_{t=\frac{T}{2}+1}^{T} \sum_{x \in D} 4\left(\frac{1}{\pi t}\right)^2 e^{-\frac{||x-a_0||^2 + ||x-b_0||^2}{t}}.$$

By bounding $||x - a_0||^2$ and $||x - b_0||^2$ from above with T in the formula, easy calculations show that $R(a_0, b_0, D, T) = \Omega(1)$. Similarly, using the fact that there are no more than $4i$ nodes at distance exactly i from x, we have:

$$\max_x R(x, x, D, T) \leq 1 + \sum_{t=1}^{T} \sum_{i=1}^{t} 4i \cdot 4\left(\frac{1}{\pi t}\right)^2 2e^{-\frac{i^2}{t}}$$
$$\leq 1 + \left(\frac{4}{\pi}\right)^2 \sum_{t=1}^{T} \frac{1}{t^2} \left(\left(\sum_{i=1}^{\sqrt{t}} i\right) + \left(\sum_{i=1+\sqrt{t}}^{t} i e^{-i^2/t}\right)\right)$$
$$\leq 1 + \left(\frac{4}{\pi}\right)^2 \sum_{t=1}^{T} \frac{1}{t^2} \left(\frac{t}{2} + \left(\sum_{i=1+\sqrt{t}}^{t} i^2 e^{-i^2/t}\right)\right)$$
$$\leq 1 + \left(\frac{4}{\pi}\right)^2 \sum_{t=1}^{T} \frac{1}{t^2} \left(\frac{t}{2} + \frac{e}{(e-1)^2}t\right) = O(\log T).$$

We conclude that there is a constant $c_3 > 0$ such that $P_{\bar{a},\bar{b}}(T) \geq c_3/\log d$. $\square$

Observe that considering the difference random walk $\bar{a} - \bar{b} = \langle a_0 - b_0, a_1 - b_1, \ldots \rangle$ and computing the probability that it hits the origin in the prescribed number of steps does not provide any information about the place where the meeting occurs, hence it is not immediate to derive the above result through that approach.

The remainder of this section is devoted to proving the following upper bound on the broadcast time of a single rumor m in the case $r = 0$. We assume that $M_a(0) = \{m\}$ for some $a \in A$, and $M_{a'}(0) = \emptyset$ for any other $a' \neq a$.

THEOREM 1. *Let* $r = 0$. *For any* $k \geq 2$, *with probability at least* $1 - 1/n^2$,

$$T_B = \tilde{O}\left(\frac{n}{\sqrt{k}}\right).$$

We observe that since the diameter of $\mathcal{G}_n$ is $2\sqrt{n} - 2$, we can use Lemma 3 to show that with probability at least $1 - 1/n^2$, at time $8n \log^2 n$ an agent has met all other agents walking in $\mathcal{G}_n$. Thus, the theorem trivially holds for $k = O(\text{poly}\log(n))$.

From now on we concentrate on the case $k = \Omega\left(\log^3 n\right)$. We tessellate $\mathcal{G}_n$ into *cells* of side $\ell \triangleq \sqrt{14 n \log^3 n / (c_3 k)}$, where c_3 is defined in Lemma 3. We say that a cell Q is *reached* at time t_Q if t_Q is the first time when a node of the cell hosts an agent informed of the rumor, and we call this first visitor the *explorer* of Q. We first show that, after a suitably chosen number $T_1 = O\left(\ell^2 \log^4 n\right)$ of steps past t_Q, there is a large number of informed agents within distance $O\left(\ell \log^{5/2} n\right)$ from Q. Furthermore, we show that while the rumor spreads to cells adjacent to Q, at any time $t \geq t_Q + T_1$ a large number of informed agents are at locations close to Q. These facts will imply that the exploration process proceeds smoothly and that all agents are informed of the rumor shortly after all cells are reached.

The above argument is made rigorous in the following sequence of lemmas.

LEMMA 4. *Consider an arbitrary $\ell \times \ell$ cell Q of the tessellation. Let $T_1 = 16\beta\gamma\ell^2\log^4 n$ and $c_4 = 8\sqrt{5\beta\gamma}$, where $\beta = 7/(2c_1)$ and $\gamma = 18/c_3$. By time $\tau_1 = t_Q + T_1$, at least $4\beta\log^2 n$ agents are informed and are at distance at most $2(1 + c_4 \log^{5/2} n)\ell$ from Q, with probability $1 - 1/n^8$, for sufficiently large n.*

PROOF. Since at any given time the agents are at random and independent locations, by the Chernoff bound we have that the following *density condition* holds with probability at least $1 - 1/n^9$, for sufficiently large n: for any cell Q' and any time instant $t \in [0, n\log^4 n]$, the number of agents residing in cell Q' at time t is at least $(7\log^3 n)/c_3$. In the rest of the proof, we assume that the density condition holds.

First, we prove that, by time τ_1, there are at least $4\beta\log^2 n$ informed agents in the system. We assume that at every time step $t \in [t_Q, \tau_1]$ there is always an uninformed agent in the same cell where the explorer resides (otherwise the sought property follows immediately by the density condition). For $1 \leq i \leq 4\beta\log^2 n$, let $t_i \geq t_Q$ be the time at which the explorer of Q informs the i-th agent. For notational convenience, we let $t_0 = t_Q$. To upper bound t_i, for $i > 0$, we consider a sequence of $\gamma\log^2 n$ consecutive, non-overlapping time intervals of length $4\ell^2$ beginning from time t_{i-1}. By the previous assumption, at the beginning of each interval the cell where the explorer resides contains an uninformed agent a. Hence, by Lemma 3, the probability that the explorer fails to meet an uninformed agent during all of these intervals is

$$\Pr\left(t_i > t_{i-1} + 4\gamma\ell^2\log^2 n\right) \leq (1 - c_3/\log(2\ell))^{\gamma\log^2 n}$$
$$\leq 1/n^9,$$

where the last inequality holds for sufficiently large n by our choice of γ. By iterating the argument for every i, we conclude that with probability at least $1 - 4\beta\log^2 n/n^9$, there are at least $4\beta\log^2 n$ informed agents at time τ_1. Let I denote the set of informed agents identified through the above argument, and observe that each agent of I was in the cell containing the explorer at some time step $t \in [t_Q, \tau_1]$.

To conclude the proof of the lemma, we note that, by Lemma 2, the probability that the explorer, during the interval $[t_Q, \tau_1]$, reaches a grid node at distance greater than $(c_4 \log^{5/2} n)\ell$ from its position at time t_Q is bounded by $2T_1/n^{10}$. Consider an arbitrary agent $a \in I$. As observed above, there must have been a time instant $\bar{t} \in [t_Q, \tau_1]$ when a and the explorer were in the same cell, hence at distance at

most $(2 + c_4\log^{5/2} n)\ell$ from Q. From time $\bar{t}$ until time τ_1 the random walk of agent a proceeds independently of the random walk of the explorer. By applying again Lemma 2, we can conclude that the probability that one of the agents of I is at distance greater than $2(1 + c_4\log^{5/2} n)\ell$ from Q at time τ_1 is at most $8\beta\log^2 n/n^9$. By adding up the upper bounds to the probabilities that the event stated in the lemma does not hold, we get $1/n^9 + 4\beta\log^2 n/n^9 + 2T_1/n^{10} + 8\beta\log^2 n/n^9$, which is less than $1/n^8$ for sufficiently large n. $\square$

LEMMA 5. *Consider an arbitrary $\ell \times \ell$ cell Q of the tessellation. Let T_1, τ_1, c_4 and β be defined as in Lemma 4, and let $T_2 = (2(2 + c_4\log^{5/2} n)\ell)^2$, $\tau_2 = \tau_1 + T_2$, and $c_5 = (4\sqrt{\log 16})c_4$. Then, the following two properties hold with probability at least $1 - 1/n^6$ for n sufficiently large:*

1. *For Q and for each of its adjacent cells, there exists a time t, with $\tau_1 \leq t \leq \tau_2$, at which there is an informed agent in the cell;*

2. *At any time t, with $\tau_1 \leq t \leq \tau_2 + T_1$, there are at least $\beta\log^2 n$ informed agents at distance at most $(2 + (2c_4 + c_5)\log^{5/2} n)\ell$ from Q.*

PROOF. We condition on the event stated in Lemma 4, which occurs with probability $1 - 1/n^8$. Hence, assume that by time τ_1 there are at least $4\beta\log^2 n$ informed agents at distance at most $d_4 \triangleq 2(1 + c_4\log^{5/2} n)\ell$ from Q. Consider the center node v of Q (resp., Q' adjacent to Q), so that at τ_1 there are at least $4\beta\log^2 n$ informed agents at distance at most $d_4 + 2\ell$ from v. By Lemma 1 the probability that v is not touched by an informed agent between τ_1 and τ_2 is at most $(1 - (c_1/\log(d_4 + 2\ell)))^{4\beta\log^2 n}$, which is less than $1/n^7$, for sufficiently large n, by our choice of β. Thus, Point 1 follows.

As for Point 2, consider an informed agent a which, at time τ_1, is at a node x at distance at most d_4 from Q. Fix a time $t \in [\tau_1, \tau_2 + T_1]$. By Lemma 2 the probability that at time t agent a is at distance greater than $(c_5\log^{5/2} n)\ell$ from x is at most $1/2$. Hence, at time t the average number of informed agents at distance at most $d_4 + (c_5\log^{5/2} n)\ell$ from Q is at least $2\beta\log^2 n$. Since agents move independently, Point 2 follows by applying the Chernoff bound to bound the probability that at time t there are less than $\beta\log^2 n$ informed agents at distance at most $d_4 + (c_5\log^{5/2} n)\ell$ from Q, and by applying the union bound over all time steps of the interval $[\tau_1, \tau_2 + T_1]$. $\square$

We are now ready to prove the main theorem of this subsection:

PROOF OF THEOREM 1. As observed at the beginning of the subsection, we can limit ourselves to the case $k = \Omega\left(\log^3 n\right)$. Consider the tessellation of $\mathcal{G}_n$ into $\ell \times \ell$ cells defined before, and focus on a cell Q reached for the first time at t_Q. By Lemma 5, we know that with probability at least $1 - 1/n^6$, in each time step $t \in [\tau_1, \tau_2 + T_1]$ there are at least $\beta\log^2 n$ informed agents at distance at most $d_5 \triangleq (2 + (2c_4 + c_5)\log^{5/2} n)\ell$ from Q and there exists a time $t' \in [\tau_1, \tau_2]$ such that an informed agent is again inside Q. By applying again the lemma, we can conclude that, with probability at least $(1 - 1/n^6)^2$, at any time step $t'' \in [t' + T_1, t' + 2T_1 + T_2]$ there are at least $\beta\log^2 n$ informed agents at distance at most d_5 from Q. Note that the two time intervals $[\tau_1, \tau_2 + T_1]$ and $[t' + T_1, t' + 2T_1 + T_2]$ overlap and the latter one ends at least T_1 time steps later. Thus, by applying the lemma $n \log^4 n$ times, we ensure that, with probability at least $(1 - 1/n^6)^{n \log^4 n} \geq 1 - \log^4 n / n^5$, from time τ_1 until the end of the broadcast, there are always at least $\beta \log^2 n$ informed agents at distance at most d_5 from Q.

Lemma 5 shows that each of the neighboring cells of Q is reached within time $\tau_2 = t_Q + T_1 + T_2$ with probability $1 - 1/n^6$. Therefore, all cells are reached within time $T^* = (2\sqrt{n}/\ell)(T_1 + T_2)$ with probability at least $1 - 1/n^5$. Hence, by applying a union bound over all cells, we can conclude that with probability at least $(1 - 1/n^5)(1 - \log^4 n / n^4) \geq 1 - 1/n^3$ there are at least $\beta \log^2 n$ informed agents at distance at most d_5 from each cell of the tessellation, from time $T^* + T_1$ until the end of the broadcast.

Consider now an agent a which at time $T^* + T_1$ is uninformed and resides in a certain cell Q. By an argument similar to the one used to prove Lemma 4, we can prove that a meets at least one of the informed agents around Q within $O\left(\ell^2 \log^5 n\right)$ time steps with probability at least $1 - 1/n^6$. A union bound over all uninformed agents completes the proof. $\square$

Observe that the broadcast time is a non-increasing function of the transmission radius. Therefore, the upper bound developed for the case $r = 0$ holds for any $r > 0$, as stated in the following corollary.

COROLLARY 1. *For any $k \geq 2$ and $r > 0$, $T_\mathrm{B} = \tilde{O}\left(n/\sqrt{k}\right)$ with probability at least $1 - 1/n^2$.*

As another immediate corollary of the above theorem, we can prove that the gossiping of multiple distinct rumors completes within the same time bound, with high probability.

COROLLARY 2. *For any $k \geq 2$ and $r > 0$, $T_\mathrm{G} = \tilde{O}\left(n/\sqrt{k}\right)$ with probability at least $1 - 1/n$.*

3.2 Lower Bound on the Broadcast Time

In this subsection we prove that the result of Corollary 1 is indeed tight, up to logarithmic factors, for any value r of the transmission radius below the percolation point. Note that this result is also a lower bound on T_G if there are multiple rumors in the system. First observe that with probability at least $1 - 2^{-(k-1)}$, there exists an agent placed at distance at least $\sqrt{n}/2$ from the source of m. W.l.o.g., we assume that the x-coordinates of the positions occupied by such an agent and the source agent differ by at least $\sqrt{n}/4$ and that the latter is at the left of the former. (The other cases can be dealt with through an identical argument.) In the proof, we cannot solely rely on a distance-based argument since we need to take into account the presence of "many" agents which may act as relay to deliver the rumor.

We define the *informed area* $\mathcal{I}(t)$ at time t as the set of grid nodes visited by any informed agent up to time t, and let $x(t)$ to be the rightmost grid node in $\mathcal{I}(t)$. We will show that there is a sufficiently large value T such that, at time T, there is at least one uniformed agent right of $x(T)$. We need the following definition:

DEFINITION 2 (ISLAND). *Let A be the set of agents. For any $\gamma > 0$, let $G_t(\gamma)$ be the graph with vertex set A and such that there is an edge between two vertices iff the corresponding agents are within distance γ at time t. Then*

any connected component of $G_t(\gamma)$ is called an island *of parameter γ at time t.*

Next, we prove an upper bound on the size of the islands.

LEMMA 6. *Let $\gamma = \sqrt{n/(4e^6 k)}$. Then, the probability that there exists an island of parameter γ with more than $\log n$ agents at any time t, with $0 \leq t \leq 8n \log^2 n$, is at most $1/n^2$.*

PROOF. Since at any given time the agents are uniformly distributed in $\mathcal{G}_n$, the probability that a given agent is within distance γ of another given agent at time t_0 is bounded by $4\gamma^2/n$. Fix a time t_0 and let $\mathcal{B}_w(t_0)$ denote the event that there exists an island with at least $w > \log n$ elements at time t_0. Then, recalling that w^{w-2} is the number of unrooted trees over w labeled nodes, we have that

$$\Pr\left(\mathcal{B}_w(t_0)\right) \leq \binom{k}{w} w^{w-2} \left(\frac{4\gamma^2}{n}\right)^{w-1}$$
$$\leq \left(\frac{ek}{w}\right)^w w^{w-2} \left(\frac{4\gamma^2}{n}\right)^{w-1}.$$

Using definition of γ and the bound $w \geq 1 + \log n$ and $k \leq n$, we have

$$\Pr\left(\mathcal{B}_w(t_0)\right) \leq \frac{ek}{w^2} e^{-5(w-1)} \leq \frac{en}{w^2} \frac{1}{n^5} \leq \frac{1}{n^4},$$

for a sufficiently large n. Applying the union bound over $O\left(n \log^2 n\right)$ time steps concludes the proof. $\square$

Next we show that, with high probability, for values of r below percolation, the informed area cannot expand to the right too fast.

LEMMA 7. *Suppose $r \leq \sqrt{n/(64e^6 k)}$. Let $\gamma = \sqrt{n/(4e^6 k)}$ and let t_0 and $t_1 = t_0 + \gamma^2/(144 \log n)$ be two time steps. Then, with probability $1 - 2/n^2$,*

$$\|x(t_1) - x(t_0)\| \leq \gamma \log n.$$

PROOF. By Lemma 2, with probability $1 - 2/n^3$ an agent cannot cover a distance of more than $(\gamma - r)/2$ in $\gamma^2/(144 \log n)$ time steps. Thus with probability $1 - 1/n^2$, any two agents belonging to distinct islands of $G_{t_0}(\gamma)$ cannot come within distance r of each other in the interval $[t_0, t_1]$. Therefore, in that time interval, the rumor can propagate exclusively among agents belonging to those islands of $G_{t_0}(\gamma)$ containing at least one informed agent. By Lemma 6 we conclude that with probability $1 - 2/n^2$, in the interval $[t_0, t_1]$, $x(t)$ can move to the right of at most $\gamma(\log n - 1) + (\gamma - r)/2 < \gamma \log n$ positions. $\square$

Finally, we can prove the main theorem of the subsection:

THEOREM 2. *Let $k \geq 2$ and suppose that $r \leq \sqrt{n/(64e^6 k)}$. Then, with probability $1 - (2^{-(k-1)} + 1/n + 2/n^2)$,*

$$T_\mathrm{B} = \Omega\left(\frac{n}{\sqrt{k} \log^2 n}\right).$$

PROOF. As mentioned before, with probability at least $1 - 2^{-(k-1)}$ there exists an agent a placed at distance at least $\sqrt{n}/2$ from the source of the rumor; we may assume that their x-coordinates differ by at least $\sqrt{n}/4$ and that the uninformed agent is to the right of the source agent. Let $T =$

$n/(2304e^3\sqrt{k}\log^2 n)$ and $\gamma = \sqrt{n/(4e^6 k)}$. By Lemma 7, with probability $1 - 1/n$ the frontier cannot move right in T steps more than $(\gamma \log n/2)T/(\gamma^2/(144 \log n)) < \sqrt{n}/8$. By Lemma 2, with probability $1 - 2/n^2$, agent a cannot move left more than $2\sqrt{T \log n} < \sqrt{n}/8$, so that agent a cannot be informed by time T. Hence, the broadcast time is at least $T_{\mathrm{B}} > T = \Omega\left(n/(\sqrt{k}\log^2 n)\right)$ with probability at least $1 - (2^{-(k-1)} + 1/n + 2/n^2)$. $\square$

4. FURTHER RESULTS AND FUTURE RE-SEARCH

In this work we took a step toward a better understanding of the dynamics of information spreading in mobile networks. We proved a tight bound (up to logarithmic factors) on the broadcast of a rumor in a mobile network where agents perform independent random walks on a grid and the transmission radius defines a system below the percolation point. Our results complement the work of Peres et al. [25], who studied the behavior of a similar system above the percolation point. A similar bound holds for the gossip problem in this model, where at time 0 each agent has a distinct rumor and all agents need to receive all rumors.

Our analysis techniques are applicable to some interesting related problems. For example, similar bounds on the broadcast time T_{B} can be obtained for the Frog Model [3], where only informed agents move and uninformed agents remain at their initial positions. In particular, we can show that the broadcast time in the Frog Model is upper bounded by $T_{\mathrm{B}} = \tilde{O}\left(n/\sqrt{k}\right)$. The argument is similar to the proof of Theorem 1, where Lemma 3 is replaced with Lemma 1 and the analysis of the initial phase of the information dissemination process is carried out by using Point 2 of Lemma 2. Also, a closer look at Theorem 2 reveals that the same argument employed in our dynamic model to bound T_{B} from below applies to the Frog Model. Thus, we have tight bounds, up to logarithmic factors, in this latter model as well.

Another measure of interest in systems of mobile agents is the *coverage time* T_{C}, that is, the first time at which every grid node has been visited at least once by an informed agent [25]. While in the Frog Model the broadcast time is obviously upper bounded by the coverage time, this relation is not so obvious in our dynamic model, since the coverage of the grid nodes does not imply that all agents have been informed of the rumor. Nevertheless, one can verify that, in our model, $T_{\mathrm{C}} \approx T_{\mathrm{B}} = \tilde{O}\left(n/\sqrt{k}\right)$. Indeed, by Point 2 of Lemma 5 and by Lemma 1, after $O\left(\ell^2\right)$ steps from the first time at which an informed agent reached a given cell, all the nodes of that cell have been visited by some informed agent. Hence, by the cell-by-cell spreading process devised in the proof of Theorem 1, we can conclude that the coverage time is bounded by $\tilde{O}\left(n/\sqrt{k}\right)$. (In fact, the same tight relation between T_{C} and T_{B} can be proved in the Frog Model.)

Another by-product of our techniques is a high-probability upper bound $O\left((n \log^2 n)/k + n \log n\right)$ on the *cover time* of k independent random walks on the n-grid (i.e., the time until each grid node has been touched by at least one such walk), improving on the previous results of [2, 12] which provide the same bound only for the expected value. Finally, in a closely related scenario, namely a random *predator-prey system* where $k = \Omega(\log n)$ predators are to catch moving

preys on an n-node grid by performing independent random walks [9], our techniques yield a high-probability upper bound $O\left((n \log^2 n)/k\right)$ on the extinction time of the preys.

In an effort to go beyond the pure mathematical contribution, we are now working on extending our analysis techniques to more complex scenarios that are interesting from the point of view of applications. Introducing mobility and communication barriers seems a first natural extension to be considered. Another dimension of mobile networks that we plan to further explore is the communication complexity of generic distributed computations among the moving agents of the system. Finally, the most challenging future direction leads to formulate sound analytical mobility models representing the dynamics of people travelling on road or subway networks, whereas, up to now, these types of systems have been studied by physicists, transportation scientists and engineers only by means of empirical or simulative techniques.

5. ACKNOWLEDGMENTS

Many thanks to Jeff Steif for referring us to some crucial references and to Andrea Clementi and Riccardo Silvestri for pointing out a claim not fully justified in an earlier draft of this paper.

6. REFERENCES

[1] D. Aldous and J. Fill. *Reversible Markov Chains and Random Walks on Graphs*. Unpublished manuscript, 1998.

[2] N. Alon, C. Avin, M. Koucký, G. Kozma, Z. Lotker, and M. R. Tuttle. Many random walks are faster than one. In *Proc. SPAA*, pages 119–128, 2008.

[3] O. S. M. Alves, F. P. Machado, and S. Y. Popov. The shape theorem for the frog model. *The Annals of Applied Probability*, 12(2):533–546, 2002.

[4] A. Chaintreau, P. Fraigniaud, and E. Lebhar. Opportunistic spatial gossip over mobile social networks. In *Proc. WOSN*, pages 73–78, 2008.

[5] A. Chaintreau, P. Hui, J. Crowcroft, C. Diot, R. Gass, and J. Scott. Impact of human mobility on opportunistic forwarding algorithms. *IEEE Trans. Mob. Comput.*, 6(6):606–620, 2007.

[6] F. Chierichetti, S. Lattanzi, and A. Panconesi. Almost tight bounds for rumour spreading with conductance. In *Proc. STOC*, pages 399–408, 2010.

[7] A. E. F. Clementi, A. Monti, F. Pasquale, and R. Silvestri. Information spreading in stationary markovian evolving graphs. In *Proc. IPDPS*, pages 1–12, 2009.

[8] A. E. F. Clementi, F. Pasquale, and R. Silvestri. MANETS: High mobility can make up for low transmission power. In *Proc. ICALP*, pages 387–398, 2009.

[9] C. Cooper, A. Frieze, and T. Radzik. Multiple random walks in random regular graphs. *SIAM Journal of Discrete Mathematics*, 23(4):1738–1761, 2009.

[10] T. Dimitriou, S. Nikoletseas, and P. Spirakis. The infection time of graphs. *Discrete Applied Mathematics*, 154(18):2577–2589, 2006.

[11] R. Durrett. Stochastic spatial models. *SIAM Review*, 41:677–718, 1999.

[12] R. Elsässer and T. Sauerwald. Tight bounds for the

cover time of multiple random walks. In *Proc. ICALP*, pages 415–426, 2009.

[13] W. Feller. *An Introduction to Probability Theory and Its Applications, Vol. I.* Wiley, 3 edition, 1968.

[14] M. Gerla. From battlefields to urban grids: New research challenges in ad hoc wireless networks. *Pervasive and Mobile Computing*, 1(1):77–93, 2005.

[15] M. Grossglauser and D. N. C. Tse. Mobility increases the capacity of ad hoc wireless networks. *IEEE/ACM Transactions on Networking*, 10(4):477–486, 2002.

[16] J. Hromkovic, R. Klasing, A. Pelc, P. Ruzicka, and W. Unger. *Dissemination of Information in Communication Networks.* Springer, Berlin, 2005.

[17] P. Juang, H. Oki, Y. Wang, M. Martonosi, L.-S. Peh, and D. Rubenstein. Energy-efficient computing for wildlife tracking: Design tradeoffs and early experiences with zebranet. In *Proc. ASPLOS*, pages 96–107, 2002.

[18] H. Kesten and V. Sidoravicius. A shape theorem for the spread of an infection. arXiv:math/0312511v1 [math.PR], 2003.

[19] H. Kesten and V. Sidoravicius. The spread of a rumor or infection in a moving population. *The Annals of Probability*, 33(6):2402–2462, 2005.

[20] J. Kleinberg. The wireless epidemic. *Nature*, 449(7160):287–288, 2007.

[21] G. F. Lawler. *Intersections of random walks.* Birkhäuser, Boston, 1991.

[22] M. Mitzenmacher and E. Upfal. *Probability and Computing.* Cambridge University Press, Cambridge, 2005.

[23] S. Olariu and M. C. Weigle. *Vehicular Networks: From Theory to Practice.* Chapman and Hall/CRC, 2009.

[24] M. Penrose. *Random Geometric Graphs.* Oxford University Press, Oxford, 2003.

[25] Y. Peres, A. Sinclair, P. Sousi, and A. Stauffer. Mobile geometric graphs: Detection, coverage and percolation. In *Proc. SODA*, 2011.

[26] I. Stojmenovic. *Handbook of Wireless Networks and Mobile Computing.* Wiley, 2002.

[27] D. C. Torney. Variance of the range of a random walk. *Journal of Statistical Physics*, 44(1):49–66, 1986.

[28] Y. Wang, S. Kapadia, and B. Krishnamachari. Infection spread in wireless networks with random and adversarial node mobilities. In *Proc. SIGMOBILE Workshop on Mobility Models*, pages 17–24, 2008.

Order Optimal Information Spreading Using Algebraic Gossip [*]

Chen Avin
Department of Communication
Systems Engineering
Ben Gurion University
Beer-Sheva, Israel
avin@cse.bgu.ac.il

Michael Borokhovich
Department of Communication
Systems Engineering
Ben Gurion University
Beer-Sheva, Israel
borokhom@cse.bgu.ac.il

Keren Censor-Hillel [†]
CSAIL
MIT
Cambridge, MA, United States
ckeren@csail.mit.edu

Zvi Lotker
Department of Communication
Systems Engineering
Ben Gurion University
Beer-Sheva, Israel
zvilo@cse.bgu.ac.il

ABSTRACT

In this paper we study gossip based information spreading with bounded message sizes. We use algebraic gossip to disseminate k distinct messages to all n nodes in a network. For arbitrary networks we provide a new upper bound for uniform algebraic gossip of $O((k+\log n + D)\Delta)$ rounds with high probability, where D and Δ are the diameter and the maximum degree in the network, respectively. For many topologies and selections of k this bound improves previous results, in particular, for graphs with a constant maximum degree it implies that uniform gossip is *order optimal* and the stopping time is $\Theta(k + D)$.

To eliminate the factor of Δ from the upper bound we propose a non-uniform gossip protocol, TAG, which is based on algebraic gossip and an arbitrary spanning tree protocol $\mathcal{S}$. The stopping time of TAG is $O(k+\log n + d(\mathcal{S}) + t(\mathcal{S}))$, where $t(\mathcal{S})$ is the stopping time of the spanning tree protocol, and $d(\mathcal{S})$ is the diameter of the spanning tree. We provide two general cases in which this bound leads to an order optimal protocol. The first is for $k = \Omega(n)$, where, using a simple gossip broadcast protocol that creates a spanning tree in at most linear time, we show that TAG finishes after $\Theta(n)$ rounds for any graph. The second uses a sophisticated, recent gossip protocol to build a fast spanning tree on graphs with large weak conductance. In turn, this leads to the optimally of TAG on these graphs for $k = \Omega(\text{polylog}(n))$. The technique used in our proofs relies on queuing theory, which is an interesting approach that can be useful in future gossip analysis.

Categories and Subject Descriptors

C.2.4 [**Computer Systems Organization**]: Computer-Communication Networks—*Distributed Systems*

General Terms

Algorithms, Performance

1. INTRODUCTION

One of the most basic information spreading applications is that of disseminating information stored at a subset of source nodes to a set of sink nodes. Here we consider the *k-dissemination* case: k initial messages ($k \leq n$) located at some nodes (a node can hold more than one initial message) need to reach all n nodes. The *all-to-all communication* – each of n nodes has an initial value that is needed to be disseminated to all nodes – is a special case of k-dissemination. The goal is to perform this task in the lowest possible number of time steps when messages have *limited* size (i.e., a node may not be able to send all its data in one message).

Gossiping, or rumor-spreading, is a simple stochastic process for dissemination of information across a network. In a synchronous *round* of gossip, *each* node chooses a *single* neighbor as the *communication partner* and takes an action. In an asynchronous time model a single node wake-up and chooses the *communication partner* and n consecutive steps are considered as one *round*. The *gossip communication model* defines how to select this neighbor, e.g., *uniform* gossip is when the communication partner is selected uniformly at random from the set of all neighbors. We then consider three possible actions: either the node pushes information to the partner (PUSH), pulls information from the partner (PULL), or does both (EXCHANGE), but here we mostly present results about EXCHANGE.

[*] The paper is a part of the PhD work of Michael Borokhovich. Zvi Lotker and Michael Borokhovich were supported in part by a grant from the Israel Science Foundation (894/09).

[†] Supported by the Simons Postdoctoral Fellows Program.

A *gossip protocol* uses a gossip communication model in conjunction with the choice of the particular content that is exchanged. Due to their distributed nature, gossip protocols have gained popularity in recent years and have found applications both in communication networks (for example, updating database replicated at many sites [10, 15], computation of aggregate information [16] and multicast via network coding [9], to name a few) as well as in social networks [17, 7].

In the current work we analyze *algebraic gossip* which is a type of network coding known as random linear coding (RLNC) [19, 18] that uses gossip algorithms for all-to-all communication and k-dissemination. In algebraic gossip the content of messages is the random linear combination of all messages stored at a sender. Once a node has received enough independent messages (independent linear equations) it can solve the system of linear equations and discover all the initial values of all other nodes. It has been proved [14] that network coding can improve the throughput of the network by better sharing of the network resources. Note, however, that in gossip protocols, nodes select a single partner, so for k-dissemination to succeed each node needs to receive at least k messages (of bounded size), hence at least a total of kn messages need to be sent and received. This immediately leads to a trivial lower bound of $\Omega(k)$ rounds for k-dissemination.

We study uniform and non-uniform algebraic gossip both in the synchronous and the asynchronous time models on arbitrary graph topologies. The stopping time obviously depends on the protocol, the gossip communication model, the graph topology, but also on the time model, as shown in other cases [12]. We now give an overview of our results followed by a discussion of previous work.

1.1 Overview of Our Results

Our first set of results is about the stopping time of uniform algebraic gossip. In [3] we have shown a tight bound of $\Theta(n)$ for all-to-all communication for graphs with constant maximum degree. To prove this, we used a reduction of gossip to a network of queues and analyzed the waiting times in the queues. Bounding the general k-dissemination case is significantly harder, despite some similarity in the tools used. Unless explicitly stated, all our results are for gossip using **EXCHANGE** and are with high probability*.

We provide a novel upper bound for uniform algebraic gossip of $O((k + \log n + D)\Delta)$ where D is the diameter and Δ is the maximum degree in the graph. For graphs with constant maximum degree this leads to a bound of $O(k+D)$. For the synchronous case we have a matching lower bound of $\Omega(k + D)$ which makes uniform algebraic gossip an order **optimal** gossip protocol for these graphs. We conjecture that the optimality holds for the asynchronous time model as well, but only show it when $k = \Omega(D)$.

However, there are topologies for which uniform algebraic gossip performs badly, e.g., in the barbell graph (two cliques connected with a single edge) it takes $\Omega(n^2)$ rounds to perform all-to-all communication [3]. This is usually the result of bottlenecks that exist in the graph and lead to low conductance. For such "bad" topologies we propose here a modification of the uniform algebraic gossip called *Tree based Algebraic Gossip* (TAG). The basic idea of the pro-

---

*An event occurs with high probability (*w.h.p.*) if its probability is of at least $1 - O(\frac{1}{n})$.

tocol is that it operates in two phases: first, using a gossip protocol $\mathcal{S}$ it generates a spanning tree in which each node in the tree has a single parent. In the next phase, algebraic gossip is performed on the tree where each node does **EX-CHANGE** with its parent. Let $t(\mathcal{S})$ and $d(\mathcal{S})$ be the stopping time of $\mathcal{S}$ and the diameter of the tree generated by $\mathcal{S}$, respectively. For any spanning tree gossip protocol $\mathcal{S}$ we prove for TAG an upper bound of: $O(k + \log n + d(\mathcal{S}) + t(\mathcal{S}))$ for the *synchronous* and the *asynchronous* time models. As a special case of a spanning tree protocol, one can use a gossip broadcast (or 1-dissemination) protocol $\mathcal{B}$ – a protocol in which a single message originated at some node should be disseminated to all nodes. Interestingly, using a gossip broadcast for the spanning tree construction in TAG, eliminates the dependence on the diameter of the spanning tree in the synchronous time model, i.e., if we use $\mathcal{B}$ as $\mathcal{S}$, we obtain the bound of $O(k + \log n + t(\mathcal{B}))$ rounds. For a general spanning tree protocol $\mathcal{S}$, it follows directly that if $k = \Omega(\max(\log n, d(\mathcal{S}), t(\mathcal{S})))$, TAG is an order **optimal** with a stopping time of $\Theta(k)$. We provide two examples of this scenario: the first example leads to the most significant result of the paper. Using a simple round-robin-based broadcast we show that TAG is an order optimal gossip protocol for k-*dissemination* in any topology when $k = \Omega(n)$. This imply, somewhat surprisingly, that for **any graph**, if $k = \Omega(n)$, TAG finishes in $\Theta(n)$ rounds. In the barbell graph mentioned above, TAG leads to a speedup ratio of n compared to the uniform algebraic gossip. The second example makes use of a recent non-uniform information dissemination protocol from [6] that works well on graphs G with large *weak conductance* denoted by $\Phi_c(G)$ for a parameter c (see Section 6). We provide sufficient conditions on k, c and $\Phi_c(G)$ that make TAG order optimal when using the protocol of [6] as a spanning tree protocol. Table 1 summarizes our main results of the paper and next, we discuss previous results.

1.2 Related Work

Uniform algebraic gossip was first proposed by Deb *et al.* in [9]. The authors studied uniform algebraic gossip using **PULL** and **PUSH** on the *complete graph* and showed a tight bound of $\Theta(k)$, for the case of $k = \omega(log^3(n))$ messages. Boyd *et al.* [4, 5] studied the stopping time of a gossip protocol for the *averaging problem* using the **EXCHANGE** algorithm. They gave a bound for symmetric networks that is based on the second largest eigenvalue of the transition matrix or, equally, the mixing time of a random walk on the network, and showed that the mixing time captures the behavior of the protocol. Mosk-Aoyama and Shah [21] used a similar approach to [4, 5] to first analyze algebraic gossip on arbitrary networks. They consider symmetric stochastic matrices that (may) lead to a non-uniform gossip and gave an upper bound for the **PULL** algorithm that is based on a measure of conductance of the network. As the authors mentioned, the offered bound is not tight, which indicates that their conductance-based measure does not capture the full behavior of the protocol.

In [3], we used queuing theory as a novel approach for analyzing algebraic gossip. We then gave an upper bound of $O(n\Delta)$ rounds for any graph for the case of all-to-all communication, where Δ is the maximum degree in the graph. In addition, a lower bound of $\Omega(n^2)$ was obtained for the barbell graph – the worst case graph for algebraic gossip. The

Protocol	Graph	Synchronous	Asynchronous
Uniform AG	any graph	$O((k + \log n + D)\Delta)$	
	constant max degree	$\Theta(\mathbf{k} + \mathbf{D})$	$O(k + D)$ (*)
TAG	any graph	$O(k + \log n + d(\mathcal{S}) + t(\mathcal{S}))$	
		$O(k + \log n + t(\mathcal{B}))$	$O(k + \log n + d(\mathcal{B}) + t(\mathcal{B}))$
	$k = \Omega(n)$, any graph	$\Theta(\mathbf{n})$	
	$c = O(\log^p(n))$ $k = \Omega(\log^{2p+3}(n))$	$\Theta(\mathbf{k})$	$O(k + d(IS))$ (**)

Table 1: **Overview of the main results of the paper. Bold text and Θ indicate order optimal result. (*) we prove an upper bound but conjecture it is optimal. (**) we prove the upper bound but conjecture it should be $\Theta(k)$. $\mathcal{S}$ is a spanning tree protocol, $\mathcal{B}$ is a broadcast protocol, and IS is an information dissemination gossip protocol from [6].**

bounds (upper and lower) in [3] were tight in the sense that they matched each other for the worst case scenario. The parameter Δ is simple and convenient to use, but, it does not fully capture the behavior of algebraic gossip. While it gives optimal ($\Theta(n)$) result for any constant-degree graphs (e.g., line, grid), it fails to reflect the stopping time of algebraic gossip on the complete graph, for example, by giving the $O(n^2)$ bound instead of $O(n)$.

A recent (yet, unpublished) work of Haeupler [13] is the most related to our work. Haeupler's paper makes a significant progress in analyzing the stopping time of algebraic gossip. While all previous works on algebraic gossip used the notion of *helpful message/node* to look at the rank evaluation of the matrices each node maintains (this approach was initially proposed by [9]), Haeupler used a completely different approach. Instead of looking on the growth of the node's subspace (spanned by the linear equations it has), he proposed to look at the orthogonal complement of the subspace and then analyze the process of its disappearing. This elegant and powerful approach led to very impressive results. First, a tight bound of $\Theta(n/\gamma)$ was proposed for all-to-all communication, where γ is a min-cut measure of a related graph. This bound perfectly captures algebraic gossip behavior for any network topology. For the case of k-dissemination, the author gives a conjecture that the upper bound is of the form of $O(k + T)$ where T is the time to disseminate a single message to all the nodes. But formally, the bound that is proved is $O(k/\gamma + \log^2 n/\lambda)$ where λ is a conductance-based measure of the graph (Lemma 7.6 in [13]). The work in [13] implicitly considered the uniform algebraic gossip, but could be extended to non-uniform cases. It is therefore hard to compare TAG to the results of [13], nevertheless, our bounds for the uniform algebraic gossip are better for certain families of graphs. Table 2 presents few such examples.

To give a quick summary of our results and previous work, the two main contributions of the paper are i) we prove that for graphs with constant maximum degree uniform algebraic gossip is order optimal for k-dissemination in the synchronous time model and ii) we offer a new non-uniform algebraic gossip protocol, TAG, that is order optimal for large selections of graphs and k. The rest of the paper is organized as follows: in Section 2 we give definitions. Section 3 proves results for uniform algebraic gossip and Section 4 presents the TAG protocol and its general bound. Sections 5 and 6, then, discuss cases where TAG is optimal.

2. PRELIMINARIES

We model the communication network by a connected undirected graph $G_n = G_n(V,E)$, where V is the set of vertices and E is the set of edges. The number of vertices in the graph is $|V| = n$. Let $N(v) \subseteq V$ be a set of neighbors of node v and $d_v = |N(v)|$ its degree, let $\Delta = \max_v d_v$ be the maximum degree of G_n, and let D be the diameter of the graph.

We consider two time models: asynchronous and synchronous. In the *asynchronous* time model at every **timeslot, one node** selected independently and uniformly at random, takes an action and a single pair of nodes communicates[†]. We consider n consecutive timeslots as one *round*. In the *synchronous* time model at every **round, every node** takes an action and selects a single communication partner. It is assumed that the information received in the current round will be available to a node for sending only at the beginning of the next round. A **Gossip communication model** (sometimes called gossip algorithm) defines the way information is spread in the network. In the gossip communication model, a node that wakes up (according to the time model) can initiate communication only with a single neighbor[‡] (i.e., communication partner). The model describes how the communication partner is chosen and in which direction (to – PUSH, from –PULL, or both – EXCHANGE) the message is sent. In this work we use the following communication models:

DEFINITION 1 (UNIFORM GOSSIP). *Uniform gossip is a gossip in which a communication partner is chosen randomly and uniformly among all the neighbors.*

DEFINITION 2 (ROUND-ROBIN ($\mathcal{RR}$) GOSSIP). *In round-robin gossip, the communication partner is chosen according to a fixed, cyclic list, of the nodes' neighbors. This list dictates the order in which neighbors are being contacted. If the initial partner is chosen at random, this gossip communication model is known as the* quasirandom rumor spreading *model[1, 11].*

2.1 Gossip Protocols

[†] Alternatively, this model can be seen as each node having a clock which ticks at the times of a rate 1 Poisson process and there is a total n clock ticks per round [4].

[‡] Note that this implies that in the synchronous model a node can communicate with more than a single neighbor, if other nodes initiate communication with it.

Graph	$O(k/\gamma + \log^2 n/\lambda)/n$ [13]	$O((k + \log n + D)\Delta)$ [here]	Improvement factor
Line	$O(k + n\log^2 n)$	$O(k + n)$	$\log^2 n$
Grid	$O(k + \sqrt{n}\log^2 n)$	$O(k + \sqrt{n})$	$\log^2 n$ for $k = O(\sqrt{n})$
Binary Tree	$O(k + n\log^2 n)$	$O(k + \log n)$	$\Omega(\frac{n\log n}{k})$

Table 2: Comparison of our results with [13]

Gossip protocols define the task and the message content. In turn, a gossip protocol can use any of the gossip communication models defined above (and others). We will use two types of gossip protocols here. The first is **STP Gossip** – protocols whose task is to create a *spanning tree* of the graph. The goal of a Gossip STP protocol $\mathcal{S}$ is that every node, except a node which is the *root*, will have a single neighbor called the *parent*. Note that one simple way to generate a spanning tree is by using a 1-dissemination protocol, namely a broadcast protocol.

The second protocol, is a k-dissemination protocol called **Algebraic Gossip**. In algebraic gossip, every message sent by a node is sent according to the random linear coding (RLNC) technique which is described next. As mentioned, algebraic gossip can use any of the communication models presented above.

2.2 Random Linear Network Coding (RLNC)

The random linear network coding approach is used in algebraic gossip for building outgoing messages to achieve fast information dissemination. Let $\mathbb{F}_q$ be a field of size q. There are $k \leq n$ initial messages $(x_1, ..., x_k)$ that are represented as vectors in $\mathbb{F}_q^r$. We can represent every message as an integer value bounded by M, and therefore, $r = \lceil \log_q(M) \rceil$. All transmitted messages have a fixed length and represent linear equations over $\mathbb{F}_q$. The variables (unknowns) of these equations are the initial values $x_i \in \mathbb{F}_q^r$, $1 \leq i \leq k$ and a message contains the coefficients of the variables and the result of the equation; therefore the length of each message is: $r \log_2 q + k \log_2 q$ bits (and it is usually assumed that $r \gg n$ [9]). A message is built as a random linear combination of all messages stored by the node and the coefficients are drawn uniformly at random from $\mathbb{F}_q$. A received message will be appended to the node's stored messages only if it is independent of all linear equations (messages) that are already stored by the node and otherwise it is ignored. Nodes store messages (linear equations) in a matrix form and once the dimension (or rank) of the matrix becomes k, a node can solve the linear system and discover all the k messages.

The following definition is necessary for understanding the concept of helpfulness in the analysis of algebraic gossip.

DEFINITION 3 (HELPFUL NODE AND HELPFUL MESSAGE). *We say that a node x is a **helpful node** to a node y if and only if a random linear combination constructed by x can be linearly independent with all equations (messages) stored in y. We call a message a **helpful message** if it increases the dimension (or rank) of the node (i.e., the rank of the matrix in which the node stores the messages).*

3. κ-DISSEMINATION WITH UNIFORM ALGEBRAIC GOSSIP

The main result of this section is that uniform algebraic

gossip is order optimal k-dissemination for graphs with constant maximum degree and for any selection of k. It is formally stated in Theorem 3 and is an almost direct result of the following general bound for uniform algebraic gossip:

THEOREM 1. *For any connected graph G_n, the stopping time of the uniform algebraic gossip protocol with k messages is $O((k + \log n + D)\Delta)$ rounds for synchronous and asynchronous time models w.h.p.*

The idea of the proof relies on the queuing networks technique we presented in [3]. The major steps of the proof are:

- Perform a Breath First Search (BFS) on G_n starting at an arbitrary node v. The search results in a directed shortest path spanning tree T_n rooted at v. The maximum depth $l_{\max}$ of the tree T_n rooted at v is at most D.

- Reduce the problem of algebraic gossip on a tree T_n to a simple system of queues Q_n^{tree} rooted at v, where at each node we assume an infinite queue with a single server. Every initial message becomes a customer in the queuing system. The root v finishes once all the customers arrive at it.

- Show that the stopping time of the tree topology queuing system – Q_n^{tree}, is $O((k + \log n + l_{\max})n\Delta)$ timeslots w.h.p. So, we obtain the stopping time for the node v.

- Use union bound to obtain the result for all the nodes in G_n.

Just before we start the formal proof of Theorem 1, we present an interesting theorem related to queuing theory. The theorem gives the stopping time of the feedforward queuing system [8] arranged in a tree topology. Consider the following scenario: n identical M/M/1 queues arranged in a tree topology. There are no external arrivals, and there are k customers arbitrarily distributed in the system. In the feedforward network, a customer can not enter the same queue more than once, thus, customers eventually leave the system via the queue at the root of the tree. We ask the following question: how much time will it take for the last customer to leave the system?

THEOREM 2. *Let Q_n^{tree} be a network of n nodes arranged in a tree topology, rooted at the node v. The depth of the tree is $l_{\max}$. Each node has an infinite queue, and a single exponential server with parameter μ. The total amount of customers in the system is k and they are initially distributed arbitrarily in the network. The time by which all the customers leave the network via the root node v is $t(Q_n^{tree}) = O((k + l_{\max} + \log n)/\mu)$ timeslots with probability of at least $1 - \frac{2}{n^2}$.*

The main idea of the proof is to show that the stopping time of the network Q_n^{tree} (i.e., the time by which all the customers leave the network) is stochastically[§] smaller or equal to the stopping time of the systems of $l_{\max}$ queues arranged in a line topology – $Q_{l_{\max}}^{line}$. Then, we make the system $Q_{l_{\max}}^{line}$ stochastically slower by moving all the customers out of the system and make them enter back via the farthest queue with the rate $\lambda = \mu/2$. Finally, we use Jackson's Theorem for open networks to find the stopping time of the system. See Fig. 1 for the illustration. The full proof of the above theorem can be found in the full version of the paper [2]. We can now prove Theorem 1.

PROOF PROOF OF THEOREM 1. We start the analysis of the uniform algebraic gossip with k messages and the asynchronous time model. First, we perform a Breath First Search (BFS) on G_n starting at an arbitrary node v. The search results in a directed shortest path spanning tree T_n rooted at v. The depth of T_n is $l_{\max}$, and since T_n is the shortest path tree, $l_{\max} \leq D$, where D is the diameter of the graph. On the tree T_n, consider a message flow towards the root v from all other nodes. Once k *helpful messages* arrive at v, it will reach rank k and finish the algebraic gossip protocol. We ignore messages that are not sent in the direction of v. Ignoring part of messages can only increase the stopping time of the algebraic gossip protocol.

We define a queuing system Q_n^{tree} by assuming an infinite queue with a single server at each node. The root of Q_n^{tree} is the node v. Customers of our queuing network are *helpful messages*, i.e., messages that increase the rank of a node they arrive at. This means that every customer arriving at some node increases its rank by 1. When a customer leaves a node, it arrives at the parent node. The queue length of a node represents a measure of *helpfulness* of the node to its parent, i.e., the number of *helpful messages* it can generate for it.

The service procedure at a node is a transmission of a *helpful message* towards the node v (from a node to its parent). Lemma 2.1 in [9] gives a lower bound for the probability of a message sent by a *helpful node* to be a *helpful message*, which is: $1 - \frac{1}{q}$. In the uniform gossip communication model, the communication partner of a node is chosen randomly among all the node's neighbors in the original graph G_n. The degree of each node in G_n is at most Δ. Thus, in the asynchronous time model, in a given timeslot, a *helpful message* will be sent over the edge in a specific direction with probability of at least $(1 - \frac{1}{q})/n\Delta$, where $\frac{1}{n}$ is the probability that a given node wakes up in a given timeslot, $\frac{1}{\Delta}$ is the minimal probability that a specific partner (the parent of the node) will be chosen, and $1 - \frac{1}{q}$ is the minimal probability that the message will be *helpful*. Thus, we can consider that the service time in our queuing system is geometrically distributed with parameter $p \geq (1 - \frac{1}{q})/n\Delta$, and since $q \geq 2$, we can assume the worst case: $p = \frac{1}{2n\Delta}$.

Lemma 2 in [3] shows that we can model the service time of each server as an exponential random variable with parameter $\mu = p$, since in this case, exponential servers are stochastically *slower* than geometric. Such an assumption can only increase the stopping time.

Theorem 2 with $\mu = p$ gives us an upper bound for the stopping time of the node v, $t_v = O((k + l_{\max} + \log n)2n\Delta)$

[§]For completeness, stochastic dominance is formally defined in the full version of the paper [2].

timeslots with probability of at least $1 - \frac{2}{n^2}$. Since the depth of every BFS tree is bounded by the diameter D, using a union bound we obtain the upper bound (in timeslots) for all the nodes in G_n:

$$\Pr\left(\bigcap_{v \in V} t_v = O((k + \log n + D)2n\Delta)\right) > 1 - \frac{2}{n}. \quad (1)$$

Thus we obtain the upper bound for uniform algebraic gossip: $O((k + \log n + D)\Delta)$ rounds. Next, we show that this bound holds also for the synchronous time model. The proof for the synchronous time model is almost the same as in the asynchronous case, except for the following change. Instead of dividing time into timeslots, we measure it by rounds (1 round = n timeslots). In a given **round**, a *helpful message* will be sent over the edge in a specific direction with probability $p \geq (1 - \frac{1}{q})/\Delta$, where the $\frac{1}{\Delta}$ is the minimal probability that a specific partner (the parent of the node) will be chosen, and $1 - \frac{1}{q}$ is the minimal probability that the message will be *helpful*. Since $q \geq 2$, we can assume the worst case: $p = \frac{1}{2\Delta}$. The difference from the asynchronous model is the factor of n in p, since in the synchronous model, every node wakes up exactly once in a each round. Moreover, in the synchronous case (and in the EXCHANGE gossip variation) there is a possibility to receive 2 messages from the same node in one round (in the asynchronous time model it was impossible to receive 2 messages from the same node in one timeslot). We assume that if a node receives 2 messages from the same node at the same round, it will discard the second one. Such an assumption can only increase the stopping time of the protocol, and will make our analysis simpler. From that point on, the analysis is exactly the same as in the asynchronous case since Theorem 2 does not depend on the time model. □

3.1 Optimality for Constant Maximum Degree Graphs and Synchronous Time

Following Theorem 1 we can state the main results of the section:

THEOREM 3. *For any connected graph G_n with constant maximum degree, the stopping time of the uniform algebraic gossip protocol with k messages is $\Theta(k + D)$ in the synchronous time and $O(k + D)$ in the asynchronous time w.h.p.*

PROOF. To show the upper bound the following simple claim is proved in the full version of the paper [2]:

CLAIM 1. *For any connected graph G_n with a constant maximum degree $(\Delta = O(1))$, the diameter of G_n is $\Omega(\log n)$.*

Now, using Claim 1 and fact that the maximum degree is constant the upper bound follows. For the lower bound note that in order to disseminate k messages to n nodes, at least kn transmissions should occur in the network. In synchronous time model, kn transmissions require at least $k/2$ rounds, since every round at most $2n$ messages are sent (2 transmissions per communication pair). In the asynchronous time model, kn transmissions require at least $kn/2$ timeslots, since at each timeslot at most 2 nodes transmit (due to EXCHANGE). Thus, in both time models, $\Omega(k)$ rounds are required. Moreover, in the synchronous time model, dissemination of a single message will take at least $D/2$ rounds, since in this model, a message can travel at most one hop

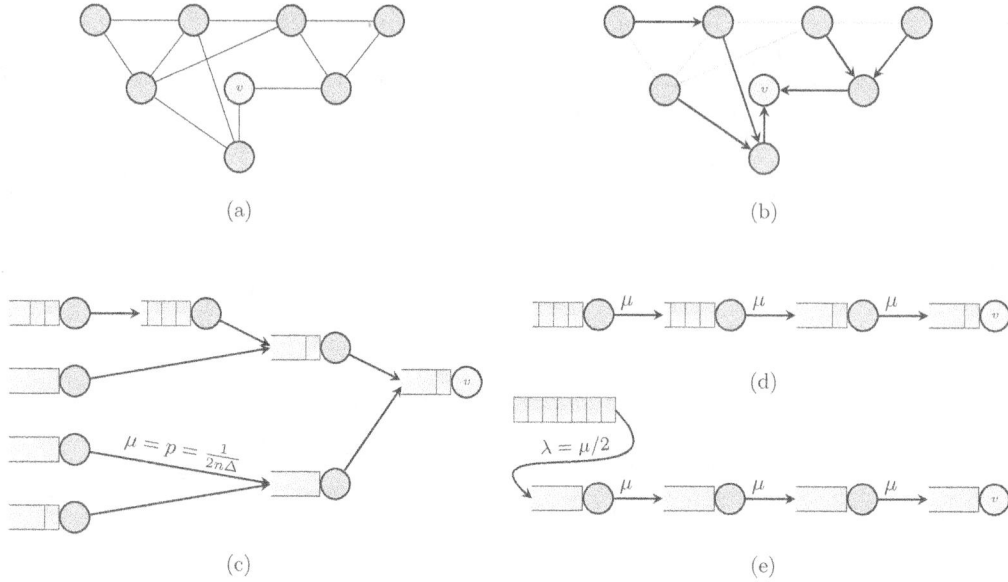

Figure 1: Reduction of AG to a system of queues. (a) – Initial graph G_n. (b) – Spanning tree T_n. (c) – System of queues Q_n^{tree}. (d) – System of queues $Q_{l_{\max}}^{line}$. Stopping time of $Q_{l_{\max}}^{line}$ is larger than of Q_n^{tree}. (e)–Taking all customers out of the system and use Jackson theorem for open networks.

Protocol TAG Pseudo code for node v. Example for asynchronous time model.

Require: $N(v)$, k, gossip spanning tree protocol $\mathcal{S}$
Initialize: $parent = null$

    On odd wakeup: // Phase 1: **EXCHANGE** gossip spanning tree protocol $\mathcal{S}$
1: choose parter $u \in N(v)$ and exchange messages with it according to $\mathcal{S}$
2: according to $\mathcal{S}$ decide if $parent = u$

    On even wakeup: // Phase 2: **EXCHANGE** algebraic gossip
3: **if** obtained $parent$ during the protocol $\mathcal{S}$ **then**
4:    exchange messages with $parent$ according to algebraic gossip (RLNC)

    On contact from other node $w \in N(v)$:
5: **if** w performs Phase 1 **then**
6:    exchange messages with w according to $\mathcal{S}$
7:    according to $\mathcal{S}$ decide if $parent = w$
8: **else**(w performs Phase 2)
9:    exchange messages with w according to algebraic gossip (RLNC)

---

in a single round. So, for the synchronous time model, the bound $\Theta(k+D)$ is tight and optimal. $\square$

4. TAG: κ-DISSEMINATION WITH TREE-BASED ALGEBRAIC GOSSIP

We now describe the protocol TAG (Tree based Algebraic Gossip), which is a k-dissemination gossip protocol that exploits algebraic gossip in conjunction with a spanning tree gossip protocol $\mathcal{S}$ (see Sec. 2). Given a connected network of

n nodes and k messages $x_1, ..., x_k$ that are initially located at some nodes, the goal of the protocol TAG is to disseminate all the k messages to all the n nodes. The protocol consists of two phases. Both phases are performed simultaneously in the following way: if a node wakes up when the total number of its wakeups until now is even, it acts according to *Phase 1* of the protocol. If the node wakes up when the total number of its wakeups until now is odd, it acts according to *Phase 2* of the protocol.

- In Phase 1, a node performs a spanning tree gossip protocol $\mathcal{S}$. Once a node becomes a part of the spanning tree, it obtains a **parent**.

- In Phase 2, a node is idle until it obtains a **parent** in Phase 1. From now on, in Phase 2, the node will perform an **EXCHANGE** algebraic gossip protocol with a fixed communication partner – its **parent**.

The following theorem gives an upper bound on the stopping time of the protocol TAG.

THEOREM 4. *Let $t(\mathcal{S})$ be the stopping time of the gossip spanning tree protocol $\mathcal{S}$ performed at Phase 1, and let $d(\mathcal{S})$ be the diameter of the spanning tree created by $\mathcal{S}$. For any connected graph G_n, the stopping time of the k-dissemination protocol TAG, is:*

$$t(TAG) = O(k + \log n + d(\mathcal{S}) + t(\mathcal{S})) \; rounds \quad (2)$$

for synchronous and asynchronous time models, and w.h.p.

PROOF. In order to prove this theorem, we will find the time needed to finish TAG, after Phase 1 is completed. Once Phase 1 is completed, every node knows its parent and thus, in Phase 2, we have the algebraic gossip **EXCHANGE** protocol on the spanning tree T_n, where communication partners of the nodes are their parents. The following lemma gives an upper bound on the stopping time of such a setting.

LEMMA 1. *Let T_n be a tree with n nodes, rooted at the node r, with depth $l_{\max}$. There are k initial messages located at some nodes in the tree. Consider algebraic gossip EXCHANGE protocol with the following communication model: the communication partner of a node is fixed to be its parent in T_n during the whole protocol. Then, the time needed for **all the nodes** to learn all the k messages is $O(k + \log n + l_{\max})$ rounds for the synchronous and asynchronous time models, with probability of at least $1 - \frac{2}{n}$.*

The proof of Lemma 1 is very similar to the proof of Theorem 1, and relies on reducing the problem of algebraic gossip to a simple system of queues. The service time is geometrically distributed with a worst-case parameter $p = \frac{1}{2n}$. The Δ is eliminated from p since each node chooses now a single communication partner. Then, using Theorem 2 we obtain the stopping time of algebraic gossip with on the tree T_n. Detailed proof of Lemma 1 can be found in the full version of the paper [2].

Since for every choice of the tree root, the depth of the tree T_n (which was created using protocol $t(\mathcal{S})$) is bounded by its diameter, we can replace the $l_{\max}$ in the bound $O(k + \log n + l_{\max})$ with $d(\mathcal{S})$. Now, we just add the stopping time of Phase 1 (the spanning tree time – $t(\mathcal{S})$) and the stopping time of Phase 2 (after Phase 1 has finished), and obtain that the number of rounds needed to complete the protocol TAG is $O(k + \log n + d(\mathcal{S}) + t(\mathcal{S}))$ w.h.p. □

4.1 TAG protocol using 1-dissemination as a spanning tree protocol

The spanning tree task can be successfully performed by a simple gossip broadcast (or 1-dissemination) protocol. When a node receives for the first time the message, it marks the sending node as its parent. In such a way we obtain a spanning tree rooted at the node that initiated the broadcast protocol. Let us denote a gossip 1-dissemination protocol as $\mathcal{B}$. Clearly, the result of Theorem 4 can be rewritten as: $t(\text{TAG}) = O(k + \log n + d(\mathcal{B}) + t(\mathcal{B}))$. An interesting observation regarding the broadcast protocol $\mathcal{B}$, is that for synchronous time model the depth of the broadcast tree cannot be larger that the broadcast time (measured in rounds), i.e., $t(\mathcal{B}) \geq d(\mathcal{B})$. The last is true since a message can not travel more than one hop in a single round. Thus, for the synchronous time model we obtain that the number of rounds needed to complete the TAG protocol w.h.p. is:

$$t(\text{TAG}) = O(k + \log n + t(\mathcal{B})). \tag{3}$$

5. OPTIMAL ALL-TO-ALL DISSEMINATION USING TAG

In this section we propose to use the TAG protocol in conjunction with a 1-dissemination (or broadcast) gossip protocol $\mathcal{B}_{\mathcal{R}\mathcal{R}}$ for spanning tree construction. For the case where $k = \Omega(n)$ messages need to be disseminated, TAG with $\mathcal{B}_{\mathcal{R}\mathcal{R}}$ achieves order optimal performance. For the case $k = \Omega(n)$ the lower bound of any gossip dissemination protocol is $\Omega(n)$ rounds. The bound from Theorem 4 gives $t(\text{TAG}) = O(k + \log n + d(\mathcal{S}) + t(\mathcal{S}))$, and if $k = n$ we obtain $O(n + t(\mathcal{S}))$. Thus, all we need to show is the existence of a gossip spanning tree protocol that finishes after $O(n)$ rounds w.h.p. on any graph.

THEOREM 5. *For any connected graph G_n, the stopping time of the broadcast protocol with the round-robin communication model - $\mathcal{B}_{\mathcal{R}\mathcal{R}}$ is $O(n)$ rounds. In the asynchronous time model, this result holds with probability of at least $1 - n(2/e)^{3n}$, and in the synchronous time model, with probability 1.*

In order to prove Theorem 5 we need the following lemma which is proved in the full version of the paper [2].

LEMMA 2. *For any connected graph G_n with n nodes, the sum of the degrees of the nodes along any shortest path between any two nodes v and u is at most $3n$.*

PROOF PROOF OF THEOREM 5. In this proof we assume the PUSH gossip variation, but it is clear that the result holds also for EXCHANGE. Without loss of generality, assume that the message that needs to be disseminated is initially located at the node v. In the *round-robin* gossip, when a node is scheduled to transmit, it transmits a message to its neighbor according to the *round robin* scheme.

Consider a shortest path between v and some other node u. On the shortest path of length l there is exactly one node at the distance i from v, where $i \in [0, \ldots, l]$, and $l \leq n - 1$. Let d_i be the degree of the node at distance i from v. In order to guarantee the delivery of the message from v to u, we need $\sum_{i=0}^{l} d_i$ transmissions in the following order: first, we need d_0 transmissions of the node v, then d_1 transmissions of the next node in the path $v \to u$, and so on until the message is delivered to u. From Theorem 2, $\sum_{i=0}^{l} d_i \leq 3n$.

In the asynchronous model, a node transmits at a given *timeslot* with probability $\frac{1}{n}$. So, the number of timeslots until some specific node transmits is a geometric random variable with parameter $\frac{1}{n}$. We define this geometric random variable as X, i.e., $X \sim \text{Geom}\left(\frac{1}{n}\right)$.

The number of timeslots until $3n$ specific transmissions occur, is the sum of $3n$ independent geometric random variables. Using a Chernoff bound we obtain $O(n^2)$ timeslots (or $O(n)$ rounds) with exponential high probability. The last allows us to perform union bound for shortest paths to all other nodes in G, thus obtaining the $O(n)$ bound for the broadcast time. We omit here the formal part of the proof which can be found in the full version of the paper [2].

It is easy to see that in the synchronous time model, $3n$ specific transmissions will occur exactly after $3n$ communication rounds. E.g., after d_0 rounds, v will perform d_0 transmissions – each one to different neighbor (according to the round-robin scheme). Thus, the message will be delivered to u after at most $3n$ rounds with probability 1. □

Using Theorems 4 and 5 we obtain the upper bound on the stopping time of TAG with $\mathcal{B}_{\mathcal{R}\mathcal{R}}$ as a spanning tree construction protocol: $O(k + \log n + d(\mathcal{S}) + n)$ which is $\Theta(n)$ for $k = \Omega(n)$.

6. GRAPHS WITH LARGE WEAK CONDUCTANCE

For values of k which are smaller than n we use the information spreading protocol (hereafter, IS) of [6], which requires only a polylogarithmic number of rounds for broadcast on graphs with large *weak conductance*. Roughly speaking, the weak conductance is a value in $[0, 1]$ that measures the connectivity of subsets of nodes of a graph. It has been used to analyze the time required for *partial* information spreading, where each message is only required to reach some fraction of the nodes. This, in turn, has been applied in the analysis of the IS protocol to show that the running time for full information spreading inversely depends on the weak conductance. The graphs with large weak conductance, for which the IS protocol is fast, form a broad family of graphs, including graphs that exhibit some (though not too many) communication bottlenecks. A simple example is the bar-bell graph, consisting of two cliques of $n/2$ nodes, connected by a single edge, which corresponds to a bottleneck since information must pass along it, but the probability of randomly choosing it is small due to large node degrees. The IS protocol overcomes this and runs in a logarithmic number of synchronous rounds on the barbell.

Formally, for an integer c, the weak conductance of a graph $G = (V, E)$ is defined as:

$$\Phi_c(G) = \min_{i \in V} \left\{ \max_{V_i \subseteq V, i \in V_i, |V_i| \geq \frac{n}{c}} \left\{ \min_{S \subseteq V_i, |S| \leq \frac{|V_i|}{2}} \varphi(S, V_i) \right\} \right\},$$

where $\varphi(S, V)$ is defined as

$$\varphi(S, V) = \frac{\sum_{i \in S, j \in V \setminus S} P_{i,j}}{|S|},$$

and P is the stochastic matrix corresponding to the communication of the nodes (i.e., $P_{i,j}$ is the probability of node i choosing to communicate with node j).

We describe the result in this section for both the synchronous and asynchronous time models considered. Although the IS protocol is designed to disseminate n messages originating one at each node, we will only use it for obtaining a spanning tree of our communication graph, while the actual information dissemination is done using algebraic gossip (i.e., we use the TAG protocol with IS as the spanning tree construction protocol). This is since the IS protocol sends large messages, while the goal of algebraic gossip is to address bandwidth concerns. The spanning tree is constructed as follows. The information sent by a node v is an n-bit string, characterizing the nodes from which v heard from, whether directly or indirectly. This corresponds to empty initial inputs, and initially the n-bit string of node v is a unit vector, characterizing only the empty input of the node v itself. The n-bit string maintained and sent by a node v is monotone, in the sense that as time passes, its entries can only change from zero to one. The spanning tree that is created corresponds to each node v declaring its parent as the first node u from which it received a message that caused its most significant bit to change from zero to one. This means that this node received the input of the node w corresponding to the most significant bit (recall that the input itself is an empty string).

The following theorem characterizes the time required for the IS protocol to complete.

THEOREM 6 ([6, THEOREM 4.1]). *For every $c > 1$ and every $\delta \in (0, 1/3c)$, the IS protocol obtains full information spreading after at most $O(c(\frac{\log(n) + \log(\delta^{-1})}{\Phi_c(G)} + c))$ rounds, with probability $\mathcal{B}$ at least $1 - 3c\delta$.*

In the synchronous model we can use the IS protocol in the TAG protocol, directly obtaining the following theorem, which shows optimality of TAG for certain families of parameters.

THEOREM 7. *Let $c = O(\log^p(n))$ for some $p \geq 0$, let G be a graph with weak conductance $\Phi_c = \Omega(\frac{1}{\log^p(n)})$, and let $k = \Omega(\log^{2p+1}(n))$. With probability at least $1 - \frac{1}{n}$, the time for disseminating k messages using protocol TAG in conjunction with the IS protocol is $\Theta(k)$ synchronous rounds.*

We show that the IS protocol works in the asynchronous model as well. While this is not a direct usage of the protocol due to some subtleties, we nevertheless show how to obtain our result as for the synchronous model. Our analysis induces an overhead of $O(\log^2(n))$ rounds.

We do not change the protocol itself to cope with asynchrony, but rather analyze the time required using additional techniques. Roughly speaking, the outline of our analysis is showing that segments of the asynchronous execution simulate synchronous rounds. This allows us to use the original analysis of the protocol for the simulated rounds, which gives our result, as stated in the following theorem, and proved in the full version of the paper [2].

THEOREM 8. *Let $c = O(\log^p(n))$ for some $p \geq 0$, let G be a graph with weak conductance $\Phi_c = \Omega(\frac{1}{\log^p(n)})$, and let $k = \Omega(\log^{2p+3}(n))$. With probability at least $1 - \frac{1}{n}$, the time for disseminating k messages using protocol TAG in conjunction with the IS protocol is $O(k + l_{\max})$ rounds for the asynchronous time model, where $l_{\max}$ is the depth of the spanning tree induced by the IS protocol.*

For completeness, we note that, in IS, during the even-numbered steps of each node the choice of neighbor is randomized. For these steps alone, adapting the analysis Mosk-Aoyama and Shah [20] for the asynchronous case to our protocol, implies that the extra $\log(n)$ timeslots can be avoided for the purpose of partial information spreading alone (as used in the proof of the information spreading protocol ([6, Theorem 2.2]). However, as this cost is required anyhow to argue about the deterministic choices, made during the odd-numbered steps, we omit going through this adjustment.

7. CONCLUSION

In this work we have studied the problem of disseminating information from a subset of k nodes to all the n nodes on connected graphs. While our previous work [3] has focused on the all-to-all dissemination problem (i.e., n-dissemination), the current paper deals with k-dissemination. We prove bounds for the uniform algebraic gossip which are optimal for some graph families (e.g., for graphs with a constant maximum degree). For some topologies, our bounds are better than any previously known results. Moreover, we propose here an altenative dissemination technique based on algebraic gossip (the TAG protocol) which is an optimal dissemination scheme for some settings (e.g., for $k = \Omega(n)$). The optimality of the bound for uniform algebraic gossip for constant maximum degree graphs is shown only for the synchronous time model, however, we conjecture that it also true for the asynchronous case. Another unproven conjecture is that the stopping time of the TAG protocol for the asynchronous time model does not depend on the diameter of the spanning tree created by the broadcast protocol $\mathcal{B}$ or, on the diameter of the spanning tree created by information dissemination protocol IS. In the future work we aim to address all the above conjectures, and also continue to analyze gossip dissemination protocols in various settings, e.g., in dynamic graphs.

8. REFERENCES

[1] S. Angelopoulos, B. Doerr, A. Huber, and K. Panagiotou. Tight bounds for quasirandom rumor spreading. *The Electronic Journal of Combinatorics*, 16(1):R102,1–R102,19, 2009.

[2] C. Avin, M. Borokhovich, K. Censor-Hillel, and Z. Lotker. Order optimal information spreading using algebraic gossip. *CoRR*, abs/1101.4372, 2011.

[3] M. Borokhovich, C. Avin, and Z. Lotker. Tight bounds for algebraic gossip on graphs. In *2010 IEEE International Symposium on Information Theory Proceedings (ISIT)*, pages 1758–1762, jun. 2010.

[4] S. Boyd, A. Ghosh, B. Prabhakar, and D. Shah. Randomized gossip algorithms. *IEEE Transactions on Information Theory*, 52(6):2508–2530, June 2006.

[5] S. P. Boyd, A. Ghosh, B. Prabhakar, and D. Shah. Gossip algorithms: design, analysis and applications. In *IEEE International Conference on Computer Communications (INFOCOM)*, pages 1653–1664, 2005.

[6] K. Censor-Hillel and H. Shachnai. Fast information spreading in graphs with large weak conductance. In *Proceedings of the 22nd ACM-SIAM Symposium on Discrete Algorithms (SODA)*, pages 440–448, 2011.

[7] A. Chaintreau, P. Fraigniaud, and E. Lebhar. Opportunistic spatial gossip over mobile social networks. In *WOSP '08: Proceedings of the first workshop on Online social networks*, pages 73–78, New York, NY, USA, 2008. ACM.

[8] H. Chen and D. Yao. *Fundamentals of Queueing Networks: Performance, Asymptotics, and Optimization*, volume 46 of *Applications of Mathematics*. Springer-Verlag, New York, first edition, 2001.

[9] S. Deb, M. Médard, and C. Choute. Algebraic gossip: a network coding approach to optimal multiple rumor mongering. *IEEE Transactions on Information Theory*, 52(6):2486–2507, 2006.

[10] A. J. Demers, D. H. Greene, C. Hauser, W. Irish, J. Larson, S. Shenker, H. E. Sturgis, D. C. Swinehart, and D. B. Terry. Epidemic algorithms for replicated database maintenance. *Operating Systems Review*, 22(1):8–32, 1988.

[11] B. Doerr, T. Friedrich, and T. Sauerwald. Quasirandom rumor spreading. In *Proceedings of the nineteenth annual ACM-SIAM symposium on Discrete algorithms*, SODA '08, pages 773–781, Philadelphia, PA, USA, 2008. Society for Industrial and Applied Mathematics.

[12] C. Georgiou, S. Gilbert, R. Guerraoui, and D. R. Kowalski. On the complexity of asynchronous gossip. In *PODC '08: Proceedings of the twenty-seventh ACM symposium on Principles of distributed computing*, pages 135–144, New York, NY, USA, 2008. ACM.

[13] B. Haeupler. Analyzing Network Coding Gossip Made Easy. To appear in the *43rd ACM Symposium on Theory of Computing (STOC)*, 2011.

[14] T. Ho, R. Koetter, M. Medard, D. R. Karger, and M. Effros. The benefits of coding over routing in a randomized setting. In *IEEE International Symposium on Information Theory (ISIT)*, page 442, 2003.

[15] R. M. Karp, C. Schindelhauer, S. Shenker, and B. Vöcking. Randomized rumor spreading. In *Annual IEEE Symposium on Foundations of Computer Science (FOCS)*, pages 565–574, 2000.

[16] D. Kempe, A. Dobra, and J. Gehrke. Gossip-based computation of aggregate information. In *Annual IEEE Symposium on Foundations of Computer Science (FOCS)*, pages 482–491, 2003.

[17] D. Kempe, J. Kleinberg, and Éva Tardos. Maximizing the spread of influence through a social network. In *KDD '03: Proceedings of the ninth ACM SIGKDD international conference on Knowledge discovery and data mining*, pages 137–146, New York, NY, USA, 2003. ACM.

[18] S.-Y. R. Li, R. W. Yeung, and N. Cai. Linear network coding. *IEEE Transactions on Information Theory*, 49(2):371–381, 2003.

[19] M. Médard and R. Koetter. Beyond routing: An algebraic approach to network coding. In *IEEE International Conference on Computer Communications (INFOCOM)*, pages 122–130, 2002.

[20] D. Mosk-Aoyama and D. Shah. Computing separable functions via gossip. In *PODC '06: Proceedings of the twenty-fifth annual ACM symposium on Principles of distributed computing*, pages 113–122, New York, NY, USA, 2006. ACM.

[21] D. Mosk-Aoyama and D. Shah. Information dissemination via network coding. In *IEEE International Symposium on Information Theory Proceedings (ISIT)*, pages 1748–1752, 2006.

Time-Efficient Randomized Multiple-Message Broadcast in Radio Networks

Majid Khabbazian[*]
Department of Applied Computer Science
University of Winnipeg, Canada
m.khabbazian@uwinnipeg.ca

Dariusz R. Kowalski[†]
Department of Computer Science
University of Liverpool, United Kingdom
D.Kowalski@liverpool.ac.uk

ABSTRACT

Multiple-message broadcast, or k-broadcast, is one of the fundamental problems in network communication. In short, there are k packets distributed across the network, each of them has to be delivered to all other nodes. We consider this task in the model of multi-hop radio network, in which n nodes interact by transmitting and receiving messages. A message transmitted at a round reaches all neighbors of the transmitter at the end of the same round, but may not be successfully received by some, or even all, of these neighbors. More specifically, a node receives a message at a round if this is the only message that has reached this node in this round. Due to this specific interference-prone nature of radio networks, many communication tasks become more challenging and more costly than in other types of networks, especially in ad-hoc setting in which each node knows only its own id and linear estimates on the basic network parameters, such as the number of nodes n, diameter D and maximum node degree Δ. We design a new randomized k-broadcast algorithm combining the best of two worlds: efficient randomized transmission schedules and network coding. We show that our algorithm accomplishes multi-broadcast in $O(\log \Delta)$ amortized number of communication rounds per packet, with high probability. This improves over the best previous solution of Bar-Yehuda, Israeli and Itai [5], which guarantees only $O(\log \Delta \log n)$ of amortized number of rounds per packet, with high probability.

Categories and Subject Descriptors

F.2.2 [**Analysis of Algorithms and Problem Complexity**]: Nonnumerical Algorithms and Problems—*Computa-*

---

[*]The work of this author was supported by the Natural Sciences and Engineering Research Council of Canada.

[†]The work of this author was supported by the Engineering and Physical Sciences Research Council [grant numbers EP/G023018/1, EP/H018816/1].

tions on discrete structures; G.2.2 [**Discrete Mathematics**]: Graph Theory—*Network problems*

General Terms

Algorithms, Theory

Keywords

radio networks, multiple-message broadcast, randomized algorithm

1. INTRODUCTION

In this work we study the problem of simultaneous broadcasting of k packets, distributed arbitrarily across the network, to all nodes in the underlying radio network. This problem is called *multiple-message broadcast*. The underlying radio network is represented by an undirected graph $G(V, E)$. Let $|V| = n$, $n \geq 2$, be the number of nodes in G, D be the network diameter, and Δ be the maximum node degree. We assume that every node knows only its own id and the basic network parameters: n, Δ and D.[1] Let k, $k \geq 1$, be the number of packets to be delivered to all other nodes in the network; this parameter is not a priori known to the nodes.[2] We denote by b the maximum size of a packet, measured in the number of bits. Since each packet specification includes at least one ID, we assume that $b \geq \log n$ and the length of each transmitted message is $\mathcal{O}(b)$. We assume that every node that initially possesses a packet wakes up at time 0, that is, before the first round. Other nodes wake up as soon as they receive a message.

Radio network is one of the classic models of wireless networks. In this setting, n nodes interact with each other by transmitting and receiving messages. A message transmitted at a round reaches all neighbors of the transmitter at the end of the same round, but may not be successfully received by some, or even all, of these neighbors. More specifically, a node receives a message at a round if this is the only message that has reached this node in this round, i.e., exactly one neighbor of this node has transmitted at the current

---

[1]In fact, throughout the paper we use slightly weaker assumptions that nodes only need to know a polynomial upper bound on n and Δ, and a linear upper bound on D.

[2]We implicitly assume that k is bounded from above by some polynomial in n, for the sake of simplicity of algorithm design and analysis. If the real number of packets is larger than some fixed polynomial, nodes locally split the initially stored packets and apply the solution for polynomial number of packets separately for each group.

round. This implies that we do not assume a collision detection mechanism hardwired at nodes, in the sense that the system does not provide a feedback to a node that allows to distinguishing between the following two cases: none of the neighbors has transmitted, or at least two neighbors have transmitted.

Our contribution.

In this paper, we propose a multiple-message broadcast algorithm and show that using this algorithm, every node receives all k packets by time $\mathcal{O}(k \log \Delta + (D + \log n) \log n \log \Delta)$, with high probability. Our solution efficiently combines the advantages of randomized techniques and simple coding in the context of radio networks. This improves over the best known result of Bar-Yehuda, Israeli and Itai [5], which guaranteed only $\mathcal{O}(k \log n \log \Delta + (D + n/\log n) \log n \log \Delta)$ completion time in expectation. In terms of per-packet amortized complexity, our solution guarantees packet delivery in amortized number of $\mathcal{O}(\log \Delta)$ rounds, with high probability, which is a substantial improvement over the previous $\mathcal{O}(\log \Delta \log n)$ amortized number of rounds per packet, in expectation. Our solution could be efficiently used as a building block of various applications, including update of routing tables, learning topology of the underlying network (in order to benefit from efficiency of centralized solutions), aggregating functions in sensor networks, etc. In all these cases, the inherited average cost per amount of information is only $\mathcal{O}(\log \Delta)$, with high probability.

Previous and related work.

Algorithmic aspects of radio communication have been widely studied in the last two decades. The formal model for multi-hop radio networks was introduced in the context of broadcasting by Chlamtac and Kutten [6]. In the early stage, the research in this area focused on basic communication primitives, such as already mentioned broadcast [1, 4] and point-to-point communication [5].

Bar-Yehuda et al. [5] were the first who considered a multi-message broadcast in radio networks. They designed the algorithm accomplishing this task in

$$\mathcal{O}(k \log n \log \Delta + (D + n/\log n) \log n \log \Delta)$$

rounds, in expectation. Khabbazian et al. [16] presented a modular approach to broadcasting in radio networks, and devised a multiple-message broadcast algorithm in this framework working in $\mathcal{O}((k\Delta \log n + D) \log \Delta)$ rounds, with high probability. The best known lower bound for randomized solutions is $\Omega(k + \log(n/D))$, in expectation [9, 19]. The best known deterministic solutions to the problem of multiple-message broadcast in ad-hoc radio networks works in time

$$\mathcal{O}(\min\{(k+n)n^{1/2} \log^3 n, (k+n^{5/2}) \log^3 n\})$$

[10, 14]. On the other hand, the best known lower bound for the time complexity of a deterministic solution is $\Omega(k + n \log n)$ [9, 10, 12, 15, 17]. A lower bound $\Omega(n \log n)$ on the length of broadcast schedule in case $k = n$ was proved by Gasieniec and Potapov [15], and it holds for any, even randomized algorithms (though this result holds under assumption that the nodes cannot look into the content of the packets).

Bar-Yehuda et al. [4] designed a randomized broadcast algorithm and showed that it accomplishes broadcasting of a single packet in $\mathcal{O}((D + \log n) \log \Delta)$ rounds, with high

probability. This result was later improved to $\mathcal{O}((D + \log n) \log(\min\{\Delta, n/D\}))$ independently by Kowalski and Pelc [17] and Czumaj and Rytter [13]. The matching lower bound was proved by Kushilevitz and Mansour [19]. Chlebus et al. [9] considered a related problem of many-to-many group communication, in which a subset of awaken nodes needs to exchange messages. In ad-hoc setting they showed

$$\mathcal{O}((d + \log p) \log^2 n + p \log p)$$

time complexity, with high probability, where p is the number of awaken nodes and d is the maximum distance between any two such nodes. Related problems of point-to-point communication and all-to-all communication in radio networks were also considered in both deterministic and randomized setting, c.f., [5, 11, 12, 13].

1.1 Mathematical Preliminaries

In the analysis of our main result we will use the following three facts. The first two lemmas estimate the probability of concentration of the sum of independent Bernoulli trials and random variables of geometric distribution, respectively (we will refer to them as Chernoff-type inequalities). The third lemma estimates the probability of achieving a full rank by a matrix with randomly chosen binary entries. These results can be easily derived from other similar results, such as presented in [2], but for the sake of completeness we attach their proofs in Appendix A (see also [16] for Lemma 1).

LEMMA 1. **(Chernoff-type bound for the sum of Bernoulli trials)** *Let $Y_q, q = 1, \ldots$ be a collection of independent $\{0, 1\}$-valued random variables, each equal to 1 with probability $p > 0$. Let d and τ be nonnegative reals, $d \geq 1$. Let $r = \lfloor \frac{1}{p}(3d + 2\tau) \rfloor$. Then*

$$Pr(\sum_{q=1}^{r} Y_q < d) \leq e^{-\tau}.$$

LEMMA 2. **(Chernoff-type bound for the sum of geometric random variables)** *For $i = 1, \ldots, k$, let X_i be independent geometric random variables with parameter p_i. Further, we define $X = \sum_{i=1}^{k} X_i$, $\mu = \mathbb{E}[X] = \sum_{i=1}^{k} 1/p_i$, and $p_{\min} = \min_{i \in [k]} p_i$. For every $\epsilon > 0$, it holds that*

$$\Pr\left(X \geq 2\mu + \frac{4\ln(1/\epsilon)}{p_{\min}}\right) \leq \epsilon.$$

LEMMA 3. **(Rank of a random binary matrix)** *Let l and w be positive integers. Suppose $l \geq 2(w + 2) + 8\ln(\frac{1}{\epsilon})$. Let $A = (a_{i,j})$ be a $(l \times w)$-binary-matrix with elements independently and identically distributed as:*

$$Pr(a_{i,j} = 0) = Pr(a_{i,j} = 1) = \frac{1}{2}.$$

Then, A has full rank with probability at least $1 - \epsilon$.

We will often use term *with high probability* (or *w.h.p.* for short) to denote probability $1 - n^{-c}$, for a sufficiently large constant $c > 1$.

2. MULTIPLE-MESSAGE BROADCAST ALGORITHM

Our proposed multiple-message broadcast algorithm consists of the following consecutive stages:

Stage 1: Leader election:

In this stage, among the nodes that have at least one packet, the node with the highest ID is selected as a leader.[3] This stage will take

$$\mathcal{O}((D + \log n) \log n \log \Delta)$$

rounds. By the end of this stage a leader is elected, w.h.p.

Stage 2: Construction of distributed BFS:

In this stage, a BFS tree with the leader as the root is constructed. The stage consists of D phases, each containing $\mathcal{O}(\log n \log \Delta)$ rounds. By the end of each phase d, where $1 \leq d \leq D$, every node at distance d from the root determines its parent in the tree as well as its distance to the root, w.h.p.

Stage 3: Packet collection:

In each phase of this stage nodes estimate the total number of packets (i.e., k) and unicast their packets to the root (along the BFS path) with some random delays. Recall that Stage 2 guarantees that each node knows its parent in the BFS path to the root. We show that in $\mathcal{O}(k + (D + \log n) \log n)$ rounds, the root collects all k packets, w.h.p.

Stage 4: Packet dissemination:

Recall that in the beginning of this stage, the root has all the packets, w.h.p. In this stage, the root broadcasts all k packets in time

$$\mathcal{O}(k \log \Delta + D \log n \log \Delta)$$

using network coding.

In the remainder of this section we describe the details of each stage of our algorithm.

2.1 Stage 1: Leader election

We say a multiple-access channel has capability of collision detection if devices using that channel can distinguish the case of no transmission from the case of multi-transmissions (i.e., transmission of more than one neighbor). Bar-Yehuda et al. [3] showed how to emulate one round of an algorithm specified for a multiple-access channel with capability of collision detection on a multi-hop radio network without collision detection, w.h.p. Using this emulation, a deterministic binary search algorithm based on collision detection can be used to select a node with maximum ID (c.f., [17]). The binary search algorithm requires $\log n$ rounds when run on a multiple-access channel with collision detection. Combining this algorithm with the emulation protocol from [3], and using union bound with respect to low probability of unsuccessful emulation of a single round on a multiple-access channel, we obtain the following result.

FACT 1. *There is a randomized algorithm electing a leader in $\mathcal{O}((D + \log n) \log n \log \Delta)$ rounds in any n-node network with diameter at most D, with high probability.*

---

[3]The reason we choose a leader from the nodes who have at least one packet is to avoid waking up other nodes if not necessary. Note however that some nodes with no packet can be involved in the next stages of the protocol to relay messages if necessary.

2.2 Stage 2: Construction of distributed BFS

We use the algorithm proposed in [4]. It proceeds in D phases, each consisting of $\mathcal{O}(\log n \log \Delta)$ rounds. At each phase d, $0 \leq d \leq D-1$, only nodes with distance d from the leader (the root of the constructed BFS tree) participate in transmitting BFS construction messages. Each construction message includes the ID of the transmitter and its distance to the leader. At each phase, the set of participating nodes use the Decay algorithm [4] to transmit its construction message. If a node receives a construction message for the first time, it selects the sender of this message as its parent in the BFS tree and sets its distance equal to the distance of its parent plus one.

THEOREM 1. *[4] The distributed BFS algorithm terminates in $\mathcal{O}(D \log n \log \Delta)$ rounds, and at the end each node knows its parent in the constructed BFS tree and its distance to the root, w.h.p.*

2.3 Stage 3: Packet collection

The objective of this stage is to collect all the packets at the leader selected in Stage 1. Recall that the leader is also a root of the BFS tree. This stage is partitioned into phases, and each phase is further split into two epochs called grabbing epoch and alarming epoch, respectively. Inside epochs, two different subroutines are used: $\mathcal{GRAB}$ and $\mathcal{ALARM}$; they will be described in detail later.

In the *grabbing epoch*, nodes with at least one packet to be delivered, unicast all their packets to the root along the BFS path using sub-routine $\mathcal{GRAB}$. In the *alarming epoch*, the nodes that have not received an acknowledgment for at least one of their packets, execute procedure $\mathcal{ALARM}$.

Since k, the total number of the packets, is not known in advance. Therefore, the nodes estimate it, starting with value $(D + \log n) \log n$ set up in the beginning of the first phase. If a node receives an alarm message in a phase, it doubles its estimate of k in the beginning of the next phase. The collection stage is finished at the end of a phase in which no alarm message is received.

2.3.1 Two main sub-routines

We define two sub-routines, which are executed in the grabbing and alarming epochs of each phase.

Sub-routine $\mathcal{GRAB}$.

Before specifying sub-routine $\mathcal{GRAB}$, we first present its main building block — procedure *One_Shot_Partial_Gather* ($\mathcal{OSPG}$ for short) — parameterized by x. In $\mathcal{OSPG}(x)$ each node that has at least one packet to be sent (except the root), chooses a random number between 1 and $6x$ for each of its packets. If the number assigned to a packet is r, then at round r of the grabbing epoch, the node starts unicasting the message towards the root along the BFS path; more precisely, in each step of the unicast a node that has received the packet in the previous round from its child, transmits it with the information that it is addressed to its parent (recall that after Stage 2, there is a BFS tree such that each node knows its parent in this tree, w.h.p.). If two or more packets stored at a node are assigned the same number, the node unicasts only one of them, selected arbitrarily. This part of procedure takes $6x + D$ rounds.

After round $6x + D$, the root unicasts acknowledgments for packets received in the current epoch, one after another, with delay of 3 to ensures that they do not collide with each other while being forwarded along their BFS paths. Each intermediate node along the path forwards an acknowledgment to the child node in the BFS tree from which it has received the corresponding packet in the grabbing epoch. This will last at most $3 \cdot (6x+D)+D$ rounds because the maximum distance to the root is D, and the root can collect at most $6x+D$ packets in that epoch (more precisely, all of them arrived during the first $6x+D$ rounds of the epoch, each in a different round). Therefore, we bound the length of procedure $\mathcal{OSPG}(x)$ by $(6x+D)+(3 \cdot (6x+D)+D) = 24x+5D$ rounds.

Note that some of the packets propagated towards the root in the first part of procedure $\mathcal{OSPG}(x)$ may get lost somewhere in the path to the root due to a collision, as we do not implement any mechanism to recover from collisions during procedure $\mathcal{OSPG}(x)$.

However, if a packet is successfully delivered to the root, the corresponding acknowledgement will be propagated backwards without any collision, and thus every successfully received packet at the root will also be acknowledged at the originator of the packet. We will also show later in this section that the root will receive at least half of all packets with high probability if x is large enough. See the proof of Lemma 4 for details. Further, we define a procedure $Multi\_Shot\_Partial\_Gather$ ($\mathcal{MSPG}(x,z)$ for short), which works similar to $\mathcal{OSPG}(x)$, with the exception that every packet selects z rounds (instead of one) from $[1,6x]$ and a copy of the packet is propagated in each of the selected rounds.

Using procedures $\mathcal{OSPG}$ and $\mathcal{MSPG}$, we define subroutine $\mathcal{GRAB}(x)$, in which $\mathcal{OSPG}(y)$ is called several times for specific values of y and followed by one execution of $\mathcal{MSPG}$ according to the sequence:

$$\mathcal{OSPG}(x), \mathcal{OSPG}\left(\frac{x}{2}\right), \ldots, \mathcal{OSPG}\left(\frac{x}{2^i}\right), \ldots$$
$$\ldots, \mathcal{OSPG}\left(c \log n\right), \mathcal{MSPG}\left(c^2 \log^2 n, c \log n\right)$$

for a sufficiently large constant c. Sub-routine $\mathcal{GRAB}$ is used in the grabbing epoch of each phase. Note that if procedure $\mathcal{OSPG}(y)$, for any y, guarantees that at least half of the remaining y packets will be collected by the root w.h.p., as we stressed above, then the resulting sub-routine $\mathcal{GRAB}(x)$ should reduce the number of non-collected packets first to at most $c \log n$, and then to 0, w.h.p. The latter reduction is based on the fact that each copy of a packet has a constant probability to be sent by its source in a unique round (and thus to be delivered to the root without a collision), and hence, every packet is delivered w.h.p., by Chernoff bound for sufficiently large c. Note that the length of sub-routine $\mathcal{GRAB}(x)$ is bounded by $(24x+5D)+(12x+5D)+\ldots+(24c \log n+5D)+(24c^2 \log^2 n+5D) = \mathcal{O}(x+D \log x + \log^2 n)$.

Sub-routine $\mathcal{ALARM}$.

The second subroutine we use is called $\mathcal{ALARM}$, and is executed in the alarming epoch of each phase. Each node that has at least one non-acknowledged packet, initializes a broadcast in order to distribute an alarm message (a single bit 1). The purpose of this broadcast is to inform all other nodes that the collection has not been completed. The BGI broadcast protocol from [4] is used in order to deliver an alarm message, consisting of a single bit 1, to all nodes in the network. Note that the original BGI protocol was analyzed in [4] in the scenario with exactly one source node, while in our alarming epoch there may be many nodes which want to initialize the process of sending the alarm message (i.e., many sources). The progress is made based on a specific procedure Decay, which guarantees that if a node has at least one neighbor who already got the source message, gets the message in $\mathcal{O}(\log \Delta)$ rounds with constant probability. In our case we have possibly many sources but still one message, therefore a simple transformation from the original graph with many alarm sources into the same graph with additional node connected to all sources justifies that the process of broadcasting alarm message in the original graph is not longer than the process of broadcasting a single message from the unique source in the latter graph of $n+1$ nodes and diameter at most $D+1$. Therefore, the BGI algorithm guarantees that each node receives an alarm message, if any, within asymptotically the same number of rounds $\mathcal{O}((D+\log n) \log \Delta)$ as in the classical setting with $n+1$ nodes and diameter $D+1$, w.h.p. Therefore, the number of rounds available in the alarm epoch of every phase is set to $\mathcal{O}((D+\log n) \log \Delta)$.

2.3.2 Analysis of Stage 3

LEMMA 4. *If $x \geq k$, the root receives all the packets using $\mathcal{GRAB}(x)$ within designated time of*

$$\mathcal{O}\left(x + D \log x + \log^2 n\right)$$

rounds, w.h.p.

PROOF. We have already estimated the length of subroutine $\mathcal{GRAB}$ right after describing it above. It remains to prove that if $x \geq k$ then the root collects all packets w.h.p.

Assume $x \geq k$. First we argue that procedure $\mathcal{OSPG}(y)$ assures that at least half of the packets are collected by the root w.h.p. when their number is at most y, for $c \log n \leq y \leq x$. Indeed, the probability that a packet is assigned a unique starting round within procedure $\mathcal{OSPG}(y)$ is at least $(1-1/(6y))^{y-1} \geq 1/2+1/4$, and since these events are independent, by the classical Chernoff bound yields that at least half of these events hold with probability at least $1 - \exp(-y(1/4)^2/3)$, which is w.h.p. as $y \geq c \log n$ and c is chosen to be sufficiently large. It follows, by the union bound, that after executing

$$\mathcal{OSPG}(x), \ldots, \mathcal{OSPG}\left(\frac{x}{2^i}\right), \ldots, \mathcal{OSPG}(c \log n)$$

where c is a sufficiently large constant, the number of non-collected packets reduces to at most $(c/2) \log n$. Here we use the fact that if a packet has been successfully delivered to the root during the execution of some $\mathcal{OSPG}(y)$, the originating node is informed about it and it will never attempt to transfer this packet in the subsequent executions. We argue that $\mathcal{MSPG}(c^2 \log^2 n, c \log n)$ assures that each copy of a packet is received by the root with constant probability, by the argument similar to the one in the analysis of procedure $\mathcal{OSPG}$ and by the fact that there are at most $c^2 \log^2 n$ packet copies in total. Therefore, at least one of the copies of any given packet will be received by the root w.h.p., by the fact that each packet has $c \log n$ copies. Hence, by the union bound, all packets are successfully collected by the root at the end of sub-routine $\mathcal{GRAB}(x)$, w.h.p. □

LEMMA 5. *The collection stage guarantees that all packets are collected by the leader within $\mathcal{O}(k + (D + \log n) \log n)$ rounds, w.h.p.*

PROOF. First note that once we run a phase for estimate y of k such that $y/2 < k \leq y$, we are guaranteed that all packets are collected at the leader and then successfully acknowledged, and thus no alarm message is launched and all nodes terminate, w.h.p.

Therefore it remains to estimate the number of rounds needed to reach the end of phase with such estimate y of the number of packets k. Each phase of the collection stage in which the estimate of k is set to x lasts

$$\mathcal{O}(x + D \log x + \log^2 n) + \mathcal{O}((D + \log n) \log \Delta)$$
$$= \mathcal{O}(x + (D + \log n) \log n) ,$$

as $x \leq k$ and k is polynomial in n. Since our initial estimate of x is $(D + \log n) \log n$, and each phase it doubles, in order to reach the end of the phase with estimate y on k we need

$$\sum_{\{i : (D + \log n) \log n \leq 2^i \leq k\}} \mathcal{O}(2^i + (D + \log n) \log n)$$

rounds. Note that each of the formulas under the sum is upper bounded by $\mathcal{O}(2^i)$. Therefore we get the final formula $\mathcal{O}(k + (D + \log n) \log n)$ on the number of rounds in Stage 3 of the algorithm, which holds w.h.p. □

2.4 Stage 4: Packet dissemination

At the end of the collection stage, the root will have all k packets, with high probability. In the dissemination stage, the root broadcasts all the packets using the following algorithm. Let $g = \lceil \frac{k}{\lceil \log n \rceil} \rceil$ be a positive integer. The dissemination stage is grouped into $g + 3D$ phases, each consisting of $\mathcal{O}(\log n \log \Delta)$ rounds. The root divides packets into g groups each with $\lceil \log n \rceil$ packets (one of the groups may have less than $\lceil \log n \rceil$ packets if $\lceil \log n \rceil$ does not divide k). Recall that b is the upper bound on the size of a packet, measured in the number of bits, and that $b \geq \log n$. Let $\mathbb{F}$ be a finite field of size 2^b. Note that every packet/message of size at most b bits can be regarded as a number in $\mathbb{F}$, and XORing messages of size at most b is equivalent of adding their corresponding numbers in $\mathbb{F}$.

Following we describe a sub-routine called $\mathcal{FORWARD}$, which is based on the Decay procedure from [4]. $\mathcal{FORWARD}$ is used in each phase of dissemination stage by the set of nodes at some distance d, where $1 \leq d \leq D-1$, from the root to forward a set of at most $\lceil \log n \rceil$ messages to the nodes at distance $d + 1$.

$\mathcal{FORWARD}$:
The sub-routine runs for $\mathcal{O}(\log n)$ epochs, each consisting of $\lceil \log \Delta \rceil$ rounds. A set T of nodes, where $|T| \geq 1$, participates. Let R be a non-empty set of nodes such that each node in R has at least one and at most Δ neighbors in T. Let $\mathcal{M}$ be a non-empty set of packets such that $|\mathcal{M}| \leq \lceil \log(n) \rceil$, and each packet in $\mathcal{M}$ has at least $\lceil \log n \rceil$ and at most b bits. Suppose every node in T knows all the messages in $\mathcal{M}$. Similar to the Decay algorithm [4], in each round $s = 1, ..., \lceil \log(\Delta) \rceil$ of every epoch, every node in T transmits with probability $p_s =$

$\frac{1}{2}, \frac{1}{4}, ..., \frac{1}{2^{\lceil \log(\Delta) \rceil}}$. Every time a node decides to transmit, it generates a new message from the set of messages $\mathcal{M}$ and transmits the new message. To generate the message, the node independently chooses each message from $\mathcal{M}$ with probability $\frac{1}{2}$ and adds their corresponding numbers in $\mathbb{F}$, where $\mathbb{F}$ is a finite field (of size 2^b) known by all the nodes in $T \cup R$. It then transmits the sum (which has b bits) together with a header of size $\lceil \log(n) \rceil$ bits indicating the set of selected messages in $\mathcal{M}$. Note that since every message in $\mathcal{M}$ has at least $\lceil \log(n) \rceil$ bits, the size of the new message is at most twice the size of any message in $\mathcal{M}$.

The sub-routine $\mathcal{FORWARD}$ lasts exactly one phase of the dissemination stage. To explain how $\mathcal{FORWARD}$ is used to disseminate messages, let us first consider a special case where $k \leq \lceil \log n \rceil$ (i.e., $g = 1$). In this case, in the first phase of the dissemination stage, the root transmits all the packets to its one-hop neighbors, one-by-one in k rounds. Since $k \leq \lceil \log n \rceil$, by the end of the first phase all the nodes with distance one from the root will receive all k packets. In the second phase of the dissemination stage, the set of nodes at distance one uses sub-routine $\mathcal{FORWARD}$ to forward all k packets to the set of nodes at distance two from the root. Note that each node with distance two has at least one and at most Δ neighbors with distance one. Therefore, as we will shortly prove in Lemma 6, all the nodes at distance two will receive all k messages by the end of the second phase, w.h.p. Similarly, in phase d, $3 \leq d \leq D-1$, nodes at distance $d - 1$ use sub-routine $\mathcal{FORWARD}$ to send all k messages to the nodes at distance d. Therefore, after D phases, all the nodes in the network will receive all messages, with high probability.

In general, when $g \geq 1$, the above process is done for each group of messages. To avoid collision between transmissions associated with different groups of messages, the dissemination of each group starts 3 phases after the start of the dissemination of the previous group of messages.

We first prove a desired property of sub-routine $\mathcal{FORWARD}$, and then conclude the analysis of Stage 4.

LEMMA 6. *Using $\mathcal{FORWARD}$, all nodes in R will receive all the messages in $\mathcal{M}$, with high probability.*

PROOF. Let u be any node in R. In each epoch, u receives a message from one of its neighbors in T with a constant probability, as guaranteed by procedure Decay [4]. Therefore, after $\mathcal{O}(\log n)$ epochs, it will receive $\mathcal{O}(\log n)$ messages, w.h.p., by Chernoff bound, c.f., Lemma 1.

We show that u can use the set of received messages to extract the set of packets in $\mathcal{M}$. Each received message is a linear combination of packets in $\mathcal{M}$ with independent random binary coefficients, each taking value 0 (or 1) with probability $\frac{1}{2}$. To extract packets in $\mathcal{M}$, node u requires to solve a set of $\mathcal{O}(\log n)$ linear equations. In other words, node u can extract all the packets in $\mathcal{M}$ if the corresponding binary matrix of linear equations has a full rank. Let M be the matrix corresponding to the set of linear equations. The elements of M are independent random binary numbers, each equal to 0 with probability $\frac{1}{2}$. Further, the matrix M has at most $\log n$ columns (i.e., the number of packets in $\mathcal{M}$) and $\mathcal{O}(\log n)$ rows (i.e., the number of rounds in which messages have been sent during the current $\mathcal{FORWARD}$ execution), with high probability. Then, by Lemma 3, M has full rank, with high probability, and consequently the set of linear equations is solvable, w.h.p. $\square$

LEMMA 7. *The root successfully broadcast all k packets stored at it in the beginning of Stage 4 during*

$$\mathcal{O}(D \log n \log \Delta + k \log \Delta)$$

rounds of that stage, w.h.p.

PROOF. The proof is by induction on the distance from the root. The first phase of the stage takes k rounds and guarantees that each node of distance 1 from the root receives all k packets. Suppose that by the end phase d, for $1 \le d \le D-1$, each node of distance at most d from the root has received all k packets. Lemma 6 applied to the execution of sub-routine $\mathcal{FORWARD}$ in phase $d+1$ guarantees that all k packets are received by any node of distance $d+1$ from the root, and thus being a neighbor of at least one and at most Δ nodes of distance d from the root, during phase $d+1$. All D inductive steps hold with high probability, therefore we conclude that all k packets are successfully delivered to all nodes within D phases of Stage 4 w.h.p.

The whole dissemination process takes $D + 3g$ phases, which consists of

$$(D + 3g) \cdot \mathcal{O}(\log n \log \Delta) = \mathcal{O}(D \log n \log \Delta + k \log \Delta)$$

rounds. $\square$

2.5 Final analysis of multi-broadcast algorithm

Combining Fact 1 and Theorem 1 with Lemmas 5 and 7, we obtain the following result.

THEOREM 2. *The multi-broadcast algorithm successfully broadcast all k packets stored in the system, for any $k > 0$, in $\mathcal{O}(k \log \Delta + (D + \log n) \log n \log \Delta)$ rounds, with high probability.*

3. CONCLUSIONS AND OPEN PROBLEMS

In this work we showed how to efficiently combine randomization techniques with network coding to obtain better multiple-message broadcast algorithm for radio networks. An interesting open question is whether a similar approach could improve design and analysis of efficient protocols in other models of wireless networks, such that geometric graphs, bounded-growth graphs or Signal-to-Interference-and-Noise-Ratio (SINR). In more practical scenario, packets appear at nodes dynamically; a challenging direction would be to adapt "static" solutions to various communication problems to such more dynamic setting.

4. REFERENCES

[1] N. Alon, A. Bar-Noy, N. Linial, and D. Peleg, A lower bound for radio broadcast, *Journal of Computer and System Sciences* 43 (1991) 290-298.

[2] N. Alon and J.H. Spencer, "The probabilistic method," (2ed). New York: Wiley-Interscience (2000).

[3] R. Bar-Yehuda, O. Goldreich, and A. Itai, Efficient emulation of single-hop radio network with collision detection on multi-hop radio network with no collision detection, *Distributed Computing*, 5 (1991) 67 - 71.

[4] R. Bar-Yehuda, O. Goldreich, and A. Itai, On the time complexity of broadcast in radio networks: An exponential gap between determinism and randomization, *Journal of Computer and System Sciences*, 45 (1992) 104 - 126.

[5] R. Bar-Yehuda, A. Israeli, and A. Itai, Multiple communication in multi-hop radio networks, *SIAM Journal on Computing*, 22 (1993) 875 - 887.

[6] I. Chlamtac and S. Kutten, Tree-based broadcasting in multihop radio networks, *IEEE Transactions on Computers* 36 (1987) 1209 - 1223.

[7] B.S. Chlebus, L. Gasieniec, A.M. Gibbons, A. Pelc, and W. Rytter, Deterministic broadcasting in ad hoc radio networks, *Distributed Computing*, 15 (2002) 27 - 38.

[8] B.S. Chlebus, L. Gasieniec, A. Östlin, and J.M. Robson, Deterministic radio broadcasting, in *Proc., 27th International Colloquium on Automata, Languages and Programming (ICALP)*, 2000, LNCS 1853, pp. 717 - 728.

[9] B. S. Chlebus, D. R. Kowalski, and T. Radzik, Many-to-many communication in radio networks, *Algorithmica*, 54(1): 118 - 139, 2009.

[10] M. Christersson, L. Gasieniec, and A. Lingas, Gossiping with bounded size messages in ad-hoc radio networks, in *Proc., 29th International Colloquium on Automata, Languages and Programming (ICALP)*, 2002, pp. 377 - 389.

[11] M. Chrobak, L. Gasieniec, and W. Rytter, Fast broadcasting and gossiping in radio networks, in *Proc., 41st Symposium on Foundations of Computer Science (FOCS)*, 2000, pp. 575 - 581.

[12] A.E.F. Clementi, A. Monti, and R. Silvestri, Distributed broadcasting in radio networks of unknown topology, *Theoretical Computer Science*, 302 (2003) 337 - 364.

[13] A. Czumaj, and W. Rytter, Broadcasting algorithms in radio networks with unknown topology, in *Proc., 44th IEEE Symposium of Foundations of Computer Science (FOCS)*, 2003, pp. 492 - 501.

[14] L. Gasieniec, E. Kranakis, A. Pelc, and Q. Xin, Deterministic m2m multicast in radio networks, in *Proc., 31st Int. Colloquium on Automata, Languages and Programming (ICALP)*, 2004, pp. 670 - 682.

[15] L. Gasieniec, I. Potapov, Gossiping with unit messages in known radio networks, in *Proc., 2nd International Conference on Theoretical Computer Science (TCS)*, 2002, pp. 193 - 205.

[16] M. Khabbazian, F. Kuhn, D.R. Kowalski, and N.A. Lynch, Decomposing broadcast algorithms using abstract MAC layers, on *Proc., 6th International Workshop on Foundations of Mobile Computing (DIALM-POMC)*, 2010, pp. 13-22.

[17] D.R. Kowalski, and A. Pelc, Broadcasting in undirected ad-hoc radio networks, *Distributed Computing*, 18 (2005) 43 - 57.

[18] D.R. Kowalski, and A. Pelc, Time of deterministic broadcasting in radio networks with local knowledge, *SIAM Journal on Computing*, 33 (2004) 870 - 891.

[19] E. Kushilevitz, and Y. Mansour, An $\Omega(D \log(N/D))$ lower bound for broadcast in radio networks, *SIAM Journal on Computing*, 27 (1998) pp. 702 - 712.

APPENDIX

A. PROOFS FROM SECTION 1.1

Proof of Lemma 1: Let $\mu = rp$. Using Chernoff, we get:

$$Pr(\sum_{q=1}^{r} Y_q < d) \leq \exp\left(-\frac{1}{2}\frac{(\mu - d)^2}{\mu}\right). \tag{1}$$

Note that the function $f(x) = \exp(-\frac{(x-d)^2}{2x})$ is non-increasing in x for $d \leq x$. Also, since $d \geq 1$, we have

$$d \leq 3d + 2\tau - p = (\frac{1}{p}(3d+2\tau) - 1)p \leq \lfloor\frac{1}{p}(3d+2\tau)\rfloor p = rp = \mu.$$

Therefore,

$$\exp\left(-\frac{1}{2}\frac{(\mu - d)^2}{\mu}\right) \leq \exp\left(-\frac{1}{2}\frac{(3d + 2\tau - p - d)^2}{3d + 2\tau - p}\right)$$

$$= \exp\left(-\frac{1}{2}\frac{(2d + 2\tau - p)^2}{3d + 2\tau - p}\right)$$

$$\leq \exp(-\tau) .$$

$\square$

Proof of Lemma 2: We prove the claim by using a Chernoff-type argument. For every $\gamma > 0$ and every $t \geq 0$, we have

$$Pr(X \geq t) = Pr\left(e^{\gamma X} \geq e^{\gamma t}\right) \leq \frac{\mathbb{E}\left[e^{\gamma X}\right]}{e^{\gamma t}} = \frac{\prod_{i=1}^{k}\mathbb{E}\left[e^{\gamma X_i}\right]}{e^{\gamma t}}, \tag{2}$$

where the inequality follows by applying Markov's inequality. Let first derive a bound on $\mathbb{E}[e^{\gamma X_i}]$. Assume that $\gamma = p_{\min}/4 \leq 1/4$, yielding $e^\gamma - 1 \leq p_{\min}/3$. For all $i \in [k]$, we get

$$\mathbb{E}\left[e^{\gamma X_i}\right] = \sum_{s=1}^{\infty} p_i(1 - p_i)^{s-1}e^{\gamma s}$$

$$= \frac{p_i e^\gamma}{1 - (1 - p_i)e^\gamma}$$

$$\overset{(1+x \leq e^x)}{\leq} e^{\frac{e^\gamma - 1}{p_i e^\gamma - (e^\gamma - 1)}}$$

$$\overset{(e^\gamma - 1 \leq \frac{p_{\min}}{3})}{\leq} e^{\frac{p_{\min}}{3p_i e^\gamma - p_{\min}}}$$

$$\overset{(e^\gamma > 1)}{\leq} e^{\frac{p_{\min}}{2p_i}} .$$

Plugging this into (2), we obtain

$$Pr(X \geq t) \leq e^{\frac{p_{\min}}{2}\cdot\sum_{i=1}^{k}\frac{1}{p_i} - \gamma t} = e^{\frac{p_{\min}}{2}\cdot(\mu - \frac{t}{2})}.$$

The lemma now follows by using $t = 2\mu + 4\ln(1/\epsilon)/p_{\min}$. $\square$

Proof of Lemma 3: Let V be the set of all binary vectors of size w. Consider the following game with possibly infinite number of rounds: At each round of the game a vector is randomly and uniformly selected from V. The game terminates if w linearly independent vectors are collected. For $i = 1, 2, \ldots, w$, let Y_i be a random variable equal to the round number at which i linearly independent vectors are collected for the first time. Let us define $X_1 = Y_1$, and $X_i = Y_i - Y_{i-1}$ for every $2 \leq i \leq w$. A set of i, $i \geq 1$, linearly independent vectors, span a vector space of dimension i and size 2^i. The probability that a uniformly selected

vector from S avoid this space is $(1 - \frac{2^i}{2^w})$. Thus, for any positive integer x, and any integer i, $1 \leq i \leq w - 1$, we get

$$Pr(X_{i+1} = x) = Pr(Y_{i+1} - Y_i = x)$$

$$= \sum_{y=1}^{\infty} Pr(Y_{i+1} = x + y | Y_i = y)Pr(Y_i = y)$$

$$= \sum_{y=1}^{\infty} \left(\frac{2^i}{2^w}\right)^{x-1}\left(1 - \frac{2^i}{2^w}\right)Pr(Y_i = y)$$

$$= \left(\frac{2^i}{2^w}\right)^{x-1}\left(1 - \frac{2^i}{2^w}\right)\sum_{y=1}^{\infty}Pr(Y_i = y)$$

$$= \left(\frac{2^i}{2^w}\right)^{x-1}\left(1 - \frac{2^i}{2^w}\right) \tag{3}$$

Also,

$$Pr(X_1 = x) = Pr(Y_1 = x) = (\frac{1}{2^w})^{x-1}(1 - \frac{1}{2^w}) \tag{4}$$

Thus, by (3) and (4), $X_1, \ldots, X_w$ are geometric random variables with parameters $p_i = 1 - \frac{2^{i-1}}{2^w}$, $1 \leq i \leq w$. By Lemma 2, we get

$$Pr\left(\sum_{i=1}^{w} X_i \geq 2\mu + \frac{4\ln(1/\epsilon)}{p_{min}}\right) \leq \epsilon,$$

where $p_{min} = 1 - \frac{2^{w-1}}{2^w} = \frac{1}{2}$ and

$$\mu = \sum_{i=1}^{w}\frac{1}{1 - \frac{2^{i-1}}{2^w}} \leq w + 2.$$

Thus,

$$Pr(\sum_{i=1}^{w} X_i \geq l) \leq \epsilon,$$

hence

$$Pr(Y_w \geq l) = Pr\left(\left(Y_1 + \sum_{i=2}^{w}(Y_i - Y_{i-1})\right) \geq l\right) \leq \epsilon$$

$$= Pr\left(\sum_{i=1}^{w} X_i \geq l\right) \tag{5}$$

$$\leq \epsilon.$$

Note that each row of matrix A is a uniformly selected vector from V. Matrix A has full rank if it has w linearly independent rows. Thus, by (5), the probability that A has full rank is at least $1 - \epsilon$. $\square$

Faster Information Dissemination in Dynamic Networks via Network Coding

Bernhard Haeupler
Massachusetts Institute of Technology
32 Vassar Street, 32-G622
Cambridge, MA 02139, USA
haeupler@mit.edu

David R. Karger
Massachusetts Institute of Technology
32 Vassar Street, 32-G592
Cambridge, MA 02139, USA
karger@mit.edu

ABSTRACT

We use *network coding* to improve the speed of distributed computation in the dynamic network model of Kuhn, Lynch and Oshman [STOC '10]. In this model an adversary adaptively chooses a new network topology in every round, making even basic distributed computations challenging.

Kuhn et al. show that n nodes, each starting with a d-bit *token*, can broadcast them to all nodes in time $O(n^2)$ using b-bit messages, where $b \geq d + \log n$. Their algorithms take the natural approach of *token forwarding*: in every round each node broadcasts some particular token it knows. They prove matching $\Omega(n^2)$ lower bounds for a natural class of token forwarding algorithms and an $\Omega(n \log n)$ lower bound that applies to all token-forwarding algorithms.

We use *network coding*, transmitting random linear combinations of tokens, to break both lower bounds. Our algorithm's performance is *quadratic* in the message size b, broadcasting the n tokens in roughly $\frac{d}{b^2} \cdot n^2$ rounds. For $b = d = \Theta(\log n)$ our algorithms use $O(n^2/\log n)$ rounds, breaking the first lower bound, while for larger message sizes we obtain linear-time algorithms. We also consider networks that change only every T rounds, and achieve an additional factor T^2 speedup. This contrasts with related lower and upper bounds of Kuhn et al. implying that for natural token-forwarding algorithms a speedup of T, but not more, can be obtained. Lastly, we give a general way to derandomize random linear network coding, that also leads to new deterministic information dissemination algorithms.

Categories and Subject Descriptors

F.2.2 [**Analysis of Algorithms and Problem Complexity**]: Nonnumerical Algorithms and Problems—*computations on discrete structures*; G.2.2 [**Discrete Mathematics**]: Graph Theory—*network problems, graph algorithms*

General Terms

Algorithms, Performance, Theory

Keywords

dynamic networks, gossip, multicast, network coding

1. INTRODUCTION

In this paper we demonstrate that *network coding* can significantly improve the efficiency of distributed computations in dynamic networks. Network coding breaks with the classical paradigm of routing atomic packets through a network and recognizes that information can be mixed and coded together in ways other (physical) quantities can not. Network coding is a relatively recent discovery that has already revolutionized information theory; it is now a crucial tool in designing robust and efficient communication protocols. We believe network coding has potential for similar impact in the distributed computing community.

We study the recently introduced *dynamic network* model of Kuhn et al. [9]. This model was designed to capture the highly dynamic and non-converging nature of many modern networks by allowing the network topology to change completely and adaptively in every round subject to the constraint that the network is always connected. In each synchronized communication round, each node chooses a message which is then broadcast to its neighbors for the round. What makes this problem particularly challenging is that the broadcast is *anonymous*, i.e., at the time a node chooses its message it does not know who its receiving neighbors for the round will be.

An important problem in such dynamic networks is k-*token dissemination*: there are k tokens initially distributed to some nodes, and the goal is to disseminate them to all nodes.

The most natural approach to solving token dissemination is *token forwarding*: in each round, each node chooses to broadcast one token it knows. Kuhn et al. [9] show how to disseminate k tokens in an n-node network in $O(nk)$ time by flooding the k tokens one by one in $O(n)$ rounds each. They also show how pipelining can improve the running time of this approach to $O(\frac{nk}{T} + n)$ in slower-changing T-*interval-connected* networks, in which for any interval of T rounds the links of some specific underlying spanning tree persist.

Kuhn et al. give evidence that this is the best one can do with token forwarding. For the natural class of *knowledge-based* token forwarding algorithms, where each node's messages depend only on the tokens it knows, they show a matching $\Omega(\frac{nk}{T} + n)$ lower bound. They also give a more general $\Omega(n \log k)$ lower bound that applies even if the algorithm is operated under "centralized control" and mention in the conclusion the "hope to strengthen [this] and obtain an $\Omega(nk/T)$ general lower bound".

Building on work of the first author [6], we show that these lower bounds cease to hold if one does not require that tokens be broadcast individually. We use network coding, sending out random linear combinations of tokens, to solve k-token dissemination of size-$O(\log n)$ tokens in $O(kn/\log n)$ time, outperforming the $\Theta(kn)$ bound [9] for knowledge-based token forwarding algorithms. We also show that, perhaps counter-intuitively, larger tokens can be disseminated faster: if the token size (and message size) is d, network coding can disseminate k tokens in $O(k(n\log n)/d)$ time. Thus, for tokens of size $n\log n$, we break the general $\Omega(n\log k)$ bound on token-forwarding algorithms.

We also consider networks that are T-stable, changing only once every T rounds. Kuhn et al. show that token-forwarding can achieve a factor-T speedup in this case, but that knowledge-based token-forwarding algorithms cannot do better. In contrast, we show network coding can achieve a factor T^2 speedup.

Finally, we show that linear network coding is not inherently randomized but that the ideas and improvements carry over to (non-uniform) deterministic algorithms as well.

2. OUR RESULTS

In this section we provide the formal statements of our main results. The model should be clear from the introduction but is also more formally described in Section 4.

2.1 The Role of Message Size

Kuhn et al. assume throughout that the message size is equal to the token size. For token-forwarding algorithms, this is quite reasonable. For fixed token size, a larger message simply allows forwarding more tokens at once, which for all their results is equivalent to executing multiple rounds in parallel. Thus, all their upper and lower bounds simply scale linearly with this message size.

Once we move beyond token forwarding this equivalence breaks down. Thus, we introduce a separate parameter, b, representing the size of a message. We will see that network coding performance improves *quadratically* with the message size. Somewhat surprisingly, this means that when the message size is equal to the token size, *larger tokens can be disseminated faster*.

Explicitly modeling b also allows us to bridge an important gap between the distributed computing and network coding communities. In distributed computing we often focus on size-$O(\log n)$ message-sizes. But in practice, most communication protocols impose a minimum message size in the thousands or tens of thousands of bits. We should therefore try to take advantage of the possibility of tokens being much smaller than the message size; with network coding we can. At the other end, the network coding community generally assumes messages are so large that overheads associated with network coding can be ignored. Our work accounts for the hidden cost of these overheads, which can be significant when messages are smaller. In summary, explicitly modeling b lets us span the range of assumptions from distributed computing's tiny messages to network coding's huge ones. We discuss this in more detail in Section 3.

2.2 Token Forwarding Algorithms

For comparison we first recall the upper- and lower-bound results of [9]:

THEOREM 2.1. *[9] There is a deterministic knowledge-based token forwarding algorithm that solves the k-token dis-*

semination problem in a T-stable dynamic network in $O(\frac{1}{T} \cdot \frac{nkd}{b} + n)$ rounds using messages of size b for tokens of size d. This is tight, i.e., for any T, any (even randomized) knowledge-based token forwarding algorithm takes at least $\Omega(\frac{1}{T} \cdot \frac{nkd}{b} + n)$ rounds in the worst case.

This is not a verbatim restatement. Indeed, Kuhn et al [9] prove this theorem for the related but stronger stability measure of T-interval connectivity. Furthermore, except for the abstract, they only describe the case of small tokens and assume that the messages size is equal to the size of the tokens, i.e., $b = d = \log n$. Lastly, for most of the paper they assume that $k = n$ or that each node starts with exactly one token. It is easy to verify that the lower bound from [9] continues to hold for our weaker T-stability model and that the algorithms also directly extend to the stated theorem: E.g., to achieve a running time of $\frac{nkd}{b}$ for $T = 1$ the nodes repeatedly flood $\frac{b}{d}$ tokens per $O(n)$ rounds instead of one.

Their second lower bound applies to deterministic centralized algorithms and shows that even if one allows such unrestricted, coordination between nodes a linear time algorithm is not achievable (in contrast to static graphs):

THEOREM 2.2. *[9] For $b = d$ any deterministic centralized token forwarding algorithm that solves the k-token dissemination problem in a dynamic network takes $\Omega(n\log k)$ rounds in the worst case.*

2.3 Network Coding

Even though the token dissemination problem is about delivering complete tokens, one can benefit from not treating the information as a physical quantity that needs to be routed through the network. We do this by providing faster (knowledge-based) algorithms for the k-token dissemination problem based on network coding. The lower bound in Theorem 2.1 pertains even if one allows the algorithms to chop up tokens into single bits and route those bits independently through the network – including concatenating bits of different tokens within one message. This shows that true (network) coding is required.

Our algorithms use *random linear network coding*, the arguably simplest form of network coding, in which messages are random linear combinations of tokens. Independent of network dynamics, nodes in our algorithm always choose a uniformly random linear combination of all received messages and can therefore also be considered knowledge-based.

Our first theorem shows that one can solve k-token dissemination roughly a factor of b faster than the lower bound for knowledge-based token forwarding algorithms:

THEOREM 2.3. *There is a randomized network coding algorithm that solves the k-token dissemination problem in a dynamic network with n nodes in*

$$O(\min\{\frac{1}{b} \cdot \frac{nkd}{b} + nb, \frac{\log n}{b} \cdot \frac{nkd}{b} + n\log n\})$$

rounds with high probability.

This means that the efficiency of token-dissemination increases at least *quadratically* with the message size, instead of the more intuitive linear increase given by Theorem 2.1. A similar result is true for the advantages coming from more stable networks. Theorem 2.1 implies that T-stability (or even T-interval connectivity) allows for a speed up of T. Our next theorem shows that with network coding the speedup of a more stable network improves to T^2. For most parameter values, this improvement can be combined with the speed-up from larger message sizes. The next theorem implies an at least $\frac{log^2 n}{bT^2}$ speed up over the $O(\frac{nkd}{b})$ rounds for most settings of the parameters b, d, k and T. This is a factor of $\frac{log^2 n}{bT}$ faster than the lower bound for knowledge-based token-forwarding algorithms:

THEOREM 2.4. *There is a randomized network coding algorithm that solves the k-token dissemination problem in a T-stable dynamic network with n nodes in*

$$O(1) \cdot \min \left\{ \begin{array}{lll} \frac{\log n}{bT^2} & \cdot \frac{nkd}{b} & + \ nbT^2 \log n \\[1.5ex] \frac{\log^2 n}{bT^2} & \cdot \frac{nkd}{b} & + \ nT \log^2 n \\[1.5ex] \frac{\log^2 n}{bT^2} & \cdot \ n^2 & + \ n \log n \end{array} \right\}$$

rounds with high probability.

All these algorithms are based on random linear network coding which seems to be inherently dependent on randomization. We show that this is not true. We give tight trade-offs between the adaptiveness of the adversary and the required coefficient size/overhead. For derandomization we must pay higher (quadratic) coefficient overhead, but we can still outperform token-forwarding algorithms. These arguments apply quite generally to the network coding framework in [6] and are interesting on their own. We defer the description of these results to Section 6 and mention here only the implications for the k-dissemination problem:

THEOREM 2.5. *There is a deterministic network coding algorithm that solves the k-token dissemination problem in a T-stable dynamic network with n nodes in*

$$O(\frac{1}{\sqrt{bT}} \cdot n \cdot \min\{k, \frac{n}{T}\} + n) \cdot 2^{O(\sqrt{\log n})}$$

rounds.

For completeness we also describe what our findings imply for centralized algorithms[1]:

COROLLARY 2.6. *There is a randomized centralized network coding algorithm that solves the k-token dissemination problem in a T-stable dynamic network with n nodes in order-optimal $\Theta(n)$ time with probability $1 - 2^{-n}$ and a deterministic centralized network coding algorithm that runs in $O(\frac{\log n}{bT} \cdot n \cdot \min\{k, \frac{n}{T}\} + n)$ rounds.*

To help interpret these general results we present a few interesting value instantiations:

- Even for $b = d = \log n$ and $k = n$, which is an important case because of its connection to counting the

---

[1] A centralized algorithm can globally coordinate nodes. Formally we define centralized algorithms as "distributed" algorithms that furthermore provide each node with knowledge about past topologies, the initial token distribution (without getting to know the tokens itself) and a source of shared randomness in case of a randomized algorithm. It is easy to verify that this extends the definition given in [9] for centralized token-forwarding algorithms to general algorithms and problems.

number of nodes in a network [9], the $n^2/\log n$ rounds needed by the network coding algorithm is a $\Theta(\log n)$-factor faster than any knowledge-based token forwarding algorithm can be.

- For the counting problem with larger message sizes, i.e., $d = \log n$ and $k = n$, Theorem 2.3 implies that a message-size of $b = \sqrt{n} \log n$ suffices to obtain an optimal linear-time randomized algorithm. For $b = n^{2/3} \log n$ this can be made deterministic. In contrast, the best known token-forwarding algorithm needs $b = n \log n$ (see Proposition 3.2 of [9]) which is tight for knowledge-based token forwarding algorithms.

- The situation is similar if one considers the question of how stable a graph needs to be to allow near-linear $n^{1+o(1)}$ time algorithms for the n-token dissemination problem. Theorems 2.4 and 2.5 show that $T = \Omega(\sqrt{n})$ suffices for randomized algorithms and $T = \Omega(n^{2/3})$ for deterministic algorithms. This means that $\sqrt{n}$ (resp. $n^{1/3}$) adversarial topology changes can be tolerated with network coding. In contrast any knowledge-based token-forwarding algorithm requires the graph to be essentially static, i.e., $T = \Omega(n^{1-o(1)})$.

- For the case that messages are of the size of a token, i.e $b = d$, the weaker but quite general lower bound for Theorem 2.2 rules out any linear time token forwarding algorithm even if a deterministic centralized algorithm is used. In contrast to this there are linear time network coding algorithms that are:
  - randomized and centralized
  - deterministic and centralized (for message and token sizes $\geq n \log n$)
  - randomized and knowledge-based (for message and token sizes $\geq n \log n$)
  - deterministic and knowledge-based (for message and token sizes $\geq n^2 \log n$)

3. RELATED WORK

While traditional distributed algorithms research has focused on computation in static networks, the analysis of dynamic network topologies has gained importance both in practice and theory. Kuhn et al. [9] offer an extensive review of this literature.

Next to [9] the line of research most relevant to this work is network coding for gossip problems [2, 4, 5, 12] and most specifically work by Haeupler [6]. Since its introduction [1, 10] network coding has revolutionized the understanding of information flow in networks and found many practical applications (see, e.g., the books [7, 14]).

Random linear network coding and its distributed implementation considered in this paper were introduced by Ho et al. [8] and shown to achieve capacity for multicast. Its performance for the distributed n-token dissemination problem has been intensively studied in combination with gossip algorithms under the name of algebraic gossip or rumor spreading. The first such analysis [4, 5] studied the performance of algebraic gossip in the random phone call model, i.e., the complete graph in which each nodes sends a message to a random neighbor in each round. Follow-on work [2, 3, 6, 12] has analyzed the distributed network coding gossip algorithm on general static networks. Haeupler [6] gives a very simple analysis technique (reviewed in Section 5) that can be used to show order optimal stopping times in practically all communication models. Most interestingly this holds true even if, as studied here and in [9], a fully adaptive adversary changes the topology in every round. In the setting considered here this would imply an optimal $O(n)$ linear time algorithm for the n-token dissemination problem. Unfortunately, these prior results do not directly apply for two subtle but important reasons:

First, [6], as well as all prior work on algebraic gossip, assumes that the additive overhead of the network coding header, which is linear in the number of coded packets, is negligible compared to the size of a packet. This assumption is backed up by many practical implementations in which this overhead is indeed less than one percent. But a rigorous theoretical treatment, like that of [9], must account for this overhead which may be significant if message-sizes are small.

Secondly, in all prior literature including [6], it is also assumed that tokens are uniquely numbered/indexed and that this index is known to any node that starts with a token. This is needed to allow nodes to specify in the coding header which packets are coded together in a message. In this paper such an assumption would be unacceptable. For example, for the task of counting the number of nodes in a dynamic network [9] having the IDs consecutively indexed would essentially amount to assuming that a solution to the counting problem is already part of the input.

In this paper we address both points explicitly. Accounting for the coding overhead leads to interesting trade-offs and poses new algorithmic challenges like the need for *gathering* many tokens in one node so that they can be grouped together to a smaller number of larger "meta-tokens" that require fewer coefficients. To this end we consider intermediate message sizes b that can range between logarithmic size [9] to (super)linear size [2–6, 12]. We furthermore do not assume any token indexing or other extra coordination between nodes but show how to bootstrap the token dissemination algorithms to find such an indexing.

4. PROBLEM DESCRIPTION

Throughout this paper we work in the dynamic network model of Kuhn et al. [9]. The following section gives a detailed description of the model and of the token dissemination problem.

4.1 The Dynamic Network Model

A *dynamic network* consists of n nodes with unique identifiers (UIDs) of size $O(\log n)$ and we assume that the number of nodes is known (up to a factor of 2) to all nodes. The network operates in synchronized *rounds*. During each round t the network's connectivity is defined by a connected undirected graph $G(t)$ chosen by an adversary. The nodes communicate via *anonymous broadcast*: At the beginning of a round each node chooses an $O(b)$-bit message, where $b \geq \log n$, without knowing to which nodes it is connected in the round. After the messages and the network $G(t)$ is fixed each node receives all messages chosen by its neighbors in $G(t)$. The model does not restrict local computations done by nodes.

We present deterministic and randomized algorithms. In the case of randomization one must carefully specify how the adversary is allowed to adapt to algorithmic actions. We cover several models in the full paper but here we assume an

adaptive adversary: in each round the adversary chooses the network topology based on all *past actions* (and the current state) of the nodes. Following this the nodes then choose random messages (still without knowing their neighbors).

Remarks:

- For randomized algorithms the assumption of $O(\log n)$ size UIDs is without loss of generality since they can be generated randomly with a high probability of success.

- In the case of n-token dissemination the assumption that all nodes know n is without loss of generality: If n is unknown one can start with guessing an upper bound $n = 2$, count the number of node IDs using n-token dissemination and repeatedly double the estimate an restart when a failure is detected. This use of the n-token dissemination prevents a termination with a too small estimate. Since the running times only depend (at least linearly) on the size of the estimate, all rounds spend on computations with too low estimates are dominated by a geometric sum and increase the overall complexity at most by a factor of two. A similar argument was given in [9]. We defer more details to the full paper.

4.2 The k-Token Dissemination Problem

In this section we describe the *k-token dissemination problem* [9]. In this problem, $k \leq n$ *tokens* of $d \leq b$ bits are located in the network and the goal is for all nodes to become aware of the union of the tokens and then terminate. We assume that the k tokens are chosen and distributed to the nodes by the adversary before the first round.

Kuhn et al. observe that k-token dissemination seems intimately connected to the problem of counting the number of nodes in a network and to simpler problems like consensus. In fact k-dissemination is "universal" as any function of the k tokens can be computed by distributing them to all nodes and the letting each node compute the function locally.

We consider only *Las Vegas* algorithms that are guaranteed to terminate with all tokens disseminated. We will bound the expected number of rounds until all nodes terminate. All stopping times actually hold with high probability.

Our algorithms for k-token dissemination solve several natural subproblems as subroutines:

gathering: nodes need to collect tokens such that a single node or a small collection of nodes knows about a specified number of tokens.

k-indexing: k tokens must be selected and a distinct *index* in the range $1, \ldots, k$ assigned to each.

k-indexed-broadcasting: k tokens with distinct indices $1, \ldots, k$ must be distributed to all nodes

5. (ANALYZING) NETWORK CODING

5.1 Random Linear Network Coding

Instead of sending the d-bit tokens as atomic entities, network coding interprets these tokens as vectors over a finite field and sends out random linear combinations of the vectors. Formally, the algorithm chooses a prime q as a field size and represents the tokens as $d' = \lceil d/\lg q \rceil$-dimensional vectors over F_q. For most of this paper one can choose $q = 2$, i.e., take the natural token representation as a bit sequence of length $d' = d$ and replace linear combinations by XORs.

Let $t_1, \ldots, t_k \in F_q^{d'}$ be k indexed tokens. We concatenate the ith basis vector e_i of F_q^k to t_i to produce a $k + d'$-dimensional vector v_i. Each node that initially knows t_i "receives" this vector v_i before the first round. Notice that if a node knows the *subspace S spanned by the* v_i, e.g, in the form of any basis of S, it can use Gaussian elimination to reconstruct the v_i, and thus the original tokens. Thus, we solve k-indexed-broadcast by delivering to every node a set of vectors that span S. The algorithm is straightforward: At each round, any node computes a *random linear combination* of any vectors received so far (if any) and broadcasts this as a message to its (unknown) neighbors. Note that the message only depends on the current knowledge of the tokens, i.e., the subspace spanned by the received vectors. This natural property was called knowledge-based in [9].

5.2 Advantages of Network Coding

To contrast network coding with token forwarding, consider the simplified setting in which a node A knows about all k tokens while another node B knows all but one token. If A does not know which token B is missing then, in a worst-case deterministic setting, k rounds of token forwarding are required. Randomized strategies can improve the expected number of rounds only to $k/2$. A better strategy is to send an XOR of all tokens: with this one piece of information B can reconstruct the missing token.

Similar situations arise frequently in the end phase of token forwarding algorithms. Here most nodes already know most of the tokens but, because of the changing topology, do not know which few tokens are not shared with their unknown neighbors of this round. Most token forwarding steps are therefore wasted. Network coding circumvents this problem, making it *highly probable* that *every* communication will carry new information.

5.3 The Network Coding Analysis

In this section we review the simple projection analysis technique that was introduced previously [6]. It shows that the full "span" of the message vectors ultimately spreads everywhere by tracking the projection of the received space in each direction separately. As argued above, a node u can recover a token t_i if and only if the first k-components of the vectors received by u span the ith unit vector of F_q^k. For the analysis we will thus solely concentrate on the first k coordinates of the vectors sent around. We track these projections using the following definition:

DEFINITION 5.1. *A node u senses a coefficient vector $\vec{\mu} \in F_q^k$ if it has received a message with a coefficient vector $\vec{\mu}'$ that is not orthogonal to $\vec{\mu}$, i.e., $\vec{\mu}' \cdot \vec{\mu} \neq 0$.*

LEMMA 5.2. *Suppose a node u senses a vector $\vec{\mu}$ and generates a new message. Any recipient of this message will then sense $\vec{\mu}$ with probability at least $1 - 1/q$.*

PROOF. This lemma simply states that a random linear combination of vectors $\vec{\mu}'_j$ that are not all perpendicular to $\vec{\mu}$ is unlikely to be perpendicular to $\vec{\mu}$. Let r_j be the random coefficient for $\vec{\mu}'_j$. Then $(\sum r_j \vec{\mu}'_j) \cdot \mu = \sum r_j (\vec{\mu}'_j \cdot \mu)$. Suppose without loss of generality that $\vec{\mu}'_0 \cdot \vec{\mu} \neq 0$. Conditioned on all other values r_j, exactly one value of r_0 will make the sum vanish. This value is taken with probability $1/q$. □

Lemma 5.2 shows that any node sensing any $\vec{\mu}$ will pass that sense to its neighbors with constant probability. Note

furthermore that sensing is monotone and that unless all nodes can already sense $\vec{\mu}$ the adversary must connect the nodes that sense $\vec{\mu}$ to those that do not. This shows that in each round the number of nodes that sense a vector $\vec{\mu}$ increases by a constant in expectation. A simple Chernoff bound shows further that the probability that after $O(n + k)$ steps not all nodes sense $\vec{\mu}$ is at most $q^{-\Omega(n+k)}$. We now apply a union bound: there are q^k distinct vectors in F_q^k, and each fails to be sensed by all nodes with probability $q^{-\Omega(n+k)}$. This shows that all vectors in F_q^k are sensed with high probability implying that all nodes are able to decode all tokens. The following lemma is immediate.

LEMMA 5.3. *The network coding algorithm with $q \geq 2$ solves the k-indexed-broadcast problem in an always connected dynamic network with probability at least $1 - q^{-n}$ in time $O(n + k)$. It uses messages of size $k \lg q + d$ where d is the size of a token.*

6. DERANDOMIZING RANDOM LINEAR NETWORK CODING

The description of network coding above might suggest that the distributed random linear network coding approach is inherently randomized. We give the novel result that this is not the case. Instead of providing a deterministic algorithm directly we first prove that even an *omniscient adversary*, which knows knows all randomness in advance, cannot prevent the fast mixing of the network coding algorithm if the field size is chosen large enough:

THEOREM 6.1. *The network coding algorithm with $q = n^{\Omega(k)}$ solves the k-indexed-broadcast problem in an always connected dynamic network against an omniscient adversary with probability at least $1 - q^{-n}$ in time $O(n + k)$. It uses messages of size $k^2 \log n + d$ where d is the size of a token.*

PROOF. (Sketch) The proof of this result is nontrivial. The obvious approach, of taking a union bound over all possible adversarial strategies expressed as a "connectivity schedule," fails because there are too many of them. Instead, we carefully map each such schedule to a small set of canonical "witnesses" that describe only the flow of new information from node to node; there are few enough of these witnesses that a union bound can be applied.

We specify a compact witness by specifying, at each time step, *which nodes learn something new* (in other words, receive a vector not already in the span of their received messages) and *which nodes they learn it from*.[2] Given all the random choices for the coefficients, this information suffices to inductively reconstruct the complete learning history (but not the complete topology sequence): By induction, we will know which subspace is spanned by each node at a given time step and, from the coefficient choices, we will know what vector it broadcasts. Given this, if we know which nodes learn something new from which nodes, we will know what vectors each received and can thus infer what their subspace will be in the next round.

The key benefit of this representation is that it is small. Note that nodes are learning a k-dimensional subspace, and

---

[2] There may be some ambiguity about which received vectors are "new" if they are not linearly independent. To remove this ambiguity, consider the vectors to arrive one at a time in some arbitrary order, and include the prior-arrived vectors of the round while evaluating newness.

that each time a node learns something new, the dimension of its subspace increases. Thus, each node can have at most k "learning events". We specify the witness by specifying, for each node, the k times and senders triggering such an events. This requires $O(k \log n)$ bits per node for a total of $O(nk \log n)$ bits to specify a witness, meaning the number of witnesses is $\exp(nk \log n)$. With a failure probability of at most q^{-n} and the given choice of q, this is sufficiently small for the union bound to apply; details will appear in the full paper. □

The proof of Theorem 6.1 can be extended to a randomized existence proof for a matrix that contains a sequence of pseudo-random choices for every possible ID; such that, no matter how the adversary assigns the IDs and decides on the network dynamics, if all nodes choose their coding coefficients according to their sequence, all vectors always spread. By giving such a matrix as a (non-uniform) advice or by computing the, e.g., lexicographically first such matrix at every node, the next corollary follows. We defer the details to the full paper.

COROLLARY 6.2. *There are uniform and non-uniform deterministic algorithms that solve the k-indexed-broadcast problem in an always connected dynamic network in time $O(n+k)$ using messages of size $k^2 \log n + d$ where d is the size of a token. The uniform deterministic algorithm performs a super-polynomial time local computation before sending the first message.*

7. TOKEN DISSEMINATION WITH NETWORK CODING

We now bridge the gap from index broadcast to token dissemination. We begin with a simple result. Combining the results from [9] and Lemma 5.3 yields the following corollary:

COROLLARY 7.1. *There is a randomized network coding algorithm that solves k-token dissemination in $O(\frac{nk \log n}{b}) = O(\frac{\log n}{d} \cdot \frac{nkd}{b})$ rounds with high probability.*

PROOF. All nodes can generate $O(\log n)$-size unique IDs for their own tokens by concatenating a sequence number to the node ID. Now all nodes flood the network repeatedly announcing the smallest $\Omega(b/\log n)$ tokens they have heard about. After n rounds all nodes will know these token IDs and can give them consistent distinct indices by sorting them. The corresponding $\Omega(b/\log n)$ tokens can then be broadcast to all nodes in $O(n)$ time using network-coded indexed broadcast. This needs to be repeated $k \frac{\log n}{b}$ times, leading to the claimed time bound. □

Unfortunately, this is only a $\frac{\log n}{d}$ factor faster than the bound for token forwarding algorithms from Theorem 2.1. Thus no improvements are achieved for $d = O(\log n)$-size tokens, even for large message sizes. This is unsurprising as the algorithm uses flooding to solve the problem of disseminating the $b/\log n$ smallest token identifiers for indexing—a $k = (b/\log n)$-token dissemination problem with the identifiers treated as tokens of size $\Omega(\log n)$. Thus if the tokens themselves are of logarithmic size relying on flooding as an indexing subroutine cannot lead to any improvement. We also note that, if $d \ll b$, the efficiency of the network coding messages is severely handicapped: The $O(b)$-size coefficient

overhead takes up nearly all the space while the coded tokens only have size d. Thus in principle one could broadcast tokens that are a factor of $\frac{b}{d}$ larger.

We solve both problems by *gathering* many tokens to one (or a small number of) nodes. If all tokens are at one node, they can all trivially be assigned distinct indices. Then, they can be grouped into blocks of $b/2d$ tokens, each of total size $b/2$, and network coding can be used to disseminate $b/2$ of these blocks simultaneously. We need an additional $b/2$ space to hold the extra $b/2$ dimensions needed to "untangle" the coded messages, but these too fit in the size-b messages. In the discussion below, we will ignore the factors of 2 mentioned here.

We have two gathering-based algorithms, one that works well as long as $b \leq k^{1/3}$ and one that works for larger message sizes. Both are based on the following simple random token forwarding algorithm:

Algorithm `random-forward`

repeat $O(n)$ times
    each node forwards b/d tokens
        chosen randomly from those it knows

Identify a node with the maximum token count
    (using $O(n)$ rounds of flooding)

LEMMA 7.2. *If initially there are k tokens in the network then, after `random-forward`, the identified node knows with high probability either all or at least $M = \sqrt{\frac{bk}{d}}$ tokens.*

PROOF. (Sketch) While there are less than M tokens at any node, a node choosing b/d random tokens to transmit will choose any *particular* token with probability at least b/dM. Since at least one node that knows the token is connected to one that do not, this implies that a token "spreads" to at least one new node each round with probability at least b/dM. Thus after n rounds each token is at $\Omega(bn/dM)$ nodes with high probability. This applies to each token so there are kbn/dM copies of tokens in the network. It follows that some node has at least kb/dM tokens. A contradiction would arise unless $M > kb/dM$; the result follows. We defer the details to the full paper. □

This lemma has a nice interpretation, if one looks how tokens spread over time. At first, the protocol is extremely efficient, but as more and more tokens become known to the nodes, there are ever more wasted broadcasts. Spreading all tokens in this way requires in expectation $O(nkd/b)$ rounds, because the wasted broadcasts occurring for the last half of the tokens dominate (see also Section 5.2). Note that this is exactly the time bound for the flooding-based algorithms of Theorem 2.1. Our first algorithm uses the efficient start phase of `random-forward` to gather tokens and then broadcasts the gathered tokens using network coded indexed-broadcast:

Algorithm `greedy-forward`

while tokens remain to be broadcast
    `random-forward`
    the identified node broadcasts up to b^2/d tokens
        (using the network coded indexed-broadcast)
    remove all broadcast tokens from consideration

THEOREM 7.3. *With high probability the* `greedy-forward` *algorithm takes* $O(nkd/b^2 + nb)$ *time to solve the k-token dissemination problem.*

PROOF. Note that it is easy to check in n rounds whether any node has any tokens to forward. Thus each iteration of the loop takes $O(n)$ rounds. Suppose that an iteration begins with k' tokens to be broadcast. Lemma 7.2 shows that at least $M = \sqrt{bk'/d}$ tokens will be gathered in one identified node by the `random-forward` process. This node can then use the network coded k-indexed-broadcast from Section 5 to broadcast these tokens in $O(n)$ rounds.

Thus, so long as $M \geq b^2/d$, meaning $k' > b^3/d$, the algorithm will broadcast b^2/d tokens every $O(n)$ rounds, which can happen at most kd/b^2 times.

Once $k' \leq b^3/d$, we no longer gather and broadcast the full b^2/d tokens. Instead, since the maximum number of tokens at a node after `random-forward` is $\sqrt{\frac{bk'}{d}}$, we have the following recurrence for the number of $O(n)$-round phases $T(k')$ performed to transmit k' items:

$$T(k') \leq 1 + T\left(k' - \sqrt{\frac{k'b}{d}}\right).$$

We conclude that it requires $O(\sqrt{k'd/b})$ phases to reduce the number of remaining items from k' to $k'/2$. Iterated halving yields a geometric series for the running time whose first term (when $k' = \Theta(b^3/d)$) dominates, giving $T(b^3/d) = O(b)$ phases of $O(n)$-time broadcasts which results in a running time of $O(nb)$ rounds in the end. Putting both parts together gives that the total time to collect all tokens is $O(nkd/b^2 + nb)$. □

Observe that this algorithm does not pay the extra $\log n$ factor introduced by the naive indexed-broadcast algorithm. Because all tokens to be broadcast are gathered to a single node, indexing is trivial. This `greedy-forward` algorithms works well for small b, but for very large $b \geq n^{1/3}$ the `random-forward` routine is not able to gather b^2/d tokens in one node efficiently. For this scenario we have a different algorithm that avoids the additive nb-round term.

Algorithm `priority-forward`

Run `greedy-forward` until no node gets b^2/d tokens
while tokens remain to be broadcast
    Nodes group tokens into blocks of size b/d
    Assign each block a random $O(\log n)$-bit priority
    Index $\Theta(b)$ random blocks in $O(n)$ time
        (using `priority-forward` recursively (*))
    Broadcast these blocks in $O(n)$ time
        (using the network coded indexed broadcast)
    remove all broadcast tokens from consideration

LEMMA 7.4. *With high probability* `priority-forward` *will terminate in* $O((1+kd/b^2)\log n)$ *iterations of its while loop.*

PROOF. The while loop starts when no node learns of more than b^2/d tokens during `random-forward`. In this case we know from the proof of Lemma 7.2 that afterwards the number of nodes c_i that know about each token i is $\Omega(\frac{n}{b})$ with high probability. Let $C = \sum c_i$.

The algorithm divides the known tokens into blocks of size b/d and picks b random blocks. There are at most $C/(b/d)$ full blocks in total and at most one partially-full block per node for a total of n partially full blocks. We consider two cases.

If $C/(b/d) < n$ then there are at most $2n$ blocks in total. Since with high probability every token is in $\Omega(n/b)$ blocks, one of these blocks is among the chosen b with probability at least $(1 - 1/2b)^b = \Omega(1)$. It follows that after $O(\log n)$ rounds involving less than n full blocks, all tokens will be chosen and disseminated with high probability.

If $C/(b/d) > n$ then the number of blocks is at most $2C/(b/d)$. We argue in this case that C decreases in expectation by a factor of $e^{-b^2/kd}$ in each iteration. If this is true then after $kd(\log n)/b^2$ rounds the expected decrease is polynomial; since C was polynomial to begin with its expected value will be polynomially small. At this point the Markov bound indicates that $C = 0$ with high probability.

To show the expected decrease, note there are at most $2C/(b/d)$ blocks of which c_i contain item i. Thus, when a random block is chosen, item i is in it with probability at least $c_i(b/d)/2C$. So item i fails to be chosen with probability at most $(1 - bc_i/2Cd)^b < \exp(-(b^2/d)c_i/2C)$. If we let $c_i' = c_i$ for tokens not chosen, and $c_i' = 0$ for tokens that are, we find $E[\sum c_i'] \leq \sum c_i \exp(-(b^2/d)c_i/C) = C \sum \alpha_i \exp(-(b^2/d)\alpha_i)$ where $\alpha_i = c_i/C$ so $\sum \alpha_i = 1$. Differentiating shows this sum is maximized when all α_i are set equal at $1/k$ (since there are at most k distinct α_i), yielding a value of $C \exp(-(b^2/kd))$. It follows that the expected value of $\sum c_i$ decreases by a factor $e^{-b^2/kd}$ in each round. □

We have shown that a small number of iterations suffices but must asses the time to implement one iteration. In particular, we must explain how line (*) in `priority-forward` can be implemented. To choose b random blocks, we give each block a random $O(\log n)$ bit priority (so collisions are unlikely) and then identify and index the b lowest priorities. Since block priorities have size $O(\log n)$, we can treat their identification as an indexing problem with $d = O(\log n)$. The naive indexing algorithm via flooding requires $O(n \log n)$ time to broadcast the b lowest priority blocks ($b/\log n$ blocks every $O(n)$ rounds). This would lead to a runtime of $O(nkd(\log^2 n)/b^2 + n \log^2 n)$. We can reduce the running time by a $\log n$ factor with a more careful approach, which calls `priority-forward` recursively to disseminate $\Theta(b)$ of the smallest size-$O(\log n)$ priorities in only $O(n)$ time on every iteration of the while loop. We defer the details to the full paper. We get the following for the performance of the `priority-forward` algorithm:

THEOREM 7.5. *For* $b \geq \log^3 n$, `priority-forward` *solves k-token dissemination in* $O(\frac{\log n}{b} \cdot \frac{nkd}{b} + n \log n)$ *rounds with high probability.*

8. EXPLOITING T-STABILITY

In this section we consider more stable networks and show how to design faster protocols in such a setting.

Kuhn et al. introduced the notion of T-*interval connectivity* to define more stable networks in which over every block of T rounds at least a spanning-subgraph is unchanging. They give algorithms with linear speedup in T and matching lower bound for knowledge-based token-forwarding algorithms. We work with our related but stronger requirement of T-*stability* which demands that the entire network changes only every T steps. Although the Kuhn et al. lower bound for token forwarding still holds in this model, we give network-coding algorithms with a quadratic speedup in T. This T^2 speedup comes from two ideas, each contributing a factor of T. The first is that in a T-stable network a node can communicate to the same neighbor T times, thus passing a message T times as large. This does cost a factor-T slowdown in the time to send a message, but the results of section 7 show that the communication rate increases as T^2. Combining these factors nets a factor-T overall improvement. The second idea, drawn from Kuhn et al., is that in T rounds pipelining enables a node to communicate its (enlarged) message to at least T nearby nodes simultaneously, yielding a second factor-T speedup. We currently need to rely on the notion of T-stability for this, but we speculate that T-interval connectivity might suffice. The technique composes with the our technique exploiting larger message sizes from the previous section and leads to quadratic speed ups in b and T for most settings of these parameters.

As previously, we begin by describing an efficient indexed-broadcast algorithm and then show how it can be used as a primitive for k-token dissemination.

Our indexed broadcast algorithm exploits T-stability to broadcast bT blocks each containing bT bits, for a total of $(bT)^2$ bits (or $(bT)^2/d$ tokens), in $O((n+bT^2)\log n)$ rounds. As before, we use network coding, treating these blocks as vectors and flooding random linear combinations of the vectors through the network. We do so by dividing the network, in each block of T stable rounds, into *patches* of size and diameter roughly T. We then spread random linear combinations of the size-bT blocks from patch to patch, taking $O(T)$ rounds to spread to each new patch but reaching T nodes in the patch each time, so that n rounds suffice for all nodes to receive all necessary linear combinations.

8.1 Patching the Graph

Our first step is to partition the graph into connected *patches* of size $\Omega(D)$ and diameter $O(D)$. It helps to think of D as approximately T; Because computing the patching takes $D\log n$ time, we will set $D = O(T/\log n)$. We will use these patches for $O(T)$ rounds, during which they will remain static. First, we argue that such patches exist. Let G^D be the Dth power of the (unchanging) connectivity graph—in other words, connect every node to any node within distance D. Consider a *maximal independent set S* in G^D. If every vertex in G is assigned to the closest vertex in S, we get patches that satisfy our criteria:

1. Consider a shortest path tree on the vertices assigned to vertex $u \in S$. If v is assigned to u, then so are the ancestors of v in the shortest paths tree. Thus, the shortest path tree connects the patch.

2. Because of the maximality of S, every vertex is adjacent in G^D to a vertex in S, since otherwise such a vertex could be added to S. In other words, any vertex is within distance D of S. It follows that the depth of each shortest paths tree, which bounds the (half of the) diameter, is at most D

3. Also by definition, no two vertices in S are adjacent in G^D—in other words, their distance in G exceeds D. Thus, any vertex within distance $D/2$ of $u \in S$ is assigned to u. It follows that every patch has at least $D/2$ vertices.

It remains to *construct* such a maximal independent set. Luby's maximal independent set permutation algorithm [11]

can be easily adapted to run in our model. In Luby's permutation algorithm, vertices talk to their "neighbors". Since we are computing in the powered graph G', we need vertices to talk to other vertices at distance D over long communication paths. We have T time, but different communication paths may overlap, causing congestion.

Fortunately, this is not a significant problem. The core step of Luby's algorithm assigns every vertex a random priority, then adds to the MIS any vertex whose priority is higher than all its neighbors and "deactivates" all its neighbors. Thus, nodes need only learn the maximum priority of any neighbor and notify neighbors of their deactivation. We can simulate the procedure. Nodes can find the highest priority within distance D by flooding the highest priority they hear for D rounds. If a node hears no higher priority than its own, then it knows it is in the MIS and can broadcast a "deactivation" message to all nodes within distance D of itself. Luby's algorithm runs in $O(\log n)$ time, which translates to $O(D\log n)$ here. We thus choose $D = O(T/\log n)$.

8.2 T-Stable Indexed-Broadcast

Given our patches of the required size and diameter, we use network coding to distribute vectors of bT bits. In a particular sequence of $O(T)$ rounds, after having computed the patches for this sequence, we do the following:

1. *share:* All nodes in a patch jointly share a random linear combination of the vectors in the *union of all* their received messages, each adding the result to its own set of received messages

2. *pass:* Each node broadcasts its patch's agreed random sum vector to its neighbors

3. *share:* The first sharing phase is repeated, including the new vectors just received from neighbors.

8.2.1 Implementation

We show how to implement all the required steps in $O(T)$ rounds. The middle pass step is trivial: each node breaks its size-bT vector into T components of size b and transmits one component in each round. Neighbors receive and reassemble all components.

Less trivial is the share step. We show how all the nodes in a given patch can compute a random sum of all the size-bT vectors in all their received messages.

For this we use the vertices in the maximal independent set S as leaders and assume that each patch has agreed on a (shortest path) tree rooted at the leader; each node knows its depth and its parent and children. This can be done by letting the leader send out an incrementing broadcast for $O(D)$ rounds. The time when this broadcast reaches a node tells it its depth and the (lowest ID) node that the broadcast was received from is the "parent".

Now we want to compute a random linear combination of the *union* of all the vectors in all the nodes of the patch. First, each node just computes a random sum of its own vectors. It remains to sum these sums. This would be easy if the vectors had dimension b—we would pass them up from children to parents, summing as we went, so that each node only passed up one vector. Since their dimension is bT we pipeline. Each node breaks its length-bT vector $(v_1, \ldots, v_{bT})$ into T length-b vectors $w_i = (v_{iT}, v_{iT+1}, \ldots, v_{(i+1)T-1})$. At step s of this phase, any node at depth j will have the cumulative sum of all the w_{s+j-T} components of the vectors from its descendants. It broadcasts this sum to its parent, and at the same time receives from its children their own cumulative $w_{s+(j+1)-T}$ sums. The receiving node adds these children's' sums to its own $w_{s+j+1+T}$ component, producing the cumulative $w_{(s+1)+j-T}$ component sum that it needs to transmit the next round. After $T + D < 2T$ time steps, the root will have received cumulative sums of all the w_i vectors from its children and added them, yielding the sum of all the vectors, which is a random sum of all the basis vectors.

This random sum, a single size bT-vector, is now distributed by the leader to all nodes in the patch via the obvious pipelined broadcast.

8.2.2 Analysis

We now analyze the share-pass-share algorithm outlined above. As before, we show that any vector μ that is *sensed* by (not perpendicular to the basis of) some node at the start is quickly sensed by all vectors.

LEMMA 8.1. *With high probability the patch-sharing network coding algorithm solves the bT-indexed-broadcast problem in a T-stable dynamic network with tokens of size bT in $O((n + bT^2) \log n)$ rounds using messages of size $O(b)$.*

This is close to the best achievable time. The n term follows from the network's possible n diameter. The bT^2 term follows from information theory: the $b^2 T^2$ bits we aim to transmit may be at a single node that broadcasts only b bits per round, implying bT^2 rounds will be necessary for that node to broadcast its information.

PROOF. To simplify our proof we assume that $bT^2 \le n$ and prove an $O(n \log n)$ bound. For if $bT^2 \ge n$, we can run our algorithm for $t < T$ such that $bt^2 = n$ and distribute $b^2 t^2$ bits in $O(n \log n)$ rounds; repeating $(T/t)^2$ times will distribute all the bits in $(T/t)^2 n \log n = (T^2 n/t^2) \log n = T^2 b \log n$ rounds.

Since we are operating on size-bT messages we can allow bT tokens of size bT, each with a $\log q = O(1)$ size coefficient. We consider share-pass-share "meta rounds" of length T where our patches are fixed, and show that $O(n/D)$ of these meta rounds suffice to disseminate all the tokens, for a total of $O(T * (n/D)) = O(n \log n)$ rounds. For a given meta round we consider two cases. The first is where there is some patch that contains no node sensing μ. In this case, the connectivity assumption implies that a node u in some such patch is adjacent to some node v in a patch containing a node that does sense μ. In the first share step v receives a random linear combination of the vectors in its patch; since some node in the patch senses μ, with probability $1 - 1/q$ node v will sense μ after the first sharing phase. In this case v transmits the same random linear combination to u in the pass phase and u will sense μ as well. If so, the final share step will deliver to all nodes in u's patch a linear combination not perpendicular to μ with probability $1 - 1/q$. Combining these arguments, we find that with probability $(1 - 1/q)^2$, the $\Omega(D)$ nodes in u's patch, which previously did not sense μ, will now do so.

The second case is where every patch contains a node that senses μ. In this case every node has a $1 - 1/q$ chance of sensing μ after the first share step. The expected number of nodes that do *not* sense μ thus shrinks by a $1/q < 1/2$ factor. The Markov bound shows that it thus shrinks by a factor $2/3$ with constant probability.

We now combine the two cases. If case 1 holds declare a success if $\Omega(D)$ new nodes sense μ; if case 2 holds declare a success if the number of nodes that do not sense μ shrinks by $2/3$. There can be only $O(n/D)$ successes of case 1 and $O(\log n)$ successes of case 2 before all nodes sense μ. A Chernoff bound shows that within $\Omega(n/D)$ occurrences of case 1 the probability that we fail to observe $O(n/D)$ successes is $e^{-\Omega(n/D)}$. Similarly, the probability of less than $\log n$ successes in $\Omega(n/D)$ occurrences of case 2 is $e^{-\Omega(n/D)}$ (this follows from the fact that $T^2 < n$, meaning $n/T > \log n$).

Finally, we apply a union bound on the above argument over all the 2^{bT} distinct vectors of size T. The probability *any* such vector fails to be sensed in $\Omega(n/D)$ phases is then at most $2^{bT} e^{-\Omega(n/D)}$ which is negligible given our assumption that $bT^2 \le n$. Thus in $\Theta(n/D)$ phases each with a running time of $O(T)$, totaling $O(n \log n)$ time, all nodes sense all vectors and can decode all tokens. $\square$

This algorithm can be derandomized using the arguments developed in Section 6 and replacing Luby's randomized MIS algorithm by the deterministic distributed MIS algorithm in [13] with a running time of $MIS(n) = 2^{O(\sqrt{\log n})}$. The larger $k^2 \log n$ coefficient overhead still allows for $\sqrt{bT/\log n}$ tokens of size $O(bT)$ being code together for a vector size of $O(bT)$. This leads to the following Lemma:

LEMMA 8.2. *The deterministic patch-sharing algorithm solves the $\sqrt{bT/\log n}$-indexed-broadcast problem with tokens of size bT in a T-stable dynamic network in $O((n + \sqrt{bT}T) \cdot MIS(n))$ rounds using messages of size $O(b)$.*

8.3 T-Stable Token Dissemination

We have given an $O(n \log n)$-time algorithm for indexed broadcast of bT vectors of bT bits. Applying the same reduction(s) as before, we might hope to achieve a k-token dissemination algorithm with running time $O(n \log n \frac{kd}{(bT)^2})$. This can be achieved for most values of k, b and T. The key, as before, is *gathering* tokens we wish to broadcast as large blocks/tokens. Since the blocks used with T-stability are larger, gathering is harder. In particular:

- Using `greedy-forward` to gather tokens yields an algorithm with running time $O(\frac{\log n}{bT^2} \cdot \frac{nkd}{b} + nbT^2 \log n)$

- Using `priority-forward` to gather tokens yields an algorithm with running time $O(\frac{\log^2 n}{bT^2} \cdot \frac{nkd}{b} + nT \log^2 n)$.

The second algorithm is near-optimal unless T is very large. In this case there is an alternative gathering algorithm we can apply: create the patches of our patch algorithm, then use pipelining to gather together the tokens in a patch to blocks of size at most bT at a single node (or, if there is more than one block, at multiple nodes) of that patch. This produces $O(n/D + kd/bT) = O(n \log n/T)$ blocks of size at most $O(bT)$ which can be much smaller than k. In phases of $O(n \log n)$ rounds we then index bT of these blocks or tokens using pipelined flooding and broadcast them out using the network coded indexed-broadcast algorithm. This leads to an $O(\frac{1}{bT} \cdot \min\{k, \frac{n \log n}{T}\} + 1) \cdot n \log n$ round algorithm for k-token dissemination. This completes the results stated in Theorem 2.4.

For deterministic algorithms gathering is much harder. Considering the limitations of token-forwarding, it seems unlikely that the gathering methods that are based on the random-forward primitive can be derandomized. Nevertheless, we can make the last gathering method deterministic by using the deterministic MIS algorithm from [13] once more. This, together with the deterministic indexed-broadcast algorithm from Lemma 8.2, leads to an $O(n/D + kd/bT)/\sqrt{bT/\log n} \cdot O(n \cdot MIS(n)) = O(\frac{MIS(n)^2 \sqrt{\log n}}{\sqrt{bTT}} \cdot n^2 + n \cdot MIS(n))$ algorithm as stated in Theorem 2.5; here $MIS(n)$ is the time needed to compute a maximum independent set in an n node graph.

Allowing centralized algorithms on the other hand alleviates many of these problems: indices can be assigned trivially and the coefficient overhead can be ignored since it is easy to infer the coefficients from knowing the past topologies. This allows a randomized centralized algorithm to distribute n blocks of size $O(b)$ in $O(n)$ time and leads to a linear time algorithm for the k-token dissemination problem as stated in Corollary 2.6. To obtain deterministic centralized algorithm we have to be more careful: A deterministic centralized algorithm that codes together k tokens requires according to Corollary 6.2 a field size $q = n^k$. In order to describe one symbol in the bT-bit size blocks, that are used in the algorithm developed in this section, at most $k = bT/\log n$ blocks of size bT can be coded together. We also note, that with central control the MIS computation becomes local and thus trivial. Putting all this together and using the third (deterministic) gathering technique leads to the results stated in Corollary 2.6.

9. CONCLUSION

We have applied *network coding* to distributed computing in dynamic networks. We provided faster algorithms for distributed information dissemination which, in several cases, work provably better than *any* non-coding algorithm.

Message size is an important parameter that was not fully accounted for in previous work: while extremely small (logarithmic size) messages are a standard assumption in distributed computing, prior work on network coding assumed exponentially larger, linear size messages. We mediate between these two assumptions using an explicit message size and show that, contrary to the natural assumption that broadcast should scale linearly with the message size, it can be made to scale *quadratically* using network coding.

We also explore the range between fully dynamic and fully static networks, showing that in T-stable networks dissemination can be sped up by a factor of T^2 using network coding. In contrast, the Kuhn et al. lower bound apply to such T-stable networks and show that knowledge-based token-forwarding algorithm can only offer a factor-T speedup. Improving our patch-sharing algorithms to avoid the computation of a maximum independent set and making them applicable to the T-interval-connectivity model remains an interesting question. So far we can achieve this goal only if the topologies chosen by the adversary are highly non-expanding.

Many of our algorithmic ideas can be extended beyond the always-connected dynamic networks discussed in this paper to other network and communication models [6]. The same is true for our results on omniscient adversaries or (non-uniformly) deterministic algorithms.

We have shown that network coding outperforms token forwarding, but it is not clear whether we have made best-possible use of this technique. Conceivably network coding can yield even better performance. Unlike for token forwarding, there are no non-trivial lower bounds for general or network-coding based algorithms for n-token dissemination in the dynamic network model. Closing this gap is an intriguing open question.

Acknowledgments

We thanks Nancy Lynch and Rotem Oshman for introducing us to the dynamic network model. We thank Muriel Médard and Lizhong Zheng for interesting discussions. Lastly, we thank the anonymous reviewers for helpful comments.

10. REFERENCES

[1] R. Ahlswede, N. Cai, S. Li, and R. Yeung. Network information flow. *Transactions on Information Theory (TransInf)*, 46(4):1204–1216, 2000.

[2] M. Borokhovich, C. Avin, and Z. Lotker. Tight bounds for algebraic gossip on graphs. In *Proc. of the International Symp. on Information Theory (ISIT)*, pages 1758–1762, 2010.

[3] K. C.-H. Chen Avin, Michael Borokhovich and Z. Lotker. Order Optimal Information Spreading Using Algebraic Gossip. In *Proc. of the 40th Symp. on Principles of Distributed Computing (PODC)*, 2011.

[4] S. Deb, M. Medard, and C. Choute. On random network coding based information dissemination. In *Proc. of the International Symp. on Information Theory (ISIT)*, pages 278 –282, 2005.

[5] S. Deb, M. Medard, and C. Choute. Algebraic gossip: a network coding approach to optimal multiple rumor mongering. *Transactions on Information Theory (TransInf)*, 52(6):2486 – 2507, 2006.

[6] B. Haeupler. Analyzing Network Coding Gossip Made Easy. In *Proc. of the 43nd Symp. on Theory of Computing (STOC)*, 2011.

[7] T. Ho and D. Lun. *Network coding: an introduction*. Cambridge Univ Pr, 2008.

[8] T. Ho, M. Medard, R. Koetter, D. Karger, M. Effros, J. Shi, and B. Leong. A random linear network coding approach to multicast. *Transactions on Information Theory (TransInf)*, 52(10):4413–4430, 2006.

[9] F. Kuhn, N. Lynch, and R. Oshman. Distributed computation in dynamic networks. In *Proc. of the 42nd Symp. on Theory of Computing (STOC)*, pages 557–570, 2010.

[10] S. Li, R. Yeung, and N. Cai. Linear network coding. *Transactions on Information Theory (TransInf)*, 49(2):371–381, 2003.

[11] M. Luby. A simple parallel algorithm for the maximal independent set problem. In *Proc. of the 17th Symp. on Theory of Computing (STOC)*, pages 1–10, 1985.

[12] D. Mosk-Aoyama and D. Shah. Information dissemination via network coding. In *Proc. of the International Symp. on Information Theory (ISIT)*, pages 1748–1752, 2006.

[13] A. Panconesi and A. Srinivasan. Improved distributed algorithms for coloring and network decomposition problems. In *Proc. of the 24th Symp. on Theory of Computing (STOC)*, pages 581–592, 1992.

[14] R. Yeung. *Information Theory and Network Coding*. Springer Verlag, 2008.

Author Index

www.ingramcontent.com/pod-product-compliance
Lightning Source LLC
Chambersburg PA
CBHW080657220326
41598CB00033B/5239